THE BARGAIN

THE
GOOD
DEAL
DIRECTORY
2001

NOELLE WALSH

First published in 1996 by
The Good Deal Directory Company Limited
P.O. Box 4, Lechlade, Glos GL7 3YB
Telephone 01367 860017

ISBN 0-9526529-9-4

Copyright © The Good Deal Directory Company Limited 1996

The right of Noelle Walsh to be identified as the author of this work
has been asserted by her in accordance with the Copyright,
Designs and Patents Act 1988.

All rights reserved. No reproduction, copy or transmission of
this publication may be made without written permission.
No paragraph of this publication may be reproduced, copied
or transmitted save with written permission or in accordance
with the provisions of the Copyright Act 1956 (as amended).
Any person who does any unauthorised act in relation to this
publication may be liable to criminal prosecution and civil claims
for damages.

Research team: Tracy Cambell, Micola Nevile, Sarah Townsend,
Richard Blake-James, Debbie Palmer, with special thanks to Alison Goldingham.

This book is sold subject to the condition that it shall not, by way
of trade or otherwise, be lent, re-sold, hired-out, or otherwise circulated
without the publisher's prior consent in any form of binding or cover
other than that in which it is published and without a similar condition
including this condition being imposed on the subsequent purchaser.

All information was correct at the time of going to press; the author and
publishers accept no responsibility for any error in detail, innaccuracy or
judgement whatsoever.

Dear Reader

We hope you enjoy reading this book,
the definitive guide to value for money shopping
in Britain.

We also run Discount Designer Fashion Sales at the
elegant Pavilion at Ascot Racecourse in Berkshire
every November and May/June.
These Sales feature up to 100 top fashion and
accessory companies selling ends of lines, last season's
stock and over-runs at fantastically reduced prices.

If you'd like to know more about how to apply
for a ticket, send us a card with your name address
to the address below and we will send you the
information you require.

Write to:
The Good Deal Directory's Fashion Sales,
PO BOX 4, Lechlade,
Gloucestershire GL7 3YB.

CONTENTS

INTRODUCTION	VI
THE GDD ON THE INTERNET	XXI
GEOGRAPHICAL BREAKDOWN OF BOOK	XXII
Bedfordshire	1
Berkshire	3
Buckinghamshire	8
Cambridgeshire	12
Cheshire	21
Co Durham	51
Cornwall	62
Cumbria	66
Derbyshire	74
Devon	90
Dorset	100
Essex	106
Gloucestershire	123
Hampshire	138
Herefordshire	150
Hertfordshire	155
Kent	169
Lancashire *(including Greater Manchester)*	184
Leicestershire	222
Lincolnshire	230
London	240
Middlesex	308
Norfolk	313
Northamptonshire	321
Northumberland	327
Nottinghamshire	340
Oxfordshire	349

Rutland	**366**
Shropshire	**368**
Somerset	**374**
Staffordshire	**393**
Suffolk	**421**
Surrey	**428**
Sussex	**445**
Warwickshire	**459**
West Midlands	**466**
Wiltshire	**481**
Worcestershire	**500**
Yorkshire	**508**
Southern Scotland	**564**
Central Scotland	**571**
Scotish Highlands and Islands	**594**
South Wales	**602**
North Wales	**624**
Northern Ireland	**630**
Channel Islands	**636**
Europe *(including Austria, Eire, France, Germany, Italy, Spain and Sweden)*	**638**
INDEX OF MAIL ORDER DISCOUNTERS	**644**
INDEX OF BRAND-NAMES	**645**
THANK YOU TO READER RESEARCHERS	**650**
REPORT FORMS	**651**

Find out how to earn yourself £10

INTRODUCTION

Welcome to the eighth edition of The Good Deal Directory, packed with even more bargain outlets than ever before.

The big discount story this year has been the response of the car trade to overseas and internet competition, although The Good Deal Directory tends not to cover this sector as it changes too quickly and is too open to individual bargaining skills. The 2001 edition, however, does include details of one or two of the more established discount car buying opportunities.

In our old stamping ground, the factory shop sector, even more factory shopping villages have opened up, those that exist have increased in size, and yet more famous brand names have taken the leap into the factory shopping sector.

For the villages, the future is now about fighting it out with each other in terms of size and the number and quality of top brand names they have. Meanwhile, individual little factory shops continue to build relationships with their customers and ensure even better bargains in order to keep them loyal.

Canny consumers now take in factory and discount shopping as part of their shopping mix. If they're looking for a fashionable outfit, the high street is their first port of call. However, for something classic, a factory shop is a good starting point for bargain hunters.

Home lovers have a more difficult choice between the high street and the discount sector. Does it really matter if the dinner service, the towel, the bedlinen or the sofa is last year's design? Leaps in style occur over a long period of time on the home front. For example, possessing a glass sink in your bathroom won't be de rigueur for a number of years yet - if at all - so you can still get away with buying an end of line ceramic sink. The high street may be the place to go for those up-to-the-minute accessories, but buying big, expensive items in the discount sector has to make sense.

This is even more true in the white goods sector *(washing machines, fridges, hobs etc)*. Manufacturers often bring out new models which are only the tiniest bit different to the old model. A new washing machine may have a top spin speed of 1100 rpm instead of 1000. This is so that the shops have something new to sell and something new to say to customers. But it makes very little difference to you, the consumer. Unless you want a bargain - in which case, you opt for the old model and get it cheaper! Occasionally, there are technological or ecological changes which might make a difference to whether you want the latest product or last season's but these are rarer than you might think.

Despite all the activity in the factory shopping sector, still shops such as Matalan and T K Maxx are thriving. Both stock fashion for all the family, homewares and an ever-changing mixed merchandise of perfumes, tights, accessories, gifts, beauty products or whatever they can buy in sufficient quantity and at very good prices. Matalan has strong brand names rather than top designer names; T K Maxx has both, although you have to be a real bargain hunter as their layout doesn't make it easy to find hot items. You can find some fabulous names at T K Maxx, though, if you're prepared to spend time and energy.

The massive amount of overstock in the world of fashion has also permeated down to permanent discount outlets and designer sales. End of line retailers are able to go over to the Continental factories where top designer labels are manufactured and buy merchandise that hasn't been bought by the big department store buyers at knockdown prices early in the selling season, bring it back to the UK and sell it at discounted prices only weeks after it has first appeared in our top boutiques and stores.

Dress agencies, those places where gently worn clothes go after their owners have tired of them, also benefit from this. The cognoscenti buy their top designer labels at discount prices and then, if they discover they've made a mistake or have only worn it once, sell it on to dress agencies. Because they got it so cheap, the mistakes don't matter so much. The growing number of dress agencies is testimony to the knock-on effect when fashion is widely discounted.

Fabrics
Some companies such as Osborne & Little, Colefax & Fowler, Sanderson and Designers Guild hold their own "warehouse" sales, reducing stock significantly to clear it to existing customers whom they mail. If you want to find out about these clearance sales, write to the company and ask for your name to be put on the mailing list *(the addresses are in the book under London, Designer Sales)*. There are hundreds of fabric discount shops countrywide: shops such as Knickerbean, which has five outlets selling Designers Guild, Anna French, Jane Churchill, Colefax & Fowler and Osborne & Little, among the scores of different fabrics. You can still find many of these famous name bargains here, but now many of their fabrics are sourced directly from the same mills and manufacturers as the top names, both here and abroad. They offer the same top quality, in the latest colours and designs, at relatively lower prices, because they are buying and selling directly and cutting out the middlemen. If you're looking for curtain fabric, try one of the many secondhand curtains businesses countrywide first. They stock a wide range of curtains, many of which are from show houses or interior designers' mistakes or simply bought by people who didn't like them once they hung them! Others are made from incredibly expensive fabric, lined, interlined and weighted and in almost-perfect condition and sold at between one third and one half of the as-new price. Most secondhand curtain shops let you take the curtains home and try them out against your windows before they cash your cheque so you, too, won't make a costly mistake.

Kitchen and dining room

Brand names such as Remington, Pifco, Moulinex and Swan are all available in factory shops where you can also buy Oneida cutlery, Swan fryers, Kenwood food mixers, kitchen knives, Russell Hobbs kettles, Tower pans, Krups kitchen applicances at discounts of at least 25%. If a new food processor comes out, shops again no longer want to sell the old one so it goes back to the factory for selling in the factory shop. Occasionally, items are returned because of damaged packaging when they are re-checked by factory technicians and then sold at discount prices.

The result of all this is that for you, the customer, there is greater choice than ever before. As long as you are prepared to wait - not to buy when an item is first on the market - you can get some great bargains. With shop rents rising, there is more and more pressure on them to change stock regularly, keep bringing in new lines - which means they have to clear out unsold stock very quickly. It's madness to try and clear old stock at discount prices in the same high-rent shop as you are also trying to sell new stock at full price - hence the increase in factory shops and discount shops.

What's New

Soon, there will be a factory shopping village within reasonable driving distance of most of us - apart from the geographical extremes of the country. By the end of 2001, there will be 35 factory shopping centres and smaller leisure-oriented factory shopping centres.

Most of the villages open in phases, so they are constantly changing as well as bringing in new shops. Even when they are completely full, some tenants may find they have taken on too large an outlet and decide to split it in two, in which case this makes room for another new tenant. Occasionally, tenants find that factory shopping doesn't work for them and close down their operations.

Factory shopping centres

Factory shopping centres - the smallest has 10 shops, the largest more than 150 - are for a different type of bargain shopper than the traditional stand-alone factory outlet. The latter attracts those who take pleasure in the hunt: in finding an out-of-the-way, sometimes unattractive shed on an industrial estate miles off the beaten track. The level of attractiveness of the site is usually directly related to the price of the goods on sale - the more unattractive the actual factory outlet is, the lower the prices. However, you can't go shopping with a list at these individual outlets. Factory shopping centres, on the other hand, offer a higher level of certainty. If there are 150-plus shops - as at the McArthurGlen Designer Outlet in Cheshire Oaks, South Wirral - you'd have to be pretty picky not to find something you like and can afford. The choice is usually enormous - most of the shops are fashion oriented although they now offer a growing selection of children's goods, luggage, jewellery, shoes, cookware, toys, glassware and electrical goods. But the choice comes at a price. On the whole, prices are higher at the factory shopping centres than at stand-alone factory shops - except at traditional sale times when the village shops also slash prices in order to clear stock. Factory shopping centres here began with the Freeport Leisure Village in Hornsea on the East Yorkshire coast in the late Eighties, early Nineties. This was followed by the first purpose-built factory shopping centre, Clarks Village in Street, Somerset, built around an already-existing shoe museum and shoe discount town. In the early Eighties, the American developers came over here, factory shopping centres in the US having reached a plateau. Many of them tied up with an existing British company in joint ventures. Being American, they thought BIG. Their centres tended to be much much bigger than the traditional British ones with twice the number of shops. Now that they have reached a plateau here, too, they have moved onto the Continent.

OUTLET VILLAGES

Bicester Outlet Shopping Village, junction 9 of M40, Pingle Drive, Bicester, Oxfordshire OX6 7WD ☎ (01869) 323200
approx 60 shops

McArthurGlen Designer Outlet Village, junction 10 of M53, Kinsey Road, Cheshire Oaks, near Ellesmere Port, South Wirral L65 9JJ
☎ (0151) 357 3633
Up to 166 shops

Jacksons Landing, The Highlight, Hartlepool Marina, Hartlepool, Cleveland TS24 OXN ☎ (01429) 866989
21 shops

K Village, Kendal junction 36 of M6, Cumbria ☎ (01539) 732363
12 shops

Clarks Village, Farm Road, Street, Somerset BA16 OBB
☎ (01458) 840064
approx 57 shops

Galleria Outlet Centre, Comet Way, Hatfield, Herts. AL10 OXR
☎ (01707) 278301
70 shops

Hornsea Freeport Shopping village, Rolston Road, Hornsea, East Yorkshire HU18 1UT ☎ (01964) 534211
over 40 shops

Freeport Shopping Village, Anchorage Road, Fleetwood, junction 3 of M55, Lancashire FY7 6AE ☎ (01253) 877377
approx 50 shops

Freeport Scotland, West Calder, West Lothian EH55 8QB
☎ (01501) 763488
40 shops

Royal Quays Factory Outlet Centre, North Shields, Newcastle-upon-Tyne
☎ (0191) 296 3743
42 shops with 60 shops planned

The Yorkshire Outlet, White Rose Way, junction 3 of M18, Doncaster, South Yorks. DN4 5JH ☎ (01302) 366444
39 shops

Village Square, Brighton Marina Village, Brighton, East Sussex BN2 5WB
☎ (01273) 818504
11 shops with more planned

McArthurGlen Designer Outlet Village, Kemble Drive, Churchward Village, junction 16 of M4, Swindon, Wilts SN2 2DY
☎ (01793) 507600
108 shops

Festival Park Factory Outlet Shopping, Festival Park, Victoria, Ebbw Vale, South Wales ☎ (01495) 350010.
36 shops

Loch Lomond Factory Outlets, Main Street, Alexandria, on the A82, Loch Lomond, near Glasgow, Scotland G83 OUG ☎ (01389) 710077
approx 22 shops

McArthurGlen Designer Outlet Wales, The Derwen, Bridgend, South Wales CF32 9SU ☎ (0800) 3164352
approx 90 shops

Clacton Common Factory Outlet Village, Clacton, Essex
☎ (01255) 430777
approx 48 shops

McArthurGlen Designer Outlet York, St Nicholas Avenue, Fulford, Junction A19 and A64, York, North Yorkshire YO19 4TA
☎ (01904) 682700
75 shops with 150 planned

McArthurGlen Designer Outlet Derbyshire, Mansfield Road, South Normanton, Alfreton, junction 28 of M1, Derbyshire DE55 2JW
☎ (01773) 545000
four themed areas: fashion, home, sport/leisure and accessories with 74 different "stores"

Peak Village, Chatsworth Road, Rowsley, on the A6 between Bakewell and Matlock, Derbyshire DE4 2JE ☎ (01629) 735326
22 factory shops and leisure facilities

Evesham Country Park, Country Park Management, Evesham,
at northern end of the Evesham by-pass at its junction with Stratford Road,
Worcestershire WR11 4TP ☎ (01386) 41661
factory shops, garden centre, leisure facilities

Sterling Mill Designer Outlet Village, Tillicoultry, near Stirling,
midway between M9 and M90, Scotland FK13 6HQ ☎ (01259) 752100
22 outlets with more planned

Gretna Gateway, Glasgow Road, Gretna DG16 6GG ☎ (01461) 339028
22 factory shops with 60 planned

Freeport Talke Outlet Mall, Pit Lane, Talke Pits, Stoke-on-Trent,
Staffordshire ST7 1XD ☎ (01782) 774113
approx 30 factory shops

Wilton Factory Shopping Village, Minster Street, Wilton, near Salisbury,
Wiltshire SP2 ORS ☎ (01722) 741211
approx 11 factory shops

Whiteley Village, off M27 between Southampton and Portsmouth,
Hampshire ☎ (01489) 886886
50 factory shops planned

Freeport Essex Village, Charter Way, Braintree, Essex CM7 8PY
☎ (01376) 348168.

Gunwharf Quays, Portsmouth, Hampshire ☎ (02392) 755940
*85 factory shops, restaurants, craft market, leisure complex,
cinema opening late 2000*

Freeport Castleford, Carrwood Road, Glasshoughton, Castleford,
off Junction 32 of M52, West Yorkshire ☎ (01977) 520153
82 factory shops with 150 eventually

McArthurGlen Designer Outlet Scotland, Almondvale Boulevard,
Livingston, junction 3 of M8, West Lothian EH54 6QX
☎ (0800) 316 4352
100 factory shops, Ferris wheel, cinema opening late 2000

DUE TO OPEN

Harwich Beacon Factory Outlet, Harwich, Essex
Planned to open in 2001, there will be forty-plus factory shops offering end of season lines and overstock at discount prices.

Lichfield, West Midlands
At time of going to press, there were a possible three villages fighting for planning permission in the Walsall, Brownhills, Lichfield area.

The Manchester Outlet Mall at the Lowry, The Quays, Salford Quays, Manchester M5 2SQ ☎ (0161) 848 1800

Factory shopping centre with seventy shops in a site next to the Manchester Ship Canal, which is due to open in October 2001. The site will include a hotel, Warner Village, Millennium Multiplex cinema, 15 cafes/restaurants, health and fitness club, indoor activity centre for children and is built alongside the £127 million Lowry Millenium Project for the Arts. The Imperial War Museum North, which opens in 2002, will be just a bridge away.

GETTING THE BEST OUT OF FACTORY SHOPPING

1. Eighty percent of factory shopping village customers visit on a weekend, leaving you with queues at the tills, parking problems and less chance of getting a table at the centre's restaurants. If you can, shop at villages during the week when they are usually quiet.

2. Although they don't advertise the fact, most factory shopping villages discount their products even further at traditional high street sale times *(January and June)*. So if you only visit villages twice a year, ring and check the sale times before you go. The disadvantage, however, is that you will be getting the last of the line in stock so colour and size choices will be limited. This is offset by the really good bargains.

3. Keep your eyes and ears open all the time. On a day trip, watch out for signs for out-of-the-way factory shops; scour the small ads of your local papers for one-day factory shop sales.

4. Put your name down on the mailing list of factory shops you visit. Fabric factory shops, for instance, often hold twice-yearly sales at their warehouses to which they invite customers and sell last year's stock at greatly reduced prices. Many fashion factory shops have one or two-day sales when even the reductions are reduced.

5. Tourist information centres are useful sources of free information on factory shops in their area.

6. If it's a particular brand name you're after, such as Jaeger, Burberry or Aquascutum, and you want a specific item *(a raincoat or blazer)* ring first and check their stock. There are certain times of year when it is very low. The staff are usually very helpful.

7. Check if the item is a second - usually there is a label on the garment stating why it is so. For example, Aquascutum label their seconds "Slightly Imperfect" and mark on an illustration of the garment where the imperfection lies. You cannot return a second if it says what's wrong with it - although all your statutory rights are in place at factory shops.

8. Never travel a long way without phoning first to check opening hours and stock levels. It's also a good idea to phone to get directions as many of the individual factory shops are in out-of-the-way, hard to find places.

9. If you're looking to be the height of fashion, factory shopping isn't for you - unless you're a natural stylist and can mix looks to modernise. Fashion factory shopping is great for children's clothes, jeans, leisure wear, sweaters, underwear and classic items such as blazers, coats and raincoats.

10. If you see something you like, buy it. You won't find it again.

11. If you want to pay by credit card, check first that some of the smaller, individual factory shops accept them.

12. If you're looking for small electrical appliances for the kitchen, it's unlikely that you will find the latest gadget, but there will be good bargains in ends of lines.

13. Whatever the condition of the outlet, your rights are just the same as if you were shopping in the mainstream.

14. Factory outlets sell limited ranges, colours and sizes so don't expect either co-ordinated ranges or to be able to exchange an item for the same thing but bigger/smaller a few days later.

15. Some of the major high street stores insist on the manufacturer cutting out their label before selling in the factory outlet, so some of the goods may be unbranded. This applies even to the washing instructions in some cases.

16. If there isn't a double price on the price tag *(ie the original selling price crossed out and replaced with the reduced one),* it may be that this item has been specially made for the factory shop from leftover fabric used in the manufacture of the original garment. Sometimes, factories are left with hundreds of a particular skirt left but very few of the matching blouses, so they make up more blouses from the same fabric. Watch out that the colours match exactly. Or it may be that the item was originally made for export and has never been on sale in the UK.

17. Don't always believe what the size tag tells you - some items are seconds because they are incorrectly marked up.

18. Before you travel, sit down with a map book and plot your journey. Often, there are three or four factory shops within a few miles of each other or on your route so you can make the most of your trip.

19. Carry room and window measurements with you if visiting carpet or fabric factory shops and children's ages and sizes with you if visiting toy or clothing outlets. What you see when you visit is all there usually is of that item.

20. In the more traditional factory shops, you may not find items as flatteringly presented as they are in department and high street stores. Be prepared to rummage.

DEFINITION OF TERMS

Factory shops
Run by the manufacturer or a representative of the manufacturer *(who may also be a retailer)* selling last season's stock as well as ends of lines, slow-selling items, returned merchandise. A few global manufacturers bring in stock from other countries which may not have been on sale here before. A few others make up clothes from the same fabric which was used to make the clothes originally on sale in high street shops. Thus, if they have hundreds of a particular skirt left over but only a few dozen of its matching jackets, but plenty of the fabric, they will make up jackets to match. They will then not be able to give two prices - an original and a discounted price - for these items. Factory shops sell manufacturer's surplus stock - cancelled orders, returned merchandise from the store, over-production, seconds or discontinued lines - at prices which are much lower than those in the high street shops which the factory supplies. Discounts vary but in general they are higher in the fashion sector where an outfit can be out of date very quickly and where markups can be as high as 280%, and lower in ceramics and glassware. There are far fewer homeware factory shops than fashion ones because for a housewares retailer whose mark-up is not very high, half-price is not profitable whereas if you're a fashion manufacturer with a high mark-up, half-price still leaves a significant profit margin. The older the item is, the cheaper the price. As a general rule, you can expect at least 30% off, and up to 80%.

Permanent discount outlets
Run by entrepreneurs who buy in stock from a variety of sources: overseas manufacturers clearance lines; bankrupt stock; fortuitous purchasing *(perhaps from a designer who needs cash quickly);* other full-price shops' slower-selling lines; returns from department stores; overstocks from the chain stores *(although these usually have the labels removed).* Those outlets selling clothes from Marks & Spencer usually have to agree to remove the St Michael label and any other identifying label such as the care label. Permanent discount outlets also include all the shops run by mail order companies clearing their old catalogue stock. These are often very good value for large electrical equipment, although these items sell out so quickly that you almost have to visit the shop every day in order to buy one. Many mail order companies now also sell designer-led merchandise and some of this makes its way into these clearance shops but you have to be willing to scour the rails. Remember that half price in these shops isn't necessarily half price in that up to 11% is added to the cost of items to cover direct marketing costs and mailing of catalogues. So half price is actually a discount of 39%.

Dress Agencies

Have you ever wondered how some women always manage to look smartly dressed? Have they just got lashings of natural style, a family member who owns a dress shop or simply money to burn? It's just as likely that they have discovered the secret of of secondhand clothes shopping. Now called dress agencies by those anxious to dispel visions of jumble sale leftovers, these recession-spawned shops are a boon both to those wishing to spend money and those wanting to earn some. As a customer, you have the opportunity to buy good quality clothes at very reasonable prices and you can also clear out your own "mistakes" and make a bit of money. Dress agency owners are very particular about which clothes they choose to sell. They have to be - the quality of their merchandise reflects how successful they - and ultimately, you if you're a seller - will be. If you're looking for designer labels, choose the best areas of town to shop in. For example if the dress agency is in London's Beauchamp Place or Hampstead, the labels will be the best: Armani, DKNY, Valentino, Bruce Oldfield. If it's the high street, Suburbia, there will probably be a good mix of labels such as Jaeger and Country Casuals as well as a sprinkling of high street favourites: Next, Principles, Marks & Spencer. But dress agency owners rely on the clients who bring them in clothes to sell so one visit may yield a goldmine of covetable clothes; another just fool's gold.

Dress agencies only accept cleaned, pressed clothes in mint condition. A price is agreed, of which most agencies take 40%-50% as their commission. The clothes are put on the rails for a set period of time - usually 6-12 weeks. If, after that time, an item hasn't sold, some proprietors will talk to the owner about reducing the price. If it still doesn't sell, it will be returned to the owner. Uncollected items are usually sent to charity shops. Dress agencies are usually friendly places - many offer coffee or tea and some even have small coffee rooms where you can relax and read a paper. The best ones build up a rapport with their regular customers, letting them know if something comes in which might be of interest.

Tips for getting the best out of dress agencies

1. If you're looking for top designer labels, choose a dress agency in an expensive neighbourhood. They're most likely to have the sort of clientele who dress in the best and then sell it on.

2. If your child is about to start a new school with all the expense of a uniform, find out if there is a dress agency dealing in childrenswear in the vicinity of the school - there's bound to be some secondhand uniforms there.

3. Clearing out your own wardrobe is a good way to find out if a dress agency is right for you. If they sift carefully through your clothes insisting on a certain quality and on the garments being dry cleaned then you know they're good enough to buy from. It's also a way of making money for yourself from clothes which you no longer wear or which were mistakes.

4. Instead of spending money hiring an evening outfit for that once-a-year special occasion, buy your evening gown/cocktail dress from a dress agency. Whether you hire or buy, you'll still be wearing a garment that's already been worn, and you might as well have use of it for another occasion!

5. Dress agencies are great places to buy almost brand new ski wear and horse riding gear, which are sold there by people who tried skiing and didn't like it or who had a short-lived passion for horses.

6. If the garment or accessory you're buying is a top designer label and that's the main reason you're buying it, insist on that fact being written on your receipt. If it turns out to be a fake, you will then have evidence that you bought what you were told was the real thing.

Architectural salvage

Someone else's rubbish could be your treasure. Architectural salvage businesses deal in reclaimed items from homes and gardens. Some specialise in, say, garden statuary or fireplaces or floorboards. They tend to be vast caverns and you need to have a keen eye. Many now offer reproduction facilities.

Showroom sales

Like any business, the fashion trade has surplus stock and precisely because it is a fashion business, they can't hang on to it for too long before it becomes unsellable. Showroom sales are held by a variety of different people: wholesalers who haven't sold in to shops all the stock they bought; agents who have lots of last season's samples which they use to show buyers *(remember last season in fashion language is usually this season in yours - thus, by May summer stock may be last season's just as the weather is hotting up sufficiently for you to buy it for this)*; designers who control the design, manufacture and wholesaling of their clothes who may have a mixture of samples, unsold items, returned goods and overstock; individuals who gather together surplus stock from a variety of different sources, hire a venue and sell it to the general public, taking a cut of the total sales.

The majority of these sales take place in London and many are advertised in the days preceding the sale in the Evening Standard newspaper. They're well worth visiting - if you don't mind a scrum and aren't over-modest as most don't boast changing rooms. *(There is a list of Designer Showroom Sales in the book in the London section under Designer Sales.)* Showroom sales at venues usually charge a small fee to cover their mailing costs. They keep a list of everyone who has visited their Sales and mail them with the date of the next one. Some Sale organisers also run sales outside London, including The Good Deal Directory, which runs the Really Good Deal Fashion Sale every November and late May/early June at the elegant Pavilion at Ascot Racecourse. This Sale was inspired by the book, The Good Deal Directory, and offers a huge range of designer and top brand-name fashion and accessories at end of the line prices. *(For more information, see Berkshire.)*

INTRODUCTION — XVII

Live Well on Less

When I first started The Good Deal Directory, I used to include tips for saving money which didn't really fall into any category. They might be things like Entertainment Guides which gave you 25% off meals at hundreds of restaurants or where lost property ends up and how you can buy some amazing bargains at the lost property auctions. Almost all of these have either been tried out by me or recommended to me by readers, so they're not just money-making schemes by some unscrupulous individual.

MORE BARGAIN HUNTING TIPS

1. Discount shopping isn't all about factory shops. There are lots of permanent discount shops all over the country, run by people who know how to find a bargain. Many of these are selling items left over from the big catalogue companies - anything from babygros to television sets, jewellery to hi-fis. Others sell Continental designers obtained direct from the manufacturers abroad.

2. Don't ignore dress agencies as a way of saving - and making - money. You can buy clothes you couldn't otherwise afford in these nearly-new shops which are springing up all over the country. Or sell off your mistakes or items you no longer like wearing and make a bit of cash yourself.

3. Someone else's rubbish may be your treasure. If you're doing up your house and want to, for example, put floorboards down instead of carpets, check out the architectural salvage experts first. They may have floors taken out of old school rooms or manor houses at very reasonable prices.

4. Visit large exhibitions such as Gardener's World or The Clothes Show Live on the afternoon of the last day. Exhibitors don't always want to take the stock on their stand home so will often sell it off at rock-bottom prices, making the ticket price well worthwhile.

5. If you buy women's magazines, always check out the small ads at the back where lots of companies advertise end of line fabrics, direct-from-the-factory spiral staircases, factory shop sofas, architectural reclamation services and the like.

6. Free information - and sometimes even samples - is widely available from supermarkets *(recipe suggestions for a new vegetable they're stocking),* large food companies, perfume and cosmetic companies launching new products.

7. If you're trying to buy curtain fabric to match sofa upholstery, bring a cushion from the sofa with you if you can. If you're trying to match curtains with your walls, paint a piece of wood with your wall colour and bring that with you.

8. The best buys at discount shops are always the most expensive items. Thus, large items such as sofas, beds and carpets offer the best bargains.

9. White goods such as fridges, washing machines and vacuum cleaners have quite small markups anyway - 20-28% compared with 110% for furniture and up to 280% for clothes - so don't expect huge discounts on these items.

10. Anything that shouts out the season will always be the better bargain: dates on T-shirts, for example. Bear in mind, though, that everyone will know what year you bought it.

11. The advice for clever bargain home buys is the same as for fashion: buy classics. The classic tin of white or cream paint; cream fabric; white tiles...you can always buy in some splashes of colour later to add interest and excitement.

12. Buy items such as evening wear. Because they're expensive to start with, you will save more. Even if you have no particular event in mind, it's much better to have that half-price bargain in your wardrobe in six months time when an unexpected invitation arrives than rush out the Saturday before and buy something expensive just to have something different to wear.

13. If you're buying shoes, trade up - buy top brand shoes at the sort of price you would normally pay for your full-price cheaper brands. Good shoes do last much longer than cheap ones. Invest in shoe trees and shoe brushes and vow to maintain them.

14. If you're trying to create a designer wardrobe from scratch, start with an anchor piece. If you've got a good coat or jacket, you will always look well dressed. Or buy a classic suit that can also be worn as separates. Go for classic colours which will stand the test of time and inject the "now" colours from the full-price high street.

15. If you need a flat pair of shoes or a handbag or a scarf in order to stretch your wardrobe and wear things that you haven't been able to, look out for that one buy which will give you a total new outfit when added to what you already have in your wardrobe.

16. Remember, the price of things can be divided by the number of times you wear it so if you can see yourself getting a lot of wear out of something that's still a bit more than you would normally pay for an item, it's probably worth it.

17. Don't buy something that looks wonderful but just doesn't go with your lifestyle.

18. Your home is as much a victim of fashion trends as your wardrobe. Because homes shops make it their business to sell the newest fabrics, the latest sofa shape, the most technologically advanced piece of kitchen equipment when, the following season, the next new designs are ready to take their place on the shop floor, the only-just arrives have to depart. Some of the unsold stock is held over in the shop's limited storage space until the twice-yearly sale; the remainder makes it way to a wide variety of disposal channels ranging from warehouse sales to factory shops. If you don't mind buying last year's trend-setting fabric to cover your Ottoman, you can pick up some exciting bargains. The same is true for almost everything you find in the home from carpets to curtains, fridges to furniture, bedlinen to breadmakers, and cutlery to ceramics.

19. Buy baby equipment such as prams, pushchairs and car seats in late October. These are all fashion items. That means the cover fabric design gets replaced every year. The big trade baby show with the new designs and colours happens at the beginning of October - after that, shops drop their prices on last year's ranges.

20. Sign on with mail order companies whose clothes you like and wait for their end-of-season sale catalogues and buy everything at reduced prices.

21. Don't go food shopping every week on the same day. Delay it by one day each week so that you're extending your shopping cycle so that instead of making 52 trips to the supermarket a year, you make 44.

22. If your child is about to start a new school with all the expense of a uniform, find out if there is a dress agency dealing in childrenswear in the vicinity of the school - there's bound to be some secondhand uniforms there.

23. Volunteers can often have a haircut for a small fee and more sophisticated treatments, such as perms or colour, for the price of the products used. There are always trained staff on hand to watch over the trainees. Ask at your local hairdresser or hair and beauty department of the nearest further education college. There, you may also be able to enjoy a wide range of free beauty treaments from foot massage and aromatherapy to waxing and a manicure from the students.

24. Don't leave gift buying until the last minute when you're tempted to pay anything just to turn up with something. Keep a list of everyone on your birthday/Christmas/wedding anniversary list and take it with you whenever you go shopping. Look over it quickly before you shop in case you find something that suits someone on your list. The right gift at the right price may not be around the week before a birthday, but it might be there six months before. Remember to keep a note of what you've bought and when it has been given.

25. Re-examine your regular expenses. For example, if you have your hair cut every six weeks, lengthening the time to six and a half or even seven weeks will cut one visit to the hairdressers a year.

26. When factory shopping for clothes if you haven't got a definite must-buy in mind, find replacements for your old favourites which are beginning to look a bit shoddy. If you've got a jacket or a pair of trousers that you wear almost every day, look out for something that fulfils the same purpose. Of if you've got a jacket in your wardrobe that you haven't worn this season because you never had the right thing to go with it, now is the time to fill in that gap.

27. Avoid outrageous outfits that people will remember you in as you won't be able to wear them more than once.

The Good Deal Directory isn't about where to find items cheaply. If it was, it would be full of details of markets and car boot sales. What it is about is buying quality goods at prices which are lower than they were originally. Most of the information has been gathered by myself and my team of researchers over the past nine or more years; now, a lot of it is also supplied by readers of The Good Deal Directory. I pay for tips: places which readers have visited and believe are good value and which I don't already know about. My readers tell me what they bought, what else was for sale there, what the discounts were and what the service was like. I couldn't ask for a better team of researchers, and all those who contributed to this book are thanked at the back of the book. If you know of somewhere that isn't in this book and which I subsequently publish, remember, I pay £10 for tips. So you could end up enjoying a free book. There are pages at the back of the book which you can fill in and send to me or if you don't want to tear pages out, simply photocopy a page and send it to me or write a letter. The address is on the pages at the back of the book.

Happy bargain hunting!

Noelle Walsh

The Good Deal Directory goes live on the internet!

www.gooddealdirectory.co.uk

Click onto our website for hot news about showroom and clearance sales taking place in the next few days. Keep the book in your car so when you're travelling you can look up discount outlets en route.
At home, meanwhile, you can check out favourite brand names or shops simply and easily on our constantly updated website and make plans for special visits to these outlets. Search by county, brand name, product or shop name.

What information will the site contain? Factory shop sales; warehouse clearances; once-in-a-lifetime special deals; factory and discount shop openings; designer showroom sales; stock sales from insurance claims due to fire or flood

What will it cost you?
Nothing. It is free to users.

Click Now!

Geographical breakdown of Book

Shops are broken down by county. For example, if you are looking for glassware in Stoke-on-Trent, you go to the chapter for Staffordshire and can then flick through picking out just the glassware shops alphabetically.

Bedfordshire

ARCHITECTURAL ANTIQUES
70 PEMBROKE STREET, BEDFORD, BEDFORDSHIRE MK40 3RQ
☎ (01234) 213131. OPEN 12 - 5 MON - FRI, 9 - 5 SAT.
Architectural Salvage • *DIY/Renovation*
Buy and sell antiques, good quality furniture, original fireplaces and all architectural salvage. They have a large selection of original Georgian, Victorian and Edwardian fireplaces in marble, slate, cast iron, mahogany, oak and pine, and provide a restoration and installation service. All types and sizes of internal and external doors and cupboards, glazed doors and bookshelves; rolltop baths, basins, glazed and stone sinks, brass taps, radiators and towel rails, stone flooring, tiles, bricks, floorboards, moulded skirting and architrave. Balustrades, chimney pots, garden edging, grates and timber; good quality antique chests of drawers, wardrobes, dressing tables, dining chairs, dressers, bookcases, mirrors, clocks, lamps radios and other unusual items.

BOYNETT & CO LTD
2 ASTON ROAD, CAMBRIDGE ROAD, BEDFORD,
BEDFORDSHIRE MK42 OJN
☎ (01234) 217788. OPEN 8.30 - 5 MON - FRI, 10 - 3 SAT.
Factory Shop • *Furniture/Soft Furnishings*
Curtain and upholstery fabrics manufactured by Boynett, who are wholesalers and distributors to the interior design market, are sold in this factory shop at discount prices for seconds and over-runs. Prices start at £2.50 per metre. There is also a large remnant bin.

D.S.& A.G. PRIGMORE & SON
MILL COTTAGE, MILL ROAD, COLMWORTH, BEDFORDSHIRE MK44 2NU
☎ (01234) 376264. OPEN 8 - 4 MON - FRI, 8 - 12 SAT.
Architectural Salvage • *DIY/Renovation*
Reclaimed building materials, oak and pine beams, slates, tiles, bricks, woodblock flooring, doors and other quality items including a good selection of 2-inch Tudor-style bricks. Also RSJs.

FREELANCE FABRICS
1 -3 HANCOCK PARADE, BUSHMEADS, LUTON, BEDFORDSHIRE L42 7SF
☎ (01582) 411522. OPEN 9.30 - 5 MON - FRI, 9 - 5 SAT, 10 - 4 SUN.
Permanent Discount Outlet • *Furniture/Soft Furnishings*
Part of a chain of shops selling well-known fabrics, curtain and upholstery weights, tracks, ready-made nets. Current fabrics are sold at reduced prices and there is a small range of end of line fabrics. For details of your local branch phone 01582 411522.

GOSSARD FACTORY SHOP
GROVEBURY ROAD, LEIGHTON BUZZARD, BEDFORDSHIRE LU7 8SN
☎ (01525) 851122. OPEN 9.30 - 5.30 MON - SAT.
Factory Shop • *Womenswear Only*
Factory shop sells seconds and discontinued ranges of Gossard and Berlei underwear including bras, briefs, suspender belts and bodies at discounted prices (no nightwear or long-line slips). Most of the stock is last year's trade catalogue styles at discounts of between 25%-75%. Large car park at rear of building; wheelchair ramp.

MATALAN
INTERCHANGE RETAIL PARK, AMPTHILL ROAD, KEMPSTON, BEDFORD, BEDFORDSHIRE MK42 7AZ
☎ (01234) 365077. OPEN 10 - 8 MON - FRI, 9 - 6 SAT, 11 - 5 SUN.
Permanent Discount Outlet • *Womenswear & Menswear Children* • *Household*
Matalan is a fashion and homewares value retailer giving customers what they claim to be unbeatable value for money with huge savings on a wide range of products including high quality fashionable clothing for men, women and children at up to 50% off high street prices. Matalan is situated out of town and stores are open seven days a week all year round.

NIGHTINGALES FACTORY SHOP
26 HIGH STREET, TODDINGTON, NEAR DUNSTABLE, HERTFORDSHIRE LU5 6BY
☎ (01525) 873888. OPEN 10 - 5 MON - SAT.
Factory Shop • *Womenswear Only*
The mail order company which sells smart but casual clothes for women - twill lined jackets in blazer stripes, button-through dresses, pinafore dresses, shirtwaisters, pure cotton blouses, lined short-sleeved jackets, polo neck sweaters, boucle jackets, blouses and skirt sets and cotton nightdresses - sells samples, ends of lines, seconds and material lengths here at discounted prices.

SIZE-UP
17 MARKET SQUARE, BIGGLESWADE, BEDFORDSHIRE SG18 8AS
☎ (01767) 314321. OPEN 9 - 5.30 MON - FRI, 8.30 - 5.30 SAT.
45 HIGH STREET, LEIGHTON BUZZARD LU7 7DN
☎ (01525) 379866. OPEN 9 - 5.30 MON - FRI, 8.30 - 5.30 SAT.
Permanent Discount Outlet • *Womenswear Only*
Top quality ladies outsize clothing, some of it from Evans, some own-label and some without labels. There are coats, dresses, suits and separates, some scarves and leisure wear. Some items cost less than half price. For example, Evans long pinstripe coat, £25, reduced from £70. All merchandise is new end of lines or last season's stock in good condition. Sizes 16-30.

THE VANITY BOX
16 CHURCH STREET, DUNSTABLE, BEDFORDSHIRE LU5 4RU
☎ (01582) 600969. OPEN 10 - 4.30 MON - SAT.
E-MAIL: enquiries@walterwright.com WEBSITE: www.walterwright.com
Dress Agency • *Womenswear Only*

Large shop on two levels which has been in operation for 24 years selling good as new seasonal ladies wear. Only items up to two years old accepted and 50% of stock is designer wear such as Jaeger, Mondi, Planet and Windsmoor in sizes 10 - 26. Both day and eveningwear, hats, shoes, jewellery and bags are also stocked. Twice yearly sales usually in July and January.

WALTER WRIGHT FACTORY SHOP
29 ALBION ROAD, LUTON, BEDFORDSHIRE LU2 0DS
☎ (01582) 721616. OPEN 10 - 6 MON - FRI BY APPOINTMENT.
Factory Shop • *Womenswear Only*

Walter Wright, family hat manufacturer since 1889, makes headwear for a variety of national and international couture milliners and dress houses, as well as one high quality partnership department store. If you are lucky, you may be able to purchase a hat from stock at a fraction of the retail price. The factory also serves the public with their own one-off couture service, normally reserved for the trade at far less cost than normal designer outlets.

Berkshire

BATHROOM WORLD
51 HIGH STREET, ASCOT, BERKSHIRE SL5 7GH
☎ (01344) 873366. FAX ☎ (01344) 626688. OPEN 9 - 6 MON - SAT,
UNTIL 8 WED. WEBSITE: www.bathrooms-showers.co.uk
Permanent Discount Outlet • *DIY/Renovation*

Fantastic, extensive bathroom showrooms pandering to any taste or budget. Many products are exclusive to the Group who are continually expanding their already large product portfolio. The buying power of the Group ensures that prices are always extremely competitive. Experienced staff and designers guide customers through styles, choices and specifications as part of a free service.

GD EVANS
331-333 HIGH STREET, SLOUGH, BERKSHIRE SL1 1TX
☎ (01753) 524188/535138. OPEN 9 - 5.30 MON - SAT.
Permanent Discount Outlet • *Electrical Equipment*

Established for over 40 years, this is the place to come for built-in appliances. Great discounts on new boxed, ex-display and discontinued models of up to 50%. Former exhibition Bosch, Neff and Siemens appliances. Phone for free brochure.

KID2KID
HIGH STREET, COOKHAM, BERKSHIRE SL6 9SH
☎ (01628) 531804. OPEN 10 - 5 MON - SAT.
Dress Agency • *Children*
Nearly-new designer clothes for children 0-10 years. Some of the most popular designer labels include Oilily, Cacherel, Ozona, Jean Bourget, Poivre Blanc, and Oshkosh, although quality items from Next, Marks & Spencer and Laura Ashley are also on sale. Prices range from £3 to £30, normally at least one-third of the original price. Own range of new children's clothes also available, as well as made-to-order bridesmaids dresses and they now also sell nearly-new baby equipment and maternity clothes. There is a large children's play area.

KNICKERBEAN
8 BARTHOLOMEW STREET, NEWBURY, BERKSHIRE RG14 5LL
☎ (01635) 529016. OPEN 9 - 5.30 MON - SAT.
Permanent Discount Outlet • *Furniture/Soft Furnishings*
Recommended by countless interior and decorating magazines and much loved by the bargain hunter, Knickerbean offers a continuous stream of stylish and sumptuous fabrics (the kind found at the Chelsea Harbour Design Centre and Decorex), but all at affordable prices. They originally specialised in top name UK designer fabrics, offering excess inventory, discontinued lines and slight imperfects, usually at about half price. You can still find many of these famous name bargains here, but now many of their fabrics are sourced directly from the same mills and manufacturers as the 'top names', both here and abroad. They offer the same top quality, in the latest colours and designs, at relatively lower prices, because they are buying and selling directly and cutting out the middlemen. Their selection of curtain and upholstery fabrics caters for both contemporary and traditional homes, with formal glazed chintzes, regal damasks, toiles de jouy and luxurious chenilles displayed next to basic neutrals, bright modern prints, airy voiles and earthy ethnic patterns. They also have large ranges of checks and stripes, self-patterned weaves, simple prints for a child's room as well as a huge range of upholstery brocades and tapestries. Prices start at £5.95 for prints to £19.95 and occasionally more for some their tapestries, chenilles and damasks. Knickerbean's outlets are bright and pleasant, more like an interior designer's showroom - there's no 'warehouse' feeling here. Their trained staff are helpful with all sorts of advice on fabrics, colours and interiors and they offer a complete home visit service with interior measuring and design advice. They have a hand finished making up service for curtains, blinds and loose covers, as well as a range of custom made furniture with footstools, sofas, etc. Twice yearly sales in January and June enable customers to snap up even bigger bargains.

BERKSHIRE 5

MARLBOROUGH TILES
BISHOP CENTRE, TAPLOW, MAIDENHEAD, BERKSHIRE SL6 ONY
☏ (01628) 667456. OPEN 10 - 5.30 MON - FRI, 9.30 - 5 SAT, 10.30 - 4.30 SUN.
Permanent Discount Outlet • *DIY/Renovation*
Wall and floor tiles from Marlborough and other top quality, specialist manufacturers. Seconds come mostly from Marlborough's own factory with discounts of up to 50% on first quality prices.

MATALAN
ROSE KILN LANE, READING, BERKSHIRE RG2 OSN
☏ (01189) 391958. OPEN 10 - 8 MON - FRI, 9 - 6 SAT, 11 - 5 SUN.
217A BATH ROAD, SLOUGH, BERKSHIRE SL1 4AA
☏ (01753) 487900. OPEN 10 - 8 MON - FRI, 9 - 6 SAT, 11 - 5 SUN.
Permanent Discount Outlet • *Womenswear & Menswear*
Children • *Household*
Matalan is a fashion and homewares value retailer giving customers what they claim to be unbeatable value for money with huge savings on a wide range of products including high quality fashionable clothing for men, women and children at up to 50% off high street prices. Matalan is situated out of town and stores are open seven days a week all year round.

SECONDS OUT DESIGNER COLLECTION
PEPPER MILL COURT, HIGH STREET, COOKHAM, BERKSHIRE SL6 9SQ
☏ (01628) 850371. OPEN 9.30 - 5 MON - SAT, 9.30 - 9 ON THUR.
Dress Agency • *Womenswear Only*
This shop, situated in a large timbered building in the riverside village of Cookham, has been in operation for 15 years, offering middle to upper range designer labels, including Laurel, Armani, Gucci, Prada, Versace and Chanel. There's casual wear and smart Ascot and wedding outfits, as well as evening wear displayed in spacious surroundings. All the clothes are colour coded by hangers. There is also a selection of brand new clearance stock and never-worn outfits and accessories including up to 80 hats at any one time, shoes and new stock handbags at unbelievable prices. Recently voted the best nearly-new in the Thames Valley and the number two Dress Agency in the UK.

SWITCHGEAR
20 ST LEONARD'S ROAD, WINDSOR, BERKSHIRE SL4 3BU
☏ (01753) 867438. OPEN 9.30 - 5 MON - SAT.
Dress Agency • *Womenswear Only*
Established in 1970, this dress agency offers many labels including Frank Usher, Betty Jackson, Gerry Weber, Paul Costelloe, Armani, Cerruti, Moschino, Versace, Patsy Seddon, Viyella, Jaeger, Mulberry and French Connection. Clothes for day, evening, Ascot, wedding outfits and leisurewear including designer jeans. There is also a good selection of hats, handbags, shoes, jewellery, scarves, belts and sunglasses, with a constant flow of reductions to two thirds of the original price. All garments are arranged in sizes from 8 - 20.

THE REALLY GOOD DEAL FASHION SALE
THE PAVILION, ASCOT RACECOURSE, ASCOT, BERKSHIRE
☎ (01367) 860017. ENQUIRIES: OPEN 9.30 - 6 MON - FRI.
Designer Sales • *Womenswear & Menswear* • *Children*
The Really Good Deal Fashion Sale takes place twice a year in the elegant Pavilion building at Ascot Racecourse. The summer sale, which is usually the last Friday and Saturday in May, features about 65 different companies; the winter sale, which is usually the first Friday and Saturday of November, features 95 different companies. The range of businesses taking part is firmly middle to upper middle end of the market, with well-known names like Mulberry, Amanda Wakeley, Kingshill Designer Collection, Dents, Paddy Campbell usually taking stands to sell their ends of lines and overstocks to the public at reduced prices. Almost anything you can think of is on sale here: coats, dresses, smart suits, wedding suits, evening wear, hats, shoes, boots, a variety of fabulous jewellery, stretch jeans, designer jeans, ties, men's shirts and sweaters, scarves, shawls, pashmina shawls, wraps, handbags, briefcases, gloves, wallets, swimwear, nightwear and although the emphasis is on womenswear there are usually one or two men's and childrenswear companies. Tickets to the event cost £5 and are only available in advance. The Sale is advertised in women's magazines three months prior to each event. To join the mailing list, phone the above telephone number or write to PO Box 4, Lechlade, Glos GL7 3YB and you will receive advance notification of each Sale and a ticket order form. The Sale is organised by the team behind this book, The Good Deal Directory.

THE STOCK EXCHANGE
1 HIGH STREET, SUNNINGHILL, ASCOT, BERKSHIRE SL5 9NQ
☎ (01344) 625420 . OPEN 9 - 5.30 MON - FRI, 9 - 4.30 SAT.
Dress Agency • *Womenswear & Menswear* • *Children*
Excellent selection of nearly-new designer and high street labels for ladies, men and children including Calvin Klein, Boss and Yves St Laurent. Rapid turnover of clothes, all very well presented, in this very busy shop with cheerful, helpful staff. Clothes are sold in season and all items are clean and up-to-date. Garments are displayed for four weeks at full price and then one week at half price. Also sell shoes, hats, handbags and belts.

TK MAXX

BROAD STREET MALL, BROAD STREET, READING, BERKSHIRE RG1 7QE
☎ (01189) 511117. OPEN 9 - 5.30 MON - FRI, 9 - 6 SAT.
THE OBSERVATORY SHOPPING CENTRE, SLOUGH
☎ (01753) 572550. OPEN 9 - 5.30 MON - FRI, 8 ON THUR, 9 - 6 SAT, 10.30 - 4.30 SUN.
6, THE MALL, THE KENNETT CENTRE, NEWBURY, BERKS. RG14 5EN
☎ (01635) 522343. OPEN 9 - 5.30 MON - WED, 9 - 7 THUR, 9 - 6 FRI, SAT, 11 - 5 SUN.

Permanent Discount Outlet • *Womenswear & Menswear Children* • *Household* • *Furniture/Soft Furnishings*

Based on an American concept, TK Maxx is situated in easily accessible, often centrally located stores and offers famous label goods with up to 60% savings off recommended retail prices. TK Maxx has fashion for the whole family - women's, men's and childrenswear - accessories, shoes, gifts, kitchenware and home goods. Everything in the store is branded with a choice of well-known high street names to designer labels, and while a small percentage might be clearly marked past season, the great majority of items in store are current season, current stock and still with phenomenal savings. There is a huge choice with 50,000 pieces in store and up to 10,000 new items arriving a week. The stores are simple and unfussy with wide aisles, shopping trolleys and baskets, and a spacious, functional feel to them but there are individual changing rooms, ramps for buggies and wheelchairs and plenty of staff on the shop floor. Every branch accepts all major credit and debit cards and has a liberal refund and return policy.

WALTON DESIGN LTD

129 HIGH STREET, HUNGERFORD, BERKSHIRE RG17 0DL
☎ (01488) 686838 . OPEN 9 - 6 MON - SAT, 10 - 4 SUN, 10 - 5 BANK HOLS.
45 SYCAMORE ROAD, AMERSHAM HP6 5EQ
☎ (01494) 723493 . OPEN 9 - 6 MON - SAT, 10 - 4 SUN, 10 - 5 BANK HOLS.
77A HIGH STREET, CHESHAM HP5 1BZ
☎ (01494) 774959. OPEN 9 - 6 MON - SAT, 10 - 4 SUN, 10 - 5 BANK HOLS.
186 HIGH STREET, BERKHAMSTED HP4 3AP
☎ (01442) 866426. OPEN 9 - 6 MON - SAT, 10 - 4 SUN, 10 - 5 BANK HOLS.

Permanent Discount Outlet • *Womenswear Only*

A chain of thirteen stores across the south of England selling well-known labels for women at greatly reduced prices. Current stock from high street stores might include Liz Claiborne, DKNY, Nougat, Ralph Lauren, Banana Republic, Calvin Klein and Tommy Hilfiger. New lines come in each week and are often one-offs, so regular customers know to buy things when they see them or risk missing out.

Buckinghamshire

ALEXON SALE SHOP
UNIT 17, CHILTERNS SHOPPING CENTRE, FROGMORE,
HIGH WYCOMBE, BUCKINGHAMSHIRE HP13 5ES
☎ (01494) 464214. OPEN 9 - 5.30 MON - SAT.
Permanent Discount Outlet • *Womenswear Only*
Alexon, Eastex, Ann Harvey and Calico from previous seasons at 40%-70% less than the original price; during sale time in January and June, the reductions are up to 70%. Stock includes separates, skirts, jackets, blouses.

BOOKENDS
22 HIGH STREET, MARLOW, BUCKINGHAMSHIRE SL7 1AW
☎ (01628) 890 007. OPEN 9.30 - 6 MON - SAT, 11 - 5 SUN.
Secondhand shop • *Food and Leisure*
Secondhand and damaged books and publishers' returns, as well as new and review copies, including recently published books, usually at half price or below.

BUMPSADAISY MATERNITY STYLE
33 WEST STREET, MARLOW, BUCKINGHAMSHIRE SL7 2LS
☎ (01628) 478487. OPEN 10 - 5.30 MON - SAT.
WEBSITE: www.bumpsadaisy.co.uk
Hire Shops • *Womenswear Only*
Franchised shops and home-based branches with large range of specialist maternity wear, from wedding outfits to ball gowns, to hire and to buy. Hire costs range from £30 to £100 for special occasion wear. To buy are lots of casual and business wear in sizes 8 - 18. For example, skirts £20-£70; dresses £40-£100. Also four branches run by young mums from their homes, specialising in hiring but also stocking a small retail range (Camberley, Edgbaston, Exeter and Southampton). Phone 0208-789 0329 for details.

DELLA FINCH DESIGNER SALE
AT THE ETHORP HOTEL, GERRARDS CROSS, BUCKINGHAMSHIRE
☎ 020-7834 9161. PHONE FOR INFORMATION ABOUT
TWICE YEARLY SALES.
Designer Sales • *Womenswear Only*
Della organises designer sales, selling top name clothes direct from the showroom at wholesale prices. The sales are unique in collecting top labels of next season clothes at least four months before they reach the shops. Some clothes are from the current season, and include evening wear, smart suits, blouses and swimwear in sizes 10 to 26. There's usually a special bargain rail from £5.
Phone and leave your name and full address for the mailing list.

ECHOES
NIGHTINGALES CORNER, LITTLE CHALFONT,
BUCKINGHAMSHIRE HP7 9PY
☎ (01494) 764174. OPEN 10 - 5.30 MON - SAT.
Dress Agency • *Womenswear Only*
A relaxed and friendly shop with a rapid turnover of stock. It offers exciting names at sensible prices. New and as-new designer names mingle together, surrounded by an eclectic mix of handbags, hats and jewellery.

HANG-UPS
1A THE SQUARE, LONG CRENDON, AYLESBURY,
BUCKINGHAMSHIRE HP18 9AA
☎ (01844) 201237. OPEN 9.30 - 5 TUE, THUR, FRI, SAT.
Dress Agency • *Womenswear Only*
Nearly new top designer labels offered at a fraction of their original price in sizes 8-22. For example, Nicole Farhi suit, worth about £350 would sell for £65. Larger sizes of Elvi clothes available. Free parking.

KINGSHILL DESIGNER COLLECTION
THE STUDIO, LITTLE KINGSHILL GRANGE, GREAT MISSENDEN,
BUCKINGHAMSHIRE HP16 0DZ
☎ (01494) 890555.
Designer Sales • *Womenswear Only*
Designer fashion mail order company which holds regular discount sales in different parts of the country. Designers on sale can include Paul Costelloe, MaxMara, Paddy Campbell and Amanda Wakeley. Phone to be put on the mailing list.

MATALAN
103 WATLING STREET, BLETCHLEY, MILTON KEYNES,
BUCKINGHAMSHIRE MK1 1HS
☎ (01908) 625400. OPEN 10 - 8 MON - FRI, 9 - 6 SAT, 10 - 4 SUN.
Permanent Discount Outlet • *Womenswear & Menswear*
Children • *Household*
Matalan is a fashion and homewares value retailer giving customers what they claim to be unbeatable value for money with huge savings on a wide range of products including high quality fashionable clothing for men, women and children at up to 50% off high street prices. Matalan is situated out of town and stores are open seven days a week all year round.

NIPPERS
CODDIMOOR FARM, WHADDON, MILTON KEYNES,
BUCKINGHAMSHIRE MK17 OIR
☎ (01908) 504506. FAX (01908) 505636. WEBSITE: www.nippers.co.uk
OPENING HOURS VARY SO PHONE FIRST.
Permanent Discount Outlet • *Children*

Nippers, the nursery equipment and toy specialists, operate from previously redundant buildings in rural areas around the country. They offer easy parking, no queues and personal service. This is on top of competitive prices on prams, cots, pushchairs, car seats, outdoor play equipment and toys, some of which are new, some seconds or secondhand and some ends of lines. Prices are low because they avoid the high overheads of traditional retail outlets and also because the successful growth of a number of branches means they can now buy in bulk and negotiate good deals. Customers are invited to try out the merchandise while the children look at the animals, mostly sheep, chicken and pigs. Also offers many brand leaders at discount, including Mamas & Papas, Cosatto, Britax, Maclaren and Bebe Confort, plus Fisher-Price and Little Tikes. You can try out the car seats in your car and there is usually a pram/pushchair repair service on site.

NUMBER TWENTY
20 HIGH STREET, OLD AMERSHAM, BUCKINGHAMSHIRE HP7 ODJ
☎ (01494) 432043. OPEN 9.30 - 5.30 TUE - SAT.
Dress Agency • *Womenswear Only*

Spacious shop in historic market town of Old Amersham which works in partnership with a Knightsbridge dress agency. Labels stocked include Chanel, Caroline Charles, Cerruti, Mondi, MaxMara, Mulberry, Joseph, Jaeger, Jasper Conran, Betty Barclay, Burberry, Episode, Escada and Armani.

ROHAN DESIGNS PLC
1 - 3 KNEBWORTH GATE, GIFFORD PARK, MILTON KEYNES,
BUCKINGHAMSHIRE MK14 5QD
☎ (01908) 615407. OPEN 9.30 - 5.30 MON - SAT.
Factory Shop • *Womenswear & Menswear* • *Sportswear & Equipment*

High performance fabrics with unique design features ranging from waterproof jackets to the famous Rohan 'bags'. Seconds and discontinued items available at discount prices. Also sells shirts, trousers, T-shirts and fleeces.

SILVER EDITIONS
PO BOX 16, CHALFONT ST GILES, BUCKINGHAMSHIRE HP8 4AU
☎ (01753) 888810/888830 FAX. MAIL ORDER
E-MAIL: sales@silver-editions.co.uk WEBSITE: www.silver-editions.co.uk
Permanent Discount Outlet • *Household*

Specialises in selling fine English sterling silver and silver-plated gifts and cutlery at wholesale prices, often half the sum for the same items in high street shops. Their catalogue features an exceptionally wide range of gifts and cutlery at prices from £2.50 to several thousand pounds. Canteens of cutlery, photo frames, desk sets, serving pieces and children's christening gifts are just a few of the categories on offer. The catalogue also carries the complete range of Hagerty silver cleaning products. Write to the address above for a copy of the catalogue.

THE CHANGING ROOM
50 HIGH STREET, CHALFONT ST GILES, BUCKINGHAMSHIRE HP8 4QQ
☎ (01494) 875933. OPEN 10 -5 TUE - SAT.
Dress Agency • *Womenswear Only*

Nearly-new fashions ranging from names such as Gerry Weber and Basler to Paul Costelloe and Armani. Generally caters to the upper end of the market. Clothes sold at one-third of the original price and bargains can always be found. Clothing tends to be very seasonal with a swift turnover of stock. Wonderful selection of hats and a wide range of special occasion wear in all sizes. A fascinating little shop - not to be missed if you like hunting for bargains.

THE CHILTERN BREWERY
NASH LEE ROAD, TERRICK, AYLESBURY, BUCKINGHAMSHIRE HP17 OTQ
☎ (01296) 613647. OPEN 9 - 5 MON - SAT.
Food and Drink Discounters

Three different types of bitter are manufactured here: Chiltern and Beechwood bitters, and Three Hundreds Old Ale. Or take your own pint container and fill with beer for £1.35 per pint. All the beers are draught except for John Hampdens Ale and Three Hundreds, which is both bottled and draught. Also stocks mustards and chutney with beer, marmalade with malt, pickled onions with hops and fruit cake with barley wine. Also three new beer sausages and beer shampoo. Free parking; museum; conducted tours on Saturdays - phone first.

THE GO BETWEEN
34B THE MARKET PLACE, OLNEY, BUCKINGHAMSHIRE MK46 4AJ
☎ (01234) 241193. OPEN 10 - 4.30 MON - SAT.
Dress Agency • *Womenswear Only*

Designer labels from Escada and Mondi to Nicole Farhi, Betty Barclay and Jaeger. Also stocks modern high street chainstore garments from Laura Ashley, Marks & Spencer and Wallis. There is a full range of accessories, shoes, hats, jewellery, bric a brac, maternity wear and perfume.

TK MAXX
THE OBSERVATORY CENTRE, SLOUGH, BUCKINGHAMSHIRE
☎ (01753) 572550. OPEN 9 - 5.30 MON - FRI, 9 - 8 THUR, 9 - 6 SAT, 10.30 - 4.30 SUN.
Permanent Discount Outlet • *Womenswear & Menswear*
Children • *Household* • *Furniture/Soft Furnishings*

Based on an American concept, TK Maxx is situated in easily accessible, often centrally located stores and offers famous label goods with up to 60% savings off recommended retail prices. TK Maxx has fashion for the whole family - women's, men's and childrenswear - accessories, shoes, gifts, kitchenware and home goods. Everything in the store is branded with a choice of well-known high street names to designer labels, and while a small percentage might be clearly marked past season, the great majority of items in store are current season, current stock and still with phenomenal savings. There is a huge choice with 50,000 pieces in store and up to 10,000 new items arriving a week. The stores are simple and unfussy with wide aisles, shopping trolleys and baskets, and a spacious, functional feel to them but there are individual changing rooms, ramps for buggies and wheelchairs and plenty of staff on the shop floor. Every branch accepts all major credit and debit cards and has a liberal refund and return policy.

WORLD OF WOOD
7 CORNWALL PLACE, BUCKINGHAM, BUCKINGHAMSHIRE MK18 1SB
☎ (01280) 822003. OPEN 9 - 5.30 MON - SAT.
Permanent Discount Outlet • *Furniture/Soft Furnishings*

Furniture for the home which offers everything except the bath! All the furniture is designed by craftsmen in Italy and much of it is made from original wood reclaimed from houses in Italy, mainly Verona, and made by small Italian manufacturers. If you're looking for modern glass-topped tables to massive semi-distressed sideboards, World of Wood has something to offer at prices which are very competitive, and in a variety of woods: chestnut, oak, cherry and walnut, to name just a few. For example, there are 200 different solid dining chairs from which to choose at prices starting from £90. You can choose your own finish for the wood or have a piece custom made.

Cambridgeshire

BARNEYS FACTORY OUTLETS
38-42 MILL ROAD, CAMBRIDGE, CAMBRIDGESHIRE CB1 2AD
☎ (01223) 369596. OPEN 9 - 6 MON - SAT, 11 - 5 SUN.
Permanent Discount Outlet • *Womenswear & Menswear*

Up to 60% off designer labels such as Calvin Klein, Ralph Lauren, Wrangler, Yves St Laurent and Marco Polo for both men and women. Closed due to fire as we went to press, but there are plans to re-open on the same site.

BOOKSALE
HEREWARD CENTRE, PETERBOROUGH, CAMBRIDGESHIRE PE1 1TA
☎ (01733) 558659. OPEN 9 - 5.30 MON - SAT.
Permanent Discount Outlet • *Food and Leisure*
Booksale now boasts more than 100 shops throughout the UK: call 0121 313 6000 for details of your nearest store. It sells books, stationery, paints, tapes, CDs and CDRoms, videos, all at enormously discounted prices. Paperbacks and hardbacks from £1.99p, children's books 49p; videos 99p, clip frames 99p - £19.95, posters £1.50 - £6.99 and classical CDs from £3.99.

CATALOGUE BARGAIN SHOP
51 WEST STREET, WISBECH, CAMBRIDGESHIRE PE13 2LY
☎ (01945) 584327. OPEN 9 - 4.30 MON - SAT, 10.30 - 4.30 SUN.
Permanent Discount Outlet • *Womenswear & Menswear Children* • *Household* • *Electrical Equipment*
Catalogue Bargain Shop is a growing national chain of stores which obtains the majority of its goods from mail order giants Great Universal and Kays, and offers a range of clothing for all the family, a wide selection of shoes, bed linen, household goods, electrical equipment and hundreds of other catalogue items at very competitive prices. The merchandise consists of ends of ranges and previous season's stock for which there is no longer storage space when the catalogues change.

CHARLTON RECYCLED AUTOPARTS LTD
VEHICLE RECYCLING CENTRE, ELY ROAD, WATERBEACH, CAMBRIDGESHIRE CB5 9PG
☎ (01223) 863386. OPEN 8.30 - 6 MON - FRI, 8.30 - 5 SAT.
Permanent Discount Outlet • *DIY/Renovation*
Sells car spares and accessories, but it's not like any usual spares or salvage yard! All parts have been checked, tagged and stored in a warehouse on a computer-controlled inventory. Examples of prices include new Nissan branded hub caps for a Micra model, £20. The shop is clean, efficient and all parts have a 101-day guarantee. Although the main business is used car parts, they also often stock brand new parts, either from bankrupt or flood damaged stock. Stock spare parts for vehicles from a Mini to a Mercedes.

CHELFORD FABRICS
CHELFORD HOUSE, STATION ROAD, GAMLINGAY, CAMBRIDGESHIRE SG19 3HQ
☎ (01767) 651888. FAX (01767) 651886. OPEN 9.30 - 5.30 MON - SAT.
Permanent Discount Outlet • *Furniture/Soft Furnishings*
A large, out-of-town showroom selling only perfect regular curtain and upholstery fabrics at greatly reduced prices, ranging from £2.99 a yard to £11.99 a yard and including everything from glazed cotton chintzes to prints, tapestries and damasks from all leading manufacturers. Choose from more than 4,000 rolls,

order from the extensive range of manufacturers pattern books or buy own-brand fabrics which are one-third less expensive than branded material. A full high quality making-up service is available. Curtain accessories, rails, tapes and hooks are also on sale at reduced prices. There is also a huge selection of towels, cushions, pillows and duvets. There is another branch in Harpenden, Hertfordshire.

CIRCLES OF YAXLEY
CHAPEL STUDIO, CHAPEL STREET, YAXLEY, PETERBOROUGH, CAMBRIDGESHIRE PE7 3LN
☎ (01733) 242539. OPEN 10 - 4 MON - SAT.
Dress Agency • *Womenswear Only* • *Children*
Circles sells ladies and children's wear. Eveningwear is stocked all year round, as are accessories such as hats, handbags and belts. Sizes range from 8 to 24. For children, labels include Marks & Spencer, Laura Ashley and Next. There are sales in January and July, during which everything except evening wear is reduced by 25%, with 40% off promotions for adult clothes during February and August.

COBBLERS
41 BRIDGE STREET, PETERBOROUGH, CAMBRIDGESHIRE PE1 1HA
☎ (01733) 891640. OPEN 9 - 5.30 MON - SAT.
Factory Shop • *Womenswear & Menswear*
Shoes from Evan Picone, Nickles, Doc Martens, Cobblers, Doc Martens Youths, sizes 2-6, £42.99; adults, £44.99; Trickers soft leather bootees, £49.99 from £63.99. Also half-price sample shoes. Ladies sizes range from three and a half to nine. For example Trickers gold leather flatties, £39.99, reduced from £53.99; Bandonino black suede shoes with buckle, £24.99 from £49.99. Leather handbags, £68.99 reduced from £91.99.

COUNTRYWIDE INTERIORS
8 TOWER CLOSE, HUNTINGDON, CAMBRIDGESHIRE PE18 7DT
☎ (01480) 52440. OPEN 9.30 - 5 MON - SAT, CLOSED WED.
Permanent Discount Outlet • *Furniture/Soft Furnishings*
Furniture including beds, carpets and three-piece suites at substantial discounts. Up to 50% off bedroom, lounge, dining room and cane furniture. Underlay is from £2.40 a square yard.

DUNELM FABRIC SHOP
UNIT 7, STUKELEY MEADOWS TRADING ESTATE, STUKELEY ROAD, HUNTINGDON, CAMBRIDGESHIRE PE18 6EB
☎ (01480) 417807. OPEN 9 - 5.30 MON - THUR, SAT, 9 - 8 FRI, 10 - 4 SUN.
MILL SHOP, 35 WESTGATE, PETERBOROUGH PE1 1PZ
☎ (01733) 349848. OPEN 9 - 5.30 MON - SAT.
Permanent Discount Outlet • *Household*
Part of a chain of shops based in the Midlands selling brand-name and chain-store curtains, masses of bedlinen, towels, wickerware, pictures and frames, all at competitive prices.

FABRIC WAREHOUSE
UNIT 15, LONDON ROAD INDUSTRIAL ESTATE, SAWSTON,
CAMBRIDGESHIRE CB2 4EE
☎ (01223) 832810. OPEN 9 - 5.30 MON - FRI, 9 - 5 SAT, 10 - 4 SUN.
Permanent Discount Outlet • *Furniture/Soft Furnishings*
Furnishing fabric, cushions and foam. Good range of printed furnishing fabrics from £4.99, with a bargain selection from £2.50; Jeff Banks prints, £8.99 instead of £16.99; wonderful Italian damasks, £13.99, usual price £18; cotton damask half price at £10.99; cotton muslins, £4.99 instead of £6.99; Belgian flat weaves and tapestries, £10.99; polycotton lining, £2.50 for 54" width. They also sell curtain rails, tiebacks, fringing, braid, chunky tassel tie backs and have their own in-house curtain making service at competitive prices.

GALLOWAY & PORTER LTD
THE PADDOCKS, CHERRY HINTON ROAD, CAMBRIDGE,
CAMBRIDGESHIRE.
☎ (01223) 367876. RING FOR SALE DATES.
MAIN BRANCH: 30 SIDNEY STREET, CAMBRIDGE CB2 3HS
☎ (01223) 367876. OPEN 8.45 - 5.30 MON - FRI, 9 - 5.15 SAT.
Permanent Discount Outlet • *Food and Leisure*
Regular book warehouse sales are held at the Cherryhinton outlet about once a month on a Saturday from 9 - 5 at which most books cost £1, regardless of the original price. There are new hardback copies in the huge variety of tomes, covering many subjects including children's. Free parking. The other branch stocks secondhand as well as new discounted books.

MATALAN
EAST STATION ROAD, PETERBOROUGH, CAMBRIDGESHIRE PE2 8AA
☎ (01733) 341229. OPEN 10 - 8 MON - FRI, 9 - 6 SAT, 11 - 5 SUN.
Permanent Discount Outlet • *Womenswear & Menswear*
Children • *Household*
Matalan is a fashion and homewares value retailer giving customers what they claim to be unbeatable value for money with huge savings on a wide range of products including high quality fashionable clothing for men, women and children at up to 50% off high street prices. Matalan is situated out of town and stores are open seven days a week all year round.

MONSOON
14 ROSE CRESCENT, CAMBRIDGE, CAMBRIDGESHIRE CB2 3CC
☎ (01223) 361507. OPEN 9.30 - 5.30 MON - SAT.
Factory Shop • *Womenswear Only*
Medium-sized outlet selling marked down current stock for some of the year as well as last year's stock and discontinued lines, including jewellery. There are also outlets at Birmingham, Bicester Village and Clarks Village in Street, Somerset.

PRETTY BRIDES
TOWN STREET, UPWELL, WISBECH, CAMBRIDGESHIRE PE14 9DA
☎ (01945) 772592. OPEN 10 - 8 MON AND THUR, 10 - 5 TUE, FRI, SAT.
Permanent Discount Outlet • *Womenswear Only*
Wedding dress shop which offers discounts on styles which have been discontinued by the manufacturer and therefore cannot be ordered in again. Also offers a limited amount of hire.

QD STORES
62 BURLEIGH STREET, CAMBRIDGE, CAMBRIDGESHIRE CB1 1DG
☎ (01223) 323174. OPEN 9 - 5.30 MON - SAT, 11 - 5 SUN.
Permanent Discount Outlet • *Womenswear & Menswear Household* • *Children*
Discount shop selling a mixture of clothes, household textiles, ceramics, kitchenware, knitting wool, garden tools, curtains, toys, stationery, dusters, Christmas decorations, masking tape, lingerie and a host of other items. Stock changes regularly because the low prices mean a quick turnover. Some items are seconds or end of season stock from the major chain stores.

RAMSEY PAINT COMPANY
19A EAST STREET, ST IVES, CAMBRIDGESHIRE PE17 2NE
☎ (01480) 465002. OPEN 8 - 5 MON - FRI, 9 - 12 SAT.
16 LITTLE WHYTE, RAMSEY, CAMBRIDGESHIRE PE17 1DS
☎ (01487) 710876. OPEN 8 - 5 MON - FRI, 9 - 12 SAT.
Permanent Discount Outlet • *DIY/Renovation*
Paints, paint accessories, wood stains and wallpapers at discounted prices. Stocks most major paint brands including Crown and holds 100 wallpaper books from which you can order at discounts of 20%. Mainly caters for the trade, but will serve the public, too. More than 6,000 colours from which to choose.

REMARK
16 TRESHAM ROAD, ORTON, SOUTHGATE, PETERBOROUGH, CAMBRIDGESHIRE PE2 6SG
☎ (01733) 231639. OPEN 8 - 6 MON - FRI.
Permanent Discount Outlet • *Electrical Equipment*
Sells new and reconditioned telecommunication systems at competitive prices. Can install equipment, voice and data networks, arrange service and maintenance.

CAMBRIDGESHIRE 17

ROTATIONS
33 ELM ROAD, FOLKSWORTH, NEAR STILTON, PETERBOROUGH, CAMBRIDGESHIRE PE7 3SX
☎ (01733) 241100. OPEN 10 - 4.30 TUE, WED, FRI, SAT, 1 - 7 THUR.
Dress Agency • *Womenswear & Menswear*
Nearly-new garments featuring designer labels and quality high street brands in sizes ranging from 8-20. There is also a small selection of wedding dresses, bridesmaids dresses, mother of the bride outfits and accessories, hats, belts, handbags, jewellery, shoes and scarves and some menswear.

SECOND GLANCE
4 BAR LANE, STAPLEFORD, CAMBRIDGE, CAMBRIDGESHIRE CB2 5BJ
☎ (01223) 844677. OPEN 10 - 5 MON - SAT.
Dress Agency • *Womenswear Only*
Sells a range of nearly-new labels from Next, Laura Ashley and M&S to Jaeger and Escada with a wide variety of dresses, ballgowns, suits, separates. A small selection of hats also available.

SIZE-UP
39 BROAD STREET, MARCH, CAMBRIDGESHIRE PE15 8PT
☎ (01354) 658656. OPEN 9 - 5.30 MON - THUR, 9 - 6 FRI, 9 - 8.30 SAT.
2 HIGH STREET, ST NEOTS PE19 1JA
☎ (01480) 403963. OPEN 9 - 5.30 MON - SAT.
5 MARKET PLACE, ELY CB7 4NB
☎ (01353) 669143. OPEN 9 - 5.30 MON - FRI, 8.30 - 5.30 SAT. 13
ST IVES PE17 4AD
☎ (01480) 493204. OPEN 9 - 5.30 MON - FRI, 8.30 - 5.30 SAT.
13 MARKET PLACE, WISBECH
☎ (01945) 584869. OPEN 9 - 5.30 MON - SAT.
Permanent Discount Outlet • *Womenswear Only*
Top quality ladies outsize clothing, some of it from Evans, some own-label and some without labels. There are coats, dresses, suits and separates, some scarves and leisure wear. Some items cost less than half price. For example, Evans long pinstripe coat, £25, reduced from £70. All merchandise is new end of lines or last season's stock in good condition. Sizes 16-30.

SOLOPARK PLC
STATION ROAD, NR PAMPISFORD, CAMBRIDGESHIRE CB2 4HB
☎ (01223) 834663. OPEN 8 - 5 MON - THUR, 8 - 4 FRI, SAT, 9 - 1 SUN.
Architectural Salvage • *DIY/Renovation*
Reclaimed bricks including soft reds, Suffolk whites, Cambridge stocks, Tudors, roofing tiles, slates, timbers, oak beams, doors, wood block, flooring, railway sleepers, chimney pots, York stone, paviors, granite setts, gates, fireplaces, statuary, garden furniture, etc.

SPOILS
5-7 SUSSEX STREET, CAMBRIDGE, CAMBRIDGESHIRE CB1 1PA
☎ (01223) 316518. OPEN 9 - 5.30 MON - SAT.
41 - 42 THE GRAFTON CENTRE, CAMBRIDGE CB1 1PS
☎ (01223) 353543. OPEN 9 - 5.30 MON - SAT.
Permanent Discount Outlet • *Household*
General domestic glassware, non-stick bakeware, kitchen gadgets, ceramic oven-to-tableware, textiles, cutting boards, aluminium non-stick cookware, bakeware, plastic kitchenware, plastic storage, woodware, coffee pots/makers, furniture, mirrors and picture frames. Rather than being discounted, all the merchandise is very competitively priced - in fact, the company carry out competitors' checks frequently in order to monitor pricing. With 38 branches, the company is able to buy in bulk and thus negotiate very good prices.

ST IVES TILES
HIGH STREET, BLUNTISHAM, HUNTINGDON,
CAMBRIDGESHIRE PE28 3LD
☎ (01487) 840471. OPEN 8.30 - 5.30 MON - FRI, 9 - 4 SAT, 10 - 1 SUN.
Permanent Discount Outlet • *DIY/Renovation*
Importers of top quality floor and wall tiles, mainly Italian and Spanish terracotta and quarry style and sold at discounts of one third on selected lines. Warehouse-type shop with a wide selection of tiles displayed and laid to give you some idea of what they look like. One reader saved 50% on their floor tiles here, having been quoted £600 elsewhere.

STAGE 2
SAVILLE ROAD, PETERBOROUGH, CAMBRIDGESHIRE PE3 6PR
☎ (01733) 263308. OPEN 10 - 8 MON - FRI, 9 - 6 SAT,
10 - 4 SUN, BANK HOLIDAYS.
Permanent Discount Outlet • *Womenswear & Menswear*
Electrical Equipment
Sells discontinued lines from Freeman's catalogues. The full range is carried, but stock depends on what has not been sold at full price from the catalogue itself, or has been returned or the packaging is damaged or soiled. Clothing discounts range from about 50% - 65%. There are also household items and electrical equipment.

SWAINE ADENEY BRIGG,
PAPWORTH LEATHER GOODS
ANSTEY HALL, MARIS LANE, TRUMPINGTON, CAMBRIDGE,
CAMBRIDGESHIRE.
☎ (01223) 843444. OPEN 10 - 5.30 MON - SAT, 11 - 4 SUN.
Permanent Discount Outlet • *Food and Leisure*
Handmade business cases and luggage in leather and leather trim, all manufactured in their own factory. Goods offered for sale here are discontinued lines or

seconds in briefcases, executive cases, folios, document cases, attache cases, suitcases, suit carriers, travel bags, holdalls, umbrellas, and small leather goods.

THE CURTAIN EXCHANGE
16 NORFOLK STREET, CAMBRIDGE, CAMBRIDGESHIRE CB1 2LF.
☎ (01223) 312500. OPEN 10 - 5 MON - SAT.
RELOCATING. RING 01376 561199 FOR NEW TELEPHONE NUMBER AND ADDRESS.

Secondhand shops • *Furniture/Soft Furnishings*

The Curtain Exchange is a franchised group of shops selling beautiful top quality secondhand curtains, blinds, pelmets, etc at between one-third and one half of the brand new price. Their stock comes from a variety of sources: people who are moving house; people who have curtains made and then feel they are wrong for the room; show houses; where the builder wants to recoup some of his outgoings; interior designers' mistakes. Stock changes constantly and ranges from rich brocades, damasks and velvets to chintzes, linens and cottons. Designer names include Colefax & Fowler, Designers Guild, Laura Ashley, Warner, Sanderson, Osborne & Little, Fortuny and Bennison. A team of fitters and alteration experts are available if required. They offer a 24-hour availability. The Curtain Exchange also supply bespoke ranges with samples of curtains hanging. These fabrics are chosen from suppliers all over the world and are an excellent buy. They also offer ready made curtains designed exclusively for them which come in lengths up to 305cm (120"). These are outstanding value, e.g. 80" wide, 120" drop start at £175 including VAT.

THE DRESS AGENCY (ST IVES)
1 THE BROADWAY, ST IVES, HUNTINGDON, CAMBRIDGESHIRE PE17 4BX
☎ (01480) 464 952.

Womenswear & Menswear • *Children*

Designer clothes and contemporary fashions up to size 26. Young designer menswear, dinner suits, ladies' eveningwear, mother of the bride outfits, special occasion hats, dancewear and children's clothing.

THE FACTORY SHOE SHOP
48 WOOLLARDS LANE, GREAT SHELFORDS, CAMBRIDGESHIRE CB2 5LZ
☎ (01223) 846723. OPEN 9.30 - 5.30 MON - FRI, 9.30 - 5 SAT.

Permanent Discount Outlet • *Womenswear & Menswear*

Slight seconds and clearance lines of Van-Dal and Holmes shoes for men and women, as well as other makes. Typical discounts include shoes which would normally cost £55 reduced to £32.50.

THE FROCK EXCHANGE
7 HIGH STREET, FENSTANTON, CAMBRIDGESHIRE PE18 9LQ
☎ (01480) 461187. OPEN 9 - 5 TUE - SAT.
Dress Agency • *Hire Shop* • *Womenswear & Menswear*

The Frock Exchange opened its doors in 1981, the first dress agency in East Anglia. 1983 saw the introduction of ballgown hire, again a first for the area. Esquire, a men's formal occasion wear business to buy or to hire, was opened in 1984. Originally in premises facing the ladies shop, Esquire has now moved above the Frock Exchange and complements the evening and special occasion wear which is such a feature of this popular and busy shop. Hat hire completes the services on offer. The Frock Exchange has been featured on The Clothes Show, Look East and About Anglia.

THE FROCK EXCHANGE
2 BAKERS MEWS, EAST STREET, KIMBOLTON, HUNTINGDON, CAMBRIDGESHIRE PE18 OHJ
☎ (01480) 860920. OPEN 10 - 5 TUE - FRI, 10 - 4 SAT.
Dress Agency • *Womenswear Only*

Located in the charming Cambridgeshire village of Kimbolton, they stock very good quality ladies wear and accessories and hire out evening wear upstairs. Mostly German designer labels such as Bianca, Ara Fink but also includes Nicole Farhi and Paul Costelloe.

THE WINDOW SCENE
105 NORFOLK STREET, WISBECH, CAMBRIDGESHIRE PE13 2LD
☎ (01945) 474335. OPEN 10 - 5 MON - FRI, CLOSED WED, 10 - 4 SAT.
Permanent Discount Outlet • *Furniture/Soft Furnishings*

Tiny, back-street shop crammed with everything to do with soft furnishings including curtain fabrics, velvets, chintzes, nets, blind tapes, linings, heading tapes, foam, track, upholstery fabrics, at very competitive prices. Brands sold include Moygashel, Nouveau, Corniche, Harmony, Prestigious, SMD Textiles, Ashley Wilde, Glen Fabrics and also Anna & Robert Swaffer.

THE WORKS
BRIDGE STREET, PETERBOROUGH, CAMBRIDGESHIRE PE1 1DW
☎ (01733) 358496. OPEN 9 - 6 MON - SAT, 8 ON THUR, 10 - 4 SUN.
Permanent Discount Outlet • *Food and Leisure*

One of 138 branches of this remainders company for books, particularly travel guides and glossy hardbacks, cards, gifts, toys, ornaments, gift wrap, stationery, videos and CDs, all discounted by at least 50%. Phone 0121 313 6000 for your local branch.

TILE CLEARING HOUSE
UNIT 1, BRASSEY CLOSE, LINCOLN ROAD, PETERBOROUGH, CAMBRIDGESHIRE PE1 2A2
☎ (01733) 553222. OPEN 8 - 6 MON - FRI, 9 - 6 SAT, 10 - 4 SUN.
Permanent Discount Outlet • *DIY/Renovation*
Over 500 ranges of top quality ceramic wall and floor tiles permanently in stock, plus a comprehensive range of grouts, adhesives, tools and accessories to complete the job. By buying direct from the manufacturer and passing the savings on to the customer, their prices are very competitive. Moreover, everything you see is in stock, so there's no waiting for orders to be processed. Save up to 75% on manufacturers' recommended selling prices.

Cheshire

A C COMPUTER WAREHOUSE
MOTTRAM STREET, MIDDLE HILLGATE, STOCKPORT, CHESHIRE SK1 3PA
☎ (0161) 476 2220. OPEN 9.30 - 6 MON - FRI, 10 - 5 SAT. MAIL ORDER.
Permanent Discount Outlet • *Electrical Equipment*
Computers, monitors, scanners and printers, all at competitive prices. Phone for a product and price list.

ADIDAS
MCARTHURGLEN OUTLET VILLAGE CHESHIRE OAKS, ELLESMERE PORT, SOUTH WIRRAL, CHESHIRE L65 9JJ
☎ (0151) 355 6893. OPEN 10 - 8 MON - THUR, 9 - 6 SAT, 10 - 5 SUN.
Factory Shop in a Factory Shopping Village
Womenswear & Menswear • *Sportswear & Equipment*
End of season products at 30% to 70% off RRP. Footwear and accessories such as bags, shinpads etc. Saloman outdoor wear and the Adidas golf range also stocked. Regular promotions run throughout the year.

ALLWEIS CHINA AND CRYSTAL
84 HIGH STREET, CHEADLE, CHESHIRE
☎ (0161) 428 7571. FAX ☎ (0161) 7959814. OPEN 9 - 5.30 MON - SAT.
Permanent Discount Outlet • *Household*
Branded china and cutlery at discount including Waterford, Wedgwood, Royal Doulton, Royal Worcester and many others. None of the stock is seconds and discounts start at 10%. Wedding lists a speciality. Names stocked in the past include Alessi, Arthur Price, Boda Nova, Bugatti, George Butler, Oneida, Rosenthal, Villeroy & Boch, and Wilkens. Many of the designers in cutlery are modern Italian and there is a variety ranging from stainless steel to silver plates.

BANNER LTD
BANNER HOUSE, GREG STREET, REDDISH, STOCKPORT,
CHESHIRE SK5 7BT
☎ (0161) 474 7600. OPEN 10 - 4 MON - THUR, 10 - 3 FRI.
Factory Shop • *Womenswear & Menswear* • *Children*
Manufactures clothes for all the family destined for top high street department stores. Seconds, overmakes and returns are sold here at discount prices, although only about 20% of the stock consists of seconds. About 80% of the merchandise sold here is made by the factory, with a further 20% manufactured within the company. Large selection of schoolwear.

BED & BATH WORKS
CHESHIRE, OAKS DESIGNER OUTLET VILLAGE, JUNCTION 10 OF M53, KINSEY ROAD, NEAR ELLESMERE PORT, CHESHIRE L65 9JJ
☎ (0151) 356 7377. OPEN 10 - 8 MON - THURS, 10 - 6 FRI, 9 - 6,
SAT, 11 - 5 SUNS AND BANK HOLS. 10 - 6 IN WINTER MONTHS.
Factory Shop in a Factory Shopping Village • *Household*
Bed & Bath Works sells bedlinen and towels from famous-name companies. Bedding companies include Vantona, Horrocks, Janet Reger, Dreams and Drapes; towels are by Christys; duvets and pillows by Fogarty and Trendsetter. There are also duvet covers, soaps, brushes, sponges, bath mitts, bath mats, flannels, cushions and throws by Opalcraft as well as lighting by Shades Unlimited. Discounts range from 30% upwards.

BENETTON
CHESHIRE OAKS OUTLET VILLAGE, ADDRESS AND OPENING HOURS ABOVE
☎ (0151) 357 3131.
Factory Shop in a Factory Shopping Village
Womenswear & Menswear • *Children*
The usual well-known range of Benetton clothes for men, women and children at discounts of up to 50%. Most are ends of lines, end of season and samples, with a few seconds.

BIG L FACTORY OUTLET
CHESHIRE OAKS OUTLET VILLAGE, ADDRESS AND OPENING HOURS ABOVE
☎ (0151) 356 8484.
Factory Shop in a Factory Shopping Village • *Womenswear & Menswear*
Men's and women's Levi jeans, jackets, cord and Sherpa fleece jackets, T-shirts and shirts but no children's, all at discount prices.

BIRTHDAYS
CHESHIRE OAKS OUTLET VILLAGE, ADDRESS AND OPENING HOURS ABOVE
☎ (0151) 356 7393.
Factory Shopping Village • *Household*
Cards, notelets, stationery sets, colouring books, soft toys, photo albums, picture frames, gifts, giftwrap, tissue paper, party packs, Christmas crackers, string puppets, fairy lights all at discounts of up to 30%. Some are special purchases, some seconds.

BRAMHALL INTERIOR DESIGN
8 -10 BUXTON ROAD, STOCKPORT, CHESHIRE SK2 6NU
☎ (0161) 477 7173. OPEN 9 - 5 MON - SAT.
Permanent Discount Outlet • *Furniture/Soft Furnishings*
Sells fabrics and wallpapers at discounts of 20%. As agents for most leading makes, you can find almost anything you want here. If you pay full price for the fabric you choose, curtains will be made free of charge.

BRITISH INDEPENDENT MOTOR TRADE ASSOCIATION
LEVER HOUSE, 9 PALMYRA SQUARE, WARRINGTON, CHESHIRE WA1 1BL
☎ (01925) 244120.
If you want to buy a car abroad but haggling with foreign dealers does not appeal, contact the BIMTA above, who will send you a list of reputable car importers. The importers make a charge, usually about £600 plus VAT. Please send a large SAE.

BURBERRY
CHESHIRE, OAKS OUTLET VILLAGE, KINSEY ROAD,
NEAR ELLESMERE PORT, CHESHIRE L65 9JJ
☎ (0151) 357 3203. OPEN 10 - 8 MON - THUR, 10 - 6 FRI, 9 - 6 SAT, 11 - 5 SUN.
Factory Shop in a Factory Shopping Village
Womenswear & Menswear
Sells a variety of Burberry and Thomas Burberry goods for men and women. Thomas Burberry jeans and polo shirts, classic men's check shirts, umbrellas, a variety of purses and wallets, handbags and travel bags; classic trench coats and overcoats and Thomas Burberry cashmere. All are discounted by about one third.

CALANGE
PO BOX 61, STOCKPORT, CHESHIRE SK3 OAP
☎ (0161) 474 7097. OPEN 9 - 5 MON - FRI.
Designer Sales • *Sportswear & Equipment*
Twice-yearly sales of adults and childrens' leisure and outdoor gear such as cycling shorts, waterproof jackets, warm hats, fleeces at incredibly cheap prices. On sale are ends of lines, imperfects and some design samples which they haven't pursued into full manufacturing. Phone or write to be put on the mailing list.

CHESHIRE, BRICK & SLATE COMPANY
BROOK HOUSE FARM, SALTERS BRIDGE, TARVIN SANDS, NR CHESTER, CHESHIRE CH3 8HL
☎ (01829) 740883. ☎ (01829) 740481 (FAX). OPEN 8 - 5.30 MON - FRI, 8 - 4.30 SAT, 10 - 4 SUN.
Architectural Salvage • *DIY/Renovation*
Reclaimed bricks, slates, setts, tiles, lampposts, doors, Victorian bathroom suites, fireplaces, ranges, garden ornaments, beams, Yorkshire paving and brass door furniture.

CHESHIRE, WORKSHOPS
BURWARDSLEY, NEAR CHESTER, CHESHIRE CH3 9PF
☎ (01829) 770401. OPEN 10 - 5 SEVEN DAYS A WEEK.
Factory Shop • *Household*
Workshops offer a day out for all the family as well as the opportunity to choose from a large range of candles at factory shop prices. You can watch skilled craftspeople carving candles by hand, and see the unique candle dipping ferris wheel, standing over thirty feet high. Most of the candles made here are exported throughout the world. There are also hundreds of other gift ideas in the shop. Candles start from 15p, much cheaper than the equivalent quality in the high street and are available in a wide range of colours, shapes and sizes. There is free parking, a play area for children and a restaurant.

CHESTER BARRIE
WESTON ROAD, CREWE, CHESHIRE CW1 6BA
☎ (01270) 508900. OPEN 9 - 5 MON - FRI, 9 - 3.30 SAT.
Factory Shop • *Womenswear & Menswear*
Busy and friendly shopping environment located just 1/4 mile from Crewe railway station and 4 miles from junction 16 on the M6. The factory shop has continued to grow in popularity with almost 8,000 people now on its mailing database. Customers who visit recognise and enjoy the value of top quality, British made products; men's and ladies tailored clothing being the speciality. The shop includes large fitting and changing areas, free parking and excellent access from the road network. Recent initiatives include a tailoring alteration service, men's and ladies bespoke tailoring, visiting tailoring to the customer's home or place or work

and the impending launch, as we went to press, of a VIP club for regular clients. Core offerings include an extensive range and selection of Chester Barrie men's ready-to-wear garments, Chester Barrie ladies tailored clothing, top quality coats, formal shirts and ladies blouses and knitwear. Regular special offers and sales are held in the factory shop as well as factory sales, held three times a year within the factory itself, which dispose of stock over-runs at reasonable prices. Details of these events can be obtained from the shop staff on the above telephone number. Chester Barrie also manufactures product for other famous brand names such as Austin Reed, Polo Ralph Lauren, Burberry, Hackett, Moss Bross, Turnbull & Asser and Harrods, to name but a few. The shop is also focussing on the accessory market with products such as belts, caps, cashmere, knitwear, cuff links, Polo shirts, Calvin Klein underwear and Grenson shoes. Bladen contry wear is available all year round. All items on display are of perfect quality, not seconds as in many outlets. The shop concentrates on the old-fashioned virtue of customer service, in particular the Bespoke Tailoring Service which offers clients an opportunity to select their own cloth and style of suit, to have a bespoke fitting and a final fitting upon completion of the garment, thus guaranteeing quality and fit.

CIRO
CHESHIRE OAKS DESIGNER OUTLET VILLAGE, JUNCTION 10 OF THE M53, NEAR ELLESMERE PORT, CHESHIRE L65 9JJ
☎ (0151) 355 4037. OPEN 10 - 8 MON - THUR, 10 - 6 FRI, 9 - 6 SAT, 11 - 5 SUN.
Factory Shop in a Factory Shopping Village • *Womenswear & Menswear*
One of more than 120 outlets, all selling brand name merchandise at discounted prices, with more outlets in the pipeline. Internationally famous jewellers Ciro sell a range of jewellery. There is a children's play area, a Garfunkels restaurant and free car parking.

CLARKS SHOP
CHESHIRE OAKS DESIGNER OUTLET VILLAGE, ADDRESS AND OPENING HOURS ABOVE
☎ (0151) 356 7492.
Factory Shop in a Factory Shopping Village
Womenswear & Menswear • *Children* • *Sportswear & Equipment*
Shoes for men and women, handbags and evening bags at discounts of at least 25%. Also luggage and coats - fleeces and waterproofs.

COLOUR ME CRAYONS
ABBEYFIELDS, LODGE ROAD, NEAR ELWORTH, CHESHIRE
☎ (01270) 753030. OPEN 8.30 - 4.30 MON - FRI.
Factory Shop • *Children*
Manufacturer of crayons, chalks, face paints, glitter, sugar paper etc, overstocks of which is sold here at discounted prices. Also on sale are card, drawing paper, sand, paint brushes, poster paints, masks, glue for papier mache, sequins, bean bags, erasers, pencils, play dough, jigsaws and bracelet kits.

CUT-PRICE WALLPAPERS
13-17 MILL STREET, CREWE, CHESHIRE CW2 7AE
☎ (01270) 250117. OPEN 9 - 5.30 MON - SAT, 10 - 4 SUN.
Permanent Discount Outlet • *DIY/Renovation*
Offers much more than the name suggests: paint, bedding, curtains, fabrics, curtain poles, pictures, mirrors and a host of other decorative and furnishing items. Brands stocked include Crown, Vymura, Shand-Kydd, Coloroll, Graham & Brown and Zen. There are two floors of wallpaper in stock but if you can't find what you want, pattern books are available.

DAKS SIMPSON
MACARTHUR GLEN DESIGNER OUTLET VILLAGE CHESHIRE OAKS, JUNCTION 10 OF M53, ELLESMERE PORT, SOUTH WIRRAL, CHESHIRE L65 9JJ
☎ (0151) 3558703. OPEN 10 - 8, MON - THUR, 10 - 6 FRI, 9 - 6 SAT, UNTIL 8 ON THUR, 11 - 5 SUNS AND BANK HOLS. OPEN 10 - 6 IN WINTER
Factory Shop in a Factory Shopping Village • *Womenswear & Menswear*
Sells previous season's stock for women and men as well as any overmakes in high quality ladies suits, jackets and skirts and men's suits, overcoats, jackets, trousers, ties and knitwear as well as belts, gloves, handbags, Simpson shirts, socks and scarves. There are good bargains to be had, but stock is very much dependent on what has not sold in the shops. Sizes from 6-20. Ladies jackets, £99, originally £279. Daks Simpson was founded in 1894 by Simeon Simpson and produced quality English tailoring for more than 100 years. His son created the Simpson store in Piccadilly in 1936 which housed the Daks range, most of which was made in Scotland.

DENBY FACTORY SHOP
CHESHIRE OAKS OUTLET VILLAGE, ELLESMERE PORT, SOUTH WIRRAL L65 9JJ
☎ (0151) 356 4943 . OPEN 10 - 8, MON - THUR, 10 - 6 FRI, 9 - 6 SAT, UNTIL 8 ON THUR, 11 - 5 SUNS AND BANK HOLS. OPEN 10 - 6 IN WINTER
Factory Shop in a Factory Shopping Village • *Household*
Denby is renowned for its striking colours and glaze effects. This outlet stocks seconds quality Denby cookware and mugs with prices starting at 20% off RRP. There are regular special offers throughout the year.

DELIA METCALFE
15A BRIDGE STREET, CONGLETON, CHESHIRE CW12 1AS
☎ (01260) 297521. OPEN 9.30 - 5 MON - THUR, 9 - 5.30 FRI, SAT.
Permanent Discount Outlet • *Womenswear Only* • *Children*
Chainstore and designer surplus stock are sold in this small town centre shop. The children's clothes are aged from 6 months to 12 years; ladies sizes from 8 to 30. Marks & Spencer merchandise is discounted by 50%, and there are many German designer labels such as Verse and Bianca.

DESIGNER WAREHOUSE
UNIT 7, DINSDALE ROAD, CROFT BUSINESS PARK, BROMBOROUGH, WIRRAL, CHESHIRE CH62 3PY
(0151) 343 9957. OPEN 10 - 5.30 MON - SAT, 11 - 4 SUN.
Permanent Discount Outlet • *Womenswear & Menswear*
Men's and women's discounted fashion items from Morgan, DKNY, Dolce & Gabanna, Moschino, Ralph Lauren, Armani, Hugo Boss and Versace Jeans.

DIESEL
CHESHIRE OAKS DESIGNER OUTLET VILLAGE, JUNCTION 10 OF THE M53, NEAR ELLESMERE PORT, CHESHIRE L65 9JJ
(0151) 355 1478. OPEN 10 - 8 MON - THUR, 10 - 6 FRI, 9 - 6 SAT, 11 - 5 SUN AND BANK HOLIDAYS, 10 - 6 IN WINTER
Factory Shop in a Factory Shopping Village • *Womenswear & Menswear*
Diesel, which claims to be the fastest growing jeans label in the world, sells Modern Basic in addition to Diesel Spare Part accessories. Based in Molvena, Italy, Diesel now distributes to 72 countries worldwide, though this is its only outlet store in the UK. Jeans seconds costs from £28 a pair or £45 for two pairs.

DISCOUNT CLOTHING
11 WOODFORD ROAD, BRAMHALL, CHESHIRE.
(0161) 439 0430. OPEN 9.30 - 5.30 MON - SAT.
19 PARK LANE, POYNTON, CHESHIRE.
(01625) 871571. OPEN 9.30 - 5.30 MON - SAT.
Permanent Discount Outlet • *Womenswear Only*
Sell perfects and seconds of chainstore and German manufacturers clothes for women, mostly made up of mix and match separates, including evening wear at Christmas time only. The Poynton branch also sells childrenswear.

DW DESIGNER WAREHOUSE
UNIT 7, DINSDALE ROAD, CROFT BUSINESS PARK, BROMBOROUGH, WIRRAL, CHESHIRE.
(0151) 343 9957. OPEN 10 - 5.30 MON - FRI, 10 - 5 SAT, 11 - 4 SUN.
7 BRIDGE STREET ROW, CHESTER.
(01244) 316110. OPEN 9.30 - 5.30 MON - SAT, 12 - 5 SUN.
Permanent Discount Outlet • *Womenswear & Menswear*
Labels such as Versace, Armani, Dolce & Gabbana, Valentino, Moschino, Hugo Boss, DKNY and Morgan at discounted prices.

E SIMPSON LTD
BUXTON ROAD, HAZEL GROVE, STOCKPORT, CHESHIRE SK7 6LZ
(0161) 483 1241. OPEN 5 - 3.45 MON - FRI, 6 - 10.45 SAT.
Factory Shop • *Food and Leisure*
Pork butchers who make sausages and cure hams. They supply top quality sausages, ham, bacon and other meats to wholesalers and supermarket chains countrywide. Overstocks sold here at greatly reduced prices.

ECCO
CHESHIRE OAKS DESIGNER OUTLET VILLAGE, KINSEY ROAD, ELLESMERE PORT, JUNCTION 10 OF M53, CHESHIRE L65 9JJ
☎ (0151) 356 3045. OPEN 10 - 8 MON - THUR, 10 - 6 FRI, 9 - 6 SAT, 11 - 5 SUN, 10 - 6 IN WINTER
Factory Shop in a Factory Shopping Village • *Children Womenswear & Menswear*
Shoes, all discounted by at least 25%. Phone 0800 387368 for a catalogue. Other outlets in South Wales, Hertfordshire, Somerset and Wiltshire.

EDINBURGH CRYSTAL
CHESHIRE OAKS OUTLET VILLAGE, ELLESMERE PORT, JUNCTION 10 OF M53, CHESHIRE L65 9JJ
☎ (0151) 357 3661. OPEN 10 - 8 MON - THUR, 10 - 6 FRI, 9 - 6 SAT, 11 - 5 SUN.
Factory Shop in a Factory Shopping Village • *Household*
Wide range of crystalware from glasses and vases to tumblers and bowls at discounts of between 30% - 40%. The shop sells firsts and seconds of crystal from one third off the normal price. There are also special promotional lines at discount prices up to 70% off seconds.

ELITE DRESS AGENCY
1 MARKET STREET, ALTRINCHAM, CHESHIRE WA14 1QE
☎ (0161) 928 5424. OPEN 10 - 5 MON - SAT.
Dress Agency • *Womenswear & Menswear*
Established since 1964, this shop sells mainly ladies wear which is less than two years old, with a small but comprehensive selection of menswear. Wide range of clothing includes some sports wear. Labels range from high street to designer and includes names such as Genny, Guy Laroche, Hardy Amies, YSL, Dior, Valentino, Ungaro, Thierry Mugler, Sonia Rykiel, Mondi, KooKai, Morgan and Ralph Lauren for women, and Boss, Versace, Armani, YSL, Cerruti and Ralph Lauren for men. Twice yearly sales at the end of June and December. A dress hire section stocks a wide selection of brand new dresses, updated twice a year (see One-Night Affair).

EMERY LIGHTING LTD
FOUNDRY BANK, CONGLETON, CHESHIRE CW12 1EE
☎ (01260) 281071. OPEN 9.30 - 4.30 MON - SAT.
Factory Shop • *Furniture/Soft Furnishings* • *Household*
Factory shop situated in an old mill selling literally thousands of lamps - bases and shades, patterned and plain. Most of the stock is seconds and reduced by about one-third. Set in a delightful market town adjacent to the town centre, this Victorian mill has recently been extensively refurbished to offer a variety of independent shops displaying a huge array of merchandise. Everything from cane furniture to chainstore merchandise, including bed, mirrors, lighting. Coffee Shop. Ample parking.

EMPORIUM
17 PILLORY STREET, NANTWICH, CHESHIRE CW5 5BZ
☎ (01270) 610144. OPEN 9.30 - 5.30 MON - SAT.
Permanent Discount Outlet • *Womenswear & Menswear*
Range of designer clothes for men and women including Moschino, Dolce and Gabbana, Armani, Lambretta, Boss, Firetrap, Chipy and Morgan, Miss Sixty and Hooch at competitive prices.

EVANS
CHESHIRE, OAKS OUTLET VILLAGE, KINSEY ROAD, JUNCTION 10 OF M53, NEAR ELLESMERE PORT, CHESHIRE L65 9JJ
☎ (01513) 554334. OPEN 10 - 6 MON - SAT, 8 ON THUR, 11 - 5 SUN.
Factory Shop in a Factory Shopping Village • *Womenswear Only*
End of season lines at discounts of between 25% and 50%, all with the normal Evans refund guarantee. The range includes tailoring, soft dressing, dresses, Profile, knitwear, East Coast (denim/jeans), lingerie/nightwear, blouses, coats, outerwear and accessories.

FAIRWAY MENSWEAR
BEAM HEATH WAY, MIDDLEWICH ROAD, NANTWICH, CHESHIRE CW5 6PQ
☎ (01270) 625900. OPEN 9 - 5 MON - SAT. OPEN BANK HOLIDAYS 10 - 4.
Factory Shop • *Menswear Only*
Men's suits, jackets, trousers and coats which are either own brand or made for chainstores such as Next and C & A but sold here under the Fairway name. Good selection in most sizes with larger sizes up to 52" now available. Suits all £89.95. Changing rooms and car park.

FAMOUS FOOTWEAR
CHESHIRE OAKS OUTLET VILLAGE, KINSEY ROAD, NEAR ELLESMERE PORT, JUNCTION 10 OF M53, CHESHIRE L65 9JJ
☎ (0151) 357 1512. OPEN 10 - 6 MON - SAT, UNTIL 8 ON THUR, 11 - 5 SUN, 10 - 8 IN SUMMER.
Factory Shop in a Factory Shopping Village • *Womenswear & Menswear*
Wide range of brand names including Stead & Simpson, Lilley & Skinner, Hobos, Hush Puppies, Lotus, Sterling & Hunt, Richleigh, Scholl, Red Tape, Flexi Country, Padders, Canaletto, Bronx, Frank Wright, Brevitt, Romba Wallace, Rieker, all at discount prices of up to 50%.

FRED PERRY UK LTD
CHESHIRE OAKS OUTLET VILLAGE, ADDRESS AND OPENING HOURS ABOVE.
☎ (0151) 357 1383.
Factory Shop in a Factory Shopping Village • *Sportswear & Equipment*
Men's and women's ranges of the famous Fred Perry active performance clothing: shorts, tennis tops, tracksuits, T-shirts. All price labels show the original and the reduced price, which usually amount to a 30% discount.

FRUIT OF THE LOOM
CHESHIRE OAKS OUTLET VILLAGE, ADDRESS AND OPENING HOURS ABOVE.
☎ (0151) 357 1745.
Factory Shop in a Factory Shopping Village • *Womenswear & Menswear*
Men's, women's and children's (ages 3-14) casual wear in the form of T-shirt, sweatshirts, shorts and tracksuits with the distinctive Fruit of the Loom logo at discounts starting at 25%.

GAP
CHESHIRE OAKS DESIGNER OUTLET VILLAGE, ADDRESS AND OPENING HOURS ABOVE.
☎ (0151) 355 2922.
Factory Shop in a Factory Shopping Village
Womenswear & Menswear • *Children*
Gap sells casual clothes for men, women and children of all ages, discounted at this factory outlet. There is a children's play area, restaurants and free car parking.

GLYN WEBB
UNIT 1C, THE BOUGHTON CENTRE, BOUGHTON, CHESTER, CHESHIRE CH3 5AF
☎ (01244) 344 144. OPEN 9 - 8 MON - SAT, 11 - 5 SUN AND BANK HOLIDAYS.
Permanent Discount Outlet • *DIY/Renovation*
Stockists of all your home improvement needs from wallpaper to paint, furniture to flooring, tiles to textiles, housewares to lighting - in fact, almost everything for your home, with 25 branches in the North-West, Midlands and Yorkshire. Specialists in discontinued mail order, slightly imperfect branded stocks as well as perfect quality superior products. They carry top brands such as Dulux, Crown Paints and Vymura and Coloroll wall coverings, Rectella and Norwood textiles and much more in store. To find your nearest branch, phone Head Office on 0161 621 4500.

GREAT NORTHERN ARCHITECTURAL ANTIQUES
NEW RUSSIA HALL, CHESTER ROAD, TATTENHALL, CHESHIRE CH3 9AH
☎ (01829) 770796. FAX (01829) 770971. OPEN 9.30 - 5 SEVEN DAYS A WEEK.
Architectural Salvage • *DIY/Renovation*
Doors, panelled rooms, sanitary fittings, stained glass, garden furniture, York stone sets and pews, gates, railings, curios, bric a brac.

HAMLET'S FAMOUS NAMES
65-69 PRINCE'S STREET, STOCKPORT, CHESHIRE SK1 1RW
☎ (0161) 476 3500. OPEN 9 - 5.30 MON - SAT, 11 - 4 SUN.
THE RIDGEDALE SK6 6AW
☎ (0161) 449 0461. OPEN 9 - 5.30 MON - SAT, CLOSED WED.
Permanent Discount Outlet • *Electrical Equipment*
Sells ends of lines and A-grade manufacturers' returns of electrical goods which dealers have sent back to suppliers as faulty and which have then been repaired to the original specification at discounts of up to 50%. These include Panasonic, Toshiba, JVC, Philips, Sony, Sharp and Aiwa television sets, videos, hi-fis, camcorders, portable audios and walkmans.

HOME AND BEAUTY DISCOUNTS
29 MILL STREET, CONGLETON, CHESHIRE
☎ (01260) 273009. OPEN 9 - 5.15 MON - SAT, 9 - 1.15 WED.
Permanent Discount Outlet • *Womenswear Only* • *Household Children*
Three-storey shop with a picture gallery also selling mirrors downstairs, cafe upstairs and in the middle a floor full of competitively-priced items for the kitchen and household. These include cleaning materials, make-up, toys, ornaments, pottery, aromatherapy oils, shampoo, toothpaste, soaps, lipsticks. They claim prices here are cheaper than in supermarkets and high street shops. Some of the brands are well-known: Flex shampoo, for instance, and Colgate toothpaste.

HOMEFREEZE FROZEN FOODS
PARK LANE, POYNTON, CHESHIRE SK12 1RE
☎ (01625) 871322. OPEN 9 - 5.30 MON - FRI, 9 - 6 FRI, 9 - 5 SAT.
28 HIGH STREET, CHEADLE, CHESHIRE SK8 5JD
☎ (0161) 428 2626. OPEN 9 - 5.30 MON - FRI, 9 - 5 SAT.
Food and Drink Discounters • *Food and Leisure*
Sell a range of brand name and low calorie ready-made meals at discounts of, on average, about one third off the normal retail price. The meals have usually been created for famous high street stores and include Marks & Spencer oven chips, individual chicken or steak pies, wholemeal quiches and pizzas. Also Romantica ice cream and Sainsbury and Tesco ready-meals, and hundreds of other lines as and when available.

JAEGER FACTORY SHOP
CHESHIRE OAKS DESIGNER OUTLET VILLAGE, ADDRESS AND OPENING HOURS AS BEFORE.
☎ (0151) 355 0022.
Factory Shop in a Factory Shopping Village • *Womenswear & Menswear*
Contemporary classics from Jaeger at excellent prices. Most of the merchandise is previous seasons' stock, but you might also find some special makes.

JAMES BARRY MENSWEAR
CHESHIRE OAKS OUTLET VILLAGE, ADDRESS AND OPENING HOURS
AS BEFORE.
☎ (0151) 357 1416.
Factory Shop in a Factory Shopping Village • *Menswear Only*
Range of men's suits, jackets, trousers, socks, belts, briefs, shirts and casual wear from James Barry and Wolsey. Some of the factory shops also stock the Double Two range of brand names. Suits from £120; casual shirts, £11.95 or two for £20; trousers reduced from £44.95 to £29.95; Pierre Cardin casual and business shirts, knitwear and trouser are available, too.

JANE SHILTON
CHESHIRE OAKS DESIGNER OUTLET VILLAGE, ADDRESS AND
OPENING HOURS AS BEFORE.
☎ (0151) 355 8266.
Factory Shop in a Factory Shopping Village • *Womenswear Only*
Merchandise from past seasons' collections or factory seconds at discounts of at least 30% and up to 70% off the original price. There is a wide range of handbags, small leather goods, shoes, luggage umbrellas and travel bags. Example of price reduction: handbags at £24.99 originally £37.

JEFFREY ROGERS
CHESHIRE OAKS OUTLET VILLAGE, ADDRESS AND OPENING HOURS
AS BEFORE.
☎ (0151) 355 6797.
Factory Shop in a Factory Shopping Village • *Womenswear Only*
Factory outlet with the emphasis on young street style: from sleeveless mini dresses to drawstring waist trousers, T-shirts, sweaters and skirts though there is also the Roger Plus range for sizes 16-24. Discount is usually around 30% and upwards.

JOE BLOGGS
CHESHIRE OAKS DESIGNER OUTLET VILLAGE, ADDRESS AND
OPENING HOURS AS BEFORE.
☎ (0151) 356 7417.
Factory Shop in a Factory Shopping Village
Womenswear & Menswear • *Children*
Range of casual clothing for men, women, children and babies which are ends of lines, imperfects or surplus ranges. Jeans, tops, long sleeved shirts and jackets at discounts of between 30% and 70%.

JOKIDS LTD
CHESHIRE, OAKS OUTLET VILLAGE, ADDRESS AND OPENING HOURS AS BEFORE.
☎ (0151) 357 1404.
Factory Shop in a Factory Shopping Village • *Children*
This shop sells childrenswear for 0-10-year-olds including everdaywear like t-shirts, jogwear, various denim styles and accessories. For special occasions there are pretty hand-smocked party dresses and rompers. Reductions are up to 40%. The village also has restaurants, children's play areas and free parking.

JUMPER
CHESHIRE OAKS DESIGNER OUTLET VILLAGE, ADDRESS AND OPENING HOURS AS BEFORE.
☎ (0151) 356 7414.
Factory Shop in a Factory Shopping Village • *Womenswear & Menswear*
A wide range of Jumper label sweaters, gloves, scarves, shirts and cardigans for men and women all at discount prices of up to 50% off. Prices start at £2.

KIDDICARE
33 THE RIDINGS, SAUGHALL, CHESTER, CHESHIRE CH1 6AX
☎ (01244) 880690.
Hire Shops • *Children*
Part of the Baby Equipment Hirers Association (BEHA), which has more than 100 members countrywide. A range of equipment can be hired from high chairs, cots and travel cots to baby car seats and buggies. Some members also hire out party equipment including child-sized tables and chairs. BEHA run an advice line which will try and answer any queries you have regarding hiring services for children. Phone the Babyline on 0831 310355.

LEE COOPER
CHESHIRE OAKS DESIGNER OUTLET VILLAGE, ADDRESS AND OPENING HOURS AS BEFORE.
☎ (0151) 355 8808.
Factory Shop in a Factory Shopping Village
Womenswear & Menswear • *Children*
Denim jeans, jackets and shirts, each ranked by size and gender at discounts of up to 30%. Casual shirts from £9.99, jeans from £14.99, T-shirts and ladieswear. Lee Cooper was founded in 1908 as a workwear manufacturer before becoming a supplier to the armed forces. Most of the stock here is current, discontinued and irregular merchandise, all of which comes straight from Lee Cooper's factories in Europe.

LITTLEWOODS CATALOGUE DISCOUNT STORE
MCARTHURGLEN OUTLET CENTRE CHESHIRE OAKS, ADDRESS AND OPENING HOURS AS BEFORE.
☎ (0151) 357 3633 (CENTRE).
Factory Shop • *Womenswear & Menswear* • *Children Electrical Equipment*
Littlewoods clearance shops offering up to 50% off the catalogue price for clothing and between 50% and 60% off for electrical goods. Stock changes constantly and varies from day to day but can include well-known brand names such as Berlei and Gossard lingerie, Vivienne Westwood, Pamplemousse leisure wear, Nike and Adidas sports shoes, Workers for Freedom, and Timberland and Caterpillar footwear. Stock depends on the size and location of the shop, so larger shops will get the longer discontinued runs and smaller shops over-runs with only a small amount of colour and size variations left. Littlewoods also run a mobile shop which operates in cities where they don't have a sale shop. For details of further venues for the sales, which usually take place once a month, contact Melanie Lamb, c/o Crosby DC Kershaw Avenue, Endbutt Lane, Crosby, Merseyside L70 1AH.

LIZ CLAIBORNE
CHESHIRE OAKS OUTLET VILLAGE, ADDRESS AND OPENING HOURS AS BEFORE.
☎ (0151) 355 9183.
Factory Shop in a Factory Shopping Village • *Womenswear Only*
An American designer, Liz Claiborne offers mid market priced smart clothes for work and casual wear.. All are ends of lines or styles which are at least one year old. Comfortable, fitting denims are reduced from £49 to £24.50 and under; plus there is a full range of co-ordinating tops from £14. Classic silk blouses cost from £35; and casual suited jackets start from £45. There is a range available in petite sizing and a wide choice of accessories, with belts from £3, and summer handbags in a large choice of colours.

MATALAN
UNIT 29, GREYHOUND RETAIL PARK, SEALAND ROAD, CHESTER, CHESHIRE CH1 1QG
☎ (01244) 380877. OPEN 9.30 - 8 MON - FRI, 9 - 6 SAT, 11 - 5 SUN.
NEW CHESTER ROAD, BROMBOROUGH, SOUTH WIRRAL L62 7EK
☎ (0151) 343 9494. OPEN 9.30 - 8 MON - FRI, 9 - 6 SAWA2 8NU
☎ (01925) 235365. OPEN 9.30 - 8 MON - FRI, 9 - 6 SAT, 11 - 5 SUN.
Permanent Discount Outlet • *Womenswear & Menswear Household* • *Children*
Matalan is a fashion and homewares value retailer giving customers what they claim to be unbeatable value for money with huge savings on a wide range of products including high quality fashionable clothing for men, women and children at up to 50% off high street prices. Matalan is situated out of town and stores are open seven days a week all year round.

MCARTHURGLEN DESIGNER OUTLET VILLAGE
JUNCTION 10 OF THE M53, KINSEY ROAD, NEAR ELLESMERE PORT,
CHESHIRE L65 9JJ
FREEPHONE INFORMATION LINE 0800 3164352.
☎ (0151) 357 3633. WEBSITE: www.mcarthurglen.com
OPEN 10 - 8 MON - THUR, 10 - 6 FRI, 9 - 6 SAT,
11 - 5 SUN AND BANK HOLIDAYS.

Factory Shopping Village • *Womenswear & Menswear* • *Children*
Household • *Electrical Equipment* • *Food and Leisure*
Sportswear & Equipment

Over 130 stores selling brand name merchandise at discounted prices. Facilities include a food court, with a choice of ten outlets, children's play area and free parking. Fashion labels for women include Adidas, Austin Reed, Benetton, Big L Levi's, Body Shop Depot, Burberrys, Cap It All, Cartoon Fashion, Ciro Pearls, Claire's Accessories, Cotton Traders, Cross Creek, Daks Simpson, Diesel, DKNY, Donna Karan (for men and women as well as DKNY Active diffusion ranges), Donnay sportswear, Dune Footwear, Ecco, Episode, Etam, Evans, Falmer Jeans, Famous Footwear, Fred Perry, Fruit of the Loom casualwear, Gap, Helly Hansen, Hobbs, Jaeger, Jeffrey Rogers, Jesire, Joe Bloggs, Jane Shilton, John Partridge, Jumper, Kangol, Karrimor Store, Kurt Geiger, La Senza, Lee Cooper, Lingerie Shop, Liz Claiborne, Littlewoods Catalogue Outlet, Mexx, Monet jewellery, Next to Nothing, Nike, Paco, Pied a Terre, Pilot, Principles, Proibito (ends of lines from Moschino, Versace, Fendi, Gianfrance Ferre, Byblos, Armani), Ravel, Red/Green, Reebok, Reiss, Richards, Russell Athletic, Shoe Studio, Soled Out, Sportsystem, Tessuti, The Designer Room, The Sweater Shop, Timberland, Tog 24 outdoorwear, U Wear I Wear, Vans footwear, Virgin Clothing, Viyella, Walker and Hall jewellery and watches, Wallis, Warehouse, Warners, Winning Line. For men, Austin Reed, Baron Jon, Benetton, Ben Sherman, Blazer, Big L Levi's, Burberrys, Cap It All, Cecil Gee, Cotton Traders, Cross Creek, Daks Simpson, Diesel, Donnay sportswear, Ecco, Eddie Bauer, Falmer Jeans, Famous Footwear, Fosters, Fred Perry, Fruit of the Loom casualwear, Gap, Helly Hansen, Jaeger, James Barry, Joe Bloggs, John Partridge, Jumper, Karrimor Store, Kurt Geiger, Lee Cooper, Mexx, Next to Nothing, Nike, Paco, Principles, Red/Green, Reebok, Russell Athletic, Shoe Studio, Soled Out, Sportsystem, Suits You, The Suit Company, The Sweater Shop, Tie Rack, Timberland, Tog 24 outdoorwear, Van Heusen, Vans footwear, Viyella, Walker and Hall watches, Woodhouse. Shops for children include Benetton, Big L Levi's, Cap It All, Cartoon Fashion, Donnay sportswear, Ecco, Falmer Jeans, Famous Footwear, Fruit of the Loom casualwear, Gap, Joe Bloggs, Jo Kids, Lee Cooper, Mexx, Mothercare, Next to Nothing, Nike, Paco, Principles, Reebok, Russell Athletic, Shoe Studio, Soled Out, Sportsystem, Thorntons, Tog 24 outdoorwear, Toyworld and Vans footwear. Shops for the home include Bed & Bath Works towels and bedlinen; Clover House tablemats and kitchenware; Denby; Edinburgh Crystal; Kitchen Store;

Onieda cutlery; Ponden Mill bedlinen, duvets and towels; Price's Candles; Royal Doulton; Royal Worcester; Villeroy & Boch; Whittard of Chelsea cafetieres, china and kitchen containers; Woods of Windsor fragrances and XS Music and Video. Electrical shops include Remington which sells everything from knives and saucepans to hairdryers and shavers and Thorn which sells TVs, videos, CD players, and small electrical equipment. Leisure shops include Antler luggage; Bookends; Card & Gift cards and small gfits; Carphone Warehouse; Thorntons and Travel Accessory Outlet which sells a range of brand name luggage, handbags and travel accessories. Sports and outdoor wear labels include Donnay sportswear, Fred Perry, Helly Hansen, John Partridge, Karrimor Store, Nike, Red/Green, Reebok, Russell Athletic, Sportsystem, Timberland, Tog 24 outdoorwear. The neighbouring Coliseum development provides lots of leisure facilities.

MEXX INTERNATIONAL
CHESHIRE OAKS DESIGNER OUTLET VILLAGE, ADDRESS AND OPENING HOURS AS BEFORE.
☎ (0151) 355 8238.
Factory Shop in a Factory Shopping Village
Womenswear & Menswear • *Children*

High street fashion at factory outlet prices for men, women, babies and kids, all of which are heavily discounted by more than 30%.

MOLLY MUMBLES
1 BOOTHBED LANE, BOOSTREY, NEAR HOLMES CHAPEL, CHESHIRE CW4 8JP
☎ (01477) 532234. OPEN 9.30 - 3 MON - SAT.
Dress Agency • *Hire Shop* • *Children*

Huge selection of top quality secondhand childrenswear and equipment at bargain prices. Labels include Mothercare, Miniman, Gap, OshKosh, Jean Bourget, Oilily, Mamas & Papas, Fisher Price Maclaren, Playmobil and Duplo. Also hires out buggies, high chairs, prams, travel cots, car seats by the day, week or month.

NEXT TO NOTHING
CHESHIRE, OAKS DESIGNER OUTLET VILLAGE, JUNCTION 10 OF M53, ELLESMERE PORT, CHESHIRE L65 9JJ
☎ (0151) 356 7404. OPEN 10 - 6 MON - SAT, 8 ON THUR, 11 - 5 SUN AND BANK HOLIDAYS.
Factory Shop in a Factory Shopping Village
Womenswear & Menswear • *Children*

Sells perfect surplus stock from Next stores and the Next Directory catalogue at discounts of 50% or more. The ranges are usually last season's and overruns but there is the odd current item if you look carefully. There are shoes, lingerie, swimwear, and clothes for men, women and children.

NIKE FACTORY STORE
CHESHIRE OAKS OUTLET VILLAGE, ADDRESS AND OPENING HOURS AS BEFORE.
☎ (0151) 357 1252.
Factory Shop in a Factory Shopping Village
Sportswear & Equipment • Children

Men's, women's and children's trainers, jackets, T-shirts, sports shirts, shorts, sleeveless T-shirts and tracksuits. Nike has been making clothes for people who live and play outdoors since 1972. This factory shop sells unsold items from previous seasons. The selection represents their worldwide collection, which means that some garments may not have been offered for sale in the UK. As ranges tend to be incomplete, they are offered at a minimum of 30% off the recommended retail price or the price they would have commanded in the UK. Occasionally, there are some slight seconds on sale, which are always marked as such. There is another factory shop in Swindon in Wiltshire.

NOSTALGIA ANTIQUE FIREPLACE
61 SHAW HEATH, STOCKPORT, CHESHIRE SK3 8BH
☎ (0161) 477 7706. FAX ☎ (0161) 477 2267.
WEBSITE: www.antique-atlas.com/nostalgia.htm
OPEN 10 - 6 TUE - FRI, 10 - 5 SAT.
Architectural Salvage • *DIY/Renovation*

A constant stock of more than 1,200 genuine antique fireplaces of all descriptions and materials dating from 1750-1920. Also lots of Victorian and Edwardian washbasins and loos. Expert restoration is carried out on this extensive stock and a wealth of advice is available.

ONE-NIGHT AFFAIR
1 MARKET STREET, ALTRINCHAM, CHESHIRE WA14 1QE
☎ (0161) 928 8477. OPEN 10 - 5 MON - SAT.
Hire Shops • *Womenswear Only*

Situated within the Elite Dress Agency, you can choose from more than 350 outfits, including cocktail wear, ball gowns, party gear and accessories to hire or to buy. Stock changes frequently. Hire costs £75-£85. No appointment necessary.

ONEIDA
CHESHIRE OAKS OUTLET VILLAGE, ADDRESS AND OPENING HOURS AS BEFORE.
☎ (0151) 356 1024.
Factory Shop in a Factory Shopping Village • *Household*

Oneida is the world's largest cutlery company and originates from the United States of America. In addition to cutlery, it sells silver and silver plate at discounts of between 30% and 50%, plus frames, candlesticks and trays. They now also have their own range of chinaware and glass, also sold here at discounts of 30%-50%.

PACO
CHESHIRE OAKS OUTLET VILLAGE, ADDRESS AND OPENING HOURS AS BEFORE.
☎ (0151) 357 3722.
Factory Shop in a Factory Shopping Village
Children • Womenswear Only • Sportswear & Equipment
Paco uses bright, distinctive colours and the knack for designing great clothes at affordable prices. For several years, they have also been creating their own brand of sports and leisurewear clothing that shows great verve and energy. This range has a much more everyday living influence. The contrast is a distinct look for the discerning wearer. If you are looking for a great T-shirt or sweatshirt, lightweight jacket or gilet, polar fleece or hooded top, three-quarter length or combat trousers, then you need look no further. Paco now competes with the very best fashion brands in the high street by offering customers high fashion combined with excellent quality, making their clothes real value for money.

PARTRIDGE COUNTRY STORE
CHESHIRE OAKS OUTLET VILLAGE, ADDRESS AND OPENING HOURS AS BEFORE.
☎ (0151) 357 1729.
Factory Shop in a Factory Shopping Village
Womenswear & Menswear • Children
Partridge specialises in fashionable outdoor clothes and accessories. Ranges include waxed jackets, Gore-tex jackets, waterproof jackets, tweeds, quilts, fleece jackets and waistcoats, knitwear, shirts, chinos, cord and moleskin trousers, hats and caps. Discontinued lines are on sale at discounted prices with a minimum of 30% and up to 70% off during promotions.

PILOT
CHESHIRE OAKS DESIGNER OUTLET VILLAGE, ADDRESS AND OPENING HOURS AS BEFORE.
☎ (0151) 355 8082.
Factory Shop in a Factory Shopping Village • *Womenswear Only*
Mainly younger-style clothes for women only. Most are end of season and end of line. Stock is mostly new and similar to high street stores at reductions of about 30%, e.g. in the summer of 1999: pedal pushers, £23 reduced to £17, short strap top £17 reduced to £10.

PONDEN MILL LINENS
CHESHIRE OAKS DESIGNER OUTLET VILLAGE, ADDRESS AND OPENING HOURS AS BEFORE.
☎ (0151) 356 4411.
Factory Shop in a Factory Shopping Village • *Household*
Famous branded products at direct from the mill prices. A fabulous assortment of towels, duvets, pillows, throws, bedspreads, up-to-the-minute coordi-

nated bed linen, from Crown, Coloroll, Jeff Banks Ports-of-Call, to name but a few. Something for every room in the house.

PRICE'S CANDLES

CHESHIRE OAKS DESIGNER OUTLET VILLAGE, ADDRESS AND OPENING HOURS AS BEFORE.

☎ (0151) 356 0248.

Factory Shop in a Factory Shopping Village • *Household*

Everything sold in this shop are seconds, discontinued sizes not available elsewhere, over-runs or candles in old packaging that has now been replaced. There are church candles, lanterns, candles in pots and glass jars, star-shaped candles, floating candles, candlestick holders, serviettes, scented candles and garden torches.

PRINCIPLES

CHESHIRE OAKS DESIGNER OUTLET VILLAGE, ADDRESS AND OPENING HOURS AS BEFORE.

☎ (0151) 357 1033.

Factory Shop in a Factory Shopping Village • *Womenswear & Menswear*

End of season lines with the normal Principles refund guarantee. The range includes, for women, dresses, blouses, coats, outerwear, knitwear, casualwear and a selection of Petite clothing for women who are 5ft 3ins and under. Also stock Amanda Wakeley at up to 50% discount. For men, there is formalwear, smart casualwear, knitwear, outerwear, PFM Sport, jeanswear and casualwear.

QS FASHION

1-5 BROAD ROAD, SALE, CHESHIRE N33 2AE

☎ (0161) 976 2747. OPEN 9 - 8 MON - FRI, 9 - 5.30 SAT, 11 - 5 SUN.

Permanent Discount Outlet • *Womenswear & Menswear* • *Children*

Although not a discount shop as such, most of the stock on sale here is cheaper than it could be found elsewhere. Fashion for all the family includes brands such as Lee Cooper, Timberland, Joe Bloggs, Fila, Nike, Reebok, Ralph Lauren.

RACING GREEN

CHESHIRE OAKS DESIGNER OUTLET VILLAGE, ADDRESS AND OPENING HOURS AS BEFORE.

☎ (0151) 351 1159.

Factory Shop in a Factory Shopping Village • *Womenswear & Menswear*

Overstocks and clearance lines from this mail order catalogue are sold here at discount prices.

RANGE DISCOUNT WAREHOUSE
9 PADGATE LANE, WARRINGTON CHESHIRE.
☎ (01925) 574943. OPEN 9 - 8 MON, THUR, 9 - 6 TUE, FRI, SAT, CLOSED WED.
Permanent Discount Outlet • *Electrical Equipment*
Everything for the kitchen in terms of large electrical equipment including ookers, hobs, microwaves, hoods, US-style fridges, range cookers at very competitive prices. The company believes in high turnover/low margins.

REDGREEN
CHESHIRE OAKS DESIGNER OUTLET VILLAGE, ADDRESS AND OPENING HOURS AS BEFORE.
☎ (0151) 356 3660. OPEN 10 - 8 MON - THUR, 10 - 6 FRI, SAT, 11 - 5 SUN.
Factory Shop in a Factory Shopping Village
Womenswear & Menswear • *Sportswear & Equipment*
RedGreen is Scandinavian leisure wear for men and women. The high quality and classic design has a nautical heritage but a stylish look. The collection includes outerwear, sweaters, shirts, trousers, skirts, dresses, sweatshirts, T-shirts, tailored jackets, footwear and accessories. In addition to the main collection, you will also find a broad RedGreen golf collection for men and women and also the younger and more casual First Gear Collection. Discounts offered are between 25% and 70%.

REMINGTON
CHESHIRE OAKS DESIGNER OUTLET VILLAGE, ADDRESS AND OPENING HOURS AS BEFORE.
☎ (0151) 357 2477.
Factory Shop in a Factory Shopping Village • *Electrical Equipment*
Lots of famous names here from Oneida and Monogram cutlery to Braun, Philips, Remington, Clairol, Wahl, Swan and small kitchen equipment as well as a wide range of hair, beauty and male grooming accessories, all at reduced prices. It's a great place to buy gifts or replenish the kitchen equipment with combi stylers, turbo travel plus hairdryers, air purifiers, liquidisers; food processors; batteries; clocks; and cutlery. Some of the packaging may be damaged but the products are in perfect working order.

ROOM SERVICE INTERIORS
38 CHARLOTTE STREET, MACCLESFIELD, CHESHIRE SK11 6JB
☎ (01625) 613955. OPEN 9.30 - 5 MON - SAT.
Permanent Discount Outlet • *Furniture/Soft Furnishings*
Sells seconds, fents (small sections of 2 yards in length), roll stock and perfect ends of lines of furnishing and upholstery fabrics from top designers at very cheap prices. The material from which the fents come would normally cost about £15-£25 a metre; here, fents are sold from £4 each. Upholstery fabric costs from £10 a metre, about one third of the normal price. Also seconds of

lace, muslins, calico and top designer trimmings from £2.50 a metre. Making-up service available.

ROYAL WORCESTER & SPODE FACTORY SHOP
CHESHIRE OAKS DESIGNER OUTLET VILLAGE, ADDRESS AND OPENING HOURS AS BEFORE.
☎ (0151) 3569199.
Factory Shop in a Factory Shopping Village • *Household*
Infinitesimally flawed porcelain and china seconds at 25% less than "perfect" prices. This outlet stocks Gleneagles, Langham Glass, Country Artists, Paw Prints, Bowbrook, Ornamenal Studio, Collectible World, Fo-Frame, Six Trees, Pimpernel table mats and Lakeland Plaques. There is a vast range with special offers throughout the year on anything from crystal decanters and bowls to figurines, cookware and dinner sets. Shipping arrangements worldwide can be organised.

RUSSELL ATHLETIC
CHESHIRE OAKS DESIGNER OUTLET VILLAGE, ADDRESS AND OPENING HOURS AS BEFORE.
☎ (0151) 356 7440.
Factory Shop in a Factory Shopping Village
Sportswear & Equipment • *Womenswear & Menswear* • *Children*
For more than 50 years, Russell Athletic has been a major supplier to American sports teams. Here they sell jogging pants, sweat tops, sports bags, caps, ski hats and T-shirts which are either discontinued or imperfects at discounts of up to 50%. Some stock is still available on the high street but is discounted here and changes constantly.

SIMON BOYD
FABRIC HOUSE, PRINCESS STREET, KNUTSFORD, CHESHIRE WA16 6DD
☎ (01565) 633855. OPEN 9.30 - 5.30 MON - SAT.
SANSBURY RETAIL PARK, CALDY VALLEY ROAD, CHESTER CH3 5QZ
☎ (01244) 311160. OPEN 9.30 - 5.30 MON - SAT, 10 - 4 SUN.
Permanent Discount Outlet • *Furniture/Soft Furnishings*
Stocks thousands of rolls of curtain fabric including chenilles, tapestries, cotton satin and chintzes from brands such as Monkwell, Sanderson and Crowson. For example a chenille costing £25 a yard costs £15.99 here. Also tie-backs, cushions, throws, ready-made curtains. Free measuring, plus making-up service available.

SOMETHING DIFFERENT
44 LOWER BRIDGE STREET, CHESTER, CHESHIRE CH1 1RS
☎ (01244) 317484. OPEN 9.30 - 5 MON - SAT.
Dress Agency • *Hire Shop* • *Womenswear Only*
Upmarket ladies clothes, with a lot of day wear from the top end of the high street names such as Alexon, Louis Feraud, Liberty and Jaeger, amongst others. There is a special events room, a hire section for ballgowns and cocktail

dresses. Casual wear is also available with some sports wear including ski clothing. There are no annual sales but there is a special couture designer rail. The shop also runs charity shows at hotels. They also sell a varied range of new clothes including German designer wear, Phool Indian summer wear, shoes, hats, bags, jewellery, belts and scarves.

SPECIAL EVENT
44 LOWER BRIDGE STREET, CHESTER, CHESHIRE CH1 1RS
☎ (01244) 340757. OPEN 9.30 - 5 MON - SAT.
Dress Agency • *Hire Shop* • *Womenswear Only*
Ball gowns and cocktail wear, with a large selection of designer dresses from sizes 8-24, jewellery, feather boas and accessories. Owned by the proprietor of the dress agency Something Different which specialises in mother of the bride outfits from Armani and Laurel to Mondi and Jaeger. All the eveningwear is new and is for sale or hire. Also an agent for men's evening wear hire by request. They sell clothing by Indian summer wear label, Phool, at competitive prices.

SPOILS
UNIT MSU4, THE PYRAMIDS CENTRE, BIRKENHEAD, CHESHIRE L41 2RA
☎ (0151) 647 5753. OPEN 9 - 5.30 MON - SAT, 10.30 - 4 SUN.
Permanent Discount Outlet • *Household*
General domestic glassware, non-stick bakeware, non-electrical kitchen gadgets, ceramic oven-to-tableware, textiles, cutting boards, aluminium non-stick cookware, bakeware, plastic kitchenware, plastic storage, woodware, coffee pots/makers, furniture, mirrors and picture frames. Rather than being discounted, all the merchandise is very competitively priced - in fact, the company carry out competitors' checks frequently in order to monitor pricing. With 38 branches, the company is able to buy in bulk and thus negotiate very good prices.

SUITS YOU
CHESHIRE OAKS DESIGNER OUTLET VILLAGE, ADDRESS AND OPENING HOURS AS BEFORE.
☎ (0151) 355 6701.
Factory Shop in a Factory Shopping Village • *Menswear Only*
Most of the suits and jackets here are sold under the Suits You label, although there are some Van Kollen jackets and Pierre Cardin suits, as well as suits by Cezan, Benvenuto and Pierre Balmain. A large sign at the door tells you the sorts of discounts you can expect. For example, you can buy two £100 suits for £180 or two £130 suits for £235. There are also cufflinks shirts, two for £26; trousers, two for £50; braces, ties and casual shirts. They also have a range of shoes by Tom English and some by Pierre Cardin with prices reduced in the same way as the clothing: buy two pairs and you get a substantial discount.

SUNRIDGE UPHOLSTERY
19 FARNWORTH ROAD, PENKETH, WARRINGTON, CHESHIRE WA5 2RZ
☎ (01925) 727610. OPEN 8 - 4 MON - FRI.
Factory Shop • *Furniture/Soft Furnishings*
A small factory with a showroom, principally making sofas and suites for showhouses. It sells three-piece suites, sofas and upholstery fabrics. Sunridge are willing to customise the sofa design based on the half dozen or so sofas they have on display. Two-seater sofas cost from £600; armchairs from £350 and foot stools from £130. There are hundreds of upholstery fabrics to choose from including Monkwell, Crowsons, Romo and John Wilman. Delivery, which is free in the northwest only, takes six weeks. They also offer a 12 months interest free credit service after paying a 10% deposit.

TELEVIEW DIRECT
CHESHIRE
☎ (0800) 900 009. WEBSITE: www.teleview-direct.co.uk
Permanent Discount Outlet • *Electrical Equipment*
Discounted TVs and videos, DVDs, hi-fis and on digital. Phone them, telling them what you are looking for, and they will send you a leaflet with a range of those products. You can buy them, rent or rent to buy.

THE BATH RE-ENAMELLING COMPANY
CHAPEL COURT, 70 HOSPITAL STREET, NANTWICH, CHESHIRE CW5 5RF
☎ (01270) 626554. WEBSITE: www.bathreenamelling.co.uk
OPEN 9 - 5 MON, TUE, THUR, FRI, 9 - 1 SAT.
Bath re-enamelling carried out by fully trained operatives in your home for £178 or baths can be collected for stove enamelling or vitreous enamelling at 1100 degrees Centigrade. Examples can be seen in the showroom here together with stimulating ideas for creating period bathrooms. Reclaimed baths for sale. The service is available throughout mainland Britain.

THE CAPE
114 FOREGATE STREET, CHESTER, CHESHIRE CH1 1HB
☎ (01244) 329880. OPEN 9 - 5.30 MON - SAT, 10.30 - 4.30 SUN.
Factory Shop • *Household* • *Furniture/Soft Furnishings*
High density pine furniture made in South Africa from trees grown in managed forests, is sold at factory direct prices with home delivery throughout the UK. The range includes beds, wardrobes, blanket boxes, chests of drawers, tallboys, dressing tables, cheval mirrors, headboards, mattresses, a kitchen range, dining room tables, Welsh dressers, hi-fi units, bookcases. Also on sale in this shops is a range of African accessories and artefacts from Zimbabwe encompassing mirrors, prints, serpentine (stone) ornaments, recylced stationery, handmade wirework, candles and other ethnic and traditional gifts. Colour brochure and price list available on 01535 650940.

THE CURTAIN EXCHANGE
3 HAWTHORN LANE, WILMSLOW, CHESHIRE SK9 1AQ
☎ (01625) 536060 OPEN 10 - 5 MON - SAT.
Secondhand shops • *Furniture/Soft Furnishings*

The Curtain Exchange is a franchised group of shops selling beautiful top quality secondhand curtains, blinds, pelmets, etc at between one-third and one half of the brand new price. Their stock comes from a variety of sources: people who are moving house; people who have curtains made and then feel they are wrong for the room; show houses where the builder wants to recoup some of his outgoings; interior designers' mistakes. Stock changes constantly and ranges from rich brocades, damasks and velvets to chintzes, linens and cottons. Designer names include Colefax & Fowler, Designers Guild, Laura Ashley, Warner, Sanderson, Osborne & Little, Fortuny and Bennison. A team of fitters and alteration experts are available if required. They offer a 24-hour availability. The Curtain Exchange also supply bespoke ranges with samples of curtains hanging. These fabrics are chosen from suppliers all over the world and are an excellent buy. They also offer ready made curtains designed exclusively for them which come in lengths up to 305cm (120"). These are outstanding value, e.g. 80" wide, 120" drop start at £175 including VAT.

THE DESIGNER WAREHOUSE
PARADISE MILL, PARK LANE, MACCLESFIELD CHESHIRE SK11 6TL
☎ (01625) 511169. OPEN 9.30 - 5.30 MON - SAT.
Permanent Discount Outlet • *Womenswear Only*

Designer warehouse has been in business for 13 years, successfully using strong contacts in Europe to sell a wide range of top quality Continental designer labels at savings of up to 50%. Clothes and suppliers change constantly so they represent up-to-the-minute fashion and they endeavour to keep sizes 8 - 20 in stock.

THE OLD SOFA WAREHOUSE
UNIT 1, 3 HAWTHORN LANE, WILMSLOW, CHESHIRE SK9 1AA
☎ (01625) 536397/(07803) 497938. OPEN 10 - 5 THUR, FRI, 10.30 - 5 SAT. OTHER TIMES BY APPOINTMENT ONLY.
Secondhand shops • *Furniture/Soft Furnishings*

The Old Sofa Warehouse buys Victorian, Edwardian and later furniture, drop-end sofas, chaise longues, winged-back armchairs or the odd dining chair in their original condition, which are all sold at very reasonable prices. They stock a selection of designer fabrics and swatches - for example, from Thomas Dare, Andrew Martin, Titley and Marr, Hill & Knowles, Ian Sanderson, Linwood and Leon Brunswick. They offer an upholstery service with customers either choosing their own fabric or the Sofa Warehouse's.

THE SUIT COMPANY
CHESHIRE OAKS OUTLET VILLAGE, ADDRESS AND OPENING HOURS AS BEFORE.
☎ (0151) 355 7473.
Factory Shop in a Factory Shopping Village • *Menswear Only*
This shop is part of the Moss Bros group and includes labels such as YSL, Pierre Cardin, Wolsey and Jockey underwear, as well as leather gloves, belts, ties, work shirts, suits, jackets.

THORNTONS
CHESHIRE OAKS OUTLET VILLAGE, ADDRESS AND OPENING HOURS AS BEFORE.
☎ (0151) 355 5637.
Factory Shop in a Factory Shopping Village • *Food and Leisure*
The UK's leading specialist confectionery retailer has more than 500 shops and franchises nationwide selling a wide range of boxed and loose, chocolate and sugar confectionery. The factory outlets sell three different categories: misshapes. discounted lines and standard lines. Misshapes are loose chocolates which are the result of new product development, product trials or end of production runs which cannot be packed as Thorntons standard lines. They are packed into assorted bags and offer a saving of 35%-55% over the recommended retail price of standard "loose line" products. Discounted lines are excess to Thorntons' normal retail requirements and can be as a result of excess seasonal or export stock, discontinued lines or packaging changes. These products, when available, are offered at a discount of 25%-50% over the standard retail price. Standard lines from the full Thorntons range are also on sale at normal prices.

TIE RACK
CHESHIRE OAKS OUTLET VILLAGE, ADDRESS AND OPENING HOURS AS BEFORE.
☎ (0151) 355 6166.
Factory Shop in a Factory Shopping Village • *Menswear Only*
Usual range of Tie Rack items including boxer shorts, silk ties, socks, silk scarves and waistcoats, all at up to 50% reductions. Customer Careline: ☎ 0208 230 2333.

TILE CLEARING HOUSE
MALBERN INDUSTRIAL ESTATE, GREF STREET, REDDISH, STOCKPORT, CHESHIRE.
☎ (0161) 476 4355. OPEN 8 - 6 MON - FRI, 9 - 6 SAT, 10 - 4 SUN.
Permanent Discount Outlet • *DIY/Renovation*
Over 500 ranges of top quality ceramic wall and floor tiles permanently in stock, plus a comprehensive range of grouts, adhesives, tools and accessories to complete the job. By buying direct from the manufacturer and passing the savings on to the customer, their prices are very competitive. Moreover, everything you see is in stock, so there's no waiting for orders to be processed. Save up to 75% on manufacturers' recommended selling prices.

TIMBERLAND
CHESHIRE OAKS OUTLET VILLAGE, ADDRESS AND OPENING HOURS AS BEFORE.
☎ (0151) 357 1359
Factory Shop in a Factory Shopping Village • *Womenswear & Menswear*
Footwear, clothing and outdoor gear from the well-known Timberland range at discounts of 30% or more. Most of the stock is last season's or discontinued lines, but not seconds. All stock is last season's excess stock in limited ranges and sizes. As most of Timberland's stock is from a core range which rarely changes, there are few discontinued lines.

TOG 24
CHESHIRE OAKS OUTLET VILLAGE, ADDRESS AND OPENING HOURS AS BEFORE.
☎ (01513) 567477.
Factory Shop in a Factory Shopping Village
Womenswear & Menswear • *Children* • *Sportswear & Equipment*
Tog 24 are the UK's fastest growing brand name in outdoor clothing and leisurewear. They utilise the world's finest performance fabrics including Gore-Tex, Polartec and Burlington MCS, catering for all the family for all seasons, with cosy fleeces and waterproofs for the winter, and trekking ranges, shorts and t-shirts for the summer. With all prices at least 30% below the recommended retail price, you can afford to enter the Tog comfort zone.

TOP NOTCH
54 HOSPITAL STREET, NANTWICH, CHESHIRE CW5 5RP
☎ (01270) 623334. OPEN 10 - 4.30 MON - FRI, 10 - 5 SAT.
Dress Agency • *Womenswear Only*
Dress agency selling names such as Betty Jackson, Louis Feraud and Paul Costelloe, as well as shoes, accessories and handbags. Specialises upstairs in a new Danish range of larger sizes from 16-30.

TOYWORLD FACTORY OUTLET LTD
CHESHIRE OAKS OUTLET VILLAGE, ADDRESS AND OPENING HOURS AS BEFORE.
☎ (0151) 355 9998. WEBSITE: www.toyworldstore.com
Factory Shop in a Factory Shopping Village • *Children*
Toyworld sell a large range of discontinued toys, manufacturers' overruns and excess stock from many famous brand names such as Barbie, Action Man, Lego, Tomy, Fisher-Price and many more at least 30-60% off high street prices.

TRAVEL ACCESSORY
CHESHIRE OAKS OUTLET VILLAGE, ADDRESS AND OPENING HOURS AS BEFORE.
☎ (0151) 357 3248.
Factory Shop in a Factory Shopping Village • *Food and Leisure*
Luggage and travel-related products and executive cases, handbags, umbrellas from leading brands such as Samsonite, Desley, Head, Taurus and GlobeTrotter. Each product is offered at a substantially reduced price compared to those found on the high street due to being production over-runs, discontinued ranges or colours and last season's products. Discounts range from 30%-75% off high street prices.

UNITED FOOTWEAR
4-6 DELAMARE STREET, CHESTER, CHESHIRE
☎ (01244) 370300. OPEN 9 - 6 MON - FRI, 9 - 5.30 SAT, 10 - 4 SUN.
Permanent Discount Outlet • *Womenswear & Menswear*
Children • *Sportswear & Equipment*
Shoes for all the family as well as clothes, handbags, sports shoes, boots, giftware and household goods, all at discounted prices. Famous brands including Clarks, K Shoes and Elmdale. Part of a national chain.

MAKING THE MOST OF SHOP SALES
Successful sales require rules which must be adhered to. First, visit the shop the week before the sale begins. Make sure you know the layout – and talk to the assistants about what might be marked down. Second, spend an evening trying on everything in your wardrobe, mixing tops with skirts you've never worn them with before. You'll be surprised how many more outfits you can make up. It will also tell you where the gaps are. Third, make a list of the item or items you really need, with sizes, colour and what you intend to wear them with. Keep the list handy and don't deviate from it. Fourth, if you've only got a limited budget and you need to replenish your wardrobe, choose big, expensive buys such as coats and suits which although they'll cost you more will also save you more. Fifth, avoid anything which will date your outfit. Logos with a year date on them are the most obvious no-nos, but designs which are very much of their year such as a particular type of braiding, or flared or palazzo trousers, should also be avoided. Seventh, if you usually live in casual trousers and T-shirts during the summer, don't suddenly buy a body-skimming all-in-one. Finally, if it says dry clean and you want to wear it for every day, it won't be such a bargain once the dry cleaning bills have been taken into account.

VELMORE LTD
UNIT 14, THORNTON ROAD INDUSTRIAL ESTATE, ELLESMERE PORT, CHESHIRE L65 9JJ
☎ (0151) 357 1212. OPEN 10.30 - 3 TUE, WED, THUR, 10.30 - 2 FRI, 9 - 1 SAT.
UNIT 52, APPIN WAY, ARGYLE INDUSTRIAL ESTATE, BIRKENHEAD
☎ (0151) 666 1579. OPEN 10.30 - 3 MON - THUR.
Factory Shop • *Womenswear Only*
Seconds of skirts, dresses, suits, shorts, jackets and trousers originally made for the most famous high street name at very cheap prices.

VICTORIA MILL RETAIL AND FACTORY OUTLETS
FOUNDRY BANK, CONGLETON, CHESHIRE CW12 1EE
☎ (01260) 297642. OPEN 10 - 5 MON - SAT.
Factory Shop • *Furniture/Soft Furnishings* • *Household*
An emporium of homewares and fashion at ex-factory prices. Set in a delightful market town adjacent to the town centre, this Victorian mill has recently been extensively refurbished to offer a variety of independent shops displaying a huge array of merchandise. Everything from cane furniture to chainstore merchandise, including bed, mirrors, lighting. Coffee Shop. Ample parking.

VILLEROY & BOCH (UK) LIMITED
CHESHIRE, OAKS OUTLET VILLAGE, KINSEY ROAD, ELLESMERE PORT, CHESHIRE L65 9JJ
☎ (0151) 355 7771. OPEN 10 - 8 MON - THUR, 10 - 6 FRI, 9 - 6 SAT, 11 - 5 SUN.
Factory Shop in a Factory Shopping Village • *Household*
One of five factory outlets for Villeroy & Boch, this shop carries an exclusive range of tableware, crystal and cutlery from Europe's largest tableware manufacturer. A varied and constantly changing stock, including seconds, hotelware and discontinued lines, on sale at excellent reductions, always makes for a worthwhile visit.

VIYELLA
CHESHIRE OAKS OUTLET VILLAGE, ADDRESS AND OPENING HOURS AS BEFORE.
☎ (0151) 357 2627.
Factory Shop in a Factory Shopping Village • *Womenswear & Menswear*
Wide range of Viyella clothing at discount prices from 30% on ladies formal wear and casual wear.

VOGUE ELEVEN

11 PARK LANE, MACCLESFIELD, CHESHIRE SK11 6TJ
☎ (01625) 427031. FAX (01625) 427031. OPEN 10 - 4 MON - FRI,
10 - 1 WED, 10 - 4 SAT.
Dress Agency • *Womenswear Only*

Small shop in 200-year old building run by the irrepressible Marjorie Potts, who dispenses advice cheerfully and knowledgeably. Marjorie wouldn't have been running the business so successfully for 20 years without being extremely good at it and the quality of the clothes and the labels prove that. There's Shiren Guild, Mani, Prada, Emporio Armani, Caroline Charles, Margaret Howell, Donna Karan, Katharine Hamnett, Workers for Freedom, Jasper Conran, Diane Fres, Jaeger, Escada, Basler, Louis Feraud and Ralph Lauren. There are also some brand new samples. Prices range from £5 to £200 in sizes from 8 to 18.

WALLIS

CHESHIRE OAKS OUTLET VILLAGE, ADDRESS AND OPENING HOURS AS BEFORE.
☎ (0151) 356 9297.
Factory Shop in a Factory Shopping Village • *Womenswear Only*

Wide range of clothes from summerwear to coats, all at discount prices of up to 30%.

WAREHOUSE

CHESHIRE OAKS OUTLET VILLAGE, ADDRESS AND OPENING HOURS AS BEFORE.
☎ (0151) 357 3168.
Factory Shop in a Factory Shopping Village • *Womenswear Only*

Wide range of clothes from summerwear to coats, all at discount prices of up to 30%.

WINDSMOOR GROUP

CHESHIRE OAKS OUTLET VILLAGE, ADDRESS AND OPENING HOURS AS BEFORE.
☎ (0151) 357 2728.
Factory Shop in a Factory Shopping Village • *Womenswear Only*

Previous season's stock as well as any returned merchandise and overmakes from the Windsmoor, Planet and Precis Petite ranges at discounts averaging about 50% off the original price.

WOODS OF WINDSOR
CHESHIRE OAKS OUTLET VILLAGE, ADDRESS AND OPENING HOURS AS BEFORE.
☎ (0151) 355 8170.
Factory Shop in a Factory Shopping Village • *Household*
This shop sells gift sets, soaps, perfume, bath gel, room fragrance sprays, hand and body lotions and talc at discounts of 30% for standard ranges and 50% for discounted ranges.

WYNSORS WORLD OF SHOES
LONDON ROAD, HAZEL GROVE, STOCKPORT, CHESHIRE SK7 4AX
☎ (0161) 456 2632. OPEN 9 - 5.30 MON, TUE, WED, SAT, 9 - 8 THUR, FRI, 10 - 4 SUN AND BANK HOLIDAYS.
Permanent Discount Outlet • *Womenswear & Menswear* • *Children*
Stocks top brand-name shoes at less than half price. Special monthly offers always available. There are shoes, trainers, slippers, sandals and boots for all the family, with a selection of bags, cleaners and polishes available.

YES STORES
207 GRANGE ROAD, BIRKENHEAD, CHESHIRE CH41 2PH
☎ (0151) 647 3050. OPEN 9 - 5.30 MON - SAT, 11 - 4 SUN
UNIT 11, PORT ARCADES, MERCER WALK, ELLESMERE PORT, SOUTH WIRRAL CHESHIRE L65 9JJ
☎ (0151) 357 3782. OPEN 9 - 5.30 MON - SAT, 10 - 4 SUN.
Permanent Discount Outlet • *Womenswear Only*
Mainly former catalogue clothes for women, with a small selection for men and children, as well as some high street store names, although the labels are often cut out. Stock changes twice-weekly as turnover is quick.

YOU & YOURS
UNIT 42, FOREST WALK, HALTON LEAS SHOPPING CENTRE, RUNCORN, CHESHIRE
☎ (01928) 795 792. OPEN 9 - 5.30 MON - SAT.
Permanent Discount Outlet • *Womenswear & Menswear* • *Children*
Electrical Equipment • *Household* • *Furniture/Soft Furnishings*
Mostly consisting of unsold lines through the Grattan mail order catalogues at the end of the season, but there is also some current season stock. Women's, men's and children's clothing, hardware, plastics and textiles, electrics and some furniture, although the majority is women's fashion, including many famous high street labels. All items in the store retail at a minimum of 30% off the catalogue price, with some items discounted by up to 50%. They also have regular promotional offers.

Co Durham

BAGGAGE DEPOT
JACKSONS LANDING, HARTLEPOOL FACTORY OUTLET SHOPPING MALL, THE HIGHLIGHT, HARTLEPOOL, CO DURHAM TS24 OXN
☎ (01429) 235998. OPEN 10 -6 MON - SAT, 11 - 5 SUN.
Factory Shop in a Factory Shopping Village • *Food and Leisure*
Luggage and travel-related products and executive cases, handbags, umbrellas from leading brands such as Samsonite, Desley, Head, Taurus and GlobeTrotter. Each product is offered at a substantially reduced price compared to those found on the high street due to being production over-runs, discontinued ranges or colours and last season's products. Discounts range from 30%-75% off high street prices.

BEST DRESS CLUB
NEW ROAD, CROOK, DURHAM DL15 8AH
☎ (01388) 764900. OPEN 10 - 5 MON - FRI, 10 - 4 SAT.
Permanent Discount Outlet • *Womenswear Only*
Ladies daywear from well-known high street names such as Dorothy Perkins, Next and Etam reduced by at least 50%. Prices for the dresses, skirts, tops, jumpers and trousers range from £7.50 to £24.95.

BMJ POWER C/O BLACK & DECKER,
SERVICE STATION, GREEN LANE, SPENNYMOOR, CO DURHAM DL16 6JG
☎ (01388) 422429. OPEN 8 - 5.30 MON, TUE, THUR, FRI, 9 - 5.30 WED, 8 - 2 SAT.
Factory Shop • *DIY/Renovation*
Predominantly an after-sales service with retail added on, this outlet sells reconditioned tools and acccessories from the famous Black & Decker range, as well as other power tools, circle saws, lawnmowers, staple guns and drills, all with full manufacturer's warranty and at discounts of about 25%. Often, stock consists of goods returned from the shops because of damaged packaging or part of a line which is being discontinued. Lots of seasonal special offers. There are more than three dozen BMJ outlets countrywide. Phone 0345 230230 and you can find out where your nearest outlet is.

CLASSY CLOTHES
USWORTH ROAD, HARTLEPOOL, CO DURHAM TS25 1YA
☎ (01429) 868553. OPEN 9 - 5 MON - FRI, 9 - 5.30 SAT.
Permanent Discount Outlet • *Womenswear Only*
Deals mostly in brand new, well-known high street names such as Wallis, Principles, BhS and Ann Harvey. All are on sale at savings of at least 40% in sizes 8 - 24. For example, trousers reduced from £28.99 to £15; jackets; £29.99 from £59.99; dresses, £15 from £49.99.

COCO
11 GRANGE ROAD, DARLINGTON, CO DURHAM DL1 5NA
☎ (01325) 383720. OPEN 10 - 5 MON - SAT.
Dress Agency • *Womenswear Only*

Small shop packed with daywear, evening wear and accessories from every kind of label - Wallis, Next and Laura Ashley to Basler, Escada and Nicole Farhi. Clothes are immaculate and often mistaken for new by window shoppers. Sizes are mostly 10-14 with some 16s, and prices range from £5 to £200.

DEWHIRST IMPRESSIONS
NORTH WEST INDUSTRIAL ESTATE, PETERLEE, CO DURHAM SR8 2HR
☎ (0191) 586 4525. OPEN 9 - 6 MON - WED, FRI, SAT, 9 - 7 THUR, 11 - 5 SUN.
PENNYWELL INDUSTRIAL ESTATE, PENNYWELL, SUNDERLAND SR4 9EN
☎ (0191) 534 642) 474210. OPEN 10 - 8 MON - FRI, 10 - 6 SAT, 10.30 - 4.30 SUN.
OWN INDUSTRIAL ESTATE, DORMANSTOWN, REDCAR TS10 5QD
☎ (01642) 474210. OPEN 10 - 8 MON - FRI, 10 - 6 SAT,10.30 - 4.30 SUN.
Factory Shop • *Children* • *Womenswear & Menswearear*

Sells garments from the manufacturing side of the business direct to the public and are part of the Dewhirst Group plc which manufactures ladies, men's and childrenswear for a leading high street retailer. You can choose from a huge selection of surplus production and slight seconds at bargain prices, making savings of more than 50% of the normal retail cost. For men there is a wide range of suits, formal shirts and casual wear. For example, suits from £60, formal and casual shirts from £7. For ladies there's a selection of blouses, smart tailoring and casual wear that includes a denim range. You can find ladies jackets from £50, skirts, trousers and blouses from £8. Children's clothes start at £3. High street quality and style at wholesale prices.

EBAC
ST HELENS TRADING ESTATE, BISHOP AUCKLAND, CO DURHAM
☎ 0800 591991. OPEN 10 - 3.30 SUMMER. HOURS CHANGEABLE DURING WINTER, PHONE FIRST.
Factory Shop • *Electrical Equipment*

Quality end of range dehumidifiers at discount prices, plus graded ex-display models which are in perfect working order. The shop itself is only open from September to the end of April but at other times you can go to reception and they will open it up for you.

EDINBURGH CRYSTAL
JACKSONS LANDING, HARTLEPOOL FACTORY OUTLET SHOPPING
MALL, HARTLEPOOL MARINA, HARTLEPOOL, CO DURHAM TS24 OXN
☎ (01429) 234335. OPEN 10 - 6 MON - SAT, 11 - 5 SUN AND
BANK HOLIDAYS.
Factory Shop in a Factory Shopping Village • *Household*
Indoor factory shopping centre with more than twenty-four outlets selling brand name items including cut-glass crystal. This shop has displays all round packed with glasses, decanters, gifts, glass picture frames, coloured glass, vases, bowls and jugs. Examples of prices include decanters reduced from £115 to £29.95; large tumblers from £14 to £5.95 for perfects; seconds wine glasses from £2.95; seconds decanters from £24.95; glass bowls from £21.50 for perfects, £14.95 for seconds. Also Arthur Price cutlery from 20% to 50% reduction. There is free parking adjacent to the centre, a coffee shop, restaurant and baby changing and disabled facilities.

ENCORE
20 FREDERICK ST, SUNDERLAND, CO DURHAM SR1 1LT
☎ (0191) 564 2227. OPEN 10- 4 MON - SAT.
Dress Agency • *Hire Shop* • *Womenswear Only*
Sells designer labels, smart day wear, evening wear, special occasion wear, wedding outfits, hats and accessories. Labels stocked include various German labels, Escada, Louis Feraud, Frank Usher, Betty Barclay, Windsmoor, Planet, Wallis and Next. One of the two rooms in this outlet specialises in special occasion wear, the other in smart daywear. There is also a hire service for evening wear only, which costs from £60-£95 a weekend. For example, a £300 dress would cost £60 to hire.

HALLMARK
JACKSONS LANDING, HARTLEPOOL FACTORY OUTLET SHOPPING
MALL, HARTLEPOOL MARINA, HARTLEPOOL, CO DURHAM TS24 OXN
☎ (01429) 275680. OPEN 10 - 6 MON - SAT AND BANK HOLIDAYS,
11 - 5 SUN.
Factory Shop in a Factory Shopping Village • *Food and Leisure*
Indoor factory shopping centre with more than twenty-four outlets selling brand name items including everything you need for celebrations at Hallmark. Most of the stock here is discounted by 50% including, stuffed toys, cards, wrapping paper and gift rosettes. Gift wrap, 30p or four sheets for £1; Christmas cards in boxed sets of 10 with envelopes, £1.99 reduced from £3.99. All the cards are half price and include the usual range of celebratory valedictions.

HONEY
JACKSONS LANDING, ADDRESS AND OPENING HOURS AS BEFORE.
☎ (01429) 260488.
Factory Shop in a Factory Shopping Village • *Womenswear Only*
Leisure-oriented women's T-shirts, leggings and sweaters at discounts of mostly 30% to 50%.

JACKSONS LANDING FACTORY OUTLETS
THE HIGHLIGHT, HARTLEPOOL MARINA, HARTLEPOOL, CLEVELAND, CO DURHAM TS24 OXN
☎ (01429) 866989 INFORMATION LINE. FAX 01249 866947.
OPEN 10 - 6 MON - SAT, 11 - 5 SUN, 10 - 6 BANK HOLIDAYS.
Factory Shopping Village • *Womenswear & Menswear* • *Children Household* • *Sportswear & Equipment*

There is now more than ever before at the Jacksons Landing Factory Outlets. The Designer Room has two floors (ladieswear - ground floor, menswear - first floor) packed with designer labels and is the biggest Designer Room in the UK with savings of up to 70%. Jacksons Landing is a purpose-built shopping mall situated on the prestigious Hartlepool Marina next to the Historic Quay and HMS Trincomalee. Around one million people visit the centre each year to take advantage of the low prices on offer. The shops sell goods direct from the factory or as excess stock and end of lines from the high street, but wherever the goods come from you will find tremendous discounts. The 21 shops include famous brands such as Benetton, Tog 24, Windsmoor Sale Shop, Edinburgh Crystal, Royal Brierley and Ponden Mill. The Designer Room stocks Ralph Lauren, DKNY, French Connection, Roman, Ghost, Jasper Conran, Diesel, John Paul Gaultier, Tommy Hilfiger, Moss Bros and many more, all with up to 70% off normal high street prices. The Designer Room also stocks perfumes and accessories to complement the range. The Designer Room Cafe on the first floor offers a wide selection of hot and cold food and drinks, making it the ideal place to take a break . Jacksons Landing has 400 free car parking spaces and is only 15 minutes from the A19. Follow the signs for Jacksons Landing and the Hartlepool Marina on the A689 or A174

JOCKEY UNDERWEAR FACTORY SHOP
EASTERN AVENUE, TEAM VALLEY TRADING ESTATE, GATESHEAD, CO DURHAM NE11 OPB
☎ (0191) 491 0088. OPEN 9 - 4 MON - FRI.
Factory Shop • *Womenswear & Menswear*

Up to 17 different types of men's underwear from Y-fronts and boxers to tangas and hipsters. Also ladies underwear: briefs, ribbed vests, cami-tops, bodies. Although well known for underwear, the factory shop also sells golfing clothing, Wolsey socks, Christy and Supreme towels, bedding, Zorbit babywear, pillows and duvets with up to 50% discount.

LABELS OF BARNARD CASTLE
8 THE BANK, BARNARD CASTLE, CO DURHAM DL12 8PQ
☎ (01833) 6905481. OPEN 10.30 - 5 MON - SAT.
Dress Agency • *Womenswear & Menswear*

Located in a historic market town with easy parking, women's clothes here range from top end Chanel and Moschino Couture to Nicole Farhi, Paul Costelloe and Joseph with a good measure of quality Italian designer labels as well. Popular men's ranges include Hugo Boss, Armani and Cerruti suits as well as casual wear. As-new clothes sell for about one third of the brand new price. New end of range clothes are sometimes available - telephone for details. Clothes sold on 50% commission; "sellers" please make appointment first.

LITTLEWOODS CATALOGUE DISCOUNT STORE
19 FAWCETT STREET, SUNDERLAND, CO DURHAM SR1 1RH
☎ (0191) 564 0684. OPEN 9.30 - 5.30 MON - THUR, 9 - 5.30 FRI, SAT.
Factory Shop • *Womenswear & Menswear* • *Children*
Electrical Equipment

Littlewoods clearance shops offering up to 50% off the catalogue price for clothing and between 50% and 60% off for electrical goods. Stock changes constantly and varies from day to day but can include well-known brand names such as Berlei and Gossard lingerie, Vivienne Westwood, Pamplemousse leisure wear, Nike and Adidas sports shoes, Workers for Freedom, and Timberland and Caterpillar footwear. Stock depends on the size and location of the shop, so larger shops will get the longer discontinued runs and smaller shops over-runs with only a small amount of colour and size variations left. Littlewoods also run a mobile shop which operates in cities where they don't have a sale shop. For details of further venues for the sales, which usually take place once a month, contact Melanie Lamb, c/o Crosby DC Kershaw Avenue, Endbutt Lane, Crosby, Merseyside L70 1AH.

MATALAN
16 GOODWOOD SQUARE, TEESSIDE RETAIL PARK, THORNABY, STOCKTON-ON-TEES.CO DURHAM TS17 7BW
☎ (01642) 633204. OPEN 10 - 8 MON - FRI, 9 - 6 SAT, 11 - 5 SUN.
ANCHOR RETAIL PARK, MARINA WAY, HARTLEPOOL TS24 0XR
☎ (01429) 855960. OPEN 10 - 8 MON - FRI, 9 - 6 SAT, 11 - 5 SUN.
UNIT 1, HYLTON RIVERSIDE RETAIL PARK, SUNDERLAND SR5 3XG
☎ (0191) 516 0141. OPEN 10 - 8 MON - FRI, 9 - 6 SAT, 11 - 5 SUN.
Permanent Discount Outlet • *Womenswear & Menswear*
Children • *Household*

Matalan is a fashion and homewares value retailer giving customers what they claim to be unbeatable value for money with huge savings on a wide range of products including high quality fashionable clothing for men, women and children at up to 50% off high street prices. Matalan is situated out of town and stores are open seven days a week all year round.

MCINTOSH'S FACTORY SHOP
UNIT 1, THE FACTORY SHOP CENTRE, TUNDRY WAY, CHAINBRIDGE INDUSTRIAL ESTATE, BLAYDON ON TYNE, CO DURHAM NE21 5SJ
☎ (0191) 414 8598. OPEN 9.30 - 5 MON - FRI, 7 ON THUR, 9 - 5 SAT, 10 - 4 SUN.
Factory Shop • *Household*
Quilts, duvet covers, towels, beach towels, bedlinen, dusters, bath mat sets and ceramic kitchenware at bargain prices. Most of the household textiles are perfect with some seconds. Parking is easy and there is a coffee shop.

NEXT ENCOUNTER
3B HOUNDGATE, DARLINGTON, CO DURHAM DL1 1RL
☎ (01325) 255033. OPEN 10 - 5 MON - SAT.
Dress Agency • *Womenswear Only*
Mostly high street labels such as Next, Principles, Oasis, Miss Selfridge, Laura Ashley and Marks & Spencer. Also sells shoes, handbags and other accessories.

NEWELL COMPANY SHOP
WEAR GLASS WORKS, OFF TRINDON STREET, MILLFIELD, SUNDERLAND, CO. DURHAM SR4 6EB
☎ (0191) 515 6500. OPEN 8.30 - 5 MON - THUR, 8.30 - 4.30 FRI.
Factory Shop • *Household*
Heat-resistant dishes for the kitchen including Pyrex cookware, bakeware and oven to tableware and Pyroflam white casserole dishes which are safe to use in the microwave, dishwasher, freezer or oven top. Also glasses, jugs, vases, lunch boxes and plastic containers. Current perfect lines are sold here at full price, but there are lots of end of line ranges, as well as surplus orders, sold at factory shop prices.

NORTHUMBRIAN FINE FOODS PLC
DUKESWAY, TEAM VALLEY INDUSTRIAL ESTATE, GATESHEAD, CO DURHAM NE11 0QP
☎ (0191) 487 0070. OPEN 9.30 - 3 MON - FRI.
Food and Drink Discounters
Value-for-money cakes, biscuits and snack foods from this north-east based company which manufactures biscuits and cakes under its own brand name, such as Cake Break, Sunwheel, Knightsbridge, Bronte, and Cakes for the Connoisseur. They also produce a selection of private label goods for many of the high street supermarkets. The factory shop sells overruns of its entire range at very reasonable prices. Availability varies but typically includes plain and chocolate biscuits, flapjacks, cookies, confectionery and cakes.

PONDEN MILL LINENS
UNITS 13-14 MILBURNGATE SHOPPING CENTRE,
CO DURHAM DH1 4SL
☎ (0191) 383 1783. OPEN 9 - 5.30 MON - SAT.
JACKSONS LANDING, THE HIGHLIGHTS, HARTLEPOOL TS24 OXN
☎ (01429) 266935. OPEN 10 - 6 MON - SAT, 11 - 5 SUN.
Factory Shop in a Factory Shopping Village • *Household Furniture/Soft Furnishings*
Famous branded products at direct from the mill prices. A fabulous assortment of towels, duvets, pillows, throws, bedspreads, up-to-the-minute coordinated bed linen, from Crown, Coloroll, Jeff Banks Ports-of-Call, to name but a few. Something for every room in the house.

POWER PLUS DIRECT
☎ (0700) 234 0700. MAIL ORDER ONLY.
If you're looking for a washing machine, fridge, freezer, tumble dryer, television set, hi-fi or camcorder, shop around, find the product you want and make a note of the product code. Then phone Power Plus Direct and they will usually beat the best price you have found. They can deliver countrywide, but there is a charge.

ROCK-A-BYE BABY
65 THE LARUM BEAT, YARM, STOCKTON-ON-TEES,
CO DURHAM TS15 9HR
☎ (01642) 898537. PHONE FIRST.
Hire Shop • *Children*
For hire: cots, travel cots, car seats, stair gates, fire guards, bed guards, portable high chairs, buggies, activity centres, door bouncers and toy packages. Terms are from one day to six months. They also specialise in a wide range of complete christening outfits and gowns in sizes 0 - 12 months from £8 to £25. Confirmation and communion dresses are also available for hire.

ROYAL BRIERLEY CRYSTAL
JACKSONS LANDING, THE HIGHLIGHT, HARTLEPOOL MARINA,
HARTLEPOOL, CLEVELAND, CO DURHAM TS24 OXN
☎ (01429) 865600. OPEN 10 - 6 MON - SAT, 11 - 5 SUN.
Factory Shop in a Factory Shopping Village • *Household*
Royal Brierley crystal seconds and Spiegelau glassware at very good prices, with a minimum of 30% off retail sold in this indoor factory shopping centre with more than twenty-four outlets and a concessions-based Emporium selling brand name items.

SEYMOUR'S OF DARLINGTON
1-3 EAST ROW, DARLINGTON, CO DURHAM DL1 5PZ
☎ (01325) 355272. OPEN 9 - 5 MON - SAT.

Permanent Discount Outlet • *Household* • *Children*
Furniture/Soft Furnishings

Seymour's of Darlington is the longest-established household linen retailer in the area and takes great pride in maintaining its loyal customer base. This unique family-owned business combines old-fashioned quality and service with the newest designs and keenest prices. There is a constantly changing, stunning variety of stock from tea towels to the latest French designer bed linens. Customers of all ages will find trendy to traditional items at prices to suit all pockets. There are always special offers giving extra value and there is a full range of duvets, pillows, tablecloths, towels, throws, cushion covers, duvet covers and curtains (ready-made and made-to-measure), and bathroom fittings include shower curtains. Seymour's have their own high quality brand of polycotton sheets, valances and pillowcases, also available in percale. More unusual items include flannelette sheets, super king-size, 4 ft and bunk-size bedding. Makes include current perfect ranges from Sanderson, Dorma, Nimbus, Snuggledown, Christy, Coloroll and Miller, plus economy lines and seconds. Chainstore seconds are often on offer and all prices are extremely competitive. For children, they stock the Sweet Dreams range, usually made from Designers Guild fabric, comprising cot quilts and bumpers, Moses baskets, baby blankets, all with matching laundry bags, lamp shades, nappy stackers, curtains, wallpapers and co-ordinating borders. Staff are friendly and obliging and will advise if required, and many items can be ordered if not in stock. Short-term parking is available right outside from Tuesday to Friday and there is wheelchair access. Debit and credit cards are accepted.

TECAZ
SWIFT 957, TECAZ HOUSE, CHIRTON INDUSTRIAL ESTATE, NORHAM ROAD, NORTH SHIELDS, CO DURHAM NE29 7TN
☎ (0191) 257 6511. OPEN 9 - 6 MON - FRI, 9 - 5 SAT, 10 - 4 SUN.
TECAZ HOUSE, RYHOPE STREET, RYHOPE, SUNDERLAND SR2 9QR.
☎ (0191) 523 8164. OPEN 9 - 6 MON - FRI, 9 - 5 SAT, 10 - 4 SUN.

Permanent Discount Outlet • *Furniture/Soft Furnishings*
DIY/Renovation

Vast area displaying over 150 bathroom suites, 50 shower cubicles from manufacturers like Heritage, Armitage Shanks, Shires, Vitra, Twyfords and Rocca, as well as 50 kitchens and bedrooms, including the electrical equipment to go in them in well-known brands. There are tiles, baths, sinks, taps, shower trays, showers, soap dishes, toilets, loo roll holders and mirrors. Because Tecaz buy in large numbers, they can get better discounts from the manufacturer, some of which they pass on to the customer.

TENSOR MARKETING LTD
LINGFIELD WAY, YARM ROAD INDUSTRIAL ESTATE, DARLINGTON,
CO DURHAM DL1 4XX
☎ (01325) 469 181. E-MAIL: TensorLimited @aol.com.
WEBSITE: www.tensormarketing.co.uk. OPEN 9 - 5 MON - FRI, 10 - 4.30 SAT.
Factory Shop • *Household* • *Children*
Sportswear & Equipment
Marketing company specialising in innovative products with a huge range of goods covering home and garden, office, motoring, gifts, novelties, pets, pest control systems, security, health and fitness, sport and leisure. The garden section has a range of items including gutter flushes, hammer and edging fencing, mole chasers, foldaway wheelbarrows, garden lighting sets, weeders, garden thermometers, corner plant stands, garden hoses and obelisks.

THE COURTAULDS FACTORY SHOP
GREENFIELDS INDUSTRIAL ESTATE, TINDALE CRESCENT,
BISHOPS AUCKLAND, CO DURHAM DL14 9TF
☎ (01388) 661703 . OPEN 9 - 5.30 MON - SAT, 11 - 5 SUN.
NORTHWEST INDUSTRIAL ESTATE, FIENNES ROAD, PETERLEE,
CO DURHAM SR8 2QH
☎ (0191) 5182267. OPEN 9 - 6 MON - SAT, 7 ON THUR, 11 - 5 SUN.
Factory Shop • *Womenswear & Menswear* • *Children* • *Household*
Sells a wide range of ladies, men's and childrens high street fashions at between 30% and 50% below high street prices. Also stocks a wide range of household textiles and accessories.

THE FACTORY SHOP
2 - 4 COMMERCIAL STREET, CROOK, CO DURHAM DL15 9HP
☎ (01388) 763211. OPEN 9 - 5.30 MON - SAT, 10.30 - 4.30 SUN.
Factory Shop • *Children* • *Womenswear & Menswear*
Household • *Furniture/Soft Furnishings* • *Sportswear & Equipment*
Wide range on sale includes men's, ladies and children's clothing and footwear; household textiles; toiletries; hardware; luggage; lighting and bedding, most of which are chainstore and high street brands at discounts of approximately 30%-50%. There are weekly deliveries and brands include many major stars such as Adidas, Nike, Joe Bloggs and Brabantia, to name just a few. Now has kitchen and furniture displays with a line of Cape Country furniture on sale. Ranges are continually changing and few factory shops offer such a variety under one roof. There is a free public car park in front of the shop.

TOG 24
THE HIGHLIGHT, JACKSONS LANDING, HARTLEPOOL FACTORY
OUTLET SHOPPING MALL, HARTLEPOOL MARINA, HARTLEPOOL,
CO DURHAM TS24 ONX
☎ (01429) 866103. OPEN 10 - 6 MON - SAT, 11 - 5 SUN AND
BANK HOLIDAYS.
Factory Shop in a Factory Shopping Village
Womenswear & Menswear • Children • Sportswear & Equipment
Tog 24 are the UK's fastest growing brand name in outdoor clothing and leisurewear. They utilise the world's finest performance fabrics including Gore-Tex, Polartec and Burlington MCS, catering for all the family for all seasons, with cosy fleeces and waterproofs for the winter, and trekking ranges, shorts and t-shirts for the summer. With all prices at least 30% below the recommended retail price, you can afford to enter the Tog comfort zone.

TOM SAYERS CLOTHING CO
JACKSONS LANDING, ADDRESS AND OPENING HOURS AS BEFORE.
☎ (01429) 861439.
Factory Shop in a Factory Shopping Village • *Menswear Only*
Tom Sayers make sweaters for some of the top high street department stores. Unusually for a factory shop, if they don't stock your size, they will try and order it for you from their factory or one of their other factory outlets and send it to you. Most of the stock here is overstock, cancelled orders or last season's and includes jumpers, trousers and shirts at discounts of 30%. The trousers and shirts are bought in to complement the sweaters which they make.

TOYMASTER FACTORY OUTLETS
50 - 51 THE CORNMILL SHOPPING CENTRE, DARLINGTON,
CO DURHAM DL1 1LT
☎ (01325) 363 222. WEBSITE: www.toyworldstore.com
OPEN 9- 5.3- MON - SAT.
Factory Shop • *Children*
A large range of the very latest toys at competitive prices plus a massive range of discontinued toys, manufacturers overruns and excess stocks from many famous brand names such as Barbie, Action Man, Lego, Tomy, Fisher Price and many more, at least 30% to 70% off normal high street prices. Also available is a full range of T.P. outdoor activity toys and play frames.

TOYWORLD FACTORY OUTLETS LTD
JACKSONS LANDING, ADDRESS AND OPENING HOURS AS BEFORE.
☎ (01429) 866606. WEBSITE: www.toyworldstore.com
Factory Shop in a Factory Shopping Village • *Children*
Toyworld sell a large range of discontinued toys, manufacturers' overruns and excess stock from many famous brand names such as Barbie, Action Man, Lego, Tomy, Fisher-Price and many more at least 30-60% off high street prices.

WARNERS UK LTD
JACKSONS LANDING, ADDRESS AND OPENING HOURS AS BEFORE.
☎ (01429) 890134.
Factory Shop in a Factory Shopping Village • *Womenswear & Menswear*
This shop sells a wide range of women's lingerie from Leisureby, Warners, with bras, slips, thongs, bodies and briefs at discounts from 25% to 70%. Each item is labelled with both the rrp and the discounted prices. For example, bikini brief, £6.99 reduced from £17; underwire bra, £14.99 reduced from £33; body, £24.99 reduced from £65. Slightly imperfect stock as well as perfect quality, end of season and discontinued merchandise and swimwear are also stocked. Underwear for men, including Calvin Klein briefs for £2.99, is on offer too.

WINDSMOOR DISTRIBUTION CENTRE
UNIT 1, NORTHERN INDUSTRIAL ESTATE, BOWBURN, DURHAM,
CO DURHAM DH6 5AT
☎ (0191) 377 9897.
Designer Sales • *Womenswear & Menswear*
Regular sales are held here (usually five or six times a year) during which first quality fashion from the Windsmoor, Planet and Precis Petite ranges are sold at discounts starting at 50%. Sometimes, there is also Dannimac rainwear for men and women. Phone or write to be put on the mailing list.

WYNSORS WORLD OF SHOES
PARKFIELD ROAD, OFF BRIDGE ROAD, STOCKTON-ON-TEES,
CLEVELAND, CO DURHAM.
☎ (01642) 672525. OPEN 9 - 5.30 MON, TUE, WED, SAT, 9 - 8 THUR, FRI, 10 - 4 SUN AND BANK HOLIDAYS.
Permanent Discount Outlet • *Children* • *Womenswear & Menswear*
Range of seconds footwear for children as well as adults. There are slippers, sandals, boots, trainers, sports shoes, leather and vinyl handbags and purses, shoe cleaners and polishes. Ladies fashion shoes start from £6 a pair. There are some well known brands, all at substantial savings on high street prices.

YOU & YOURS
UNIT 8, HYLTON RIVERSIDE RETAIL PARK, SUNDERLAND,
CO DURHAM SR5 3XG
☎ (0191) 548 7080. OPEN 10 - 8 MON - FRI, 9 - 6 SAT, 11 - 5 SUN.
Permanent Discount Outlet • *Womenswear & Menswear* • *Children Electrical Equipment* • *Household* • *Furniture/Soft Furnishings*
Mostly consisting of unsold lines through the Grattan mail order catalogues at the end of the season, but there is also some current season stock. Women's, men's and children's clothing, hardware, plastics and textiles, electrics and some furniture, although the majority is women's fashion, including many famous high street labels. All items in the store retail at a minimum of 30% off the catalogue price, with some items discounted by up to 50%. They also have regular promotional offers.

Cornwall

ART CANDLES
DUNMERE ROAD, BODMIN, CORNWALL PL31 2QN
☎ (01208) 73258. WEBSITE: www.artcandles.co.uk
OPEN 10 - 6 MON - FRI, 10 - 5 SAT, 11 - 6 SUN, EASTER TO SEPTEMBER.
Factory Shop • *Household*

A family business with a factory outlet selling candles and candleholders of every shape and design from beeswax to scented, figurative holders to pottery. They specialise in marbled candles, and there are also 3ft high stalagmite candles, owl, tortoise and Buddha-shaped candles. There are tubs of seconds at even cheaper prices. They also sell candle making materials, joss sticks and oil burners, boxes or kilos of wax, moulds, colours and wicks, and pottery. Stock changes constantly.

CORNISH MARKET WORLD
STADIUM RETAIL PARK, PAR, ST AUSTELL, CORNWALL PL25 3RR
☎ (01726) 812544. OPEN 9 - 5 SAT, SUN, BANK HOLS.

Huge indoor market that sells an enormous range of goods and food at very competitive prices - for example, a good quality breadmaker, £45. Sells clothes, fabrics, phones, bags, tools, electric equipment, motability equipment, jewellery, furniture. There is a good butcher's, fish and fruit and veg stands.

DARTINGTON CRYSTAL
KERNOW MILL, TRERULEFOOT, NR SALTASH, CORNWALL PL12 5BL
☎ (01752) 851161. OPEN 9.30 - 5.30 MON - SAT, 11 - 5 SUN.
Factory Shop • *Household*

An extensive range of Dartington Crystal seconds at greatly reduced prices as well as some perfect crystal at full price. Range includes wine suites, sherry glasses, tankards, decanters, rippled glass, fruit and salad bowls.

JUST FABRICS AT INSCAPE
THE BRIDEWELL, DOCKACRE ROAD, LAUNCESTON,
CORNWALL PL15 8YY
☎ (01566) 776279. OPEN 9 - 5 MON - SAT. MAIL ORDER ALSO.
Permanent Discount Outlet • *Furniture/Soft Furnishings*

Based in a very attractive converted stone-built warehouse, Just Fabrics hold the largest sample library in the country for all types of furnishing fabrics, trimmings and fittings as well as wallpapers, borders and Heritage paints. Most top brand names are represented and a substantial discount off the recommended retail price is available on most items. The company undertakes to despatch orders to customers worldwide. The showroom carries extensive stock of the very best designer fabrics plus all making-up accessories at unbeatable prices. The helpful and expert staff are able to demonstrate the appearance of a chosen decoration scheme with the help of a sophisticated computer aided design scheme.

NO FRILLS DIY STORE
STADIUM PARK, ST AUSTELL, CORNWALL PL25 3RR
☎ (01726) 814791. OPEN 9 - 8 MON - SAT, 10 - 4 SUN.

Permanent Discount Outlet • *Household Furniture/Soft Furnishings* • *Electrical Equipment*

Not a discount operator as such but a great place for bargains. Useful if doing up a holiday home. They stock everything you would find in B&Q or Homebase but at cheaper prices. Paints, tiles, bathroom equipment, patio furniture, toiletries, sheds, lighting, crockery, bedding, pans, kitchen units, barbecues in season. Large car park.

REDRUTH BREWERY (1792) LTD
THE BREWERY, FOUNDRY ROW, REDRUTH, CORNWALL TR15 1RB
☎ (01209) 212244. OPEN 12 - 6 MON - FRI, 10 - 4 SAT.

Factory Shop • *Food and Leisure*

Factory shop selling beers and lagers with damaged labels, as well as trial brews and those which are close to last-sell-by date.

SCENT TO YOU
6 CATHEDRAL LANE, TRURO, CORNWALL TR1 2QS
☎ (01872) 263663. PHONE FOR OPENING TIMES.

Permanent Discount Outlet • *Womenswear Only*

Discounted perfume, cosmetics and accessories including body lotions and gels. The company, which has more than thirty branches, buys in bulk and sells more cheaply, relying on a high turnover for profit. Discounts range from 5% to 60%, with greater savings during their twice-yearly sales (phone for details). Most of the leading brand names in perfume are stocked including Christian Lacroix, Armani, Charlie, Givenchy, Anais Anais from Cacherel, Charlie from Revlon, Coco Chanel, Christian Dior, Elizabeth Taylor, Blue Grass from Elizabeth Arden, Aramis, Lagerfeld. Plus cosmetics from Revlon and Spectacular and skincare from Clarins and Lancome as well as Scent To You's own range of bags, watches, hair brushes and brushkits which is sold under the name S.T.Y. Designs. Stock varies greatly due to the fast turnover and varying supplies so more than one visit may be necessary to obtain the scent of your choice. Or phone first to avoid disappointment.

SILKEN LADDER
VICTORIA SQUARE, NEAR ROCHE, CORNWALL PL26 8LX
☎ (01726) 891092. OPEN 9.30 - 5.30 MON - SAT, 10 - 5 SUN,
BANK HOLIDAYS.
Factory Shop • *Womenswear & Menswear*
Silken Ladder originally specialised in the design, manufacture and wholesale of ladies' blouses and tops in a myriad of options, both pretty and classic. Now their ranges extend to four labels. They still produce two complete new ranges of blouses every six months, one under the Silken Ladder label whilst La Scala di Seta is their upmarket label for evening wear and special occasions. Newly available are Sanderson Hall, classic and contemporary shirts for men, and the exciting ladieswear range, Victoria Roche - coordinating jackets, skirts, trousers, knitwear, dresses and shorts for women on the fast track. The factory shop sells the prototypes, samples, ends of lines, overmakes, less-than-perfects at appropriately reduced prices. There is an enormous selection of really super garments and some of the latest range is often available too - but this only, of course, at the full retail price. Bargains range from only £3 up to £100 although there is a very wide selection of blouses in particular in all sorts of fabrics, both natural and man-made, a selection of colours to die for and all sizes from 8 to 30. The shop also sells excess stock from other companies such as Kinloch Anderson, who are kiltmakers to the Queen and Duke of Cornwall (as well as Sean Connery) and Hourihan's of Ireland - tailors of ladies jackets and skirts. To complement the men's shirts Silken Ladder carry a wide range of ties, both classical and fun, as well as silk boxer shorts and kimonos. For ladies the accessories selection covers jewellery, scarves, hair decorations and other giftwear. A good selection of nightwear features their own ever-popular beautiful cotton nighties and silk, satin and cotton lingerie. Find it on Cornwall's main arterial road, the A30, six miles west of Bodmin and six miles north of St Austell, next to a BP petrol station and opposite Victoria Business Park and the Victoria Inn. Definitely different.

THE CURTAIN EXCHANGE
UNIT 3, NEWPORT INDUSTRIAL ESTATE, LAUNCESTON,
CORNWALL PL15 8EX
☎ (01566) 776001. OPEN 10 - 5 MON - SAT.
Secondhand shops • *Furniture/Soft Furnishings*
The Curtain Exchange is a franchised group of shops selling beautiful top quality secondhand curtains, blinds, pelmets, etc at between one-third and one half of the brand new price. Their stock comes from a variety of sources: people who are moving house; people who have curtains made and then feel they are wrong for the room show houses where the builder wants to recoup some of his outgoings; interior designers' mistakes. Stock changes constantly and ranges from rich brocades, damasks and velvets to chintzes, linens and cottons. Designer names include Colefax & Fowler, Designers Guild, Laura Ashley, Warner, Sanderson, Osborne & Little, Fortuny and Bennison. A team

of fitters and alteration experts are available if required. They offer a 24-hour availability. The Curtain Exchange also supply bespoke ranges with samples of curtains hanging. These fabrics are chosen from suppliers all over the world and are an excellent buy. They also offer ready made curtains designed exclusively for them which come in lengths up to 305cm (120"). These are outstanding value, e.g. 80" wide, 120" drop start at £175 including VAT.

THE FACTORY SHOP

MOUNT AMBROSE, SCORRIER, REDRUTH, CORNWALL TR15 1QT
☎ (01209) 219116. OPEN 9.30 - 5.30 MON - SAT, 10 - 4 SUN.
OLD STATION YARD, BERRYCOMBE ROAD, BODMIN, CORNWALL PL31 2NF
☎ (01208) 78492. OPEN 9 - 5.30 MON - SAT, 10.30 - 4.30 SUN.

Factory Shop • *Children* • *Womenswear ear & Menswear*
Household • *Furniture/Soft Furnishings* • *Sportswear & Equipment*

Wide range on sale includes men's, ladies and children's clothing and footwear; household textiles; toiletries; hardware; luggage; lighting and bedding, most of which are chainstore and high street brands at discounts of approximately 30%-50%. There are weekly deliveries and brands include many major stars such as Adidas, Nike, Joe Bloggs and Brabantia, to name just a few. Now has kitchen and furniture displays with a line of Cape Country furniture on sale. Ranges are continually changing and few factory shops offer such a variety under one roof. Both stores have their own free car parks and tea rooms offering freshly prepared hot and cold homemade food.

TRAGO MILLS

TWOWATERSFOOT, LISKEARD, CORNWALL PL14 6HY
☎ (01579) 348877. OPEN 9 - 5.30 MON - SAT, 10.45- 4.45 SUN.
ARWENACK STREET, FALMOUTH, CORNWALL TR11 3LF
☎ (01326) 315738. OPEN 9 - 5.30 MON - SAT, 10.45 - 4.45 SUN.

Permanent Discount Outlet • *Children* • *Womenswear & Menswear*
Household • *Furniture/Soft Furnishings* • *Food and Leisure*

Trago's original Cornish site is in the Glynn Valley on the A38 between Liskeard and Bodmin. You can bargain hunt here for brand name art materials, bathrooms and bedrooms and ceramics, carpets and rugs, clothing, diy and home improvement, furniture, garden accessories, gifts, textiles, lighting, pet care, saddlery, stationery, tools, motoring products, toys and sport equipment and much more. There's a restaurant and picnic area by the beautiful Fowey river bank, free parking and disabled access. The Falmouth store is smaller, with only limited free car parking outside, but there is a public car park adjacent.

TRIPLE M FASHION
NEW PORTREATH ROAD, JUST OUTSIDE REDRUTH,
CORNWALL TR16 4QL
☎ (01209) 842931. OPEN 10 - 5.30 SEVEN DAYS A WEEK.
Permanent Discount Outlet • *Womenswear & Menswear*
Children • *Household*

Large permanent discount shop selling men's and women's clothes, toys, bedding, footwear, bags, children's clothes. The clothes are not by well-known or high street names.

WILLIAMSON'S FACTORY SHOP
NEW PORTREATH ROAD, REDRUTH, CORNWALL TR16 4QL
☎ (01209) 842915. OPEN 10 - 5 SEVEN DAYS A WEEK.
Factory Shop • *Womenswear & Menswear* • *Household*

Two factory shops in one, the smaller one sells shoes and household goods, mainly textiles, in equal quantities. The shoes are very reasonably priced and include some designer trainers and deck shoes. The household textiles include bedlinen, tea towels, towels, duvets and pillows. The larger shop opposite sells men's and women's middle market clothes including coats, underwear and socks from names such as Regatta, Wrangler, Outdoor Scene, Ben Sherman and HJ socks.

Cumbria

BRIGGS SHOES
SOUTHEND ROAD, PENRITH, CUMBRIA
☎ (01768) 899001. OPEN 9.30 - 5.30 MON - SAT.
Permanent Discount Outlet • *Womenswear & Menswear* • *Children*

Vast selection of well-known brands of shoes with permanent clearance lines always on display. Some of the brands stocked include Van-Del, Gabor and the wider-fitting Elmdale range.

CUMBRIA ARCHITECTURAL SALVAGE
BIRKS HILL, RAUGHTON HEAD, CARLISLE, CUMBRIA CA5 7DH
☎ (01697) 476420. OPEN 9 - 5 MON - FRI, 9 - 12 SAT.
Architectural Salvage • *DIY/Renovation*

Period fireplaces, ranges, old free-standing baths, re-claimed doors, oak beams, building materials and general fittings from old houses.

DARTINGTON CRYSTAL
K VILLAGE, KENDAL, CUMBRIA LA9 7BT
☎ (01539) 737834. OPEN 9.30 - 6 MON - FRI, 9 - 6 SAT, 11 - 5 SUN.
Factory Shop in a Factory Shopping Village • *Household*
An extensive range of Dartington Crystal seconds at greatly reduced prices as well as some perfect crystal at full price. Range includes wine suites, sherry glasses, tankards, decanters, rippled glass, fruit and salad bowls.

DENBY FACTORY SHOP
K VILLAGE, KENDAL, CUMBRIA LA9 7DA
☎ (01539) 735418. OPEN 9.30 - 5.30 MON - FRI (WINTER), 9.30 - 6 MON, TUE, WED, FRI (SUMMER), 9.30 - 8 THUR (SUMMER) 9 -6 SAT, 11 - 5 SUN.
Factory Shop in a Factory Shopping Village • *Household*
Denby is renowned for its striking colours and glaze effects. The Factory Shops stock first and second quality with seconds discounts starting at 20% off RRP. There are regular "mega bargains" with up to 75% off throughout the year.

FACTORY BEDDING SHOP
ATLAS HOUSE, NELSON STREET, DENTON HOLME, CARLISLE, CUMBRIA CA2 5NB
☎ (01228) 514703. OPEN 10 - 5.30 MON - FRI, 9 - 5 SAT.
Factory Shop • *Household* • *Furniture/Soft Furnishings*
Bedding, curtains, duvets, duvet covers, pillows, towels, cushions, and curtain fabrics bought in direct from the manufacturer at factory shop prices. No brand names, but all sold in high street department stores. Pillows from £1.99; quilts from £5.99; curtains from £10.99; double fitted sheet from £6.49; double duvet cover, £12.99; double valances, £8.99. Wide range of curtain fabrics from £1.99 a metre and a curtain making service.

FINE FEATHERS
6 LIBRARY ROAD, KENDAL, CUMBRIA LA9 4QB
☎ (01539) 727241. OPEN 10 - 5 MON - SAT.
Dress Agency • *Womenswear Only*
Wide range of middle of the market names such as Country Casuals and Lakelands, with mix of in-season styles. Also Jacques Vert, Principles, Next, and Jaeger. More than 6,000 clients sell their as-new clothes here.

FURNESS FOOTWEAR FACTORY SHOP
LONG LANE, DALTON-IN-FURNESS, CUMBRIA.
☎ (01229) 468837. OPEN 9 - 5.30 MON - SAT, 9 - 8 ON FRI, 10 - 4 SUN.
Permanent Discount Outlet • *Womenswear & Menswear* • *Children*
Stocks a wide range of branded footwear for children as well as adults. There are slippers, sandals, boots, leather and vinyl handbags, shoe cleaners and polishes. Ladies fashion shoes start from £6 a pair. There are some well known brands, all at substantial savings on high street prices. Free parking.

HI-PENNINE OUTDOOR SHOP
MARKET SQUARE, ALSTON, CUMBRIA CA9 3QN
☎ (01434) 381389. OPEN 9.30 - 4.30 MON - FRI, 9 - 5 SAT.
Permanent Discount Outlet • *Sportswear & Equipment*
Permanent discount outlet selling Gore-tex and Polartec fleece clothing including jackets, windproof trousers, mitts, gaitors, scarves, headbands and hats all manufactured under the Mountain Range label. The Outdoor Shop acts as a factory shop on behalf of the Mountain Range factory, selling seconds and ends of lines at discounts of up to 25%. There is a mail order service; for details call (01434) 381389.

K SHOES
K VILLAGE, NETHERFIELD, KENDAL, CUMBRIA LA9 7BT
☎ (01539) 734347. OPEN 9.30 - 6 MON - SAT, 8 ON THUR, 11 - 5 SUN.
Factory Shop in a Factory Shopping Village • *Children Womenswear & Menswear*
Clarks International operate a chain of factory shops nationally which specialise in selling discontinued lines and slight sub-standards for children, women and men from Clarks, K Shoes and other famous brands. These shops trade under the name of Crockers, K Shoes Factory shop or Clarks Factory Shop and while not all are physically attached to a shoe factory, these shops are treated as factory shops by the company. Customers can expect to find an extensive range of quality shoes, sandals, walking boots, slippers, trainers, handbags, accessories and gifts, while their major outlets also offer luggage, sports clothing, sports equipment and outdoor clothing. Brands stocked include Clarks, K Shoes, Springer, CICA, Hi-Tec, Puma, Mercury, Fila, Mizuno, Slazenger, Samsonite, Delsey, Antler and Carlton, although not all are sold in every outlet. Discounts are on average 30% off the normal high street price for perfect stock.

K VILLAGE FACTORY SHOPPING
LOUND ROAD, KENDAL, NEAR JUNCTION 36 OF M6, CUMBRIA LA9 7DA
☎ (01539) 732363. E-MAIL: Outletcentres@mepc.co.uk
WEBSITE: www.kvillage.co.uk
OPEN 9.30 - 6 MON - FRI, 9 - 6 SAT, 11 - 5 SUN.
Factory Shopping Village • *Womenswear & Menswear* • *Children Sportswear & Equipment* • *Household*
Twelve outlets including Cotton Traders, Crabtree & Evelyn, Dartington Crystal selling Cloverleaf as well as glassware, Van Heusen, Denby Pottery, The Food Factory, Ponden Mill, Prices Candles, Tog 24, National Trust Gift Shop and a giant K Shoes factory shop selling a wide range of labels from K Shoes, Clarks, Cica, Delsey, and Antler, as well as a full-price K shop. There is also a heritage centre where you can discover the history of shoemaking, a 150-seater restaurant, a coffee shop, childrens play area, baby changing facili-

ties, a picnic area next to a river, disabled facilities and free parking. Take the South Kendal exit and follow the signs for K Village.

KANGOL FACTORY SHOP
CLEATOR, ON THE A5086 BETWEEN COCKERMOUTH AND EGREMONT, CUMBRIA CA23 3DJ
☎ (01946) 810312. OPEN 9 - 5 MON - SAT, 11 - 4 SUN. PLEASE RING FOR XMAS, EASTER AND BANK HOLIDAY OPENING HOURS.
Factory Shop • *Womenswear & Menswear*
This shop has a huge selection of headwear and millinery, plus branded clothing and accessories at factory prices. There's also a coffee shop for drinks and light snacks.

KIT4KIDS
99 SERPENTINE ROAD, KENDAL, CUMBRIA LA9 4PD
☎ (01539) 724920.
Hire Shop • *Children*
Part of the Baby Equipment Hirers Association (BEHA), which has more than 100 members countrywide. A range of equipment can be hired from high chairs, cots and travel cots to baby car seats and buggies. Short or long term hire can be arranged. They also sell three-wheel all-terrain Land Rover pushchairs and buggies. BEHA run an advice line which will try and answer any queries you have regarding hiring services for children. Phone the Babyline on 0831 310355.

LINTON TWEEDS LTD
SHADDON MILLS, CARLISLE, CUMBRIA CA2 5TZ
☎ (01228) 527569. OPEN 9.30 - 5 MON - SAT. MAIL ORDER.
Factory Shop • *Womenswear Only*
Eighty percent of Linton Tweeds Ltd's business is for the couture trade for export and includes exclusive fabrics for Chanel, Ann Klein, Ungaro, Courreges, Bill Blass and Escada. British designers to whom it supplies fabrics include Jean Muir, Windsmoor, Aquascutum, Jaeger and Liberty, and ranges from fancy yarns to silk and wool crepes. The mill shop has a large selection of ends of lines and remnants at prices ranging from £15-£25 per metre. You have to buy the fabric when you see it as there are no repeat orders. Also offer an exclusive designer knitwear section sold at discounted prices. There is an exhibition section, small museum and restaurant on site with hands-on display for adults and children. The site also has its own car park.

LITTLEWOODS CATALOGUE DISCOUNT STORE
RAWLINSON STREET, BARROW-IN-FURNESS, CUMBRIA LA14 1BS
☎ (01229) 870668. OPEN 8.45 - 5.30 MON - SAT, 11 - 5 SUN.
Permanent Discount Outlet • *Womenswear & Menswear*
Children • *Electrical Equipment*

Littlewoods clearance shops offering up to 50% off the catalogue price for clothing and between 50% and 60% off for electrical goods. Stock changes constantly and varies from day to day but can include well-known brand names such as Berlei and Gossard lingerie, Vivienne Westwood, Pamplemousse leisure wear, Nike and Adidas sports shoes, Workers for Freedom, and Timberland and Caterpillar footwear. Stock depends on the size and location of the shop, so larger shops will get the longer discontinued runs and smaller shops over-runs with only a small amount of colour and size variations left. Littlewoods also run a mobile shop which operates in cities where they don't have a sale shop. For details of further venues for the sales, which usually take place once a month, contact Melanie Lamb, c/o Crosby DC Kershaw Avenue, Endbutt Lane, Crosby, Merseyside L70 1AH.

MATALAN
PLOT 12, DERWENT HOUSE, SOLWAY ROAD, WORKINGTON, CUMBRIA CA14 3YA
☎ (01900) 870966. OPEN 9.30 - 8 MON - FRI, 9 - 6 SAT, 11 - 5 SUN.
WALNEY ROAD, BARROW LA14 5UN
☎ (01229) 430899. OPEN 9.30 - 8 MON - FRI, 9 - 6 SAT, 11 - 5 SUN.
Permanent Discount Outlet • *Womenswear & Menswear*
Household • *Children*

Matalan is a fashion and homewares value retailer giving customers what they claim to be unbeatable value for money with huge savings on a wide range of products including high quality fashionable clothing for men, women and children at up to 50% off high street prices. Matalan is situated out of town and stores are open seven days a week all year round.

NEW TO YOU
1 BOUNDARY ROAD, CURROCK, CARLISLE, CUMBRIA CA2 4RS
☎ (01228) 592669. OPEN 10 - 5 MON - FRI, 10 - 4 SAT.
Dress Agency • *Hire Shop* • *Womenswear Only*

Classic clothing, shoes and bags from Louis Feraud, Mansfield, Frank Usher and Mondi to Kanga, Next and Laura Ashley at anything from one half to one quarter of the original price. Sizes range from 10 - 24. Also sells and hires hats from a range of about forty for £12 with a refundable £2.

PONDEN MILL LINENS
K VILLAGE, LOUND ROAD, KENDAL, CUMBRIA LA9 7DA
☎ (01539) 737116. OPEN 9.30 - 6 MON - FRI, 9 - 6 SAT, 11 - 5 SUN.
Factory Shop in a Factory Shopping Village • *Household*

Famous branded products at direct from the mill prices. A fabulous assortment of towels, duvets, pillows, throws, bedspreads, up-to-the-minute coordinated bed linen, from Crown, Coloroll, Jeff Banks Ports-of-Call, to name but a few. Something for every room in the house.

PRICE'S CANDLES
K VILLAGE, KENDAL, NEAR JUNCTION 36 OF M6, CUMBRIA LA9 7DA
☎ (01539) 733736. OPEN 9.30 - 6 MON - FRI, 9 - 6 SAT, 11 - 5 SUN,
9 - 6 BANK HOLIDAYS (END OCT-EASTER OPEN 9.30 - 5.30 MON - FRI).
Factory Shop in a Factory Shopping Village • *Household*

Everything sold in this shop are seconds, discontinued sizes not available elsewhere, over-runs or candles in old packaging that has now been replaced. There are church candles, lanterns, candles in pots and glass jars, star-shaped candles, floating candles, candlestick holders, serviettes, scented candles and garden torches.

SEKERS FABRICS
HENSINGHAM, WHITEHAVEN, CUMBRIA CA28 8TR
☎ (01946) 692691. OPEN 9 - 7 THUR, 9 - 3 FRI, 9 - 1 SAT ONCE A MONTH ONLY.
Factory Shop • *Furniture/Soft Furnishings*

Discontinued curtain and upholstery fabrics and braiding sold off at monthly sales, usually held on the second Thursday, Friday and Saturday of each month. There are 5,000-6,000 metres to choose from at discounts of up to 75% off normal retail prices. Please phone for sale times before travelling.

STEAD McALPIN & CO LTD
CUMMERSDALE PRINT WORKS, CARLISLE, CUMBRIA CA2 6BT
☎ (01228) 599589. OPEN 9 - 4.30 MON - SAT, 9.30 - 4.30 WED,
BANK HOLIDAY MONDAY.
Factory Shop • *Furniture/Soft Furnishings*

This genuine factory shop has been refurbished and expanded over the last 3 years. There is a wide variety of prints in traditional and modern designs from £6.50 per metre produced in the factory, together with plain dyed fabrics and upholstery weaves from a sister company in Lancashire, priced from £7.50. The mill prints fabric for the top end of the furnishing trade. The fabrics are seconds but are checked for suitability before sale. The staff are always pleased to help you with calculations for making up. Also available are curtain poles, haberdashery, pillows and cushions, duvets, bed linen and occasional specials such as wallpaper or ready-made curtains. The stock varies according to factory production, so ring before travelling if there is something special you are looking for.

THE COLONY COUNTRY STORE
LINDAL-IN-FURNESS, ULVERSTON, CUMBRIA LA12 OLL
☎ (01229) 461102. OPEN 9 - 5 MON - SAT, 12 - 5 SUN.
Factory Shop • *Household*

This is one of the biggest outlets for factory price candles, scented candles, candle holders and lamps in Britain, with some stock selling at between 10% and 50% of the normal retail price. There are normally 3,000 candles on display, both perfect and seconds. Waxworks is the name of the special section offering goods at a fracton of their usual retail price. The store also sells pot pourri and gift soaps. The Christmas shop with Santa's grotto on site is open from September to January. You can watch the candles being made from a viewing gallery.

THE FACTORY SHOP
EMPIRE BUILDINGS, MAIN STREET, EGREMONT, CUMBRIA CA22 2BD
☎ (01946) 820434. OPEN 9 - 5 MON - SAT. 10 - 4 SUN.
THE GILL, ULVERSTON, CUMBRIA LA12 7BN
☎ (01229) 583360. OPEN 9 - 5.30 MON - SAT, 10.30 - 4.30 SUN.
5 MARKET PLACE, WIGTON, CUMBRIA CA7 9NW
☎ (01697) 342171. OPEN 9 - 5.30 MON - SAT, 10.30 - 4.30 SUN.
Factory Shop • *Children* • *Womenswear & Menswear*
Household • *Furniture/Soft Furnishings*

Wide range on sale includes men's, ladies' and children's clothing and footwear; household textiles; toiletries; hardware; luggage; lighting and bedding, most of which are chainstore and high street brands at discounts of approximately 30%-50%. There are weekly deliveries and brands include many major stars such as Adidas, Nike, Joe Bloggs and Brabantia, to name just a few. Now has kitchen and furniture displays with a line of Cape Country furniture on sale. Ranges are continually changing and few factory shops offer such a variety under one roof. The Egremont and Wigton branches have their own free car park, in Ulverston there is a large pay and display car park in front of the shop.

THE SPORTS FACTORY
K SHOE FACTORY SHOP, K VILLAGE, KENDAL, JUNCTION 36 OF M6, CUMBRIA LA9 6DA
☎ (01539) 721892. OPEN 9.30 - 6 MON - FRI, 9 - 6 SAT, 11 - 5 SUN.
Factory Shop in a Factory Shopping Village
Sportswear & Equipment • *Womenswear & Menswear* • *Children*

Wide range of sports clothes, equipment and accessories, some of which are only stocked in season (for example, cricket bats and tennis rackets in summer only). All are discontinued lines and are cheaper than in the high street by between 10%-40%.

THE TEA POTTERY
CENTRAL CAR PARK ROAD, KESWICK, CUMBRIA CA12 5DF
☎ (017687) 73983. OPEN 9 - 5 SEVEN DAYS A WEEK.
Factory Shop • *Household*
Paradise for collectors of novelty teapots, all of which are manufactured on site in up to 50 different designs and in sizes from one cup to five cups. Designs include Welsh dressers, caravans, Agas, cookers, bellboys with luggage, can-can girls, washbasins and a host of others, many of which are collectors' items. Prices range from £9.95 - £45 for perfects, which represents a 10% - 20% savings on retail prices, and up to 50% discounts on seconds. This factory shop is smaller than its sister shop in Leyburn and has no refreshments or disabled facilities.

TK MAXX
THE EDEN CENTRE & MARKET FISHER STREET, CARLISLE, CUMBRIA CA3 8JB
☎ (01228) 819292. OPEN 9 - 5.30 MON - THUR, 8.30 - 5.30 FRI, SAT, 11 - 5 SUN.
Permanent Discount Outlet • *Womenswear & Menswear Children* • *Household* • *Furniture/Soft Furnishings*
Based on an American concept, TK Maxx is situated in easily accessible, often centrally located stores and offers famous label goods with up to 60% savings off recommended retail prices. TK Maxx has fashion for the whole family - women's, men's and childrenswear - accessories, shoes, gifts, kitchenware and home goods. Everything in the store is branded with a choice of well-known high street names to designer labels, and while a small percentage might be clearly marked past season, the great majority of items in store are current season, current stock and still with phenomenal savings. There is a huge choice with 50,000 pieces in store and up to 10,000 new items arriving a week. The stores are simple and unfussy with wide aisles, shopping trolleys and baskets, and a spacious, functional feel to them but there are individual changing rooms, ramps for buggies and wheelchairs and plenty of staff on the shop floor. Every branch accepts all major credit and debit cards and has a liberal refund and return policy.

TOG 24
UNIT 4, MARKET CROSS, AMBLESIDE, CUMBRIA LA22 9BT
☎ (01539) 433913. OPEN 10 - 6.30 SEVEN DAYS A WEEK.
10 CRAG BOW, BOWNESS, CUMBRIA LA23 3BX
☎ (01539) 488656. OPEN 9.30 - 6 MON - SAT, 10 - 6 SUN.
K VILLAGE, LOUND ROAD, KENDAL, CUMBRIA LA9 7DA
☎ (01539) 721555. OPEN 9.30 - 6 MON - FRI, 9 - 6 SAT, 11 - 5.30 SUN.
Factory Shop and Factory Shop in a Factory Shopping Village
Sportswear & Equipment
Tog 24 are the UK's fastest growing brand name in outdoor clothing and leisurewear. They utilise the world's finest performance fabrics including

Gore-Tex, Polartec and Burlington MCS, catering for all the family for all seasons, with cosy fleeces and waterproofs for the winter, and trekking ranges, shorts and t-shirts for the summer. With all prices at least 30% below the recommended retail price, you can afford to enter the Tog comfort zone.

WILSON RECLAMATION SERVICES
YEW TREE BARN, LOW NEWTON IN CARTMEL, GRANGE-OVER-SANDS, CUMBRIA LA11 6JP
☎ (0153 95) 31498. OPEN 10 - 5 MON - SAT, 12 - 5 SUN.
Architectural Salvage • *DIY/Renovation*
Fireplaces, oak beams, doors, bathroom fittings, flagstones, chimney pots, quoins and antiques. There's also a soft furnishing department, antique restoration and upholstery service and cafe.

WYNSORS WORLD OF SHOES
FURNESS FOOTWEAR, LONG LANE, DALTON-IN-FURNESS, CUMBRIA LA15 8PB
☎ (01229) 468837. OPEN 9 - 5.30 MON, TUE, WED, SAT, 9 - 8 THUR, FRI, 10 - 4 SUN AND BANK HOLIDAYS.
Permanent Discount Outlet • *Womenswear & Menswear* • *Children*
Stocks top brand-name shoes at less than half price. Special monthly offers always available. There are shoes, trainers, slippers, sandals and boots for all the family, with a selection of bags, cleaners and polishes available.

Derbyshire

ABRIS OUTDOOR CLOTHING FACTORY SHOP
94, HIGH STREET WEST, GLOSSOP, DERBYSHIRE SK13 8EB
☎ (01457) 853145. FAX 865333. OPEN 9.30 - 5 TUE - SAT.
Factory Shop • *Sportswear & Equipment*
Outdoor clothing for hillwalkers and backpackers and tops suitable for snowboarders, all of which are made in the on-site factory and sold at prices which are up to 60% cheaper than in the high street. For example, walking trousers, £24.99 which would normally sell for £39.99 in the high street; breathable waterproofs from £69.99, fleece jackets from £49.99. Sizes range from extra small to double extra large; ladies from 10 - 18; men's trousers from 28-inch to 40-inch waist.

ANDREW SHANE LTD
157 NOTTINGHAM ROAD, SOMERCOTES, ALFRETON, DERBYSHIRE DE55 4JH
☎ (01773) 541414. OPEN 9 - 3 SAT.
Factory shop • *Womenswear & Menswear*
Men,s and ladies shirts (polo, rugby, sport), fleece tops, jackets and assorted children,s wear.

ARMSTRONG'S MILL
MIDDLETON STREET, OFF STATION ROAD, ILKESTON,
DERBYSHIRE DE7 5TT
☎ (0115) 932 4913. OPEN 9.15 - 5 MON, TUE, THUR, FRI, 9.15 - 6 WED,
9.30 - 5.30 SAT, 10.30 - 4.30 SUN.
Factory Shop • *Menswear Only*
Just 10 mins from M1 Junction 26, follow signs for Ilkeston A610, carry on over railway bridge and turn immediately sharp left, the mill car park is straight ahead. Armstrong's manufactures high quality men's suits, jackets and trousers. You can also find offers from Wolsey, Pierre Cardin and Double Two, all at factory prices.

BIG L FACTORY OUTLET
BUILDING 3, DERBYSHIRE DESIGNER OUTLET, MANSFIELD ROAD,
SOUTH NORMANTON, DERBYSHIRE DE55 2ER
☎ (01773) 545000. OPEN 10 - 6 MON, TUE, WED, FRI, 10 - 8 THUR,
9 - 6 SAT, 11 - 5 SUN.
Factory Shop in a Factory Shopping Village • *Womenswear & Menswear*
Men's and women's Levi jeans, jackets, cord and Sherpa fleece jackets, T-shirts and shirts but no children's, all at discount prices.

BOOK THRIFT
44 SADDLEGATE, DERBY, DERBYSHIRE DE1 3NQ
☎ (01332) 290912. OPEN 9.30 - 5.30 MON - SAT.
Permanent Discount Outlet • *Food and Leisure*
One of many outlets supplied by a central warehouse with remaindered books, all first hand, sold at around half price. Most are the result of over buying on the part of bookshops and overprints by publishers and they include hard and soft backs, fiction, fact, reference and academic. They sell some stationery and local ordnance maps at full price. Also stock a wide range of current bestselling titles at discounted prices of up to 25%, sometimes more. A 10% discount is given on all customer orders. Stores in Kendal, Macclesfield, Ilkeston, Southwold, Hebden Bridge, Ashbourne, Nantwich and a London branch that specialises in art, design and architecture. Phone 01625 576890 for details of your nearest outlet.

BROUGHTON SHOE WAREHOUSE
7 CROWN SQUARE, MATLOCK DERBYSHIRE DE4 3AT
☎ (01629) 55616. OPEN 9 - 5.30 MON - SAT, 10 - 4 SUN.
Permanent Discount Outlet • *Womenswear & Menswear* • *Children*
Sells ladies boots, shoes, sandals and slippers as well as men's and children's footwear. Savings can be between 20% and 50% here. There are shoes by Kappa, Timberland, Hi-Tec, Trickers, Caterpillar, Kickers and some Italian and Spanish designers. Deliveries are made every Tuesday.

BUDGET FABRICS
6 EAGLE STREET, HEAGE, DERBYSHIRE DE56 2AJ
☎ (01773) 853552. OPEN 9 - 4.30 MON - FRI, 9.30 - 4.30 SAT, 10 - 3 SUN.
Factory Shop • *Furniture/Soft Furnishings*
Fabrics and haberdashery including curtaining, upholstery and dress fabrics at discounted prices. Remnants are a speciality. They also manufacture scatter cushions from a huge choice of designer fabrics.

CHARNOS
CORPORATION ROAD, ILKESTON, DERBYSHIRE DE7 4BP
☎ (0115) 9440301. OPEN 10 - 4 TUE - FRI, 9.30 - 1 SAT.
Factory Shop • *Womenswear & Menswear* • *Children* • *Household*
About 25% of the shop is given over to discontinued perfects of the famous Charnos lingerie at discounts of 25%-50%. Current ladies lingerie is discounted by 25%, discontinued lingerie by 50%. The rest of the shop stocks wool, acrylic and cotton knitwear for women and men at factory shop prices, and babywear, cards and giftwrap at very competitive prices. Some stock is grade B quality. Each garment is marked to show normal retail and reduced prices.

DARTINGTON CRYSTAL
DENBY POTTERY CO, DENBY, DERBYSHIRE DE5 8NX
☎ (01773) 513116. OPEN 9.30 - 5 MON - SAT, 11 - 5 SUN.
POOLE POTTERY, MASSON MILL SHOPPING CENTRE, DERBY ROAD, MATLOCK BATH DE4 3PY
☎ (01629) 582441. OPEN
MCARTHURGLEN OUTLET VILLAGE, MANSFIELD ROAD, SOUTH NORMANTON DE55 2ER
☎ (01773) 545216. OPEN 10 - 6 MON - FRI, 8 ON THUR, 9 - 6 SAT, 11 - 5 SUN.
Factory Shop and Factory Shop in a Factory Shopping Village
Household
Factory Shop in a Factory Shopping Village in a Factory Shopping Villageof Dartington Crystal seconds at greatly reduced prices as well as some perfect crystal at full price. Range includes wine suites, sherry glasses, tankards, decanters, rippled glass, fruit and salad bowls.

DAVID NIEPER
NOTTINGHAM ROAD, ALFRETON, DERBYSHIRE DE55 7LE
☎ (01773) 833335. OPEN 9 - 5 MON - SAT AND BANK HOLIDAYS.
Factory Shop • *Womenswear Only*
Classic ladies clothing and specialists in nightwear/lingerie. David Nieper is an internationally acclaimed designer and from this factory in Alfreton private customers order directly from all over the world. The factory shop has design room samples including beautiful silk fabrics and laces; pure cotton nightdresses; silk/satin slips; luxury velvet housegowns; Liberty blouses and skirts. There is also an amazing range of lingerie from well-known designers. Free car park.

DE BRADELEI MILL SHOPS LTD
DE BRADELEI HOUSE, CHAPEL STREET, BELPER, DERBYSHIRE DE56 1AR
☎ (01773) 829830. OPEN 9.30 - 5.30 MON - FRI, 9.30 - 6 SAT, 11 - 5 SUN.
Permanent Discount Outlet • *Womenswear & Menswear*
Household • *Furniture/Soft Furnishings*

A delightful Mill centre with individual shops based round a central courtyard, each one selling top brand names in fashions and footwear for men and women, along with soft furnishings and giftware. The ladieswear includes such names as Windsmoor, Planet, Precis Petite, Jaeger Knitwear Shop, French Connection, Elle, Virgin, Jackpot, Phase Eight, Country Casuals, Elvi, top American and German designer labels, plus many more. The menswear range includes underwear, socks, sweaters, trousers, jackets, coats and suits from labels such as Wolsey, French Connection, Virgin, Jaeger Knitwear Shop and Glenmuir. Robert Leonard's Menswear provides Pierre Cardin, Gabicci, Gurteen, Oakman and many more. There is a large shoe department with a superb range of shoes and accessories for men and women. Soft Furnishings from Ponden Mill includes duvets, bedlinen, pillows, towels and much more. The giftware department offers a superb collection of Liberty giftware with scented candles, Dart Valley Foods and chocolates from Italo Suisse. Chevin Coffee Shop serves delicious home-cooked food throughout the day. De Bradelei Mill Shop has its own car park with alternative parking nearby; coach parties are always welcome though booking is preferred.

DEMAGLASS FACTORY SHOP
POTTERY LANE WEST, CHESTERFIELD, DERBYSHIRE S41 9BN
☎ (01246) 545193. OPEN 9.30 - 4.15 MON - FRI, UNTIL 8 ON THUR, 9.30 - 1 SAT.
Factory Shop • *Household*

Manufacturers of cut, plain and decorated glasses only, they sell glassware manufactured on site as well as bought-in giftware and some pottery at its seconds factory shop at the rear of the building. Glasses start at around 30p each to £1.99. Crystal modern flutes cost £3.99 each or £19.50 in boxes of 6, crystal tumblers, £3.99 each or £15.50 in boxes of 6. The factory shop also sells Royal Scot Crystal and Edinburgh Crystal seconds. There are also gifts, china, crockery, tablemats, candles, silverplated gifts, photoframes and christening presents. Three main sales a year are held - usually over the Easter weekend, August and November - at which prices are discounted still further.

DENBY POTTERY VISITOR CENTRE
DERBY ROAD, DENBY, NR RIPLEY, DERBYSHIRE DE5 8NX
☎ (01773) 740 799. OPEN 9.30 - 5 MON - SAT, 10 - 5 SUN (CENTRE), 11 - 5 SUN (FACTORY SHOP).
Factory Shop • *Household* • *Food and Leisure*

Renowned for its striking colours and glaze effects, Denby has been inviting people to tour and visit the pottery for more than thirty years. Their own factory shop warehouse sells both seconds and best quality products. Second discounts start at 20% off RRP. There are regular "mega bargains" with up to 75% off individual items, plus mid season and main sales throughout the year. The attractive Visitor Centre also features a Dartington Factory shop and an excellent Cookery Emporium which stocks over 3,000 pots, pans and gadgets. In the adjacent Demonstration Theatre you can see the latest equipment put to the test - then taste the results! Demonstrations are held twice daily (normally 12.30pm and 2.30pm) and are free of charge. The centre also includes Courtyard Restaurant, garden centre shop, gift shop, ample parking facilities and a children's play area. Full guided factory tours are offered from Monday to Thursday. You can also 'have a go' yourself - paint a plate and make a Denby Frog any day of the week.

DERWENT CRYSTAL LTD
SHAWCROFT, ASHBOURNE, DERBYSHIRE DE6 1GH
☎ (01335) 345219. OPEN 9 - 5 MON - SAT.
LITTLE BRIDGE STREET, DERBY, DERBYSHIRE DE1 3LE
☎ (01332) 360186. OPEN 9 - 5 MON - SAT.
Factory Shop • *Household*
A wide selection of glassware and fancy items at factory shop prices. Full English lead crystal from liqueur glasses to vases and bowls, ringstands and dressing-table novelties. More than 200 different items on sale. Gift wrap service available.

DIRECT SPECS LTD
30 OSMASTON ROAD, DERBY DERBYSHIRE DE1 2HR
☎ (01332) 295384. OPEN 9 - 5 MON - SAT.
Permanent Discount Outlet • *Womenswear & Menswear*
Spectacles and sunglasses at prices which the owner claims beat any competitor's. Most designer names are stocked at one time or another, though if you have a favourite, check first. Bring along your prescription and glasses will be found to suit. No eye tests conducted.

END OF THE LINE FURNITURE
32 DERBY ROAD, AMBERGATE, DERBYSHIRE DE56 2GE
☎ (01773) 856082. OPEN 10 - 5 THUR, FRI, SAT, 1 - 5 SUN.
Factory Shop • *Furniture/Soft Furnishings*
Factory direct upholstery at discounted prices.

FABRIC DESIGN
10-12 NORTH PARADE, MATLOCK BATH, DERBYSHIRE DE4 3NS
☎ (01629) 584747. OPEN 1.30 - 5 MON, THUR, SUN, 11 - 5 TUE, WED, FRI, SAT, CLOSED BANK HOLIDAYS.
Permanent Discount Outlet • *Furniture/Soft Furnishings*
Situated in a beautiful spa town, the Matlock Bath outlet is a busy, exciting Victorian shop on the parade by the river, which carries a huge range of design-

er clearance fabrics from £4.25 per metre, heavy linens from £5.99 per metre and an ever-changing range of bargain one-off buys such as £42 per metre fabric reduced to £9.99 per metre. Fabrics sold in the shop include such names as Sanderson, Monkwell, Jane Churchill, Warner, Anna French and Liberty, but there is also available a range of natural fabrics - calico, twills and cream weaves. Those looking for good quality fabric for upholstery and curtaining should be prepared to buy on the day as the good deals don't stay in the shop for long. Huge range of discounted one-off end of lines and a discount is also offered on perfect fabrics and wallpapers ordered from pattern books in store.

FACTORY SHOP OUTLET, COATS VIYELLA CLOTHING,

STEVENSONS, DROVERS WAY, BULLBRIDGE, AMBERGATE, DERBYSHIRE DE5 2EX
☎ (01773) 853473. OPEN 10 - 5.30 MON - FRI, 10 - 5 SAT, SUN AND BANK HOLIDAYS, 10 - 4
THE FACTORY SHOP, CV CLOTHING, RETFORD ROAD, MANTON, WORKSOP S80 2PX
☎ (01909) 483898. OPEN 10 - 5 MON - SAT.

Factory Shop • *Womenswear & Menswear* • *Children*

Part of the Coats Viyella group, which makes quality clothing for many of the major high street stores, overstocks and clearance lines are sold through more than 30 of the group's factory shops. Many of you will recognise the garments on sale, despite the lack of well-known labels. Ladieswear includes dresses, blouses, jumpers, cardigans, trousers, nightwear, underwear, lingerie, hosiery, coats and swimwear. Menswear includes trousers, belts, shirts, ties, pullovers, cardigans, T-shirts, underwear, nightwear, hosiery and jackets. Childrenswear includes jackets, trousers, T-shirts, underwear, hosiery, jumpers and babywear. There are regular deliveries to constantly update the range.

FILIGREE

CARTER LANE EAST, SOUTH NORMANTON, (JCT 28 OF M1), DERBYSHIRE DE55 2EG
☎ (01773) 811630 EXT 296. OPEN 9 - 4.30 MON - THUR, 9 - 5 FRI, 9 - 1.30 SAT, 10 - 2 SUN.

Factory Shop • *Furniture/Soft Furnishings*

Real factory shop behind factory makes filigree and Stiebel of Nottingham lace curtain and printed curtains. Makes net curtains on the premises for well-known high street department stores and mail order companies and sells them at reduced prices. Nets range from 50p a metre to £6 with fabric from £1.99 a metre to £5.99 a metre and remnants from 50p. Also readymade curtains, curtain accessories and bedding.

GILLIVERS FOOTWEAR AND CLOTHING WAREHOUSE
1-3 ASHBY ROAD, MOIRA, SWADLINCOTE, DERBYSHIRE DE12 6DJ
☎ (01283) 214255. OPEN 9 - 8 MON - FRI, 9 - 5.30 SAT, 10 - 5 SUN.
Permanent Discount Outlet • *Womenswear & Menswear*

Shoes from £1.99 to £40, at much reduced prices. The clothes are mainly from BhS and Marks & Spencer, although the labels are removed, and are discounted by between 25% and 50%. There are also bags, accessories and jewellery. Refreshments available.

GLYN WEBB
ASCOT DRIVE, DERBY, DERBYSHIRE DE24 8QZ
☎ (01332) 204282. OPEN 9 - 8 MON - SAT, 11 - 5 SUN AND BANK HOLIDAYS.
Permanent Discount Outlet • *DIY/Renovation*

Stockists of all your home improvement needs from wallpaper to paint, furniture to flooring, tiles to textiles, housewares to lighting - in fact, almost everything for your home, with 25 branches in the North-West, Midlands and Yorkshire. Specialists in discontinued mail order, slightly imperfect branded stocks as well as perfect quality superior products. They carry top brands such as Dulux, Crown Paints and Vymura and Coloroll wall coverings, Rectella and Norwood textiles and much more in store. To find your nearest branch, phone Head Office on 0161 621 4500.

JAEGER FACTORY SHOP
JAEGER DEPT, VIYELLA HOUSE, NOTTINGHAM ROAD, SOMERCOTES, DERBYSHIRE DE55 4SB
☎ (01773) 541183. OPEN 9 - 5 MON - SAT, 10.30 - 4.30 SUN.
Factory Shop • *Womenswear & Menswear*

Contemporary classics from Jaeger at excellent prices. Most of the merchandise is previous seasons' stock, but you might also find some special makes. The shops at King's Lynn in Norfolk and here at Somercotes shops stock tailoring and knitwear for women and men; the Coalville, Leicestershire shop stocks womenswear only.

JAMES BARRY MENSWEAR
ARMSTRONG'S MILL, MIDDLETON STREET, OFF STATION ROAD, ILKESTON, DERBYSHIRE DE7 5TT
☎ (0115) 932 4913. OPEN 9.15 - 5 MON - FRI, UNTIL 6 WED, 9.15 - 5.30 SAT, 10.30 - 4 SUN.
Factory Shop • *Menswear Only*

Designer mensear and ladieswear available at discount of up to 50% off rrp. Join the mailing list at any of the James Barry outlets which will give you advanced warning of any promotions (your details will not be passed on to anyone else).

JOHN SMEDLEY LTD
LEA MILLS, LEA BRIDGE, MATLOCK, DERBYSHIRE DE4 5AG
☎ (01629) 534571. OPEN 10 - 4 SEVEN DAYS A WEEK AND MOST BANK HOLIDAYS.
Factory Shop • *Womenswear & Menswear*
Sells John Smedley high quality knitwear which are ends of ranges or seconds, all at substantial discounts. There are more than 5,000 garments to choose from in cotton and wool, including cardigans and sweaters for ladies and men; own range underwear and an assortment of accessories. Childrenswear is not stocked. There is another outlet in Doncaster.

JUMPER
DERBYSHIRE DESIGNER OUTLET VILLAGE, MANSFIELD ROAD, SOUTH NORMANTON, DERBYSHIRE DE55 2EF
☎ (01773) 545251. OPEN 9.30 - 5.30 MON - SAT, 11 - 5 SUN.
Factory Shop in a Factory Shopping Village • *Womenswear & Menswear*
A wide range of Jumper label sweaters, gloves, scarves, shirts and cardigans for men and women all at discount prices of up to 50% off. Prices start at £2.

LABELS OF BASLOW
CHURCH STREET, BASLOW, DERBYSHIRE PEAK DISTRICT, DERBYSHIRE.
☎ (01246) 582971.
Dress Agency • *Womenswear Only*
Friendly and accommodating shop, selling ladies' upmarket and designer labels in immaculate condition. Business terms are 60:40% and only quality items less than two years' old are accepted for sale. The range includes beachwear to designer evening wear and includes a huge stock of accessories to complement any outfit.

LANGLEY FURNITURE
DELVES ROAD, HEANOR GATE INDUSTRIAL ESTATE, HEANOR, DERBYSHIRE DE75 7SJ
☎ (01773) 765544. FAX ☎ (01773) 531322. WEBSITE: www.langleypine.co.uk
OPEN 9 - 5.30 MON - FRI, 9 - 5 SAT, 10.30 - 4 SUN AND BANK HOLIDAYS.
Factory Shop • *Furniture/Soft Furnishings*
A comprehensive and distinctive range of furniture individually manufactured by craftsmen in Langley's own factories using selected quality pine and traditional carpentry methods. Each piece of furniture is stained to customers' choice of colour using exclusive mixes of natural pigments and then finished with dressings of high quality wax polish. The Langley collection offers a complete range of bedroom, lounge and dining-room furniture, and individually designed kitchen units, fitted or free standing. In addition, Langely offer a made-to-measure service, producing items to customers' own designs and dimensions. For commercial customers, Langely design, manufacture and supply stand-alone display and merchandiser units and other specialist shop fixtures. Free brochure and price list available on request.

LEE COOPER
DESIGNER OUTLET CENTRE, MANSFIELD ROAD, SOUTH
NORMANTON, ALFRETON, JUNCTION 28 OF M1, FOLLOW SIGNS FOR
A38, DERBYSHIRE DE55 2ER
☎ (01773) 545153. OPEN 10 - 6 MON - FRI, 8 ON THUR, 9 - 6 SAT, 11 - 5 SUN.
Factory Shop in a Factory Shopping Village
Womenswear & Menswear • *Children*

Denim jeans, jackets and shirts, each ranked by size and gender at discounts of up to 30%. Casual shirts from £9.99, jeans from £14.99, T-shirts and ladieswear. Lee Cooper was founded in 1908 as a workwear manufacturer before becoming a supplier to the armed forces. Most of the stock here is current, discontinued and irregular merchandise, all of which comes straight from Lee Cooper's factories in Europe.

LITTLEWOODS CATALOGUE DISCOUNT STORE
MANSFIELD ROAD, SOUTH NORMANTON, ALFRETON, JUNCTION 28
OF M1, DERBYSHIRE DE55 2ER
☎ (01773) 545105. OPEN 10 - 6 MON - FRI, 8 ON THUR, 9 - 6 SAT,
11 - 5 SUN.
Factory Shop • *Womenswear & Menswear* • *Children*
Electrical Equipment

Littlewoods clearance shops offering up to 50% off the catalogue price for clothing and between 50% and 60% off for electrical goods. Stock changes constantly and varies from day to day but can include well-known brand names such as Berlei and Gossard lingerie, Vivienne Westwood, Pamplemousse leisure wear, Nike and Adidas sports shoes, Workers for Freedom, and Timberland and Caterpillar footwear. Stock depends on the size and location of the shop, so larger shops will get the longer discontinued runs and smaller shops over-runs with only a small amount of colour and size variations left. Littlewoods also run a mobile shop which operates in cities where they don't have a sale shop. For details of further venues for the sales, which usually take place once a month, contact Melanie Lamb, c/o Crosby DC Kershaw Avenue, Endbutt Lane, Crosby, Merseyside L70 1AH.

LUGGAGE & BAGS
THE PEAK VILLAGE, CHATSWORTH ROAD, ROWSLEY,
DERBYSHIRE DE4 2JE
☎ (01629) 732 883. OPEN 9.30 - 5.30 MON - SAT, 10 - 5 SUN.
Factory Shop in a Factory Shopping Village • *Food and Leisure*

Luggage and travel-related products and executive cases, handbags, umbrellas from leading brands such as Samsonite, Desley, Head, Taurus and GlobeTrotter. Each product is offered at a substantially reduced price compared to those found on the high street due to being production over-runs, discontinued ranges or colours and last season's products. Discounts range from 30%-75% off high street prices.

MASSONS MILL
NEAR MATLOCK, PEAK DISTRICT, DERBYSHIRE DE4 3PY
☎ (01629) 760208. OPEN 9.30 - 5.30 MON - FRI, 9.30 - 6 SAT, 11 - 5 SUN.
Factory Shopping Village • *Womenswear & Menswear* • *Children Household* • *Sportswear & Equipment*
Anchored by Edinburgh Woollen Mills, this shopping village has a heritage attraction in the setting of this regenerated 18th century mill building with working textile museum and conference facilities. Other shops sell fashion, golfwear and equipment, gifts, speciality foods and country goods and include Julian Graves food items, Woods of Windsor, Ponden Mill selling bedlinen and towels, Colony Candles, Dartington Crystal, Siaparlane tableware and gifts.

MATLOCK SHOE SALES
SLACK'S FOOTWEAR LTD, PAXTON WAREHOUSE, MATLOCK GREEN, MATLOCK, DERBYSHIRE DE4 3BX
☎ (01629) 583105. OPEN 9 - 5.30 MON - SAT, 10 - 5 SUN.
Permanent Discount Outlet • *Womenswear & Menswear*
Sells discounted men's and women's shoes in sizes 3 - 8 for women and 5 - 12 for men. The shoes range from ladies Italian leather shoes and wide fitting lines from Equity, Jenny and Elmdale, to Hi-Tec trainers, Ecco, walking boots, hiking boots, leather boots and a range of Rombah Wallace shoes.

MCARTHURGLEN DESIGNER OUTLET
MANSFIELD ROAD, SOUTH NORMANTON, ALFRETON, JUNCTION 28 OF M1, FOLLOW SIGNS FOR A38, DERBYSHIRE DE55 2JW
☎ (0800) 3164352 FREEPHONE INFORMATION LINE.
☎ (01773) 545000. WEBSITE: www.mcarthurglen.com
OPEN 10 - 6 MON - FRI, 8 ON THUR, 9 - 6 SAT, 11 - 5 SUN.
Factory Shopping Village • *Womenswear & Menswear* • *Children Household* • *Food and Leisure* • *Sportswear & Equipment* *Electrical Equipment* • *Furniture/Soft Furnishings*
Unusually, this outlet centre is set out in department store format with four distinct merchandise areas: fashion, homewares, sport/leisure and accessories. Sited 400 metres from the M1, there are 74 different stores selling a variety of brand names at discount prices of between 30% and 50%, a Sherwood Forest themed food court with seven different food outlets, a children's play area and free parking for 1,100 cars. The House & Home building has Banana Books, Bed & Bath Works, Birthdays, Churchill China, Coloroll, Dartington Crystal, Edinburgh Crystal, Fabric Corner, Littlewoods Electrical, Room, Oneida, Oven 2 Table, Portmerion Potteries, Prices Candles, The Professional Cookware Co., Remington, Royal Doulton, Royal Worcester, Speigelau, TTC Colour for Living, Toyworld, Whittards, XS music, and the Xmas Shop. The Women's and Men's Fashion building houses Baird, Big L, Camille, Chilli Pepper, Ciro jewellery, Cotton Traders, Double Two, Erdos, Fans of London,

Fruit of the Loom, Haggar, Harbi, Jaeger, Jumper, Knickerbox, Lee Cooper, Littlewoods, Marilyn Moore, Nickelbys, Petroleum, Pilot, Roman Originals, Suits You, The Brand Store, Tom Sayers, Ton Sur Ton, Viyella, Van Heusen, and Winning Line. Jewellery and Accessories include Antler Luggage, Ciro Pearls, Claires Accessories, Monet, The Jewellery Outlet, Travel Accessory Outlet and the Watch Store selling men's and women's watches. The Children's Wear and Sportswear area caters for both sexes with Fat Face, Fruit of the Loom, Jokids, Karrimor, Littlewoods Catalogue Outlet, Tog 24, Speedo and Sportsmill. Pavers and Soled Out provide footwear and Julian Graves and Thorntons sustenance.

ONEIDA

MCARTHURGLEN DESIGNER OUTLET CENTRE, ADDRESS AND OPENING HOURS AS BEFORE.
☎ (01773) 545130.
Factory Shop in a Factory Shopping Village • *Household*
Oneida is the world's largest cutlery company and originates from the United States of America. In addition to cutlery, it sells silver and silver plate at discounts of between 30% and 50%, plus frames, candlesticks and trays. They now also have their own range of chinaware and glass, also sold here at discounts of 30%-50%.

PEAK VILLAGE

CHATSWORTH ROAD, ROWSLEY, (ON THE A6 BETWEEN BAKEWELL AND MATLOCK) DERBYSHIRE DE4 2JE
☎ (01629) 735326. OPEN 9.30 - 5.30 MON - SAT, 10 - 5 SUN, EXCEPT CHRISTMAS DAY.
Factory Shopping Village • *Womenswear & Menswear* • *Children Household* • *Furniture/Soft Furnishings* • *Food and Leisure Sportswear & Equipment*
Twenty-two factory outlets including Leading Labels, Winning Line, Luggage & Bags, The Book Depot, Because It's There, Yeoman Outdoors outdoor wear and equipment, Famous Shoes 4U, Ponden Mill, De Bradelei Mill Shop and The Garden Outlet, just 30 minutes from the M1 at the entrance to the Peak National Park. On-site catering includes a choice of the Gold Restaurant, which offers everything from an ice cream sundae to a traditional Sunday roast. The Wind in the Willows Attraction is a magical journey through the world of Ratty, Badger, Mole and of course the irrepressible Mr Toad. The latest sound and lighting effects bring Kenneth Grahame's classic tale to life in an enchanting recreation that's not just for kids! Free parking for up to 400 cars. Recently opened the Woodlands Fitness Centre.

PONDEN MILL LINENS
PEAK VILLAGE, CHATSWORTH ROAD, ROWSEY, DERBYSHIRE DE4 2JE
☎ (01629) 733857. OPEN 9.30 - 5.30 MON - SAT, 10 - 5 SUN.
PONDEN MILL FACTORY SHOP, DE BRADELEI MILL SHOPS,
DE BRADELEI HOUSE, CHAPEL STREET, BELPER DE56 1AR
☎ (01773) 882815. OPEN 9.30 - 5.30 MON - FRI, 9.30 - 6 SAT, 11 - 5 SUN.
Factory Shop in a Factory Shopping Village • *Household*
Famous branded products at direct from the mill prices. A fabulous assortment of towels, duvets, pillows, throws, bedspreads, up-to-the-minute coordinated bed linen, from Crown, Coloroll, Jeff Banks Ports-of-Call, to name but a few. Something for every room in the house.

PRETTY PERFECTS
78 HIGH STREET, ALFRETON, DERBYSHIRE DE55 7BE
☎ (01773) 521929. OPEN 9 - 5 MON - SAT, CLOSED 1 ON WED.
Factory Shop • *Womenswear only*
Playtex and Pretty Polly lingerie, hosiery, socks and branded toiletries.

PRICE'S CANDLES
MCARTHURGLEN DESIGNER OUTLET DERBYSHIRE,
MANSFIELD ROAD, SOUTH NORMANTON, JUNCTION 28 OF M1,
DERBYSHIRE DE55 2ER
☎ (01773) 545202. OPEN 10 - 6 MON - FRI, 8 ON THUR, 9 - 6 SAT,
11 - 5 SUN.
Factory Shop in a Factory Shopping Village • *Household*
Everything sold in this shop are seconds, discontinued sizes not available elsewhere, over-runs or candles in old packaging that has now been replaced. There are church candles, lanterns, candles in pots and glass jars, star-shaped candles, floating candles, candlestick holders, serviettes, scented candles and garden torches.

R S SPORTS & LEISUREWEAR
192-194 NORMAN STREET, COTMANHAY, ILKESTON,
DERBYSHIRE DE7 8NR
☎ (0115) 932 3865. FAX ☎ (0115) 930 1919.
E-MAIL: roger@sweatshirtsdirect.co.uk
OPEN 9.30 - 3.30 MON - FRI. SAT: PHONE TO CONFIRM.
Permanent Discount Outlet • *Womenswear & Menswear*
Children • *Sportswear & Equipment*
Sports, leisurewear and sweatshirts and cardigans for schoolwear in sizes from 1 year to XXXXL (60" waist) at discounts of up to 50%. Ladies cardigans, sweatshirts and ski pants plus a variety of clothes, but no shoes, ranging from £1 to £12. All the merchandise is made up of overmakes, slight imperfects and end of season lines. There is a permanent sale rail.

REMINGTON
MCARTHURGLEN OUTLET CENTRE, MANSFIELD ROAD,
SOUTH NORMANTON, ALFRETON, JUNCTION 28 OF M1 DE55 2JW
☎ (01773) 545062. OPEN 10 - 6 MON - FRI, UNTIL 8 ON THUR,
9 - 6 SAT, 11 - 5 SUN.
Factory Shop in a Factory Shopping Village • *Electrical Equipment*
Specialise in haircare, personal hygiene and small kitchen items at 30% off high street prices. Lots of famous names here from Monogram cutlery to Braun, Philips, Remington, Clairol, Wahl, Krups and Kenwood small kitchen equipment. It's a great place to buy gifts or replenish the kitchen equipment with combi stylers, turbo travel plus hairdryers, air purifiers, liquidisers; food processors; batteries; clocks; and cutlery. Some of the packaging may be damaged but the products are in perfect working order.

ROYAL CROWN DERBY
194 OSMASTON ROAD, DERBY, DERBYSHIRE DE23 8JZ
☎ (01332) 712833. OPEN 9 - 5 MON - SAT, 11 - 5 SUN.
Factory Shop • *Household*
One third of the stock in this shop is made up of seconds of bone china at discount prices of about one third off normal retail. This includes giftware, tableware and paperweights. Factory tours can be arranged on weekdays, while a new seven-day-a-week visitor centre allows you to see Royal Crown Derby being made and have a go at it yourself

STEVENSON'S OF AMBERGATE
BULLBRIDGE, AMBERGATE, DERBYSHIRE DE56 2HH
☎ (01773) 853473. OPEN 10 - 5.30 MON - FRI, 10 - 5 SAT,
10 - 4 SUN AND BANK HOLIDAYS.
Factory Shop • *Womenswear & Menswear* • *Children* • *Household*
Sells a wide range of ladies knitwear, blouses, skirts, dresses, underwear, nightdresses, hosiery, men's trousers, outerwear, knitwear and childrenswear, as well as towels, face cloths and tea towels. Ladies clothes range from 8-22 in size, men's from 28" waist to 44" in season. There is a huge range of underwear, as well as wool coats, macs and anoraks in the outerwear. Childrenswear ranges from babies to teenwear.

T G GREEN POTTERY FACTORY OUTLET
JOHN STREET, CHURCH GRESLEY, DERBYSHIRE DE11 8EF
☎ (01283) 226696. OPEN 9.30 - 4.30 MON - FRI, 9.30 - 4 SAT,
10 - 3.30 SUN. AND MAIL ORDER.
Factory Shop • *Household*
Part of the Clover Leaf group, this factory shop sells table mats, dinner sets, clocks, linen, towels, tablecloths, pottery and aprons, most of which are either discontinued lines of seconds of ongoing ranges. Many items are half the normal retail price. They will send you a price list and catalogue for £2.50 and you can order by phone. For more details contact Brenda Maddock on 01283 226696.

TDP FACTORY SHOP
TDP HOUSE, RAWDON ROAD, MOIRA, SWADLINCOTE,
DERBYSHIRE DE12 6DT
☎ (01283) 550400. WEBSITE: www.tdptex-promotions.com
OPEN 9.30 - 5.30 MON - FRI, 10 - 4 SAT, SUN.
Factory Shop • *Children* • *Womenswear & Menswear*
Disney character clothes for children, mainly nightwear and underwear, at good discounts. Also ladies and menswear at reasonable prices.

THE COURTAULDS TEXTILES FACTORY SHOP
NIX HILL INDUSTRIAL ESTATE, ALFRETON, DERBYSHIRE DE55 7FQ
☎ (01773) 831035. OPEN 9 - 5.30 MON - SAT, 10.30 - 4.30 SUN.
Factory Shop • *Womenswear & Menswear* • *Children* • *Household*
Sells a wide range of ladies, men's and childrens high street fashions at between 30% and 50% below high street prices. Also stocks a wide range of household textiles, shoes, luggage and accessories.

THE FABRIC FACTORY
LOSCOE ROAD, HEANOR, DERBYSHIRE DE75 7FF
☎ (01773) 718911. OPEN 9.30 - 5.30 MON - SAT, 10 - 2 SUN.
Factory Shop • *Furniture/Soft Furnishings*
Furnishing and dress fabrics at prices from £1.99 to £9.99 a metre. Furnishing fabrics include Prestigious, SMD, Fairfield Mills, Claremont and Villa Nova. Dress fabrics include Derby House clearance lines.

THE SHOE FACTORY SHOP
UNIT 6, TRAFFIC STREET, EAGLE CENTRE, DERBY,
DERBYSHIRE DE1 2NL
☎ (01332) 372823. OPEN 9 - 5 MON - SAT, 10.30 - 4.30 SUN.
Factory Shop • *Womenswear & Menswear* • *Children*
Men's, women's and children's shoes and accessories which are bought in from other manufacturers including Spanish, Portuguese and Italian companies. All are unbranded. The range covers from mocassins to dressy shoes. Ladies shoes which would cost £35 retail are £29. Children's shoes from size 6 to adult size 5 from £10 upwards. Slippers start at baby size 4 to junior size 2 from £3.50 - £6.50.

THORNTONS
MCARTHURGLEN DESIGNER OUTLET VILLAGE, MANSFIELD ROAD,
SOUTH NORMANTON, ALFRETON, DERBYSHIRE DE55 2JW
☎ (01773) 545289. OPEN 10 - 6 MON - FRI, 8 ON THUR, 9 - 6 SAT,
11 - 5 SUN.
Factory Shop in a Factory Shopping Village • *Food and Leisure*
The UK's leading specialist confectionery retailer has more than 500 shops and franchises nationwide selling a wide range of boxed and loose, chocolate and sugar confectionery. The factory outlets sell three different categories:

misshapes. discounted lines and standard lines. Misshapes are loose chocolates which are the result of new product development, product trials or end of production runs which cannot be packed as Thorntons standard lines. They are packed into assorted bags and offer a saving of 35%-55% over the recommended retail price of standard "loose line" products. Discounted lines are excess to Thorntons' normal retail requirements and can be as a result of excess seasonal or export stock, discontinued lines or packaging changes. These products, when available, are offered at a discount of 25%-50% over the standard retail price. Standard lines from the full Thorntons range are also on sale at normal prices.

TOYWORLD FACTORY OUTLET LTD

MCARTHURGLEN DESIGNER OUTLETS, ADDRESS AND OPENING HOURS AS BEFORE.

☎ (01773) 545 333. WEBSITE: www.toyworldstore.com

Factory Shop in a Factory Shopping Village • *Children*

Toyworld sell a large range of discontinued toys, manufacturers' overruns and excess stock from many famous brand names such as Barbie, Action Man, Lego, Tomy, Fisher-Price and many more at least 30-60% off high street prices.

TRADE PRICES

3 NOTTINGHAM ROAD, RIPLEY, DERBYSHIRE DE5 3DJ

☎ (01773) 513483. OPEN 9 - 5.30 MON - FRI, 9 - 5 SAT, 10 - 4 SUN.

Permanent Discount Outlet • *Womenswear & Menswear*
Children • *Household* • *Sportswear & Equipment*

Men's, women's and children's clothes as well as household goods and giftware. Two floors of brand name perfects and chainstore items, the latter consisting of factory over-runs, ends of lines and slight seconds, with up to 50% off high street prices. Brand names include Farah, Wrangler, Lyle & Scott, Wolsey, Naturana, Adidas, Reebok, Nike and Fruit of the Loom. Chainstore clothes have the labels cut out, but many are still recognisable as current high street stock. Names such as Marks & Spencer, BhS, Principles, Etam, Dorothy Perkins, New Look, Richards and Mothercare are available, to name just a few. There is a lift available for pushchairs and disabled customers.

TRAVEL ACCESSORY

MCARTHURGLEN DESIGNER OUTLETS, ADDRESS AND OPENING HOURS AS BEFORE.

☎ (01773) 545255.

Factory Shop in a Factory Shopping Village • *Food and Leisure*

Luggage and travel-related products and executive cases, handbags, umbrellas from leading brands such as Samsonite, Desley, Head, Taurus and GlobeTrotter. Each product is offered at a substantially reduced price compared to those found on the high street due to being production over-runs, discontinued ranges or colours and last season's products. Discounts range from 30%-75% off high street prices.

WEBB IVORY LTD
36 HIGH STREET, SWADLINCOTE, DERBYSHIRE DE11 8HY
☎ (01283) 226700. OPEN 9 - 5 MON - SAT.
38 MAIN CENTRE, DERBY, DERBYSHIRE DE1 2DE
☎ (01332) 204078. OPEN 9 - 5 MON - SAT.
Factory Shop • *Household* • *Womenswear & Menswear* • *Children*
Items from the Webb Ivory catalogue at reduced prices including cards, gifts, soft toys, books, pens, lamps, kitchenware, garden furniture and clothes. Discounts range from at least 50%.

WIRKSWORTH FACTORY SHOP
BENCO HOSIERY, NORTH END MILLS, WIRKSWORTH, DERBYSHIRE DE4 4FG
☎ (01629) 824731. OPEN 9 - 5 SEVEN DAYS A WEEK, 8 ON THUR.
Factory Shop • *Womenswear & Menswear* • *Children* • *Household*
Wide selection of clothes for the family, household goods, giftware and linen. There are T-shirts, shorts, sun vests, skirts, blouses, shirts, sweatshirts, jeans, trousers, dresses, work shirts, swimwear, jog suits, underwear, babywear, socks, tea towels, pillows, duvets and towels. There is a children's play corner and snacks facility. Men's shirts are up to 19 inch collar. For women, the stockings are less than half the shop prices and there are cotton, thermal and woollen underwear. Large, free car park. Working machines making socks in operation most days.

WYNSORS WORLD OF SHOES
SHEFFIELD ROAD, CHESTERFIELD, DERBYSHIRE S41 8JT
☎ (01246) 276690. OPEN 9 - 5.30 MON, TUE, WED, SAT, 9 - 8 THUR, FRI, 10 - 4 SUN AND BANK HOLIDAYS.
Permanent Discount Outlet • *Womenswear & Menswear* • *Children*
Stocks a wide range of footwear for children as well as adults, including some seconds. There are slippers, sandals, boots, sports shoes, trainers, leather and vinyl handbags and purses, shoe cleaners and polishes. Ladies fashion shoes start from £6 a pair. There are some well known brands, all at substantial savings on high street prices.

Devon

ASHBURTON MARBLES
GREAT HALL, NORTH STREET, ASHBURTON, DEVON TQ13 7QD
☎ (01364) 653189. OPEN 8 - 5 MON - FRI, 10 - 4 SAT.
Architectural Salvage • *DIY/Renovation*

Ashburton Marbles offers an extensive array of items at their 18th century showrooms including period marble and wood chimney pieces, cast iron inserts, fire baskets, fenders, guards, etc and anything related to your fireplace spanning 250 years. There is also a varied selection of furnishings, including Art Deco suites, Victorian chaise longues, comfortable Victorian sofas, gilt overmantels and mirrors, chandeliers and wall lights from country-made cast iron to French ormolu. For the garden, there are cast iron fountains, stone bird baths, sun dials, staddle stones, Moroccan pots, reconstituted stone bird baths, stone sundial stands, lead planters, massive olive jars, planters, garden statuary and furniture. Delivery can be arranged throughout the UK.

ATLANTIC VILLAGE OUTLET CENTRE
BIDEFORD, DEVON EX39 3QU
☎ (01237) 422544. E-MAIL: Outletcentres@mepc.co.uk
WEBSITE: www.atlanticvillage.co.uk
OPEN JULY - MID SEPT, 9.30 - 8 MON - SAT, 11 - 5 SUN,
MID SEPT - MID OCT, EASTER TO JULY 9.30 - 6.30 MON - SAT,
11 - 5 SUN, MID OCT - EASTER 9.30 - 5 MON - SAT, 11 - 5 SUN.
Factory Shopping Village • *Womenswear & Menswear* • *Children Household* • *Furniture/Soft Furnishings* • *Food and Leisure Sportswear & Equipment* • *Electrical Equipment*

Over 40 shops with famous names and Devon,s largest interactive maze make this village a good family day out. Shops include Banana Books; Camille; Carlton luggage; Claire,s Accessories; Colony Candles; Cotton Traders, Designer Room, Ecco; Edinburgh Woollen Mill; Eurocall; Event jewellery; Fruit of the Loom; Jane Shilton; Jean Scene; Julian Graves; Kids Play Factory; Nickelby,s, Outdoor Centre; Paco; Pavers Shoes; Pilot Ladieswear; Ponden Mill; Puma; Roman Originals; Room selling accessories for the home and fabrics and soft furnishings; Sportsmill; Suits You; Tog 24; Toyzone; Triumph; Warners; Windsmoor; XS Sound & Media. Free car parking, disabled and baby changing facilities. Atlantic Village also features an attractive piazza, cafes, food court, visitor garden, arts and crafts market, open-air amphitheatre, and an adventure park set in an additional three-acre site linked to the shopping area by the piazza and amphitheatre. The Adventure Park features a mystery maze, adventure golf, wrecker,s cove and adventure play boat.

BABE-EQUIP
9 LEAT STREET, TIVERTON, DEVON EX16 5LG
☎ (01884) 257938.

HUSH-A-BYE-HIRE
16 WHITCHURCH AVENUE, EXETER, DEVON EX2 5NU
☎ (01392) 257636.

BABY EQUIPMENT HIRE
HEATHERTON, FIR HILL, WOODBURY, EXETER, DEVON EX5 1JX
☎ (01395) 233057.

BABE-EQUIP
27 JOHN STREET, TIVERTON, DEVON EX16 5JP
☎ (01884) 259042.
Hire Shops • *Children*
Cots, highchairs, buggies, car seats and safety gates. All items are bought new specially for hire. Both businesses are members of the Baby Equipment Hire Association, which has more than 100 members countrywide who can also provide you with a travel cot, back pack or almost anything a parent of young children might want. Phone 0831 310355 to find your nearest BEHA member. Hush-a-Bye Hire supplies ball pools, bouncy castles etc. for children's parties.

C H BRANNAM LTD
ROUNDSWELL INDUSTRIAL ESTATE, BARNSTAPLE, DEVON EX31 3NJ
☎ (01271) 376853. OPEN 9 - 5 MON - SAT, 10 - 4 SUN
FROM MAY - SEPT ONLY.
Factory Shop • *Household*
On-site factory shop selling terracotta gardening and cookware, including many different forms of pots, especially glazed pots. Seconds are usually available. Phone for details of factory tours.

CHILD'S PLAY
28 ALBION STREET, EXMOUTH, DEVON EX8 1JJ
☎ (01395) 276975. OPEN 10 - 4 MON, TUE, THUR-SAT, 10 - 1 WED, CLOSED 1 - 2 DAILY.
Dress Agency • *Children*
Secondhand and new baby equipment and clothes for ages 0 - 6 years. Babygros cost from 50p to £3; prams from £5 to £100. Also offers hire service. For example, cot or buggy, £1.50 a day or £10 a week per item.

CLARKS SHOES
SHOE VALUE, 22 THE CROSSWAYS, HYDE ROAD, PAIGNTON, DEVON TQ4 5BL
☎ (01803) 553444. OPEN 9 - 5.30 MON - SAT, 10 - 4 BANK HOLIDAYS.
Factory Shop • *Womenswear & Menswear* • *Children*
Clarks International operate a chain of factory shops nationally which specialise in selling discontinued lines and slight sub-standards for men, women and children from Clarks, K Shoes and other famous brands. These shops trade under the name of Crockers, K Shoes Factory shop or Clarks Factory Shop and while not all are physically attached to a shoe factory, these shops are treated as factory shops by the company. Customers can expect to find an extensive range of quality shoes, sandals, walking boots, slippers, trainers, handbags, accessories and gifts, while their major outlets also offer luggage, sports clothing, sports equipment and outdoor clothing. Brands stocked include Clarks, K Shoes, Springer, CICA, Hi-Tec, Puma, Mercury, Fila, Mizuno, Slazenger, Samsonite, Delsey, Antler and Carlton, although not all are sold in every outlet. Discounts are from 30% to 60% off the normal high street price for perfect stock.

CLASSIC COUNTRY RANGES
4 WEBBERS YARD, DARTINGTON, NR TOTNES, DEVON TQ9 6JY
☎ (01803) 865555. FAX 867267. OPEN 9 - 5 MON - FRI, 9 - 2 SAT.
Secondhand Shop • *DIY/Renovation* • *Household*
Specialist suppliers of factory renovated Aga and Rayburn cookers, plus a range of new appliances for cooking or central heating, all at very competitive prices. Main agent for Nobel and Sandyford products, spares and discount heating materials especially flue products. Installations undertaken at competitive prices. Also sell a range of Bridgewater pottery and stainless steel kitchenware.

COLIN BAKER
CROWN HILL, HALBERTON, TIVERTON, DEVON EX16 7AY
☎ (01884) 820152. OPEN 8.30 - 5 MON - FRI.
Architectural Salvage • *DIY/Renovation*
Reclaimed oak beams and joists, oak floorboards and period joinery. Quality timber for furniture making and flooring, doors, mullioned windows. Also new kiln-dried seasoned oak floorboards.

CURTAIN TRADER
187 HIGH STREET, HONITON, DEVON EX14 1LQ
☎ (01404) 45451. OPEN 9.30 - 4.30 TUE - SAT, 9.30 - 1 THUR.
Secondhand shops • *Furniture/Soft Furnishings*
Secondhand curtain agency, they are also specialists in discontinued and seconds designer fabrics and sale stock from £2 to £20 a metre, selling curtain fabrics, linings and accessories from many different labels.

DARTINGTON CRYSTAL
LINDEN CLOSE, SCHOOL LANE, GREAT TORRINGTON,
DEVON EX38 7AN
☎ (01805) 626262. OPEN 9.30 - 5 MON - SAT, 10.30 - 4.30 SUN.
MAIL ORDER.
BARBICAN GLASSWORKS, THE OLD FISH MARKET, THE BARBICAN,
PLYMOUTH, DEVON PL1 2LT
☎ (01752) 224777. OPEN 9 - 6 MON - SAT, 11 - 5 SUN.
ATLANTIC VILLAGE, CLOVELLY ROAD, BIDEFORD EX39 3QU
☎ (01237) 473998. OPENING HOURS VARY SEASONALLY.
KERNOW MILL, TGEREULEFOOT, NEAR SALTASH PL12 5BL
☎ (01752) 851161.
Factory Shop • *Household*
The factory shop at Torrington has an extensive range of Dartington Crystal seconds at greatly reduced prices. Shopping opportunities include a giftware shop selling Portmeirion, Wedgwood, Clover Leaf and Denby, locally produced quality goods, gifts and candles as well as The Edinburgh Woollen Mill with a large selection of classic knitwear and co-ordinated clothing. For a small charge, there are factory tours where you can watch skilled craftsmen blowing and shaping beautiful crystal. The Visitor Centre now includes a family activity centre where you can try your hand at Glass Art, paint or engrave your own designs on a piece of glass. There is a restaurant serving hot and cold meals. The other outlets sell crystal of first and second quality, all at discounted prices.

DARTMOUTH POTTERY
WARFLEET, DARTMOUTH, DEVON TQ6 9BY
☎ (01803) 832258. OPEN 10 - 5 SEVEN DAYS A WEEK.
Factory Shop • *Household*
Discontinued lines and some perfects of Dartmouth pottery at varied discounts. Always some special offers on; prices range from 50p to £15. Cafe, gallery retail area and factory walk through on site.

EXETER SURPLUS
BAKERS YARD, ALPHINBROOK ROAD, MARSH BARTON INDUSTRIAL
ESTATE, EXETER, DEVON EX2 8SS
☎ (01392) 427508. OPEN 10 - 5 MON - FRI.
**Permanent Discount Outlet • *Household* • *Sportswear & Equipment*
Furniture/Soft Furnishings • *Food and Leisure***
Operates from a 4,000 sq ft retail unit and a 10,000 sq ft trade site half a mile away on Christow Road, the latter specialising in quality nearly new office furniture and shelving. Retail goods include engineering equipment, hand tools, clothing, a large range of outdoor goods, chandlery, a range of tents, bedding and domestic furniture, kayaks, rope and chain, canvas sheets, rucksacks, boots and shoes, overalls, ceremonial clothing and an enormous amount of miscellaneous one-off items, all very competitively price. The outdoor leisure market is their new specialisation, particularly ex-government supplies.

HARVEY BAKER DESIGNS
RODGERS INDUSTRIAL ESTATE, YALBERTON ROAD, PAIGNTON, DEVON TQ4 7PJ
☎ (01803) 521515. PHONE BEFORE VISITING.
Factory Shop • *Furniture/Soft Furnishings*
Studio/showroom where you can buy both painted and unpainted MDF furniture and gift items to decorate yourself. There are chests of drawers, wardrobes, beds and bedheads, cabinets as well as unusual items such as Gothic chairs made to order. Hands-on instruction is given on the spot and there is a telephone advice service from the owners who run courses and do demonstrations for the BBC Good Homes Show. Also available are paints, glazes, varnishes, brushes, stencils and mosaics. Send £1 and SAE for a brochure.

HONITON REMNANT SHOP
52 HIGH STREET, HONITON, DEVON EX14 9PW
☎ (01404) 43004. OPEN 9 - 5 MON - SAT.
Permanent Discount Outlet • *Furniture/Soft Furnishings*
Packed full of ends of lines and seconds from famous name furnishing manufacturers. Lining, £2.20 a metre, upholstery fabrics, velvet, from £3.99 a metre for seconds. Curtain fabrics stocked include those from famous names such as Hardy, Sanderson, Derby House, Prestigious, Curtaina, Crowsons and many others. Fabrics start at £2.99 a yard or £3.20 a metre.

HOUSE OF MARBLES & TEIGN VALLEY GLASS
POTTERY ROAD, BOVEY TRACEY, DEVON TQ13 9DS
☎ (01626) 835358. OPEN 9 - 5 SEVEN DAYS A WEEK.
Factory Shop • *Household*
Traditional games, glassware and gifts for all occasions, with lots of discounted seconds at up to 50% off. There are museums of pottery, glass marbles and games and a coffee shop and licensed restaurant. Glass blowing can be viewed from 9am - 4.30pm Monday to Friday and from 10am - 3pm on Sundays all year round. No entrance charge and free parking.

KIDS PLAY FACTORY
ATLANTIC VILLAGE, BIDEFORD, DEVON.
☎ (01237) 422544 (VILLAGE TEL NUMBER). OPENING HOURS VARY.
Factory Shop in a Factory Shopping Village • *Children*
This shop sells a wide range of well-known children's brand names: Little Tikes, Corgi, Crayola, Tomy, Lego, Hasbro, Playskool, Mattel and Fisher-Price at discounts of up to 50%. They also stock a wide range of soft toys including TY Beanie Babies. The village also has a cafe, children's play area and free parking.

M C SLATES
BOW STATION YARD, BOW, NEAR CREDITON, DEVON EX17 6JD
☎ (01363) 82598. OPEN 8 - 4.30 MON - FRI, 9 - 1 SAT.
Architectural Salvage • *DIY/Renovation*
Reclaimed roofing slates and new terracotta flooring - natural not ceramic.

MATALAN
UNIT 2, HAVEN BANKS, WATER LANE, EXETER, DEVON EX2 8DW
☎ (01392) 413375. OPEN 10 - 8 MON - FRI, 9 - 6 SAT, 11 - 5 SUN.
TRANSIT WAY, PLYMOUTH, DEVON PL5 3TN
☎ (01752) 772313. OPEN 10 - 8 MON - FRI, 9 - 6 SAT, 10 - 4 SUN.
Permanent Discount Outlet • *Womenswear & Menswear*
Children • *Household*
Matalan is a fashion and homewares value retailer giving customers what they claim to be unbeatable value for money with huge savings on a wide range of products including high quality fashionable clothing for men, women and children at up to 50% off high street prices. Matalan is situated out of town and stores are open seven days a week all year round.

ORIGIN
STATION ROAD INDUSTRIAL ESTATE, BAMPTON, NEAR TIVERTON, DEVON EX16 9NG
☎ (01398) 331704. OPEN 9 - 5 MON - FRI, 9 - 1 SAT.
Factory Shop • *Womenswear Only*
The Origin factory shop offers a large range of womenswear (dresses, soft suits and separates) suitable for casual and special occasions at approximately 50% less than the recommended retail price. The fabrics used are of a high quality, predominantly natural fibres, including Liberty of London and Rose & Hubble. Situated in the attractive town of Bampton on the edge of Exmoor, the factory offers parking, wheelchair access and a friendly, relaxed atmosphere. Dresses and skirts can be shortened free of charge.

SCENT TO YOU
THE DESIGNER ROOM, ATLANTIC VILLAGE OUTLET CENTRE, BIDEFORD, NORTH DEVON EX39 3QU
☎ (01237) 422544 (CENTRE TEL NO). OPEN JULY - MID SEPT, 9.30 - 8, MON - SAT, 11 - 5 SUN, MID SEPT - MID OCT, EASTER TO JULY 9.30 - 6.30 MON - SAT, 11 - 5 SUN, MID OCT - EASTER 9.30 - 5 MON - SAT, 11 - 5 SUN.
Factory Shop in a Factory Shopping Village • *Womenswear Only*
Operating within The Designer Room at this outlet village, Scent to You sells discounted perfume, cosmetics and accessories including body lotions and gels. The company, which has more than thirty branches, buys in bulk and sells more cheaply, relying on a high turnover for profit. Discounts range from 5% to 60%, with greater savings during their twice-yearly sales (phone for details). Most of the lead-

ing brand names in perfume are stocked including Christian Lacroix, Armani, Charlie, Givenchy, Anais Anais from Cacherel, Charlie from Revlon, Coco Chanel, Christian Dior, Elizabeth Taylor, Blue Grass from Elizabeth Arden, Aramis, Lagerfeld. Plus cosmetics from Revlon and Spectacular and skincare from Clarins and Lancome as well as Scent To You's own range of bags, watches, hair brushes and brushkits which is sold under the name S.T.Y. Designs. Stock varies greatly due to the fast turnover and varying supplies so more than one visit may be necessary to obtain the scent of your choice. Or phone first to avoid disappointment.

SHERIDAN SECONDS SHOP

KENNEDY WAY INDUSTRIAL ESTATE, MOUNTBATTEN ROAD, TIVERTON, DEVON EX16 6SW
☎ (01884) 255997. OPEN 10 - 5 MON - SAT.
Permanent Discount Outlet • *Household*

Sells bed linen from Australia, which is superb quality, to 60 concessions countrywide. Fitted and flat sheets, duvet covers, pillow cases, bath towels, valances and quilt covers. Manufactured and designed in Australia, the designs are unusual, some requiring up to 16 screens. With a high thread count, they are made to last. The shop is sited behind Safeways store (second exit off Devon Link Road North).

STEWART'S

58-60 FORE STREET, BRIXHAM, DEVON TQ5 8DZ
☎ (01803) 852000. OPEN 9 - 5.30 MON - SAT.
9-15 STATION ROAD, TEIGNMOUTH, DEVON TQ14 8PE
☎ (01626) 773963. OPEN 9 - 5.30 MON - SAT.
Factory Shop • *Household* • *Womenswear & Menswear* • *Children Sportswear & Equipment*

Branded merchandise from most of the major UK chain stores, all well-known high street department store names, offered at a discount of 40%-70% off normal high street prices. The garments are selected with great care by experienced buyers direct from factories worldwide to bring customers top quality merchandise at highly competitive prices.

SUSSMAN FACTORY SHOP

POTTINGTON BUSINESS PARK, BARNSTAPLE, DEVON EX31 1NA
☎ (01271) 379305. OPEN 9 - 4.30 MON - FRI, 9 - 4 SAT.
Factory Shop • *Womenswear & Menswear*

Sussman make men's shirts which they sell in this factory shop together with other items of clothing bought in from other manufacturers such as Farah trousers, bedding and textiles. Having recently acquired a business that makes outdoor play equipment for the garden, they now also sell bikes for all the family, swings, gazebo pools, climbing frames and slides, most of which were made for Argos and ToysRUs. These are usually last year's stock or have some slight scratches or marks on them, but are very cheap.

THE CARDEW TEAPOT POTTERY
NEWTON ROAD, BOVEY TRACEY, DEVON TQ13 9DX
☎ (01626) 832172. OPEN 10 - 5.30 SEVEN DAYS A WEEK.
Factory Shop • *Household*

It's said that Josiah Wedgwood used to personally smash any pottery which didn't come up to his exacting standards - Paul Cardew has much the same philosophy. As Cardew don't sell anything other than first quality perfect goods to retailers, here in Bovey Tracey they sell a selected range of slightly imperfect teapots, miniature teapots and other ceramics at up to 50% less than half the normal price. Their shop is also a Mecca for all other things to do with tea - from tea itself to teatowels, books about tea, tea cosies etc. There are free tours when you can see these collectable teapots being made. Large free car park and tea room.

THE EXETER FABRIC WAREHOUSE
UNIT 1, MERRIOTT HOUSE, HENNOCK ROAD, MARSH BARTON
TRADING ESTATE, EXETER, DEVON EX2 8NJ
☎ (01392) 422881. OPEN 9 - 5.30 MON - SAT, 10 - 4 SUN.
7/9 FARADAY MILL, PRINCE ROCK, PLYMOUTH PL4 0ST
☎ (01752) 253351. OPEN 9 - 5 MON - SAT, 10 - 4 SUN.
Permanent Discount Outlet • *Furniture/Soft Furnishings*

By buying vast quantities of fabric direct from the factory, they are able to sell the material at discounts averaging 25%. There is a large selection of fabrics from £2.99 a metre for curtaining to £16.99 for upholstery. They also sell zips, brass hooks, curtain tracks and accessories, Velcro, pillow and cushion covering, pelmets, foam, nets and bean bags and offer a competitive curtain making service. Dress fabrics are also sold at a discount.

THE FROCK EXCHANGE
9 SEAWAY ROAD, PRESTON, PAIGNTON, DEVON TQ3 2NX
☎ (01803) 522951. OPEN 10 - 4.30 TUE - SAT. CLOSED 1 - 2.
Dress Agency • *Womenswear & Menswear*

Women's and menswear with a cross section of clothes from designer labels to high street names and chain stores: Jacques Vert, Louis Feraud, YSL, Christian Dior, Hodges and Dunns. Suits range from £18-£60, and there are hundreds of ties, some shoes from Barkers and Church's, morning suits, blazers, flannels and grey suits. One-third of the shop is taken up with menswear; two thirds with women's.

TK MAXX
YEO BUILDING, 28 ROYAL PARADE, PLYMOUTH, DEVON PL1 1SA
☎ (01752) 255081. OPEN 9 - 5.30 MON FRI, UNTIL 8 THUR, 9 - 6 SAT,
11 - 5 SUN.
Permanent Discount Outlet • *Womenswear & Menswear
Children* • *Household* • *Furniture/Soft Furnishings*

Based on an American concept, TK Maxx is situated in easily accessible, often centrally located stores and offers famous label goods with up to 60% savings off recommended retail prices. TK Maxx has fashion for the whole family - women's, men's and childrenswear - accessories, shoes, gifts, kitchenware and home goods. Everything in the store is branded with a choice of well-known high street names to designer labels, and while a small percentage might be clearly marked past season, the great majority of items in store are current season, current stock and still with phenomenal savings. There is a huge choice with 50,000 pieces in store and up to 10,000 new items arriving a week. The stores are simple and unfussy with wide aisles, shopping trolleys and baskets, and a spacious, functional feel to them but there are individual changing rooms, ramps for buggies and wheelchairs and plenty of staff on the shop floor. Every branch accepts all major credit and debit cards and has a liberal refund and return policy.

TOBYS
(THE OLD BUILDERS YARD AND STORE)
EXMINSTER STATION, EXMINSTER, EXETER, DEVON EX6 8DZ
☎ (01392) 833499. OPEN 9 - 5 MON - FRI, 9.30 - 4.30 SAT, 10.30 - 4.30 SUN.
BRUNEL ROAD INDUSTRIAL ESTATE, NEWTON ABBOT,
DEVON TQ12 4PB
☎ (01626) 351767. OPEN 8.30 - 4.30 MON - FRI, 9.30 - 4.30 SAT.
TORRE STATION, TORQUAY ROAD, TORQUAY, DEVON
☎ (01803) 212222. OPEN 10 - 5 MON - SAT, 10.30 - 4.30 SUN,
BANK HOLIDAYS.
Architectural Salvage • *DIY/Renovation*

Ten thousand square feet of reclaimed doors, windows, slates, sanitaryware, bricks, chimney pots, roof tiles, timber and pine stripping. Also sell antique and imported furniture, bric a brac and much more.

TOG 24
ATLANTIC VILLAGE, CLOVELLY ROAD, BIDEFORD, DEVON EX39 3QU
☎ (01237) 473799. OPENING HOURS VARY SEASONALLY.
Factory Shop in a Factory Shopping Village
Womenswear & Menswear • *Children* • *Sportswear & Equipment*

Tog 24 are the UK's fastest growing brand name in outdoor clothing and leisurewear. They utilise the world's finest performance fabrics including Gore-Tex, Polartec and Burlington MCS, catering for all the family for all seasons, with cosy fleeces and waterproofs for the winter, and trekking ranges, shorts and t-shirts for the summer. With all prices at least 30% below the recommended retail price, you can afford to enter the Tog comfort zone.

TRAGO MILLS
REGIONAL SHOPPING CENTRE, LIVERTON, NEWTON ABBOT
DEVON TQ12 6JD
☎ (01626) 821111. OPEN 9 - 5.30 MON - SAT, 10.45 - 4.45 SUN.
Permanent Discount Outlet • *Children* • *Womenswear & Menswear*
Household • *DIY/Renovation* • *Food and Leisure*
Furniture/Soft Furnishings

The biggest range of discounted goods in the West Country, with a whole range of activities to keep the family amused on the 100 acre site. Sells virtually everything from men's, women's and children's wear, gardening equipment and cookware to wallpaper, carpets and fitted kitchens. Most are branded goods and there is a cafe, pizza bar and petrol station. The women's fashion has a reasonable amount coming from high street multiples. The menswear offers Lee Cooper jeans, Joe Bloggs jeans, Farah trousers, Pierre Cardin, all-leather classic brogues and Oxford shoes, and Doc Martens. Vast car parking areas, lots of outdoor picnic spots. For the home, there are Black & Decker Dustbusters, Hotpoint dryers and washing machines with cosmetic blemishes; curtain fabrics by the metre from Monkwell, Sekers, Filigree, Laura Ashley as well as Janet Reger for Vantona double quilt covers, with matching sheets, pillow cases and valances. There is a vast range of tiles including Pilkington seconds. A separate building houses garden equipment and plant life while the home decorating department has a vast selection of paint, brushes and wallpapers. For example, Crown vinyl emulsion, Magicoat non-drip gloss. An excellent leisure section offers bicycles and accessories, golf gear, keep-fit systems, fishing rods and flies. A separate building houses garden equipment and plant life while the home decorating department has a vast selection of paint, brushes and wallpapers. Comparison prices are not given here, although staff say most items are discounted by up to 50%, so if you're looking for a bargain, make sure you've done your homework on the high street first. The best deals are in fabrics, carpeTs, tiles and diy. There is a Leisure park with a giant free fall slide, Supakart and family go-Kart circuit, dodgems, bumper boats, trawler rides, swan pedalos, pirate ship, aquablasters, orbiters, shooting gallery, remote control cars and cruisers, forklifts and mini-diggers, fun dungeon, animal park, model railway, narrow gauge steam railway, nature reserve, coarse fishing , Edwardian Penny Arcade and plenty of space to picnic and to park.

WINDSMOOR SALE SHOP
34 FLEET STREET, TORQUAY, DEVON TQ2 5DJ
☎ (01803) 201081. OPEN 9 - 5.30 MON - SAT.
ATLANTIC VILLAGE OUTLET CENTRE, BIDEFORD, DEVON EX39 3QU
☎ (01237) 422544 CENTRE TEL. OPENING HOURS VARY SEASONALLY.
Permanent Discount Outlet • *Womenswear Only*
Previous season's stock as well as any returned merchandise and overmakes from the Windsmoor, Planet and Precis Petite ranges. Also rainwear brands including Danimac, Cloud Nine, Telemac, at discounts averaging about 50% off the original price.

WINKLEIGH TIMBER
SECKINGTON CROSS, INDUSTRIAL ESTATE, WINKLEIGH,
DEVON EX19 8DQ
YARD ☎ (01837) 83573. OPEN 9 - 5 MON - FRI, 9 - 12.30 SAT.
SHOWROOM ☎ (01837) 83832. OPEN 9 - 5 MON - FRI, 8 - 12.30 SAT.
Architectural Salvage • *DIY/Renovation* • *Furniture/Soft Furnishings*
Largest source of reclaimed timber in the South of England, including pine, oak and pitch pine planks. Parquet flooring in oak, mahogany, maple, meranti; strip flooring in maple, mahogany, oak and pitch pine. Joinery grade timber, beams and new random width oak and elm. Large stocks of handmade furniture in reclaimed timber always on display in showroom. Also now includes a small range of slate, stone and granite cobbles.

Dorset

BALMAIN & BALMAIN
DORSET DT9 4SB
☎ (01963) 220247. PHONE FOR APPOINTMENT.
Factory Shop • *Furniture/Soft Furnishings*
Buying a sofa is one of the biggest home purchases you make, particularly for good quality. Balmain & Balmain offer traditional handmade furniture which is custom made and can be delivered throughout the country at workshop direct prices. The sofas and chairs are built on best beechwood frames, with coil-sprung seats and feather cushions and carry a ten-year guarantee. Prices are 20%-30% less than the equivalent quality in the high street.

BROWSERS
35 CHEAP STREET, SHERBORNE, DORSET DT9 3PU
☎ (01935) 813326. OPEN 10 - 5 MON - SAT.
Dress Agency • *Womenswear Only*
An upmarket dress agency selling nearly-new labels from Jaeger to Mondi, Viyella to Valentino. Whilst most of their range consists of designer labels, some better quality high street names are also available. This shop is renowned

for brand new clearance stock, overmakes and sample sales. It has a large stock which turns over very quickly. They also stock belts, hats, handbags, jewellery and other accessories.

CD & BOOK & VIDEO SELECTIONS
DORCHESTER, DORSET DT2 7YG
☎ (01305) 848725. MAIL ORDER ONLY.
E-MAIL: sales@cdselections.com   WEBSITE: www.cdselections.com
Permanent Discount Outlet • *Food and Leisure*

CD, Book & Video Selections publishes their bargain selection of CDs, tapes, books and videos five times a year. Two editions are 56 or more pages; three editions are sale supplements. These full-colour guides offer a remarkable range of classical, opera, jazz, easy listening and popular CDs with prices starting at 99p. Overstocks, deletions and ongoing titles are selected for value for money. All sales are backed by a full refund guarantee. CD, Book & Video Selections also sells popular and general interest videos, and bargain books. They publish specialist catalogues for opera and jazz. All stock is now available at the internet site at www.cdselections.com

CURTAINS ENCORE
62 SALISBURY STREET, BLANDFORD FORUM, DORSET DT11 7PR
☎ (01258) 458871. OPEN 9.30 - 1.30 MON - SAT OR BY APPOINTMENT.
Secondhand shops • *Furniture/Soft Furnishings*

Quality new and secondhand curtains, lined and interlined, as well as headboards, tablecloths, bedspreads, stencils, blanks and decoupage materials. Also sells lined and interlined calico curtains for DIY patterning. Alteration service also available.

DAMART
ADELINE ROAD, OFF CHRISTCHURCH ROAD, BOSCOMBE,
BOURNEMOUTH, DORSET
☎ (01202) 301627. OPEN 9 - 5 MON - SAT.
Factory Shop • *Womenswear & Menswear*

Damart underwear and merchandise - anything from tights, socks and gloves to dresses, coats, cardigans and jumpers - some of which is current stock sold at full price, some discontinued and ends of lines sold at discount. There several shops selling some discounted stock from the Damart range, known as Damart Extra.

DARTINGTON CRYSTAL
POOLE POTTERY, THE QUAY, POOLE, DORSET BH15 1RP
☎ (01202) 668615. OPEN 9.30 - 5.30 MON - FRI, 9.30 - 6 SAT, 11 - 5 SUN.
Factory Shop • *Household*

An extensive range of Dartington Crystal seconds at greatly reduced prices as well as some perfect crystal at full price. Range includes wine suites, sherry glasses, tankards, decanters, rippled glass, fruit and salad bowls.

DORSET RECLAMATION
COW DROVE, BERE REGIS, NEAR WAREHAM, DORSET BH20 7JZ
☎ (01929) 472200. E-MAIL: info@dorsetrec.u-net.com
WEBSITE: www.dorset-reclamation.co.uk   OPEN 8 - 5 MON - FRI, 9 - 4 SAT
Architectural Salvage • *DIY/Renovation*

Bathroom fittings, fireplaces, stained glass, Dorset bricks, flagstones, quarry tiles, clay Peg and ridge tiles, doors, oak beams, reclaimed wood flooring, garden statuary, chimney pots, and lead garden figures. Take business park exit off A31/A35 roundabout at Bere Regis.

FABRIC WAREHOUSE
50-52 COMMERCIAL ROAD, POOLE, DORSET BH14 OJT
☎ (01202) 740459. OPEN 9.30 - 5.30 MON - SAT.
58-60 BRIDGE STREET, CHRISTCHURCH, DORSET BH23 1EB
☎ (01202) 481188. OPEN 9.30 - 5.30 MON - SAT.
89 COMMERCIAL ROAD, POOLE, DORSET BH14 OJD
☎ (01202) 723544. OPEN 9.30 - 2 MON - SAT.
Permanent Discount Outlet • *Furniture/Soft Furnishings*

More than 900 different rolls of curtaining fabrics, all well-known brand names, from £4.50 to £14.50 a metre. Expert and friendly curtain making service using traditional methods. Foam and upholstery centre at 89 Commercial Road, Poole.

GEMMA
422 LYMINGTON ROAD, HIGHCLIFFE, CHRISTCHURCH, DORSET BH23 5HE
☎ (01425) 276928. OPEN 10 -5 MON - SAT, 10 - 1 WED.
Dress Agency • *Womenswear* • *Children*

Stocks anything from Marks & Spencer to Ralph Lauren in sizes 8-20, with a wide range of shoes available. Childrenswear is also stocked up to the age of 8 and there is a separate play area for kids. Bargain rail of older stock sold at half-price; sales in the summer and after Christmas. Large range of hats, handbags, scarves and jewellery.

HANSONS FABRICS
STATION ROAD, STURMINSTER NEWTON, DORSET DT10 1BD
☎ (01258) 472698. OPEN 9 - 5 MON - SAT.
Permanent Discount Outlet • *Furniture/Soft Furnishings*

Fashion and curtaining fabric specialist which also sells sewing machines, haberdashery, craft items, patterns and knitting wools. It stocks all the well-known names and the full range of fabric weights. Lots of choice for wedding dress fabric: polyester, satin, silk dupion, taffeta, tulles, veiling and lining and plenty of bridal pattern books available. If you spend more than £25, you get a 5% discount; more than £125 and you receive a seven and a half percent discount; more than £250 and your discount is 10%. All leading makes of sewing machines, including Bernina and Brother, are very competitively priced and machines can also be repaired. Stocks specialist craft books and sells seasonal fabrics out of season. Sewing and craft workshops throughout the year - send for brochure.

LORI'S BOUTIQUE
MILLSTREAM CLOSE, EAST STREET, WIMBORNE, DORSET BH21 1DX
☎ (01202) 889575. open 10 - 5 mon, TUE, THUR, fri, 10 - 1 WED, 10 - 4 SAT.
Dress Agency • *Womenswear Only*
Quality high street names such as Country Casuals, Windsmoor, Jaeger as well as designer names, mostly German, such as Gerry Webber and Bianca. Also sell hats from £10 - £60 and competitively priced shoes, handbags and accessories.

LYME REGIS REMNANT SHOP
16 MARINE PARADE, THE COBB, LYME REGIS, DORSET DT7 3JF
☎ (01297) 442706. OPEN 10 - 5 SEVEN DAYS A WEEK.
Permanent Discount Outlet • *Furniture/Soft Furnishings*
Packed full of ends of lines and seconds from famous name furnishing manufacturers. Lining, £2.20 a metre, upholstery fabrics, velvet, from £3.99 a metre for seconds. Curtain fabrics stocked include those from famous names such as Hardy, Sanderson, Derby House, Prestigious, Curtaina, Crowsons and many others. Fabrics start at £2.99 a yard or £3.20 a metre.

MATALAN
TURBARY RETAIL PARK, RINGWOOD ROAD, POOLE, DORSET PH12 3JJ
☎ (01202) 590686. OPEN 10 - 8 MON - FRI, 9 - 6 SAT, 10 - 4 SUN.
JUBILEE RETAIL PARK, RADIPOLE DRIVE, WEYMOUTH DT4 7BG
☎ (01305) 831300. OPEN 10 - 8 MON - FRI, 9 - 6 SAT, 11 - 5 SUN.
Permanent Discount Outlet • *Womenswear & Menswear*
Children • *Household*
Matalan is a fashion and homewares value retailer giving customers what they claim to be unbeatable value for money with huge savings on a wide range of products including high quality fashionable clothing for men, women and children at up to 50% off high street prices. Matalan is situated out of town and stores are open seven days a week all year round.

PILKINGTON'S TILES FACTORY SHOP
BLANDFORD ROAD, HAMWORTHY, POOLE, DORSET BH15 4AR
☎ (01202) 675200. OPEN 8.30 - 5.30 MON - FRI, 9 - 5 SAT, 10 - 4 SUN.
Factory Shop • *DIY/Renovation*
Sells seconds of the well-known Pilkington's bathroom and kitchen wall and floor tiles and DIY tiling equipment at discount prices of up to 75% off manufacturers' prices. Two hundred and fifty ranges of wall and floor tiles from which to choose. Now also have laminate wood floor and glazed floor tiles.

PONDEN MILL LINENS

POOLE POTTERY, THE QUAY, POOLE, DORSET BH15 1RF
☎ (01202) 684024. OPEN 9 - 5.30 MON - SAT, 10 - 5 SUN. .
Factory Shop • *Household*

Famous branded products at direct from the mill prices. A fabulous assortment of towels, duvets, pillows, throws, bedspreads, up-to-the-minute coordinated bed linen, from Crown, Coloroll, Jeff Banks Ports-of-Call, to name but a few. Something for every room in the house.

POOLE POTTERY LTD

THE QUAY, POOLE, DORSET BH15 1RF
☎ (01202) 666200. FAX ☎ (01202) 682894. OPEN 9 - 5 MON - SAT, 10 - 5 SUN. PHONE FOR LATE OPENING SEASONAL TIMES.
Factory Shop • *Household*

The Poole Pottery Factory Shop is still the cheapest place to buy the widest selection of Poole Pottery. All the old favourite ranges such as Dorset Fruit, Vincent and Vineyard are joined by new exciting ranges like Fresco. The critically acclaimed new "Living Glaze" gift range which uses a glazing method pioneered at Poole nearly forty years ago is now also available. However, it has long since ceased to be just an outlet for Poole Pottery firsts and seconds. It now boasts some of the top brands in giftware such as Dartington and Stuart Crystal, Colony, Spiegalau, Candles and Edinburgh Woollen Mill and more recently, Julian Graves, Book Ends, Nauticalia and Sia Parlane. All these plus the new cook shop makes it the perfect place for the first-time housebuyer to buy practically all their home essentials - it is fast becoming the biggest gift shop in the South. Poole Pottery has recently undertaken an extensive site redevelopment responding to their own research which suggested that both parents and children prefer a separate area to paint plates, throw pots and learn the ancient skills of the potter. The activity area can now be found on a floor of its own offering more freedom and security. The Have-A-Go area has also increased in size from 3,000 sq ft to 6,000 sq ft. Glass blowing demonstrations are regularly held, and a tour of the superb museum together with the factory provides a stimulating and interesting experience. In addition you can enjoy an a la carte, table d'hote meal with fine wines and with unique harbour views at Carters restaurant, or opt for a light snack in the tea room or self-service area.

S. MOORES

THE BISCUIT BAKERY, MORCOMBELAKE, NEAR BRIDPORT, DORSET DT6 6ES
☎ (01297) 489253. OPEN 9 - 5 MON - FRI, 9 - 1 SAT (SUMMER ONLY).
Food and Drink Discounters

Broken biscuits including shortbreads, walnut crunch, chocolate chip and ginger biscuits sold in 800 gram bags at 30% saving. Tend to sell out very early in the day, so don't leave your visit until late in the afternoon. There is also a small gallery of West Country paintings and bakery bygones and a new viewing gallery for visitors to look around the factory.

THE CATALOGUE SHOP
401 LYMINGTON ROAD, HIGHCLIFFE, DORSET BH23 5HE
☎ (01425) 271202. FAX ☎ (01425) 278478. OPEN 9 - 5 MON - SAT, 10 - 5 SUN.
Permanent Discount Outlet • *Womenswear & Menswear* • *Children*
Household • *Furniture/Soft Furnishings* • *Sportswear & Equipment*

Returns, damaged and worn goods as well as clearance lines and ends of lines of branded merchandise from mail order catalogues. This includes men's, women's and children's wear, footwear, bedding, curtains, furniture, exercise equipment and leather coats. These items are always in stock but the shop also has an ever-changing range of items as well. Turnover is very fast with new deliveries every day. All items are sold at less than 50% of the catalogue price starting at 99p, with branded trainers from £14.99.

THE OLD MILL FACTORY SHOP
PYMORE MILLS, BRIDPORT, DORSET DT6 5PJ
☎ (01308) 420969. E-MAIL: info@oldmillshop.co.uk
WEBSITE: www.oldmillshop.co.uk
OPEN 9.30 - 5 MON - SAT. CLOSED BANK HOLIDAYS.
Factory Shop • *Furniture/Soft Furnishings*

Traditional-style brass, cast and forged headboards and bedsteads, top quality handmade sofa beds and mattresses, designer fabric and period wooden furniture, slight seconds and discontinued lines of which are on sale at huge discounts. The beds are from a well-known brand name, Relyon, made for top quality stores. Now also sell three piece suites and brass curtain poles.

TK MAXX
QUADRANT ARCADE, OLD CHRISTCHURCH ROAD, BOURNEMOUTH, DORSET BH1 2BX
☎ (01202) 316367. OPEN 9 - 5.30 MON - FRI, 9 - 6 SAT, 11 - 5 SUN, UNTIL 8 ON THUR.
Permanent Discount Outlet • *Womenswear & Menswear*
Children • *Household*

Based on an American concept, TK Maxx is situated in easily accessible, often centrally located stores and offers famous label goods with up to 60% savings off recommended retail prices. TK Maxx has fashion for the whole family - women's, men's and childrenswear - accessories, shoes, gifts, kitchenware and home goods. Everything in the store is branded with a choice of well-known high street names to designer labels, and while a small percentage might be clearly marked past season, the great majority of items in store are current season, current stock and still with phenomenal savings. There is a huge choice with 50,000 pieces in store and up to 10,000 new items arriving a week. The stores are simple and unfussy with wide aisles, shopping trolleys and baskets, and a spacious, functional feel to them but there are individual changing rooms, ramps for buggies and wheelchairs and plenty of staff on the shop floor. Every branch accepts all major credit and debit cards and has a liberal refund and return policy.

TRAVELMATE
52 YORK PLACE, BOURNEMOUTH DORSET BH7 6JN
☎ (01202) 431520.
This company keeps a database of people looking for travel companions and wishing to avoid single supplements. They will send you details of those wanting to go to the same area or who have the same holiday interest or wish to go on holiday and are willing to share a room with a stranger but still keep their independence. Golden Friends is a new service for the over-50s to introduce prospective travelling companions or simply those looking for friendship.

TRIO
179 NEW ROAD, WEST PARLEY, DORSET BH22 8ED
☎ (01202) 594242. OPEN 10 - 5 MON - SAT.
Dress Agency • *Womenswear Only*
Good high street labels such as Country Casuals, Jaeger, Viyella, Betty Barclay, in a selection that includes day and evening wear, handbags, belts, scarves, shoes and jewellery. Free parking outside.

Essex

BABY DIRECT DISCOUNT WAREHOUSE
BABY DIRECT, CROMWELL CENTRE, RIVER ROAD, BARKING, ESSEX 1G11 0JE
☎ 020-8507 0572. OPEN 9.30 - 5.30 MON - SAT, 10 - 2 SUN.
Permanent Discount Outlet • *Children*
Sells baby goods including cots from £49.95; high chairs from £19.95; walkers from £19.95; gates from £16.95; playpens from £39.95; quilt sets from £9.95; cot beds from £139.95; travel cots from £29.95. All cots come with free mattresses. Baby Direct is a Mamas & Papas main stockist and offers sales, service and spares. Items can be paid for in instalments.

BAGGAGE DEPOT
VICARAGE FIELDS SHOPPING CENTRE, BARKING, ESSEX IG11 0LZ
☎ 020-8591 1961. OPEN 9 - 5.30 MON - SAT.
Permanent Discount Outlet • *Food and Leisure*
Luggage and travel-related products and executive cases, handbags, umbrellas from leading brands such as Samsonite, Desley, Head, Taurus and GlobeTrotter. Each product is offered at a substantially reduced price compared to those found on the high street due to being production over-runs, discontinued ranges or colours and last season's products. Discounts range from 30%-75% off high street prices.

BRANDED STOCKS
SHARP HOUSE, 2-3 ARTERIAL ROAD, LAINDON, ESSEX SS15 6DR
☎ (01268) 418000. OPEN 9 - 4.30 MON - SAT.
Permanent Discount Outlet • *Womenswear & Menswear*
Men's and ladies casual wear from Thomas Burberry, Burberry, Versace, Armani, Ralph Lauren, Romeo Gigli, Diesel, Aquascutum, Moschino, Gucci, MaxMara Weekend, Jean Paul Gaultier, Iceberg and Calvin Klein.

BRANDLER GALLERIES
1 COPTFOLD ROAD, BRENTWOOD, ESSEX CM14 4BN
☎ (01277) 222269. E-MAIL: Art-British@Dial.Pipex.com.
WEBSITE: www.brandler-galleries.com OPEN 10 - 5.30 TUE - SAT.
PHONE FIRST IF LOOKING FOR A PARTICULAR ITEM.
Permanent Discount Outlet • *Food and Leisure*
Prints, sculptures and paintings of a high standard at prices which reflect the low overheads outside London. Works by Diana Armfield, Bill Bowyer, Fred Cuming, Bernard Dunstan, Mary Fedden, David Tindle, Carel Weight, Andy Warhol, David Hockney, Picasso and others of a similar calibre. Prices range from £45-£20,000. Recently they sold a Turner watercolour for £18,500 which would have cost as much as £75,000 in Bond Street. There are original book illustrations for Noddy, Postman Pat, Pugwash, Rupert etc. Also offer a framing service and free car park.

CHARLES CLINKARD
CLACTON COMMON FACTORY SHOPPING VILLAGE,
STEPHENSON ROAD WEST, CLACTON ON SEA, ESSEX CO15 4TL
☎ (01255) 220384. OPEN 10 - 6 MON - SAT, 11 - 5 SUN.
Factory Shop in a Factory Shopping Village • *Children*
Womenswear & Menswear
Footwear for the family at discounts of between 20% and 50%. Labels on sale here include Rockport, Loake, Church's, Ecco, Gabor, Rohde, Van-Dal, Kickers, Clarks, Grensons, Elefanten, K Shoes, Lotus and Renata.

CHOICE DISCOUNT STORES LIMITED
14-20 RECTORY ROAD, HADLEIGH, BENFLEET, ESSEX SS7 2ND
☎ (01702) 555245. OPEN 9 - 5.30 MON - THUR, 9 - 6 FRI, SAT.
26-28 HIGH STREET, BARKINGSIDE, ILFORD, ESSEX IG6 2DQ
☎ 0208-551 2125. OPEN 9 - 5.30 MON - FRI, 9 - 6 SAT, 11 - 5 SUN.
10-11 LADYGATE CENTRE, HIGH STREET, WICKFORD, ESSEX SS12 9AJ
☎ (01268) 764893. OPEN 9 - 5.30 MON - FRI, 9 - 6 SAT.
UNIT 6A, MAYFLOWER RETAIL PARK, GARDINERS LINK, BASILDON, ESSEX SS14 3AP
☎ (01268) 288331. OPEN 9 - 6 MON - SAT, 7 ON THUR, FRI, 11 - 5 SUN.
14-16 HIGH STREET, GRAYS, ESSEX RM17 6LU
☎ (01375) 385780. OPEN 9 - 5.30 MON - SAT.

CLACTON COMMON FACTORY SHOPPING VILLAGE, STEPHENSON
ROAD WEST, CLACTON-ON-SEA, ESSEX CO15 4TL
☎ (01255) 474786. OPEN 10 - 6 MON - SAT, 11 - 5 SUN.
Permanent Discount Outlet • *Womenswear & Menswear* • *Children*
Surplus stock including women's, men's and children's fashions from Next plc, Next Directory and other high street fashion houses, Next Interiors and footwear. You can save up to 50% off normal retail prices for first quality; up to two thirds for seconds. There are special sales each January and September. Easy access for wheelchairs and pushchairs. The Watford and Wickford stores are known as Next 2 Choice; the former specialises in ladies and menswear only from Next plc and Next Directory.

CHRISTMAS IN THE EASTERS
EASTER HALL, AYTHORPE RODING, GREAT DUNMOW, ESSEX CM6 1PE
☎ (01245) 231628. WEBSITE: wwwachristmastree.co.uk
OPEN 8 - 8 SEVEN DAYS A WEEK. MID OCT - CHRISTMAS EVE.
Permanent Discount Outlet • *Household*
Christmas tree farm with a seasonal discount outlet in the form of a themed Christmas barn selling everything you could need for the festive season. Good quality Christmas trees, both home-grown and artificial; a fantastic selection of tree and wall decorations; home-made decorated noble fir wreaths and artificial wreaths, fresh garlands to trail down staircases and above mantelpieces. Plus they sell all the accessories to make your own wreath such as orange slices, dried roses and limes. Well-known names sold here include Gisela Graham and Hollywell Designs. A Santa's Grotto is open at weekends.

CLACTON COMMON FACTORY SHOPPING VILLAGE
STEPHENSON ROAD WEST, CLACTON-ON-SEA, ESSEX CO15 4TL
☎ (01255) 479595 INFORMATION OR (01255) 430777.
OPEN 10 - 6 MON - SAT, 11 - 5 SUN.
Factory Shopping Village • *Womenswear & Menswear* • *Children*
Household • *Electrical Equipment* • *Food and Leisure*
Sportswear & Equipment
Forty-eight units centred around a Victorian winter garden comprising the following: Banana Bookshop selling books, games and stationery; Bairdwear, selling ladies and men's fashions; Bed & Bath Works, a homeware outlet with discounted branded linens and housewares from Janet Reger, Sheridan, Christy and Kingsley; Benetton selling men's, women's and children's casual wear; Birthdays, stocking mainstream cards and gifts from manufacturers such as Andrew Brownsword, Disney, Parker, Galt and Warner Brothers; Braveoffer; Camille lingerie; Caterpillar selling foorwear from the Cat range; Choice, which sells family clothing from Next; Claire's Accessories; Clinkards family footwear from Church's, Gabor, Bally and Loake; Cook & Dine kitchenware, glass and ceramics; Cotton Traders casual wear; Dannimac out-

door wear; Designer Room selling designer fashion from Christian Lacroix and Louis Feraud for men and women; Event fashion costume jewellery and watches from Accurist, Timberland, Seiko and Timex; Eye Zone fashion sunglasses and accessories; Garden Store selling garden furniture, barbecues and equipment; Globetrotter, with travel goods from Delsey and Samsonite; Haggar selling menswear; Honey, a manufacturer which supplies the major high street stores with women's knitwear and co-ordinated separates; Jacques Vert selling ladies dresses, skirts, suits, blouses, hats, belts and scarves; JD Sports selling branded sports merchandise from Adidas, Nike, Reebok, Ellesse and Le Coq Sportif; Jean Scene for men, women and children; Joanna Hall selling handbags from the Jane Shilton range; Joe Bloggs jeans and casualwear for men, women and children; JoKids; Julian Graves foods and nut mixes; Kids Play Factory with toys from ranges such as Fisher-Price and Lego; Leading Labels, with men's and women's fashions from Bruna Fashions, Gemini, Cote a Cote, Ben Sherman, Farah and Double Two; Millano selling men's, women's and children's leatherwear; Mobile Phone Shop; Nicklebys fashion wear for men and women; Olli Moda selling branded jeans and casual wear; Pilot, a young women's fashion outlet; Price's Candles; Roman Originals ladieswear; R S Shoes with shoes for all the family; Spotlight, a young woman's fashion outlet; Suits You men's shirts, suits, and casual separates as well as wedding hire; The Great Outdoors selling outdoor clothing and equipment: Thorntons chocolates; Tog 24 outdoor and activity wear; Tom Sayer men's knitwear and co-ordinated separates; Windsmoor; and Woods of Windsor toiletries and gift items; XS Music CDs and videos. There are also be two restaurants, a tourist information centre, parking for 1,000 cars and a bus service link to Clacton town centre and railway station.

DESIGNER SHADES

FREEPORT DESIGNER OUTLET VILLAGE, CHAPEL HILL, BRAINTREE, ESSEX CM7 8YH
☎ (01376) 334007. OPEN 10 - 6 MON - SAT, UNTIL 8 ON THUR, 11 - 5 SUN.

Permanent Discount Outlet • *Womenswear & Menswear* • *Children*

Designer Shades offer a wide selection of top-notch sunglasses at more than 30% off typical high street prices. The frames are invitingly displayed on backlit columns - no locked cabinets, messy stickers or hanging labels to contend with. Gucci, Polo Ralph Lauren, Jean Paul Gaultier, Valentino, Police, Christian Dior and Diesel are included in the ever-changing stock of top international brand names. Designer Shades ensure that all their sunglasses have quality lenses which protect against UVA and UVB rays, as well as filtering out damaging reflective blue light. They plan to have 20 shops throughout Europe by the end of 2001. For details of other locations, ring 01423 858007 or email info@designer-shades.net.

FAIRHEADS
60-64 CRANBROOK ROAD, ILFORD, ESSEX IG1 4NQ
☎ 020-84780328. OPEN 9 - 5.30 MON - SAT.
Permanent Discount Outlet • *Household*

There are thirteen different departments at Fairheads, including household, linen, soft furnishings, lingerie, fashion, hosiery, craft and haberdashery. There are often 'blue ticket' specials where if, for example, you bought three pairs of Sloggi briefs you get the fourth for free. Best quality stock at the lowest price possible and always special offers and reduced lines throughout the store. At sale time stock is half price or less. There are two genuine sales a year: after Christmas and at the end of June, telephone for details.

FREEPORT BRAINTREE DESIGNER OUTLET VILLAGE
CHARTER WAY, CHAPEL HILL, BRAINTREE ESSEX CM7 8YH
☎ (01376) 348168. OPEN 10 - 6 MON - SAT, 8 ON THUR, 11 - 5 SUN.
Factory Shopping Village • *Womenswear & Menswear Children* • *Household* • *Electrical Equipment* • *Furniture/Soft Furnishings* • *Food and Leisure* • *Sportswear & Equipment*

A terrific range of designer products selling at up to 50% off high street prices: from big name fashion brands to kitchenware and china. Outlets include Armani, Calvin Klein, Christian Lacroix, Moschino, Nike, Reebok, Versace, Burberry, Iceberg, Boxfresh, Tommy Hilfiger, Wedgwood and Denby. Clothes for all the family including lingerie, casualwear, accessories, sportswear and outdoorwear, luggage, glass, house and home ideas. There's free parking, several places to eat and play areas for children. Freeport Braintree is located off juction 8 of the M11, join the A120 to Braintree and follow the sights to Freeport. It has its own station with a direct rail link to London's Liverpool Street.

GLYN WEBB
ST ANDREW AVENUE, COLCHESTER, ESSEX CO4 3BQ
☎ (01206) 798407. OPEN 9 - 8 MON - SAT, 11 - 5 SUN AND BANK HOLIDAYS.
Permanent Discount Outlet • *DIY/Renovation*

Stockists of all your home improvement needs from wallpaper to paint, furniture to flooring, tiles to textiles, housewares to lighting - in fact, almost everything for your home, with 25 branches in the North-West, Midlands and Yorkshire. Specialists in discontinued mail order, slightly imperfect branded stocks as well as perfect quality superior products. They carry top brands such as Dulux, Crown Paints and Vymura and Coloroll wall coverings, Rectella and Norwood textiles and much more in store. To find your nearest branch, phone Head Office on 0161 621 4500.

HARWICH BEACON FACTORY OUTLET CENTRE
HARWICH, ESSEX, DUE TO OPEN IN 2001.
Factory Shopping Village • *Womenswear & Menswear* • *Children Household* • *Sportswear & Equipment* • *Food and Leisure*

Planned to open in 2001, there will be forty-plus factory shops offering end of season lines and overstock at discount prices. If you live locally, watch out for opening notices in the local press.

HUBBINET REPRODUCTIONS
UNIT 7, HUBBINET INDUSTRIAL ESTATE, EASTERN AVENUE WEST, HAINAULT ROAD, ROMFORD, ESSEX RM7 7NU
☎ (01708) 762212. OPEN 9 - 5 MON - FRI, 10 - 4 SAT.
Factory Shop • *Furniture/Soft Furnishings*

Manufacturers of reproduction furniture in mahogany and yew, all of which are sold in the factory shop at discounts of about 20%. Seconds in dining room suites, bookcases, video cabinets, display cabinets, desks, computer desks and cupboards at factory shop prices. Free parking and refreshments available. Staff are willing to take customers round the factory.

JANE SHILTON
FREEPORT BRAINTREE OUTLET VILLAGE, CHARTER WAY, CHAPEL HILL, BRAINTREE, ESSEX CM7 8YH
☎ (01376) 341696. OPEN 10 - 6 MON - SAT, 10 - 8 THUR, 11 - 5 SUN.
Factory Shop in a Factory Shopping Village • *Womenswear Only*

Merchandise from past seasons' collections or factory seconds at discounts of at least 30% and up to 70% off the original price. There is a wide range of handbags, small leather goods, shoes, luggage umbrellas and travel bags. Example of price reduction: handbags at £24.99 originally £37.

JOE BLOGGS
CLACTON FACTORY SHOPPING VILLAGE, CLACTON-ON-SEA, ESSEX CO15 4TL
☎ (01255) 428288. OPEN 10 - 6 MON - SAT, 11 - 5 SUN AND BANK HOLS.
Factory Shop in a Factory Shopping Village
Womenswear & Menswear • *Children*

Range of casual clothing for men, women, children and babies which are ends of lines, imperfects or surplus ranges. Jeans, tops, long sleeved shirts and jackets at discounts of between 30% and 70%.

JOKIDS LTD
CLACTON COMMON FACTORY SHOPPING VILLAGE,
STEPHENSON ROAD WEST, CLACTON ON SEA, ESSEX CO16 9HB
☎ (01255) 421311. OPEN 10 - 6 MON - SAT, 11 - 5 SUN.
Factory Shop in a Factory Shopping Village • *Children*
JoKids is the factory shop trading name for Jeffrey Ohrenstein which sells unusual and attractive clothes for children aged from birth to ten years. This includes pretty party dresses for girls at reductions of up to 40%, all-in-one smocked playsuits, T-shirts, denim shirts, denim dresses, sunhats, shorts, and accessories.

JUST FABRICS
102 HIGH STREET, MALDON, ESSEX CN9 5ET
☎ (01621) 852552. OPEN 9 - 5.30 MON - SAT.
Permanent Discount Outlet • *Furniture/Soft Furnishings*
This fabric shop sells discounted fabric from dress material to net curtains, fleece, tapestry, curtaining, voile, cushion covers, toy making fabric, buttons, zips, tapes and a full range of haberdashery. If it's not end of line, it's always reasonably priced. For example, at time of writing, they had Sanderson fabric at £2.99 per metre, cotton satine at £1.99 a metre and fabric which would normally cost between £8 and £17.99 at £2.99. Upholstery weight fabric which would retail at £9.99 to £25.99 a metre is available at £6.99.

KIDS COLLECTIONS
176C QUEEN ROAD, BUCKHURST HILL, ESSEX IG9 5BD
☎ 020-8502 9600. OPEN 10 - 5.30 MON - SAT.
Dress Agency • *Children*
Nearly-new designer wear children's clothes. Labels on sale at about one third of the retail price include Kenzo, Portofino, Oilily, Chipie and Levi's and all are in excellent condition. There are also new shoes, high chairs and a range of First Holy Communion accessories for sale.

KIDS PLAY FACTORY
CLACTON COMMON FACTORY SHOPPING VILLAGE,
STEPHENSON ROAD WEST, CLACTON ON SEA, ESSEX CO15 4TL
☎ (01255) 222219. OPEN 10 - 6 MON - SAT, 11 - 5 SUN.
Factory Shop in a Factory Shopping Village • *Children*
This shop sells a wide range of well-known children's brand names: Little Tikes, Corgi, Crayola, Tomy, Lego, Hasbro, Playskool, Mattel and Fisher-Price at discounts of up to 50%. They also stock a wide range of soft toys including TY Beanie Babies. The village also has a cafe, children's play area and free parking.

LABELS FOR LESS
THE COCKPIT, EMSON CLOSE, SAFFRON WALDEN, ESSEX CB10 1HF
☎ (01799) 523533. OPEN 9.45 - 5.30 MON - FRI, 10 - 5.30 SAT.
Permanent Discount Outlet • *Womenswear & Menswear*

Designer ladieswear, menswear and footwear including labels such as Calvin Klein, Ralph Lauren, Moschino, Versace, YSL, Timberland, Ton Sur Ton, Lacoste and Armani at discount prices.

LE CREUSET
FREEPORT VILLAGE, CHARTER WAY, CHAPEL HILL, BRAINTREE, ESSEX
☎ (01376) 329584. OPEN 10 - 6 MON - SAT, 10 - 8 THUR, 11 - 5 SUN.
Factory Shop in a Factory Shopping Village • *Household*

Items from the famous Le Creuset range - casseroles, saucepans, fry pans etc - plus their pottery collection at discounts of at least 30%.

LEATHER FOR LESS
7 MARKET ROW, SAFFRON WALDEN, ESSEX
☎ (01799) 516711. OPEN 10 - 5.30 MON - SAT.
Permanent Discount Outlet • *Womenswear Only*

Leather bags, shoes, belts and hats at discount prices.

LEE COOPER
FREEPORT OUTLET VILLAGE, CHARTER WAY, CHAPEL HILL, BRAINTREE, ESSEX CM7 8YH
☎ (01376) 554684. OPEN 10 - 6 MON - SAT, 8 ON THUR, 11 - 5 SUN.
Factory Shop in a Factory Shopping Village
Womenswear & Menswear • *Children*

Denim jeans, jackets and shirts, each ranked by size and gender at discounts of up to 30%. Casual shirts from £9.99, jeans from £14.99, T-shirts and ladieswear. Lee Cooper was founded in 1908 as a workwear manufacturer before becoming a supplier to the armed forces. Most of the stock here is current, discontinued and irregular merchandise, all of which comes straight from Lee Cooper's factories in Europe.

LEIGH LIGHTING COMPANY
1593 LONDON ROAD, LEIGH-ON-SEA, ESSEX SS9 2SG
☎ (01702) 477633/470112 FAX. OPEN 9 - 5 MON - FRI, CLOSED 1 ON WED, 9 - 5 SAT. MAIL ORDER.
Factory Shop • *Electrical Equipment*

Thousands of lighting fixtures at between 20-50% below normal retail prices. Selling to both the commercial and domestic market, they offer recessed lights, table lamps, chandeliers, wall lights and outdoor security lighting, all of which are bought direct from the manufacturer. They can supply virtually any lighting seen elsewhere at very competitive prices. Catalogues available for mail order.

LILLEY & SKINNER
FREEPORT DESIGNER OUTLET VILLAGE, CHARTER WAY,
CHAPEL HILL, BRAINTREE ESSEX CM7 8YH
- (01376) 327490. OPEN 10 - 6 MON - SAT, 10 - 8 THUR, 11 - 5 SUN.

Factory Shop in a Factory Shopping Village
Womenswear & Menswear • *Children*

Wide range of brand names including Stead & Simpson, Lilley & Skinner, Hobos, Hush Puppies, Lotus, Sterling & Hunt, Richleigh, Scholl, Red Tape, Flexi Country, Padders, Canaletto, Bronx, Frank Wright, Brevitt, Romba Wallace, Rieker, all at discount prices of up to 50%.

MATALAN
UNIT 4B, THE TUNNEL ESTATE, WESTERN AVENUE, LAKESIDE RETAIL PARK, WEST THURROCK, ESSEX RM16 1HH
- (01708) 864350. OPEN 10 - 8 MON - FRI, 9 - 6 SAT, 11 - 5 SUN.
UNIT 4, RIVERSIDE RETAIL PARK, VICTORIA ROAD, CHELMSFORD, ESSEX EM2 6LL
- (01245) 348787. OPEN 10 - 8 MON - FRI, 9 - 6 SAT, 11 - 5 SUN.
UNIT E, COLCHESTER RETAIL PARK, SHEEPHEN ROAD, COLCHESTER CO3 3LE
- (01206) 812400. OPEN 10 - 8 MON - FRI, 9 - 6 SAT, 11 - 5 SUN.
CRAYFORD RETAIL PARK, CRAYFORD DA1 4LA
- (01322) 552140. OPEN 9 -8 MON - FRI, 9 -6 SAT, 10 - 4 SUN.
THE GREYHOUND RETAIL PARK, SUTTON ROAD, SOUTHEND SS2 5PY
- (01702) 466248. OPEN 10 -8 MON - FRI, 9 -6 SAT, 10 - 4 SUN.
117 NORTH STREET, ROMFORD RM1 1EX
- (01708) 759780. OPEN 10 - 8 MON - FRI, 9 - 6 SAT, 10 - 4 SUN.

Permanent Discount Outlet • *Womenswear & Menswear*
Children • *Household*

Matalan is a fashion and homewares value retailer giving customers what they claim to be unbeatable value for money with huge savings on a wide range of products including high quality fashionable clothing for men, women and children at up to 50% off high street prices. Matalan is situated out of town and stores are open seven days a week all year round.

NATIONAL WEDDING INFORMATION SERVICES
121-123 HIGH STREET, EPPING ESSEX CM16 4BD
- (01992) 576461. OPEN 8.30 - 9.30 MON - FRI, 9 - 5.30 SAT.

Free information on a range of facilities in your area from car hire to bridal wear, hall decoration to marquee hire. Phone them and tell them where your wedding is taking place and they will send you, free, a list of services local to you. Obviously, the quality of the list depends on which local businesses have registered with the Information Service.

NEW HALL VINEYARDS
CHELMSFORD ROAD, PURLEIGH, CHELMSFORD, ESSEX CM3 6PN
☎ (01621) 828343. OPEN 10 - 5 MON - FRI, 10 - 1.30 SAT, SUN.
Food and Drink Discounters • *Food and Leisure*

Specialises in white wine - Muller, Bacchus, Huxelrebe and Chardonnay - on which it offers discounts of up to 10% depending on the quantities you buy. There is an annual English wine festival on the weekend before August Bank Holiday and guided tours are available from May to September. Book in advance - phone for details.

NIPPERS
WHITES FARM, BURES ROAD, WHITE COLNE, COLCHESTER, ESSEX CO6 2QF
☎ (01787) 228000. FAX (01787) 228560. E-MAIL: colchester@nipprs.co.uk
WEBSITE: www.nippers.co.uk   OPENING HOURS VARY SO PHONE FIRST.
Permanent Discount Outlet • *Children*

Nippers, the nursery equipment and toy specialists, operate from previously redundant buildings in rural areas around the country. They offer easy parking, no queues and personal service. This is on top of competitive prices on prams, cots, pushchairs, car seats, outdoor play equipment and toys, some of which are new, some seconds or secondhand and some ends of lines. Prices are low because they avoid the high overheads of traditional retail outlets and also because the successful growth of a number of branches means they can now buy in bulk and negotiate good deals. Customers are invited to try out the merchandise while the children look at the animals, mostly sheep, chicken and pigs. Also offers many brand leaders at discount, including Mamas & Papas, Cosatto, Britax, Maclaren and Bebe Confort, plus Fisher-Price and Little Tikes. You can try out the car seats in your car and there is usually a pram/pushchair repair service on site.

PACO
FREEPORT BRAINTREE DESIGNER OUTLET VILLAGE, CHARTER WAY, CHAPEL HILL, BRAINTREE ESSEX CM7 8YH
☎ (01376) 553820. OPEN 10 - 6 SEVEN DAYS A WEEK, 10 - 8 THUR, 11 - 5 SUN.
Factory Shop in a Factory Shopping Village
Womenswear & Menswear • *Children* • *Sportswear & Equipment*

Paco uses bright, distinctive colours and the knack for designing great clothes at affordable prices. For several years, they have also been creating their own brand of sports and leisurewear clothing that shows great verve and energy. This range has a much more everyday living influence. The contrast is a distinct look for the discerning wearer. If you are looking for a great T-shirt or sweatshirt, lightweight jacket or gilet, polar fleece or hooded top, three-quarter length or combat trousers, then you need look no further. Paco now competes with the very best fashion brands in the high street by offering customers high fashion combined with excellent quality, making their clothes real value for money.

PARTRIDGE
FREEPORT BRAINTREE ADDRESS AND OPENING HOURS AS BEFORE.
☎ (01376) 554994.
Factory Shop in a Factory Shopping Village
Womenswear & Menswear • *Children*

Partridge specialises in fashionable outdoor clothes and accessories. Ranges include waxed jackets, Gore-tex jackets, waterproof jackets, tweeds, quilts, fleece jackets and waistcoats, knitwear, shirts, chinos, cord and moleskin trousers, hats and caps. Discontinued lines are on sale at discounted prices with a minimum of 30% and up to 70% off during promotions.

PRICE'S CANDLES
CLACTON COMMON OUTLET VILLAGE, STEPHENSON ROAD WEST, CLACTON ON SEA, ESSEX CO15 4TL
☎ (01255) 426331. OPEN 10 - 6 MON - SAT, 11 - 5 SUN.
Factory Shop in a Factory Shopping Village • *Household*

Everything sold in this shop are seconds, discontinued sizes not available elsewhere, over-runs or candles in old packaging that has now been replaced. There are church candles, lanterns, candles in pots and glass jars, star-shaped candles, floating candles, candlestick holders, serviettes, scented candles and garden torches.

SCENT TO YOU
THE DESIGNER ROOM, FREEPORT BRAINTREE DESIGNER OUTLET VILLAGE, CHARTER WAY, CHAPEL HILL, BRAINTREE, ESSEX CM7 8YH
☎ (01376) 554642. OPEN 10 - 6 SEVEN DAYS A WEEK, 10 - 8 THUR, 11 - 5 SUN.
THE DESIGNER ROOM, CLACTON COMMON FACTORY SHOPPING VILLAGE, STEPHENSON ROAD WEST, CLACTON-ON-SEA, ESSEX CO15 4TL
☎ (01255) 479779. OPEN 10 - 6 MON - SAT, 11 - 5 SUN.
Factory Shop in a Factory Shopping Village • *Womenswear Only*

Operating within The Designer Room at these outlet villages, Scent to You sells discounted perfume, cosmetics and accessories including body lotions and gels. The company, which has more than thirty branches, buys in bulk and sells more cheaply, relying on a high turnover for profit. Discounts range from 5% to 60%, with greater savings during their twice-yearly sales (phone for details). Most of the leading brand names in perfume are stocked including Christian Lacroix, Armani, Charlie, Givenchy, Anais Anais from Cacherel, Charlie from Revlon, Coco Chanel, Christian Dior, Elizabeth Taylor, Blue Grass from Elizabeth Arden, Aramis, Lagerfeld. Plus cosmetics from REvlon and Spectacular and skincare from Clarins and Lancome as well as Scent To You's own range of bags, watches, hair brushes and brushkits which is sold under the name S.T.Y. Designs. Stock varies greatly due to the fast turnover and varying supplies so more than one visit may be necessary to obtain the scent of your choice. Or phone first to avoid disappointment.

SIZE-UP

3 MARKET HILL, SAFFRON WALDEN, ESSEX CB10 1HQ
☎ (01799) 516536. OPEN 9 - 5.30 MON - FRI, 8.30 - 5.30 SAT.
54-56 HIGH STREET, BILLERICAY CM12 9BS
☎ (01277) 636337. OPEN 9 - 5.30 MON - SAT.
12 GEORGE YARD, BRAINTREE CM7 1UR
☎ (01376) 554728. OPEN 9 - 5.30 MON - SAT.

Permanent Discount Outlet • *Womenswear Only*

Top quality ladies outsize clothing, some of it from Evans, some own-label and some without labels. There are coats, dresses, suits and separates, some scarves and leisure wear. Some items cost less than half price. For example, Evans long pinstripe coat, £25, reduced from £70. All merchandise is new end of lines or last season's stock in good condition. Sizes 16-30.

SPOILS

253-254 LAKESIDE SHOPPING CENTRE, WEST THURROCK, GRAYS, ESSEX RM16 1ZQ
☎ (01708) 890298. OPEN 10 - 10 MON - FRI, 9 - 7.30 SAT, 11 - 5 SUN.
UNIT 21/22 CULVER STREET WEST, CULVER SQUARE, COLCHESTER, ESSEX CO1 1PB
☎ (01206) 763411. OPEN 9 - 5.30 MON - SAT, 11 - 4 SUN.
145 HIGH STREET, SOUTHEND, ESSEX SS1 1LL
☎ (01702) 352733. OPEN 9 - 5.30 MON - SAT.
UNIT 22, LIBERTY 2, ROMFORD, ESSEX RM1 3EE
☎ (01708) 751413. OPEN 9 - 5.30 MON - SAT.
UNITS 85, 86 AND 87, THE EXCHANGE SHOPPING CENTRE, ILFORD, ESSEX IG1 1AT
☎ 0208-514 5894. OPEN 9.30 - 6 MON - FRI, 8 ON WED, 9 - 6 SAT, 11 - 5 SUN.
82/84 EASTGATE CENTRE, BASILDON, ESSEX SS14 1AE
☎ (01268) 520827. OPEN 9 - 5.30 MON - FRI, 9 - 6 SAT, 11 - 4.30 SUN.

Permanent Discount Outlet • *Household*

General domestic glassware, non-stick bakeware, kitchen gadgets, ceramic oven-to-tableware, textiles, cutting boards, aluminium non-stick cookware, bakeware, plastic kitchenware, plastic storage, woodware, coffee pots/makers, furniture, mirrors and picture frames. Rather than being discounted, all the merchandise is very competitively priced - in fact, the company carry out competitors' checks frequently in order to monitor pricing. With 38 branches, the company is able to buy in bulk and thus negotiate very good prices.

STELLISONS LTD

350 HARWICH ROAD, COLCHESTER, ESSEX CO4 3HP
☎ (01206) 871151. OPEN 9 - 6 MON - SAT, 10 - 4 SUN.

Permanent Discount Outlet • *Electrical Equipment*

Excellent display of electrical goods from television sets and videos to cookers, fridges, freezers, washing machines, tumble dryers and fitted kitchens by Comera and Arthur Bonnet . They claim to sell at prices which are lower than any other shop in Essex. Sell only mainstream brands and local delivery is free.

THE CURTAIN EXCHANGE
11 MARKET HILL, COGGESHALL, ESSEX CO6 1TS
☎ (01376) 561199. OPEN 10 - 5 MON - SAT.
Secondhand shops • *Furniture/Soft Furnishings*
The Curtain Exchange is a franchised group of shops selling beautiful top quality secondhand curtains, blinds, pelmets, etc at between one-third and one half of the brand new price. Their stock comes from a variety of sources: people who are moving house; people who have curtains made and then feel they are wrong for the room; show houses where the builder wants to recoup some of his outgoings; interior designers' mistakes. Stock changes constantly and ranges from rich brocades, damasks and velvets to chintzes, linens and cottons. Designer names include Colefax & Fowler, Designers Guild, Laura Ashley, Warner, Sanderson, Osborne & Little, Fortuny and Bennison. A team of fitters and alteration experts are available if required. They offer a 24-hour availability. The Curtain Exchange also supply bespoke ranges with samples of curtains hanging. These fabrics are chosen from suppliers all over the world and are an excellent buy. They also offer ready made curtains designed exclusively for them which come in lengths up to 305cm (120"). These are outstanding value, e.g. 80" wide, 120" drop start at £175 including VAT.

THE DESIGN HOUSE
FREEPORT DESIGNER OUTLET VILLAGE, CHAPEL HILL, BRAINTREE, ESSEX CM7 8YH
☎ (01376) 343004. OPEN 10 - 6 MON - SAT, TILL 8 ON THUR11 - 5 SUN.
Factory Shop in a Factory Shopping Village • *Household*
Famous branded products at direct from the mill prices. A fabulous assortment of towels, duvets, pillows, throws, bedspreads, up-to-the-minute coordinated bed linen, from Crown, Coloroll, Jeff Banks Ports-of-Call, to name but a few. Something for every room in the house.

THE FABRIC FACTORY
33-35 EAST WALK, BASILDON, ESSEX CM9 5ET
☎ (01268) 521887. OPEN 9 - 5.30 MON - SAT.
Permanent Discount Outlet • *Furniture/Soft Furnishings*
The Fabric Factory sells dress and furnishing fabrics at discounted prices. Stock is regular and clearance, and they also sell tracks, poles, and offer a made-to-measure service.

THE FACTORY SHOP (ESSEX) LTD
THE GLOUCESTERS, LUCKYN LANE, PIPPS HILL INDUSTRIAL ESTATE, BASILDON, ESSEX SS14 3AX
☎ (01268) 520546. OPEN 9 - 6 MON - SAT, 10 - 5 SUN.
PURDEY'S INDUSTRIAL ESTATE, 1 MAGNOLIA WAY, ROCKFORD, ESSEX SS4 1ND
☎ (01702) 531153. OPEN 9 - 6 MON - SAT, 10 - 5 SUN.
Factory Shop • *Womenswear & Menswear* • *Children* • *Household*
No-frills factory shop selling seconds, discontinued lines and some perfect current stock from department and chain store high street names, as well as direct from the manufacturer. This is not the place to look for high fashion, but it has an enormous amount of middle-of-the-range men's, women's and children's clothes, as well as bedlinen, towels, toys, food, kitchen utensils, disposable cutlery and partyware, short-dated food, garden furniture, tools, sportswear, china, glass and barbecues within its 8,000 square feet of selling space. A large pet and aquatic department has recently opened. Everything is sold at between 30% and 50% of the retail price. Parking is easy, the M25 is near and there's good wheelchair/pushchair access.

THE FACTORY SHOP LTD
THE CROSS ROADS, KELVEDON ROAD, TIPTREE, ESSEX CO5 OLJ
☎ (01621) 817662. OPEN 9 - 5.30 MON - SAT, 10 - 4 SUN.
Factory Shop • *Womenswear & Menswear* • *Children* • *Household* *Furniture/Soft Furnishings* • *Sportswear & Equipment*
High street chainstore seconds and ends of ranges from clothes for all the family, bedding, toiletries, kitchenware, glassware, footwear, lighting, cosmetics, jewellery, and luggage at discounts of approximately 30%-50%. There are weekly deliveries and brands include many major stars: Joe Bloggs, Nike, Adidas and Brabantia, to name just four. Lines are continually changing and few factory shops offer such a variety under one roof. There are furniture displays and a new line of Cape Country Furniture is now on sale. This high quality pine furniture made exclusively for The Factory Shop in the new South Africa is sold at factory direct prices with home delivery throughout the UK. Colour brochure and price list available. This branch has its own free car park.

THE LIGHTING AND FURNITURE FACTORY SHOP
UNIT 1, HASTINGWOOD ROAD, HASTINGWOOD, NEAR HARLOW, ESSEX CM17 9JH
☎ (01279) 413466. OPEN 9 - 4.30 MON - FRI, 10 - 4 SAT.
Factory Shop • *Furniture/Soft Furnishings*
Outdoor lights, lamps, chandeliers, bulbs, lamp bases, shades, all at factory shop prices. Makes lamp bases and fabric shades with coordinating trims. Also sells reproduction and pine furniture.

THE REMNANT SHOP
12 - 14 HEAD STREET, COLCHESTER, ESSEX CO1 1NY
☎ (01206) 763432. OPEN 9 - 5.30 MON - SAT.
Permanent Discount Outlet • *Furniture/Soft Furnishings*
Although not strictly a discount fabric shop, they sell cut-price ends of rolls and remnants in curtain materials, dressmaking fabrics (satins, silks, dupions, polyesters) and patterns. They always have a good range of curtain fabrics and hold thousands of rolls of fabric in stock. Lines change constantly so you should always find something to suit. Also hold a substantial stock of haberdashery at very competitive prices.

THE WAREHOUSE (BOOKSALE) COMPANY
EDWARD'S WALK, MALDON, ESSEX CM9 5PS
☎ (01621) 841292. OPEN 9 - 5 MON - SAT, CLOSES AT 2 ON WED.
Permanent Discount Outlet • *Food and Leisure*
Booksale now boasts more than 100 shops throughout the UK: call 0121 313 6000 for details of your nearest store. It sells books, stationery, paints, tapes, CDs and CDRoms, videos, all at enormously discounted prices. Paperbacks and hardbacks from £1.99p, children's books 49p; videos 99p, clip frames 99p - £19.95, posters £1.50 - £6.99 and classical CDs from £3.99.

THORNTONS
CLACTON COMMON FACTORY VILLAGE, CLACTON ON SEA,
ESSEX CO16 9HB
☎ (01255) 220527. OPEN 10 - 6 MON - SAT, 11 - 5 SUN.
UNIT B4 FREEPORT BRAINTREE, DESIGNER OUTLET VILLAGE,
CHARTER WAY,CHAPEL HILL, BRAINTREE, ESSEX CM7 8YH.
☎ (01376) 347242. OPEN 10 - 6 MON - SAT, 8 ON THUR, 11 - 5 SUN.
Factory Shop in a Factory Shopping Village • *Food and Leisure*
The UK's leading specialist confectionery retailer has more than 500 shops and franchises nationwide selling a wide range of boxed and loose, chocolate and sugar confectionery. The factory outlets sell three different categories: misshapes. discounted lines and standard lines. Misshapes are loose chocolates which are the result of new product development, product trials or end of production runs which cannot be packed as Thorntons standard lines. They are packed into assorted bags and offer a saving of 35%-55% over the recommended retail price of standard Òloose line" products. Discounted lines are excess to Thorntons' normal retail requirements and can be as a result of excess seasonal or export stock, discontinued lines or packaging changes. These products, when available, are offered at a discount of 25%-50% over the standard retail price. Standard lines from the full Thorntons range are also on sale at normal prices.

TK MAXX

THE EXCHANGE, ILFORD, ESSEX.
☎ 020-8514 1288. OPEN 9.30 - 6 MON - FRI, 8 ON WED, 9 - 6 SAT, 11 - 5 SUN.
EASTGATE SHOPPING CENTRE, BASILDON, ESSEX
☎ (01268) 273604. OPEN 9 - 5.30 MON - FRI, 9 - 6 SAT, 11 - 5 SUN.
THE ROYAL SHOPPING CENTRE, HIGH STREET, SOUTHEND SS1
☎ (01702) 600020.

Permanent Discount Outlet • *Womenswear & Menswear*
Children • *Household* • *Furniture/Soft Furnishings*

Based on an American concept, TK Maxx is situated in easily accessible, often centrally located stores and offers famous label goods with up to 60% savings off recommended retail prices. TK Maxx has fashion for the whole family - women's, men's and childrenswear - accessories, shoes, gifts, kitchenware and home goods. Everything in the store is branded with a choice of well-known high street names to designer labels, and while a small percentage might be clearly marked past season, the great majority of items in store are current season, current stock and still with phenomenal savings. There is a huge choice with 50,000 pieces in store and up to 10,000 new items arriving a week. The stores are simple and unfussy with wide aisles, shopping trolleys and baskets, and a spacious, functional feel to them but there are individual changing rooms, ramps for buggies and wheelchairs and plenty of staff on the shop floor. Every branch accepts all major credit and debit cards and has a liberal refund and return policy.

TOG 24

CLACTON COMMON FACTORY OUTLET, STEPHENSON ROAD,
CLACTON ON SEA ESSEX CO15 4TL
☎ (01255) 435035. OPEN 10 - 6 MON - SAT, 8 ON THUR, 11 - 5 SUN.

Factory Shop in a Factory Shopping Village
Womenswear & Menswear • *Children* • *Sportswear & Equipment*

Tog 24 are the UK's fastest growing brand name in outdoor clothing and leisurewear. They utilise the world's finest performance fabrics including Gore-Tex, Polartec and Burlington MCS, catering for all the family for all seasons, with cosy fleeces and waterproofs for the winter, and trekking ranges, shorts and t-shirts for the summer. With all prices at least 30% below the recommended retail price, you can afford to enter the Tog comfort zone.

TOM SAYERS CLOTHING CO
CLACTON COMMON FACTORY OUTLET VILLAGE, STEPHENSON
ROAD WEST, CLACTON ON SEA, ESSEX CO13 4T4
☎ (01255) 221860. OPEN 10 - 6 MON - SAT, 11 - 5 SUN.
Factory Shop in a Factory Shopping Village • *Menswear Only*
Tom Sayers make sweaters for some of the top high street department stores. Unusually for a factory shop, if they don't stock your size, they will try and order it for you from their factory or one of their other factory outlets and send it to you. Most of the stock here is overstock, cancelled orders or last season's and includes jumpers, trousers and shirts at discounts of 30%. The trousers and shirts are bought in to complement the sweaters which they make.

TRAVEL ACCESSORY
CLACTON COMMON OUTLET VILLAGE, STEPHENSON ROAD,
CLACTON-ON-SEA, ESSEX CO15 4TL
☎ (01255) 221500. OPEN 10 -6 MON - SAT, 11 - 5 SUN.
Factory Shop in a Factory Shopping Village • *Food and Leisure*
Luggage and travel-related products and executive cases, handbags, umbrellas from leading brands such as Samsonite, Desley, Head, Taurus and GlobeTrotter. Each product is offered at a substantially reduced price compared to those found on the high street due to being production over-runs, discontinued ranges or colours and last season's products. Discounts range from 30%-75% off high street prices.

TSAR SOLUTIONS LTD
120 ELM ROAD, LEIGH-ON-SEA, ESSEX SS9 1SQ
☎ (01702) 480505. OPEN 9.30 - 1 WED - SAT.
Factory Shop • *Womenswear Only*
As manufacturers of top quality ladies clothes, which are sold only in this retail showroom, prices are extremely competitive as there is no wholesaler to add his margin. Wide range of womenswear from dresses, jackets and tops to skirts, shorts and blouses - everything except swimwear, nightwear and coats. The range covers casual and dressy - in particular for mother of the bride/groom outfits.

VALROSE
610 CHIGWELL ROAD, WOODFORD BRIDGE, ESSEX 1G8 8AA
☎ 020-8506 1667. OPEN 9.30 - 5 TUE - SAT.
Dress Agency • *Womenswear* • *Children*
Valrose is a well-established dress agency dealing mostly in womenswear for the past 15 years. Labels in the adult section include anything from high street chainstore makes to DKNY, Ouiset, Windsmoor, Next, Jaeger, Escada, Valentino, Calvin Klein, Betty Barclay and Moschino. Labels in the children's section include Oilily, Next and Gap. There is always plenty of stock available and friendly, helpful staff. Clothing is sectioned into skirts, trousers, blouses, jumpers, coats, swimwear, suits, bags, hats and shoes and then divided into sizes.

Gloucestershire

ANCILLA
15 LECKHAMPTON ROAD, CHELTENHAM,
GLOUCESTERSHIRE GL53 0A2
☎ (01242) 242799. OPEN 10 - 5 TUE, THUR, FRI, 10 - 1 WED AND SAT.
Dress Agency • *Womenswear Only*
Wide selection of womenswear from casual to occasion wear; good range of separates and acessories. Caters for ages 18-80 in sizes 8 - 20. Examples of labels sold inclue Windsmoor, Planet, Paul Costelloe and Louis Feraud, Armani, Jaeger.

AU TEMPS PERDU
28 - 30 MIDLAND ROAD, ST PHILIPS, BRISTOL,
GLOUCESTERSHIRE BS2 0JY
☎ (0117) 9299143. MOBILE 0374 486648. OPEN 10 - 5 TUE - SAT.
Architectural Salvage • *DIY/Renovation*
General architectural salvage with French and English stock: bathroom fittings, fire surrounds, cooking ranges, door and furniture stripping, landscaping materials, paving, flagstones and Victorian fireplaces.

BABY EQUIPMENT HIRERS ASSOCIATION
☎ (0831) 310355. PHONE 9 - 5 MON - FRI.
Expecting a visit from grandchildren or friends with young babies? Save them the bother of bringing cots and high chairs with them - hire the equipment instead. Or having your first baby and want to splash out on all the latest equipment? You may only use a few items for a couple of months at most and even if you put it away for the next child, it will be out of date very quickly. The BEHA has more than 100 members countrywide who can provide you with a travel cot, high chair, buggy, back pack, cot, baby walker, electric breast pump Moses basket, play pen, auto swing or almost anything a parent of young children might want. Phone (tel no above) to find your nearest BEHA member.

BOOKENDS
26 WESTGATE STREET, GLOUCESTER, GLOUCESTERSHIRE GL1 2NW
☎ (01452) 331011. OPEN 9 - 5.30 MON - SAT.
43 PARK STREET, BRISTOL BS1 5PB
☎ (0117) 926 5565. OPEN 9 - 6 MON - SAT, 1 - 5 SUN.
UNIT 23, EASTWALK, YATE SHOPPING CENTRE, BRISTOL BS17 4AS
☎ (01454) 312359. OPEN 9 - 5.30 MON - SAT.
Secondhand shops • *Food and Leisure*
Damaged books and publishers' returns, as well as new and review copies, including recently published books, usually at half price or below.

CASTAWAY
HIGH STREET, MORETON-IN-MARSH, GLOUCESTERSHIRE GL56 OAD
☎ (01608) 652683. OPEN 10 - 5 MON - SAT.
Dress Agency • *Womenswear Only*
Sells suits, separates, evening wear, shoes and accessories by names such as Monsoon and Laura Ashley, with some designer wear from labels such as Mondi, Louis Feraud, Christian Dior and Mulberry. A rocking horse and a selection of newspapers keeps the rest of the family entertained.

CATALOGUE BARGAIN SHOP
1/6 GROSVENOR HOUSE, STATION ROAD, GLOUCESTER, GLOUCESTERSHIRE.
☎ (01452) 308779. OPEN 9 - 5.30 MON - SAT, 10.30 - 4.30 SUN.
Permanent Discount Outlet • *Womenswear & Menswear Children* • *Household* • *Electrical Equipment*
Catalogue Bargain Shop is a growing national chain of stores which obtains the majority of its goods from mail order giants Great Universal and Kays, and offers a range of clothing for all the family, a wide selection of shoes, bed linen, beds, household goods, electrical equipment and hundreds of other catalogue items at very competitive prices. For example, double bed, £99.99, wardrobes and three-piece suites. The merchandise consists of ends of ranges and previous season's stock for which there is no longer storage space when the catalogues change.

CHANTILLY
65 GREAT NORWOOD STREET, CHELTENHAM, GLOUCESTERSHIRE GL50 2BQ
☎ (01242) 512639. OPEN 10 - 4.45 TUE - FRI, 10 - 3 SAT.
Dress Agency • *Womenswear Only*
Medium-sized shop with up to 3,000 items on two floors including a selection of clothes perfect for a working wardrobe from Marks & Spencer, Next and Wallis to Monsoon and Jigsaw with some designer labels such as Windsmoor, Eastex and MaxMara. There are also shoes, handbags and jewellery. Examples of average prices include blouses, £12.99; jackets £28; skirts from £12-£14. Free parking.

COTSWOLD FABRIC WAREHOUSE
TEWKESBURY ROAD, CHELTENHAM, GLOUCESTERSHIRE GL51 9AH
☎ (01242) 255959. E-MAIL: wool.weavers@dial.pipex.com
WEBSITE: www.naturalbest.co.uk
OPEN 9 - 5.30 MON - FRI, 9 - 5 SAT, 10 - 4 SUN.
Permanent Discount Outlet • *Furniture/Soft Furnishings*
Huge range of well-known designer label furnishing fabric in very large premises. Fabrics start at £2.99 per metre. Beautiful Indian linen checks, bargain remnants at £1 per metre; as well as a selection of dress fabrics, curtain poles and accessories. Stock changes constantly so buy when you see.

COTSWOLD WOOLLEN WEAVERS
FILKINS, OFF A361, NEAR LECHLADE, GLOUCESTERSHIRE GL7 3JJ
☎ (01367) 860491. OPEN 10 - 6 MON - SAT, 2 - 6 SUN.
Factory Shop • *Household*
Cotswold Woollen Weavers make their blankets on site using Dobcross looms. Regarded as the elite of looms, their slow action is gentler on yarns than modern machines, resulting in cloth with more depth, resilience and texture. CWW also produce "organic" blankets, rugs and cloth made from merino yarn which is naturally coloured and washed using soap rather than synthetic detergent. The on-site shop sells blankets for £25 which are on sale in the high street for up to £80 as well as a range of clothes, throws, candles.

COURTAULDS BODYWEAR FACTORY SHOP
THE GARDEN FACTORY, SIGNAL ROAD, STAPLE HILL, BRISTOL, GLOUCESTERSHIRE BS16 5PG
☎ (0117) 975 5599. OPEN 1.15 - 3 FRI ONLY.
Factory Shop • *Womenswear & Menswear*
Lingerie seconds from the factory, mainly for women but with some men's underwear and a small children's selection. Briefs, camisoles, bodyshapers, swimwear, Y-front and vests.

COX'S YARD
10 FOSSE WAY BUSINESS CENTRE, MORETON IN MARSH, GLOUCESTERSHIRE GL56 9NQ
☎ (01608) 652505. E-MAIL: cox@fsbdial.co.uk   OPEN 8.30 - 6 MON - SAT.
Architectural Salvage • *DIY/Renovation*
Architectural antiques, reclamation oak, pine, elm and pitch beams and boards. Can make traditional oak doors from reclaimed oak to your dimensions.

CROCK SHOP
DIGBETH STREET, STOW ON THE WOLD, GLOUCESTERSHIRE GL54 1BN
☎ (01451) 870340. OPEN 9.30 - 6 SEVEN DAYS A WEEK.
Permanent Discount Outlet • *Household*
China, glass and cookware and giftware direct from the factories of the manufacturers of Churchill, BhS, Wood and Sons and Portmeirion at discounts of up to 50%. Now in bigger premises so an even wider range is available.

DAMART
LISTER BUILDINGS STATION ROAD, GLOUCESTER, GLOUCESTERSHIRE.
☎ (01452) 526510. OPEN 9.30 - 5 MON - SAT.
Factory Shop • *Womenswear & Menswear*
Damart underwear and merchandise - anything from tights, socks and gloves to dresses, coats, cardigans and jumpers - some of which is current stock sold at full price, some discontinued and ends of lines sold at discount. There are several shops selling some discounted stock from the Damart range, known as Damart Extra.

DISCOUNT CHINA
HIGH STREET, BOURTON-ON-THE-WATER, NEAR CHELTENHAM,
GLOUCESTERSHIRE GL54 2AP
☎ (01451) 820662. OPEN 10 - 5 SEVEN DAYS A WEEK.
Permanent Discount Outlet • *Household*
Retailers of china and cookware direct from the factories of Staffordshire. Supplies are sourced from different manufacturers so varies according to what is available at the time, but includes china fancies, beakers, cookware, planters, Portmerion cookware and dinner sets.

DUNELM MILL SHOPS LTD
CARRIAGE BUILDINGS, BRUTON WAY, GLOUCESTER,
GLOUCESTERSHIRE GL1 1BZ
☎ (01452) 385063. OPEN 9 - 5 MON - THUR, 9 - 5.30 FRI, SAT,
10.30 - 4.30 SUN.
Permanent Discount Outlet • *Household*
Part of a chain of shops based in the Midlands selling brand-name and chain-store curtains, masses of bedlinen, towels, wickerware, pictures and frames, all at competitive prices.

ENCORE
8 SWAN YARD, WEST MARKET PLACE, CIRENCESTER,
GLOUCESTERSHIRE GL7 2NH
☎ (01285) 885223. OPEN 10 - 4 MON - FRI, 10 - 5 SAT.
Dress Agency • *Womenswear Only*
Using their celebrity and TV presenter contacts, the owners of this relatively new dress agency sell top-name, up-to-date, hardly worn clothes at very reasonable prices. Current stock usually includes Armani, Alexon, Escada, Maxmara, Joseph, Jaeger, Planet, Valentino, Amanda Wakeley as well as items from smaller fashion chains such as Karen Millen, Jigsaw, Kookai, Hobbs, Warehouse, etc.

ENGLISH COUNTRY POTTERY
STATION ROAD, WICKWAR, WOTTON-UNDER-EDGE,
GLOUCESTERSHIRE GL12 8NB
☎ (01454) 299100. FAX 01454 294053. OPEN 9 - 4 MON - FRI.
MAIL ORDER.
Factory Shop • *Household*
English Country Pottery has a factory shop on site just down the stairs from where the large range of pottery is made. Each pot is taken through eight traditional processes, before being handpainted and signed by the painters. Finally, the pattern is sealed under the glaze and fired, making it very durable: oven, dishwasher and microwave proof. Here, seconds and discontinued pottery from their own ranges are sold at discounted prices. Some of the pottery has been made by special commission for department stores, galleries and mail

order companies, some is wholesaled to the independent gift trade. Because of this, and the fact that they design and manufacture their own pottery, the variety of styles is very wide, resulting in a vibrant, individualistic and very English style of pottery. The designs include farm animals, brightly coloured geometric and floral designs. The range includes tableware, children's items, giftware and bathroom accessories, as well as a large range of wall tiles, hand decorated with sea, animal and floral motifs with co-ordinating plain coloured tiles.

FOX & CHAVE
27 THE CIRCUS, BATH, GLOUCESTERSHIRE BA1 2EU
☎ (0709) 202 7033. BY APPOINTMENT ONLY.
Factory Shop • *Menswear Only*
Fox & Chave, who are wholesalers of the largest silk tie collection in the UK, have a showroom where the public can purchase from their complete range and receive a 50% discount on the recommended retail price. Phone for an appointment and a chance to pay just £10 for a hand-made silk tie.

GERALD ANTHONY FASHIONS
1 WEST WAY, OFF CRICKLADE STREET, CIRENCESTER,
GLOUCESTERSHIRE GL7 1JA
☎ (01285) 656100. OPEN 9.30 - 5 MON - SAT.
Permanent Discount Outlet • *Womenswear & Menswear*
Chainstore clothes for ladies and men at reduced prices. Discontinued lines and Grade A garments are reduced by about one third. There are skirts, trousers, socks, underwear, nightwear, sweaters, blouses, dressing gowns, shorts, T-shirts and swimwear. Primarily Marks & Spencers' merchandise (with labels removed), Principles, Next, BHS and well known brands.

GRACEFUL GOWNS
69 BELL HILL ROAD, ST GEORGE, BRISTOL
GLOUCESTERSHIRE BS5 7LY
☎ (0117) 9557166. SHOP OPEN BY APPOINTMENT
SEVEN DAYS A WEEK.
Permanent Discount Outlet • *Womenswear Only*
Wedding dresses, shoes, veils, head-dresses - dresses from £50 - £1,000; bridesmaids' dresses from £20-£150. Labels include Alfred Angelo, Dreammaker and Sincerity by Sweetheart. Large selection of bridal headdresses and veils including Trudy Lee and Richards. Nicholas House handmade veils made to order and alterations by hand.

HAWICK CASHMERE COMPANY
2 BREWERY YARD, SHEEP STREET, STOW-ON-THE-WOLD,
COTSWOLDS, GLOUCESTERSHIRE GL54 1AA
☎ (01451) 870840. OPEN 9.30 - 5.30 MON - SAT.
Factory Shop • *Womenswear & Menswear*
Hawick offers you the luxury of Scottish knitwear direct from the Scottish borders at prices which are below normal retail prices. You can choose from cashmere, cashmere/silk, merino and lambswool for men and women. Also some trousers, gloves, scarves and handbags.

INDEX
THE PROMENADE, CHELTENHAM, GLOUCESTERSHIRE GL50 1LN
☎ (01242) 226674. OPEN 9 - 5.30 MON - SAT.
31-33 NORTHGATE STREET, GLOUCESTER
☎ (01452) 300357. OPEN 9 - 5.30 MON - SAT.
Permanent Discount Outlet • *Electrical Equipment* • *Household*
There are 12 'bargain zones' within Index stores countrywide selling catalogue clearance items from toys to electrical goods at discounts of 30%-70%. Ring 0345 444444 to find your nearest department.

JAMES GAUNT
33 SOUTHGATE STREET, GLOUCESTER GLOUCESTERSHIRE GL1 1TX
☎ (01452) 311 709. OPEN 9 - 5.30 MON - SAT.
Permanent Discount Outlet • *Furniture/Soft Furnishings*
Specialist interior designers James Gaunt sells regular lines and some clearance fabrics. The range includes well known names such as Nina Campbell, Jane Churchill, Malabar and Warners and the emphasis throughout this shop is on designer stock at bargain prices.

JUST THOUGHTS
56 CHURCH STREET, TEWKESBURY, GLOUCESTERSHIRE GL20 5RZ
☎ (01684) 293037. OPEN 10 - 5 TUE - SAT,
CLOSED 1.30 - 2.30 DAILY AND ALL DAY MONDAYS.
Dress Agency • *Womenswear Only*
Wide selection of labels, mostly middle to upmarket including many designer names. For example, MaxMara, Marella, Escada, Paul Costelloe, Frank Usher and Betty Barclay usually selling at a third of the original retail price. Situated opposite Tewkesbury Abbey.

JUST-IN LIMITED
2 HAILES STREET, WINCHCOMBE, GLOUCESTERSHIRE GL54 5HU
☎ (01242) 603204. OPEN 10 - 5.30 MON - SAT, 12 - 5 SUN.
21 ST JOHNS AVENUE, CHURCHDOWN, GLOUCESTERSHIRE GL3 2DG
☎ (01452) 530530. OPEN 10 - 5 MON - SAT.
Dress Agency • *Womenswear & Menswear*
Both branches sell quality fashion seconds, continental designer wear, a range of nearly-new clothes and incorporate Nightingales Ltd. The Churchdown

shop is small but well stocked with a large car park. The Winchcombe branch is made up of three shops and also carries a large stock. The latter consists of anything from Marks & Spencer to designer labels and there is also a new section of designer clothes, mostly German makes, in sizes 8-30. Alterations can be carried out on the premises. Wax jackets are sold from the Oxford range from £25-£85 and there is an evening dress hire service for men and women. Accessories such as handbags, jewellery, scarves and hats are also stocked.

KIDS' STUFF MAIL ORDER LTD
10 HENSMANS HILL, CLIFTON, BRISTOL GLOUCESTERSHIRE BS8 4PE
☎ (0117) 970 6095. OPEN 9 - 5 MON - FRI, 9.30 - 5.30 SAT.
☎ (0870) 0763763 MAIL ORDER LINE.
Factory Shop • *Children*
In operation for over 20 years, Kids' Stuff sells high quality children's clothes (no coats), almost all of which are 100% cotton, for ages one to 12-years. Sited under the factory where the clothes are made, the factory shop sells over-runs, discontinued lines and ex-catalogue items at up to 50% discount, as well as clothing from current ranges. Phone for a mail order catalogue: (0870) 0763763 .

L C TRADING
QUEDGELEY URBAN VILLAGE, NAAS LANE, QUEDGELEY, NR GLOUCESTER, GLOUCESTERSHIRE GL2 5ZZ
☎ (01452) 720735. OPEN 9 - 3 MON - FRI.
Permanent Discount Outlet • *Furniture/Soft Furnishings*
The Ministry of Defence's Disposal Sales Agency (DSA) runs the largest disposal operation of its kind in the UK, selling off anything from frigates and aircraft to spanners, clothing and furniture through nineteen different contractors countrywide. In four warehouses in Quedgeley, Gloucester, one of the contractors, LC Trading, houses more than 12,000 items of both new and secondhand domestic and office furniture from beds and mattresses to desks, chests of drawers, dining tables and settees. Their refurbishment department modernises ex-ministry furniture, while the upholstery section has long experience of the ministry's high quality hardwood beech frames. Double beds, with mattress, cost from £95; solid mahogany chests of drawers, £50; sideboards, from £35. Although open from 9am-3pm on weekdays, they recommend you don't arrive later than 1pm as it takes at least two hours to walk round the warehouses. Brand new items are now also on sale in growing numbers, as government stock is depleted. These include carpet from £3 a metre, brand name beds, three-piece suites and office furniture.

LADY CLARE LTD
OLDENDS LANE INDUSTRIAL ESTATE, STONEHOUSE,
GLOUCESTERSHIRE GL10 3RQ
☎ (01453) 824482. OPEN 9 - 4 MON - THUR, 9 - 3 FRI, CLOSED 12 - 1.
Factory Shop • *Household*
Tiny shop attached to the factory that makes the placemats, trays, coasters, glass boards and chopping boards. Stock varies, depending on whether there are any overmakes, cancelled orders, seconds or discontinued lines. Prices are extremely good: from 50p for small chopping boards with slight mistakes; £4.99 for huge chopping boards. Most items are under £5.

MAGPIE
41 LYFIELD ROAD WEST, CHARLTON KINGS, CHELTENHAM,
GLOUCESTERSHIRE GL53 AT2
☎ (01242) 573909. OPEN 10 - 5 MON - FRI AND 10 - 3 SAT.
Dress Agency • *Womenswear Only*
A dress agency with three rooms selling a good selection of designer wear and high street names. A good selection of handbags, hats and shoes.

MARLBOROUGH TILES
14 MONTPELLIER STREET, CHELTENHAM,
GLOUCESTERSHIRE GL50 1SX
☎ (01242) 224870. OPEN 9.30 - 5, MON - SAT.
Permanent Discount Outlet • *DIY/Renovation*
Wall and floor tiles from Marlborough and other top quality, specialist manufacturers. Seconds come mostly from Marlborough's own factory with discounts of up to 50% on first quality prices.

MASH
INNSWORTH TECHNOLOGY PARK, INNSWORTH LANE, GLOUCESTER,
GLOUCESTERSHIRE GL3 1DL
☎ (01452) 730577. OPEN 8.30 - 5.30 MON - FRI, 8.30 - 5 SAT,
10 - 4 SUN, BANK HOLIDAYS.
Secondhand shops • *Sportswear & Equipment*
Warehouse/shop carrying an extensive range of backpacking and camping equipment, outdoor clothing, tools and government/camping surplus stock at discount prices.

MATALAN
ALDERMOOR WAY, LONGWELL GREEN, BRISTOL
GLOUCESTERSHIRE BS15 7AD
☎ (0117) 935 2828. OPEN 10 - 8 MON - FRI, 9 - 6 SAT, 11 - 5 SUN.
GALLAGHER RETAIL PARK, TEWKESBURY ROAD, CHELTENHAM,
GLOUCESTERSHIRE GL51 9RR
☎ (01242) 254001. EN 10 - 8 MON - FRI, 9 - 6 SAT, 11 - 5 SUN.

ABBEY RETAIL PARK, STATION ROAD, FILTON, BRISTOL BS12 7JW
☎ (0117) 974 8000. OPEN 10 - 8 MON - FRI, 9 - 6 SAT, 11 - 5 SUN.
Permanent Discount Outlet • *Womenswear & Menswear*
Children • *Household*

Matalan is a fashion and homewares value retailer giving customers what they claim to be unbeatable value for money with huge savings on a wide range of products including high quality fashionable clothing for men, women and children at up to 50% off high street prices. Matalan is situated out of town and stores are open seven days a week all year round.

MINCHINHAMPTON ARCHITECTURAL SALVAGE CO

NEW CATBRAIN CIRENCESTER ROAD, MINCHINHAMPTON, NEAR STROUD, GLOUCESTERSHIRE.
☎ (01452) 814064. FAX ☎ (01452) 813634. WEBSITE: www.recserv.demon.co.uk
PHONE FOR OPENING TIMES.
Architectural Salvage • *DIY/Renovation*

Antique statuary, chimney pieces, fireplaces, oak panelled rooms doors, columns, arches, cornice, pediments, porches, mullions, capitals, gargoyles, sundials, troughs, staddlestones, coping, ridge, stone tiles, quarry tiles, stone walling, flagstones, setts, bricks, floorboards, building stone, woodstrip, pine beams, boarding, baths, basins and taps. Specialists in hardwood floors.

PAINSWICK FABRICS

NEW STREET, PAINSWICK, GLOUCESTERSHIRE GL6 6XH
☎ (01452) 812616. OPEN 9.30 - 5 WED - FRI, 9.30 - 5.30 SAT.
Permanent Discount Outlet • *Furniture/Soft Furnishings*

Sells curtain and upholstery fabric from G P & J Baker, Warner and Andrew Martin, among many other designer names, at discounts of up to 70%. You can find chenilles, linens and chintzes in lengths from half a metre to 50 metres, most of which is current season stock, hand picked by the shop owner. There is also a limited selection of trimmings and braids. Constantly changing stock - come with an open mind.

PRIMARK

53 EASTGATE STREET, GLOUCESTER GLOUCESTERSHIRE GL1 1NN
☎ (01452) 424 174. OPEN 9 - 5.30 MON - SAT, 10 - 4 SUN.
Permanent Discount Outlet • *Womenswear & Menswear* • *Children*

Not a discount shop as such, but with extremely low prices, Primark sells women's, men's and childrenswear, swimwear, lingerie, hosiery, shoes and accessories.

RAGS TO RICHES
7 GOSDITCH STREET, CIRENCESTER, GLOUCESTERSHIRE GL7 2AG
☎ (01285) 656864. OPEN 10 - 4 MON - FRI, 10 - 5 SAT.
Dress Agency • *Womenswear Only*
Sells a mixture of high street and designer labels; featuring Paul Costelloe, MaxMara and Nicole Farhi, among other leading labels. Also sells accessories.

REVIVAL
BURFORD STREET, LECHLADE, GLOUCESTERSHIRE GL7 3AP
☎ (01367) 253803. OPEN 10 - 5 TUE - SAT, CLOSED 1 - 2 DAILY.
Dress Agency • *Womenswear Only*
Revival sells blouses, dresses, trousers, skirts, shoes, wedding outfits, some evening wear, and jewellery. Sizes range from 8-20. There are also hats, shoes, scarves, handbags. Labels include MaxMara, Jaeger, Jacques Vert, Calvin Klein, Jasper Conran, Nicole Farhi and Marks & Spencer.

SECOND TO NONE
61 HENLEAZE ROAD, (ADULTS)
95 HENLEAZE ROAD, (CHILDREN)
HENLEAZE, BRISTOL, GLOUCESTERSHIRE BS9 3AW
☎ (0117) 962 1365. OPEN 9 - 5 MON - SAT.
792 FISHPONDS ROAD, FISHPONDS, BRISTOL BS16 3TE
☎ (0117) 965 9852. OPEN 9 - 5 MON - SAT.
2 SOMERSET SQUARE, NAILSEA, BRISTOL BS9 2EU
☎ (01275) 851333. OPEN 9 - 5 MON - SAT, SOME BANK HOLS.
42A HIGH STREET, KEYNSHAM, BRISTOL BS31 1DX
☎ (0117) 986 8627. OPEN 9 - 5 MON - SAT.
95 HENLEAZE ROAD, HENLEAZE, BRISTOL BS9
☎ (0117) 962 8354. OPEN 9 - 5 MON - SATT
Permanent Discount Outlet • *Womenswear & Menswear* • *Children*
Established in the South West for twenty-seven years, this company has built a reputation for giving excellent customer service and for selling goods which are of a quality and value second to none! The famous chainstore and branded clearing lines include surplus stocks of branded goods such as Fabrizio, Zorbit, Naturana and many more. They stock a large range of ladies and children's and baby wear (including baby bedding and accessories), leisurewear, sports clothes and some menswear, and an extensive range of underwear and nightwear for all the family. You can save up to 75% off recommended retail prices and they offer a seven-day money back guarantee.

SEQUELS
DIGBETH STREET, STOW ON THE WOLD GLOUCESTERSHIRE GL54 1BN
☎ (01451) 870041. OPEN 10 - 5 MON - SAT, CLOSED 1 - 2 DAILY.
Dress Agency • *Womenswear Only*
One of the best agencies in central England. They always have an excellent range of labels at competitive prices from MaxMara, August Silk, Jaeger to plenty of good high street brands. Also sell new samples and designer discount lines for day and evening.

SMALL TALK EQUIPMENT HIRE
204 OLD BATH ROAD, CHELTENHAM, GLOUCESTERSHIRE GL53 9EQ
☎ (01242) 231231. FAX ☎ (01242) 231919. E-MAIL: sheathers@zoo.co.uk.
Hire Shop • *Children*
Exciting inflatable play structures for parties and special events. New shapes include Nessie the Sea Monster - 40 feet of adventure - the first in the UK. Also Balloon Typhoons and Bouncy Castles. Cots, car seats, highchairs, buggies etc also for hire from 1 day to 3 months. In fact everything you need for kids.

SOUTH WEST ARCHITECTURAL SALVAGE
28-30 MIDLAND ROAD, ST PHILIPS, BRISTOL,
GLOUCESTERSHIRE BS2 0JY
☎ (0117) 929 9143. OPEN 10 - 5 TUE - SAT.
Architectural Salvage • *DIY/Renovation*
Established for more than 20 years, this architectural salvage specialist stocks more than 300 stripped doors and general salvage. Au Temps Perdu is also located on this site selling fireplaces, bathroom ware and general fixtures and fittings for period houses.

SPRING GRAND SALE
SUDELEY CASTLE, WINCHCOMBE, NEAR CHELTENHAM,
GLOUCESTERSHIRE.
ORGANISER: DAVID HESLAM, PO BOX 4, LECHLADE, GLOS GL7 3YB.
☎ (01367) 860017.
Designer Sale • *Household* • *Furniture/Soft Furnishings*
There are now three annual Grand Sales taking place countrywide. The Christmas Grand Sale in London, with over 120 different small companies selling their merchandise to the public, is the largest. This takes place in mid-November each year. Quality is high and covers everything from dried flowers to bath accessories, Amish quilts to silverware, wooden toys to hand-painted kitchenware, often at discount because they are ends of lines. There is a Spring Grand Sale at Sudeley Castle, Winchcombe, near Cheltenham, Glos, from 26th - 28th April 2001, and a Summer Grand Sale at Ripley Castle, near Harrogate, North Yorkshire, from 7th - 10th June, both of which feature gardening furniture and equipment as well as decorative homes accessories. Phone the above number for more details; a proportion of the ticket revenue goes to charity.

STOCK EXCHANGE
14 CHURCH STREET, NEWENT, GLOUCESTER,
GLOUCESTERSHIRE GL18 1PP
☎ (01531) 821681. OPEN 9 - 1 AND 2 - 5 MON, TUE, THUR, FRI, SAT,
9 - 1 WED.
Dress Agency • *Womenswear* • *Children*
Dress Agency stocking labels from Mondi to Marks & Spencer, Laura Ashley, Next, Wallis and Principles. Also childrenswear from babygros to clothes for 14-year-olds, family videos and books, curtains, jewellery, children's and ladies' shoes and hats.

THE CAPE
10 MERCHANT STREET, BROADMEAD, BRISTOL ,
GLOUCESTERSHIRE BS1 3ET
☎ (0117) 929 7919. OPEN 9 - 5.30 MON - FRI, 9 - 6 SAT, 11 - 5 SUN.
25 REGENT ARCADE, CHELTENHAM, GLOUCESTERSHIRE, GL50 1JZ
☎ (01242) 519021. OPEN 9 - 5.30 MON - SAT, 10.30 - 4.30 SUN.
Factory Shop • *Furniture/Soft Furnishings* • *Household*
High quality, high density pine furniture made in South Africa from trees grown in managed forests, is sold at factory direct prices with home delivery throughout the UK. The range includes beds, wardrobes, blanket boxes, chests of drawers, tallboys, dressing tables, cheval mirrors, headboards, mattresses, a kitchen range, dining room tables, Welsh dressers, hi-fi units, bookcases. Also on sale in this shops is a range of African accessories and artefacts from Zimbabwe encompassing mirrors, prints, serpentine (stone) ornaments, recylced stationery, handmade wirework, candles and other ethnic and traditional gifts. Colour brochure and price list available on 01535 650940.

THE CONTINENTAL CLOTHES WAREHOUSE,
13 REGENT STREET, CLIFTON VILLAGE, BRISTOL,
GLOUCESTERSHIRE BS8 4HW
☎ (0468) 738116. OPEN 10 - 5.30 TUE - SAT.
Dress Agency • *Womenswear & Menswear*
Unusual dress agency in that the stock is sourced from the Continent, mainly from Germany. Labels such as Betty Barclay, Jil Sander and Gil Brett feature constantly and there is a good men's range of linen jackets, shirts and trousers as well as wonderful winter coats and raincoats. Also new evening wear and 50s, 60s, 70s as new evening wear. Hire for fancy dress is available.

THE FACTORY SHOP LTD

WESTWARD ROAD, CAINSCROSS, STROUD,
GLOUCESTERSHIRE GL5 4JE
☎ (01453) 756655. OPEN 9 - 5 MON - SAT, 10 - 4 SUN.

Factory Shop • *Household* • *Womenswear & Menswear* • *Children Furniture/Soft Furnishings* • *Sportswear & Equipment*

Wide range on sale includes men's, ladies and children's clothing and footwear; household textiles, toiletries, hardware, luggage, lighting and bedding, most of which are chainstore and high street brands at discounts of approximately 30%-50%. There are weekly deliveries and brands include many major stars such as Adidas, Nike, Joe Bloggs and Brabantia, to name just four. Lines are continually changing and few factory shops offer such a variety under one roof. This branch also displays furniture and sells the Cape Country Furniture range. This high quality pine furniture made exclusively for The Factory Shop in the new South Africa is sold at factory direct prices with home delivery throughout the UK. Colour brochure and price list available. It also has its own free car park.

THE NEARLY NEW SHOP (TETBURY) LTD

53 CHURCH STREET, TETBURY, GLOUCESTERSHIRE GL8 8JG
☎ (01666) 502297. OPEN 10 - 4 MON - FRI, 10 - 12.30 SAT.

Dress Agency • *Womenswear Only*

Dress agency set up to support a charity, The National Star Centre, a specialist residential college for students with a physical disability. It sells high quality ladies nearly-new clothes, shoes, hats, handbags and sportswear.

THE ORIGINAL ARCHITECTURAL ANTIQUES CO LTD

22 ELLIOT ROAD, LOVE LANE INDUSTRIAL ESTATE, CIRENCESTER,
GLOUCESTERSHIRE GL7 1YS
☎ (01285) 653532. OPEN 9 - 5 MON - SAT, 10 - 4 SUN.

Architectural Salvage • *DIY/Renovation* • *Household Furniture/Soft Furnishings*

Architectural antiques including period fireplaces and doors, floor tiles, chairs, doors, baths, beams, beds, busts, fire surrounds, kitchen ranges, marble fireplaces, mirrors, oak floorboards, objets d'art, painting, pews, prints, radiators, shutters, sinks, stained glass, taps, towel rails. Also gardenware, including stone troughs, flagstones, stone artefacts, sundials, terracotta pots, weather vanes, windows, wrought ironwork, gates, lead cisterns and many other one-off architectural features.

TK MAXX

THIRD FLOOR, THE GALLERIES, BRISTOL,
GLOUCESTERSHIRE BS1 3XE
☎ (0117) 930 4404. OPEN 9 - 5.30 MON - SAT, 11 - 5 SUN,
UNTIL 7 ON THUR.
REGENT ARCADE SHOPPING CENTRE, CHELTENHAM
☎ (01242) 513848. OPEN 9 - 5.30 MON - WED, 9 - 8 THUR, 9 - 6 FRI, SAT,
11 - 5 SUN.
Permanent Discount Outlet • *Womenswear & Menswear
Children* • *Household* • *Furniture/Soft Furnishings*

Based on an American concept, TK Maxx is situated in easily accessible, often centrally located stores and offers famous label goods with up to 60% savings off recommended retail prices. TK Maxx has fashion for the whole family - women's, men's and childrenswear - accessories, shoes, gifts, kitchenware and home goods. Everything in the store is branded with a choice of well-known high street names to designer labels, and while a small percentage might be clearly marked past season, the great majority of items in store are current season, current stock and still with phenomenal savings. There is a huge choice with 50,000 pieces in store and up to 10,000 new items arriving a week. The stores are simple and unfussy with wide aisles, shopping trolleys and baskets, and a spacious, functional feel to them but there are individual changing rooms, ramps for buggies and wheelchairs and plenty of staff on the shop floor. Every branch accepts all major credit and debit cards and has a liberal refund and return policy.

TOAD HALL: THE DRESS AGENCY

7 ROTUNDA TERRACE, MONTPELLIER, CHELTENHAM,
GLOUCESTERSHIRE GL50 1SW
☎ (01242) 255214. OPEN 9 - 5.30 MON - SAT.
Dress Agency • *Womenswear Only*

Large shop with two floors, almost exclusively filled with designer names. This is a top quality shop: Emporio Armani, MaxMara, Chanel, Givenchy, Caroline Charles, Escada and Nicole Farhi. The first floor is devoted to daywear and there's lots of it well set out and presented. Suits, jackets, trousers, blouses, bags, hats, sweaters, cardigans. There is an extensive range of evening wear including evening wraps and coats, plus day coats and jackets and a good range of shoes. Toad Hall has been extensively refurbished, adding extra changing rooms and display areas. Situated in fashionable Montpellier, it has free parking facilities.

TOP MARKS
23 HIGH STREET, MORETON-IN-MARSH,
GLOUCESTERSHIRE GL56 OAF
☎ (01608) 651272. OPEN 9 - 5.30 MON - FRI, 9 - 5 SAT.
Permanent Discount Outlet • *Womenswear & Menswear* • *Children*
Sells seconds from leading chain stores for all the family. Most of the stock is made up of men's and women's wear, with some childrenswear. The clothes are mainly Marks & Spencer seconds, sold at about one third cheaper than in the high street. Wide range of stock in various sizes with new stock arriving twice a week. They also stock Debenhams' and Richards' stock when available. There are other branches at Banbury and Chipping Norton in Oxfordshire.

WALTON DESIGN LTD
7 LONG STREET, TETBURY, GLOUCESTERSHIRE GL8 8AA
☎ (01666) 505671. OPEN 9 - 6 MON - SAT, 10 - 4 SUN, 10 - 5 BANK HOLS.
20 MARKET PLACE, CIRENCESTER GL7 2NW.
☎ (01258) 655400. OPEN 9 - 6 MON - SAT, 10 - 4 SUN, 10 - 5 BANK HOLS.
Permanent Discount Outlet • *Womenswear Only*
A chain of thirteen stores across the south of England selling well-known labels for women at greatly reduced prices. Current stock from high street stores might include Liz Claiborne, DKNY, Nougat, Ralph Lauren, Banana Republic, Calvin Klein and Tommy Hilfiger. New lines come in each week and are often one-offs, so regular customers know to buy things when they see them or risk missing out.

WOOSTERS & CO
2 BATH ROAD, OFF HIGH STREET, CHELTENHAM
GLOUCESTERSHIRE GL53 7HA
☎ (01242) 256855. OPEN 10 - 5 TUE - SAT.
Dress Agency • *Womenswear & Menswear*
Busy shop in town centre location with a brisk turnover so there's always something new to see. One of the very few in the area which also sells men's nearly-new, which has resulted in Woosters cornering the market in the good quality clothes. Ground level packed with very stylish ladieswear, with an excellent selection of designer labels such as Nicole Farhi, Armani, Mulberry etc, plus accessories to complement any outfit. The lower ground floor houses good quality menswear, country tweeds, business and dinner suits with designer labels such as Boss, Paul Smith and many more. Friendly atmosphere in which to browse, with expert advice if needed.

Hampshire

ADIDAS
GUNWHARF QUAYS, PORTSMOUTH, HAMPSHIRE
☎ (023 92 755940) INFORMATION LINE.
Factory Shop in a Factory Shopping Village
Womenswear & Menswear • Sportswear & Equipment

Factory shop within a new outlet centre due to open in late 2000 selling end of season products at 30% to 70% off RRP. Footwear and accessories such as bags, shinpads etc. Saloman outdoor wear and the Adidas golf range also stocked. Regular promotions run throughout the year.

ALEXON SALE SHOP
HART SHOPPING CENTRE, FLEET, HAMPSHIRE
☎ (01252) 815055. OPEN 9 - 5.30 MON - SAT.
Permanent Discount Outlet • *Womenswear Only*

Alexon, Eastex, Ann Harvey and Calico from previous seasons at 40%-70% less than the original price; during sale time in January and June, the reductions are up to 70%. Stock includes separates, skirts, jackets, blouses. Current stock at 10%-40% discounts.

ANCORA DRESS AGENCY
275 CHARMINSTER ROAD, BOURNEMOUTH, HAMPSHIRE BH8 9QJ
☎ (01202) 523848. OPEN 9.30 - 5 MON - SAT.
Dress Agency • *Womenswear Only*

Top designer labels including Armani, Escada, Caroline Charles, Christian Dior, Versace, Christian Le Croix, Jaeger, Country Casuals, Viyella, Louis Feraud. Clothes to suit all ages from sizes 8 - 24.

ARTIGIANO
49 HIGH STREET, COWES, ISLE OF WIGHT, HAMPSHIRE PO31 7RR
☎ (01983) 297773. WEBSITE: www.artigiano.com   OPEN 10 - 5 MON - SAT.
Permanent Discount Outlet • *Womenswear Only*

Artigiano, the mail order company, has a shop which sells overstocks from the previous catalogues at discounted prices. Artigiano is known for its ladies fashion exclusively made in Italy. The beautiful and elegant outfits range from cool wool suits to angora sweaters and silk scarves. Available in sizes 10 - 26.

C J ROGERS DEMOLITION AND SALVAGE
33 - 43 EMPRESS ROAD, BEVOIS VALLEY, PORTSWOOD,
SOUTHAMPTON, HAMPSHIRE SO14 0JU
☎ (023 80) 235777. OPEN 8 - 5.45 MON - FRI, 8 - 4 SAT.
Architectural Salvage • *DIY/Renovation*

Literally anything that can be salvaged from architectural demolition, including sheds, barns, gates and railings. Huge selection of timber as well as fireplaces, bricks and tiles.

CAMEO OF COWES
16 BATH ROAD, THE PARADE, COWES, ISLE OF WIGHT,
HAMPSHIRE PO31 7QN
☎ (01983) 297907. OPEN 10 - 5 SEVEN DAYS A WEEK.
Secondhand shops • *Womenswear & Menswear*

Buy and sell unclaimed lost property from British Airways, Royal Mail, London Transport and police departments. This can include anything from clothes and shoes to umbrellas and jewellery; make-up and perfume to purses and designer items.

CAMEO KIDZ
306 SHIRLEY ROAD, SOUTHAMPTON, HANTS SO15 2HL
☎ (02380) 777 277. OPEN 10 - 5 MON - SAT.
Secondhand shops • *Children*

Specialises in baby and childrenswear all new items from uncollected parcels. Baby Gap, Next etc.

CAMEO SPORT AND LEISURE
92 HIGH STREET, COWES, ISLE OF WIGHT, HAMPSHIRE PO31 7AW
☎ (01983) 297219. OPEN 10 - 5 SEVEN DAYS A WEEK.
Secondhand shops • *Sportswear & Equipment*

Run by the son of the owner of Cameo of Cowes, this shop also specialises in buying and selling unclaimed lost property and bankrupt stock but with the emphasis on sportswear: tennis rackets, wet suits, surf boards and anything to do with sports generally.

CHINAMATCHING
23 KILN ROAD, FAREHAM, HAMPSHIRE PO16 7UA
☎ (01329) 282785. E-MAIL: Sue.holder@talk21.com
WEBSITE: www.btinternet.com/-china.matching
OPEN 8 - 8 SEVEN DAYS A WEEK.

Stocks and searches for English and some European patterns from the 1940s to the present. Brands stocked include Wedgwood, Colclough, Denby, Royal Doulton, Royal Worcester and Hornsea. There is no registration fee.

CURTAIN UP

STONEFIELD PARK, MARTINS LANE, CHILBOLTON, STOCKBRIDGE,
HAMPSHIRE SO20 6BL
(01264) 339800. OPEN 2 - 5 MON, WED, THUR, 10 - 1 SAT,
AND BY APPOINTMENT.

Secondhand shops • *Furniture/Soft Furnishings*

Now in its tenth year and in larger premises, this shops stocks an even greater choice of top quality and designer secondhand curtains at a fraction of their original cost. Names such as Colefax & Fowler, Designers Guild, GP & J Baker, Warners and Sanderson feature prominently. Stock changes constantly and there is a huge range of sizes and prices, from £20 for a small pair through to £400 for large, grand drapes. Alteration and making-up services are also available, as are a selection of bedspreads, cushions, circular cloths, lamps and tie-backs. Just off the A30, close to the village of Stockbridge; do phone for directions.

DARTINGTON CRYSTAL

CLOVERLEAF LTD, WHITELEY SHOPPING VILLAGE,
FAREHAM, HAMPSHIRE PO15 7BS
(01489) 571021.

Factory Shop in a Factory Shopping Village • *Household*

An extensive range of Dartington Crystal seconds at greatly reduced prices as well as some perfect crystal at full price. Range includes wine suites, sherry glasses, tankards, decanters, rippled glass, fruit and salad bowls.

DESIGNER SHADES

GUNWHARF QUAYS, PORTSMOUTH, HAMPSHIRE PO1 3TA
(023) 92 755940 CENTRE INFORMATION LINE.
OPEN 9 - 5 SEVEN DAYS A WEEK.

Factory Shop in a Factory Shopping Village
Womenswear & Menswear • *Children*

Designer Shades offer a wide selection of top-notch sunglasses at more than 30% off typical high street prices. The frames are invitingly displayed on back-lit columns - no locked cabinets, messy stickers or hanging labels to contend with. Gucci, Polo Ralph Lauren, Jean Paul Gaultier, Valentino, Police, Christian Dior and Diesel are included in the ever-changing stock of top international brand names. Designer Shades ensure that all their sunglasses have quality lenses which protect against UVA and UVB rays, as well as filtering out damaging reflective blue light. They plan to have 20 shops throughout Europe by the end of 2001. For details of other locations, ring 01423 858007 or email info@designer-shades.net.

DIRECT ELECTRICAL
UNIT 2, FAREHAM ENTERPRISE CENTRE, NEWGATE LANE, FAREHAM, HAMPSHIRE PO14 1TH
☎ (01329) 319999. OPEN 10 - 4 TUE - SAT, CLOSED MON.
Permanent Discount Outlet • *Electrical Equipment*

Small warehouse specialising in very competitively priced cordless telephones, answerphones, fax machines, 10 - 46 inch television sets and music centres. For example, 28 inch Nicam stereo TV, £199; Philips 14 inch Televideo, £150 (RRP £229), Hitachi camcorder £199.

GIEVES & HAWKES
GUNWHARF QUAYS FACTORY OUTLET VILLAGE, PORTSMOUTH, HAMPSHIRE
☎ (023) 92 826648 ENQUIRIES.
Factory Shop in a Factory Shopping Village • *Womenswear & Menswear*

This Savile Row retailer's clearance shop sells Gieves & Hawkes menswear at exceptional discounts. As we went to press, the outlet was sited at 22 The Hard, Portsmouth, prior to moving into the new factory outlet centre in autumn 2000.

GLOBETROTTER
ARLINGTON GALLERIES, WELLINGTON CENTRE, LITTLE WELLINGTON STREET, ALDERSHOT, HAMPSHIRE GU11 1DB
☎ (01252) 329696. OPEN 9 - 6 MON - SAT, 10 - 4 SUN.
Factory Shop in a Factory Shopping Village • *Food and Leisure*

Luggage and travel-related products and executive cases, handbags, umbrellas from leading brands such as Samsonite, Desley, Head, Taurus and GlobeTrotter. Each product is offered at a substantially reduced price compared to those found on the high street due to being production over-runs, discontinued ranges or colours and last season's products. Discounts range from 30%-75% off high street prices.

GRANDFORD CARPET MILLS
UNIT 11, BRIDGE INDUSTRIES, BROAD CUT, FAREHAM, HAMPSHIRE PO16 8ST
☎ (01329) 289612. FREEPHONE 0500 717124. OPEN 9 - 4.30 MON - FRI, 10 - 3.30 SAT.
Factory Shop • *Furniture/Soft Furnishings*

Family-run factory shop which sells the majority of their carpets direct to the consumer. Good quality carpets at half the price you would pay in high street shops. The top price is £15.95 a square yard for carpet which you would pay at least £30 for in the high street. Seconds, which may be due to uneven dyeing, are £6.50 per square yard. Carpets can be dyed and made to customer's own colour requirements in 80/20 twist, minimum order 50 square yards. Measuring and fitting can be undertaken and underlay and accessories are available.

GUNWHARF QUAYS
PORTSMOUTH, HAMPSHIRE.
☎ (023) 92 755940. INFORMATION LINE.
Factory Shopping Village • *Womenswear & Menswear* • *Children Household* • *Sportswear & Equipment* • *Food and Leisure*

Due to open in late 2000, there are plans for 85 factory shops on this site next to historic Portsmouth harbour, home to HMS Victory and the Mary Rose. As well as the factory shops, including Adidas, Benetton, Bookends, Crabtree & Evelyn, Ecco, Gap, Gieves & Hawkes, Nike, Stefanel, Villeroy & Boch, Wedgwood/Waterford, Whittard, XS Music and Video, there will be 20 restaurants, a craft market, a leisure complex, a 14-screen cinema, bowling centre, comedy club, casino and 300 Berkeley homes.

JAMES MEADE LTD
48 CHARLTON ROAD, ANDOVER, HAMPSHIRE SP10 3JL
☎ (01264) 387700. FAX ☎ (01264) 363200.
E-MAIL: classicstyle@jamesmeade.com WEBSITE: www.jamesmeade.com
OPEN 9 - 5.30 MON - FRI.
Factory Shop • *Womenswear & Menswear*

Discontinued lines from the well-known mail order catalogues, James Meade Ltd, Jake and Cashmere by James Meade, are available at discounted prices at this factory shop. Classic clothing for men and women on display including shirts, jackets, skirts, trousers, ties and knitwear. Items in the current catalogues can also be bought at normal prices - including cashmere. Displays are good and there are facilities for trying on clothes.

JOHN JENKINS & SON LTD
NYEWOOD, ROGATE, PETERSFIELD, HAMPSHIRE GU31 5HZ
☎ (01730) 821811. OPEN 9.30 - 5 MON - SAT.
Factory Shop • *Household*

Factory shop situated next door to the factory selling cut crystal, plain glass and porcelain.

KENWOOD SERVICE SHOP
NEW LANE, HAVANT, HAMPSHIRE PO9 2NH
☎ (023 92) 476000. OPEN 9 - 4 MON - THUR, 9 - 12 FRI.
Factory Shop • *Household*

Wide range of Kenwood items from food processors, coffee makers and deep fryers to irons, can openers, water filters, juice extractors and toasters at factory prices. This usually means 20% off the normal retail price. All items are in perfect condition and come with a one year's guarantee. On-site parking available.

MATALAN
STATION STREET, PORTSMOUTH, HAMPSHIRE PO1 1BE
☎ (023 92) 851967. OPEN 9 - 7 MON - WED, FRI, 9 - 8 THUR, 9 - 6 SAT, 11 - 5 SUN.
CHANNON RETAIL PARK, WOODSIDE AVENUE, EASTLEIGH SO50 9ER
☎ (023 92) 626150. OPEN 9.30 - 8 MON - FRI, 10 - 8 SAT, 10 - 4 SUN.
Permanent Discount Outlet • *Womenswear & Menswear*
Children • *Household*
Matalan is a fashion and homewares value retailer giving customers what they claim to be unbeatable value for money with huge savings on a wide range of products including high quality fashionable clothing for men, women and children at up to 50% off high street prices. Matalan is situated out of town and stores are open seven days a week all year round.

MOUNTJOY PICTURE FRAMES
61 WINCHESTER ROAD, FOUR MARKS, ALTON, HAMPSHIRE GU34 5HR
☎ (01420) 561220. OPEN 9 - 5 TUE - FRI, 9 - 4.30 SAT.
Factory Shop • *Household*
Sells ready-made picture frames, framed chalkboards and letter boards, manufactured on the premises, at about 20% less than high street retail. There's now a growing range of lap-trays starting at £15.75, also available mail order.

PONDEN MILL LINENS
WHITELEY VILLAGE DESIGNER OUTLET, SWANWICK,
HAMPSHIRE PO15 7BS
☎ (01489) 571075. OPEN 10 - 6 MON - SAT, 11 - 5 SUN. .
Factory Shop in a Factory Shopping Village • *Household*
Famous branded products at direct from the mill prices. A fabulous assortment of towels, duvets, pillows, throws, bedspreads, up-to-the-minute coordinated bed linen, from Crown, Coloroll, Jeff Banks Ports-of-Call, to name but a few. Something for every room in the house.

PRET A PORTER
SHOP ONE, 18-20 HIGH STREET, RINGWOOD, HAMPSHIRE BH24 1AF
☎ (01425) 476090. OPEN 10 - 5 MON - SAT.
Dress Agency • *Sportswear & Equipment*
Womenswear & Menswear • *Children*
Sells nearly new designer ladies and menswear. Labels include Frank Usher, Jacques Vert, Betty Barclay, Escada, Eastex, M&S and Alexon. Examples of prices include Frank Usher ballgown, £80; Jacques Vert suits, £34. Also, from January to Easter, a huge selection of ski wear for women and children is kept. They specialise in cruise wear and mother of the bride/groom outfits. There are hats galore and evening wear, all at a fraction of the original price.

PRICE'S PATENT CANDLE CO
WHITELEY VILLAGE, WHITELEY WAY, FAREHAM, PORTSMOUTH,
HAMPSHIRE PO15 5BS
☎ (01489) 565150. OPEN 10 - 6 MON - SAT, 11 - 5 SUN.
Factory Shop in a Factory Shopping Village • *Household*
Everything sold in this shop are seconds, discontinued sizes not available elsewhere, over-runs or candles in old packaging that has now been replaced. There are church candles, lanterns, candles in pots and glass jars, star-shaped candles, floating candles, candlestick holders, serviettes, scented candles and garden torches.

PRIVATE COLLECTION
SHOEMAKERS COTTAGE, 7 UNION STREET, FAREHAM,
HAMPSHIRE PO16 7XX
☎ (01329) 826123. OPEN 10 - 5 MON - SAT.
Dress Agency • *Womenswear Only*
Exclusive dress agency with no chainstore items. Sells wedding outfits, evening dresses, day wear, casualwear, hats, belts and bags. Labels include MaxMara, Gerry Weber and Jaeger. Eveningwear hire also available for women.

ROMSEY RECLAMATION
STATION APPROACH, RAILWAY STATION, ROMSEY,
HAMPSHIRE SO51 8DU
☎ (01794) 524174/515486. OPEN 8 - 5 MON - FRI, 8.30 - 12 SAT.
Architectural Salvage • *DIY/Renovation*
Reclaimed slates, railway sleepers, bricks, tiles and oak beams, Yorkshire flags, quarry tiles, and telegraph poles and other reclaimed materials.

SCENT TO YOU
THE DESIGNER ROOM, WHITELEY VILLAGE DESIGNER OUTLET
CENTRE, WHITELEY WAY, FAREHAM, JUNCTION 9 OF M27,
HAMPSHIRE PO15 7BS
☎ (01489) 580509. OPEN 10 - 6 MON - SAT, 11 - 5 SUN.
ALDERSHOT GALLERIES, THE WELLINGTON CENTRE, LITTLE
WELLINGTON STREET, ALDERSHOT HAMPSHIRE GU11 1DB
☎ (01252) 328894. OPEN 9 - 6 MON - SAT, 10 - 4 SUN.
Factory Shop in a Factory Shopping Village • *Womenswear Only*
Operating within The Designer Room at this outlet village, Scent To You sells discounted perfume, cosmetics and accessories including body lotions and gels. The company, which has more than thirty branches, buys in bulk and sells more cheaply, relying on a high turnover for profit. Discounts range from 5% to 60%, with greater savings during their twice-yearly sales (phone for details). Most of the leading brand names in perfume are stocked including Christian Lacroix, Armani, Charlie, Givenchy, Anais Anais from Cacherel, Charlie from Revlon, Coco Chanel, Christian Dior, Elizabeth Taylor, Blue

Grass from Elizabeth Arden, Aramis, Lagerfeld. Plus cosmetics from REvlon and Spectacular and skincare from Clarins and Lancome as well as Scent To You's own range of bags, watches, hair brushes and brushkits which is sold under the name S.T.Y. Designs. Stock varies greatly due to the fast turnover and varying supplies so more than one visit may be necessary to obtain the scent of your choice. Or phone first to avoid disappointment.

SOUTHERN DOMESTIC ELECTRICAL SERVICES
4-6 BRIDGE ROAD, WOOLSTON, SOUTHAMPTON,
HAMPSHIRE SO19 7GQ
☎ (023 80) 421021. WAREHOUSE: ☎ (01703) 328428.
OPEN 8.30 - 6 MON - FRI, 9 - 5 SAT.
Permanent Discount Outlet • *Electrical Equipment*
Domestic electrical kitchen goods - washing machines, fridges, cookers, tumble dryers, freezers - sold at prices which are usually 10%-25% below competitors. Also sell goods that are slight seconds with damaged boxes or a small scratch, which are priced even lower from Bosch, Neff and Siemens. Other makes include Creda, Zanussi, Lacanche, Amana, White Knight, Baumatic, Cannon, Belling, Hotpoint, Flavel Leisure, Miele, Electrolux, Panasonic, Technic, Britannia, Amana, Liebherr De Dietrich, AEG, Stoves, Elica, Fisher-Paykel, Gaggenau, Norcool, Maytag and all other leading brands. Free local delivery.

SPOILS
UNIT F7-11, THE MARLANDS, SOUTHAMPTON, HAMPSHIRE SO14 7SJ
☎ (023 80) 332019. OPEN 9 - 5.30 MON - SAT.
Permanent Discount Outlet • *Household*
General domestic glassware, non-stick bakeware, kitchen gadgets, ceramic oven-to-tableware, textiles, cutting boards, aluminium non-stick cookware, bakeware, plastic kitchenware, plastic storage, woodware, coffee pots/makers, furniture, mirrors and picture frames. Rather than being discounted, all the merchandise is very competitively priced - in fact, the company carry out competitors' checks frequently in order to monitor pricing. With 38 branches, the company is able to buy in bulk and thus negotiate very good prices.

SUE FOSTER FABRICS
14 QUEENS STREET, EMSWORTH, HAMPSHIRE PO10 7YA
☎ (01243) 378831. OPEN 9.30 - 5 MON - FRI, 9.30 - 1 WED, 9.30 - 4 SAT.
Permanent Discount Outlet • *Furniture/Soft Furnishings*
Supplies top name furnishing fabrics at discounts. Her showroom has one of the widest ranges of pattern books outside London, where customers can choose perfect fabrics and wallpapers, usually 15%-20% below retail price and where they can also find trimmings, cushions, sofas and chairs. Also takes orders over the phone and sends out samples and undertakes sample searches - send for the questionnaire. E-mail: suefoster@cwcom.net.

THE BATHROOM WAREHOUSE WINCHESTER LTD
UNIT 3, WYKEHAM ESTATE, MOORSIDE ROAD, WINNALL,
NEAR WINCHESTER HAMPSHIRE SO23 7RX
☎ (01962) 862554. FAX ☎ (01962) 840927.
WEBSITE: www.bathrooms-showers.co.uk
OPEN 9 - 6 MON - SAT, UNTIL 8 WED.
BATHROOM WORLD, 9 SOLARTRON ROAD, FARNBOROUGH,
HAMPSHIRE GU14 7QL
☎ (01252) 373366. FAX ☎ (01252) 370333. OPEN 9 - 6 MON - SAT,
UNTIL 8 WED.
Permanent Discount Outlet • *DIY/Renovation*

Fantastic, extensive bathroom showrooms pandering to any taste or budget. Many products are exclusive to the Group who are continually expanding their already large product portfolio. The buying power of the Group ensures that prices are always extremely competitive. Experienced staff and designers guide customers through styles, choices and specifications as part of a free service.

THE CATALOGUE SHOP
6 CHURCH STREET, ROMSEY, HAMPSHIRE SO51 8BU
☎ (01794) 518522. OPEN 9 - 5 MON - SAT.
Permanent Discount Outlet • *Womenswear & Menswear* • *Children Household* • *Furniture/Soft Furnishings* • *Sportswear & Equipment*

Returns, damaged and worn goods as well as clearance lines and ends of lines of branded merchandise from mail order catalogues. This includes men's, women's and children's wear, footwear, bedding, curtains, furniture, exercise equipment and leather coats. These items are always in stock but the shop also has an ever-changing range of items as well. Turnover is very fast with new deliveries every day. All items are sold at less than 50% of the catalogue price, starting at 99p with branded trainers from £14.99.

THE CLOTHES LINE
171 HIGH STREET, WINCHESTER, HAMPSHIRE SO23 9BQ
☎ (01962) 868892. OPEN 10 - 4 MON - SAT, CLOSED 1 ON WED.
Dress Agency • *Womenswear Only*

Designer and high street labels from Next and Laura Ashley to Frank Usher, Laurel, YSL, Marella and Jacques Vert, Ramsay of Dublin, Yarell, Paul Costelloe, Nicole Farhi, Moschino and Max Mara, plus accessories: hats, costume jewellery and shoes. The shop is situated below King Alfred's statue before Chesil Bridge.

THE GALLERIES
HIGH STREET, ALDERSHOT, HAMPSHIRE GU11 1PE
☎ (01252) 341 111. WEBSITE: www.offprice.co.uk
OPEN 10 - 6 MON - SAT, 10 - 4 SUN.

Factory Shopping Village • *Womenswear & Menswear*

Formerly a full-price town centre shopping mall, the Shopping Centre now has 18 discount shops on two levels such as Bed & Bath Works, a homeware outlet with branded linens, towels and housewares; Cotton Traders casual wear; Designer Room selling ladies and men's branded fashion; Globetrotter's luggage and travel accessories; Jean Scene; JJB Sports selling branded sportswear and equipment; Julian Graves selling food and nut mixes; Kids Play Factory with children's toys and games; Kitchen Kiosk with branded kitchen and homewares; Leading Labels selling men's, ladies and childrens wear; Nicklebys, with men's and ladies fashions; Optisave, an optician selling designer branded glasses; Pilot selling young ladies fashions; Pocket Phone selling mobile telephones and accessories; Roman Originals ladieswear; Tog 24's outdoor and activity wear; Suits You's men's shirts, suits and casual separates; and XS Music's CDs and videos.

THE MALTHOUSE
CHURCH LANE, BOTLEY, HAMPSHIRE SO30 2EJ
☎ (01489) 786272. OPEN 9 - 5 MON - SAT.

Permanent Discount Outlet • *DIY/Renovation*

On the ground floor, the Malthouse, which incorporates the Botley Bathroom Centre, sells anything from carving knives and strimmers to toilet seats, shower hoses, basins, garden umbrellas, discontinued taps, DIY materials, screws, nails, worktops, bric-a-brac; on the first floor, there are 20 displays of bathroom furniture including everything from toilet roll holders to Jacuzzis, some of which are discontinued lines. They can match up, for example, windows to a Wimpey house or replace parts of a broken avocado suite. Their basins range from those that are the size of a table mat to those the size of a coffee table.

THE SHOE SHED
UNIT 9, QUADRANT ARCADE, HINTON ROAD, BOURNEMOUTH
HAMPSHIRE BH1 2AD
☎ (01202) 292992. OPEN 9 - 5.30 MON - SAT, 10 - 4 SUN.

Factory Shop • *Womenswear & Menswear* • *Children*

Large factory shop selling a vast range of all types of men's, women's and children's shoes, all of which are perfects, at up to 30% below normal high street prices. Men's shoes from £10; sports shoes from £10. Ladies sandals cost from £5; ladies shoes from £7.50.

TK MAXX

173-178 HIGH STREET (BELOW BAR), SOUTHAMPTON,
HAMPSHIRE SO14 2BY

☎ (023 80) 631600. OPEN 9 - 5.30 MON - FRI, 9 - 6 SAT, 11 - 5 SUN,
UNTIL 7 ON THUR.

Permanent Discount Outlet • *Womenswear & Menswear*
Children • *Household* • *Furniture/Soft Furnishings*

Based on an American concept, TK Maxx is situated in easily accessible, often centrally located stores and offers famous label goods with up to 60% savings off recommended retail prices. TK Maxx has fashion for the whole family - women's, men's and childrenswear - accessories, shoes, gifts, kitchenware and home goods. Everything in the store is branded with a choice of well-known high street names to designer labels, and while a small percentage might be clearly marked past season, the great majority of items in store are current season, current stock and still with phenomenal savings. There is a huge choice with 50,000 pieces in store and up to 10,000 new items arriving a week. The stores are simple and unfussy with wide aisles, shopping trolleys and baskets, and a spacious, functional feel to them but there are individual changing rooms, ramps for buggies and wheelchairs and plenty of staff on the shop floor. Every branch accepts all major credit and debit cards and has a liberal refund and return policy.

TOG 24

CANUTES PAVILION, OCEAN VILLAGE, SOUTHAMPTON,
HAMPSHIRE SO14 3JS

☎ (0238) 033 7383. OPEN 9.30 - 5.30 SEVEN DAYS A WEEK.

UNIT SU29, 10 THE GALLERIES, HIGH STREET, ALDERSHOT, GU11 1PF

☎ (0125) 232 9387. OPEN 9 - 6 MON - SAT, 10 - 4 SUN.

Factory Shop • *Womenswear & Menswear* • *Children*
Sportswear & Equipment

Tog 24 are the UK's fastest growing brand name in outdoor clothing and leisurewear. They utilise the world's finest performance fabrics including Gore-Tex, Polartec and Burlington MCS, catering for all the family for all seasons, with cosy fleeces and waterproofs for the winter, and trekking ranges, shorts and t-shirts for the summer. With all prices at least 30% below the recommended retail price, you can afford to enter the Tog comfort zone.

TOYZONE

WHITELEY VILLAGE, FAREHAM, JUNCTION 10 OFF M27,
SOUTHAMPTON, HAMPSHIRE PO15 7BS

☎ (01489) 565226. OPEN 10 - 6 MON - SAT, 11 - 5 SUN.

ALDERSHOT GALLERIES, THE WELLINGTON CENTRE, HIGH STREET,
ALDERSHOT, HAMPSHIRE GU11 1DB

☎ (01252) 329652. OPEN 10 - 6 MON - SAT, 10 - 4 SUN.

GUNWHARF QUAYS, PORTSMOUTH, HAMPSHIRE.
OPENING NOVEMBER 2000
Factory Shop in a Factory Shopping Village • *Children*
This shop sells a wide range of well-known children's brand names: Little Tikes, Corgi, Crayola, Tomy, Lego, Hasbro, Playskool, Mattel and Fisher-Price at discounts of up to 50%. They also stock a wide range of soft toys including TY Beanie Babies. The village also has a cafe, children's play area and free parking.

UNITED FOOTWEAR
117-125 FRATTON ROAD, PORTSMOUTH, HAMPSHIRE
☎ (023 92) 826799. OPEN OPEN 9 - 5.30 MON - SAT, 10 - 4 SUN.
Permanent Discount Outlet • *Womenswear & Menswear*
Children • *Sportswear & Equipment*
Shoes for all the family as well as clothes, handbags, sports shoes, boots, giftware and household goods, all at discounted prices. Famous brands including Clarks, K Shoes and Elmdale. Part of a national chain.

VILLEROY & BOCH (UK) LIMITED
GUNWHARF QUAYS, PORTSMOUTH, HAMPSHIRE.
☎ (023) 9275 5940 CENTRE INFORMATION LINE.
DUE TO OPEN AUTUMN 2000.
Factory Shop in a Factory Shopping Village • *Household*
One of five factory outlets for Villeroy & Boch, this shop carries an exclusive range of tableware, crystal and cutlery from Europe's largest tableware manufacturer. A varied and constantly changing stock, including seconds, hotelware and discontinued lines, on sale at excellent reductions, always makes for a worthwhile visit.

WESTHOUSE TEXTILES
CORNWALL ROAD, FRATTON, PORTSMOUTH, HAMPSHIRE PO1 5AA
☎ (023) 9285 1275. OPEN 9 - 5 MON - SAT.
103-105 LYNCHFORD ROAD, NORTH CAMP, FARNBOROUGH,
HAMPSHIRE GU14 6ET
☎ (01252) 372701. OPEN 9 - 5 MON - SAT.
Permanent Discount Outlet • *Furniture/Soft Furnishings*
Sells quality fabrics, curtaining, sheeting, dress fabrics, haberdashery and houses one of the biggest ranges of craft fabrics in the South. Most of the major fabric names are sold here. Half the stock is clearance, ends of lines and seconds sold at discounts of 50%; half is perfect stock sold at discounts of about 20%. Also offers a curtain making service.

WHITELEY VILLAGE DESIGNER OUTLET CENTRE

OFF THE M27 BETWEEN SOUTHAMPTON AND PORTSMOUTH, JUNCTION 9 OF M27, HAMPSHIRE

☎ (01489) 886886. OPEN 10 - 6 MON - SAT, 11 - 5 SUN.

Factory Shopping Village • *Womenswear & Menswear*

Factory shopping village with plans for 50 factory shops, cafes, and car parking for 1,400 cars. Shops include Banana Book; Carlton Luggage; Claire's Accessories; Cloverleaf; Cotton Traders; Designer Room; Elle; Jane Shilton; John Jenkins; Julian Graves; Moss Bros; Nachtmann (the world's largest crystal manufacturer); Outdoor Direct; Pilot; Ponden Mill; Price's Candles; Proibito; The Shoe Collection; Toyzone. There is a Tesco superstore on site.

Herefordshire

AFFORDABLE FABRICS

THE GRANARY, LOWER COURT, CLIFFORD, HAY-ON-WYE, HEREFORDSHIRE HR3 5ER

☎ (01497) 831309. E-MAIL: affordablefabrics.co.uk
WEBSITE: www.affordablefabrics.co.uk OPEN 10 - 5 MON - SAT.

Permanent Discount Outlet • *Furniture/Soft Furnishings*

Ends of lines and overstocks of designer fabrics (traditional designs and hand embroidered) from names such as Zoffany, Monkwell, Malibar and G P & J Baker at discounted prices. They specialise in crewel work imported direct from India at affordable prices and provide a full curtain making and design service.

BAILEYS HOME & GARDEN

THE ENGINE SHED, STATION APPROACH, ROSS-ON-WYE, HEREFORDSHIRE HR9 7BW

☎ (01989) 563015. FAX (01989) 768172.
E-MAIL: sales@baileys-home-garden.co.uk   OPEN 9 - 5 MON - SAT.

Architectural Salvage • *DIY/Renovation*

Bathroom fittings, fireplaces, stonework, garden furniture, gates ironwork, lighting, Belfast sinks and dressers. They also sell a range of garden statuary and items made from reconstituted stone as well as original troughs, saddles stones, original oak benches, repro Regency-style distressed metal benches with Gothic arched backs, French folding chairs, and lots of terracotta plant pots. This company specialise in antique garden tools and horticultural antiques.

BOOKENDS
THE PAVEMENT, HAY-ON-WYE HEREFORDSHIRE HR3 5BU
☎ (01497) 821341. OPEN 9 - 8 MON - SAT, 11 - 5 SUN.
9 CASTLE STREET, HAY-ON-WYE, HEREFORDSHIRE HR3 5BU
☎ (01497) 821572. OPEN 9 - 5.30 SEVEN DAYS A WEEK.
Secondhand shops • *Food and Leisure*

Damaged books and publishers' returns, as well as new and review copies, including recently published books, usually at half price or below.

CHAMELEON DRESS AGENCY
123 EIGN STREET, HEREFORD, HEREFORDSHIRE HR4 0RJ
☎ (01432) 353436. OPEN 10 - 5 TUE - SAT.
Dress Agency • *Womenswear Only*

Very friendly shop, which is light and well stocked. Customers are encouraged to exchange views - if it doesn't suit, the owner says they don't sell it to you. Sited near Sainsbury's, it stocks a wide range of clothes, from Marks & Spencer, Jaeger, Country Casuals, Alexon, Berkertex and Eastex to Yarrell, Nicole Farhi, Bianca, Ralph Lauren and Joseph. There is plenty of day wear, wedding outfits and evening wear, as well as accessories. Prices range from £10 upwards to about £100. A Bianca jacket would sell for about £45, Jaeger jacket, £55, Nicole Farhi two-piece, £75, Joseph leggings, £30. There is also a huge selection of hats.

DARTINGTON CRYSTAL
ROSS LABELS LTD, OVERROSS, ROSS-ON-WYE, HEREFORD,
HEREFORDSHIRE HR9 7QJ
☎ (01989) 769000. OPEN 10 - 6 MON - SAT, 11 - 5 SUN.
Factory Shop • *Household*

An extensive range of Dartington Crystal seconds at greatly reduced prices as well as some perfect crystal at full price. Range includes wine suites, sherry glasses, tankards, decanters, rippled glass, fruit and salad bowls.

DESIGNER DISCOUNT CLUB
UNIT E, ASHBURTON ESTATE, ROSS-ON-WYE,
HEREFORDSHIRE HR9 7BW
☎ (01989) 564357. OPEN 9.30 - 5 MON - FRI, 10 - 5 SAT.
Permanent Discount Outlet • *Womenswear Only*

This designer discount business has a retail outlet in Ross-on-Wye where members can come and purchase top quality German clothes at wholesale prices. Provides classic, smart clothes for work or daywear and plenty of special occasion wear and evening clothes. Members are kept up-to-date by post of special offers. You can join during your first visit when you will be issued with your own card and membership number at a cost of £5.

DUNELM MILL SHOPS LTD
2/3A UNION WALK, HEREFORD HEREFORDSHIRE HR1 2EP
☎ (01432) 266466. OPEN 9 - 5 MON - THUR, 9 - 5.30 FRI, SAT,
10.30 - 4.30 SUN.
Permanent Discount Outlet • *Household*
Part of a chain of shops based in the Midlands selling brand-name and chain-store curtains, masses of bedlinen, towels, wickerware, pictures and frames, all at competitive prices.

E WALTERS FACTORY SHOP
STATION YARD, LEOMINSTER, HEREFORDSHIRE HR6 8TW
☎ (01568) 616127. OPEN 9 - 5 MON - FRI, 9 - 4 SAT.
Factory Shop • *Children*
Europe's largest trouser manufacturer sells ends of lines, cancelled orders and samples of jeans, trousers and shorts for all the family at factory direct prices. Also available ancillary lines of casual wear at bargain prices.

M & M SPORTS
CLINTON ROAD, LEOMINSTER, HEREFORDSHIRE HR6 0SP
☎ (01568) 616161. FAX (01568) 619555. WEBSITE: www.mandmsports.com
OPEN 9 - 10 MON - FRI, 9 - 7 SAT, SUN. MAIL ORDER ONLY.
FACTORY SHOP: LEOMINSTER INDUSTRIAL ESTATE, SOUTHERN AVENUE, LEOMINSTER
OPEN 10 - 8 THUR, 10 - 5 FRI, SAT, 10 - 4 SUN.
Permanent Discount Outlet • *Sportswear & Equipment*
Children • *Womenswear & Menswear*
M and M Sports is the UK's largest sports and leisurewear mail order company, offering quality brand names at huge discounts including Nike, Adidas, Reebok, Fila, Ellesse, Berghaus and Rockport. Five catalogues a year are packed with all types of sports footwear and clothing, equipment, eyewear and watches. M & M buys up huge quantities of 'end-of-line' ranges direct from the manufacturers and passes on the massive savings to its customers. The factory shop sells discontinued catalogue items. To order a catalogue, phone or fax the above numbers or visit their website. They also offer a Team Kit range. Phone 01568 616262 for a catalogue (answerphone out of office hours).

PONDEN MILL LINENS
ROSS LABELS LTD, OVEROSS, ROSS-ON-WYE,
HEREFORDSHIRE HR9 7AS
☎ (01989) 564348. OPEN 10 - 6 MON - SAT, 11 - 5 SUN.
Permanent Discount Outlet • *Household*
Famous branded products at direct from the mill prices. A fabulous assortment of towels, duvets, pillows, throws, bedspreads, up-to-the-minute coordinated bed linen, from Crown, Coloroll, Jeff Banks, Ports-of-Call, to name but a few. Something for every room in the house.

ROSS LABELS LTD
OVERROSS HOUSE, ROSS ON WYE, HEREFORDSHIRE HR9 7QJ
☎ (01989) 769000. OPEN 10 - 6 MON - SAT, 11 - 5 SUN.
Permanent Discount Outlet • *Womenswear & Menswear* • *Children* • *Household*

Women's, mens and children's wear from underwear and jeans to good, middle-of-the-road brand name outfits and suits bought direct from the manufacturer. Some of the labels on sale include Aquascutum, Lee Cooper, Wolsey, Double Two and Telemac. Stock is usually one year old, while current merchandise consists of overmakes. Discounts range from 20% to 50%. There is also a Ponden Mill linen department selling at discounted prices.

STEWART SECONDS
33 HIGH STREET, ROSS-ON-WYE, HEREFORDSHIRE HR9 5HD
☎ (01989) 762403. OPEN 9.30 - 5.30 MON - SAT.
Factory Shop • *Children* • *Womenswear & Menswear* • *Household*

Branded merchandise from most of the major UK chain stores, all well-known high street department store names, offered at a discount of 40%-70% off normal high street prices. The garments are selected with great care by experienced buyers direct from factories worldwide to bring customers top quality merchandise at highly competitive prices.

STEWART'S
33 HIGH STREET, ROSS ON WYE, HEREFORDSHIRE HR9 5HD
☎ (01989) 762403 OPEN 9 - 5.30 MON - SAT.
Factory Shop • *Household* • *Womenswear & Menswear* • *Children* • *Sportswear & Equipment*

Branded merchandise from most of the major UK chain stores, all well-known high street department store names, offered at a discount of 40%-70% off normal high street prices. The garments are selected with great care by experienced buyers direct from factories worldwide to bring customers top quality merchandise at highly competitive prices.

TK MAXX

5 TRINITY SQUARE, MAYLORD ORCHARD, HEREFORD HR1 2BX
☎ (01432) 35500. OPEN 10 - 8 MON - FRI, 9 - 6 SAT, 11 - 5 SUN.
Permanent Discount Outlet • *Womenswear & Menswear Children* • *Household* • *Furniture/Soft Furnishings*

Based on an American concept, TK Maxx is situated in easily accessible, often centrally located stores and offers famous label goods with up to 60% savings off recommended retail prices. TK Maxx has fashion for the whole family - women's, men's and childrenswear - accessories, shoes, gifts, kitchenware and home goods. Everything in the store is branded with a choice of well-known high street names to designer labels, and while a small percentage might be clearly marked past season, the great majority of items in store are current season, current stock and still with phenomenal savings. There is a huge choice with 50,000 pieces in store and up to 10,000 new items arriving a week. The stores are simple and unfussy with wide aisles, shopping trolleys and baskets, and a spacious, functional feel to them but there are individual changing rooms, ramps for buggies and wheelchairs and plenty of staff on the shop floor. Every branch accepts all major credit and debit cards and has a liberal refund and return policy.

THE FACTORY SHOP

52 BROAD STREET, LEOMINSTER, HEREFORDSHIRE HR6 8BS
☎ (01568) 613944. OPEN 9 - 5.30 MON - SAT, 10 - 4 SUN.
Factory Shop • *Household* • *Womenswear & Menswear* • *Children Furniture/Soft Furnishings* • *Sportswear & Equipment*

Wide range on sale includes men's, ladies' and children's clothing and footwear; household textiles, toiletries, hardware, luggage, lighting and bedding, most of which are chainstore and high street brands at discounts of approximately 30%-50%. There are weekly deliveries and brands include many major stars such as Adidas, Nike, Joe Bloggs and Brabantia, to name just four. Lines are continually changing and few factory shops offer such a variety under one roof. This branch also display furniture and sells the Cape Country Furniture range. This high quality pine furniture made exclusively for The Factory Shop in the new South Africa is sold at factory direct prices with home delivery throughout the UK. Colour brochure and price list available. There is a small free car park with a large free public car park adjacent.

TWYFORD COOKERS

UNITS 4 - 6, LUGG VIEW INDUSTRIAL ESTATE, MORETON-ON-LUGG, HEREFORD, HEREFORDSHIRE HR4 8DP
☎ (01432) 761686. OPEN 9 - 5 MON - FRI.
Renovated Agas at prices which are very competitive with other similar outlets. They also supply Aga parts and re-fit lids with new chrome parts while you wait. Also supply gas CE-approved Agas and offer an installation service.

Hertfordshire

AQUASCUTUM
CLEVELAND ROAD, MAYLANDS WOOD ESTATE, HEMEL HEMPSTEAD,
HERTFORDSHIRE HP2 7EY
☎ (01442) 248333. OPEN 10 - 5 MON - SAT.
Factory Shop • *Womenswear & Menswear*
Previous season's stock and seconds for women and men at greatly reduced prices. For men, blazers, suits and silk ties. Examples include 20% off men's raincoats and half-price ladies silk blouses. Different promotions take place throughout the year with an average 50% reduction.

BHS FOR LESS
GALLERIA OUTLET CENTRE, COMET WAY, HATFIELD,
HERTFORDSHIRE AL10 0XT
☎ (01707) 258351. OPEN 10 - 8 MON - FRI, 10 - 6 SAT, 11 - 5 SUN.
Factory Shop in a Factory Shopping Village • *Womenswear & Menswear Children* • *Electrical Equipment* • *Household*
BhS for Less sells the high street chain's men's, women's and childrenswear ranges, plus selections from its home and lighting ranges, at discounts of at least thirty percent and up to seventy percent.

CAMEO
150 HIGH STREET, BERKHAMSTED, HERTFORDSHIRE HP4 3AT
☎ (01442) 865791. OPEN 9.30 - 5.15 MON - FRI, 9.30 - 5 SAT.
Dress Agency • *Womenswear Only* • *Children*
Cameo is a well-known shop in Berkhamsted High Street that sells ladies and children's nearly-new clothes and accessories with lots of designer wear. Famous makes include Osh Kosh, Oilily, Benetton, Absorba, Gap, Next, Windsmoor, Jacques Vert, Mondi, Bellino, Patsy Seddon, Benny Ong, Betty Barclay and many more. All clothes are in immaculate condition and are sold at very affordable prices. Cameo has been trading successfully for more than twenty years under the present owner and is well worth a visit. The shop is opposite the King's Arms.

CARA
GARSTON, WATFORD, HERTFORDSHIRE WD2 6PZ
☎ (01923) 670853. BY APPOINTMENT ONLY.
Dress Agency • *Womenswear Only*
Cara is a home-based business selling a range of designers including Mondi, Betty Barclay, Krizia, Escada, Jacques Vert, Maxmara, Jaeger, Windsmoor and Planet as well as lots of French and Italian designers. Sizes range from 10-18. Evening wear is stocked all year round as well as accessories, bags, shoes, belts and hats. Prices range from £5 - £75.

CATALOGUE BARGAIN SHOP (CBS)
GALLERIA OUTLET CENTRE, COMET WAY, HATFIELD, HERTFORDSHIRE AL10 OXR
☎ (01707) 267067. OPEN 10 - 8 MON - FRI, 10 - 6 SAT, 11 - 5 SUN.
Permanent Discount Outlet • *Womenswear & Menswear Children* • *Household* • *Electrical Equipment*
Catalogue Bargain Shop is a growing national chain of stores which obtains the majority of its goods from mail order giants Great Universal and Kays, and offers a range of clothing for all the family, a wide selection of shoes, bed linen, household goods, electrical equipment and hundreds of other catalogue items at very competitive prices. The merchandise consists of ends of ranges and previous season's stock for which there is no longer storage space when the catalogues change.

CENTRAL PARK
88 HIGH STREET BARNET, HERTFORDSHIRE EN5 5SN
☎ 020-8440 9950. OPEN 9.30 - 5.30 MON - SAT.
Permanent Discount Outlet • *Womenswear Only*
Large multiple group stocking cancelled orders and over runs for women, most of the clothes are de-labelled before they come here. There are dresses, suits, skirts, trousers and tops. Prices are very cheap.

CHAMBERLAIN
GALLERIA OUTLET CENTRE, COMET WAY, HATFIELD, HERTFORDSHIRE AL10 0YA
☎ (01707) 268433. OPEN 10 - 8 MON - FRI, 10 - 6 SAT, 11 - 5 SUN.
Factory Shop in a Factory Shopping Village • *Food and Leisure*
Sells GT, Dawes and Raleigh bikes for adults and children, helmets, baskets and tyres. Stock changes constantly and the owner says that their prices will not be beaten.

CHARLES CLINKARD
THE GALLERIA, COMET WAY, HATFIELD, HERTFORDSHIRE AL10 OXS
☎ (01707) 258653 . OPEN 10 - 8 MON - FRI, 9 - 6 SAT, 11 - 5 SUN.
Factory Shop in a Factory Shopping Village • *Children Womenswear & Menswear*
Shoes for all the family at discounts of between 20% and 50%. Labels on sale here include Rockport, Loake, Camel, Church's, Ecco, Gabor, Rohde, Van-Dal, Kickers, Clarks, Start-Rite, Elefanten, K Shoes, Lotus and Renata. The telephone number given here is for the centre, not the shop.

CHELFORD FABRICS LTD
CHELFORD HOUSE, COLDHARBOUR LANE, HARPENDEN, HERTFORDSHIRE AL5 4SR
☎ (01582) 763636. FAX ☎ (01582) 461114. OPEN 9.30 - 5.30 MON - SAT.
Permanent Discount Outlet • *Furniture/Soft Furnishings*
A large, out-of-town showroom selling only perfect regular curtain and upholstery fabrics at greatly reduced prices, ranging from £2.99 a yard to £11.99 a yard and including everything from glazed cotton chintzes to prints, tapestries and damasks from all leading manufacturers. Choose from more than 4,000 rolls, order from the extensive range of manufacturers pattern books or buy own-brand fabrics which are one-third less expensive than branded material. A full high quality making-up service is available. Curtain accessories, rails, tapes and hooks are also on sale at reduced prices. There is also a huge selection of towels, cushions, pillows and duvets. This branch also sells high-quality three-piece suites and occasional chairs at very reasonable prices. A wide selection of ready made curtains is also available. (There is another branch in Gamlingay, Cambridgeshire.)

CHOICE DISCOUNT STORES LIMITED
44-46 HIGH STREET, WATFORD, HERTFORDSHIRE WD1 2BS
☎ (01923) 233255. OPEN 9 - 5.30 MON - FRI, 9 - 6 SAT.
UNIT 45, GALLERIA OUTLET CENTRE, COMET WAY, HATFIELD, HERTFORDSHIRE AL10 0XR
☎ (01707) 258545. OPEN 10 - 8 MON - FRI, 10 - 6 SAT, 11 - 5 SUN.
Permanent Discount Outlet • *Womenswear & Menswear* • *Children*
Surplus stock including women's, men's and children's fashions from Next plc, Next Directory and other high street fashion houses, Next Interiors and footwear. You can save up to 50% off normal retail prices for first quality; up to two thirds for seconds. The Watford store is known as Next 2 Choice and specialises in ladies and menswear only from Next plc and Next Directory.

COURTAULDS TEXTILES
ORCHARD ROAD, ROYSTON, HERTFORDSHIRE SG8 5HA
☎ (01763) 249941. OPEN 9 - 5.30 MON, TUE, WED, SAT, 9 - 6 THUR, FRI, 10 - 4 SUN.
Factory Shop • *Womenswear & Menswear* • *Household* • *Children*
Sells extensive range of casual wear for girls and boys from birth to twelve years, men's and women's clothes, as well as seconds and bought-in stock in bedding, towels, duvets and pillows, luggage, accessories and shoes at discounts of 30%-50%. About half the stock is perfect, the other half seconds, stocks Christian Marcos, Kushi, Wolsey, Lyle and Scott. Childrenswear includes tights and underwear from 60p, cord trousers, knitwear, coats, socks, sweatshirts from £5.99, joggers from £3.99, and shirts, £3.99.

DISCOUNT CARS
THE CONSUMERS ASSOCIATION, PO BOX 44, HERTFORD,
HERTFORDSHIRE SG14 1LH WEBSITE: www.carbusters.com
Permanent discount website whereby you can receive overseas quotes on car prices via the Internet. Select the make, model and specification and you then pay £10 for an exact quote from an overseas dealer, which will include delivery charges, legal costs and VAT registration. You are put in touch with the dealers and make payments direct to them. It takes an average of three months for cars to be delivered.

DISCOUNT DRESSING
GALLERIA OUTLET CENTRE, COMET WAY, HATFIELD,
HERTFORDSHIRE AL10 OXR
☎ (01707) 259925. OPEN 10 - 8 MON - FRI, 10 - 6 SAT, 11 - 5 SUN.
Factory Shop in a Factory Shopping Village • *Womenswear Only*
A veritable Aladdin's Cave of designer bargains, Discount Dressing sells mostly German, Italian and French designer labels at prices at least 50% and up to 90% below those in normal retail outlets. All items are brand new and perfect. A team of buyers all over Europe purchase stock directly from the manufacturer for this growing chain of discount shops. This enables Discount Dressing to by-pass the importers and wholesalers and, of course, their mark-up. They also buy bankrupt stock in this country. Their agreement with their suppliers means that they are not able to advertise brand names for obvious reasons, but they are all well-known for their top quality and style. So confident is Discount Dressing that you will be unable to find the same item cheaper elsewhere, that they guarantee to give the outfit to you free of charge should you perform this miracle. Merchandise includes raincoats, dresses, suits, trousers, blouses, evening wear, special occasion outfits and jackets, in sizes 6-24 and in some cases larger. GDD readers can obtain a further 10% discount if they visit the shop taking a copy of this book with them. There are other branches in Lincolnshire, Northern Ireland and London.

ECCO
GALLERIA OUTLET CENTRE, COMET WAY, HATFIELD,
HERTFORDSHIRE AL10 0XR
☎ (01707) 258399. OPEN 10 - 8 MON - FRI, 10 - 6 SAT, 11 - 5 SUN.
Factory Shop in a Factory Shopping Village
Womenswear & Menswear • *Children*
Ladies', men's and children's shoes, all discounted by at least 25%. Phone 0800 387368 for a catalogue. Other outlets at South Wales, Wiltshire, Somerset and Cheshire.

FABRIC WAREHOUSE
184 EAST BARNET ROAD, NEW BARNET, HERTFORDSHIRE EN4 8RD
☎ 020-8441 3114. OPEN 10 - 6 MON - SAT.
Permanent Discount Outlet • *Furniture/Soft Furnishings*

Furnishing fabric, cushions and foam. Good range of printed furnishing fabrics from £4.99, with a bargain selection from £2.50; Jeff Banks prints, £8.99 instead of £16.99; wonderful Italian damasks, £13.99, usual price £18; cotton damask half price at £10.99; cotton muslins, £4.99 instead of £6.99; Belgian flat weaves and tapestries, £10.99; polycotton lining, £2.50 for 54" width. They also sell curtain rails, tiebacks, fringing, braid, chunky tassel tie backs and have their own in-house curtain making service at competitive prices.

GLASERS FACTORY SHOP
REMBRANDT HOUSE, WHIPPENDELL ROAD, WATFORD,
HERTFORDSHIRE WD1 7QN
☎ (01923) 234067 FOR SALE DETAILS.
Designer Sale • *Womenswear Only*

End of season sales of well-made ladies smart knitted suits, dresses and dress and jacket sets. Skirts tend to be knee-length, although some suits also have long skirts.

IMPRESSIONS
THE GALLERIA OUTLET CENTRE, HATFIELD,
HERTFORDSHIRE AL10 OXR
☎ (01707) 268755. OPEN 10 - 8 MON - FRI, 10 - 6 SAT, 11 - 5 SUN.
Factory Shop in a Factory Shopping Village • *Womenswear & Menswear*

Impressions, clothing direct from the factory, sells garments from the manufacturing side of the Dewhirst Group plc. The Dewhirst Group plc manufactures ladies and menswear for a leading high street retailer. You can choose from a huge selection of surplus production and slight seconds at bargain prices, making savings of more than 50% of the normal retail cost. For men, there is a wide range of suits, formal shirts and casualwear. For example, suits from £60, formal and casual shirts from £7. For ladies, a selection of blouses, smart tailoring and casualwear that includes a denim range. For example ladies jackets from £50, skirts, trousers and blouses from £8.

JUST BETWEEN US
29 HILLSIDE ROAD, ST ALBANS, HERTFORDSHIRE AL1 3QW
☎ (01727) 811172. BY APPOINTMENT ONLY.
Hire Shop • *Womenswear Only*

Offers an enormous selection of evening wear from 150 long and zappy party dresses to formal ballgowns and cocktail dresses in sizes 8-24, wraps, coats and boleros. Hire fee £69 plus £50 deposit for a flexible number of days. By appointment only, including evenings. The entire stock is changed every season and brand new stock is introduced. The old stock is then put into twice-yearly sales. Phone for dates. The sales are exceedingly popular as dresses can go for less than £50.

KIDS PLAY FACTORY
GALLERIA OUTLET CENTRE, COMET WAY, HATFIELD,
HERTFORDSHIRE AL10 OXR
☎ (01707) 258720. OPEN 10 - 8 MON - FRI, 10 - 6 SAT, 11 - 5 SUN.
Factory Shop in a Factory Shopping Village • *Children*
This shop sells a wide range of well-known children's brand names: Little Tikes, Corgi, Crayola, Tomy, Lego, Hasbro, Playskool, Mattel and Fisher-Price at discounts of up to 50%. They also stock a wide range of soft toys including TY Beanie Babies. The village also has a cafe, children's play area and free parking.

KNICKERBEAN
11 HOLYWELL HILL, ST ALBANS, HERTFORDSHIRE AL1 1EZ
☎ (01727) 866662. OPEN 9 - 5.30 MON - SAT.
Permanent Discount Outlet • *Furniture/Soft Furnishings*
Recommended by countless interior and decorating magazines and much loved by the bargain hunter, Knickerbean offers a continuous stream of stylish and sumptuous fabrics (the kind found at the Chelsea Harbour Design Centre and Decorex), but all at affordable prices. They originally specialised in top name UK designer fabrics, offering excess inventory, discontinued lines and slight imperfects, usually at about half price. You can still find many of these famous name bargains here, but now many of their fabrics are sourced directly from the same mills and manufacturers as the 'top names', both here and abroad. They offer the same top quality, in the latest colours and designs, at relatively lower prices, because they are buying and selling directly and cutting out the middlemen. Their selection of curtain and upholstery fabrics caters for both contemporary and traditional homes, with formal glazed chintzes, regal damasks, toiles de jouy and luxurious chenilles displayed next to basic neutrals, bright modern prints, airy voiles and earthy ethnic patterns. They also have large ranges of checks and stripes, self-patterned weaves, simple prints for a child's room as well as a huge range of upholstery brocades and tapestries. Prices start at £5.95 for prints to £19.95 and occasionally more for some their tapestries, chenilles and damasks. Knickerbean's outlets are bright and pleasant, more like an interior designer's showroom - there's no 'warehouse' feeling here. Their trained staff are helpful with all sorts of advice on fabrics, colours and interiors and they offer a complete home visit service with interior measuring and design advice. They have a hand finished making up service for curtains, blinds and loose covers, as well as a range of custom made funiture with footstools, sofas, etc. Twice yearly sales in January and June enable customers to snap up even bigger bargains.

LITTLEWOODS CATALOGUE DISCOUNT STORE
GALLERIA OUTLET CENTRE, COMET WAY, HATFIELD,
HERTFORDSHIRE AL10 0XA
☎ (01707) 258536. OPEN 10 - 8 MON - FRI, 9- 6 SAT, 11 - 5 SUN.
Factory Shop • *Womenswear & Menswear* • **Children**
Electrical Equipment
Littlewoods clearance shops offering up to 50% off the catalogue price for clothing and between 50% and 60% off for electrical goods. Stock changes constantly and varies from day to day but can include well-known brand names such as Berlei and Gossard lingerie, Vivienne Westwood, Pamplemousse leisure wear, Nike and Adidas sports shoes, Workers for Freedom, and Timberland and Caterpillar footwear. Stock depends on the size and location of the shop, so larger shops will get the longer discontinued runs and smaller shops over-runs with only a small amount of colour and size variations left. Littlewoods also run a mobile shop which operates in cities where they don't have a sale shop. For details of further venues for the sales, which usually take place once a month, contact Melanie Lamb, c/o Crosby DC Kershaw Avenue, Endbutt Lane, Crosby, Merseyside L70 1AH.

MATALAN
DANESTRETE, STEVENAGE, HERTFORDSHIRE SG1 1XB
☎ (01438) 312433. OPEN 9 - 6 MON - SAT, 10 - 4 SUN.
Permanent Discount Outlet • *Womenswear & Menswear*
Children • *Household*
Matalan is a fashion and homewares value retailer giving customers what they claim to be unbeatable value for money with huge savings on a wide range of products including high quality fashionable clothing for men, women and children at up to 50% off high street prices. Matalan is situated out of town and stores are open seven days a week all year round.

MILLANO
GALLERIA OUTLET CENTRE, COMET WAY, HATFIELD,
HERTFORDSHIRE AL10 0XR
☎ (01707) 259199. OPEN 10 - 8 MON - FRI, 10 - 6 SAT, 11 - 5 SUN.
Factory Shop in a Factory Shopping Village
Womenswear & Menswear • *Children*
One of more than 70 shops in this glass and steel factory shopping centre straddling the A1. This outlet sells designer suede, leather and sheepskin jackets, coats, trousers etc for men, women and children at discount prices. Larger than average sizes can sometimes be made on request. Prices can be up to 60% cheaper than in the high street, with samples, over-runs or slight seconds as well as a selection of last and current season's perfects.

NAZEING GLASS
NAZEING NEW ROAD, BROXBOURNE, HERTFORDSHIRE EM10 6SU
☎ (01992) 464485. OPEN 9.30 - 4.30 MON - FRI, 9.30 - 3 SAT.
Factory Shop • *Household*
Bespoke handmade glass makers since 1610, Nazeing don't design their own ranges but make to other companies' designs, many of them limited edition or exclusive ranges. The factory shop sells ends of lines and seconds at discounted prices. You can find 24% lead crystal, thin-stemmed and very thin-stemmed elegant plain glass, coloured glass, reproduction glass in eighteenth century styles and Bristol blue glassware in chapagne flutes, red and white wine glasses, water goblets and decanters.

NIPPERS
LEYHILL FARM, BRIDGE STREET, NR ROYSTON
HERTFORDSHIRE SG8 5SQ
☎ (01223) 207071. FAX ☎ (01223) 208666. E-MAIL: royston@nippers.co.uk
WEBSITE: www.nippers.co.uk OPENING HOURS VARY SO PHONE FIRST.
Permanent Discount Outlet • *Children*
Nippers, the nursery equipment and toy specialists, operate from previously redundant buildings in rural areas around the country. They offer easy parking, no queues and personal service. This is on top of competitive prices on prams, cots, pushchairs, car seats, outdoor play equipment and toys, some of which are new, some seconds or secondhand and some ends of lines. Prices are low because they avoid the high overheads of traditional retail outlets and also because the successful growth of a number of branches means they can now buy in bulk and negotiate good deals. Customers are invited to try out the merchandise while the children look at the animals, mostly sheep, chicken and pigs. Also offers many brand leaders at discount, including Mamas & Papas, Cosatto, Britax, Maclaren and Bebe Confort, plus Fisher-Price and Little Tikes. You can try out the car seats in your car and there is usually a pram/pushchair repair service on site.

OUTDOOR TRADING POST
GALLERIA OUTLET CENTRE, COMET WAY, HATFIELD,
HERTFORDSHIRE AL10 OXR
☎ (01707) 256606. OPEN 10 - 8 MON - FRI, 10 - 6 SAT, 11 - 5 SUN.
Factory Shop in a Factory Shopping Village • *Sportswear & Equipment*
Specialist outdoor sports factory shop for skiers and urban hikers selling top quality brands such as Patagonia, Salamon, SOS, Lowe Alpine and North Face at reductions which average 30%-40%. In the summer, they stock mostly outdoor and trekking gear and equipment with some lines in skiwear and equipment at final clearance prices. In the winter, from September to March, they carry the full range of premium brands in skiwear at the sort of prices you would pay for lower quality brands. Ski outfits which would normally retail for £399 cost £249; ski boots which normally cost £200 are £129.

OUTDOOR WEAR
10 - 14 POTTER STREET, BISHOPS STORTFORD,
HERTFORDSHIRE CM23 3UL
☎ (01279) 653694. OPEN 9 - 6 MON - SAT.
Permanent Discount Outlet • *Sportswear & Equipment* • *Children*
Ends of lines from Karrimor, Berghaus, Tenson, Barbour, Levi's, Rohan and Drizabone in shirts, jeans, hats, and skiwear.

PILOT
GALLERIA OUTLET CENTRE, COMET WAY, HATFIELD,
HERTFORDSHIRE AL10 0XU
☎ (01707) 258144. OPEN 10 - 8 MON - FRI, 10 - 6 SAT, 11 - 5 SUN.
Factory Shop in a Factory Shopping Village • *Womenswear Only*
Mainly younger-style clothes for women only. Most are end of season and end of line. Stock is mostly new and similar to high street stores at reductions of about 30%, e.g. in the summer of 1999: pedal pushers, £23 reduced to £17, short strap top £17 reduced to £10.

PONDEN MILL LINENS
GALLERIA OUTLET CENTRE, COMET WAY, HATFIELD,
HERTFORDSHIRE AL10 OXS
☎ (01707) 270053. OPEN 10 - 8 MON - FRI, 10 - 6 SAT, 11 - 5 SUN.
Factory Shop in a Factory Shopping Village • *Household*
Famous branded products at direct from the mill prices. A fabulous assortment of towels, duvets, pillows, throws, bedspreads, up-to-the-minute coordinated bed linen, from Crown, Coloroll, Jeff Banks Ports-of-Call, to name but a few. Something for every room in the house.

R S SHOES
GALLERIA OUTLET CENTRE, COMET WAY, HATFIELD,
HERTFORDSHIRE AL10 OXR
☎ (01707) 258021. OPEN 10 - 8 MON - FRI, 10 - 6 SAT, 11 - 5 SUN.
Factory Shop in a Factory Shopping Village • *Womenswear & Menswear*
Sells men's, women's and children's shoes including Dr Martens, Kickers, Wrangler, Levi's LSCO and branded clothes for men and women in this glass and steel factory shopping centre straddling the A1.

RECOLLECTIONS
48 CHURCH STREET, WARE, HERTFORDSHIRE SG12 9EW
☎ (01920) 461188. OPEN 10 - 4 TUE - SAT.
Dress Agency • *Womenswear & Menswear* • *Hire Shop*
On two floors, this pretty little shop in Ware's town centre specialises in once-worn wedding gowns and holds about 150 gowns at any one time, together with accessories. Labels include Benjamin Roberts, Stevie, Ellis, Mon Cherie, with constantly changing stock. Prices from £100. Also sell evening dresses, ballgowns, bridesmaides dresses, shoes, veils, mother of the bride and groom outfits and a selection of christening wear. Also offers formal wear hire for men and boys, as well as wedding dress hire.

SCENT TO YOU
THE DESIGNER ROOM, THE GALLERIA OUTLET CENTRE, COMET WAY, HATFIELD, HERTFORDSHIRE AL10 OXR
☎ (01707) 275014. OPEN 10 - 8 MON - FRI, 10 - 6 SAT, 11 - 5 SUN.
UNIT 142A, HARLEQUIN CENTRE, WATFORD, HERTFORDSHIRE WD1 2TL
☎ (01923) 225712. OPEN 9.30 - 5.30 MON - SAT.
Factory Shop in a Factory Shopping Village and Permanent Discount Outlet • *Womenswear Only*

Operating within The Designer Room at the Galleria, Scent to You sells discounted perfume, cosmetics and accessories including body lotions and gels. The company, which has more than thirty branches, buys in bulk and sells more cheaply, relying on a high turnover for profit. Discounts range from 5% to 60%, with greater savings during their twice-yearly sales (phone for details). Most of the leading brand names in perfume are stocked including Christian Lacroix, Armani, Charlie, Givenchy, Anais Anais from Cacherel, Charlie from Revlon, Coco Chanel, Christian Dior, Elizabeth Taylor, Blue Grass from Elizabeth Arden, Aramis, Lagerfeld. Plus cosmetics from REvlon and Spectacular and skincare from Clarins and Lancome as well as Scent To You's own range of bags, watches, hair brushes and brushkits which is sold under the name S.T.Y. Designs. Stock varies greatly due to the fast turnover and varying supplies so more than one visit may be necessary to obtain the scent of your choice. Or phone first to avoid disappointment.

SIZE-UP
27C HIGH STREET, ROYSTON, HERTFORDSHIRE SG8 9AA
☎ (01763) 246034. OPEN 9 - 5.30 MON - SAT.
Permanent Discount Outlet • *Womenswear Only*

Top quality ladies outsize clothing, some of it from Evans, some own-label and some without labels. There are coats, dresses, suits and separates, some scarves and leisure wear. Some items cost less than half price. For example, Evans long pinstripe coat, £25, reduced from £70. All merchandise is new end of lines or last season's stock in good condition. Sizes 16-30.

SPOILS
UNIT D, THE MARLOWES CENTRE, HEMEL HEMPSTEAD, HERTFORDSHIRE HP1 1DY
☎ (01442) 235018. OPEN 9 - 5.30 MON - SAT, UNTIL 8 ON THUR.
Permanent Discount Outlet • *Household*

General domestic glassware, non-stick bakeware, kitchen gadgets, ceramic oven-to-tableware, textiles, cutting boards, aluminium non-stick cookware, bakeware, plastic kitchenware, plastic storage, woodware, coffee pots/makers, furniture, mirrors and picture frames. Rather than being discounted, all the merchandise is very competitively priced - in fact, the company carry out competitors' checks frequently in order to monitor pricing. With 38 branches, the company is able to buy in bulk and thus negotiate very good prices.

THE BAGGAGE FACTORY
GALLERIA OUTLET CENTRE, COMET WAY, HATFIELD,
HERTFORDSHIRE AL10 0XR
☎ (01707) 257779. WEBSITE: www.baggagefactory.co.uk
OPEN 10 - 8 MON - FRI, 10 - 6 SAT, 11 - 5 SUN.
Factory Shop in a Factory Shopping Village
Food and Leisure
One of more than 70 shops in this glass and steel shopping centre straddling the A1. This outlet sells bags, cases and wallets, some well-known brand names such as Delsey and Samsonite, at discount prices.

THE CURTAIN CONNECTION LTD
108 LONDON ROAD, ST ALBANS, HERTFORDSHIRE AL1 1NX
☎ (01727) 868368. FAX (01727) 874515.
PLEASE TELEPHONE FOR OPENING HOURS.
Secondhand shops • *Furniture/Soft Furnishings*
A secondhand curtain shop with a well-deserved reputation for service and value for money. The shop is now in its seventh year and has recently been extended with currently over 450 pairs of good quality curtains, as well as a wide range of soft furnishings and accessories. Designer fabrics from all the main labels are represented here, including Liberty, Designers Guild, Anna French, Colefax & Fowler and Laura Ashley. Prices generally vary from £20 to £400 for a full-length pair of top-name interlined curtains complete with pelmet and tie-backs. At the back of the shop there is a special section which caters for the growing number of clients who are renting out properties. The curtains represented here, at the lower end of the price scale, are excellent value for money. To get the best out of your visit, bring your measurements with you together with a sample of fabric, if possible.

THE CURTAIN MILL
19 GREYCAINE ROAD, WATFORD, HERTFORDSHIRE WD2 4JP
☎ (01923) 220339. OPEN 9 - 5.30 SEVEN DAYS A WEEK.
Permanent Discount Outlet • *Furniture/Soft Furnishings*
Huge choice of fabrics at really low prices - from £1.99p a metre and including excellent discounts on many designer labels. A large warehouse, it stocks Ashley Wilde and Swatchbox, among other leading names at discount prices. Also supplies ready made curtains, bespoke curtains, blinds, venetian verticals, all types of window treatments and has its own in-house making up service.

THE GALLERIA OUTLET CENTRE
COMET WAY, HATFIELD, HERTFORDSHIRE AL10 OXR
☎ (01707) 278301. OPEN 10 - 8 MON - FRI, 10 - 6 SAT, 11 - 5 SUN.
Factory Shopping Village • *Womenswear & Menswear* • *Children*
Household • *Furniture/Soft Furnishings* • *Food and Leisure*
Sportswear & Equipment

The outlet centre for North London houses more than 70 outlets: Active Venture sells designer casual menswear including Timberland and YSL; Alphamarque specialise in mobility and easier living; the Baggage Factory has luggage, travel accessories and handbags including Samsonite. Bed & Bath Works sell bedlinen, towels and soaps; BhS for Less sell the Storehouse owned chain's men's, women's and childrenswear ranges, plus selections from its home and lighting ranges, at discounts of at least 30%; The Big Picture sells modern and classical prints including originals. B52 for adult casualwear; Blazer selling men's clothes and accessories; Bow Bangles offering jewellery, hair accessories, sunglasses and bags; Card Crazy seling collector cards; the Candle Store; Carlton Luggage; Casino Roma - an amusement arcade; CBS selling a huge range of products synonymous with the UK's largest catalogue company, GUS; Chamberlaine's bicycles; Charles Kinkard sells footwear, belts and handbags; Chinacraft specialise in glass, china and giftware from names such as Wedgwood and Royal Doulton; Choice selling Next and other retailers' clothes for men, women and children; Ciro Citterio and City Menswear for vast selections of suits, shirts and leisure wear; Class Cosmetics sell top name beauty and skincare products including Elizabeth Arden, Lancome, Revlon, Max Factor, L'Oreal, Almay, Cover Girl and Yardley at between 30%-75% off normal retail prices; Cook Ware House; Cotton Traders specialises in sports and leisure wear; Country Bookshop; Deep pan Pizza; Designer Room ladieswear for Dolce & Gabbana, Calvin Klein, Maska and Versace; Designer Room Menswear for Cerruti 1881, Dolce & Gabbana, Valentino, Ralph Lauren, Nicole Farhi and Calvin Klein; Discount Dressing for designer womenswear; Dorothy Perkins; Double Two; Ecco Shoes; Erdos Cashmere; Furniture and Furnishings is a special section selling sofas, pine, cherry spruce and reproduction furniture; Fantasy Arcade; Fatty Arbuckles, American Diner; Impressions which sells quality mens' and ladieswear; Haggar specialises in American casual menswear; Jane Shilton sells handbags, shoes, luggage and accessories; Julian Graves sells dried fruits and nuts; Kidcraft sells childrenswear and accessories; Littlewoods catalogue outlet selling a wide range of designer and non-designer label leisure wear and shoes; Madisons sandwich bar; Millano sells a designer collection of real leather goods; Moist sells women's and men's club wear including Quiksilver and Trigger Happy; MPC sells formal and casula designer men's and ladieswear; Oddysey Communications sells mobile phones and accessories; Outdoor Trading Post for famous-name fleeces, jackets, waterproofs and skiwear; Petroleum, the menswear specialist; Pilot; Ponden Mill for bedlinen, duvets, towels, kitchen linen; RBC for fomal and casual ladieswear; Room for home furnishings; RS Shoes for fashion footwear; Soled Out shoes; Suits You for menswear; The Baggage Factory stocks luggage, briefcases, handbags and accessories; The Garden Store sells pots, garden furniture, parasols, fountains and gazebos; Tog 24 for outdoor wear; Tom Sayers knitwear and menswear; Tool Warehouse; Whittard of Chelsea; Winning Line fashions. Walker and Hall for jewellery and watches which include Tag, Gucci and Well. There is a good range of stores for children: Chamberlaine's bikes and Kids Play Factory stock an enviable range of branded toys including Duplo, Lego, Raleigh and Scalextric. For clothes, Kidcraft sells branded fashion for 2-12-year-olds. Littlewoods, TK Maxx and Choice all offer a full range of childrenswear complimented by RS Shoes, Soled Out and Ecco. For the home, TK Maxx always has an exciting array of decorative vases, cookware, glassware and crockery from famous manufacturers; BhS for Less sells the Storehouse-owned chain's men's, women's and childrenswear ranges, plus selections from its home and lighting ranges, at discounts of at least 30 percent; Ponden Mill has bedlinen, towels, duvets and bathroom accessories, while Bed & Bath Works will compliment any home with range of towels, duvets, pillows, bathroom accessories, lampshades and dried flowers. There are lots of restaurants and a multiplex cinema on site with masses of free car parking.

TK MAXX

THE GALLERIA OUTLET CENTRE, COMET WAY, JUNCTION 3 OFF THE A1, HATFIELD HERTFORDSHIRE AL10 OXR
☎ (01707) 260066. OPEN 10 - 8 MON - THUR, 10 - 8.30 FRI, 10 - 6 SAT, 11 - 5 SUN.
UNIT 50, 18 THE MALTINGS, ST ALBANS AL1 3HL
☎ (01727) 855999. OPEN 9 - 5.30 MON - WED, 9 - 8 THUR, 9 - 6 FRI, SAT, 11 - 5 SUN.

Permanent Discount Outlet • *Womenswear & Menswear*
Children • *Household* • *Furniture/Soft Furnishings*

Based on an American concept, TK Maxx is situated in easily accessible, often centrally located stores and offers famous label goods with up to 60% savings off recommended retail prices. TK Maxx has fashion for the whole family - women's, men's and childrenswear - accessories, shoes, gifts, kitchenware and home goods. Everything in the store is branded with a choice of well-known high street names to designer labels, and while a small percentage might be clearly marked past season, the great majority of items in store are current season, current stock and still with phenomenal savings. There is a huge choice with 50,000 pieces in store and up to 10,000 new items arriving a week. The stores are simple and unfussy with wide aisles, shopping trolleys and baskets, and a spacious, functional feel to them but there are individual changing rooms, ramps for buggies and wheelchairs and plenty of staff on the shop floor. Every branch accepts all major credit and debit cards and has a liberal refund and return policy.

TOG 24
GALLERIA OUTLET CENTRE, ADDRESS AND OPENING TIMES AS BEFORE.
☎ (01707) 258088.
Factory Shop in a Factory Shopping Village
Womenswear & Menswear • Children • Sportswear & Equipment

Tog 24 are the UK's fastest growing brand name in outdoor clothing and leisurewear. They utilise the world's finest performance fabrics including Gore-Tex, Polartec and Burlington MCS, catering for all the family for all seasons, with cosy fleeces and waterproofs for the winter, and trekking ranges, shorts and t-shirts for the summer. With all prices at least 30% below the recommended retail price, you can afford to enter the Tog comfort zone.

TOM SAYERS CLOTHING CO
GALLERIA OUTLET CENTRE, ADDRESS AND OPENING TIMES AS BEFORE.
☎ (01707) 257729.
Factory Shop in a Factory Shopping Village • *Menswear Only*

Tom Sayers make sweaters for some of the top high street department stores. Unusually for a factory shop, if they don't stock your size, they will try and order it for you from their factory or one of their other factory outlets and send it to you. Most of the stock here is overstock, cancelled orders or last season's and includes jumpers, trousers, jackets and shirts. The trousers and shirts are bought in to complement the sweaters which they make.

WALKER & HALL
GALLERIA OUTLET CENTRE, ADDRESS AND OPENING TIMES AS BEFORE.
☎ (01707) 270121.
Factory Shop in a Factory Shopping Village • *Womenswear & Menswear*

One of more than 70 shops in this glass and steel factory shopping centre straddling the A1. This outlet sells Raymond Weil watches, reduced from £550 to £385; Longines, Gucci, Maurice Lacroix and Tag Heuer. Some ranges reduced from 20% up to 50%.

WATFORD BATHROOMS AND INTERIORS
60-62 QUEEN'S ROAD, WATFORD, HERTFORDSHIRE WD17 2LA
☎ (01923) 250663. OPEN 9 - 5.30 MON - SAT, 10.30 - 4 SUN.
Permanent Discount Outlet • *DIY/Renovation*

Good quality bathrooms at discounted prices including Sottini, Heritage, Daryl, Showerlux and Aqualisa. Discounts represents about 25% off normal retail prices. Bathrooms accessories are also discounted. Free parking.

WHITTARD
GALLERIA OUTLET CENTRE, ADDRESS AND OPENING TIMES AS BEFORE.
☎ (01707) 273930.
Factory Shop in a Factory Shopping Village • *Food and Leisure*

Sells tea, coffee, coffee-making equipment (cafetieres and stove-top espressos) and wide range of china at discount prices.

Kent

ALEXON AND EASTEX SALE SHOP
64 HIGH STREET, RAMSGATE, KENT CT11 9RS
☎ (01843) 589860. OPEN 9 - 5.30 MON - SAT.
Permanent Discount Outlet • *Womenswear Only*
Eastex, Dash and Alexon clothing at reduced prices. Savings are between 20% and 75% and there are short term offers such as jackets for £19.99 reduced from £139. Stock is mostly last year's and at least half the original price.

AMAZON
20 HIGH STREET, CANTERBURY, KENT.
Permanent Discount Outlet • *Womenswear & Menswear*
The most common labels seen here are In Wear, French Connection, Great Plains, Fenn Wright & Manson, Nicole Farhi and Sticky Fingers. There's always plenty of stock in good condition and very reasonable prices. For example, Fenn Wright & Manson long dress, £29.99 reduced from £105; James Lakeland shirt, £22, reduced from £80; cashmere blend sweater, £19.99, was £180; French Connection boat neck striped jersey, £20, instead of £65. Caters for office, weekend and party wear. Shoes at number 7 are very cheap: Velcro dolly shoe, £19.99 reduced from £50; wedge boot, £42.95 reduced from £78.95; evening shoes, £14.99 was £49.99.

B & A WHELAN
52 HIGH STREET, BLUE TOWN, SHEERNESS, KENT ME12 1RW
☎ (01795) 663879. OPEN 9 - 6 SEVEN DAYS A WEEK.
Permanent Discount Outlet • *Food and Leisure*
Manufacturers of concrete garden ornaments, they sell more than 1,300 different items including benches, gnomes, bird baths and sundials, all sold at prices which are about 75% less than those charged in most garden centres. Parking.

BAGGINS BOOK BAZAAR
19 HIGH STREET, ROCHESTER, KENT ME1 1PY
☎ (01634) 811651. FAX 840591. OPEN 10 - 5.50 SEVEN DAYS A WEEK.
Secondhand shops • *Food and Leisure*
Largest secondhand bookshop in England with prices from 50p to £500. Deals in rare and secondhand books, but also sells some brand new review copies at substantial discounts. Prices of the older books depend on their condition. Book search service also offered.

BE-WISE
5 GLOUCESTER PARADE, BLACKFEN ROAD, SIDCUP, KENT DA15 8PS
☎ 020-8859 2658. OPEN 10 - 5 MON - SAT, CLOSED THUR.
Dress Agency • *Womenswear Only*
Middle market names including Principles, Berkertex, Marks & Spencer and Next as well as the occasional designer label.

BELL HOUSE FABRICS
HIGH STREET, CRANBROOK, KENT TN17 3DN
☎ (01580) 712555. OPEN 9 - 5.30 MON - SAT.
Permanent Discount Outlet • *Furniture/Soft Furnishings*
Cranbrook is a two-storey shop which is a Sanderson specialist, but also offers an extensive range of beautiful fabrics from manufacturers such as Anne Swaffer, Jane Churchill, Monkwell and John Wilman, with 400 books to order from other well-known suppliers. Everything is sold at competitive prices, with current, seconds and discontinued lines at less than half price. Printed cottons from £6.99; upholstery fabrics - brocades, tapestries and damasks - from £13.99; Sanderson's linens from £10.99; dress fabrics from £2.99 and silks from £8. They also offer a quality design, make-up and fitting service. Haberdashery, wallpapers and all soft furnishing accessories either in stock or to order.

BON MARCHE
47 NORTHGATE, CANTERBURY, KENT CT1 1BE
☎ (01227) 764823. OPEN 10 - 5.30 MON - FRI, 9.30 - 5.30 SAT.
Dress Agency • *Womenswear Only*
A large, well-established dress agency which offers across-the-board labels from Marks & Spencer up to YSL, with plenty of Jaeger, Maxmara, Mondi, Alexon and Caroline Charles. Prices range from £10 for an M&S top quality outfit to £189, though most items are in the £20 - £69 price range. Day and evening wear as well as shoes, jewellery, bags, scarves and hats are stocked. The owner says that style is more important than the label and is as likely to stock Dorothy Perkins as Dior. After one month in the shop, stock is reduced by one third.

BROMLEY DEMOLITION
75 SIWARD ROAD, BROMLEY, KENT BR2 9JY
☎ 020-8464 3610. OPEN 9 - 5 MON - FRI.
Architectural Salvage • *DIY/Renovation*
Bromley Demolition reclaim whatever is usable from demolished properties including doors, old bricks, assorted sizes of timbers, fireplaces.

CATALOGUE BARGAIN SHOP
19A PRESTON STREET, FAVERSHAM, KENT ME13 8NX
☎ (01795) 591203. OPEN 9 - 5.30 MON - SAT, 10 - 4 SUN.
Permanent Discount Outlet • *Womenswear & Menswear*
Children • *Household* • *Electrical Equipment*
Catalogue Bargain Shop is a growing national chain of stores which obtains the majority of its goods from mail order giants Great Universal and Kays, and offers a range of clothing for all the family, a wide selection of shoes, bed linen, household goods, electrical equipment and hundreds of other catalogue items at very competitive prices. The merchandise consists of ends of ranges and previous season's stock for which there is no longer storage space when the catalogues change.

CLOTHESLINE
58 UNION STREET, MAIDSTONE, KENT ME14 1ED
☎ (01622) 758439. OPEN 10 - 5 TUE - SAT.
Dress Agency • *Womenswear Only*
Designer labels of not more than two years in age in mint condition. Labels include Mondi, Jaeger, Laurel, Jacques Vert, Yarrell, Escada, Betty Barclay, Frank Usher, Tom Bowker and MaxMara.

CLOVER LEAF
DE BRADELEI WHARF,CAMBRIDGE ROAD, DOVER, KENT CT17 9BY
☎ (01304) 226616. OPEN 9.30 - 5.30 MON - FRI, 9.30 - 6 SAT, 11 - 5 SUN.
Factory Shop • *Household*
Part of the large household department at this large factory shopping complex, one section sells a range of melamine products, such as place mats, coasters and trays, oven to tableware and bathroom accessories. Seconds and discontinued lines are sold here at reduced prices.

DAVID EVANS WORLD OF SILK
BOURNE ROAD, CRAYFORD, KENT DA1 4BP
☎ (01322) 559401. OPEN 9.30 - 5 MON - SAT.
Factory Shop • *Womenswear & Menswear* • *Household*
Silk ties, silk fabric, purses, wallets, handbags, photo frames, silk cosmetic bags, seconds in scarves, silk dressing gowns, visitors books, silk waistcoats and cravats are all on sale here at what are described as "real factory shop prices". Silk fabric sold by the metre. Occasional clearance sales make for even better bargains. Now also ladieswear from top fashion designer Paul Costelloe factory shop selling his ends of lines, seconds and samples at up to 70% off the usual shop prices. Museum and coffee shop, ample parking; also guided tours - please book. The shop is on the A223, five minutes from the A2 to London and 15 minutes from junction 2 of the M25.

DE BRADELEI WHARF

DE BRADELEI MILL SHOPS (DOVER) LTD, CAMBRIDGE ROAD, DOVER, KENT CT17 9BY
☎ (01304) 226616. OPEN 9.30 - 5.30 MON - FRI, 9.30 - 6 SAT, 11 - 5 SUN.
Permanent Discount Outlet • *Womenswear & Menswear*
Household • *Furniture/Soft Furnishings* • *Children*

Large outlet in superb maritime setting just off the Dover Seafront, selling top brand names for all the family, including shoes. The ladieswear includes such names as Windsmoor, Planet, Precis Petite, Elle, French Connection, Virgin, Jackpot, Phase Eight, Gerard Pasquier, plus top American and German designer labels, handbags and much more. The menswear range includes underwear, socks, coats, sweaters, jackets, suits and trousers from labels such as Wolsey, Countrywear, French Connection, Virgin and Tog 24. Robert Leonard's Menswear provide Greiff, Pierre Cardin, Gabicci, Gurteen, Oakman, Saville Row, John Slim and many more. There is a large shoe department featuring international shoes for all the family and a wonderful Home Furnishings Department. The Interior Design shops sell bedding, towels, top-name furnishing fabric, cushions, throws, furniture and curtains. The Glass and China Department has an amazing selection from Waterford Wedgwood, Stuart Crystal, Royal Doulton, Arthur Price of England Silverware, Staffordshire Tableware, Churchill, Cloverleaf, Hornsea Pottery, Cristal d'Arques and much more. There is superb Liberty stock in the giftware department. Parking is easy with a large car park behind the store. The Waves Coffee Shop is open all day, serving delicious home-cooked food. Coach parties are welcome.

DEJA VU

OLD SEAL HOUSE, 19 CHURCH STREET, SEAL, NEAR SEVENOAKS, KENT TN15 0DA
☎ (01732) 762155. OPEN 10 - 4.30 TUE - SAT.
Dress Agency • *Womenswear* • *Children*

In this small, friendly shop, established in 1977, you will find British and European designers such as Paul Costelloe, Gerry Weber, Betty Barclay, Liz Claiborne, Patsy Seddon and Ouiset as well as old favourites such as Jaeger, Marks & Spencer and Laura Ashley. The price range is from £10 to £200. There is also a small range of children's dresses, and from September each year, ski wear for adults and children. After six to eight weeks, clothes which haven't sold or been collected are sent to charity. An alteration service is also offered for clothes purchased here.

ELITE LIGHTING

7 GOODWOOD PARADE, UPPER ELMERS END ROAD, BECKENHAM, KENT BR3 3QZ
☎ 020-8639 0050. E-MAIL: sales@elitelighting.co.uk
WEBSITE: www.elitelighting.co.uk
OPEN 9.30 - 5.30 MON - SAT. ALSO MAIL ORDER.
Permanent Discount Outlet • *Household* • *Furniture/Soft Furnishings*

Spectacular range of crystal chandeliers and wall brackets, all with 24 carat gold plated frames and dressed with Swarovski strass crystal. Their prices are very competitive because they buy direct from leading importers. Also offers a mail order service.

EUROBE
STATION APPROACH, ST MARY CRAY STATION, KENT BR5 2NB
☎ (01689) 822722. FAX (01869) 876517.
PHONE FOR DETAILS OF OPENING HOURS.
Permanent Discount Outlet • *Womenswear Only*

Wholesale warehouse open to the public for limited times offering labels such as Olsen, Gerry Weber, Michelle trousers, Delores knitwear, Duo and many more. Stock varies from current originals, showroom samples, late deliveries and some items of second quality. All clothes are sold at the wholesale price plus VAT. Features extensive coordinated ranges, separates, holiday and evening wear and outerwear.

FROCK FOLLIES
49 HIGH STREET, BECKENHAM, KENT BR3 1DA
☎ 020-8650 9283. OPEN 9.30 - 5.30 MON - SAT.
Dress Agency • *Womenswear Only*

Middle market labels from Marks & Spencer to Armani with some new samples. Specialises in hats, with more than 100 to choose from, as well as swimwear, shoes, hat pins, belts and scarves. The hats and jewellery are new. Plenty of evening wear, particularly ball gowns, especially from September to Christmas.

GAP
MCARTHURGLEN DESIGNER OUTLET VILLAGE, ROMNEY MARSH ROAD, ASHFORD, KENT TM23 1EL
☎ (01233) 663951. OPEN 10 - 6 MON - SAT, UNTIL 8 ON THUR, 11 - 5 SUN AND BANK HOLIDAYS.
Factory Shop in a Factory Shopping Village
Womenswear & Menswear • *Children*

Gap sells casual clothes for men, women and children of all ages, discounted at this factory outlet. There is a children's play area, restaurants and free car parking.

HANGERS
53 CROYDON ROAD, BECKENHAM, KENT BR4 4AB
☎ 020-8658 5386. OPEN 9.30 - 5.30 MON - SAT.
Dress Agency • *Womenswear & Menswear*

Mixture of high street and designer labels including Valentino, Boss, Windsmoor, Planet and Country Casuals. For men, there are suits, jackets, coats, shirts, trousers, ties and shoes. For women, day and evening wear, dresses, skirts, tops, hats, shoes and accessories. Prices range from £5 - £100.

HANRO OF SWITZERLAND
MCARTHURGLEN DESIGNER OUTLET VILLAGE, ASHFORD. ADDRESS AND OPENING HOURS AS BEFORE.
☎ (01233) 626660.
Factory Shop in a Factory Shopping Village • *Womenswear & Menswear*
Luxury lingerie for men and women which is normally sold through Harvey Nichols, Harrods and Selfridges is available here at reduced prices. For example, a bra which normally retails for £100 would be reduced by 35% - 50%. Sizes range from extra small to extra large and the company specialises in garments for smaller busts, although D-cups are also stocked. Very well known for their mercerised cottons which never fade or shrink.

IN DOORS
BEECHINWOOD LANE, PLATT, SEVENOAKS, KENT TN15 8QN
☎ (01732) 887445. OPEN 9 - 5 MON - FRI, 9 - 12.30 SAT.
Architectural Salvage • *DIY/Renovation*
Reclaimed pine and some oak doors and new doors made from reclaimed wood for the kitchen, wardrobe or door frames. Reclaimed pine doors £60, for small kitchen door, £100 for wardrobe door, £150 for large door. Free parking.

JANE SHILTON
MCARTHURGLEN DESIGNER OUTLET VILLAGE, ASHFORD. ADDRESS AND OPENING HOURS AS BEFORE.
☎ (01233) 625030. FAX (01233) 625033.
Factory Shop in a Factory Shopping Village • *Womenswear Only*
Merchandise from past seasons' collections or factory seconds at discounts of at least 30% and up to 70% off the original price. There is a wide range of handbags, small leather goods, shoes, luggage umbrellas and travel bags. Example of price reduction: handbags at £24.99 originally £37.

JOKIDS
MCARTHURGLEN DESIGNER OUTLET VILLAGE, ASHFORD. ADDRESS AND OPENING HOURS AS BEFORE.
☎ (0800) 316 4352 CENTRE INFORMATION LINE.
Factory Shop in a Factory Shopping Village • *Children*
This shop sells childrenswear for 0-10-year-olds including everdaywear like t-shirts, jogwear, various denim styles and accessories. For special occasions there are pretty hand-smocked party dresses and rompers. Reductions are up to 40%. The village also has restaurants, children's play areas and free parking.

KIDS PLAY FACTORY
MCARTHURGLEN DESIGNER OUTLET VILLAGE, ASHFORD. ADDRESS AND OPENING HOURS AS BEFORE.
Factory Shop in a Factory Shopping Village • *Children*
This shop sells a wide range of well-known children's brand names: Little Tikes, Corgi, Crayola, Tomy, Lego, Hasbro, Playskool, Mattel and Fisher-Price at discounts of up to 50%. They also stock a wide range of soft toys including TY Beanie Babies.

KNICKERBEAN
87 HIGH STREET, TUNBRIDGE WELLS, KENT TN1 1XZ
☎ (01892) 520883. OPEN 9 - 5.30 MON - SAT.
Permanent Discount Outlet • *Furniture/Soft Furnishings*
Recommended by countless interior and decorating magazines and much loved by the bargain hunter, Knickerbean offers a continuous stream of stylish and sumptuous fabrics (the kind found at the Chelsea Harbour Design Centre and Decorex), but all at affordable prices. They originally specialised in top name UK designer fabrics, offering excess inventory, discontinued lines and slight imperfects, usually at about half price. You can still find many of these famous name bargains here, but now many of their fabrics are sourced directly from the same mills and manufacturers as the 'top names', both here and abroad. They offer the same top quality, in the latest colours and designs, at relatively lower prices, because they are buying and selling directly and cutting out the middlemen. Their selection of curtain and upholstery fabrics caters for both contemporary and traditional homes, with formal glazed chintzes, regal damasks, toiles de jouy and luxurious chenilles displayed next to basic neutrals, bright modern prints, airy voiles and earthy ethnic patterns. They also have large ranges of checks and stripes, self-patterned weaves, simple prints for a child's room as well as a huge range of upholstery brocades and tapestries. Prices start at £5.95 for prints to £19.95 and occasionally more for some their tapestries, chenilles and damasks. Knickerbean's outlets are bright and pleasant, more like an interior designer's showroom - there's no 'warehouse' feeling here. Their trained staff are helpful with all sorts of advice on fabrics, colours and interiors and they offer a complete home visit service with interior measuring and design advice. They have a hand finished making up service for curtains, blinds and loose covers, as well as a range of custom made funiture with footstools, sofas, etc. Twice yearly sales in January and June enable customers to snap up even bigger bargains.

LE CREUSET
MCARTHURGLEN OUTLET VILLAGE, ASHFORD, KENT TM23 1EL
☎ (01233) 611635 . OPEN 10 - 6 MON - WED, 10 - 8 THUR, 10 - 6 SAT, 11 - 5 SUN.
Factory Shop in a Factory Shopping Village • *Household*
Items from the famous Le Creuset range - casseroles, saucepans, fry pans etc - plus their pottery collection at discounts of at least 30%.

LEE COOPER
MCARTHURGLEN DESIGNER OUTLET VILLAGE, ASHFORD. ADDRESS AND OPENING HOURS AS BEFORE.
☎ (01233) 611186.
Factory Shop in a Factory Shopping Village
Womenswear & Menswear • *Children*

Denim jeans, jackets and shirts, each ranked by size and gender at discounts of up to 30%. Casual shirts from £9.99, jeans from £14.99, T-shirts and ladieswear. Lee Cooper was founded in 1908 as a workwear manufacturer before becoming a supplier to the armed forces. Most of the stock here is current, discontinued and irregular merchandise, all of which comes straight from Lee Cooper's factories in Europe.

LILLEY & SKINNER
MCARTHURGLEN DESIGNER OUTLET VILLAGE, ASHFORD. ADDRESS AND OPENING HOURS AS BEFORE.
☎ (01233) 623963.
Factory Shop in a Factory Shopping Village • *Household*
Womenswear & Menswear

Wide range of brand names including Stead & Simpson, Lilley & Skinner, Hobos, Hush Puppies, Lotus, Sterling & Hunt, Richleigh, Scholl, Red Tape, Flexi Country, Padders, Canaletto, Bronx, Frank Wright, Brevitt, Romba Wallace, Rieker, all at discount prices of up to 50%.

LITTLEWOODS CATALOGUE OUTLET STORE
MCARTHURGLEN DESIGNER OUTLET VILLAGE, ASHFORD. ADDRESS AND OPENING HOURS AS BEFORE.
☎ (0800) 316 4352 CENTRE INFORMATION LINE.
Factory Shop in a Factory Shopping Village
Womenswear & Menswear • *Electrical Equipment* • *Children*

Ends of line and surplus stock from the Littlewoods catalogue at discounts of 30-50%. Sels clothing, footwear and electricals.

MATALAN
BROADWAY SHOPPING CENTRE, THE BROADWAY, MAIDSTONE, KENT ME16 8PS
☎ (01622) 675153. OPEN 10 - 8 MON - FRI, 9 - 6 SAT, 10 - 4 SUN.
WESTWOOD RETAIL PARK, WESTWOOD ROAD, RAMSGATE, THANET CT10 2RQ
☎ (01843) 608700. OPEN 10 - 8 MON - FRI, 9 - 6 SAT, 11 - 5 SUN.
Permanent Discount Outlet • *Womenswear & Menswear*
Children • *Household*

Matalan is a fashion and homewares value retailer giving customers what they claim to be unbeatable value for money with huge savings on a wide range of products including high quality fashionable clothing for men, women and children at up to 50% off high street prices. Matalan is situated out of town and stores are open seven days a week all year round.

MCARTHURGLEN DESIGNER OUTLET CENTRE
KIMBERLEY WAY, ASHFORD, JUNCTION 10 OF M20, KENT TN24 OSD
☎ (0800) 316 4352 FREEPHONE INFORMATION LINE.
WEBSITE: www.mcarthurglen.com
OPEN 10 - 6 MON - SAT, 8 ON THUR, 11 - 5 SUN.
Factory Shopping Village • *Household* • *War & Menswear* • *Children Food and Leisure* • *Sportswear & Equipment* • *Electrical Equipment*

Opened in March 2000, this outlet centre was designed by Millennium Dome architect Richard Rogers and takes the form of a leaf-shaped tented structure, one kilometre in circumference. It includes a covered children's play area, food court, cafes and parking for 1,500 cars. Almost all of the parking is in the centre of the piazza so that shoppers can see all the shops immediately they leave their car. Located alongside the Ashford International Rail Station on the Channel Tunnel rail link, from where there is a shuttle bus every eight minutes. Over 60 stores sell top brands and designer labels, offering a discount of between 30% and 50% off regular retail prices. Shops include Antler, Bed & Bath Works, Bookends, China Place, Claire's Accessories, Clarks, Cotton Traders, Le Creuset, Donnay, Ecco, Edinburgh Crystal, European Fashion House, Gap, Hanro, Tommy Hilfiger, Jokids, Lee Cooper, Levi's, Lilley and Skinner, Littlewoods Catalogue Outlet, Nike, Paco, Pink, Pilot, Polo, Prices Candles, Professional Cookware Company, Reebok, Roman Originals, Samsonite, Ben Sherman, Jane Shilton, Soled Out, Spiegelau, The Suit Company, Suits You, Thomas Pink, Tog 24, Toyzone, Waterford Wedgwood, Woodhouse, XS Music and Video.

MICHELSONS
STAPLEHURST ROAD, SITTINGBOURNE KENT ME10 2NH
☎ (01795) 426821. OPEN 9 - 12 FRI.
Factory Shop • *Menswear Only*

Michelsons, one of the largest tie manufacturers in Europe, has a small factory shop attached to the factory selling silk neckties, bowties, handkerchiefs, scarves and cravats. All the stock is current or last season's or ends of lines and is discounted by at least 30%. There is a choice of more than 1,000 ties in silk at maximum prices of £6.

NIPPERS
MANSERS, NIZELS LANE, HILDENBOROUGH, KENT TN11 8NX
☎ (01732) 832253. FAX ☎ (01732) 833658. E-MAIL: tonbridge@nippers.co.uk
OPENING HOURS VARY SO PHONE FIRST.
CHALKPIT FARM, SCHOOL LANE, BEKESBOURNE,
CANTERBURY, KENT CT4 5EU
☎ (01227) 832008. FAX ☎ (01227) 831496.
WEBSITE: www.nippers.co.uk   OPENING HOURS VARY SO PHONE FIRST.
Permanent Discount Outlet • *Children*

Nippers, the nursery equipment and toy specialists, operate from previously redundant buildings in rural areas around the country. They offer easy parking, no queues and personal service. This is on top of competitive prices on prams, cots, pushchairs, car seats, outdoor play equipment and toys, some of which are new, some seconds or secondhand and some ends of lines. Prices are low because they avoid the high overheads of traditional retail outlets and also because the successful growth of a number of branches means they can now buy in bulk and negotiate good deals. Customers are invited to try out the merchandise while the children look at the animals, mostly sheep, chicken and pigs. Also offers many brand leaders at discount, including Mamas & Papas, Cosatto, Britax, Maclaren and Bebe Confort, plus Fisher-Price and Little Tikes. You can try out the car seats in your car and there is usually a pram/pushchair repair service on site.

PACO
MCARTHURGLEN DESIGNER OUTLET CENTRE, KIMBERLEY WAY,
ASHFORD, JUNCTION 10 OF M20, KENT TN24 OSD
☎ (01233) 626262. OPEN 10 - 6 MON - SAT, 10 - 8 THUR, 11 - 5 SUN.
Factory Shop in a Factory Shopping Village
Womenswear & Menswear • *Children* • *Sportswear & Equipment*

Paco uses bright, distinctive colours and the knack for designing great clothes at affordable prices. For several years, they have also been creating their own brand of sports and leisurewear clothing that shows great verve and energy. This range has a much more everyday living influence. The contrast is a distinct look for the discerning wearer. If you are looking for a great T-shirt or sweatshirt, lightweight jacket or gilet, polar fleece or hooded top, three-quarter length or combat trousers, then you need look no further. Paco now competes with the very best fashion brands in the high street by offering customers high fashion combined with excellent quality, making their clothes real value for money.

PANACHE
90 - 92 HIGH STREET, ROYAL TUNBRIDGE WELLS, KENT TN1 1YF
☎ (01892) 522 883. OPEN 10 - 5 MON - SAT.
Dress Agency • *Womenswear Only* • *Children*

On two floors, Panache sells women's nearly-new at savings of up to 50% on high street prices. The agency stocks a wide range of labels from Marks and Spencer and Viyella to Jacques Vert, MaxMara and Escada. They also sell hats, a large selection of evening wear, coats, shoes, jackets, handbags and belts.

PETER NEWMAN FACTORY SHOP
UNIT IB, EDDINGTON BUSINESS PARK, THANET WAY, HERNE BAY, KENT CT6 5TT
☎ (01227) 741112. OPEN 9 - 5.30 MON - SAT, 10 - 4 SUN.
Factory Shop • *Womenswear & Menswear* • *Children*

Discontinued styles, slight seconds and end of line adult and children's shoes. Clarks, Timberland, Lee, Pods, Lotus, Equity, Hush Puppies and Hi-Tec sportswear are typical names, available at up to 35% reductions. A GDD reader bought a pair of Clarks children's shoes for £20, usual price £29; and two pairs of sandals for £10 and £12, usual price, £29.95 and £34.95. Also sell bags. Small refreshment area, car parking and wheelchair accessibility.

PHASE EIGHT
11 BUTCHERY LANE, CANTERBURY, KENT CT1 2JR
☎ (01227) 786581. OPEN 9 - 5.30 MON - SAT.
DE BRADELEI WHARF, CAMBRIDGE ROAD, DOVER, KENT CT17 9BY
☎ (01304) 226616. OPEN 9.30 - 5.30 MON - FRI, 9.30 - 6 SAT, 11 - 5 SUN.
Permanent Discount Outlet • *Womenswear Only*

Phase Eight, the 24-strong chain which sells smart workwear and wearable special occasion outfits, has a Sale Shop in Canterbury and a department in Dover's De Bradelei outlet. Here, end of season merchandise, samples and seconds are sold at discount prices, including tailored trouser suits, dresses, skirts, knitwear and tops as well as more formal outfits for special occasions and casual weekend wear.

PONDEN MILL LINENS
DE BRADELEI WHARF, CAMBRIDGE ROAD, DOVER, KENT CT17 9BY
☎ (01304) 225821. OPEN 9.30 - 5.30 MON - FRI, 9.30 - 6 SAT, 11 - 5 SUN.
Factory Shop • *Household*

Famous branded products at direct from the mill prices. A fabulous assortment of towels, duvets, pillows, throws, bedspreads, up-to-the-minute coordinated bed linen, from Crown, Coloroll, Jeff Banks Ports-of-Call, to name but a few. Something for every room in the house.

PRICE'S PATENT CANDLE CO
MCARTHURGLEN OUTLET VILLAGE, KIMBERLEY WAY, ASHFORD, KENT TN24 OSD
☎ (01233) 611828. OPEN 10 - 6 MON - SAT, 8 ON THUR, 11 - 5 SUN.
Factory Shop • *Household*

Everything sold in this shop are seconds, discontinued sizes not available elsewhere, over-runs or candles in old packaging that has now been replaced. There are church candles, lanterns, candles in pots and glass jars, star-shaped candles, floating candles, candlestick holders, serviettes, scented candles and garden torches.

RAMSGATE BOULEVARD DESIGNER OUTLET VILLAGE
RAMSGATE HARBOUR RAILWAY STATION, MARINE ESPLANADE, RAMSGATE, KENT
Factory Shopping Village • *Womenswear & Menswear*
65,000 sq ft retail development set in the magnificent Victorian structure of the old Ramsgate Harbour Railways Station located on Marine Esplanade which is due to open in late 2000.

ROYAL WORCESTER & SPODE FACTORY SHOP
MCARTHURGLEN DESIGNER OUTLET VILLAGE, ASHFORD. ADDRESS AND OPENING HOURS AS BEFORE.
☎ (01233) 621640.
Factory Shop • *Household*
Infinitesimally flawed porcelain and china seconds at 25% less than "perfect" prices. This outlet also sells Edinburgh Crystal, Mayflower, Pimpernel Table Mats, Lakeland Plaques, Paw Prints, Collectible World Studios, Fo Frame, Chadda Glass, Country Artists, Six Trees. There is a vast range with special offers throughout the year on anything from crystal decanters and bowls to figurines, cookware and dinner sets. Shipping arrangements worldwide can be organised.

SNIPS IN FASHION
234 HIGH STREET, ORPINGTON, KENT BR6 OLS
☎ (01689) 828288. OPEN 9.30 - 5.30 MON - SAT.
Permanent Discount Outlet • *Womenswear Only*
Women's clearance outlet featuring labels such as Olsen, Michelle, Dolores, Gerry Weber, Cavita and Aspa at less than half the original price. Some are current stock, others samples from showrooms, yet others discontinued lines, seconds or late deliveries. Sizes from 8 - 20 usually available. The whole range of clothing is stocked from ballgowns and coats to jeans and beach wear, but no accessories.

SPOILS
M323-324 CHEQUERS CENTRE, DUKES WALK, MAIDSTONE, KENT ME15 6AS
☎ (01622) 678916. OPEN 9 - 5.30 MON - SAT, 9.30 - 5.30 TUE.
Permanent Discount Outlet • *Household*
General domestic glassware, non-stick bakeware, kitchen gadgets, ceramic oven-to-tableware, textiles, cutting boards, aluminium non-stick cookware, bakeware, plastic kitchenware, plastic storage, woodware, coffee pots/makers, furniture, mirrors and picture frames. Rather than being discounted, all the merchandise is very competitively priced - in fact, the company carry out competitors' checks frequently in order to monitor pricing. With 38 branches, the company is able to buy in bulk and thus negotiate very good prices.

THE CURTAIN SHOP
12 GOODS STATION ROAD, TUNBRIDGE WELLS, KENT TN1 2BL
☎ (01892) 527202. FAX ☎ (01892) 522682. OPEN 9.30 - 5.30 MON - SAT.
Secondhand shops • *Furniture/Soft Furnishings*
The seven show rooms are festooned with fine quality secondhand and new curtains at reasonable prices. Designer fabrics are available on the roll at discount prices and the shop provides a making-up and track-fitting service. Curtain prices range from as little as £30 for a pair of cottage curtains to more than £1,000 for a pair of antique silk velvet curtains. Typically, a wide pair of long, lined and interlined damask curtains covering nine feet of track would cost around £440, and a pair of curtains suitable for the spare room can cost as little as £185. They also offer a design service for either machine-made or handmade new curtains and pelmets.

THE DESIGN HOUSE
MCARTHURGLEN DESIGNER OUTLET VILLAGE, ASHFORD. ADDRESS AND OPENING HOURS AS BEFORE.
☎ (01233) 620106.
Factory Shop in a Factory Shopping Village • *Household*
Famous branded products at direct from the mill prices. A fabulous assortment of towels, duvets, pillows, throws, bedspreads, up-to-the-minute coordinated bed linen, from Crown, Coloroll, Jeff Banks Ports-of-Call, to name but a few. Something for every room in the house.

THE DRESS AGENCY
5 BOURNE ROAD, BEXLEY, KENT DA5 1LG
☎ (01322) 523451. OPEN 10.30 - 5 TUE - SAT.
Dress Agency • *Womenswear Only*
Mixed selection of chainstore clothes and secondhand designer wear in sizes 6 - 22 plus a large selection of shoes, hats and other accessories. Labels range from Richards to Rodier and Betty Barclay.

THE FACTORY SHOP LTD
THE FOREMAN CENTRE, HIGH STREET, HEADCORN, KENT TN27 9NE
☎ (01622) 891651. OPEN 9 - 5.30 MON - SAT, 10 - 4 SUN.
Factory Shop • *Womenswear & Menswear* • *Children* • *Household* *Furniture/Soft Furnishings* • *Sportswear & Equipment*
High street chainstore seconds and ends of ranges from clothes for all the family, bedding, toiletries, kitchenware, glassware, footwear, lighting, cosmetics, jewellery, and luggage at discounts of approximately 30%-50%. There are weekly deliveries and brands include many major stars: Joe Bloggs, Nike, Adidas and Brabantia, to name just four. Lines are continually changing and few factory shops offer such a variety under one roof, with at the Brighton branch, a large number of clothing concessions in addition to The Factory Shop range. On display is a new line of Cape Country Furniture has recently

been introduced at all four South East branches. This high quality pine furniture made exclusively for The Factory Shop in the new South Africa is sold at factory direct prices with home delivery throughout the UK. Colour brochure and price list available. Free car park.

THE FROCK EXCHANGE
7 WALDEN PARADE, WALDEN ROAD, CHISLEHURST, KENT BR7 5DW
OPEN 9.30 - 4.30 MON - SAT, CLOSED WED.
Dress Agency • *Womenswear Only*
Located less than one miles from Chislehurst high street, with easy free parking, the Frock Exchange sells an extensive range of nearly-new clothes from the high street chains, plus Mondi, Karen Millen, Giorgio Armani, Mansfield, Betty Barclay and Jacques Vert etc. From time to time, there are also wonderful outfits from top houses such as Jean Muir, Bruce Oldfield, Escada and Valentino. Apart from frocks and separates, the shop also has a wide selection of bags, belts, jewellery (real diamonds as well as fakes), hats, scarves and footwear. Most clothing is not more than two years old and there is a rapid turnover with new stock constantly arriving each day. There is a small bric-a-brac area with pretty china, photo frames and ornaments, as well as second-hand curtain and other textiles.

TILE CLEARING HOUSE
UNIT A5, NUGENT INDUSTRIAL ESTATE, CRAY WAY, ST MARY CRAY, ORPINGTON, KENT BR5 3RP
☎ (01689) 890 511. OPEN 8 - 6 MON - FRI, 9 - 6 SAT, 10 - 4 SUN.
Permanent Discount Outlet • *DIY/Renovation*
Over 500 ranges of top quality ceramic wall and floor tiles permanently in stock, plus a comprehensive range of grouts, adhesives, tools and accessories to complete the job. By buying direct from the manufacturer and passing the savings on to the customer, their prices are very competitive. Moreover, everything you see is in stock, so there's no waiting for orders to be processed. Save up to 75% on manufacturers' recommended selling prices.

TOG 24
DE BRADLEI WHARF, CAMBRIDGE ROAD, DOVER, KENT CT17 9BY
☎ (01304) 216126. OPEN 9.30 - 5.30 MON - FRI, 9.30 - 6 SAT, 11 - 5 SUN.
MCARTHURGLEN OUTLET VILLAGE, KIMBERLEY WAY,
ASHFORD TN24 0SD
☎ (01233) 647357. OPEN 10 - 6 MON - SAT, 8 ON THUR, 11 - 5 SUN.
Factory Shop in a Factory Shopping Village
Womenswear & Menswear • *Children* • *Sportswear & Equipment*
Tog 24 are the UK's fastest growing brand name in outdoor clothing and leisurewear. They utilise the world's finest performance fabrics including Gore-Tex, Polartec and Burlington MCS, catering for all the family for all seasons, with cosy fleeces and waterproofs for the winter, and trekking ranges,

shorts and t-shirts for the summer. With all prices at least 30% below the recommended retail price, you can afford to enter the Tog comfort zone.

TOYTIME
MEOPHAM BANK FARM, LEIGH ROAD, HILDENBOROUGH, NEAR TONBRIDGE, KENT TN11 9AQ
☎ (01732) 833695/832416. OPEN 9 - 12 AND 7.30 - 8.30 TUE, 9 - 12 THUR, 9 - 4 SAT.
Permanent Discount Outlet • *Children*
Sells both new and secondhand toys - anything from a rattle to a climbing frame. The stock is always changing as you can get immediate cash for your used toys in good condition. There is a huge selection in three barns including bikes, trikes, doll's prams, doll's houses, trampolines, slides, sandpits, to mention just a few. In addition, party bag fillers and baby toys abound. All the outdoor equipment (as well as Brio, Playmobil and Lego) is new and is sold at discounted prices. Climbing frames and swings are on display outside (and some animals) and advice is given, when required.

TRACKS AND TRIMMINGS
50 THE PANTILES, TUNBRIDGE WELLS, KENT TN2 5TN
☎ (01892) 515288. OPEN 9.30 - 5.30 MON - SAT, 9.30 - 1 WED.
MAIL ORDER.
Permanent Discount Outlet • *Furniture/Soft Furnishings*
Small shop with a lot of stock - what they don't have you can order. Everything for the curtain maker and upholsterer, as well as roller and Venetian blinds and exterior awnings. Tracks and trimmings, upholstery and curtains, cushions, tie-backs, from £3.95 each, compared with £18 in the high street; plaited and rope tie-backs, from £9.99; cushion covers, £3.95; pelmet boards and handmade lampshades. Extensive fabric and pole ranges. Cafe clips (decorative or plain), cafe clip hooks, swag creators, rings and brackets in all sizes, pelmet brackets, weights, tieback hooks, silicon lubricant, soil guard, new tab inserts, roller and Austrian blind kits, Velcro, nail studs, net wire, webbing, curved/mattress/spring needles, key tassels, nail strips. Clearance lines of trimmings and tie-backs can be discounted by up to 50%.

WINDSMOOR GROUP
MCARTHURGLEN OUTLET CENTRE, ASHFORD, JUNCTION 10 OF M20, KENT TN24 OSD
☎ (0800) 316 4352 CENTRE INFORMATION LINE.
OPEN 10 - 6 MON - SAT, 8 ON THUR, 11 - 5 SUN.
Factory Shop in a Factory Shopping Village • *Womenswear Only*
Previous season's stock as well as any returned merchandise and overmakes from the Windsmoor, Planet and Precis ranges at discounts averaging about 50% off the original price.

WORLDWIDE HOME EXCHANGE CLUB
PO BOX 27, TUNBRIDGE WELLS, KENT TN1 2WQ
☎ (01892) 619300. FAX 01892 619311.

Home exchange and rental is a great way to see the world at a fraction of the cost. Mainly aimed at seasoned travellers who eschew package holidays and prefer to stay in a private home rather than a hotel room or bleak apartment, you pay for travel, food and holiday spending only and you get to taste someone else's lifestyle! They have 450 quality homes on their books in places, as well as properties in Europe, the USA and worldwide. Exchange guidelines are provided, sample agreements and general useful information. They publish an annual directory at the beginning of December with a supplement in April. Contact them for more details.

Lancashire

ABAKHAN FABRICS
111-115 OLDHAM STREET, MANCHESTER, LANCASHIRE
☎ (0161) 839 3229. OPEN 9.30 - 5.15 MON - SAT.
34-44 STAFFORD STREET, LIVERPOOL
☎ (0151) 207 4029. OPEN 9.30 - 5 MON - SAT
8-12 GREENWAY ROAD, BIRKENHEAD, MERSEYSIDE
☎ (0151) 652 5195. OPEN 9 - 5 MON - SAT, UNTIL 8 ON THUR, 10 - 4 SUN.
65-67 CHURCH ROAD, BIRKENHEAD, MERSEYSIDE
☎ (0151) 647 6983. OPEN 9 - 5 MON - SAT.

Factory Shop • *Furniture/Soft Furnishings* • *DIY/Renovation*
Food and Leisure

With five outlets in the North West, Abakhan Fabrics are as well known for the emphasis they put on value for money as they are for the huge variety of fabrics, needlecrafts, haberdashery, gifts and knitting yarns, soft furnishings, all gathered from around the world. The large mill shop complex in Clwyd (see Wales) has has a new Home and Garden Department, baskets of remnant fabrics, wools, yarns and unrivalled selections of fabrics sold by the metre from evening wear, bridal wear and crepe de Chine to curtaining, nets and velvets. Here in this historic building, there are more than ten tonnes of remnant fabrics and 10,000 rolls, all at mill shop prices. Abakhan is able to offer such bargains through bulk buying, or selling clearance lines, job lots and seconds. There is a coffee shop and free parking at the Flintshire outlet and coach parties are welcome provided they pre-book. The Manchester and Liverpool outlets do not have free parking facilities or a coffee shop. The Greenway Road, Birkenhead, outlet has a bridal fabric and accessories shop, and the Church Road branch also supplies craft fabrics. Free information pack available: ring 01745 562100.

AFFLECK'S PALACE
52 CHURCH STREET, MANCHESTER, LANCASHIRE M4 1PW
☎ (0161) 834 2039. OPEN 10 - 5.30 MON - FRI, 10 - 6 SAT.
Secondhand and Vintage Clothes • *Womenswear & Menswear*
Indor fashion market specialising in street fashion and alternative fashion such as Seventies' fashion including platform shoes, Fifties' and Sixties' nostalgia, outfits from the Twenties' to the present day and new designer clothes. Also jewellery, rubber clothes, body piercing, tattooing (and exclusively black henna tattooing) and hair extensions. Two cafes and two hairdressers, offering hair beading, on site.

ALLSPORTS
99 ALBANY WAY, SALFORD 6, GREATER MANCHESTER M6 5JA
☎ (0161) 736 8582. OPEN 9 - 5.30 MON - SAT.
Permanent Discount Outlet • *Sportswear & Equipment*
Allsports is a standard shop but at the rear, it has a dedicated area of marked-down goods. These are all damaged or end of season and there are great bargains to be had. Goods can be one-offs to particular items in various sizes. Stock varies from day to day so you could be delighted one day and disappointed the next. Typical bargains are British and foreign football shirts at between one quarter and one half of the normal perfect price. There are also trainers, sports goods, clothing, football boots, including some Man. United merchandise. There are fresh deliveries every day.

AL MURAD DIY
94 CHORLTON ROAD, OLD TRAFFORD, MANCHESTER,
LANCASHIRE M15 4AL
☎ (0161) 226 3929. OPEN 9.30 - 5.30 MON - THUR, SAT.
Permanent Discount Outlet • *DIY/Renovation*
Sells a wide range of branded paints - Dulux, Crown and Johnsons - at discount prices. With 35 shops in Yorkshire, Lancashire and Lincolnshire, they bulk buy and pass on savings to customers. They also offer a range of discounted wallpapers from Vymura, Crown, Super Fresco, Pride and Knightsbridge which, if not in stock, can be ordered from their range of books, as well as ceramic tiles, grouting and grouting tools.

ALEXON SALE SHOP
469 LORD STREET, SOUTHPORT, LANCASHIRE.
☎ (01704) 531281. OPEN 9 - 5.15MON - SAT.
71 BANK HEY STREET, BLACKPOOL, LANCASHIRE.
☎ (01253) 622528. OPEN 9 - 5.30 MON - SAT.
Permanent Discount Outlet • *Womenswear Only*
Alexon and Eastex from last season at 40% less than the original price; during sale time in January and June, the reductions are 70%. Stock includes separates, skirts, jackets, blouses; there is no underwear or night clothes.

ALLWEIS CHINA AND CRYSTAL
GEORGE STREET, BURY OLD ROAD, CHEETHAM HILL VILLAGE,
MANCHESTER M7 4PX,
☎ (0161) 740 2409. OPEN 9.15 - 5.30 MON - SAT, 11 - 2 SUN.
Permanent Discount Outlet • *Household*
Branded china and cutlery at discount including Waterford, Wedgwood, Royal Doulton, Royal Worcester and many others. None of the stock is seconds and discounts start at 10%. Wedding lists a speciality. Names stocked in the past include Alessi, Arthur Price, Boda Nova, Bugatti, George Butler, Oneida, Rosenthal, Villeroy & Boch, and Wilkens. Many of the designers in cutlery are modern Italian and there is a variety ranging from stainless steel to silver plates.

ANTLER LTD
ALFRED STREET, BURY, LANCASHIRE BL9 9EF
☎ (0161) 764 5241. OPEN 10 - 4 EVERY DAY.
Factory Shop • *Food and Leisure*
Factory shop selling leather goods: handbags, business cases, wallets, purses, as well as travel aids and suitcases; also soft luggage and tool cases which tend not to be made out of leather. All the products are quality seconds and ends of lines. Free parking.

ARCHITECTURAL WALL AND FLOOR CO.
UNIT 3, PREMIER MILL, BEGONIA STREET, DARWEN,
LANCASHIRE BB3 2DR
☎ (01254) 873994. OPEN 9 - 5 MON - FRI, 9 - 2 SAT.
Architectural Salvage • *DIY/Renovation*
Ceramics, terracotta, floor coverings, traditional sanitaryware, glazed brick, Belfast sinks, architectural antiques, reclaimed building materials, timber, stone, slate, pine stripping.

ARENA KITCHENS AND APPLIANCES LTD
2A HEAVILY GROVE, HEAVILY, STOCKPORT, LANCASHIRE SK2 6HQ
☎ (0161) 456 1187. OPEN 9.30 - 5.30 MON - FRI, 9 - 5 SAT, 11 - 2 SUN.
Permanent Discount Outlet • *Electrical Equipment*
Specialists in Smeg, De Dietrich, Bosch, Neff, stainless steel and American appliances, there are discounts, particularly for cash purchasers.

BARDEN MILL
BARDEN LANE, BURNLEY, LANCASHIRE BB12 0DX
☎ (01282) 420333. OPEN 10 - 6 MON - SAT, 11 - 5 SUN
(LATE NIGHTS TILL 8 THUR APRIL - SEPTEMBER).
Factory Shop • *Womenswear & Menswear* • *Household*
Furniture/Soft Furnishings • *Children*
A true working mill which operates a manufacturing and finishing plant handling all kinds of textiles, especially clothing. Prices are, they claim, unbeat-

able because the retailer is being cut out and you are buying direct. On offer is a full range of branded ladieswear, most of which is overmakes for chainstores. The menswear, ladieswear and childrenswear departments have a huge range of fashionable clothes and everyday wear at a fraction of high street prices. Some items are de-labelled but there are no seconds. Current and surplus high street stock arrives every week. Merchandise includes clothes for all the family; Musbury fabrics and curtains; Briggs Shoes department selling Clarks, K Shoes, Hotter, Sterling & Hunt; great gift ideas in the Hothouse Department, as well as books, luggage, wool, pictures, mirrors and furniture. Shopping takes place on one floor and there is free parking and excellent disabled access.

BARNEYS

JULIA STREET, MANCHESTER M3 1LN

☎ (0161) 833 0533. OPEN 9.30 - 5.30 MON, TUE, WED, FRI, 9.30 - 7 THUR, 10 - 6 SAT, 11 - 5 SUN.

Permanent Discount Outlet • *Womenswear & Menswear*

Versace, Prada, Paul Smith, Armani, Boss, Diesel, Calvin Klein, Iceberg, Moschino, Gianfranco Ferre and Gucci at around half their normal retail value. Prices range from about £20 for a pair of designer sunglasses up to as much as £500 for a Versace suit.

BCP AIRPORT PARKING AND TRAVEL SERVICES

MANCHESTER

☎ (0870) 0134586. WEBSITE: www.bcponline.co.uk

8AM - 9 PM, 7 DAYS A WEEK.

BCP provides secure, value-for-money car parking at Gatwick, Heathrow, luton, Manchester, Glasgow, Bristol, Birmingham, Cardiff, East Midlands, Southampton, Newcastle, Leeds Bradford, Edinburgh, Prestwick and Belfast, with prices from just £2.50 NET per day. For an extra £24.95 (£28.95 at Prestwick and Heathrow), you can save time by being met at the airport terminal on your departure and return as part of BCP's Meet and Greet Parking service. Your car is then taken to the BCP.Co.UK secure car park nearby. Or you can pre-book a chauffeur-driven airport car to and from the airport. This service is ideal if you live within 30 miles of your departure airport - prices start from about £60 return. To book and save at least 15% on the car park gate prices and 10% on lounges and chauffeur-driven cars, phone the BCP reservations line quoting reference 'GDD'. BCP will confirm your booking by post with directions to your car park or details of the pick-up or meeting arrangements as appropriate.

BOHEMIA PERIOD CLOTHING
11 WARNER STREET, ACCRINGTON, LANCASHIRE BB51HW
☎ (01254) 231119. OPEN 10.30 - 5 TUE, THUR - SAT,
CLOSED MON, WED.
Secondhand and Vintage Clothes • *Womenswear & Menswear*
Specialises in Sixties and Seventies gear, although their clothing and accessories dates from the Forties.

BOTTOMS MILL CO LTD
ROCHDALE ROAD, WALSDEN, LANCASHIRE OL14 7UB
☎ (01706) 812691. OPEN 9.30 - 5 MON - SAT, 10.30 - 4.30 SUN.
Factory Shop • *Household* • *Electrical Equipment*
Cotton textile manufacturers, the factory shop sells a wide range of household textiles, pottery, tea towels, sheets, cleaning cloths, lighting and fabrics. Opposite the Gordon Rigg's Garden Centre.

BOUNCING BABES
NEWBROOK COTTAGE, LANDSDOWNE ROAD, ATHERTON,
MANCHESTER, LANCASHIRE M46 9HL
☎ (01942) 894729.
Hire Shops • *Children*
Part of the Baby Equipment Hirers Association (BEHA), which has more than 100 members countrywide. A range of equipment can be hired from high chairs, cots and travel cots to baby car seats and buggies. Some members also hire out party equipment including child-sized tables and chairs. BEHA run an advice line which will try and answer any queries you have regarding hiring services for children. Phone the Babyline on 0831 310355.

BOUNDARY MILL STORES
BURNLEY ROAD, COLNE, LANCASHIRE BB8 8LS
☎ (01282) 865229. OPEN 10 - 6 MON - SAT, 8 ON THUR, 11 - 5 SUN,
10 - 6 BANK HOLS.
Permanent Discount Outlet • *Womenswear & Menswear* • *Children*
Household • *Furniture/Soft Furnishings* • *Sportswear & Equipment*
One of the largest clearance stores in Britain, it covers more than 70,000 sq ft. Some of the top end of the high street designer labels are on sale here for both women and men. The women and men's departments are very extensive - not to mention impressive - and cover the whole range from casual to evening wear, with reductions of between 30% and 70%. There is also a large shoe department; jeans and luggage sections; and a lingerie department. A 25,000 sq ft building next door to the Fashion store sells brand-name home furnishings, glass and china, including Dartington Crystal. Four times a year there are special sales at which prices are discounted still further. Most of the stock is perfect clearance and ends of lines with the occasional marked seconds. There is a large coffee shop, TV lounge and restaurant, and free parking. A recent addition is an adjoining Polo Ralph Lauren factory shop on two storeys selling homeware, childrenswear and men's and women's fashions at discounted prices.

BROOKS FACTORY OUTLET STORES
CAROLINE STREET, WIGAN LANCASHIRE WN3 4HW
☎ (01942) 231205 . OPEN 9.30 - 6 MON - SAT, 11 - 5 SUN.
Permanent Discount Outlet • *Womenswear & Menswear*
Household • *Children* • *Furniture/Soft Furnishings*
Food and Leisure • *Sportswear & Equipment*
Walk through the store and you can't fail to find a bargain. New stock arrives daily from well-known names such as Nike, Reebok, Antler, Gabicci, Gossard, Tommy Hilfiger and Ralph Lauren. Apart from clothes, they sell sportswear, linens, lingerie, accessories, luggge, towels, co-ordinated bed linen, household textiles, duvets, pillows and lots more from names such as Vantona, Hamilton McBride, Helena Springfield, Broomhill, Monogram, Chortex, Zorbit and Christy. Everything under one roof at up to 50% off high street prices.

BRUCE KILNER ARCHITECTURAL SALVAGE
ASHTON'S FIELD FARM, WINDMILL ROAD, WALKDEN, WORSLEY, LANCASHIRE M28 3RP
☎ (0161) 702 8604. OPEN EVERY DAY.
PHONE FOR DETAILS OF OPENING HOURS.
Architectural Salvage • *DIY/Renovation*
Original doors, baths, radiators, sinks, sash windows, Victorian stable fittings, cart wheels, troughs.

BUILT-IN KITCHEN APPLIANCES
70 - 88 BRECK ROAD, LIVERPOOL, MERSEYSIDE LANCASHIRE L4 2RB
☎ (0151) 263 8966. WEBSITE: www.builtinkitchenappliances.com
OPEN 9 - 5 MON - FRI, 9 - 4.30 SAT, 10 - 4 SUN.
Permanent Discount Outlet • *Electrical Equipment*
Hobs, ovens, dishwashers, fridges, freezers, sinks from top brand names such as AEG, Neff, Bosch, Canon, Franke, all at prices which can be up to 30% off top department store prices. If you know the make and model number of the item you want, phone and find out their best price.

BUMPSADAISY MATERNITY STYLE
6 DAMSIDE STREET, LANCASTER, LANCASHIRE LA1 1PB
☎ (01524) 382 022. WEBSITE: www.bumpsadaisy.co.uk
OPEN 9.30 - 5 MON - SAT.
Hire Shop • *Womenswear Only*
Franchised shops and home-based branches with large range of specialist maternity wear, from wedding outfits to ball gowns, to hire and to buy. Hire costs range from £30 to £100 for special occasion wear. To buy are lots of casual and business wear in sizes 8 - 18. For example, skirts £20-£70; dresses £40-£100. Also four branches run by young mums from their homes, specialising in hiring but also stocking a small retail range (Camberley, Edgbaston, Exeter and Southampton). Phone 0208-789 0329 for details.

CATALOGUE BARGAIN SHOP
THE BEEHIVE MILL, CRESCENT ROAD, GREAT WEAVER, BOLTON
☎ (01204) 361159. OPEN 10 - 5 MON - FRI, 9 - 4.30 SAT.
LORNE STREET, FARNWORTH, BOLTON BL1 2DY
☎ (01204) 573511. OPEN 10 - 4.30 MON - FRI, 7 ON TUE, WED, THUR, 9 - 4.30 SAT, 10.30 - 4.30 SUN.
KINGSWAY, BURNLEY BB11 1AB
☎ (01282) 420202. OPEN 9 - 5 MON - SAT, 6.45 ON THUR, 10.30 - 4 SUN.
40-42 MARKET STREET, CHORLEY, LANCASHIRE BB11 1AA
☎ (012572) 68325. OPEN 9 - 5.30 MON - SAT, 10.30 - 4.30 SUN.
HALL BANK, WORSLEY, ECCLES, MANCHESTER, LANCASHIRE M30 8NR
☎ (0161) 787 7726. OPEN 10 - 5.30 MON - FRI, 8 ON THUR, 9 - 5 SAT, 10 - 4.30 SUN.
82/83 EGARTON WALK, ELLESMERE CENTRE, WALKDEN, MANCHESTER M28 3ZD
☎ (0161) 703 9311. OPEN 9 - 5.30 MON - SAT.
Permanent Discount Outlet • *Womenswear & Menswear Children • Household • Electrical Equipment*
Catalogue Bargain Shop is a growing national chain of stores which obtains the majority of its goods from mail order giants Great Universal and Kays, and offers a range of clothing for all the family, a wide selection of shoes, bed linen, household goods, electrical equipment and hundreds of other catalogue items at very competitive prices. The merchandise consists of ends of ranges and previous season's stock for which there is no longer storage space when the catalogues change.

CHATLEYS
14 CHATLEY STREET, MANCHESTER LANCASHIRE M3 1HX
☎ (0161) 833 3230. OPEN 10 - 6 MON - FRI, 7 ON THUR, 10 - 5 SAT, SUN.
Permanent Discount Outlet • *Menswear Only*
Classic clothes for men from Gabicci, Oakman and Peter England. Shirts, trousers, ties, coats and shoes are all discounted by 20%.

CHILTON ARCHITECTURAL ANTIQUES
36 INGLEWHITE ROAD, LONGRIDGE, NEAR PRESTON, LANCASHIRE PR3 3JS
☎ (01257) 273095. OPEN 10 - 4 MON - SAT, CLOSED WED.
Architectural Salvage • *DIY/Renovation* • *Furniture/Soft Furnishingst*
Freestanding furniture for the kitchen; sets of shelves made from the Bible rests on the back of old church pews; dressers made from old wood; tables, pottery; old church pews also for sale, as well as Belfast sinks and old brass taps.

CHORTEX TOWEL MILL SHOP
VICTORIA MILL, CHORLEY NEW ROAD, HORWICH, NEAR BOLTON, LANCASHIRE BL6 6ER
☎ (01204) 695611. OPEN 9 - 4.45 MON - FRI, 7 ON THUR, 10 - 3 SAT.
Factory Shop • *Household*
Sells top quality plain dyed towels in every colour imaginable, produced in their own factory in Horwich. Embellished towels, towelling robes, beach towels, duvets, pillows, bleached 100% Egyptian cotton sheets, easy-care polyester cotton sheets, double ended oven gloves, dusters, dishcloths, handkerchiefs, bath mats and shower curtains are also stocked, together with other bathroom accessories.

CHURCHILL CHINA
FREEPORT SHOPPING VILLAGE, FLEETWOOD, LANCASHIRE FY7 6AE
☎ (01253) 773927. OPEN 10 - 6 SEVEN DAYS A WEEK, 8 ON THUR, FRI.
Factory Shop in a Factory Shopping Village • *Household*
Top quality fine bone china, tableware and mugs from Queens and Churchill at discount prices of up to 30%. All are seconds.

CLARKSON FABRIC
VIVARY MILL, NORTH VALLEY ROAD, COLNE, LANCASHIRE BB8 9RG
☎ (01282) 871947. OPEN 10 - 5 MON - SAT, UNTIL 7 ON THUR, 10.30 - 4 SUN.
Permanent Discount Outlet • *Furniture/Soft Furnishings*
Sells a wide range of curtain fabric as well as three-piece suites and upholstery fabric. They stock at least 200 different voiles, as well as cotton prints, jacquards, damasks, linens and chenille by brands such as Swatch Box, SMD and Ashley Wilde. Prices range between £1.50 and £18 a metre.

CRESTA FURNITURE
RIBBLETON LANE, PRESTON, LANCASHIRE PR1 5LB
☎ (01772) 797474. OPEN 9 - 6 MON - SAT, 11 - 5 SUN.
Permanent Discount Outlet • *Furniture/Soft Furnishings*
Permanent discount outlet which endeavours to offer top of the range leather furniture at competive prices by buying large quantities from the largest manufacturers. They offer both "family" leather sofas made of a coarser grade of leather, designed to withstand heavy usage and the softer, supple aniline leathers, which are more expensive. Their range starts at £389 for a three-seater Chesterfield up to £4,000.

CROFT MILL
LOWTHER LANE, FOULRIDGE, COLNE, LANCASHIRE BB8 7NG
☎ (01282) 869625. OPEN 10 - 4 SEVEN DAYS A WEEK.
ALSO MAIL ORDER.

Factory Shop • *Womenswear Only* • *Furniture/Soft Furnishings*

Sells fabric, dress and furnishing, haberdashery and sheeting material, both in the shop and by mail order. Also stock high quality upholstery fabrics and chenilles and offer a home make up service. Most of the fabrics are over-runs, samples, ends of lines, bankrupt stock and some seconds. Nearly all, including the dress fabrics, are 60" (150cm) wide and range in price from £1.50 to £6.95 or so a metre. They include cottons, jerseys, sweatshirting, drills, linings, anorak fabric, coatings, and suitings. They send out a catalogue describing their current stock every two months or so and will supply samples up to ten items for £1; up to 30 items for £2; up to 50 items for £5, all of which is refundable if you make a purchase. Most have been manufactured for high street store clothes for shops such as Marks & Spencer, BhS, Laura Ashley and for Dorma. There are also pillows, cushion pads, tea towels and quilts, all at factory shop prices.

DALE BATHROOM AND TILE FACTORY
77 DALE STREET, MANCHESTER, LANCASHIRE M1 2HG
☎ (0161) 236 4645. OPEN 9 - 5 MON - FRI, 10 - 4 SAT, SUN.

Factory Shop • *DIY/Renovation*

Makes baths which it sells direct to the public at competitive prices. Unlike most acrylic baths which are made from 5m deep sheets of acrylic, Dale's baths are handmade from 10ml sheets, making them strong, durable and heat retentive. The factory shop also sells a full range of bathroom and shower accessories, sinks, stone resin shower trays, shower cubicles, showers which work off a standard hot water system, and tiles which are imported directly from the factory in Spain.

DALE MILL DISCOUNTS
DALE STREET, MILNROW, NEAR ROCHDALE, LANCASHIRE OL16 3NJ
☎ (01706) 359737. OPEN 9.30 - 6 MON - WED, FRI, 9.30 - 8 THUR, 9.30 - 5.30 SAT, 10 - 5.30 SUN.

Permanent Discount Outlet • *Womenswear & Menswear* • *Children Household* • *Electrical Equipment* • *Furniture/Soft Furnishings*

A wide range of items from clothes and shoes for all the family to kitchenware, furniture, tablecloths, beds and bedding, TVs and general electrical goods, fridges, cookers, microwaves, kitchen and bedroom fittings and units, all on sale at discounted prices. On site there is also a designer clothes store and sportswear outlet.

DAMART
85-87 DEANE ROAD, BOLTON, LANCASHIRE
☎ (0120) 452 4608. OPEN 9.30 - 5 MON - SAT.
Factory Shop • *Womenswear & Menswear*

Damart underwear and merchandise - anything from tights, socks and gloves to dresses, coats, cardigans and jumpers - some of which is current stock sold at full price, some discontinued and ends of lines sold at discount. There several shops selling some discounted stock from the Damart range, known as Damart Extra.

DARTINGTON CRYSTAL
BOUNDARY MILL, BURNLEY ROAD, COLNE, LANCASHIRE BB8 8LS
☎ (01282) 865229. OPEN 10 - 6 MON - SAT, 8 ON THUR, 11 - 5 SUN.
FREEPORT VILLAGE, ANCHORAGE ROAD, FLEETWOOD FY7 6AE
☎ (01253) 872272. OPEN 10 - 6 SEVEN DAYS A WEEK, 8 ON THUR, FRI.
Factory Shop in a Factory Shopping Village • *Household*

An extensive range of Dartington Crystal seconds at greatly reduced prices as well as some perfect crystal at full price. Range includes wine suites, sherry glasses, tankards, decanters, rippled glass, fruit and salad bowls.

DESIGNER FINE FRAGRANCES
PO BOX 231, BOLTON, LANCASHIRE BL3 4FF
☎ (01204) 650132. E-MAIL: sale@design-r-co.uk   MAIL ORDER ONLY.
Permanent Discount Outlet • *Womenswear Only*

Up to 75% off well-known fragrances. Specialises in the newer lines from Calvin Klein, Dolce & Gabbana, Armani, Versace and Polo Sport.

DOUBLE TWO
FREEPORT SHOPPING VILLAGE, FLEETWOOD, LANCASHIRE
☎ (01253) 777117. OPEN 10 - 6 SEVEN DAYS A WEEK,
UNTIL 8 THUR, FRI.
Factory Shop in a Factory Shopping Village • *Womenswear & Menswear*

Men's shirts (both casual and formal), belts, ties, jeans and dress shirts and women's blouses, co-ordinates, dresses, trousers, skirts and waistcoats at discount prices of about 30%-50%.

ECHOES
650A HALIFAX ROAD, EASTWOOD, TODMORDEN,
LANCASHIRE OL14 6DW
☎ (01706) 817505. OPEN 11 - 6 WED - SAT, 12 - 5 SUN.
Secondhand and Vintage Clothes • *Womenswear & Menswear*

Stocks period clothing for men and women from the Victorian era to the 1960s. Also stocks accessories such as hats, bags, scarves, shoes and jewellery.

EVANS
FREEPORT VILLAGE FLEETWOOD, ANCHORAGE ROAD,
JUNCTION 12 OF M55, LANCASHIRE FY7 6AE
☎ (01253) 878554. OPEN 10 - 6 SEVEN DAYS A WEEK, 8 ON THUR, FRI.
Factory Shop in a Factory Shopping Village • *Womenswear Only*
End of season lines with the normal Evans refund guarantee. The range includes tailoring, soft dressing, dresses, Profile, knitwear, East Coast (denim/jeans), lingerie/nightwear, blouses, coats, outerwear and accessories.

FELICITY HAT HIRE
22 THURNHAM STREET, LANCASTER, LANCASHIRE LA1 1XY
☎ (01524) 381822. OPEN 10 - 5 MON - SAT.
Hire Shops • *Womenswear Only*
Elegant hats to hire from £15 - £45, including some by Frederick Fox. Ascot hats and wedding hats a speciality. Also hires out unusual bags for the evening.

FINSLEY MILL SHOP
FINSLEY GATE, BURNLEY, LANCASHIRE.
☎ (01282) 471283. OPEN 9.30 - 5 MON - FRI, 9 - 4 SAT.
Permanent Discount Outlet • *Children* • *Womenswear & Menswear Household*
High Street brand name mens' ladies' and some children's shoes at discounts of up to 50% from toddlers' size upwards. Slippers, trainers, Wellingtons, school and party shoes, as well as a small range of ladies clothes, some pottery and towels, all this season's chainstore seconds, mostly made for Marks & Spencer. As we went to press, there was a possibility of the shop relocating, so do phone before making a special journey.

FOUR SEASONS
154 COLLEGE ROAD, CROSBY, LIVERPOOL, LANCASHIRE L23 3DP
☎ (0151) 924 2863. OPEN 9.30 - 5.30 MON - SAT.
Hire Shop • *Womenswear Only*
Specialists in hiring and selling hats, Four Seasons has been in business for 15 years and has more than 450 hats from which to choose. The main business is in hiring hats for all occasions - customers can bring their outfit to find the perfect match, and trimmings can be added from as little as £2.50. Hire fees start from £10 up to £30 for a period of 4 days or longer by arrangement. There are also accessories for sale, particularly jewellery, scarves, gloves and handbags. Ex-hire hats are sold off at reasonable prices.

FREEPORT FLEETWOOD OUTLET VILLAGE
ANCHORAGE ROAD, FLEETWOOD, 12 MILES FROM JUNCTION 3 OF M55, LANCASHIRE FY7 6AE
☎ (01253) 877377. OPEN 10 - 6 SEVEN DAYS A WEEK, 8 ON THUR, FRI.
Factory Shopping Village • *Womenswear & Menswear* • *Children*

Household • Food and Leisure • Sportswear & Equipment
Furniture/Soft Furnishings

Large, brightly-coloured seaside shopping village with New England fishing village theme complete with authentic American Diner. There are more than 50 shops selling at up to 50% off high street prices, as well as restaurants, family attractions, free parking and free entry. Women's fashions include Next to Nothing, Spotlight, Honey, Easy Jeans, VF Corp, Double Two, Evans, Warner's, Jane Shilton, Edinburgh Woollen Mill, The Designer Room, Giorgio, BHS for Less and Roman Originals. For men, there is The Suit Company, Petroleum, Ciro Citterio, Double Two, Giorgio, VF Corp, Easy Jeans and BHS for Less. Sportswear and outdoor wear shops include The Sports Mill, Craghoppers, Regatta and London Leathers. Footwear outlets comprise Briggs Shoes, Jane Shilton, Shoe Sellers, Next to Nothing and The Sports Mill. Sweet-toothed visitors can indulge at Thornton's factory shop, The Sweet Shop, and for snacks and savouries, there is Julian Graves. Household outlets include Bed & Bath Works, Churchill China, Ponden Mill, Dartington Crystal and China Traders. Childrenswear stockists include Next to Nothing, BhS for Less, Vecopri, VF Corp and Giorgio, while for teenage girls there is Spotlight, Claire's Accessories and Pilot. Other stores include Woods of Windsor, Hallmark Cards and Gifts, XS Music & Video, Luggage & Bags and Book Depot.

GARDENERS CHOICE MILL SHOP

STANDROYD MILL, COTTONTREE, COLNE, LANCASHIRE BB8 7BW
☎ (01282) 873341. OPEN 9 - 5 MON - FRI, 9 - 4 SAT, 10 - 4 SUN.

Factory Shop • *Food and Leisure*

Horticultural and garden sundries specialists catering for the smaller garden. You can visit the small factory shop or go next door and buy in bulk. Items on sale include spades, gloves, bulbs, seeds, benches, cloches, hanging baskets, cane trellis, secateurs, wheelbarrows, pergolas, garden furniture, fertiliser, weedkiller, insecticide, hose pipes, poly tunnels. They don't sell electrical gardening instruments or plants.

GDS DISCOUNT FURNITURE STORE

GREAT DUCIE STREET, MANCHESTER.
☎ (0161) 834 8375. OPEN 0 - 5.30 MON - THUR, 9.30 - 5 FRI,
10 - 5 SAT, 10.30 - 4.30 SUN.

Permanent Discount Outlet • *Furniture/Soft Furnishings*

Up to seventy suites on show at this store which features both top of the market and mass market suites. By buying over-runs and cancelled orders from the main manufacturers, they are able to stock some of the best names including Lebus, Christie Tyler, Lifestyle and Pendragon, the leather specialists. Suites range from £490 to £2,000.

GERARDS FROZEN FOOD CENTRE
WILLIAM STREET, ARDWICK, MANCHESTER M12 5FX
☏ (0161) 274 3622. PHONE FOR OPENING TIMES. MAIL ORDER.
Food and Drink Discounters

Branded foods at low prices which, they claim, are lower than Iceland except when the latter is running a special offer. You will find anything here that you would find in a freezer centre from oven chips and fish fingers to frozen desserts. During the summer, the outlet reverts to an ice cream shop.

GIFT TREE
REEDYFORD MILL, WESTFIELD ROAD, NELSON, LANCASHIRE BB9 7TT
☏ (01282) 619540. OPEN 9 - 5 MON - SAT.
Permanent Discount Outlet • *Household* • *Children*
Food and Leisure • *Furniture/Soft Furnishings*
Womenswear & Menswear

Permanent discount outlet selling ex-catalogue stock including a wide range of cards and gifts, a mixture of toys and children's equipment with household goods, Royal Doulton collectables, pixtures, teapots, furniture, towels and clothes. There is always a good range of cards, especially around Christmas, and toys including jigsaws, babies toys and Galt toys.

GLYN WEBB
UNIT A, ORLANDO STREET, OFF MANCHESTER ROAD, BOLTON, LANCASHIRE BL2 1DY
☏ (01204) 365806. OPEN 9 - 8 MON - SAT, 11 - 5 SUN AND OPEN ALL BANK HOLIDAYS.
144-146 BLACKBURN ROAD, ACCRINGTON BB5 OAB
☏ (01254) 236831. OPEN 9 - 8 MON - SAT, 11 - 5 SUN AND OPEN ALL BANK HOLIDAYS.
HILL STREET, OFF HUDDERSFIELD ROAD, OLDHAM OL4 2AG
☏ (0161) 620 4415. OPEN 9 - 8 MON - SAT, 11 - 5 SUN AND BANK HOLS.
126 RIBBLETON LANE, PRESTON PR1 5LB
☏ (01772) 794373. OPEN 9 - 8 MON - SAT, 10 - 4 SUN AND BANK HOLS.
DENTONS GREEN LANE, DENTONS GREEN, ST HELENS, MERSEYSIDE WA10 2QB
☏ (01744) 454798. OPEN 9 - 8 MON - SAT, 10 - 4 SUN AND BANK HOLS.
BRIGHTON MILL, SPENCER STREET, OLDHAM OL1 3QF
☏ (0161) 620 4415. OPEN 9 - 8 MON - SAT, 10 - 4 SUN AND BANK HOLS.
UNIT A, THE NEW MERSEY WAY RETAIL PARK, SPEKE ROAD, SPEKE, LIVERPOOL L24 8QB
☏ (0151) 494 0421. OPEN 9 - 8 MON - SAT, 10 - 4 SUN AND BANK HOLS.
641 HYDE ROAD, BELLEVUE, MANCHESTER M12 5PS
☏ (0161) 230 8099. OPEN 9 - 8 MON - SAT, 10 - 4 SUN AND BANK HOLS.
231 VICARAGE LANE, BLACKPOOL FX4 4NG
☏ (01253) 692549. OPEN 9 - 8 MON - SAT, 10 - 4 SUN AND BANK HOLS.
Permanent Discount Outlet • *DIY/Renovation*

Stockists of all your home improvement needs from wallpaper to paint, furniture to flooring, tiles to textiles, housewares to lighting - in fact, almost everything for your home, with 25 branches in the North-West, Midlands and Yorkshire. Specialists in discontinued mail order, slightly imperfect branded stocks as well as perfect quality superior products, they carry top brands such as Dulux, Crown Paints and Vymura and Coloroll wall coverings, Rectella and Norwood textiles and much more in store. To find your nearest branch, phone Head Office on 0161 621 4500.

GORSE MILL LIGHTING
GORDON STREET, OFF JARDINE WAY, BROADWAY, CHADDERTON, OLDHAM, LANCASHIRE OL9 9RJ
☎ (0161) 628 4202. FAX (0161) 6520945. OPEN 9.30 - 5 MON - FRI, 7 ON THUR, 10 - 5 SAT, 11 - 5 SUN.
Permanent Discount Outlet • *Electrical Equipment* • *Household*
240,000 sq feet dedicated to lighting up your home. One of Britain's largest decorative light manufacturers, this shop claims to house the biggest display of lighting, halogen, garden and security lights as well as crystal fittings at savings averaging 30% off high street prices. Lamp shades start at as little as 50p and also come in a variety of sizes, patterns and colours. Gorse Mill supplies major chain stores and has vast ranges of decorative lighting, outdoor lighting, crystal chandeliers, as well as Chinese and Portuguese pottery. Coffee shop, parking for 300 cars, disabled facilities.

GREENBRIDGE FACTORY SHOP
GREEN WORKS, GREENBRIDGE, FALLBARN ROAD, RAWTENSTALL, ROSSENDALE, LANCASHIRE BB4 7NX
☎ (01706) 235160. OPEN 9.30 - 5 MON - FRI, 9 - 4 SAT, 10 - 4 SUN.
Factory Shop • *Womenswear & Menswear*
High street chainstore seconds specialising in footwear. Also sells ladies clothes, towels, handbags, pottery and a small selection of menswear.

HALLMARK
FREEPORT SHOPPING VILLAGE, ANCHORAGE ROAD, FLEETWOOD, LANCASHIRE FY7 6AE
☎ (01253) 773854. OPEN 10 - 6 SEVEN DAYS A WEEK, UNTIL 8 THUR, FRI.
Factory Shop • *Food and Leisure*
A wide range of cards to suit every occasion, as well as stuffed toys, wrapping paper, rosettes, gift cards from names such as Andrew Brownswood and Gordon Fraser. Almost all the stock here is ends of lines as the card business demands constant change and therefore some unsold lines. Most of the items are half price. Cafes on site as well as children's play areas; free parking.

HAMLET'S FAMOUS NAMES
32 STAVELEIGH WAY, LADYSMITH CENTRE, ASHTON,
LANCASHIRE OL6 7JJ
☎ (0161) 343 5127. OPEN 9 - 5.30 MON - SAT.
Permanent Discount Outlet • *Electrical Equipment*
Sells ends of lines and A-grade manufacturers' returns of electrical goods which dealers have sent back to suppliers as faulty and which have then been repaired to the original specification at discounts of up to 50%. These include Panasonic, Toshiba, JVC, Philips, Sony, Sharp and Aiwa television sets, videos, hi-fis, camcorders, portable audios and walkmans.

HARTLEYS MAIL ORDER LTD
REGENT HOUSE, WHITEWALLS INDUSTRIAL ESTATE, COLNE,
LANCASHIRE BB8 8LJ
☎ (01282) 861350. E-MAIL: regenthouse@whitewalls,fsnet,co.uk.
OPEN 9.30 - 4.30 MON - FRI AND MAIL ORDER
(UK ORDERS C & H CHARGE ONLY £3.50).
Permanent Discount Outlet • *Household* • *Furniture/Soft Furnishings*
Fragrance lines from manufacturers who supply well-known high street names, this company, which has been established for 35 years, sells calico, voile, muslin, sheeting, pillows, dress fabric, towels, quilts, ready made bedding, curtaining, many of which are well-known brand names, as well as selected kitchenware and garden furniture. Curtaining is available from £2 to £20 a metre, dress fabrics from 99p a yard; plus a large stock of poly/cottons, cottons and wool and silks. Curtaining can also be ordered from the curtain range books in the shop which include Crowson and Moygashel. Prices are the same whether you buy through the on-site shop or by mail order, although many offers are available through the shop only. Parking available. Send five 2nd class stamps for samples and a free copy of Hartleys' most recent offers.

HI-LIFE DINERS CLUB
THE EPICENTRE, 5 HARDHORN ROAD, POULTON, NEAR BLACKPOOL,
LANCASHIRE FY6 7SR
☎ (01253) 884477. 24-HOUR MEMBERSHIP LINE.
The Hi-Life Club has been operating for more than 15 years in the north-west of England and is the biggest diners' club of its type, with more than 25,000 members. Members can choose from among 700 Lancashire restaurants, most of which now give two meals for the price of one. Restaurants included vary and include Nico Central, Gary Rhodes & Co, Mash & Air, Cafe Rouge, Henry's table, Beefeaters, Brewers' Fare, Millers' Kitchen, TGI Fridays etc. Every cuisine is covered form French to Indian, English or Mexican. The club literature says that most people save £100s or even £1000s per year and there's a no-quibbble money back guarantee if you're not delighted with your membership. Membership costs £35.95 per annum.

HOLLIN HALL CRAFT & SEWING CENTRE

EMPRESS MILLS (1927) LTD, HOLLIN HALL MILL, TRAWDEN, COLNE,
LANCASHIRE BB8 8SS
☎ (01282) 863181. FAX ☎ (01282) 870935.
E-MAIL: chris@empressmills.co.uk   WEBSITE: www.empressmills.co.uk
OPEN 9 - 5 MON - FRI, 10 - 4 SAT, SUN. MAIL ORDER.

Factory Shop • *Furniture/Soft Furnishings*

At Hollin Craft & Sewing Centre, you will find a modern, working thread mill. The Centre houses all the threads and yarns previously only available to industry. Here, you can buy extraordinary threads at factory prices. Hand and machine quilting, endless overlocking types, tailoring, household textiles, tacking, speciality bookbinding, machine and hand embroidery are all on show. The haberdashery section stocks a similarly huge variety including many types of zip fastener. In the large, two-floor shop, they also accommodate the Thread Collection, plus books, kits, and innumerable crafts including stencilling, stamping & embossing, American innovations, decoupage, beading, hardanger, dolls houses and furniture. There are also ceramics, glassware, wood, candles and wicker in the exclusive Gift and Homewares section. All this is available by mail order, worldwide. Set in the heart of the countryside, there are workshops, demos and good walking routes nearby.

HONEY

FREEPORT SHOPPING VILLAGE, ANCHORAGE ROAD, FLEETWOOD,
LANCASHIRE FY7 6AE
☎ (01253) 777123. OPEN 10 - 6 SEVEN DAYS A WEEK, 8 ON THUR, FRI.

Factory Shop in a Factory Shopping Village • *Womenswear Only*

Leisure-oriented women's T-shirts, leggings and sweaters at discounts of mostly 30% TO 50%.

IN SITU

TALBOT MILL, 44 ELLESMERE STREET, HULME,
LANCASHIRE M15 4JY
☎ (0161) 839 5525. OPEN 10 - 5.30 MON - SAT, 11 - 4 SUN.
149 BARTON ROAD, STRETFORD, MANCHESTER M32 8DB
OPEN 9 - 5.30, 10 - 4 SUN.

Architectural Salvage • *DIY/Renovation*

Church interiors, period fireplaces, doors, leaded glass, antique bathrooms, garden ware, staircases, chimney pots, furniture, flooring. Deliver anywhere. Period fireplaces cost from £50 for a small cast-iron bedroom fireplace; baths from £100; reclaimed maple strip flooring from £18 per square yard.

J B CARPETS LTD
UNIT F2, TOLLBAR BUSINESS PARK, NEW CHURCH ROAD, STACKSTEADS, BACUP, LANCASHIRE OL13 ONA
☎ (01706) 875709. OPEN 9 - 5 MON - FRI, 9 - 4.30 SAT, 10 - 4 SUN.
Permanent Discount Outlet • *Furniture/Soft Furnishings*

Most of the stock here is clearance stock from middle of the road brand names such as Berbers, Axminster Wilton, Saxony, at discounts of at least 50%. 80/20 twists and 50/50 wool twists from £4.99-£8.99, free delivery. Bigger, better and cheaper than before: the more you spend, the bigger the discount.

JAEGER FACTORY SHOP
BOUNDARY MILLS, BURNLEY ROAD, COLNE, LANCASHIRE BB8 8LS
☎ (01282) 865229. OPEN 10 - 6 MON - SAT, 10 - 8 THUR, 11 - 5 SUN.
Factory Shop • *Womenswear & Menswear*

Contemporary classics from Jaeger at excellent prices. Most of the merchandise is previous seasons' stock, but you might also find some special makes. This shop stocks tailoring and knitwear for women only.

JANE SHILTON
FREEPORT SHOPPING VILLAGE, ANCHORAGE ROAD, FLEETWOOD, LANCASHIRE FY7 6AE
☎ (01253) 773875. OPEN 10 - 6 SEVEN DAYS A WEEK, UNTIL 8 THUR, FRI.
Factory Shop in a Factory Shopping Village • *Womenswear Only*

Merchandise from past seasons' collections or factory seconds at discounts of at least 30% and up to 70% off the original price. There is a wide range of handbags, small leather goods, shoes, luggage umbrellas and travel bags. Example of price reduction: handbags at £24.99 originally £37.

JORGUS CARPETS
GRIMEFORD MILL, GRIMEFORD LANE, ANDERTON, NEAR CHORLEY, LANCASHIRE PR6 9HL
☎ (01257) 482636. OPEN 8 - 5 MON - FRI, 8.30 - 3 SAT, 11 - 3 SUN, CLOSED 12 - 1 WEEKDAYS.
Factory Shop • *Furniture/Soft Furnishings*

Manufacture twist, plain, tweed and wool carpets at discounted prices, although most of the stock is plain. Bedroom quality carpets 80% wool/20% nylon costs £7.99 a sq yd. Lounge quality carpet, 40 ounce twist pile, costs £9.99 a sq yd, which represents a 50% discount.

JUMPER
BRIDGE MILL, COWAN BRIDGE, CARNFORTH, LANCASHIRE LA6 2HS
☎ (015242) 71071. OPEN 10 - 4 SEVEN DAYS A WEEK IN WINTER, 10 - 5 SUMMER.
BOUNDARY MILL 65229. OPEN 9 - 6 MON - SAT, 11 - 5 SUN. B8 8LS
☎ (01282) 865229. OPEN 9 - 6 MON - SAT, 11 - 5 SUN.

Factory Shop • *Womenswear & Menswear*

A wide range of Jumper label sweaters, gloves, scarves, shirts and cardigans for men and women all at discount prices of up to 50% off. Prices start at £2.

K SHOES

UNIT 3, CLIFTON ROAD RETAIL PARK, BLACKPOOL,
LANCASHIRE FY4 4RA
☎ (01253) 699380. OPEN 9.30 - 7.30 MON - FRI AND BANK HOLIDAYS,
9 - 5.30 SAT, 10 - 4 SUN, 9.30 - 6 BANK HOLIDAYS.
18/19 WILLIAMSON SQUARE, LIVERPOOL, MERSEYSIDE L1 1EJ
☎ (0151) 708 7564. OPEN 9 - 5.30 MON - SAT.
21 CHURCH STREET, ECCLES, GREATER MANCHESTER M30 OAF
☎ (0161) 788 7039. OPEN 9 - 5.30 MON - SAT, 10 - 3.30 WED.

Factory Shop • *Womenswear & Menswear* • *Children*

Clarks International operate a chain of factory shops nationally which specialise in selling discontinued lines and slight sub-standards for children, women and men from Clarks, K Shoes and other famous brands. These shops trade under the name of Crockers, K Shoes Factory shop or Clarks Factory Shop and while not all are physically attached to a shoe factory, these shops are treated as factory shops by the company. Customers can expect to find an extensive range of quality shoes, sandals, walking boots, slippers, trainers, handbags, accessories and gifts, while their major outlets also offer luggage, sports clothing, sports equipment and outdoor clothing. Brands stocked include Clarks, K Shoes, Springer, CICA, Hi-Tec, Puma, Mercury, Fila, Mizuno, Slazenger, Samsonite, Delsey, Antler and Carlton, although not all are sold in every outlet. Discounts are on average 30% off the normal high street price for perfect stock.

KARRIMOR

PETRE ROAD, CLAYTON-LE-MOORS, ACCRINGTON,
LANCASHIRE BB5 5JZ
☎ (01254) 893134. OPEN 10 - 5 MON - FRI, 7.30 ON THUR, 10 - 4 SAT.

Factory Shop • *Sportswear & Equipment*

Best known for their comprehensive range of rucksacks, Karrimor also make an outstanding range of outdoor equipment for walkers, climbers and campers. The factory shop sells seconds, former display items and clearance stock at discounts of between 15% and 25% and always stocks the current range for the season.

KIPPAX BISCUITS

FACTORY SHOP, KING STREET, COLNE, LANCASHIRE BB8 9HU
☎ (01282) 864 198. OPEN 10 - 3.45 MON, WED, FRI, SAT, CLOSED 1 - 1.15.

Food and Drink Discounters

More than 100 different types of biscuits from ginger wafers and shortbread to plain assorted and chocolate sold in packets, tins or loose. Broken biscuits also sold very cheaply. Coach parties welcome by prior appointment only.

LAMBERT HOWARTH FOOTWEAR
GREENBRIDGE WORKS, FALBARN ROAD, OFF BOCHOLT WAY,
RAWTENSTAL, ROSSENDALE, LANCASHIRE.
☎ (01706) 235160. OPEN 10.30 - 5 MON - THUR, 10 - 1 FRI, 9.30 - 3.30 SAT.
Factory Shop • *Womenswear & Menswear* • *Children* • *Household*
A real mixture of seconds from their own factories and perfects from other sources - footwear, clothes, handbags and towels. The seconds in footwear are from shoes made for major high street chainstores and all are at discounted prices. These include slippers, walking boots, flat shoes and sandals for men, women and children. The perfects in clothes, towels and bags are two-thirds of the high street prices. Also large selection of pottery.

LAURA ASHLEY
BOUNDARY MILL STORES, BURNLEY ROAD, COLNE,
LANCASHIRE BB8 8LS
☎ (01282) 867511. OPEN 10 - 6 MON - WED, FRI AND SAT, 10 - 8 THUR,
11 - 5 SUN.
Permanent Discount Outlet • *Furniture/Soft Furnishings*
At Boundary Mill Stores, Laura Ashley furnishings are housed in a special homewares building next to the huge high quality clearance warehouse for men and women's clothes. Most of the merchandise is made up of perfect carry-overs from the high street shops around the country, though there are also some discontinued lines. Stock reflects the normal high street variety, though at least one season later and with less choice in colours.

LBS HORTICULTURE
COTTON TREE, NEAR TRAWDEN, COLNE, LANCASHIRE BB8 7BW
☎ (01282) 871777. OPEN 9 - 5 MON - FRI, 9 - 4 SAT, 10 - 4 SUN.
MAIL ORDER.
Factory Shop • *Household* • *Food and Leisure*
Suppliers of all gardening equipment from wheelbarrows to gardening gloves by both mail order and in the on-site shop. Sells grass seed, plant pots, furniture and trugs, wheelbarrows, hose pipes, cloches, fertiliser, plant labels and padded jackets. Prices are trade plus VAT. Car parking, disabled access.

LITTLEWOODS CATALOGUE DISCOUNT STORE
160 MARINE ROAD, CENTRAL MORECAMBE, LANCASHIRE LA4 4BU
☎ (01524) 412074. OPEN 9.30 - 5.30 MON, 9 - 5.30 TUE - SAT,
10.30 - 4.30 SUN.
69-74 LORD STREET, FLEETWOOD FY7 6DS
☎ (01253) 773418. OPEN 9 - 5.30 MON - SAT, 11 - 5 SUN.
UNIT 3, MONUMENT BUILDINGS, LONDON ROAD, LIVERPOOL L3 8JY
☎ (0151) 708 6118. OPEN 9 - 5.30 MON - SAT.
UNIT 2, KINGS STREET, FARNWORTH BL4 7AZ
☎ (01204) 861464. OPEN 9 - 5.30 MON - SAT, 7 ON THUR, FRI,
11 - 5 SUN.

LANCASHIRE

102 DEANSGATE, BOLTON BL1 1 BD
☎ (01204) 527 669. OPEN 9.30 - 5.30 MON - WED, 9 - 5.30 THUR - SAT.
185 STAMFORD STREET, ASHTON-UNDER-LYME,
GREATER MANCHESTER OL6 7PY
☎ (0161) 339 0966. OPEN 9.30 - 5.30 MON - SAT.
Permanent Discount Outlet • *Womenswear & Menswear*
Electrical Equipment • *Children*
Littlewoods clearance shops offering up to 50% off the catalogue price for clothing and between 50% and 60% off for electrical goods. Stock changes constantly and varies from day to day but can include well-known brand names such as Berlei and Gossard lingerie, Vivienne Westwood, Pamplemousse leisure wear, Nike and Adidas sports shoes, Workers for Freedom, and Timberland and Caterpillar footwear. Stock depends on the size and location of the shop, so larger shops will get the longer discontinued runs and smaller shops over-runs with only a small amount of colour and size variations left. Littlewoods also run a mobile shop which operates in cities where they don't have a sale shop. For details of further venues for the sales, which usually take place once a month, contact Melanie Lamb, c/o Crosby DC Kershaw Avenue, Endbutt Lane, Crosby, Merseyside L70 1AH.

LONDON LEATHERS DIRECT
FREEPORT VILLAGE, ANCHORAGE ROAD, FLEETWOOD,
LANCASHIRE FY7 6AE
☎ (01253) 779090. OPEN 10 - 6 SEVEN DAYS A WEEK, 8 THUR, FRI.
Factory Shop in a Factory Shopping Village • *Womenswear & Menswear*
Very good quality leather nubuck and suede jackets and coats at discounts of at least 30%, with most at 50% off in this village which features lots of restaurants and fun things for the family to take part in.

LUGGAGE & BAGS
BOUNDARY MILL STORES, BURNLEY ROAD, COLNE,
LANCASHIRE BB8 8LS
☎ (01282) 865 229. OPEN 10 - 6 MON - SAT, 8 ON THUR, 11 - 5 SUN,
10 - 5 BANK HOLS.
FREEPORT LEISURE SHOPPING VILLAGE, ANCHORAGE ROAD,
FLEETWOOD, LANCASHIRE FY7 6AE
☎ (01253) 773 548. OPEN 10 - 6 SEVEN DAYS A WEEK,
UNTIL 8 THUR, FRI.
Factory Shop in a Factory Shopping Village • *Food and Leisure*
Luggage and travel-related products and executive cases, handbags, umbrellas from leading brands such as Samsonite, Desley, Head, Taurus and GlobeTrotter. Each product is offered at a substantially reduced price compared to those found on the high street due to being production over-runs, discontinued ranges or colours and last season's products. Discounts range from 30%-75% off high street prices.

MATALAN
HOLME ROAD, BAMBER BRIDGE, PRESTON, LANCASHIRE PR5 6BP
☎ (01772) 627365. OPEN 9.30 - 8 MON - FRI, 9 - 6 SAT, 11 - 5 SUN.
UNIT 3, ALEXANDRA CENTRE, PARK ROAD, OLDHAM, LANCASHIRE OL4 1SG
☎ (0161) 620 6686. OPEN 10 - 8 MON - FRI, 9 - 6 SAT, 11 - 5 SUN.
UNIT 2, CLIFTON RETAIL PARK, CLIFTON ROAD, BLACKPOOL FY4 4US
☎ (01253) 697850. OPEN 9.30 - 8 MON - FRI, 9 - 6 SAT, 11 - 5 SUN.
UNITS G & H, THE TRIUMPH CENTRE, HUNTS CROSS, LIVERPOOL L24 9GB
☎ (0151) 486 0325. OPEN 9.30 - 8 MON - FRI, 9 - 6 SAT, 11 - 5 SUN.
ROBIN RETAIL PARK, 35 LOIRE DRIVE, ROBIN PARK, WIGAN WN5 0UH
☎ (01942) 629500. OPEN 9.30 - 6 MON - FRI, 8.30 - 6 SAT, 11 - 5 SUN.
FOUNTAIN RETAIL PARK, HYNDBURN ROAD, ACCRINGTON BB5 4AA
☎ (01254) 356100. OPEN 9.30 - 8 MON - FRI, 9 - 6 SAT, 11 - 5 SUN.
BROOKWAY RETAIL PARK, ALTRINCHAM ROAD, BAUGHLEY, MANCHESTER M23 9BP
☎ (0161) 902 2500. OPEN 10 - 8 MON - FRI, 9 - 6 SAT, 11 - 5 SUN.
WESTOVER STREET, OFF STATION ROAD, SWINTON N27 2AH
☎ (0161) 794 3441. OPEN 9.30 - 8 MON - FRI, 9 - 6 SAT, 11 - 5 SUN.
SEFTON RETAIL PARK, DUNNINGS BRIDGE ROAD, BOOTLE, LIVERPOOL L30 6UU
☎ (0151) 525 1190. OPEN 9.30 - 8 MON - FRI, 9 - 6 SAT, 11 - 5 SUN.
TONGE MOOR ROAD, BOLTON, LANCASHIRE BL2 2DJ
☎ (01204) 383733. OPEN 10 - 8 MON - FRI, 9 - 6 SAT, 11 - 5 SUN.
Permanent Discount Outlet • *Womenswear & Menswear*
Children • *Household*

Matalan is a fashion and homewares value retailer giving customers what they claim to be unbeatable value for money with huge savings on a wide range of products including high quality fashionable clothing for men, women and children at up to 50% off high street prices. Matalan is situated out of town and stores are open seven days a week all year round.

MILLENIUM FURNITURE IMPORTERS LTD
80 OLDHAM STREET, MANCHESTER.
☎ (0161) 228 2377. OPEN 9.30 - 5.30 MON - FRI, 11 - 5 SUN.
Permanent Discount Outlet • *Furniture/Soft Furnishings*

Imports furniture, predominantly dining room and bedroom furniture, from Italy and sofas and chairs from Belgium. By buying directly from the Continental manufacturers, they can sell at very competitive prices. For example, they claim you can buy a complete set of bedroom furniture for £1,000. They also sell 23 different types of leather suites. They are situated opposite Abakhan Fabrics.

MUSBURY FABRICS MILL SHOP
PARK MILL, HOLCOMBE ROAD, HELMSHORE, ROSSENDALE,
LANCASHIRE BB4 4NP
☎ (01706) 221318. OPEN 9.30 - 4.30 MON - FRI, 9.30 - 4.30 SAT, 10 - 4 SUN.
Permanent Discount Outlet • *Household* • *Furniture/Soft Furnishings*
Bedlinen by Dorma and Horrockses; fabric from Fairfield Mills and SMD, all at discount prices. There are thousands of metres of fabric on sale here. Examples of prices include pillows, £1.50 reduced from £8; fitted sheet, £3.95 reduced from £17; single duvet cover, £7.95 reduced from £25.

NELSON INTIMATE APPAREL
WHITEWALLS INDUSTRIAL ESTATE, COLNE, LANCASHIRE.
☎ (01282) 868575. OPEN 10 - 4.30 WED, THUR, 10 - 3.30 FRI, 8.30 - 12 SAT.
Factory Shop • *Womenswear Only*
Manufacturers of lingerie, the factory shop sells mainly bras and pants made on site with some other underwear, dressing gowns, pyjamas, thermal wear and nightwear, mostly from chainstores and priced very reasonably. The stock room is used as a fitting room. Car park.

NEW ENGLAND FACTORY SHOP
SLADEN WOOD MILL, TODMORDEN ROAD, LITTLEBOROUGH,
LANCASHIRE OL15 9EW
☎ (01706) 813563.
Factory Shop • *Furniture/Soft Furnishings*
Manufacturers of furniture, they sell beds, sofas and three-piece suites.

NEWBOLD TEXTILES
SHAW ROAD, ROCHDALE, LANCASHIRE OL16 4SQ
☎ (01706) 640211. OPEN 9 - 3 MON - FRI, 8 ON THUR, 10 - 2 SAT.
Permanent Discount Outlet • *Furniture/Soft Furnishings*
Two-storey mill shop in residential area at the back of a house which sells an enormous variety of different types of fabric: curtaining, dress material, voiles, sheeting, towelling. Names on sale include Jane Shilton, Crowsons and Montgomery. Swatches are available and if they don't stock what you want you can order it, though it will cost a little more. Open to trade and public.

NEXT TO NOTHING
FREEPORT SHOPPING VILLAGE, FLEETWOOD, LANCASHIRE L65 9JJ
☎ (01253) 779826. OPEN 10 - 6 MON - SAT, 8 ON THUR, FRI, 12 - 6 SUN.
Factory Shop in a Factory Shopping Village
Womenswear & Menswear • *Children*
Sells perfect surplus stock from Next stores and the Next Directory catalogue at discounts of 50% or more. The ranges are usually last season's and overruns but there is the odd current item if you look carefully. There are shoes, lingerie, swimwear, and clothes for men, women and children.

ONEIDA

BOUNDARY MILL, BURNLEY ROAD, COLNE, LANCASHIRE BB8 8LS
☎ (01282) 865 229. OPEN 10 - 6 MON - SAT, 8 ON THUR, 11 - 5 SUN,
10 - 5 BANK HOLS.
Factory Shop • *Household*
Oneida is the world's largest cutlery company and originates from the United States of America. In addition to cutlery, it sells silver and silver plate at discounts of between 30% and 50%, plus frames, candlesticks and trays. Boundary Mill is one of the country's largest clearance stores for fashion and homewares.

OSWALDTWISTLE MILLS

MOSCOW MILL, COLLIER ST, OSWALDTWISTLE, ACCRINGTON,
LANCASHIRE BB5 3DF
☎ (01254) 871025. OPEN 9 - 5 MON - SAT, 11 - 5 SUN, UNTIL 8 ON THUR.
Factory Shop • *Household*
A working mill which manufactures for top hotels and restaurants within the UK, with lots of attractions for families, apart from the bargains on offer. There are landscaped grounds with mini golf, Wendy House village, Gnomeland, wildfowl reserve and picnic area. Musbury Fabrics sell bedding, quilts, sheets and towels; Hot House sell dried flowers, mirrors, ceramics, kitchenware and pictures. Also sells a selection of women's clothes plus cards and books. Craft House sell everything from salt dough to decoupage; Body Shop sells shampoo and bathroom products; and there are other shops selling furniture, handicrafts, jewellery sweets (made on the premises), all at competitive prices. There is also a weaver, silk painting, garden centre and a children's play area. Part of the Oswaldtwistle Mills complex sells everything from Egyptian cotton to household textiles, plus everything you need to keep the house clean, including brand-names such as JIF, Comfort and Flash - and you don't have to bulk buy.

PIFCO GROUP FACTORY SHOP

PRINCESS STREET, FAILSWORTH, ON THE A62 MANCHESTER TO
OLDHAM ROAD, LANCASHIRE M35 OHS
☎ (0161) 947 3000. OPEN 9 - 5.30 MON, WED - FRI, CLOSED TUE,
9 - 1 SAT,
Factory Shop • *Electrical Equipment*
Discontinued lines and seconds of Pifco, Carmen, Salton, Russell Hobbs, Mountain Breeze and Tower, as well as some perfect lines. For example, kettles, haircare, saucepan sets, slow cookers, mini ovens, air cleaners, ionisers and aromatherapy products. Also Christmas tree lights in season.

PILKINGTON'S TILES FACTORY SHOP
BURY FACTORY SHOP, 1 DERBY STREET, ROCHDALE ROAD, BURY,
LANCASHIRE BL9 ONW
☎ (0161) 761 7771. OPEN 8.30 - 5.30 MON - FRI, UNTIL 8 THUR,
9 - 5 SAT, 10 - 4 SUN.
RAKE LANE, CLIFTON JUNCTION, MANCHESTER,
LANCASHIRE M27 8LP
☎ (0161) 727 7088. OPEN 8.30 - 5.30 MON - FRI, 9 - 5 SAT, 10 - 4 SUN.
Factory Shop • *DIY/Renovation*
Sells seconds of the well-known Pilkington's bathroom and kitchen wall and floor tiles and DIY tiling equipment at discount prices of up to 75% off manufacturers' prices. Two hundred and fifty ranges of wall and floor tiles from which to choose. Now also have laminate wood floor and glazed floor tiles.

PONDEN MILL LINENS
FREEPORT SHOPPING VILLAGE, ANCHORAGE ROAD, FLEETWOOD,
LANCASHIRE FY7 6AE
☎ (01253) 777252. OPEN 10 - 6 SEVEN DAYS A WEEK, 8 ON THUR, FRI.
Factory Shop in a Factory Shopping Village • *Household*
Famous branded products at direct from the mill prices. A fabulous assortment of towels, duvets, pillows, throws, bedspreads, up-to-the-minute coordinated bed linen, from Crown, Coloroll, Jeff Banks, Ports-of-Call, to name but a few. Something for every room in the house.

PRO IMAGE LTD
20 BRIDDON STREET, STRANGEWAYS, MANCHESTER,
LANCASHIRE M3 1LS
☎ (0161) 839 2845. OPEN 10 - 6 MON - WED, 10 - 8 THUR, FRI,
10 - 5 SAT, SUN.
Permanent Discount Outlet • *Sportswear & Equipment*
Discount designer sportswear: golf wear, breathable waterproof suits, shoes, track suits, sports shoes from Adidas and Nike.

PUMPKIN DRESS HIRE
14 ST MARY STREET, MANCHESTER, LANCASHIRE M3 2LB
☎ (0161) 831 7610. OPEN 10 - 5 MON - SAT, UNTIL 7 ON THUR.
Hire Shop • *Womenswear & Menswear*
There are more than 2,000 outfits available at any one time at this shop which is well known to Granada TV, whose stars often make use of its hire service. The shop offers a choice of more than 450 garments in evening wear, cocktail wear, ballgowns, wedding outfits (for men only) and men's dinner suits. Costs range from £40 for up to one week to a maximum of £95. There is a discount for students of 15% as well as a discount for nurses and a corporate discount. Sizes range from 8-26 and there are also handbags and jewellery for hire.

QUIGGINS CENTRE
12-16 SCHOOL LANE, LIVERPOOL, LANCASHIRE L1 3BT
☎ (0151) 709 2462. OPEN 10 - 6 MON - SAT.
Secondhand and Vintage Clothes • *Womenswear & Menswear*
There are 45 different shops at the Quiggins Centre, the second biggest market in Liverpool, selling a variety of goods including theatrical and period costumes, secondhand clothes, furniture, bric-a-brac, jewellery, antiques, a cafe and a music shop.

RANGE DISCOUNT WAREHOUSE
52 COLLEGE ROAD, WHALLEY RANGE, MANCHESTER.
☎ (0161) 861 9648. OPEN 9 - 8 MON, THUR, 9 - 6 TUE, WED, FRI, CLOSED SAT.
OLDHAM ROAD, FAILSWORTH
☎ (0161) 682 1919. OPEN 9 - 8 MON, THUR, 9 - 6 WED, FRI, SAT, CLOSED TUE.
Permanent Discount Outlet • *Electrical Equipment*
Everything for the kitchen in terms of large electrical equipment including ookers, hobs, microwaves, hoods, US-style fridges, range cookers at very competitive prices. The company believes in high turnover/low margins.

REDDISH DEMOLITION LTD
ALBION HOUSE, UNDER LANE, CHADDERTON, NEAR OLDHAM, LANCASHIRE OL9 7PP
☎ (0161) 682 6660. OPEN 7.30 - 5 MON - FRI, 7.30 - 12 SAT.
Architectural Salvage • *DIY/Renovation*
Reclaimed bricks, slates, beams and Yorkshire flags.

REGATTA
FREEPORT SHOPPING VILLAGE, ANCHORAGE ROAD, FLEETWOOD, LANCASHIRE FY7 6AE
☎ (01253) 777705. OPEN 10 - 6 MON, TUE, WED, SAT, SUN, 10 - 8 THUR, FRI.
Factory Shop in a Factory Shopping Village
Sportswear & Equipment • *Womenswear & Menswear* • *Children*
Clothing for the great outdoors including fleeces, waterproof jackets, quilted gilets, hiker shirts, rucksacks, socks, hats, scarves and balaclavas at discounts of at least 30%.

REVIVAL
34 WARNER STREET, ACCRINGTON, LANCASHIRE BB5 1HN
☎ (01254) 382316. OPEN 10.30 - 5 MON - SAT, CLOSED WED.
Secondhand and Vintage Clothes • *Womenswear & Menswear*
Vintage clothes from the beginning of the century to the Seventies including men and women's flares, £8 - £12, tank tops and shirts from £4, cheesecloth tops, Biba trousers. Levi jeans, from £9 up to £18; Levi jackets, £10-£35;

Adidas and Lacoste T-shirts from £5-£12; cocktail dresses from £14-£28; ballgowns from £20-£75; Fifties-style shirts, £6-£12; dinner suits, £24. They also keep accessories, shoes, hats, gloves and costume jewellery.

ROYAL WORCESTER & SPODE FACTORY SHOP
BOUNDARY MILL, BURNLEY ROAD, COLNE, LANCASHIRE BB8 8LS
☎ (01282) 862793. OPEN 10 - 6 MON - SAT, 8 ON THUR, 11 - 5 SUN.
Factory Shop • *Household*
Infinitesimally flawed porcelain and china seconds at 25% less than "perfect" prices. This outlet also sells Fo-Frame, Mayflower, Collectible World, Lakeland Plaques, FrameMaker, Mug Mates and Six Trees. There is a vast range with special offers throughout the year on anything from crystal decanters and bowls to figurines, cookware and dinner sets. Shipping arrangements worldwide can be organised.

SANDERSON CLEARANCE OUTLET SHOP
2 POLLARD STREET, ANCOATS, MANCHESTER, LANCASHIRE M4 7DS
☎ (0161) 272 8501. FAX ☎ (0161) 272 8628. OPEN 10 - 6 MON - SAT,
10 - 4 SUN.
Factory Shop • *Furniture/Soft Furnishings*
Seconds in furnishing fabrics from discontinued patterns, lines and end of ranges; wallpapers and ready made curtains, duvet covers, most of which cost about half price. Lots of remnants and ends of ranges and slight seconds of bedding. Free parking.

SCENT TO YOU
BOUNDARY MILLS, BURNLEY ROAD, COLNE, LANCASHIRE BB8 8LS
☎ (01282) 865229. OPEN 10 - 6 MON - SAT, 8 ON THUR, 11 - 5 SUN,
10 - 6 BANK HOLS.
THE DESIGNER ROOM, FREEPORT FLEETWOOD OUTLET VILLAGE,
ANCHORAGE ROAD, FLEETWOOD, 12 MILES FROM JUNCTION 3 OF
M55, LANCASHIRE FY7 6AE
☎ (01253) 770080. OPEN 10 - 6 SEVEN DAYS A WEEK,
UNTIL 8 THUR, FRI.
Factory Shop in a Factory Shopping Village • *Womenswear Only*
A concession within this large men's and women's fashion and homewares discount store selling discounted perfume, cosmetics and accessories including body lotions and gels. The company, which has more than thirty branches, buys in bulk and sells more cheaply, relying on a high turnover for profit. Discounts range from 5% to 60%, with greater savings during their twice-yearly sales (phone for details). Most of the leading brand names in perfume are stocked including Christian Lacroix, Armani, Charlie, Givenchy, Anais Anais from Cacherel, Charlie from Revlon, Coco Chanel, Christian Dior, Elizabeth Taylor, Blue Grass from Elizabeth Arden, Aramis, Lagerfeld. Plus cosmetics from Revlon and Spectacular and skincare from Clarins and Lancome as well as Scent To You's own range of bags, watches, hair brushes

and brushkits which is sold under the name S.T.Y. Designs. Stock varies greatly due to the fast turnover and varying supplies so more than one visit may be necessary to obtain the scent of your choice. Or phone first to avoid disappointment.

SCOOPS

C/O DISCOUNT GIANT, SISSONS STREET, OFF OLDHAM ROAD, FAILSWORTH LANCASHIRE M35 OEJ
☎ (0161) 682 5684. OPEN 9 - 6 MON, TUE, SAT, 9 - 7 WED, 9 - 8 THUR, 9 -7 FRI, 10 - 4 SUN.
UNIT 56, ARNDALE CENTRE, MIDDLETON, MANCHESTER M24 4EL
☎ (0161) 653 5435. OPEN 9 - 5.30 MON - SAT.
984 STOCKPORT ROAD, LEVENSHULME, MANCHESTER M19 3NN
☎ (0161) 257 3515. OPEN 9 - 5.30 MON - SAT.
1318-1324 ASHTON OLD ROAD, OPENSHAW, MANCHESTER M11 1JG
☎ (0161) 371 8243. OPEN 9 - 5.30 MON - SAT.
UNIT 102, CONCOURSE SHOPPING CENTRE, SOUTH WAY, SKELMERSDALE, LANCS WN8 6LJ
☎ (01695) 50965. OPEN 9 - 5.30 MON - SAT.
THE IN SHOP CENTRE, TELEGRAPH WAY, KIRKBY, MERSEYSIDE L32 8YS
☎ (0151) 545 0226. OPEN 9.30 - 5.30 MON - SAT.
Permanent Discount Outlet • *Children* • *Womenswear & Menswear*
Grattan catalogue shops. There is a selection of items from those featured in the catalogue, which can consist of anything from children's clothes and toys to bedding, electrical equipment and nursery accessories. Each shop sells a slightly different range, so always ring first to check they stock what you want. All items are discounted by up to 50%.

SECOND CHANCE

8 PORTLAND STREET, SOUTHPORT, LANCASHIRE PR8 1JU
☎ (01704) 538329. OPEN 9.30 - 5.30 MON - SAT.
Permanent Discount Outlet • *Household*
Sells mostly good quality seconds in English bone china. For example, Queens cups and saucers, £3.99, list price approx £8.99; Queens mugs, £2.99, list price £5.99; Royal Stafford china 10" plate, £2.99, list price £7.26; teapot, £10, list price £30.70. Also stocks Burgess & Leigh seconds at 30% discounts, cut glass tableware, oven to table cookware, drinking glasses from 75p and giftware.

SLATERS MENSWEAR

7 DALE STREET, MANCHESTER M1 1JA
☎ (0161) 228 6482. OPEN 8.30 - 5.30 MON - SAT, 7.30 ON THUR.
Permanent Discount Outlet • *Menswear Only*
Full range of men's clothes from underwear and shoes to casualwear, suits and dresswear and including labels such as Odermark, Bulmer, Valentino, Charlie's Co, and Charlton Gray. Men's suits from £79.

SPOILS
48-50 UPPER MALL, MARKET PLACE, BOLTON, LANCASHIRE BL1 2AL
☎ (01204) 528860.
UNIT R10YAGERS WALK, ARNDALE CENTRE, MANCHESTER M3 1AP
☎ (0161) 819 2633. OPEN 9 - 5.30 MON - SAT, 8 ON THUR.
UNIT 16/17 THE SPINDLES, OLDHAM, LANCASHIRE OL1 1HE
☎ (0161) 628 6967. OPEN 9 - 5.30 MON - SAT, 8 ON THUR.
UNIT L36/37 TRAFFORD CENTRE, TRAFFORD, MANCHESTER
☎ (0161) 202 9364.
UNIT 1 WILLIAMSON SQUARE, LIVERPOOL
☎ (0151) 709 0075. 0075.
Permanent Discount Outlet • *Household*

General domestic glassware, non-stick bakeware, non-electrical kitchen gadgets, ceramic oven-to-tableware, textiles, cutting boards, aluminium non-stick cookware, bakeware, plastic kitchenware, plastic storage, woodware, coffee pots/makers, furniture, mirrors and picture frames. Rather than being discounted, all the merchandise is very competitively priced - in fact, the company carry out competitors' checks frequently in order to monitor pricing. With 38 branches, the company is able to buy in bulk and thus negotiate very good prices.

SPRINGVALE LEATHER FURNITURE
UNIT 2, HOLMEBANK WORKS, FOUNDRY STREET, RAWTENSTALL, ROSSENDALE, LANCASHIRE BB4 6HQ
☎ (01706) 225005. E-MAIL: springv@springvaleleather.co.uk
WEBSITE: www.springvaleleatherco.uk
OPEN 9 - 5 MON - FRI, 9 - 1 SAT. MAIL ORDER.
Permanent Discount Outlet • *Furniture/Soft Furnishings*

Manufacturers of leather sofas and chairs which are sold either by mail order or from the factory shop. Frames are made from seasoned European hardwood, constructed to withstand warping and cracking. The joints are screwed, doweled and glued together in the traditional style of centuries past. Chairs start at £609; recliners, £926; 3-seater sofas, £933.

STANDFAST FACTORY FABRIC SHOP
CATON ROAD, LANCASTER, LANCASHIRE LA1 3PA
☎ (01524) 64334. OPEN 9.30 - 1 MON - FRI, 10 - 12.30 SAT.
Factory Shop • *Furniture/Soft Furnishings*

Genuine factory shop selling a wide range of well-known designer named fabrics, which are suitable for all soft furnishings, at discounted prices. Stocks vary according to factory production and all fabrics are seconds. Prices range from £2 to £7 per metre. They always stock plenty of pieces for cushion covers and patchwork from 30p each to £3 for small sackful. Usually they have some fabrics on special offer, ranging from £1.50 per metre to £7 a metre. None of the fabric is flame retardant but once treated, can be used for upholstery. Seconds of top brand towels are also for sale.

STAMPER ENTERPRISES & CO LTD
ALMA HOUSE, GRIMSHAW LANE, MIDDLETON,
GREATER MANCHESTER.
☎ (0161) 655 1000. WEBSITE: www.sales@stamper.co.uk
OPEN 9 - 5.30 MON - FRI.
Permanent Discount Outlet • *Womenswear & Menswear* • *Children*
Permanent discount outlet selling vast stocks of high street names for men, women and children from shops such as M&S, BhS, Debenhams, Gap, Next, Ladybird and Mothercare. All the items are end of season or slight seconds and are sold without labels.

STAPLES
UNIT 4, TRINITY RETAIL PARK, BOLTON, LANCASHIRE BL2 1HY
☎ (01204) 365307. OPEN 8 - 8 MON - FRI, 9 - 6 SAT, 11 - 5 SUN.
Permanent Discount Outlet • *Furniture/Soft Furnishings*
Office equipment and furniture supplier which is aimed at businesses, but is also open to the public. The owner buys in bulk and so is able to sell at very competitive prices a range of goods from paper clips to personal computers. Customers do not have to buy in bulk to make savings. A mail order catalogue is available and delivery is free on purchases over £30 (area permitting). There are more than 70 branches countrywide - for your nearest store, phone Talking Pages on 0800 600 900.

SUTTONS FACTORY SHOP
NEW CHURCH ROAD, BACUP, LANCASHIRE
☎ (01706) 875578. OPEN 10 - 5.30 MON - FRI, 9 - 5.30 SAT, 10 - 4 SUN.
Permanent Discount Outlet • *Womenswear & Menswear* • *Children*
Stocks a wide range of footwear for children as well as adults. There are slippers, sandals, boots, leather and vinyl handbags and shoe cleaners and polishes. Ladies fashion shoes start from £6 a pair. There are some well known brands, all at substantial savings on high street prices.

T J HUGHES
FISHERGATE CENTRE, PRESTON, LANCASHIRE PR1 8HJ
☎ (01772) 887326. OPEN 9 - 5.30 MON - FRI, SAT, 8 ON WED, 11 - 5 SUN.
Permanent Discount Outlet • *Womenswear & Menswear*
Children • *Household* • *Electrical Equipment*
Expanding chain of shops offering, not discounts as such, but very competitively priced goods from clothes for all the family to china, towels, bedlinen, duvets, pots and pans, kettles, vacuum cleaners, television sets, CDs, toasters, many from top brand names There are branches around the country, mostly in the Midlands and North West: Birkenhead, Bootle, Ellesmere Port, Oldham, Wolverhampton, Macclesfield, Kidderminster, Stretford, Lichfield, Chester, Widnes, Salford, Rochdale, Shrewsbury, Blackburn, Sheffield, Liverpool, Warrington, Eastbourne, Wrexham, Middlesbrough, Bournemouth, Crawley, Weston-Super-Mare and Burnley.

TARLETON MILL FACTORY OUTLET
UNIT 8-10, CROWLAND STREET INDUSTRIAL ESTATE, CROWLAND STREET, SOUTHPORT, LANCASHIRE PR9 7RG
☎ (01704) 541543. OPEN 10 - 7 THUR, FRI, 10 - 5 SAT, 10 - 4 SUN. 10 - 5 BANK HOLIDAYS.
Factory Shop • *Household* • *Furniture/Soft Furnishings*
This factory shop sells only merchandise which is manufactured by Tarleton Mill who make household textiles for major high street stores, using only top quality fabrics. The shop sells upholstery fabric, duvet sets, throwovers, curtains (cotton, velvet), pelmets, tie-backs, Austrian blinds, cushion covers and pads, seat pads, bean bags, top-up beans, floor cushions, conservatory cushion and patchwork pieces. All stock is discontinued lines or surplus of current lines and seconds, so in some cases it is possible to purchase a whole matching range for a fraction of the high street price. They also hold factory sales here throughout the year.

TERRY'S STORES URMSTON LTD
47 STATION ROAD, URMSTON, MANCHESTER, LANCASHIRE M41 9JG
☎ (0161) 748 6011. OPEN 9.30 - 5 MON - SAT, CLOSED WED.
Permanent Discount Outlet • *Womenswear & Menswear*
Furniture/Soft Furnishings • *Children* • *Electrical Equipment*
The "final resting-place for ex-catalogue stock", it sells everything that is normally available by catalogue at half price. This includes leather jackets, jeans, dress and curtaining fabric, watnot stands, nests of tables, dining table and chairs, bedlinen, curtains, electrical goods, wedding and bridesmaids dresses. Delivery is free locally. The company has been in operation for 45 years and is privately owned.

THE BOOK PEOPLE LTD
HALL WOOD AVENUE, HAYDOCK, ST HELENS, LANCASHIRE WA11 9UR
ORDER LINE ☎ 0870 607 7740. FAX 0870 6077720.
Permanent Discount Outlet • *Food and Leisure*
The catalogue promises no membership, no contract to sign, no further obligation, savings of up to 75% off high street prices, phone, fax or post ordering, guaranteed delivery within seven working days, and reduced price p&p for pensioners. There are 13 pages of children's books, a variety of romantic novels; gardening and cookery titles; some sports books and contemporary autobiographies. Package and posting costs £2.95 regardless of the size of order.

THE EAST LANCASHIRE TOWEL COMPANY
PARK MILL, HOLSTEAD LANE, BARROWFORD, NELSON,
LANCASHIRE BB9 6HJ
☎ (01282) 612193. OPEN 8.30 - 5 MON - FRI. MAIL ORDER.
Factory Shop • *Household*
The East Lancashire Towel Company still produces towels by the traditional method - making them both highly absorbent and hard wearing - and are able to keep costs down by selling direct to the general public. They produce a wide variety of towels: bath sheets, jacquard woven with intricate floral patterns in a variety of designs, children's daisy duck bath towels, kitchen and terry roller towels, souvenir and promotional towels, football club towels, etc. Towels, dish cloths, tea towels, sheets, duvets, pillows, face cloths, dusters and hankies, all at about half price. Toilets and car parking.

THE ELITE DRESS AGENCY
35 KINGS STREET WEST, MANCHESTER, LANCASHIRE M3 2PW
☎ (0161) 832 3670. OPEN 9.30 - 5.30 MON - SAT, 11 - 4 SUN.
Dress Agency • *Womenswear & Menswear* • *Children*
Three floors of good quality men's, women's and children's clothing, many with a Continental flavour. Among womenswear can be found labels such as Moschino as well as Escada, Prada, Armani, DKNY to name but a few, with lots of chainstore makes, too. For men, there are Italian designer suits from £50-£150, including Boss, Paul Smith and Armani. There are lots of hats from £8; also shoes, handbags, accessories and a selection of unwanted gifts for sale.

THE FABRIC WAREHOUSE
UNIT 2B, QUEENS RETAIL PARK, QUEENS STREET, PRESTON,
LANCASHIRE PR1 4HZ
☎ (01772) 202066. OPEN 9 - 5.30 MON - SAT, 8 ON WED, 11 - 5 SUN.
Permanent Discount Outlet • *Furniture/Soft Furnishings*
Massive outlet, heaving with shelves of fabric, net, voiles, as well as haberdashery from needles and cotton to braid and Velcro. Brand names on sale here include Prestigious, Ashley Wilde, Fairfield Mills, Rectella and Style. Ready-made curtains also for sale with an express service available in which curtains can be made in five days.

THE FACTORY SHOP
LANCASTER LEISURE PARK, WYRESDALE ROAD, LANCASTER,
LANCASHIRE LA1 3LA
☎ (01524) 846079. OPEN 10 - 5 MON - SAT, 11 - 5 SUN.
SHAWBRIDGE STREET, CLITHEROE, LANCASHIRE BB7 1NA
☎ (01200) 428784. OPEN 9 - 5.30 MON - SAT, 10.30 - 4.30 SUN.
Factory Shop • *Children* • *Womenswear & Menswear*
Household • *Sportswear & Equipment* • *Furniture/Soft Furnishings*
Wide range on sale includes men's, ladies and children's clothing and footwear; household textiles; toiletries; hardware; luggage; lighting and bedding, most of

which are chainstore and high street brands at discounts of approximately 30%-50%. There are weekly deliveries and brands include many major stars such as Adidas, Nike, Joe Bloggs and Brabantia, to name just a few. There are furniture displays and a new line in Cape Country furniture is on sale. Ranges are continually changing and few factory shops offer such a variety under one roof. The Lancaster outlet is also part of the family Leisure Park with antique centres, restaurant and children's leisure facilities. Both branches have their own free car park.

THE FASHION AGENCY
FIRST FLOOR, 21 QUEEN STREET, BLACKPOOL LANCASHIRE FY1 1LN
☎ (01253) 628679. OPEN 10.30 - 4.30 TUE - FRI, 10.30 - 4 SAT.
Dress Agency • *Womenswear Only*
A spacious showroom above a fashion shop called Elizabeth Todd. In business for more than 20 years, it offers top end of the market nearly-new outfits and continental separates. A large and constantly-changing selection of labels such as YSL, Escada, Chanel, Morgan, Versace and Moschino make this a very popular shop. It caters for all ages and from casual to cocktail wear. It also sells shoes, handbags and jewellery; there is a permanent half-price sale rail.

THE MANCHESTER OUTLET MALL AT THE LOWRY
THE QUAYS, SALFORD QUAYS, NEAR MANCHESTER, LANCASHIRE M5 2SQ
☎ (0161) 848 1800 FOR MORE DETAILS.
Factory Shopping Village • *Womenswear & Menswear* • *Household*
Factory shopping centre with seventy shops in a site next to the Manchester Ship Canal, which is due to open in October 2001. The site will include a hotel, Warner Village, Millenium Multiplex cinema, 15 cafes/restaurants, health and fitness club, indoor activity centre for children and is built alongside the £127 million Lowry Millenium Project for the Arts. The Imperial War Museum North, which opens in 2002, will be just a bridge away.

THE SALVAGE SHOP
71-77 NEWPORT STREET, BOLTON, LANCASHIRE
☎ (01204) 528528. OPEN 9 - 5.30 MON - SAT.
Permanent Discount Outlet • *Womenswear & Menswear*
Furniture/Soft Furnishings • *Children* • *Household*
Electrical Equipment • *DIY/Renovation* • *Food and Leisure*
Sportswear & Equipment
Sister shop to the Middlesex outlet which is an Aladdin's cave of "salvaged" stock for the avid bargain hunter, most of which has been the subject of bankruptcy, insurance claims, fire or flood. Regular visitors have found anything from half-price Kenwood Chefs, typewriters and telephones to furniture, kitchen items and designer clothes. Yves St Laurent, Ungaro, MaxMara, Chloe,

Agnes B and Mondi are just some the labels (though they are often cut out) to appear. Discounts range from 50%-75%. Stock is constantly changing with a new designer name every week, so phone first to check what is available.

THE SUIT COMPANY
FREEPORT SHOPPING VILLAGE, ANCHORAGE ROAD, FLEETWOOD, LANCASHIRE FY7 6AE
☎ (01253) 773998. OPEN 10 - 6 SEVEN DAYS A WEEK, 8 ON THUR, FRI.
Factory Shop in a Factory Shopping Village • *Menswear Only*
This shop is part of the Moss Bros group and includes labels such as YSL, Pierre Cardin, Wolsey and Jockey underwear, as well as leather gloves, belts, ties, work shirts, suits, jackets.

THOMAS WITTER LTD
PO BOX 16, FROOM STREET, CHORLEY, LANCASHIRE PR6 9AU
☎ (01257) 263031. OPEN 9 - 4.30 MON - FRI, 10 - 4 SAT.
Factory Shop • *Furniture/Soft Furnishings*
Small outlet containing a lot of stock: quality and middle of the range carpets from £4.50 a sq metre. Only plain carpets are sold, either 50% wool/polyproplene and 80% wool/polyproplene. Nationwide delivery can be arranged.

THORNTONS
FREEPORT VILLAGE, ANCHORAGE ROAD, FLEETWOOD, LANCASHIRE FY7 6AE
☎ (01253) 770710. OPEN 10 - 6 SEVEN DAYS A WEEK, 8 ON THUR, FRI.
Factory Shop in a Factory Shopping Village • *Food and Leisure*
The UK's leading specialist confectionery retailer has more than 500 shops and franchises nationwide selling a wide range of boxed and loose, chocolate and sugar confectionery. The factory outlets sell three different categories: misshapes, discounted lines and standard lines. Misshapes are loose chocolates which are the result of new product development, product trials or end of production runs which cannot be packed as Thorntons standard lines. They are packed into assorted bags and offer a saving of 35%-55% over the recommended retail price of standard "loose line" products. Discounted lines are excess to Thorntons' normal retail requirements and can be as a result of excess seasonal or export stock, discontinued lines or packaging changes. These products, when available, are offered at a discount of 25%-50% over the standard retail price. Standard lines from the full Thorntons range are also on sale at normal prices.

TILE CLEARING HOUSE
1326 ASHTON OLD ROAD, HIGHER OPENSHAW, GREATER MANCHESTER M11 1LG
☎ (0161) 370 6449. OPEN 8 - 6 MON - FRI, 9 - 6 SAT, 10 - 4 SUN.
UNIT 2, RIBBLETON LANE, PRESTON, LANCASHIRE PR1 5LR
☎ (01772) 705 990. OPEN 8 - 6 MON - FRI, 9 - 6 SAT, 10 - 4 SUN.
13A CROSBY ROAD NORTH, WATERLOO, LIVERPOOL,

LANCASHIRE L22 OLD
☎ (0151) 920 3400. OPEN 8 - 6 MON - FRI, 9 - 6 SAT, 10 - 4 SUN.
Permanent Discount Outlet • *DIY/Renovation*
Over 500 ranges of top quality ceramic wall and floor tiles permanently in stock, plus a comprehensive range of grouts, adhesives, tools and accessories to complete the job. By buying direct from the manufacturer and passing the savings on to the customer, their prices are very competitive. Moreover, everything you see is in stock, so there's no waiting for orders to be processed. Save up to 75% on manufacturers' recommended selling prices.

TILE WIZARD
UNIT 39, ELLESMERE RETAIL PARK, WALKDEN,
GREATER MANCHESTER.
☎ (0161) 702 8886. OPEN 9 - 5.30 MON - SAT, 10 - 4 SUN.
Permanent Discount Outlet • *DIY/Renovation*
Floor and wall tiles both English and Continental at discounted prices. There are ten branches: Warrington, St Helen's, Northwich, Crewe, Chester, Southport, Preston, Morecambe and Blackpool.

TOP MARKS
149-151 HOLLAND STREET, DENTON, GREATER MANCHESTER M34 3GE
☎ (0161) 336 1279. OPEN 9.30 - 5.30 MON - SAT,
UNTIL 8 ON THUR, 11 - 5 SUN.
Permanent Discount Outlet • *Womenswear & Menswear*
Children • *Household*
Sells grade A fashion seconds from high street stores, as well as end of season and ends of lines in homeware and giftware, towels, homeware, handbags, shoes, underwear, hosiery, jackets and evening wear. Hand towels, £3.25; bath towels, £6.50; bath sheets, £10.50; face cloths, £1; tea towels, £1.50; hosiery, from 75p. Ladies sizes range from 8-18; men's from small to XXL, 30"-42" waist and 29" to 33" leg. Evening wear is stocked from October until Christmas at one third off the retail price. There are also branches at Walkden, Urmston and Monton.

TIMBERLAND
BOUNDARY MILL STORES, BURNLEY ROAD, COLNE,
LANCASHIRE BB8 8LS
☎ (01282) 865229. OPEN 10 - 6 MON - SAT, 8 ON THUR, 11 - 5 SUN.
Factory Shop in a Factory Shopping Village • *Womenswear & Menswear*
Footwear, clothing and outdoor gear from the well-known Timberland range at discounts of 30% or more. Most of the stock is last season's or discontinued lines, but not seconds. All stock is last season's excess stock in limited ranges and sizes. As most of Timberland's stock is from a core range which rarely changes, there are few discontinued lines.

TK MAXX

UNIT 1 & 2, ANGOULEME RETAIL PARK, BURY, LANCASHIRE.
- ☏ (0161) 7611700. OPEN 9 - 5.30 MON - WED, 9 - 6 SAT, 9 - 7 THUR, FRI, 11- 5 SUN.

1ST FLOOR, 15 PARKER ST, OFF CLAYTON SQUARE, LIVERPOOL, LANCASHIRE L1 1DP
- ☏ (0151) 708 9919. OPEN 9 - 6 MON - SAT, 11 - 5 SUN.

UNIT 16, TELFORD FORGE RETAIL PARK, ORDSALL LANE, TELFORD, MANCHESTER, LANCASHIRE TF3 4AG
- ☏ (01952) 210200. OPEN 10 - 8 MON - FRI, 9 - 6 SAT, 11 - 5 SUN.

UNIT A1, REGENT ROAD RETAIL PARK, ODSALL LANE, MANCHESTER M5 3TP
- ☏ (0161) 8332200 . OPEN 9.30 - 8 MON ,THUR, FRI, 9 - 6 TUE, WED, SAT, 11 - 5 SUN.

FISHERGATE SHOPPING CENTRE, PRESTON, LANCASHIRE
- ☏ (01772) 253220. OPEN 9 - 5.30 MON - FRI, 9 - 8 WED, 9 - 6 SAT, 11 - 5 SUN.

7 - 9 MARBLE PLACE SHOPPING CENTRE, SOUTHPORT PR8 1DF
- ☏ (01704) 501900. 9 - 5.30 MON - FRI, 9 - 6 SAT, 11 - 5 SUN.

GRANGE ROAD, BIRKENHEAD, MERSEYSIDE.

Permanent Discount Outlet • *Womenswear & Menswear Children* • *Household*

Based on an American concept, TK Maxx is situated in easily accessible, often centrally located stores and offers famous label goods with up to 60% savings off recommended retail prices. TK Maxx has fashion for the whole family - women's, men's and childrenswear - accessories, shoes, gifts, kitchenware and home goods. Everything in the store is branded with a choice of well-known high street names to designer labels, and while a small percentage might be clearly marked past season, the great majority of items in store are current season, current stock and still with phenomenal savings. There is a huge choice with 50,000 pieces in store and up to 10,000 new items arriving a week. The stores are simple and unfussy with wide aisles, shopping trolleys and baskets, and a spacious, functional feel to them but there are individual changing rooms, ramps for buggies and wheelchairs and plenty of staff on the shop floor. Every branch accepts all major credit and debit cards and has a liberal refund and return policy.

TOG 24

7, THE LINKWAY, MIDDLEBROOK PARK, HORWICH, BOLTON, LANCASHIRE BL6 6JA
- ☏ (01204) 469899. OPEN 10 - 6 MON - FRI, SAT, 8 ON WED, THUR, 11 - 5 SUN.

12 REGENT CRESCENT, TRAFFORD CENTRE, MANCHESTER LANCASHIRE M17 8AP
- ☏ (01612) 029960. OPEN 10 - 9 MON - FRI, 9 - 7 SAT, 11 - 5 SUN.

BOUNDARY MILLS STORE, BURNLEY ROAD, COLNE,
LANCASHIRE BB8 8JN
☎ (01282) 865229. OPEN 10 - 6 MON - SAT, 8 ON THUR, 11 - 5 SUN.
Factory Shop in a Factory Shopping Village • *Sportswear & Equipment*
Tog 24 are the UK's fastest growing brand name in outdoor clothing and leisurewear. They utilise the world's finest performance fabrics including Gore-Tex, Polartec and Burlington MCS, catering for all the family for all seasons, with cosy fleeces and waterproofs for the winter, and trekking ranges, shorts and t-shirts for the summer. With all prices at least 30% below the recommended retail price, you can afford to enter the Tog comfort zone.

TOMMY BALLS
HART STREET MILL, BLACKBURN, LANCASHIRE BB11HW
☎ (01254) 261910. OPEN 10 - 5 MON - SAT, 11 - 5 SUN.
Permanent Discount Outlet • *Womenswear & Menswear* • *Children*
A large discount shoe warehouse selling quality shoes from leading British manufacturers for the whole family. Some are seconds, all are brand new. There is also a store at Eanam, which sells reconditioned footwear (01254) 261910.

TOYWORLD FACTORY OUTLET LTD
FREEPORT SHOPPING VILLAGE, ANCHORAGE ROAD, FLEETWOOD,
FYLDE LANCASHIRE FY7 6AE
☎ (01253) 773776. WEBSITE: www.toyworldstore.com
OPEN 10 - 6 SEVEN DAYS A WEEK, 8 ON THUR, FRI.
Factory Shop in a Factory Shopping Village • *Children*
Toyworld sell a large range of discontinued toys, manufacturers' overruns and excess stock from many famous brand names such as Barbie, Action Man, Lego, Tomy, Fisher-Price and many more at least 30-60% off high street prices.

UNITED FOOTWEAR
68-70 OLDHAM STREET, MANCHESTER.
☎ (0161) 228 1706. OPEN 9 - 5.30 MON - SAT.
12 LORD STREET, LEIGH, LANCASHIRE.
☎ (01942) 604440. OPEN 9 - 5.30 MON - WED, 9 - 8 THUR, 9 - 6 FRI,
9 - 5.30 SAT.
CARRMILL ROAD, OFF EAST LANCS. ROAD, ST HELENS, LANCASHIRE.
☎ (01744) 737777. OPEN 9 - 6 MON - WED, 9 - 8 THUR, FRI, 9 - 5.30 SAT,
10 - 4 SUN.
126 FRIARGATE BROW, PRESTON, LANCASHIRE.
☎ (01772) 204410. OPEN 9 - 5.30 MON - SAT, 11 - 4.30 SUN.
Permanent Discount Outlet • *Womenswear & Menswear*
Children • *Sportswear & Equipment*
Shoes for all the family as well as clothes, handbags, sports shoes, boots, giftware and household goods, all at discounted prices. Famous brands including Clarks, K Shoes and Elmdale. Part of a national chain.

VF OUTLETS
FREEPORT SHOPPING VILLAGE, ANCHORAGE ROAD, FLEETWOOD,
LANCASHIRE FY7 6AE
☎ (01253) 773988. OPEN 10 - 6 MON - WED, SAT, 10 - 8 THUR, FRI,
11 - 5 SUN.
Factory Shop in a Factory Shopping Village
Womenswear & Menswear • *Children*
Men's, women's and children's denim jeans and jackets, cords, T-shirts, shirts, most of which are irregular (ie seconds). T-shirts and shirts are all perfects, as are some jeans. Discounts are at least one-third off the normal price. Brand names on sale include Lee, Wrangler and Sedgefield. Children's range starts at two years. Also sells French underwear by Variance, Jan Sport bags, caps and hats.

VIYELLA
BOUNDARY MILL STORES, BURNLEY ROAD, COLNE,
LANCASHIRE BB8 8LS
☎ (01282) 865229. OPEN 10 - 6 MON - SAT, 11 - 5 SUN.
Factory Shop • *Womenswear & Menswear*
Wide range of Viyella clothing at discount prices from 30% on ladies formal wear and casual wear.

WARNERS
FREEPORT SHOPPING VILLAGE, ANCHORAGE ROAD, FLEETWOOD,
LANCASHIRE FY7 6AE
☎ (01253) 773770. OPEN 10 - 6 SEVEN DAYS A WEEK,
UNTIL 8 THUR, FRI.
Factory Shop in a Factory Shopping Village • *Womenswear & Menswear*
This shop sells a wide range of women's lingerie from Leisureby, Warners, with bras, slips, thongs, bodies and briefs at discounts from 25% to 70%. Each item is labelled with both the rrp and the discounted prices. For example, bikini brief, £6.99 reduced from £17; underwire bra, £14.99 reduced from £33; body, £24.99 reduced from £65. Slightly imperfect stock as well as perfect quality, end of season and discontinued merchandise and swimwear are also stocked. Underwear for men, including Calvin Klein briefs for £2.99, is on offer too.

WILLSMART FACTORY SHOP
LANGLEY MILL, LANGLEY ROAD, SALFORD,
GREATER MANCHESTER M6 6JP
☎ (0161) 737 9056. E-MAIL: Rsimon@wills.gb.com
WEBSITE: www.willsmart.co.uk
OPEN 9.30 - 5 MON - FRI, 10 - 4 SAT, SUN, BANK HOLIDAYS.
STONEBRIDGE MILL, SHED STREET, OFF UNION ROAD,
OSWALDTWISTLE, LANCASHIRE BB5 3HY
☎ (01254) 384289. E-MAIL: Rsimon@wills.gb.com
WEBSITE: www.willsmart.co.uk
OPEN 9.30 - 5 MON - FRI, 10 - 4 SAT, SUN, BANK HOLIDAYS.

135/139 BRADSHAWGATE, BOLTON, LANCASHIRE BL2 1BJ
☎ (01204) 527227. E-MAIL: Rsimon@wills.gb.com
WEBSITE: www.willsmart.co.uk
OPEN 9.30 - 5 MON - FRI, 10 - 4 SAT, SUN, BANK HOLIDAYS.
ST PAULS MILL, CAROLINE STREET, BOLTON, LANCS BL3 6UQ
☎ (01204) 64215.

Factory Shop • *Furniture/Soft Furnishings* • *Household*

Willsmart manufactures bedding and curtains for the high street and mail order. The shops have an extensive range of bedding and curtains as well as quilts, pillows, towels, nets, cushions, throws and lampshades, subject to availability. There's a minimum discount of 50% off all merchandise and during sales and promotions this can increase to 65% and 75% off bedding and curtains. The Willsmart Discount and Loyalty card gives cardholders an extra 10% off all bedding and curtains (up to a maximum of 75% off) and you can apply for a card by e-mailing your full name and address to the e-mail address above. The website is updated with news and special offers at all shops.

WINDSMOOR SALE SHOP

21-23 MARKET PLACE, WIGAN, LANCASHIRE.
☎ (01942) 820050. OPEN 9 - 5.30 MON - SAT.
BOUNDARY MILL, BURNLEY ROAD, COLNE BB8 8LS
☎ (01282) 865229. OPEN 10 - 6 MON - SAT, 8 ON THUR, 11 - 5 SUN.

Factory Shop • *Womenswear Only*

Previous season's stock as well as any returned merchandise and overmakes from the Windsmoor, Planet and Precis ranges at discounts averaging about 50% off the original price.

WINFIELDS

HAZEL MILL, BLACKBURN ROAD, HASLINGDEN, ROSSENDALE,
LANCASHIRE BB4 5DD
☎ (01706) 227916. OPEN 10 - 5.30 MON - WED, 10 - 8 THUR,
FRI, 9 - 5.30 SAT, 11 - 5 SUN.

Permanent Discount Outlet • *Womenswear & Menswear* • *Household Sportswear & Equipment* • *Electrical Equipment*

Clothing and housewares, some of which was made for Marks & Spencer, as well as catalogue seconds and surplus, are sold in this 70,000 sq ft mill. The footwear department houses over 100,000 pairs of shoes, many at half price. The ladieswear and lingerie store boasts a wide range of beautiful garments for all occasions at a fraction of the high street price. For outdoors, a wide choice of jackets, fleeces, rucksacks, gloves and footwear. A massive range of sports goods includes many famous name clothes, training shoes and accessories. Homewares range from electrical appliances to crockery. Large car park with space for more than 800 cars and large restaurant.

WYNSORS WORLD OF SHOES
BOUNDARY ROAD, ST HELENS, MERSEYSIDE. LANCASHIRE.
☎ (01744) 454983. OPEN 9 - 5.30 MON, TUE, WED, SAT, 9 - 8 THUR, FRI, 10 - 4 SUN AND BANK HOLIDAYS.
WARRINGTON ROAD, PENKETH, NR WARRINGTON, MERSEYSIDE.
☎ (01925) 727481. OPEN 9 - 5.30 MON, TUE, WED, SAT, 9 - 8 THUR, FRI, 10 - 4 SUN AND BANK HOLIDAYS.
DOCK STREET, FLEETWOOD, NEAR BLACKPOOL
☎ (01253) 779871. OPEN 9 - 5.30 MON - SAT, 8 ON THUR, FRI, 10 - 5 SUN AND BANK HOLIDAYS.
E. SUTTON & SON LTD, NEWCHURCH ROAD, BACUP, LANCASHIRE.
☎ (01706) 875578.
EAST PRESCOTT ROAD, KNOTTY ASH, LIVERPOOL.
☎ (0151) 228 6673. OPEN 9 - 5.30 MON, TUE, SAT, 9 - 8 WED, THUR, FRI, 10 - 4 SUN, BANK HOLS.
Permanent Discount Outlet • *Womenswear & Menswear* • *Children*
Stocks top brand-name shoes at less than half price. Special monthly offers always available. There are shoes, trainers, slippers, sandals and boots for all the family, with a selection of bags, cleaners and polishes available.

Leicestershire

APPLIANCE CENTRE
87 LOTHAIR ROAD, LEICESTER, LEICESTERSHIRE LE2 7QE
☎ (0116) 244 0150. OPEN 7.45 - 5.45 MON - FRI.
Permanent Discount Outlet • *Electrical Equipment*
Small shop which holds brochures from most of the leading manufacturers of large appliances (cookers, range cookers, ovens, hobs, hoods, washing machines, dishwashers, fridges, freezers, sinks, etc) from which you can order at very competitive prices. Dealing mainly in seconds or graded products, these usually consist of slightly imperfect goods damaged in transit or ex-display. Other items are service or catalogue returns which have been in use for a very short period of time. All goods come with a full 12-month guarantee. Perfect goods are also readily available at discounted rates. All prices include home delivery (mainland GB only). Before ordering any of your appliances/sinks for your fitted kitchen, it's worth talking to Appliance Centre who can save you a lot of money compared with kitchen showroom prices. Phone before travelling to ascertain the current stock availability of the appliances you require as there is a high turn around of goods.

BECK MILL FACTORY SHOP
33 KINGS ROAD, MELTON MOWBRAY, LEICESTERSHIRE LE13 1QF
☎ (01664) 501105. OPEN 12 - 5 MON, 10 - 5 TUE - SAT, 11 - 5 SUN.
Factory Shop • *Womenswear & Menswear* • *Household*

Top high street women's and menswear at discounts of up to 70%. For women, there is Roman Originals, Dannimac, Legs and Co Swimwear, Double Two, Blast, Imogen, Spicy and Silhouette by Susan Jon. For men, there is Double Two, Dannimac, Barracuta, Wolsey, and David Andrews Ratcatcher Moleskins. Excellent selection of towels and giftware. There is easy parking at the side of the shop.

BLUNTS
128-132 GRAMBY STREET, LEICESTER, LEICESTERSHIRE LE1 1DL
☎ (0116) 255 5959. OPEN 8.30 - 6 MON - SAT, 11 - 5 SUN.
UNITED FOOTWEAR, 114 MAIN CS.
☎ (01455) 822407. OPEN 9 - 8 MON - FRI, 9 - 5.30 SAT, 10 - 4 SUN.
4 SUN.30 SAT, 10 - 4 SUN.

Permanent Discount Outlet • *Womenswear & Menswear*

Well-known brand name shoes for women and men at big discounts for discontinued stock, seconds and ends of ranges. Men's shoes, £5.99 - £79.99; women's shoes from £2.99 - £45.

BOOKENDS
49 GALLOWTREE GATE, LEICESTER, LEICESTERSHIRE LE1 5AD
☎ (0116) 253 2093. OPEN 9 - 5.30 MON - SAT, 11 - 4 SUN.

Secondhand shops • *Food and Leisure*

Secondhand and damaged books and publishers' returns, as well as new and review copies, including recently published books, all sold at £1 or below.

CHARTERHOUSE HOLDINGS
173 CHARNWOOD ROAD, SHEPSHED, LOUGHBOROUGH,
LEICESTERSHIRE LE12 9NN
☎ (01509) 505050. OPEN 10 - 5.30 MON - SAT, 8 ON THUR, FRI,
11 - 5 SUN. HELPLINE (01509) 600006.

Factory Shop • *Womenswear & Menswear* • *Children*
Household • *Sportswear & Equipment*

The Charterhouse Retail Outlet was established 30 years ago and now enjoys its reputation as probably the largest of its kind in the UK. With over £1 million worth of stock always available, Charterhouse offers family clothing, fashion, footwear, giftware, kitchenware, homeware and more - all ex chain and branded products at a fraction of high street prices. Ladieswear includes casual, evening, swimwear and lingerie - all styles and sizes. Childrenswear ranges from babies upwards with a special department for the early teens. Men will also find an excellent selection of sportswear, casual clothing and footwear. The recently expanded kitchenware and household department stocks a huge selection of present ideas. The outlet also offers a Reward Card scheme earning you free shopping vouchers on every average spend. There is free parking, a children's play area, parent and baby room, wheelchair access and cafe area. Open seven days a week, the outlet is only one mile from Junction 23 of the MI.

CREATIVE CARPETS LTD
UNIT 8, MILL HILL INDUSTRIAL ESTATE, QUARRY LANE, ENDERBY, LEICESTERSHIRE LE9 5AU
☎ (0116) 2841455. OPEN 9 - 3 SAT, WEEKDAYS BY APPOINTMENT ONLY. CLOSED CHRISTMAS.
Factory Shop • *Furniture/Soft Furnishings*
Genuine factory shop where carpets are manufactured on the premises. All carpets are quality heavy domestic, 80/20 wool, hessian backed. There is a large choice of colour including plain dyed, Berbers and heather tweeds. Savings of 50% can be made by buying direct from the factory. Prices for the perfects start at about £9.50 a sq yd; seconds also available.

CURTAINS COMPLETE
THE STABLES, EAST FARNDON HALL, MARKET HARBOROUGH, LEICESTERSHIRE LE16 9SE
☎ (01858) 466671. OPEN 9.30 - 3 TUE, OTHER TIMES BY APPOINTMENT.
Secondhand shops • *Furniture/Soft Furnishings*
Owner Caroline Everard spent a five-year apprenticeship in London making for most of the top interior decorators, and twenty years making top quality hand-made curtains and soft furnishings for private clients. Now, the stables at her home, East Farndon Hall, house more than 200 pairs of nearly-new curtains ranging in price from £35 to £800, many in top quality fabrics such as Colefax & Fowler, Jane Churchill and Designers Guild. A large number are in almost perfect condition, but for those needing repairs or alterations, these can be easily organised. Linings, interlinings, hooks and tapes are also available for those wishing to do their own alterations. She also sells new made-to-measure curtains from a wide range of fabrics. Curtains can also be taken home on approval.

DIRECT COSMETICS LTD
LONG ROW, OAKHAM, LEICESTERSHIRE LE15 6LN
☎ (01572) 724477/756805. MAIL ORDER.
E-MAIL: customercare@directcosmetics.com WEBSITE: www.directcosmetics.com
Permanent Discount Outlet • *Womenswear Only*
This mail order and now internet business has been supplying international brands of cosmetics, perfumes, skincare and beauty products direct to the public since 1977. Brands available include Max Factor, Revlon, Elizabeth Arden, Estee Lauder, Clinique, Clarins, Coppertone, Cacharel, Givenchy, YSL and Crown Perfumery at prices up to 90% off the UK retail price. Phone for a price list with more than 400 offers to be sent direct to you free of charge. Alternatively, look at the website which features more than 1,500 product lines. Direct Cosmetics is a Which? Web Trader authorised site and has been featured in the Daily Mail, Essentials magazine and Shop@Home.

DUNELM FABRIC SHOP
25 EAST STREET, LEICESTER, LEICESTERSHIRE LE1 6NB
☎ (0116) 247 1524. OPEN 9 - 5.30 MON - SAT, 9 - 5 FRI, 11 - 5 SUN.
BRITANNIA CENTRE, HINCKLEY LE10 MON - FRI, 9 - 5.30 SAT.
MILL SHOP, THE REX, MARLBOROUGH SQUARE, COALVILLE LE67 3LT
☎ (01530) 510004. OPEN 9 - 5 MON - SAT, 10.30 - 4.30 SUN.
40-44 CASTLE STREET, HINCKLEY LE10 1DD
☎ (01455) 234908. OPEN 9 - 5 MON - FRI, 9 - 5.30 SAT.
MILL SHOP, 74 CHURCHGATE, LEICESTER LE1 4AL
☎ (0116) 253 7293. OPEN 9 - 5 MON - FRI, 9 - 5.30 SAT.
17-23 EAST STREET, LEICESTER LE1 6NB
☎ (0116) 247 0592/247 1524 (FABRIC SHOP). OPEN 9 - 5.30 MON - SAT, 11 - 5 SUN.
3-6 THE RUSHES, LOUGHBOROUGH, LEICESTE RUSHES, LOUGHBOROUGH, LEICESTERSHIRE LE11 OBJ
☎ (01509) 234717. OPEN 9 - 5 MON - THUR, 9 - 5.30 FRI, SAT.
Permanent Discount Outlet • *Household*

Part of a chain of shops based in the Midlands selling brand-name and chain-store curtains, masses of bedlinen, towels, wickerware, pictures and frames, all at competitive prices.

GEOFF'S TOYS
30 HIGH STREET, COALVILLE, LEICESTERSHIRE LE67 3ED
☎ (01530) 832795. OPEN 9 - 5 MON - SAT, 9- 12.45 WED.
20 HIGH STREEET, LOUGHBOROUGH, LEICESTERSHIRE LE11
☎ (01509) 216966. OPEN 9 - 5.30 MON - FRI, 9 - 5 SAT.
Permanent Discount Outlet • *Children*

Vast array of toys at very low prices.

GILLIVERS FOOTWEAR AND CLOTHING WAREHOUSE
MARKET STREET, COALVILLE, LEICESTERSHIRE.
☎ (01530) 811452. OPEN 9 - 5 MON - SAT.
Permanent Discount Outlet • *Womenswear & Menswear*

Shoes from £1.99 to £40, at much reduced prices. The clothes are mainly from BhS and Marks & Spencer, although the labels are removed, and are discounted by between 25% and 50%. There are also bags, accessories and jewellery. Refreshments available.

GLYN WEBB
10A BURTON ROAD, HUMBERSTONE GATE, LEICESTER, LEICESTERSHIRE LE1 1TE
☎ (0116) 251 6622. OPEN 9 - 8 MON - SAT, 11 - 5 SUN AND BANK HOLS.
Permanent Discount Outlet • *DIY/Renovation*

Stockists of all your home improvement needs from wallpaper to paint, furniture to flooring, tiles to textiles, housewares to lighting - in fact, almost everything for your home, with 25 branches in the North-West, Midlands and

Yorkshire. Specialists in discontinued mail order, slightly imperfect branded stocks as well as perfect quality superior products. They carry top brands such as Dulux, Crown Paints and Vymura and Coloroll wall coverings, Rectella and Norwood textiles and much more in store. To find your nearest branch, phone Head Office on 0161 621 4500.

INTO CLOTHING
45 CASTLE STREET, HINCKLEY, LEICESTERSHIRE
☎ (01455) 611558. OPEN 9 - 5 MON - SAT.
Permanent Discount Outlet • *Womenswear Only*
Sells ladies clothing, cotton knitwear, separates and jackets at factory direct prices, which can be as much as 70% off the normal retail prices. The shop is small but well stocked and organised to make the maximum use of the space. Most of the stock is leading chainstore makes and includes dresses, jackets, rainwear, shoes, underwear, tights, suits, blouses, sweaters, nightwear, leggings, trousers, jeans, anoraks, with dressing gowns and eveningwear at Christmas only. There is another branch in Leamington Spa, Warwickshire.

JAEGER FACTORY SHOP
C/O R H N GRIEVE LTD, WOLSLEY ROAD, COALVILLE,
LEICESTERSHIRE LE6 7ET
☎ (01530) 835506. OPEN 10 - 5 MON - SAT.
Factory Shop • *Womenswear Only*
Contemporary classics from Jaeger at excellent prices. Most of the merchandise is previous seasons' stock, but you might also find some special makes.

JILLY'S DRESS AGENCY
THE SONDEES BARN, MAIN STREET, ROCKINGHAM, NEAR MARKET HARBOROUGH, LEICESTERSHIRE LE16 8TG
☎ (01536) 770352. OPEN 10.30 - 4 MON - SAT.
Dress Agency • *Womenswear Only*
Designer dress agency and evening wear hire. Labels tend to be designer oriented - the high street names stocked regularly include Windsmoor, Wallis, Monsoon and Marks & Spencer. Hire costs from £35 - £75 for designer ballgowns. Also sells shoes, bags and jewellery and hat hire is now available from £20 to £55.

LADY CLARE LTD
LEICESTER ROAD, LUTTERWORTH, LEICESTERSHIRE LE17 4HF
☎ (01455) 558427. OPEN 9 - 4.45 MON - THUR, 9 - 3.45 FRI,
CLOSED 1 - 1.30 DAILY. THEY ARE MOVING TOWARDS THE END OF 2000 SO RING BEFORE MAKING A SPECIAL TRIP.
Factory Shop • *Household*
Lady Clare supplies high class gift shops and top department stores with table mats, trays, coasters, wastepaper bins, picture frames and paper weights. Most of the stock in this small shop adjacent to the factory is seconds, cancelled orders or ends of lines with one third to one half off the normal price. Trays,

bins and table mats are all hand lacquered, hand gilded and felt-backed with central designs. Perfect place mats which would cost £11 are about £5 here.

MATALAN
100 CHURCHGATE, VAUGHAN WAY, LEICESTER,
LEICESTERSHIRE LE1 4AL
☎ (0116) 242 6700. OPEN 9 - 8 MON - FRI, 9 - 6 SAT, 11 - 5 SUN.
Permanent Discount Outlet • *Womenswear & Menswear*

Matalan is a fashion and homewares value retailer giving customers what they claim to be unbeatable value for money with huge savings on a wide range of products including high quality fashionable clothing for men, women and children at up to 50% off high street prices. Matalan is situated out of town and stores are open seven days a week all year round.

MAX SHOES
44-46 BELVOIR STREET, LEICESTERSHIRE LE1 6QC
☎ (0116) 254 4394. OPEN 9 - 5.30 MON - SAT.
Permanent Discount Outlet • *Menswear Only*

Large shop selling clearance lines of English and Italian top quality men's all-leather dress and leisure shoes. Often, there are brand names, but the shop will not divulge these beforehand. Shoes which cost £60 in high street retail outlets cost from £20-£40 here. Stocks sizes 6 - 11.

PIC A CHIC
FACTORY SHOP, NOTTINGHAM ROAD INDUSTRIAL ESTATE,
ASHBY DE LA ZOUCH, LEICESTERSHIRE LE6 51DR
☎ (01530) 413077. OPEN 9 - 4 MON - FRI, 9 - 12 SAT.
Food and Drink Discounters • *Food and Leisure*

Frozen chicken pieces sold in packets of 40 (either legs, breasts or a mixture of both) at savings of 20%. Also 10% savings on steak and kidney pies sold in packs of 12. Frozen gateaux sells for an average of £3 a cake and has 18 portions. Many lines three for £1, e.g. tagliatelli ready meals, family-sized chicken and mushroom pies, fish in sauce, etc. Products always changing.

SPOILS
UNITS 11 AND 12, THE SHIRES, HIGH STREET, LEICESTER,
LEICESTERSHIRE LE1 4FR
☎ (0116) 262 4002. OPEN 9 - 5.30 MON - FRI, UNTIL 8 ON WED, 9 - 6 SAT.
Permanent Discount Outlet • *Household*

General domestic glassware, non-stick bakeware, kitchen gadgets, ceramic oven-to-tableware, textiles, cutting boards, aluminium non-stick cookware, bakeware, plastic kitchenware, plastic storage, woodware, coffee pots/makers, furniture, mirrors and picture frames. Rather than being discounted, all the merchandise is very competitively priced - in fact, the company carry out competitors' checks frequently in order to monitor pricing. With 38 branches, the company is able to buy in bulk and thus negotiate very good prices.

THE DOC SHOP
BRUCE WAY, CAMBRIDGE ROAD INDUSTRIAL ESTATE, WHETSTONE, LEICESTERSHIRE LE8 6HP
☎ (0116) 286 5958. OPEN 9 - 5 MON - SAT.
Permanent Discount Outlet • *Womenswear & Menswear* • *Children*
Sells Doc Martens shoes and boots, as well as clothing and a vast range of accessories at discounted prices.

THE DRESS AGENCY
THE SQUARE, CROSS STREET, ENDERBY, LEICESTERSHIRE LE9 5NJ
☎ (0116) 275 0501. WEBSITE: www.thedressagency.co.uk
OPEN 10.30 - 3 MON - FRI, 10 - 4 SAT.
Dress Agency • *Womenswear Only*
Nearly-new shop selling mostly high street names such as Next, M&S, Richards, Debenhams, Wallis, with a small amount of menswear and childrenswear. Some of the designer labels stocked include Paul Costelloe, Betty Jackson and Yves St Laurent. They also sell accessories such as shoes and bags.

THE FACTORY SHOP LTD
NEWBOLD FOOTWEAR, BROOK STREET, SILEBY, LEICESTERSHIRE LE12 7RF
☎ (01509) 813514. OPEN 9 - 5 MON - SAT. CLOSED SUN.
Factory Shop • *Household* • *Womenswear & Menswear*
Children • *Furniture/Soft Furnishings* • *Sportswear & Equipment*
Wide range on sale includes men's, ladies and children's clothing and footwear; household textiles; toiletries; hardware; luggage; lighting and bedding, most of which are chainstore and high street brands at discounts of approximately 30%-50% as well as the Cape Country Furniture range with free-standing kitchens, and living, bedroom and dining furniture. There are weekly deliveries and brands include many major stars such as Adidas, Nike, Joe Bloggs and Brabantia, to name just a few. Lines are continually changing and few factory shops offer such a variety under one roof. This outlet has its own free car park.

TK MAXX
HAYMARKET CENTRE, LEICESTER, LEICESTERSHIRE LE1 3YD
☎ (0116) 251 0155. OPEN 9 - 5.30 MON - FRI, 9 - 6 SAT, 10 - 4 SUN.
Permanent Discount Outlet • *Womenswear & Menswear*
Children • *Household* • *Furniture/Soft Furnishings*
Based on an American concept, TK Maxx is situated in easily accessible, often centrally located stores and offers famous label goods with up to 60% savings off recommended retail prices. TK Maxx has fashion for the whole family - women's, men's and childrenswear - accessories, shoes, gifts, kitchenware and home goods. Everything in the store is branded with a choice of well-known high street names to designer labels, and while a small percentage might be clearly marked past season, the great majority of items in store are current sea-

son, current stock and still with phenomenal savings. There is a huge choice with 50,000 pieces in store and up to 10,000 new items arriving a week. The stores are simple and unfussy with wide aisles, shopping trolleys and baskets, and a spacious, functional feel to them but there are individual changing rooms, ramps for buggies and wheelchairs and plenty of staff on the shop floor. Every branch accepts all major credit and debit cards and has a liberal refund and return policy.

TWEEDIES
MARLBOROUGH SQUARE, COALVILLE, LEICESTERSHIRE LE67 2WD
☎ (01530) 510227. OPEN 9 - 5 MON - SAT, 10 - 4 SUN.
NOTTINGHAM STREET, MELTON MOWBRAY, LEICESTERSHIRE
☎ (01664) 501072. OPEN 9 - 5 MON - SAT.
Permanent Discount Outlet • *Womenswear & Menswear*
Children • *Household* • *Sportswear & Equipment*
Three-storey building full of menswear, womenswear, children's clothes, luggage and gifts, which consist of a mixture of perfects, seconds and ends of lines, all sold at discounted prices. Top brand names and favourite high street labels are sold at up to 50% off. Brand names include Wrangler, Wolsey, Lyle & Scott, Nike, Adidas, Fruit of the Loom, Peter England, Farah and many more, plus high street names such as Marks & Spencer, Dorothy Perkins, Evans, Top Shop, BhS and Richards, to name just a few. A men's leisurewear department sells Burberry, Puma and much more. Plus on the first floor there's a European designerwear department with outfits for every occasion and a fabulous ladies golf department selling Lyle & Scott and Burberry golf accessories and luggage.

UNITED FOOTWEAR
114 MAIN STREET, NEWBOLD VERDON, LEICESTERSHIRE
☎ (01455) 822407. OPEN 9 - 8 MON - FRI, 9 - 5.30 SAT, 10 - 4 SUN.
Permanent Discount Outlet • *Womenswear & Menswear*
Children • *Household*
Shoes for all the family as well as clothes, handbags, sports shoes, boots, giftware and household goods, all at discounted prices. Famous brands including Clarks, K Shoes and Elmdale. Part of a national chain.

WEBB IVORY LTD
BRITANNIA CENTRE, HINCKLEY, LEICESTERSHIRE LE10 1RU
☎ (01455) 891920. OPEN 9 - 5 MON - SAT.
Factory Shop • *Household* • *Womenswear & Menswear* • *Children*
Items from the Webb Ivory catalogue at reduced prices including cards, gifts, soft toys, books, pens, lamps, kitchenware, garden furniture and clothes. Discounts range from at least 50%.

Lincolnshire

ALEXON SALE SHOP
ST BENEDICTS SQUARE, LINCOLN, LINCOLNSHIRE
☎ (01522) 545220. OPEN 9 - 5.30 MON - SAT.
THE ALEXON DEPARTMENT, GONERBY MOOR, GRANTHAM, LINCS. NG32 2AB
☎ (01476) 591001. OPEN 9.30 - 5.30 MON - SAT, 11 - 5 SUN.
Permanent Discount Outlet • *Womenswear Only*
Alexon and Eastex from last season at 40% less than the original price; during sale time in January and June, the reductions are as much as 70%. Stock includes separates, skirts, jackets, blouses; there is no underwear or night clothes.

BEDLAM
15 STEEP HILL, LINCOLN, LINCOLNSHIRE LN2 1LT.
☎ (01522) 545498. OPEN 11 - 5 MON - SAT.
Secondhand and Vintage Clothes • *Womenswear & Menswear*
Secondhand period clothes from the Twenties to the Seventies, some of which are available to hire. Dresses cost from £8-£30, coats from £15-£25 and eveningwear, £20-£35, as well as some women's designer wear. Women's sizes range from 8-16.

BOUNDARY MILL STORES
AT DOWNTOWN SUPER STORE, GONERBY MOOR, A1 GRANTHAM, LINCOLNSHIRE NG32 2AB
☎ (01476) 591001. OPEN 9.30 - 5.30 MON - SAT, 11 - 5 SUN.
Permanent Discount Outlet • *Womenswear & Menswear* • *Children*
Sister to the very large clearance store in Colne, Lancashire, the newly extended Grantham store takes up 45,000 sq ft of the Downtown Super store, selling ladies and men's top quality clothes, shoes and lingerie. Some of the top end of the high street designer labels are on sale here from casual to evening wear, with reductions of between 30% and 70%. Four times a year there are special sales at which prices are discounted still further. Most of the stock is perfect clearance and ends of lines with the occasional marked seconds. There is a coffee shop and free parking.

CATALOGUE BARGAIN SHOP
12-14 SILVER STREET, GAINSBOROUGH, LINCOLNSHIRE DN21 2DP
☎ (01427) 810604. OPEN 9 - 5.30 MON, THUR, FRI, 8.30 - 5 TUE, 9 - 5 WED, 8.30 - 5.30 SAT, 10 - 4 SUN.
29-31 THE STRAIT, LINCOLN LN1 1JD
☎ (01522) 527276. OPEN 9 - 5.30 MON - SAT, 10.30 - 4.30 SUN.
Permanent Discount Outlet • *Womenswear & Menswear*
Children • *Household* • *Electrical Equipment*

Catalogue Bargain Shop is a growing national chain of stores which obtains the majority of its goods from mail order giants Great Universal and Kays, and offers a range of clothing for all the family, a wide selection of shoes, bed linen, household goods, electrical equipment and hundreds of other catalogue items at very competitive prices. The merchandise consists of ends of ranges and previous season's stock for which there is no longer storage space when the catalogues change.

CLOTH MARKET
UNIT 5, STAMFORD WALK, ST MARY'S STREET, STAMFORD, LINCOLNSHIRE PE9 2JE
☎ (01780) 753409. FAX 01780 757535. OPEN 9.30 - 5.30 MON - SAT, CLOSED THUR.
Permanent Discount Outlet • *Furniture/Soft Furnishings*
Small shop selling upholstery and furnishing fabric by Liberty, Sanderson, G P & J Baker, Monkwell and other good quality makes. Apart from offering a cut-length service on new collections, they specialise in discontinued designs and seconds in current designs, including undyed natural weaves and damasks, at prices starting at £3.90 a yard. Here, customers can see it all in stock, check out the good prices and walk away with it. Some even borrow a roll to look at against their home colours. There is also a marvellous stock of dress fabrics, with couture wools at a quarter of the regular price, starting at £10 a yard. Friendly, personal service.

COSALT INTERNATIONAL LTD
WICKHAM ROAD, GRIMSBY, LINCOLNSHIRE DN31 3SL
☎ (01472) 504293 . OPEN 8.30 - 5 MON - FRI.
Permanent Discount Outlet • *Womenswear & Menswear*
Specialises in workwear, safety clothing and marine wear but some of the merchandise is eminently wearable for everyday and is sold at very reasonable prices. There is plenty of stock on the shelves, but you can also order some lines from the catalogue. There is a wide selection of leisure and outdoor clothes from Doc Martens to padded jackets and denim shirts, dungarees and donkey jackets. VAT has to be added to prices. They also provide marine safety and life-raft servicing.

DESIGNER FABRIC SUPERSTORE
UNIT 5, GREYFRIARS, GRANTHAM, LINCOLNSHIRE NG31 6PG
☎ (01476) 570022. OPEN 9.30 - 5.30 MON - SAT, 10 - 4 SUN.
HUCKNALL LANE, BULWELL, NOTTINGHAM NG6 8AJ
☎ (0115) 975 3311. OPEN 9.30 - 5.30 MON - SAT, 10 - 4 SUN.
Permanent Discount Outlet • *Furniture/Soft Furnishings*
Stocks up to 8,000 rolls of fabric from £2.99 a metre with remnants at £1 per metre. There are also made-up curtains, lampshades, cushions, pillows, net curtains, tassle tie-backs at £2.50 a pair, curtain poles, tracks, lining, braid, bean

bags, upholstery and dress fabrics, some pottery and giftware. They will also take orders for fabric. There is a coffee shop at the Grantham branch, car parking and disabled facilities. In spring 1997, they introduced upholstery and dress fabrics. The Bulwell branch does not sell pottery, dress fabrics or giftware.

DISCOUNT DRESSING
45 STEEP HILL, LINCOLN, LINCOLNSHIRE LN2 1LU
☎ (01522) 532239. OPEN 10 - 6 MON - SAT.
Permanent Discount Outlet • *Womenswear Only*
A veritable Aladdin's Cave of designer bargains, Discount Dressing sells mostly German, Italian and French designer labels at prices at least 50% and up to 90% below those in normal retail outlets. All items are brand new and perfect. A team of buyers all over Europe purchase stock directly from the manufacturer for this growing chain of discount shops. This enables Discount Dressing to by-pass the importers and wholesalers and, of course, their mark-up. They also buy bankrupt stock in this country. Their agreement with their suppliers means that they are not able to advertise brand names for obvious reasons, but they are all well-known for their top quality and style. So confident is Discount Dressing that you will be unable to find the same item cheaper elsewhere, that they guarantee to give the outfit to you free of charge should you perform this miracle. Merchandise includes raincoats, dresses, suits, trousers, blouses, evening wear, special occasion outfits and jackets, in sizes 6-24 and in some cases larger. GDD readers can obtain a further 10% discount if they visit the shop taking a copy of this book with them. There are other branches in London, Northern Ireland and Hertfordshire.

DUNELM FABRIC SHOP
LAWRENCE LANE, BOSTON, LINCOLNSHIRE PE21 8QD
☎ (01205) 353787. OPEN 9 - 5 MON, TUE, THUR, FRI, 9 - 5.30 WED, SAT, 10.30 - 4.30 SUN.
PROCTERS ROAD, OUTER CIRCLE ROAD, LINCOLN LN2 4LA
☎ (01522) 589737. OPEN 9 - 5.30 MON - WED, FRI, 9 - 8 THUR, 9 - 6 SAT, 10.30 - 4.30 SUN.
6-8 WATERGATE, GRANTHAM NG31 6NS
☎ (01476) 574447. OPEN 9 - 5 MON - SAT.
Permanent Discount Outlet • *Household*
Part of a chain of shops based in the Midlands selling brand-name and chain-store curtains, masses of bedlinen, towels, wickerware, pictures and frames, all at competitive prices.

GLYN WEBB
TRITTON ROAD, LINCOLN, LINCOLNSHIRE LN6 7QY
☎ (01522) 575252. OPEN 9 - 8 MON - SAT, 11 - 5 SUN AND OPEN ALL BANK HOLIDAYS.
Permanent Discount Outlet • *DIY/Renovation*
Stockists of all your home improvement needs from wallpaper to paint, furniture to flooring, tiles to textiles, housewares to lighting - in fact, almost every-

thing for your home, with 25 branches in the North-West, Midlands and Yorkshire. Specialists in discontinued mail order, slightly imperfect branded stocks as well as perfect quality superior products. They carry top brands such as Dulux, Crown Paints and Vymura and Coloroll wall coverings, Rectella and Norwood textiles and much more in store. To find your nearest branch, phone Head Office on 0161 621 4500.

GYMPHLEX SPORTSWEAR
BOSTON ROAD, HORNCASTLE, LINCOLNSHIRE LN9 6HU
☎ (01507) 523243.
Designer Sale • *Sportswear & Equipment* • *Children Womenswear & Menswear*
Holds a one day factory shop sale just once a year, please phone 01507 523243 for details. Your chance to buy a huge range of sportswear for all the family: jogging pants, tracksuits, rugby and football shirts, rugby shorts, T-shirts, polo shirts, Lycra swimwear, leotards, tights, socks. Some of the stock is seconds, some overmakes. The rest is freshly-made stock which is specially reduced for the sale.

HEMSWELL CLIFF ANTIQUE AND CRAFTS CENTRE
NEAR CAENBY CORNER, HEMSWELL, LINCOLNSHIRE
☎ (01427) 668389. OPEN 10 - 5 SEVEN DAYS A WEEK.
Secondhand shops • *Furniture/Soft Furnishings*
Created from the former RAF Hemswell, it claims to be the largest centre for antiques, collectables and retro items in Europe, with about 300 stalls spread over three separate buildings. There is also a major craft centre, a wallpaper factory shop, pine and garden furniture manufacturers, pottery and a tools/diy centre. Many of the antiques are of high quality though the prices seem to be below most recognised major centres. Avoid Sundays when there is a very popular car boot sale/market making car parking difficult.

JAKEMANS
46 WORMGATE, BOSTON, LINCOLNSHIRE PE21 6NS
☎ (01205) 362052. OPEN 9 - 5 MON - FRI, 9 - 4 SAT.
Factory Shop • *Food and Leisure*
Sweets factory shop which sells way out sweets at discount prices from boiled sweets to chocolates and liquorice allsorts. Jakemans Throat and Chest cough sweet is a particular favourite. Discounted bulk £1 bags available.

JUMPER
BOUNDARY MILL STORES, GRANTHAM, LINCOLNSHIRE NG3 2AB
☎ (01476) 591001. OPEN 9 - 6 MON - SAT, 11 - 5 SUN.
Factory Shop • *Womenswear & Menswear*
A wide range of Jumper label sweaters, gloves, scarves, shirts and cardigans for men and women all at discount prices of up to 50% off. Prices start at £2.

LITTLEWOODS CATALOGUE DISCOUNT STORE
7 HIGH STREET, GRANTHAM, LINCOLNSHIRE NG31 6PN
☎ (01476) 590552. OPEN 9.30 - 5.30 MON, 9 - 5.30 TUE - SAT.
Permanent Discount Outlet • *Womenswear & Menswear*
Children • *Electrical Equipment*
Littlewoods clearance shops offering up to 50% off the catalogue price for clothing and between 50% and 60% off for electrical goods. Stock changes constantly and varies from day to day but can include well-known brand names such as Berlei and Gossard lingerie, Vivienne Westwood, Pamplemousse leisure wear, Nike and Adidas sports shoes, Workers for Freedom, and Timberland and Caterpillar footwear. Stock depends on the size and location of the shop, so larger shops will get the longer discontinued runs and smaller shops over-runs with only a small amount of colour and size variations left. Littlewoods also run a mobile shop which operates in cities where they don't have a sale shop. For details of further venues for the sales, which usually take place once a month, contact Melanie Lamb, c/o Crosby DC Kershaw Avenue, Endbutt Lane, Crosby, Merseyside L70 1AH.

MAGPIE FABRICS
22 BRIDGE STREET, SAXILBY, LINCOLN, LINCOLNSHIRE LN1 2PZ
☎ (01522) 702137. OPEN 10 - 1 MON, WED, 10 - 5 TUE, THUR, FRI, 10 - 4 SAT.
Permanent Discount Outlet • *Furniture/Soft Furnishings*
Sells quality low-priced fabrics for curtaining and upholstery as well as fabrics and wallpapers to order from Blendworth, Malthouse, John Wilman, Nouveau, Wemyss, Sanderson, Dovedale and others at competitive prices. Curtaining from £7.50 per yard, upholstery from £8.50 per yard. Also stocks lining fabric (100% cotton sateen), heading tapes (from standard to diamond and pinch pleat), cording, haberdashery, tassels, tiebacks, wooden holdbacks and cotton thread. Phone for the price of any of the fabrics you want. Making-up service available. The shop is five minutes out of Lincoln on the A57, with easy parking.

MATALAN
LINDIS RETAIL PARK, TRITTON ROAD, LINCOLN, LINCOLNSHIRE LN6 7QY
☎ (01522) 696541. OPEN 10 - 8 MON - FRI, 9 - 6 SAT, 11 - 5 SUN.
DUDLEY ROAD, SCUNTHORPE DN16 1BA
☎ (01724) 270958. OPEN 9.30 - 8 MON - FRI, 9 - 6 SAT, 11 - 5 SUN.

JOHN ADAMS WAY, BOSTON PE21 6TY
☎ (01205) 312040. OPEN 10 - 8 MON - FRI, 9 - 6 SAT, 11 - 5 SUN.
UNIT 1, HEWITTS CIRCUS, CLEETHORPES, GRIMSBY DN35 9QH
☎ (01472) 200255. OPEN 9 - 8 MON - FRI, 9 - 6 SAT, 11 - 5 SUN.
Permanent Discount Outlet • *Womenswear & Menswear*
Children • *Household*

Matalan is a fashion and homewares value retailer giving customers what they claim to be unbeatable value for money with huge savings on a wide range of products including high quality fashionable clothing for men, women and children at up to 50% off high street prices. Matalan is situated out of town and stores are open seven days a week all year round.

REVIVE DRESS AGENCY
4 ST MARY'S STREET, LINCOLN, LINCOLNSHIRE LN5 7EQ
☎ (01522) 527619. OPEN 9.30 - 5 MON - FRI, 9.30 - 4.30 SAT.
Dress Agency • *Womenswear Only*

Pleasant and friendly shop on two floors in central Lincoln opposite the train station. Good quality nearly-new clothes, evening wear, shoes and handbags from names such as Next, Wallis, Principles, Planet, Jasper Conran, Eastex, Windsmoor and M&S to Moschino and Versace.

RUTLAND LIGHTING
10-12 WATERGATE, GRANTHAM, LINCOLNSHIRE
☎ (01476) 591049. OPEN 9 - 5.30 MON - SAT.
Permanent Discount Outlet • *Household*

Sells a full range of lampshades, table and floor lamps, chandeliers, bulbs, outdoor and indoor lights, plus other manufacturers' ends of lines and chainstore seconds. Most lines have genuine reductions on normal retail prices. This shop, unlike its sister shop in Market Overton, Leicestershire, is large and on the high street.

STAGE 2
UNIT 3, TRITTON RETAIL PARK, TRITTON ROAD, LINCOLN
LINCOLNSHIRE LN6 7YA
☎ (01522) 560303. OPEN 10 - 8 MON - FRI, 9 - 6 SAT, 11 - 5 SUN AND BANK HOLIDAYS.
Permanent Discount Outlet • *Womenswear & Menswear*
Children • *Household* • *Electrical Equipment*

Sells discontinued lines from Freeman's Catalogues. The full range is carried, but stock depends on what has not been sold at full price from the catalogue itself, or has been returned or the packaging is damaged or soiled. Clothing discounts range from about 50% - 65%. There are also household items and electrical equipment.

SUNDAES SANDALS
THE CHASE, 18 HIGH STREET, MOULTON, SPALDING,
LINCOLNSHIRE PE12 6QB
☎ (01406) 371370. OPEN 9 - 3.30 MON - FRI, SAT BY APPOINTMENT.
FREE COLOUR MAIL ORDER CATALOGUE AVAILABLE.
Factory Shop • *Womenswear & Menswear* • *Children*
Handmade shoes and sandals in bright summer colours, top quality materials, including leather uppers, insoles and linings. There are 35 styles for all the family, with some women's shoes up to size 9 and sandals to size 10. Their small, informal factory shop sells the full range of Sundaes made on the premises and usually has a selection of discontinued styles, colours and slight seconds at bargain prices. Visitors are always welcome, but do phone first.

TALLINGTON DRESS AGENCY
LODGE FARM, TALLINGTON, STAMFORD, LINCOLNSHIRE PE9 4RJ
☎ (01778) 342792. OPEN 10 - 5 EVERY DAY EXCEPT WED.
Dress Agency • *Womenswear Only*
Stocks everything from high street names such as Wallis to designer names such as Mondi, Escada, and Yarell. Sizes range up to 22. There is also a wedding dress hire service including veils and shoes. New shoes, hats and jewellery are also stocked.

THE CAPE
UNIT 1A, 233-235 HIGH STREET, LINCOLN, LINCOLNSHIRE LNZ 1AT
☎ (01522) 522462. OPEN 9 - 5.30 MON - FRI, 9 - 6 SAT, 11 - 5 SUN.
Factory Shop • *Furniture/Soft Furnishings* • *Household*
High quality, high density pine furniture made in South Africa from trees grown in managed forests, is sold at factory direct prices with home delivery throughout the UK. The range includes beds, wardrobes, blanket boxes, chests of drawers, tallboys, dressing tables, cheval mirrors, headboards, mattresses, a kitchen range, dining room tables, Welsh dressers, hi-fi units, bookcases. Also on sale in this shops is a range of African accessories and artefacts from Zimbabwe encompassing mirrors, prints, serpentine (stone) ornaments, recylced stationery, handmade wirework, candles and other ethnic and traditional gifts. Colour brochure and price list available on 01535 650940.

THE FACTORY SHOP, COATS VIYELLA CLOTHING
CV CLOTHING LADIES AND CHILDRENSWEAR, SCOTTER ROAD,
SCUNTHORPE, LINCOLNSHIRE DN15 8AT
☎ (01724) 270426. OPEN 9 - 5 MON - FRI, 9 - 4 SAT, 10 - 4 SUN.
WASHDYKE ROAD, IMMINGHAM, HUMBERSIDE DN40 2AA
☎ (01469) 574310. OPEN 9 - 5.30 MON - SAT, 10 - 4 SUN.
Factory Shop • *Womenswear & Menswear* • *Children*
Part of the Coats Viyella group, which makes quality clothing for many of the

major high street stores, overstocks and clearance lines are sold through more than 30 of the group's factory shops. Many of you will recognise the garments on sale, despite the lack of well-known labels. Ladieswear includes dresses, blouses, jumpers, cardigans, trousers, nightwear, underwear, lingerie, hosiery, coats and swimwear. Menswear includes trousers, belts, shirts, ties, pullovers, cardigans, T-shirts, underwear, nightwear, hosiery and jackets. Childrenswear includes jackets, trousers, T-shirts, underwear, hosiery, jumpers and babywear. There are regular deliveries to constantly update the range.

THE FACTORY SHOP

MALT KILN ROAD, BARTON ON HUMBER, LINCOLNSHIRE DN18 5JT
☎ (01652) 636701. OPEN 9 - 7 MON, TUE, WED, 9 - 8 THUR, FRI,
8.30 - 7 SAT, 10 - 4 SUN.
51 FLEET STREET, HOLBEACH, SPALDING, LINCOLNSHIRE PE12 7AU
☎ (01406) 422180. OPEN 9 - 5 MON - SAT, 10 - 4 SUN.
CARRE STREET, SLEAFORD, LINCOLNSHIRE NG34 7TW
☎ (01529) 410155. OPEN 9 - 5.30 MON - SAT, 10 - 4 SUN.
43 HIGH STREET, MABLETHORPE, LINCOLNSHIRE LN12 1XA
☎ (01507) 473705. OPEN 9.30 - 6 MON - SAT, 10.30 - 4.30 SUN.

Factory Shop • *Household* • *Womenswear & Menswear* • *Children Furniture/Soft Furnishings* • *Sportswear & Equipment*

Wide range on sale includes men's, ladies and children's clothing and footwear; household textiles; toiletries; hardware; luggage; lighting and bedding, most of which are chainstore and high street brands at discounts of approximately 30%-50%. Now has kitchen and furniture displays and the Cape Country Furniture range is on sale with free-standing kitchens, as well as living, bedroom and dining furniture. There are weekly deliveries and brands include many major stars such as Adidas, Nike, Joe Bloggs and Brabantia, to name just a few. Lines are continually changing and few factory shops offer such a variety under one roof. There is free car parking at all outlets and a cafe at Barton.

THE SHOE FACTORY SHOP

21 WELLOWGATE, GRIMSBY, LINCOLNSHIRE DN32 ORA
☎ (01472) 342415. OPEN 9 - 5 MON - SAT, 9 - 7 THUR.

Factory Shop • *Womenswear & Menswear* • *Children*

Men's, women's and children's shoes and accessories which are bought in from other manufacturers including Spanish, Portuguese and Italian companies. All are unbranded. The range covers from mocassins to dressy shoes. Ladies shoes which would cost £35 retail are £29. Children's shoes from size 6 to adult size 5 from £10 upwards. Slippers start at baby size 4 to junior size 2 from £3.50 - £6.50.

TILE CLEARING HOUSE

UNIT 1, SPRONBROUGH ROAD, OFF YORK ROAD, DONCASTER, LINCOLNSHIRE DN5 8BN

☎ (01302) 787 000. OPEN 8 - 6 MON - FRI, 9 - 6 SAT, 10 - 4 SUN.

Permanent Discount Outlet • *DIY/Renovation*

Over 500 ranges of top quality ceramic wall and floor tiles permanently in stock, plus a comprehensive range of grouts, adhesives, tools and accessories to complete the job. By buying direct from the manufacturer and passing the savings on to the customer, their prices are very competitive. Moreover, everything you see is in stock, so there's no waiting for orders to be processed. Save up to 75% on manufacturers' recommended selling prices.

TK MAXX

UNIT 16, ST MARK'S CENTRE, LINCOLN, LINCOLNSHIRE

☎ (01522) 530933. OPEN 9 - 6 MON - SAT, 8 ON THUR, 11 - 5 SUN.

Permanent Discount Outlet • *Womenswear & Menswear*
Children • *Household*

Based on an American concept, TK Maxx is situated in easily accessible, often centrally located stores and offers famous label goods with up to 60% savings off recommended retail prices. TK Maxx has fashion for the whole family - women's, men's and childrenswear - accessories, shoes, gifts, kitchenware and home goods. Everything in the store is branded with a choice of well-known high street names to designer labels, and while a small percentage might be clearly marked past season, the great majority of items in store are current season, current stock and still with phenomenal savings. There is a huge choice with 50,000 pieces in store and up to 10,000 new items arriving a week. The stores are simple and unfussy with wide aisles, shopping trolleys and baskets, and a spacious, functional feel to them but there are individual changing rooms, ramps for buggies and wheelchairs and plenty of staff on the shop floor. Every branch accepts all major credit and debit cards and has a liberal refund and return policy.

TOG 24

BOUNDARY MILL STORES, GONERBY MOOR, ON THE A1, GRANTHAM, LINCOLNSHIRE NG32 2AB

☎ (01476) 591001. OPEN 9.30 - 5.30 MON - SAT, 11 - 5 SUN.

Factory Shop in a Factory Shopping Village
Womenswear & Menswear • *Children* • *Sportswear & Equipment*

Tog 24 are the UK's fastest growing brand name in outdoor clothing and leisurewear. They utilise the world's finest performance fabrics including Gore-Tex, Polartec and Burlington MCS, catering for all the family for all seasons, with cosy fleeces and waterproofs for the winter, and trekking ranges, shorts and t-shirts for the summer. With all prices at least 30% below the recommended retail price, you can afford to enter the Tog comfort zone.

VOGUE CLOTHING AGENCY
94 EASTGATE, LOUTH, LINCOLNSHIRE LN11 9AA
☎ (01507) 604233. OPEN 10 - 5 MON - FRI, 9.30 - 5 SAT.
Dress Agency • *Hire Shops* • *Womenswear & Menswear*
Sportswear & Equipment
Trading for 25 years, this shop stocks a wide range of middle to high quality designer women's clothing. Consisting of two floors situated next to Curry's on the main street, it offers day wear, wedding and evening outfits with appropriate accessories including shoes and handbags. Labels include Escada, Jaeger, Laurel, Mondi and Wallis. There is a well-stocked hat hire department. Since 1996 a separate men's department has been established within the premises offering designer clothes such as Daks, Aquascutum, Armani and Hugo Boss plus casual wear separates. There is also a range of dinner suits and accessories. More recently the shop has diversified again, with a further department carrying a range of skiwear and motorcycle clothing, including one piece and two piece suits and boots.

WINDSMOOR GROUP
BOUNDARY MILL, DOWNTOWN SUPERSTORE, GONERBY MOOR, GRANTHAM, LINCOLNSHIRE NG32 2AB
☎ (01476) 591001. OPEN 9.30 - 5.30 MON - SAT, 11 - 5 SUN.
Factory Shop in a Factory Shopping Village • *Womenswear Only*
Previous season's stock as well as any returned merchandise and overmakes from the Windsmoor, Planet and Precis ranges at discounts averaging about 50% off the original price.

WYNSORS WORLD OF SHOES
CROMWELL ROAD, GRIMSBY, LINCOLNSHIRE
☎ (01472) 251627. OPEN 9 - 5.30 MON, TUE, WED, SAT, 9 - 8 THUR, FRI, 10 - 4 SUN AND BANK HOLIDAYS.
Permanent Discount Outlet • *Womenswear & Menswear* • *Children*
Stocks top brand-name shoes at less than half price. Special monthly offers always available. There are shoes, trainers, slippers, sandals and boots for all the family, with a selection of bags, cleaners and polishes available.

London

ADAM RICHWOOD
5 GARDEN WALK, LONDON EC2A 3EQ
☎ 020-7729 0976. OPEN 7 - 4 MON - FRI.
Furniture/Soft Furnishings

Makers of fine period furniture, Adam Richwood sells direct from their factory, top quality pieces at savings of between 75% and 100% on shop prices. (VAT is extra and delivery can be arranged at a nominal cost.) A 5ft mahogany sideboard with solid brass fittings costs £644; a 30in yew wood Regency bureau costs £473; a burr walnut Queen Anne 4ft by 2ft desk with solid brass handles costs £802. They also make chests, hi-fi and television cabinets, as well as open bookcases made to any size, the most popular being 6 ft by 3 ft and costing £260 in mahogany. Prices change in January each year.

ALADDINS
47 FULHAM HIGH STREET, LONDON SW6
☎ 020-7731 2345. OPEN 10 - 6 MON - FRI, 10 - 5.30 SAT.
Permanent Discount Outlet • *Household*

Clearing house for a whole range of household items from electrical equipment, gardening tools, binoculaurs, clothes, pots and pans to cast iron barbecues, fans, storage containers, brushes, air mattresses. Stock changes constantly so it's worth popping in regularly if you live nearby.

ALEXANDER FURNISHINGS
51-61 WIGMORE STREET, LONDON W1H 9LF
☎ 020-7935 2624. OPEN 9 - 6 MON - SAT, UNTIL 7 ON THUR.
Permanent Discount Outlet • *Furniture/Soft Furnishings*

The largest independent curtain retailer in the UK, Alexander Furnishings has been operating from the same base for nearly 50 years. Famous for curtaining, they also sell upholstery fabric and wallpapers and trimmings. There's always a discount on fabrics and the biggest bargains are the discontinued lines which can be discounted by up to 50%. There is also a trimming shop on the premises and sofas and sofabeds are on sale. Fabric prices can start as low as £1.95 and there is a vast selection below £10 but this varies over the year.

AMAZON
1,3,7,22 KENSINGTON CHURCH STREET, LONDON W8
☎ 020-7937 4692.
Permanent Discount Outlet • *Womenswear & Menswear*

Amazon ranges over five shops at the Kensington High Street end of Kensington Church Street. Numbers 1, 3 and 22 feature much the same merchandise which changes from one week to the next according to what the buyers can get hold of. Number 7 features menswear in the left hand shop, ladies shoes and childrenswear on the right. The most common labels seen here are In Wear, French Connection, Great Plains, Fenn, Wright & Manson, Nicole

Farhi and Sticky Fingers. There's always plenty of stock in good condition and very reasonable prices. For example, Fenn, Wright & Manson long dress £29.99 reduced from £105; James Lakeland shirt £22 reduced from £80; cashmere blend sweater £19.99, was £180; French Connection boat neck striped jersey £20, insted of £65. Caters for office, weekend and party wear. Shoes at number 7 are very cheap: Velcro dolly shoe £19.99 reduced from £50; wedge boot, £24.95 reduced from £78.95; evening shoes £14.99 from £49.99.

ANDREW'S OFFICE FURNITURE
97-101 HACKNEY ROAD, LONDON E2
☎ 020-7256 1269. OPEN 7.30 - 5.30 MON - FRI, 8 - 2 SAT.
Secondhand shops • *Furniture/Soft Furnishings*
Two floors and a labyrinthian courtyard packed with really cheap office furniture. Stock is mostly from bankrupt companies or comprises new but discontinued styles, with prices 50% lower than at usual retail outlets. Outdoors, there is a huge selection of stacking chairs and old rickety desks.

ANGELS FANCY DRESS
119 SHAFTESBURY AVENUE, LONDON WC2H 8AE
☎ 020-7836 5678. FAX 0207-240 9527 E-MAIL: party@fancydress.com
WEBSITE: www.fancydress.com
OPEN 9 - 5.30 MON - FRI, LAST COSTUME FITTING 4.30.
Hire Shops • *Womenswear & Menswear*
Angels hires the best costumes for parties and sells accessories, wigs, masks, make-up and tiaras. You can party like a star dressed in a Georgian, Victorian, 1970s, Halloween, Christmas, animal or space costume. Angels has been dressing the entertainment industry for 160 years, recently supplying films such as Topsy-Turvy, Shakespeare in Love and Titanic.

ANNIES
10 CAMDEN PASSAGE, ISLINGTON, LONDON N1 8ED
☎ 020-7359 0796. OPEN 11- 6 MON - SAT, MARKET DAYS.
Secondhand and Vintage Clothes • *Womenswear Only*
Mainly women's clothes from late Victorian times to the Forties, specialising in Twenties beaded garments, as well as ballgowns, silk lingerie, Forties suits and blouses, table linen, cushions, curtains, textiles and bed linen.

APPLIANCE DIRECT
86 WESTBOURNE GROVE, BAYSWATER, LONDON W2 5RT
☎ 020-7221 1144. FAX 0207-221 7770. WEBSITE: www.appliancedirectuk.com
OPEN 9.30 - 5.30 MON - FRI, TILL 7 THUR, 10 - 5.30 SAT.
Permanent Discount Outlet • *Electrical Equipment*
Specialise in ex-display and graded white electrical goods. For example new, cosmetically damaged washing machines from £160. They also sell fridges, cookers, ranges, deep fat fryers, blenders, vacuum cleaners, toasters, irons, food processors and American fridges.

ART IN IRON
UNIT F, BRIDGES WHARF, BRIDGES COURT, OFF YORK ROAD,
BATTERSEA, LONDON SW11 3AD
☎ 020-7924 2332. E-MAIL: sales@artiniron.demon.co.uk
WEBSITE: www.zzz4v.com   OPEN 10 - 6 MON - FRI, 11 - 5 SAT, SUN.
66A PADDENSWICK ROAD, LONDON W6.
☎ 020-8735 1800. OPEN 9 - 6 MON - FRI, 11 - 5 SAT, SUN.
Factory Shop • *Furniture/Soft Furnishings*
Make all their wrought iron beds on site in a construction area to the side of the showroom at the Battersea outlet. They specialise in simple, unfussy, contemporary designs, some with Gothic elements. New to the range are iron beds incorporating wood. Single beds cost from £260-£360; doubles and three-quarters from £320-£600; kings from £340-£660 and superkings from £390-£750. A four-poster option is available on most styles for an extra £220. Prices here are lower than the same beds would cost in department stores.

AUDIO GOLD
31 PARK ROAD, CROUCH END, LONDON N8 8TE
☎ 020-8341 9007. OPEN 11 - 6 MON - SAT, CLOSED WED, THUR.
Secondhand shops • *Electrical Equipment*
Small shop with friendly, unintimidating atmosphere where old, loved music machines get a second life. Catering for the run-of-the-mill end of the secondhand hi-fi market as well as the esoteric and expensive end. Particular bargains can be found in the imposing speaker areas as most people trading in equipment tend to trade down, not up, in size. Most equipment is guaranteed for three months. One of the few places left in London where you can still get a good range of turntables.

BATHROOMS @ SOURCE,
517-519 BATTERSEA PARK ROAD, LONDON SW11 3BN
☎ 020-7738 0808. PHONE FOR OPENING HOURS.
128 GARRETT LANE, LONDON SW18 3DJ.
PHONE FOR OPENING HOURS. ☎ 020-8870 0066
Permanent Discount Outlet • *DIY/Renovation*
Retailers of discounted bathrooms, selling a very extensive range to suit all tastes and budgets. Quality service and installation.

BENNY DEE (CITY) LTD
74-80 MIDDLESEX STREET, LONDON E1
☎ 020-7377 9067. OPEN 9.30 - 6 MON, 8.30 - 6 TUE - FRI, 10 - 4 SAT, 9.30 - 4.30 SUN.
136-138 WALTHAMSTOW HIGH STREET, LONDON E17 1JS
☎ 020-8520 4637. OPEN 9 - 6 MON - SAT.
110-114 KILBURN HIGH ROAD, LONDON NW6 4HY
☎ 020-7624 2995. OPEN 9 - 6 MON - SAT, 10 - 4 SUN.

4-6 HIGH ROAD, WOOD GREEN, LONDON N22 6BX
☎ 020-8881 8101. OPEN 9 - 6 MON - SAT, 10 - 4 SUN.
Permanent Discount Outlet • *Womenswear & Menswear Children* • *Household*

This branch is on two floors with children's clothes and baby bedding in the basement, most of which are end of lines or bankrupt stock with the labels cut out. Some of the brands there include Zorbit, Mothercare, Baby Gap, Baby Togs and Grasshopper. The ground floor contains predominantly ladies lingerie with masses of bras, all brand names such as Marks & Spencer, Berlei, Gossard, Triumph and Warner and some clothing. For men there are socks, ties, underwear, shirts, T shirts, jogging bottoms and occasionally suits.

BERTIE GOLIGHTLY (UK) LTD
48 BEAUCHAMP PLACE, NEAR HARRODS, LONDON SW3 1NX
☎ 020-7584 7270. OPEN 10 - 6 MON - SAT.
Dress Agency • *Womenswear Only*

Former stunt girl, Roberta Gibbs, opened Bertie Golightly in 1980 and sells a richly diverse selection of the world's most famous labels including Chanel, Valentino, Armani, Yves St Laurent. To complete your outfit, there are also hats, scarves, costume jewellery and shoes from Hermes, Philip Somerville and Gucci, etc. Ballgowns and evening wear are Bertie's speciality - a whole floor full awaits you. Many samples are 50% of the normal price. All items are immaculate and in season.

BERTIE WOOSTER
284 FULHAM ROAD, LONDON SW10 9EW
☎ 020-7352 5662. WEBSITE: www.bertie-wooster.co.uk
OPEN 10 - 6 MON, WED, FRI, 10 - 7 TUE, THUR, 10 - 5 SAT.
Dress Agency • *Menswear Only*

High street shop with two floors of the finest quality secondhand and new clothes and good luggage. New clothes are excellent quality at low prices - suits cost £320 made to measure. Secondhand clothes are of the quality rarely seen outside bespoke tailoring and includes suits, ties, blazers, waistcoats, and hankies at extremely attractive prices. The new and made-to-measure clothing includes morning coats, morning coat trousers, full backed waistcoats, dinner and sports jackets.

BIBLIOPHILE BOOKS
5 THOMAS ROAD, LONDON E14 7BN
☎ 020-7515 9222/538 4115 FAX. OPERATES 8.30 - 5 MON - FRI.
WEBSITE: www.bibliophilebooks.com   MAIL ORDER ONLY.
Permanent Discount Outlet • *Food and Leisure*

Mail order books from biographies and art, to literature and general tomes at half price or less. Stock is brand new remainders, plus reprints, rare and sometimes signed editions. Send for free catalogue or shop online.

BLACKOUT II
51 ENDELL STREET, COVENT GARDEN, LONDON WC2
☎ 020-7240 5006. OPEN 11 - 7 MON - FRI, 11.30 - 6.30 SAT.
Secondhand and Vintage Clothes • *Womenswear & Menswear*

Twenties and upwards gear, plus accessories, for sale and to hire at reasonable prices. Specialises in Sixties and Seventies gear.

BODIE & GIBBS
16 MOTCOMB STREET, LONDON SW1
☎ 020-7259 6620. OPEN 10 - 6 MON - FRI, 11 - 5 SAT.
Hire Shop • *Womenswear Only*

Designer and couture dresses to hire. Long evening dresses from Bruce Oldfield, Calvin Klein, Tomasz Starzewski and Amanda Wakeley are just some of the 300 dresses from which to choose in sizes up to 16. Also a selection of evening bags, jewellery and pashminas to buy or to hire.

BOOKENDS
108 CHARING CROSS ROAD LONDON WC2H OBP
☎ 020-7836 3457. OPEN 9 - 8 MON - SAT, 12 - 6 SUN.
Secondhand shops • *Food and Leisure*

Damaged books and publishers' returns, as well as new and review copies, including recently published books, usually at half price or below.

BOOKS FOR AMNESTY
139 KING STREET, HAMMERSMITH, LONDON W6
☎ 020-8746 3172. OPEN 10 - 6 MON - FRI, 10 - 4 SAT.
Secondhand shops • *Food and Leisure*

New books hot off the presses, many of which are critics' copies, at reductions of 25%-30%. Also remainders, secondhand and some antiquarian books, secondhand CDs, records and videos.

BOOMERANG
2 LEVERTON PLACE, LONDON NW5 2PL
☎ 020-7284 3967. OPEN 10 - 6 TUE, WED, FRI, SAT, 10 - 3 THUR.
Dress Agency • *Womenswear & Menswear* • *Children*

Boomerang is a very full shop with constantly changing stock. Split into a front area and a back area, the front is for adults - mainly womenswear but with some menswear from the 1920s to today, including M&S, Nicole Farhi, Whistles, Karen Millen etc. The rear of the shop is packed with children's clothes sizes 0-12 years, as well as equipment, books and other paraphernalia. Run by Becky Bain, formerly a fashion editor with twenty years experience, she will be on hand to offer expert advice, if requested and is also willing to help stylists and props buyers.

BRITISH DESIGNERS SALE FOR WOMEN AND MEN

42 YORK MANSIONS, PRINCE OF WALES DRIVE, LONDON SW11 4BP
☎ 020-7228 5314. OPEN 10 - 4 MON - FRI.
SALES ARE HELD AT CHELSEA TOWN HALL, KINGS ROAD, LONDON SW3.

Designer Sale • *Womenswear & Menswear*

The first top end of the market designer sale - now a booming industry - the British Designers Sale was started by Deborah Hodges, a former PR, more than eighteen years ago. Because of her contacts, it offers top British, Italian, German and French labels you won't find at other designer sales - but no names mentioned or those publicity-shy designers would not be happy to let Debbie sell their overstocks. Labels are the sort you would expect to find in the designer rooms at Harrods or Harvey Nichols. The women's sales, held twice a year in Edinburgh and five times a year in London, are open to members only. Membership costs £32 per year. Please enclose an SAE when writing to Debbie or contact her at the above telephone number or by fax (0171 498 6956) for further information. There is no membership required for the Men's Sale, which takes place twice a year, also at Chelsea Town Hall. They also hold twice yearly sales in Edinburgh.

BRONDESBURY ARCHITECTURAL RECLAMATION

THE YARD, 136 WILLESDEN LANE, LONDON NW6 7TE
☎ 020-7328 0820. OPEN 10 - 6 MON - SAT, 10 - 4 SUN.

Architectural Salvage • *DIY/Renovation*

Architectural salvage up to the Thirties including Art Deco, Victorian, Edwardian and Georgian with the occasional French piece. Lots of fireplaces, baths, sinks, taps, towel rails, kitchen ranges, marble surrounds, cast-iron. Garden department stocks garden tables, sun dials, bird baths, chimney pots. Everything you could want to convert a modernised house back to its former glory - all originals, no copies.

BROWNS LABELS FOR LESS

50 SOUTH MOLTON STREET, LONDON W1Y 1DA
☎ 020-7514 0052. OPEN 10 - 6.30 MON - WED, 10 - 7 THUR, FRI, 10 - 6.30 SAT.

Permanent Discount Outlet • *Womenswear & Menswear*

This designer sale shop supplies rails of clothes which, if you're a keen bargain hunter and don't mind rummaging, offers exciting names for bargain prices. Designers on sale here include most of those sold in the main, full-price shop including Jil Sander, Helmut Lang, Sonia Rykiel, Missoni, Comme Des Garcons, and Browns Focus. Men's rails are at the front of the narrow, winding shop; women's at the back near the six changing rooms. Prices are advertised as representing reductions of 50%-80%. We saw Jil Sander lace evening top reduced from £305 to £75; Browns Own cardigan, £155 instead of £310; Comme des Garcons unstructured suit, £165 reduced from £545. Assistants are helpful and there's always lots of stock.

BUCKS
125 EVELYN STREET, DEPTFORD, LONDON SE8 5RJ
☎ 020-8692 4447. OPEN SEVEN DAYS A WEEK, 10 - 7 MON - FRI,
10 - 5 SAT, 10 - 4 SUN.
Permanent Discount Outlet • *Furniture/Soft Furnishings* • *Household*
20,000 sq foot warehouse selling cancelled orders, ex-display and ex-photo shoot furniture from famous department stores and other well-known brand names. Some of the department store furniture is from the current catalogue. Some has been marked or damaged during display or photography, but they are all clearly signposted. A lot of stock is brand new. Furniture includes three-piece suites, wardrobes, a very large stock of beds, tables, chairs, dressing tables. Most of the three-piece suites are reduced by 40%-50% and the other items are all substantially discounted. They now stock a range of homewares including duvets and lamps. Free car parking.

BUMPSADAISY MATERNITY STYLE
43 COVENT GARDEN MARKET, LONDON WC2E 8HA
☎ 020-7379 9831. WEBSITE: www.bumpsadaisy.co.uk
OPEN 10 - 6 MON - SAT, UNTIL 7.30 ON THUR.
157 LOWER RICHMOND ROAD, LONDON SW15 1H
OPEN 9.30 - 5.30 MON - SAT.- 5.30 MON - SAT.
Hire Shop • *Womenswear Only*
Franchised shops and home-based branches with large range of specialist maternity wear, from wedding outfits to ball gowns, to hire and to buy. Hire costs range from £30 to £100 for special occasion wear. To buy are lots of casual and business wear in sizes 8 - 18. For example, skirts £20-£70; dresses £40-£100. Also four branches run by young mums from their homes, specialising in hiring but also stocking a small retail range (Camberley, Edgbaston, Exeter and Southampton). Phone 0208-789 0329 for details.

BURBERRY
29-53 CHATHAM PLACE, LONDON E9 6LP
☎ 020-8985 3344. OPEN 11 - 6 MON - FRI, 10 - 5 SAT, 11 - 4 SUN.
Factory Shop • *Children* • *Womenswear & Menswear*
Factory shop sells the full range of Burberry merchandise, none of which is current. It stocks seconds and overmakes of the famous name raincoats and duffle coats as well as accessories such as the distinctive umbrellas, scarves and handbags. All carry the Burberry label and discounts are about one third off the normal retail price. Childrenswear tends to be thin on the ground, but there are plenty of gift items such as Burberry brand name teas, coffees and marmalade. A large warehouse with clothes set out on dozens of rails, surroundings are relatively spartan and the outlet is often full of tourists.

BUTTERFLY
28A PONSONBY PLACE, LONDON SW1
☎ 020-7821 1983. OPEN 12 - 6.30 WED, FRI, 12 - 7.30 THUR.
28 OLD BAILEY, LONDON EC4M 7HS
☎ 020-7489 8288. OPEN 12 - 6.30 MON, TUE, 12 - 4 WED, THUR, FRI.
Permanent Discount Outlet • *Womenswear Only*
Sells fashion samples obtained through extensive contacts in the industry at wholesale price or less. Stock is from the current season and the following season so that you can be ahead of the fashion - but only if you are a size 10 or 12 as samples are mostly model-sizes with a few sizes 14 and 16. As well as some British designers, the shop has a lot of French and Italian labels, many of which can be seen in Harrods designer department. There's Dusk, Diana Gee, Caroline Roumer, Character, and Frank Usher, Krizia, Blue Time, as well as silk shirts and skirts from Fenn Wright & Manson and raincoats and rain jackets from Savannah and Freetex, at less than half price.

BUTTERFLY,
3 LOWER RICHMOND ROAD, PUTNEY BRIDGE, LONDON SW15
☎ 020-8788 8304. OPEN 10.30 - 6.30 MON - FRI, 10 - 5 SAT.
Dress Agency • *Womenswear Only*
Selling middle to upper range nearly-new designer clothes, new samples and end of ranges, this shop has been going since 1981. Selection includes Armani, Rifat Ozbek, Chanel, Nicole Farhi, French Connection, Jigsaw and Hobbs. Lots of linen, silks, cashmere, wool and natural fibres. Also some samples and clothes used for modelling, handbags, scarves, new jewellery and purses.

BUYERS & SELLERS LTD
120-122 LADBROKE GROVE, LONDON W10 5NE
☎ 020-7229 1947/8468. FAX ☎ 020-7221 4113.
OPEN 9.30 - 5.30 MON - FRI, 9.30 - 4.30 SAT, 10 - 5.30 WED.
Permanent Discount Outlet • *Electrical Equipment*
Buyers & Sellers has been in business for more than 40 years, selling brand name domestic equipment at bargain prices. Everything from fridges and freezers, ovens and microwaves, hobs and vacuum cleaners, washing machines and dishwashers, tumble dryers and cookers, all new and guaranteed and in perfect working order. They stock and can obtain almost any make and model currently available. Nationwide delivery service. Telephone orders taken. Advice line and brochures are part of the service. Credit cards accepted.

CAROLINE CHARLES
9 ST JOHN'S WOOD HIGH STREET, LONDON NW8
☎ 020-7483 0080. OPEN 10 - 5.30 MON - SAT.
Permanent Discount Outlet • *Womenswear Only*
This shop has stock at full price and a sale basement for Caroline Charles merchandise. Here, end of season outfits, samples and one-offs which never made it into production are sold at discounts of at least 30%. Daywear to evening wear is covered as well as handbags, belts, jewellery, scarves and hats.

CARPET TILE CENTRE
227-229 WOODHOUSE ROAD, NORTH FINCHLEY, LONDON N12 9BD
☎ 020-8361 1261. OPEN 9 - 5 MON - FRI, 9 - 1 SAT.
Permanent Discount Outlet • *Furniture/Soft Furnishings DIY/Renovation*
Offers a wide range of seconds as well as end of line carpet tiles, specials and non-standard colours of Heuga and Interface brands. Prices start at £1.95-£2.95 for tiles which normally cost £5. Even the perfect tiles are competitively priced.

CATALOGUE BARGAIN SHOP
252 GREEN LANES, PALMERS GREEN, LONDON N13 5TU
☎ 020-8886 9532. OPEN 9 - 5.30 MON - SAT, 10 - 4 SUN.
Permanent Discount Outlet • *Womenswear & Menswear* • *Household Electrical Equipment* • *Children* • *Sportswear & Equipment*
Catalogue Bargain Shop is a growing national chain of stores which obtains the majority of its goods from mail order giants Great Universal and Kays, and offers a range of clothing for all the family, a wide selection of shoes, bed linen, household goods, electrical equipment (TVs, videos, hi-fis) and hundreds of other catalogue items at very competitive prices. The merchandise consists of ends of ranges and previous season's stock for which there is no longer storage space when the catalogues change.

CATHERINE GROSVENOR DESIGNS
3 ELYSTAN STREET, CHELSEA GREEN, LONDON SW3 3NT
☎ 020-7584 2112. OPEN 10 - 5.30 MON - FRI, 10 - 4 SAT.
Permanent Discount Outlet • *Womenswear Only*
Own designer knitwear at competitive prices. There are pashminas, cottons, cashmere and merino wools, and linens, jumpers, cardigans, jackets, skirts, designer jewellery and accessories. Offers made-to-measure service.

CATWALK NEARLY-NEW DESIGNER CLOTHES
52 BLANDFORD STREET, LONDON W1H 3HD
☎ 020-7935 1052. OPEN 12.30 - 6 MON, 11.15 - 6 TUE, WED, THUR, FRI, 11.15 - 5 SAT.
Dress Agency • *Womenswear Only*
Nearly-new designer clothes from Chanel to Ghost, Gucci to Whistles and including Prada, Armani and Jil Sander. Has a good range of young funky designer gear such as Dolce & Gabbana, Joseph, Mui Mui, DKNY and Katherine Hamnett. Always has a wide variety of jackets and separates as well as jewellery, hats, shoes, belts, scarves and handbags. For example, Emporio Armani suit £129; Gucci trousers, £50; Mui Mui dress £69; Nicole Farhi silk blouse, £32.

CD WAREHOUSE
5IA, NEW BROADWAY, EALING, LONDON W5 5AH
☎ 020-8567 2122. OPEN 10 - 7 SEVEN DAYS A WEEK.
Compact Discs • Food and Leisure
CDs at discounted prices. Branches also in Watford (01923 252 300) and Wimbledon (0208 543 2355)

CENCI
31 MONMOUTH STREET, LONDON WC2 9DD
☎ 020-7836 1400. OPEN 11 - 6.30 MON - SAT.
Secondhand and Vintage Clothes • *Womenswear & Menswear*
Small shop selling vintage clothing from the Forties to the Seventies from America and Europe. There are about 10,000 items in the shop at any one time, many of which are bought from a factory in Italy devoted to the recycling of old style, quality clothing. As well as 1960s sweaters from £16 to £125, Forties' and Sixties' suits from £75 and a large selection of cashmere, there are also accessories such as luggage, watches, rings, hats, cufflinks and glasses from the 1920s to the 1960s and a small selection of shoes.

CENTRAL PARK
152 MUSWELL HILL BROADWAY, MUSWELL HILL, LONDON N10
☎ 020-8883 9122. OPEN 9.30 - 6 MON - SAT, 1 - 5 SUN.
67, MALL, EALING, LONDON W5 5LS.
☎ 020-8567 2250. OPEN 10 - 7 MON - SAT, 11 - 5 SUN.
9, EALING BROADWAY, EALING, LONDON W5 2NH
☎ 020-8567 0503. OPEN 10 - 7 MON - SAT, 11 - 5 SUN.
WEST 1 SHOPPING CENTRE, LOWER GROUND FLOOR, BOND STREET STATION, LONDON W1
☎ 020-7495 5097. OPEN 10 -7 MON - SAT, 1 - 5 SUN.
5 ST CHRISTOPHER'S PLACE, OXFORD CIRCUS, LONDON W1
☎ 020-7487 3442. OPEN 10 - 6 MON - SAT.
HAMMERSMITH BROADWAY STATION, LONDON W6 9YE
☎ 020-8563 1700. OPEN 10 - 7 MON - SAT, 1 - 6 SUN.
UNIT B & C, BAKER STREET STATION, BAKERLOO TICKET HALL, LONDON NW1
☎ 020-7935 2820. OPEN 10 - 8 MON - SAT, 12 - 6 SUN.
54 GOLDERS GREEN ROAD, LONDON
☎ 020-8731 6200. OPEN 10 - 5.45 MON - SAT.
Permanent Discount Outlet • *Womenswear Only*
Large multiple group stocking cancelled orders and over runs for women, although most of the clothes are de-labelled before they come here. There are dresses, suits, skirts, trousers and tops. Prices are very cheap. A new store at 168 Muswell Hill "Size Plus" was opening as we went to press. It caters especially for more mature women and larger sizes. For more details phone 0181-883 9122. Formerly called The Outlet, the shops are now being changed to Central Park.

CERRUTI 1881
6, CAVENDISH PLACE, LONDON W1M 0NB
☎ 020-7580 6066.
Designer Sale • *Womenswear Only*
Phone or write to put your name down on the mailing list for an automatic invitation to the showroom sales at which prices are considerably reduced.

CHANGE OF HABIT
65 ABBEVILLE ROAD, CLAPHAM, LONDON SW4 9JW
☎ 020-8675 9475. OPEN 10 - 5.30 MON - SAT.
Dress Agency • *Womenswear Only* • *Children*
Furniture/Soft Furnishings
Day and evening wear as good as new from high street to designer label. Also nearly-new clothes for babies and children up to the age of 8. Described by the owner as "everyday clothes for everyday people at realistic prices". Very high turnover. Also has mothers-to-be wear and a range of brand new clothes and accessories and recently added antiques and home furnishing.

CHANGE OF HEART
THE OLD SCHOOL, 59B & C PARK ROAD, LONDON N8 8DP
☎ 020-8341 1575. OPEN 10 - 6 MON - SAT.
Dress Agency • *Womenswear & Menswear* • *Furniture/Soft Furnishings*
Sells a mixture of designer and good high street labels for women and men including labels such as DKNY, Ghost, Betty Jackson, Armani, Jigsaw, Next, Whistles, MaxMara, Oilily, Joseph and Paul Smith. Prices vary from £20 for a pair of Armani shorts to £50 for a Nicole Farhi silk two-piece suit. They now offer new and nearly new contemporary home furnishings.

CHARLES TYRWHITT SHIRTS
UNIT 13, SILVER ROAD, LONDON W12 7RR
☎ 020-8735 1000. OPEN 8 - 8 MON - FRI, 10 - 4 SAT. MAIL ORDER ONLY.
Permanent Discount Outlet • *Menswear Only*
Traditional, top quality Jermyn-Street shirts at high street prices. Selling through mail order, overheads are low and the price is kept down by a policy of high volume and low margins. The comparison with Jermyn Street comes not just from the cut of the shirts, but also from the fabric: longstaple Egyptian cotton, which produces a soft, silky finish which washes well and is hard-wearing. All shirts come with brass collar stiffeners. The mail order catalogue also includes cufflinks, £5-£60; a range of silk ties; and felt and many other accessories. Call for details of the introductory offer.

CHESNEY'S ANTIQUE FIREPLACE WAREHOUSE LTD
194-202 BATTERSEA PARK ROAD, LONDON SW11 4ND
☎ 020-7627 1410. OPEN 9 - 5.30 MON - FRI, 10 - 5 SAT.
Architectural Salvage • *DIY/Renovation*
Antique and reproduction fireplaces with at least 120 in stock at any one time. Full fitting service. Marble fireplaces range from £450 to £6,000; stone from £495 to £3,000; pine from £230 to £900.

CHINA MATCHING SERVICE
4 QUEEN'S PARADE CLOSE, FRIERN BARNETT, LONDON N11 3FY
☎ 020-8361 6111. E-MAIL: tablewhere @globalnet.co.uk
WEBSITE: www.tablewhere.co.uk   OPEN 9 - 5.30 MON - FRI, 9 - 5 SAT.
Discontinued china, tableware, earthenware, stoneware and pottery from over 250 manufacturers - English and foreign.

CHLOE BROMLEY FASHIONS LTD
21 MONTPELIER VALE, BLACKHEATH VILLAGE, LONDON SE3 0TJ
☎ 020-8318 4300. OPEN 9.30 - 6 MON - SAT, 11 - 5 SUN.
Permanent Discount Outlet • *Womenswear Only*
Chloe has been trading in top quality fashion for more than 30 years, specialising in special occasion outfits in sizes 8-22. Chloe 2, on the lower ground floor, stocks thousands of samples and seconds from Chloe's usual suppliers, specialising in Frank Usher's and Joseph Ribkoff's factory rejects and seconds. This enables customers to buy top quality clothes at prices which range from 25%-75% off the usual retail price. There is always a batch clearance rail for under £40; hats at half price; jewellery from £6; but no shoes.

CHOICE DISCOUNT STORES LIMITED
67 GOLDERS GREEN ROAD, GOLDERS GREEN, LONDON NW11 8EL
☎ 020-8458 8247. OPEN 9 - 6 MON - SAT, 11 - 5 SUN.
Permanent Discount Outlet • *Womenswear & Menswear*
Surplus ladies and men's fashions and accessories from Next plc and the Next Directory. You can save up to 50% off normal retail prices for first quality; up to two thirds for seconds. There are no changing rooms but the shop offers refunds if goods are returned in perfect condition within 28 days. There are special sales each January and July.

CHOMETTE
307 MERTON ROAD, LONDON SW18 5JS
☎ 020-8871 4116. WEBSITE: www.chomette.co.uk   OPEN 10 - 5 TUE - SAT.
Factory Shop • *Household*
Cookware factory shop selling Pillivuyt, De Buyer, SKK, Langenthal and Deglon, near the Villeroy & Boch factory shop. Massive savings to be made on oven to tableware: microwave and diswasher safe.

CHRISTMAS GRAND SALE
ROYAL HORTICULTURAL HALLS, VICTORIA, LONDON SW1
ORGANISER: DAVID HESLAM, PO BOX 4, LECHLADE, GLOS GL7 3YB.
☎ (01367) 860017. ENQUIRIES: OPEN 9.30 - 5.30 MON - FRI.
Designer Sale • *Household & Giftwear*
There are now three annual Grand Sales taking place countrywide. The Christmas Grand Sale in London, with over 120 different small companies selling their merchandise to the public, is the largest. This takes place in mid-November each year. Quality is high and covers everything from dried flowers to bath accessories, Amish quilts to silverware, wooden toys to hand-painted kitchenware, often at discount because they are ends of lines. There is a Spring Grand Sale at Sudeley Castle, Winchcombe, near Cheltenham, Glos every April/May and a Summer Grand Sale at Ripley Castle, near Harrogate, North Yorkshire, in June, both of which feature gardening equipment as well as decorative homes accessories. Phone the above number for more details; a proportion of the ticket revenue goes to charity.

CITY BEDS
17-39 GIBBINS ROAD, OFF CARPENTER'S ROAD, LONDON E15 2HU
☎ 020-8534 9000. OPEN 8.30 - 5 MON - SAT, 10 - 3.30 SUN.
Permanent Discount Outlet • *Furniture/Soft Furnishings*
Family-owned bed specialist selling mostly UK-made brand names quality beds such as Sealy, Sprung Slumber, Silent Night, Nestledown and Hypnos, although the metal beds are imported from Holland and Malaysia. Single beds cost from £65 to top of the range beds, £1.600, normal price £2,300. Also branches at Hainault, Brimsdown and Rayleigh.

CITY MENSWEAR
1-5 BREAD STREET, CHEAPSIDE, LONDON EC4
☎ 020-7248 1809. OPEN 9 - 6 MON - FRI.
Permanent Discount Outlet • *Menswear Only*
Part of the Moss Bros Group, this shop mostly hires out dinner and morning suits and sells at full price everything from suits, shirts, wedding suits and dinner suits to overcoats and ties from many different brands. From time to time, ex-hire wear from the other Moss Bros hire shops are sold off here at greatly reduced prices. For example, ex-hire morning tails - including jacket, trousers and waistcoat - which would normally cost £249 when new are sold here for £90. Ring first to check ex-hire availability. Remember when trying on that the ex-hire stock has been dry cleaned every time it's been hired out so there will be some shrinkage, so look out for sizes above your normal size. Suits, shirts, dinner suits, wedding suits, overcoats and ties from many different brands, all at discount prices.

CLOTHES DIRECT
48B HENDON LANE, FINCHLEY, LONDON N3 1TT
☎ 020-8343 4072. OPEN 10 - 6 TUES - SAT, 10 - 2 SUN.
Permanent Discount Outlet • *Menswear Only*
Warehouse selling Italian brand name clothes for men at discount prices.

COLEFAX & FOWLER
19 - 23 GROSVENOR HILL, LONDON W1X 9HG
☎ 020-7493 2231.
Designer Sale • *Furniture/Soft Furnishings*
Annual sales of Colefax & Fowler and Jane Churchill ranges, held at the Royal Horticultural Halls in London's SW1 usually in January. Ask for Trade and put your name on the mailing list.

CORNUCOPIA
12 UPPER TACHBROOK STREET, LONDON SW1
☎ 020-7828 5752. OPEN 11 - 6 SEVEN DAYS A WEEK.
Secondhand and Vintage Clothes • *Womenswear Only*
This marvellous vintage clothes shop has been established for more than 28 years. It specialises in glamorous evening wear for women from the Twenties to modern day. Huge selection of eveningwear, some evening shoes, some designer samples, silk suits and hats, shoes, accessories, handbags, jewellery.

DAVE'S DIY
294 & 296 FIRS LANE, LONDON N13 5QQ
☎ 020-8807 3539. OPEN 8.30 - 5 MON - FRI, 9 - 1 SAT.
Permanent Discount Outlet • *DIY/Renovation*
Aimed at the trade, it will cater for members of the public who benefit from the discounts. Carries wallpaper brands from Kingfisher, Mayfair, Crown and Vymura, among others, from a range of 300 wallpaper books at discounts of up to 40%. Next day ordering for wallpapers. Also carries a large stock of paint, with three computerised mixing machines that offer thousands of combinations of colours.

DAVID CHARLES
2 - 4 THANE WORKS, THANE VILLAS LONDON N7 7NU
☎ 020-7609 4797.
Designer Sale • *Children*
Twice yearly showroom sale of this children's range at which prices are considerably reduced. Phone or write to put your name down on the mailing list for an automatic invitation.

DAVID J WILKINS
27 PRINCESS ROAD, LONDON NW1 8JR
☎ 020-7722 7608. OPEN BY APPOINTMENT.
Permanent Discount Outlet • *Furniture/Soft Furnishings*
Handmade rugs from Iran, Turkey, Afghanistan and Russia at what are claimed to be wholesale prices, giving members of the public average discounts of 25% compared with normal retail prices. Customers can spend the whole morning or afternoon looking at stock at this huge, bonded warehouse which specialises in large and unusual sizes. Car parking nearby.

DAVID RICHARDS & SONS
10 NEW CAVENDISH STREET, LONDON W1M 7LJ
☎ 020-7935 3206. OPEN 9.30 - 6 MON - FRI.
Permanent Discount Outlet • *Household & Giftwear*
David Richards & Sons are really wholesalers, but they are pleased to help retail customers from their showroom. Their shop is stacked high with solid silver, silver plate and silver picture frames, christening presents, models of animals, candlesticks, salvers and silver jewellery. Also, they can provide wedding lists, personalised corporate gifts, customers repairs and valuations. Service is well informed and courteous, and prices are much more reasonable than comparable prices in the high street. This is due to the fact that because the shop wholesales in Britain and Europe, it buys enormous quantities and is thus able to pass on bulk-buying savings to customers.

DELLA FINCH DESIGNER SALE
LONDON
☎ 020-7834 9161.
Designer Sale • *Womenswear Only*
Della organises designer sales, usually in London, selling top name clothes direct from the showroom at wholesale prices. The sale is unique in collecting top labels of next season clothes at least four months before they reach the shops. Some clothes are from the current season, and include evening wear, smart suits, blouses and swimwear in sizes 10 to 26. There's usually a special bargain rail from £5. Phone and leave your name and full address for the mailing list. The sale takes place four times a year.

DENNER CASHMERE
PO BOX 8551, LONDON SW11 1ZP
☎ (0870) 1200055. OPEN 9 - 7 MON - SAT. MAIL ORDER ONLY.
Permanent Discount Outlet • *Womenswear Only*
Finest quality designer cashmere and silk/cashmere knitwear similar to TSE and N Peal, from as little as one third of shop prices. Because they only sell through mail order and occasional sales at well-known venues, overheads are low and profit margins can be kept to a minimum. Only the best quality yarns are used and the finishing is impeccable. They produce two collections a year:

the spring/summer consists of garments made from silk/cashmere; the autumn/winter features items made of 100% cashmere. Styles include long cardigans, dresses, twinsets, cable knits, wraps, scarves, skinny ribs, tunics, classic V, round and polo neck sweaters. Each collection is designed so that pieces can be worn together to create a whole outfit or bought separately to mix and match with basics from a typical wardrobe. Prices from £39.90. Phone for the list of forthcoming sales, special offers and up-to-date brochure.

DESIGNER BARGAINS
29 KENSINGTON CHURCH STREET, LONDON W8 4LL
☎ 020-7795 6777. OPEN 10 - 6.30 MON - SAT.
Dress Agency • *Womenswear Only*
There are lots of top labels on sale here, as befits the catchment area, with hundreds of garments. Labels on sale include Thierry Mugler, Armani, Escada, Chanel, Dolce e Gabbana, Gucci, Moschino, Prada and Versace.

DESIGNERS FOR LESS
203 UXBRIDGE ROAD, WEST EALING, LONDON W13 9AA
☎ 020-8579 5954. FAX 020 8579 4463
E-MAIL: designersforless@villaroma. freeserve.co.uk   OPEN 9.30 - 6 MON - SAT.
Permanent Discount Outlet • *Hire Shops* • *Menswear Only*
High street shop, established since 1973, which sells 'top quality designer menswear at rock bottom prices': factory seconds, ends of ranges, samples and previous season's stock in a range of men's clothes. Their main attractions are suits from Germany, although the labels have to be removed from their best contacts' merchandise. Suits that normally retail for £350 sell here for as little as £135, 'Super 100' trousers usually £49.50 sell at £22.50. Italian knitwear by Point of Italy which normally sells at £75 - £100 is just £19.50. Italian shoes by Panelli from £25, pure wool suits normally sold for £295 are £99. Cotton shirts normally retailing at £35 sell for £14.50. Jockey or giant, they promise to kit you out with a king size department up to size 60. There are two clearance sales a year - phone or e-mail Roy or Malcolm in the shop for details and to be put on the mailing list and receive mailings of latest offers. There is also an extensive dresswear hire department.

DESIGNERS' GUILD
RELAY ROAD, OFF ARIEL WAY, WOOD LANE, LONDON W12
☎ 020-7351 5775 TO BE PUT ON MAILING LIST.
Designer Sale • *Furniture/Soft Furnishings*
Twice-yearly warehouse clearance sale which is usually advertised in London newspapers. Stock usually comprises some large furniture - sofas, chairs - masses of rolls of fabric at greatly reduced prices, wallpaper borders, cushion covers and upholstery fabrics. Come armed with measurements and exact lengths required as it can be very busy.

DESIGNS
60 ROSSLYN HILL, LONDON NW3 1ND
☎ 020-7435 0100. OPEN 10 - 5.45 MON - SAT, UNTIL 6.30 ON THUR.
Dress Agency • *Womenswear* • *Children*
Designs has been established for more than eighteen years, selling ladies designer clothes and accessories. Their most sought-after labels include Hermes, Chanel, Donna Karan, Ralph Lauren, Giorgio Armani, Prada, Gucci, Joseph, Issey Miyake and Jil Sander and they have a constant supply of covetable Gucci and Prada handbags and shoes. They only accept perfect merchandise under two years old and have a rapid turnover with the most exciting pieces coming their way. Regular customers talk about the spacious, relaxed atmosphere and prices remain keenly competitive: ranging from £5 to £500. They have more than 6,000 clients and take in stock from the UK, America and Italy. They also keep a range of girls' clothes from 0 - 8 years.

DISCOUNT COOKERS
97 RUSHEY GREEN, CATFORD, LONDON SE6 4AF
☎ 020-8461 5273. OPEN 9 - 6 MON - SAT.
Permanent Discount Outlet • *Electrical Equipment*
New and reconditioned models from New World, Whirlpool, Canon with more than 2,000 new cookers in stock at any one time. Because they buy in bulk to supply their five south-east London shops, they can offer competitive prices - although they say that the more expensive the cooker you buy, the better the discount. They also stock between 400-500 reconditioned cookers at prices from £100 upwards - which works out at between 25%-50% cheaper than when new - as well as some new ex-display models. All the cookers come with a six month guarantee and there is free delivery within the M25 area. Countrywide delivery is by courier.

DISCOUNT DECORATING
157-159 RYE LANE, PECKHAM, LONDON SE15 4TL
☎ 020-7732 3986. OPEN 8 - 5.30 MON - FRI, 9 - 5.30 SAT.
Permanent Discount Outlet • *DIY/Renovation*
Three thousand square foot warehouse selling top of the range wallpapers including Contour, Crown, Sanderson, Vymura, Hill & Knowles at between 10% and 50% discount. Also mainly Dulux paints and decorating equipment at low prices. All current, last season's or discontinued stock - no seconds sold.

DISCOUNT DRESSING
58 BAKER STREET, LONDON W1
☎ 020-7486 7230. OPEN 10 - 6 SEVEN DAYS A WEEK.
16 SUSSEX RING, WOODSIDE PARK, LONDON N12
☎ 020-8343 8343. OPEN 10 - 6 SEVEN DAYS A WEEK.
Permanent Discount Outlet • *Womenswear Only*
A veritable Aladdin's Cave of designer bargains, Discount Dressing sells mostly German, Italian and French designer labels at prices at least 50% and up to

90% below those in normal retail outlets. All items are brand new and perfect. A team of buyers all over Europe purchase stock directly from the manufacturer for this growing chain of discount shops. This enables Discount Dressing to by-pass the importers and wholesalers and, of course, their mark-up. They also buy bankrupt stock in this country. Their agreement with their suppliers means that they are not able to advertise brand names for obvious reasons, but they are all well-known for their top quality and style. So confident is Discount Dressing that you will be unable to find the same item cheaper elsewhere, that they guarantee to give the outfit to you free of charge should you perform this miracle. Merchandise includes raincoats, dresses, suits, trousers, blouses, evening wear, special occasion outfits and jackets, in sizes 6-24 and in some cases larger. GDD readers can obtain a further 10% discount if they visit the shop taking a copy of this book with them. There are other branches in Lincolnshire, Northern Ireland and Hertfordshire.

DISPOSAL SALES AGENCY (DSA)
ROOM 727, MINISTRY OF DEFENCE, 6 HERCULES ROAD, LONDON SE1 7DJ
☎ 020-7261 8968. WEBSITE: www.disposalsales.agency.mod.uk

The Disposal Sales Agency is an agency of the Ministry of Defence set up to dispose of surplus equipment. It runs the largest disposal operation in the UK, organising the sale of both military equipment and commodities in use commercially, such as embassy furniture, government department office furniture, closed-down RAF base vehicles and housing stock, ex-marine boats, ex-army tents, boots and ski equipment, medical and dental equipment, clothing, ship and aircraft spares, scrap metal and IT equipment. The DSA uses 19 companies throughout the UK, each with their own specialist area, to dispose of stock. These companies also dispose of stock from a host of other, usually public sector, organisations varying from fire brigades and hospitals to health authorities and the police. Equipment from these companies varies from kitchen equipment and fax machines to mobile radios, cars, generators, jewellery, telecommunications equipment to food trolleys, X-ray equipment, telephones, uniforms, dinghies, fishing nets, photocopiers and chair lifts. Visit the website to find out which companies sell which products and how to contact them direct.

DRUG STORE
583 ROMAN ROAD, LONDON E3 5EL
☎ 020-7493 4156. OPEN 9 - 5 MON - SAT.

Permanent Discount Outlet • *Womenswear Only*

Formerly the South Molton Street Drug Store, now relocated, this permanent discount shop selling a wide range of cosmetics, some of which is current season, at discount prices. They usually stock Elizabeth Arden, Revlon, Ultima 11 and Max Factor as well as some of the more trendy brands. Also sells hair accessories, make-up brushes, mirrors, nail equipment toiletries and special purchases such as make-up cases, £9.99.

DYNASTY
12A TURNHAM GREEN TERRACE, CHISWICK LONDON W4
☎ 020-8995 3846. OPEN 10.30 - 5 MON - SAT.
Dress Agency • *Womenswear Only*
Sells good quality secondhand clothes. Labels include Edina Ronay, Louis Feraud, Joseph, Moschino, as well as occasionally La Perla swimwear. Examples of outfits for sale include an Edina Ronay suit, £175, a Christian Lacroix dress, £99, and a Paul Costelloe dress, £49; La Perla swimsuits from £25-£39; Valentino three-piece, £220, originally £1,000.

DYNASTY MAN
12 TURNHAM GREEN TERRACE, CHISWICK LONDON W4 1QP
☎ 020-8994 4450. OPEN 10.30 - 5.30 MON - SAT.
Dress Agency • *Menswear Only*
Small dress agency which sells only labels from Jaeger upwards and including Boss suits and jackets, Yves St Laurent and Armani suits, Jean Paul Gaultier, business shirts, pure silk ties, sweaters, leathers, Burberry raincoats and wool and cashmere coats. No separate trousers sold at all. Alterations can be undertaken.

EDWARD SYMMONS & PARTNERS
2 SOUTHWARK STREET, LONDON BRIDGE, LONDON SE1 1RQ
☎ 020-7955 8454. OPEN 9.30 - 5.30 MON - FRI.
Permanent Discount Outlet • *Furniture/Soft Furnishings*
Auctioneers dealing mainly in plant and machine tools for liquidated companies but they have sold almost everything from aeroplanes to offices and restaurants. Some equipment is sold by private treaty or tender. Prices depend on how long they have available to market the sale; the shorter the time, the more your chances of picking up a bargain.

EMPORIUM
330-332 CREEK ROAD, GREENWICH, LONDON SE10
☎ 020-8305 1670. OPEN 10.30 - 6 TUE - SUN.
Secondhand Shop • *Hire Shop* • *Secondhand and Vintage Clothes*
One of London's vintage clothes stores selling high quality vintage wear from the Thirties to the Seventies. Supplies film, theatre and pop promo companies as well as members of the public. Also hires out ballgowns, and evening wear for men. Near to another good vintage shop, The Observatory.

ENCORE
53 STOKE NEWINGTON CHURCH STREET, LONDON N16 0AR
☎ 020-7254 5329. OPEN 10 - 5.30 TUE -SAT.
Dress Agency • *Children*
Well-organised children's shoe and clothes shop. Selling Start-Rite, Bundgaard (a Danish brand) and French and German designs. All assistants are trained in fitting children's feet. Also offers nearly new clothes with OshKosh, Oilily and

other good makes at about one third of their original price and an exclusive range of new clothes.

EXCLUSIVO
24 HAMPSTEAD HIGH STREET, HAMPSTEAD, LONDON NW3
☎ 020-7431 8618. OPEN 11.30 - 6 SEVEN DAYS A WEEK.
Dress Agency • *Womenswear Only*
A small shop stocked high with every kind of label from Jaeger and Windsmoor to YSL, Prada, Gucci, Dior, Chanel, Donna Karan and Nicole Farhi. Prices range from £50-£500. For example, Alaia dress £120, as new £450. Specialise in accessories: for example Chanel handbags, £250 usually £750; Prada bags, from £85; Moschino bags, from £50. Good range of footwear such as Donna Karan shoes, £89, originally £200; Hermes scarves, £49; Chanel earrings, from £50; Donna Karan earrings, from £29. There are usually about 1,500 outfits from which to choose.

FACTORY DIRECT
17 STRUTTON GROUND, VICTORIA, LONDON SW1 P2H
☎ 020-7799 2651. OPEN 10.30 - 6 MON - FRI, 10 - 4 SAT.
Permanent Discount Outlet • *Womenswear Only*
Fashion for ladies which mostly consists of day and work wear: coats, suits, dresses, tops, skirts. Bought direct from a variety of different factories, there are no labels in any of these clothes.

FELICITY HAT HIRE
226 MUNSTER ROAD, LONDON SW6
☎ 020-7381 5128. OPEN 10 - 7 MON, THUR, FRI, 10 - 5 TUE,
10 - 2 WED, SAT.
Hire Shop • *Womenswear Only*
The alternative to spending a fortune on a hat for a formal occasion. Choose from more than 400 hats of which many are new, bought directly from milliners each season. Styles vary from Frederick Fox straw hats to more contemporary styles from Caroline Hickman.

FENS RESTORATION
46 LOTS ROAD, CHELSEA, LONDON SW10 0QF
☎ 020-7352 9883. OPEN 9 - 5 MON - FRI, BY APPOINTMENT SAT.
Architectural Salvage • *DIY/Renovation*
Sells reclaimed doors, bathroom fittings and mouldings. Also sells furniture and carries out restoration work and repairs, french polishing and metal polishing and (caustic) pine stripping.

FOFO CLUB
23 OLD BOND STREET, LONDON W1X 3DA
☎ 020-7499 5132.
Designer Sale • *Womenswear & Menswear*

Regular sales of top designer names which in the past have included Mondi, Kasper, Maska and Louis Feraud at fantastically reduced prices. However, designers stocked do change regularly. Entrance by membership only with different degrees of membership at different prices. The top degree of membership, Gold, allows you to bring unlimited guests to the sales and gain entry to the preview day; Silver means you can bring two guests and gain entry on preview day; Basic means you can bring only one friend and only on general day. Contact Olivia Smart at FOFO at the above address for more details.

FRANK USHER
66 GROSVENOR STREET, LONDON W1
☎ 020-76299696.
Designer Sales • *Womenswear Only*

Phone or write to put your name down on the mailing list for an automatic invitation to the showroom sales at which prices are considerably reduced.

FREDERICK FOX
1ST FLOOR, 17 AVERY ROW, BROOK STREET, LONDON W1
☎ 020-7629 5706.
Designer Sales • *Womenswear only*

Twice-yearly sale with end of season hats which usually include a selection of boutique hats from as little as £15 and model hats from £60. Credit cards not taken. Phone to put your name on the mailing list.

FROCK BROKERS
47-49 BRUSHFIELD STREET, SPITALFIELDS, LONDON E1 6AA
☎ 020-7247 4222. OPEN 11 - 6.30, MON - FRI, 11 - 8 ON WED, 11 - 5.30 SUN.
Permanent Discount Outlet • *Womenswear Only*

A contemporary designer boutique with a difference. Ninety per cent of stock is new young designers or end of season/sample pieces that either come directly from the designers or from independent shops. The remaining 10% is dress agency which can range from clothes used in photo shoots or catwalk shows to unwanted presents or expensive mistakes. All designer labels are in perfect condition and absolute bargains. All staff offer personal shopping and free styling advice. Labels range from Gharani Strok and Ruti Danan to Gucci, Prada and Manolo Blahnik. Located in the heart of the city - two minutes from Liverpool Street station. A second store was due to open as we went to press in West India Quay, Canary Wharf. Phone above telephone number for address.

FROCK FOLLIES
18 THE GRANGEWAY, GRANGE PARK, LONDON N21 2HG
☎ 020-8360 3447. OPEN 9.30 - 5 TUE - SAT.
Dress Agency • *Womenswear Only*

Recommended by one of our readers who says that the owner is so helpful that shopping here is a pleasure. Double-fronted shop with more than 2,000 items in stock including costume jewellery, handbags, swimwear and shoes. Labels include Escade, Frank Usher, Karen Millen, Jacques Vert, Basler, Betty Barclay, Betty Jackson, Principles, Next and Monsoon - in other words, across the fashion spectrum. One of the cheapest second hand clothes shops you will find.

FROCKS
33 WESTFIELDS AVENUE, BARNES, LONDON SW13 0AT
☎ 020-8392 1123. OPEN 9 - 8 MON - FRI, 10 - 2 SAT.
BY APPOINTMENT ONLY.
Hire Shop • *Womenswear Only*

Home-based business offering a wide range of evening wear to hire and for sale. Party frocks, cocktail dresses and ballgowns, in sizes 8-20, can be hired from £40 to £75 for up to five days. Jewellery, bags, stoles and capes are also available for hire or sale.

G THORNFIELD LTD
321 GRAY'S INN ROAD, LONDON WC1X 8PX
☎ 020-7837 2996. OPEN 8 - 6 MON - FRI, 9 - 2 SAT.
Permanent Discount Outlet • *DIY/Renovation*
Furniture/Soft Furnishings • *Household*

Offers from 20%-50% off wallcovering brands such as Sanderson and Kingfisher. The more you buy, the greater your discount. Also up to one-third off co-ordinating fabrics. Doesn't hold stocks of wallpapers and fabrics but you can order from their books. Next day delivery. Also sells frames, prints and posters at very low prices. Access to nearly 10,000 picture and prints from stock or to order, including Limited Editions. Dulux paint colours mixed on the premises, with 1800 shades to choose from.

GEORGIANA GRIMSTON
18 EDNA STREET, LONDON SW11 3DP
☎ 020-7978 6161. BY APPOINTMENT ONLY.

Georgiana Grimston bespoke tailoring service is perfectly suited to workaholic men and women who barely have time to go home, let alone to the tailor. She and her team of Savile Row cutters produce high quality clothes at prices considerably lower than Savile Row (starting at £675) and conduct fittings almost anywhere: at the office, at home or in Savile Row. All patterns are individually designed, cut in the traditional method and are 100% handmade and handstitched. Ring for an appointment.

GERTRUDE FASHIONS
84 WILTON ROAD, VICTORIA, LONDON SW1V 1DL
☎ 020-7834 6933. OPEN 10 - 5.30 MON - SAT.
Permanent Discount Outlet • *Womenswear Only*
Jackets, skirts, blouses, suits, dresses, trousers and coats. German designers as well as some Italian and French names at very competitive prices. Discounts from 35% off original prices.

GHOST LTD
263 KENSAL ROAD, LONDON W10 5DB
☎ 020-8960 3121.
Designer Sale • *Womenswear Only*
Annual warehouse sale of famous Ghost label which consists of old stock, current season damaged stock, show pieces and one-off samples usually takes place in first or second week of December. Write to put your name down on the mailing list.

GLOUCESTER ROAD BOOKSHOP
123 GLOUCESTER ROAD, LONDON SW7
☎ 020-7370 3503. OPEN 8.30 - 10.30 MON - FRI, 10.30 - 6.30 SAT, SUN AND BANK HOLIDAYS.
Permanent Discount Outlet • *Food and Leisure*
Secondhand books including review copies, also catalogues in modern First Editions and rare antiquarian books. A reader who recommended this shop said they are strong on all areas: literature, arts, travel, gardening etc, all in good condition, well displayed and categorised. Book prices range from 20p - £200.

GOLD'S FACTORY OUTLET
108-114 GOLDERS GREEN ROAD, LONDON NW11 8HB
☎ 020-8905 5721. OPEN 10 - 6 MON- FRI, SUN, CLOSED SAT.
Permanent Discount Outlet • *Womenswear & Menswear*
Famous men's and women's clothing and shoes. Labels on sale include Vandal and Loake shoes and Hugo James and Austin Reed clothing.

GOTTELIER LTD
103 BERMONDSEY STREET, LONDON SE1 3XB
☎ 020-7403 6332. PHONE TO BE PUT ON MAILING LIST.
Designer Sales • *Womenswear Only*
Twice-yearly showroom sales of distinctive chunky knits, denim dresses, skirts, leggings and sweatshirts - all made from cotton and usually half price or less here. Sales are usually June and November. Parking outside. Phone to put your name on the mailing list.

HALF-PRICE POTS
340 FULHAM ROAD, LONDON SW10 9UH
☎ 020-7376 4808. OPEN 10 - 5.30 SEVEN DAYS A WEEK.
Permanent Discount Outlet • *Food and Leisure*
Terracotta pots from around the world at extremely competitive prices. The pots come in all shapes and sizes from China, Spain, Morocco, Mexico and Tunisia, Egypt, Turkey and India. Prices range from 20p to £1,000 and include antique pots and storage jars reclaimed from the desert. Stock changes constantly.

HALF-PRICE TICKET BOOTH
THE BOOKING HALL, LEICESTER SQUARE STATION, LONDON WC2
THE CRITERION THEATRE, PICCADILLY CIRCUS, LONDON W1
☎ 020 8427 6566. WEBSITE: www.uktickets.co.uk
Here's where you can pick up official half-price and discounted theatre tickets for many of the popular West End musicals and plays, usually for that day's performance. Also tickets for sold out musicals and plays. Turn up in person at the two outlets, or call 020 8427 6566. Beware of ticket touts!

HANG UPS
366 FULHAM ROAD, LONDON SW10 9UU
☎ 020-7351 0047. OPEN 11 - 6 MON - SAT, 10.30 - 6 SAT, 1 - 4 SOME SUNS, PHONE FIRST.
Dress Agency • *Womenswear Only*
High fashion designer labels plus vintage clothes, Seventies gear and accessories for women. Designers include Azzedine Aliai, Ghost, Gaultier, Moschino, Joseph, Gucci, Vivienne Westwood, Whistles. Prices range from £1 for a t-shirt to £500 for a Gucci jacket. Plenty of daywear, evening wear, casual clothes, shoes, handbags, as well as lingerie and a selection of new designer clothing at discounted prices.

HAZLE CERAMICS
JUBILEE HALL, COVENT GARDEN MARKET, LONDON WC2
OPEN 9 - 5.
WORKSHOP: HAZLE CERAMICS, STALLIONS YARD, COOdHAM HALL, GREAT WARLEY, BRENTWOOD ESSEX CM13 3JT.
☎ (01277) 220892. OPEN TO PUBLIC 11 - 5 FRI, SAT, SUN.
Permanent Discount Outlet • *Household*
Covent Garden: Collectable Nation of Shopkeeper ceramic wall plaques in a wide variety of different designs. Seconds are sold off here at weekends at about one third off the normal prices. **Workshop:** Tour available with tea, coffee, access to gift shop and ceramics available.

HENRY BUTCHER INTERNATIONAL LTD
BROWNLOW HOUSE, 50-51 HIGH HOLBORN, LONDON WC1V 6EG
☎ 020-7405 8411. OPEN 9.15 - 6 MON - FRI.
Furniture/Soft Furnishings
Established more than 100 years ago, Henry Butcher International are global auctioneers and valuers, dealing with all types of industrial plant, machinery and equipment. They have a mailing list of some 30,000 names under the categories of equipment which they are looking for from heavy engineering to office furniture and computers. They sell anything from boardroom tables to typists' chairs, computers to manufacturing plants. Put your name on their mailing list for a colour flysheet of sales which you might be interested in.

HITACHI FACTORY SHOP
166 HIGH STREET NORTH, LONDON E6
☎ 020-8472 1373. OPEN 9 - 6 MON - FRI, 10 - 6 SAT.
Factory Shop • *Electrical Equipment*
Hitachi's factory outlet sells returned and former display items at discounts averaging 25%. For example, a Hitachi digital 28" TV, £700, usual price £1,200. They also sell CD players and hi-fis starting at £200 from Panasonic and Technics and some cheaper Daewoo CD players such as a three-disk, twin tape with a silver front and remote control, £130.

HOT & COLD INC
13-15 GOLBORNE ROAD, LONDON W10 5NY
☎ 020-8960 1200/1300. OPEN 10 - 5 MON - FRI, 10 - 5 SAT.
Permanent Discount Outlet • *Electrical Equipment* • *Household*
Supplies domestic appliances from nearly one hundred brands. Range now includes American fridge freezers and range cookers. A total of about 10,000 different items - at prices which they claim will beat any genuine competitor's. In fact, they are so sure of this that they promise to refund the difference if you find you could have bought the same product elsewhere at the same time for a lower price, provided you give them proof of that within two weeks of purchase. All goods are brand new, perfect and guaranteed. Their strength is in built-in equipment, but they can also supply freestanding appliances. Also ends of lines, some at less than half the original price. Prices include VAT. Delivery can be arranged countrywide.

HOUSE OF STEEL
400 CALEDONIAN ROAD, LONDON N1 1DN
☎ 020-7607 5889. OPEN 11.30 - 5 MON - FRI, BY APPOINTMENT ON SAT.
Architectural Salvage • *DIY/Renovation*
Five thousand square foot warehouse devoted to reclaimed metalwork of every kind including wrought-iron gates, old grilles, wrought-iron panels, arched gates, beds, staircases, balconies and lighting. Also designs and makes a range of steel furniture. Anything in metal custom made or cast - from a pin to an anchor. Repairs and restoration undertaken.

I KINN
80 GEORGE LANE, SOUTH WOODFORD, LONDON E18 1JJ
☎ 020-8989 2927. OPEN 10 - 5.30 MON - FRI, 10 - 5 SAT, 10.30 - 1 SUN.
Permanent Discount Outlet • *Womenswear Only*
Large showroom selling classic store merchandise such as is found in Allders, John Lewis, House of Fraser groups at bargain prices. There are plenty of ladies jackets, suits, dresses and skirts plus designer clothes from time to time at about half the normal retail price.

ICELAND CLEARANCE WAREHOUSE
120-132 CAMBERWELL ROAD, LONDON SE5
☎ 020-7708 4347. OPEN 9 - 7 MON - FRI, 9 - 5.30 SAT, 10 - 4 SUN.
Factory Shop • *Electrical Equipment*
Iceland's showroom near Camberwell Green has a clearance section which sells a wide range of "shop-soiled" or damaged packaging kitchen equipment from large US-style fridges to microwaves, kettles, tumble dryers, washing machines, dishwashers and ovens at discounts of about 20%. The showroom also has brand new stock at full price. Items in the clearance section could be there as a result of being damaged on delivery, because it broke down within two weeks of being purchased and has been reconditioned, because it is part of a range or a manufacturer no longer being sold by Iceland's 600-plus branches or because of Iceland's policy of lending appliances to customers whose machines have broken down within one year of purchase. The loaned machine, which may only have been used for a few days, is then sold off at discount. The clearance section is at the back of the Iceland showroom.

IN WEAR FACTORY OUTLET
100 GARRATT LANE, WANDSWORTH, LONDON SW18 4DJ
☎ 020-8871 2155. OPEN 10 - 5.30 MON - SAT, 11 - 5 SUN.
Factory Shop • *Womenswear & Menswear*
In Wear for women and Matinique for men as well as Part Two for both men and women at discounts of between 30%-70% for last season's stock, ends of lines and seconds. All the stock is made up of separates and tends to be stylishly casual and includes blazers, jeans, trousers, dresses, knitwear, suits and outerwear. Twice-yearly designer sample sale is held here. Phone for details. There is another factory shop at Bicester Village.

JOEL & SON FABRICS
75-83 CHURCH STREET, LONDON NW8 8EU
☎ 020-7724 6895.   E-MAIL: info@JoelandSonfabrics.co.uk
OPEN 8.30 - 5.30 MON - SAT.
Permanent Discount Outlet • *Womenswear Only*
London's foremost designer fabric store sells up-to-date fabrics used by the top catwalk designers and couturiers from St Laurent and Cerruti to Versace and Gianfranco Ferre. Prices are very competitive, and the fabric is exceptional.

Also carries a wide range of supplies for bridal wear including embroidered laces, beaded fabrics, Jacquards, Duchess satins, as well as veils in silk and silk mixes. Good range of designer lookalike buttons. Mr Joel & Son have been in the business for 45 years and at the same premises for 20 years. Staff are always on hand to advise and are proud of their personal service.

JOSEPH CLEARANCE SHOP
53 KING'S ROAD, LONDON SW3 1QN
☎ 020-7730 7562. OPEN 10.30 - 6.30 MON - SAT, UNTIL 7 ON WED, 12 - 5 SUN.
Permanent Discount Outlet • *Womenswear Only*
End of season and clearance lines from the Joseph label at reductions of up to 70%. Several concessions include Gucci and Helmut Lang. Faulty stock from the current season at 30% off.

KEW ARCHITECTURAL ANTIQUES
4 KEWBRIDGE ARCHES, STRAND ON THE GREEN, LONDON W4 3NG
☎ 020-8987 2610. OPEN 10 - 6.30 MON - FRI, 9.30 - 5 SAT, 11 - 4 SUN.
Architectural Salvage • *DIY/Renovation* • *Furniture/Soft Furnishings*
Lots of door fittings, door knobs, door knockers, coat hooks, finger plates, period bathroom fittings, cast iron radiators, wood flooring and antique furniture (Edwardian and Victorian) etc. Also shades and refurbished French light fittings. If you are looking for something special, it's worth ringing first to see what they have in stock.

KING'S CROSS TILES
3-13 PANCRAS ROAD, KING'S CROSS, LONDON NW1 2QB
☎ 020-7833 3884. OPEN 8 - 7 MON - FRI, 9 - 5 SAT.
Permanent Discount Outlet • *DIY/Renovation*
Wall tiles, floor tiles, mosaics, slates, marbles, borders, stick-ons and bathroom suites, all at very competitive prices. The tiles are imported directly from Spain and Italy so there is no middleman taking a cut, which is why prices are so good. The company don't produce glossy brochures so can offer the bathroom suites at prices lower than most of their competitors. Full range of exterior patio tiles also good value.

L'HOMME DESIGNER EXCHANGE
50 BLANDFORD STREET, LONDON W1H 3HD
☎ 020-7224 3266. OPEN 11 - 6 MON - THUR, 11.30 - 6 FRI, 11 - 5 SAT.
Dress Agency • *Menswear Only*
This shop sells designer menswear from the outrageous to the classic for the beach, the office, the nightclub and special evenings out. Designers in stock vary, but usually include Versace (couture jackets from £180) and Armani (suits from £180), Boss (suits and coats from £140) and Prada, Gucci and Gaultier. All stock is less than two years old. Sales in July and December see the sell-off of hire stock.

LA SCALA
39 ELYSTAN STREET, LONDON SW3 3NT
☎ 020-7589 2784. OPEN 10 - 5.30 MON - SAT.
Dress Agency • *Womenswear & Menswear* • *Children*
La Scala sells women's nearly-new clothes, accessories, men's and children's clothes under the same roof. There is a separate room full of top designer men's clothes including Armani, Valentino and Boss, and large quantities of women and men's cashmere as well as a range of shoes in immaculate condition. Owner Sandy Reid lived for 14 years in Northern Italy and uses her experience there in her shop behind the Conran Shop in Chelsea. There, she sells end of season Italian designer wear and current top designer nearly-new outfits from Armani, Mani, DKNY, Paddy Campbell, Valentino, Voyage and MaxMara. Italian is spoken in the shop which has a large Italian clientele. There's an emphasis on younger lines and the price reductions are fantastic.

LABELS
146 FLEET ROAD, HAMPSTEAD, LONDON NW3 2QX
☎ 020-7267 8521. OPEN 10 - 6 TUE - SAT.
Permanent Discount Outlet • *Womenswear Only*
A comprehensive selection of clothing from mid-market labels, Nicole Farhi, Escada, Ghost, Betty Barclay and Gap as well as Marks & Spencer, Options and French Connection. There are also accessories - shoes, handbags and costume jewellery - on sale. Prices range from £10-£150.

LASSCO FLOORING
41 MALTBY STREET, LONDON SE1 3PA
☎ 020-7237 4488.
E-MAIL: flooring@lassco.co.uk   WEBSITE: www.lassco.co.uk
OPEN 10 - 5 MON - SAT.
Architectural Salvage • *DIY/Renovation*
Supplies over 150 lines of reclaimed, antique and new timber flooring in parquet strip and board. Two galleries in Bermondsey display finished samples. Recent stocks are burgeoning with the arrival of 1/4 million feet of Oregon pine salvaged from Whitfield Barracks, Dover, dating from the 1930s. The Tate & Lyle building in Silvertown has also yielded enormous quantities of Muhuhu parquet, an unusual East African hardwood of extreme durability in a marbled, honeyed colour. LASSCO's sawmill has produced a new range of traditional French chevron flooring as an alternative to the English herringbone style parquet. Mainland delivery and worldwide export can be arranged.

LASSCO RBK
BRITANNIA WALK, ISLINGTON, LONDON N1 7LU
☎ 020-7336 8221. OPEN 9.30 - 5.30 MON - SAT.
LASSCO TRADE WAREHOUSE, BRITANNIA WALK, ISLINGTON,
LONDON N1 7LU
☎ 020-7490 1000.
E-MAIL: lasscorbk@aol.com
Architectural Salvage • *DIY/Renovation*
Lassco RBK has an eclectic stock of reclaimed cast iron radiators, many with decorative casting and unusual examples. Radiators restored, guaranteed and finished to order. Many finishes are available including burnishing, priming and powder coating. Continually changing and expanding stocks of bathtubs in enamel, porcelain, tin and copper; Art Deco suites, Edwardian shower units, original and antique taps, sinks, nauticalia plus much more. A colour brochure is available. Lassco Trade Warehouse next door offers discounted architectural elements, door panelling, marine salvage, counters, shop fittings, etc, many sourced from famous hotels, museums, theatres, department stores and public buildings.

LASSCO ST MICHAEL'S
ST MICHAEL'S CHURCH, MARK STREET, OFF PAUL STREET,
LONDON EC2M 4ER
☎ 020-7739 0448. WEBSITE: www.lassco.co.uk.
OPEN 10 - 5 SEVEN DAYS A WEEK.
Architectural Salvage • *DIY/Renovation*
Fine architectural antiques, chimney pieces, panelled rooms, garden ornaments, lighting, door furniture and much more. See also LASSCO Flooring at Maltby Street, Bermondsey and LASSCO RBK (radiators, bathrooms, kitchens) in Islington.

LAUREL HERMAN
18A LAMBOLLE PLACE, LONDON NW3 4PG
☎ 020-7586 7925. FAX 020-7586 7926. E-MAIL: info@pospres.co.uk
WEBSITE: www.pospres.co.uk
BY APPOINTMENT ONLY.
Permanent Discount Outlet • *Womenswear Only*
Established for over 25 years, and with 2,000 regular clients, this is London's best-kept secret in order to maintain its exclusivity. Housed in a spacious, airy "concealed" Hampstead showroom is an ever-changing melange of 6,000 upmarket designer items (Armani, Escada, MaxMara, Donna Karan, Valentino, etc) at a fraction of their original price. Both brand new and "gently-worn" but sourced only from Laurel's own personal contacts who shop the world to answer all requirements for day or evening, casual or formal, business or leisure. This unique concept is ideal for those who normally hate shopping, need a new look, have figure problems - or just clothesaholics. Many clients work towards the ultimate wardrobe solution, ie Laurel Herman's "Wardrobe That Works" but all advice is totally objective, free of

charge, and based on personal lifestyle, shape, personality and budget. (There is a brochure to explain the concept in more detail.) In order to maintain the peaceful, relaxed ambience, appointments are compulsory, from 10am Monday to Saturday, but extending to 11pm in the evening twice weekly for working women. Be warned, customers usually stay three or four hours! The collection is taken twice yearly to Southampton in June and November. Workshops and seminars are available for improving personal style and business image. Laurel Herman also creates women's events for the corporate market, professional organisations and groups such as golf clubs and charities. The sister company, Positive Presence, offers a wide range of consultancy for men, women and organisations on all issues relating to appearance and presentation - including "real" life makeovers, metamorphosis, personal shopping, workshops, seminars and "talks".

LAURENCE CORNER
62-64 HAMPSTEAD ROAD, LONDON NW1
☎ 020-7813 1010. OPEN 9.30 - 6 MON - SAT.
Secondhand and Vintage Clothes • *Womenswear & Menswear*
Secondhand clothing shop specialising in uniforms and army surplus. Stock varies from string vests to Chinese military great coats.

LAZDAN
218 BOW COMMON LANE, LONDON E3 4HH
☎ 020-8981 4632. OPEN 8 - 5 MON - FRI, 8 - 12.30 SAT.
Architectural Salvage • *DIY/Renovation*
Secondhand bricks, reclaimed slates, sash weights and chimney pots.

LETTERBOX LIBRARY
71-73 ALLEN ROAD, LONDON N16 8RY
☎ 020-7503 4801 FAX: 0207-503 4800.
OPEN 10 - 5 MON - FRI AND OCCASIONAL SATURDAYS.
Permanent Discount Outlet • *Children*
Run by a co-operative, Letterbox offers non-sexist, non-racist, multi-cultural books, as well as those about the environment, citizenship and disabilty for children of all ages. Books are sold at discounts of between 5% and 12%. Phone or fax for catalogue at the address above.

LEVY AND FRIEND
9 EBURY BRIDGE ROAD, LONDON SW1W 8QX
☎ 020-7730 5695. OPEN 11 - 6 MON - SAT, CLOSED WEDS.
Dress Agency • *Womenswear Only*
Well presented garments in pristine condition are sold in a relaxed atmosphere in this ground floor shop. Specialising in day wear, the shop offers fashionable, functional, affordable modern clothing from labels such as Prada, Joseph, Dolce e Gabbanna, Margaret Howell and Gucci, as well as lots of accessories, designer bags, belts, shoes and boots. Established for fourteen years, the shop has a clientele from around the world and the owner is ready with advice, if needed. Prices range from £10 - £200. Payment can be made by Switch, American Express, Mastercard, Visa or Barclaycard.

LEYLAND SDM

43-45 FARRINGDON ROAD, LONDON EC1M 3JB
- 020-76242 5791. OPEN 7 - 6 MON - SAT.
- 020-7828 8695. 7 - 6 MON - SAT.
683-685 FINCHLEY ROAD, LONDON NW2
- 020-7794 5927. 7 - 6 MON - SAT.
9 THE MALL, EALING BROADWAY, EALING, LONDON W5
- 020-8566 0481. OPEN 7 - 6 MON - SAT.
335-337 KING'S ROAD, LONDON SW3 5EU
- 020-7352 4742. OPEN 7 - 6 MON - SAT, 9 - 3 SUN.
361-365 KENSINGTON HIGH STREET, LONDON W14 8QY
- 020-7602 9099. OPEN 7 - 6 MON - SAT.
7 - 15 CAMDEN ROAD, LONDON NW1
- 020-7284 4366. OPEN 7 - 6 MON - SAT, 9 - 3 SUN.
371-373 EDGWARE ROAD, LONDON W2
- 020-7723 8048. OPEN 7 - 6 MON - SAT, 9 - 3 SUN.
167-169 SHAFTESBURY AVENUE, LONDON WC2H
- 020-7836 7337. OPEN 7 - 6 MON - SAT.

Permanent Discount Outlet • DIY/Renovation

Everything the enthusiastic diy-er could require, from tools and equipment to wallpapers, cornicing, moulding, brace fittings and paint. In fact, there are four thousand colours from which to choose which can be mixed to match fabric or carpets, all at trade prices. Also special offers such as 40% off power tools. There are nine branches of Leyland SDM Londonwide; for details of your local branch, freephone 0800 454 484.

LIGHT AND SOUND

166 HIGH STREET NORTH, LONDON E6
- 020-8472 1373. OPEN 9 - 6 MON - FRI, 10-6 SAT.

Factory Shop • Electrical Equipment

Hitachi's factory outlet sells returned and former display items at discounts averaging 25%. This can include CD players, TVs, videos, hi-fis, fridges, microwaves, vacuum cleaners, radio cassettes, Walkmans and accessories.

LIPMANS HIRE DEPARTMENT

22 CHARING CROSS RD, LONDON WC2
- 020-7240 2310. OPEN 9 -8 MON - FRI, 9 - 6 SAT.

Hire Shop • Secondhand and Vintage Clothes

Hires and sells ex-hire outfits. For example, dinner suits which would normally cost £160 to buy are £110 while those which have seen more wear cost from £50. New business suits in pure wool cost from £149. They also hire out dinner suits and top and tails from £27.95 to £43. Separates, dinner jackets and trousers can be hired from £22.95.

LLOYDS INTERNATIONAL AUCTION GALLERIES
118 PUTNEY BRIDGE ROAD, LONDON SW15 2NQ
☎ 020-8788 7777. VIEWING 10.30 - 5 WED, 10.30 - 7 FRI,
SALE STARTS 5 WED. TIMES VARY, PHONE FIRST.
Auctioneers who specialise in Victorian and Edwardian furniture and carpets as well as china, glass, art and collectables, also offer unclaimed goods from the Customs department and lost property which is sold here by auction. Furniture Sales are held fortnightly on a Saturday, viewing is on the Friday. Miscellaneous Sales are held fortnightly on a Wednesday with viewing on the same day. Phone for the date of the next auction.

LONDON FOR LESS
222 KENSAL ROAD, LONDON W10 5BN
☎ 020-8964 4242.
Anyone who likes visiting London may like to take advantage of London for Less. Usually promoted to American visitors, it has recently been launched to the domestic British market. For just £12.95, you get a package which includes a discount card providing discounts at over 250 places in central London, plus a 288-page full colour guidebook and a fold-out map. Discounts are applicable for up to four people for up to eight days. Example of discounts include: 20%-50% off 45 attractions and museums such as Madame Tussaud's; 25%-75% off ticket prices at shows, concerts, operas and ballets; such as The London Philharmonic; 20%-50% off rack rates at 42 hotels such as The Rochester Hotel; 25% off the total bill at 90 restaurants; and 20% off all goods at 50 shops. Restaurants included range from Bella Pasta for very inexpensive meals, to Cafe Lazeez for award-winning Indian food. Shops included range from Piccadilly Souvenirs, situated right next to Piccadilly Circus to House of Cashmere on Oxford Street selling famous brand-name clothes. Books are also available at £5.95 for European cities: Amsterdam, Athens, Barcelona, Berlin, Bruges, Brussels, Budapest, Copenhagen, Dublin, Florence, Hamburg, Iceland, Istanbul, Lisbon, London, Madrid, Milan, Munich, New York, Paris, Prague, Rome, Salzburg, Venice, Verona, Vienna and Washington D.C. and for the USA guides on: California, Florida, Hawaii, Las Vegas, Los Angeles, Orlando, San Francisco and the Far East and Thailand. All For Less titles can be purchased at good book shops and at the British Travel Centre on Lower Regent Stree or via the above telephone number.

LONDON WAREHOUSES LTD
UNIT 2A, ENDEAVOUR WAY, WIMBLEDON, LONDON SW19 8UH
☎ 020-8947 9878. OPEN 10 - 5 SAT, SUN.
Permanent Discount Outlet • *Furniture/Soft Furnishings*
Sales every weekend of ex-showhouse furniture direct from designers and national house builders, plus manufacturers end of line and surplus stocks. Three-piece suites, tables, chairs, bedroom furniture plus much much more, all at affordable prices.

LOSNERS DRESS HIRE
232 STAMFORD HILL, LONDON N16 6TT
☎ 020-8800 7466. OPEN 9 - 5.30 MON - SAT, UNTIL 7 ON THUR.
Hire Shop • *Womenswear & Menswear*
Specialises in top end of the market wedding outfits to hire and to buy. Basic hire costs anything from £100 to £300; you can choose from a huge range that includes new and nearly-new bridal outfits. Labels include Ronald Joyce, Ellis, Alfred Angelo, Mori Lee. Can also make dresses to order. All the accessories are to buy only and they offer a shoe-dyeing service. There are also morning and dinner suits to hire from £40-£200. Other branches in Dunstable, Ilford, Edgware, Gants Hill, Enfield, Ealing and St Albans, however these are all menswear outlets with the exception of St Albans which also carries the bridal range.

LUNN ANTIQUES LTD
86 NEW KING'S ROAD, PARSONS GREEN, LONDON SW6 4LU
☎ 020-7736 4638. OPEN 10 - 6 MON - SAT.
UNIT 8, ADMIRAL VERNON ARCADE, PORTOBELLO ROAD,
LONDON W11
OPEN 7.30 - 3.30 SAT ONLY.
Secondhand and Vintage Clothes • *Household*
Stockists of antique and modern linen and lace. Its headquarters are at the New King's Road shop where it specialises in antique and modern bedlinen, sheets, duvet covers and bedcovers. Here, they also sell top quality antique christening robes and modern reproductions and there is an expert laundry and restoration service for antique linen and lace. Period clothing includes Victorian nightwear, Edwardian camisoles and blouses, 1920s beaded dresses, 1930s silk chiffon and 40s, 50s and 60s outfits. Also risque silk lingerie, luxurious lace and elaborate embroidery and a rich profusion of antique textiles. All wholesale and trade enquiries should be made here. The Portobello Road shop is Lunn Antique's lace outlet with a good selection from four centuries: 17th century needlepoints: 18th century Brussels, Mechlin, Valenciennes and White work; 19th century Alencon, Point de Gaze, Chantilly, Honiton and Youghal, plus 20th century bed and table linen decorated with filet, cutwork, drawnwork, embroidery and needlepoint.

MASSIMO FIORUCCI
43A COMMERCIAL STREET, LONDON E1 6BD
☎ 020-7247 3220. OPEN 10.30 - 5.30 MON - FRI, 12 - 3.30 SUN.
Permanent Discount Outlet • *Womenswear & Menswear*
There's a vetted entry system to this large, glass fronted warehouse-type shop. Best buys here are jeans from Moschino, Versace and Armani, although they also stock knitwear, T-shirts, jackets, cocktail dresses, ties and shoes by Dolce & Gabbana, Valentino, Hugo Boss, Gianfranco Ferre and Zegna. Items aren't priced, which leaves room for a bit of haggling, but they're generally about 30-40% cheaper than the high streeet. For example, ladies Versace long-sleeved sweater, £65; Moschino T-shirt, £30; Versus cocktail dress, £65. Merchandise is 50/50 for men and women. The shop has now been refurbished and has changing rooms.

MATALAN
EDGWARE ROAD, CRICKLEWOOD BROADWAY, CRICKLEWOOD, LONDON NW2 6PH
☎ 020-8450 5667. OPEN 9 - 8 MON - FRI, 9 - 6 SAT, 11 - 5 SUN.
30-59 BUGSBY WAY, LONDON SE7 7SE
☎ 020-8269 4290. OPEN 9 - 8 MON - FRI, 9 - 6 SAT, 11 - 5 SUN.
THURSTON ROAD, LOANPIT VALE, LEWISHAM SE13 7SN
☎ 020-8463 9830. OPEN 10 - 8 MON - SAT, 10 - 4 SUN.
Permanent Discount Outlet • *Womenswear & Menswear*
Children • *Household*
Matalan is a fashion and homewares value retailer giving customers what they claim to be unbeatable value for money with huge savings on a wide range of products including high quality fashionable clothing for men, women and children at up to 50% off high street prices. Matalan is situated out of town and stores are open seven days a week all year round.

MAXFIELD PARRISH
TEMPO HOUSE, 5 CONGREVE STREET, LONDON SE17 1TJ
☎ 020-7252 5225.
Designer Sale • *Womenswear Only*
Phone or write to put your name down on the mailing list for an invitation to the showroom sales at which prices of these fabulous leather and suede jackets and coats are considerably reduced. Sales are normally three times a year.

MODERN AGE VINTAGE CLOTHING
65 CHALK FARM ROAD, LONDON NW1 8AN
☎ 020-7482 3787. OPEN 10.30 - 6 MON - FRI, 10 - 6 SAT, SUN.
Secondhand and Vintage Clothes • *Womenswear & Menswear*
American secondhand clothing, particularly from the Fifties, Sixties and Seventies to hire and to buy. Average price for any garment is £25; men's shirts from £8 - £50, dinner suits for hire at £25. Women's eveningwear for hire from £25.

MORRY'S
22 NORTH MALL, EDMONTON, LONDON N9 OEJ
☎ 020-8807 6747. OPEN 8.30 - 5 MON - SAT, CLOSED 1 ON THUR.
Permanent Discount Outlet • *Womenswear & Menswear*
Electrical Equipment • *Children*

Liquidation stock which includes some famous makes and can comprise anything from gardening equipment (shovels, forks and hoses) and household items to electrical equipment (CDs, radios, TVs, radio alarms) and clothing for men, women and children. Everything is at least half the retail price. If you live nearby, drop in frequently.

MOSS BROS
27 - 28 KING STREET, COVENT GARDEN, LONDON WC2E 8JD
☎ 020-7632 9700. OPEN 9 - 6 MON - SAT, UNTIL 7 ON THUR AND SAT.
Permanent Discount Outlet • *Menswear Only*

This Moss Bros London store has a permanent own-label ex-hire department. Morning suits from £205, black morning coats from £165, top hats from £40, dinner suits from £79, trousers £30, kilts £199, white tuxedos £79: prices depend on age and condition of garments.

NATIONAL ART COLLECTIONS FUND
MEMBERSHIP SECRETARY, MILLAIS HOUSE, 7 CROMWELL PLACE, LONDON SW7 2JN
☎ 020-7225 4800.
Food and Leisure

Join this fund and get a whole host of benefits. It costs £27 to join (£18 for concessions) and you get free admission to about 200 permanent collections including the Imperial War Museum, The Royal Pavilion in Brighton, National Maritime Museum and the Christ Church Picture Gallery in Oxford. You also get the Art Quarterly magazine and Review catalogue, first choice of tours at home and abroad and talks by artists and experts and visits to historic private houses. Your subscription will enable you to become a patron of the arts as it is used to help galleries buy works of art.

NETWORTH ENTERPRISES LTD
LONDON
☎ 020-8888 9499/0961 939973. OPEN BY APPOINTMENT.
Permanent Discount Outlet • *Furniture/Soft Furnishings*

Sole agents of a company in Romania producing wicker baskets and garden furniture of the highest quality and workmanship. They have in stock a large variety of both of these ranges of products. Non-stock items can be delivered direct from the factory within 40 days. Other items can be delivered the following day. As they sell direct from the factory, their prices are very competitive. Bespoke items can also be made, depending on the quantity ordered. Relocating as we went to press, phone for details of their new warehouse.

NEXT TO NOTHING
UNIT 11, ARCADIA CENTRE, EALING BROADWAY,
LONDON, W5 2ND
☎ 020-8567 2747. OPEN 9.30 - 6 MON - SAT.

Permanent Discount Outlet • *Womenswear & Menswear* • **Children**

Sells perfect surplus stock from Next stores and the Next Directory catalogue - from belts, jewellery and underwear to day and evening wear - at discounts of 50% or more. The ranges are usually last season's and overruns but there is the odd current item if you look carefully. Stock consists of men's, women's and children's clothing, and shoes. Stock is replenished three times a week and there is plenty of it. This branch does not stock a lot of homes items and has only a small amount of accessories.

NICOLE FARHI/FRENCH CONNECTION OUTLET SHOP
3 HANCOCK ROAD, BROMLEY-BY-BOW,
LONDON E3 3DA
☎ 020-7399 7125. OPEN 10 - 3 TUE, WED, SAT, 11 - 6.30 THUR, 10 - 5.30 FRI.

Factory Shop • *Womenswear & Menswear*

Nicole Farhi/French Connection's Outlet Shop in Bow, next door to the warehouse, may be small but it's packed with rails of clothes for women and men. Stock is mainly made up of previous season merchandise, samples and seconds from Nicole Farhi and French Connection, with some Great Plains merchandise. There's a selection of blouses, knitwear, trousers, skirts, coats, jackets, bags, leather and suede wear, some shoes and boots, and a small amount of evening wear, although stock varies. Womenswear makes up about 80% of the shop's contents. Great finds include a cream cashmere longline polo neck sweater, £60; chunky grey roll neck fisherman's jumper with a snag in the collar, £99, reduced from £279; grey pinstripe classic suit, £70; Great Plains sample blouse, £15; little black sleeveless dress, £20 reduced from £99 because of a torn seam; long black leather skirt, £150. Seconds are marked and faults are also pointed out at the cash desk as you can't return goods. Discounts vary according to how old the stock is so some outfits may only be reduced from £179 to £150; others are practically given away. There are two changing rooms. There is also a Nicole Farhi/French Connection factory shop at Bicester Village designer outlet centre in Oxfordshire.

NORTON & TOWNSEND
71 BONDWAY, LONDON SW8 1SQ
☎ 020-7735 4701. OPEN 9 - 5 MON - FRI.

Norton & Townsend offer bespoke tailoring at off-the-peg prices with all the traditional hand-finishing and attention to detail that you expect from a quality tailor. You can buy a hand cut and finished, perfectly fitting, 100% wool/worsted suit in four to six weeks for as little as £425. The tailor will visit you at home or at work to help you choose from a range of hundreds of cloths. They carry a range of cloths that are bought straight from mills as well as well known merchants such as Dormeuil and Holland & Sherry. They will also tailor suits or jackets using the customer's own fabric. Phone the above telephone number for a list of their regional offices.

NOT QUITE NEW
159 BRENT STREET, HENDON, LONDON NW4 4DH
☎ 020-8203 4691. OPEN 10 - 4.30 MON - FRI, CLOSED WED, 10 - 1 SAT.
Dress Agency • *Womenswear & Menswear*

Personal service are the key words to this unique boutique which sells beautiful garments in pristine condition. In business for more than 20 years, Not Quite New sells top Italian, French and German designer names including Basler, Louis Feraud, Valentino, Yarell, Mondi, Betty Baclay and Jaeger, as well as shoes and bags of the highest quality. Sizes stocked range from 8-20 and most items cost less than £100. They now include menswear of the highest quality including Boss and Armani.

NOTTING HILL HOUSING TRUST
309 FULHAM ROAD, LONDON SW10 9QH
☎ 020-7352 7986. OPEN 10 - 6 MON - SAT, 12 - 4 SUN.
Dress Agency • *Womenswear & Menswear*

Charity shop featuring Betty Barclay, Mondi, Versace, Paul Costelloe and Moschino. Examples of prices include a Versus (Versace Diffusion) dress, unworn, for £75 and a Moschino jacket, slightly worn, £75. Men's clothes are also stocked including Ralph Lauren, Paul Smith and Conran. The shop accepts credit cards.

OAKVILLE
FIFTH FLOOR, 32-36 GREAT PORTLAND STREET, LONDON W1N 5AD
☎ 020-7580 3686.
Designer Sale • *Womenswear Only*

Phone or write to put your name down on the mailing list for an automatic invitation to the showroom sales at which prices are considerably reduced. Designers include Fendi and Ungaro and stock covers mother of the bride, evening and day wear.

OCEAN WAREHOUSE
OCEAN HOME SHOPPING, 9 HARDWICKS WAY, WANDSWORTH, LONDON SW18 4AW
☎ 020-7670 1222. OPEN MON - SAT 10 - 6.
Factory Shop • *Household*
Based at the head office, this factory shop clears old stock from this catalogue company as well as selling imperfect returns. This could be anything from chrome soap dispensers or corkscrews to sofas and stainless steel laundry bins. Past bargains have included plastic hangers and flower pots from 50p, Alessi bins at half price, beech bath racks at £15, reduced from £35; breakfast trays, £39, reduced from £139.

ONE NIGHT STAND
44 PIMLICO ROAD, LONDON SW1W 8LP
☎ 020-7730 8708. OPEN 10 - 6.30 MON - FRI, 10 - 5 SAT.
Hire Shop • *Womenswear Only*
More than 500 designer dresses in stock, sizes 8-18. Also hires jewellery, evening bags, capes and jackets. Cost £130-£180 for four days with a small number of more expensive items. Retail section with lingerie to complement clothes. Appointments preferred.

ORIENT EXPRESSIONS
STUDIO 3B2, COOPER HOUSE, 2 MICHAEL ROAD, LONDON SW6 2AD
☎ 020-7610 9311. WEBSITE: www.antiquesbulletin.com/orientexpressions
OPEN 9 - 1, 2 - 5 MON - FRI, AND BY APPOINTMENT.
Permanent Discount Outlet • *Furniture/Soft Furnishings*
Specialises in buying genuine antiques from China. The majority of the stock is from the early to mid-19th century, although the rarer 18th century pieces are bought when possible. Shipments are regular but small. Each piece is handpicked by the owners who both lived and worked in Hong Kong for many years. They are chosen carefully for their appearance, character and practical potential. Pieces are left in their original condition as much as possible. Any restoration is kept to a minimum to retain the character of the piece. The furniture comes mostly from the rural provinces of China and offers a variety of looks: simple, quite chunky, country pieces in elm and beech; more sophisticated pieces in huali or dark lacquer; highly decorative, lacquered and gilded items. Whether a piece is plain and simple or wild and whacky, the criteria for buying it is always the same - it must be beautiful, useful, genuine and, of course, the price must be right. Orient Expressions keeps overheads to a minimum and offers really good value, undercutting all its main competitors. Its major outlet is a spacious shop in Bath, but it is worth visiting the London showroom for the excellent trade prices. A further selection is available at Great Grooms Antique Centre in Hungerford, Berkshire.

OSBORNE & LITTLE
LONDON
☎ 020-8675 2255.
Designer Sale • *Furniture/Soft Furnishings*
Annual sales of fabrics, wallpapers and accessories from O & L, Nina Campbell and Liberty Furnishings ranges, usually held at London's Battersea Town Hall. Invitations are sent out to trade customers only but if you phone customer relations on the above telephone number, they will tell you the date of the next sale - normally in March.

OXFAM ORIGINAL
26 GANTON STREET, LONDON W1
☎ 020-7437 7338. OPEN 11.30 - 6.30 MON - SAT.
Secondhand and Vintage Clothes • *Womenswear & Menswear*
Secondhand shop famous in the past for its one-off designs made up by fashion students using donated fabric from top designers, this shop sells trendy high-street clothes with a mixture of retro and funky fashion. Motto 'Original clothes for original people'. All stock has been pre-sorted to contain only desirable garments, contemporary designer labels and a few tasteful high street basics.

OXFAM SUPER SAVING SHOP
570 KINGSLAND ROAD, LONDON E8
☎ 020-7923 1532. OPEN 9.15 - 5.30 MON - SAT.
Secondhand shops • *Household* • *Children*
Womenswear & Menswear • *Food and Leisure*
Vast secondhand shop selling loads of cheap bric a brac, records and clothes. Stock is made up of unsold items from Oxfam's other shops in London so it's very cheap indeed. For example, bric a brac items, £1; items of clothing, £2. Other end of the line Oxfam shops include Kilburn, Burnt Oak and Tooting.

P N JONES
18 HOLLY GROVE, LONDON SE15 5DF
☎ 020-7639 2113. OPEN 2 - 4 MON - WED AND BY APPOINTMENT.
Permanent Discount Outlet • *Furniture/Soft Furnishings*
Packed with natural-fibre fabrics, all hand-woven Indian cotton and silks, at trade prices. More than fifty-two different colours in checks and stripes, and voiles as well as curtaining and upholstery fabrics. VAT extra. Ring for stock cuttings and prices.

PAMELA'S
16 BEAUCHAMP PLACE, LONDON SW3 1MQ
☎ 020-7589 6852. OPEN 10- 5 MON - SAT.
Dress Agency • *Womenswear Only*
Selection of mostly French and Italian designer labels ‹ Chanel, Valentino ‹ as well as middle range names such as Jaeger and Country Casuals. There is plenty to choose from for weddings and balls, as well as lots of accessories.

PANDORA
16-22 CHEVAL PLACE, LONDON SW7 1ES
☎ 020-7589 5289. OPEN 9 - 6 MON-SAT AND MOST BANK HOLIDAYS.
Dress Agency • *Womenswear Only*
Based around the corner from Harrods, this large shop with more than 5,000 items in stock sells only the top, well-known designer names: Donna Karan, Emporio Armani, Thierry Mugler, Hardy Amies, Chanel, Bruce Oldfield, Valentino, Escada, Ghost. They sell everything to do with a woman's wardrobe but it has to be in good condition and sport a top label. Also stocks a range of size 16 plus, as well as handbags, belts, hats and shoes. Shoes have to be mistakes (ie new) though bags can be older eg crocodile, Hermes, Gucci. Everything is categorised into daywear, evening wear, trousers, skirts, etc so it is easy to browse. December/January and July/August clear-out sales see everything reduced by 30% with a further 20% reduction in February and September of previous season items.

PAUL SMITH SALE SHOP
23 AVERY ROW, LONDON W1X 9HB
☎ 020-7493 1287. OPEN 10 - 6 MON - SAT, UNTIL 7 ON THUR.
Permanent Discount Outlet • *Menswear Only*
Offers year-round seconds, ends of lines and sample stock in the heart of London's West End. This sale shop sells last season's stock from the main shop at discounts of 40%-50%, including R Newbold workwear range, jeans, shirts, knitwear, hats, gloves, suits, trousers and sportswear. There are lots of bargains with reductions of 75% off original retail price, and a wide selection of accessories from belts to cuff links. As with all permanent sale shops, stock varies, so more than one visit may be necessary.

PENGUIN SOCIETY
144 WEST END LANE, LONDON NW6 1SD
☎ 020-7625 7778. OPEN 11.OO - 7 MON - FRI, SAT 10.30 - 5.30
Dress Agency • *Womenswear & Menswear*
New and "gently worn" designer ladies and mens wear. Designers range from Valentino and Ghost to Jigsaw and Warehouse in the womens' range and from Armani to John Richmond and Boss in the men's. The clothes stocked cover both casual working day and evening wear, though they tend towards the former. Prices range from £10 - £200. Twice yearly sales in summer and winter. Clothing styles range from current to classical. Also ladies' and men's accessories: belts, jewellery, sunglasses etc. Quick turnover and deposits accepted on items of clothing.

POETSTYLE LTD
UNIT 1, BAYFORD STREET INDUSTRIAL CENTRE, LONDON E8 3SE
☎ 020-8533 0915. OPEN 7 - 6 MON - FRI, 10 - 5 SAT, 10 - 3 SUN.
1A CLEVELAND WAY, MILE END ROAD, LONDON E1 4TZ
☎ 020-7790 4233. OPEN 9-5 MON, THUR, FRI 10-2.30 SAT, SUN.
Permanent Discount Outlet • *Furniture/Soft Furnishings*
Established for more than 15 years, these shops sell ex-display model sofas and sofabeds at greatly reduced prices, as well as made to order sofas at reduced prices, upholstered using Sanderson, Liberty and Parkertex fabric. Also Ottomans, stools, armchairs. All goods sold here are manufactured on the premises using traditional methods. They will undertake contract upholstery.

PORTOBELLO CURTAIN SHOP
UNIT 22, ACKLAM WORKSHOPS, 10 ACKLAM ROAD,
LONDON W10 5QZ
☎ 020-8968 0078. OPEN 9.30 - 5.30 MON - SAT.
Permanent Discount Outlet • *Furniture/Soft Furnishings*
Quality upholstery and soft furnishing fabrics at very competitive prices, usually at least 25% cheaper than in the haberdashery and soft furnishings departments of stores. Also advises on curtains, fits tracks, makes blinds and curtains and makes up using customer's own fabric. Free estimates. By appointment only - moving premises as we went to press; phone for new address.

POSNERS: THE FLOOR STORE
35A-37 FAIRFAX ROAD, SWISS COTTAGE, LONDON NW6 4EW
☎ 020-7625 8899. OPEN 9 - 6 MON - SAT.
Permanent Discount Outlet • *Furniture/Soft Furnishings*
Posners - The Floor Store is London's largest hardwood flooring showroom where you will get unbiased advice based on three generations of experience in timber and carpets. Posners, an independent family business since 1946, specialises in fitted carpets and pre-finished hardwood floors. Recommended installers for all major brands, you will find most brands supplied at trade prices. Posners are the London stockist for Pergo - the high pressure laminate floor that's difficult to distinguish from real wood and which is scratch, dent and burn resistant. Posners have more than 2,000 ranges of flooring and carpeting, with various promotional ranges available at any time from £11.99 (incl VAT) for carpet and £22 net for 14/15mm pre-finished flooring from stock. Posners are unique for the almost overwhelming choice on offer and for the in-house fitting service available.

POSTSCRIPT
24 LANGROYD ROAD, LONDON SW17 7PL
☎ 020-8767 7421. FAX 0208-682 0280. E-MAIL: enquiries@postscriptbooks.co.uk
MAIL ORDER ONLY 9 - 5.30 MON - FRI.
Permanent Discount Outlet • *Food and Leisure*
Specialises in high quality books by mail at greatly reduced prices. Unlike the big book clubs, you are under no obligation to buy any books at any time. The

selection covers a huge range of interests from art, gardening, cookery, biography, travel and reference to history, philosophy, psychology and literature - from classic works to the frankly esoteric - many of which cannot be found in bookshops and all priced at a fraction of publishers' latest prices. Telephone for free catalogue.

POT LUCK
84 COLUMBIA ROAD, LONDON E2
☎ 020-7722 6892. OPEN 8 - 2.30 SUN.
Permanent Discount Outlet • *Household*

A great variety of seconds, discontinued ranges and ends of lines of china and vitreous porcelain (ovenproof hotelware). Sells English bone china from £2.50 and also Portmeirion cookware seconds such as oval dishes, £6.50 and 13" pasta bowls, £8.50. Among the well-known china names here are Thomas Goode and Wedgwood and stock changes constantly. They also stock Flokati rugs.

PRICE'S PATENT CANDLE CO
110 YORK ROAD, LONDON SW11 3RU
☎ 020-7801 2030. OPEN 9.30 - 5.30 MON - SAT, 11 - 5 SUN.
Factory Shop • *Household*

Everything sold in this shop are seconds, discontinued sizes not available elsewhere, over-runs or candles in old packaging that has now been replaced. There are church candles, lanterns, candles in pots and glass jars, star-shaped candles, floating candles, candlestick holders, serviettes, scented candles and garden torches.

PROIBITO
42 SOUTH MOLTON STREET, LONDON W17 1HB
☎ 020-7491 3244. OPEN 10 - 6.30 MON - FRI, UNTIL 7.30 THUR,
10 - 7 SAT, 12 - 6 SUN.
9 GEES COURT, OFF OXFORD STREET, W1
☎ 020-7409 2769. OPEN 10 - 6.30 MON - FRI, UNTIL 7.30 THUR,
10 - 7 SAT, 12 - 6 SUN.
93 NEW BOND STREET W1.
☎ 020-7491 7292. OPEN 10 - 6.30 MON - FRI, UNTIL 7.30 THUR,
10 - 7 SAT, 12 - 6 SUN.
Permanent Discount Outlet • *Womenswear Only*

The South Molton Street branch is a two-storey outlet with women's clothes on the ground floor, men's downstairs. Labels seen at all the branches include Moschino, Iceberg, Armani Jeans, Gianfranco Ferre, Dolce & Gabbana, Christian Lacroix and Valentino. Good for casual wear - it has racks of designer jeans, jackets and T-shirts - it also caters for the office market with smart suits, too. Versace jeans are £35 or two for £60; Versace Jeans Couture jacket, £40; Iceberg cocktail dress, £25; while at the top end, Versace dogtooth jacket and skirt costs £700 reduced from £900. Phone before visiting as many discount shops now take on short leases and move around a lot.

R F GREASBY LONDON LTD
211 LONGLEY ROAD, TOOTING, LONDON SW17 9LG
☎ 020-8672 2972/0208-682 4564. WEBSITE: www.greasbys.co.uk
OPEN 9 - 5 MON - THUR, 9 - 4 FRI, VIEWING 4 - 8.30 MON.
Furniture/Soft Furnishings
Want to buy a computer for £30, a leather briefcase for £20, a dozen umbrellas for the price of one good one? R F Greasby Ltd (Public Auctioneers) deal in goods from London Transport's and major airlines' lost property offices, Customs & Excise, among others, plus those obtained because of outstanding debt. Merchandise has included Nepal rugs, cases of good quality wine, built-in ovens, fridges and freezers, office equipment, clothing, computers, furniture, coffins, garden and agricultural equipment, television sets and hi-fis. This is the place where dealers get great bargains, but there's still some left for members of the public. Regular buyers are admitted first, then entry is on a first-come, first-served basis every second Tuesday. The catalogue can be obtained by annual subscription (phone 0208 672 2972 or visit the website for details), or from the premises for £1.50.

RAINBOW
249 & 253 ARCHWAY ROAD, HIGHGATE, LONDON N6 5BS
☎ 020-8340 8003. OPEN 10.30 - 5.30 MON - SAT.
Dress Agency • *Children* • *Womenswear & Menswear*
Household • *Food and Leisure*
Number 249 sells secondhand items, while 253 is new merchandise. Nearly-new consists of a wide range of well-known baby and children's clothes - from Osh Kosh and Oilily to Baby Gap and Marks & Spencer - as well as good quality women's clothing. Designer clothes sell here at a fraction of their original cost. There is also good condition baby equipment from cots and high chairs to car seats and playpens and many bargains in the big range of second hand toys, games and books. The shop at 253 has a large and interesting selection of new toys at reasonable prices. They stock traditional wooden toys such as rocking horses, trains, forts, garages and doll's houses from amongst others, Galt, Brio, Escor and John Crane. They also sell Lego, Playmobile, T.Y. Beanies, Dressing Up, books, creative kits, nostalgic pocket money toys and lots more. End of lines are discounted throughout the year. Highgate tube and buses are nearby and there's free parking in the side streets.

REAL NAPPY ASSOCIATION
PO BOX 3704, LONDON SE26 4RX
☎ (0121) 693 4949 WEBSITE: www.realnappy.com.
Encourages the use of real nappies which, compared to disposable ones, are much cheaper. Plus, they argue, your baby stays comfortable and healthy and you save resources and minimise pollution. Over two and a half years, or 5,020 nappy changes, disposables cost between £705 and £1050 whereas real nappies can cost as little as £250 including all accessories, washing agents, energy and £150 wear and tear on a washing machine. Nappy washing services are especially good value for families with two or more children in nappies. Send large SAE with two stamps for free information pack.

RECYCLE
176-178 CROYDON ROAD, ANNERLEY, LONDON SE20 7YU
☎ 020-8676 0900. OPEN 10 - 5.30 MON - FRI, 9.30 - 5.30 SAT.
Permanent Discount Outlet • *Sportswear & Equipment*

Recycle is based in two adjacent shops, one selling new bikes and equipment, the other selling good quality secondhand and reconditioned bikes, most of which are mountain bikes from £100 up to £4000. Some of the "secondhand" bikes are actually test bikes which have been barely used. Prices are discounted, but there are some serious bikes here for the real enthusiast as well as some smaller ones for children aged 8 and above.

REJECT CHINA SHOP
183 BROMPTON ROAD, LONDON SW3 1NF
☎ 020-7581 0739. OPEN 9 - 6 MON - SAT, 11 - 5.30 SUN.
Permanent Discount Outlet • *Household*

Sells china, crystal and gifts of overstocks and imperfect lines from mainly well-known makes. The majority of the stock is first quality, but sold at discounted prices and includes Portmerion, Wedgwood, Crown Derby and Royal Doulton. Also seconds dinner sets from Spode, Royal Doulton, Aynsley, and Royal Worcester at up to 50% off. For example, a Royal Doulton dinner service, £215, normally £430 when perfect; half a dozen Bohemian crystal glasses, £32.50, normally £63.00. Other manufacturers' available.

REJECT POT SHOP
56 CHALK FARM ROAD, LONDON NW1
☎ 020-7485 2326. OPEN 11 - 5.30 TUE - SUN.
Permanent Discount Outlet • *Household*

Reject shop selling white china seconds and some decorated china seconds at great prices. The china comes from a variety of manufacturers including Royal Stafford, Royal Doulton and Wedgwood, although there are no manufacturers' names on the underside of the china. Most are rejected before stamping. White china seconds are in greater abundance because faults are not as discernible as on patterned china.

RENAISSANCE LONDON
193-195 CITY ROAD, LONDON E1
☎ 020-7251 8844.
Architectural Salvage • *DIY/Renovation*

Specialist in antique, reproduction and contemporary fireplaces. On show is a large selection of antique stone fireplaces, with at least 20 on display at any one time. The showroom boasts seven rooms and a warehouse packed with fireplaces from 16th century Art Nouveau and Art Deco originals to reproduction pieces and stunning modern versions. There are also displays of crucifixed original doors, shutters, radiators, chairs, gates, grates, chandeliers, window boxes and decorative objects, as well as on-site restoration services and bespoke designing.

RENUBATH SERVICES
248 LILLIE ROAD, LONDON SW6 7QA
☎ 020-7381 8337. OPEN 9 - 5.30 MON - THUR, 9 - 5 FRI.
If you've got a good quality bath that looks a bit tatty and chipped, why not have it resurfaced, polished or cleaned by the experts? They also sell cast iron baths from £525 plus VAT.

ROCHELLE
LONDON NW7
☎ 020-8906 2158. PHONE FOR APPOINTMENT.
Designer Sale • *Children*
Home-based business selling designer childrenswear at discount prices including Osh Kosh B'Gosh, Double Dutch and Coco. Dresses, jeans, tracksuits, pinafores, leggings for boys and girls aged 0-8.

ROCOCO FRAMES
19 JERDAN PLACE, ON FULHAM ROAD, LONDON SW6 1BE
☎ 020-7386 0506. OPEN 10 - 6 MON - SAT, 11 - 4 SUN.
Permanent Discount Outlet • *Household*
Furniture/Soft Furnishings
A fantastic sprawling shop with seven rooms decorated like a real house, near Fulham Broadway. One of the biggest ranges of gorgeous frames and mirrors in London in masses of styles from simple to ornate, in all standard sizes - at amazingly low prices (4ft x 3ft mirror £79). Everything is made by Rococo in London and sold direct to the public. Weekly delivery of offcut frames, seconds and bargain lines at clearance prices. Also sells prints from £4, photo frames from 3 for £10, pictures, cards, interior accessories, gifts and has a highly experienced picture framing workshop for public, trade and artists. The nearest tube is Fulham Broadway or you can park at the Safeway supermarket at the junction of Fulham Road/North End Road.

ROGER LASCELLES CLOCKS LTD
29 CARNWATH ROAD, LONDON SW6 3HR
☎ 020-7731 0072. FAX ☎ 020-7384 1957. OPEN 11 - 4 MON - THUR.
Permanent Discount Outlet • *Household*
Established for sixteen years, Mr Lascelles makes an inspiring selection of clocks from tickers in a tin to traditional styles which replicate covetable antiques. There are wall clocks, table clocks, kitchen ranges, mantle clocks and even tin clocks with nursery rhyme designs, all with quartz battery movement. At his factory in London, there are usually seconds and ends of lines available at about half the retail price and display items at discounts of up to 50%. For example, mantel clocks from £20. New for the millennium, the factory shop has just been extended to embrace a whole range of well-known, branded gift items including candles, tablemats, china, glassware, toys and games, at well below normal retail prices. Overlooking the Thames in Fulham, this factory shop is near a number

of picturesque riverside pubs and is easily accessible. However, there were plans as we went to press to relocate, so do phone first before travelling.

ROKIT
225 CAMDEN HIGH STREET, LONDON NW1
☎ 020-7267 3046. OPEN 10 - 6.30 MON - SUN.
Secondhand and Vintage Clothes • *Womenswear & Menswear*

Vintage and original clothing from 1920s through to the present day. You can find vintage sportswear, denim, designer and reptile handbags.

ROYAL NATIONAL THEATRE
HIRE DEPARTMENT, CHICHESTER HOUSE, 1-3 BRIXTON ROAD, LONDON SW9 6DE
☎ 020-7735 4774. OPEN 10 - 6 MON - FRI BY APPOINTMENT ONLY, CLOSED 1-2 DAILY.
Hire Shop • *Womenswear & Menswear*

Stocks up to 100,000 theatrical costumes from Roman togas to leather biker jackets which have been worn in past RNT productions. A warning note, however: some of the costumes looked better on stage than they do in the full glare of daylight. Also hires out props and furniture.

RUG CONNECTIONS
13 PRIOR STREET, GREENWICH, LONDON SE10 8SF
☎ 020-8853 3358. E-MAIL: rugs@greenwich.demon.co.uk
PHONE FOR APPOINTMENT.
Permanent Discount Outlet • *Furniture/Soft Furnishings*

Carpet broking service set up to provide independent advice on purchasing an Oriental rug. By providing clients with access to the rarified atmosphere of London's bonded warehouses which are never usually open to the public, they can offer the largest selection of rugs from Persia, Afghanistan, India, Turkey, China, Iran and many more countries in styles from traditional to contemporary. The prices are significantly below retail, saving hundreds of pounds. Based in Greenwich, Rug Connections operates on a one-to-one by appointment basis, offering Home Counties customers their professional skills. Customers who are too busy to visit the warehouses will be visited at home, day or evening, with a carefully chosen selection of carpets.

RUSSELL & CHAPPLE LTD
68 DRURY LANE, LONDON WC2B 5SP
☎ 020-7836 7521. OPEN 9 - 5.30 MON - FRI, CLOSED WEEKENDS.
Permanent Discount Outlet • *Furniture/Soft Furnishings*

Specialists in artists' and theatrical supplies, they also sell natural upholstery fabrics at rock bottom prices for hessians, calicos and muslins. Prices from £1.25 per metre for muslin to £20.64 per metre for linen which is 120 inches wide. The more you buy, the bigger the discount. There are also flame retardant materials on sale.

S & B EVANS & SONS
7A EZRA STREET, LONDON E2 7RH
☎ 020-7729 6635. OPEN 9.30 - 5 FRI, 9 - 1.30 FIRST SUN EACH MONTH, OTHER TIMES BY APPOINTMENT.
Permanent Discount Outlet • *Household*
Seconds from the kiln are half price on the first Sunday of each month. The rest of the time, the shop is full-priced. Their stock is mostly for the garden and ranges from flower pots to terracotta ware, mugs, jugs and bowls. Situated near to Colombia Road Flower Market which is open from 8am-2pm every Sunday.

S & M MYERS LTD
100-106 MACKENZIE ROAD, HOLLOWAY, LONDON N7 8RG
☎ 020-7609 0091. OPEN 10 - 5.30 MON, WED, FRI, 10 - 5 TUE, THUR, 9.30 - 2 SAT.
81-85 EAST END ROAD, EAST FINCHLEY, LONDON N2 OST
☎ 020-8444 3457. OPEN 9.30 - 5.30 MON - SAT.
Permanent Discount Outlet • *Furniture/Soft Furnishings*
Permanent discount outlet specialising in plain wool carpets. This company, which was established in 1819, offers end of range carpets at discount prices, as well as value-for-money perfect quality carpets by buying direct from the manufacturer or selling liquidated stock. Mainly 80% wool twist carpets and English makes such as BMK, Westex, Wilton Royal and Berber with some ranges of wool blends and manmade velvet piles.

SALLY HAIR AND BEAUTY SUPPLIES
81 SHAFTESBURY AVENUE, LONDON W1V 7AD
☎ 020-7434 0064. OPEN 8 - 8 MON - SAT, 11 -5 SUN.
Permanent Discount Outlet • *Womenswear Only*
Sells a huge range of hair products and hair styling and beauty equipment (including a wide range of nail products but no make-up) from cheap and cheerful curling tongs at around £4.95 to top-of-the-range professional hair driers at more than £100. You won't find any of the recognisable brands advertised on television here, but what you will find are products which professional hairdressers use - which means they're likely to last a long time and be well-priced. The curling tongs are sold with different barrel widths so you can give yourself a tight or a loose curl. Sells all but its chemical products to individual members of the public. There are 120 branches countrywide. Phone 0800 525118 for your nearest store.

SALOU
6 CHEVAL PLACE, LONDON SW7 1ES
☎ 020-7581 2380. OPEN 10 - 5 MON - SAT
Dress Agency • *Womenswear Only*
Two-storey shop which sells evening wear and separates downstairs, suits upstairs, as well as jewellery, hats and accessories. Labels include Giorgio

Armani, Valentino, Gucci, Prada, Christian Lacroix, Chanel and Jean Paul Gaultier. Prices from £10-£600 for a Chanel suit. The average price for a suit is between £60 and £120; the top end of the market averages £200-£400. Loads of shoes from £30 including Gucci, Prada and Chanel.

SCENT TO YOU
UNIT 25B, CENTRE COURT SHOPPING CENTRE, 4 QUEENS ROAD, WIMBLEDON, LONDON SW19 8YA
☎ 020-8944 0122. PHONE FOR OPENING TIMES.
Permanent Discount Outlet • *Womenswear Only*

Discounted perfume, cosmetics and accessories including body lotions and gels. The company, which has more than thirty branches, buys in bulk and sells more cheaply, relying on a high turnover for profit. Discounts range from 5% to 60%, with greater savings during their twice-yearly sales (phone for details). Most of the leading brand names in perfume are stocked including Christian Lacroix, Armani, Charlie, Givenchy, Anais Anais from Cacherel, Charlie from Revlon, Coco Chanel, Christian Dior, Elizabeth Taylor, Blue Grass from Elizabeth Arden, Aramis, Lagerfeld. Plus cosmetics from Revlon and Spectacular and skincare from Clarins and Lancome as well as Scent To You's own range of bags, watches, hair brushes and brushkits which is sold under the name S.T.Y. Designs. Stock varies greatly due to the fast turnover and varying supplies so more than one visit may be necessary to obtain the scent of your choice. Or phone first to avoid disappointment.

SCREENFACE
20 & 24 POWIS TERRACE, LONDON W11 1JH
☎ 020-7221 8289. OPEN 9 - 6 MON - SAT. MAIL ORDER.
48 MONMOUTH STREET, LONDON WC2 9EP
☎ 020-7836 3955. OPEN 10 - 7 MON - SAT, 12 - 5 SUN.
Permanent Discount Outlet • *Womenswear Only*

Stocks the largest selection of make-up in the UK and is open to individuals as well as professionals. The shop has collected together the very best from all over the world. In addition to everyday make-up, they stock body paints, eyelashes, temporary tattoos, camouflage products, shaders, highlighters, eye colours, glittering powders and a vast selection of accessory items. Their huge selection of brushes include retractable lip, eyeline and mascara brushes, perfect for the handbag. They make bags from UV proof PVC that will not crack or split and stock a huge range of powder puffs and sponges. Now stock airbrush systems which you can use to apply body paint or fake tan. All the products are available by mail order using a credit card. Or you could have a make-up lesson, £45 for one hour. Screenface also runs a business renting out mirrors and make-up chairs for location shoots.

SEERS ANTIQUES
THE CONSERVATORY, 238A BATTERSEA PARK ROAD,
LONDON SW11 4NG
☎ 020-7720 0263. OPEN 10 - 6 TUE - SAT, 10 - 5 SUN.
THE BANK, 213 TRAFALGAR ROAD, GREENWICH SE10 9EQ
☎ 020-8293 0293. OPEN 10 - 6 TUE - SAT, 10 - 5 SUN.
49 NEW KINGS ROAD, FULHAM SW6
☎ 020-7371 8999. OPEN 10 - 6 TUE - SAT, 10 - 5 SUN.
Secondhand shops • *Furniture/Soft Furnishings*

Brimming with largely undiscovered bargains that you would never imagine were available in today's well-trodden market. The furniture is a mixture of antique and reproduction intermingling with a vast array of frames and mirrors and a selection of gifts all at bargain prices. Original bedroom fireplaces are priced from around £125 with reproduction dining tables varying between £75 and £175 and low-priced antiques such as Pembrokes starting at £95. Prices are competitive because they have a policy of quick turnover and low profit margins. All the prices are clearly displayed and the friendly atmosphere, along with the bustle and bargains, is in stark contrast to the hush usually associated with antique shops.

SHEILA WARREN-HILL
THE GARDEN FLAT, 63 SHEPHERDS HILL, HIGHGATE,
LONDON N6 5RE
☎ 020-8348 8282. BY APPOINTMENT ONLY.
Dress Agency • *Womenswear Only*

Sheila is a lovely, lively character who operates from her garden flat in London's Highgate, offering open house on Sundays when lunch and drinks are served while customers try on couture outfits. Many of her outfits were originally owned by rich and famous personalities. Having worn a dress to a special event, they can't be seen wearing the same outfit twice and so pass it on to Sheila to dispose of discreetly and enable them to recoup some of the costs and buy another dazzling creation for the next outing. The labels are top range - Jasper Conran, Giorgio Armani, Yves St Laurent, Chanel, Tomasz Starzewski, Place Vendome, Gianfranco Ferre, Escada. The atmosphere is relaxed, with Sheila on hand to dispense advice if wanted. She also sells daywear, designer shoes, swimwear and jewellery. Sheila also has an arrangement with other nearly-new businesses around the country, who take some of her stock, which means that she always has a very good supply. Customers can also have clothes delivered to their home by chauffeur-driven Bentley. Phone her for details of her regular sales and for details of other shops taking her stock.

SHIPTON & HENEAGE
117 QUEENSTOWN ROAD, LONDON SW8 3RH
☎ 020-7738 8484. WEBSITE: www.shiphen.com
OPEN 9 - 6 MON - FRI, 10 - 2 SAT. MAIL ORDER.
Permanent Discount Outlet • *Womenswear & Menswear*
Traditional men's and ladies shoes, loafers, half brogues, Oxfords, and Chelsea boots manufactured and supplied by the very best factories in Northampton, the traditional home of British footwear, and stocked typically by Savile Row outfitters and Jermyn Street tailors but sold here at discounts of up to 30% off shop prices. Their premium range is made from the finest hides from the best tanneries in Europe, while their grade range shoes are from sides of more mature hides. These are priced at £149 and £89 respectively. Additionally, they also sell a comprehensive range of deck shoes, plus a range of slippers equally discounted. Any style can be ordered from the catalogue and because there is no retail outlet, prices are low.

SIGN OF THE TIMES
17 ELYSTAN STREET, LONDON SW3 3NT
☎ 020-7589 4774. OPEN 10 - 6 MON - FRI, 10 - 5.30 SAT.
Dress Agency • *Womenswear Only*
A broad range of clothes from casual to evening wear which includes Prada, Gucci, Donna Karan, Voyage, Fendi, Louis Vuitton, Chanel and Armani among its range of nearly new bargains. Also lots of hats (Frederick Fox, Gilly Forge), handbags and shoes (Manolo Blahnik, Christian Laubourton, Gucci, J P Todds, Joseph Azurgary) in sizes 3 to 8.

SIZE PLUS
168 MUSWELL HILL BROADWAY, MUSWELL HILL, LONDON N10
☎ 020-8444 5748. OPEN 9.30 - 5.30 MON - SUN.
Permanent Discount Outlet • *Womenswear Only*
An offshoot of the Central Park group, this store caters especially for more mature women and larger sizes. Stock is mostly cancelled orders and over runs with very good prices.

SOVIET CARPET AND ART GALLERIES
303-305 CRICKLEWOOD BROADWAY, LONDON NW2 6PG
☎ 020-8452 2445. OPEN 10.30 - 5.30 SUN ONLY,
BY APPOINTMENT MON - FRI.
Permanent Discount Outlet • *Furniture/Soft Furnishings* • *Household*
Sells Oriental rugs and Russian art at trade prices, giving savings of about 50% on high street prices. The company has only been open to the public since 1992 and then only on Sundays (established in 1983, it was exclusively a wholesale operation for the first nine years of its existence). It imports handmade rugs directly from all the main rug-producing centres of the East (Persia, Turkey, Afghanistan, Pakistan, China) and is one of the principal world distributors of rugs from the former Soviet Union. This explains why the superb

Caucasian and Turkmenian (Bukhara) rugs are a speciality. They also stock one of the largest collections of quality Russian art in Europe. Only a small fraction of this is displayed, the remaining thousands of paintings can be chosen from photographs, and will then be brought out from storage. All styles in Russian art are covered from museum-quality greatest names of the 19th century through propaganda art of the Stalin years to leading contemporary artists. All works are offered at prices well below retail/auction price levels, and in extreme cases paintings sold in West End galleries for thousands can be picked up here for a few hundred pounds.

STEINBERG & TOLKIEN
193 KING'S ROAD, LONDON SW3 5EQ
☎ 020-7376 3660. OPEN 11 - 7 MON - SAT, 12 - 6 SUN.

Secondhand and Vintage Clothes • *Womenswear & Menswear*

London's most famous vintage clothes store is situated on two floors. One floor is devoted totally to jewellery, handbags, scarves, shoes and accessories, the other floor to American vintage and European couture clothing from the Twenties and Thirties to the Seventies. Some of the more interesting items were worn by movie stars of the Thirties and Forties and the garment is often seen on the original wearer in photographs around the shop. Popular with those looking for something unusual for a theme evening or a gala event, it's also frequented by those searching for an individual look in a style and quality unmatched even by couture designers today. Here, you can find Halston suede button-through dresses from the Seventies alongside heavily beaded cardigans from the Fifties, Pucci shirts and Gucci bags, bias-cut slips from the Thirties, shirtwaisters from the Seventies, Fortuny gowns and Ossie Clark outfits. There is also a selection of men's clothes. Many of the clothes are now featured in the book: Vintage: The Art of Dressing Up by Tracy Tolkein, published by Pavilion and sold here in the shop, £19.99.

STOCKHOUSE
101-105 GOSWELL ROAD, LONDON EC1V 7EZ
☎ 020-7253 5761. OPEN 9 - 5 MON, TUE, FRI, 9 - 6 WED, THUR, 9 - 2 SUN, CLOSED SAT.

Permanent Discount Outlet • *Menswear Only*

Formerly known as Goldsmith & Company, in late 1994 Stockhouse expanded from a purely wholesale warehouse into a trade discount centre for branded menswear that is also open to the public. It stocks more than 3,500 men's suits, from stylish business suits, formal dresswear and comfortable lounge suits to famous brand men's shirts, silk ties, blazers, sports jackets, casual jackets, overcoats, designer swimwear, underwear, socks and branded sportswear. Sizes range from 36" chest to 54". By purchasing cancelled orders and broken ranges from famous manufacturers at clearing prices, they are able to offer famous brands at greatly reduced prices without compromising on quality or style. Suits include many famous labels and everything shows a considerable saving off normal shop prices. Stock is constantly changing. Well worth a visit.

SURPRISE SURPRISE
18 GOLDERS GREEN ROAD, LONDON NW11 9PU
- 020-8209 0003. OPEN 9 - 6 MON - SAT, 10 - 6 SUN.

299 WALWORTH ROAD SE17 2TG
- 020-7703 5164. OPEN 9 - 6 MON - SAT, 6.IGH STREET SE13 5JH
- 020-8297 2444. OPEN 9 - 6.30 MON - SAT, 10 - 5 SUN.

414 MARE STREET E8 1HP
- 020-8533 4453. OPEN 9 - 6 MON - SAT, 10 - 5 SUN.

167 FINCHLEY ROAD NW3 6LB
- 020-7624 9988. OPEN 9 - 7 MON - SAT, 10 - 6 SUN.

52 CHAPEL MARKET N1 9EW
- 020-7833 3171. OPEN 9 - 6.30 MON - SAT, 9 - 4 SUN.

13 CHEAPSIDE, WOOD GREEN N22 6HH
- 020-8888 5189. OPEN 9 - 6 MON - SAT, 10 - 5 SUN.

752 HIGH ROAD, NORTH FINCHLEY N12 9QG
- 020-8445 4766. OPEN 9 - 6.30 MON - SAT, 10 - 6 SUN. W2 1DH.

61 HARLESDEN HIGH STREET, NW10 4NJ
- 020-8838 3331. OPEN 9 - 6 SEVEN DAYS A WEEK.

57 HIGH STREET, WALTHAMSTOW E17 7AD
- 020-8223 0386. OPEN 10 - 6.30 MON - SAT, 10 - 5 SUN.

527 OXFORD STREET W1R 1DD
- 020-7495 7161. OPEN 9 - 9 MON - SAT, 10 - 8 SUN.

146 OXFORD STREET W1N 9DL
- 020-7323 1124. OPEN 9 - 7.30 MON - SAT, 8 ON THUR, 10 - 6.30 SUN.

175-179 VICTORIA STREET SW1E 5NE
- 020-7233 5421. OPEN 9 - 7 MON - SAT, 10 - 6.30 SUN.

226 EDGWARE ROAD W2 1DH
- 020-7724 4650. OPEN 9 - 11 MON - SAT, 10 - 10 SUN.

3 RYE LANE, PECKHAM SE15 5EW
- 020-7639 0434. OPEN 9 - 6 MON - SAT, 10 - 5 SUN.

Permanent Discount Outlet • *Menswear Only*

Men's shirts, ties and socks at very reasonable prices. For example, polo shirts, £3.99 each or three for £10; silk ties, £3.99 or three for £10; socks from £3.99 to £6.99 for a pack of six. Ladies' mid range fashion. The Oxford Street, Victoria Street and Edgware Road shops also sell women's clothing.

SURPRISE SURPRISE FOR WOMEN
51 GOLDERS GREEN ROAD, LONDON NW11 8EL
- 020-8209 0042. OPEN 9 - 6.30 MON - SAT, 10 - 6 SUN.

Permanent Discount Outlet • *Womenswear Only*

Women's clothes at very reasonable prices.

SWALLOWS & AMAZONS
91 NIGHTINGALE LANE, LONDON SW12 8NX
☎ 020-8673 0275. OPEN 10 - 5.30 MON - SAT.
Dress Agency • *Children*

Probably the largest good-as-new children's shop in London, S & A has a ground floor full of quality clothes for 0-12 year olds: OshKosh, Oilily, Jean Le Bourget, Mexx etc, as well as a large basement with toys, books and baby equipment. The stock is constantly changing and they pride themselves on keeping standards high, but prices low - from 90p to £99. There is also children's hairdressing (with videos) on most afternoons and on Saturdays (appointments necessary) and a play area. Friendly, helpful staff.

SWIMGEAR
11 STATION ROAD, FINCHLEY, LONDON N3 2SB
☎ 020-8346 6106. OPEN 9.30 - 5 MON - SAT. MAIL ORDER.
Permanent Discount Outlet • *Sportswear & Equipment*
Children • *Womenswear & Menswear*

A mail order company which also operates via a retail outlet next to Finchley Central station. As well as selling their swimwear at less than the normal retail price by not putting the full markup on their products, they also sell discontinued and ends of line ranges of swimwear for men, women and children at between 20%-30% less than normal retail prices. They also stock goggles and flippers in adult and children's sizes. Flippers normally cost about £18.50, but can be bought here for about £8 in black rubber; Lycra trunks, plain £7.35 up to £10 for patterned ones. Bikinis are on sale all year round, with women's swimwear ranging up to size 46. The catalogues are full colour and carry the names Adidas, Tyr, Moontide, Tweeka and Maru, as well as Swimgear's own brand full colour Mark One brochure. Prices are lower than would be offered at swim meets and retail shops. As part of their service, they do not cash your cheque until your full order has been completed. P&p extra. Orders over £20 are post free, excluding heavy items such as flippers and shampoo on which p&p is charged.

TABLEWHERE?
4 QUEEN'S PARADE CLOSE, FRIERN BARNET, LONDON N11 3FY
☎ 020-8361 6111. E-MAIL: tablewhere@globalnet.co.uk
WEBSITE: www.tablewhere.co.uk   MAIL ORDER.

The UK's largest china matching service, they stock thousands of patterns from the world's leading manufacturers including Wedgwood, Royal Doulton, Spode, Denby, Minton, Royal Albert, Johnson Bros., Royal Worcester and Aynsley, some of which go back 40 or 50 years. By buying up discontinued lines from all over the country, Tablewhere? has built up a stock of over one million pieces which are available through the London-based mail order service. Specialist staff maintain detailed computer and photographic records of all the patterns and shapes in stock so that they can locate any replacement pieces from egg cups to soup tureens, although tea cups and dinner plates are in most demand. Replacement pieces usually cost around the equivalent of today's retail prices. There is no charge to register requirements - phone or write with details of the manufacturer, pattern name and the replacement pieces needed. If there is no pattern name on the service, then a photograph or colour photocopy showing both sides of a dinner plate with a colour description will help identification. You can also visit their website or e mail them.

TEMPTATION ALLEY
359-361 PORTOBELLO ROAD, LONDON W10 5SA
☎ 020-8964 2004. OPEN 10 - 5.30 MON - SAT.
Permanent Discount Outlet • *Furniture/Soft Furnishings*

A trade warehouse which is also open to the public selling a wide range of tie-backs, trimmings(2,000 different types of upholstery trimmings), fabric, cords, braids and general haberdashery. Tie-backs cost from £2.50 to £28, the latter normally costing £60 in top department stores. Fabrics are mostly plain ranging from calico and muslin at £1.50 a metre to velvets, basic cotton drills, silks, organza and slub cotton imported from India to their own design.

THE CANDLE SHOP
50 NEW KING'S ROAD, LONDON SW6 4LS
☎ 020-7736 0740. E-MAIL: CGCC@candles-sales.com
WEBSITE: www.candles-sales.com   OPEN 10 - 6 MON - SAT, 11 - 5 SUN.
Permanent Discount Outlet • *Household*

Warehouse outlet servicing the shop in Covent Garden's Piazza which sells candles at what they claim are the lowest prices in the country. You can buy anything from bulk boxes of two hundred 8" cream candles from £29.95 to church candles at wholesale prices, as well as floating, scented and novelty candles. Candle-making supplies are also available. Mail order catalogue on request. Or visit the website to compare prices.

THE CASH EXCHANGE
352 HOLLOWAY ROAD, LONDON N7
☎ 020-7609 2022. OPEN 10 - 6 MON - SAT.
Permanent Discount Outlet • *Household*
Electrical Equipment

Discount outlet which operates rather like a pawn brokers. It takes unwanted household and electrical items and gives you cash. Unredeemed items are sold off at very low prices. For example, laptop computers from £200, top of the range TVs, worth £1,500, for £900.

THE CHANGING ROOM
148 ARTHUR ROAD, WIMBLEDON PARK, LONDON SW19 8AQ
☎ 020-8947 1258. OPEN 10 - 6 TUES - FRI.
Dress Agency • *Womenswear Only*
Fast-moving stock of designer samples, end of line and secondhand lables including: Ghost, Whistles, Jigsaw, Kenzo, Moschino, Armani, Resource, Romeo Gigli. Also shoes and accessories. Sample and second-hand childrenswear: Gap, Parsisal, Kenzo, Monsoon, Jigsaw, Petit Bateau, Armani.

THE CLOTH SHOP
290 PORTOBELLO ROAD, LONDON W10 5TE
☎ 020-8968 6001. OPEN 10 - 6 MON - SAT.
Permanent Discount Outlet • *Furniture/Soft Furnishings*
Discounted fabric from good tweeds and cottons, muslin and calico to Lycra, as well as brand name ends of rolls, sample lengths and former window drapes. There is also a large range of Indian furnishing fabrics at reduced prices, plain linens and antique sheets and fabrics. Turnover is high and stock changes constantly. Most fabrics are under £10 per metre.

THE CORRIDOR
309A KING'S ROAD, CHELSEA, LONDON SW3 5EP
☎ 020-7351 0772. OPEN 10.30 - 6.30 MON - SAT.
Dress Agency • *Womenswear Only*
Small, personalised boutique providing women's nearly-new and sample high quality designer clothing, handbags and jewellery. Names include Chanel, Prada, Valentino, Ralph Lauren, Alberta Ferretti and Max Mara, sold seasonally. Clothing is taken in on a sale or return basis. An alteration service is also available.

THE COSTUME STUDIO
MONTGOMERY HOUSE, 159-161 BALLS POND ROAD, ISLINGTON, LONDON N1 4BG
☎ 020-7388 4481/275 9614. OPEN 9.30 - 6 MON - FRI, 10 -5 SAT.
Hire Shop • *Womenswear & Menswear*
Twenty thousand costumes from medieval times to the 70s. Clients include TV and video companies. Individual hiring costs from £30 - £75 plus VAT for one week. There are plenty of accessories from shoes and hats to bags and gloves to complete an outfit.

THE CURTAIN EXCHANGE
131-133 STEPHENDALE ROAD, LONDON SW6 2PF
☎ 020-7-731 8316/7. OPEN 10 - 5 MON - SAT.
54 ABBEY GARDENS, LONDON NW8 9HT
☎ 020-7-372 1044. OPEN 10 - 5 MON - SAT.

80 PARK HALL ROAD, DULWICH, LONDON SE21 8BW
☎ 020-8670 5570. OPEN 10 - 5 MON - SAT.
Secondhand shops • *Furniture/Soft Furnishings*
The Curtain Exchange is a franchised group of shops selling beautiful top quality secondhand curtains, blinds, pelmets, etc at between one-third and one half of the brand new price. Their stock comes from a variety of sources: people who are moving house; people who have curtains made and then feel they are wrong for the room; show houses where the builder wants to recoup some of his outgoings; interior designers' mistakes. Stock changes constantly and ranges from rich brocades, damasks and velvets to chintzes, linens and cottons. Designer names include Colefax & Fowler, Designers Guild, Laura Ashley, Warner, Sanderson, Osborne & Little, Fortuny and Bennison. A team of fitters and alteration experts are available if required. They offer a 24-hour availability. The Curtain Exchange also supply bespoke ranges with samples of curtains hanging. These fabrics are chosen from suppliers all over the world and are an excellent buy. They also offer ready made curtains designed exclusively for them which come in lengths up to 305cm (120"). These are outstanding value, e.g. 80" wide, 120" drop start at £175 including VAT.

THE CURTAIN FABRIC FACTORY SHOP
230-236 NORTH END ROAD, LONDON W14 9NU
☎ 020-7381 1777. FAX 020-7381 8879. E-MAIL: cfpolytrad@aol.com
WEBSITE: www.curtainfabricfactory.co.uk OPEN 9.30 - 5.30 MON - SAT.
Factory Shop • *Furniture/Soft Furnishings*
Genuine factory shop which prints curtain fabric on site and sells overstocks, seconds and cancelled orders at trade prices here - there are 1,000 rolls in stock. Makes for hundreds of shops countrywide and exports to twelve different countries. There are hundreds of different designs and qualities from which to choose at prices starting at £1.99 a metre. There are also quilted bedspreads available to match the fabrics, and a curtain making and track fitting service.

THE CURTAIN MILL
46-52 FAIRFIELD ROAD, BOW, LONDON E3 2QB
☎ 020-8980 9000. OPEN 9 - 5.30 SEVEN DAYS A WEEK.
2 THE VALE, ACTON, LONDON W3 7SB
☎ 020-8743 2299. OPEN 9 - 5.30 SEVEN DAYS A WEEK.
UNIT 75, CAPITOL INDUSTRIAL PARK, CAPITOL WAY, COLINDALE, LONDON NW9 0EQ
☎ 020-8205 2220. OPEN 9 - 5.30 SEVEN DAYS A WEEK.
Permanent Discount Outlet • *Furniture/Soft Furnishings*
Huge choice of fabrics at really low prices - from £1.99p a metre and including excellent discounts on many designer labels. A large warehouse, it stocks Ashley Wilde and Swatchbox, among other leading names at discount prices. Also supplies ready made curtains, bespoke curtains, blinds, venetian verticals, all types of window treatments and has its own in-house making up service.

THE DESIGNER FABRICS WAREHOUSE SALES

DWS LTD, STUDIO 6, THE IVORIES, 6-8 NORTHAMPTON STREET, LONDON N1 2HY
☎ 020-7704 1064. E-MAIL: dwslondon@aol.com
WEBSITE: www.dwslondon.co.uk

Designer Sale • *Furniture/Soft Furnishings*

The two totally unique Designer Fabric Warehouse Sales are sister of the 10 annual Womenswear and Menswear Designer Warehouse Sales (see following entry). Held in spacious photographic studios at The Worx, 45 Balfe Street in central London, these three-day Sales are like an Aladdin's cave of sample lengths and ends of rolls from more than 40 top designers including names such as Amanda Wakeley, Mulberry, Nicole Farhi, Vivienne Westwood, Boyd, Elspeth Gibson and textile queen Georgina von Etzdorf. Not only an opportunity to invest in exclusive fabrics not normally available to the general public but a treasure trove of trimmings such as braiding, fringing and feathers. Prices start at 50p a metre. Although most of the lengths are dress and clothing fabrics the astute bargain hunter will find many are suitable (and cheaper) for soft funishings such as curtains, cushions and throws. Admission is £2, students £1. Register for regular invitations to the Sales by e-mail or phone or browse their website.

THE DESIGNER WAREHOUSE SALES FOR WOMEN AND MEN

DWS LTD, STUDIO 6, THE IVORIES, 6-8 NORTHAMPTON STREET, LONDON N1 2HY
☎ 020-7704 1064. FAX 020-7704 1379. E-MAIL: dwslondon@aol.com
WEBSITE: www.dwslondon.co.uk
SALES USUALLY OPEN 10 - 8 FRI, 10 - 6 SAT, 11 - 5 SUN.

Designer Sale • *Womenswear & Menswear*

The Designer Warehouse Sales probably boast more London Fashion Week award-winning labels than can be found under one roof anywhere else in the country - and all at around two thirds off the retail price. From Designer of the Year Hussein Chalayan, to past winners Katharine Hamnett and Betty Jackson, to newcomers such as Boyd, Elspeth Gibson and Lewis Sterling and fashion favourites Paul Smith, John Smedley, Nicole Farhi, Dolce & Gabanna, Donna Karan, Strenesse and Victor Victoria, the three day Sales offer men and women a host of over 80 labels. The Designer Warehouse Sales pride themselves on stocking many of the contemporary labels exclusively, especially catwalk one-offs and studio samples which nestle amongst current collections. Accessories from established names are also on offer. Held in spacious photographic studios at The Worx, 45 Balfe Street in London's Kings Cross area, there are five Designer Menswear and five Designer Womenswear Sales every year. The atmosphere is relaxed and communal changing rooms add to the fun of the 'must have' ambience. Register for regular invitations to the Sales by e-mail or phone or browse their website. Unique Designer Fabric Sales take place twice a year (see previous entry).

THE DRESS BOX
8-10 CHEVAL PLACE, LONDON SW7 1ES
☎ 020-7589 2240. OPEN 10 - 6 MON - FRI, 10.30 - 6 SAT.
Dress Agency • *Womenswear & Menswear*

Operating for more than 50 years, the Dress Box caters for the top end of the market including new and nearly-new couture - YSL, Chanel, Gucci, Hermes, Valentino, Prada and Pierre Cardin. Those looking for special occasion wear, evening outfits or ball gowns are well catered for. Among the 500 or so outfits in the shop at any one time are Chanel suits from £425 and Valentino and Ungaro suits from £295. Wonderful collection of YSL suits, some Chanel jackets and suits. Prices range from £150-£1,000 for suits though most outfits cost £200-£400. There is also a collection of hats from £45 (Philip Somerville, Philip Treacy) and shoes from £25. Alterations service available. There are also Chanel handbags, scarves from £95, costume jewellery, as well as a small selection of menswear. You can buy a whole wardrobe here from swimwear to coats. Also offers an in-house couture alteration service.

THE DRESSER
10 PORCHESTER PLACE, LONDON W2 2BS
☎ 020-7724 7212. OPEN 11 - 5.30 MON - FRI, 11 - 5 SAT.
Dress Agency • *Womenswear & Menswear*

Nearly-new couture and contemporary women's and men's clothes including Armani, Donna Karan, Jil Sander, Dolce & Gabanna, Gucci, Prada, Comme des Garcons, at prices ranging from £50-£400. The men's department has such as Paul Smith, Yohji Yamamoto, Jasper Conran, Armani, Gaultier and Comme des Garcons at prices ranging from £30-£400. There is more women's merchandise than men's, with lots of separates and some accessories.

THE EXCHANGE DRESS AGENCY
30 ELIZABETH STREET, BELGRAVIA, LONDON SW1
☎ 020-7730 3334. OPEN 10 - 4 MON - SAT, 10 - 6 THUR.
Dress Agency • *Womenswear Only*

Set up in aid of The National Kidney Research Fund, to whom all the profits are donated, it stocks a range of women's clothing including Paul Costelloe, Valentino, Flyte Ostell, Moschino, Guy Laroche, Givenchy, Caroline Charles and Rifat Ozbek. Customers bringing in clothes to sell receive 50% of the selling price; the charity receives the other 50%.

THE GALLERY OF ANTIQUE COSTUME & TEXTILES
2 CHURCH STREET, MARYLEBONE, LONDON NW8 8ED
☎ 020-7723 9981. OPEN 10 - 5.30 MON - SAT.
Secondhand and Vintage Clothes • *Womenswear & Menswear*
Original costumes from Victorian times to the 1940s and waistcoats and fabrics from the early textiles to mid nineteenth century. Cushions from £65-£500; table covers from £100-£400; curtains from £300; Edwardian tea dresses from £100; Twenties and Thirties evening wear from £200 upwards.

THE HARDWOOD FLOORING CO LTD
146-152 WEST END LANE, WEST HAMPSTEAD, LONDON NW6 1SD
☎ 020-7328 8481. WEBSITE: www.hardwood-flooring.uk.com
OPEN 8.30 - 5.30 MON - FRI, UNTIL 8 ON THUR.
Architectural Salvage • *DIY/Renovation*
Situated in West Hampstead, this outlet has been established for more than 14 years. It has the largest showrooms with customer parking in London for over 200 different types of new hardwood floorings ranging from pre-finished strip and blocks to American white oak wide board planking. full installation service is available, if required.

THE HOUSE HOSPITAL
UNIT 9, FERRIER STREET INDUSTRIAL ESTATE, WANDSWORTH, LONDON SW18 1SW
☎ 020-8870 8202. 10 - 5 MON - SAT.
Architectural Salvage • *DIY/Renovation*
Cast iron radiators, bathroom fittings, brass mixer taps, doors, door handles, fireplaces and stone flooring.

THE LOFT
35 MONMOUTH STREET, COVENT GARDEN, LONDON WC2H 9DD
☎ 020-7240 3807. WEBSITE: www.the-loft.co.uk
OPEN 11 - 6 MON - SAT, 1 - 5 SUN.
Dress Agency • *Hire Shop* • *Womenswear & Menswear*
One-offs, ends of lines, nearly-new for men and women from the likes of Vivienne Westwood, Jean-Paul Gaultier, DKNY, Versace, Paul Smith, Gucci, Prada and Armani and many more. A hire service is also available in this two-storey shop which is packed with bargains. Denise Van Outen, Bjork and George Michael have all been kitted out in The Loft's designer outfits at a fraction of their original price. Fed up with some of your own designer outfits? Take them here and turn them into cash.

storey shop which is packed with bargains. Denise Van Outen, Bjork and George Michael have all been kitted out in The Loft's designer outfits at a fraction of their original price. Fed up with some of your own designer outfits? Take them here and turn them into cash.

THE LONDON PICTURE CENTRE
709 FULHAM ROAD, LONDON SW6 5UL
☎ 020-7371 5737. OPEN 9 - 5.30 MON - FRI, 10 - 6 SAT 11 - 3 SUN.
152 HACKNEY ROAD, LONDON E2 1QL
☎ 020-7729 0881. OPEN 9 - 5 MON - FRI, 10 - 2 SAT.
75 LEATHER LANE, LONDON EC1 7UJ. OPEN 9 - 4 MON - FRI.
☎ 020-7404 4110. OPEN 9.30 - 5.30 MON - FRN.
THE LONDON PICTURE GALLERY 287-9 HACKNEY ROAD,
LONDON E2 8NA.
☎ 020-7739 6624. OPEN 8 - 5 MON - FRI, 10 - 4 SAT, 10 - 2 SUN.
MON - FRI, 10 - 6 SAT, 11 - 3 SUN.
THE LONDON PICTURE GALLERY 287-9 HACKNEY ROAD,
LONDON E2 8NA.
☎ 020-7739 6624. OPEN 8 - 5 MON - FRI, 10 - 4 SAT, 10 - 2 SUN.

Permanent Discount Outlet • *Furniture/Soft Furnishings*

Manufacturers and global importers of mirrors and frames with large wholesale premises with own retail showroom offering an enormous selection of mirrors in all sizes and types from gilt frames to baroque style, as well as oil paintings and framed prints. Prices range from £2-£1,000. Framing is very reasonable, too, and the service is used regularly by local artists. The branch at 709 Fulham Road is a mirror gallery offering competitively priced mirrors to any specification. 723 Fulham Foad has a large selection of oil paintings by local artists from £10-£1000. At 152 Hackney Road, there is a prints and posters showroom offering a huge selection of prints - flowers, impressionist, abstracts and many more - at unbeatable prices. 287-289 Hackney Road has now been established for over 25 years. Picture framing is available at all branches.

THE MAKE-UP CENTRE
52A WALHAM GROVE, FULHAM, LONDON SW6 1QR
☎ 020-7381 0213. OPEN 10 - 4 MON - FRI.

Womenswear Only

Sells own brands of matt eyeshadow, foundation, and blusher which are twice the size of ones you can buy in department stores. Also good sable brushes which are cheaper than those found in artists' shops. Also do makeovers and offer make-up lessons for £125 for one and a half hours. With more than thirty years experience in the business, they have not only trained the best make-up artists, but made up prime ministers, film stars and tv presenters. Full wedding makeovers from £125.

THE NAPPY EXPRESS
128 HIGH ROAD, NEW SOUTHGATE, LONDON N11 1PG
☎ 020-8361 4040. PHONE FIRST FOR BROCHURE.
Hire Shop • *Children* • *Food and Leisure*
A member of the Baby Equipment Hirers Association (BEHA), which has more than 100 members countrywide. A range of equipment can be hired from high chairs, cots and travel cots to baby car seats and buggies. BEHA run an advice line which will try and answer any queries you have regarding hiring services for children. Phone the Babyline on 0831 310355. There is also a free home delivery service aimed at new mothers in north, central and south London for Pampers and Huggies nappies, baby foods (including organic), baby toiletries, also large household items like washing powders, toilet rolls, bottled waters, fizzy drinks, beer etc, all at supermarket prices.

THE NATURAL WOOD FLOOR COMPANY
20 SMUGGLERS WAY, WANDSWORTH, LONDON SW18 1EQ
☎ 020-8871 9771. OPEN 9 - 6 MON - FRI, 9 - 4 SAT.
Architectural Salvage • *DIY/Renovation*
Up to 170 different wood-flooring materials including reclaimed wooden floorboards: pine, douglas fir, woodblock and pitch pine. Pine floorboards cost from £21 sq metre; beechwood woodblock from £18, while oak starts at £18 a sq metre. Also sells new solid wood floors at prices which they claim are cheaper than anything offered in the same style. For example, 20 ml thick redwood, £18.13 per square metre.

THE OBSERVATORY
20 GREENWICH CHURCH STREET, GREENWICH, LONDON SE10 9BJ
☎ 020-8305 1998. OPEN 10 - 6 EVERY DAY
Secondhand and Vintage Clothes • *Womenswear & Menswear*
This retrospective clothing shops (combining retro with new) has been established for over ten years. It sells turn-of-the-century fashion as well as Fifties, Sixties, Seventies and early Eighties gear. Women's frocks, shoes, hats and jewellery as well as lots of leather, suede and denim garments. Men's suits, jackets, trousers and shoes.

THE OLD CINEMA
157 TOWER BRIDGE ROAD, LONDON SE1 3LW
☎ 020-7407 5371. OPEN 9.30 - 5.30 MON - SAT, 12 - 5 SUN.
160 CHISWICK HIGH ROAD, LONDON W4 1PR
☎ 020-8995 4166. OPEN 9.30 - 6 MON - SAT, 12 - 5 SUN.
Secondhand shops • *Furniture/Soft Furnishings*
The Tower Bridge branch is a thirty thousand square foot warehouse with antique furniture, some from pub fittings, garden furniture, and pine furniture. Periods include art deco, art nouveau, Victoriana and Americana. There's everything from kitchen sinks to veteran cars. Chairs start at £20, art deco

dining room suites from £400 to £2,000, Victorian dining tables from £900. The Chiswick branch holds ten thousand square feet of antique furniture, some in complete room settings. Wide range of Victorian, Georgian, Edwardian and art nouveau. Items range from light fittings and mirrors to dining tables and room panelling.

THE OLD DRAGON
UNIT 7B, IMPERIAL STUDIOS, 3-11 IMPERIAL ROAD, FULHAM, LONDON SW6 2AG
☎ 020-7731 8802. E-MAIL: vicki@olddragon.co.uk OPEN BY APPOINTMENT.

Permanent Discount Outlet • *Furniture/Soft Furnishings*

Classical and unusual items from China, Tibet and the East, with soft furnishings of needlepoint and Aubusson carpets and cushion covers, ceramics, gold and silver leaf ginger jars, blue and white and Celadon vases, 18th and 19th century Buddhas in alabaster, marble and stone from Burma, tea caddies and charger plates. Each piece is hand picked and chosen for originality and design. New items are constantly being sourced and introduced to keep up with demand.

THE OLD STATION
72 LOAMPIT HILL, LEWISHAM, LONDON SE13
☎ 020-8694 6540. OPEN 10 - 6 MON - SAT, SOME SUNS.

Architectural Salvage • *DIY/Renovation*

The Old Station in Lewisham is a salvage yard based in a converted station with a garden at the rear. While the salvage yard section houses Victorian reclaimed items from roll-top baths and original and reproduction fireplaces to Butler sinks, doors and radiators, the garden features repro garden statues which start at £30; urns on plinths, £300; garden railings, old slate sculptures and Victorian chimney pots from £20.

THE OUTLET
5 KENSINGTON CHURCH STREET, LONDON W8
☎ 020-7708 5522. OPEN 10 - 7 MON - FRI, 9 - 7 SAT, 11 - 6 SUN.

Permanent Discount Outlet • *Womenswear Only*

The Outlet is a new chain of shops selling top Italian labels at discount prices. Twice-monthly buying trips to the best-known Italian manufacturers means you can visit and find the shops brimming with DKNY, DKNY Signature range, Versace, Armani, Dolce & Gabbana and Calvin Klein or you could be unlucky and hit the end of the fortnight and find very little. It's worth trying again for the great prices. For example, Armani Jeans jacket, £49.99 reduced from £200; DKNY jackets £79.99 reduced from £240. Discounts are usually at least 70%. There are branches in Wimbledon, Richmond, Hounslow, Walworth Road and Peckham, although most of the shops are on short leases, which is why they can offer such good prices, so do ring before visiting in case they've moved on. Or call the above telephone number for locations of other stores.

THE REJECT TILE SHOP
178 WANDSWORTH BRIDGE ROAD, LONDON SW6 2UQ
☎ 020-7731 6098. OPEN 9.30 - 5.30 MON - FRI, 9.30 - 5 SAT.
2A ENGLANDS LANE, LONDON NW3 4TG
☎ 020-7483 2608. OPEN 10 - 6 MON - FRI, 10 - 5 SAT.
Permanent Discount Outlet • *DIY/Renovation*

Specialises in second quality and low cost ceramic wall and floor tiles as well as terracotta and quarry tiles. Most tiles are sold at approximately half the cost of first quality equivalent products. Quality control is so tight nowadays that seconds are usually given this status due to minor glazing defects, barely perceptible pinholing in the glaze or slightly "off-standard" colour shades. Many tiles are imported exclusively from Italy and there is also a wide selection of fine quality English and Victorian style decorated tiles, borders and dados, as well as a wide choice of discontinued and special purchase first quality tiles. They also have a large range of handmade Mexican tiles to clear.

TILE CLEARING HOUSE
ACE CORNER, STONEBRIDGE PARK, NORTH CIRCULAR ROAD, LONDON NW10 7UI
☎ 020-8965 8062. FAX 0181-453 0392. OPEN 8 - 6 MON - FRI, 9 - 6 SAT, 10 - 4 SUN.
NEW SOUTHGATE INDUSTRIAL ESTATE, LOWER PARK ROAD, LONDON N11 1HT
☎ 020-8361. OPEN 8 - 6 MON - FRI, 9 - 6 SAT, 10 - 4 SUN.
MARITIME INDUSTRIAL ESTATE, HORIZON WAY, CHARLTON, LONDON SE7 7SW
☎ 020-8858 9955. OPEN 8 - 6 MON - FRI, 9 - 6 SAT, 10 - 4 SUN.
Permanent Discount Outlet • *DIY/Renovation*

Over 500 ranges of top quality ceramic wall and floor tiles permanently in stock, plus a comprehensive range of grouts, adhesives, tools and accessories to complete the job. By buying direct from the manufacturer and passing the savings on to the customer, their prices are very competitive. Moreover, everything you see is in stock, so there's no waiting for orders to be processed. Save up to 75% on manufacturers' recommended selling prices.

TILES GALORE
GRACEFIELD GARDENS, STREATHAM, LONDON SW16 2ST
☎ 020-8677 6068. OPEN 8 - 5.30 MON - SAT.
1 CROSS WAYS PARADE, SELSDON PARK ROAD, ADDINGTON, LONDON CR2 8JJ
☎ 020-8651 3782. OPEN 7.30 - 5 MON - SAT.
Permanent Discount Outlet • *DIY/Renovation*

Sells perfect tiles from round the world at discount prices by buying direct from the factories, unlike the large department stores which buy from distributors. There are hundreds of designs to choose from. The Addington Shop is small, whereas the Streatham shop has 10,000 sq ft of tiles. All necessary equipment is also stocked and staff give helpful advice and tips.

TIMOTHY EVEREST
32 ELDER STREET LONDON E1 6BT
☎ 020-7377 5770. OPEN 9 - 5.30 MON - FRI, 9 - 4 SAT.
PHONE FOR AN APPOINTMENT.

Having trained at Tommy Nutter in Savile Row, Timothy now offers bespoke tailoring at accessible prices. A suit selling in Savile Row for £2,000 can be made from £995 for full bespoke, £899 for semi-bespoke. Jackets, trousers, shirts, overcoats and silk ties can also be bought. Everything is made on the premises of this unusual eighteenth century building.

TK MAXX
THE ARCADIA CENTRE, EALING, LONDON
☎ 020-8566 0447. OPEN 9.30 - 6 MON - SAT, TILL 8 THUR, 11 - 5 SUN.
UNIT 31, ST GEORGE'S CENTRE, ST ANNE'S ROAD, HARROW HA1 1HS
☎ 020-8863 2921. OPEN 9 - 6 MON - WED, FRI, SAT, 9 - 8 THUR, 11 - 5 SUN.

Permanent Discount Outlet • *Womenswear & Menswear*
Children • *Household* • *Furniture/Soft Furnishings*

Based on an American concept, TK Maxx is situated in easily accessible, often centrally located stores and offers famous label goods with up to 60% savings off recommended retail prices. TK Maxx has fashion for the whole family - women's, men's and childrenswear - accessories, shoes, gifts, kitchenware and home goods. Everything in the store is branded with a choice of well-known high street names to designer labels, and while a small percentage might be clearly marked past season, the great majority of items in store are current season, current stock and still with phenomenal savings. There is a huge choice with 50,000 pieces in store and up to 10,000 new items arriving a week. The stores are simple and unfussy with wide aisles, shopping trolleys and baskets, and a spacious, functional feel to them but there are individual changing rooms, ramps for buggies and wheelchairs and plenty of staff on the shop floor. Every branch accepts all major credit and debit cards and has a liberal refund and return policy.

TOG 24
PUTNEY EXCHANGE SHOPPING CENTRE, PUTNEY HIGH STREET, LONDON SW15 1TW
☎ 020-8785 3565. OPEN 9 - 6 MON - SAT, 7 ON THUR, 11 - 5 SUN.

Factory Shop • *Womenswear & Menswear* • *Children*
Sportswear & Equipment

Tog 24 are the UK's fastest growing brand name in outdoor clothing and leisurewear. They utilise the world's finest performance fabrics including Gore-Tex, Polartec and Burlington MCS, catering for all the family for all seasons, with cosy fleeces and waterproofs for the winter, and trekking ranges, shorts and t-shirts for the summer. With all prices at least 30% below the recommended retail price, you can afford to enter the Tog comfort zone.

TOP VALUE DRUGSTORE
23 TEMPLE FORTUNE PARADE, OPPOSITE MARKS & SPENCERS, FINCHLEY ROAD, LONDON NW11 OQS
☎ 020-8905 5448. OPEN 8.30 - 6 MON - SAT, 9.30 - 1.30 SUN.

Permanent Discount Outlet • *Food and Leisure* • *Household*

One of those rare, family-run businesses which manages to undercut the competition including, with many items, Boots and Superdrug. Well-stocked shop which is divided into sections such as haircare, skincare, toiletries, baby equipment, household cleaning (Jif, Comfort, Pledge, Flash, Dettol, Ajax, Mr Muscle, Astonish etc.), bathroom cleaning products, oven cleaners, window cleaning products, polishes, scourers, brushes, cloths, sponges, air fresheners etc, bakeware, non-pharmaceutical drugs. The shop also stocks a selection of cards, toys and fancy goods and offers same-day developing for £2.99 for up to 40 prints with an extra set costing £1.99 if ordered at time of processing. Prices are generally 25%-30% cheaper than other chemist chains. You can phone your order through and there is a delivery service if you spend a minimum of £35.

TOWNSENDS
81 ABBEY ROAD, LONDON NW8 0AE
☎ 020-7624 4756. OPEN 10 - 6 MON - FRI, 10 - 5 SAT.
106 BOUNDARY ROAD, LONDON NW8 ORH
☎ 020-7372 4327. OPEN 10 - 6 MON - FRI, 10 - 5 SAT.

Architectural Salvage • *DIY/Renovation*

Antique fireplaces and related items, and antique stained glass at the Boundary Road branch just down the road. More than 200 fireplaces in stock at prices from £250 to £15,000 in wood, marble, cast-iron and natural stone. This business has been established for more than 20 years and offers a full survey and fitting service and free delivery in the London area. They also restore antique stained glass, acid-etched and sandblasted glass from £30 per square foot to £100.

TWENTIETH CENTURY FROX
614 FULHAM ROAD, LONDON SW6 5RP
☎ 020-7731 3242. OPEN 10 - 7 MON , WED, THUR, 10 - 6 TUE, FRI, SAT.

Hire Shop • *Womenswear Only*

Two hundred dresses, mainly ballgowns and cocktail dresses, to hire or to buy. Costs £75 - £95 for three days' hire. No appointment necessary. Also new and ex-hire stock available to buy.

UNIVERSITY VISION
UNIVERSITY OF LONDON UNION BUILDING, MALET STREET, LONDON WC1
☎ 020-7636 8925. OPEN 9 - 5.30 MON - FRI, 10 - 2 SAT.

Permanent Discount Outlet • *Womenswear & Menswear*

Permanent discount outlet used mostly by students but available for use by the general public selling spectacles and contact lenses at very competitive prices. Students get an even bigger discount.

UPSTAIRS DOWNSTAIRS
8 MALCOLM COURT, MALCOLM CRESCENT, HENDON,
LONDON NW4 4PJ
☎ 020-8202 7720. BY APPOINTMENT ONLY.
Dress Agency • *Womenswear Only*
Features top designer makes in perfect condition on uncluttered rails which makes for unhurried browsing. Accessories are for sale as well as day clothes. Customers come from all over the country and clothes from all over the world, where they both enjoy personal attention. Designers include Louis Feraud, Valentino, Jobis, Yarell, MaxMara and Cerruti. There is also an alterations service.

USA FASHION
111 & 117 FONTHILL ROAD, LONDON N4 3HH
☎ 020-7272 3992. OPEN 9.30 - 5.30 MON - FRI, 9 - 4 SAT.
Permanent Discount Outlet • *Womenswear Only*
Specialises in a wide size-range in womenswear (8 to 26), including familiar high street names and American designers, all at discount prices. For example, a garment which would normally retail at £170 costs only £60 here. All the stock is brand new. They also specialise in a large range of eveningwear (more than 300 different styles) in sizes 8 to 26, and childrenswear aged 12 upwards.

VICTORIAN WOOD WORKS
INTERNATIONAL HOUSE, LONDON INTERNATIONAL FREIGHT
TERMINAL, TEMPLE MILLS LANE, LONDON E15 2ES
☎ 020-8534 1000. OPEN 8.30 - 5.30 MON - FRI, 10 - 2 SAT.
Architectural Salvage • *DIY/Renovation*
Reclaimed or new hardwood flooring manufacturers and suppliers.

VIDAL SASSOON SCHOOL OF HAIRDRESSING
56 DAVIES MEWS, LONDON W1Y 1AS
☎ 020-7318 5205. OPEN 10 - 3 MON - FRI.
VIDAL SASSOON STAFF TRAINING, WHITELEYS OF BAYSWATER,
151 QUEENSWAY, LONDON W2 4SB
☎ 020-7792 5540. OPEN 10 - 3 MON - SAT.
VIDAL SASSOON ADVANCED ACADEMY, 20 GROSVENOR STREET W1
☎ 020-7491 0030.
Cuts and styles undertaken by students at the School of Hairdressing for £16.50 or £8.25 if you're a student, nurse, unemployed or an OAP. Appointment must be made at least one week in advance. At the Staff Training School in Bayswater, you can pay between £15 and £29, £42 if tinting or colouring, depending on the level of experience of the staff. Again, appointments must be made. The Grosvenor Street school is for hairdressers who have trained for at least seven years so you are assured of a high level of competence.

VILLEROY & BOCH (UK) LIMITED
267 MERTON ROAD, LONDON SW18 5JS
☎ 020-8875 6006. OPEN 10 - 5 SEVEN DAYS A WEEK.
Factory Shop • *Household*
The UK's main factory outlet for Villeroy & Boch carries an exclusive range of tableware, crystal and cutlery from Europe's largest tableware manufacturer. Convenient parking and pleasant surroundings make for a pleasurable and unhurried shopping experience. A varied and constantly changing stock, including seconds, hotelware and discontinued lines, on sale at excellent reductions, always makes for a worthwhile visit.

VIRGINIA
98 PORTLAND ROAD, HOLLAND PARK, LONDON W11 4LQ
☎ 020-7727 9908. OPEN 11 - 6 MON - SAT.
Secondhand and Vintage Clothes • *Womenswear Only*
Antique clothing from the turn of this century to the 1940s. Nightgowns, beaded dresses, chiffon, hats and accessories. Everything is a one-off and top quality.

WAHL FASHIONS
4 GREAT PORTLAND STREET, LONDON W1N 5AA
☎ 020-7580 8050. FAX 0207-758 01330   E-MAIL: sales@wahlfashions.co.uk
Designer Sale • *Womenswear Only*
Agents for Blacky Dress, Beppi, Bondi, Pleinsud Jeans, Tuzzi, they hold showroom sales regularly. Write or phone to be put on the mailing list.

WALL TO WALL
549 BATTERSEA PARK ROAD, BATTERSEA, LONDON SW11 3BL
☎ 020-7585 3335. FAX 020-7228 5080. OPEN 10 - 6 MON - SAT.
Permanent Discount Outlet • *Furniture/Soft Furnishings*
Top name designer brand wallpaper, all at £7.95 a roll, with 450 different designs from which to choose. All their bargain lines are discontinued patterns, or ends of ranges so you have to buy the right quantity when you see it as there won't be any more. Names on sale include Anna French, Monkwell, Hill & Knowles and GP&J Baker. Also designer-name fabrics at clearance prices from £9.95 a metre - 10,000 metres always in stock. Full making-up and fitting service, which is particularly good for people who want to do places up quickly as there is a very fast free measuring and estimating service. There's also a free design service on the premises.

WALLERS
21-24 NEWPORT COURT, CHARING CROSS ROAD, LONDON WC2H 7JS
☎ 020-7437 1665. OPEN 9 - 5.30 MON - FRI, 9 - 4.30 SAT.
Permanent Discount Outlet • *Womenswear & Menswear*
Wallers is a family firm established at the same address for more than 70 years. They specialise in famous name suits, sports jackets, blazers, trousers, coats

and morning and evening dress wear at greatly reduced prices. Well known to TV and film designers, who appreciate the value of choice, their Chinatown shop looks small on the outside but inside is a rabbit warren, full to the brim. Wallers clothes have been seen in Inspector Morse, Minder, Yes Minister, The Bill, Between The Lines, Only Fools and Horses and even blockbuster Hollywood films such as Mission Impossible. There are usually at least 5,000 items in stock at any one time, in all sizes, most of which are ends of ranges, cancelled orders, seconds (clearly marked as such) or bought as a result of liquidations. Examples of prices include suits, £125, usual price £225; jackets, £79.50, usual price £125; trousers, £25, usual price £59.50; raincoats and overcoats, from £79.50; dinner suits, from £110; three-piece morning suits, from £165. They also have a smart range of business clothes for women.

WARD & STEVENS
248 HIGH STREET NORTH, MANOR PARK, LONDON E12 6SB
☎ 020-8472 4067. FAX 020-8470 9091. OPEN 9 - 5.30 MON - SAT, 11 - 4 SUN.

Permanent Discount Outlet • *DIY/Renovation*

Budget ranges of floor and wall tiles including standard quality and excellent seconds. Specialise in low cost quarry floor tiles at prices starting from £6.80 per square metre plus VAT. Also 300x300 floors in a wide range available from stock. Wall tiles from £2 per metre to £25 per metre. Budget range of wallcoverings from stock. Full range of British Standard and NCS paints (10,000 plus colours) at less than trade prices. Also sells mirrors cut to size.

WELLINGTONS
1 WELLINGTON PLACE, LONDON NW8 7PE
☎ 020-7483 0688. OPEN 11 - 5 MON - SAT.

Dress Agency • *Womenswear & Menswear*

Stunning selection of Gucci, Prada, Chanel, MaxMara, Armani and Joseph. Ladies suits from £18, jackets from £28. There's also a bargain basement full of high street names such as Marks & Spencer and Karen Millen as well as reduced designer clothing. Also sells menswear such as Armani, Boss, Kenzo, Versace, Ralph Lauren.

WINDSMOOR WAREHOUSE
WINDSMOOR HOUSE, 83 LAWRENCE ROAD, TOTTENHAM, LONDON N15 4EP
☎ 020-8800 8022.

Designer Sale • *Womenswear & Menswear*

Regular sales are held here (usually four times a year) during which first quality fashion from the Windsmoor, Planet and Precis Petite ranges are sold at discounts of up to 75%. Sometimes, there is also Dannimac rainwear for men and women. Phone or write to be put on the mailing list.

ZEON
39 WATERLOO ROAD, LONDON NW2 7TT
☎ 020-8208 1833. PHONE BEFORE VISITING.
Factory Shop • *Household*

Zeon is the UK's largest timepiece importer. Brands include Zeon, Ingersoll, Elle, Head, Speedo and Wrangler. Zeon is also a specialist in children's and young people's watches and clocks such as Disney, Barbie, Action Man, Furby, MTV, Steps, Five and B*witched. The products on sale here include watches of all types, clocks and executive gifts.

Middlesex

ARTHUR SANDERSON & SONS LTD
100 ACRES, SANDERSON ROAD, UXBRIDGE, MIDDLESEX UB8 1DH
☎ (01895) 238244.
Designer Sale • *Furniture/Soft Furnishings*

This world-renowned furnishing house holds an annual warehouse clearance sale on one of the May bank holidays at its factory shop in Uxbridge of seconds and discontinued fabrics and accessories at reduced prices. Whatever time the sale starts, get there at least an hour earlier as there is usually a queue. Phone at the end of April to find out the date.

BCP AIRPORT PARKING AND TRANSFER SERVICE
HEATHROW, MIDDLESEX
☎ (0870) 0134586. 8AM - 9 PM, 7 DAYS A WEEK.

BCP provides secure, value-for-money car parking at Gatwick, Heathrow, luton, Manchester, Glasgow, Bristol, Birmingham, Cardiff, East Midlands, Southampton, Newcastle, Leeds Bradford, Edinburgh, Prestwick and Belfast, with prices from just £2.50 net per day. For an extra £24.95 (£28.95 at Prestwick and Heathrow), you can save time by being met at the airport terminal on your departure and return as part of BCP's Meet and Greet Parking service. Your car is then taken to the BCP.Co.Uk secure car park nearby. Or you can pre-book a chauffeur-driven airport car to and from the airport. This service is ideal if you live within 30 miles of your departure airport - prices start from about £60 return. To book and save at least 15% on the car park gae prices and 10% on lounges and chauffeur-driven cars, phone the BCP reservations line quoting reference 'GDD'. BCP will confirm your booking by post with directions to your car park or details of the pick-up or meeting arrangements as appropriate.

CHILDREN'S PARTY HIRE
STANMORE, MIDDLESEX
☎ 020-8952 8130. PHONE FOR DETAILS.
Hire Shop • *Children*

Small tables and chairs for hire for children's parties. Examples of prices include three tables and 14 chairs, £7; six tables and 26 chairs, £12. Also offers small-scale adult party hire.

DAMART
63-67 HIGH STREET, HOUNSLOW, MIDDLESEX
☎ 020-8570 6796. OPEN 9 - 5 MON - SAT.
Factory Shop • *Womenswear & Menswear*

Damart underwear and merchandise - anything from tights, socks and gloves to dresses, coats, cardigans and jumpers - some of which is current stock sold at full price, some discontinued and ends of lines sold at discount. There several shops selling some discounted stock from the Damart range, known as Damart Extra.

DAVE'S DIY
4 ENFIELD ROAD, ENFIELD, MIDDLESEX
☎ 020-8363 1680. OPEN 8.30 - 5 MON - FRI, 9 - 5 SAT.
Permanent Discount Outlet • *DIY/Renovation*

Aimed at the trade, it will cater for members of the public who benefit from the discounts. Carries wallpaper brands from Kingfisher, Mayfair, Crown and Vymura, among others, from a range of 300 wallpaper books at discounts of up to 40%. Next day ordering for wallpapers. Also carries a large stock of paint, with a computerised mixing machine that offers thousands of combinations of colours.

EUROTILES
UNIT 2C, TWICKENHAM TRADING ESTATE, RUGBY ROAD,
MIDDLESEX TW1 1DG
☎ 020-8744 0088. OPEN 8 - 5 MON - FRI, 9 - 4 SAT, 11 - 3 SUN.
Permanent Discount Outlet • *DIY/Renovation*

Opposite the main entrance to Twickenham Rugby Ground, this showroom displays tiles and some bathroom suites. There are regular changes of merchandise which are good deals.

GORDONS CONNECTIONS
92-100 HIGH STREET, YEWSLEY, WEST DRAYTON,
MIDDLESEX UB7 7DU
☎ (01895) 441846. OPEN 9 - 6 TUE, WED, THUR, SAT, 9 - 7 FRI.
SEVEN DAYS A WEEK FROM NOVEMBER TO CHRISTMAS.
Permanent Discount Outlet • *Womenswear & Menswear*

Well-known high street brands including Marks & Spencer and Principles, at discounts of up to 70%. Rapid turnover of stock.

JUST TILES
142 KENTON ROAD, HARROW, MIDDLESEX HA3 8BL
☎ 020-8907 3020. OPEN 9 - 5.30 MON - SAT, 10 - 4 SUN AND BANK HOLIDAYS, CLOSED WED.
Permanent Discount Outlet • *DIY/Renovation*
Specialise in discount tiles for both floor and wall. Trends are towards larger tiles and design printing can be carried out in house. Very large selection, including many Continental tiles, all at competitive prices.

KENTON WAREHOUSE SUPERSTORE
2A CHARLTON ROAD, KENTON, MIDDLESEX HA3 9HF
☎ 020-8732 2525. OPEN 9.30 - 5.30 MON - SAT.
Permanent Discount Outlet • *Furniture/Soft Furnishings*
Carpet and bed warehouse which sells Sealy beds up to 30% off the recommended retail price; Relyon beds up to 35% off RRP, brand name carpets at highly competitive prices, as well as carpet rolls, room size ends of rolls, laminate flooring and remnants. Free delivery inside M25 area if you spend £250.

LITTLE STARS
33 ROYSTON PARK ROAD, HATCH END, MIDDLESEX HA5 4AA
☎ 020-8537 0980. PHONE FIRST.
8, ANSELM ROAD, HATCH END, MIDDLESEX HA5 4LJ
☎ 020-8621 4378. PHONE FIRST.
Hire Shops • *Children*
Part of the Baby Equipment Hirers Association (BEHA), which has more than 100 members countrywide. A range of equipment can be hired from high chairs, cots and travel cots to baby car seats and buggies. Some members also hire out party equipment including child-sized tables and chairs. They also sell branded and unbranded equipment competitively, price list available by phone request. BEHA run an advice line which will try and answer any queries you have regarding hiring services for children. Phone the Babyline on 0831 310355.

LONDON WAREHOUSES LTD
802 FIELDEND ROAD, SOUTH RUISLIP, MIDDLESEX
☎ 020-8422 7326. OPEN 10 - 5 SAT, SUN.
Permanent Discount Outlet • *Furniture/Soft Furnishings*
Sales every weekend of ex-showhouse furniture direct from designers and national house builders, plus manufacturers end of line and surplus stocks. Three-piece suites, tables, chairs, bedroom furniture plus much much more, all at affordable prices.

OCEAN

ST ANN'S ROAD, HARROW, MIDDLESEX HA1 11G
☎ 020-8861 3554. OPEN 9 - 6 MON - SAT, 7 ON THUR, 11 - 5 SUN,
10 - 5 BANK HOLIDAYS.

Permanent Discount Outlet • *Womenswear Only*

Manufacturers of ladies fashion, they sell everydaywear at very cheap price: tops, £2.50; dresses £10; suits, £20; eveningwear from £20; skirts and trousers, £10 each.

PECO

72 STATION ROAD, HAMPTON, MIDDLESEX TW12 2BT
☎ 020-8979 8310. FAX 0181-941 3319. OPEN 8.15 - 5.15 MON - SAT.

Architectural Salvage • *DIY/Renovation*

One of the largest door and fireplace warehouse in the country with two floors of display area and three additional shops featuring at least 600 fireplaces, 100 in marble and slate. Stocks about 2,000 period doors up to 1930s as well as oak beams, pot stoves from France and cast-iron fireplaces. Offers marble restoration and pine-stripping.

SESSION

GARDEN ROOM, SYON PARK, BRENTFORD, MIDDLESEX
☎ 020-8994 4983.

Designer Sale • *Womenswear Only*

Designer sales run by fashion trade insider and featuring big-name British and international labels, all at discounted prices. There are usually about 8 sales per year, each one featuring a variety of different names which can't be mentioned here as the designers are very sensitive about their names being used in promoting discount sales. Membership costs £29.50 a year which also entitles you to other concessions, which were being put together as we went to press. Phone for more details. Also offers exclusive one-day showroom sales for members.

SEVALS

21 GARNAULT ROAD, ENFIELD, MIDDLESEX EN1 4TS
☎ 020-8342 1988. OPEN 9 - 6 MON - SAT.
17 SILVER STREET, ENFIELD, MIDDLESEX
☎ 020 8363 7059. OPEN 9 - 5.30 MON - SAT.

Permanent Discount Outlet • *Children* • *Womenswear*

Warehouse at Garnault Road selling mostly women's quality clothing, with some children's; the Silver Street branch is a shop. Most are one-off samples or current stock of well-known brand names, although some of the labels are cut out. Discounts can be up to 50% on high street pices.

STEWART & YOUNG
30 & 105-107 HIGH STREET, HAMPTON HILL, MIDDLESEX TW12 1NJ
☎ 020-8979 1178. OPEN 9 - 5.30 MON - FRI, 9 - 4.30 SAT.
Permanent Discount Outlet • *Electrical Equipment*
Sells domestic household goods as well as servicing them. As they belong to the Euronics group, the biggest buying group in Europe, prices match those of big stores. Where Stewart & Young have the edge is that they include delivery, installation to existing fitting and removal of any old machine in their price. The branch at 30 High Street specialises in cookers, refrigeration and built-in appliances. Washing machines, tumble dryers, vacuum cleaners, dishwashers etc. are to be found at the 105 High Street address.

THE TALK SERVICE
☎ (0800) 107 0139, WEBSITE: www.talksense.com
An "intelligent" box which, when attached to your telephone, traces the cheapest rate for any call. It is updated automatically every 24 hours to pick up any new call costs. The size of a paperback book, it plugs into your wall socket. You don't have to change your telephone number, dial extra codes or leave your existing provider.

THE CLOTHES HORSE
166 HIGH STREET, TEDDINGTON, MIDDLESEX TW11
☎ 020-8977 1887. OPEN 11 - 6 TUE - SAT.
Dress Agency • *Womenswear Only*
Nearly-new outfits from dresses, jackets, suits, coats to shoes, handbags, belts and jewellery. Labels include Whistles, Ghost, Gap, Hobbs and Next and LK Bennett shoes.

THE CURTAIN MILL
13-19 LONDON ROAD, ENFIELD, MIDDLESEX EN2 6BS
☎ 020-8364 6515. OPEN 9 - 5.30 SEVEN DAYS A WEEK.
Permanent Discount Outlet • *Furniture/Soft Furnishings*
Huge choice of fabrics at really low prices - from £1.99p a metre and including excellent discounts on many designer labels. A large warehouse, it stocks Ashley Wilde and Swatchbox, among other leading names at discount prices. Also supplies ready made curtains, bespoke curtains, blinds, venetian verticals, all types of window treatments and has its own in-house making up service.

THE SALVAGE SHOP
34-40 WATLING AVENUE, BURNT OAK, MIDDLESEX HA8 0LR
☎ 020-8952 4353. OPEN 9 - 5.30 MON - SAT, 10 - 4 SUN.
Permanent Discount Outlet • *Womenswear & Menswear* • *Children Electrical Equipment* • *DIY/Renovation* • *Furniture/Soft Furnishings Food and Leisure* • *Sportswear & Equipment* • *Household*
An Aladdin's cave of "salvaged" stock for the avid bargain hunter, most of which has been the subject of bankruptcy, insurance claims, fire or flood.

Regular visitors have found anything from half-price Kenwood Chefs, typewriters and telephones to furniture, kitchen items and designer clothes. Yves St Laurent, Ungaro, MaxMara, Chloe, Agnes B and Mondi are just some the labels (though they are often cut out) to appear. Discounts range from 50%-75%. Stock is constantly changing with a new designer name every week, so phone first to check what is available.

WHEELHOUSE LTD
9-21 BELL ROAD, HOUNSLOW, MIDDLESEX TW3 3NS
☎ 020-8570 3501. OPEN 8.30 - 5.30 MON - SAT, 10 - 4.30 SUN.
Permanent Discount Outlet • *Household*

Sells all sorts of household goods (plates, cups, cutlery, Addis bins, tea towels etc), DIY, garden equipment (flowers, plants, lawn seed), everything to do with cars, etc. There is an extensive tool section on the upper floor - everything for the DIY enthusiast. You need to visit it regularly as items change each time, but it's very cheap with easy access and helpful staff. They buy in bulk and job lots of branded products, adding new lines every week. Plenty of car parking.

Norfolk

ALEXON SALE SHOP
THEATRE PLAIN, GREAT YARMOUTH, NORFOLK
☎ (01493) 332146. OPEN 9 - 5.30 MON - SAT.
Permanent Discount Outlet • *Womenswear Only*

Alexon and Eastex from last season at 40% less than the original price; during sale time in January and June, the reductions are as much as 70%. Stock includes separates, skirts, jackets, blouses; there is no underwear or night clothes.

AYLSHAM BATHROOM & KITCHEN
BURGH ROAD, AYLSHAM, NORFOLK NR11 6AR
☎ (01263) 735396. OPEN 8.30 - 5 MON - FRI, 9 - 5 SAT, 10 - 4 SUN.
Permanent Discount Outlet • *DIY/Renovation*

Bathroom equipment, kitchen displays, all at reduced prices of at least 20%-25% less than normal retail prices. Top brands such as Dalton, Ideal Standard, Armitage Shanks and Shires are some of the 70 bathrooms displayed here; and there are 30 display kitchens with appliances by Neff, Philips, Whirlpool and Zanussi.

BALLY OUTLET STORE
HALL ROAD, NORWICH, NORFOLK NR4 6DP
☎ (01603) 226040. OPEN 9.30 - 5.30 MON - FRI, 9 - 5.30 SAT,
11 - 5 SUN AND MOST BANK HOLIDAYS. PHONE FIRST.
Factory Shop • *Womenswear & Menswear*
The Bally Outlet Store is located on the outskirts of Norwich, and sells women's and men's footwear, clothing, handbags, and accessories. Other items are also available such as socks, scarves, silk ties, shoe horns and shoe care products. Most of the merchandise is ex-sale, reject or substandard and is priced from £5-£400. A saving of at least one-third off the recommended retail price can usually be made. Also on the same site is a coffee shop which serves morning coffee, light lunches and afternoon teas in a pleasant and relaxing atmosphere. Toilet facilities and ample free parking are available. Coach parties are welcome by prior arrangement.

BOOKSALE
31 GENTLEMANS WALK, NORWICH, NORFOLK NR2 1NB
☎ (01603) 667209. OPEN 9 - 6 MON - SAT, 8 ON THUR, 10.30 - 4.30 SUN.
Permanent Discount Outlet • *Food and Leisure*
Booksale now boasts more than 100 shops throughout the UK: call 0121 313 6000 for details of your nearest store. It sells books, stationery, paints, tapes, CDs and CDRoms, videos, all at enormously discounted prices. Paperbacks and hardbacks from £1.99p, children's books 49p; videos 99p, clip frames 99p - £19.95, posters £1.50 - £6.99 and classical CDs from £3.99.

CAITHNESS CRYSTAL
8 - 12 PAXMAN ROAD, HARDWICK INDUSTRIAL ESTATE, KINGS LYNN, NORFOLK, PE30 4NE
☎ (01553) 765111. OPEN 9 - 5 MON - SAT, 10.15 - 4.15 SUN.
Factory Shop • *Household*
Well stocked factory shop with many bargains all year round in glass and crystal, giftware and tableware. Also selection of Royal Doulton products and other great gift ideas to choose from.

ESSENTIAL COLLECTION
63 SUSSEX STREET, NORWICH, NORFOLK NR3 3BP
☎ (0421) 391909. OPEN 10 - 4 MON - SAT.
Dress Agency • *Womenswear Only*
Two-storey shop just out of the city centre with a marble entrance and staircase. It specialises in bridal wear, mother of the bride, evening wear and ballgowns, plus a good selection of casual daywear. Labels range from high street to designer: Frank Usher, Jacques Vert, Mark Angelo, Bianca, Wallis, Next, M&S, Monsoon as well as some one-off samples and large sizes. There is a large selection of shoes, bags, belts, scarves and jewellery. A special room is set aside with hundreds of fancy dress costumes, and there is a hat hire and seamstress service available.

GILCHRIST CONFECTIONERY LTD
UNITS 1 & 2, OXBOROUGH LANE, FAKENHAM, NORFOLK NR21 8AF
☎ (01328) 862632. OPEN 8 .30 - 4.30 MON - WED, 7.30 - 4.30 THUR, 8.30 - 4 FRI, 9 - 12 SAT
Food and Drink Discounters

Factory shop underneath the offices sells all sorts of chocolate items - walnut whips, petit fours, mints, Thomas the Tank Engine chocolates, Christmas chocolate tree decorations - to well-known department stores. Seconds and misshapes are sold in bags for £1; overmakes at half price. Stock varies from week to week.

GLADRAGS
THE BARN, HUNTS FARM, HILLS ROAD, SAHAM TONEY, WATTON, NORFOLK
☎ (01953) 885210. OPEN 10 - 4 TUE - THUR AND SAT.
Dress Agency • *Womenswear Only*

Sells women's new and nearly-new outfits, including ballgowns. Accessories also on sale range from hats and bags to shoes and belts.

JAEGER FACTORY SHOP
1 HANSA ROAD, KING'S LYNN, NORFOLK PE30 4HZ
☎ (01553) 732132. OPEN 9 - 5.30 MON - SAT, 11 - 4 SUN.
Factory Shop • *Womenswear & Menswear*

Contemporary classics from Jaeger at excellent prices. Most of the merchandise is previous seasons' stock, but you might also find some special makes.

LATHAMS
BRIDGE STREET, POTTER HEIGHAM, GREAT YARMOUTH, NORFOLK NR29 5JE
☎ (01692) 670080. OPEN 9 - 5.30 MON - SAT, 10 - 4 SUN.
Factory Shop • *Womenswear & Menswear* • *Children Household* • *Sportswear & Equipment*

Sell a wide range of fashions, hardware, china, fishing tackle, books, gardening equipment, linen, groceries and Christmas gifts at very reasonable prices. Most of the makes are high street labels and consist of discontinued lines and seconds. Also jewellery concessions, shoes, photo developing in-store coffee shop and garden centre.

MARSTON & LANGINGER FACTORY SHOP
GEORGE EDWARDS ROAD, FAKENHAM, NORFOLK NR21 8NL
☎ (01328) 852540. WEBSITE: www.marston-and-langinger.com
OPEN 9 - 1 AND 2 - 5 MON - FRI, 9 - 1 SAT.
Factory Shop • *Furniture/Soft Furnishings*

Marston & Langinger, top quality conservatory manufacturers and designers, with a showroom in London's Ebury Street, operate a factory shop in Norfolk selling former display stock from exhibitions such as the Chelsea Flower Show, as well as ends of ranges and prototypes. Because they offer a complete design service from making conservatories to supplying blinds, floors, lighting, furniture and furnishings, the factory shop section of their mail order warehouse can feature a variety of items: doors, windows and conservatory accessories, hurricane and zinc lanterns, willow furniture, metal dining chairs, brass trombone sprays, terracotta pots, glassware, rugs, interior and exterior lighting, cushions, lampshades. Books and smaller items can be purchased on line.

MATALAN
BLACKFRIARS ROAD, KINGS LYNN, NORFOLK PE30 1RX
☎ (01553) 765696. OPEN 10 - 8 MON - FRI, 9 - 6 SAT, 11 - 5 SUN.
SOUTHTOWN ROAD, GREAT YARMOUTH NR31 OJB
☎ (01493) 444734. OPEN 9 - 8 MON - FRI, 9 - 6, 11 - 5 SUN.
Permanent Discount Outlet • *Womenswear & Menswear Children • Household*
Matalan is a fashion and homewares value retailer giving customers what they claim to be unbeatable value for money with huge savings on a wide range of products including high quality fashionable clothing for men, women and children at up to 50% off high street prices. Matalan is situated out of town and stores are open seven days a week all year round.

MONEY £ACTS
MONEY FACTS HOUSE, 66-70 THORPE ROAD, NORWICH NR1 1BJ
☎ (01603) 476476.
Food and Leisure
Very little in this life comes free and often saving money involves spending some first. This is true in the case of Money £acts, the guide to savings, investment and mortgage rates, guaranteed income bonds, national savings and annuities, which operates an update by fax. Whether you want to find out what the interest rates are on mortgages or where to open your savings account to get the best rates, you simply dial the relevant fax number and wait for the information to appear at your end. Commercial and residential mortgage information is updated daily, as is savings information. Cost is not more than 75p per minute.

MR SHOE'S FACTORY SHOP
YAXHAM ROAD, DEREHAM, NORFOLK NR19 1HD
☎ (01362) 699599. OPEN 9 - 6 MON - SAT, 10.30 - 4.30 SUN.
Permanent Discount Outlet • *Womenswear & Menswear* • *Children*
Shoes for all the family, including well-known brands, at discounted prices.

MRS PICKERING'S DOLLS' CLOTHES
THE PINES, DECOY ROAD, POTTER HEIGHAM, GREAT YARMOUTH, NORFOLK NR29 5LX
☎ (01692) 670407. WEBSITE: www.freespace.virgin.net/dolls.clothes/index.html.
MAIL ORDER.
Permanent Discount Outlet • *Children*
A wide selection of well-made dolls' clothes which are easy to put on and take

off and, especially for smaller children, will help them learn to use various methods of fastening. All the popular dolls are catered for including Tiny Tears, Timmy, Baby Born, Baby Annabell, Katie, Action Man, Sindy, Paul, Barbie, Ken, Skipper, Stacie and Shelly as well as Teddies. Special outfits, such as school uniforms to match the child's, can be made on request. Prices range from 40p for a Barbie-sized skirt to £3 for a wedding dress and £1.25 for a nappy to £2.25 for a Tiny Tears-sized dress. Please send a stamped, self-addressed envelope for a catalogue and mention The Good Deal Directory.

NORWICH CAMPING SPORTS AND LEISURE

54-56 MAGDALEN STREET, NORWICH, NORFOLK NR3 1JE
☎ (01603) 615525. OPEN 9 - 5.45 MON - SAT.

Permanent Discount Outlet • *Sportswear & Equipment* • *Children*

Reductions of up to 50% on skiing jackets, one-pieces and salopettes all year round. This includes brand names such as Berghaus, O'Neill and Quicksilver, in children's sizes too. Also many ends of lines and last year's colours in fleeces, cagoules and waterproofs, as well as some reductions on ski boots and tents.

REAL FACTORY SHOP (CARTWRIGHT & BUTLER)

HEMPSTEAD ROAD INDUSTRIAL ESTATE, HOLT, NORFOLK NR25 6EC
☎ (01263) 711447. FAX ☎ (01263) 711595. WEBSITE: www.realfactoryshop.co.uk
OPEN 9 - 5 MON - SAT, 10 - 4 SUN.

Food and Drink Discounters

Sells overstocks of the full range of famous Cartwright & Butler foods: preserves, pickles, chutneys, marmalades, biscuits, seasonings and spices, as well as over-runs of own-label product. There's a wide range of non-foods including candles, fragrant products, toys, baskets etc. and they specialise in producing unique gift boxes, baskets and hampers containing a combination of goodies.

ROMBAH WALLACE FACTORY SHOP

14-17 IRONSIDE WAY, NORWICH ROAD, HINGHAM, NORFOLK NR9 4LF
☎ (01953) 851106. OPEN 9 - 5 MON - SAT, 10 - 4 SUN.

Factory Shop • *Womenswear & Menswear*

Good selection of shoes for women and men at discounted prices (ladies courts from £19.95 - £65). Sandals, court shoes, smart or casual. Rombah Wallace shoes are on sale at discounts of 30%. Also sells shirts, ties, handbags and jewellery at competitive prices.

ROYS OF WROXHAM LTD
WROXHAM, NORWICH, NORFOLK NR12 8DB
☎ (01603) 782131. OPEN 9 - 5.30 MON, TUE, 9 - 8 WED, THUR, FRI,
9 - 6 SAT, 10.30 - 4.30 SUN.
ROYS VARIETY STORE, 10 YARMOUTH ROAD, NORTH WALSHAM,
NORFOLK NR28 9BW
☎ (01692) 501058. OPEN 9 - 5.30 MON, TUE, 9 - 8 WED,3) 761696.
OPEN 9 - 6 MON - SAT, 10 - 4 SUN.
ROYS VARIETY STORE, YAXHAM ROAD, DEREHAM NR19 1HD
☎ (01362) 690555. OPEN 9 - 8 MON - FRI, 9 - 6 SAT, 11 - 5 SUN.
ROYS VARIETY STORE, GOODALL STREET, THETFORD,
NORFOLK IP24 2DP
☎ (01842) 766161. OPEN 9 - 5.30 MON - SAT, 10 - 4 SUN.
ROYS BOWTHORPE CENTRE, WENDENE, BOWTHORPE,
NORWICH NR5 9HA
☎ (01603) 746622. OPEN 8.30 - 8 MON - THUR, 8.30 - 9 FRI, 8 - 6 SAT,
10 WENDENE, BOWTHORPE, NORWICH NR5 9HA
☎ (01603) 746622. OPEN 8.30 - 8 MON - THUR, 8.30 - 9 FRI, 8 - 6 SAT,
10 - 4 SUN.
Permanent Discount Outlet • *Womenswear & Menswear* • *Children*
Reputed to be the largest village shop in the world, they sell branded household goods at what they call "valued prices". The Save 'N Wear Department deals with the cheaper end of the clothing market for men, women and children. Other departments include DIY, gardening, electrical, housewares and gifts. There is also a pharmacy department that deals with photography, records and toiletries, all at competitive prices, and a large food hall.

SECONDHAND LAND
113-117 MAGDALEN STREET, NORWICH, NORFOLK NR3 1LN
☎ (01603) 611922. OPEN 9 - 6 MON - SAT.
Secondhand shops • *Electrical Equipment*
Sells tvs, videos, computers, hi-fi systems, recording equipment - all of which are, as the name suggests, second-hand. Some are reconditioned, all come with a six or twelve month guarantee. A two-year-old 26-inch standard tv set with remote control and Teletext costs between £125-£175. Also sells household furniture and white goods. For example, reconditioned washing machine with a 3-month guarantee, £100. Free local delivery.

SIZE-UP
5 HIGH STREET, EAST DEREHAM, NORFOLK NR19 1DZ
☎ (01362) 699641. OPEN 9 - 5.30 MON - SAT.
47 MARKET PLACE, SWAFFHAM PE37 7LE
☎ (01760) 725035. OPEN 9 - 5.30 MON - FRI, 8.30 - 5.30 SAT.
19-23 KING STREET, THETFORD IP24 2AN
☎ (01842) 754821. OPEN 9 - 5.30 MON - SAT.

34 MARKET PLACE, GREAT YARMOUTH NR30 1LX
☎ (01493) 332187. OPEN 9 - 5.30 MON - SAT, 10 - 4 SUN.
Permanent Discount Outlet • *Womenswear Only*
Top quality ladies outsize clothing, some of it from Evans, some own-label and some without labels. There are coats, dresses, suits and separates, some scarves and leisure wear. Some items cost less than half price. For example, Evans long pinstripe coat, £25, reduced from £70. All merchandise is new end of lines or last season's stock in good condition. Sizes 16-30.

SPOILS
UNIT LS2, CASTLE MALL, ST JOHN'S WALK, NORWICH,
NORFOLK NR1 3DD
☎ (01603) 762052. OPEN 9 - 5.30 MON - FRI, UNTIL 8 ON THUR,
9 - 6 SAT.
Permanent Discount Outlet • *Household*
General domestic glassware, non-stick bakeware, kitchen gadgets, ceramic oven-to-tableware, textiles, cutting boards, aluminium non-stick cookware, bakeware, plastic kitchenware, plastic storage, woodware, coffee pots/makers, furniture, mirrors and picture frames. Rather than being discounted, all the merchandise is very competitively priced - in fact, the company carry out competitors' checks frequently in order to monitor pricing. With 38 branches, the company is able to buy in bulk and thus negotiate very good prices.

START-RITE
8 HIGH STREET, KING'S LYNN, NORFOLK P30 1BX
☎ (01553) 760786. OPEN 9 - 5.30 MON - SAT.
Factory Shop • *Children* • *Womenswear & Menswear*
The children's shoe experts have a large factory shop selling clearance lines at discounts of one third, and rejects at discounts of 50%. They don't stock the full range - it's a matter of choosing from what's available. Rejects are sold at at least half price; end of sales stock with not quite such a high discount. There are also some senior sizes up to 9. Feet are expertly measured by trained staff.

SUE MEBBREY FABRICS
4 POST OFFICE ROAD, DERSINGHAM, NEAR KING'S LYNN,
NORFOLK PE31 6HP
☎ (01485) 541111. OPEN 9 - 5 TUE - SAT.
Permanent Discount Outlet • *Furniture/Soft Furnishings*
Sells curtain and upholstery fabrics, with a good selection of top brands, at discount prices. There is a full making-up service for curtains, blinds, valances, cushions and loose covers. Names include Advanced, Crowsons, Blendworth, A & R Swaffer, Warwick, Harlequin and Fibre Naturelle. The most expensive fabric in this shop costs £19.95 a metre.

THE FACTORY SHOE SHOP
ESDELL WORKS, DRAYTON ROAD, NORWICH, NORFOLK NR3 2DB
☎ (01603) 493185. OPEN 10 - 4 MON - SAT.
Permanent Discount Outlet • *Womenswear & Menswear*
Slight seconds and clearance lines of Van-Dal and Holmes shoes for men and women, as well as other makes. Typical discounts include shoes which would normally cost £55 reduced to £32.50. Large free car park.

THE FACTORY SHOP LTD
NORWICH STREET, EAST DEREHAM, NORFOLK NR19 1AD
☎ (01362) 691868. OPEN 9 - 5.30 MON - SAT, 10 - 4 SUN.
52 LONDON ROAD, HARLESTON, NORFOLK IP20 9BZ
☎ (01379) 854860. OPEN 9 - 5.30 MON - SAT, 10.30 - 4 SUN.
LYNN ROAD, SNETTISHAM, NORFOLK PE31 7QG
☎ (01485) 544441. OPEN 9 - 5.30 MON - SAT, 10 - 4 SUN.
Factory Shop • *Household* • *Womenswear & Menswear* • *Children Furniture/Soft Furnishings* • *Sportswear & Equipment*
Wide range on sale includes men's, ladies and children's clothing and footwear; household textiles; toiletries; hardware; luggage; lighting and bedding, most of which are chainstore and high street brands at discounts of approximately 30%-50%. There are kitchen and furniture displays and on sale is the Cape Country Furniture range with free-standing kitchens, as well as living, bedroom and dining furniture. There are weekly deliveries and brands include many major stars such as Adidas, Nike, Joe Bloggs and Brabantia, to name just a few. Lines are continually changing and few factory shops offer such a variety under one roof.

TONY HODGSON & PARTNERS
THE FORGE, 2 WESLEY ROAD, TERRINGTON ST CLEMENT,
NR KING'S LYNN, NORFOLK PE34 4NG
☎ (01553) 828637. OPEN 8 - 5 MON - FRI,
WEEKENDS BY APPOINTMENT.
Architectural Salvage • *DIY/Renovation*
Hand-forged wrought iron work, including restoration. Anything from fenders and fire irons to finials and gates.

Northamptonshire

AQUASCUTUM
PRINCEWOOD ROAD, EARLSTREE INDUSTRIAL ESTATE, CORBY,
NORTHAMPTONSHIRE NN17 4XD
☎ (01536) 205086. OPEN 10 - 5.30 MON - FRI, 10 - 4 SAT.
Factory Shop • *Womenswear & Menswear*
Previous season's stock and seconds for women and men at greatly reduced prices. For men, blazers, suits and silk ties. Examples include 20% off men's raincoats and half-price ladies silk blouses.

ARCHITECTURAL HERITAGE
HEART OF THE SHIRES, A5, NR WEEDON,
NORTHAMPTONSHIRE NN7 4LB
☎ (01327) 349249. OPEN 10 - 5 TUE - FRI.
Architectural Salvage • *DIY/Renovation*
Situated in converted farm buildings and dealing in architectural antiques, particularly Victorian shop fittings, church interiors and large gates. There is a tea room and gift shop on site, and a shop selling cookware. On A5, two miles north of Weedon.

BARKER SHOES LTD
STATION ROAD, EARLS BARTON, NORTHAMPTON,
NORTHAMPTONSHIRE NN6 0NT
☎ (01604) 810387. WEBSITE: www.barker-shoes.co.uk
OPEN 10 - 5 MON - FRI, 10 - 4 SAT.
Factory Shop • *Womenswear & Menswear*
Discontinued lines of shoes at about 30% off the retail price, and rejects at 40% off the normal retail price. Sells shoes manufactured by its own factory which include brogues, smart day shoes for men and women, but no trainers. There are men's high grade, traditional shoes which sell to top stores, casual shoes and moccasins.

BARRATT'S SALE SHOP
BARRACK ROAD, KINGSTHORPE HOLLOW, NORTHAMPTON,
NORTHAMPTONSHIRE NN2 6EL
☎ (01604) 718632. OPEN 9 - 5.30 MON - SAT.
Factory Shop • *Womenswear & Menswear* • *Children*
Reject trainers and ex-window display shoes for men, women and children at factory prices among a range of perfect shoes, the latter of which are sold at sale prices. Discounts of up to at least 50% compared to normal retail prices.

BATHCRAFT
4A HAVELOCK STREET, KETTERING, NORTHAMPTONSHIRE NN16 9PZ
☎ (01536) 417009. WEBSITE: www.antiquebaths.co.uk
OPEN 9.30 - 5.30 WED - SAT.
Architectural Salvage • *DIY/Renovation*
Old fashioned rolltop baths, taps, bath fittings, reproduction showers, re-enamelling.

BELLE OF THE BALL
42 LONDON ROAD, KETTERING, NORTHAMPTONSHIRE NN15 7QA
☎ (01536) 484949. OPEN 10 - 4 TUE - SAT.
Dress Agency • *Womenswear Only*
Sells both new and secondhand clothes for women, as well as wedding dresses and hats. High street names as well as some designer labels: wedding dresses include Ronald Joyce, Hilary Morgan and Dante, with head-dresses, veils and shoes.

BIG L FACTORY OUTLET
34 COMMERCIAL STREET, NORTHAMPTON,
NORTHAMPTONSHIRE NN1 1PJ
☎ (01604) 603022. OPEN 10 - 8 MON - THUR, 9 - 6 SAT.
Factory Shop • *Womenswear & Menswear*
This store retails a large range of Levi jeans, shirts, jackets, sweatshirts and t-shirts, all at discounted prices and a large selection of ladieswear. Most of the stock is seconds or end-of-line.

ELEGANZ
66 BIRCHFIELD ROAD, CORNER OF COLLINGWOOD ROAD,
NORTHAMPTON, NORTHAMPTONSHIRE
☎ (01604) 712820. OPEN 9.30 - 5.30 MON - SAT.
Factory Shop • *Womenswear Only*
Ladies designer shoes and boots at great reduced prices, plus the Shoe Boutique, showing high quality, latest fashion German footwear.

FINEDON DRESS AGENCY
23 HIGH STREET, FINEDON, (OFF A14 JCT 10 TO A6),
NORTHAMPTONSHIRE NN9 5JN
☎ (01933) 680080. FAX (01933) 680714. OPEN 9.30 - 5 TUE - FRI,
9.30 - 4.30 SAT. CLOSED MON.
Dress Agency • *Womenswear Only*
Pretty shop which specialises in good quality bridal wear and brides mothers outfits, hats, smart guest wear and evening wear in sizes 8-24. Wedding dress designers include Ronald Joyce, Margaret Lee, Benjamin Roberts, Hilary Morgan, Sally Bee, Brides of Paradise and Angelo Dreammaker in sizes 8-30. Prices range form £75-£800. Also veils, headdresses, flowers and shoes, all beautifully presented and an enormous range of hats from £25-£150. Other outfits include designers such as Coterie, Basler and Condici up to size 24 and priced from £55. There are lots of samples at good prices and lots of larger sizes. Friendly service in air conditioned comfort and easy parking.

JANE'S DESIGNER EVENING WEAR
69 ST LEONARD'S ROAD, NORTHAMPTON,
NORTHAMPTONSHIRE NN4 8DL
☎ (01604) 705256. OPEN 11 - 2 MON - SAT OR BY APPOINTMENT.
Permanent Discount Outlet • *Hire Shop*
Hire or buy evening wear from names such as House of Nicholas, Roots, Cinderella and Consortium at a cost of £40-£55 for up to six days. There are usually rails of ex-hire for sale at bargain prices as well as brand-new merchandise at competitive prices.

LITTLESTONE & GOODWIN
VICTORIA STREET, DESBOROUGH, NORTHAMPTONSHIRE NN14 2LX
☎ (01536) 760084. OPEN 1.30 - 5 FRI, 9 - 1 SAT.
Permanent Discount Outlet • *Womenswear Only*
First class ladies handbags, accessories and a large range of evening bags at very reasonable prices.

MATALAN
UNIT 1, WEEDON ROAD INDUSTRIAL ESTATE, TYNE ROAD,
NORTHAMPTON, NORTHAMPTONSHIRE NN5 5BE
☎ (01604) 589119. OPEN 9 - 8 MON - FRI, 9 - 6 SAT, 11 - 5 SUN.
UNIT 1, PHOENIX RETAIL PARK, PHEONIX PARKWAY, CORBY,
NORTHAMPTONSHIRE NN17 5DT
☎ (01536) 408042. OPEN 9 - 8 MON - FRI, 9 - 6 SAT, 10 - 4 SUN.
Permanent Discount Outlet • *Womenswear & Menswear*
Children • *Household*
Matalan is a fashion and homewares value retailer giving customers what they claim to be unbeatable value for money with huge savings on a wide range of products including high quality fashionable clothing for men, women and children at up to 50% off high street prices. Matalan is situated out of town and stores are open seven days a week all year round.

NORTHAMPTON FOOTWEAR DISTRIBUTORS LTD
SUMMERHOUSE ROAD, MOULTON PARK,
NORTHAMPTONSHIRE NN3 1WD
☎ (01604) 790 827. OPEN 9 - 12 AND 2 - 4 MON - FRI FOR PHONE
ENQUIRIES. MAIL ORDER.
Permanent Discount Outlet • *Womenswear & Menswear*
Direct mail clearance brochures featuring a wide range of footwear at incredible prices. There is no minimum order, although there is p & p for orders under £200. Size ranges are limited, but not overly so. If they don't fit you get your money refunded if returned within 10 days. Spring, Summer and Autumn catalogues are available.

OCCASIONS
9A HIGH STREET, HIGHAM FERRERS,
NORTHAMPTONSHIRE NN10 8BW
☎ (01933) 314970. OPEN 10 - 2 TUE, 10 - 4 WED - SAT.
Dress Agency • *Womenswear Only*
Small, friendly shop selling names from BhS and Marks & Spencer to Betty Barclay, Givenchy and Jacques Vert. Good selection of bridal wear and mother of the bride outfits, as well as evening wear. Seamstress service available. Also hire out hats and a large range of jewellery.

ORCHIDS
3 PARK STREET, TOWCESTER, NORTHAMPTONSHIRE NH12 6DQ
☎ (01327) 358455. OPEN 9.30 - 5 MON - SAT.
Dress Agency • *Womenswear* • *Children*
Sells women's and children's new and as-new clothes. The ladies wear includes a range of good quality accessories: belts, tights and stockings, socks, scarves, costume jewellery and hair accessories. Labels sold include Marks & Spencer, Jaeger, Betty Barclay, Mondi and Alexon. Nothing is more than two years old and sizes range from 8-20. Occasionally, there are free open sessions with a colour consultant who will help to co-ordinate your wardrobe. The children's range is from birth to twelve years, with more girl's outfits than boy's, and includes snowsuits and coats, with labels from Marks & Spencer, Mothercare and Gap to Osh Kosh and Oilily.

REGENT BELT COMPANY
UNIT B, LEO HOUSE, ROSS ROAD, WEEDON ROAD INDUSTRIAL
ESTATE, NORTHAMPTON, NORTHAMPTONSHIRE NN5 5AX
☎ (01604) 684708. OPEN 9.30 - 4 WED - FRI.
Factory Shop • *Womenswear & Menswear*
Leather belts, bags, luggage, hip flasks, wallets, purses, key fobs, ties and braces all at substantially reduced prices. Bi-annual clearance sales offer even better value with leather belts from £5. Weedon Road Industrial Estate is approximately one mile west of Northampton centre. From the town centre aim for the A45 to Coventry, follow signs to M1 North, pass the Saints Rugby Football ground on the left and go left into Ross Road. From the M1 get off at junction 16 and follow the A45 towards Northampton. After the fourth roundabout take a right hand turn into Ross Road and the RBC is a quarter of a mile along this road on the right hand side.

RIGBY & PELLER & FANTASIE FACTORY SHOP
ROTHWELL ROAD, DESBOROUGH, NORTHAMPTONSHIRE NN1 42PG
☎ (01536) 761252. OPEN 10 - 4 TUE - FRI, 9 - 1 SAT.
Factory Shop • *Womenswear Only*
Range of Fantasie swimwear and Rigby & Peller underwear including bras, pants, thongs, suspender belts at discounted prices. Specialises in larger cup

sizes up to J cup fitting. For example Fantasie swimsuit, £15.99, usually £55; matching pareo, £15.99, usually £50. Some of the stock is made up of seconds but most is perfect, redundant stock.

ROBERTS FACTORY OUTLET SHOP
114 PRINCES STREET, KETTERING, NORTHAMPTONSHIRE
☎ (01536) 513769. OPEN 12.30 - 4.30 TUES - FRI, 10 - 4.30 SAT.

Permanent Discount Outlet • *Womenswear Only*

Men's suits for all occasions: dinner suits, morning suits, loung suits and blazers. Made to measure and alterations also available.

SHOWHOME WAREHOUSE
11-17 FRANCIS COURT, WELLINGBOROUGH ROAD, RUSHDEN, NORTHAMPTONSHIRE NN10 6AY
☎ (01933) 411695. OPEN 10 - 5 TUE - SUN, 11 - 3 MON.

Permanent Discount Outlet • *Furniture/Soft Furnishings*
Household • *Electrical Equipment* • *DIY/Renovation*

Weekly warehouse clearance of the contents of quality show homes by warehouse clearance. The contents of the show houses are sold seven days a week at this 20,000 ft warehouse. There is normally an average of between 50%-70% savings on the prices seen in the stores. About 50% of their stock is sold each week and different stock arrives daily. Choose from a range of kitchen appliances, lounge furniture, three-piece suites, dining tables and chairs, rugs, study and bedroom furniture, oil paintings, mirrors, ornaments, TVs and videos, patio and garden furniture and gym equipment. The range is eclectic: from suits of armour to lion's heads, Tiffany lampshades to leather zebras, handpainted furniture to mahogany classics, alien-shaped CD racks to antique carts made into bookcases or sets of oars turned into coat racks. Prices exclude VAT but still represent very good value for money. For example, elaborate metal bed, £175, normally £750; dining room table and chairs, £350, normally £1,500; washer-dryer, £300, usually £500-600. Occasional auctions take place during the year, phone for details.

SIZE-UP
57 HIGH STREET, RUSHDEN, NORTHAMPTONSHIRE NN10 0QE
☎ (01933) 411990. OPEN 9 - 5.30 MON - SAT, 10 - 4 SUN.
8 THE MALL, NEWLANDS CENTRE, KETTERING NN16 8JL
☎ (01536) 412770. OPEN 9 - 5.30 MON - FRI, 8.30 - 5.30 SAT.

Permanent Discount Outlet • *Womenswear Only*

Top quality ladies outsize clothing, some of it from Evans, some own-label and some without labels. There are coats, dresses, suits and separates, some scarves and leisure wear. Some items cost less than half price. For example, Evans long pinstripe coat, £25, reduced from £70. All merchandise is new end of lines or last season's stock in good condition. Sizes 16-30.

STUART BUGLASS INTERIOR DESIGN IRONWORK
THE BUGLASS METALWORK GALLERY, CLIFFORD MILL HOUSE, LITTLE HOUGHTON, NORTHAMPTONSHIRE NN7 1AL
☎ (01604) 890366. OPEN 10 - 5 MON - SAT, 11 - 4 SUN.
26, REGENT STREET, LEAMINGTON SPA, WARWICKSHIRE CV 32 5EH
☎ (01926) 426900. OPEN 10 - 5 TUES - SAT.
Factory Shop • *Furniture/Soft Furnishings* • *Household*
Hand-crafted interior design wrought-iron work from candleholders, wine racks, electric lighting (including wall sconces and chandeliers) to curtain poles, and furniture including beds, tables, chairs and shelving, are all on sale in this converted barn at direct-to-the-public prices. The showroom was extended in 1998 and is now twice the size. There is now a high street outlet in Leamington Spa.

T GROOCOCK & CO LTD
GORDON STREET, ROTHWELL, NORTHAMPTONSHIRE NN14 6BJ
☎ (01536) 714115. OPEN 10 - 5 MON - FRI, 9 - 1 SAT.
Factory Shop • *Womenswear & Menswear*
New 3000 sq ft shop selling high quality men's and women's leather shoes including padders youth shoes in sizes11 - 5 . Comfortable, stylish leisure walking shoes: women's sizes 3-9, men's sizes 6-14. Easy access for wheelchairs. Credit cards accepted.

TANDEE NURSERIES
BARNWELL ROAD, THURNING, NEAR OUNDLE, NORTHAMPTONSHIRE PE8 5RJ
☎ (01832) 293755. OPEN 9 - 5 SEVEN DAYS A WEEK.
Factory Shop • *Food and Leisure*
A grower of quality nursery stock, sells direct to the public at trade prices. You can buy shrubs, conifers, trees, perennials, bedding plants, climbers, hedging and fruit trees at this large centre. Climbers which normally cost £7 are £3.95 here; trees which cost £35 are £15.95 while conifers are 4 for £10 and shrubs cost from £2.95 to £8.95.

THE DOC SHOP
RUSHDEN & DIAMONDS FOOTBALL CLUB, NENE PARK, DIAMOND WAY, IRTHLINGBOROUGH, NORTHAMPTONSHIRE NN9 5QF
☎ (01933) 652000. OPEN 9 - 5.30 MON - FRI, 9 - 5 SAT, 10 - 4 SUN.
71 HIGH STREET, WOLLASTON, NORTHAMPTONSHIRE
☎ (01933) 666144. OPEN 9 - 5.30 MON - FRI, 9 - 5 SAT, 11 - 4 SUN.
Permanent Discount Outlet • *Womenswear & Menswear* • *Children*
Sells Doc Martens shoes and boots, as well as clothing and a vast range of accessories at discounted prices. Nene Park is the only official outlet for Rushden and Diamonds' merchandise.

UNITED FOOTWEAR

75-79 STAMFORD ROAD, KETTERING, NORTHAMPTONSHIRE
☎ (01536) 481855. OPEN 9 - 5.30 MON - SAT, 10 - 4 SUN.
Permanent Discount Outlet • *Womenswear & Menswear*
Children • *Sportswear & Equipment*

Shoes for all the family as well as clothes, handbags, sports shoes, boots, giftware and household goods, all at discounted prices. Famous brands including Clarks, K Shoes and Elmdale. Part of a national chain.

Northumberland

ASHINGTON BEDDING CENTRE

UNIT 10A, NORTH SEATON INDUSTRIAL ESTATE, ASHINGTON, NORTHUMBERLAND NE63 OYB
☎ (01670) 852522. OPEN 9.30 - 5.30 MON - FRI, 9.30 - 5.15 SAT, 11 - 3 SUN.
Permanent Discount Outlet • *Furniture/Soft Furnishings*

Sells a wide variety of beds from the bottom end of the market to the pocket sprung top end, ranging in price from £75 to £750. Prices have the edge over the same beds sold elsewhere, with one bed costing £499 here on sale for £799 in a local department store. Brands sold here include Millbrook, fSilent Night, Rest Assured and Airsprung.

ATTICA

2 OLD GEORGE YARD, BIGG MARKET, NEWCASTLE-UPON-TYNE, NORTHUMBERLAND NE1 1EZ
☎ (0191) 261 4062. OPEN 10.30 - 5.30 MON - SAT.
Secondhand and Vintage Clothes • *Womenswear & Menswear*

Two floors of vintage clothes from Twenties to Seventies with most of the stock coming from the Sixties and Seventies. Blouses, lots of suede, Sixties mini-skirts and dresses, jewellery, hats and shoes as well as men's formalwear including dinner suits. Also large range of Fifties to Seventies furnishings, lamps and decor.

BARGAIN BAGGAGE FACTORY SHOP

BUGATTI HOUSE, NORHAM ROAD, NORTH SHIELDS NE2 7HA
☎ (0191) 258 4451. OPEN 10 - 2 TUES, 10 - 3 WED, THUR, FRI.
Factory Shop • *Food and Leisure*

Leather goods from Pierre Cardin, Gina Ferrari, Cardin Weekender and Executive Essentials at discounts of up to 50%. Suitcases, weekend bags, handbags, wallets, purses, briefcases, attache cases, suiters. Situated next door to Welch's sweet factory.

BIRTHDAYS
ROYAL QUAYS OUTLET VILLAGE, HAYHOLD ROAD, NORTH SHIELDS, NORTHUMBERLAND NE29 6DW
☎ (0191) 2574767. OPEN 10 - 6 MON - SAT, 11 - 5 SUN.
Factory Shop in a Factory Shopping Village • *Household*
Cards, notelets, stationery sets, colouring books, soft toys, photo albums, picture frames, gifts, giftwrap, tissue paper, party packs, Christmas crackers, string puppets, fairy lights all at discounts of up to 30%. Some are special purchases, some seconds.

BURBERRY
KITTY BREWSTER INDUSTRIAL ESTATE, BLYTH, NORTHUMBERLAND NE24 4RG
☎ (01670) 352524. OPEN 10 - 4 MON, 9.30 - 4 TUE - FRI, 8.45 - 3.30 SAT.
Factory Shop • *Womenswear & Menswear* • *Children*
This Burberry factory shop sells seconds and overmakes of the famous name raincoats and duffle coats as well as accessories such as the distinctive umbrellas, scarves and handbags. It also sells childrens duffle coats, knitwear and shirts, as well as some of the Burberry range of food: jams, biscuits, tea, coffee and chocolate. All carry the Burberry label and discounts are about one third off the normal retail price.

CATALOGUE BARGAIN SHOP
51 SHIELDS ROAD, BYKER, NEWCASTLE-UPON-TYNE NE6 1DJ
☎ (0191) 265 6033. OPEN 9 - 5 MON - SAT, 10.30 - 4.30 SUN.
Permanent Discount Outlet • *Womenswear & Menswear*
Children • *Household* • *Electrical Equipment*
Catalogue Bargain Shop is a growing national chain of stores which obtains the majority of its goods from mail order giants Great Universal and Kays, and offers a range of clothing for all the family, a wide selection of shoes, bed linen, household goods, electrical equipment and hundreds of other catalogue items at very competitive prices. The merchandise consists of ends of ranges and previous season's stock for which there is no longer storage space when the catalogues change.

CHINA TIME
FENWICK STEAD, BELFORD, NORTHUMBERLAND NE70 7PL
☎ (01289) 381363.
Specialises in fine bone china as individual pieces or complete antique tea and coffee sets.

CRAMLINGTON TEXTILES
NELSON WAY, NORTH NELSON INDUSTRIAL ESTATE, CRAMLINGTON, NORTHUMBERLAND NE23 9JT
- (01670) 713434. OPEN 10 - 5 MON - FRI, 9.30 - 5 SAT.

Factory Shop • *Household*

Perfects and seconds in bedlinen, curtains, bath sets, bedspreads, duvets and pillows including polycotton flat sheets, curtain tie backs and pelmets, valances and throwover bedspreads.

CURTAIN FABRICS FACTORY SHOP
36 GRASSMER WAY, KITTY BREWSTER INDUSTRIAL ESTATE, BLYTH, NORTHUMBERLAND NE24 4RR
- (01670) 540240. OPEN 10 - 3 MON - SAT.

Permanent Discount Outlet • *Furniture/Soft Furnishings*

Low prices on curtains, fabrics, made-to-measure curtains or ready-made curtains. Lots of fabrics on the roll or you can order through books, though this is not as god value as buying from the rolls.

DEWHIRST IMPRESSIONS
PENNYWELL INDUSTRIAL ESTATE, PENNYWELL, SUNDERLAND, NORTHUMBERLAND SR4 9EN
- (0191) 534 7928. OPEN 9 - 6 MON - SAT, 11 - 5 SUN.

NORTH SEATON INDUSTRIAL ESTATE, OFF NEWBIGGIN ROAD, ASHINGTON, NORTHUMBERLAND NE63 OYB
- (01670) 813493. OPEN 10 - 8 MON - FRI, 9 - 6 SAT, 10.30 - 4.30 SUN.

Factory Shop • *Children* • *Womenswear & Menswearear*

Dewhirst Impressions sell garments from the manufacturing side of the business direct to the public and are part of the Dewhirst Group plc which manufactures ladies, men's and childrenswear for a leading high street retailer. You can choose from a huge selection of surplus production and slight seconds at bargain prices, making savings of more than 50% of the normal retail cost. For men there is a wide range of suits, formal shirts and casual wear. For example, suits from £60, formal and casual shirts from £7. For ladies there's a selection of blouses, smart tailoring and casual wear that includes a denim range. You can find ladies jackets from £50, skirts, trousers and blouses from £8. Children's clothes start at £3. High street quality and style at wholesale prices.

DISCOUNT CLOTHING STORE
19 KINGSTON PARK CENTRE, KINGSTON PARK, NORTHUMBERLAND NE3 2FP
- (0191) 271 4126. OPEN 9.30 - 5.30 MON - SAT.

Permanent Discount Outlet • *Womenswear & Menswear* • *Children*

Seconds and overstock in ladies, men's and childrenswear from Next and other well-known high street names. A good selection of jackets, skirts, trousers, dresses and tops for ladies with a small selection of men's trousers, jackets, shirt and ties. There are a few rails of childrenswear. All are at half price or less.

DISCOUNT CLOTHING STORE
UNIT 1, MORPETH ROAD, ASHINGTON,
NORTHUMBERLAND NE53 8PX
☎ (01670) 858300. OPEN 9.30 - 5.30 MON - SAT.
Permanent Discount Outlet • *Household*
Womenswear & Menswear • *Children*
Wide range of clothes for all the family and some bedlinen and towels, most of which is from high street stores.

ERRINGTON REAY POTTERY,
TYNESIDE POTTERY WORKS, HEXHAM,
NORTHUMBERLAND NE47 7HU
☎ (01434) 344245. OPEN 9 - 5 MON - FRI, 10 - 4.30 SAT, SUN.
Factory Shop • *Household*
Large, salt-glazed garden and domestic clay pots in all sizes from £7.50. Lots of storage pot seconds available from this supplier to garden centres from £6 to £45.

FACTORY SHOP CENTRE
CHAINBRIDGE INDUSTRIAL ESTATE, BLAYDON,
NORTHUMBERLAND NE21 5SJ
UNIT 23 & 24 FACTORY FABRIC CENTRE
☎ (0191) 414 4515. OPEN 10 - 5 MON - FRI, 7 ON THUR, 9 - 5 SAT, 10 - 4 SUN.
UNIT 5 CUT PRICE WALLPAPER
☎ (0191) 414 6716. OPEN 9.30 - 5 MON - SAT, 7 ON THUR, 10 - 4 SUN.
UNIT 2 MCINTOSH FACTORY BEDDING SHOP
☎ (0191) 414 8969. OPEN 10 - 5 MON - FRI, 7 ON THUR, 9 - 5 SAT, 10 - 4 SUN.
FACTORY BEDS
☎ (0191) 414 6331. OPEN 9 - 5 MON - SAT 7 ON THUR, 10 - 4 SUN.
FACTORY CARPETS
☎ (0191) 414 5887. OPEN 9 - 5 MON - FRI, 7 ON THUR, 10 - 4 SUN.
Permanent Discount Outlet • *Furniture/Soft Furnishings*
Large industrial estate on which a variety of discount shops operate selling everything from brand-name wallpaper and paint, fire surrounds, gas fires and back boilers, curtains, bedding, towels, upholstery fabrics and textiles to Axminster and Wilton carpets, Rest Assured and Silent Night beds.

GLADRAGS
51 BONDGATE WITHIN, ALNWICK, NORTHUMBERLAND NE66 1HZ
☎ (01665) 602396. OPEN 10 - 4 MON - SAT, CLOSED WED.
Dress Agency • *Womenswear Only*
High quality nearly-new ladies clothing with labels such as Alexon, Planet and Donna Karan.

J BARBOUR & SONS LTD
CUSTOMER SERVICE DEPARTMENT, MONKSWAY, JARROW,
NORTHUMBERLAND NE32 3HQ
☎ (0191) 428 4707. OPEN 10 - 5 MON - THUR, 10 - 4 FRI, 10 - 2 SAT.
Factory Shop • *Womenswear & Menswear* • *Children*

The famous waterproof waxed jackets and outdoor wear, all of which are seconds or discontinued lines, at discounts of 20%-25%. Jackets come in fifteen different styles from short to full-length and in various colours, but you may not find the style, colour and size you want as quantities vary. There are also shooting jackets, tweed hats and caps, linings for coats, bags, waxed trousers, waders and some children's waxed jackets, breathable jackets for men and women, fleeces, knitwear and quilted jackets. There is also a new range of Barbour shoes and a small selection of children's jackets. Free parking.

JAMES BARRY MENSWEAR
ROYAL QUAYS, NORTH SHIELDS, NEWCASTLE-UPON-TYNE,
NORTHUMBERLAND NE29 6DW
☎ (0191) 296 4821. OPEN 10 - 6 MON - SAT, 11 - 5 SUN.
Factory Shop in a Factory Shopping Village • *Menswear Only*

James Barry sells branded menswear including Double Two casual shirts, two for £20; James Barry shirts, £11.95, or two for £20; 100% cotton Savile Row shirts reduced to £20 each or two for £30; Lancers trousers, £34.95, or two for £60; jackets from £69.95; belts from £7.95 to £15.95; single breasted suits from £99; dinner suits, £139.

JAMES SHOES
369 WEST ROAD, NEWCASTLE-UPON-TYNE,
NORTHUMBERLAND NE15 7NL
☎ (0191) 274 3690. OPEN 9 - 5 MON - SAT.
Permanent Discount Outlet • *Womenswear & Menswear*

Discontinued perfects and seconds footwear, most of which is either Italian or Spanish makes. All the ladies shoes are perfects, the men's Loake shoes are slight seconds and cost between £40 and £50 for shoes that would normally cost £75.

JANE SHILTON
ROYAL QUAYS, NORTH SHIELDS, NEAR A19, NORTH SHIELDS
NORTHUMBERLAND NE29 6DW
☎ (0191) 257 3672. OPEN 10 - 6 MON - SAT, 11 - 5 SUN.
Factory Shop in a Factory Shopping Village • *Womenswear Only*

Merchandise from past seasons' collections or factory seconds at discounts of at least 30% and up to 70% off the original price. There is a wide range of handbags, small leather goods, shoes, luggage umbrellas and travel bags. Example of price reduction: handbags at £24.99 originally £37.

JOHN ELIOT FOOTWEAR,
53 BONDGATE WITHIN, ALNWICK, NORTHUMBERLAND
☎ (01665) 602286. OPEN 9 - 5.30 MON - SAT.
Permanent Discount Outlet • *Womenswear & Menswear*
Shoe shop with cut-price shoes upstairs from the likes of Clarks, Laoke, Elmdale and Rohde. Children's shoes, Wellingtons and trainers stocked.

KARRIMOR
8 - 10 FENKLE STREET, ALNWICK, NORTHUMBERLAND NE66 1HR
☎ (01665) 510753. OPEN 9.30 - 5 MON - SAT, 10 - 4 SUN.
Factory Shop • *Sportswear & Equipment*
Best known for their comprehensive range of rucksacks, Karrimor also make an outstanding range of outdoor equipment for walkers, climbers and campers including rucksacks waterproofs, walking boots and fleeces. The factory shop sells seconds, former display items, samples and clearance stock at discounts of between 15% and 25% and always stocks the current range for the season.

LUGGAGE & BAGS
ROYAL QUAY OUTLET VILLAGE, 5 COBLE DEAN, NORTH SHIELDS, NORTHUMBERLAND NE29 6DW
☎ (0191) 257 4458. OPEN 10 - 6 MON - SAT, 11 - 5 SUN.
Factory Shop in a Factory Shopping Village • *Food and Leisure*
Luggage and travel-related products and executive cases, handbags, umbrellas from leading brands such as Samsonite, Desley, Head, Taurus and GlobeTrotter. Each product is offered at a substantially reduced price compared to those found on the high street due to being production over-runs, discontinued ranges or colours and last season's products. Discounts range from 30%-75% off high street prices.

MARGARET WILLIAMS DRESS AGENCY
21 EAST STREET, WHITBURN, TYNE & WEAR,
NORTHUMBERLAND SR6 7BY
☎ (0191) 529 2247 OPEN 10 - 5 MON - SAT.
Dress Agency • *Womenswear Only*
Large shop selling mainly designer labels, varying from Frank Usher, Jean Muir and Mondi to the occasional selection of Marks & Spencer, Laura Ashley and Next. Stocks both day wear and special occasion outfits, including hats, costume jewellery and shoes. Also holds seasonal stock such as shorts and T-shirts, as well as antiques, prints, paintings, porcelain and a large selection of reproduction furniture.

MATALAN
CAMERON PARK, METRO CENTRE, GATESHEAD,
NEWCASTLE-UPON-TYNE, NORTHUMBERLAND NE11 9XU
☎ (0191) 461 0880. OPEN 10 - 8 MON - FRI, 9 - 6 SAT, 11 - 5 SUN.

BELVEDERE RETAIL PARK, BRUNTON LANE,
NEWCASTLE UPON TYNE NE3 2PA
☎ (0191) 214 0352. OPEN 10 - 8 MON - FRI, 9 - 6 SAT, 11 - 5 SUN.
Permanent Discount Outlet • *Womenswear & Menswear*
Children • *Household*
Matalan is a fashion and homewares value retailer giving customers what they claim to be unbeatable value for money with huge savings on a wide range of products including high quality fashionable clothing for men, women and children at up to 50% off high street prices. Matalan is situated out of town and stores are open seven days a week all year round.

MEXX INTERNATIONAL
ROYAL QUAYS FACTORY OUTLET CENTRE, NORTH SHIELDS,
NEWCASTLE-UPON-TYNE, NEAR A19, TYNE & WEAR,
NORTHUMBERLAND
☎ (0191) 257 5001. OPEN 10 - 6 MON - SAT, 11 - 5 SUN.
Factory Shop in a Factory Shopping Village
Womenswear & Menswear • *Children*
High street fashion at factory outlet prices for men, women, babies and kids, all of which are heavily discounted by more than 30%.

OMEGA OUTDOOR FACTORY SHOP
COQUET ENTERPRISE PARK, AMBLE, MORPETH,
NORTHUMBERLAND NE65 OPE
☎ (01665) 710080. OPEN 10 - 5 MON - SAT.
Factory Shop • *Sportswear & Equipment*
High-performance outdoor clothing, including samples and ends of runs, as well as ski wear and lightweight tents, at value-for-money factory prices. Omega was the manufacturer of clothing for the officials of the 1999/2000 Tour de France and also produced garments for the James Bond film, The World Is Not Enough.

PENNY PLAIN
10 MARLBOROUGH CRESCENT, NEWCASTLE UPON TYNE,
TYNE & WEAR, NORTHUMBERLAND NE1 4EE
☎ (0191) 232 1124. OPEN 10 - 4 FRI, SAT.
ROYAL QUAYS FACTORY OUTLET, ADDRESS AND OPENING HOURS AS BEFORE.
☎ (0191) 258 1954.
Permanent Discount Outlet
Factory Shop in a Factory Shopping Village • *Womenswear Only*
Overstocks and ends of lines from Penny Plain mail order collections; also designer samples and slight seconds. High quality, well made clothes. Superb savings on original prices. Ladies separates and knitwear in smart and casual, summer and winter styles. Garments are made in colourful, luxurious fabrics, especially natural fibres: pure cotton, linen, silk, wool, velvet and cupro. Sizes 8 - 22.

PONDEN MILL LINENS
ROYAL QUAYS FACTORY OUTLET, ADDRESS AND OPENING HOURS AS BEFORE.
☎ (0191) 257 4607.
Factory Shop in a Factory Shopping Village • *Household*
Famous branded products at direct from the mill prices. A fabulous assortment of towels, duvets, pillows, throws, bedspreads, up-to-the-minute coordinated bed linen, from Crown, Coloroll, Jeff Banks Ports-of-Call, to name but a few. Something for every room in the house.

REMINGTON
ROYAL QUAYS FACTORY OUTLET, ADDRESS AND OPENING HOURS AS BEFORE.
☎ (0191) 258 3622.
Factory Shop in a Factory Shopping Village • *Electrical Equipment*
Lots of famous names at this outlet in the Royal Quays factory outlet village from Monogram cutlery to Braun, Philips, Remington, Wahl, Prima and Morphy Richards, small kitchen equipment and grooming tools for men and women.

ROYAL QUAYS FACTORY OUTLET CENTRE
COBLE DENE, NORTH SHIELDS, NEWCASTLE-UPON-TYNE, NEAR A19, NORTH SHIELDS NORTHUMBERLAND NE29 6DW
☎ (0191) 296 3743. E-MAIL: Outletcentres@mepc.co.uk
WEBSITE: www.royalquaysoutletcentre.co.uk
OPEN 10 - 6 MON - SAT, 11 - 5 SUN.
Factory Shopping Village • *Womenswear & Menswear* • *Children Household* • *Sportswear & Equipment* • *Electrical Equipment*
Forty-two shops with leisure facilities nearby including a full-scale steam railway, working harbour, Roman Ruins and the usual seaside attractions. Adjacent to the Wet and Wild water park which has 350,000 visitors a year and next door to an international ferry terminal, the village has a nautical feel to it. Shops here include: Academy; Alice Collins; August Silk; Bed & Bath Works linen and bathroom accessories; Black & Decker; Broughton Shoe Warehouse; Cards and Gifts selling, as their name suggests, cards, soft toys, wrapping paper and mugs; CBS for fashion for the whole family; The Chainstore Outlet; Ciro Citterio menswear; Cotton Traders; Delifrance; Diamonds Direct; Direct Design womenswear (mostly knits and tops) with some children,s clothes; Discount Clothing Store, which sells lots of cheaper styles for women and children; Easy Jeans for men, women and children; Honey ladieswear; James Barry men,s suits, trousers, and coats; Jane Shilton shoes for women, handbags, scarves, jewellery, gloves and luggage; Joe Bloggs for men, women and children; John Jenkins crystal and porcelain; Leading Labels for men and women, a large shop with, for women, Roman Originals, Alexara, Blast leisurewear, Katherine Hamnett Denim, Cote a Cote Paris,

Klass coats and jackets, Jersey Masters and Just Elegance and, for men, Pringle, Farah trousers, Kangol, Double Two shirts, Tommy Hilfiger, Calvin Klein, Ralph Lauren, Oakman, Lee Cooper, Fruit of the Loom and Wolsey, Luggage and Bags; Mexx for men, women and children, Pavers Branded Shoes for men, women and children; Penny Plain womenswear; Picture Port; Pilot womenswear; Ponden Mill bedlinen, duvets, towels, curtains and tea towels from Dorma, Coloroll, Horrockses, Vantona and Sheridan; Puma selling Dunlop, Slazenger, Carlton, Maxfli and Goudi; Remington branded electrical goods from hairdryers to kitchen knives; Sports Mill; Sports Unlimited with Head rucksacks, Le Coq Sportif clothes, Wilson, Arena ladies swimwear, Hi-Tec gym shoes, Trespass ski clothes and Fila; SU214, which stocks Ben Sherman, Chipie, Red or Dead and Top Man; Tom Sayers menswear; Tog 24 outdoor clothes, shoes and equipment for men, women and children; Lee jeans for men and women, with a youth section; The Designer Room; The Suit Company (Moss Bros) for men selling Pierre Cardin suits, Moss Bros dress shirts, Baumler and Daks shirts; Suits You menswear including Van Kollem, Pierre Cardin, Pierre Balmain, Tom English, Daniel Hechter, Ralph Lauren and Ben Sherman; Luggage & Bags including Tula handbags, Samsonite, Delsey and Pierre Balmain; Thorntons chocolates; The Book Depot; Toyworld selling Matchbox, Lego, Little Tikes, Tyco, Tomy and Waddingtons; The Chainstore Outlet, which sells clothes from leading chainstores, many with their labels cut out, for men, women and children - uncut labels seen here include Next, Adams, Gossard, Farah, Wallis; The Mountain Outlet, a ski and walkers shop for men, women and children with walking boots, Nevica ski jackets, ski luggage; Suits You; Thorntons; Warners underwear; XS Music & Video.

SECOND TIME AROUND

1 - 3 WOOL MARKET, BERWICK-UPON-TWEED,
NORTHUMBERLAND TD15 1DH
☎ (01289) 307875 10 - 5 MON - SAT.
Dress Agency • *Womenswear & Menswear*

High quality, nearly new clothes with designers ranging from Jacques Vert to Marks & Spencer and Laura Ashley. Established for more than seven years, this two-storey shop now caters for the whole family with an across the board selection of clothing from casual daywear to wedding outfits, babywear to men's outfits. There is usually a bargain rail with skirts going for as little as £4, and twice yearly sales in the summer and winter. A varied selection of clothes can be found year round as the stock is not necessarily seasonal. Accessories include shoes, hats, handbags and a small amount of jewellery. Menswear includes Armani, Hugo Boss and other Continental designers. Childrenswear ranges from babies to teenagers and there is also a selecton of baby equipment such as high chairs and buggies as well as toys, games and books. Rest area and refreshments always available in thie friendly, spacious shop.

SHARK GROUP
NORDSTROM HOUSE, NORTH BROOMHILL, NEAR AMBLE, MORPETH, NORTHUMBERLAND NE65 9UJ
☎ (01670) 760365. OPEN 2 - 4 MON - FRI (ALL YEAR ROUND), 10 - 12 SAT (APRIL - MID-DEC).
Factory Shop • *Sportswear & Equipment* • *Children Womenswear & Menswear*
Manufactures and sells in the factory shop wetsuits, dry suits, cag tops, sailing suits, boots and gloves, for men, women and children at factory prices. Children's one-piece wetsuits, £42.50 - £47.50 and adult two-piece wetsuits, from £80, adult one-piece wetsuits, £65. Also sell specialist outdoor clothing from Real Tree and Loden Green jackets and trousers. Special sales are held occasionally. The factory shop closes for the usual factory holidays in late July/early August and late October as well as bank holidays.

SLATERS MENSWEAR
10 GRAINGER STREET, NEWCASTLE-UPON-TYNE, TYNE & WEAR, NORTHUMBERLAND NE1 5EW
☎ (0191) 232 5557. OPEN 8.30 - 5.30 MON - SAT, 7.30 ON THUR.
Permanent Discount Outlet • *Menswear Only*
Full range of men's clothes from underwear and shoes to casualwear, suits and dresswear and including labels such as Odermark, Bulmer, Valentino, Charlie's Co, and Charlton Gray. Men's suits from £79.

SPOILS
17-19 WHITE ROSE WAY, ELDON SQUARE, NEWCASTLE UPON TYNE, TYNE & WEAR, NORTHUMBERLAND NE1 7XN
☎ (0191) 222 0184. OPEN 9 - 5.30 MON - SAT, 8 ON THUR, 11 - 5 SUN.
METRO CENTRE, NEWCASTLE, TYNE & WEAR
☎ (0191) 460 7573.
Permanent Discount Outlet • *Household*
General domestic glassware, non-stick bakeware, kitchen gadgets, ceramic oven-to-tableware, textiles, cutting boards, aluminium non-stick cookware, bakeware, plastic kitchenware, plastic storage, woodware, coffee pots/makers, furniture, mirrors and picture frames. Rather than being discounted, all the merchandise is very competitively priced - in fact, the company carry out competitors' checks frequently in order to monitor pricing. With 38 branches, the company is able to buy in bulk and thus negotiate very good prices.

THE CAPE
UNIT F43, THE FORUM, METRO CENTRE, GATESHEAD, TYNE & WEAR, NORTHUMBERLAND NE11 9XR
☎ (0191) 493 2379. OPEN 10 - 8 MON - WED, 10 - 9 THUR, 10 - 8 FRI, 9 - 7 SAT, 11 - 5 SUN.
Factory Shop • *Household* • *Furniture/Soft Furnishings*
High density pine furniture made in South Africa from trees grown in managed forests, is sold at factory direct prices with home delivery throughout the UK. The range includes beds, wardrobes, blanket boxes, chests of drawers, tallboys, dressing tables, cheval mirrors, headboards, mattresses, a kitchen range, dining room tables, Welsh dressers, hi-fi units, bookcases. Also on sale in this shops is a range of African accessories and artefacts from Zimbabwe encompassing mirrors, prints, serpentine (stone) ornaments, recylced stationery, handmade wirework, candles and other ethnic and traditional gifts. Colour brochure and price list available on 01535 650940.

THE FABRIC AND TAPESTRY SHOP
SYDGATE HOUSE, MIDDLE STREET, CORBRIDGE, NORTHUMBERLAND NE45 5AT
☎ (01434) 632902. OPEN 10 - 5 MON -SAT.
Permanent Discount Outlet • *Secondhand shops*
Furniture/Soft Furnishings
Designer discount fabric in 2 - 3 metre lengths from £8, including names such as Colefax & Fowler and Ramm Son & Crocker. Also good quality secondhand curtains as well as leading brand tapestry kits, such as Elizabeth Bradley, the latter at full price.

THORNTONS
SOUTH PARADE, ROYAL QUAYS SHOPPING CENTRE, COBLE DENE, NORTH SHIELDS, NORTHUMBERLAND NE29 6DN
☎ (0191) 258 0623. OPEN 10 - 6 MON - SAT, 11 - 5 SUN.
Factory Shop in a Factory Shopping Village
Food and Leisure • *Household*
The UK's leading specialist confectionery retailer has more than 500 shops and franchises nationwide selling a wide range of boxed and loose, chocolate and sugar confectionery. The factory outlets sell three different categories: misshapes. discounted lines and standard lines. Misshapes are loose chocolates which are the result of new product development, product trials or end of production runs which cannot be packed as Thorntons standard lines. They are packed into assorted bags and offer a saving of 35%-55% over the recommended retail price of standard "loose line" products. Discounted lines are excess to Thorntons' normal retail requirements and can be as a result of excess seasonal or export stock, discontinued lines or packaging changes. These products, when available, are offered at a discount of 25%-50% over the standard retail price. Standard lines from the full Thorntons range are also on sale at normal prices.

TK MAXX
LOWER GROUND FLOOR, MONUMENT MALL SHOPPING CENTRE, NEWCASTLE-UPON-TYNE, TYNE & WEAR, NORTHUMBERLAND NE1 7AL
☎ (0191) 261 0404. OPEN 9 - 5.30 MON - SAT, UNTIL 8 ON THUR, 11 - 5 SUN.
UNIT 13A, TEAM VALLEY RETAIL WORLD, GATESHEAD, NE11 0BD
☎ (0191) 487 4468. OPEN10 - 8 MON, TUE, WED, FRI, UNTIL 8 THUR, 11 - 5 SUN.
UNIT 3, THE HIGHLIGHT RETAIL PARK, HARTLEPOOL MARINA, MARINA WAY, HARTLEPOOL TS24 OUX
☎ (01429) 222296. OPEN 10 - 8 MON - FRI, 9 - 6 SAT, 11 - 5 SUN.
12 CAPTAIN COOK SQUARE, MIDDLESBROUGH 5UB
☎ (01642) 222220. OPEN 9 - 5.30 MON - WED, FRI, 9 - 7 FRI, 9 - 6 SAT, 11 - 5 SUN.
THE BRIDGES SHOPPING CENTRE, 34 CROWTREE ROAD, SUNDERLAND SR3 3JU
☎ (0191) 5144484.

Permanent Discount Outlet • *Womenswear & Menswear Children* • *Household* • *Furniture/Soft Furnishings*

Based on an American concept, TK Maxx is situated in easily accessible, often centrally located stores and offers famous label goods with up to 60% savings off recommended retail prices. TK Maxx has fashion for the whole family - women's, men's and childrenswear - accessories, shoes, gifts, kitchenware and home goods. Everything in the store is branded with a choice of well-known high street names to designer labels, and while a small percentage might be clearly marked past season, the great majority of items in store are current season, current stock and still with phenomenal savings. There is a huge choice with 50,000 pieces in store and up to 10,000 new items arriving a week. The stores are simple and unfussy with wide aisles, shopping trolleys and baskets, and a spacious, functional feel to them but there are individual changing rooms, ramps for buggies and wheelchairs and plenty of staff on the shop floor. Every branch accepts all major credit and debit cards and has a liberal refund and return policy.

TOG 24
ROYAL QUAYS FACTORY OUTLET, ADDRESS AND OPENING HOURS AS BEFORE.
☎ (0191) 258 3754.
32 HIGH FRIARS, ELDON SQUARE, NEWCASTLE, TYNE & WEAR NE1 7XG
☎ (01912) 602810. OPEN 9 - 5.30 MON - FRI, 8 ON THUR, 9 - 6 SAT, 11 - 5 SUN.

Factory Shop in a Factory Shopping Village • *Factory Shop Womenswear & Menswear* • *Children* • *Sportswear & Equipment*

Tog 24 are the UK's fastest growing brand name in outdoor clothing and leisurewear. They utilise the world's finest performance fabrics including Gore-Tex, Polartec and Burlington MCS, catering for all the family for all seasons, with cosy fleeces and waterproofs for the winter, and trekking ranges, shorts and t-shirts for the summer. With all prices at least 30% below the recommended retail price, you can afford to enter the Tog comfort zone.

TOM SAYERS CLOTHING CO
ROYAL QUAYS FACTORY OUTLET, ADDRESS AND OPENING HOURS AS BEFORE.
☎ (0191) 257 3369.
Factory Shop in a Factory Shopping Village • *Menswear Only*
Tom Sayers make sweaters for some of the top high street department stores. Unusually for a factory shop, if they don't stock your size, they will try and order it for you from their factory or one of their other factory outlets and send it to you. Most of the stock here is overstock, cancelled orders or last season's and includes jumpers, trousers and shirts at discounts of 30%. The trousers and shirts are bought in to complement the sweaters which they make.

TOYWORLD FACTORY OUTLETS LTD
ROYAL QUAYS FACTORY OUTLET, ADDRESS AND OPENING HOURS AS BEFORE.
☎ (0191) 257 3333. WEBSITE: www.toyworldstore.com
Factory Shop in a Factory Shopping Village • *Children*
Toyworld sell a large range of discontinued toys, manufacturers' overruns and excess stock from many famous brand names such as Barbie, Action Man, Lego, Tomy, Fisher-Price and many more at least 30-60% off high street prices. The Cornmill Shopping Centre outlet also has a large range of TP Outdoor Activity Toys.

TYNEDALE PARK
HEXHAM, NORTHUMBERLAND NE46 3PG
☎ (01434) 607788. OPEN 10 - 6 MON - FRI, 9.30 - 6 SAT, 11 - 5 SUN.
Permanent Discount Outlet • *Womenswear & Menswear*
Food and Leisure • *Household* • *Furniture/Soft Furnishings*
Large discount outlet selling overstock and clearance lines. There are lots of good names here in fashion (Windsmoor, Dannimac, Berlei, Pringle), furniture, electrical items, toys, gifts, and diy equipment. The main section is a garden centre and there is also a pets, golf, sports and a large outdoorwear department, linens and bathshop. Clothing is just for adults but there are shoes for children too. Readers have found sandals at £5, anoraks at £35. There is a restaurant upstairs, lifts, and lots of free parking.

Nottinghamshire

ABSOLUTE BEGINNERS NURSERY HIRE
162 RADCLIFFE ROAD, WEST BRIDGFORD, NOTTINGHAM, NOTTINGHAMSHIRE NG2 5HF
☎ (0115) 981 8135, 0115 846 8967.
FLEXIBLE OPENING HOURS. PHONE FOR APPOINTMENT.
Hire Shop • *Children*
Hires out a wide range of good quality baby and nursery equipment, such as travel cots, car seats and highchairs at competitive prices. Part of the Baby Equipment Hirers Association (BEHA), which has more than 100 members countrywide. BEHA run an advice line which will try and answer any queries you have regarding hiring services for children. Phone the Babyline on 0831 310355.

BROUGHTON SHOE WAREHOUSE
6 QUEENS COURT, LENTON LANE, NOTTINGHAM NG7 2NR
☎ (0115) 986 1945. OPEN 10 - 6 MON - SAT, 10 - 4 SUN.
32 KING STREET, SOUTHWELL, NOTTINGHAMSHIRE NG25 OEN
☎ (01636) 812078. OPEN 9.30 - 5 MON - SAT.
Permanent Discount Outlet • *Womenswear & Menswear* • *Children*
Sells ladies boots, shoes, sandals, handbags and slippers seasonally as well as men's footwear. Savings can be between 20% and 50% here. Brands include Trickers and some Italian and Spanish designers. Deliveries are made every Tuesday.

BUNNY APPLIANCE WAREHOUSE
UNIT 1 & 2, BUNNY TRADING ESTATE, GOTHAM LANE, BUNNY, NOTTINGHAM NG11 6QJ
☎ (0115) 9844357. WEBSITE: www.bunnyuk.com
OPEN 10 - 5 MON - FRI, 10 - 4 SAT, 11 - 3 SUN.
Permanent Discount Outlet • *Electrical Equipment*
Large warehouse with 10,000 fitted kitchen appliances. They specialise in built-in kitchen appliances, stocking all leading brands from AEG to Zanussi at up to 60% discounts. There is a large showroom displaying 60 gas and electric single and double ovens, and 200 ceramic, halogen, gas and electric hobs are always in stock. Specialise in American fridges and fridge freezers with up to £500 off, and range cookers. They offer excellent advice and service.

CATALOGUE BARGAIN SHOP
50 MAIN STREET, BULWELL, NOTTINGHAM, NOTTINGHAMSHIRE NG6 8EY
☎ (0115) 927 8373. OPEN 9 - 5.30 MON - SAT, 10 - 4 SUN.
24-28 LEEMING STREET, MANSFIELD, NG18 1NE
☎ (01623) 623353. OPEN 9 - 5.30 MON - SAT, 10 - 4 SUN.

Permanent Discount Outlet • *Womenswear & Menswear Children* • *Household* • *Electrical Equipment*

Catalogue Bargain Shop is a growing national chain of stores which obtains the majority of its goods from mail order giants Great Universal and Kays, and offers a range of clothing for all the family, a wide selection of shoes, bed linen, household goods, electrical equipment and hundreds of other catalogue items at very competitive prices. The merchandise consists of ends of ranges and previous season's stock for which there is no longer storage space when the catalogues change.

CHANGE OF A DRESS

294 BROXTOWE LANE, NOTTINGHAM NG8 5NB
☎ (0115) 929 1531. ☎ (0115) 929 6888 FAX. OPEN 9.30 - 5 TUE - SAT
Dress Agency • *Womenswear Only*

This must be the country's most glamorous dress agency, as its appearance on TV can testify. Where else could you find Chanel, Armani, Moschino and Escada modelled by the agency's "in house" mannequin, whilst accompanied by their resident pianist at a grand piano? The owner imports clothing from Hollywood and has sold garments from Joan Collins, Priscilla Presley and Zsa Zsa Gabor. The extensive salon is decorated with 15 chandeliers and ornate gilded mirrors, with a coffee lounge for customers' comfort; alterations can be undertaken on site. Clients travel far and wide to this mecca for the fashion-conscious and penny-wise.

CLARKS FACTORY SHOP

111 FRONT STREET, ARNOLD, NOTTINGHAMSHIRE NG5 7ED
☎ (0115) 967 4212. OPEN 9 - 6 MON - SAT, 10 - 4 SUN, BANK HOLIDAYS.
Factory Shop • *Children* • *Womenswear & Menswear*

Clarks International operate a chain of factory shops nationally which specialise in selling discontinued lines and slight sub-standards for children, women and men from Clarks, K Shoes and other famous brands. These shops trade under the name of K Shoes Factory shop or Clarks Factory Shop and while not all are physically attached to a shoe factory, they are treated as factory shops by the company. Customers can expect to find an extensive range of quality shoes, sandals, walking boots, slippers, trainers, handbags, accessories and gifts, while their major outlets also offer luggage, sports clothing, sports equipment and outdoor clothing. Brands stocked include Clarks, K Shoes, Springer, CICA, Hi-Tec, Puma, Mercury, Dr Martens, Nike, LA Gear, Fila, Mizuno, Slazenger, Weider, Antler and Carlton, although not all are sold in every outlet. Discounts are on average 30% off the normal high street price for perfect stock.

COOPER & ROE FACTORY SHOP
KIRKBY ROAD, SUTTON-IN-ASHFIELD, NOTTINGHAMSHIRE NG17 1GP
☎ (01623) 554026. OPEN 9 - 5 MON - FRI, 9 - 4 SAT, 10 - 4 SUN.
Factory Shop • *Household* • *Womenswear & Menswear* • *Children*
Part of a larger chain of shops catering for a manufacturer for the popular high street chains, including Marks & Spencer and Next. Merchandise includes fashion for all the family, underwear, pyjamas, evening wear, coats, gifts, towels, bedding, socks. Free face painting for children on Saturdays.

DAYCLEAR LIGHTING LTD
85A CROMFORD ROAD, LANGLEY MILL, NOTTINGHAM,
NOTTINGHAMSHIRE NG16 4DP
☎ (01773) 763787. OPEN 9 - 5 MON - FRI, 9 - 4 SAT.
Factory Shop • *Electrical Equipment*
Lampshades, table lamps, chandeliers and decorative lighting at manufacturers prices. There are usually at least 300 lines in stock at any one time. For example, 12" table lamps with pleated shades, £6.99; three-arm solid brass chandelier, £68; standard lamp, £27.95. There is parking at the rear of the building.

DENBY FACTORY SHOP
DURY WALK, BROADMARSH SHOPPING CENTRE, NOTTINGHAM,
NOTTINGHAMSHIRE NG1 7LP
☎ (0115) 948 3932. OPEN 9 - 5.30 SEVEN DAYS A WEEK.
Factory Shop • *Household*
Denby is renowned for its striking colours and glaze effects. The Factory Shops stock first and second quality with seconds discounts starting at 20% off RRP. There are regular "mega bargains" with up to 75% off throughout the year.

DIRECT SPECS LTD
UNIT 12, ACORN SHOPPING CENTRE, STATION ROAD,
LANGLEY MILL, NOTTINGHAMSHIRE NG16 4AF
☎ (01773 711911) . OPEN 9 - 5 MON - SAT.
Permanent Discount Outlet • *Womenswear & Menswear*
Spectacles and sunglasses at prices which the owner claims beat any competitor's. Most designer names are stocked at one time or another, though if you have a favourite, check first. Bring along your prescription and glasses will be found to suit. No eye tests conducted.

EDWARDIAN CONFECTIONERY LTD
HUTHWAITE, BARKER STREET, NOTTINGHAMSHIRE NG17 2LG
☎ (01623) 554712. OPEN 8 - 6 MON - FRI, 9 - 1 SAT.
Food and Drink Discounters • *Food and Leisure*
Sweets and rock sold at two-thirds of the shop price. Range includes peanut brittle, treacle slab, caramel slab and chocolate, all of which can be bought either whole or broken up. Approximately 70 types of boiled sweets made on the premises.

ESSENTIAL ITEMS
CHURCH HOUSE, PLUNGAR, NOTTINGHAMSHIRE NG13 0JA
☎ (0194) 9861172. FAX (0194) 9861320.
E-MAIL: cross@plungarfsbusiness.co.uk
OPEN 8 - 8 SEVEN DAYS A WEEK. MAIL ORDER.
Permanent Discount Outlet • *Furniture/Soft Furnishings*

Essential Items is one of the country's most established companies manufacturing and designing stools and ottomans. Other items new to their range are elegant window seats and bed-end stools, all made to order and covered in the customers' own fabric. Because of their low overheads, their mail order service offers much more competitive prices than similar items bought in department stores. Although items can be covered in calico, most lines are covered in customers' own material at no extra charge. Now specialising in hand made curtains as well as re-upholstery. The upholstered filing cabinet Ottoman is one of their best sellers - either as a single at £195 or as a double at £250.

FACTORY SHOP OUTLET, COATS VIYELLA CLOTHING,
CV CLOTHING LADIES AND CHILDRENSWEAR, SLEAFORD ROAD, NEWARK, NOTTINGHAMSHIRE NG24 1NG
☎ (01636) 701390. OPEN 10 - 5 MON - SAT, 10 - 4 SUN, BANK HOLS.
THE FACTORY SHOP OUTLET, COATS VIYELLA CLOTHING, NORTH STREET, HUTHWAITE, NOTTINGHAM NG17 QPS
☎ (01623) 515808. OPEN 9 - 5.30 MON - FRI, 9 - 5 SAT, 10 - 4 SUN.
Factory Shop • *Womenswear & Menswear* • *Children*

Part of the Coats Viyella group, which makes quality clothing for many of the major high street stores, overstocks and clearance lines are sold through more than 30 of the group's factory shops. Many of you will recognise the garments on sale, despite the lack of well-known labels. Ladieswear includes dresses, blouses, jumpers, cardigans, trousers, nightwear, underwear, lingerie, hosiery, coats and swimwear. Menswear includes trousers, belts, shirts, ties, pullovers, cardigans, T-shirts, underwear, nightwear, hosiery and jackets. Childrenswear includes jackets, trousers, T-shirts, underwear, hosiery, jumpers and babywear. There are regular deliveries to constantly update the range.

JUST A SECOND FABRICS
7 KIRKSTALL LODGE, HIGH ST, EDWINSTOWE, MANSFIELD, NOTTINGHAMSHIRE NG21 9QS
☎ (01623) 825156. OPEN 9.30 - 4.30 MON - FRI, 10 - 4 SAT, CLOSED WED.
Permanent Discount Outlet • *Furniture/Soft Furnishings*

Specialists in all aspects of soft furnishings, all products (fabrics, wallpaper, carpets, laminated flooring etc) are carefully sourced to provide individual designs of exceptional quality at affordable prices. Home design service available with first class making up service, fitting service, upholstery, loose covers, quilting and much more. Hand-finished poles, tassle tie-backs, fringes and braids offer the perfect finishing touches. These are price leaders at an average of 20% off brand names.

LABELS OF EDWINSTOWE
25 HIGH STREET, EDWINSTOWE, NOTTINGHAMSHIRE NG21 9QP
☎ (01623) 825479. 10 - 5.30 MON - SAT.
Dress Agency • *Womenswear Only* • *Household Furniture/Soft Furnishings*

Friendly and accommodating shop, concentrating on barely worn upmarket and designer labels, stocking garments, accessories and jewellery in immaculate condition. The emporium at Edwinstone is set on two floors and also incorporates gifts, beauty salon and sought after pieces for the home such as Persian rugs, old olive jars and other decorative items. In addition, a range of imported Indonesian and Asian furniture is also displayed, although the main part of the business is still women's clothes from beachwear to designer evening and day wear. (Business terms = 60:40%).

LIQUIDATION SUPPLIES
26 LONDON ROAD, RETFORD, NOTTINGHAMSHIRE DN22 6AY
☎ (01777) 711151. OPEN 9 - 5 MON - SAT, 11 - 4 SUN.
Permanent Discount Outlet • *Electrical Equipment*

Factory soiled, new dishwashers, cookers, fridges, washing machines and built-in ovens, all with a one-year guarantee, at discount prices.

MARTIN LINDSAY LTD
UNIT 24, NOTTINGHAM FASHION CENTRE, HUNTINGDON STREET, NOTTINGHAM, NOTTINGHAMSHIRE NG1 3LH
☎ (0115) 941 7838.
Designer Sale • *Womenswear Only*

Accessories and clothing made from exquisite, hand-printed fabrics including velvets, devore, silks and satins under the Jan Lindsay label which is sold in top department stores countrywide. New studio showroom is well worth a visit. Write or ring to put your name on the mailing list for an invitation to special events.

MATALAN
CHILWELL RETAIL PARK, EAST WEST LINK ROAD, BEESTON, NOTTINGHAM, NOTTINGHAMSHIRE N69 6DS
☎ (0115) 946 9354. OPEN 10 - 8 MON - FRI, 9 - 6 SAT, 11 - 5 SUN.
SPRINGFIELD RETAIL PARK, HUCKNALL LANE, BULWELL, NOTTINGHAM NG6 8AJ
☎ (0115) 977 7800. OPEN 10 - 8 MON - FRI, 9 - 6 SAT, 10 - 4 SUN.
Permanent Discount Outlet • *Womenswear & Menswear Children* • *Household*

Matalan is a fashion and homewares value retailer giving customers what they claim to be unbeatable value for money with huge savings on a wide range of products including high quality fashionable clothing for men, women and children at up to 50% off high street prices. Matalan is situated out of town and stores are open seven days a week all year round.

NOTTINGHAM ARCHITECTURAL ANTIQUES
531 WOODBOROUGH ROAD, NOTTINGHAM,
NOTTINGHAMSHIRE NG3 5FR
☎ (0115) 960 5665. OPEN 9 - 5 MON - SAT, CLOSED WED.
Architectural Salvage • *DIY/Renovation*
Garden ornaments, bathroom fittings, Victorian fireplaces, doors, stained and etched glass.

P W SHEPHERD UPHOLSTERY
195 STATION ROAD, LANGLEY MILL, NOTTINGHAMSHIRE NG16 4AF
☎ (01773) 769395. OPEN 9 - 5.30 MON - FRI, 9 - 5 SAT, 10 - 2 SUN.
Factory Shop • *Furniture/Soft Furnishings*
Three-piece suites, storage boxes, cushions and curtains.

RENAISSANCE
31 WOLLATON ROAD, BEESTON, NOTTINGHAM,
NOTTINGHAMSHIRE NG9 2NG
☎ (0115) 9220653. OPEN 9 - 5.30 MON - THUR, SAT, 9 - 7 FRI, 11 - 4 SUN.
Dress Agency • *Womenswear & Menswear*
Ever-changing stock of labels from M&S to Moschino, Next to Nicole Farhi, Jigsaw to Jacques Vert, Laura Ashley to Ralph Lauren, Gap to Gaultier, Austin Reed to Armani. Prices from £5 to £300. About one quarter of the space is devoted to men's clothes including a regular stock of Paul Smith, and there is also some secondhand jewellery. All clothes and accessories are pristine and imaginatively presented, in delightful, relaxed surroundings. Credit/Debit cards welcome.

SPOILS
2B HIGH STREET, NOTTINGHAM, NOTTINGHAMSHIRE NG1 2ET
☎ (0115) 9584 753. OPEN 9 - 5.30 MON - SAT.
309 VICTORIA CENTRE, NOTTINGHAM NG1 1QN
☎ (0115) 9581 210. OPEN 9 - 5.30 MON - SAT.
Permanent Discount Outlet • *Household*
General domestic glassware, non-stick bakeware, kitchen gadgets, ceramic oven-to-tableware, textiles, cutting boards, aluminium non-stick cookware, bakeware, plastic kitchenware, plastic storage, woodware, coffee pots/makers, furniture, mirrors and picture frames. Rather than being discounted, all the merchandise is very competitively priced - in fact, the company carry out competitors' checks frequently in order to monitor pricing. With 38 branches, the company is able to buy in bulk and thus negotiate very good prices.

THE COURTAULDS FACTORY SHOP
RAYMOTH LANE, WORKSOP, NOTTINGHAMSIRE S81 7LT
☎ (01909) 501716. OPEN 9 - 5.30 MON - SAT, SUN 10.30 - 4.30.
HAYDN ROAD, NOTTINGHAM, NOTTINGHAMSHIRE NG5 1DH
☎ (0115) 924 6100 . OPEN 9 - 5.30 MON - SAT, 7.30 ON WED,
10.30 - 4.30 SUN.
ELLIS STREET, KIRKBY IN ASHFIELD, NOTTINGHAM NG17 7AL
☎ (01623) 754193. OPEN 9 - 5.30 MON - SAT, 10.30 - 4.30 SUN.
SHERWOOD DRIVE, NEW ALLERTON, NEAR NEWARK,
NOTTINGHAMSHIRE NG 22 9PN
☎ (01623) 836335. OPEN 9 - 5 MON - SAT.
Factory Shop • *Womenswear & Menswear* • *Children* • *Household*
Sells a wide range of ladies, men's and childrens high street fashions at between 30% and 50% below high street prices. Also stocks a wide range of household textiles, luggage, shoes and accessories.

THE DESIGNER WAREHOUSE
CASTLE BUILDINGS, CASTLE BOULEVARD, NOTTINGHAM
☎ (0115) 948 0100. OPEN 9 - 6 MON - SAT, 10 - 5 SUN.
Permanent Discount Outlet • *Menswear Only*
Wholesalers who buy surplus stock in a wide variety of sizes and sell it to the public at this clearance shop. Most of the stock is for men and features Ralph Lauren, Versace, Armani, Calvin Klein, Cerruti jeans, leather jackets and sweatshirts at about half price.

THE FACTORY SHOP
DONCASTER ROAD, LANGOLD, WORKSOP,
NOTTINGHAMSHIRE DN22 7HY
☎ (01909) 731115. OPEN 9 -5.30 MON - SAT, 10 - 4.30 SUN.
Factory Shop • *Household* • *Womenswear & Menswear*
Children • *Furniture/Soft Furnishings* • *Sportswear & Equipment*
Wide range on sale includes men's, ladies' and children's clothing and footwear; household textiles, toiletries, hardware, luggage, lighting and bedding, most of which are chainstore and high street brands at discounts of approximately 30%-50%. There are weekly deliveries and brands include many major stars such as Adidas, Nike, Joe Bloggs and Brabantia, to name just four. Lines are continually changing and few factory shops offer such a variety under one roof. This branch also display furniture and sells the Cape Country Furniture range. This high quality pine furniture made exclusively for The Factory Shop in the new South Africa is sold at factory direct prices with home delivery throughout the UK. Colour brochure and price list available. There is a free car park.

THE SHOE FACTORY SHOP
20 BROAD STREET, NOTTINGHAM, NOTTINGHAMSHIRE NG1 3AL
☎ (0115) 924 2390. OPEN 10 - 5 MON - FRI, 9.30 - 5.30 SAT.
Factory Shop • *Womenswear & Menswear* • *Children*
Men's, women's and children's shoes and accessories which are bought in from other manufacturers including Spanish, Portuguese and Italian companies. All are unbranded. The range covers from mocassins to dressy shoes. Ladies shoes which would cost £35 retail are £29. Children's shoes from size 6 to adult size 5 from £10 upwards. Slippers start at baby size 4 to junior size 2 from £3.50 - £6.50.

THE SHOE SHED
COURTAULDS TEXTILES FACTORY SHOP, ELLIS STREET, KIRKBY-IN-ASHFIELD, NOTTINGHAMSHIRE NG17 7AL
☎ (01623) 723083. OPEN 9 - 5.30 MON - SAT, 10.30 - 4.30 SUN.
Factory Shop • *Womenswear & Menswear* • *Children*
Large factory shop selling a vast range of all types of women's, men's and children's shoes, all of which are perfects, at up to 30% below normal high street prices. Ladies sandals cost from £5; ladies shoes from £7.50. Men's shoes from £10; sports shoes from £10.

TILE CLEARING HOUSE
POULTON DRIVE, OFF DALESIDE ROAD, NOTTINGHAM, NOTTINGHAMSHIRE NG4 4DH
☎ (01159) 851 921. OPEN 8 - 6 MON - FRI, 9 - 6 SAT, 10 - 4 SUN.
Permanent Discount Outlet • *DIY/Renovation*
Over 500 ranges of top quality ceramic wall and floor tiles permanently in stock, plus a comprehensive range of grouts, adhesives, tools and accessories to complete the job. By buying direct from the manufacturer and passing the savings on to the customer, their prices are very competitive. Moreover, everything you see is in stock, so there's no waiting for orders to be processed. Save up to 75% on manufacturers' recommended selling prices.

TWEEDIES
OGLE STREET, HUCKNALL, NOTTINGHAMSHIRE NG15 NFR
☎ (0115) 963 6662. OPEN 9 - 5 MON - SAT.
THE AVENUE, WEST BRIDGFORD, NOTTINGHAMSHIRE NG2 5GR
☎ (0115) 981 8752. OPEN 9 - 5.30 MON RE NG9 2JH
☎ (0115) 943 0054. OPEN 9 - 5.30 MON - FRI, 9 - 5 SAT.
NOTTINGHAM ROAD, KEYWORTH, NOTTINGHAMSHIRE NG12 5GS
☎ (0115) 937 5067. OPEN 9 - 5.30 MON - FRI, 9 - 5 SAT.
HIGH STREET, LONG EATON
☎ (0115) 946 5820. OPEN 9 - 5.30 MON - FRI, 9 - 5 SAT.
Permanent Discount Outlet • *Womenswear & Menswear*
Children • *Household*

Top brand names and favourite high street labels, all at discount prices of up to 50%. Family fashions plus some household goods and giftware to suit all budgets and ages. Although some of the labels are cut out, names you will recognise include Marks & Spencer, Evans, Wallis, Dorothy Perkins, Next and Etam, plus brands such as Farah, Wolsey, Fruit of the Loom, Nike, Adidas and Lyle & Scott. They now also have a range of top European designer labels like Stielman and Hucke.

UNITED FOOTWEAR
BEECH AVENUE, OFF SHERWOOD RISE, OFF A60, NOTTINGHAM, NOTTINGHAMSHIRE
☎ (0115) 979 2799. OPEN 9 - 6.30 MON - FRI, 9 - 5.30 SAT, 10 - 4 SUN.
Permanent Discount Outlet • *Womenswear & Menswear*

Shoes for all the family as well as clothes, handbags, sports shoes, boots, giftware and household goods, all at discounted prices. Famous brands including Clarks, K Shoes and Elmdale. Part of a national chain.

WARNERS UK LTD
DABELL AVENUE, BLENHEIM INDUSTRIAL PARK, BULWELL, NOTTINGHAMSHIRE NG6 8WA
☎ (0115) 979 5796. OPEN 10 - 5 TUE - SAT.
Factory Shop • *Womenswear & Menswear*

This shop sells a wide range of women's lingerie from Leisureby, Warners, with bras, slips, thongs, bodies and briefs at discounts from 25% to 70%. Each item is labelled with both the rrp and the discounted prices. For example, bikini brief, £6.99 reduced from £17; underwire bra, £14.99 reduced from £33; body, £24.99 reduced from £65. Slightly imperfect stock as well as perfect quality, end of season and discontinued merchandise and swimwear are also stocked. Underwear for men, including Calvin Klein briefs for £2.99, is on offer too.

WEBB IVORY LTD
34 HIGH STREET, LONG EATON, NOTTINGHAMSHIRE NG10 1LL
☎ (0115) 973661. OPEN 9 - 5.30 MON - SAT.
Factory Shop • *Household* • *Womenswear & Menswear* • *Children*
Items from the Webb Ivory catalogue at reduced prices including cards, gifts, soft toys, books, pens, lamps, kitchenware, garden furniture and clothes. Discounts range from at least 50%.

WESTON MILL POTTERY
NAVIGATION YARD, MILLGATE, NEWARK,
NOTTINGHAMSHIRE NG24 4TY
☎ (01636) 676835. OPEN 9 - 4.30 MON - FRI, 9.30 - 4.30 SAT,
11 - 4.30 SUN, BANK HOLIDAYS.
Factory Shop • *Food and Leisure* • *Household*
Manufacturer of terracotta wares which they supply to many high street retailers. Garden pots in a variety of shapes and sizes are handthrown on the premises. Quality clay and high-firing make these frost resistant. A range of imported troughs, urns and large pots are also available at discounted prices. Weston Mill also produces items for the kitchen and home, including bread bins, chicken roasters, egg racks, candle pots and perfume burners. Seconds and discounted items are always on sale at bargain prices.

WILLIS OWEN LTD:
THE BUILDING SOCIETY SHOP
98 MANSFIELD ROAD, NOTTINGHAM, NOTTINGHAMSHIRE NG1 3HD
☎ (0115) 947 2595.
They will send you free guides to investing in ISAs, With Profit Bonds, Investment Bonds etc. Top discounts available on all investments. Fully independent recommendations.

Oxfordshire

AQUASCUTUM
BICESTER OUTLET SHOPPING VILLAGE, PINGLE DRIVE, BICESTER,
OXFORDSHIRE OX6 7WD
☎ (01869) 325943. OPEN 10 - 6 SEVEN DAYS A WEEK.
Factory Shop in a Factory Shopping Village • *Womenswear & Menswear*
Ends of ranges and last season's stock for women and men from the complete Aquascutum range sold in this factory shopping village with 58 other factory shops, food facilities and a children's play area. There is a minimum 25% discount against normal retail prices, and up to 50% on some lines.

BENETTON
BICESTER OUTLET SHOPPING VILLAGE, ADDRESS AND OPENING HOURS AS BEFORE.
☎ (01869) 320030.
Factory Shop in a Factory Shopping Village
Womenswear & Menswear • Children

Benetton stocks a wide range of clothes for women, men and children including colourful T-shirts, sweatshirts, men's button-neck T-shirts, swimwear, jeans, children's jackets, stretch shorts and all-in-one shorts. Some of the stock is marked seconds, but it is often difficult to tell why.

BICESTER OUTLET SHOPPING VILLAGE
PINGLE DRIVE, BICESTER, JUNCTION 9 OF M40,
OXFORDSHIRE OX6 7WD
☎ (01869) 323200. OPEN 10 - 6 SEVEN DAYS A WEEK.
Factory Shopping Village • *Womenswear & Menswear*
Children • Household • Sportswear & Equipment

Described as 'Bond Street comes to Bicester', when it opened, Bicester Village has established itself as the UK's leading outlet shopping destination with by far the largest selection of international Bond Street names to choose from. Currently there are 60 shops offering quality merchandise at discounts of up to 60%, sometimes even more. The choice of famous brands at Bicester Village is second to none. International star names include a Polo Ralph Lauren store, which now stocks more goods from their Sport and Home collections, Donna Karan, Versace, Christian Lacroix, Cerruti 1881 and TSE Cashmere. New arrivals from the international fashion scene are Escada, Tod's, MaxMara, Salvatore Ferragamo, Gianfranco Ferre and Alta Moda, a shop which stocks Valentino among its other brands. Both of Britain's leading designers, Nicole Farhi and Paul Smith, have shops with goods from their men's and women's collections. Karen Millen and Whistles both cater for the younger set with much more women's fashion to be found in The Designer Room, Episode, Hobbs, Jigsaw and Inwear Matinique. Top high street names are also well represented by Benetton, Principles, French Connection, Monsoon, Pepe Jeans and Racing Green. The more classic customer also has an unequalled choice with Burberry, Aquascutum, Jaeger and the Scandinavian company Red/Green, whose yachting style of casualwear is very popular. Rugged outdoor wear can be found at Helly Hansen, Tog 24, the climbing and walking specialist and John Partridge for traditional countrywear. Active sportswear, represented by Fred Perry and Reebok, has now been joined by one of America's most famous sports shoe brands, Vans. A comprehensive collection of shoes, including many ranges for children, can be found in Clarks, with elegant high fashion styles in Charles Jourdan from Paris and Joan & David from New York. Also, for ladies shoes, handbags and accessories, there is Jane Shilton; for luggage, there is the Samsonite shop, plus the exciting addition of the first TAG-Heuer outlet, which stocks end-of-line designer watches, all fully guaranteed, at very attractive prices. Lingerie and underwear is to be found at Warners and Triumph, with HOM, the French brand, for the men; and the finest French childrenswear at Petit Bateau; English fragrances at Penhaligon's; make-up, bath and body therapies at Molton Brown and soaps and gifts at Woods of Windsor. For the home, there are Price's candles and towels and duvets from another leading French brand, Descamps; cutlery from Oneida; china and crystal from Villeroy & Boch and Waterford Wedgwood. Another exciting addition is The Cosmetic Company, which stocks well-known skincare products, cosmetics and fragrances for men and women. Bicester Village likes to see itself as something akin to a 'one-floor department store' and menswear, which can often be found in the designer shops, is also well represented in its own right with Blazer, Savoy Taylors Guild, Jigsaw Menswear and Dockers, plus another international touch being provided by Cerruti Menswear, all offering good size ranges in a wide choice from very casual through to traditional business clothes. To complete the day out at Bicester Village, take home some popular titles from Sapphire Books, the outlet shop of the Borders/Books Etc. Group, get to know more about the location for a return visit from the Tourist Information Centre, and regain strength with top quality refreshment at Pret-A-Manger. There are cash machines, a children's play area, free parking and a shuttle bus and taxi connection to Bicester North Station, which is on the Chiltern Railways line, and runs between Marylebone and Birmingham. Bicester Village is about one hour's drive from London, two miles from Junction 9 on the M40. Take the A41and follow signs for Village Retail Park.

BURBERRYS LTD

BICESTER OUTLET SHOPPING VILLAGE, ADDRESS AND OPENING HOURS AS BEFORE.
☎ (01869) 323522.

Factory Shop in a Factory Shopping Village • *Womenswear & Menswear*

Sells a variety of Burberry and Thomas Burberry goods for men and women. Thomas Burberry jeans and polo shirts, classic men's check shirts, umbrellas, a variety of purses and wallets, handbags and travel bags; classic trench coats and overcoats and Thomas Burberry cashmere.

CERRUTI 1881-FEMME LTD

BICESTER OUTLET SHOPPING VILLAGE, ADDRESS AND OPENING HOURS AS BEFORE.
☎ (01869) 325519.

Factory Shop in a Factory Shopping Village • *Womenswear Only*

Cerruti has a very stylish shop in this designer village, offering a range of their women's clothes at discounts of up to 60%. Examples of prices include jackets reduced from £499 to £299; silk blouses reduced from £159 to £89; linen dresses reduced from £229 to £115; trousers suits reduced from £625 to £339; trousers reduced from £199 to £99.

CLARKS FACTORY SHOP
BICESTER OUTLET SHOPPING VILLAGE, ADDRESS AND OPENING HOURS AS BEFORE.
☎ (01869) 325646.
Factory Shop in a Factory Shopping Village
Womenswear & Menswear • Children • Sportswear & Equipment
Clarks International operate a chain of factory shops nationally which specialise in selling discontinued lines and slight sub-standards for men, women and children from Clarks, K Shoes and other famous brands. These shops trade under the name of Crockers, K Shoes Factory shop or Clarks Factory Shop and while not all are physically attached to a shoe factory, these shops are treated as factory shops by the company. Customers can expect to find an extensive range of quality shoes, sandals, walking boots, slippers, trainers, handbags, accessories and gifts, while their major outlets also offer luggage, sports clothing, sports equipment and outdoor clothing. Brands stocked include Clarks, K Shoes, Springer, CICA, Hi-Tec, Puma, Mercury, Dr Martens, Nike, LA Gear, Fila, Mizuno, Slazenger, Weider, Antler and Carlton, although not all are sold in every outlet. Discounts are from 30% to 60% off the normal high street price for perfect stock.

CURTAIN WORLD
276 BANBURY ROAD, SUMMERTOWN, OXFORD, OXFORDSHIRE OX2 7ED
☎ (01865) 516181. OPEN 9.30 - 5 MON - FRI, 9.30 - 4 SAT.
Permanent Discount Outlet • *Furniture/Soft Furnishings*
Brand name fabrics at bargain prices including Osborne & Little, Malabar, Sanderson, Crowson and Monkwell. The average discount is between 40%-50% and they also sell a wide range of chintzes from £2.99 a yard, curtain poles and accessories. The company has been in operation for more than 20 years and can offers lots of helpful advice. Up to 900 rolls of fabric at any one time sold at about half price including lots of natural and Indian fabrics.

DAKOTA MARKETING
PO BOX 121, WITNEY, OXFORDSHIRE OX8 1YU
☎ (01865) 880024. MAIL ORDER ONLY.
Permanent Discount Outlet • *Food and Leisure*
Best-selling paperbacks, audio books and a few CD Roms at discounted prices. A reader who has used this service a few times tells the GDD that the books can take up to four weeks to arrive. Audiobook cassettes, from £3.50; paperbacks, from £1.95; children's books, from £1.65; CD Roms, from £2.

DESCAMPS
BICESTER OUTLET SHOPPING VILLAGE, ADDRESS AND OPENING HOURS AS BEFORE.
☎ (01869) 323636.
Factory Shop in a Factory Shopping Village • *Household*
French designer range of bedlinen, towels and dressing gowns. By using a very

high cotton count (the amount of thread used per square metre), their bedlinen is very soft. The higher the density of cotton, the better the quality.

DISCOUNT CHINA
HIGH STREET, BURFORD, OXFORDSHIRE OX18 4QA
☎ (01993) 823452. OPEN 10 - 5 SEVEN DAYS A WEEK.
Permanent Discount Outlet • *Household*
Retailers of china and cookware direct from the factories of Staffordshire. Supplies are sourced from different manufacturers so varies according to what is available at the time, but includes china fancies, beakers, cookware, planters, Portmerion cookware and dinner sets.

EARLY'S OF WITNEY
WITNEY MILL, BURFORD ROAD, WITNEY, OXFORDSHIRE OX8 5EB
☎ (01993) 703131. OPEN 10 - 4.45 MON - FRI, 10 - 3.45 SAT.
Factory Shop • *Household*
Having moved to a different position on the same site, the shop is now bigger and sells a wider range of stock. Blankets in pure new Merino wool, traditional cellular blankets, new designs in cotton blankets in a myriad selection of colours, economy priced acrylic blankets, baby blankets, the famous Witney Point blankets, white cotton embroidered bedlinen, pram blankets, table cloths, teacloths, at factory prices. Blanket stock is made in the next door factory and depends on what is available from there. There are also some seconds, but most of the goods are perfects. Great place to shop for new bedlinen and bedspreads. There were some exceptional bargains in clearance items when we visited. The shop also stocks Coloroll bedlinen at 20% discount; a wide range of perfect and imperfect towels from Chortex, plus towelling robes, and duvets and pilows from Polywarm, including Horrockses branded products.

FIRED EARTH
TWYFORD MILL, OXFORD ROAD, ADDERBURY,
OXFORDSHIRE OX5 3HP
☎ (01295) 814399. OPEN 9.30 - 5.30 MON - SAT, 12 - 4 SUN.
Factory Shop • *DIY/Renovation*
Fired Earth sell seconds and discontinued ranges of tiles, fabric and natural fibre floor coverings from their countryside venue, as well as rugs, kelims, gabbehs and other tribal weaving at full price. Terracotta and slate floor tiles are sold from around £15 a square metre upwards: some glazed tiles from around £5 a square metre. Typical bargains in fabric range from prototype tartans (unique because they have not been put into production) to slightly soiled crewel works (which simply need dry cleaning) often at less than cost price. Fired Earth also produce the V&A range of historic and traditional paints and dented paints tins are sold at a discount alongside other "bruised" accessories.

FRED PERRY LTD
BICESTER OUTLET SHOPPING VILLAGE, ADDRESS AND OPENING HOURS AS BEFORE.
☎ (01869) 325504.
Factory Shop in a Factory Shopping Village • *Sportswear & Equipment*
Sells men's and women's ranges of the famous Fred Perry active performance clothing: shorts, tennis tops, tracksuits, T-shirts. All price labels show the original and the reduced price.

GOOD AS NEW
21 NEWBURY STREET, WANTAGE, OXFORDSHIRE OX12 8BU
☎ (01235) 769526 OPEN 10 - 4 TUE - SAT.
Dress Agency • *Womenswear Only*
High street, medium sized shop selling ladies designer wear ranging from Marks & Spencer to Armani, though the majority of clothes come from Jaeger, Windsmoor and Planet. All nearly-new clothes are under two years old and come in a wide range of sizes. The full range from coats, dresses, separates, evening wear and hats to shoes and handbags are sold.

HILARY'S HAT HIRE
THE OVEN, 1 HIGH STREET, BODICOTE, OXFORDSHIRE OX15 4BZ
☎ (01295) 263880. OPEN 9.30 - 7 MON - FRI, BY APPOINTMENT ONLY.
Hire Shop • *Womenswear Only*
Home-based business in a converted barn with more than 500 hats from which to choose. £15, £20 and £25 hires a hat for a weekend. Whether you're looking for something for a wedding, funeral or graduation, regattas or race events, you'll find something suitable here, whatever your age.

HOBBS
BICESTER OUTLET SHOPPING VILLAGE, ADDRESS AND OPENING HOURS AS BEFORE.
☎ (01869) 325660.
Factory Shop in a Factory Shopping Village • *Womenswear Only*
Hobbs has a range of clothes for women and a large shoe selection. All carry reductions of between 30% and 70%. Styles include business suits, evening wear and fashionable high street designs.

IMPS
34 MARKET SQUARE, WITNEY, OXFORDSHIRE OX8 58A
☎ (01993) 779875. OPEN 9 - 5.30 MON - SAT.
40 UPPER HIGH STREET, THAME, OXFORDSHIRE OX9 E OX9 3AG
☎ (01844) 212985. OPEN 9 - 5 MON - SAT.
52 SHEEP STREET, BICESTER, OXFORDSHIRE
☎ (01869) 243455. OPEN 9 - 5 MON - SAT.
Permanent Discount Outlets • *Womenswear & Menswear*

Children • Household
High street shops selling popular chainstore seconds fashion for all the family as well as towels, china, trays and flower cachepots. Men's women's and childrenswear from designer brands such as Ralph Lauren, Tommy Hilfiger, Timberland and Gap. Sportswear from Umbro, Adidas and Nike all at up to 50% off high street prices.

IN WEAR FACTORY OUTLET
BICESTER VILLAGE, PINGLE DRIVE, JUNCTION 9 OF M40,
OXFORDSHIRE OX6 7WD
☎ (01869) 369415. OPEN 10 - 6 SEVEN DAYS A WEEK.
Factory Shop in a Factory Shopping Village • *Womenswear & Menswear*
In Wear for women and Matinique for men and Part Two for both men and women at discounts of between 30%-70% for last season's stock, ends of lines and seconds. All the stock is made up of separates and tends to be stylishly casual and includes blazers, jeans, trousers, dresses, knitwear, suits and outerwear.

ISIS CERAMICS
THE OLD TOFFEE FACTORY, 120A MARLBOROUGH RD, OXFORD,
OXFORDSHIRE OX1 4LS
☎ (01865) 722729. OPEN 10 - 4 MON -FRI, SAT BY APPOINTMENT.
Factory Shop • *Household*
Makers of ceramics which are handpainted in the style of seventeenth and eighteenth century Delftware, Isis has a range of cut-price seconds on sale at its workshops and showroom set in an old toffee factory in Oxford. Their most popular seller is the flower brick followed by lamps and colander bowls, all painted in traditional colours - blue, green, plum, sepia, black, saffron and pink. They also do complete dinner services, platters with tulips, birds and farmyard animals, dessert plates with scalloped edges, teapots and cream jugs, vases, baluster vases and cachepots. Seconds range from £15, high quality seconds enjoy discounts of at least 25%. There are twice-yearly clearance sales in January and July. Best to phone ahead for weekend opening times.

JAEGER FACTORY SHOP
BICESTER VILLAGE, 35 PINGLE DRIVE, BICESTER (JUNCTION 9 OF M40), OXFORDSHIRE OX6 7WD
☎ (01869) 369220. OPEN 10 - 6 MON - SUN.
Factory Shop in a Factory Shopping Village • *Womenswear & Menswear*
Contemporary classics from Jaeger at excellent prices. Most of the merchandise is previous seasons' stock, but you might also find some special makes. Both shops stock tailoring and knitwear for women and men.

JANE AND STEPHEN BAUGHAN
THE STABLE, KINGSWAY FARM, ASTON, OXFORDSHIRE OX18 2BT
☎ (01993) 852031. OPEN 9 - 5 MON - SAT, 10.30 - 4.30 SUN, BANK HOLS.
Factory Shop • *Household*
Set in a converted barn next to their workshop, Jane and Stephen Baughan's factory shop sells seconds and overmakes of their hand decorated pottery. The pottery is made using traditional methods of slip-casting and jollying before being decorated by hand using a combination of fresh colours and a wide variety of surface designs. They have also developed their own specialised technique of hand stencilling on pottery. Designs range from Sunflower and Blue Wild Clematis to birds and animals, and all products are microwave and dishwasher safe. Stephen and Jane usually supply more than 200 shops, as well as the National Trust. There is now a visitors' centre open on weekdays from 9 to 5. Tours take place four times a day at £1.50 for adults and £1 for children, with the chance to decorate your own piece. Coffee shop and free parking for 250 cars.

JANE SHILTON
☎ (01869) 325387.
Factory Shop in a Factory Shopping Village • *Womenswear Only*
Merchandise from past seasons' collections or factory seconds at discounts of at least 30% and up to 70% off the original price. There is a wide range of handbags, small leather goods, shoes, luggage umbrellas and travel bags. Example of price reduction: handbags at £24.99 originally £37.

JEFFREY ROGERS
☎ (01869) 323567.
Factory Shop in a Factory Shopping Village • *Womenswear Only*
Jeffrey Rogers stocks fashions for the younger, trendy end of the market . There is also the Rogers Plus range for sizes 16-24. Twenty five percent of the stock is discounted by 75%. The village also has a restaurant, a children's play area and free parking.

JOAN & DAVID
BICESTER OUTLET SHOPPING VILLAGE, ADDRESS AND OPENING HOURS AS BEFORE.
☎ (01869) 323387.
Factory Shop in a Factory Shopping Village • *Womenswear Only*
This is a very stylish shop now catering for women only. The stock comprises 25% classic clothing and 15% accessories. J & D's divine shoes are reduced by about 50%, though they are still mostly above the £60 mark. The village also has a cafe, children's play area and free parking.

JUST FABRICS
BURFORD ANTIQUES CENTRE, CHELTENHAM ROAD, BURFORD, OXFORDSHIRE OX18 4JA
☎ (01993) 823391. E-MAIL: fabrics@justfabrics.co.uk
WEBSITE: www.justfabrics.co.uk   MAIL ORDER ON LINE.

OPEN 9.30 - 5.30 MON - SAT, 12 - 4 SUN AND BANK HOLIDAYS.
Permanent Discount Outlet • *Furniture/Soft Furnishings*
Just Fabrics offers huge savings on a comprehensive selection of quality furnishing fabrics from stock. Whether choosing a leading designer name, clearance or from their own range of linen unions or checks and stripe collection, all are very competitively priced. Their telephone enquiry service is also very popular. After discussing your fabric requirements, stock fabric cuttings are then despatched. A mail order service is available. They do not order from pattern books. The enquiry line is 01993 823391, open during shop hours, with an answerphone out of hours.

LOOSE ENDS
78 HIGH STREET, WITNEY, OXFORDSHIRE OX8 6HL
☎ (01993) 773508. OPEN 9.30 - 5 MON - SAT.
Permanent Discount Outlet • *Furniture/Soft Furnishings*
Selected seconds in furnishing fabrics from well-known designers. Budget ranges of first quality fabrics in cotton prints and natural fabrics, damasks and madras checks from about £5 a metre. Medium-sized shop in busy high street with double yellow lines outside, although there is a car park nearby. Full making up service is available.

MATALAN
UNIT 5, THE JOHN ALLEN CENTRE, COWLEY, OXFORD, OXFORDSHIRE OX4 3UP
☎ (01865) 747400. OPEN 10 - 8 MON - FRI, 9 - 6 SAT, 10 - 4 SUN.
Permanent Discount Outlet • *Womenswear & Menswear*
Children • *Household*
Matalan is a fashion and homewares value retailer giving customers what they claim to be unbeatable value for money with huge savings on a wide range of products including high quality fashionable clothing for men, women and children at up to 50% off high street prices. Matalan is situated out of town and stores are open seven days a week all year round.

MILL OUTLETS LTD
51 HIGH STREET, BANBURY, OXFORDSHIRE OX16 BLA
☎ (01295) 264455. OPEN 9 - 5 MON - SAT.
Permanent Discount Outlet • *Household*
Specialises in curtains, net curtains, bedding, bed linens, towels, kitchen textiles and other household textiles. They also offer ranges of hand knitting yarns, men's and ladies socks, hosiery and underwear. Merchandise comes direct from the manufacturers, often made up of clearance stock or chainstore overmakes and seconds. Prices are very competitive with savings of up to 50% and more off manufacturer's recommended prices.

MONSOON
UNIT 3, BICESTER VILLAGE, JUNCTION 9 OF M40, BICESTER,
OXFORDSHIRE OX6 7WD
☎ (01869) 323286. OPEN 10 - 6 SEVEN DAYS A WEEK.
Factory Shop in a Factory Shopping Village • *Womenswear Only*
Medium-sized outlet selling marked down current stock for some of the year as well as last year's stock and discontinued lines, including jewellery. There are also outlets at Birmingham, Cambridge and Clarks Village in Street, Somerset.

NICOLE FARHI AND FRENCH CONNECTION
BICESTER VILLAGE, JUNCTION 9 OF M40, BICESTER
OXFORDSHIRE OX26 6WD
☎ (01869) 252346 NICOLE FARHI.
☎ (01869) 369582 FRENCH CONNECTION.
OPEN 10 - 6 SEVEN DAYS A WEEK.
Factory Shop • *Womenswear & Menswear*
Separate shops selling previous season merchandise, samples and seconds from Nicole Farhi and French Connection at 30% - 80% less than retail price. There is also a Nicole Farhi/French Connection factory shop in London.

ONEIDA
BICESTER OUTLET SHOPPING VILLAGE, ADDRESS AND OPENING HOURS AS BEFORE.
☎ (01869) 324789.
Factory Shop in a Factory Shopping Village • *Household*
Oneida is the world's largest cutlery company and originates from the United States of America. In addition to cutlery, it sells silver and silver plate at discounts of between 30% and 50%, plus frames, candlesticks and trays. They also have their own range of chinaware and glass, also sold here at discounts of 30%-50%.

PARTRIDGE
BICESTER OUTLET SHOPPING VILLAGE, ADDRESS AND OPENING HOURS AS BEFORE.
☎ (01869) 325332.
Factory Shop in a Factory Shopping Village
Womenswear & Menswear • *Children*
Partridge specialises in fashionable outdoor clothes and accessories. Ranges include waxed jackets, Gore-tex jackets, waterproof jackets, tweeds, quilts, fleece jackets and waistcoats, knitwear, shirts, chinos, cord and moleskin trousers, hats and caps. Discontinued lines are on sale at discounted prices with a minimum of 30% and up to 70% off during promotions.

PEPE JEANS LONDON
BICESTER OUTLET SHOPPING VILLAGE, ADDRESS AND OPENING HOURS AS BEFORE.
☎ (01869) 325378.
Factory Shop in a Factory Shopping Village
Womenswear & Menswear • *Children*
Pepe Jeans is a European fashion jean company stocking a wide range of casual wear including men's, women's and children's jeans, all of which are end of season or fragmented ranges. Free alteration service and exchange policy offered. There's also a postal service - phone for details. Bicester Village also has a cafe, children's play area and free parking.

PERUVIAN CONNECTION
28 HART STREET, HENLEY ON THAMES, OXFORDSHIRE RG9 2AU
☎ (01491) 414446. OPEN 9.30 - 5.30 MON - SAT.
Permanent Discount Outlet • *Womenswear & Menswear*
Last season's stock from the well-known Peruvian Connection catalogue. Alpaca and pima cotton sweaters, lighter weight polo necks, cardigans and pullovers for men and women at discounted prices.

POLO RALPH LAUREN FACTORY STORE
BICESTER OUTLET SHOPPING VILLAGE, PINGLE DRIVE, BICESTER, JUNCTION 9 OF M40, OXFORDSHIRE OX6 7WD
☎ (01869) 325200. OPEN 10 - 6 MON - SAT, 12 - 6 SUN.
Factory Shop in a Factory Shopping Village • *Womenswear & Menswear*
Polo Ralph Lauren, the largest shop in this factory shopping village with the prime spot, has discounted items by between 30% and 60% for men, women and boys. For men wool jackets, jackets, sports jackets, Polo T-shirts, rugby shirts, trousers, jeans, ties, as well as accessories. For women, outerwear, skirts, jackets, dresses, trousers, knits, T-shirts and accessories. Also home collections and fragrances discounted by between 15% and 50%.

PRICE'S CANDLES
BICESTER OUTLET SHOPPING VILLAGE, ADDRESS AND OPENING HOURS AS BEFORE.
☎ (01869) 325520.
Factory Shop in a Factory Shopping Village • *Household*
Everything sold in this shop are seconds, discontinued sizes not available elsewhere, over-runs or candles in old packaging that has now been replaced. There are church candles, lanterns, candles in pots and glass jars, star-shaped candles, floating candles, candlestick holders, serviettes, scented candles and garden torches.

PRINCIPLES
BICESTER OUTLET SHOPPING VILLAGE, ADDRESS AND OPENING HOURS AS BEFORE.
☎ (01869) 325300.
Factory Shop in a Factory Shopping Village • *Womenswear & Menswear*
End of season lines with the normal Principles refund guarantee. The range includes, for women, dresses, blouses, coats, outerwear, knitwear, casualwear and a selection of Petite clothing for women who are 5ft 3ins and under. For men, there is formalwear, smart casualwear, knitwear, outerwear, PFM Sport, jeanswear and casualwear.

RACING GREEN
BICESTER OUTLET SHOPPING VILLAGE, ADDRESS AND OPENING HOURS AS BEFORE.
☎ (01869) 325484.
Factory Shop in a Factory Shopping Village • *Womenswear & Menswear*
Overstocks and clearance lines from this mail order catalogue are sold here at discount prices.

REDGREEN
BICESTER OUTLET SHOPPING VILLAGE, ADDRESS AND OPENING HOURS AS BEFORE.
☎ (01869) 323324.
Factory Shop in a Factory Shopping Village • *Womenswear & Menswear Sportswear & Equipment*
RedGreen is Scandinavian leisure wear for men and women. The high quality and classic design has a nautical heritage but a stylish look. The collection includes outerwear, sweaters, shirts, trousers, skirts, dresses, sweatshirts, T-shirts, tailored jackets, footwear and accessories. In addition to the main collection, you will also find a broad RedGreen golf collection for men and women and also the younger and more casual First Gear Collection. Discounts offered are between 25% and 70%.

REVIVAL CLOTHES AGENCY
60 ST CLEMENT'S, OXFORD OXFORDSHIRE OX4 1AH
☎ (01865) 251005, OPEN 10 - 4 TUE, WED, THUR, 10 - 5 FRI, SAT.
Dress Agency • *Womenswear & Menswear* • *Children Furniture/Soft Furnishings*
A large shop containing two spacious rooms behind a showroom. All stock is less than two years' old. The ladies section includes labels from Wallis and Next to Whistles, Nicole Farhi, Jaeger and Karen Millen. There are also accessories such as hats and jewellery. All prices are well under half the original price and sizes range from 8 - 24. The Wedding dress section has dresses from £90 - £600 including Ronald Joyce and Anna Belinda. The evening dresses range from £30 - £100 and include many Monsoon ballgowns. The menswear is not

extensive but includes Armani, Next and Jaeger suits and dinner suits. Childrenswear includes Next, OshKosh and Laura Ashley. Soft furnishings and curtains are also stocked and hat hire is now available at £15.

SAPPHIRE BOOKS
BICESTER OUTLET SHOPPING VILLAGE, ADDRESS AND OPENING HOURS AS BEFORE.
☎ (01869) 325417.
Factory Shop in a Factory Shopping Village • *Food and Leisure*
This shop sells a wide range of books, including popular paperback and hardback fiction, classics, cookery titles, children's books and reference tomes, as well as wrapping paper and greetings cards. All books are sold at a discount of at least 30% from the reccommended retail price and many are available at even greater savings.

SCOOP
77 BELL STREET, HENLEY-ON-THAMES, OXFORDSHIRE RG9 2BD
☎ (01491) 572962. OPEN 10 - 5 MON - SAT.
Dress Agency • *Womenswear Only*
Nearly-new ladies wear from designers at the top end of the market, including Max Mara, Gucci, Escada, Betty Barclay, Valentino, Armani, Emanuel, Louis Feraud. Often stocks seasonal wear for Ascot and Derby Day, as well as cocktail and wedding outfits. Also has a supply of holidaywear, shoes, hats, jewellery and other accessories.

THE BALLROOM
5-6 THE PLAIN, OXFORD, OXFORDSHIRE OX4 1AS
☎ (01865) 241054. ☎ (01865) 202303 FOR MENSWEAR. OPEN 9.15 - 5.45 MON - SAT.
Hire Shops • *Womenswear & Menswear*
Hundreds of bridal gowns, including designer clearance from £50 - £500. Over 2000 ballgowns and slinky dresses including clearance. Short dresses from £15, long dresses from £35. Extensive accessories and most items to hire or buy. Menswear and mens' clearance formal wear includes DJ's from £15 to £200, £29.80 to hire.

THE CURTAIN EXCHANGE
85 HIGH STREET, THAME, OXFORDSHIRE OX9 3EH
☎ (01844) 261566. OPEN 9.30 - 5 MON - SAT.
Secondhand shops • *Furniture/Soft Furnishings*
The Curtain Exchange is a franchised group of shops selling beautiful top quality secondhand curtains, blinds, pelmets, etc at between one-third and one half of the brand new price. Their stock comes from a variety of sources: people who are moving house; people who have curtains made and then feel they are wrong for the room; show houses where the builder wants to recoup

some of his outgoings; interior designers' mistakes. Stock changes constantly and ranges from rich brocades, damasks and velvets to chintzes, linens and cottons. Designer names include Colefax & Fowler, Designers Guild, Laura Ashley, Warner, Sanderson, Osborne & Little, Fortuny and Bennison. A team of fitters and alteration experts are available if required. They offer a 24-hour availability. The Curtain Exchange also supply bespoke ranges with samples of curtains hanging. These fabrics are chosen from suppliers all over the world and are an excellent buy. They also offer ready made curtains designed exclusively for them which come in lengths up to 305cm (120"). These are outstanding value, e.g. 80" wide, 120" drop start at £175 including VAT.

THE DESIGNER ROOM
BICESTER VILLAGE, BICESTER, JUNCTION 9 OF M40,
OXFORDSHIRE OX6 7WD
☎ (01869) 320052. OPEN 10 - 6 MON - SAT, 11 - 5 SUN.
Factory Shop in a Factory Shopping Village • *Womenswear Only*
Ever-changing range of top designer clothes including Jean-Paul Gaultier, Jasper Conran, Calvin Klein, Dolce and Gabbana and The Maska Group. Discounts vary from 30%-70%.

THE PAMELA HOWARD FASHION CONSULTANCY
WOODLAND, BEDWELLS HEATH, BOARS HILL,
OXFORDSHIRE OX1 5JE
☎ (01865) 735735. BY APPOINTMENT ONLY.
Dress Agency • *Hire Shop* • *Womenswear Only*
Pamela Howard holds successful Open Days of new and nearly-new designer clothes, shoes and accessories including Armani, Valentino, Joseph, Chanel, Moschino, Nicole Farhi etc. Prices range from £25 - £400. The Open Days have become extremely popular over a number of years, and have been described as fun and a totally different concept of shopping in a relaxed and friendly atmosphere. For shopaholics it is an Aladdins Cave, but ladies who hate clothes shopping also save time and gain confidence by trying different colours and styles that are not just in the current season's fashion. The Hire Service - Prelude - for Designer evening wear, ball gowns and outfits for Ascot and Henley, is available by appointment. Write or telephone to go on the mailing list, or if you are visiting Oxford, phone and arrange to view the wide selection of clothes.

THE RED HOUSE
WINDRUSH PARK, WITNEY, OXFORDSHIRE OX8 5YF
☎ (01993) 893456. WEBSITE: www.redhouse.co.uk   MAIL ORDER.
Permanent Discount Outlet • *Children*
An excellent catalogue of children's books. The Red House covers both educational matters, from reading skills to history, and practical activity books as well as fiction. The books are a mixture of hardback and paperback from a

variety of different publishers, and good savings are to be made. Occasionally some CD Roms are available. They hold end of season sales about twice a year at their warehouse in Witney, Oxfordshire. Telephone for dates.

THE SUIT COMPANY
BICESTER OUTLET SHOPPING VILLAGE, PINGLE DRIVE, BICESTER, JUNCTION 9 OF M40, OXFORDSHIRE OX6 7WD
☎ (01869) 324321. OPEN 10 - 6 SEVEN DAYS A WEEK.
Factory Shop in a Factory Shopping Village • *Menswear Only*
Part of the Moss Bros group, every item has a large price tag with the old and the new price, also leather gloves, belts, ties, work shirts, suits, jackets. The village also has a cafe, children's play area and free parking.

TK MAXX
CALTHORPE STREET, OFF HIGH STREET, BANBURY, OXFORDSHIRE
☎ (01295) 277022. OPEN 9 - 5.30 MON - WED, 9 - 7 THUR,
9 - 6 FRI, SAT 10 - 4 SUN.
Permanent Discount Outlet • *Womenswear & Menswear*
Children • *Household* • *Furniture/Soft Furnishings*
Based on an American concept, TK Maxx is situated in easily accessible, often centrally located stores and offers famous label goods with up to 60% savings off recommended retail prices. TK Maxx has fashion for the whole family - women's, men's and childrenswear - accessories, shoes, gifts, kitchenware and home goods. Everything in the store is branded with a choice of well-known high street names to designer labels, and while a small percentage might be clearly marked past season, the great majority of items in store are current season, current stock and still with phenomenal savings. There is a huge choice with 50,000 pieces in store and up to 10,000 new items arriving a week. The stores are simple and unfussy with wide aisles, shopping trolleys and baskets, and a spacious, functional feel to them but there are individual changing rooms, ramps for buggies and wheelchairs and plenty of staff on the shop floor. Every branch accepts all major credit and debit cards and has a liberal refund and return policy.

TOG 24
BICESTER OUTLET SHOPPING VILLAGE, PINGLE DRIVE, BICESTER, JUNCTION 9 OF M40, OXFORDSHIRE OX6 7WD
☎ (01869) 323278. OPEN 10 - 6 SEVEN DAYS A WEEK.
Factory Shop in a Factory Shopping Village
Womenswear & Menswear • *Children* • *Sportswear & Equipment*
Tog 24 are the UK's fastest growing brand name in outdoor clothing and leisurewear. They utilise the world's finest performance fabrics including Gore-Tex, Polartec and Burlington MCS, catering for all the family for all seasons, with cosy fleeces and waterproofs for the winter, and trekking ranges, shorts and t-shirts for the summer. With all prices at least 30% below the recommended retail price, you can afford to enter the Tog comfort zone.

TOGS
13 HIGH STREET, THAME, OXFORDSHIRE OX9 2BZ
☎ (01844) 215002. OPEN 9.30 - 5 MON - SAT.
36 STERT STREET, ABINGDON, OXFORDSHIRE
☎ (01235) 524989. OPEN 9.30 - 5 MON - SAT.
Permanent Discount Outlet • *Womenswear Only*

Togs elegant shop front on Thame High Street has been established for more than 15 years and suggests something of the quality fashions you will find inside. What may not be apparent is the value-for-money ladies separates on offer, most of which are priced beween £10 and £15. This policy extends to Togs other outlet Monmouth. Catering for all ages, they introduce new lines frequently. Regulars drop in often to see what's new or just for a chat. Staff are friendly and helpful and will always advise honestly on what suits each customer. Each of the three shops is situated in a building full of character with dark green paintwork and a distinctive oval signboard. Wide range of casual wear for women at competitive prices, including labels such as Viz-A-Viz, Adini and Poppy. Sizes range from 10 - 18 for women. All items are perfects and current fashion.

TOP MARKS
8 HIGH STREET, CHIPPING NORTON, OXFORDSHIRE OX7 5ND
☎ (01608) 642653. OPEN 9 - 5.30 MON - FRI, 9 - 5 SAT.
60 PARSON STREET, BANBURY, OXFORDSHIRE OX16 8NB
☎ (01295) 270530. OPEN 9 - 5.30 MON - FRI, 9 - 5 SAT.
Permanent Discount Outlet • *Womenswear & Menswear* • *Children*

Sells seconds from leading chain stores for all the family. Most of the stock is made up of men's and women's wear, with some childrenswear. The clothes are mainly Marks & Spencer seconds, sold at about one third cheaper than in the high street. Wide range of stock in various sizes with new stock arriving twice a week. They also stock Debenhams' and Richards' stock when available. There is another branch at Moreton-in-Marsh, Gloucestershire.

TRIUMPH INTERNATIONAL LTD
BICESTER OUTLET SHOPPING VILLAGE, ADDRESS AND OPENING HOURS AS BEFORE.
☎ (01869) 329930.
Factory Shop in a Factory Shopping Village • *Womenswear & Menswear*

This shop sells Hom swimwear and underwear for men, outerwear including shirts as well as nightwear. For women, there is the Triumph range of lingerie, swimwear and nightwear.

VILLEROY & BOCH (UK) LIMITED
BICESTER OUTLET SHOPPING VILLAGE, ADDRESS AND OPENING HOURS AS BEFORE.
☎ (01869) 324646.
Factory Shop in a Factory Shopping Village • *Household*

An exclusive range of tableware, crystal and cutlery from Europe's largest tableware manufacturer. Convenient parking and pleasant surroundings make for a pleasurable and unhurried shopping experience. A varied and constantly changing stock, including seconds, hotelware and discontinued lines, on sale at excellent reductions, always makes for a worthwhile visit.

WALTON DESIGN LTD
9 MARKET PLACE, CHIPPING NORTON, OXFORDSHIRE OX7 5NA
☎ (01608) 642153. OPEN 9 - 6 MON - SAT, 10 - 4 SUN, 10 - 5 BANK HOLS.
6 MARKET PLACE, WANTAGE OX12 8AB
☎ (01235) 771115. OPEN 9 - 6 MON - SAT, 10 - 4 SUN, 10 - 5 BANK HOLS.
14 MARKET PLACE, WALLINGFORD OX10 0AD
☎ (01491) 832797. OPEN 9 - 6 MON - SAT, 10 - 4 SUN, 10 - 5 BANK HOLS.
3 DUKE STREET, HENLEY-ON-THAMES RG9 1UR
☎ (01491) 412636. OPEN 9 - 6 MON - SAT, 10 - 4 SUN, 10 - 5 BANK HOLS.

Permanent Discount Outlet • *Womenswear Only*

A chain of thirteen stores across the south of England selling well-known labels for women at greatly reduced prices. Current stock from high street stores might include Liz Claiborne, DKNY, Nougat, Ralph Lauren, Banana Republic, Calvin Klein and Tommy Hilfiger. New lines come in each week and are often one-offs, so regular customers know to buy things when they see them or risk missing out.

WARNERS
BICESTER OUTLET SHOPPING VILLAGE, PINGLE DRIVE, BICESTER, JUNCTION 9 OF M40, OXFORDSHIRE OX6 7WD
☎ (01869) 324401. OPEN 10 - 6 SEVEN DAYS A WEEK.

Factory Shop in a Factory Shopping Village • *Womenswear & Menswear*

This shop sells a wide range of women's lingerie from Leisureby, Warners, with bras, slips, thongs, bodies and briefs at discounts from 25% to 70%. Each item is labelled with both the rrp and the discounted prices. For example, bikini brief, £6.99 reduced from £17; underwire bra, £14.99 reduced from £33; body, £24.99 reduced from £65. Slightly imperfect stock as well as perfect quality, end of season and discontinued merchandise and swimwear are also stocked. Underwear for men, including Calvin Klein briefs for £2.99, is on offer too.

WOODS OF WINDSOR
BICESTER OUTLET SHOPPING VILLAGE, ADDRESS AND OPENING HOURS AS BEFORE.
☎ (01869) 325307.

Factory Shop in a Factory Shopping Village • *Household*

Sells traditional gift sets, soaps, perfume, and talc at discounts of 25% for standard ranges and 50% for discontinued ranges. The village also has a cafe, children's play area and free parking.

Rutland

COTTESMORE DRESS AGENCY
MAIN STREET, COTTESMORE, NR OAKHAM, RUTLAND LE15 7DJ
☎ (01572) 813247. OPEN 10 - 5 TUE - SAT.
Dress Agency • *Womenswear Only*
Middle market to high quality designer clothes including labels such as Basler, Escada, Bianca, Jaeger, Louis Feraud, Mansfield. Also high quality evening wear and costume jewellery to buy, sizes 8 - 24. Please phone before making a special journey during holiday periods.

LANDS' END DIRECT MERCHANTS
LANDS' END WAY, OAKHAM, RUTLAND LE15 6US
☎ (01572) 722553. OPEN 10 - 6 MON - SAT, 10 - 4 SUN AND BANK HOLIDAYS.
Factory Shop • *Womenswear & Menswear*
Lands' End, a US mail order company, moved its headquarters and factory outlet to a larger site in summer 1998. Their factory outlet store is now 25% larger and only a few minutes walk down the road from the old location. Modelled on the dozen or so clearance outlets they operate in and around their US headquarters in Dodgeville, Wisconsin, this factory shop is designed to sell warehouse overstocks, obsolete lines and a range of "not quite perfect" products. There will normally be about 3,000 items in the store from jeans to jumpers, leggings to luggage, turtlenecks to trousers. Genuine overstocks are priced at 25%-40% below normal catalogue prices; catalogue returns and near-perfect seconds are reduced by between 40%-85%. All overstock items are guaranteed, first quality Lands' End label products, all of which have been offered previously in their catalogues at regular prices. There is ample free parking, easy wheelchair and pushchair access and changing facilities. You cannot buy current catalogue merchandise from the clearance outlet.

NIKKI'S NURSERY HIRE
1 RECTORY FARM COTTAGE, ROOKERY ROAD, STRETTON,
OAKHAM, RUTLAND LE15 7RA
☎ (01780) 410359.
Hire Shop • *Children*
Part of the Baby Equipment Hirers Association (BEHA), which has more than 100 members countrywide. BEHA run an advice line which will try and answer any queries you have regarding hiring services for children. Phone the Babyline on 0831 310355.

RUTLAND LIGHTING
THISTLETON ROAD INDUSTRIAL ESTATE, MARKET OVERTON,
OAKHAM, RUTLAND LE15 7PP
☎ (01572) 767587. OPEN 9 - 4 MON - SAT.
Permanent Discount Outlet • *Household*
Sells a full range of lampshades, table and floor lamps, chandeliers, bulbs, outdoor and indoor lights, plus other manufacturers' ends of lines and chainstore seconds. Most lines have genuine reductions on normal retail prices. This shop is small and within the factory itself unlike the Grantham, Lincolnshire shop which is large and on the high street.

THE CURTAIN EXCHANGE
4 CROWN WALK, HIGH STREET, OAKHAM, RUTLAND LE15 6BZ
☎ (01572) 770990. OPEN 10 - 4 TUE - SAT.
Secondhand shop • *Furniture/Soft Furnishings*
The Curtain Exchange is a franchised group of shops selling beautiful top quality secondhand curtains, blinds, pelmets, etc at between one-third and one half of the brand new price. Their stock comes from a variety of sources: people who are moving house; people who have curtains made and then feel they are wrong for the room; show houses where the builder wants to recoup some of his outgoings; interior designers' mistakes. Stock changes constantly and ranges from rich brocades, damasks and velvets to chintzes, linens and cottons. Designer names include Colefax & Fowler, Designers Guild, Laura Ashley, Warner, Sanderson, Osborne & Little, Fortuny and Bennison. A team of fitters and alteration experts are available if required. They offer a 24-hour availability. The Curtain Exchange also supply bespoke ranges with samples of curtains hanging. These fabrics are chosen from suppliers all over the world and are an excellent buy. They also offer ready made curtains designed exclusively for them which come in lengths up to 305cm (120"). These are outstanding value, e.g. 80" wide, 120" drop start at £175 including vat.

THE UPPINGHAM DRESS AGENCY
2-6 ORANGE STREET, UPPINGHAM, RUTLAND LE15 9SQ
☎ (01572) 823276. FAX ☎ (01572) 823815. WEBSITE: www.dressagency.co.uk
OPEN 9 - 5 MON - SAT, 12 - 4 SUN AND BANK HOLS.
Dress Agency • *Womenswear & Menswear* • *Children*
One of Britain's largest, longest established and most reputable dress agencies with ten rooms packed with over 4000 quality nearly-new and end of line garments from famous high street names to top designer labels. Featured on TV and in numerous national newspapers and magazines, this agency, situated in a picturesque market town has everything from casuals to occasion wear, evening wear, suits and separates, hats, shoes, handbags, scarves and costume jewellery. There are departments for men, women and children, seven changing rooms and a small coffee lounge where the coffee and biscuits are free.

Shropshire

BARN BOOKS
PEAR TREE FARM, NORBURY, WHITCHURCH, SHROPSHIRE SY13 4HZ
☎ (01948) 663742. E-MAIL: barnbooks@barnbooks.co.uk
WEBSITE: www.barnbooks.co.uk   OPEN 10 - 5.30 FRI - SUN, BANK HOLIDAYS.
Permanent Discount Outlet • *Food and Leisure*
Remainders, publishers' returns and secondhand books of an excellent quality and range. Comprehensive gardening, architecture and countryside selection as well as children's books. The bookshop is set in beautiful countryside with ample parking, visit the website for more information and a map.

CANE AND WICKER FACTORY SHOP
MONKMOOR INDUSTRIAL ESTATE, SHREWSBURY, SHROPSHIRE SY2 5ST
☎ (01743) 240261. OPEN 9.30 - 5 MON - SAT, CLOSED SUN.
Factory Shop • *Furniture/Soft Furnishings*
The UK's largest importer of cane and wicker furniture has a huge factory shop with over 60 suites on display at prices starting from £199. There are more than 1,000 fabrics from which to choose. This importer and wholesaler runs two factory shops (here and a larger outlet in Walsall, West Midlands). The furniture comes in part-assembled and is finished, stuffed and upholstered on site. It comes in a wide range of finishes including light and dark antique, honey, mahogany and walnut. Furniture is all perfect stock unless otherwise stated, end of lines, protoypes as well as many current models. There is also a Mexican pine furniture range and fabric for curtains (though because the fabric is back coated for fire retardancy, it is very heavy). The cheapest cane suites cost from £199, the most expensive, £2,500. This represents a saving of about 15% - 20% on normal retail prices. Matching dining sets and occasional furniture also available. There is immediate delivery for furniture in stock; orders will be fulfilled within about one week.

CATALOGUE SURPLUS CENTRE LTD
28-30 ST MARY'S STREET, NEWPORT, SHROPSHIRE TF10 7AB
☎ (01952) 825889. OPEN 9 - 5 MON - SAT.
Permanent Discount Outlet • *Womenswear & Menswear*
Children • *Household*
Ex-catalogue clothes for men, women and children as well as shoes and bedlinen, with occasional supplies of cookware and china - in fact some of everything a large catalogue sells, all at half price. There are other outlets at Telford, Oswestry, Shrewsbury and Stoke.

CLASSIC FURNITURE
CLASSIC FURNITURE GROUP PLC, AUDLEY AVENUE, NEWPORT,
SHROPSHIRE TF10 7BX
- (01952) 825000. OPEN 9 - 5 MON - FRI, 9 - 12 SAT.

Factory Shop • *Furniture/Soft Furnishings*

A clearance warehouse of furniture from pubs, clubs and restaurants, leading to most of the stock here being made up of chairs and tables. Most of the furniture is suitable for dining rooms.

CLASSICAL PASSIONS
PO BOX 7, OSWESTRY, SHROPSHIRE SY10 9WF
- (01691) 670 750. FAX (01691) 670 747.
E-MAIL: classical-passions@yahoo.co.uk   MAIL ORDER.

Permanent Discount Outlet • *Food and Leisure*

Mail order company which claims to better most prices for CDs, cassettes, DVDs and videos. Rather than operating by catalogue, you simply phone up - having checked prices locally - and find out what their best price is. Their name suggests they are classical specialists, but they deal in any type of music and any video on general release. Postage free over £25.

DICKINSONS ARCHITECTURAL ANTIQUES
140 CORVE STREET, LUDLOW, SHROPSHIRE SY8 2PG
- (01584) 876207. 9.30 - 5 MON - SAT.

Architectural Salvage • *DIY/Renovation*

Specialise in genuine period bathrooms, fireplaces, architectural fittings, doors, lighting and fenders.

DUNELM MILL SHOPS LTD
18 MARKET STREET, SHREWSBURY, SHROPSHIRE SY1 1LE
- (01743) 271478. OPEN 9 - 5 MON - THUR, 9 - 5.30 FRI, SAT, 10 - 4 SUN.
BRIDGE ROAD, WELLINGTON TF1 1ED
- (01952) 245593. OPEN 9 - 5.30 MON - THUR, 9 - 8 FRI, 9 - 6 SAT,
10.30 - 4.30 SUN.

Permanent Discount Outlet • *Household*

Part of a chain of shops based in the Midlands selling brand-name and chain-store curtains, masses of bedlinen, towels, wickerware, pictures and frames, all at competitive prices.

E WALTERS FACTORY SHOP
CHAPEL WORKS, OLD STREET, LUDLOW, SHROPSHIRE SY8 1NR
- (01584) 875595. OPEN 9 - 5 MON - FRI, 9 - 4 SAT 11 - 5 SUN,
EASTER - XMAS.

Factory Shop • *Womenswear & Menswear* • *Children*

Europe's largest trouser manufacturer sells ends of lines, cancelled orders and samples of jeans, trousers and shorts for all the family at factory direct prices. Also available ancillary lines of casual wear at bargain prices.

FASHION FACTORY
THE MALTINGS, KING STREET, WELLINGTON, TELFORD,
SHROPSHIRE TF1 3AE
☎ (01952) 260489. OPEN 9.30 - 5.30 MON - SAT, 11 - 5 SUN.
Permanent Discount Outlet • *Womenswear & Menswear*

At the Fashion Factory stores in Cannock (see Staffordshire) and Telford, you'll find a comprehensive selection of quality branded and designer fashions for men and women, all reduced by up to 70% off the normal high street prices. Stock is made up of excess production, cancelled orders and ends of season ranges from dozens of UK and international clothing manufacturers. This means a constantly changing selection from lingerie and basic fashion essentials to dresses, suits and separates, all at a fraction of the prices you'd normally expect to pay. The boutique-style store in Telford features two floors packed with a huge variety of ladieswear, while the Cannock superstore boasts possibly one of the largest selection of discounted clothing and footwear under one roof in the Midlands, with between 50,000-60,000 garments on display in a massive 20,000 sq ft of retail space. Parking outside.

GLYN WEBB
UNIT 3, SUNDORNE RETAIL PARK, SHREWSBURY,
SHROPSHIRE SY1 4YA
☎ (01743) 460993. OPEN 9 - 8 MON - SAT, 11 - 5 SUN AND OPEN ALL BANK HOLIDAYS.
Permanent Discount Outlet • *DIY/Renovation*

Stockists of all your home improvement needs from wallpaper to paint, furniture to flooring, tiles to textiles, housewares to lighting - in fact, almost everything for your home, with 25 branches in the North-West, Midlands and Yorkshire. Specialists in discontinued mail order, slightly imperfect branded stocks as well as perfect quality superior products. They carry top brands such as Dulux, Crown Paints and Vymura and Coloroll wall coverings, Rectella and Norwood textiles and much more in store. To find your nearest branch, phone Head Office on 0161 621 4500.

HARRY TUFFINS SUPERMARKET
CRAVEN ARMS, SHROPSHIRE
☎ (01588) 672202. OPEN 8 - 6 MON - WED, SAT, 8 - 8 THUR, FRI, 10 - 4 SUN.
Permanent Discount Outlet • *Food and Leisure*

Supermarket selling foodstuffs, garden furniture, household goods at incredibly competitive prices. Newly refurbished with the looks and service of a Sainsbury's and the prices are better. There's a vast range of tinned food, pickles, sauces, dried foods, soups, cereals, wine, household cleaning products, kitchen equipment, stationery and diy. The fruit and veg sections outside the main shop are not run by Tuffins and are not always a bargain.

MATALAN
WREKIN RETAIL PARK, WELLINGTON, TELFORD,
SHROPSHIRE TF1 2DE
☎ (01952) 641080. OPEN 10 - 8 MON - FRI, 9 - 6 SAT, 11 - 5 SUN.
MEOLE BRACE RETAIL PARK, HEREFORD ROAD, SHREWSBURY SY3 9NB
☎ (01743) 363240. OPEN 10 - 8 MON - FRI, 9 - 6 SAT, 11 - 5 SUN.
Permanent Discount Outlet • *Womenswear & Menswear*
Household • *Children*

Matalan is a fashion and homewares value retailer giving customers what they claim to be unbeatable value for money with huge savings on a wide range of products including high quality fashionable clothing for men, women and children at up to 50% off high street prices. Matalan is situated out of town and stores are open seven days a week all year round.

NIGHTINGALES FACTORY SHOP
NIGHTINGALES HOUSE, LONG LANE, CRAVEN ARMS,
SHROPSHIRE SY7 8DU
☎ (01588) 674108. OPEN 9.30 - 4.30 MON - FRI.
Factory Shop • *Womenswear Only*

The mail order company which sells smart but casual clothes for women - twill lined jackets in blazer stripes, button-through dresses, pinafore dresses, shirtwaisters, pure cotton blouses, lined short-sleeved jackets, polo neck sweaters, boucle jackets, blouses and skirt sets and cotton nightdresses - sells samples, ends of lines, seconds and material lengths here at discounted prices.

SIMON BOYD
SMITHFIELD ROAD, SHREWSBURY, SHROPSHIRE SY1 1PB
☎ (01743) 363006. OPEN 9 - 5.30 MON - SAT.
Permanent Discount Outlet • *Furniture/Soft Furnishings*

Stocks thousands of rolls of curtain fabric including chenilles, tapestries, cotton satin and chintzes from brands such as Monkwell, Sanderson and Crowson. For example a chenille costing £25 a yard costs £15.99 here. Also tie-backs, cushions, throws, ready-made curtains. Free measuring, plus making-up service available.

STANWAY FABRICS AND INTERIORS
SHIPTON HALL BARN, SHIPTON, NEAR MUCH WENLOCK,
SHROPSHIRE TF13 6JZ
☎ (01746) 785151. WEBSITE: www.stanwayfabrics.co.uk
OPEN 10 - 4 MON - SAT.
Permanent Discount Outlet • *Furniture/Soft Furnishings*

Leading suppliers of top designer fabric seconds and clearances at prices from as little as £3.95 per metre for fabrics which would normally retail between £25 and £35. Thousands of metres of curtain and upholstery fabrics always in stock, together with linings, interlinings, tape etc, at extremely competitive prices. They stock a wide range of tassels, tie-backs, trimmings and accessories, with many more available to order. Curtains, cushions, loose covers and headboards can be made to customers' specification by their experienced in house team at affordable prices. They also have a swap shop where customers can buy or sell beautiful curtains. Situated in a converted barn next to the sixteenth century Shipton Hall in the beautiful Corvedale area of South Shropshire, close to the historic towns of Ludlow, Much Wenlock and Shrewsbury, there is also a coffee shop within the barn and parking is right outside the door.

STEWART'S
19-21 CROSS STREET, ELLESMERE, SHROPSHIRE SY12 0AW
☎ (01691) 624478. OPEN 9 - 5.30 MON - SAT.
Factory Shop • *Household* • *Womenswear & Menswear* • *Children Sportswear & Equipment*
Branded merchandise from most of the major UK chain stores, all well-known high street department store names, offered at a discount of 40%-70% off normal high street prices. The garments are selected with great care by experienced buyers direct from factories worldwide to bring customers top quality merchandise at highly competitive prices.

TEXTILE EXPRESS
42 CHURCH STREET, OSWESTRY, SHROPSHIRE
☎ (01691) 670277. E-MAIL: pauline@textileexpress.co.uk
WEBSITE: www.textile-express.co.uk OPEN 9 - 5 MON - FRI, 9 - 5.30 SAT.
Permanent Discount Outlet • *Furniture/Soft Furnishings*
Regular line first quality fabrics sold alongside clearance fabrics suitable for bedding, curtaining, upholstery, bridal, craft and dressmaking - from hessian to silk. Large remnant department where prices start at £2 a metre. Curtain accessories also sold such as poles and blinds and a making up service is available. The large stock at this business which wholesales and exports is constantly changing. The mill shop across the road also stocks rolls of fabrics from £2-£4 a metre.

THE ART BOOKSHOP
3 QUALITY SQUARE, LUDLOW, SHROPSHIRE SY8 1AR
☎ (01584) 872758. OPEN 10 - 5 FRI, SAT.
Permanent Discount Outlet • *Food and Leisure*
Superb range of specialist stock of new art, design and architecture books as well as secondhand books. Some books are reduced by 25%-50%, while there is a bargain box of books at £2 each.

THE FABRIC BARN
UPPER ASTON FARM, CLAVERLEY, SHROPSHIRE WV5 7EE
☎ (01746) 710237. OPEN 9 - 5 MON - SAT.
Permanent Discount Outlet • *Furniture/Soft Furnishings*
Top quality designer curtain and upholstery fabrics from £3.50 a metre as well as linings from £2 a metre, craft poles and tracks. Lots of trimmings, tie backs and accessories.

TK MAXX
DARWIN SHOPPING CENTRE, SHREWSBURY, SHROPSHIRE
☎ (01743) 341370. OPEN 9 - 5.30 MON - SAT, 9 - 7 WED, 11 - 5 SUN.
FORGE RETAIL PARK, TELFORD
Permanent Discount Outlet • *Womenswear & Menswear*
Children • *Household* • *Furniture/Soft Furnishings*
Based on an American concept, TK Maxx is situated in easily accessible, often centrally located stores and offers famous label goods with up to 60% savings off recommended retail prices. TK Maxx has fashion for the whole family - women's, men's and childrenswear - accessories, shoes, gifts, kitchenware and home goods. Everything in the store is branded with a choice of well-known high street names to designer labels, and while a small percentage might be clearly marked past season, the great majority of items in store are current season, current stock and still with phenomenal savings. There is a huge choice with 50,000 pieces in store and up to 10,000 new items arriving a week. The stores are simple and unfussy with wide aisles, shopping trolleys and baskets, and a spacious, functional feel to them but there are individual changing rooms, ramps for buggies and wheelchairs and plenty of staff on the shop floor. Every branch accepts all major credit and debit cards and has a liberal refund and return policy.

WREKIN WORKWEAR LTD
UNIT 26, SNEDSHILL TRADING ESTATE, TELFORD,
SHROPSHIRE TF2 9NH
☎ (01952) 615976. OPEN 9 - 5 MON, TUE, WED, THUR, 9 - 3.30 FRI.
Permanent Discount Outlet • *Womenswear & Menswear*
Fleece jackets, workwear trousers and jackets, dust coats, work shirts, dry suits, dry socks for walkers, waterproofs, Wellingtons, safety footwear, polo shirts, T-shirts, all at discounted prices. For example, end of line Polar fleece jacket, £19.99, originally £59.99.

Somerset

ABSENT LABELS
51B ST JAMES' STREET, TAUNTON, SOMERSET TA1 IJH
☎ (01823) 330242. OPEN 9.30 - 5.30 MON - FRI, SAT, 9 - 5.30.
CHURCH HOUSE, CHURCH STREET, YEOVIL BA20 1HE
☎ (01935) 478183. OPEN 9.30 - 5 MON - SAT.
Permanent Discount Outlet • *Womenswear & Menswear*
Good deals direct from the manufacturer of clothes designed for Marks & Spencer, Next, Principles etc., for ladies and men at reduced prices. Discontinued lines and Grade A garments are reduced by about one third. There are skirts, trousers, socks, underwear, nightwear, sweaters, blouses, dressing gowns, shorts, T-shirts and swimwear.

BLACK & DECKER
UNIT 25, CLARKS VILLAGE, FARM ROAD, STREET, SOMERSET BA16 OBB
☎ (01458) 840205. OPEN 9 - 5.30 MON - SAT OCT - APRIL, 11 - 5 SUN,
9 - 6 MAY - OCT 11 - 5 SUN.
Factory Shop in a Factory Shopping Village • *DIY/Renovation*
Reconditioned tools and acccessories from the famous Black & Decker range, all with full manufacturer's warranty. Often, stock consists of goods returned from the shops because of damaged packaging or are part of a line which is being discontinued. Lots of seasonal special offers.

BRIDGWATER RECLAMATION
THE OLD CO-OP DAIRY, MONMOUTH STREET, BRIDGWATER,
SOMERSET TA6 5EJ
☎ (01278) 424636. OPEN 8 - 5 MON - FRI, 8 - 12 SAT.
Architectural Salvage • *DIY/Renovation*
Building materials: reclaimed bricks, Bridgwater-made clay roof and ridge tiles, natural Welsh slates, flagstones, chimney pots, doors, baths, fireplaces, reproduction furniture, purpose-made joinery from the on-site workshop - in fact everything!

BROWSERS
THE BOROUGH, WEDMORE, SOMERSET BS28 4EB
☎ (01934) 713663. OPEN 10 - 5 MON - SAT.
Dress Agency • *Womenswear Only*
An upmarket dress agency selling nearly-new labels from Jaeger to Mondi, Viyella to Valentino. Whilst most of their range consists of designer labels, some better quality high street names are also available. This shop is renowned for brand new clearance stock, overmakes and sample sales. It has a large stock which turns over very quickly. They also stock belts, hats, handbags, jewellery and accessories.

CLARKS FACTORY SHOP
UNIT 13, CLARKS VILLAGE, FARM ROAD, STREET,
SOMERSET BA16 OBB
☎ (01458) 843161. OPEN 9 - 6 MON - SAT, 9 - 5.30 WINTER, 11 - 5 SUN.
2 EASTOVER, BRIDGWATER, SOMERSET TA6 5AB
☎ (01278) 452617. OPEN 9 - 5.30 MON - SAT.
10A HIGH STREET, BURNHAM-ON-SEA, SOMERSET TA8 1NX
☎ (01278) 794668. OPEN 9 - 5.30 MON - SAT, 11 - 5 SUN,
10 - 5 BANK HOLIDAYS.
112-114 HIGH STREET, STREET, SOMERSET BA16 OEW
☎ (01458) 442055. OPEN 9 - 5.30 MON - SAT AND BANK HOLIDAYS,
11 - 5 SUN.
UNIT 2, SAINSBURYS PRECINCT, QUEENSWAY SHOPPING CENTRE,
WORLE, SOMERSET BS22 OBT
☎ (01934) 521693. OPEN 9 - 6 MON - SAT, 10.30 - 4.30 SUN,
10 - 5 BANK HOLIDAYS.
Factory Shop in a Factory Shopping Village • *Children*
Womenswear & Menswear • *Sportswear & Equipment*
Clarks International operate a chain of factory shops nationally which specialise in selling discontinued lines and slight sub-standards for children, women and men from Clarks, K Shoes and other famous brands. These shops trade under the name of Crockers, K Shoes Factory shop or Clarks Factory Shop and while not all are physically attached to a shoe factory, these shops are treated as factory shops by the company. Customers can expect to find an extensive range of quality shoes, sandals, walking boots, slippers, trainers, handbags, accessories and gifts, while their major outlets such as at here at Clarks Village also offer luggage, sports clothing, sports equipment and outdoor clothing. Brands stocked include Clarks, K Shoes, Springer, CICA, Hi-Tec, Puma, Mercury, Dr Martens, Nike, LA Gear, Fila, Mizuno, Slazenger, Weider, Antler and Carlton, although not all are sold in every outlet. Discounts are from 30% to 60% off the normal high street price for perfect stock. This shop also incorporates Sports Factory and Baggage Factory.

CLARKS VILLAGE FACTORY SHOPPING
FARM ROAD, STREET, JUNCTION 23 OF M5, THEN A39,
SOMERSET BA16 OBB
☎ (01458) 840064. OPEN APRIL - OCTOBER 9 - 5.30 MON - SAT,
11 - 5 SUN, NOVEMBER - MARCH 10 - 6, MON - SAT, 11 - 5 SUN.
Factory Shopping Village • *Womenswear & Menswear*
Household • *Children* • *Food and Leisure*
Purpose-built village of brick-built shops with extensive car parking facilities. Restaurant, fast food stands, carousel, indoor and outdoor play areas, and working village pottery and artists, studio. Here, there are 57 shops with more planned. Shops include: Body Shop, Reebok selling the Reebok brand, Rockport and the Greg Norman Collection; Monsoon/Accessorize, Laura

Ashley, Benetton, Wrangler, The Designer Room, Jaeger, Viyella, Alexon/Eastex, Triumph/Hom, Jacques Vert, Gossard, JoKids, Clarks Factory Shop, Woolea (which also sells Aquascutum, Lyle & Scott and Barbour), Rohan, Paco, Windsmoor (which also sells Planet, Berkertex, Precis and Genesis), Liz Claiborne, Jumper, Centaur, Calvin Klein, Van Heusen, Next, Warehouse, Tom Sayers men,s sweaters and trousers, Warner,s lingerie, Tog 24 outerwear, Jane Shilton handbags, luggage and shoes, The Suit Company and Blazer and Event jewellery. Other shops include: Royal Brierley, Royal Worcester, Denby Pottery, Dartington Crystal, Edinburgh Crystal; Crabtree & Evelyn, Clarks Baggage Factory, Clarks Sports Factory, The Linen Cupboard, Thorntons Chocolates, Clarks Sports Factory, Black & Decker, Hallmark Cards, Remington, Whittard of Chelsea, XS CDs and videos, Price,s Candles, Cadbury,s, Bookends, The Kitchen Cupboard (Cloverleaf table mats, trays and caddies, Hackman cutlery, Chasseur cookware), Stuart Crystal, Poole Pottery, Village Pottery, Waterford/Wedgwood, The Pot People, Gardeners, Gate, Michael Cooper,s Studio, The National Trust Gift Shop, and Kid,s Play Factory children,s toys.

COURTAULDS TEXTILE

NORTH WORLE DISTRICT CENTRE, QUEENSWAY, WORLE, WESTON SUPER MARE, SOMERSET BS22 7BT
☎ (01934) 522065. OPEN 9 - 5.30 MON - THUR, 9 - 6 FRI, SAT, 10 - 4 SUN.
Factory Shop • *Womenswear & Menswear* • *Children*
Manufacturers for Marks & Spencers, this shop sells men's, ladies and children's clothing and household goods including towels, bedding and duvets at discounts of up to 50%.

CRAFTS

16 CHEAP STREET, BATH, SOMERSET BA1 1NA
☎ (01225) 464397. OPEN 9.30 - 5.30 MON - SAT, 10.30 - 4.30 SUN.
Factory Shop • *Household*
Crafts is a cooperative selling direct to the public at makers' direct prices. Items range from ceramics to wood, clocks, musical intruments and glassware. Everything is hand made and commissions are welcome. They also sell a small amount of English Country Pottery.

DARTINGTON CRYSTAL

CLARKS OUTLET VILLAGE, FARM ROAD, STREET, SOMERSET BA16 OBB
☎ (01458) 841618. OPENING HOURS VARY.
Factory Shop in a Factory Shopping Village • *Household*
An extensive range of Dartington Crystal seconds at greatly reduced prices as well as some perfect crystal at full price. Range includes wine suites, sherry glasses, tankards, decanters, rippled glass, fruit and salad bowls.

DENBY FACTORY SHOP
CLARKS VILLAGE, FARM ROAD, STREET, SOMERSET BA16 0BB
☎ (01458) 840940. OPEN 9 - 5.30 MON - SAT (WINTER),
9 - 6 MON - SAT (SUMMER), 11 - 5 SUN.
Factory Shop in a Factory Shopping Village • *Household*
Denby is renowned for its striking colours and glaze effects. The Factory Shops stock first and second quality with seconds discounts starting at 20% off RRP. There are regular "mega bargains" with up to 75% off throughout the year.

DICKIES UK LTD
CHARLTON LANE, MIDSOMER NORTON, NEAR BATH,
SOMERSET BA3 4BH
☎ (01761) 410732. FAX ☎ (01761) 418786. OPEN 9 - 5 MON - SAT,
10 - 4 SUN.
Factory Shop • *Womenswear & Menswear*
Casual outdoor wear, workwear, footwear and waterproof clothing: many end of lines at bargain prices from £2.50.

ECCO
82 HIGH STREET, STREET, SOMERSET BA16 0EN
☎ (01458) 443950. 9 - 5.30 MON -SAT.
Factory Shop • *Womenswear & Menswear* • *Children*
Ladies', men's and children's shoes, all discounted by at least 25%. Phone 0800 387368 for a catalogue. Other outlets at South Wales, Hertfordshire, Wiltshire and Cheshire.

FINE SHOES
31-34 HIGH STREET, WELLS, SOMERSET
☎ (01749) 679090. open 9.30 - 5.30 mon - fri, 9 - 5.30 SAT, 10.30 - 4.30 SUN.
Permanent Discount Outlet • *Womenswear & Menswear* • *Children*
Men's and women's shoes, boots, plimsolls, sandals and trainers, with some children's merchandise up to size 5. Most of the shoes are from Bellina, but other brands on sale here include Roder, Hogl, Flexi, Dubarry, Hush Puppy, Barkers, Lec boots for men, Grensons and DB wider shoes for men.

FOX'S MILL SHOP
TONEDALE MILLS, WELLINGTON, SOMERSET TA21 0AW
☎ (01823) 662271. OPEN 10 - 5 FRI AND SAT ONLY.
Factory Shop • *Womenswear & Menswear*
Newly refurbished, this shop sells wool and cashmere fabrics for men and women made up of seconds and perfect quality but end of season lines at very low prices starting at £5 a metre for material that would normally retail at £25-£35, cashmere jumpers, silk ties, woollen scarves, umbrellas and fashion accessories. Cloth can be bought and taken away or the in-situ tailor will make

up garments at a fraction of the London charges. The shop sells woollen and worsted cloth, wool and cashmere seconds and perfect quality and there's a bargain basket with fabric at silly prices. The tailor is on site on both days and will make men's and women's suits.

GEAR CHANGE
8 CLAVERTON BUILDINGS, WIDCOMBE, BATH, SOMERSET
☎ (01225) 442188. 0PEN 10.30 - 4.30 MON - SAT.
Dress Agency • *Womenswear Only*

Dress agency selling high quality ladies wear and accessories including good shoes, leather bags and costume jewellery. Labels range from M&S to Versace, depending on what is brought into the shop.

HALLMARK
CLARKS VILLAGE, STREET, SOMERSET BA16 OBB
☎ (01458) 447005. OPEN 9 - 6 MON - SAT SUMMER,
9 - 5.30 MON - SAT WINTER, 11 - 5 SUN.
Factory Shop • *Food and Leisure*

A wide range of cards to suit every occasion, as well as stuffed toys, wrapping paper, rosettes, gift cards from names such as Andrew Brownswood, Gordon Fraser and Sharpe's Classics. Almost all the stock here is ends of lines as the card business demands constant change and therefore some unsold lines. Most of the items are half price. Cafes on site as well as children's play areas; free parking.

HYBURY CHINA
27B NORTH STREET, CREWKERNE, SOMERSET TA18 7AL
☎ (08707) 380380. FAX (08707) 353637. MAIL ORDER ONLY.
Permanent Discount Outlet • *Household*

Sells pure white English bone china seconds, all from famous manufacturers. Brilliant value at very competitive prices. All items are dishwasher safe and available delivered to your door by mail order. All the china is ideal for hand painting. There are several ranges which offer a wide selection of cups and saucers, plates, vegetable dishes, teapots, tureens etc. The china comes from major English companies prior to being stamped by the manufacturer. A perfect bone china dinner plate would normally cost £17-£35; Hybury offer their dinner plates from £4.50. The china is ideal for use at home or in restaurants, rented properties, B&Bs, boardrooms and offices. Call for a free brochure.

JAEGER
CLARKS VILLAGE, FARM ROAD, STREET, SOMERSET BA16 OBB
☎ (01458) 447215. OPEN 9 - 6 MON - SAT, 11 - 5 SUN.
Factory Shop in a Factory Shopping Village • *Womenswear & Menswear*

Contemporary classics from Jaeger at excellent prices. Most of the merchandise is previous seasons' stock, but you might also find some special makes. Both shops stock tailoring and knitwear for women and men.

JAMES GAUNT
1 CHURCH STREET, FROME, SOMERSET BA11 1PW
☎ (01373) 452344. OPEN 9 - 5.30 MON - SAT.
Permanent Discount Outlet • *Furniture/Soft Furnishings*
Specialist interior designers James Gaunt sells regular lines and some clearance fabrics. The range includes well known names such as Nina Campbell, Jane Churchill, Malabar and Warners and the emphasis throughout this shop is on designer stock at bargain prices.

JANE'S DRESS AGENCY
THE TRIANGLE, SOMERTON, SOMERSET TA11 6QJ
☎ (01458) 273711. OPEN 9.30 - 5 MON - FRI, 9.30 - 4.30 SAT.
Dress Agency • *Womenswear Only*
Small, well-stocked shop selling high street and designer labels, Viyella, Bianca Country Casuals, and German labels such as Escada and Betty Barclay Also sells belts, secondhand jewellery, shoes, scarves, handbags and lots of hats. Evening wear and cruise wear stocked - will help put together outfits for weddings and special occasions.

JOKIDS
CLARKS FACTORY SHOPPING VILLAGE, FARM ROAD, STREET, SOMERSET BA16 OBB
☎ (01458) 841909. OPEN 9 - 6 MON - SAT, 9 - 5.30 WINTER, 11 - 5 SUN.
Factory Shop in a Factory Shopping Village • *Children*
This shop sells childrenswear for 0-10-year-olds including everdaywear like t-shirts, jogwear, various denim styles and accessories. For special occasions there are pretty hand-smocked party dresses and rompers. Reductions are up to 40%.

JPS FOOTWEAR LTD
2 HIGH STREET, BURNHAM-ON-SEA, SOMERSET TA8 1NX
☎ (01278) 780141. OPEN 9 - 5.30 MON - SAT, 11 - 5.30 SUN.
Factory Shop • *Womenswear & Menswear* • *Children*
Stock over 10,000 pairs of shoes for men, women and children. The men's sizes range from 6-12; and women's from 4-9. Most of the stock consists of warehouse clearance lines and ends of lines.

JUMPER
CLARKS VILLAGE, FARM ROAD, STREET, SOMERSET BA16 OBB
☎ (01458) 840320. OPEN 9 - 6 MON - SAT, 9 - 5.30 WINTER, 11 - 5 SUN.
Factory Shop in a Factory Shopping Village • *Womenswear & Menswear*
A wide range of Jumper label sweaters, gloves, socks, scarves, shirts and cardigans for men and women all at discount prices of up to 50% off. Prices start at £2.

KNICKERBEAN
5 WALCOT STREET, BATH, SOMERSET BA1 5BN
☎ (01225) 445741. OPEN 9 - 5.30 MON - SAT.
Permanent Discount Outlet • *Furniture/Soft Furnishings*

Recommended by countless interior and decorating magazines and much loved by the bargain hunter, Knickerbean offers a continuous stream of stylish and sumptuous fabrics (the kind found at the Chelsea Harbour Design Centre and Decorex), but all at affordable prices. They originally specialised in top name UK designer fabrics, offering excess inventory, discontinued lines and slight imperfects, usually at about half price. You can still find many of these famous name bargains here, but now many of their fabrics are sourced directly from the same mills and manufacturers as the 'top names', both here and abroad. They offer the same top quality, in the latest colours and designs, at relatively lower prices, because they are buying and selling directly and cutting out the middlemen. Their selection of curtain and upholstery fabrics caters for both contemporary and traditional homes, with formal glazed chintzes, regal damasks, toiles de jouy and luxurious chenilles displayed next to basic neutrals, bright modern prints, airy voiles and earthy ethnic patterns. They also have large ranges of checks and stripes, self-patterned weaves, simple prints for a child's room as well as a huge range of upholstery brocades and tapestries. Prices start at £5.95 for prints to £19.95 and occasionally more for some their tapestries, chenilles and damasks. Knickerbean's outlets are bright and pleasant, more like an interior designer's showroom - there's no 'warehouse' feeling here. Their trained staff are helpful with all sorts of advice on fabrics, colours and interiors and they offer a complete home visit service with interior measuring and design advice. They have a hand finished making up service for curtains, blinds and loose covers, as well as a range of custom made funiture with footstools, sofas, etc. Twice yearly sales in January and June enable customers to snap up even bigger bargains.

LAURA ASHLEY
CLARKS VILLAGE, ADDRESS AND OPENING HOURS AS BEFORE.
☎ (01458) 840405.

Factory Shop in a Factory Shopping Village
Furniture/Soft Furnishings • *Womenswear Only*

Laura Ashley home furnishings and fashion at Clarks. Most of the merchandise is made up of perfect carry-overs from the high street shops around the country, though there are also some discontinued lines. Stock reflects the normal high street variety, though at least one season later and with less choice in colours and sizes.

LIZ CLAIBORNE UK
CLARKS VILLAGE, ADDRESS AND OPENING HOURS AS BEFORE.
☎ (01458) 840912.
Factory Shop • *Womenswear Only*
American designer Liz Claiborne's factory shop at Clarks Factory Shopping Village offers middle of the range, mid-priced smart clothes for work and casual wear. All are end of lines or styles which are at least one year old. Stock quantities and sizes vary, depending on whether there has recently been a delivery, so it's worth making frequent visits. Suited jackets start from £45; casual trousers, £15; skirts from £15. A range is available in Petite sizing and there is a good selection of discounted accessories. Most items are reduced by 50% with further reductions always on offer.

MATALAN
LOCKING CASTLE DISTRICT CENTRE, WORLE, WESTON SUPER MARE, SOMERSET
☎ (01934) 529830. OPEN 9.30 - 8 MON - FRI, 9 - 6 SAT, 11 - 5 SUN.
Permanent Discount Outlet • *Womenswear & Menswear*
Children • *Household*
Matalan is a fashion and homewares value retailer giving customers what they claim to be unbeatable value for money with huge savings on a wide range of products including high quality fashionable clothing for men, women and children at up to 50% off high street prices. Matalan is situated out of town and stores are open seven days a week all year round.

MINEHEAD SHOE CO LTD
1 NORTH ROAD, MINEHEAD, SOMERSET TA24 5QW
☎ (01643) 705591. OPEN 9 - 5 MON - THUR, 9 - 4 FRI, 10 - 1 SAT.
CLOSED FOR LUNCH 1 - 2 EVERYDAY.
Permanent Discount Outlet • *Womenswear & Menswear*
Specialists in made-to-measure footwear for wide fittings, including some bowling shoes. Goods are supplied by the factory next door and sold at factory prices. Mail order available.

MONSOON
CLARKS VILLAGE, FARM ROAD, STREET, SOMERSET BA16 OBB
☎ (01458) 840890. OPEN 9 - 6 MON - SAT, 9 - 5.30 WINTER, 11 - 5 SUN.
Factory Shop in a Factory Shopping Village • *Womenswear Only*
Medium-sized outlet selling marked down current stock for some of the year as well as last year's stock and discontinued lines, including jewellery. There are also outlets at Bicester Village in Oxfordshire, Cambridge and Birmingham.

MORLANDS (GLASTONBURY)
NORTHOVER, BETWEEN GLASTONBURY & STREET, GLASTONBURY,
SOMERSET BA6 9YA
☎ (01458) 835042. OPEN 9.30 - 5 MON - SAT AND MOST
BANK HOLIDAYS.
Factory Shop • *Womenswear & Menswear*
Established in 1870, Morlands are the leading brand name in quality sheepskin garments and footwear. The Factory Shop on the A39 (just north of Clarks Village) offers the opportunity to buy both men's and women's sheepskin coats, slippers and ladies boots at attractive prices. Ranges include first quality design samples, ends of runs and overstock, together with slight seconds. There is also a wide range of rugs, hats, mitts, handbags, belts, leatherwear and gifts.

MULBERRY
THE OLD SCHOOL HOUSE, KILVER STREET ON THE A37,
SHEPTON MALLET, SOMERSET BA4 5NF
☎ (01749) 340583. OPEN 10 - 6 MON - SAT, 11 - 5 SUN AND
BANK HOLIDAYS.
Factory Shop • *Womenswear & Menswear*
Furniture/Soft Furnishishings • *Household*
A very popular large, attractive, factory outlet situated in an old school house with parking outside, which sells last season's and slightly substandard items from the famous Mulberry leather handbags, briefcases, filofaxes and wallets at discounted prices. The factory shop is sufficiently large also to display ends of lines from the homes range of sofas, fabrics, occasional tables, lamps, rugs, throws, cushions, china, decanters, glass. Also rails of last season's clothes including men's jackets, waxed jackets, trousers, shirts, waistcoats, braces and shoes; and women's jackets, handknitted sweaters and cardigans, jackets and coats. There are also umbrellas, pewter napkin rings, golfing and fishing gifts, shaving kits, and a skincare range. Discontinued lines are discounted from 30%; current seconds, many of which come direct from the factory, are discounted by 30%. Examples of prices include cashmere from £89, fabric clippers at £79. Small coffee shop and toilet and disabled facilities.

NEXT TO NOTHING
CLARKS VILLAGE, FARM ROAD, STREET, SOMERSET BA16 OBB
☎ (01458) 840828. OPEN 10 - 6 MON - SAT, 11 - 5 SUN.
Factory Shop in a Factory Shopping Village
Womenswear & Menswear • *Children*
Sells perfect surplus stock from Next stores and the Next Directory catalogue - from belts, jewellery and underwear to day and evening wear - at discounts of 50% or more. The ranges are usually last season's and overruns. Stock consists of women's, men's and children's clothing, with some homeware and shoes. Stock is replenished three times a week and there is plenty of it.

NIPPERS
YARDE FARM, LANGFORD LANE, NORTON FITZWARREN, TAUNTON,
SOMERSET TA2 6PA
☎ (01823) 350005. FAX ☎ (01823) 350119. WEBSITE: www.nippers.co.uk
OPENING HOURS VARY SO PHONE FIRST.
Permanent Discount Outlet • *Children*

Nippers, the nursery equipment and toy specialists, operate from previously redundant buildings in rural areas around the country. They offer easy parking, no queues and personal service. This is on top of competitive prices on prams, cots, pushchairs, car seats, outdoor play equipment and toys, some of which are new, some seconds or secondhand and some ends of lines. Prices are low because they avoid the high overheads of traditional retail outlets and also because the successful growth of a number of branches means they can now buy in bulk and negotiate good deals. Customers are invited to try out the merchandise while the children look at the animals, mostly sheep, chicken and pigs. Also offers many brand leaders at discount, including Mamas & Papas, Cosatto, Britax, Maclaren and Bebe Confort, plus Fisher-Price and Little Tikes. You can try out the car seats in your car and there is usually a pram/pushchair repair service on site.

OLD HARRY'S RECLAMATION LTD
FAIRWATER YARD, HIGHER PALMERSTON ROAD, OFF STAPLEGROVE ROAD, TAUNTON, SOMERSET TA1 1DP
☎ (01823) 337035. WEBSITE: www.oldharrys.co.uk:8181/
OPEN 9.5.30 MON - FRI, 10 - 12 SAT.
Architectural Salvage • *DIY/Renovation*

Tiles, slates, bricks, chimney pots, recycled timber, floorboards, fireplaces, windows, doors, sanitaryware, staircases, RSJ's, channel-crushed concrete and interesting curios discovered during demolition.

ORIENT EXPRESSIONS
ASSEMBLY ANTIQUES CENTRE, 5-8 SAVILLE ROW,
BATH SOMERSET BA1 2QP
☎ (01225) 313399. WEBSITE: www.antiquesbulletin.com/orientexpressions
OPEN 10 -5 MON - SAT, AND BY APPOINTMENT.
Permanent Discount Outlet • *Furniture/Soft Furnishings*

Specialises in buying genuine antiques from China. The majority of the stock is from the early to mid-19th century, although the rarer 18th century pieces are bought when possible. Shipments are regular but small. Each piece is handpicked by the owners who both lived and worked in Hong Kong for many years. They are chosen carefully for their appearance, character and practical potential. Pieces are left in their original condition as much as possible. Any restoration is kept to a minimum to retain the character of the piece. The furniture comes mostly from the rural provinces of China and offers a variety of looks: simple, quite chunky, country pieces in elm and beech; more sophisticated pieces in huali or dark lacquer; highly decorative, lacquered and gilded items. Whether a piece is plain and simple or wild and whacky, the criteria for buying it is always the same - it must be beautiful, useful, genuine and, of course, the price must be right. Orient Expressions keeps overheads to a minimum and offers really good value, undercutting all its main competitors. Its major outlet is this spacious shop in Bath, but it is worth visiting the London showroom (see LONDON for address) for the excellent trade prices. A further selection is available at Great Grooms Antique Centre in Hungerford, Berkshire.

PACO
CLARKS VILLAGE, FARM ROAD, STREET, SOMERSET BA16 0BB
☎ (01458) 440222. OPEN 9 - 6 MON - SAT, 11 - 5 SUN.
Factory Shop in a Factory Shopping Village • *Children Womenswear Only* • *Sportswear & Equipment*

Paco uses bright, distinctive colours and the knack for designing great clothes at affordable prices. For several years, they have also been creating their own brand of sports and leisurewear clothing that shows great verve and energy. This range has a much more everyday living influence. The contrast is a distinct look for the discerning wearer. If you are looking for a great T-shirt or sweatshirt, lightweight jacket or gilet, polar fleece or hooded top, three-quarter length or combat trousers, then you need look no further. Paco now competes with the very best fashion brands in the high street by offering customers high fashion combined with excellent quality, making their clothes real value for money.

PENNYWISE
10 WESTMINSTER STREET, YEOVIL, SOMERSET BA21 3PE
☎ (01935) 423938. OPEN 9.15 - 5 MON - SAT.
Dress Agency • *Womenswear & Menswear* • *Children*

Dress agency selling men's and women's day and evening business and casual clothes, shoes and accessories. Good quality and designer labels. There is no parking available but the shop is near a large Tesco car park.

PRICE'S CANDLES
CLARKS VILLAGE, ADDRESS AND OPENING HOURS AS BEFORE.
☎ (01458) 440006.
Factory Shop in a Factory Shopping Village • *Household*

Everything sold in this shop are seconds, discontinued sizes not available elsewhere, over-runs or candles in old packaging that has now been replaced. There are church candles, lanterns, candles in pots and glass jars, star-shaped candles, floating candles, candlestick holders, serviettes, scented candles and garden torches.

REMINGTON
CLARKS VILLAGE, ADDRESS AND OPENING HOURS AS BEFORE.
☎ (01458) 840209.
Factory Shop in a Factory Shopping Village • *Electrical Equipment*
Lots of famous names here from Monogram cutlery to Braun, Philips, Remington, Clairol, Philips, Stellar, Global, Prima, Wahl and Kenwood small kitchen equipment.

ROUNDABOUT
2 PRIOR PARK ROAD, WIDCOMBE, BATH, SOMERSET BA2 4NG
☎ (01225) 316696. OPEN 9 - 5 MON - SAT.
Dress Agency • *Children*
Newly refurbished side by side shops, one selling nearly-new and sample childrenswear from Oilily to Cakewalk at discounts of about 45%, the other selling womenswear such as Gap. Roundabout has half-price brand new samples from Cakewalk and Oilily as well as nearly-new Laura Ashley, Gap, Next and Petit Bateau. They now also stock nearly-new nursery equipment, prams, cots, buggies, high chairs etc.

ROYAL WORCESTER & SPODE FACTORY SHOP
CLARKS VILLAGE, FARM ROAD, STREET, SOMERSET BA16 OBB
☎ (01458) 840554. OPEN 9 - 6 MON - SAT, 9 - 5.30 WINTER, 11 - 5 SUN.
Factory Shop in a Factory Shopping Village • *Household*
Infinitesimally flawed porcelain and china seconds at 25% less than "perfect" prices. This outlet also sells Edinburgh Crystal, Fo-Frame, Country Artists, Mayflower, Pimpernel table mats, Lakeland Plaques, Leeds Display, Arthur Price cutlery, Paw Prints and Collectible World Studios. There is a vast range with special offers throughout the year on anything from crystal decanters and bowls to figurines, cookware and dinner sets. Shipping arrangements worldwide can be organised.

SALA DESIGN LTD
THE WORKS, BOWER HINTON, MARTOCK, SOMERSET TA12 6LG
☎ (01935) 827050. OPEN 9 - 5 FRI, 10-5 SAT, 11 - 4 SUN.
PHONE FOR SALE DATES.
Permanent Discount Outlet • *Furniture/Soft Furnishings*
Sala supplies top London interiors shops and department stores countrywide with imported furniture from India, rattan and wooden furniture from Thailand and metal pieces from the Philippines, as well as furniture from Africa, Afghanistan, Nepal and China; Aghanistan and Persian kelims; and Persian and Baluchi carpets. Their warehouse outlet, which is open to the public, also sells unusual ornaments, candles, rugs, glasses and cutlery, and one-off antique pieces and artefacts. There are twice-yearly warehouse sales where prices are cut dramatically, sometimes by up to 75%. Otherwise, prices here represent savings of about 40-50%.

SANDPITS HEATING CENTRE
HIGH STREET, CURRY RIVEL, LANGPORT, SOMERSET TA10 ONG
☎ (01458) 251476. OPEN 8 - 5.30 MON - FRI, 8 - 4.30 SAT.

A Rayburn Cooking Centre specialising in new and reconditioned Rayburns and Agas. The reconditioned models are considerably cheaper than the new and some can incorporate a domestic heating system for hot water and radiators. They also stock Stanley, Alpha and Nobel cookers at full price and a selection of wood burning stoves. Check before travelling, as they are moving premises in December 2000.

SCENT TO YOU
THE DESIGNER ROOM, CLARKS VILLAGE FACTORY SHOPPING, FARM ROAD, STREET, JUNCTION 23 OF M5, THEN A39, SOMERSET BA16 OBB
☎ (01458) 440626. OPEN APRIL - OCTOBER 9 - 5.30 MON - SAT, 11 - 5 SUN, NOVEMBER - MARCH 10 - 6, MON - SAT, 11 - 5 SUN.

Factory Shop in a Factory Shopping Village • *Womenswear Only*

Operating within The Designer Room at this outlet village, Scent to You sells discounted perfume, cosmetics and accessories including body lotions and gels. The company, which has more than thirty branches, buys in bulk and sells more cheaply, relying on a high turnover for profit. Discounts range from 5% to 60%, with greater savings during their twice-yearly sales (phone for details). Most of the leading brand names in perfume are stocked including Christian Lacroix, Armani, Charlie, Givenchy, Anais Anais from Cacherel, Charlie from Revlon, Coco Chanel, Christian Dior, Elizabeth Taylor, Blue Grass from Elizabeth Arden, Aramis, Lagerfeld. Plus cosmetics from REvlon and Spectacular and skincare from Clarins and Lancome as well as Scent To You's own range of bags, watches, hair brushes and brushkits which is sold under the name S.T.Y. Designs. Stock varies greatly due to the fast turnover and varying supplies so more than one visit may be necessary to obtain the scent of your choice. Or phone first to avoid disappointment.

SCREWFIX DIRECT
SHOP: HOUNDSTONE BUSINESS PARK, YEOVIL, SOMERSET BA22 8RT
☎ (0500) 414141. WEBSITE: www.screwfix.com MAIL ORDER FREEPOST: ADDRESS, SCREWFIX DIRECT, FREEPOST, YEOVIL BA22 8BF.
SHOP: OPEN 7 - 6 MON - WED, 7 - 8 THUR, FRI, 8 - 6 SAT, SUN.

Permanent Discount Outlet • *DIY/Renovation*

DIY materials by mail order - everything including the kitchen sink from nails, screws, torches and bulbs to electric screwdrivers, plumbing materials and sealants - at prices which, one reader claims, are lower than the local diy superstore. Send for a 144 page catalogue, which is updated and expanded quarterly. All products are available for next working day delivery. Warehouse shop on site also sells ends of lines and one-off samples at discounted prices.

SECOND TO NONE
85 HIGH STREET, BURNHAM-ON-SEA, SOMERSET TA8 1PE
☎ (01278) 787457. OPEN 9 - 5 MON - SAT AND BANK HOLIDAYS.
UNIT 2, CHESTERFIELD HOUSE, HIGH STREET, MIDSOMER NORTON,
BATH BA3 2DD
☎ (01761) 415545. OPEN 9 - 5 MON - SAT.

Permanent Discount Outlet • *Womenswear & Menswear* • *Children*

Established in the South West for twenty-seven years, this company has built a reputation for giving excellent customer service and for selling goods which are of a quality and value second to none! This Famous chainstore and branded clearing lines include surplus stocks of branded goods such as Fabrizio, Zorbit, Naturana and many more. They stock a large range of ladies and children's and baby wear (including baby bedding and accessories), leisurewear, sports clothes and some menswear, and an extensive range of underwear and nightwear for all the family. You can save up to 75% off recommended retail prices and they offer a seven-day money back guarantee.

SOMERSET CREATIVE PRODUCTS
SOMERSET DESIGN, LAUREL FARM, WESTHAM, WEDMORE,
SOMERSET BS28 4UZ
☎ (01934) 712416. OPEN BY APPOINTMENT ONLY.

Factory Shop • *Furniture/Soft Furnishings*

A large range of garden furniture and accessories made from reclaimed timber furniture in "ocean drift" and "honey" finishes. Stock depends on finding the right kind of timber so it's best to ring before making a long journey. They also stock a selection of traditional mild steel benches with curled arms and legs, from £200. Seconds are on sale here at discount prices. Westham is about 8 miles from Clarks Village Factory Shopping Centre in Street; telephone for directions.

SPOILS
UNIT CG9, THE GALLERIES SHOPPING CENTRE, BROADMEAD,
BRISTOL, SOMERSET BS1 3XD
☎ (0117) 922 5955. OPEN 9 - 5.30 MON - FRI, 7 ON THUR,
9 - 6 SAT, 11 - 5 SUN.

Permanent Discount Outlet • *Household*

General domestic glassware, non-stick bakeware, kitchen gadgets (but no electricals), ceramic oven-to-tableware, textiles, cutting boards, aluminium non-stick cookware, bakeware, plastic kitchenware, plastic storage, woodware, coffee pots/makers, furniture, mirrors and picture frames. Rather than being discounted, all the merchandise is very competitively priced - in fact, the company carry out competitors' checks frequently in order to monitor pricing. With 38 branches, the company is able to buy in bulk and thus negotiate very good prices.

TAUNTON REMNANT SHOP
9A EASTREACH, TAUNTON, SOMERSET TA1 3EN
☎ (01823) 323932. OPEN 9 - 5 MON - SAT.
Permanent Discount Outlet • *Furniture/Soft Furnishings*
Packed full of ends of lines and seconds from famous name furnishing manufacturers. Lining, £2.20 a metre, upholstery fabrics, velvet, from £3.99 a metre for seconds. Curtain fabrics stocked include those from famous names such as Hardy, Sanderson, Derby House, Prestigious, Curtaina, Crowsons and many others. Fabrics start at £2.99 a yard or £3.20 a metre.

TAYLORS OF TAUNTON
RICHMOND ROAD, OFF STAPLEGROVE ROAD, TAUNTON, SOMERSET TA1 1EN
☎ (01823) 272961. OPEN 9 - 5.30 MON - SAT.
Permanent Discount Outlet • *Household*
Large shop with a free car park and a coffee shop which sells both perfect and seconds in a wide range of china and glassware, as well as cutlery, cooking utensils, baskets, wrapping paper, cards, napkins, table mats, garden pots, logs and pet baskets and sundials. There are always special offers in the china and glassware sections such as Denby Pottery reduced by 20%, Johnson Bros dinner services reduced by 25%, seconds of Churchill tableware; George Butler stainless steel 44-piece canteens reduced from £390 to £195, special offers on Edinburgh crystal and half-price offers on Dartington Crystal as well as run of kiln Spode Blue Italian at reductions of 30% (run of kiln means the factory hasn't checked the products - while there is certain to be a few seconds, the majority of the products are fine).

THE CURTAIN EXCHANGE
LONGALLER MILL, BISHOPS HULL, TAUNTON, SOMERSET TA4 1AD
☎ (01823) 326071. OPEN 10 - 4 WED - SAT OR BY APPOINTMENT.
11 WIDCOMBE PARADE, BATH BA2 4JT
☎ (01225) 422078. OPEN 9.30 - 1 MON, 10 - 4 TUE - SAT.
Secondhand shops • *Furniture/Soft Furnishings*
The Curtain Exchange is a franchised group of shops selling beautiful top quality secondhand curtains, blinds, pelmets, etc at between one-third and one half of the brand new price. Their stock comes from a variety of sources: people who are moving house; people who have curtains made and then feel they are wrong for the room; show houses where the builder wants to recoup some of his outgoings; interior designers' mistakes. Stock changes constantly and ranges from rich brocades, damasks and velvets to chintzes, linens and cottons. Designer names include Colefax & Fowler, Designers Guild, Laura Ashley, Warner, Sanderson, Osborne & Little, Fortuny and Bennison. A team of fitters and alteration experts are available if required. They offer a 24-hour availability. The Curtain Exchange also supply bespoke ranges with samples of curtains hanging. These fabrics are chosen from suppliers all over the world and are an excellent buy. They also offer ready made curtains designed exclu-

sively for them which come in lengths up to 305cm (120"). These are outstanding value, e.g. 80" wide, 120" drop start at £175 including vat.

THE DESIGN HOUSE
CLARKS VILLAGE, STREET, SOMERSET BA16 0BB
☎ (01458) 448470. OPEN 9 - 6 MON - SAT, 11 - 5 SUN. .
Factory Shop in a Factory Shopping Village • *Household*
Famous branded products at direct from the mill prices. A fabulous assortment of towels, duvets, pillows, throws, bedspreads, up-to-the-minute coordinated bed linen, from Crown, Coloroll, Jeff Banks Ports-of-Call, to name but a few. Something for every room in the house.

THE DOC SHOP
TOWNSEND ROAD, SHEPTON MALLET, SOMERSET BA4 5SB
☎ (01794) 347081. OPEN 9 - 5.30 MON - FRI, 9 - 5 SAT.
Permanent Discount Outlet • *Womenswear & Menswear* • *Children*
Sells Doc Martens shoes and boots, as well as clothing and a vast range of accessories at discounted prices.

THE FABRIC BARN
CLOCK HOUSE, QUEEN CAMEL, YEOVIL, SOMERSET BA22 7NB
☎ (01935) 851025. OPEN 10 - 4 TUE - FRI OR BY APPOINTMENT ON SATURDAY.
Permanent Discount Outlet • *Furniture/Soft Furnishings*
Designer furnishing fabrics off the roll from Monkwell, Malabar, Warwick, G P & J Baker and Swaffer, amongst others. All at clearance prices at discounts of up to 50% and many available in 40 - 50 metre rolls. Sited in a converted barn in a farmyard setting and run by two former curtain makers who can offer advice and recommend a local making-up service.

THE FACTORY SHOP LTD
MART ROAD, MINEHEAD, SOMERSET TA24 5BJ
☎ (01643) 705911. OPEN 9.30 - 5.30 MON - SAT, 11 - 5 SUN.
Factory Shop • *Household* • *Womenswear & Menswear*
Children • *Furniture/Soft Furnishings* • *Sportswear & Equipment*
Wide range on sale includes men's, ladies and children's clothing and footwear; household textiles, toiletries, hardware, luggage, lighting and bedding, most of which are chainstore and high street brands at discounts of approximately 30%-50%. There are weekly deliveries and brands include many major stars such as Adidas, Nike, Joe Bloggs and Brabantia, to name just four. Lines are continually changing and few factory shops offer such a variety under one roof. This branch also display kitchens and furniture and sells the Cape Country Furniture range. This high quality pine furniture made exclusively for The Factory Shop in the new South Africa is sold at factory direct prices with home delivery throughout the UK. Colour brochure and price list available. It also has its own free car park.

THE POT PEOPLE
CLARKS VILLAGE, STREET, SOMERSET BA16 OBB
☎ (01458) 840652. OPEN SUMMER 9 - 6 MON - SAT,
WINTER 9 - 5.30, 11 - 5 SUN.
Factory Shop in a Factory Shopping Village • *Food and Leisure*
A family-run business, the Pot People have years of experience producing a wide variety of pots and ornaments for garden centres and retails all round the country. In 1993, they started selling their garden stoneware directly to the public at wholesale prices, about half what you might expect to pay for similar stoneware products. When shopping at Clarks Village, they will happily deliver your purchase directly to your car, wrapped in sacking to help prevent damage en route. Ornaments include cherub bird baths, £18, normal price, £36; swag pots, £12, usually £25; plumed tubs, £11, usually £20.95; lion's head troughs, £18, usually £36; sundials, £35, usually £77.75.

THE SPORTS FACTORY
CLARKS VILLAGE, ADDRESS AND OPENING HOURS AS BEFORE.
☎ (01458) 843156.
Factory Shop in a Factory Shopping Village
Sportswear & Equipment • *Womenswear & Menswear* • *Children*
Wide range of sports clothes and accessories, some of which are only stocked in season (for example, cricket bats and tennis rackets in summer only). There are also tennis rackets, cricket gear, leisure clothing (Kicker, Kangol, Timberland, Mizuno, Champion, and Reggatta). All are discontinued lines and are cheaper than in the high street by between 10% - 40%.

THORNTONS
CLARKS VILLAGE, ADDRESS AND OPENING HOURS AS BEFORE.
☎ (01458) 841553.
Factory Shop in a Factory Shopping Village
Food and Leisure • *Household*
The UK's leading specialist confectionery retailer has more than 500 shops and franchises nationwide selling a wide range of boxed and loose, chocolate and sugar confectionery. The factory outlets sell three different categories: misshapes. discounted lines and standard lines. Misshapes are loose chocolates which are the result of new product development, product trials or end of production runs which cannot be packed as Thorntons standard lines. They are packed into assorted bags and offer a saving of 35%-55% over the recommended retail price of standard "loose line" products. Discounted lines are excess to Thorntons' normal retail requirements and can be as a result of excess seasonal or export stock, discontinued lines or packaging changes. These products, when available, are offered at a discount of 25%-50% over the standard retail price. Standard lines from the full Thorntons range are also on sale at normal prices.

TOG 24
CLARKS VILLAGE, ADDRESS AND OPENING HOURS AS BEFORE.
☎ (01458) 840468.
Factory Shop in a Factory Shopping Village
Womenswear & Menswear • Children • Sportswear & Equipment

Tog 24 are the UK's fastest growing brand name in outdoor clothing and leisurewear. They utilise the world's finest performance fabrics including Gore-Tex, Polartec and Burlington MCS, catering for all the family for all seasons, with cosy fleeces and waterproofs for the winter, and trekking ranges, shorts and t-shirts for the summer. With all prices at least 30% below the recommended retail price, you can afford to enter the Tog comfort zone.

TOM SAYERS CLOTHING CO
CLARKS VILLAGE, ADDRESS AND OPENING HOURS AS BEFORE.
☎ (01458) 448874.
Factory Shop in a Factory Shopping Village • *Menswear Only*

Tom Sayers make sweaters for some of the top high street department stores. Unusually for a factory shop, if they don't stock your size, they will try and order it for you from their factory or one of their other factory outlets and send it to you. Most of the stock here is overstock, cancelled orders or last season's and includes jumpers, trousers and shirts at discounts of 30%. The trousers and shirts are bought in to complement the sweaters which they make.

TOYZONE
CLARKS VILLAGE, ADDRESS AND OPENING HOURS AS BEFORE.
☎ (01458) 440771.
Factory Shop in a Factory Shopping Village • *Children*

This shop sells a wide range of well-known children's brand names: Little Tikes, Corgi, Crayola, Tomy, Lego, Hasbro, Playskool, Mattel and Fisher-Price at discounts of up to 50%. They also stock a wide range of soft toys including TY Beanie Babies. The village also has a cafe, children's play area and free parking.

TRIUMPH INTERNATIONAL LTD
CLARKS VILLAGE, ADDRESS AND OPENING HOURS AS BEFORE.
☎ (01458) 840700.
Factory Shop in a Factory Shopping Village • *Womenswear & Menswear*

Factory shop selling a wide and ever-changing range of Triumph lingerie, a French range: Valisere, and swimwear which are last season's stock or discontinued lines. Also stocks Sloggi underwear for men and women. The smaller department for men includes shirts, T-shirts, socks, underwear and swimwear from the Hom range.

VIYELLA
CLARKS VILLAGE, ADDRESS AND OPENING HOURS AS BEFORE.
☎ (01458) 448533.
Factory Shop • *Womenswear & Menswear*
Wide range of Viyella clothing at discount prices from 30% on ladies formal wear and casual wear.

WALCOT RECLAMATION
108 WALCOT STREET, BATH, SOMERSET BA1 5BG
☎ (01225) 444404. OPEN 8.30 - 5.30 MON - FRI, 9 - 5 SAT.
Architectural Salvage • *DIY/Renovation*
Ideas and advice for the period house owner. Everything from panelling to paving, doors, flagstones, flooring, bathroom fittings, fireplaces, radiators, garden ornaments, railings and gates. High quality replicas also available from ÒThe Repro Shop". Stone carving, wood and metal-working restoration workshops on site.

WELLS RECLAMATION COMPANY
COXLEY, NR WELLS, SOMERSET BA5 1RQ
☎ (01749) 677087. FAX (01749) 671089.
OPEN 8.30 - 5.30 MON - FRI, 9 - 4 SAT.
Architectural Salvage • *DIY/Renovation*
Reclaimed timber: pine and oak beams, pine doors, flooring; bathroom accessories, quarry tiles and flagstones (pennent and blue lias), fireplaces and bricks sold from this four-acre site.

WINDSMOOR SALE SHOP
CLARKS VILLAGE, ADDRESS AND OPENING HOURS AS BEFORE.
☎ (01458) 840888.
Factory Shop in a Factory Shopping Village • *Womenswear Only*
Previous season's stock as well as any returned merchandise and overmakes from the Windsmoor, Planet and Precis Petite ranges at discounts averaging about 50% off the original price.

Staffordshire

ALEXON SALE SHOP
34 GEORGE STREET, TAMWORTH, STAFFORDSHIRE
☎ (01827) 310041. OPEN 9 - 5.30 MON - SAT.
Permanent Discount Outlet • *Womenswear Only*
Alexon, Eastex and Ann Harvey from last season at 40% less than the original price; during sale time in January and June, the reductions are as much as 70%. Stock includes separates, skirts, jackets, blouses; there is no underwear or night clothes.

ALLSORTS EX-CATALOGUE AND SURPLUS STOCK
23 HAMILL ROAD, BURSLEM, STOKE-ON-TRENT, STAFFORDSHIRE ST6 1AJ
☎ (01782) 833006. OPEN 10 - 5 MON - SAT.
Permanent Discount Outlet • *Furniture/Soft Furnishings*
Household • *Sportswear & Equipment*
Household goods, furniture and exercise equipment at discounts of 40%-60%. Furniture includes new three-piece suites, pine tables and chairs, TV cabinets, nests of tables, kitchen furniture. Household goods include pots and pans, ovenware, casserole dishes kettles etc. There are also suitcases, exercise bikes, step striders, walking and running machines, but no clothes, fabrics or curtains.

AMBER LEISURE
PEARSON STREET, WOLVERHAMPTON STAFFORDSHIRE WV2 4HP
☎ (01902) 871301. E-MAIL: sales@saunabuild.demon.uk
WEBSITE: www.saunabuild.demon.co.uk OPEN 9 - 5 MON - FRI, 9 - 1 SAT.
Factory Shop • *Sportswear & Equipment*
Mail order company which also has a factory shop selling sunbeds, steam baths and saunas at factory prices. Delivery extra.

AMERICAN DISCOUNT GOLF
75-81 NEWCASTLE ROAD, TRENT VALE, STOKE-ON-TRENT, STAFFORDSHIRE ST4 6QE
☎ (01782) 747787. OPEN 9.30 - 6.30 MON - SAT, 8 ON THUR, 10 - 4 SUN.
Permanent Discount Outlet • *Sportswear & Equipment*
A wide selection of discounted golf equipment and apparel: sweaters, rainsuits, gloves, clubs, balls - everything you need for a golf game. Stocks all the top names including Wilson, MacGregor, Callaway, Links and Mizuno. This is just one of 48 stores around the UK; telephone their Head Office on 01925 488 400 for more information.

ARTHUR PRICE OF ENGLAND
BRITANNIA WAY, BRITANNIA ENTERPRISE PARK, LICHFIELD,
STAFFORDSHIRE WS14 9UY
☎ (01543) 257775. OPEN 9 - 5 MON - FRI, 10 - 1 SAT.
Factory Shop • *Household*
This factory shop in Lichfield sells seconds, discontinued lines and shop-soiled samples of silver-plated and stainless steel cutlery. There are sets as well as loose items on sale at half price or less. Also on sale is giftware consisting of candelabras, cruet sets, tea services, tankards and trays, most at half price. There are usually four sales a year - in March, June, September and December - when there is up to 50% off.

AYNSLEY CHINA
SUTHERLAND ROAD, LONGTON, STOKE-ON-TRENT,
STAFFORDSHIRE ST3 1HS
☎ (01782) 339420. OPEN 9 - 5.30 MON - SAT, 11 - 4 SUN. MAIL ORDER.
UNIT 14, LOWER MALL, POTTERIES SHOPPING CENTRE, HANLEY,
STOKE-ON-TRENT, STAFFORDSHIRE ST1 1PS
☎ (01782) 204108. OPEN 9 - 5.30 MON - SAT, TILL 8 THUR.
Factory Shop • *Household*
The chance to buy beautiful fine bone china at affordable prices from a selection of seconds and discontinued lines at factory shop prices. The giftware range includes handmade china flowers, clocks, table lamps, vases, photograph frames and trinket boxes. For formal or informal dining, Aynsley China has a tableware pattern for every occasion.

BALERAS INTERNATIONAL
STAFFORDSHIRE
☎ (01782) 273335.
Secondhand shops • *Electrical Equipment* • *Household*
Clearance company for businesses which relocate or shut down, specialising in the catering market, especially pubs, clubs, restaurants and supermarkets. When they go in, they take everything from bulbs to desks, chairs, computers, racking and shelving. You can find almost anything here, but if you're looking for anything to do with preparing food, there are fridges, freezers, cookers, microwaves, plates, saucepans, stainless steel sinks and tables. Cookers range from domestic size to commercial 6-burner versions; freezers from domestic to 20ft by 18ft walk-in types, stainless steel sinks from 6ft to 14 ft. Relocating as we went to press, phone the above number for details of their new warehouses.

BDF NEWLIFE
MARTINDALE, HAWK'S GREEN, CANNOCK,
STAFFORDSHIRE WS11 2XN
☎ (01543) 468888. OPEN 9.30 - 10 MON - SAT, 10 - 4 SUN,
10 - 5 BANK HOLS.
Permanent Discount Outlet • *Womenswear & Menswear* • *Children Household* • *Furniture/Soft Furnishings* • *Sportswear & Equipment*

8,000 sq feet charity superstore which sells both new merchandise donated by most of the top high street stores and nearly-new. This is the sort of shop where you can find anything from a girl's party dress to a two-seater rowing boat, men's shoes to a cooler bag and in between towels, jewellery, family clothes, furniture, mattresses (new with damaged packaging), beds, clocks, golf bags, umbrellas, wallpaper and designer dresses. Stock changes every 45 minutes. All the profits go to charity. You have to be a supporter of the charity which entails bringing two forms of printed ID with you showing your name and address. Cost is by donation averaging £2, renewable annually. The shop is on one floor so is very accessible and has disabled toilet facilities. As the store also takes counterfeit goods from Trading Standards Departments' seizures nationally, stress is put on not believing any labelling or assuring authenticity. There are also branches in Kirkby in Ashfield, Nottinghamshire and Stoke Aldermoor, Coventry.

BRIDGEWATER
EASTWOOD WORKS, LICHFIELD STREET, HANLEY, STOKE-ON-TRENT,
STAFFORDSHIRE ST1 3EJ
☎ (01782) 201328. OPEN 9.30 - 5.30 MON - SAT, 11 - 4 SUN. MAIL ORDER.
Factory Shop • *Household*

Emma Bridgewater's distinctive hand decorated and sponge painted pottery, textiles and cookware ranges at discounts of 30% for seconds and discontinued lines. All the pottery on sale here has been made on site. Also on sale across the courtyard at the Bridgewater Pottery Cafe (not open on Sundays) is the equally distinctive Matthew Rice range of stationery, boxes, tins and recipe boxes, some of which are discounted, though the current range is on sale at full price. A mail order system operates for both sides of the business. For Matthew Rice's mail order, phone 01782 269682. For Bridgewater, phone above.

BRITISH TRIMMINGS LTD
BALL HAYE ROAD, LEEK, STAFFORDSHIRE ST13 6AU
☎ (01538) 383634. OPEN 9.30 - 4.30 MON - FRI,
10 - 2 FIRST SAT EACH MONTH (EXCL AUG).
Factory Shop • *Furniture/Soft Furnishings*

An exciting range of trimmings, braids, tie-backs cord and fringing, all made originally for department stores with seconds reduced here by one third to one half. £1 bargain bags of oddments set out in boxes for those who like to rummage. Prices range from 25p to £11 per metre.

CANNOCK GATES FACTORY SHOP
MARTINDALE INDUSTRIAL ESTATE, HAWKS GREEN, CANNOCK, STAFFORDSHIRE WS11 2XT
☎ (01543) 462500. WEBSITE: www.cannockbeds.co.uk
OPEN 9 - 6 MON - FRI, 9 - 5 SAT, 10 - 4 SUN. MAIL ORDER.
Factory Shop • *Furniture/Soft Furnishings*
Small shop next to the factory selling garden gates in wrought iron and timber, garden furniture, adult swings, timber gazebos, arbours with swings, decking, heavy-duty trellis, parasols, cast iron planters, bird baths, urns, fountains, beds, furniture, gazebos, arches, gifts and accessories, all sold at direct to the public prices. Most of the items are manufactured on site.

CANNOCK GATES LTD
MARTINDALE INDUSTRIAL ESTATE, HAWKS GREEN, CANNOCK, STAFFORDSHIRE WS11 2XT
☎ (01543) 462500. WEBSITE: www.cannockbeds.co.uk
MAIL ORDER FOR CANNOCK GATES AND THE GARDEN FACTORY.
☎ (01543) 438 200. MAIL ORDER FOR CANNOCK BEDS.
Permanent Discount Outlet • *Food and Leisure*
Three mail order companies under the umbrella of Cannock Gates Ltd: Cannock Gates, Cannock Beds and The Garden Factory. All offer a mail order catalogue and customers are sent regular updates and special offers. There are special deals in a wide range of wrought iron and wooden gates, as well as an ever-growing selection of garden loungers, wrought iron beds, gazebos, parasols, summer houses, garden arches, wooden planters, cast-iron garden furniture, gifts and accessories.

CARPET MILL FACTORY SHOP
WATERLOO ROAD, BURSLEM, STOKE-ON-TRENT, STAFFORDSHIRE ST6 2QB
☎ (01782) 833823. OPEN 9 - 8 MON, FRI, 9 - 6 TUE - THUR, SAT, 10 - 4 SUN.
Factory Shop • *Furniture/Soft Furnishings*
The biggest carpet warehouse in Stoke-on-Trent, it usually has at least 1,000 remnants in all sizes as well as a big selection of roll stock - all one-offs and non-repeatable - and samples from which customers can order. They don't stock Axminsters, but there is a good selection of Wiltons (from £10 a yard), Berbers and Saxony, both plain and patterned. Prices are obviously cheaper for the remnants and roll stock, although carpets to order are still very competitive. Also stock laminate wood flooring and a wide selection of imported cane furniture.

CARPETS TO GO
VINE LANE, CANNOCK, STAFFORDSHIRE WS11 3XF
☎ (01543) 500546. OPEN 10 - 8 MON, FRI, 9 - 6 TUE - THUR, SAT, 10 - 4 SUN.
Factory Shop • *Furniture/Soft Furnishings*
Allied Carpets clearance outlet for selling cheap roll-stock, underlay and remnants for customers to install themselves. Laminate flooring also stocked and carpets now available to order.

CATALOGUE SURPLUS CENTRE LTD
5 HIDE STREET, STOKE-ON-TRENT, STAFFORDSHIRE
☎ (01782) 744445. OPEN 9 - 5 MON - SAT.
Permanent Discount Outlet • *Womenswear & Menswear*
Children • *Electrical Equipment* • *Household*
Surplus catalogue goods from Kays, Littlewoods, Great Mills and Empire at discounted prices. This is limited to clothing, including the catalogues' designer ranges, shoes and bedding.

CATERING RESALES
MEADOW STREET, CHESTERTON, NEWCASTLE-UNDER LYME, STAFFORDSHIRE
☎ (01782) 564563. OPEN 9 - 5 MON - FRI, 9 - 1 SAT. PHONE FIRST.
Secondhand shops • *Electrical Equipment*
Secondhand and reconditioned catering equipment. Stainless steel sinks and tables, 6-burner cookers, fryers, griddles, both gas and electric, but no saucepans or pans.

CAWARDEN BRICK COMPANY
CAWARDEN SPRINGS FARM, BLITHBURY ROAD, RUGELEY, STAFFORDSHIRE WS15 3HL
☎ (01889) 574066. OPEN 8 - 5 MON - FRI, 8 - 4 SAT, 9 - 3 SUN.
Architectural Salvage • *DIY/Renovation*
New showroom with fireplaces, large quantities of reclaimed handmade bricks, also tiles, flagstone and block stone. Oak flooring, doors, cupboards, garden ornaments and oak beams.

CHARLES CLINKARD
FREEPORT OUTLET MALL, TALKE PITS, STOKE ON TRENT, STAFFORDSHIRE ST7 1QE
☎ (01782) 787016. OPEN 10 - 8 MON - SAT, 11 - 4 SUN.
Factory Shop in a Factory Shopping Village • *Children*
Womenswear & Menswear
Shoes for the family at discounts of between 20% and 50%. Labels on sale here include Rockport, Loake, Camel, Ecco, Gabor, Rohde, Van-Dal, Kickers, Clarks, Dr Martens, K Shoes, Lotus and Renata. The telephone number given here is for the centre, not the shop.

CHINACAVE
LEWIS'S ARCADE, THE POTTERIES SHOPPING CENTRE, HANLEY, STOKE-ON-TRENT, STAFFORDSHIRE ST1 1PS
☎ (01782) 204156. OPEN 9 - 5.30 MON - SAT, 8 ON THUR, 11 - 4 SUN.
Factory Shop • *Household*
This outlet sells seconds in Royal Doulton, Royal Albert crystal, Beatrix Potter figurines and Royal Minton at discounts of up to 50%. In the same complex is Royal Aynsley and the general discount shop, TK Maxx.

CHROMAVISION
29 LONSDALE STREET, STOKE-ON-TRENT, STAFFORDSHIRE
☎ (01782) 848153. OPEN 10 - 5 MON - SAT.
Permanent Discount Outlet • *Electrical Equipment*
Ex-rental and former display models in TVs, videos and satellites at bargain prices. Mostly stocks Ferguson with some Sony and Philips models.

CJ DOMESTICS
92 HIGH STREET, TUNSTALL, STOKE-ON-TRENT, STAFFORDSHIRE
☎ (01782) 833303. OPEN 9 - 5 MON - SAT.
Permanent Discount Outlet • *Electrical Equipment*
Furniture/Soft Furnishings
Reconditioned Hotpoint washing machines, £85, as well as fridge freezers, tumble dryers and cookers from different manufacturers. Also new repro tables, beds and chairs imported from abroad and sold at low profit margins.

COLOURS
3 PEPPER STREET, NEWCASTLE UNDER LYME, STAFFORDSHIRE ST5 1PR
☎ (01782) 714164. OPEN 9 - 5 MON - SAT.
Dress Agency • *Womenswear & Menswear*
Dress agency catering for men, women and children. Men's labels include Armani, Boss, Josef, Calvin Klein, Thomas Burberry and Ralph Lauren. Women's labels: Armani, Betty Barclay, Paul Costelloe, Nicole Farhi, Wallis and Next. Children's labels include Osh Kosh, Jean Le Borget and Next. There is always a marvellous selection of shoes in sizes 3-8.

DARTINGTON CRYSTAL
WEDGWOOD GROUP FACTORY SHOP, KING STREET, FENTON, STOKE-ON-TRENT, STAFFORDSHIRE ST4 3DQ
☎ (01782) 361161. OPEN 9 - 5.30 MON - SAT, 11 - 5 SUN.
Factory Shop • *Household*
An extensive range of Dartington Crystal seconds at greatly reduced prices as well as some perfect crystal at full price. Range includes wine suites, sherry glasses, tankards, decanters, rippled glass, fruit and salad bowls.

DEAN'S FURNITURE WORLD
LEEK ROAD, HANLEY, STOKE-ON-TRENT, STAFFORDSHIRE ST1 6AT
☎ (01782) 286677. OPEN 9.30 - 5.30 MON - SAT, 11 - 5 SUN.
Permanent Discount Outlet • *Furniture/Soft Furnishings*
Furniture at discounted prices. They specialise in three-piece suites, beds and dining sets, some of which are recognisable brand names. A 5 ft double divan bed costs £199.

DIRECT SPECS LTD
39 LOWER GUNGATE, TAMWORTH, STAFFORDSHIRE B79 7AS
☎ (01827) 50233. OPEN 9 - 5 MON - SAT.
1 CHURCH HOUSE, OLD HALL STREET, HANLEY, STOKE-ON-TRENLEY, STOKE-ON-TRENT ST1 3AU
☎ (01782) 263038. OPEN 9 - 5 MON - SAT.
3 LICHFIELD ROAD, STAFFORD ST17 4JX
☎ (01785) 212 001. OPEN 9 - 5 MON - SAT.
8 BERKELEY COURT, BOROUGH ROAD, NEWCASTLE ST5 1TT
☎ (01782) 620 663. OPEN 9 - 5 MON - SAT.
UNIT 9, NORTHSIDE BUSINESS PARK, HAWKINS LANE, BURTON ON TRENT D14 1DB
☎ (01283) 563 782. OPEN 9 - 5 MON - SAT.
UNIT 3, 179 QUEEN STREET, WALSALL WS2 9NX
☎ (01922) 635 301. OPEN 9 - 5 MON - SAT.
Womenswear & Menswear
Spectacles and sunglasses at prices which the owner claims beat any competitor's. Most designer names are stocked at one time or another, though if you have a favourite, check first. Bring along your prescription and glasses will be found to suit. No eye tests conducted.

DISCOUNT CERAMICS
7 MILLFIELDS ROAD, BILSTON, WOLVERHAMPTON, STAFFORDSHIRE WV1 0QS
☎ (01902) 405526. OPEN 8 - 6 MON - FRI, 8 - 5.30 SAT, 10 - 4 SUN.
Permanent Discount Outlet • *DIY/Renovation*
Stocks a vast range of imported wall and floor tiles. As they buy direct from the importer, they can cut costs to below that of most of their competition, though in areas with a wide selection of tile shops, prices will be on a par.

DUNELM MILL SHOP
98-104 HIGH STREET, NEWCASTLE UNDER LYME, STAFFORDSHIRE ST5 1QQ
☎ (01782) 713400. OPEN 9 - 5.30 MON - SAT.
UNIT 3, QUEENSVILLE RETAIL PARK, SILKMORE LANE, STAFFORD ST17 4SU
☎ (01785) 248433. OPEN 10 - 6 MON - WED, 10 - 8 THUR, FRI, 9 - 6 SAT, 11 - 5 SUN.

GUNGATE PRECINCT, LOWER GUNGATE, TAMWORTH B79 7AG
☎ (01827) 69504. OPEN 9 - 5 MON - FRI, 9 - 5.30 SAT.
FABRIC SHOP, 81 HIGH GREEN, CANNOCK WS1 1BH
☎ (01543) 503437. OPEN 9 - 5 MON - FRI, 9 - 5.30 SAT, 10 - 4 SUN.
4 WORTHINGTON WALK, BURTON-ON-TRENT,
STAFFORDSHIRE DE14 1BU
☎ (01283) 512803. OPEN 9 - 5 MON - FRI, 9 - 5.30 SAT.
Permanent Discount Outlet • *Household*
Part of a chain of shops based in the Midlands selling brand-name and chain-store curtains, masses of bedlinen, towels, wickerware, pictures and frames, all at competitive prices. Some of the shops well fabric on the roll.

ELECTRIC LIGHT CO
135 NEWCASTLE STREET, BURSLEM, STOKE-ON-TRENT,
STAFFORDSHIRE
☎ (01782) 812821. OPEN 8 - 5.30 MON - FRI, 8.30 - 1 SAT.
Permanent Discount Outlet • *Electrical Equipment*
A permanent discount outlet, the Electric Light Company don't keep stock in store, but allow customers to take away the catalogue, browsing at their leisure at home, before ringing them with a product number. As a general rule, discounts are 15% for the range of glass, ceramic, plaster, centre, wall, and outside lights, although gold and crystal lights, which can cost £1,000, will attract a higher discount. Halogen downlighters are sold with individual transformers and bulbs rather than in kits and cost £4 plus bulb and transformer.

FASHION FACTORY
WYRLEY BROOK PARK, VINE LANE, BRIDGETOWN, CANNOCK,
STAFFORDSHIRE WS11 3XF
☎ (01543) 466000. OPEN 9.30 - 5.30 MON - SAT, 11 - 5 SUN.
Permanent Discount Outlet • *Womenswear & Menswear*
At the Fashion Factory stores in Cannock and Telford (see Shropshire) you'll find a comprehensive selection of quality branded and designer fashions for men and women, all reduced by up to 70% off the normal high street prices. Stock is made up of excess production, cancelled orders and ends of season ranges from dozens of UK and international clothing manufacturers. This means a constantly changing selection from lingerie and basic fashion essentials to dresses, suits and separates, all at a fraction of the prices you'd normally expect to pay. The boutique-style store in Telford features two floors packed with a huge variety of ladieswear, while the Cannock superstore boasts possibly one of the largest selection of discounted clothing and footwear under one roof in the Midlands, with between 50,000-60,000 garments on display in a massive 20,000 sq ft of retail space. Parking outside.

FIVE STAR DRESS AGENCY
7 - 8 BRIDGTOWN BUSINESS CENTRE, NORTH STREET, BRIDGTOWN,
CANNOCK, STAFFORDSHIRE WS11 3AZ
☎ (01543) 571397. OPEN 10 - 4 MON - SAT.
Dress Agency • *Womenswear Only*
Good range of designer wear as well as high street names. For example, Planet, Laura Ashley, Next, Wallis and Windsmoor to Frank Usher, Betty Barclay, Klass and Louis Feraud. Offers small selection of evening wear, mother of the bride/groom outfits including hats, also large selection of day wear.

FRAYLING FURNITURE
SALEM STREET, ETRURIA, NEAR HANLEY, STOKE-ON-TRENT,
STAFFORDSHIRE ST1 5PR
☎ (01782) 811041. open 2 - 8 fri, 10 - 4 sat, sun.
Designer Sale • *Furniture/Soft Furnishings*
Quarterly sales are held at this anufacturers of leather furniture to clear overstocks. Prices are discounted by up to 50%. Telephone for the next dates.

FREEPORT TALKE OUTLET MALL
TALKE, NEAR STOKE-ON-TRENT, NEWCASTLE UNDER LYME,
PIT LANE, TALKE PITS, STOKE ON TRENT
☎ (01782) 774113. OPEN 10 - 8 MON - SAT, 11 - 5 SUN.
Factory Shopping Village • *Womenswear & Menswear* • *Children Household* • *Furniture/Soft Furnishings* • *Food and Leisure Sportswear & Equipment*
Fully covered indoor outlet mall. Ladieswear: Alice Collins, Designer Room, Edinburgh Woollen Mill, Giorgio, Honey, Iceberg, London Leathers, Nickelbys, Pilot, Spotlight, The Suit Company. Menswear: Watson's Heavies, Leading Labels, Easy Jeans, Cotton Traders, Jean Scene, Double Two, Petroleum, Nicklebys. Childrenswear: Giorgio and Used Co. Kids, Luggage and Accessories: Carlton, Claire's Outlet. Footwear: Charles Clinkard, Jane Shilton and Rhode Shoes. Sports and outdoorwear: Tog 24, Trespass, Streetwise Sports. Also, Thornton's confectionery, Birthdays, Mobile Phone Shop, Book Depot, Pictureport, Ponden Mill, XS Music and Video, three cafes (Cafe Ritazza, Jacket Junction, burger KIng) and a childrens' play area - Cheeky Chimps.

GABBIES
59 THE STRAND, LONGTON, STOKE-ON-TRENT, STAFFORDSHIRE
☎ (01782) 501102. OPEN 9 - 5.30 MON - SAT.
Permanent Discount Outlet • *Household*
Discounted toiletries from toothpaste, shampoo and hairspray to household cleaners, toilet rolls and medical items such as Nurofen tablets or Aspirin.

GEORGIAN CRYSTAL FACTORY SHOP
SILK MILL LANE, TUTBURY, BURTON-ON-TRENT,
STAFFORDSHIRE DE13 9LE
☎ (01283) 814534. OPEN 9 - 5 MON - SAT, 10 - 4 SUN.
Factory Shop • *Household*
The only retail outlet for the lead crystal glassware manufactured on site. One of the few manufacturers in the UK of English handmade full lead crystal, you can buy first quality lead crystal only here at 75% less than the high street price for the same quality, with seconds at even bigger discounts. Full lead crystal English handmade sherry glasses cost £5.50 each compared with between £15-£20 in department stores. The range extends from liqueur glasses to 16-inch chalices, and includes decanters and salad bowls. Call and see a free demonstration of glass being made on the premises - from Monday to Thursday.

GLYN WEBB
122-126 BROAD STREET, HANLEY, STOKE-ON-TRENT,
STAFFORDSHIRE ST1 4EQ
☎ (01782) 214471. OPEN 9 - 8 MON - SAT, 11 - 5 SUN.
Permanent Discount Outlet • *DIY/Renovation*
Stockists of all your home improvement needs from wallpaper to paint, furniture to flooring, tiles to textiles, housewares to lighting - in fact, almost everything for your home, with 25 branches in the North-West, Midlands and Yorkshire. Specialists in discontinued mail order, slightly imperfect branded stocks as well as perfect quality superior products. They carry top brands such as Dulux, Crown Paints and Vymura and Coloroll wall coverings, Rectella and Norwood textiles and much more in store. To find your nearest branch, phone Head Office on 0161 621 4500.

GOODMANS CARPETS
MILL CLEARANCE WAREHOUSE, UNIT 1, HEATHCOTE STREET,
CHESTERTON, NEWCASTLE-UNDER-LYME, STAFFORDSHIRE
☎ (01782) 563060. OPEN 11 - 6 MON - SAT, CLOSED THUR.
Factory Shop • *Furniture/Soft Furnishings*
Carpets sold direct to the public at sale prices.

H L LINEN BAZAARS
9 WULFRUN WAY, WULFRUN CENTRE, WOLVERHAMPTON,
STAFFORDSHIRE WV1 3HG
☎ (01902) 714083. OPEN 9 - 5.30 MON - SAT.
Permanent Discount Outlet • *Household* • *Furniture/Soft Furnishings*
The mail order catalogue of this company which sells bedlinen, duvets, towels and sheets is very busy and hides some of the gems which are on sale, ends of lines of which can be found in their warehouse outlets both here and in the West Midlands. Hunt carefully at these outlets and you will find many famous

brand names such as Early's of Witney, Vantona and Slumberdown. Their warehouse sells ends of lines, slight seconds and bulk purchases of duvets, pillows, cotton sheets (usually hotel over-orders) at discounts of up to 50%.

H & R JOHNSON FACTORY SHOP
HAREWOOD STREET, TUNSTALL, STOKE-ON-TRENT, STAFFORDSHIRE ST6 4JX
☎ (01782) 524040. Open 8.30 - 4 Mon - Sat, 10 - 4 Sun.

Permanent Discount Outlet • *DIY/Renovation*

Seconds of wall tiles from many of the biggest manufacturers in the UK, as well as best quality imported ceramic floor tiles. The flaws in the wall tiles are visual only - there are no cracks or chips. There is a vast selection including plain and patterned tiles, borders, white tiles and 400mm x 300mm marble effect bathroom tiles. Free parking.

HADIDA BATHROOM INTERIORS
OLD FOLEY POTTERY, KING STREET, FENTON, STOKE-ON-TRENT, STAFFORDSHIRE ST4 3DH
☎ (01782) 597739. OPEN 9 - 4.30 MON - SAT, 11 - 5 SUN.

Factory Shop • *Household* • *Furniture/Soft Furnishings*

Hadida Bathroom Interiors sells shower curtains, Roman and Austrian bathroom blinds, towels, a ceramic range of toothbrush holders and soap dishes and waterproof window drapes, all of which are discontinued lines or seconds. Shower curtains and blinds are specially treated to make them mildew resistant and some curtains have matching tie-backs. The range varies from 100% cotton, polycotton to PVC and costs £8.50 for a curtain which would normally cost £40. Toilet roll holders are £7.95, normal price £23.50. Austrian blinds come in 2ft, 4ft and 6ft sizes.

HARRY HANCOCK LTD
NEWFIELD CHINA WAREHOUSE, SUMMERBANK ROAD, TUNSTALL, STOKE-ON-TRENT, STAFFORDSHIRE
☎ (01782) 837303. OPEN 8.30 - 4.45 MON - FRI, CLOSED 1 - 2 DAILY, 9.30 - 11.30 SAT.

Permanent Discount Outlet • *Household*

Trade warehouse also dealing with members of the public. The majority of the stock here is lead crystal from Czechoslovakia and Poland, although there is also imported china, some English bone china, giftware such as figurines and ornaments, and earthenware dinner sets. All sold at trade prices. Open to the public.

HEART OF THE COUNTRY
SWINFEN, NEAR LICHFIELD, STAFFORDSHIRE WS14 9QR
☎ (01543) 481612. PHONE FOR SALE DATES.
Permanent Discount Outlet • *Furniture/Soft Furnishings*
This wholesaler of American textiles and gift items who usually supplies garden centres and gift shops, holds sales of discontinued stock in a barn. These sales are normally held at weekends - ring for details.

HYDE PARK TILES
UNIT 6, HYDE PARK INDUSTRIAL ESTATE, CITY ROAD,
STOKE-ON-TRENT, STAFFORDSHIRE ST4 1DS
☎ (01782) 747547. OPEN 8.30 - 5.30 MON, WED, FRI, 8.30 - 8 TUE, THUR, 8.30 - 5 SAT, 10 - 2 SUN.
Permanent Discount Outlet • *DIY/Renovation*
Part of a tile distribution company, which means that when they sell the tiles themselves, they are their own middleman and can cut out most of that cost to pass savings on to their customers. For example, they sell tiles at £16.95 a sq yard which are on sale at other tile shops for £29.50. They specialise in top Italian and Spanish companies such as Apperici, Richetti and Gomez Gomez and deal in sizes from 10cms x 10cms to 45cms x 45cms.

JOHN TAMS
SUTHERLAND ROAD, LONGTON, STOKE-ON-TRENT,
STAFFORDSHIRE ST3 1JB
☎ (01782) 599667. OPEN 9 - 4.30 MON - FRI, 9 - 3 SAT. 11 - 4 SUN.
Factory Shop • *Household*
Discounted prices of between 50%-75% for seconds and discontinued lines of Royal Grafton, Duchess, John Tams and other chinaware.

KEYSTONES
PO BOX 387, STAFFORD, STAFFORDSHIRE ST16 3FG
☎ (01785) 256648. E-MAIL: gkey@keystones.demon.co.uk
WEBSITE: www.keystones.demon.co.uk   MAIL ORDER.
A long-established business operated by Graham and Alva Key, leading specialists in old Denby pottery for the last decade. They will save you from wasting your old dinner/tea service by supplying replacement items for discontinued designs. A free, no-obligation search sevice is provided if they cannot supply from existing stocks. A worldwide ordering service is available and deliveries are by post or private carrier. Retail outlets are situated at Unit 3, First Floor, Gloucester Antiques' Centre (situated in the Historic Docks) and also at Stables Antiques' Centre, Hatton Country World, near Warwick. They provide value-for-money and combine traditional values with personal service for customers.

STAFFORDSHIRE

L FOR LEATHER
THE QUADRANT, TOWN ROAD, HANLEY, STOKE-ON-TRENT, STAFFORDSHIRE
☎ (01782) 274242. OPEN 10 - 5 MON - SAT.
Permanent Discount Outlet • *Furniture/Soft Furnishings*
L for Leather specialises in Italian products from lighting to sofas as well as a full range of divan, single, double and kingsize beds. The frames for the ceiling lights, which are available with 3 or 5 pendants, are made in Naples while the glass shades are handmade in Venice. Exclusive to L for Leather, their price is dictated by the fact that they buy direct from the Italian makers and many come with matching wall lights. Handmade Italian three-piece suites in beech or oak start at £995. Handmade clocks, burnished and varnished and made in Derbyshire, come with old 17th century pictures. There are also pine mirrors exclusive to the store at low prices.

LEW-WAYS FACTORY SHOP
WATLING STREET, CANNOCK, STAFFORDSHIRE WS11 3NB
☎ (01543) 363711. OPEN 9.30 - 6 MON - SAT, 10 - 4 SUN IN SUMMER, BANK HOLIDAYS.
Factory Shop • *Children* • *Womenswear & Menswear*
Sportswear & Equipment
Wide range of children's outdoor and indoor play equipment and bicycles. There are trikes from as little as £9.99, children's bicycles, scooters, as well as slides, climbing frames, sand pits, play sand, pools and baby swings. Adult equipment includes cycles, car roof boxes and camping trailers.

LONDON LEATHERS DIRECT
FREEPORT OUTLET MALL, JAMADGE ROAD, TALKE, STOKE ON TRENT, STAFFORDSHIRE ST7 1QE
☎ (01782) 788288 . OPEN 10 - 8 MON - SAT, 11 - 5 SUN.
Factory Shop in a Factory Shopping Village • *Womenswear & Menswear*
Very good quality leather and suede jackets, coats and trousers, at discounts of at least 30%, with most at 50% off in this village which features lots of restaurants and fun things for the family to take part in.

MATALAN
VENTURA SHOPPING CENTRE, VENTURA PLACE ROAD, BONE HILL, TAMWORTH, STAFFORDSHIRE B78 3HB
☎ (01827) 50900. OPEN 10 - 8 MON - FRI, 9 - 6 SAT, 10 - 6 SUN.
QUEENSDALE RETAIL PARK, SILKMORE LANE, STAFFORD ST17 4SU
☎ (01785) 226211. OPEN 10 - 8 MON - FRI, 9 - 6 SAT, 11 - 5 SUN.
UNIT A, LICHFIELD STREET, BURTON-ON-TRENT, STAFFORDSHIRE DE14 3QZ
☎ (01283) 540856. OPEN 10 - 8 MON - FRI, 9 - 6 SAT, 11 - 5 SUN.
WOLSTANTON RETAIL PARK, WOLSTANTON, STOKE, STAFFORDSHIRE ST5 1DY
☎ (01782) 711731. OPEN 9.30 - 8 MON - FRI, 9 - 6 SAT, 11 - 5 SUN.
Permanent Discount Outlet • *Womenswear & Menswear Children* • *Household*

Matalan is a fashion and homewares value retailer giving customers what they claim to be unbeatable value for money with huge savings on a wide range of products including high quality fashionable clothing for men, women and children at up to 50% off high street prices. Matalan is situated out of town and stores are open seven days a week all year round.

MINTON FACTORY SHOP
LONDON ROAD, STOKE-ON-TRENT, STAFFORDSHIRE ST4 7QD
☎ (01782) 292121. OPEN 9 - 5.30 MON - SAT.
Factory Shop • *Household*

Part of the Royal Doulton company which operates several factory shops. As well as selling at normal retail prices, the factory shops also offer a variety of discontinued and slightly imperfect pieces at reduced prices. Most of the shops sell the company's other three main brands as well: Royal Crown Derby, Royal Albert and Royal Doulton itself. For a tour of china factory shops in this area, go to the railway station and take the Potteries tour. There is an information service on: 01782 292292.

MOORLAND POTTERY
CHELSEA WORKS, 72A MOORLAND ROAD, BURSLEM, STOKE-ON-TRENT, STAFFORDSHIRE ST6 1DY
☎ (01782) 834631. WEBSITE: www.moorlandpottery.co.uk
OPEN 9 - 5 MON - FRI, 10 -4 SAT.
Factory Shop • *Household*

The place where Susie Cooper started her business, Moorland Pottery is one of the few art ware potteries still producing hand thrown, hand turned and hand painted pottery for the modern collector. The small factory shop sells tableware, giftware, reproduction Art Deco, reproduction Staffordshire dogs, and flatbacks and hand decorated spongeware - all manufactured at the works - at reasonable prices. There is a Collectors Club which produces exclusive products for members and there are plans for a complete restoration of this 19th century building complete with original bottle kiln and enclosed cobbled yard.

PAINT N PAPER
CLOUGH STREET, HANLEY, STOKE-ON-TRENT, STAFFORDSHIRE
☎ (01782) 205201. OPEN 9 - 6 MON - FRI, 9 - 5.30 SAT, 10 - 4 SUN.
Permanent Discount Outlet • *DIY/Renovation*
Leyland paint, Coloroll wallpaper, borders, vinyls at discount prices.

PARK LANE TILES
UNIT 7, EMERALD WAY, STONE BUSINESS PARK, STONE, STAFFORDSHIRE ST15 0SR
☎ (01785) 816161. OPEN 9 - 5.30 MON - FRI, 9 - 5 SAT.
Permanent Discount Outlet • *DIY/Renovation*
Retail shop for Creta Ceramica, a company which imports good quality Italian and Spanish wall and floor tiles. You can find their tiles in shops countrywide, but at varying prices depending on the local competition and almost always more expensive than they are in this shop, which is on the same industrial estate as the wholesale warehouse. For the floor, they offer terracotta look-alike tiles averaging £14 a square yard, quarry tiles, porcelain tiles, both glazed and unglazed, octagon, dot, hexagon, square and lozenge shaped. For walls, the tiles are glazed in a variety of finishes from satin and glossy to eggshell and come in sizes from four inches square to 14 inches square by nine inches. They also offer a range of glass mosaic tiles on sheets in 10 different colours with 144 tiles to a one foot square sheet.

PARTRIDGE ENGLAND LTD
POWER STATION ROAD, TRENT MEADOWS, RUGELEY, STAFFORDSHIRE WS15 2HS
☎ (01889) 584438. OPEN 9 - 5 MON - FRI, 9 - 4 SAT.
Factory Shop • *Womenswear & Menswear* • *Children Sportswear & Equipment*
Partridge specialises in fashionable outdoor clothes and accessories. Ranges include waxed jackets, Gore-tex jackets, waterproof jackets, tweeds, quilts, fleece jackets and waistcoats, knitwear, shirts, chinos, cord and moleskin trousers, hats and caps. Discontinued lines are on sale at discounted prices with a minimum of 30% and up to 70% off during promotions.

PATTENS
HIGH STREET, WOLSTANTON, NEWCASTLE, STAFFORDSHIRE
☎ (01782) 719101. OPEN 9 - 5.30 MON - SAT.
Permanent Discount Outlet • *Furniture/Soft Furnishings*
Ex-catalogue (Kays, Freemans, Argos) furniture including chairs, beds, wardrobes, wall units, three-piece suites, coffee tables, console tables.

PONDEN MILL LINENS
FREEPORT OUTLET MALL, PIT LANE, TALKE PITS, STOKE-ON-TRENT, STAFFORDSHIRE ST7 1XD
☎ (01782) 787150. OPEN 10 - 8 MON - SAT, 11 - 5 SUN.
Factory Shop in a Factory Shopping Village • *Household*
Famous branded products at direct from the mill prices. A fabulous assortment of towels, duvets, pillows, throws, bedspreads, up-to-the-minute coordinated bed linen, from Crown, Coloroll, Jeff Banks Ports-of-Call, to name but a few. Something for every room in the house.

PORTMEIRION
SILVAN WORKS, NORMACOTT ROAD, LONGTON, STOKE-ON-TRENT, STAFFORDSHIRE ST3 1PW
☎ (01782) 326412. OPEN 9.30 - 5.30 MON - SAT, 10 - 4 SUN.
VICTORIA ROAD, FENTON, STOKE-ON-TRENT, STAFFORDSHIRE ST4 2TE
☎ (01782) 743460. OPEN 9 - 5.30 MON - SAT, 10 - 4 SUN.
LONDON ROAD, STOKE, STAFFORDSHIRE ST4 7QQ
☎ (01782) 411756. OPEN 9 - 5.30 MON - SAT, 10 - 4 SUN.
NORMACOTT ROAD, LONGTON, STAFFORDSHIRE
☎ (01782) 326412. OPEN 9.30 - 5.30 MON - SAT, 10 - 4 SUN.
Factory Shop • *Household*
Factory shops selling Portmeirion seconds in all patterns. The selection includes tableware (tea, coffee and dinner set); giftware (vases, planters, mugs, candlesticks, salad and fruit bowls) and co-ordinating accessories (placemats, cookware, textiles, tumblers). Discounts are approximately one third but vary from item to item.

PRICE AND KENSINGTON POTTERIES
TRUBSHAW CROSS, LONGPORT, STOKE-ON-TRENT, STAFFORDSHIRE ST6 4LR
☎ (01782) 838631. OPEN 9.15 - 5 MON - FRI, 9.30 - 4.30 SAT.
Factory Shop • *Household*
Price & Kensington Pottery is renowned for its traditionally hand-decorated spongeware, novelty teapots and cottageware, although it now also produces an extensive selection of quality earthenware kitchen items. The on-site factory shop boasts a wide selection of selected seconds from both Price and Kensington and its parent company, Arthur Wood and Son.

PRIMA
FINCHFIELD ROAD, WOLVERHAMPTON, STAFFORDSHIRE WV3 8AY
☎ (01902) 380398. OPEN 9.30 - 5 MON - SAT.
Dress Agency • *Womenswear Only*
Elegant shop with friendly owner selling a good selection of nearly-new designer clothes for women, with a small selection for children. Accessories include shoes, handbags, hats and some jewellery.

PROBUS MAYFAIR LTD
FACTORY SHOP, 15A SELSPAR ROAD, AMINGTON, TAMWORTH,
STAFFORDSHIRE B78 4DP
☎ (01827) 312891.
Factory Shop • *Household*
Probus Mayfair plc manufacture a wide range of small items for the kitchen for top Knightsbridge and mail order names. Kitchenware overstocks and seconds are sold off at their factory shop at substantial discounts. The shop also stocks some cookware imported from the Far East. As well as utensils, oven gloves, cookware and chopping boards, there are aprons, tea towels, breadbins, icing cookware and tablecloths.

RACING GREEN
THE POTTERIES SHOPPING CENTRE, HANLEY, STOKE -ON-TRENT,
STAFFORDSHIRE ST1 1PS
☎ (01782) 265763 . OPEN 9 - 5.30 MON - WED, FRI, SAT, 9 - 8 THUR,
11 - 4 SUN.
Factory Shop • *Womenswear & Menswear*
Overstocks and clearance lines from this mail order catalogue are sold here at discount prices.

REVIVAL DRESS & BRIDAL AGENCY
10 ALBION STREET, HANLEY, STOKE-ON-TRENT,
STAFFORDSHIRE ST1 1QH
☎ (01782) 202195. OPEN 10 - 4 TUE, WED, FRI, SAT, 11.30 - 4 THUR.
BRIDAL SECTION CLOSED ON MONDAYS
BUT DRESS AGENCY IS OPEN 10 - 4.
Dress Agency • *Womenswear Only*
More than 200 once-worn bridal gowns in stock at any one time, plus bridesmaids dresses from children's sizes to adults and some page boys outfits. There is a dress agency downstairs, with hats, shoes, casual wear and clothes from Jacques Vert, Frank Usher and well knownhigh street stores. Alterations can be arranged and carried out on site.

REVUE DRESS AGENCY
12 FORSTER STREET, TUNSTALL, STOKE-ON-TRENT,
STAFFORDSHIRE ST6 5AQ
☎ (01782) 813939. OPEN 10 - 4 MON, TUE, 9.30 - 4.30 WED - SAT.
Dress Agency • *Womenswear Only*
A wide selection of nearly-new women's clothes. The labels are middle of the market and more inclined to the high street - names such as Laura Ashley, Morgan and Wallis - and there are also shoes, bags, jewellery and perfume.

ROYAL BRIERLEY SPODE FACTORY SHOP
SPODE, CHURCH STREET, STOKE ON TRENT ST4 1BX
OPEN 9 - 5 MON - SAT, 10 - 4 SUN.
Factory Shop • *Household*
Sells seconds of Royal Brierley crystal at 30%-50% off retail price, with two special sales. Also Royal Worcester porcelain available at seconds prices.

ROYAL DOULTON
MINTON HOUSE, LONDON ROAD, STOKE-ON-TRENT,
STAFFORDSHIRE ST4 7QD
☎ (01782) 292292. OPEN 9 - 5.30 MON - SAT, 11 - 5 SUN.
NILE STREET, BURSLEM, STOKE-ON-TRENT
☎ (01782) 291700. OPEN 9.- 5.30 MON - SAT, 11 - 5 SUN.
VICTORIA ROAD, FENTON
☎ (01782) 291869. OPEN 9.- 5.30 MON - SAT, 10 - 4 SUN.
REGENT WORKS, LAWLEY STREET, LONGTON, STOKE-ON-TRENT,
STAFFORDSHIRE ST3 2PH
☎ (01782) 291172. OPEN 9 - 5.30 MON - SAT, 10.30 - 4.30 SUN.
BESWICK FACTORY SHOP, BARFORD STREET,
STOKE-ON-TRENT ST3 2NN
☎ (01782) 291237. OPEN 9 - 5.30 MON - SAT, 10 - 4 SUN.ORD STREET,
STOKE-ON-TRENT ST3 2NN
☎ (01782) 291237. OPEN 9 - 5.30 MON - SAT, 10 - 4 SUN.
Factory Shop • *Household*
Royal Doulton's factory shops which, as well as selling at normal retail prices, also offer a variety of discontinued and slightly imperfect pieces at reduced prices. The shops sell the company's four main brands: Royal Crown Derby, Minton, Royal Albert and Royal Doulton itself. For a tour of china factory shops in this area, go to the railway station and take the Potteries tour. There is an information service on: 01782 292292.

SCENT TO YOU
THE DESIGNER ROOM, FREEPORT TALKE OUTLET MALL, TALKE,
NEAR STOKE-ON-TRENT, NEWCASTLE UNDER LYME, PIT LANE,
TALKE PITS, STOKE ON TRENT STAFFORDSHIRE ST7 1QE
☎ (01782) 784997. OPEN 10 - 8 MON - SAT, 11 - 5 SUN.
Factory Shop in a Factory Shopping Village • *Womenswear Only*
Operating within The Designer Room at this outlet village, Scent to You sells discounted perfume, cosmetics and accessories including body lotions and gels. The company, which has more than thirty branches, buys in bulk and sells more cheaply, relying on a high turnover for profit. Discounts range from 5% to 60%, with greater savings during their twice-yearly sales (phone for details). Most of the leading brand names in perfume are stocked including Christian Lacroix, Armani, Charlie, Givenchy, Anais Anais from Cacherel, Charlie from Revlon, Coco Chanel, Christian Dior, Elizabeth Taylor, Blue Grass from Elizabeth Arden, Aramis, Lagerfeld. Plus cosmetics from Revlon

and Spectacular and skincare from Clarins and Lancome as well as Scent To You's own range of bags, watches, hair brushes and brushkits which is sold under the name S.T.Y. Designs. Stock varies greatly due to the fast turnover and varying supplies so more than one visit may be necessary to obtain the scent of your choice. Or phone first to avoid disappointment.

SECONDS 2 NONE
86 HIGH STREET, CHEADLE, STOKE-ON-TRENT, STAFFORDSHIRE
☎ (01538) 751000. OPEN 9.30 - 5 MON, TUE, THUR, FRI, 9.30 - 4 WED, SAT.
Permanent Discount Outlet • *Womenswear Only*
Suits, blouses, tops, knitwear, dresses, jackets and trousers from well-known high street stores at discounted prices. Labels on sale include Dorothy Perkins, M&S, Principles, River Island and Next.

SEVARG FINE BONE CHINA
CHILTON STREET, HERON CROSS, STOKE-ON-TRENT,
STAFFORDSHIRE ST4 3AU
☎ (01782) 599722. OPEN 8.30 - 4.30 MON - FRI.
Factory Shop • *Household*
Sevarg Fine Bone China makes all its tableware and dinner services on site, where it also operates a seconds shop. Selling mainly to Abbies, Cathedrals, Palaces and top department stores under the stamp "Royal Crown Duchy", the seconds shop advertises no prices. Customers choose from entire dinner services or parts of dinner services in plain white and patterns or tableware and then ask for the price. The shop also sells giftware such as soap dishes and trinket boxes.

SLIMMA
JAMES STREET, LEEK, STAFFORDSHIRE ST13 8BQ
☎ (01538) 388096. OPEN 9 - 5 MON - FRI, 9 - 3 SAT.
7 CROSS STREET, CHEADLE, STAFFORDSHIRE ST10 1NP
☎ (01538) 751455. OPEN 9 - 5 MON, TUE, THUR, FRI, 9 - 1 WED, 9 - 4 SAT.
Factory Shop • *Womenswear Only*
Manufacturers for 850 independent retailers countrywide of smart, tailored clothing, the factory shops stock over-runs and seconds from the Slimma ranges as well as chainstore seconds. Examples of prices include, skirts from £4; trousers from £5; swimwear from £8. Co-ordinated ranges available.

SPECTRUM SERVICES
11-13 HIGH STREET, TUNSTALL, STOKE-ON-TRENT,
STAFFORDSHIRE ST6 5TE
☎ (01782) 826162. OPEN 9 - 5.30 MON - FRI, 9 - 3.30 SAT.
Permanent Discount Outlet • *Electrical Equipment*
Graded electrical items which have either been returned because of a slight cosmetic mark or because the packaging is broken. Cookers, fridges, freezers, vacuum cleaners, spin dryers etc from Zanussi, Electrolux, Hoover, Creda, Hotpoint.

SPODE
CHURCH STREET, STOKE-ON-TRENT, STAFFORDSHIRE ST4 1BX
☎ (01782) 744011. OPEN 9 - 5 MON - SAT, 10 - 4 SUN.
Factory Shop • *Household*
This is the oldest pottery in England, still on its original site and the factory shop sells Spode china and earthenware at about 25% below the normal retail price, as well as holding regular sales at which further discounts are available on some discontinued lines. All the stock, including seconds, are current patterns and include tableware, wall plaques, fine bone china dinner sets, tea and coffee sets and giftware. Also exceptional bargains in the whiteware shop. There is a Museum and Visitor Centre which is open seven days a week with fully guided factory tours running every week day. There are conference facilities and an Italian restuarant on site and new for 2001 a selection of national and international concession shops.

ST GEORGES FINE BONE CHINA FACTORY SHOP
HUNTBACH STREET, HANLEY, STOKE-ON-TRENT, STAFFORDSHIRE
☎ (01782) 263709. OPEN 9 - 5.30 MON - FRI, 9 - 3.30 SAT.
Factory Shop • *Household*
This factory shop sells seconds or thirds of any item manufactured here from teapots and mugs to Victorian planters, vases and giftware. The patterns are old-fashioned and chintzy. Firsts are made for export and are also sold to department stores.

SUITES DIRECT
MINSTER MILLS, WALLEY STREET, BIDDULPH, STOKE-ON-TRENT, STAFFORDSHIRE ST8 6EA
☎ (01782) 510007. OPEN 9 - 5 MON - FRI, 10 - 5 SAT, 11 - 4 SUN.
Factory Shop • *Furniture/Soft Furnishings*
Manufacturers of three-piece suites mainly, as well as some beds, they sell to the public at excellent prices as there is no middleman. There are three showrooms here so you can see lots of examples of their products or choose to have something unique made up - perhaps a three and a half seater sofa. Sofas can be manufactured and delivered within 10 days. Plenty of fabric from which to choose covers.

T J HUGHES
BAKERS LANE, 3 SPIRES SHOPPING CENTRE, LICHFIELD, STAFFORDSHIRE WS13 6JF
☎ (01543) 418181. OPEN 9 - 5.30 MON - SAT.
Permanent Discount Outlet • *Womenswear & Menswear Children* • *Household*
Expanding chain of shops offering, not discounts as such, but very competitively priced goods from clothes for all the family to china, towels, bedlinen,

duvets, pots and pans, kettles, vacuum cleaners, television sets, CDs, toasters, many from top brand names There are branches around the country, mostly in the Midlands and North West: Birkenhead, Bootle, Ellesmere Port, Oldham, Wolverhampton, Macclesfield, Kidderminster, Stretford, Lichfield, Chester, Widnes, Salford, Rochdale, Shrewsbury, Blackburn, Sheffield, Liverpool, Warrington, Eastbourne, Wrexham, Middlesbrough, Bournemouth, Crawley, Weston-Super-Mare and Burnley.

TELETRONIX
21 HIGHERLAND, NEWCASTLE, STAFFORDSHIRE
☎ (01782) 661925. OPEN 9.15 - 5.30 MON - FRI, 9.15 - 5 SAT.
Permanent Discount Outlet • *Electrical Equipment*
Ex-hotel, ex-catalogue and A-grade TV and video sets, the latter only used a few times while demonstrating, at good prices. All sets carry a 12-month guarantee. New sets costs from £89 for a 20-inch set from Alba or Bush with Fastext; ex-catalogue videos from Hitachi cost from £79 with remote control.

TERRY'S FABRIC WAREHOUSE
CARTLIDGE STREET, OFF SHELTON NEW ROAD, NEWCASTLE, STAFFORDSHIRE ST4 6DJ
☎ (01782) 710777. OPEN 9 - 5.30 MON - SAT, 11 - 5 SUN.
Permanent Discount Outlet • *Furniture/Soft Furnishings*
Fabric warehouse with thousands of rolls on sale from £1 to £17 a metre. The most popular name stocked here is Prestigious, but there is also some Crowson. Parking outside.

THE AYNSLEY FACTORY SHOP
UNIT 14, LOWER MALL, THE POTTERY SHOPPING CENTRE, HANLEY STAFFORDSHIRE ST1 1PS
☎ (01782) 204108. OPEN 9 - 5.30 MON - SAT, 8 ON THUR.
Factory Shop • *Household*
Next door to the Chinacave shop, this sells dinner services, lamps, tableware, gifts, vases, bells mugs and clocks from the Aynsley range at up to 50% discount.

THE DISCOUNT KITCHEN FACTORY
UNIT 3, CANNOCK INDUSTRIAL CENTRE, WALKMILL LANE, BRIDGTOWN, NEAR CANNOCK, STAFFORDSHIRE
☎ (01543) 506423. OPEN 10 - 4 MON - SAT.
Factory Shop • *Furniture/Soft Furnishings*
Sells the branded kitchen, likes, made by one of the biggest kitchen manufacturers in the country, Bernstein. Available in oak, pine and white. The company operates a high turnover/low margins policy to keep prices down.

THE FACTORY SHOP
QUEEN STREET CAR PARK, QUEEN STREET, MARKET DRAYTON,
STAFFORDSHIRE TF9 1EQ
☎ (01630) 655673. OPEN 9 - 5 MON - SAT, 10 - 4 SUN.
Factory Shop • *Children* • *Womenswear & Menswear*
Household • *Furniture/Soft Furnishings*

Wide range on sale includes men's, ladies and children's clothing and footwear; household textiles; toiletries; hardware; luggage; lighting and bedding, most of which are chainstore and high street brands at discounts of approximately 30%-50%. There are weekly deliveries and brands include many major stars such as Adidas, Nike, Joe Bloggs and Brabantia, to name just a few. Now has kitchen and furniture displays with a line of Cape Country furniture on sale. Ranges are continually changing and few factory shops offer such a variety under one roof. There is a free public car park in front of the shop.

THE GARDEN FACTORY
MARTINDALE INDUSTRIAL ESTATE, HAWKS GREEN, CANNOCK,
STAFFORDSHIRE WS11 2XT
☎ (01543) 462500. WEBSITE: www.cannockbeds.co.uk
MAIL ORDER FOR THE GARDEN FACTORY AND CANNOCK GATES.
☎ (01543) 438 200. MAIL ORDER FOR CANNOCK BEDS.
Permanent Discount Outlet • *Food and Leisure*

Three mail order companies under the umbrella of Cannock Gates Ltd: Cannock Gates, Cannock Beds and The Garden Factory. All offer a mail order catalogue and customers are sent regular updates and special offers. There are special deals in a wide range of wrought iron and wooden gates, as well as an ever-growing selection of garden loungers, wrought iron beds, gazebos, parasols, summer houses, garden arches, wooden planters, cast-iron garden furniture, gifts and accessories.

THE PINE WAREHOUSE
UNIT 2, ETRUSCAN TRADING ESTATE, ETRURIA ROAD, HANLEY,
STOKE-ON-TRENT, STAFFORDSHIRE ST1 5NH
☎ (01782 204500). OPEN 10 - 5.30 MON - SAT, 11 - 4 SUN.
Permanent Discount Outlet • *Furniture/Soft Furnishings*

The Pine Warehouse sells stained and finished furniture made from redwood pine. There are five or six bedroom ranges, as well as tables, chairs, dressers and hi-fi units in ten different finishes. Unlike more expensive competitors, they aren't able to incorporate intricate design details, but their prices are very reasonable. Free delivery locally.

THE SHOE SHED
CASTLEFIELDS, NEWPORT ROAD, STAFFORD,
STAFFORDSHIRE ST16 1BQ
☎ (01785) 211311. OPEN 9 - 5.30 MON - SAT, 10 - 4 SUN.
Factory Shop • *Children* • *Womenswear & Menswear* • *Household*
Large factory shop selling a vast range of all types of women's, men's and children's shoes, all of which are perfects, at up to 30% below normal high street prices. Ladies sandals cost from £5; shoes from £7.50. Men's shoes cost from £10; sports shoes from £10. A large range of casualwear, including T-shirts and tracksuits for women, men and children, plus a selection of ladies underwear. Kitchenware, ceramics, household goods and giftware are also stocked at discounted prices.

THE STOCK EXCHANGE
49 MAIN STREET, BARTON-UNDER-NEEDWOOD,
STAFFORDSHIRE D13 8AA
☎ (01283) 713177. OPEN 10 - 5 TUE - SAT.
Dress Agency • *Womenswear Only*
Situated in the main street of this olde worlde village, you can park outside this shop selling designer and good quality womenswear. Labels on sale include Country Casuals, Laurel and Bianca. There are also new belts, shoes, bags and hats.

THORNTONS
FREEPORT OUTLET MALL, PIT LANE, TALKE PITS, STOKE-ON-TRENT,
STAFFORDSHIRE ST7 1QE
☎ (01782) 787793. OPEN 10 - 8 MON - SAT, 11 - 5 SUN.
Factory Shop in a Factory Shopping Village • *Food and Leisure*
The UK's leading specialist confectionery retailer has more than 500 shops and franchises nationwide selling a wide range of boxed and loose, chocolate and sugar confectionery. The factory outlets sell three different categories: misshapes. discounted lines and standard lines. Misshapes are loose chocolates which are the result of new product development, product trials or end of production runs which cannot be packed as Thorntons standard lines. They are packed into assorted bags and offer a saving of 35%-55% over the recommended retail price of standard "loose line" products. Discounted lines are excess to Thorntons' normal retail requirements and can be as a result of excess seasonal or export stock, discontinued lines or packaging changes. These products, when available, are offered at a discount of 25%-50% over the standard retail price. Standard lines from the full Thorntons range are also on sale at normal prices.

TILE CLEARING HOUSE
104 - 106 CITY ROAD, FENTON, STOKE ON TRENT,
STAFFORDSHIRE ST4 2PH
☎ (01782) 849966 . OPEN 8 - 6 MON - FRI, 9 - 6 SAT, 10 - 4 SUN.
BROWN HILL ROAD, TUNSTALL, STOKE ON TRENT ST6 4JY
☎ (01782) 833248. OPEN 8 - 6 MON - FRI, 9 - 6 SAT, 10 - 4 SUN.
Permanent Discount Outlet • *DIY/Renovation*

Over 500 ranges of top quality ceramic wall and floor tiles permanently in stock, plus a comprehensive range of grouts, adhesives, tools and accessories to complete the job. By buying direct from the manufacturer and passing the savings on to the customer, their prices are very competitive. Moreover, everything you see is in stock, so there's no waiting for orders to be processed. Save up to 75% on manufacturers' recommended selling prices.

TK MAXX
THE POTTERIES SHOPPING CENTRE, HANLEY, STOKE-ON-TRENT,
STAFFORDSHIRE ST1 1PP
☎ (01782) 207509. OPEN 9 - 5.30 MON - FRI, 9 - 6 SAT, 11 - 5 SUN,
UNTIL 8 ON THUR.
OCTAGON CENTRE, BURTON-UPON-TRENT
NO OTHER DETAILS AS WE WENT TO PRESS.
Permanent Discount Outlet • *Womenswear & Menswear*
Children • *Household* • *Furniture/Soft Furnishings*

Based on an American concept, TK Maxx is situated in easily accessible, often centrally located stores and offers famous label goods with up to 60% savings off recommended retail prices. TK Maxx has fashion for the whole family - women's, men's and childrenswear - accessories, shoes, gifts, kitchenware and home goods. Everything in the store is branded with a choice of well-known high street names to designer labels, and while a small percentage might be clearly marked past season, the great majority of items in store are current season, current stock and still with phenomenal savings. There is a huge choice with 50,000 pieces in store and up to 10,000 new items arriving a week. The stores are simple and unfussy with wide aisles, shopping trolleys and baskets, and a spacious, functional feel to them but there are individual changing rooms, ramps for buggies and wheelchairs and plenty of staff on the shop floor. Every branch accepts all major credit and debit cards and has a liberal refund and return policy.

TOG 24
FREEPORT OUTLET CENTRE, JAMAGE ROAD, TALKE PITS,
STOKE-ON-TRENT STAFFORDSHIRE ST7 1QE
☎ (01782) 787558. OPEN 10 - 8 MON - SAT, 11 - 5 SUN.
Factory Shop in a Factory Shopping Village
Womenswear & Menswear • *Children* • *Sportswear & Equipment*
Tog 24 are the UK's fastest growing brand name in outdoor clothing and leisurewear. They utilise the world's finest performance fabrics including Gore-Tex, Polartec and Burlington MCS, catering for all the family for all seasons, with cosy fleeces and waterproofs for the winter, and trekking ranges, shorts and t-shirts for the summer. With all prices at least 30% below the recommended retail price, you can afford to enter the Tog comfort zone.

TOPPS TILES
UNIT B, SCOTIA ROAD, BURSLEM, STOKE-ON-TRENT,
STAFFORDSHIRE ST6 4HE
☎ (01782) 819111. OPEN 8 - 6 MON - FRI, 8 ON THUR, 8.30 - 5.30 SAT,
10 -4 SUN.
Permanent Discount Outlet • *DIY/Renovation*
Owners of the Tile Clearing House whose shops are detailed in this book, their main business also offers tiles at competitive prices. They sell wall and floor tiles from names such as Johnsons, Pilkington's and Candy as well as Spanish and Bulgarian tiles. Here, if you buy more than four square metres, you get a discount of 30%. They also sell laminate flooring. There is a catalogue available on freephone 0800 783 6262.

TOYWORLD FACTORY OUTLETS LTD
FREEPORT OUTLET MALL, TALKE, STOKE-ON-TRENT,
STAFFORDSHIRE ST7 1QE
☎ (01782) 777744. WEBSITE: www.toyworldstore.com
OPEN 10 - 8 MON - SAT, 11 - 5 SUN.
Factory Shop in a Factory Shopping Village • *Children*
Toyworld sell a large range of discontinued toys, manufacturers' overruns and excess stock from many famous brand names such as Barbie, Action Man, Lego, Tomy, Fisher-Price and many more at least 30-60% off high street prices.

TUTBURY CRYSTAL FACTORY SHOP
BURTON STREET, TUTBURY, BURTON-ON-TRENT,
STAFFORDSHIRE DE13 9NG
☎ (01283) 813281. OPEN 9 - 5 MON - SAT, 10 - 4 SUN.
Factory Shop • *Household*
Cut-glass from liqueur glasses and goblets to tumblers, jugs, decanters, rose bowls and vases, seconds of which are sold at discounts of up to 50%. There is also a tea room and large free car park with wheelchair access.

TV WAREHOUSE
UNIT 5, IMEX BUSINESS PARK, ORMOND STREET, OFF DUKE STREET, FENTON, STAFFORDSHIRE
☎ (01782) 593303. PHONE FOR OPENING TIMES.
Permanent Discount Outlet • *Electrical Equipment*
Sells both new, reconditioned and graded (manufacturers' returns) TV sets, videos, CD players and hi-fis at either reduced or very competitive prices. They cover both ends of the market from less well-known names such as Thomson, Daewoo and Beko at very reasonable prices - a 28-inch Beko set costs just £249 - to 32-inch Nicam stereo wide screen Philips sets at £799 which competitors sell for more than £1,000. A 21-inch brand new Sharp or Ferguson costs £169, while a 28-inch Thomson wide screen costs just £549. Their TVs start at £39 while a 28-inch Nicam wide flat scrren TV costs £229.

UNIT DISCOUNT
53 UPPER HUNTBACK STREET, HANLEY, STOKE-ON-TRENT, STAFFORDSHIRE ST1 2BX
☎ (01782) 268977. OPEN 9 - 5.30 MON - SAT.
Permanent Discount Outlet • *DIY/Renovation*
Unit Discount sell competitively priced baths, sinks, toilets, bidets, shower trays, kitchen sink units, as well as the plumbing materials to complete your own diy installation: copper tubes and plastic waste pipes.

VISION X
8 LAMB STREET, HANLEY, STOKE-ON-TRENT, STAFFORDSHIRE
☎ (01782) 205122. OPEN 9 - 5.30 MON - SAT.
Permanent Discount Outlet • *Electrical Equipment*
Specialise in ex-rental TV sets, all with a 6-month guarantee. Stock Philips, Ferguson and Panasonic. Also vidoes, Sky digital, satellite, hi-fis and widescreen TVs.

VOGUE CARPETS
11 BRUNSWICK STREET, NEWCASTLE UNDER LYME, STAFFORDSHIRE ST5 1HF
☎ (01782) 630569. OPEN 9 - 5 MON - SAT.
Factory Shop • *Furniture/Soft Furnishings*
All types and styles of carpets including Axminsters and Wilton at very competitive prices. Vogue work on small margins and buy direct as part of a large group from the manufacturers, thereby buying in at good prices. Also now sell laminate and wood flooring at competitive prices.

WATERFORD WEDGWOOD FACTORY SHOP
KING STREET, FENTON, STOKE-ON-TRENT, STAFFORDSHIRE ST4 3DQ
☎ (01782) 316161. OPEN 9 - 5.30 MON - SAT, 11 - 5 SUN,
9 - 5.30 BANK HOLIDAYS.
Factory Shop • *Household*
Now incorporating ranges from Wedgwood, Johnson Brothers, Dartington Crystal, Masons Ironstone, Coalport, Waterford and Dartington, and Arthur Price cutlery. Masons' decorative tableware and giftware and Stuart Crystal at factory shop prices with seconds starting at 30% off the first quality prices. There's a nursery range of Wedgwood Peter Rabbit, and a selection of Coalport figurines. The Johnson Brothers department has some imperfect china, while others are ends of lines or discontinued patterns. There is a wide variety on sale. Large car park and facilities for the disabled.

WEBB IVORY LTD
QUEENSBRIDGE WORKS, QUEEN STREET, BURTON-ON-TRENT,
STAFFORDSHIRE DE14 3LP
☎ (01283) 506371. OPEN 9 - 5 MON - FRI, 9 - 2 SAT.
POTTERIES SHOPPING CENTRE, HANLEY, STOKE-ON-TRENT,
STAFFORDSHIRE ST1 1PP
☎ (01782) 202570. OPEN 9 - 5.30 MON - SAT, 8 ON THUR.
6 MARKET STREET, TAMWORTH, STAFFORDSHIRE
☎ (01827) 60266. OPEN 9 - 5 MON - SAT.
Factory Shop • *Womenswear & Menswear* • *Children* • *Household*
Items from the Webb Ivory catalogue at reduced prices including cards, gifts, soft toys, books, pens, lamps, kitchenware, garden furniture and clothes. Discounts range from at least 50%. The Burton shop now also has clothing and textiles at discounts up to 75%.

WILKINSONS HOME AND GARDEN STORES
OLD HALL STREET, HANLEY, STOKE-ON-TRENT, STAFFORDSHIRE
☎ (01782) 279225. WEBSITE: www.wilko.co.uk
OPEN 8.30 - 6 MON - FRI, UNTIL 8 ON THUR, 11 - 5 SUN. MAIL ORDER.
CASTLE HOUSE, 47-48 IRONMARKET, NEWCASTLE-UNDER-LYME,
STAFFORDSHIRE ST5 1PD.
☎ (01782) 714334. OPEN 8.30 - 5.30 MON - SAT.
UNIT 27, SMITHFIELD CENTRE, LEEK, STAFFORDSHIRE
☎ (01538) 386669. OPEN 9 - 5.30 MON, TUE, THUR,
8.30 - 5.30 WED, FRI, SAT.
THE MARKET CENTRE, CREWE, CHESHIRE
☎ (01270) 250754.
Permanent Discount Outlet • *Food and Leisure*
Family-owned business offering value on the high street through its 179 stores, selling 25,000 high quality, low-priced essential everyday products for all the family including kitchenware, household disposables, clothing, DIY decoration, confectionery and seasonal goods. It also caters for the ardent gardener with

fertiliser, grass seed - loose or boxed - plants, insecticides, composts - both multi-purpose or tub and basket - garden tools, strimmers, hoses and attachments, watering cans, water butts, wheelbarrows, and reels on wheels. In season, they sell bedding plants, garden lights, coolboxes, paint, paint brushes and rollers, climbing plants, honeysuckle but as the summer progresses, these are replaced by barbecues and picnic ranges. Own-brand seeds such as sweet peas cost from 49p per packet and they also stock Unwins; tub and basket compost costs 99p. Summer mail order brochure has suntan lotion, luggage, beach sandals, loungers, and garden toys. Phone 01909 505505 for details of your local outlet.

WYNSOR SHOES
151-153 MARSH STREET, HANLEY, STOKE-ON-TRENT, STAFFORDSHIRE ST1 5HR
☎ (01782) 266660.
Permanent Discount Outlet • *Womenswear & Menswear* • *Children*
Stocks top brand-name shoes at less than half price. Special monthly offers always available. There are shoes, trainers, slippers, sandals and boots for all the family, with a selection of bags, cleaners and polishes available.

YEWS FARM BABY EQUIPMENT
MIDLAND RAILWAY GRAIN WAREHOUSE, DERBY STREET, BURTON-ON-TRENT, STAFFORDSHIRE
☎ (01283) 531689. OPEN 9.30 - 5 MON - SAT, CLOSED WED AT 1.
Permanent Discount Outlet • *Children*
Sells a wide range of equipment for babies, including all leading makes of pushchairs, prams, cots, cot beds and toys, all at discounted prices. They also carry out repairs to most makes of buggies. The shop is situated in a small village outside Rugby on a deer farm, where you can also buy country fresh produce such as eggs. There is car parking, a cafe, public toilets and baby changing facilities.

Suffolk

DINDY'S
HAWSTEAD HOUSE, HAWSTEAD, BURY ST EDMUNDS, SUFFOLK IP29 5NL
☎ (01284) 388276. OPEN 10 - 4 TUE & THUR, 10 - 1 SAT.
CLOSED DURING STATE SCHOOL HOLIDAYS.
Dress Agency • *Womenswear Only*
Set in a converted stables, Dindy's sells high quality second hand clothes ranging from Marks & Spencer to Yves St Laurent, Betty Barclay, Escada, Louis Feraud, Tom Bowker, etc. Well respected for evening dresses, cocktail wear and wedding outfits, they also sell a selection of new, top label clothes at less than 50% of the normal retail price. There's a wide range of new gifts and a dress agency.

FIRST STOP DISCOUNT FOOD STORE
71 ST ANDREW'S STREET NORTH, OFF RISBEYGATE,
BURY ST EDMUNDS, SUFFOLK IP33 1TZ
☎ (01284) 754585. OPEN 9 - 5.30 MON - SAT.
Permanent Discount Outlet • *Food and Leisure*
Gourmet food close to its sell-by date. For example, Irish truffles, Lloyd Grossman sauces and boxed Ribena soft drinks, four for 50p. Discounted lines constantly changing.

GLAD RAGS
24 HIGH STREET, HADLEIGH, IPSWICH, SUFFOLK
☎ (01473) 827768. OPEN 9.30 - 4.30 TUE, THUR - SAT
(CLOSED MON, WED, SUN).
Dress Agency • *Womenswear* • *Children*
Established for more than 18 years, this shop sells a range of nearly-new outfits including Monsoon, Gerry Weber, Viyella, Jacques Vert, Betty Barclay, Caroline Charles, Windsmoor and Alexon as well as American, Italian and German designers. Accessories on sale include belts, scarves, hats and shoes. Prices vary according to design and wear. Childrenswear - both English and Continental for 0 to 14-year-olds - is sold very quickly.

GREENS CLOTHING COMPANY
GAOL LANE, SUDBURY, SUFFOLK
☎ (01787) 881500. OPEN 10 - 4 MON - FRI, 9 - 1 SAT.
Permanent Discount Outlet • *Womenswear Only*
Ladies clothes made by Frank Green, all brand new and at very cheap prices. For example, 100% cotton dresses, £12, jackets, £6, skirts, £6. Some in flowery prints, some plain.

KNICKERBEAN
4 OUT NORTHGATE, BURY ST EDMUNDS, SUFFOLK IP33 1JQ
☎ (01284) 704055. OPEN 9 - 5.30 MON - SAT.
Permanent Discount Outlet • *Furniture/Soft Furnishings*
Recommended by countless interior and decorating magazines and much loved by the bargain hunter, Knickerbean offers a continuous stream of stylish and sumptuous fabrics (the kind found at the Chelsea Harbour Design Centre and Decorex), but all at affordable prices. They originally specialised in top name UK designer fabrics, offering excess inventory, discontinued lines and slight imperfects, usually at about half price. You can still find many of these famous name bargains here, but now many of their fabrics are sourced directly from the same mills and manufacturers as the 'top names', both here and abroad. They offer the same top quality, in the latest colours and designs, at relatively lower prices, because they are buying and selling directly and cutting out the middlemen. Their selection of curtain and upholstery fabrics caters for both contemporary and traditional homes, with formal glazed

chintzes, regal damasks, toiles de jouy and luxurious chenilles displayed next to basic neutrals, bright modern prints, airy voiles and earthy ethnic patterns. They also have large ranges of checks and stripes, self-patterned weaves, simple prints for a child's room as well as a huge range of upholstery brocades and tapestries. Prices start at £5.95 for prints to £19.95 and occasionally more for some their tapestries, chenilles and damasks. Knickerbean's outlets are bright and pleasant, more like an interior designer's showroom - there's no 'warehouse' feeling here. Their trained staff are helpful with all sorts of advice on fabrics, colours and interiors and they offer a complete home visit service with interior measuring and design advice. They have a hand finished making up service for curtains, blinds and loose covers, as well as a range of custom made funiture with footstools, sofas, etc. Twice yearly sales in January and June enable customers to snap up even bigger bargains.

LAMBOURNE CLOTHING
15 CHRISTCHURCH STREET, IPSWICH, SUFFOLK IP4 2DP
☎ (01473) 250404. OPEN 10 - 3 TUE - FRI.
Factory Shop • *Womenswear & Menswear*

Manufactures and sells own brand skirts, trousers, and jackets. The clothes, for men and women, are overmakes and seconds and are usually discounted by about 50%.

MATALAN
EASLEA ROAD, BURY ST EDMUNDS, SUFFOLK IP32 7BY
☎ (01284) 748300. OPEN 9 - 8 MON - FRI, 9 - 6 SAT, 11 - 5 SUN.
Permanent Discount Outlet • *Womenswear & Menswear*

Matalan is a fashion and homewares value retailer giving customers what they claim to be unbeatable value for money with huge savings on a wide range of products including high quality fashionable clothing for men, women and children at up to 50% off high street prices. Matalan is situated out of town and stores are open seven days a week all year round.

ORWELL PINE CO LTD
HALIFAX MILL, 427 WHERSTEAD ROAD, IPSWICH, SUFFOLK IP2 8LH
☎ (01473) 680091. OPEN 8.30 - 5.30 MON - FRI, 8 - 4 SAT.
Architectural Salvage • *DIY/Renovation*

Buys old pine floorboards and joists to make new "old" pine furniture, including kitchens, with usually 1,000 doors in stock in old pine. Also strips doors for £16 plus VAT (£12.90 plus VAT for more than one door), as well as making bedroom furniture and selling fireplaces and restored house clearance furniture. 100-year-old pine doors cost from £55.

PUFFA
UNIT 2, BRICETT BUSINESS PARK, GREAT BRICETT, IPSWICH, SUFFOLK IP7 7DZ
☎ (01473) 657338. WEBSITE: www.puffa.com

OPEN 10 - 4 TUE - THUR, 10 - 1 FRI.
Factory Shop • *Womenswear & Menswear*
Original genuine Puffa clothing some of which are samples, some production over-runs, others discontinued lines or seconds plus a bargain rail where garments are priced at 50% off rrp.

ROYS VARIETY STORE
GREAT EASTERN ROAD, SUDBURY, SUFFOLK CO10 6TJ
☎ (01787) 882800. OPEN 9 - 6 MON, TUE, WED, 8.30 - 8 THUR, FRI, 8.30 - 6 SAT, 10 - 4 SUN.
Permanent Discount Outlet • *Womenswear & Menswear* • *Children*
Reputed to be the largest village shop in the world, it sells branded household goods at what it calls "valued prices". The Save 'N Wear Department deals with the cheaper end of the clothing market for men, women and children. Other departments include DIY, gardening, electrical, housewares and gifts. There is also a pharmacy department that deals with photography, records and toiletries, all at competitive prices, and a large food hall.

SHUFFLES
16 OXFORD STREET, EXNING, NEWMARKET, SUFFOLK CB8 7EW
☎ (01638) 578297. OPEN 10 - 4 TUE - SAT.
Dress Agency • *Womenswear Only*
Friendly little shop in village location selling day dresses, suits, separates and evening gowns and a small selection of accessories. Labels include Gerry Weber, Escada, Betty Barclay, Mondi, Jaeger, Paul Costelloe and Windsmoor.

SIZE-UP
8 THE CHAUNTRY CENTRE, HIGH STREET, HAVERHILL,
SUFFOLK CB9 8BE
☎ (01440) 762738. OPEN 9 - 5.30 MON - SAT.
THE ROOKERY CENTRE, NEWMARKET CB8 8EQ
☎ (01638) 560790. OPEN 9 - 5.30 MON - SAT.
10 IPSWICH ROAD, STOWMARKET IP14 1AQ
☎ (01449) 674777. OPEN 9 - 5.30 MON - SAT.
75 HAMILTON ROAD, FELIXSTOWE IP11 7BE
☎ (01394) 279846. OPEN 9 - 5 MON - SAT.
20 MARKET HILL, SUDBURY CO10 8NN
☎ (01787) 319257. OPEN 9 - 5.30 MON - FRI, 8.30 - 5.30 SAT.
Permanent Discount Outlet • *Womenswear Only*
Top quality ladies outsize clothing, some of it from Evans, some own-label and some without labels. There are coats, dresses, suits and separates, some scarves and leisure wear. Some items cost less than half price. For example, Evans long pinstripe coat, £25, reduced from £70. All merchandise is new end of lines or last season's stock in good condition. Sizes 16-30.

SPOILS
24 ST MATTHEW'S STREET, IPSWICH, SUFFOLK IP1 3EU
☎ (01473) 252020. OPEN 9 - 5.30 MON -SAT.
29 - 33 UPPER BROOK STREET, IPSWICH, SUFFOLK IP4 1ED
☎ (01473) 236646. OPEN 9 - 5.30 MON -SAT.
Permanent Discount Outlet • *Household*

General domestic glassware, non-stick bakeware, kitchen gadgets, ceramic oven-to-tableware, textiles, cutting boards, aluminium non-stick cookware, bakeware, plastic kitchenware, plastic storage, woodware, coffee pots/makers, furniture, mirrors and picture frames. Rather than being discounted, all the merchandise is very competitively priced - in fact, the company carry out competitors' checks frequently in order to monitor pricing. With 38 branches, the company is able to buy in bulk and thus negotiate very good prices.

TERRACOTTA DIRECT
PINFORD END FARM, PINFORD END, HAWSTEAD, BURY ST EDMUNDS, SUFFOLK IP29 5NU
☎ (01284) 388002.   E-MAIL: info@terracottadirect.com
WEBSITE: www.terracottadirect.com   BY APPOINTMENT ONLY.
Permanent Discount Outlet • *DIY/Renovation*

Handmade Spanish terracotta floor tiles in different sizes and shades at prices which are discounted by one third. Delivery within three days. Colour brochure available.

THE CROCKERY BARN
ASHLEIGH FARM, ASHBOCKING, IPSWICH, SUFFOLK IP6 9JS
☎ (01473) 890123. WEBSITE: www.thecrockerybarn.co.uk
OPEN 10 - 5 SEVEN DAYS A WEEK.
Permanent Discount Outlet • *Household*

Mountains of white tableware, huge stocks of Portmerion, Spode, Emma Bridgewater and imported ceramics. Stock bought directly from Italy and Portugal can be found nowhere else in the UK and is good value. Fresh deliveries arrive weekly so there is always something new to see.

THE CURTAIN AGENCY AND PERIOD HOUSE INTERIORS
73 HIGH STREET, NEEDHAM MARKET, IPSWICH, SUFFOLK IP6 8AN
☎ (01449) 722885. OPEN 10 - 5 MON - FRI, 10 - 1 SAT.
Secondhand shops • *Furniture/Soft Furnishings • Household Electrical Equipment*

An emporium of quality secondhand and new made-to-measure or ready-to-hang curtains. Classic fabrics by the metre include brocades, Toile de Jouy, Gainsborough silks, Country house chintz's, Crewel work, Cath Kidston, Ramm Son & Crocker and Bernard Thorp hand-printed designs (half price seconds as well as affordable stock lines). A wide range of fabulous old and new continental accessories, including tie backs and trimmings. Tapestries, handmade finials, reeded, plain and antique gilt curtain poles. Elegant secondhand period lighting: crystal brass and ceramic chandeliers and pretty glass shades; new traditional fittings - switches, ceiling roses and flex complete the look. Lovely French linen, lace voiles and 19th Century tapestry curtains and textiles. Decorative furniture and original French beds - all at sensible prices.

THE CURTAIN EXCHANGE
75 ST JOHN'S STREET, BURY ST EDMUNDS, SUFFOLK IP33 1SN
☎ (01284) 760059. OPEN 10 - 5 MON - SAT.
Secondhand shops • *Furniture/Soft Furnishings*

The Curtain Exchange is a franchised group of shops selling beautiful top quality secondhand curtains, blinds, pelmets, etc at between one-third and one half of the brand new price. Their stock comes from a variety of sources: people who are moving house; people who have curtains made and then feel they are wrong for the room; show houses where the builder wants to recoup some of his outgoings; interior designers' mistakes. Stock changes constantly and ranges from rich brocades, damasks and velvets to chintzes, linens and cottons. Designer names include Colefax & Fowler, Designers Guild, Laura Ashley, Warner, Sanderson, Osborne & Little, Fortuny and Bennison. A team of fitters and alteration experts are available if required. They offer a 24-hour availability. The Curtain Exchange also supply bespoke ranges with samples of curtains hanging. These fabrics are chosen from suppliers all over the world and are an excellent buy. They also offer ready made curtains designed exclusively for them which come in lengths up to 305cm (120"). These are outstanding value, e.g. 80" wide, 120" drop start at £175 including VAT.

THE DRESS CIRCLE
64 UPPER ORWELL STREET, IPSWICH, SUFFOLK IT4 1HR
☎ (01473) 258513. OPEN 10 - 5 MON - SAT.
Dress Agency • *Womenswear Only*

Sells nearly-new labels from Next and Principles to Nicole Farhi and Jasper Conran in sizes 8-20. A Caroline Charles evening dress, size 12, £75; a Jaeger spring suit, size 18, £40; Ally Cappellino dress, size 10, £30. Evening wear and accessories are stocked all year round.

THE DRESSING ROOM
22 ST JOHN'S STREET, BURY ST EDMUNDS, SUFFOLK 1P33 1SJ
☎ (01284) 723700. OPEN 11 - 5 MON, THUR, 10 - 5 TUE, WED, FRI, SAT.
CLOSED AT 4 DURING WINTER MONTHS.
Dress Agency • *Womenswear Only*

Excellent selection of evening wear with daywear labels such as Ouiset, Mondi, Jaeger, Windsmoor, Betty Barclay, Ara, Planet and designer names such as Gucci, YSL, Louis Feraud. Some as new shoes, lots of hats and a few handbags.

THE FACTORY SHOP
BARTON BUSINESS CENTRE, BARTON ROAD, BURY ST EDMUNDS,
SUFFOLK IP32 7BQ
☎ (01284) 701578. OPEN 9.30 - 5 MON - FRI, 10 - 6 SAT, 10 - 4 SUN.
LONDON ROAD, WRENTHAM, NR BECCLES, SUFFOLK NR34 7HJ
☎ (01502) 676100. OPEN 9 - 5.30 MON - SAT, 10.30 - 4.30 SUN.
Factory Shop • *Children* • *Womenswear & Menswear*
Household • *Furniture/Soft Furnishings*
Wide range on sale includes men's, ladies and children's clothing and footwear; household textiles; toiletries; hardware; luggage; lighting and bedding, most of which are chainstore and high street brands at discounts of approximately 30%-50%. There are weekly deliveries and brands include many major stars such as Adidas, Nike, Joe Bloggs and Brabantia, to name just a few. Now has kitchen and furniture displays with a line of Cape Country furniture on sale. Ranges are continually changing and few factory shops offer such a variety under one roof. Both branches has their own free car parks.

THE REMNANT SHOP
3-5 HAMILTON ROAD, FELIXSTOWE, SUFFOLK IP11 7AX
☎ (01394) 283186. OPEN 9 -5.30 MON - SAT.
Permanent Discount Outlet • *Furniture/Soft Furnishings*
Although not strictly a discount fabric shop, they sell cut-price ends of rolls and remnants in curtain materials, dressmaking fabrics (satins, silks, dupions, polyesters) and patterns. They always have a good range of curtain fabrics and hold thousands of rolls of fabric in stock. Lines change constantly so you should always find something to suit. Also hold a substantial stock of haberdashery at very competitive prices.

THE TOOL SHOP
78 HIGH STREET, NEEDHAM MARKET, SUFFOLK IP6 8AW
☎ (01449) 722992. FAX ☎ (01449) 722683.
E-MAIL: tony@toolshop.demon.co.uk   WEBSITE: www.toolshop.demon.co.uk
OPEN 10 - 5 MON - SAT. MAIL ORDER.
Secondhand shops • *DIY/Renovation*
Specialises in antique and usable tools with a vast selection always in stock and 25 new types added each week. They always have more than 1,500 carving tools (planes, chisels, gauges) at the shop as well as many tools associated with other trades. They also send tools by mail all over the world and will always try and find a specific tool. Four times a year, they hold tool auctions at the Limes Hotel, opposite the shop. Three of these auctions contain tools of mixed quality, ranging from tools in "as found condition" to items of collectable quality. There is also a fishing tackle section and a "bygones" section containing items of interest, kitchenalia, old golf clubs etc. Once a year, there is also an International Tool Sale. This comprises more than 1,500 lots of superior quality tools for the user and collector. In order to qualify for this sale, the

tools have to be in superb condition and are presented in a large format colour catalogue. Also now sells a fine range of new Japanese tools and French Auriou handmade chisels.

TK MAXX
BUTTERMARKET SHOPPING CENTRE, IPSWICH, SUFFOLK
☎ (01473) 226800. OPEN 9 - 5.30 MON - FRI, 9 - 6 SAT, CLOSED SUN.
UNIT 14, THE HOWARD CENTRE, BEDFORD MK40 1UH
☎ (01234) 270787. OPEN 9 - 5.30 MON, TUE, THUR,
FRI, 8.30 - 6 WED, SAT.

Permanent Discount Outlet • *Womenswear & Menswear Children* • *Household* • *Furniture/Soft Furnishings*

Based on an American concept, TK Maxx is situated in easily accessible, often centrally located stores and offers famous label goods with up to 60% savings off recommended retail prices. TK Maxx has fashion for the whole family - women's, men's and childrenswear - accessories, shoes, gifts, kitchenware and home goods. Everything in the store is branded with a choice of well-known high street names to designer labels, and while a small percentage might be clearly marked past season, the great majority of items in store are current season, current stock and still with phenomenal savings. There is a huge choice with 50,000 pieces in store and up to 10,000 new items arriving a week. The stores are simple and unfussy with wide aisles, shopping trolleys and baskets, and a spacious, functional feel to them but there are individual changing rooms, ramps for buggies and wheelchairs and plenty of staff on the shop floor. Every branch accepts all major credit and debit cards and has a liberal refund and return policy.

TOP DRAWER
21A THORO'FARE, WOODBRIDGE, SUFFOLK 1P12 1AA
☎ (01394) 388775. OPEN 9.30 - 5 MON - SAT.

Dress Agency • *Womenswear Only*

Dress agency selling a mixture of labels from high street names to Armani, Escada, Paul Costelloe and Jaeger. All the shoes are new, although there are nearly-new hats and accessories.

VANNERS MILL SHOP
GREGORY STREET, SUDBURY, SUFFOLK CO10 6BB
☎ (01787) 313933. OPEN 9 - 5 MON - FRI, 9 - 12 SAT.

Factory Shop • *Household*

Silk ties, silk fabric, purses, wallets, handbags, photo frames, silk cosmetic bags and dressing gowns, and seconds in scarves are all on sale here at incredibly low prices, also printed woven silks by the metre. Twice-yearly clearance sales make for even better bargains. Phone for details.

WASTEWATCH WASTELINE
☎ (0870) 243 0136. OPERATES 10 - 5 MON - FRI.
That old washing machine, the sofa that needs recovering, the printer that you've updated may just be junk to you but they are of real value in the right hands. There are hundreds of charities in the UK which want your old furniture and white goods. Household items can be repaired and passed on to people in need or sold for cash and given to charity. Passing on your old things to a good cause also benefits the environment because you are reducing the amount of material going into waste dumps. Waste Watch can tell you which organisation in your area wants to give your old things new life. Smaller items are probably best given to a local charity shop, though.

Surrey

ABACUS BABY HIRE
LONG LODGE, NIGHTINGALE AVENUE, WEST HORSLEY,
SURREY KT24 6PA
☎ (01483) 285142. PHONE FIRST.
Hire Shop • *Children*
Part of the Baby Equipment Hirers Association (BEHA) which has more than 100 members countrywide. A range of equipment can be hired from one day to several months, including buggies, car seats, double buggies, baby swings, cots, travel cots, highchairs. Also party equipment, small tables and chairs, ball pond, roller coaster (suitable age 1 - 5), outdoor and indoor play equipment, pop up play equipment including castle, ride on cars, space hoppers, goal post plus many other items. Just ask if you want something special. For adults they hire out patio tables, chairs, umbrellas and gazebos.

ALAN PAINE KNITWEAR LTD
SCATS COUNTRY STORE, BRIGHTON ROAD, GODALMING,
SURREY GU7 1NS
☎ (01483) 419962. OPEN 9 - 5 MON - FRI, 9.30 - 4 SAT.
Factory Shop • *Womenswear & Menswear*
Knitwear, made in Derbyshire and sold here at factory shop prices. Although the majority of the jumpers and cardigans are made for men and start at size 38-inch chest, they are just as likely to be bought by women. They do also have a selection of styles specially for women. Choose from cotton, cashmere, lambswool, camel hair, merino and merino and silk mix. The factory makes most of its stock for export, and sells to some of the top shops in London.

ALFRED G. CAWLEY
HAVERING FARM, GUILDFORD ROAD, SUTTON GREEN, SURREY GU4 7QA
☎ (01483) 232398. OPEN 8 - 5 MON - FRI, 8 - 1 SAT.
Architectural Salvage • *DIY/Renovation*
Demolition experts, they stock bathroom fittings, floorboards, roof tiles, bricks, windows, doors and beams.

AMAZON
3 & 7 THE QUADRANT, RICHMOND, SURREY
Permanent Discount Outlet • *Womenswear & Menswear*

The most common labels seen here are In Wear, French Connection, Great Plains, Fenn Wright & Manson, Nicole Farhi and Sticky Fingers. There's always plenty of stock in good condition and very reasonable prices. For example, Fenn Wright & Manson long dress, £29.99 reduced from £105; James Lakeland shirt, £22, reduced from £80; cashmere blend sweater, £19.99, was £180; French Connection boat neck striped jersey, £20, instead of £65. Caters for office, weekend and party wear. Shoes at number 7 are very cheap: Velcro dolly shoe, £19.99 reduced from £50; wedge boot, £42.95 reduced from £78.95; evening shoes, £14.99 was £49.99.

ANCORA BAMBINI
27 CHURCH STREET, WEYBRIDGE, SURREY KT13 8DG
☎ (01932) 857665. OPEN 9.30 - 5 MON - THUR, SAT, 9.30 - 4.30 FRI.
Dress Agency • *Children*

Up the road from the women's dress agency, Ancora, Ancora Bambini sells middle of the road to designer labels for children aged from birth to 10 years, including Next, Gap, Miniman, M & S, Levis, Osh Kosh and Benetton.

ANCORA DRESS AGENCY
74 CHURCH STREET, WEYBRIDGE, SURREY KT13 8DL
☎ (01932) 855267. OPEN 9.30 - 5.30 MON, TUE, THUR, FRI, 9.30 - 5 WED, SAT.
Dress Agency • *Womenswear Only*

Middle to upper range designer outfits from Alexon, Monsoon and Wallis to Betty Barclay, Mondi, Yarell and Frank Usher. Also stocks a small selection of maternity wear.

ANGELA MARBER'S PRIVATE BUY
FIVEMARCH, COOMBE PARK, KINGSTON HILL, SURREY KT2 7JA
☎ 020-8549 8453. FAX 0208-541 5049.
Designer Sales • *Womenswear Only* • *Furniture/Soft Furnishings*

Private Buy arranges for its club members to purchase current and next season's top label European and American samples and stock in the Agents' intimate and friendly showrooms, most of which are in London, ahead of the season at half the cost. Also available at trade prices are household linens, fabrics, wallpapers - even holidays. Usually a recommendation-only club; due to this exclusivity, some personal references may be required. Membership costs £70 a year and includes a regular newsletter informing you of future showroom visits, restaurant reviews and member-to-member recommendations.

ANTIQUE BUILDINGS LIMITED
ALFOLD ROAD, DUNSFOLD, GODALMING, SURREY GU8 4NP
☎ (01483) 200477. E-MAIL: antiquebuildings.com
WEBSITE: www.antiquebuildings.com
OPEN 8.15 - 4.30 MON - FRI, OR BY APPOINTMENT.
Architectural Salvage • *DIY/Renovation*
Stock an immense number of ancient oak beams, ceiling joists, bressumes, handmade clay tiles, bricks and walling stone, reclaimed handmade bricks and peg tiles. Specialises in ancient timber framed buildings, with more than thirty-five barns, cartsheds, hovels, granary and house frames available for re-erection, each of which has been measured, drawn and photographed before being dismantled.

APRES VOUS
2 STATION APPROACH, CHIPSTEAD, SURREY CR3 3TD
☎ (01737) 556791. OPEN 10 - 4.30 TUE, THUR, FRI, 10 - 1 SAT.
Dress Agency • *Womenswear Only*
Beautifully presented nearly-new shop with a wide selection of good quality day and evening wear in all sizes. Also hats, handbags, shoes, belts and some jewellery. Suits all budgets from high street brands to Bianco, Betty Barclay, MaxMara, Jaeger and Jacques Vert. Parking in front, and close to Chipstead station.

BEANOS
MIDDLE STREET, CROYDON, SURREY CR0 1RE
☎ 020-8680 1202.FAX 020-8680 1203.
E-MAIL: enquiries@beanos.co.uk   WEBSITE: www.beanos.co.uk
OPEN 10 - 6 MON - FRI, 9 - 6 SAT. ALSO MAIL ORDER.
Secondhand shops • *Food and Leisure*
The largest secondhand record store in Europe with more than two and a quarter million items on display in this three-storey shop. The three floors of nostalgia cover all formats and styles of music, a Sixties-style cafe and minicine on the top floor and a small stage on the middle floor with live bands performing every Saturday. They also run a mail order service which endeavours to search out and provide all musical requirements. A GDD reader says they have a wide choice of CDs at an average price of £7.

BROWSERS OF RICHMOND
36 FRIARS STILE ROAD, RICHMOND, SURREY TW10 6QN
☎ 020-8332 0875. OPEN 10 - 5.30 MON - SAT.
Dress Agency • *Womenswear Only*
The largest dress agency in Surrey, Browsers carries a wide range of top designer labels at realistic and irresistible prices. The owners keep up to date with fashion trends and are experienced at both pricing and merchandising their stock at a realistic level. They have a large volume of stock and a fast turnover and are therefore constantly looking for new stock.

C H FURNITURE LTD
19-21 NORTH STREET, GUILDFORD, SURREY GU1 4TB
☎ (01483) 573405. FAX 539094. OPEN 9 - 5.30 MON - SAT.
Permanent Discount Outlet • *Furniture/Soft Furnishings*
Privately owned by the same owner since 1932, this shop sells better end furniture of the same sort of quality as seen in Furniture Village. They stock cabinets, beds, upholstery, dining tables (both modern and traditional in glass, wicker, iron and painted), sofas, wardrobes, etc at very competitive prices. The cabinets are all imported, the upholstery English. Most of the furniture comes from Italy, Denmark and France with some from Germany, India, Belgium and Holland. There is a small section of cane conservatory furniture, while the metal tables and chairs and the Mexican mosaic range can be used outdoors as long as they're not left out in winter.

CHANTERELLE
95-99 STATION ROAD EAST, OXTED, SURREY RH8 OAX
☎ (01883) 714389. OPEN 9.30 - 5.30 MON - SAT, 11 - 5 SUN AND BANK HOLIDAYS.
Permanent Discount Outlet • *Womenswear Only*
At Chanterelle, you will find a huge range of famous fashion labels - all under one roof - and all with massive discounts. One of the largest ladies' fashion discounters in the South East, Chanterelle occupies a spacious and beautifully fitted emporium packed with bargains. Most of the stock consists of current season ranges, including well-known high street brands at excellent discounts - a bargain hunter's paradise. All the ranges are fully co-ordinated and merchandised and cover everything from casual wear, daytime, executive suits, special occasion and evening wear. New collections arrive daily. Sizes range from 10-24. Stock is sourced from all over Europe and the USA. The shop is only five minutes from junction 6 of the M25 and there is free car parking nearby.

CHINA MATCHING REPLACEMENTS
29 GREENHILL ROAD, CAMBERLEY, SURREY GU15 1HE
☎ (01276) 64587. OPEN 9 - 1 MON - FRI, THEN ON ANSWERPHONE AND FAX. MAIL ORDER.
Specialist stockists and finders of discontinued English twentieth century tableware such as Royal Doulton, Wedgwood, Royal Worcester, Spode, Denby etc. Single or multiple pieces bought and sold. Mail order or collections close to M3 Junction 3/M4. Don't buy an entire new service when you can replenish your treasured collection.

CHOICE DISCOUNT STORES LIMITED
1 WARWICK QUADRANT, LONDON ROAD, REDHILL, SURREY RH1 1NN
☎ (01737) 772777. OPEN 9 - 6 MON - WED, SAT, 9 - 7 THUR, FRI.
Permanent Discount Outlet • *Womenswear & Menswear* • *Children*
Surplus stock including women's, men's and children's fashions from Next plc, Next Directory and other high street fashion houses, Next Interiors and footwear. You can save up to 50% off normal retail prices for first quality; up to two thirds for seconds. There are no changing rooms but the shop offers refunds if goods are returned in perfect condition within 28 days. There are special sales each January and September. Easy access for wheelchairs and pushchairs. The Watford and Wickford stores are known as Next 2 Choice; the former specialises in ladies and menswear only from Next plc and Next Directory.

CITY MENSWEAR
3-5 HIGH STREET, CROYDON, SURREY CR0 1QA
☎ 020-8686 5047. OPEN 9 - 6 MON - SAT, 10 - 4 SUN, 8 ON THUR.
Permanent Discount Outlet • *Womenswear & Menswear*
City Menswear is Moss Bros's permanent sale shop and this two-storey shop is rumoured to be "the biggest quality menswear discount store in the South East". It now also has some ladieswear and perfumes for both sexes. With 5,000 square feet of space on two levels, it sells 150 suits every week in a wide range of sizes at discounts of up to 50%, as well as the full range of Moss Bros merchandise: Pierre Cardin shirts; YSL shirts; Dior shirts at half price. As well as suits, there are also jackets and blazers.

CLOTHES LINE
KILNHANGER, FARLEY HEATH, ALBURY, NEAR GUILDFORD, SURREY GU5 9EW
☎ (01483) 898855. BY APPOINTMENT ONLY.
Dress Agency • *Hire Shop* • *Womenswear Only*
Beautifully cut jackets, infinitely wearable skirts and trousers, modern tailoring from business suits to special occasion wear. Designers include Jasper Conran, Edina Ronay, Ghost, Betty Jackson and Nicole Farhi. Most are nearly new, although some are one-off samples from designer ranges. There is also an evening wear hire service from designers such as Belville Sassoon, David Fielden and Roland Klein at prices ranging from £25-£45.

CORCORAN & MAY'S FABRIC SUPERSTORE
31-35 BLAGDON ROAD, NEW MALDEN, SURREY KT3 4AH
☎ 020-8949 0234. OPEN 9.30 - 5.30 MON - SAT, 11 - 5 SUN, BANK HOLS.
Permanent Discount Outlet • *Furniture/Soft Furnishings*
Huge fabric superstore drawing on Corcoran & May's long years of expertise in the industry where they are known for getting the best of seconds and overstocks from a whole host of designers such as Andrew Martin, Anna French, Monkwell and the Malabar Cotton Company. They also have a vast range of

repeatable designs from the brightest newcomers, as well as traditional damasks, plains and weaves. Prices range from £1.99 to £19.99 per metre, and there's everything in-store for the home curtain maker, plus an expert curtain making service, ready-made curtains and blinds, and plenty of friendly advice.

CURTAIN CALL
52 FRIARS STILE ROAD, RICHMOND, SURREY TW10 6NQ
☎ 020-8332 6250. WEBSITE: www.curtain-call.co.uk
OPEN 9.30 - 5.30 MON - FRI, 10 - 6 SAT, CLOSED WED.
Secondhand shops • *Furniture/Soft Furnishings*
Curtain Call offers nearly-new curtains for at least half of their original price. The current stock of more than 300 pairs includes Colefax & Fowler, Osborne & Little and Designers Guild fabrics. They range in price from £50 to £1,250 for sets which include valances and swags and tails, etc. An alteration service is also available on the premises, as well as a making-up service using customers' own fabric. They also have a large selection of made-to-measure fabrics which can be made up in three weeks. This range comprises natural textured cottons through to more elaborate toiles, crewel and chenille, damasks, velvets and silks. The samples are made as curtains for customers to take home and try before ordering. Also sell a large range of textured silks in checks and stripes as well as plains in 60 colours. Curtain Call also now have a selection of new luxurious tapestry and velvet cushions as well as a range of small gifts such beaded handbags and picture frames.

DESIGNER FASHION SALE
79 GROSVENOR ROAD, LANGLEY VALE, EPSOM DOWNS,
SURREY KT18 6JF
☎ (01372) 278194.
Designer Sale • *Womenswear & Menswear*
British, Continental and American designer label clothes at wholesale prices or less - most items less than half the price you would pay in the shops. Established for six years, the Designer Fashion Sale allows you to buy samples, cancelled orders and current season stock at regular one, two or three-day events throughout the year. There are usually 15 to 20 designers at each womenswear sale including names such as Bruce Oldfield, Edina Ronay, Mondi, Escada, Ozbek, Joseph Ribkoff, Sara Sturgeon and Workers for Freedom. The Menswear Sales have collections from Versace, Armani, Valentino and Boss. There are also Shoe Sales and Bag and Accessory Sales where you will find top quality Italian and Spanish designer merchandise at wholesale prices. Attendance is by invitation only for which there is a £5 registration fee.

DESIGNER NEARLY NEW
109 SANDERSTEAD ROAD, SOUTH CROYDON, SURREY CR2 OPJ
☎ 020-8680 5734. OPEN 10 - 5.30 MON - SAT.
121 STATION ROAD EAST, OXTED, SURREY RH8 OQE
☎ (01883) 717604. OPEN 10 - 5.30 MON - SUN.
Dress Agency • *Womenswear Only*
Upmarket ladies designer wear such as Escada and Laurel, as well as YSL, Chanel, Donna Karan and Nicole Farhi. The Croydon branch also offers ballgown and hat hire.

DRUMMONDS ARCHITECTURAL ANTIQUES LTD,
KIRKPATRICK BUILDINGS, 25 LONDON ROAD, HINDHEAD, NEAR A3, SURREY GU26 6AB
☎ (01428) 605444. E-MAIL: info@drummonds-arch.co.uk
WEBSITE: www.drummonds-arch.co.uk OPEN 9 - 6 MON - FRI, 10 - 5 SAT.
Architectural Salvage • *DIY/Renovation*
Now in new, larger premises, Drummonds cover the complete spectrum of architectural antiques from chimney pots to the gamekeeper's gate. Their speciality is in period bathrooms, including proper vitreous enamelling of antique baths. Also manufacture their own range of cast iron baths and accessories. Specialises in period flooring.

ENCORE
22-23 VICTORIA STREET, ENGLEFIELD GREEN, SURREY TW20 OQY
☎ (01784) 439475. OPEN 10 - 5.30 TUE, FRI, SAT, 10 - 4 WED, 10 - 7 THUR.
Dress Agency • *Hire Shop* • *Womenswear Only*
The service is friendly and the shop is bright, giving you the impression of being in a high class dress shop. The prices are reasonable as the owner is prepared to negotiate on commission rates for more expensive items. There is a large range of end of lines and designer samples including exclusive evening and special occasion wear from Milan, as well as nearly-new. Labels include Moschino, Mondi, Betty Barclay, Armani and many more. Encore can also offer colour analysis, image consultancy and a range of beauty treatments and alternative therapies. They also offer an evening wear hire service.

FABRIC WAREHOUSE
UNIT F2, FELNEX TRADING ESTATE, 190 LONDON ROAD, OFF HACKBRIDGE ROAD, WALLINGTON, NEAR SUTTON, SURREY SM6 7EL
☎ 020-8647 3313. OPEN 9 - 5 MON - SAT, 10 - 4 SUN.
Permanent Discount Outlet • *Furniture/Soft Furnishings*
Large warehouse chain, now with 39 other outlets countrywide, selling upholstery fabric, furnishing fabric, cushions, ready-made curtains and net curtains. Most of the merchandise is made up of clearance material from mills and manufacturers. Free car parking. Phone the telephone number above for details of other outlets.

FABRIC WORLD
287-289 HIGH STREET, SUTTON, SURREY SM1 1LL
☎ 020-8643 5127. E-MAIL: info@fabricworldlondon.co.uk
WEBSITE: www.fabricworldlondon.co.uk   OPEN 9 - 5.30 MON - SAT.
6-10 BRIGHTON ROAD, SOUTH CROYDON, SURREY CR2 6AA
☎ 020-8688 6282. OPEN 9 - 5.30 MON - SAT.
Permanent Discount Outlet • *Furniture/Soft Furnishings*
A family business which claims to be the largest factory warehouse of designer curtain and upholstery fabrics in England. It stocks at least 2,000 rolls of material, most selling at between £5 and £20 a metre for fabric which would normally cost between £22 and £55 a metre. Designer names on sale include Warners and Sandersons, and stock is all perfect and includes current lines. The company imports from all over the world: tapestries, damasks, natural fabrics, checks, stripes, linens, cottons and satins. There is a making-up service available.

FLAIR OF ASHTEAD
11 CRADDOCKS PARADE, CRADDOCKS AVENUE, LOWER ASHTEAD, SURREY KT21 1QL
☎ (01372) 277207 OPEN 9.30 - 5 MON - SAT.
Dress Agency • *Hire Shop* • *Womenswear Only*
Nearly new ladies wear with a wide variety of good labels to choose from. Strong on seasonal event clothing as well as wedding outfits. Friendly and well informed, will alter garments and assist in wardrobe selection, even keeping an eye out for suitable outfits for regular customers. Some costume jewellery, as well as shoes, handbags and belts. Hat hire service offering a variety of more than 150 hats at £7 to £25 per hiring. Ex-hire hats also sold at bargain prices.

FLAIR OF COBHAM
15 CHURCH STREET, COBHAM, SURREY KT11 3EG
☎ (01932) 865825 OPEN 9.30 - 5 MON - SAT
Dress Agency • *Womenswear Only*
Nearly-new ladies wear with a wide variety of good labels to choose from ie; Caroline Charles, Jaeger, etc. Strong on seasonal event clothing as well as wedding outfits. Friendly and well informed, will alter garments and assist in wardrobe selection, even keeping an eye out for suitable outfits for regular customers. Many accessories, including handbags, shoes, hats, jewellery and scarves.

GENEVIEVE THE GALLERY
13 VICTORIA STREET, ENGLEFIELD GREEN, SURREY TW20 OQY
☎ (01784) 430516. OPEN 10 - 5 TUE - SAT 10 - 8 THUR.
Factory Shop • *Household*
A ceramicist of handmade and handpainted items with bright floral, fruit and foliage designs, Genevieve Neilson is now manufacturing and retailing from the same outlet. At the back is the workshop; at the front, the shop where she sells her own products at factory direct prices. Among other items on sale are mirrors, candles, candlesticks, clocks, soft toys, cards and gift wrap and a slipware range was recently introduced. Commissions taken for specific orders.

HABITAT OUTLET
1 DRURY CRESCENT, PURLEY WAY, CROYDON, SURREY CR9 4PE
☎ 020-8649 9312. OPEN 9.30 - 6 MON, WED - SAT, 8 ON THUR, FRI, 10 - 6 TUE, 11 - 5 SUN.
Permanent Discount Outlet • *Household Furniture/Soft Furnishingse*

Ends of ranges and slightly damaged stock from the famous Habitat stores including sofas, tables, kitchenware, plates, glasses, upholstery and cookware, discounted by 20%-40%. Discontinued perfects also available at similarly reduced prices. The main floor is taken up mostly with cut-price sofas - ex-display, discontinued lines and customer returns - reduced by 30-50%. Some of the stock needs a bit of tender loving care so handy customers can get even better bargains.

HOMELINK INTERNATIONAL
LINFIELD HOUSE, GORSE HILL ROAD, VIRGINIA WATER, SURREY GU25 4AS,
☎ (01344) 842642. WEBSITE: www.homelink.org.uk

Home exchange is a great way to see the world, have a holiday and save money. You pay for travel, food and holiday spending only and you get to taste someone else's lifestyle! Homelink publishes a worldwide directory listing members interested in exchanging homes for holidays. £89 annual subscription brings five directories a year. Phone them for more details or try their website.

KENT & CURWEN
21 FARNCOMBE STREET, FARNCOMBE, GODALMING, SURREY GU7 3AY
☎ (01483) 426917. OPEN 10 - 5 THUR, FRI, SAT ONLY.
Permanent Discount Outlet • *Menswear Only*

Sells high quality menswear - shirts, ties, jackets, suits, blazers and sportswear including golfwear. Samples and ends of ranges are priced at one third to one half of the london shop prices. Suits from £150, that normally retail for £400; cotton shirts from £29, usually £60; pure silk ties from £5 and pique shirts from £15 that normally retail at £40.

LINDA AMARNANI
21 STANLEY GARDENS, WALTON-ON-THAMES, SURREY KT12 4HB
☎ (01932) 224368. PHONE FOR APPOINTMENT.
Permanent Discount Outlet • *Womenswear Only*

Made to measure cashmere knitwear in a variety of colours to Linda's own designs in a choice of colourways.

LONDON CURTAIN AGENCY
298 SANDYCOMBE ROAD, KEW, SURREY TW9 3NG
☎ 020-8940 5959. OPEN 10 - 4 TUE - FRI 10 - 5 SAT.
Secondhand shops • *Furniture/Soft Furnishings*

A mixture of new and secondhand curtains. Some of the curtains are refurbishment stock from London's five-star hotels, others designer samples and former display stock from fabric houses and interior designers. Stock ranges from curtains for small windows for £50 up to £800 for drapes for huge bay windows with swags and tails. Designer fabrics include Designer's Guild, Osborne & Little and Colefax & Fowler. There are also curtain rails, cushions, bedheads, lamps, blinds, tie-backs and pelmets. All the curtains are lined or interlined. Fantastic bargains at approximately one third of the original cost. Their made-to-measure collection of calico and cream cotton damask curtains handmade to individual requirements, as recommended in Homes & Gardens magazine, are at competitive prices.

MATALAN
268-278 HIGH STREET, SUTTON, SURREY SM1 1PG
☎ 020-8652 9600. OPEN 9 - 8 MON - FRI, 9 - 6 SAT, 11 - 5 SUN.
Permanent Discount Outlet • *Womenswear & Menswear*

Matalan is a fashion and homewares value retailer giving customers what they claim to be unbeatable value for money with huge savings on a wide range of products including high quality fashionable clothing for men, women and children at up to 50% off high street prices. Matalan is situated out of town and stores are open seven days a week all year round.

MUMS2BE
3 MORTLAKE TERRACE, MORTLAKE ROAD, KEW, RICHMOND, SURREY TW9 3DT
☎ 020-8332 6506. OPEN 10 - 6 MON - SAT.
Hire Shop • *Womenswear Only*

Offers retail and evening wear hire from businesswear to leisure wear during your pregnancy. Whether you want suits or trousers, dresses or skirts, blouses or jumpers, leggings, miniskirts, wedding outfits or evening gowns, Mums2Be can kit you out. Evening wear is £60 to hire. After you have given birth, suits can be re-tailored for you for a small fee. They also offer bra fittings and petite collections.

NIPPERS
THE SAFFRONS, WOODSTOCK LANE SOUTH, CHESSINGTON, SURREY KT9 1UF
☎ 020-8398 3114. FAX 020-8398 7553.
E-MAIL: chessington@nippers.co.uk WEBSITE: www.nippers.co.uk
OPENING HOURS VARY SO PHONE FIRST.
Permanent Discount Outlet • *Children*

Nippers, the nursery equipment and toy specialists, operate from previously redundant buildings in rural areas around the country. They offer easy parking, no queues and personal service. This is on top of competitive prices on prams, cots, pushchairs, car seats, outdoor play equipment and toys, some of which are new, some seconds or secondhand and some ends of lines. Prices are low because they avoid the high overheads of traditional retail outlets and also because the successful growth of a number of branches means they can now buy in bulk and negotiate good deals. Customers are invited to try out the merchandise while the children look at the animals, mostly sheep, chicken and pigs. Also offers many brand leaders at discount, including Mamas & Papas, Cosatto, Britax, Maclaren and Bebe Confort, plus Fisher-Price and Little Tikes. You can try out the car seats in your car and there is usually a pram/pushchair repair service on site.

OPTILABS
109 STAFFORD ROAD, CROYDON, SURREY CR0 4BB
☎ 020-8686 5708. OPEN 8 - 5.30 MON - FRI, 8 - 12.30 SAT. MAIL ORDER.
Permanent Discount Outlet • *Womenswear & Menswear*

Spectacle frames and lenses, sunglasses, prescription sunglasses and sports frames, including designer frames, at factory prices, making them about half the high street price. Designers on sale include Calvin Klein, Giorgio Armani, Jaguar, Paco Rabanne and Dolce & Gabbana. Sports frames are used by professional sportsmen and women worldwide. The showroom is on the first floor at which sight tests are available, or you can take your own prescription. They stock a wide range of lenses which are made on the premises and are often available while you wait. Or they offer a mail order service to your prescription.

PEW CORNER LTD
ARTINGTON MANOR FARM, OLD PORTSMOUTH ROAD, GUILDFORD, SURREY GU3 1LP
☎ (01483) 533337. WEBSITE: www.pewcorner.co.uk OPEN 10 - 5 MON - SAt.
Architectural Salvage • *DIY/Renovation*

Showroom with over 10,000 sq ft of floor space filled with scores of styles of church pews and chairs in pine, oak, elm and mahogany. Also pulpits, lecterns, fonts, panelling. Also creates fine bespoke furniture from reclaimed timber. Phone for brochure and map.

PHOENIX
5 CHURCH STREET, COBHAM, SURREY KT11 3EG
☎ (01932) 862147. OPEN 9.30 - 5 MON - SAT.
Dress Agency • *Womenswear Only*

This black and pink cottage devotes two floors and four rooms to middle to upmarket labels, usually no more than two years old, from M & S to Escada, Laurel, Mondi, Simon Ellis and Parigi. There are plenty of accessories from jewellery and hats to belts and shoes, as well as a bargain rail.

RAFF RADIO
1 STATION APPROACH, HINCHLEY WOOD, SURREY KT10 0SR
☎ 020-8398 0987. OPEN 9.15 - 5.30 MON - SAT.
Permanent Discount Outlet • *Electrical Equipment*

Kitchen appliances from leading brand names at prices which are cheaper than most other white goods retailers. Fridges, freezers, washing machines, etc from AEG, Electrolux, Hotpoint, Creda, Neff, Bosch. Stainless steel specialists, they also offer a good selection of range-style cookers from Lacanche, Stoves, Leisure, Britannia and Belling, and US-style fridges from Admiral and Amana.

RDO KITCHEN APPLIANCES
BANCROFT ROAD, REIGATE, SURREY RH2 7RP
☎ (01737) 240403. OPEN 9 - 5.30 MON - FRI, 9 - 4.30 SAT.
Permanent Discount Outlet • *Electrical Equipment*

Any kitchen appliance you can think of with up to 6,000 items to choose from. Specialises in British, French and German brand names - Gaggenau, Zanussi, De Dietrich, Britannia, Neff, Bosch, AEG, Smeg, Falcon, Creda - at trade prices. There are continuous special offers - phone for details. Delivery nationwide. Range of more than 300 appliances constantly on show, including built-in and freestanding appliances. Access/Visa phone orders accepted. Huge discounts available.

RICHE
87 HIGH STREET, EWELL, SURREY KT17 1RX
☎ 020-8393 2256. OPEN 9.30 - 5 MON - SAT.
Dress Agency • *Womenswear Only*

Riche has made its name selling current top quality designer wear at much reduced prices. The owner is a former model and fashion buyer and has brought a wealth of experience to this small high street shop, making it more than just another nearly-new agency. Escada, Yves St Laurent, Mondi, Gucci, Chanel and Krizia are just a few of the regular labels. While most of the stock is nearly-new, some is ex-fashion show samples and ends of lines and stock is constantly changing. There's an extensive range of new accessories such as jewellery and hats at reasonable prices.

RICHMOND BOOK SHOP
20 RED LION STREET, RICHMOND, SURREY TW9 1RW
☎ 020-8940 5512. OPEN 9.30 - 6 FRI AND SAT.
Permanent Discount Outlet • *Food and Leisure*
A wide selection second hand books including many recent publications. Subject areas include, Art, Architecture, Aviation, Biography, Cookery, English Literature, Fiction, Film, History, Military, Nautical, Poetry, Plays, and Travel.

SEQUEL
181 CHESSINGTON ROAD, WEST EWELL, SURREY KT19 9XE
☎ 020-8786 7552. OPEN 10 - 5 MON- SAT, CLOSED WED.
Dress Agency • *Womenswear Only*
Sells new and nearly-new womenswear including ends of lines and samples in sizes 8-18. There is always a good cross-section of garments to be found on the rails with labels such as Armani, Moschino, Escada, Mondi, Betty Barclay, Gerry Weber, Jaeger, Betty Barclay, Jigsaw, DKNY and Karen Millen, complemented by a wide range of hats, handbags, new scarves and jewellery. Nothing is more than two seasons old.

SIESTA CORK TILES
UNIT 21, TAIT ROAD, CROYDON, SURREY CR0 2DP
☎ 020-8683 4055. FAX: 0181-683 4480. OPEN 9 - 5 MON - FRI.
CLOSED BETWEEN 1 AND 2. MAIL ORDER
Permanent Discount Outlet • *DIY/Renovation*
Cork importers, who supply on a mail order basis, a complete range of cork floor tiles in all thicknesses - unsealed, acrylic varnished, hard wax or PVC surfaced, plus a coloured range. Special offers usually available. Details and samples sent on request. They also sell cork for walls and ceilings, decoration, insulation and for noticeboards. Large range tiles are stocked in thicknesses of 3mm, 6mm, 8mm and 10mm and in sizes 300x300mm and 600x300mm. Composition cork (fine grain) comes in rolls up to 1.22mx5m in a variety of thicknesses: 2mm, 3mm and 6mm, ideal for large noticeboards. Remember that unsealed floor cork can be coloured using diluted water-based paints then clear varnish when laid with quick-dry water-based floor sealant.

SILVERLAND STONE
HOLLOWAY HILL, CHERTSEY, SURREY KT16 0AE
☎ (01932) 569277. OPEN 8 - 5 MON - FRI, 9 - 1 SAT, SUN.
Architectural Salvage • *DIY/Renovation*
Natural stone floors for both interior and exterior and fireplaces. Extensive range of hard landscaping materials sold including rockery and pebbles.

SPECIAL OCCASIONS
1 OLD WOKING ROAD, WEST BYFLEET, SURREY KT14 6LW
☎ (019323) 54907. OPEN 10 - 4 MON - SAT.
EVENINGS AND IN AUGUST BY APPOINTMENT.
Hire Shop • *Womenswear & Menswear*
Established for more than 12 years, Special Occasions has more than 400 evening dresses in sizes 8 - 20 and accessories for hire. There is always a rail of dresses for sale in the shop. Also agents for men's dress hire.

SPOILS
UNIT 17, THE DRUMMOND CENTRE, CROYDON, SURREY CR0 1TQ
☎ 020-8688 8717. OPEN 9.30 - 6 MON - SAT, 9 ON THUR, 1 - 6 SUN.
UNIT S12, THE BENTALL CENTRE, KINGSTON-UPON-THAMES, SURREY KT1 1TP
☎ 020-8974 9303. OPEN 9.30 - 6 MON - WED & FRI, 9 - 8 THUR, 9 - 6 SAT, 11 - 5 SUN.
UNITS 9-11, ST NICHOLAS CENTRE, SUTTON, SURREY SM1 1AW
☎ 020-8642 4450. OPEN 9 - 5.30 MON - FRI, 8 ON THUR, 9 - 6 SAT, 10.30 - 4.30 SUN.
Permanent Discount Outlet • *Household*
General domestic glassware, non-stick bakeware, kitchen gadgets, ceramic oven-to-tableware, textiles, cutting boards, aluminium non-stick cookware, bakeware, plastic kitchenware, plastic storage, woodware, coffee pots/makers, furniture, mirrors and picture frames. Rather than being discounted, all the merchandise is very competitively priced - in fact, the company carry out competitors' checks frequently in order to monitor pricing. With 38 branches, the company is able to buy in bulk and thus negotiate very good prices.

SUIT CITY
15 HOLMETHORPE AVENUE, HOLMETHORPE INDUSTRIAL ESTATE, REDHILL, SURREY RH1 2NB
☎ (0173) 778 9963. OPEN 11 - 3 FRI, 10 - 4 SAT, SUN.
Permanent Discount Outlet • *Menswear Only*
Quality menswear: suits, blazers, trousers and overcoats at discounts of up to 65% in sizes to fit 36 inch to 60 inch chests.

THE CURTAIN AGENCY
231 LONDON ROAD, CAMBERLEY, SURREY GU15 3EY
☎ (01276) 671672. OPEN 10 - 5 MON - SAT.
103 WEST STREET, FARNHAM, SURREY GU9 7EN
☎ (01252) 714711. OPEN 10 - 5 MON - SAT.
Secondhand shops • *Furniture/Soft Furnishings* • *Electrical Equipment*
Two shops in Surrey offering a wide range of quality secondhand curtains from designer elegance to practical and functional. Many are from shops' display stock and executive home relocations. All the curtains are ready to hang, but if alter-

ations are needed an excellent service is available and a 24 hour sale or return option can be requested at both shops. A good range of quality fabrics is stocked for making up to customers' own requirements, with a delivery time of five weeks. A unique selection of antique and decorative lighting is also available. Poles and rings, antique or new, metal or wood, tiebacks and holdbacks, door furnishing knobs and knockers, cushions and kilims are all found here under one roof.

THE DRESS AGENCY
5B RECTORY LANE, ASHTEAD, SURREY KT21 2BA
☎ (01372) 271677. WEBSITE: www.business.virgin.net/d.agency
OPEN 9 - 5 MON - FRI, 9 - 3 WED, 9 - 4 SAT.
Dress Agency • *Womenswear Only*
Double-fronted shop, half of which is devoted to daywear, the other of which has nearly-new bridal dresses. The daywear includes good quality names such as Planet, Basler, Jaeger, Jigsaw, Mondi, Frank Usher, Betty Barclay and Episode. The bridal section has about 50 wedding dresses at any one time from £100-£700, plus veils, tiaras, shoes and evening jewellery. They also have a large range of ballgowns sizes 8-22 for hire.

THE DRESS CIRCLE
6 WOOLMEAD WALK, FARNHAM, SURREY GU9 7SH
☎ (01252) 716540 OPEN 9.30 - 4.30 MON - SAT.
Dress Agency • *Womenswear Only*
Renowned designer labels in good condition - Parigi, Betty Barclay, Louis Feraud - as well as good high street names such as Marks & Spencer, Laura Ashley, Next and Benetton. Caters for seasonal events such as Ascot and towards Christmas supplies a wide variety of good evening wear. also stocks hats and some shoes but no jewellery.

THE FACTORY SHOP LTD
THE ENGINE SHED, CONSORT WAY EAST, HORLEY, SURREY RH6 7AU
☎ (01293) 823883. OPEN 9 - 5.30 MON - SAT, 10 - 4 SUN.
Factory Shop • *Womenswear & Menswear* • *Children*
Household • *Furniture/Soft Furnishings*
High street chainstore seconds and ends of ranges from clothes for all the family, bedding, toiletries, kitchenware, glassware, footwear, lighting, cosmetics, jewellery, and luggage at discounts of approximately 30%-50%. There are weekly deliveries and brands include many major stars: Joe Bloggs, Nike, Adidas and Brabantia, to name just four. Lines are continually changing and few factory shops offer such a variety under one roof, with at the Brighton branch, a large number of clothing concessions in addition to The Factory Shop range. There are kitchen and furniture displays and a new line of Cape Country Furniture has recently been introduced at all four South East branches. This high quality pine furniture made exclusively for The Factory Shop in the new South Africa is sold at factory direct prices with home delivery throughout the UK. Colour brochure and price list available. Own free car park.

THE LIGHTING AGENCY & TRADING COMPANY
LION & LAMB YARD, FARNHAM, SURREY TU9 7LL
☎ (01252) 719192. OPEN 10 - 5.30 MON - SAT.
Permanent Discount Outlet • *Household* • *Electrical Equipment Furniture/Soft Furnishings*

Classical and contemporary lighting: tablelamps, standard lamps, chandeliers, centre lights, desk lights, picture lights, wall lights shades and carriers. Many of these are quality seconds or ex-display stock sold at extremely competitive prices. They also sell antique and continental chandeliers and offer a rewiring service. Old and new furniture is for sale as well as antique and unusual garden pots and ornaments.

TIM MARTIN INTERIORS
76 LOWER MORTLAKE ROAD, RICHMOND, SURREY TW9 2JG
☎ 020-8332 6712. OPEN 10 - 6 MON - SAT.
Permanent Discount Outlet • *Furniture/Soft Furnishings*

Sells complete interiors packages, made up of a mixture of new and secondhand, most of which are the result of five-star hotel refurbishments. Their speciality is country-house style hotels so items tend towards the traditional. The contents of a hotel bedroom can be bought for £1,500 compared with the original cost of £5,000. New items include rolls of fabrics, cream interlined curtains and lighting, from table lamps to chandeliers, the latter of which are bought in bulk for hotel clients and sold at trade price at the Richmond site. Secondhands items sold at half price include top quality interlined curtains, mirrors and oil paintings.

TINKERS
17 OLD OAK AVENUE, CHIPSTEAD, SURREY CR5 3PG
☎ (01737) 553761. PHONE FIRST.
Hire Shop • *Children*

Part of the Baby Equipment Hirers Association (BEHA), which has more than 100 members countrywide. This member only hires out child sized tables and chairs. BEHA run an advice line which will try and answer any queries you have regarding hiring services for children. Phone the Babyline on 0831 310355.

TK MAXX
TIMES SQUARE SHOPPING CENTRE, HIGH STREET, SUTTON, SURREY SM1 1LF
☎ 020-8770 7786. OPEN 9 - 5.30 MON - FRI, 9 - 6 SAT, 11 - 5 SUN, UNTIL 8 ON THUR.
THE DRUMMOND CENTRE, CROYDON, SURREY CR0 1TY
☎ 020-8686 9753. OPEN 9 - 6 MON - WED, SAT, 9 - 6 THUR, 9 - 7 FRI, 11 - 5 SUN.
THE PEACOCKS CENTRE, WOKING, SURREY
☎ (01483) 771660. OPEN 9.30 - 6 MON - FRI, 9.30 - 8 THUR, 9.30 - 6 SAT, 11 - 5 SUN.

Permanent Discount Outlet • *Womenswear & Menswear Children* • *Household* • *Furniture/Soft Furnishings*

Based on an American concept, TK Maxx is situated in easily accessible, often centrally located stores and offers famous label goods with up to 60% savings off recommended retail prices. TK Maxx has fashion for the whole family - women's, men's and childrenswear - accessories, shoes, gifts, kitchenware and home goods. Everything in the store is branded with a choice of well-known high street names to designer labels, and while a small percentage might be clearly marked past season, the great majority of items in store are current season, current stock and still with phenomenal savings. There is a huge choice with 50,000 pieces in store and up to 10,000 new items arriving a week. The stores are simple and unfussy with wide aisles, shopping trolleys and baskets, and a spacious, functional feel to them but there are individual changing rooms, ramps for buggies and wheelchairs and plenty of staff on the shop floor. Every branch accepts all major credit and debit cards and has a liberal refund and return policy.

WALTON DESIGN LTD
108 HIGH STREET, GODALMING, SURREY GU7 1DW
☎ (01483) 423855. OPEN 9 - 6 MON - SAT, 10 - 4 SUN, 10 - 5 BANK HOLS.

Permanent Discount Outlet • *Womenswear Only*

A chain of thirteen stores across the south of England selling well-known labels for women at greatly reduced prices. Current stock from high street stores might include Liz Claiborne, DKNY, Nougat, Ralph Lauren, Banana Republic, Calvin Klein and Tommy Hilfiger. New lines come in each week and are often one-offs, so regular customers know to buy things when they see them or risk missing out.

Sussex

ALWAYS IN VOGUE
1 THE OLD MILL, RIVER ROAD, ARUNDEL, WEST SUSSEX BN18 9DH
☎ (01903) 883192. OPEN 10 - 5 MON - SAT, 10 - 4 WINTER.
Dress Agency • *Womenswear Only*
Founded in 1993 by former model, Lisa Knight, Always in Vogue now has a reputation for being one of the best dress agencies in the south. No high street labels are taken and all garments must be dry cleaned and no more than three years old. Planet, Jacques Vert and Country Casuals form the bottom line of the stock, and you can generally find Jaeger, Windsmoor, Alexon, Condici, Nicole Farhi, Louis Feraud, Chanel, Karl Lagerfeld, Armani, Thierry Mugler, Escada, Gaultier, Ralph Lauren, Frank Usher and Gina Bacconi at between one quarter and one half of the as-new price. There is also new Gottex at about half price. Such is the quality of the merchandise, much of it unworn and still carrying the original price labels, that customers come here for outfits and accessories for Ascot, Goodwood, Henley, polo matches, weddings or simply for a blouse and skirt. Because the client base covers ten counties, customers are unlikely to buy an item that originated from their next door neighbour. Now also offering brand new end of line garments from top British designers at 50% discounts. Always in Vogue continues to set new standards both in the stock it carries and its service to clients.

ANSELL'S FURNITURE WAREHOUSE
KIRDFORD ROAD, WISBOROUGH GREEN, NR BILLINGSHURST, SUSSEX RH14 0DD
☎ (01403) 700359. OPEN 10 - 4 SAT.
Permanent Discount Outlet • *Furniture/Soft Furnishings*
Established for 40 years, Ansell's specialises in three-piece suites and beds from most of the leading names such as Collins & Hayes, Heirloom Wade, G-Plan, Durestur, Christy Tyler, Peter Guild, Derwent and beds from Dorlux, Rest Assured and Relyon. This is the only warehouse in the UK allowed to sell these brands direct. There are ten big buildings full of sofas and beds so come prepared to spend some time walking round. Offers excellent value for money all year round.

BCP AIRPORT PARKING AND TRANSFER SERVICE
GATWICK , EAST SUSSEX
(0870) 0134586. 8AM - 9 PM, 7 DAYS A WEEK.
BCP provides secure, value-for-money car parking at Gatwick, Heathrow, luton, Manchester, Glasgow, Bristol, Birmingham, Cardiff, East Midlands, Southampton, Newcastle, Leeds Bradford, Edinburgh, Prestwick and Belfast, with prices from just £2.50 net per day. For an extra £24.95 (£28.95 at

Prestwick and Heathrow), you can save time by being met at the airport terminal on your departure and return as part of BCP's Meet and Greet Parking service. Your car is then taken to the BCP.Co.Uk secure car park nearby. Or you can pre-book a chauffeur-driven airport car to and from the airport. This service is ideal if you live within 30 miles of your departure airport - prices start from about £60 return. To book and save at least 15% on the car park gate prices and 10% on lounges and chauffeur-driven cars, phone the BCP reservations line quoting reference 'GDD'. BCP will confirm your booking by post with directions to your car park or details of the pick-up or meeting arrangements as appropriate.

BATH SHIELD
BLENHEIM STUDIO, LONDON ROAD, FOREST ROW, SUSSEX RH18 5EZ
☎ (01342) 823243. WEBSITE: www.chadder.com
OPEN 8.30 - 5.30 MON - FRI, 8.30 - 2 SAT.
PHONE FIRST FOR AN APPOINTMENT.
If you've got a good quality bath which is looking a bit tatty, have it re-enamelled in situ or in the workshop. While it will cost from £275 plus VAT, just think of the savings made by not having to rip out an old bath, hire a plumber, redo tiling etc. And because the re-enamelled bath is baked with infra-red lamps and polished, it will repel calcium and dirt and be easier to clean in the future. Also provides traditional and victorian bathroom equipment, taps, shower roses and fittings and old-fashioned bathrooms. Up to 150 different baths and accessories on display at any one time at the retail shop, Chadder & Co. Delivers in the London area and abroad.

BRIGHTON ARCHITECTURAL SALVAGE
33-34 GLOUCESTER ROAD, BRIGHTON, EAST SUSSEX BN1 4AQ
☎ (01273) 681656. OPEN 10 - 5 MON - SAT.
Architectural Salvage • *DIY/Renovation*
Lots of fireplaces including marble, cast iron and wood surrounds; reclaimed flooring; cast-iron inserts from Regency to Art Nouveau; doors, pine furniture, columns, stained and etched glass, panelling, railings and garden ornaments.

BRIGHTON MARINA
VILLAGE SQUARE, BRIGHTON, EAST SUSSEX BN2 5WB
☎ (01273) 818504. OPEN 10 - 6 SEVEN DAYS A WEEK.
Factory Shopping Village • *Womenswear & Menswear* • *Children Household* • *Food and Leisure* • *Sportswear & Equipment*
Eleven factory shops including Baggage Factory, Book Depot, Giovanna (ladies fashions, jewellery, sunglasses, some beauty products), Leading Labels, Leave It To Jeeves (pictures and frames), Pulse (sports shop for skaters), Sanctuary Cove (gifts, lava lamps, candles), The Factory Shop, Toorak, Tog 24 outdoor wear, and Tom Sayers. There are also pubs and restaurants, most offering al fresco eating, and a selection of specialist yachting shops, gifts shops

and boutiques. There is an ASDA superstore, an 8-screen cinema complex, a 26-lane Bowlplex bowling alley and a David Lloyd health and fitness centre. All this is based around the working marina and picturesque village square. There are 1,600 free parking spaces in the multi-storey car park. Further developments are planned including more factory outlet shops, nightclub, casino, 100-room hotel, pubs and restaurants.

BROWNS
SUSSEX ROAD, HAYWARDS HEATH WEST SUSSEX RH16 4OZ
☎ (01444) 458295. OPEN 10 - 4.30 MON - SAT, 10 - 4 THUR.
32 EAST STREET, HORSHAM, WEST SUSSEX
☎ (01403) 259 711. OPEN 10 - 4.30 MON - SAT.
Dress Agency • *Womenswear Only*
Sell everything from T-shirts to ballgowns from high street names to designer labels. Sizes range from 8-20. Designs by Jaeger, Country Casuals, Betty Barclay, Yarell and Gerry Weber.

CANCER RESEARCH CAMPAIGN
172 TERMINUS ROAD, EASTBOURNE, EAST SUSSEX BN21 3BB
☎ (01323) 739703. OPEN 9 - 5 MON - SAT.
Dress Agency • *Hire Shops* • *Womenswear Only*
Shop with a department specifically aimed at the bridal market which sells or hires wedding dresses and bridesmaids dresses, with accessories. Most of the stock is either donated or straight from the manufacturer.

COLLINS AND HAYES
PONSWOOD INDUSTRIAL ESTATE, MENZIES ROAD, ST LEONARDS, HASTINGS, EAST SUSSEX, TN34 1XF
☎ (01424) 443834. OPEN 9 - 5 MON - SAT.
Factory Shop • *Furniture/Soft Furnishings*
Manufacturers of upholstered furniture and with their own collection of fabrics, this is Collins and Hayes only factory shop. Here, they sell ends of lines, discontinued models and cancelled orders of sofas and chairs, as well as fabrics, at half price or less. Upholstered furniture is a fashion industry and accordingly new collections are brought out once or twice a year, so there is a steady supply of ends of lines.

COUNTRY TRADITIONALS
FOREST ROW, ASHURST WOOD, WEST SUSSEX
☎ (01342) 822622. OPEN 9 - 12.30 FIRST SAT EACH MONTH.
Designer Sale • *Household*
Original Bunzlau ceramics from Poland are sold at London shows countrywide or at monthly warehouse sales which offer savings of 5 - 10% off show and shop prices. Phone 01342 822622 for a catalogue and directions. There is aslo a shop in London. Phone 0207-486 1101 for details.

DAISY DAISY
33 NORTH ROAD, BRIGHTON, EAST SUSSEX BN1 1YB
☎ (01273) 689108. OPEN 10.30 - 5 MON - SAT.
Dress Agency • *Children*
Only the best quality secondhand children's clothes are sold here: both designer and high street names including Oilily, Jean Bourget, Osh Kosh and Nipper alongside Baby Gap, Next, Laura Ashley and Monsoon. All are priced at between one quarter and one half of the original price. There are also plenty of accessories including shoes, hats, socks, tights and swimwear. They now also stock a selection of new wooden toys and dolls houses. As there's so much to choose from, toys are provided to keep the children amused while parents browse. There's also a toilet if needed.

DESIGNER SALE UK
STUDIO 6, STAR GALLERY, CASTLE DITCH LANE, LEWES,
EAST SUSSEX BN7 1YJ
☎ (01273) 470 880. FAX ☎ (01273) 470 881
E-MAIL: Kaa54@dial.pipex.com   WEBSITE: www.fashionweb.co.uk/designer-sales/
Designer Sales • *Womenswear & Menswear*
During its 11 years in operation, Designer Sale UK has established itself as an increasingly popular way to buy desirable designer gear. Whether you are looking for something really offbeat or that classic item to complement your wardrobe, there are many bargains to be had at prices discounted by 80% to 90% off the normal shop price. Cerruti men's suits £900 now £220; an Armani shirt normally £115 is £39; a Burro £80 shirt for £20; Vivienne Westwood jacket £500 now £75; Duffer of St George items start at £5 and Joe Caseley Hayford jackets go from a retail value of £290 to £55. Neisha Crosland scarves start a t£10 and William Hunt suits were £850 now £250.There are countless bargains on names like D&G, Griffin, Mickey Brazil, Bella Freud, Victor Victoria, Marc Jacobs and Alberta Ferretti. They now represent over 50 different fashion companies. The sale venue is within the Old Truman Brewery Complex in Brick Lane, East London. They hold five sales a year: February, March/April, May, September and November/December. Each sale is four days from Thursday to Sunday with an extra day (Wednesday) for mailing list customers. Phone to join the mailing list and for information on upcoming sales.

DEXAM INTERNATIONAL LTD
HOLMBUSH WAY, MIDHURST WEST SUSSEX GU29 9HX
☎ (01730) 814188. OPEN 10 - 3 MON - FRI, 10 - 1 SAT
(CLOSED BANK HOLIDAY SATURDAYS).
Permanent Discount Outlet • *Household*
Sells figurines, glass, china, gifts, cookware, kitchen gadgets and housewares at well below normal retail prices.

DIAMONDS DRESS AGENCY
4 SCHOOL HILL, STORRINGTON, WEST SUSSEX RH20 4NB
☎ (01903) 746824. OPEN 10 - 5 MON - SAT.
Dress Agency • *Womenswear Only*
Ground floor shop in the middle of the village selling everything from daywear to, in the winter, ballgowns. Designer labels such as MaxMara, Yves St Laurent, Valentino, Escada, Mondi, Betty Barclay, as well as good high street names, and accessories: belts, shoes and bags.

EDGCUMBE TEA AND COFFEE
WICKS HOUSE, FORD LANE, FORD, ARUNDEL, WEST SUSSEX BN18 0DF
☎ (01243) 555775. E-MAIL: sales@edgcumbes.co.uk
WEBSITE: www.edgcumbes.co.uk
OPEN 9 - 6 MONDAY TO FRIDAY. MAIL ORDER.
Food and Drink Discounters
Primarily trade suppliers, Edgcumbe sell direct to personal shoppers and have some very good bargains in ends of lines. They offer top quality tea blends in tea bag or loose form and a "roast and post" coffee service by mail order - within 24 hours of ordering, you will find fresh coffee on your doorstep. They roast and blend their own coffee on site to order, and you can enjoy a range of flavoured coffee from amaretto to choc-mint. Because of their low overheads, the prices are very competitive. For example, £25 for 3,000 tea bags of English Breakfast blend. They also sell Cobra Indian Beer and premium bottled lager in half pint and pint measures. Van delivery service to local areas.

FURNITURE WAREHOUSE
UNIT 1, QUAY SIDE, BASIN ROAD SOUTH, PORTSLADE, HOVE, BRIGHTON, EAST SUSSEX BN41 1NS
☎ (01273) 541500. OPEN 9 - 6 MON - SAT, 10 - 5 SUN.
UNIT 1, QUAY SIDE, BASIN ROAD SOUTH, PORTSLADE, HOVE, BRIGHTON BN41 1NF
Permanent Discount Outlet • *Furniture/Soft Furnishings*
High street quality furniture at warehouse prices. Also antique pine furniture, wardrobes, chests of drawers and a range of repro furniture. Local delivery.

GOLF FACTORY SHOP
BRIGHTON ROAD, PEASE POTTAGE, CRAWLEY, SUSSEX RH11 9AD
☎ (01444) 400219. OPEN 10 - 6 MON - FRI, 10 - 5 SAT, 10 - 2 SUN.
Permanent Discount Outlet • *Sportswear & Equipment*
Golf clubs and full range of accessories such as trolleys and clothing. Made to measure golf clubs start at £56 per set up to £218. Left-handed sets available. Trolleys from £19.99 to £50. Canon Golf at Shotters Hill, also offers part exchange for old clubs.

GOOSEBERRY BUSH
2 BARNHAM ROAD, BARNHAM, NR BOGNOR, SUSSEX PO22 OES
☎ (01243) 554552 OPEN 10 - 4 MON - SAT
Dress Agency • *Children*
Nearly-new largely high street fashions for children ie Next, Gap, Osh Kosh. Stock ranges from a good selection of maternity wear and toys to all baby equipment including cots, pushchairs and stairgates. Stock changes daily. New items at reasonable prices.

HEIRLOOMS LTD
2 ARUN BUSINESS PARK, BOGNOR REGIS, WEST SUSSEX PO22 9SX
☎ (01243) 820252. OPEN 10 - 5 EVERY FRIDAY AND ONE SAT MORNING EACH MONTH.
Factory Shop • *Household* • *Furniture/Soft Furnishings*
Sleep like a king, dine like a lord or lounge like a lady....the Heirlooms factory shop is brimming with luxury at affordable prices, the majority of which are made on the premises. Elegant and exceptionally high quality bed linens in Egyptian cotton, cotton percale and the finest polycotton percale, in four sizes up to super-king, are sold in this 1,200 sq ft outlet, together with the very best Egyptian cotton towels. There's also table linens using classic hem stitching or handmade laces, a cornucopia of gifts with exquisite laces and embroideries, and handmade christening and baby wear. Sterling silver frames, waterproof picnic rugs, candles, Isis ceramics and seasonal variations complete the diverse selection of really high quality products. Normally only found in the most exclusive shops, homes and palaces all over the world, here you can buy ends of lines and slight seconds at between 30% and 65% off the recommended retail price. This busy exporting company only opens the factory shop about once a week, so check before making what will be a worthwhile journey. As they manufacture, they can make bedlinen and tablecloths to order in any size. Free parking.

IMPULSE
LONDON ROAD, HICKSTEAD, WEST SUSSEX RH17 5RL
☎ (01444) 881255. OPEN 10 - 5 MON - SAT.
Permanent Discount Outlet • *Womenswear & Menswear*
Men's trousers, jackets and shoes and a large selection of ladies shoes and handbags - all at up to 50% discount. Next door to the ladies designer fashion warehouse, M & G Designer Fashions.

JAEGER AND VIYELLA FACTORY SHOP
UNIT B, 208-216 LONDON ROAD, BURGESS HILL, WEST SUSSEX RH15 9NF
☎ (01444) 333100. OPEN 10 - 6 MON - FRI, 9 - 6 SAT, 11 - 5 SUN.
Factory Shop • *Womenswear & Menswear*
Purpose-built factory shop selling contemporary classics from Jaeger and Viyella at excellent prices. Most of the merchandise is previous seasons' stock,

but you might also find some special makes. This shop stocks tailoring and knitwear for women and men.

M & G DESIGNER FASHIONS
OLD LONDON ROAD (OLD A23), NEAR HICKSTEAD VILLAGE,
WEST SUSSEX RH17 5 RL
☎ (01444) 881511. OPEN 10 - 5 MON - SAT.
Permanent Discount Outlet • *Womenswear & Menswear*

A large fashion warehouse selling designer and famous high-street name clothes at discounted prices from 20% to 80% less than the normal retail price. Because they carry many famous high street and designer labels in the 3,400 sq ft outlet, they are unable to advertise these names. Many of the clothes are the current season's fashions, discontinued lines, late deliveries, bankrupt stock and cancelled orders. Twice a year, they hold "Silly" sales where no garment is over £30. They also hold winter and summer clearance sales. Their range covers everything from T-shirts to ballgowns in sizes 10-24. There is ample parking, free coffee or tea, easy access for wheelchairs and individual changing rooms. They have recently started selling menswear, millinery and ladies shoes in the next door shop. (Follow the signs to Ricebridge and Hickstead Village.) Please phone for Christmas and bank holiday hours. Amex, Mastercard, Switch and Visa cards accepted.

MATALAN
THE CRUMBLES RETAIL PARK, PEVENSEY BAY ROAD, EASTBOURNE,
SUSSEX BN23 6JH
☎ (01323) 470347. OPEN 10 - 8 MON - FRI, 9 - 6 SAT, 10.30 - 4.30 SUN.
CARDEN AVENUE, HOLLINGBURY, BRIGHTON BN1 8NS
☎ (01273) 543800. OPEN 10 - 8 MON - FRI, 9 - 6 SAT, 11 - 5 SUN.
Permanent Discount Outlet • *Womenswear & Menswear*
Household • *Children*

Matalan is a fashion and homewares value retailer giving customers what they claim to be unbeatable value for money with huge savings on a wide range of products including high quality fashionable clothing for men, women and children at up to 50% off high street prices. Matalan is situated out of town and stores are open seven days a week all year round.

NAPIER FACTORY SHOP
3 COURTLANDS ROAD, EASTBOURNE, SUSSEX BN22 8SW
☎ (01323) 644511. OPEN 9.30 - 5.30 MON - FRI, 10 - 6 SAT, 10 - 4 SUN.
Permanent Discount Outlet • *Womenswear Only*

Ends of lines and limited edition designer fashion jewellery in classic and contemporary styles direct from US manufacturers. Stock includes classic chains, necklaces, brooches, earrings, rings, chokers and bracelets at up to 75% discount. Prices range from £2.50 to £500. Parking available.

PANACHE
5 STANFORD SQUARE, WARWICK ST, WORTHING, SUSSEX BN11 3EZ
☎ (01903) 212503. OPEN 10 - 5 MON - SAT.
Dress Agency • *Womenswear* • *Children*

Two shops in one: Panache sells women's nearly-new at savings of up to 50% on high street prices; Smarties sells childrenswear up to the age of nine. The children's selection ranges from Petite Bateau, Laura Ashley and Oilily to Matrise and Osh Kosh. They do not stock children's sleepwear or underwear. The adult dress agency stocks a wide range of labels from Marks and Spencer and Viyella to Jacques Vert, MaxMara and Escada. They also sell hats, evening wear, coats, shoes, jackets, handbags and belts.

POWER WAREHOUSE
53-59 LINGFIELD ROAD, EAST GRINSTEAD, WEST SUSSEX RH19 2EU
☎ (01342) 410444. OPEN 9 - 5.30 MON - FRI, 9 - 4 SAT.
Permanent Discount Outlet • *Electrical Equipment*

Small showroom displaying all major domestic kitchen appliances (from fridges and washing machines to hobs and ovens and including American washing and refrigeration units) from Creda, Neff, Bosch, Miele, AEG, Hotpoint, Zanussi, Siemens, De Dietrich, Smeg, etc, both free-standing and built-in appliances. They claim to be able to beat any competitor's price. Offer a phone service whereby you can ring them with the make and model number of your chosen piece of equipment and they will quote you a more competitive price. Small charge for UK delivery may apply.

QUONTUM
3, NILE PAVILIONS, 10 NILE STREET, BRIGHTON, SUSSEX BN1 1HW
☎ (01273) 321509. WEBSITE: www.quontum.com
OPEN 10 - 6 MON - SAT, 12 - 5 SUN. AND BANK HOLS.
Dress Agency • *Womenswear Only*

Original own-label designs sold at high street prices, with the emphasis on a directional look. Prices are very reasonable: a cashmere jumper for £35 which would cost £250 new. Also sell shoes.

RENAHALL LTD
1 SCIENCE SQUARE, FALMER, SUSSEX BN1 9SB
☎ (01788) 811454. MAIL ORDER ONLY.
Permanent Discount Outlet • *Food and Leisure*

Vitamins and similar products such as evening primrose oil, fish oil are sold by mail order only (post paid) usually within 48 hours of receipt of order. Vitamin C is sold in powder form (also as Calcium Ascorbate) to avoid unwanted fillers and binders (and the cost of tabletting) in packs of 240 grams. It is pure ascorbic acid and costs £9.25 for 240 grams compared with £7 for 60 grams at a high street chain chemist. Vitamin E is sold in both powder and capsule form, from d-alpha tocopheryl ex soya beans and other vegetable oils. Send for price list by return. Telephone orders are accepted from established customers.

REVIVAL DRESS AGENCY
24 GROVE ROAD, EASTBOURNE, EAST SUSSEX BN21 4TR
☎ (01323) 649552. OPEN 9.30 - 4.30 MON - FRI, 9 - 5.30 SAT.
Dress Agency • *Womenswear Only*
Excellent selection of good chainstore labels such as Principles, Monsoon, Wallis, Jaeger, Country Casuals and some designer stock such as Giorgio Armani, Calvin Klein and Nicole Farhi. The majority of items are less than two years old. Shoes and accessories are also available. A relaxed and comfortable environment with friendly staff. Browsers are more than welcome.

RICARA
12 SURREY STREET, LITTLEHAMPTON, WEST SUSSEX BN17 5BG
☎ (01903) 723843. OPEN 9 - 5 MON - SAT, 10 - 4 SUN.
42 SOUTH STREET, CHICHESTER, WEST SUSSEX PO19 1DR
☎ (01243) 778850. OPEN 9 - 5 MON - SAT.
Factory Shop • *Womenswear & Menswear* • *Children*
Sportswear & Equipment
Sells mainly schoolwear and men's casualwear, and branded sportswear such as unisex cycling shorts, track suits and leggings at very reasonable prices - discounts can be up to 50%. Brands include Nike and Adidas and specialised outfits for karate, weight lifting, ballet etc are also available.

ROBINA BABY EQUIPMENT HIRE
10 DOWNSWAY, SHOREHAM-BY-SEA, WEST SUSSEX BN43 5GH
☎ (01273) 453548. PHONE FIRST.
Hire Shop • *Children*
Part of the Baby Equipment Hirers Association (BEHA), which has more than 100 members countrywide. A range of equipment can be hired from high chairs, cots and travel cots to baby car seats and buggies. Some members also hire out party equipment including child-sized tables and chairs. BEHA run an advice line which will try and answer any queries you have regarding hiring services for children. Phone the Babyline on 0831 310355.

ROUNDABOUT
31 CLIFFE HIGH STREET, LEWES, EAST SUSSEX BN7 2AN
☎ (01273) 471325. OPEN 9.30 - 4.30 MON, TUE, THUR, FRI, SAT.
Dress Agency • *Womenswear Only*
Good quality clothes. Also small selection of hats, some jewellery, shoes and handbags.

RYE POTTERY LTD
77 FERRY ROAD, RYE, EAST SUSSEX TN31 7DJ
☎ (01797) 223038. OPEN 9.30 - 12.30, 1.30 - 4 SAT.
Factory Shop • *Household*
There is always a selection of seconds available in distinctive, hand-decorated designs. No two items of this 'majolica' or 'delft' decorated pottery are the same. Choose from Chaucer figures, American folk heroes or Pastoral Primitives; seconds are usually two-thirds of retail price.

SECOND EDITION
46-48 HIGH STREET, BOGNOR REGIS, WEST SUSSEX PO21 1SP
☎ (01243) 868319. OPEN 9.30 - 5 MON - SAT.
Permanent Discount Outlet • *Household*
Second Edition sells a wide range of household goods including lamps, china ornaments, tablecloths, giftware, garden ornaments, cushion covers, duvets, pillows and kitchenware. Some are seconds, some perfects and discounts range from 25%-50%. There's a wide range of high street and chainstore brand names. Kitchenware includes storage jars, assorted mugs, assorted melamine and various designs in kitchen linens.

SECOND LOOK
166 HIGH STREET, UCKFIELD, EAST SUSSEX TN22 1AT
☎ (01825) 768622. OPEN 9.30 - 5 MON - FRI, 10 - 5 SAT.
Dress Agency • *Children*
Children's nearly-new clothes from 0 - 6 years, as well as maternity wear. Also stocks new prams, strollers, nursery and baby equipment at very competitive prices - you can pay by instalment or credit card.

SNIPS IN FASHION
40 CHURCH ROAD, HOVE, SUSSEX BN3 2NF
☎ (01273) 729059. OPEN 9.30 - 5.30 TUE - SAT.
Permanent Discount Outlet • *Womenswear Only*
Women's clearance outlet featuring labels such as Olsen, Michelle, Dolores, Gerry Weber, Cavita and Aspa at less than half the original price. Some are current stock, others samples from showrooms, yet others discontinued lines, seconds or late deliveries. Sizes from 8 - 20 usually available. The whole range of clothing is stocked from ballgowns and coats to jeans and beach wear, but no accessories.

SOMETHING SPECIAL
15 ARDSHEAL ROAD, BROADWATER GREEN, WORTHING,
SUSSEX BN14 7RN
☎ (01903) 217317. OPEN 9.30 - 5 MON - SAT.
Dress Agency • *Hire Shop* • *Womenswear Only*

Sells good-as-new clothes for women at discount prices from Marks & Spencer to designer labels, as well as manufacturers' samples, once-worn bridal gowns and hats. The shop also hires out bridesmaids dresses and evening wear.

SPOILS
85, 86 & PART 87, COUNTY MALL, CRAWLEY, WEST SUSSEX RH10 1FD
☎ (01293) 539941. OPEN 9 - 5.30 MON - WED, 9 - 8 THUR, 9 - 6 FRI, SAT.
UNITS 88-90 CHURCHILL SQUARE, BRIGHTON
☎ (01273) 735 097. OPEN 9 - 6 MON - SAT, 8 ON THUR, 11 - 5 SUN
Permanent Discount Outlet • *Household*

General domestic glassware, non-stick bakeware, kitchen gadgets, ceramic oven-to-tableware, textiles, cutting boards, aluminium non-stick cookware, bakeware, plastic kitchenware, plastic storage, woodware, coffee pots/makers, furniture, mirrors and picture frames. Rather than being discounted, all the merchandise is very competitively priced - in fact, the company carry out competitors' checks frequently in order to monitor pricing. With 38 branches, the company is able to buy in bulk and thus negotiate very good prices.

STOCKLEY TRADING
UNIT N10/11, RIVERSIDE INDUSTRIAL ESTATE, LITTLEHAMPTON,
WEST SUSSEX BN17 5DF
☎ (01903) 732392. OPEN 9 - 6 TUE - FRI, 9.30 - 5 SAT, 10 - 4 SUN.
Permanent Discount Outlet • *Sportswear & Equipment*
Children • *Womenswear & Menswear*

Warehouse shop which operates as a wholesaler and retailer, but which is open to members of the public. The outlet sells a range of sportswear which changes depending on what they are able to buy in at good prices. There is a good selection of trainers, including brand names Adidas, Nike and Reebok, tracksuits, and lots of equestrian wear including accessories, boots and hats for riders, and saddles for horses.

THE CURTAIN EXCHANGE
45 HIGH STREET, CUCKFIELD, WEST SUSSEX RH17 5JU
☎ (01444) 417000. OPEN 10 - 4 MON - SAT
Secondhand shops • *Furniture/Soft Furnishings*

The Curtain Exchange is a franchised group of shops selling beautiful top quality secondhand curtains, blinds, pelmets, etc at between one-third and one half of the brand new price. Their stock comes from a variety of sources: people who are moving house; people who have curtains made and then feel they are wrong for the room; show houses where the builder wants to recoup some of his outgoings; interior designers' mistakes. Stock changes constantly and ranges from rich brocades, damasks and velvets to chintzes, linens and cottons. Designer names include Colefax & Fowler, Designers Guild, Laura Ashley, Warner, Sanderson, Osborne & Little, Fortuny and Bennison. A team of fitters and alteration experts are available if required. They offer a 24-hour availability. The Curtain Exchange also supply bespoke ranges with samples of curtains hanging. These fabrics are chosen from suppliers all over the world and are an excellent buy. They also offer ready made curtains designed exclusively for them which come in lengths up to 305cm (120"). These are outstanding value, e.g. 80" wide, 120" drop start at £175 including VAT.

THE DENBY SHOWROOM
BROWNINGS FARM, BLACKBOYS, UCKFIELD, EAST SUSSEX TN22 5HG
☎ (01825) 890 664. OPEN 10 - 4 MON - SAT.
Buys and sells discontinued tableware from Denby, Poole and Marks & Spencer, among others.

THE FABRIC WAREHOUSE
42 GEORGE STREET, BRIGHTON, EAST SUSSEX BN2 1RJ
☎ (01273) 620744. OPEN 9.30 - 5 MON - SAT.
Permanent Discount Outlet • *Furniture/Soft Furnishings*
Curtain and upholstery fabric including names such as Monkwell, Voyager, Whiteheads, Prestigious, Washington DC. Stock depends on what is available on the end of line market so changes constantly. If you are particularly interested in one label, phone first to check they have it in stock.

THE FACTORY SHOP LTD
BRIGHTON MARINA, THE VILLAGE SQUARE, BRIGHTON
SUSSEX BN2 5WA
☎ (01273) 818590. OPEN 10 - 6 MON - FRI, 10 - 6 SAT, 10.30 - 4.30 SUN.
Factory Shop in a Factory Shopping Village
Womenswear & Menswear • *Children* • *Household*
Furniture/Soft Furnishings • *Sportswear & Equipment*
High street chainstore seconds and ends of ranges from clothes for all the family, bedding, toiletries, kitchenware, glassware, footwear, lighting, cosmetics, jewellery, and luggage at discounts of approximately 30%-50%. There are weekly deliveries and brands include many major stars: Joe Bloggs, Nike, Adidas and Brabantia, to name just four. Lines are continually changing and few factory shops offer such a variety under one roof, with at this branch, a large number of clothing concessions in addition to The Factory Shop range. There are furniture displays and a line of Cape Country Furniture is on sale. This high quality pine furniture made exclusively for The Factory Shop in the new South Africa is sold at factory direct prices with home delivery throughout the UK. Colour brochure and price list available.

THE OLD LOOM MILL
MULBROOKS FARM, ERSHAM ROAD, HAILSHAM,
EAST SUSSEX BN27 2RH
☎ (01323) 848007. OPEN 9 - 5 MON - SAT, 10 - 5 SUN & BANK HOLIDAYS.
Factory Shop • *Furniture/Soft Furnishings*
One of the largest stockists in the area selling fabric and wool, curtaining, sheeting, lining and dress fabric. Curtaining ranges from £1.99 - £5 per meter; sheeting is £5.99 per kilo, £1.50 per metre; 54" wide lining £1.99 per metre; dress fabrics from £1 - £4.50. All material is perfect unless otherwise stated. There are lots of well-known brands here, adding up to savings of about 60% on the high street. The outlet also offers a curtain-making service, a tea room and a craft hall. Easy off road free parking and wheelchair access makes this a lovely place in the countryside for a visit to browse or buy.

THE SHOE SHED
3 THE ARCADE, BOGNOR REGIS, WEST SUSSEX PO21 1LH
☎ (01243) 829600. OPEN 9 - 5.30 MON - SAT, 10 - 4 SUN.
Factory Shop • *Womenswear & Menswear* • *Children*
Large factory shop selling a vast range of all types of men's, women's and children's shoes, all of which are perfects, at up to 30% below normal high street prices. Men's shoes from £10; sports shoes from £10. Ladies sandals cost from £5; ladies shoes from £7.50.

THE TRUGGERY
COOPERS CROFT, HERSTMONCEUX, EAST SUSSEX BN27 1QL
☎ (01323) 832314. OPEN 10 - 5 TUE - FRI, SAT 10 - 1.
Factory Shop • *Household*
Manufacturers of traditional Sussex trugs, shallow wooden gardening baskets made from sweet chestnut and willow and particular to the region. Prices range from £15 to £50. Also supply English willow baskets, all shapes and sizes from £15 - £40, kitchen storage shelf baskets, prawning baskets, duck nesters, and local wooden crafts such as hay rakes, dibbers and miniature sheep hurdles to use as borders. Parking provided.

THE WEST SUSSEX ANTIQUE TIMBER COMPANY LTD
RELIANCE WORKS, NEWPOUND, WISBOROUGH GREEN,
WEST SUSSEX RH14 0AZ
☎ (01403) 700139. FAX (01403) 700936. OPEN 8.30 - 5 MON - FRI,
9 - 1 SAT.
Architectural Salvage • *DIY/Renovation*
Specialists in old pine, oak beams, oak flooring and mouldings (the oak flooring is supplied and laid). Also sells pine and oak doors and old timber furniture. Kit form pine door £95, made up doors £185, oak doors from £250 plus vat. Undertakes barn restoration and conversion too.

TK MAXX

36/37 NORTH STREET, BRIGHTON, EAST SUSSEX BN1 1EB
☎ (01273) 727483. OPEN 9 - 6 MON - SAT, 8 ON THUR, 11 - 5 SUN.
Permanent Discount Outlet • *Womenswear & Menswear*
Children • *Household* • *Furniture/Soft Furnishings*

Based on an American concept, TK Maxx is situated in easily accessible, often centrally located stores and offers famous label goods with up to 60% savings off recommended retail prices. TK Maxx has fashion for the whole family - women's, men's and childrenswear - accessories, shoes, gifts, kitchenware and home goods. Everything in the store is branded with a choice of well-known high street names to designer labels, and while a small percentage might be clearly marked past season, the great majority of items in store are current season, current stock and still with phenomenal savings. There is a huge choice with 50,000 pieces in store and up to 10,000 new items arriving a week. The stores are simple and unfussy with wide aisles, shopping trolleys and baskets, and a spacious, functional feel to them but there are individual changing rooms, ramps for buggies and wheelchairs and plenty of staff on the shop floor. Every branch accepts all major credit and debit cards and has a liberal refund and return policy.

TOG 24

BRIGHTON MARINA, THE VILLAGE SQUARE, BRIGHTON,
EAST SUSSEX BN2 5UF
☎ (01273) 818759. OPEN 10 - 6 SEVEN DAYS A WEEK.
Factory Shop in a Factory Shopping Village
Womenswear & Menswear • *Children* • *Sportswear & Equipment*

Tog 24 are the UK's fastest growing brand name in outdoor clothing and leisurewear. They utilise the world's finest performance fabrics including Gore-Tex, Polartec and Burlington MCS, catering for all the family for all seasons, with cosy fleeces and waterproofs for the winter, and trekking ranges, shorts and t-shirts for the summer. With all prices at least 30% below the recommended retail price, you can afford to enter the Tog comfort zone.

Warwickshire

ARKWRIGHTS MILL
HATTON COUNTRY WORLD, DARK LANE, HATTON, NEAR WARWICK, WARWICKSHIRE CV35 8XA
☎ (01926) 843022. FAX (01926) 842761. OPEN 10 - 5.30
(CLOSES 5 MON - FRI DURING WINTER) SEVEN DAYS A WEEK
Factory Shop • *Womenswear & Menswear*

Claims to be the most interesting clothes store in the Midlands. Brand names available direct from the factories at big discounts incude: French Connection, Chilli Pepper, Morgan, Elle, Joe Bloggs plus many other factory outlet brands. Hatton Country World is home to one of the biggest Craft Centres in the UK and provides plenty to amuse both adults and children alike, including 20 craft shops, factory shops, farm animals, pets' corner, 20 antique dealers, cafe/bar and free car parking.

CHINASEARCH
P.O. BOX 1202, KENILWORTH, WARWICKSHIRE CV8 2WW
☎ (01926) 512402. FAX: (01926) 859311. MAIL ORDER. VISITORS BY APPOINTMENT ONLY.
E-MAIL: jackie@chinasearch.uk.com   E-MAIL: helen@chinasearch.uk.com
WEBSITE: www.chinasearch.uk.com

During the past decade, Chinasearch has built up a stock of around 2000 patterns of china and pottery which have been discontinued over the last 30 years or more. This stock changes daily, and due to ever-increasing business, they have moved to a warehouse. The manufacturers whose products they keep in stock include Royal Doulton, Minton, Crown Derby, Royal Albert, Paragon, Colclough and Booths, Wedgwood, Coalport, Susie Cooper, Adams, Johnsons, Masons, Meakin and Midwinter, Royal Worcester, Palissey and Copeland Spode, Aynsley, Denby, Hornsea, Marks & Spencer, Poole, Portmeirion and Villeroy & Boch. Friendly staff are always willing to help: If they don't have the items you require, whether it be one tea saucer, a complete dinner service, a china egg or a miniature coffee pot, they will keep details on file until they find them. They do not charge a registration fee and there is no obligation to buy. They are always pleased to hear from people who wish to sell unwanted tableware or collectables and can arrange collection countrywide. Please enclose an SAE with correspondence.

DUNELM MILL SHOP
CLOCK TOWERS CENTRE, MANNINGS WALK, RUGBY,
WARWICKSHIRE CV21 2JT
☎ (01788) 541171. OPEN 9 - 5.30 MON - SAT.
20 QUEENS ROAD, NUNEATON CV11 5JW
☎ (024 76) 344711. OPEN 9 - 5 MON - SAT, UNTIL 5.30 ON FRI.
Permanent Discount Outlet • *Household*
Part of a chain of shops based in the Midlands selling brand-name and chain-store curtains, masses of bedlinen, towels, wickerware, pictures and frames, all at competitive prices.

FORGET-ME-NOT DESIGNER BRIDAL WEAR
THE WEDDING CENTRE, 5 - 7 LUTTERWORTH ROAD,
ATTLEBOROUGH GREEN, NUNEATON, 3 MILES EAST OF JUNCTION 3
ON THE M6, WARWICKSHIRE CV11 4LD
☎ (024 76) 375555 BRIDAL. (024 76) 375544 HIRE.
WEBSITE: www.theweddingcentre.co.uk
OPEN 9.30 - 5 MON - FRI, 9.30 - 5 SAT OR BY APPOINTMENT.
Dress Agency • *Hire Shop* • *Womenswear Only*
The complete wedding shop. Forget-Me-Not Designer Bridalwear operates from a dedicated Wedding Centre where, as well as being able to choose from a stunning collection of both new and immaculate once-worn wedding dresses (mainly to buy but also to hire) there are also some designers' samples at very affordable prices. There is a gent's formal wear hire service with a massive selection of frock coats in brocade velvets and silks, highland wear and a choice of 100 waistcoats; wedding florist specialist, photographic studio, on-site beautician, wedding stationers and wedding cake business. You can find tiaras, balloons and a bridal register of caterers, musicians, pipers, vocalists and video specialists. There are more than 200 dresses on display at any one time, with 600 more on computer, many of which are in larger sizes. Designers on sale here include Anna Christina, Ave Marie, Donna Salado, Beverley Lister, Alfred Angelo, Prettymades, Ellis, Paloma Blanca, Pronovias, Mon Cheri, Sincerity, Ronald Joyce, Kelsey Rose, Tous Les Jours and Sweetheart. If bridesmaids' dresses need sorting out, too, there is a made-to-measure service with such leading firms as Prettymades and Catherine Jane. Forget-me-Not can also make bridesmaids dresses themselves in a choice of over 100 silks and fabrics, provide accessories including shoes and hats and even personalised wedding wines and champagne.

GAMES CAROUSEL
129 REGENT STREET, LEAMINGTON SPA, WARWICKSHIRE CV32 4NX
☎ (01926) 335600. OPEN 10 - 5.30 MON - SAT.
Permanent Discount Outlet • *Children*
Offer part-exchange deals and sells both new and used computer leisure and games software. All are in their original boxes with the original manuals and

in good condition and savings of over half price are available. These include PCs, Play Station and Play Station II, Dreamcast and Nintendo entertainment.

HATTON COUNTRY WORLD
DARK LANE, HATTON, WARWICK, WARWICKSHIRE CV35 8XA
☎ (01926) 843411. E-MAIL: hatton@hattonworld.com
WEBSITE: www.hattonworld.com   OPEN 10 - 5 SEVEN DAYS A WEEK.
Factory Shop • *Household* • *Womenswear & Menswear Food and Leisure*

Hatton is a totally unique blend of shopping and leisure carved out 19th centruy farm buildings in the heart of the Warwickshire countryside. It's home to England's biggest craft centre and incorporates 25 craft and gift shops including a toy shop, wood turner, fam and butcher's shops, Soft Play centre, cafebar, three factory shops selling china, glass, kitchenware, books and cards and clothes for men and women. The Farm Park contains 40 different breeds of animals, pets corner, falconry and farming demonstrations, adventure playground, guinea pig village and nature trail to Hatton locks. Parking is free. Admission is only charged to enter the Farm Park and Soft Play.

INTO CLOTHING
144 THE PARADE, LEAMINGTON SPA, WARWICKSHIRE CV32 0AG
☎ (01926) 430407. OPEN 9 - 5 MON - SAT.
Permanent Discount Outlet • *Womenswear Only*

Sells ladies clothing, cotton knitwear, separates and jackets at factory direct prices, which can be as much as 70% off the normal retail prices. The shop is small but well stocked and organised to make the maximum use of the space. Most of the stock is leading chainstore makes and includes dresses, jackets, rainwear, shoes, underwear, tights, suits, blouses, sweaters, nightwear, leggings, trousers, jeans, anoraks, with dressing gowns and eveningwear at Christmas only. There is another branch at Hinckley, Leicestershire.

JAMES GILBERT FACTORY OUTLET
5/6 ST MATTHEWS STREET, RUGBY, WARWICKSHIRE CV21 3BY
☎ (01788) 333888. WEBSITE: www.james-gilbert.com   OPEN 9 - 5 MON - SAT.
Factory Shop • *Sportswear & Equipment*

Attached to the James Gilbert Rugby Football Museum selling rugby goods, outdoor wear and souvenirs and gifts. There are lots of clearance lines including their own catalogue goods at reduced prices such as last season's football boots at 50% discount.

LILLIPUT
63 AVON CRESCENT, STRATFORD-UPON-AVON, WARWICKSHIRE CV37 7EZ
☎ (01789) 267991. OPEN 10 - 4.30 TUE - SAT.
Dress Agency • *Hire Shop* • *Children*
Children's toys, secondhand clothes, and secondhand baby equipment from 0 - 10 years as well as some maternity wear. Most of the children's merchandise is baby and toddler equipment and toys, though there is some end of line branded clothing and equipment, including quality secondhand and shop seconds. Short term hire is available on most equipment.

LITTLEWOODS CATALOGUE DISCOUNT STORE
14-16 NORTH STREET, RUGBY, WARWICKSHIRE CV21 2AF
☎ (01788) 565116. OPEN 9.30 - 5.30 MON - WED, 9 - 5.30 THUR - SAT.
Permanent Discount Outlet • *Womenswear & Menswear*
Electrical Equipment • *Children*
Littlewoods clearance shops offering up to 50% off the catalogue price for clothing and between 50% and 60% off for electrical goods. Stock changes constantly and varies from day to day but can include well-known brand names such as Berlei and Gossard lingerie, Vivienne Westwood, Pamplemousse leisure wear, Nike and Adidas sports shoes, Workers for Freedom, and Timberland and Caterpillar footwear. Stock depends on the size and location of the shop, so larger shops will get the longer discontinued runs and smaller shops over-runs with only a small amount of colour and size variations left. Littlewoods also run a mobile shop which operates in cities where they don't have a sale shop. For details of further venues for the sales, which usually take place once a month, contact Melanie Lamb, c/o Crosby DC Kershaw Avenue, Endbutt Lane, Crosby, Merseyside L70 1AH.

MAID OF CHINA
HATTON COUNTRY WORLD, DARK LANE, HATTON, NEAR WARWICK, WARWICKSHIRE CV35 8XA
☎ (01926) 842789. E-MAIL: hatton@hattonworld.com
WEBSITE: www.hattonworld.com   OPEN 10 - 5 SEVEN DAYS A WEEK
Factory Shop • *Household*
Set in the centre of the shopping village and leisure complex, these rambling 19th century farm buildings are full of character, as well as great bargains in china and glassware from famous names. The 3000 sq ft premises offer first-quality, select seconds and ends of lines at 30% or more off list price as well as a fabulous cookshop stuffed full of those hard-to-find gadgets you thought had disappeared years ago. Look out for bargains from Arthur Price International, Gleneagles Crystal, Hornsea, Royal Stafford, Henry Watson, Mondian, Poole Pottery, Cloverleaf, and many more. Hatton Country World is home to the biggest craft centre in the UK and provides plenty to amuse both adults and children, including more than 20 craft shops, 3 factory shops, farm animals, pets' corner, 20 antique dealers, cafe/bar and free car parking.

MATALAN
MAYBIRD CENTRE, BIRMINGHAM ROAD, STRATFORD-UPON-AVON,
WARWICKSHIRE CV37 OHZ
☎ (01789) 262223. OPEN 10 - 8 MON - FRI, 9 - 6 SAT, 10 - 6 SUN.
Permanent Discount Outlet • *Womenswear & Menswear*
Children • *Household*

Matalan is a fashion and homewares value retailer giving customers what they claim to be unbeatable value for money with huge savings on a wide range of products including high quality fashionable clothing for men, women and children at up to 50% off high street prices. Matalan is situated out of town and stores are open seven days a week all year round.

MERCIA SAFETY
WARBORO FARM, HENLEY ROAD, NEAR WARWICK,
WARWICKSHIRE CV38 8QX
☎ (01926) 411388.
Hire Shop • *Children*

Part of the Baby Equipment Hirers Association (BEHA), which has more than 100 members countrywide. A range of equipment can be hired from high chairs, cots and travel cots to baby car seats and buggies. Some members also hire out party equipment including child-sized tables and chairs. BEHA run an advice line which will try and answer any queries you have regarding hiring services for children. Phone the Babyline on 0831 310355.

MESDAME'S COLLECTION
HATTON COUNTRY WORLD, DARK LANE, HATTON, NEAR WARWICK,
WARWICKSHIRE CV35 8XA
☎ (01926) 842021. E-MAIL: hatton@hattonworld.com
WEBSITE: www.hattonworld.com   OPEN 10 - 5 SEVEN DAYS A WEEK
Factory Shop • *Food and Leisure* • *Household*

A large range of discount books (many at less than half price) are tucked discreetly into this converted barn cheek by jowl with a full range of picture framing services and supplies and a huge selection of greetings cards.

MILL OUTLETS LTD
33 SOUTHAM ROAD, DUNCHURCH, RUGBY, WARWICKSHIRE CV22 6NL
☎ (01788) 816008. OPEN 9 - 5 MON - SAT, 10 - 4 SUN.
3 ALBERT STREET, RUGBY, WARWICKSHIRE CV21 2R7
☎ (01788) 542947. OPEN 9 - 5 MON - SAT.
2 CANNON PARK CENTRE, CANLEY, COVENTRY CV4 7AY
☎ (01203) 418441. OPEN 9 - 5.30 MON - WED, 9 - 6 THUR,
FRI, 8.30 - 5 SAT, 10 - 4 SUN.
14 FAIRFAX STREET, COVENTRY CV1 5RY
(024 76) 223508. OPEN 9 - 5.30 MON - SAT.

134 THE PARADE, LEAMINGTON SPA, WARWICKSHIRE CV32 4AG
☎ (01926) 470015. OPEN 9 - 5.30 MON - SAT.
Permanent Discount Outlet • *Household*
Specialises in curtains, net curtains, bedding, bed linens, towels, kitchen textiles and other household textiles. They also offer ranges of hand knitting yarns, men's and ladies socks, hosiery and underwear. Merchandise comes direct from the manufacturers, often made up of clearance stock or chainstore overmakes and seconds. Prices are very competitive with savings of up to 50% and more off manufacturer's recommended prices.

NIPPERS
FIELDS FARM, MARTON, NEAR RUGBY, WARWICKSHIRE CV23 9RS
☎ (01926) 633100. FAX ☎ (01926) 633007. WEBSITE: www.nippers.co.uk
OPENING HOURS VARY SO PHONE FIRST.
Permanent Discount Outlet • *Children*
Nippers, the nursery equipment and toy specialists, operate from previously redundant buildings in rural areas around the country. They offer easy parking, no queues and personal service. This is on top of competitive prices on prams, cots, pushchairs, car seats, outdoor play equipment and toys, some of which are new, some seconds or secondhand and some ends of lines. Prices are low because they avoid the high overheads of traditional retail outlets and also because the successful growth of a number of branches means they can now buy in bulk and negotiate good deals. Customers are invited to try out the merchandise while the children look at the animals, mostly sheep, chicken and pigs. Also offers many brand leaders at discount, including Mamas & Papas, Cosatto, Britax, Maclaren and Bebe Confort, plus Fisher-Price and Little Tikes. You can try out the car seats in your car and there is usually a pram/pushchair repair service on site.

ROBERTSON & PARTNERS LTD
JODRELL STREET, NUNEATON, WARWICKSHIRE CV11 5EH
☎ (024 76) 384110. FAX 01203 642403. OPEN 9 - 5 MON - FRI, 9 - 1 SAT.
Architectural Salvage • *DIY/Renovation*
Reclaimed materials from demolition sites, including doors, chimney pots, staircase parts, baths, steel shelving, slabs, reclaimed timber, reinforced steel joists, roof tiles and slates. In fact anything from a demolished building will be available her.

SCOTTS CLOTHING EXCHANGE
43 PARK STREET, LEAMINGTON SPA, WARWICKSHIRE CV32 4QN
☎ (01926) 337868. OPEN 11.30 - 6 MON - SAT.
Dress Agency • *Womenswear & Menswear*
Good quality ladies and men's clothes and shoes with original and reduced prices marked. Merchandise comes from both the top end of the market and the high street end with labels from Top Shop to MaxMara, Marella and

Armani for women and Zegna, Boss, Hilton and Yves St Laurent for men. There is also a selection of designer jeans such as those by Calvin Klein, handbags and jewellery.

THE CRAFT COMPANY
23 COTEN END, WARWICK, WARWICKSHIRE CV34 4NT
☎ (01926) 492505. OPEN 9 - 5.30 MON - SAT. MAIL ORDER ALSO.
Permanent Discount Outlet • *Household*
Needlecraft warehouse which also operates a mail order leaflet. Due to bulk buying, savings are between 5% and 10%. There is every type of thread, tapestry wool, stranded cotton, shade cards, metallic threads, crochet cotton, flexihoops, needles, tapestry frames, scissors, beads, anchor accessories such as organiser boxes, as well as fabrics (Aida, Evenweave and Zweigart linens).

THE CUCKOO'S NEST
70 SMITH STREET, WARWICK, WARWICKSHIRE CV34 4HU
☎ (01926) 496804. OPEN 9.30 - 5 TUE - SAT.
Dress Agency • *Womenswear Only*
Wide range of ladies clothing from Marks & Spencer to Margaret Howell, Workers for Freedom and John Rocha. Prices equally variable, anything from £8 to £250. For example, a Margaret Howell suit retailing at £600 was sold for £210. Limited stock of evening wear, although there are usually some special occasion outfits including once-worn mother-of-the-bride outfits. A lot of casual wear, suits and jackets, as well as classical tailored wear. The varied contents of the shop is reflected in the rapid turnover and age range - between 14 and 95 - of those who visit. No garment is more than two years old.

THE FACTORY SHOP OUTLET, COATS VIYELLA CLOTHING
CV CLOTHING LADIES AND CHILDRENSWEAR, BOSWORTH ROAD, BARLESTONE, NEAR NUNEATON, WARWICKSHIRE CV13 OEL
☎ (01455) 290685. OPEN 10 - 5 MON - SAT.
Factory Shop • *Womenswear & Menswear* • *Children*
Part of the Coats Viyella group, which makes quality clothing for many of the major high street stores, overstocks and clearance lines are sold through more than 30 of the group's factory shops. Many of you will recognise the garments on sale, despite the lack of well-known labels. Ladieswear includes dresses, blouses, jumpers, cardigans, trousers, nightwear, underwear, lingerie, hosiery, coats and swimwear. Menswear includes trousers, belts, shirts, ties, pullovers, cardigans, T-shirts, underwear, nightwear, hosiery and jackets. Childrenswear includes jackets, trousers, T-shirts, underwear, hosiery, jumpers and babywear. There are regular deliveries to constantly update the range.

TOP DRAWER AS NEW
19-20 WOOD STREET, STRATFORD-UPON-AVON,
WARWICKSHIRE CV37 6JF
☎ (01789) 269766. OPEN 10 - 4.30 TUE - SAT
Dress Agency • *Womenswear Only*
"Clothes and acccesories for the discerning woman". Top Drawer, established in 1978, has hundreds of Ògently used" top quality and designer ladies wear. Proprietor Joanne Hastie carefully selects her collection which boasts amongst others, labels such as Valentino and Escada. It's an adventure in itself setting out to find this pretty shop with its Tudor beams and friendly atmosphere, discreetly tucked away above Bottoms Up.

YEWS FARM BABY EQUIPMENT
RUGBY ROAD, PAILTON, RUGBY, WARWICKSHIRE CV23 OQH
☎ (01788) 832219. OPEN 9 - 5.30 MON - SAT, CLOSED WED.
Permanent Discount Outlet • *Children*
Sells a wide range of equipment for babies, including all leading makes of pushchairs, prams, cots, cot beds and toys, as well as new clothes, all at discounted prices. They also carry out repairs to most makes of buggies. The shop is situated in a small village outside Rugby on a deer farm, where you can also buy country fresh produce such as eggs. There is car parking, a cafe, public toilets and baby changing facilities.

West Midlands

BEVERLEY'S DRESS AGENCY
211 TRYSULL ROAD, WOLVERHAMPTON, WEST MIDLANDS WV3 7JP
☎ (01902) 839111. OPEN 10 - 5 TUE - SAT.
Dress Agency • *Womenswear Only*
Good quality designer clothes at realistic prices including Moschino jeans, Jacques Vert, Alexon, Jaeger, Versace jeans and high street labels such as Wallis and Windsmoor. Shoes, hats, bags and jewellery also stocked.

BLUNTS
112 -124 HOLBROOK LANE, COVENTRY, WEST MIDLANDS
☎ (024 76) 581838. OPEN 9 - 8 MON - FRI, 9 - 5.30 SAT, 10 - 4 SUN.
Permanent Discount Outlet • *Womenswear & Menswear*
Well-known brand name shoes for women and men at big discounts for discontinued stock, seconds and ends of ranges. Men's shoes, £5.99 - £79.99; women's shoes from £2.99 - £45.

BMJ POWER
LONG ACRE, BIRMINGHAM, WEST MIDLANDS B7 5SL
☎ (0121) 327 3411. OPEN 8 - 5.30 MON - FRI, 8 - 2 SAT.
Factory Shop • *DIY/Renovation*
Reconditioned tools and acccessories from the famous Black & Decker range, as well as other power tools from well-known brands such as Makita, Flymo and Kress, all with full manufacturer's warranty. This is essentially an after-sales service with a retail outlet. Often, stock consists of goods returned from the shops because of damaged packaging or are part of a line which is being discontinued. Lots of seasonal special offers. There are more than three dozen BMJ service outlets countrywide. Phone 0345 230230 and you can find out where your nearest outlet is.

BORSHCH ELECTRIC
NEPTUNE HOUSE, UPPER TRINITY STREET, BORDESLEY,
BIRMINGHAM, WEST MIDLANDS B9 4EG
☎ (0121) 773 6361/771 0453 FAX. OPEN 9 - 5.30 MON - SAT, 10 - 4 SUN AND BANK HOLIDAYS.
Permanent Discount Outlet • *Electrical Equipment*
Sells gas and electric items which include fridges, freezers, fridge/freezers, washing machines, microwaves, dishwashers, ovens, vacuum cleaners and a small selection of smaller electrical items for the kitchen such as toasters and kettles which are manufacturers' new graded returns from this 10,000 sq ft showroom. These are not A grade and therefore cannot be sold in high street stores. All are guaranteed for parts and service. Examples of prices include fridges, from £89; cookers from £149; microwaves from £59; washing machines from £150; fridge/freezers from £139; gas fires, £129; tumble dryers from £89; built-in ovens £109. Manufacturers on sale include Zanussi, Candy, Servis, Hotpoint, Bosch, Leisure, Canon, Creda, Baumatic, White Knight. Full delivery service is available, which is free to pensioners.

CADBURY WORLD
LINDEN ROAD, BOURNEVILLE, BIRMINGHAM,
WEST MIDLANDS B30 2LD
☎ (0121) 451 4159. OPENING HOURS VARY.
Food and Drink Discounters
Bargains all year round such as 500g bags of misshapes of Milk Tray, Roses, etc, from £2.25 as well as regular buy-one-get-one-free offers on Cadbury's chocolates and biscuits. Also exceptional seasonal reductions. Novelty and exclusive lines also available.

CANE AND WICKER FACTORY SHOP
TAME BRIDGE, WEST BROMWICH ROAD, WALSALL,
WEST MIDLANDS WS5 4AN
☎ (01922) 63 63 64. OPEN 10 - 5 MON - SAT, 11 - 4 SUN.
Factory Shop • *Furniture/Soft Furnishings*
The largest cane and wicker furniture showroom in the country, with over 80 suites on display at any one time. This importer and wholesaler runs two factory shops (here and a smaller outlet in Shrewsbury) to clear stock which has been returned by retailers. There may be nothing wrong with the furniture other than a change of mind on the part of the original customer, but the furniture has probably been unwrapped, delivered and handled so cannot be sold to other retailers to sell on to full-price customers. The furniture comes in part-assembled and is finished, stuffed and upholstered on site. It comes in a wide range of finishes including light and dark antique, honey, mahogany and walnut. There is also a Mexican pine furniture range and fabric for curtains (though because the fabric is back coated for fire retardancy, it is very heavy). The cheapest cane suites cost from £199, the most expensive, £2,500. This represents a saving of about 15% - 20% on normal retail prices. Matching dining sets and occasional furniture also available. There is immediate delivery for furniture in stock; orders will be fulfilled within about one week.

CATALOGUE BARGAIN SHOP
95 CHURCH STREET, BILSTON, WEST MIDLANDS WV14 OBJ
☎ (01902) 353624. OPEN 9 - 5.30 MON - SAT, 9.30 - 3.30 SUN.
78 HIGH STREET, STOURBRIDGE, WEST MIDLANDS DY8 1DX
☎ (01384) 374544. OPEN 9 - 5.30 MON - SAT, 10.30 - 4.30 SUN.
17 BRADFORD STREET, WALSALL WS1 1PB
☎ (01922) 722286. OPEN 9 - 5.30 MON - SAT, 10.30 - 4.30 SUN.
Permanent Discount Outlet • *Womenswear & Menswear*
Household • *Electrical Equipment* • *Children*
Catalogue Bargain Shop is a growing national chain of stores which obtains the majority of its goods from mail order giants Great Universal and Kays, and offers a range of clothing for all the family, a wide selection of shoes, bed linen, household goods, electrical equipment and hundreds of other catalogue items at very competitive prices. The merchandise consists of ends of ranges and previous season's stock for which there is no longer storage space when the catalogues change.

CONSERVATION BUILDING PRODUCTS LTD
FORGE WORKS, FORGE LANE, CRADLEY HEATH, WARLEY,
WEST MIDLANDS B64 5AL
☎ (01384) 564219. WEBSITE: www.conservationbuildingproducts.co.uk
8 - 4 MON - FRI, 8 - 12 SAT.
Architectural Salvage • *DIY/Renovation*
Bricks, roof tiles, slates, quarry tiles, flooring beams, decorative ironwork,

staircase parts, complete oak-framed buildings, garden statuary and interesting artefacts.

DEJA VU
5 BOLDMERE ROAD, SUTTON COLDFIELD WEST MIDLANDS B73 5UY
☎ (0121) 321 3110. OPEN 10 - 5 MON - SAT.
Dress Agency • *Womenswear Only*
Stock anything from Marks & Spencer to top designer labels, all at very reasonable prices. Names include Mondi, Escada, Windsmoor and Country Casuals. All sizes from 10-22. Also offers ranges of new samples at discounts of one third and has 150 pairs of good quality shoes, as well as belts, handbags, hats and costume jewellery.

DIRECT SPECS LTD
312 WALSGRAVE ROAD, COVENTRY, WEST MIDLANDS CV2 4PL
☎ (019024) 7645 5555 . OPEN 9 - 5 MON - SAT.
UNIT 12, WULFRUN TRADING ESTATE, STAFFORD ROAD, WOLVERHAMPTON WV10 6HH.
☎ (01902) 717744.SAT.
2288 COVENTRY ROAD, SHELDON B26 3JR
☎ (0121) 742 3861. OPEN 9 - 5 MON - SAT.
111 STRATFORD ROAD, SHIRLEY BD90 3ND
☎ (0120) 744 9372. OPEN 9 - 5 MON - SAT.
UNIT 3, 179 QUEEN STREET, WALSALL WS2 9NX
☎ (01922) 635301. OPEN 9 - 5 MON - SAT. - 5 MON - SAT.
UNIT 3, 179 QUEEN STREET, WALSALL WS2 9NX
☎ (01922) 635301. OPEN 9 - 5 MON - SAT.
Permanent Discount Outlet • *Womenswear & Menswear*
Spectacles and sunglasses at prices which the owner claims beat any competitor's. Most designer names are stocked at one time or another, though if you have a favourite, check first. Bring along your prescription and glasses will be found to suit. No eye tests conducted.

DRESS EXCHANGE
1003 ALCESTER ROAD (ABOVE THREE COOKS), THE MAYPOLE, BIRMINGHAM, WEST MIDLANDS B14 5JA
☎ (0121) 474 5707. OPEN 10 - 5 MON - SAT
Dress Agency • *Womenswear Only*
Middle to up market designer wear, with accessories to match, at prices ranging from £10-£200. Designers range from Marks & Spencer upwards and include MaxMara, Escada, Ghost, Jasper Conran, Moschino, Armani and Valentino. Occasionally stocks wedding outfits, as well as seasonal event wear. Casual wear is stocked.

ELIZA'S DRESS AGENCY
18 PARK STREET, KINGSWIMFORD, WEST MIDLANDS DY6 9LX
☎ (01384) 402638. OPEN 10 - 4.30 MON - WED, FRI, 10 - 4 SAT.
Dress Agency • *Womenswear Only*
Designer nearly-new clothes as well as high street names from Marks & Spencer to Jean Muir, Versace, Condicci and Cara. Also evening wear, wedding outfits, shoes, handbags and jewellery.

ENCORE
48-52A ST MARY'S ROW, MOSELEY, BIRMINGHAM,
WEST MIDLANDS B13 8JG
☎ (0121) 442 4888. OPEN 9.30 - 5 MON - FRI, 9.30 - 4.45 SAT
Dress Agency • *Womenswear & Menswear*
Middle to up market designer wear and accessories for both men and women with formal and casual clothing for all occasions. Labels include Armani, Max Mara, Ferretti, Hugo Boss, Moschino, Calvin Klein, alongside High Street names like Mondi, Betty Barclay, Windsmoor, Principles and Next. New stock arrives daily. Prices range from £5 to £200. The shop welcomes customers wishing to sell their own quality clothing.

GOWNS GALORE
1 OLD WARWICK ROAD, HOCKLEY HEATH, SOLIHULL, WEST MIDLANDS B94 6HH
☎ (01564) 783003. OPEN 9 - 5 MON - SAT, UNTIL 8 ON TUE.
Hire Shop • *Womenswear Only*
Specialises in the hire of designer ball gowns, cocktail wear and accessories. A three-day hire, including alterations and VAT, costs from £39.

HAROLD BIRD & SON
NORTHGATE, ALDRIDGE, WALSALL, WEST MIDLANDS WS9 8UB
☎ (01922) 451444. OPEN 8 - 5 MON - THUR, 8 - 3.45 FRI, 9 - 12 SAT.
Factory Shop • *Sportswear & Equipment*
Golf club manufacturers for some of the mail order catalogues such as Kays and Littlewoods, the brands sold in the factory shop here aren't well known but the prices are very keen indeed. They also sell waterproofs. Free parking.

HAWK FACTORY CYCLE STORES
FORGE LANE, CRADLEY HEATH, WEST MIDLANDS B64 5AL
☎ (01384) 636535. OPEN 9 - 6 MON - SAT, 9 - 4.30 SUN.
Factory Shop • *Children*
Sportswear & Equipmentear & Equipments of adult's and children's bikes direct to the public at factory prices. Children's trikes start at £26.99, adult mountain bikes at £89.99, normally £149.99. There are also clearance shops in South Yardley, Birmingham ☎ (0121 742 3332), Nottingham ☎ (0115 958 5900) and Derby ☎ (01332) 756666 with the same opening hours.

H L LINEN BAZAARS
41 NEW BARTHOLOMEW STREET, BIRMINGHAM B5 5QS
☎ (0121) 541 1918. OPEN 9 - 5.30 MON - FRI, RING FOR SAT OPENING.
14 MARKET SQUARE, CRADLEY HEATH, WEST MIDLANDS B64 5HH
☎ (01384) 565548. OPEN 9 - 5.30 MON - SAT.
225 MARKET PLACE, DUDLEY, WEST MIDLANDS
☎ (01384) 239776. OPEN 9 - 5.30 MON - SAT.
Permanent Discount Outlet • *Household* • *Furniture/Soft Furnishings*
The mail order catalogue of this company which sells bedlinen, duvets, towels and sheets is very busy and hides some of the gems which are on sale, ends of lines of which can be found in their warehouse outlets both here and in Staffordshire. Hunt carefully at these outlets and you will find many famous brand names such as Early's of Witney, Vantona and Slumberdown. Their warehouse sells ends of lines, slight seconds and bulk purchases of duvets, pillows, cotton sheets (usually hotel over-orders) at discounts of up to 50%.

INTERNATIONAL STOCK LTD
1 - 17 SILVER STREET, KINGS HEATH, BIRMINGHAM,
WEST MIDLANDS B14 7QX
☎ (0121) 443 3232. OPEN 9 - 6 MON - SAT, CLOSED 1 ON WED.
95-100 REA STREET, DIGBETH, BIRMINGHAM B5 6HA
☎ (0121) 622 3232. OPEN 9 - 5 MON - SAT, CLOSED 1 ON WED.
Permanent Discount Outlet • *Household* • *Furniture/Soft Furnishings*
DIY/Renovation • *Electrical Equipment* • *Womenswear & Menswear*
Children
Bankrupt, fire and flood damaged articles from CDs and videos, household goods and clothes to diy tools and television sets, carpets and cookers. The King's Heath branch is a two-storey warehouse with ever-changing stock. The upper floor is devoted to electrical goods, some marked down to 30% of their normal retail cost. The Digbeth branch sells bigger items such as kitchens, flooring, tiles, dining room and lounge furniture, central heating radiators and a large clothing section for all the family, all of which is sold below wholesale price and in some cases below manufacturers' cost price. Top brand name kitchens, when in stock, are discounted by 75%.

JEWELLERY QUARTER
NORTH-WEST BIRMINGHAM, WEST MIDLANDS
Britain's biggest centre of jewellery manufacture is home to scores of jobbing jewellers, whose family have been in this area for generations, and contemporary designers. You can find discounts of 15%-25% off a wide range of good quality jewellery and watches. The Big Peg is a seven-storey block in the quarter that provides a base for contemporary designers and small-scale creative enterprises.

LEGS CLOTHING CO
42 HIGH STREET, BLACKHEATH, ROWLEY REGIS,
WEST MIDLANDS B65 0DR
☎ (0121) 559 0774. OPEN 9 - 5 MON - FRI, 9 - 4 SAT.
Factory Shop • *Womenswear & Menswear* • *Children*
Exclusive outlet for Europe's largest trouser manufacturer sells ends of lines, cancelled orders and samples of jeans, trousers and shorts for all the family at factory direct prices. Also available ancillary lines of casual wear at bargain prices.

LITTLEWOODS CATALOGUE DISCOUNT STORE
299-303 COVENTRY ROAD, BIRMINGHAM, WEST MIDLANDS B10 0RA
☎ (0121) 772 1637. OPEN 9.30 - 5.30 MON - SAT, 11 - 4 SUN.
236 HAWTHORN ROAD, KINGSTANDING, BIRMINGHAM,
WEST MIDLANDS B44 8PP
☎ (0121) 373 1276. OPEN 9.15 - 5.30 MON - SAT.
Permanent Discount Outlet • *Womenswear & Menswear*
Children • *Electrical Equipment*
Littlewoods clearance shops offering up to 50% off the catalogue price for clothing and between 50% and 60% off for electrical goods. Stock changes constantly and varies from day to day but can include well-known brand names such as Berlei and Gossard lingerie, Vivienne Westwood, Pamplemousse leisure wear, Nike and Adidas sports shoes, Workers for Freedom, and Timberland and Caterpillar footwear. Stock depends on the size and location of the shop, so larger shops will get the longer discontinued runs and smaller shops over-runs with only a small amount of colour and size variations left. Littlewoods also run a mobile shop which operates in cities where they don't have a sale shop. For details of further venues for the sales, which usually take place once a month, contact Melanie Lamb, c/o Crosby DC Kershaw Avenue, Endbutt Lane, Crosby, Merseyside L70 1AH.

M LATIF & SONS
NEW CANAL STREET, DIGBETH, BIRMINGHAM,
WEST MIDLANDS B5 5PL
☎ (0121) 643 2822. OPEN 9.30 - 5.30 MON - SAT, 8 ON THUR,
10 - 2.30 SUN.
Permanent Discount Outlet • *Womenswear & Menswear*
Household • *Children*
Household and electrical goods, bedding, linens, ready-made curtains, clothes for all the family, pictures, garden equipment, toys, gifts and silk flowers, which are ex-catalogue and department store seconds from shops such as Marks & Spencer.

MAGNET LTD CLEARANCE CENTRE
CHESTON ROAD, ASTON, BIRMINGHAM, WEST MIDLANDS B7 5EL
☎ (0121) 327 3201. OPEN 8 - 5 MON - FRI, 9 - 1 SAT.
Factory Shop • *Furniture/Soft Furnishings*
With more than 200 branches countrywide, when Magnet Kitchens discontinue one of their ranges, there are always some shops with spare stock they can no longer sell. This applies to equipment such as ovens, hob, hoods, washing machines, tumble dryers and fridges, too as when manufacturers upgrade their ranges, Magnet customers don't want to buy the old model currently in situ in the showroom. Old stock is sent to three sites in Birmingham, Darlington and the head office factory site in Keighley, West Yorkshire. Prices on average are about 70% less than the high street price. If you are looking for a particular kitchen from the current catalogue, you may need to make three or four trips to buy sufficient quantities. The Birmingham outlet has more stock than the Keighley one, but less than Darlington. Electrical equipment is all top brands - Neff and Smeg ovens, as well as Magnet's own brand range which is made by Whirlpool. Some is ex-display, some discontinued models, some just overstock which is still boxed. Ovens cost from £120-£400. There are also wood and PVC glazed window frames, conservatory panels (from £25 for panels which normally cost £100), patio doors and French doors.

MATALAN
BIRMINGHAM ROAD, HOWARD STREET, WOLVERHAMPTON,
WEST MIDLANDS WV2 2LQ
☎ (01902) 352813. OPEN 10 - 8 MON - FRI, 9 - 6 SAT, 10 - 6 SUN.
UNIT 9, BROADWAY RETAIL PARK, BESCOT CRESCENT, WALSALL,
WEST MIDLANDS WS1 4DK
☎ (01922) 615188. OPEN 9.30 - 8 MON - FRI, 9 - 6 SAT, 11 - 5 SUN.
GALLAGHER RETAIL PARK, STONEY STANTON ROAD, COVENTRY,
WEST MIDLANDS CV6 5QQ.
(024 76) 637320. OPEN 10 - 8 MON - FRI, 9 - 6 SAT, 11 - 5 SUN.
PORTWAY ROAD, PORTWAY GREEN, OLDBURY,
WEST MIDLANDS B69 2BZ
☎ (0121) 544 4899. OPEN 10 - 8 MON - FRI, 9 - 6 SAT, 11 - 5 SUN.
STECHFORD RETAIL PARK, STATION ROAD, STECHFORD,
BIRMINGHAM B33 8BB
☎ (0121) 789 5950. OPEN 10 - 8 MON - FRI, 9 - 6 SAT, 11 - 5 SUN.
Permanent Discount Outlet • *Womenswear & Menswear*
Children • *Household*
Matalan is a fashion and homewares value retailer giving customers what they claim to be unbeatable value for money with huge savings on a wide range of products including high quality fashionable clothing for men, women and children at up to 50% off high street prices. Matalan is situated out of town and stores are open seven days a week all year round.

MERRY-GO-ROUND
24 BOLDMERE ROAD, SUTTON COLDFIELD, WEST MIDLANDS B73 5UY
☎ (0121) 354 2098. OPEN 10 - 5 MON - SAT.
Dress Agency • *Children*
Sells top quality secondhand childrenswear: from M & S, Next, Baby Gap etc. as well as designer names from birth to age eight.

MINOR MATTERS
54 ST MARY'S ROW, MOSELEY, BIRMINGHAM, WEST MIDLANDS B13 8JG
☎ (0121) 449 3553. OPEN 9.30 - 5 MON - SAT.
Dress Agency • *Children*
Good quality childrenswear from birth to pre-teens. Labels include Oilily and Osh Kosh as well as high street names, equipment such as prams, cots and pushchairs, books, toys, games and maternity wear as well as new equipment. Also sells beanie Babies. This shop has two floors and is next door to Encore ladies and men's dress agency.

MONSOON
BIRMINGHAM PLAZA, UG5 CITY PLAZA, CANON STREET, BIRMINGHAM, WEST MIDLANDS B2 5EF
☎ (0121) 643 1927. OPEN 9.30 - 5.30 MON - SAT.
Factory Shop • *Womenswear Only*
Medium-sized outlet selling mid-season stock for some of the year as well as last year's stock and discontinued lines, including jewellery. There are also outlets at Bicester Village in Oxfordshire, Cambridge and Clarks Village in Street, Somerset.

NEXT TO NOTHING
104 CORPORATION STREET, BIRMINGHAM, WEST MIDLANDS B2 6SZ
☎ (0121) 233 0022. OPEN 9 - 5.30 MON - SAT, 11 - 5 SUN.
Permanent Discount Outlet • *Womenswear & Menswear* • *Children*
Sells perfect surplus stock from Next stores and the Next Directory catalogue - from belts, jewellery and underwear to day and evening wear - at discounts of 50% or more. The ranges are usually last season's and overruns but there is the odd current item if you look carefully. Stock, which consists of men's, women's and children's clothing, some homeware and shoes, is replenished three times a week and there is plenty of it.

NURSERY TO LEISURE
35 SANDWELL CENTRE, QUEENS SQUARE, WEST BROMWICH, WEST MIDLANDS B70 7NG
☎ (0121) 553 5948. OPEN 9 - 5.30 MON - SAT, CLOSED WED.
Has a shop and a mail order arm called prams direct. The shop specialises in Maclaren pushchairs, but also sells reconditioned prams and pushchairs, as well as ends of lines which are particularly prevalent around the end of

October after the nursery trade fair when fabric designs change. It also sells baby monitors, Zorbit baby cot linen, cots and mattresses and is a stockist for Jack Horner corner cots.

PJ GOLD DEPOT LTD
37 VYSE STREET, BIRMINGHAM, WEST MIDLANDS B18 6JY
☎ (0121) 554 6165/2438 FAX. OPEN 9 - 4 MON - SAT,
SUN BEFORE CHRISTMAS ONLY.
Permanent Discount Outlet • *Womenswear Only*
Manufacturers of wedding rings, engagement rings, bracelets and necklets, which are sold here at savings of about 30% compared with high street prices. Gold jewellery can be made to customer's own design with any gem stones. Also sells glassware and pewter items.

PROBUS MAYFAIR LTD
UNION STREET, KENRICK WAY, WEST BROMWICH,
WEST MIDLANDS B70 6DB
☎ (0121) 553 2741. OPEN 10 - 4 THUR - SUN.
Factory Shop • *Household*
Probus Mayfair plc manufacture a wide range of small items for the kitchen for top Knightsbridge and mail order names. Kitchenware overstocks and seconds are sold off at their factory shop in Tamworth, Staffordshire, at substantial discounts. The shop also stocks some cookware imported from the Far East. As well as utensils, oven gloves, cookware and chopping boards, there are aprons, tea towels, breadbins, icing cookware and tablecloths. Most of the stock they make is textile-based and there are no ceramics or saucepans.

RMJ (ALLOYS) LTD
46-48 BAYTON ROAD, COVENTRY, WEST MIDLANDS CV7 9EJ
☎ (02476) 367508. OPEN 9 - 4.30 MON - THUR, 9 - 3.30 FRI.
Factory Shop • *Furniture/Soft Furnishings*
Made to measure staircases in metal or wood for indoors or outdoors - spiral, straight or fire escapes - at factory prices.

ROYAL BRIERLEY CRYSTAL
MOOR STREET, OFF NORTH STREET, BRIERLEY HILL,
WEST MIDLANDS DY5 3SJ
☎ (01384) 573580. OPEN 9 - 5 MON - SAT, 10 - 4 SUN.
Factory Shop • *Household*
Sells seconds of Royal Brierley crystal at 30%-50% off retail price, with two special sales. Also Royal Worcester porcelain available at seconds prices.

ROYAL DOULTON
CRYSTAL GLASS CENTRE, CHURTON HOUSE, STOURBRIDGE,
WEST MIDLANDS DY8 4AJ
☎ (01384) 354400. OPEN 9 - 5.30 MON - SAT.
Factory Shop • *Household*
Royal Doulton factory shop which, as well as selling at normal retail prices, also offers a variety of discontinued and slightly imperfect pieces at reduced prices. The shop sells the company's four main brands: Royal Crown Derby, Minton, Royal Albert and Royal Doulton itself.

ROYAL WORCESTER & SPODE FACTORY SHOP
ROYAL BRIERLEY CRYSTAL, NORTH STREET, BRIERLEY HILL,
WEST MIDLANDS DY5 3SJ
☎ (01384) 573580. OPEN 9 - 5 MON - SAT, 10 - 4 SUN.
Factory Shop • *Household*
Infinitesimally flawed porcelain and china seconds at 25% less than "perfect" prices. This outlet also sells Crummles, Country Artists, Clover Leaf, Lakeland Plaques, Fo-Frame, Leeds Display, Paw Prints and Collectible World Studios. There is a vast range with special offers throughout the year on anything from crystal decanters and bowls to figurines, cookware and dinner sets. Shipping arrangements worldwide can be organised.

RUSSELL HOBBS FACTORY SHOP
BRIDGNORTH ROAD, WOMBOURNE, WOLVERHAMPTON,
WEST MIDLANDS WV5 8AQ
☎ (0161) 947 3000. OPEN 9 - 4.30 TUE - FRI, 9 - 12.30 SAT.
Factory Shop • *Electrical Equipment*
Discontinued lines and seconds of Pifco, Carmen, Salton, Russell Hobbs, Mountain Breeze and Tower, as well as some perfect lines. For example, kettles, haircare, saucepan sets, slow cookers, mini ovens, air cleaners, ionisers and aromatherapy products. Also Christmas tree lights in season and Hi-Tec torches and batteries.

SCOOPS
63 HIGH STREET, BROWNHILLS, WEST MIDLANDS WS8 6HH
☎ (01543) 372933. OPEN 9 - 5.30 MON - SAT.
SWAN CENTRE, COVENTRY ROAD, YARDLEY, BIRMINGHAM B26 1AJ.
☎ (0121) 707 6585. OPEN 9 - 5.30 MON - SAT.
UNIT 67, THE MOOR CENTRE, BRIERLEY HILL, DUDLEY DY5 3AH
☎ (01384) 262537. OPEN 9 - 5.30 MON - SAT.
Permanent Discount Outlet • *Womenswear & Menswear*
Electrical Equipment • *Household* • *Children*
Grattan catalogue shop. There is a selection of items from those featured in the catalogue, which can consist of anything from children's clothes and toys to bedding, electrical equipment and nursery accessories. Each shop sells a

slightly different range, so always ring first to check they stock what you want. All items are discounted by up to 50%.

SLATERS MENSWEAR
3 CANNON STREET, BIRMINGHAM, WEST MIDLANDS B2 5EP
☎ (0121) 633 3855. OPEN 8.30 - 5.30 MON - SAT, 7.30 ON THUR, 11 - 4 SUN.
Permanent Discount Outlet • *Menswear Only*
Full range of men's clothes from underwear and shoes to casualwear, suits and dresswear and including labels such as Odermark, Bulmer, Valentino, Charlie's Co, and Charlton Gray. Men's suits from £79.

SPOILS
UNIT 38 MERRY HILL CENTRE, PEDMORE ROAD, BRIERLEY HILL, DUDLEY, WEST MIDLANDS DY5 1QX
☎ (01384) 77325. OPEN 10 - 8 MON - FRI, 9 ON THUR, 9 - 7 SAT, 11 - 5 SUN.
UNIT 41, WEST TERRACE, THE PALLASADES
OPEN 9 - 5.30 MON - SAT, 11 - 5 SUN. EN 9 - 5.30 MON - SAT, 11 - 5 SUN.
Permanent Discount Outlet • *Household*
General domestic glassware, non-stick bakeware, kitchen gadgets (but no electricals), ceramic oven-to-tableware, textiles, cutting boards, aluminium non-stick cookware, bakeware, plastic kitchenware, plastic storage, woodware, coffee pots/makers, furniture, mirrors and picture frames. Rather than being discounted, all the merchandise is very competitively priced - in fact, the company carry out competitors' checks frequently in order to monitor pricing. With 38 branches, the company is able to buy in bulk and thus negotiate very good prices.

STAGE 2
AUSTIN DRIVE, COURTHOUSE GREEN, COVENTRY,
WEST MIDLANDS CB6 7NS
☎ (024 76) 681520. OPEN 10 - 8 MON - FRI, 9 - 6 SAT, 11 - 5 SUN.
Permanent Discount Outlet • *Electrical Equipment*
Household • *Womenswear & Menswear* • *Children*
Sells discontinued lines from Freeman's catalogues. The full range is carried, but stock depends on what has not been sold at full price from the catalogue itself, or has been returned or the packaging is damaged or soiled. Clothing discounts range from about 50% - 65%. There are also household items and electrical equipment.

STUART CRYSTAL
RED HOUSE GLASSWORKS, WORDSLEY, STOURBRIDGE,
WEST MIDLANDS DY8 4AA
☎ (01384) 261777. OPEN 9 - 5 MON - SAT, BANK HOLS, 10 - 4 SUN.
Factory Shop • *Household*
Seconds of Stuart Crystal sold at about 25% discount. The selection includes wine glasses, flower holders, perfume holders, everyday tableware, salt and pepper sets, ice buckets, wine coolers, cutlery and candle lamps. Also seasonal special offers. First quality is also for sale at the appropriate price.

THE CHANGING ROOM AT FOUR OAKS
11 MERE GREEN RD, FOUR OAKS, SUTTON COLDFIELD,
WEST MIDLANDS B75 5BL
☎ (0121) 308 1848. OPEN 10 - 5 MON - SAT.
Dress Agency • *Womenswear Only*
A very exclusive dress agency selling such labels as Versace, Moschino, Armani, Prada, George Rech, Louis Feraud and Christian Dior. The shop itself occupies two floors and is full to the brim with constantly changing stock including accessories such as jewellery, belts, shoes, hats and handbags. Also hats to hire.

THE DRESS EXCHANGE
1003 ALCESTER ROAD, MAYPOLE, BIRMINGHAM,
WEST MIDLANDS B14 5JA
☎ (0121) 474 5707. OPEN 10 - 5 MON - SAT.
Dress Agency • *Womenswear Only*
New and nearly-new from Marks & Spencer to Valentino. Labels on sale in the past have included Maxmara, Reldan, Jaeger, Betty Barclay, Yarell, Mani and Mondi

THE MOULINEX SWAN FACTORY SHOP
UNIT 3 MERLIN PARK, WOOD LANE, ERDINGTON, BIRMINGHAM,
WEST MIDLANDS B24 9LZ
☎ (0121) 380 0635. OPEN 10 - 4 MON - FRI, 9 - 1 SAT.
Factory Shop • *Electrical Equipment*
Moulinex, Swan and Krups kitchen appliances including microwaves, kettles, toasters, electric knives, and irons. All are seconds or discontinued items with some slight imperfections but electrically sound. An Ovatio food processor which would cost £83.99 in department stores sells for £46.99 here; kettles from £6.99; toasters from £4.99. All come with a one-year guarantee.

TILE CLEARING HOUSE
UNIT 1, OLD WALSALL ROAD, GREAT BARR, BIRMINGHAM,
WEST MIDLANDS B42 1EA
☎ (0121) 357 1247. OPEN 8 - 6 MON - FRI, 9 - 6 SAT, 10 - 4 SUN.
Permanent Discount Outlet • *DIY/Renovation*
Over 500 ranges of top quality ceramic wall and floor tiles permanently in stock, plus a comprehensive range of grouts, adhesives, tools and accessories to complete the job. By buying direct from the manufacturer and passing the savings on to the customer, their prices are very competitive. Moreover, everything you see is in stock, so there's no waiting for orders to be processed. Save up to 75% on manufacturers' recommended selling prices.

TK MAXX
UPPER MALL, MERRYHILL SHOPPING CENTRE, DUDLEY,
WEST MIDLANDS DY10 3UY
☎ (01384) 77878. OPEN 10 - 8 MON - FRI, 10 - 9 THUR, 9 - 7 SAT, 11 - 5 SUN.
TOWN WHARF RETAIL PARK, WALSALL
TELEPHONE NUMBER AND OPENING HOURS
NOT AVAILABLE AS WE WENT TO PRESS.
Permanent Discount Outlet • *Womenswear & Menswear*
Children • *Household* • *Furniture/Soft Furnishings*
Based on an American concept, TK Maxx is situated in easily accessible, often centrally located stores and offers famous label goods with up to 60% savings off recommended retail prices. TK Maxx has fashion for the whole family - women's, men's and childrenswear - accessories, shoes, gifts, kitchenware and home goods. Everything in the store is branded with a choice of well-known high street names to designer labels, and while a small percentage might be clearly marked past season, the great majority of items in store are current season, current stock and still with phenomenal savings. There is a huge choice with 50,000 pieces in store and up to 10,000 new items arriving a week. The stores are simple and unfussy with wide aisles, shopping trolleys and baskets, and a spacious, functional feel to them but there are individual changing rooms, ramps for buggies and wheelchairs and plenty of staff on the shop floor. Every branch accepts all major credit and debit cards and has a liberal refund and return policy.

UNITED FOOTWEAR
926-928 STRATFORD ROAD, BIRMINGHAM, WEST MIDLANDS
☎ (0121) 778 1978 . OPEN 9 - 5.30 MON - SAT, 10 - 4 SUN.
74 BRADFORD STREET, WALSALL, WEST MIDLANDS
☎ (01922) 641577. OPEN 9 - 5.30 M ON - SAT, 10 - 4 SUN.
114-124 HOLBROOK LANE, COVENTRY, WEST MIDLANDS
☎ (024 76) 581838. OPEN 9 - 8 MON - FRI, 9 - 5.30 SAT, 10 - 4 SUN.
80-81 HIGH STREET, DUDLEY, WEST MIDLANDS
☎ (01384) 238492. OPEN 9 - 5.30 MON - SAT, 10 - 4 SUN.
Permanent Discount Outlet • *Womenswear & Menswear Children* • *Sportswear & Equipment*

Shoes for all the family as well as clothes, handbags, sports shoes, boots, giftware and household goods, all at discounted prices. Famous brands including Clarks, K Shoes and Elmdale. Part of a national chain.

V & F PARKER LTD
(ARDEN JEWELLERY), 51 VYSE STREET, OFF GREAT HAMPTON STREET, BIRMINGHAM, WEST MIDLANDS B18 6HS
☎ (0121) 554 3587. OPEN 9 - 4.30 MON - FRI, 9.30 - 2 SAT. MAIL ORDER.
Factory Shop • *Womenswear Only*

Part of Birmingham's famous jewellery quarter, V & F Parker are specialists in making rings, bangles and earrings. They are suppliers to jewellers, stocking more than 3,000 lines and hold stocks of major patterns enabling them to make or remake old rings. As manufacturers with a small showroom, personal customers obviously miss out on the middleman's cut. They have a small range of lockets and silver and gold chains which are not made on the premises. They also sell loose stones. They claim to be able to sell at "best prices available". Repairs also carried out.

WELWYN LIGHTING DESIGN
UNIT 15B, CRANMORE DRIVE, CRANMORE INDUSTRIAL ESTATE, SHIRLEY, WEST MIDLANDS B90 4PG
☎ (0121) 705 8222. OPEN 8.30 - 4.30 MON - THUR, 8.30 - 3 FRI, 8 - 12 SAT.
Factory Shop • *Electrical Equipment*

Small factory showroom with a selection of lampshades and indoor lights for the home including bathroom lights, wall lights, chandeliers, nursery shades, table lamps.

Wiltshire

ALEXON SALE SHOP
MCARTHURGLEN GREAT WESTERN DESIGNER OUTLET VILLAGE, KEMBLE DRIVE, SWINDON, WILTSHIRE SN2 2DY
☎ (01793) 431854. OPEN 10 - 6 MON - WED, FRI, 10 - 8 THUR, 9 - 6 SAT, 11 - 5 SUN.

Permanent Discount Outlet • *Womenswear Only*

Alexon and Eastex from last season at 40% less than the original price; during sale time in January and June, the reductions are as much as 70%. Stock includes separates, skirts, jackets, blouses; there is no underwear or night clothes.

AQUASCUTUM
MCARTHURGLEN GREAT WESTERN DESIGNER OUTLET VILLAGE, ADDRESS AND OPENING HOURS AS BEFORE.
☎ 01793 693073.

Factory Shop in a Factory Shopping Village • *Womenswear & Menswear*

Ends of ranges and last season's stock for women and men from the complete Aquascutum range in this factory shopping village with other shops, food facilities and a children's play area. There is a minimum 25% discount against normal retail prices, and up to 50% on some lines.

BIG L FACTORY OUTLET
MCARTHURGLEN GREAT WESTERN DESIGNER OUTLET VILLAGE, ADDRESS AND OPENING HOURS AS BEFORE.
☎ (01793) 693339.

Factory Shop in a Factory Shopping Village • *Womenswear & Menswear*

Men's and women's Levi jeans, jackets, cord and Sherpa fleece jackets, T-shirts and shirts but no children's, all at discount prices.

BIRTHDAYS
MCARTHURGLEN GREAT WESTERN DESIGNER OUTLET VILLAGE, ADDRESS AND OPENING HOURS AS BEFORE.
☎ (01793) 719751.

Factory Shop in a Factory Shopping Village • *Household*

Cards, notelets, stationery sets, colouring books, soft toys, photo albums, picture frames, gifts, giftwrap, tissue paper, party packs, Christmas crackers, string puppets, fairy lights all at discounts of up to 30%. Some are special purchases, some seconds.

BLACKWELL BROS INTERNATIONAL PLANTS LTD
MCARTHURGLEN GREAT WESTERN DESIGNER OUTLET VILLAGE, ADDRESS AND OPENING HOURS AS BEFORE.
☎ (01793) 706275.
Factory Shop • *Food and Leisure*
Reasonably priced plants, plant pots, terracotta ware and plant giftware of good quality. The company's core business is house plants and planted arrangements which they supply to the high street and grocery chains and sell in this retail shop at factory prices. Terracotta pots start at £1.99, bulbs, bedding plants and shrubs sold at great reductions on the high street prices. Planted arrangements can be made up on request.

BURBERRYS LTD
MCARTHURGLEN GREAT WESTERN DESIGNER OUTLET VILLAGE, ADDRESS AND OPENING HOURS AS BEFORE.
☎ (01793) 486861.
Factory Shop in a Factory Shopping Village • *Womenswear & Menswear*
Sells a variety of Burberry and Thomas Burberry goods for men and women. Thomas Burberry jeans and polo shirts, classic men's check shirts, umbrellas, a variety of purses and wallets, handbags and travel bags; classic trench coats and overcoats and Thomas Burberry cashmere.

CASTAWAYS
THE GRANGE, GRANGE LANE, MALMESBURY, WILTSHIRE SN16 OEP
☎ (01666) 824288. OPEN 9.30 -3 TUE AND WED,
9.30 - 12.30 FRIST SAT OF EACH MONTH.
Dress Agency • *Womenswear* • *Children*
Children's top quality nearly new designer wear plus nursery equipment and toys. Also do fittings for maternity bras, agency for Kingswood nursery equipment (all new) and Pollyotter float suits.

CLARKS SHOES
UNITS 1A AND G13, WEST SWINDON DISTRICT CENTRE, SWINDON, WILTSHIRE SN5 7DI
☎ (01793) 873662. OPEN 9 - 6 MON - WED, SAT, 9 - 8 THUR, FRI, 10 - 4 SUN, 10 - 5 BANK HOLIDAYS.
MCARTHURGLEN GREAT WESTERN DESIGNER OUTLET VILLAGE, ADDRESS AND OPENING HOURS AS BEFORE.
☎ (01793) 507600 (VILLAGE TEL NO).
Factory Shop • *Womenswear & Menswear* • *Children*
Clarks International operate a chain of factory shops nationally which specialise in selling discontinued lines and slight sub-standards for men, women and children from Clarks, K Shoes and other famous brands. These shops trade under the name of Crockers, K Shoes Factory shop or Clarks Factory Shop and while not all are physically attached to a shoe factory, these shops

are treated as factory shops by the company. Customers can expect to find an extensive range of quality shoes, sandals, walking boots, slippers, trainers, handbags, accessories and gifts, while their major outlets also offer luggage, sports clothing, sports equipment and outdoor clothing. Brands stocked include Clarks, K Shoes, Springer, CICA, Hi-Tec, Puma, Mercury, Fila, Mizuno, Slazenger, Samsonite, Delsey, Antler and Carlton, although not all are sold in every outlet. Discounts are from 30% to 60% off the normal high street price for perfect stock.

CLOVER LEAF
ARKWRIGHT ROAD, GROUNDWELL INDUSTRIAL ESTATE, SWINDON, WILTSHIRE SN2 5BB
☎ (01793) 720709. OPEN 9.30 - 4.30 MON - SAT, 10 - 4 SUN, BANK HOLIDAYS.
Factory Shop • *Household*
Sells a good range of kitchen and oven to tableware, place mats, teapot stands, teabag tidies, chopping bords, ceramic pottery, beech trays, kitchen clocks and coasters. There are usually about 48 different designs of table mat in stock at any one time. Seconds and discontinued lines are sold here at reduced prices.

DAKS SIMPSON
MCARTHURGLEN GREAT WESTERN DESIGNER OUTLET VILLAGE, ADDRESS AND OPENING HOURS AS BEFORE.
☎ (01793) 530618.
Factory Shop in a Factory Shopping Village • *Womenswear & Menswear*
Sells previous season's stock for women and men as well as any overmakes in high quality ladies suits, jackets and skirts and men's suits, overcoats, jackets, trousers, ties and knitwear as well as belts, gloves, handbags, Simpson shirts, socks and scarves. There are good bargains to be had, but stock is very much dependent on what has not sold in the shops. Sizes from 6-20. Ladies jackets, £99, originally £279. Daks Simpson was founded in 1894 by Simeon Simpson and produced quality English tailoring for more than 100 years. His son created the Simpson store in Piccadilly in 1936 which housed the Daks range, most of which was made in Scotland.

DARTINGTON CRYSTAL
CLOVERLEAF RETAIL SHOP, ARKWRIGHT ROAD, GROUNDWELL, SWINDON, WILTSHIRE SN2 5BB
☎ (01793) 720709. OPEN 9.30 - 4.30 MON - SAT, 10 - 4 SUN.
POOLE PDRIVE, SWINDON SNW 2DY
☎ (01793) 530222. OPEN 10 - 6 MON - FRI, 8 ON THUR, 9 - 6 SAT,
11 - 5 SUN. , 8 ON THUR, 9 - 6 SAT, 11 - 5 SUN. 11 - 5 SUN.
Factory Shop • *Household*
An extensive range of Dartington Crystal seconds at greatly reduced prices as well as some perfect crystal at full price. Range includes wine suites, sherry glasses, tankards, decanters, rippled glass, fruit and salad bowls.

DENTS
FAIRFIELD ROAD, WARMINSTER, WILTSHIRE BA12 9DL
☎ (01985) 212291. OPEN 9.30 - 5 TUE - SAT.
Factory Shop • *Womenswear & Menswear*
The accessories company which produces covetable gloves, belts, handbags, leather wallets and purses for most of the big department stores has a factory outlet near Salisbury. Most of the stock in this reasonably-sized warehouse shop consists of gloves, sold at at least 50% discount, but there is also a wonderful selection of leather briefcases, handbags, silk ties, leather belts, leather card holders and key fobs. The range of handbags come from three sources: ends of ranges from last season and discontinued ranges; returned sample stock for the current season from their two dozen agents; and prototypes for next season. Some of the briefcases are in English bridle leather, full hide or split hide. Stock from the discontinued and end of ranges changes constantly.

DESIGNER ROOM
MCARTHURGLEN GREAT WESTERN DESIGNER OUTLET VILLAGE, ADDRESS AND OPENING HOURS AS BEFORE.
☎ (01793) 436941.
Factory Shop in a Factory Shopping Village • *Womenswear Only*
Sells international designers such as Moschino, Armani, Cerruti, Dolce e Gabanna, Yves St Laurent, Byblos, Gucci and Louis Feraud. Designers vary according to how much overstock or ends of line they have; don't expect to find your favourites here every visit.

DOROTHY PERKINS
MCARTHURGLEN GREAT WESTERN DESIGNER OUTLET VILLAGE, ADDRESS AND OPENING HOURS AS BEFORE.
☎ (01793) 693796.
Factory Shop in a Factory Shopping Village • *Womenswear Only*
End of season lines with the normal Dorothy Perkins refund guarantee. The range includes knickers, scarves, suits, blouses, sweaters, coats, jackets, dresses and jewellery.

ECCO
MCARTHURGLEN GREAT WESTERN DESIGNER OUTLET VILLAGE, ADDRESS AND OPENING HOURS AS BEFORE.
☎ (01793) 422240.
Factory Shop in a Factory Shopping Village
Womenswear & Menswear • *Children*
Ladies, men's and children's shoes, all discounted by at least 25%. Phone 0800 387368 for a catalogue. Other outlets in South Somerset, Cheshire, and Hertfordshire.

ENCORE
42 GEORGE STREET, WARMINSTER, WILTSHIRE BA12 8QB
☎ (01985) 846022. OPEN 9.30 - 5 MON - SAT.
Dress Agency • *Womenswear Only*
Sells nearly-new ballgowns, handbags, shoes, hats, accessories and many Italian designer labels. Labels on sale include Liz Claiborne, Country Casuals, Mondi, Windsmoor, Jacques Vert and Jaeger. At Christmas, there is evening wear and for the New Year and summer ball season, ballgowns and cocktail wear. Examples of prices include Laura Ashley two-piece £30, evening wear from £20-£200. Sizes range from 8-26.

FRED PERRY LTD
MCARTHURGLEN GREAT WESTERN DESIGNER OUTLET VILLAGE, ADDRESS AND OPENING HOURS AS BEFORE.
☎ (01793) 481900
Factory Shop in a Factory Shopping Village
Sportswear & Equipment • *Womenswear & Menswear*
Men's, women's and children's ranges of the famous Fred Perry active performance clothing: shorts, tennis tops, tracksuits, T-shirts. All price labels show the original and the reduced price, which usually amount to a 30% discount.

GAP
MCARTHURGLEN GREAT WESTERN DESIGNER OUTLET VILLAGE, ADDRESS AND OPENING HOURS AS BEFORE.
☎ (01793) 486696.
Factory Shop in a Factory Shopping Village
Womenswear & Menswear • *Children*
Gap sells casual clothes for men, women and children of all ages, discounted at this factory outlet. There is a children's play area, restaurants and free car parking.

GEORGINA VON ETZDORF
ODSTOCK ROAD, SALISBURY, WILTSHIRE SP5 4NZ
☎ (01722) 343005. OPEN 10 - 5 MON - SAT, 12 - 5 SUN AND BANK HOLS.
Factory Shop • *Womenswear & Menswear*
Based on the edge of the village of Odstock lies the Georgina von Etzdorf factory shop, A purpose designed building which itself has won eight design awards, overlooking the beautiful Chalke Valley. Here you will find an extensive range of scarves and accessories at considerably reduced prices from their London flagship shop. Fabric by the metre is also available: velvets, silks, wools, linens and jacquards, printed, woven, knitted, embroidered, embellished and adorned. From classic chiffons to futuristic fibre optics, the collection will have a broad appeal to both men and women.

HANRO OF SWITZERLAND

MCARTHURGLEN GREAT WESTERN DESIGNER OUTLET VILLAGE, ADDRESS AND OPENING HOURS AS BEFORE.
☎ (01793) 480118.
Factory Shop in a Factory Shopping Village • *Womenswear & Menswear*
Luxury lingerie for men and women which is normally sold through Harvey Nichols, Harrods and Selfridges is available here at reduced prices. For example, a bra which normally retails for £100 would be reduced by 35% - 50%. Sizes range from extra small to extra large and the company specialises in garments for smaller busts, although D-cups are also stocked. Very well known for their mercerised cottons which never fade or shrink.

IN EXCESS

131 NETHERHAMPTON ROAD, SALISBURY, WILTSHIRE SP2 8NA
☎ (01722) 414444. OPEN 9 - 5.30 MON - SAT.
Permanent Discount Outlet • *Household*
In Excess is stacked full of bankrupt stock from stationery and paint to diy tools and cleaning materials, plumbing materials, screws, bolts, nuts, telephone accessories. It also houses, in season, garden furniture and pots aimed at the starter garden lover. Plastic tables and chairs start at £2.95 for a chair and from £5.95 to £12.95 for a table; terracotta pots start from 50p and there are also "antiqued" stone pots.

INTERVAC INTERNATIONAL HOME EXCHANGE

COXES HILL BARN, NORTH WRAXALL WILTSHIRE SN14 7AD
☎ (01225) 892208. FAX ☎ (01225) 892011.
E-MAIL: intervac-gb@email.msn.com   WEBSITE: www.intervac.co.uk
Home exchange is a great way to see the world, have a holiday and save money. You pay for travel, food and holiday spending only and make hotel bills a thing of the past! You also take on a home that has all the facilities and comforts you take for granted and sample another lifestyle and region from a better perspective: not as a tourist, but as part of the community. Subscribe at £85 per annum to receive an up-to-date listing of 11,500 homes in 67 countries, including your own personal listing. The directory is updated five times a year. Information is also published on the Internet.

JAEGER

MCARTHURGLEN GREAT WESTERN DESIGNER OUTLET VILLAGE, ADDRESS AND OPENING HOURS AS BEFORE.
☎ (01793) 484660.
Factory Shop in a Factory Shopping Village • *Womenswear & Menswear*
Contemporary classics from Jaeger at excellent prices. Most of the merchandise is previous seasons' stock, but you might also find some special makes. Both shops stock tailoring and knitwear for women and men.

JANE SHILTON
MCARTHURGLEN GREAT WESTERN DESIGNER OUTLET VILLAGE, ADDRESS AND OPENING HOURS AS BEFORE.
☎ (01793) 430356.
Factory Shop in a Factory Shopping Village • *Womenswear Only*
Merchandise from past seasons' collections or factory seconds at discounts of at least 30% and up to 70% off the original price. There is a wide range of handbags, small leather goods, shoes, luggage umbrellas and travel bags. Examples of price reduction: handbags at £24.99 originally £37, shoes reduced from £39.99 to £19.99.

JOKIDS LTD
MCARTHURGLEN GREAT WESTERN DESIGNER OUTLET VILLAGE, ADDRESS AND OPENING HOURS AS BEFORE.
☎ (01793) 436944.
Factory Shop in a Factory Shopping Village • *Children*
JoKids is the factory shop trading name for Jeffrey Ohrenstein which sells unusual and attractive clothes for children aged from birth to ten years. This includes pretty party dresses for girls at reductions of up to 40%, all-in-one smocked playsuits, T-shirts, denim shirts, denim dresses, sunhats, shorts, and accessories.

KARALYNE'S
20 WEST STREET, WILTON, WILTSHIRE SP2 0DF
☎ (01722) 742802. OPEN 9.30 - 4.30 TUE, THUR - SAT.
Dress Agency • *Womenswear Only*
This tiny but full shop sells nearly-new clothing and accessories for women at bargain prices, including evening wear. Stocks more than 1,000 items at a time with top designer labels and a constant flow of new arrivals and very popular "special rails" selling top makes including shoes, handbags, hats and belts. Permanent half-price rails added to weekly, plus two "everything half price" sales each year in February and August. If required, they will help to put together a special outfit or keep an eye out for something specific. They cater for all ages and sizes from 8 to 20+.

KIDS PLAY FACTORY
MCARTHURGLEN GREAT WESTERN DESIGNER OUTLET VILLAGE, ADDRESS AND OPENING HOURS AS BEFORE.
☎ (01793) 695550.
Factory Shop in a Factory Shopping Village • *Children*
This shop sells a wide range of well-known children's brand names: Little Tikes, Corgi, Crayola, Tomy, Lego, Hasbro, Playskool, Mattel and Fisher-Price at discounts of up to 50%. They also stock a wide range of soft toys including TY Beanie Babies. The village also has a cafe, children's play area and free parking.

LE CREUSET
MCARTHURGLEN GREAT WESTERN DESIGNER OUTLET VILLAGE, ADDRESS AND OPENING HOURS AS BEFORE.
☎ (01793) 641587.
Factory Shop in a Factory Shopping Village • *Household*
Items from the famous Le Creuset range - casseroles, saucepans, fry pans etc - plus their pottery collection at discounts of at least 30%.

LONG TALL SALLY
MCARTHURGLEN GREAT WESTERN DESIGNER OUTLET VILLAGE, ADDRESS AND OPENING HOURS AS BEFORE.
☎ (01793) 527228.
Factory Shop in a Factory Shopping Village • *Womenswear Only*
Targeted at women 5' 9" - 6' 4" between sizes 10 and 20, this shop offers discounts of at least 30% over high street stores.

LOOSE ENDS
GILES GREEN, BRINKWORTH, CHIPPENHAM, WILTSHIRE SN15 5DQ
☎ (01666) 510685. OPEN 9 - 1 MON - SAT OR BY APPOINTMENT.
Permanent Discount Outlet • *Furniture/Soft Furnishings*
Operating from two large converted barns in the grounds of the proprietor's house, Loose Ends offers top quality discontinued lines of fabric and textured and plain upholstery fabrics which they obtain from the best manufacturers in England and sell at about one third of the normal price. They hold very large stocks of all types of furnishing fabrics including lining, interlining and wallpapers which you can buy on the spot.

MARLBOROUGH TILES FACTORY SHOP
16 HIGH STREET, MARLBOROUGH, WILTSHIRE SN8 1AA
☎ (01672) 515287. OPEN 9.30 -5 MON - SAT.
MARLBOROUGH TILES 13 MILFORD STREET, SALISBURY, WILTSHIRE SP1 2AJ
☎ (01722) 328010. OPEN 9.30 - 5 MON - SAT.
Permanent Discount Outlet • *DIY/Renovation*
Wall and floor tiles from Marlborough and other top quality, specialist manufacturers. Seconds come mostly from Marlborough's own factory with discounts of up to 50% on first quality prices.

MATALAN
MANNINGTON RETAIL PARK, WOOTTON BASSETT ROAD, SWINDON, WILTSHIRE SN5 9NP
☎ (01793) 649500. OPEN 10 - 8 MON - FRI, 9 - 6 SAT, 10 - 4 SUN.
Permanent Discount Outlet • *Womenswear & Menswear*
Children • *Household*
Matalan is a fashion and homewares value retailer giving customers what they claim to be unbeatable value for money with huge savings on a wide range of products including high quality fashionable clothing for men, women and children at up to 50% off high street prices. Matalan is situated out of town and stores are open seven days a week all year round.

MCARTHURGLEN DESIGNER OUTLET
KEMBLE DRIVE, CHURCHWARD VILLAGE, (JUNCTION 16 OF M4) SWINDON, WILTSHIRE SN2 2DY
☎ (0800) 316 4352. FREEPHONE INFORMATION LINE .
☎ (01793) 507600. WEBSITE: www.mcarthurglen.com
OPEN 10 - 6 MON - FRI, 8 ON THUR, 9 - 6 SAT,
11 - 5 SUN AND BANK HOLIDAYS.
Factory Shopping Village • *Womenswear & Menswear* • *Children*
Household • *Furniture/Soft Furnishings* • *Food and Leisure*
Electrical Equipment • *Sportswear & Equipment*
More than 100 individual factory shops, a themed food court, licensed creche, indoor and outdoor play area, all built in the restored Great Western Railway buildings designed by Isambard Kingdom Brunel. Housed next door to the new interactive railway museum. Discounts are between 30% and 50% off regular retail prices. There is parking for 1,900 cars, which is free if you spend more than £10 in the centre and also a regular shuttle bus from Swindon station. Incorporates a large Homes Department with over 15 well-known names selling everything from glasses and cookware to decorative items and heavy Far Eastern-style furniture. Shops here include Alexon, Antler, Aquascutum, Austin Reed, Baron Jon menswear (Moschino, Versace, Romeo Gigli, Polo Ralph Lauren, Calvin Klein jeans, Kenzo), Ben Sherman, Birthdays, Bookends, Boots (selling only homewares such as glasses, china, beach towels, toys and brand-name kettles, toasters, steamers), Burberrys, Ciro Citterio, Claire,s Accessories, Clarks Shoes for all the family, Daks Simpson, Dorothy Perkins, Easy Jeans, Ecco shoes, Edinburgh Crystal, Episode, Fred Perry, French Connection, Gap selling Gap and GapKids, Gleneagles Crystal, Hanro lingerie, Henri Lloyd, Iceberg (children,s designerwear), Jacques Vert, Jaeger, Jane Shilton, Jigsaw, Jokids, Julian Graves herbs and dried food, Just Sweets, Le Creuset, Levi,s The Big L, Liz Claiborne, Long Tall Sally, Mexx, Mondian glass and gifts, Next to Nothing, Nike, Olsen ladies fashion, Oneida cutlery, Overland, Paco, Pilot womenswear, Ponden Mill, Poole Pottery, Price,s Candles, Principles for men and women, Professional Cookware, Quiksilver beach and casualwear, Remington small electrical appliances and

cutlery, Sheridan Australian towels and bedlinen, Sia vases and ceramics, Sofa Works, Soled Out footwear, Spiegelau glass, Staffordshire Pottery, Stuart Crystal, Suit Co, Suits You, Ted Baker selling men,s and womenswear, Tefal/Rowenta, the Designer Room selling international designers such as Moschino, Armani, Cerruti, Dolce & Gabbana, Yves St Laurent, Gucci, Jasper Conran and Louis Feraud; Thomas Pink men,s shirts, The Karrimor Store, Thorntons, Tie Rack, Timberland, Tog 24 outerwear, Toyzone, Triumph swimwear and underwear for women, Van Heusen, Villeroy & Boch, Viyella, Walker & Hall jewellery, Warners lingerie, Waterford/Wedgwood, Whittard of Chelsea, Windsmoor, Woods of Windsor, XS music and video (CDs and videos). Shops here selling items for children include Birthdays, Bookends, Easy Jeans, Ecco shoes, Jokids, Just Sweets, Mexx, Next to Nothing, Principles, Soled Out footwear, Thorntons and Toyzone. Shops here for the home include Birthdays, Bookends, Cloverleaf, Edinburgh Crystal, Garden Outlet, Gleneagles Crystal, Jane Heath House, Le Creuset, Mondian glass and gifts, Oneida cutlery, Ponden Mill duvets, towels and bedlinen, Poole Pottery, Price,s Candles, Professional Cookware, Sheridan Australia towels and bedlinen, Sia vases and ceramics, Spiegelau glass, Staffordshire Pottery, Stuart Crystal, Tefal/Rowenta, Villeroy & Boch, Waterford/Wedgwood, Whittard of Chelsea and Woods of Windsor. Furniture and furnishing shops here include Sofa Works. Shops here selling electrical equipment include Remington which has everything from hairdryers to kitchen knives, foot spas to kettles. Sports shops here include Fred Perry, Nike, The Karrimor Store, Tog 24 outerwear, Triumph swimwear and underwear. Leisure shops include Antler luggage and Jane Shilton luggage and handbags. Restaurants include McDonalds, Villa Pizza, Singapore Sam, Fat Jackets, Harry Ramsdens, Nana Massarella,s, Starbucks Coffee and the Baker,s Oven.

MEXX INTERNATIONAL
MCARTHURGLEN GREAT WESTERN DESIGNER OUTLET VILLAGE, ADDRESS AND OPENING HOURS AS BEFORE.
☎ (01793) 692205.
Factory Shop in a Factory Shopping Village
Womenswear & Menswear • *Children*

High street fashion at factory outlet prices for men, women, babies and kids, all of which are heavily discounted by more than 30%.

MUMS AND TOTS
2 & 4 SOUTH STREET, WILTON, NEAR SALISBURY, WILTSHIRE SP2 OJS
☎ (01722) 744582. OPEN 9.30 - 5 MON - FRI, 9.30 - 2 SAT.
Dress Agency • *Hire Shops* • *Children*

Factory seconds and new nursery equipment and bedding including prams and pushchairs are sold and hired out in this shop which also sells children's clothes, soft toys and traditional wooden toys.

NEXT TO NOTHING
MCARTHURGLEN GREAT WESTERN DESIGNER OUTLET VILLAGE, ADDRESS AND OPENING HOURS AS BEFORE.
☎ (01793) 525555.
Factory Shop in a Factory Shopping Village
Womenswear & Menswear • Children

Sells perfect surplus stock from Next stores and the Next Directory catalogue - from belts, jewellery and underwear to day and evening wear - at discounts of 50% or more. The ranges are usually last season's and overruns. Stock consists of women's, men's and children's clothing, with some homeware and shoes. Stock is replenished three times a week and there is plenty of it.

NIKE FACTORY STORE
MCARTHURGLEN GREAT WESTERN DESIGNER OUTLET VILLAGE, ADDRESS AND OPENING HOURS AS BEFORE.
☎ (01793) 484440.
Factory Shop in a Factory Shopping Village
Sportswear & Equipment • Children • Womenswear & Menswear

Men's, women's and children's trainers, jackets, T-shirts, sports shirts, shorts, sleeveless T-shirts and tracksuits. Nike has been making clothes for people who live and play outdoors since 1972. This factory shop sells unsold items from previous seasons. The selection represents their worldwide collection, which means that some garments may not have been offered for sale in the UK. As ranges tend to be incomplete, they are offered at a minimum off 30% off the recommended retail price or the price they would have commanded in the UK. Occasionally, there are some slight seconds on sale, which are always marked as such. There is another factory shop at Cheshire, Oaks in Lancashire.

OFF THE RAILS
15 NORTH STREET, WILTON, WILTSHIRE SP2 OHA
☎ (01722) 744966. OPEN 10 - 4 THUR - SAT.
Secondhand shops • *Furniture/Soft Furnishings*

Secondhand curtain shop which sells drapes made from fabric by Designers Guild, Colefax & Fowler, Osborne & Little, etc, allowing you to take them home and try before buying. Quality is Marks & Spencer upwards with curtains at £15 to £685. Alterations can be undertaken and curtains are made up at very good prices. Also sells anything to do with furnishing fabrics, including lampshades from £4 for pleated ones to £59 for silk ones, cushions, curtain poles, cut-price fabric, Indian crewel work. The poles selection covers everything from plain natural untreated wooden ones to antique gilt poles. There are also baskets of finials, and bundles of secondhand tie-backs in all shapes and sizes.

OLD DAIRY SADDLERY LTD
GREENWAY FARM, TOCKENHAM, SWINDON, WILTSHIRE SN4 7PP
☎ (01793) 849284. OPEN 9.30 - 5.30 MON - SAT, 9.30 - 1 SUN.
Permanent Discount Outlet • *Womenswear & Menswear*
Sportswear & Equipment
Normal-priced large shop on a farm selling outdoor wear, horse blankets, country clothing etc at competitive prices. Cliff Barnsby, Maintain Horse and Kyra K saddlewear has also been included. Phone first to check stock levels.

ONEIDA
MCARTHURGLEN GREAT WESTERN DESIGNER OUTLET VILLAGE, ADDRESS AND OPENING HOURS AS BEFORE.
☎ (01793) 514103.
Factory Shop in a Factory Shopping Village • *Household*
Oneida is the world's largest cutlery company and originates from the United States of America. In addition to cutlery, it sells silver and silver plate at discounts of between 30% and 50%, plus frames, candlesticks and trays. They now also have their own range of chinaware and glass, also sold here at discounts of 30%-50%.

OXFAM BRIDAL BOUTIQUE
FIRST FLOOR, 5 THE BRIDGE, CHIPPENHAM, WILTSHIRE SN15 1HA
☎ (01249) 447061. BY APPOINTMENT ONLY.
Hire Shops • **Permanent Discount Outlet**
Bridal clothes and accessories including up to 200 gowns for brides, as well as bridesmaids and page boys outfits; artificial flowers, shoes, headdresses, veils, foundation garments, petticoats. Many of these items have been donated by manufacturers after being used in catwalk shows so have only been worn by a model though that does mean they tend to be smaller sizes. Some clothes are to buy, some to hire. Prices from £20-£250. Make an appointment with the Oxfam charity shop situated on the ground floor.

PACO
MCARTHURGLEN GREAT WESTERN DESIGNER OUTLET VILLAGE, ADDRESS AND OPENING HOURS AS BEFORE.
☎ (01793) 536936.
Factory Shop in a Factory Shopping Village
Children • *Womenswear Only* • *Sportswear & Equipment*
Paco uses bright, distinctive colours and the knack for designing great clothes at affordable prices. For several years, they have also been creating their own brand of sports and leisurewear clothing that shows great verve and energy. This range has a much more everyday living influence. The contrast is a distinct look for the discerning wearer. If you are looking for a great T-shirt or sweatshirt, lightweight jacket or gilet, polar fleece or hooded top, three-quar-

ter length or combat trousers, then you need look no further. Paco now competes with the very best fashion brands in the high street by offering customers high fashion combined with excellent quality, making their clothes real value for money.

PONDEN MILL LINENS
WILTON SHOPPING VILLAGE, KING STREET, WILTON,
NEAR SALISBURY, WILTSHIRE SP2 0RS
☎ (01722) 741271. OPEN 9.30 - 5.30 MON - SAT, 11 - 5 SUN.
MCARTHURGLEN GREAT WESTERN DESIGNER OUTLET VILLAGE,
ADDRESS AND OPENING HOURS AS BEFORE.
☎ (01793) 531880.
Factory Shop in a Factory Shopping Village • *Household*
Famous branded products at direct from the mill prices. A fabulous assortment of towels, duvets, pillows, throws, bedspreads, up-to-the-minute coordinated bed linen, from Crown, Coloroll, Jeff Banks Ports-of-Call, to name but a few. Something for every room in the house.

PRICE'S CANDLES
MCARTHURGLEN GREAT WESTERN DESIGNER OUTLET VILLAGE,
ADDRESS AND OPENING HOURS AS BEFORE.
☎ (01793) 693745.
Factory Shop in a Factory Shopping Village • *Household*
Everything sold in this shop are seconds, discontinued sizes not available elsewhere, over-runs or candles in old packaging that has now been replaced. There are church candles, lanterns, candles in pots and glass jars, star-shaped candles, floating candles, candlestick holders, serviettes, scented candles and garden torches.

PRINCIPLES
MCARTHURGLEN GREAT WESTERN DESIGNER OUTLET VILLAGE,
ADDRESS AND OPENING HOURS AS BEFORE.
☎ (01793) 693890.
Factory Shop in a Factory Shopping Village • *Womenswear & Menswear*
End of season lines with the normal Principles refund guarantee. The range includes, for women, dresses, blouses, coats, outerwear, knitwear, casualwear and a selection of Petite clothing for women who are 5ft 3ins and under. For men, there is formalwear, smart casualwear, knitwear, outerwear, PFM Sport, jeanswear and casualwear.

REMINGTON
MCARTHURGLEN GREAT WESTERN DESIGNER OUTLET VILLAGE, ADDRESS AND OPENING HOURS AS BEFORE.
☎ (01793) 430515.
Factory Shop in a Factory Shopping Village • *Electrical Equipment*
Lots of famous names here from Monogram cutlery to Braun, Philips, Remington, Wahl, Krups, Swan and Kenwood small kitchen equipment. There are usually hair, beauty and male grooming accessories as well as kitchen equipment, all at reduced prices. A great place to buy gifts or replenish the kitchen equipment with combi stylers, turbo travel plus hairdryers, air purifiers, liquidisers; food processors; batteries; clocks; and cutlery. Some of the packaging may be damaged but the products are in perfect working order.

ROYAL WORCESTER & SPODE FACTORY SHOP
MCARTHURGLEN GREAT WESTERN DESIGNER OUTLET VILLAGE, ADDRESS AND OPENING HOURS AS BEFORE.
☎ (01793) 692311.
Factory Shop • *Household*
Infinitesimally flawed porcelain and china seconds at 25% less than "perfect" prices. This outlet also sells Edinburgh Crystal, Fo Frame, Country Artists, Langham Glass, Paw Prints and Collectible World. There is a vast range with special offers throughout the year on anything from crystal decanters and bowls to figurines, cookware and dinner sets. Shipping arrangements worldwide can be organised.

SECOND TO NONE
13 THE BRIDGE, CHIPPENHAM, WILTSHIRE SN15 1HA
☎ (01249) 656456. OPEN 9 - 5 MON - SAT.
Permanent Discount Outlet • *Womenswear & Menswear*
Established in the South West for twenty-seven years, this company has built a reputation for giving excellent customer service and for selling goods which are of a quality and value second to none! This Famous chainstore and branded clearing lines include surplus stocks of branded goods such as Fabrizio, Zorbit, Naturana and many more. They stock a large range of ladies and children's and baby wear (including baby bedding and accessories), leisurewear, sports clothes and some menswear, and an extensive range of underwear and nightwear for all the family. You can save up to 75% off recommended retail prices and they offer a seven-day money back guarantee.

SMART CHOICE
32-34 GLOUCESTER STREET, MALMESBURY, WILTSHIRE SN16 OAA
☎ (01666) 822327. OPEN 10 - 5 MON - SAT, CLOSED THUR.
Dress Agency • *Hire Shop* • *Womenswear Only*
Dress agency selling designer ladies wear, shoes and accessories, including some larger sizes. Labels on sale vary from Jigsaw, Planet and Escada to

Cerruti, Valentino, Pirigi and Armani. They also sell new Gossard underwear and Levantie tights and hire out designer hats.

THE CURTAIN TRADERS

123 HIGH STREET, MARLBOROUGH, WILTSHIRE SN8 1LZ
☎ (01672) 516994. FAX ☎ (01672) 512400. E-MAIL: pl@curtaintradersuk.com
WEBSITE: www.curtaintraders.uk.com
OPEN 10 - 4.30 MON - FRI, 10 - 2.30 SAT.

Secondhand shops • *Furniture/Soft Furnishings*

Specialises in value for money, selling high quality, pre-loved curtains and accessories at rock-bottom prices. With two floors of constantly-changing stock, they offer an extensive variety to suit most tastes and needs and most fabrics can be obtained on request. They stock many designer names such as Osborne & Little, Colefax & Fowler, Sanderson, Warner and Designers Guild in natural linens, cottons, damasks, brocades, designer chintzes and velvets. They have extended their range of services to provide a fast make-up, alterations and fitting team and can source most materials. They also offer a design service at their in-house workshop which does not involve expensive interior design prices.

THE FACTORY SHOP LTD

36-37 ROUNDSTONE STREET, TROWBRIDGE, WILTSHIRE BA14 8DE
☎ (01225) 751399. OPEN 9 - 5 MON - SAT.
24 MARKET PLACE, WARMINSTER, WILTSHIRE BA12 9AN
☎ (01985) 217532. OPEN 9 - 5 MON - SAT.
23-25 NEW PLACE, CORSHAM, WILTSHIRE SN13 OHL
☎ (01249) 712160. OPEN 9 - 5.30 MON - SAT, 10 - 4 SUN.

Factory Shop • *Household* • *Womenswear & Menswear* • *Children Furniture/Soft Furnishings* • *Sportswear & Equipment*

Wide range on sale includes men's, ladies and children's clothing and footwear; household textiles, toiletries, hardware, luggage, lighting and bedding, most of which are chainstore and high street brands at discounts of approximately 30%-50%. There are weekly deliveries and brands include many major stars such as Adidas, Nike, Joe Bloggs and Brabantia, to name just four. Lines are continually changing and few factory shops offer such a variety under one roof. The Trowbridge branch also sells the Cape Country Furniture range. This high quality pine furniture made exclusively for The Factory Shop in the new South Africa is sold at factory direct prices with home delivery throughout the UK. Colour brochure and price list available.

THE MAGNIFICENT MATERIAL COMPANY
CHITTERNE LODGE, CHITTERNE, WARMINSTER, WILTSHIRE BA12 OLQ
☎ (01985) 850501. OPEN 9.30 - 12.30 MON, THUR AND
BY APPOINTMENT.
Permanent Discount Outlet • *Furniture/Soft Furnishings*
Sells a wide variety of discontinued lines, overstocks, first and seconds, including traditional chintzes, linens, damasks, checks and upholstery, and a small selection of wallpaper. These fabrics come from many of the top designer warehouse and are sold at less than half the retail price.

THE SHOESTRING
5 APSLEY HOUSE ARCADE, WOOTTON BASSETT, SWINDON,
WILTSHIRE SN4 7AQ
☎ (01793) 850106. OPEN 9.30 - 4.30 MON - SAT, CLOSED THUR.
Dress Agency • *Womenswear Only*
Small shop full of fahionable clothes from casual to eveningwear which are a mixture of high street and designer labels, Frank Usher, Jaeger, Windsmoor etc. Also sells accessories such as bags, belts and shoes. There is also a sales rail with clothes reduced even further for clearance items.

THORNTONS
MCARTHURGLEN GREAT WESTERN DESIGNER OUTLET VILLAGE,
ADDRESS AND OPENING HOURS AS BEFORE.
☎ (01793) 692438.
Factory Shop in a Factory Shopping Village • *Food and Leisure*
The UK's leading specialist confectionery retailer has more than 500 shops and franchises nationwide selling a wide range of boxed and loose, chocolate and sugar confectionery. The factory outlets sell three different categories: misshapes. discounted lines and standard lines. Misshapes are loose chocolates which are the result of new product development, product trials or end of production runs which cannot be packed as Thorntons standard lines. They are packed into assorted bags and offer a saving of 35%-55% over the recommended retail price of standard "loose line" products. Discounted lines are excess to Thorntons' normal retail requirements and can be as a result of excess seasonal or export stock, discontinued lines or packaging changes. These products, when available, are offered at a discount of 25%-50% over the standard retail price. Standard lines from the full Thorntons range are also on sale at normal prices.

TIE RACK
MCARTHURGLEN GREAT WESTERN DESIGNER OUTLET VILLAGE,
ADDRESS AND OPENING HOURS AS BEFORE.
☎ (01793) 531070.
Factory Shop in a Factory Shopping Village • *Menswear Only*
Usual range of Tie Rack items including boxer shorts, silk ties, socks, silk scarves and waistcoats, all at up to 50% reductions.
Customer Careline: 0208 230 2333.

TIMBERLAND
MCARTHURGLEN GREAT WESTERN DESIGNER OUTLET VILLAGE, ADDRESS AND OPENING HOURS AS BEFORE.
☎ (01793) 480156.
Factory Shop in a Factory Shopping Village • *Womenswear & Menswear*
Footwear, clothing and outdoor gear from the well-known Timberland range at discounts of 30% or more. Most of the stock is last season's or discontinued lines, but not seconds. All stock is last season's excess stock in limited ranges and sizes. As most of Timberland's stock is from a core range which rarely changes, there are few discontinued lines.

TK MAXX
CROSS KEYS SHOPPING CENTRE, SALISBURY, WILTSHIRE
☎ (01722) 320644. OPEN 9 - 5.30 MON - FRI, 9 - 8 THUR, 9 - 8 SAT, 10 - 4 SUN.
Permanent Discount Outlet • *Womenswear & Menswear*
Children • *Household* • *Furniture/Soft Furnishings*
Based on an American concept, TK Maxx is situated in easily accessible, often centrally located stores and offers famous label goods with up to 60% savings off recommended retail prices. TK Maxx has fashion for the whole family - women's, men's and childrenswear - accessories, shoes, gifts, kitchenware and home goods. Everything in the store is branded with a choice of well-known high street names to designer labels, and while a small percentage might be clearly marked past season, the great majority of items in store are current season, current stock and still with phenomenal savings. There is a huge choice with 50,000 pieces in store and up to 10,000 new items arriving a week. The stores are simple and unfussy with wide aisles, shopping trolleys and baskets, and a spacious, functional feel to them but there are individual changing rooms, ramps for buggies and wheelchairs and plenty of staff on the shop floor. Every branch accepts all major credit and debit cards and has a liberal refund and return policy.

TOG 24
MCARTHURGLEN GREAT WESTERN DESIGNER OUTLET VILLAGE, ADDRESS AND OPENING HOURS AS BEFORE.
☎ (01793) 695966.
Factory Shop in a Factory Shopping Village
Womenswear & Menswear • *Children* • *Sportswear & Equipment*
Tog 24 are the UK's fastest growing brand name in outdoor clothing and leisurewear. They utilise the world's finest performance fabrics including Gore-Tex, Polartec and Burlington MCS, catering for all the family for all seasons, with cosy fleeces and waterproofs for the winter, and trekking ranges, shorts and t-shirts for the summer. With all prices at least 30% below the recommended retail price, you can afford to enter the Tog comfort zone.

TRIUMPH INTERNATIONAL LTD
MCARTHURGLEN GREAT WESTERN DESIGNER OUTLET VILLAGE,
ADDRESS AND OPENING HOURS AS BEFORE.
☎ (01793) 480892.
Factory Shop in a Factory Shopping Village • *Womenswear & Menswear*
Factory shop selling a wide and ever-changing range of Triumph lingerie, a French range, Valisere, and swimwear which are last season's stock or discontinued lines at discounts of between 30% - 50%. Also women's and men's Sloggi underwear and underwear and swimwear from the Hom range for men.

UNITED FOOTWEAR
HORHAM CRESCENT, PARK SOUTH, SWINDON, WILTSHIRE SN3 2LX
☎ (01793) 435238. OPEN 9 - 5.30 MON - SAT, 10 - 4 SUN.
Permanent Discount Outlet • *Womenswear & Menswear*
Children • *Household*
Shoes for all the family as well as clothes, handbags, sports shoes, boots, giftware and household goods, all at discounted prices. Famous brands including Clarks, K Shoes and Elmdale. Part of a national chain.

VILLEROY & BOCH (UK) LIMITED
MCARTHURGLEN GREAT WESTERN DESIGNER OUTLET VILLAGE,
ADDRESS AND OPENING HOURS AS BEFORE.
☎ (01793) 480944.
Factory Shop in a Factory Shopping Village • *Household*
One of ffive factory outlets for Villeroy & Boch, this shop carries an exclusive range of tableware, crystal and cutlery from Europe's largest tableware manufacturer. A varied and constantly changing stock, including seconds, hotelware and discontinued lines, on sale at excellent reductions, always makes for a worthwhile visit.

VIVM
FIRST FLOOR, ABOVE PRIMROSE LANE, 137 HIGH STREET,
MARLBOROUGH, WILTSHIRE SN8 1HN
☎ (01672) 519143. OPEN 9.30 - 5.30 MON - FRI, 9.30 - 3 SAT.
Permanent Discount Outlet • *Womenswear Only*
Permanent discount shop operating at the top end of the fashion market. They specialise in samples, end of line and returned orders, working directly with designers and manufacturers. This enables them to offer customers designer labels for less. Stock changes regularly according to availability.

VIYELLA
MCARTHURGLEN GREAT WESTERN DESIGNER OUTLET VILLAGE, ADDRESS AND OPENING HOURS AS BEFORE.
☎ (01793) 484450.
Factory Shop • *Womenswear & Menswear*
Wide range of Viyella clothing at discount prices from 30% on ladies formal wear and casual wear.

WALTON DESIGN LTD
22A HIGH STREET, MALMESBURY, WILTSHIRE SN16 9AA
☎ (01666) 825994. OPEN 9 - 6 MON - SAT, 10 - 4 SUN, 10 - 5 BANK HOLS.
119 HIGH STREET, MARLBOROUGH, SN8 1LZ
☎ (01672) 516954. OPEN 9 - 6 MON - SAT, 10 - 4 SUN, 10 - 5 BANK HOLS.
Permanent Discount Outlet • *Womenswear Only*
A chain of thirteen stores across the south of England selling well-known labels for women at greatly reduced prices. Current stock from high street stores might include Liz Claiborne, DKNY, Nougat, Ralph Lauren, Banana Republic, Calvin Klein and Tommy Hilfiger. New lines come in each week and are often one-offs, so regular customers know to buy things when they see them or risk missing out.

WEAR IT WELL
59 NORTH STREET, OFF EASTCOTT HILL, OLD TOWN, SWINDON, WILTSHIRE SN1 3JY
☎ (01793) 695223. OPEN 10 - 4.30 TUE, THUR, FRI, SAT.
Dress Agency • *Womenswear Only*
Two-storey shop, established for eight years, selling many high street labels in "as new" condition, including Wallis, Principles, as well as Precis, Windsmoor, Alexon, Louis Feraud, Betty Barclay and Rodier. There is also a selection of bridal wear, £900 down to £300, often ex-exhibition, maternity wear, evening wear, hats, bags, shoes, mother-of-the-bride outfits, groom outfits. New stock arrives daily. Also caters for the younger, trendier market with outfits from Oasis, Morgan and some high street labels.

WILTON SHOPPING VILLAGE
MINSTER STREET, WILTON, SALISBURY, WILTSHIRE SP2 0RS
☎ (01722) 741 211. OPEN 9.30 - 5.30 MON - SAT, 11 - 5 SUN.
Factory Shopping Village • *Womenswear & Menswear*
Food and Leisure • *Household* • *Furniture/Soft Furnishings*
On the former site of the Royal Wilton Carpet Factory, this village uses the refurbished original factory dye houses and 300-year old listed historic courtyard buildings to house factory shops selling fashion and homewares at discounted prices. It includes shops such as Cotton Traders, Double Two, Edinburgh Woollen Mill, Julian Graves, Old Traditions, Ponden Mill, Remainders Books, Roman Originals, Scotts of Stow and the Wilton Carpet Factory Shop.

WINDSMOOR GROUP
MCARTHURGLEN GREAT WESTERN DESIGNER OUTLET VILLAGE,
ADDRESS AND OPENING HOURS AS BEFORE.
☎ (01793) 693615.
Factory Shop in a Factory Shopping Village • *Womenswear Only*
Previous season's stock as well as any returned merchandise and overmakes from the Windsmoor, Planet and Precis Petite ranges at discounts averaging about 50% off the original price.

Worcestershire

BABY BARN
GANNOW GREEN FARM, GANNOW GREEN LANE, ROMSLEY,
WORCESTERSHIRE B45 9AS
☎ (01562) 710220. OPEN 10 - 5 THUR - SAT, 11 - 4 SUN. MAIL ORDER.
Permanent Discount Outlet • *Children*
Permanent discount outlet catering for nursery equipment and accessories. You can visit their outlet or phone for a leaflet outlining all the products they sell. These include buggies, prams, pram sheets, cotton blankets, foot muffs, baby nests, pushchair liners, shawls, pram bags, rain covers, net bag and clips, insect nets, cots, mattresses, Moses baskets, musical mobiles, nursery sheets, quilts, bumpers, valances with matching curtains, nappy stackers, waterproof sheets, travel cots, baby walkers door bouncers, baby swings, arm bands, baby floats, rocking horses, car seats, car window sunshades, sterilisers, fireguards, high chairs, harnesses, baby food mixers, disposable bottles, non-spill cups, portable gates, baby monitors, rompers, mitts, christening gowns, nappies, changing mats, layette boxes, toilet steps, nursery furniture potty and step stools, changing bags, changing mats, bath and carrycot stands, bath thermometer, shampoo shields, brush and comb sets and baby clothes hangers. Most of the merchandise is branded with names such as Cosatto, Chicco, Britax, Pegasus, Maclaren, Mamas & Papas, Zorbit, Klippan, Avent, Kiddiproof and Tomy. They will also hire out some items such as travel cots. If you see what you want cheaper elsewhere, you can phone them and see if they can beat the price.

BOOKENDS
9-13 PUMP STREET, WORCESTER WR1 2QT
☎ (01905) 24389. OPEN 9 - 5.30 MON - SAT, 11 - 5 SUN.
Secondhand shops • *Food and Leisure*
Damaged books and publishers' returns, as well as new and review copies, including recently published books, usually at half price or below.

BUMPSADAISY MATERNITY STYLE
25 FRIARS STREET, WORCESTER
☎ (01905) 28993. WEBSITE: www.bumpsadaisy.co.uk
OPEN 10 - 5.30 MON - SAT.
Hire Shop • *Womenswear Only*

Franchised shops and home-based branches with large range of specialist maternity wear, from wedding outfits to ball gowns, to hire and to buy. Hire costs range from £30 to £100 for special occasion wear. To buy are lots of casual and business wear in sizes 8 - 18. For example, skirts £20-£70; dresses £40-£100. Also four branches run by young mums from their homes, specialising inhiring but also stocking a small retail range (Camberley, Edgbaston, Exeter and Southampton). Phone 0208-789 0329 for details.

CARPETS OF WORTH LTD
SEVERN VALLEY MILLS, SEVERN ROAD, STOURPORT-ON-SEVERN, WORCESTERSHIRE DY13 9HA
☎ (01299) 872411/872400. E-MAIL: sales@carpetsofworth.co.uk
WEBSITE: www.carpetsofworth.co.uk   OPEN 8.30 - 5 MON - FRI, 8 - 1 SAT.
Factory Shop • *Furniture/Soft Furnishings*

Sells Axminster tufted carpets and rugs, both patterned or plain. These are usually seconds or overmakes, discontinued lines or end of contract rolls. Credit cards accepted. There is another, smaller outlet, at Stroud.

CATALOGUE BARGAIN SHOP
WEST BANK, BERRY HILL INDUSTRIAL ESTATE, DROITWICH, WORCESTERSHIRE WR9 9AP
☎ (01905) 615521. OPEN 9 - 8 MON - FRI, 9 - 5.30 SAT, 10.30 - 4.30 SUN.
233 WORCESTER ROAD, MALVERN LINK, MALVERN WR14 1SY
☎ (01684) 893062. OPEN 9 - 5.30 MON - SAT, 10.30 - 4.30 SUN.
15 PUMP STREET, WORCESTER WR1 2QX
☎ (01905) 617211. OPEN 9 - 5.30 MON - SAT, 10.30 - 4.30 SUN.
Permanent Discount Outlet • *Womenswear & Menswear*
Household • *Electrical Equipment* • *Children*

Catalogue Bargain Shop is a growing national chain of stores which obtains the majority of its goods from mail order giants Great Universal and Kays, and offers a range of clothing for all the family, a wide selection of shoes, bed linen, household goods, electrical equipment and hundreds of other catalogue items at very competitive prices. The merchandise consists of ends of ranges and previous season's stock for which there is no longer storage space when the catalogues change.

CHINAMATCH
P.O. BOX 30, DROITWICH L.D.O. WORCESTERSHIRE WR9 7ZJ
☎ (01905) 391520/391520 FAX. MAIL ORDER.
WEBSITE: www.chinamatch-uk@compuserve.com

Would you like to add to your dinner or tea service or replace breakages, but find the pattern is no longer available? Or perhaps you want to buy a new service but need to sell on your old service first. China Match registers your requirements and checks them constantly against existing and incoming stock: they stock most English manufacturers and Noritake. There are no registration fees. The company buys stock daily and only supplies pieces in new or little used condition. Most customers are supplied with their requirements from stock, but in those instances where stock is not available, every effort is made to find your particular need as quickly as possible, although success cannot be guaranteed. Established since 1980, this company prides itself on its proactive, personal service.

CONTINENTAL COLLEXTION
48 HEWELL ROAD, BARNT GREEN, WORCESTERSHIRE B45 8NF
☎ (0121) 447 7544. OPEN 10 - 5 TUE - SAT.
Dress Agency • *Womenswear Only*

Stock includes some designer samples, evening wear, wedding outfits, ball gowns, hats and accessories, though the shop specialises in cocktail wear, ballgowns, hats and wedding outfits. Examples of recent prices include a Simon Ellis wedding outfit, £180 original price, £350. Ballgowns and hats are available for hire.

D & C REYNOLDS
EDWIN AVENUE, HOO FARM TRADING ESTATE, WORCESTER ROAD, KIDDERMINSTER, WORCESTERSHIRE DY11 7RA
☎ (01562) 67187. OPEN 9 - 5 MON - SAT, 11 - 4 BANK HOLS.
Permanent Discount Outlet • *Womenswear & Menswear*

Well-established trade shop offering a huge selection of imported ladies clothing, some lingerie and some men's suits at incredible prices. The ladies clothes are the German brand, Madeleine, and include macintoshes, suits, jackets, trousers, dresses, skirts in a range of sizes, with lots of larger sizes. The men's suits are German and Dutch. Open to the public though you have to become a member, which is free. VAT is added at the till.

DARTINGTON CRYSTAL
SECONDS SHOP, ROYAL WORCESTER PORCELAIN, SEVERN STREET, WORCESTER, WORCESTERSHIRE WR1 2NE
☎ (01905) 23221. OPEN 9 - 5.30 MON - SAT, 11 - 5 SUN.
Factory Shop • *Household*

An extensive range of Dartington Crystal seconds at greatly reduced prices as well as some perfect crystal at full price. Range includes wine suites, sherry glasses, tankards, decanters, rippled glass, fruit and salad bowls.

DESIGNER DEPOT
UNIT 5, CHARLES HOUSE, CHARLES STREET, WORCESTER,
WORCESTERSHIRE WR1 2AQ
☎ (01905) 611568. OPEN 9 - 5.30 MON - SAT.
Permanent Discount Outlet • *Womenswear Only*
At Designer Depot, you'll find one of the best selections of top quality branded fashions for women anywhere with amazing discounts of up to 50% off the normal retail price. With new stock arriving weekly, you'll always find something special here.

DIRECT SPECS LTD
23 ANGEL PLACE, WORCESTER, WORCESTERSHIRE WR1 3QN
☎ (01905) 729313 . OPEN 9 - 5 MON - SAT.
Permanent Discount Outlet • *Womenswear & Menswear*
Spectacles and sunglasses at prices which the owner claims beat any competitor's. Most designer names are stocked at one time or another, though if you have a favourite, check first. Bring along your prescription and glasses will be found to suit. No eye tests conducted.

DUNELM MILL SHOPS LTD
F17 CROWNGATE SHOPPING CENTRE, FRIARY WALK, WORCESTER,
WORCESTERSHIRE WR1 3LE
☎ (01905) 611159. OPEN 9 - 5 MON - SAT.
Permanent Discount Outlet • *Household*
Part of a chain of shops based in the Midlands selling brand-name and chainstore curtains, masses of bedlinen, towels, wickerware, pictures and frames, all at competitive prices.

EVESHAM COUNTRY PARK
COUNTRY PARK MANAGEMENT, EVESHAM, AT THE NORTHERN END OF THE EVESHAM BY-PASS AT ITS JUNCTION WITH THE STRATFORD ROAD
☎ (01386) 41661
SHOPPING & GARDEN CENTRE
☎ (01386) 761888. OPEN 9 - 6 MON - SAT (WINTER 5.30), 10.30 - 4.30 SUN.
APPLE BARN RESTAURANT
☎ (01386) 761333
VALE WILDLIFE VISITOR CENTRE
☎ (01386) 443348
COARSE FISHING/GOTTFRIED
☎ (0973) 147323
Factory Shopping Village • *Womenswear & Menswear* • *Children*
Food and Leisure • *Sportswear & Equipment* • *Household*
Courtyard shops and garden centre providing a wide variety of goods at bargain prices. Designer and brand name men's and women's fashions from

Leading Labels, leisurewear from Cotton Traders, co-ordinated soft furnishings, bedlinen and duvets from Ponden Mill, dried fuits and nuts and packaged herbs from Julien Graves, an extensive range of books from The Book Depot, quality plants, colourful pots, garden equipment, pets and fish and Luggage and Bags sells a range of quality branded luggage and travel goods at great prices. Also restaurant, wildlife centre and coarse fishing on the River Avon for a real country day out.

EXCHANGE & SMART
45 NEW STREET, WORCESTER, WORCESTERSHIRE WR1 2DL
☎ (01905) 611522. OPEN 10 - 4.30 MON - FRI, 10 - 5 SAT.
Dress Agency • *Womenswear Only*

Lovely, relaxed shopping with a huge amount of stock on two floors of excellent quality clothing, bags and shoes. The stock includes designer labels such as Nicole Farhi, MaxMara, Armani, and high street labels such as Marks & Spencer, Jaeger and Principles.

G R PRATLEY & SONS
THE SHAMBLES, WORCESTER WR1 2RG
☎ (01905) 22678/28642. FAX: 745031. OPEN 9 - 5.30 MON - SAT, CLOSES AT 1 ON THUR.
Permanent Discount Outlet • *Household*

A family business which specialises in bone china and earthenware, selling famous designer names at 15% lower than normal retail prices. Manufacturers include Royal Worcester, Spode, Royal Doulton, Wedgwood, Johnsons and many others, and individual pieces as well as sets can be bought. Good country furniture, tribal rugs and carpet specialists.

HOLLOWAYS
LOWER COURT, SUCKLEY, WORCESTERSHIRE WR6 5DE
☎ (01886) 884665. WEBSITE: www.holloways.co.uk OPEN 9 - 5 MON - SAT.
Architectural Salvage • *DIY/Renovation*

Conservatory furniture specialists, with perhaps the best range of furniture and garden furniture in the country. They also sell antique and reproduction garden statuary, urns, troughs, gates, old and new Coalbrookdale benches, cider mills, staddle stones. The conservatory furniture includes a wide selection of rattan, English willow, metal and Lloyd loom. Amongst the huge choice they have an exclusive range of rattan with elegant sofas, chairs and dining furniture with driftwood-coloured frames, leather bindings and woven banana fibre panels. The cushions can be covered in any fabric. There is also more rustic casual furniture made from unpeeled woven rattan which is waxed to a deep patina and traditional English willow with deep feather cushions. They also sell Plantation teak garden furniture - steamer chairs, folding chairs, loungers, benches, rectangular and round tables - plus a good selection of other hardwood and cast-aluminium furniture. Among the antique and reproduction garden items are antique stone benches, sundials, urns and figures, 19th century Coalbrookdale cast iron seats and farm artefacts such as stone troughs, staddle stones and cider mills. Other ornaments like stone vases, urns, birdbaths and statues, are made from reconstituted limestone with a surface texture like Portland stone and coloured to resemble Portland, Bath or Cotswold stone or terracotta. This stone soon develops a covering of moss and lichen to look genuinely old. Original Coalbrookdale benches cost from £1,250, repro ones from £300; antique cider mills from £1,200.

LUGGAGE & BAGS
EVESHAM COUNTRY PARK SHOPPING AND GARDEN CENTRE,
EVESHAM, WORCESTERSHIRE WR11
☎ (01386) 47393. OPEN 9 - 6 MON - SAT, 10.30 - 4.30 SUN.
Factory Shop in a Factory Shopping Village • *Food and Leisure*
Luggage and travel-related products and executive cases, handbags, umbrellas from leading brands such as Samsonite, Desley, Head, Taurus and GlobeTrotter. Each product is offered at a substantially reduced price compared to those found on the high street due to being production over-runs, discontinued ranges or colours and last season's products. Discounts range from 30%-75% off high street prices.

NIPPERS
ORCHARD COTTAGE FARM, CROOME ROAD, DEFFORD, WORCESTER
WORCESTERSHIRE WR8 9AS
☎ (01386) 750888. FAX (01386) 750333. E-MAIL: worcester@nippers.co.uk
WEBSITE: www.nippers.co.uk OPENING HOURS VARY SO PHONE FIRST.
Permanent Discount Outlet • *Children*
Nippers, the nursery equipment and toy specialists, operate from previously redundant buildings in rural areas around the country. They offer easy parking, no queues and personal service. This is on top of competitive prices on prams, cots, pushchairs, car seats, outdoor play equipment and toys, some of which are new, some seconds or secondhand and some ends of lines. Prices are low because they avoid the high overheads of traditional retail outlets and also because the successful growth of a number of branches means they can now buy in bulk and negotiate good deals. Customers are invited to try out the merchandise while the children look at the animals, mostly sheep, chicken and pigs. Also offers many brand leaders at discount, including Mamas & Papas, Cosatto, Britax, Maclaren and Bebe Confort, plus Fisher-Price and Little Tikes. You can try out the car seats in your car and there is usually a pram/pushchair repair service on site.

PONDEN MILL
ROYAL WORCESTER FACTORY SHOP, SEVERN STREET, WORCESTER, WORCESTERSHIRE WR1 2NE
☎ (01905) 726708. OPEN 9 - 5.30 MON - SAT, 11 - 5 SUN.
Factory Shop • *Household*
Bedlinen, sheets, valances, duvet covers, pillowcases, duvets, eiderdowns, towels and bath mats from leading brands all at discount prices. Also nursery bedding, lampshades and cushions, bean bags and sleeping bags.

PONDEN MILL LINENS
EVESHAM COUNTRY PARK, EVESHAM, WORCESTERSHIRE WR11 4TP
☎ (01386) 47407. OPEN 9 - 6 MON - SAT, 10.30 - 4.30 SUN.
Factory Shop in a Factory Shopping Village • *Household*
Famous branded products at direct from the mill prices. A fabulous assortment of towels, duvets, pillows, throws, bedspreads, up-to-the-minute coordinated bed linen, from Crown, Coloroll, Jeff Banks Ports-of-Call, to name but a few. Something for every room in the house.

POSTERITY ARCHITECTURAL ANTIQUES
UNDERHILL FARM, LITTLE MALVERN, WORCESTERSHIRE WR14 4JN
☎ (01684) 541254. OPEN 9 - 5 MON - SAT.
Architectural Salvage • *DIY/Renovation*
Sells all types of old building materials and artefacts, internal fittings, bathrooms, fireplaces, kitchen church pews, stained glass, doors, lighting, garden urns, benches, mouldings and radiators. Whether it's a lamp post for the garden, a butler's sink, a 17th century doorway or a pile of handmade bricks, you're bound to find what you're looking for here.

ROYAL WORCESTER PORCELAIN
SEVERN STREET, WORCESTER, WORCESTERSHIRE WR1 2NE
☎ (01905) 23221. OPEN 9 - 5.30 MON - SAT, 11 - 5 SUN. MAIL ORDER.
Factory Shop • *Household*
The Victorian buildings of Royal Worcester's Visitor Centre lead into the heart of a world famous porcelain industry that was founded in 1751. Royal Worcester's factory shops carry an extensive range of quality bone china tableware, porcelain oven-to-tableware, giftware and figurines. The factory seconds shop offers quality seconds ware at greatly reduced prices. Visitors can also shop in Wigornia Court where a myriad of home accessories and factory outlets selling cutlery, crystal, candles, linen, kitchen utensils, rugs and giftware can be found. Parking and disabled facilities available.

STUDIO
11 ABBEY ROAD, MALVERN, WORCESTERSHIRE WR14 3ES
☎ (01684) 576253. OPEN 9 - 5.30 MON - SAT.
Permanent Discount Outlet • *Womenswear Only*
Finest designer clothes from the Continent (mostly Germany) at discounts of

50%. The company's team of buyers search out and secure considerable discounts on top European name ranges which include both this season's stock and next. The names are well-known but they cannot be divulged here - suffice it to say that they are excellent labels. All stock is perfect, and the vast range covers from casual wear to special occasion outfits.

THE CURTAIN RACK
25 HIGH STREET, PERSHORE, WORCESTERSHIRE WR10 1AA
☎ (01386) 556105. OPEN 10 - 5 MON - FRI, 9.30 - 5.30 SAT.
Secondhand shops • *Furniture/Soft Furnishings*
Three large showrooms specialising in good quality secondhand curtains, readymades and fabrics. The curtains vary from some cheap and cheerful through to lined curtains, some with matching valances, cushion covers etc. One section of the shop has a large variety of brocades and damask fabrics sold by the metre or they tailor at very competitive prices. They also offer a choice of six companies for a selection of top quality ready-made lined curtains at discounted prices, all of which have optional accessories. There is also a large showroom, packed with sumptuous designer curtains, some interlined, some with swags, tails, tiebacks and others beautifully fringed. They can cater for extremely large windows, all at unbeatable prices.

THE FACTORY SHOP LTD
NEW ROAD, PERSHORE, WORCESTERSHIRE WR10 1BY
☎ (01386) 556467. OPEN 9 - 5 MON - FRI, 9 - 5.30 SAT, 10.30 - 4.30 SUN.
Factory Shop • *Womenswear & Menswear* • *Children*
Household • *Furniture/Soft Furnishings*
Wide range on sale includes men's, ladies and children's clothing and footwear; household textiles, toiletries, hardware, luggage, lighting and bedding, most of which are chainstore and high street brands at discounts of approximately 30%-50%. There are weekly deliveries and brands include many of the major stars such as Adidas, Nike, Joe Bloggs and Brabantia, to name just four. There are also kitchen and furniture displays and a line of Cape Country furniture on sale. Ranges are continually changing and few factory shops offer such a variety under one roof. Excellent tea rooms offer hot and cold freshly-prepared homemade food and drinks and has its own free car park.

THE WEAVERS SHOP
DUKE PLACE, KIDDERMINSTER, WORCESTERSHIRE DY10 9HB
☎ (01562) 820680/820030 FAX. OPEN 9 - 5 MON - FRI, 9 - 12.30 SAT.
Factory Shop • *Furniture/Soft Furnishings* • *Household*
Offers a large selection of tufted and Axminster plain and patterned carpets from the factory. Also now has a wide collection of natural floor coverings and rugs at a considerable discount off high street prices. All goods sold here are returns, discontinued, contract overmakes, ends or slight seconds and therefore represent excellent value for money. Fitters can be suggested and delivery arranged.

TOP DRAWER
THE OLD MALT HOUSE, CHADDESLEY CORBETT,
WORCESTERSHIRE DY10 4FD
☎ (01562) 777808. OPEN 10 - 4 TUE - FRI, 10 - 1 SAT.
Dress Agency • *Womenswear Only*
Upmarket dress agency whose labels include Workers for Freedom, Amanda Wakeley, Bed de Lisi, MaxMara, Betty Jackson, Paul Costelloe, Nicole Farhi. Situated in a very pretty village in a delightful old building. Also sell accessories, shoes, hats, scarves, jewellery etc.

TP ACTIVITY TOYS FACTORY SHOP
SEVERN ROAD, STOURPORT-ON-SEVERN, WORCESTERSHIRE DY13 9EX
☎ (01299) 872872. 9 - 5 MON - FRI, 9 - 4.30 SAT.
Factory Shop • *Children*
A full range of outdoor and indoor play equipment from swings and climbing frames to sand trays, some of which are discounted at certain times of the year as they are used as display items and aren't as pristine. There is usually one big factory site sale every year as well, which is well worth going to. This usually takes place in April. Discounts for seconds are 20% on outdoor items only. Site shop has Lego, Playmobil and Brio at competitive prices.

UNITED FOOTWEAR
NEW ROAD, KIDDERMINSTER, WORCESTERSHIRE
☎ (01562) 744022. OPEN 9 - 6 MON - SAT, 8 ON THUR, 9 - 1 SUN.
OPEN 9 - 5.30 MON - SAT, 10 - 4 SUN.
☎ (01905) 27738. OPEN 9 - 5.30 MON - SAT, 10 - 4 SUN.
Permanent Discount Outlet • *Womenswear & Menswear*
Children • *Household*
Shoes for all the family as well as clothes, handbags, sports shoes, boots, giftware and household goods, all at discounted prices. Famous brands including Clarks, K Shoes and Elmdale. Part of a national chain.

Yorkshire

ADIDAS
MCARTHURGLEN OUTLET VILLAGE, ST NICHOLAS AVENUE, FULFORD, JUNCTION OF A19 AND A64, YORK, NORTH YORKSHIRE YO19 4TA
☎ (01904) 655 811. OPEN 10 - 6 MON - WED, FRI, SAT, 10 - 8 THUR, 11 - 5 SUN.
Factory Shop in a Factory Shopping Village • *Womenswear & Menswear*
Sportswear & Equipmentntnd of season products at 30% to 70% off RRP. Footwear and accessories such as bags, shinpads etc. Saloman outdoor wear and the Adidas golf range also stocked. Regular promotions run throughout the year.

ALADDIN'S CAVE
19 QUEEN'S ARCADE, LEEDS, WEST YORKSHIRE LS1 6LF
☎ (0113) 245 7903. OPEN 10 - 5 MON - SAT.
Dress Agency • *Womenswear Only*
Two-storey shop with a working jeweller on the premises (jewellery repaired in an hour) and an array of antique jewellery, silver, and teddy bears on the ground floor.

ALEXON SALE SHOP
HORNSEA FREEPORT SHOPPING VILLAGE, HORNSEA,
EAST YORKSHIRE HU18 1UJ
☎ (01964) 535441. OPEN 9.30 - 6 SEVEN DAYS A WEEK.
10-14 BRIDGEGATE, ROTHERHAM, SOUTH YORKSHIRE S60 1PQ
☎ (01709) 382491. OPEN 9 - 5.30 MON - SAT.
Permanent Discount Outlet • *Womenswear Only*
Alexon and Eastex from last season at 40% less than the original price; during sale time in January and June, the reductions are 70%. Stock includes separates, skirts, jackets, blouses; there is no underwear or night clothes. The Hornsea shop also sells the Dash and Calico ranges.

ALLDERS AT HOME
2 BRIDGE ROAD, KIRKSTALL, LEEDS, WEST YORKSHIRE LS5 3BL
☎ (0113) 230 5800. OPEN 10 - 5.30 MON - WED, 10 - 8 THUR, FRI, 9.30 - 5.30 SAT, 10.30 - 4.30 SUN.
Permanent Discount Outlet • *Womenswear & Menswear* • *Children*
The fashion centre within the Allders department store is a clearance outlet for Allders stores selling men's, ladies and children's reduced stock. Famous names include Morgan, Benetton, Planet, Precis, Windsmoor, Frank Usher, Jumper, Dannimac, Fenn Wright & Manson, French Connection, Gabicci, O'Neil, Matinique, YSL, Shoe Studio. Samples are also available at competitive prices twice a year from Gerry Webber, Taifun, She, Ravens, Sigrid Olsen, Erfo and Samoon. The Sports Department sells a mix of reduced and full price stock.

ANDY THORNTON ARCHITECTURAL ANTIQUES LTD
VICTORIA MILLS, STAINLAND ROAD, GREETLAND, HALIFAX,
WEST YORKSHIRE HX4 8AD
☎ (01422) 377314. OPEN 8.30 - 5.30 MON - FRI, 9 - 5 SAT, 10 - 4.30 SUN.
Architectural Salvage • *DIY/Renovation*
Doors, fireplaces, panelled rooms, church interiors, radiators, balustrades, chandeliers, stained glass, marble, pews and light-fittings all situated in an enormous converted mill. If you can't find the original piece you want, they will make you a reproduction. One of the five floors is devoted to reproductions with a huge range of Tiffany lamps. The top floor houses Americana and outside are plenty of garden urns, statuary and cast-iron gates.

ANTA SCOTLAND LTD,
12 SWINEGATE, YORK, NORTH YORKSHIRE
☎ (01904) 670 900. E-MAIL: sales@anta.co.uk WEBSITE: www.anta.co.uk
OPEN 9.30 - 5.30 MON - SAT, 12 - 4 SUN. ALSO MAIL ORDER.
Factory Shop • *Furniture/Soft Furnishings*
Anta design everything on site, using tartan check designs in traditional Scottish landscape colours and there are usually seconds and ends of lines available at discounted prices. There are jazzy check woollen rugs, carpets, fabrics, throws, blankets and ceramics (also made on site) on sale at greatly discounted prices. Mail order is not at discount prices.

ARKWRIGHTS MILL
HORNSEA FREEPORT, ROLSTON ROAD, HORNSEA,
EAST YORKSHIRE HU18 1PG
☎ (01964) 535040. OPEN 9.30 - 6 MON - SAT, 11 - 5 SUN.
Factory Shop • *Womenswear & Menswear*
Factory discount outlet selling a wide range of brandnames in men's and women's clothing.

BABY HIRE
25 FARLEA DRIVE, ECCLESHILL, BRADFORD, WEST YORKSHIRE BD2 3RJ
☎ (01274) 642140.
Hire Shop • *Children*
Part of the Baby Equipment Hirers Association (BEHA), which has more than 100 members countrywide. A range of equipment can be hired from high chairs, cots and travel cots to baby car seats and buggies. Some members also hire out party equipment including child-sized tables and chairs. BEHA run an advice line which will try and answer any queries you have regarding hiring services for children. Phone the Babyline on 0831 310355 for your nearest BEHA shop.

BECOMING MATERNITY WEAR
11 THE CRESCENT, RIPON, NORTH YORKSHIRE HG4 2JB
☎ (01765) 601895. BY APPOINTMENT ONLY.
Hire Shop • *Womenswear Only*
One of a growing chain of home-based businesses hiring out practical, stylish and affordable outfits for expectant mothers for home, work or play. Separates cost from £10 to hire, with ballgowns at £50. Also offers made to order business wear. There are other outlets in Barnsley, Brentwood, Burnley, Carlisle, London and Saffron Walden. Phone the above number for further details.

BIG L FACTORY OUTLET
THE YORKSHIRE OUTLET, WHITE ROSE WAY, DONCASTER,
SOUTH YORKSHIRE DN4 5JH
☎ (01302) 367043. OPEN 10 - 6 MON - SAT, 11 - 5 SUN.
Factory Shop in a Factory Shopping Village • *Womenswear & Menswear*
Men's and women's Levi jeans, jackets, cord and Sherpa fleece jackets, T-shirts and shirts but no children's, all at discount prices.

BIRTHDAYS
UNIT 25, THE YORKSHIRE OUTLET, WHITE ROSE WAY, DONCASTER,
SOUTH YORKSHIRE DN4 5JY
☎ (01302) 325803. OPEN 10 - 6 MON - SAT, 11 - 5 SUN.
Factory Shopping Village • *Household*
Cards, notelets, stationery sets, colouring books, soft toys, photo albums, picture frames, gifts, giftwrap, tissue paper, party packs, Christmas crackers, string puppets, fairy lights all at discounts of up to 30%. Some are special purchases, some seconds.

BLACK & DECKER
THE YORKSHIRE OUTLET, WHITE ROSE WAY, DONCASTER,
SOUTH YORKSHIRE DN4 5JH
☎ (01302) 344488. OPEN 10 - 6 MON - SAT, 11 - 5 SUN.
Factory Shop in a Factory Shopping Village • *DIY/Renovation*
Reconditioned tools and acccessories from the famous Black & Decker range, all with full manufacturer's warranty. Often, stock consists of goods returned from the shops because of damaged packaging or are part of a line which is being discontinued. Lots of seasonal special offers.

BRETT HARRIS LTD
WATERLOO MILLS, HOWDEN ROAD, SILSDEN, YORKSHIRE BD20 OHA
☎ (01535) 654479. HOLDS OCCASIONAL FACTORY SALES.
Factory Shop • *Sportswear & Equipment*
Manufacturers of sleeping bags, cold weather clothing, camping accessories, compression sacks and outdoor accessories, most of which are exported, they sell discontinued lines, demo models and slight seconds at occasional sales. These sales, which are usually held on Saturday mornings, offer stock discounted by up to 50%. Phone for the date of their next sale.

BRITISH MOHAIR SPINNERS
LOWER HOLME MILLS, SHIPLEY, WEST YORKSHIRE BD17 7EU
☎ (01274) 583111. OPEN 9 - 4 MON - FRI.
Factory Shop • *Womenswear & Menswear*
Hand knitting yarns in mohair, British wool, arrans, as well as a small selection of quality knitwear. Knitting service allows you to choose the yarn and have an item knitted up to your pattern.

BROOKS FACTORY OUTLET STORES
SOUTH LANE, ELLAND, NEAR HALIFAX, WEST YORKSHIRE HX5 OHQ
☎ (01422) 377337. OPEN 9.30 - 5.30 MON - SAT, 11 - 5 SUN.
BUYWELL RETAIL PARK, THORP ARCH, WETHERBY,
NORTH YORKSHIRE LS23 7BJ
☎ (01937) 541895. OPEN 9.30 - 5.30 MON - SAT, 11 - 5 SUN.

Permanent Discount Outlet • *Womenswear & Menswear* • *Household Children* • *Furniture/Soft Furnishings* • *Food and Leisure Sportswear & Equipment*

Walk through the store and you can't fail to find a bargain. New stock arrives daily from well-known names such as Nike, Reebok, Antler, Gabicci, Gossard, Tommy Hilfiger and Ralph Lauren. Apart from clothes, they sell sportswear, linens, lingerie, shoes, accessories, luggge, towels, co-ordinated bed linen, household textiles, duvets, pillows and lots more from names such as Vantona, Hamilton McBride, Helena Springfield, Broomhill, Monogram, Chortex, Zorbit and Christy. Everything under one roof at up to 50% off high street prices. The Elland store has a coffee shop.

BUMPSADAISY MATERNITY STYLE
14 BANK STREET, WETHERBY, LEEDS, WEST YORKSHIRE LS22 6NQ
☎ (01937) 580641. WEBSITE: www.bumpsadaisy.co.uk
OPEN 9.30 - 5.30 MON - SAT, 9.30 - 1 WED.

Hire Shop • *Womenswear Only*

Franchised shops and home-based branches with large range of specialist maternity wear, from wedding outfits to ball gowns, to hire and to buy. Hire costs range from £30 to £100 for special occasion wear. To buy are lots of casual and business wear in sizes 8 - 18. For example, skirts £20-£70; dresses £40-£100. Also four branches run by young mums from their homes, specialising in hiring but also stocking a small retail range (Camberley, Edgbaston, Exeter and Southampton). Phone 0208-789 0329 for details.

BURBERRY
WOODROW UNIVERSAL, JUNCTION MILLS, CROSS HILLS,
NEAR KEIGHLEY, WEST YORKSHIRE BD20 7SE
☎ (01535) 631991. OPEN 10 - 4 MON - SAT.
CORONATION MILLS, ALBION STREET, CASTLEFORD, WEST YORKSHIRE
☎ (01977) 554411. OPEN 10 - 4.30 MON - FRI, 9.30 - 3 SAT.
MIDLAND ROAD, ROYSTON, NEAR BARNSLEY, SOUTH YORKSHIRE
☎ (01226) 728030. OPEN 10 - 4.30 MON - FRI, 9.30 - 3.30 SAT,
ONCE A MONTH ON SUNS.
OLD MARKET TAVERN, MARKET PLACE, WHITBY, NORTH YORKSHIRE
☎ (01947) 606161. OPEN 9.30 - 4.30 MON - SAT, 11 - 4 SUN.
CHESHIRE, OAKS OUTLET VILLAGE, KINSEY ROAD, NEAR ELLESMERE
PORT, SOUTH WIRRAL L65 9JJ
☎ (0151) 357 3203. OPEN 10 - 6 MON - SAT, UNTIL 8 ON THUR,
11 - 5 SUN.

Factory Shop • *Womenswear & Menswear* • *Children*

These Burberry factory shops sell seconds and overmakes of the famous name raincoats and duffle coats as well as accessories such as the distinctive umbrellas, scarves and handbags. They also sell children's duffle coats, knitwear and shirts, as well as some of the Burberry range of food: jams, biscuits, tea and chocolate. All carry the Burberry label and discounts are about one third off the normal retail price.

BURMATEX LTD
VICTORIA MILLS, THE GREEN, OSSETT, WEST YORKSHIRE WF5 OAN
☎ (01924) 276 333. OPEN 9.30 - 4 MON - FRI. 8 - 11.45 SAT.
Factory Shop • *Furniture/Soft Furnishings*

A factory shop selling B quality carpet tiles at prices that are significantly less than high street prices and which range from £1.65 to £2.

BYWORTH FABRIC WAREHOUSE
36 CEMETERY ROAD, 4 LANE ENDS, BRADFORD,
WEST YORKSHIRE BD8 9RY
☎ (01274) 481800. OPEN 9 - 5 MON - SAT, 10 - 4 SUN.
Permanent Discount Outlet • *Furniture/Soft Furnishings*

Stocks over 6,000 rolls of curtain and furnishing fabrics in its 14,000 sq ft outlet, including muslins, linings and all accessories - tracks, poles and brassware. Most are department store brands, but at warehouse prices. Soft furnishing fabric costs from £1.99 a metre, lining from £1.99; upholstery fabrics from £4.99 a metre. There is free on-site parking and easy access for the disabled. Professional staff are on hand with advice.

CARD & GIFT
DAWSON LANE, DUDLEY HILL, BRADFORD,
WEST YORKSHIRE BD4 6HW
☎ (01274) 689399. OPEN 10 - 5.30 MON - FRI, 10 - 5 SAT.
Factory Shop • *Household*

Wedding novelties, cards, gift wrap, toys, soft toys, banners, balloons, badges, candle sticks, stationery, all of which is perfect stock at reduced prices.

CATALOGUE BARGAIN SHOP
BOOTHFERRY ROAD, GOOLE, EAST YORKSHIRE DN14 6BB
☎ (01405) 765138. OPEN 9 - 8 MON - WED, SAT, 9 - 9 THUR, FRI,
10 - 4 SUN.
28 NEW BRIGGATE, BRIGGATE, LEEDS, WEST YORKSHIRE LS1 6NU
☎ (0113) 243 6425. OPEN 9 - 5.30 MON - SAT, 11 - 5 SUN.
57-59 MARKET PLACE, HECKMONDWIKE, WEST YORKSHIRE WF16 OEZ
☎ (01924) 402674. OPEN 9 - 5.30 MON - SAT, 10 - 4 SUN.
42 JOHN WILLIAM STREET, HUDDERSFIELD,
WEST YORKSHIRE HD1 1ER
☎ (01484) 535112. OPEN 9 - 5.30 MON - SAT, 10.30 - 4.30 SUN.

20 ST THOMAS STREET, SCARBOROUGH YO11 1DR
☎ (01723) 371733. OPEN 9 - 5.30 MON - SAT, 10.30 - 4.30 SUN.
51 ACKLAM ROAD, MIDDLESBROUGH, YORKSHIRE TS5 5HA
☎ (01642) 825925. OPEN 9 - 5 MON - SAT, 10.30 - 4.30 SUN.
Permanent Discount Outlet • *Womenswear & Menswear
Children* • *Household* • *Electrical Equipment*
Catalogue Bargain Shop is a growing national chain of stores which obtains the majority of its goods from mail order giants Great Universal and Kays, and offers a range of clothing for all the family, a wide selection of shoes, bed linen, household goods, electrical equipment and hundreds of other catalogue items at very competitive prices. The merchandise consists of ends of ranges and previous season's stock for which there is no longer storage space when the catalogues change.

CHAPEL HOUSE FIREPLACES
ST GEORGE'S ROAD, SCHOLES, HOLMFIRTH, HUDDERSFIELD,
WEST YORKSHIRE HD7 1UH
☎ (01484) 682275. OPEN TUE - SAT BY APPOINTMENT ONLY.
Architectural Salvage • *DIY/Renovation*
Period fireplaces with correct grates, baskets and inserts, including French fireplaces dating from 1750-1910.

CHARLES CLINKARD
FREEPORT CASTLEFORD DESIGNER OUTLET VILLAGE, CARRWOOD
ROAD, GLASSHOUGHTON, WEST YORKSHIRE WF10 4SB
☎ (01977) 515391. OPEN 10 - 8 MON - FRI, 10 - 6 SAT, 11 - 4 SUN.
Factory Shop in a Factory Shopping Village • *Children
Womenswear & Menswear*
Footwear for the family at discounts of between 20% and 50%. Labels on sale here include Rockport, Loake, Camel, Bally, Church's, Ecco, Gabor, Rohde, Van-Dal, Kickers, Clarks, Dr Martens, K Shoes, Lotus and Renata. The telephone number given here is for the centre, not the shop.

CLARKS FACTORY SHOP
THE YORKSHIRE OUTLET, WHITE ROSE WAY, DONCASTER,
SOUTH YORKSHIRE DN4 5JH
☎ (01302) 322663. OPEN 10 - 6 MON - SAT, 11 - 5 SUN.
Factory Shop in a Factory Shopping Village
Womenswear & Menswear • *Children* • *Sportswear & Equipment*
Clarks International operate a chain of factory shops nationally which specialise in selling discontinued lines and slight sub-standards for men, women and children from Clarks, K Shoes and other famous brands. These shops trade under the name of Crockers, K Shoes Factory shop or Clarks Factory Shop and while not all are physically attached to a shoe factory, these shops are treated as factory shops by the company. Customers can expect to find an

extensive range of quality shoes, sandals, walking boots, slippers, trainers, handbags, accessories and gifts, while their major outlets such as here also offer luggage, sports clothing, sports equipment and outdoor clothing. Brands stocked include Clarks, K Shoes, Springer, CICA, Hi-Tec, Puma, Mercury, Dr Martens, Nike, LA Gear, Fila, Mizuno, Slazenger, Weider, Antler and Carlton, although not all are sold in every outlet. Discounts are from 30% to 60% off the normal high street price for perfect stock. This shop also incorporates Sports Factory and Baggage Factory.

CLOVER LEAF

THE YORKSHIRE OUTLET, ADDRESS AND OPENING HOURS AS BEFORE.
☎ (01302) 367021.
Factory Shop in a Factory Shopping Village • *Household*
Sells a good range of kitchen and oven to tableware, place mats, teapot stands, teabag tidies, chopping bords, ceramic pottery, beech trays, kitchen clocks and coasters. There are usually about 48 different designs of table mat in stock at any one time. Seconds and discontinued lines are sold here at reduced prices.

COLDSPRING MILL

HAWORTH ROAD, CULLINGWORTH, BRADFORD, (NEAR HAWORTH), WEST YORKSHIRE BD13 5EE
☎ (01535) 275646. OPEN 10 - 4 SEVEN DAYS A WEEK.
Factory Shop • *Womenswear Only* • *Food and Leisure*
Sells high quality branded knitting wool and mohair from local manufacturers at vastly discounted prices. As the yarns come direct from the spinner, Coldspring always has the latest shades. Also Yorkshire tweed skirt lengths at very good prices and fleeces from £9.99. There are bargain packs of knitting wools and shoppers receive 10 free patterns of their choice with their purchase. Examples of prices include 1,000 grams of Arran wool, £7.99; skirt lengths, £7.99. Situated in Emily Bronte country, it makes a marvellous day out as you drive over the bleak heights near Haworth. There is a tea room and plenty of parking. Just ten minutes away is the Denholme Velvets Factory Shop with Ponden Mill nearby, too.

CONVERSE EMEA LTD

THE YORKSHIRE OUTLET, ADDRESS AND OPENING HOURS AS BEFORE.
☎ (01302) 367088.
Factory Shop in a Factory Shopping Village • *Womenswear & Menswear*
Founded in 1908, Converse is the largest manufacturer of sports footwear in the U.S. They are a leading designer, manufacturer and marketer of high quality athletic footwear and clothing, specialising in Baseball, Action Sports and Athletic Originals. Stock is sold with a minimum discount of 25% for ends of lines and discounted ranges. For example, Canvas All Star Chuck Taylor, £19.99, reduced from £29.99.

COSALT INTERNATIONAL LTD
UNIT 12, HEADWAY BUSINESS PARK, DENBY DALE ROAD, WAKEFIELD,
WEST YORKSHIRE WF2 7AZ
☎ (01924) 880770 . OPEN 8.30 - 5 MON - FRI.
Permanent Discount Outlet • *Womenswear & Menswear*
The company specialises in workwear, safety clothing and marine wear but some of the merchandise is eminently wearable for everyday and is sold at very reasonable prices. This particular outlet specialises in ropes, and ratchet straps. VAT has to be added to prices. There are catalogues available for you to order from if what you want isn't in stock. They also provide marine safety and life-raft servicing.

COTTON TRADERS
MCARTHURGLEN DESIGNER VILLAGE, OLD HABURN HOSPITAL SITE,
FULFORD, YORK, NORTH YORKSHIRE Y01 4RE
☎ (01904) 625490. OPEN 10 - 6 MON - SAT, TILL 8 THUR, 11 - 5 SUN.
Factory Shop in a Factory Shopping Village • *Womenswear & Menswear*
Sells own label leisurewear for men, women and children.

CREAM
27 HALIFAX ROAD, HIPPERHOLME, HALIFAX,
WEST YORKSHIRE HX3 8HQ
☎ (01422) 205080. OPEN 9 - 5.30 MON - SAT.
Dress Agency • *Womenswear & Menswear*
Three-storey shop selling a large selection of constantly changing stock: ladies daywear, evening wear, accessories and menswear. Labels on sale include Moschino, Frank Usher, Rifat Ozbek and Betty Barclay. Menswear includes labels such as Armani and Boss.

CURTAIN TRANSFER
THE OLD STABLE, BACK TEWIT WELL ROAD, OFF SOUTH DRIVE,
HARROGATE, NORTH YORKSHIRE HG2 8JF
☎ (01423) 505520. WEBSITE: www.curtain-transfer.com
OPEN 10 - 6 TUE - SAT, WED BY APPOINTMENT.
Secondhand shops • *Furniture/Soft Furnishings*
Curtain Transfer opened in Harrogate in 1992. The showroom in a converted stable in a courtyard opposite the owner's own home is a treasure trove of secondhand curtains, blinds, bedcovers and all kinds of upmarket furnishing accessories - pictures, lamps and lampshades, cushions and rugs. Goods are taken in on sale-or-return agency terms. There is always a good selection of long lined or interlined curtains - from Monkwell, Sanderson and G P & J Baker, as well as current designer names. Buyers can take goods home overnight on approval. Parking is in the courtyard and children are welcome. To get there from Leeds going towards the town centre, take a right at St George's Roundabout on South Drive, over Tewit Well Road, left by railway

bridge. From the by-pass, go into Harrogate to the Empress roundabout, turn left on York Place, left again on Stray Rein to just over the railway bridge on the right.

DALESOX
6 SWADFORD STREET, SKIPTON, YORKSHIRE BD23 1JA
☎ (01756) 796509. OPEN 9 - 5 SEVEN DAYS A WEEK.
Factory Shop • *Womenswear & Menswear* • *Children*
Based in Skipton's main shopping area, Dalesox sells quality hosiery and accessories. Most are perfect ladies, men's and children's socks made for the best high street chainstores and cost about £1-£2.99 a pair, normal retail price up to £4.99. There is lots of design choice from Disney character socks to Christmas character socks. There are also ties, ski socks made for famous department stores, unusual design Swedish polyester ties, knickers, boxer shorts, pyjamas and nightshirts. Most of the stock is bought in from other manufacturers, cutting out the middleman.

DALESWEAR FACTORY OUTLET
LAUNDRY LANE, INGLETON, YORKSHIRE LA6 3DF
☎ (015242) 42373. OPEN 9 - 5 MON - SAT, 9.30 - 5 SUN.
Factory Shop • *Womenswear & Menswear* • *Children*
Sportswear & Equipment
Manufacturer of fleeces and waterproofs using Polartec. They sell breathable waterproof trousers and jackets and a vast range of fleece pullovers and tops. Also a small selection of Rohan socks and hats. There are two shops in Ingleton, here and in the high street.

DAMART
BOWLING GREEN MILLS, BINGLEY, WEST YORKSHIRE BD16 4BH
☎ (01274) 567152. OPEN 9.30 - 5 MON - SAT.
HORNSEA FREEPORT SHOPPING VILLAGE, HORNSEA,
EAST YORKSHIRE
☎ (01964) 536581. OPEN 10 - 5 MON - SAT, 10 - 6 SUN.
Factory Shop • *Womenswear & Menswear*
Damart underwear and merchandise - anything from tights, socks and gloves to dresses, coats, cardigans and jumpers - some of which is current stock sold at full price, some discontinued and ends of lines sold at discount. There several shops selling some discounted stock from the Damart range, known as Damart Extra.

DARTINGTON CRYSTAL
FREEPORT VILLAGE, CARRWOOD ROAD, GLASSHOUGHTON,
CASTLEFORD, WEST YORKSHIRE WF10 4SB
☎ (01977) 519617. OPEN
HORNSEA FREEPORT ROLSTON ROAD, HORNSEA,
EAST YORKSHIRE HU18 1UT
☎ (01964) 536201. OPEN 9.30 AT BATLEY, BRADFORD ROAD WF17 5LZ
☎ (01924) 424000. OPEN 9.30 - 5.30 MON - SAT, 11 - 5 SUN.
Factory Shop in a Factory Shopping Village • *Household*

An extensive range of Dartington Crystal seconds at greatly reduced prices as well as some perfect crystal at full price. Range includes wine suites, sherry glasses, tankards, decanters, rippled glass, fruit and salad bowls.

DEJA VU
8 BOWER ROAD, HARROGATE, NORTH YORKSHIRE HG1 1BA
☎ (01423) 503535. OPEN 10.30 - 4 MON - SAT.
Dress Agency • *Womenswear & Menswear*

Two roomed shop full of good quality men's and women's clothes from sweaters to coats, scarves to costume jewellery with a large selection of evening wear. Labels on sale include Paul Costelloe, Betty Barclay and Nicole Farhi.

DENHOLME VELVETS MILL SHOP
HALIFAX ROAD, DENHOLME, BRADFORD, WEST YORKSHIRE BD13 4EZ
☎ (01274) 839108. OPEN 1 - 5 MON - FRI, 9.30 - 4.30 SAT.
Factory Shop • *Womenswear Only*

Claims to be the only factory producing dress velvet in Britain, most of which is for export. Lots of remnants as well as slight seconds. They also sell rayon and cotton, all at huge savings, and a range of velvet cushions. Opening hours may vary during the summer holidays. Free parking.

DESIGNER SHADES
MCARTHURGLEN DESIGNER OUTLET, FULFORD, YORK,
NORTH YORKSHIRE YO19 4TA
☎ (01904) 679007. OPEN 10 - 6 MON - SAT, TILL 8 THUR, 11 - 5 SUN.
Permanent Discount Outlet • *Womenswear & Menswear* • *Children*

Designer Shades offer a wide selection of top-notch sunglasses at more than 30% off typical high street prices. The frames are invitingly displayed on back-lit columns - no locked cabinets, messy stickers or hanging labels to contend with. Gucci, Polo Ralph Lauren, Jean Paul Gaultier, Valentino, Police, Christian Dior and Diesel are included in the ever-changing stock of top international brand names. Designer Shades ensure that all their sunglasses have quality lenses which protect against UVA and UVB rays, as well as filtering out damaging reflective blue light. They plan to have 20 shops throughout Europe by the end of 2001. For details of other locations, ring 01423 858007 or email info@designer-shades.net.

DESIGNER WAREHOUSE
20 CUMBERLAND ROAD, MIDDLESBROUGH,
NORTH YORKSHIRE TS5 6HZ
☎ (01642) 850651. OPEN 9 - 5 MON - WED, 9 - 6 THUR - SAT, 11 - 5 SUN.
Permanent Discount Outlet • *Womenswear & Menswear*
Brand new top designer labels for men and women including Armani men's suits, £200 instead of £600; Versace dresses, £49.99 instead of £100; Calvin klein jeans, £29.99 instead of £59; Armani PK T-shirts, £19 instead of £45.

DEWHIRST IMPRESSIONS
42 MIDDLE STREET NORTH, DRIFFIELD, EAST YORKSHIRE YO25 7SS
☎ (01377) 256209. OPEN 9 - 5.30 MON - SAT.
5 WELHAM ROAD, MALTON YO10 9DP
☎ (01653) 690141. OPEN 9 - 5.30 MON - SAT, 10.30 - 4.30 SUN.
AMSTERDAM ROAD, SUTTON FIELD INDUSTRIAL ESTATE,
HULL HU8 OXF
☎ (01482) 820166. OPEN 9 - 5.30 MON - WED, 9 - 7.30 THUR,
9 - 6 FRI, 9 - 5.30 SAT, 10.30 - 4.30 SUN.
WEST COTHAM LANE, DORMANSTOWN INDUSTRIAL ESTATE,
DORMANSTOWN, REDCAR, NORTH YORKSHIRE TS10 5QD
☎ (01642) 474210. OPEN 9 - 5.30 MON - SAT, 10.30 - 4.30 SUN.
Factory Shop • *Womenswear & Menswear*
Dewhirst Impressions sell garments from the manufacturing side of the business direct to the public and are part of the Dewhirst Group plc which manufactures ladies, men's and childrenswear for a leading high street retailer. You can choose from a huge selection of surplus production and slight seconds at bargain prices, making savings of more than 50% of the normal retail cost. For men there is a wide range of suits, formal shirts and casual wear. For example, suits from £60, formal and casual shirts from £7. For ladies there's a selection of blouses, smart tailoring and casual wear that includes a denim range. You can find ladies jackets from £50, skirts, trousers and blouses from £8. Children's clothes start at £3 (not available at Driffield and Malton). High street quality and style at wholesale prices.

DOLMENS
79 LATHAM LANE, GOMERSAL, CLECKHEATON, YORKSHIRE BD19 4AP
☎ (01274) 872368. FAX (01274) 869953. BY APPOINTMENT ONLY.
Architectural Salvage • *DIY/Renovation*
Old and new York stone paving flags. Various prices and quality. Worldwide delivery.

DOUBLE TWO
FREEPORT CASTLEFORD, CARRWOOD ROAD, GLASSHOUGHTON,
WEST YORKSHIRE WF10 4SB
☎ (01977) 519122. OPENING HOURS 10 - 8 MON - FRI, 10 - 6 SAT,
11 - 5 SUN.
HORNSEA FREEPORT SHOPPING VILLAGE, ROLSTON ROAD,
HORNSEA, EAST YORKSHIRE HU18 1UT
☎ (01964) 533339. OPEN 9.30 - 6 SEVEN DAYS A WEEK.
THE YORKSHIRE OUTLET, WHITE ROSE WAY, DONCASTER,
SOUTH YORKSHIRE DN4 5PH
☎ (01302) 367156. OPEN 10 - 6 MON - SAT, 11 - 5 SUN.
Factory Shop • *Womenswear & Menswear*
Men's shirts (both casual and formal), belts, ties, jeans and dress shirts and women's blouses, co-ordinates, dresses, trousers, skirts and waistcoats at discount prices of about 30%-50%.

DRESS FOR LESS FASHIONS
THE OLD SUNDAY SCHOOL, LIDGET SE, LINDLEY, HUDDERSFIELD,
WEST YORKSHIRE HD3 3JF
☎ (01484) 640498. OPEN 10 - 5 MON - SAT, PHONE FOR OPENING
HOURS ON SUN.
Permanent Discount Outlet • *Womenswear & Menswear*
Enviable classic labels at a discount of up to 75%. They specialise in German and other European manufacturers in sizes 10-24 with a choice of up to 15,000 garments. Now based in a beautifully restored old school room with fresh filter coffee offered free.

DUNELM MILL SHOP
151 BRADFIELD ROAD, HILLSBOROUGH, SHEFFIELD,
SOUTH YORKSHIRE S6 2BY
☎ (01142) 315600. OPEN 9 - 5 MON - SAT, 10 - 4 SUN.
UNIT 3, CANKLOW MEADOWS, WEST BAWTRY ROAD,
ROTHERHAM S60 2XL
☎ (01709) 820374. OPEN 10 - 8 MON - FRI, 9 - 6 SAT, 11 - 5 SUN.
Permanent Discount Outlet • *Household*
Part of a chain of shops based in the Midlands selling brand-name and chain-store curtains, masses of bedlinen, towels, wickerware, pictures and frames, all at competitive prices.

DUNSFORD WELSEY MENSWEAR
OXFORD STREET, CASTLEFORD, WEST YORKSHIRE WF10 5SZ
☎ (01977) 710200. OPEN 10 - 5 WED, THUR, 10 - 6 FRI, 10 - 4 SAT.
Factory Shop • *Menswear Only*
Sells men's suits, trousers from £8, shirts, sweaters, and a few ladies oddments as well as leather handbags and small leather goods. The garments are good quality at affordable prices. Suits from £50 to £95; leather belts, £6.99-£9.99;

shirts from £10 to £20; sweaters from £15-£20; leather handbags from £5 upwards; purses and wallets from £5.

EDINBURGH CRYSTAL
HORNSEA FREEPORT SHOPPING VILLAGE, HORNSEA,
EAST YORKSHIRE HU18 1UT
☎ (01964) 534260. OPEN 9.30 - 6 SEVEN DAYS A WEEK.
Factory Shop in a Factory Shopping Village • *Household*
Wide range of crystalware from glasses and vases to tumblers and bowls at discounts of between 33% - 50%. The shop sells firsts and seconds of crystal from one third off the normal price. There are also special promotional lines at discount prices up to 70% off seconds. Hornsea has plenty to entertain the family with an adventure playground, an indoor play centre, restaurants and butterfly world.

ELEANOR
14 CHELTENHAM MOUNT, HARROGATE, NORTH YORKSHIRE
☎ (01423) 524787. OPEN 10 - 2 AND 2.30 - 4.30 TUE - SAT.
Dress Agency • *Womenswear Only*
Dress agency selling only the top end of the market women's fashions including Armani, Jil Sanders, Caroline Charles, Louis Feraud, Escada.

EVERYTHING BUT THE BABY
19 KNARESBOROUGH RD, HARROGATE, NORTH YORKSHIRE HG2 7SR
☎ (01423) 888292. OPEN 10 - 4 MON - SAT, 10 - 1 WED.
Dress Agency • *Children*
Sells a wide range of nearly-new babywear from birth to ten years, as well as baby equipment, bedding, toys and maternity wear. There is an extensive range of pushchairs. All the equipment is fully checked and the clothes range from mothercare and ladybird to Oshkosh, Oilily and some French designers.

EXECICHEF
19 MOOR ROAD, WATH-UPON-DEARNE, ROTHERHAM,
SOUTH YORKSHIRE S63 7RS
☎ (01709) 878364. OPEN 9 - 5 MON - THUR, 9 - 12 FRI, 10 - 1 SAT.
Factory Shop • *Sportswear & Equipment* • *Children*
Sells mostly Pulse 8 brand-name fleece jackets at half-price and also stocks some sweatshirts, waterproof jackets, chef's trousers and jackets. All are current season perfects offered at 50% discounts to men, women and children.

FABRICS FROM THE MILLS
ARCH 9, VIADUCT STREET, HUDDERSFIELD,
WEST YORKSHIRE HD1 5DL
☎ (01484) 450509. OPEN 9.30 - 6 MON - SAT, 9.30 - 5.30 WED.
Permanent Discount Outlet • *Furniture/Soft Furnishings*
A place where you can change that room without breaking the bank! There's a huge choice of quality curtain and upholstery fabric in as many designs and colours. The stock is mainly first quality, but there are clearances and seconds of famous labels such as Next, Marks & Spencer, Prestigious, etc: all at a fraction of their original price. There's also a speedy, professional made to measure service.

FAMOUS FOOTWEAR
MCARTHURGLEN DESIGNER OUTLET VILLAGE, SELBY ROAD,
NABURN, YORK, NORTH YORKSHIRE YO19 4TA
☎ (01904) 678997. OPEN 10 - 6 MON, TUE, WED, FRI, SAT, 10 - 8 THUR, 11 - 5 SUN.
HORNSEA FREEPORT, ROLSTON ROAD, HORNSEA YORKSHIRE HU18 1UT
☎ (01964) 536503. OPEN 10 - 5 SEVEN DAYS A WEEK (WINTER),
10 - 5 MON - FRI, 10 - 6 SAT, SUN (SUMMER).
Factory Shop in a Factory Shopping Village • *Womenswear & Menswear*
Wide range of brand names including Stead & Simpson, Lilley & Skinner, Hobos, Hush Puppies, Lotus, Sterling & Hunt, Richleigh, Scholl, Red Tape, Flexi Country, Padders, Canaletto, Bronx, Frank Wright, Brevitt, Romba Wallace, Rieker, all at discount prices of up to 50%.

FROCKS DRESS AGENCY,
16 DENHOLME GATE ROAD, HIPPERHOLME, HALIFAX,
WEST YORKSHIRE
☎ (01422) 202085. OPEN 9.30 - 3.30 MON,TUE, FRI, SAT,
9.30 - 3.30 & 5 - 7.30 THUR, - SAT (CLOSED WED).
Dress Agency • *Womenswear Only*
Day and evening wear with designer labels. Constantly changing stock and new stock.

FREEPORT CASTLEFORD DESIGNER OUTLET VILLAGE
CARRWOOD ROAD, GLASSHOUGHTON, CASTLEFORD, OFF JUNCTION 32 OF M52, CARRWOOD ROAD, GLASSHOUGHTON, CASTLEFORD, WEST YORKSHIRE WF10 4SB
☎ (01977) 520153. OPEN 10 - 8 MON - FRI, 10 - 6 SAT, 11 - 5 SUN.
Factory Shopping Village • *Womenswear & Menswear* • *Children Household* • *Electrical Equipment* • *Furniture/Soft Furnishings Food and Leisure* • *Sportswear & Equipment*
Factory shopping village with 82 shops (150 eventually), indoor and outdoor children's play areas and restaurants. Shops include Alice Collins, Bakers

Oven, Baron Jon, BBs Coffee & Muffins, BhS, Bradwells Restaurant, Burger King, Camille, Cromwells, Churchill, Ciro Citterio, Craghoppers, CBS, Carlton, Clinkards, Company, Claire's Accessories, Cotton Traders, Damart, Dartington Crystal, Dockers, Donnay, Double Two, Event Jewellery, Easy Jeans, Edinburgh Woollen Mill, Elle, Fila, Giorgio, Gossard, Harbi, Honey, ITs Music and Video, Jane Shilton, Jacques Heim, Jean Scene, John Partridge, Kappa, Kitchen and Table, Kurt Muller, Leading Labels, Lee Cooper, Littlewoods, London Leathers, Mexx, Mobile Phone Store, Mondian, Nike, Next, Outrage, Paco, Petroleum, Picture Port, Pilot, Ponden Mill, Proibito, Review, Rio Jewellery, Roman Originals, Room (selling tables and lamps), Royal Brierley, Sports Mill, Spotlight, Stead & Simpson, Suit Company, The Book Depot, The Designer Room, The Garden Outlet, The Great Outdoors, The Jewellery Outlet, The Oasis, The Shoe Collection, The Toy Factory, Time, The X Catalogue Store, Thorntons, Trespass, UBI, Used Co For Kids, Venezzen, Waterford/Wedgwood, Windsmoor.

FREEPORT HORNSEA OUTLET VILLAGE

ROLSTON ROAD, HORNSEA, EAST YORKSHIRE HU18 1UT
☎ (01964) 534211. OPEN 9.30 - 6 SEVEN DAYS A WEEK.

Factory Shopping Village • *Womenswear & Menswear* • *Children Household* • *Sportswear & Equipment*

The original British factory shopping village with over 40 shops offering discounts of 50% and more below high street prices, plenty of places to eat in a relaxed rural setting with free parking and entry. Womenswear labels include Alexon, Kaliko, Dash and Eastex, Designer Room with Jasper Conran, Paul La Porte and Scent to You, Roman Originals for Blast and Sloggi. At Arkwright Mill you can find Morgan and French Connection, there's also Honey, Damart, Select, Laura Ashley, Mexx and London Leathers with Tog 24 and Sports Mill offering family outdoor/sports clothing. Footwear is sold by Famous Footwear, Shoe Sellers and Sports Mills and for accessories visit Claire's Accessories. Woods of Windsor stock traditional English fragrances and Evans Jewellers have a lovely range of jewellery. Childrens' clothing can be found in Mexx, Laura Ashley, Giorgio and Wrangler and the men are spoilt for choice with VF Northern stocking Wrangler and Lee, The Suit Co has Ben Sherman in their range, Double Two, Greenwoods, Mexx and Giorgio. Shops selling household goods from bed linen to pot pourri include Ponden Mill, Churchill China and Hornsea Pottery. For crystal try Royal Brierley, Edinburgh Crystal and Waterford/Wedgwood. Visit Thorntons for chocolate, Book Depot for books, The Gadget Shop for gadgets and Luggage and Bags with every item from a handbag to a suitcase. To keep the children amused there's the model village, Butterfly World, Frontierland, Bouncy Castles, Orbitors and Go-Karts and indoor Ball Pools along with a great range of games machines.

GLYN WEBB

UNIT 2, THORNE RETAIL PARK, OGDEN ROAD, DONCASTER, SOUTH YORKSHIRE DN2 4SG
☎ (01302) 556556. OPEN 9 - 8 MON - SAT, 11 - 5 SUN AND OPEN ALL BANK HOLIDAYS.
SHAY SYKE, HALIFAX, WEST YORKSHIRE HX1 2ND
☎ (01422) 349249. OPEN 9 - 8 MON - SAT, 11 - 5 SUN AND OPEN ALL BANK HOLIDAYS.
100 WAKEFIELD ROAD, HUDDERSFIELD, WEST YORKSHIRE HD1 3PD
☎ (01484) 539330. OPEN 9 - 8 MON - SAT, 11 - 5 SUN AND BANK HOLS.
JOSLO ROAD, SUTTON FIELDS, HULL HU8 0JY
☎ (01484) 836344. OPEN 9 - 8 MON - SAT, 11 - 5 SUN AND OPEN ALL BANK HOLIDAYS.
INGS ROAD, WAKEFIELD, WEST YORKSHIRE WF1 1RN
☎ (01924) 298600. OPEN 9 - 8 MON - SAT, 11 - 5 SUN AND OPEN ALL BANK HOLIDAYS.
UNIT C KILNER WAY, OFF HALIFAX ROAD, SHEFFIELD, SOUTH YORKSHIRE S6 1NN
☎ (0114) 2312665. OPEN 9 - 8 MON - SAT, 11 - 5 SUN AND OPEN ALL BANK HOLIDAYS.
KINGS ROAD, BRADFORD, WEST YORKSHIRE BD1 1EX
☎ (01274) 722 122. OPEN 9 - 8 MONANK HOLIDAYS.
BRIDGE ROAD, CHANDLERS WHARF, STOCKTON ON TEES, NORTH YORKSHIRE TS18 3BA
☎ (01642) 606699. OPEN 9 - 8 MON - SAT, 11 - 5 SUN AND OPEN ALL BANK HOLIDAYS.

Permanent Discount Outlet • *DIY/Renovation*

Stockists of all your home improvement needs from wallpaper to paint, furniture to flooring, tiles to textiles, housewares to lighting - in fact, almost everything for your home, with 25 branches in the North-West, Midlands and Yorkshire. Specialists in discontinued mail order, slightly imperfect branded stocks as well as perfect quality superior products. They carry top brands such as Dulux, Crown Paints and Vymura and Coloroll wall coverings, Rectella and Norwood textiles and much more in store. To find your nearest branch, phone Head Office on 0161 621 4500.

GREENWOODS WHITE CROSS DISCOUNT SHOPPING

WHITE CROSS, GUISELEY, LEEDS, WEST YORKSHIRE LS20 8ND
☎ (01943) 875414. VISITOR CENTRE OPEN 9 - 5.30 MON - SAT, 11 - 5 SUN, BANK HOLIDAYS. CLUB OPEN 9 - 5 WED, THUR, FRI, SAT, 11 - 5 SUN AND BANK HOLIDAYS.

Factory Shop • *Menswear Only*

Specialists in menswear, the Visitor Centre and Warehouse Club withing 150 yards of each other both stock what one reader calls "the best men's clothing in the area". There are shirts from £5, jackets from £20, trousers from £10; knitwear from

£12; suits from £40; casuals, £20; socks and briefs. Sizes range from 38-54 inch chest and 32-52 inch waist. Wedding and evening wear hire service available here plus famous brands. Now also have Yorkshire Linen Co, Designer Warehouse, a chainstore reject department and sports shoe warehouse within the Club. Combine this with a trip to Harry Ramsden's Fish Shop, only 100 yards away.

HALLMARK
HORNSEA FREEPORT, HORNSEA, YORKSHIRE HU18 1UT
☎ (01964) 533080. OPEN 9.30 - 6 SEVEN DAYS A WEEK.

Factory Shop • *Food and Leisure*

A wide range of cards to suit every occasion, as well as stuffed toys, wrapping paper, rosettes, gift cards from names such as Andrew Brownswood, Gordon Fraser and Sharpe's Classics. Almost all the stock here is ends of lines as the card business demands constant change and therefore some unsold lines. Most of the items are half price. Cafes on site as well as children's play areas; free parking.

HANRO OF SWITZERLAND
MCARTHURGLEN DESIGNER OUTLET VILLAGE, NABURN, YORK YO19 4TA
☎ (01904) 610782 . OPEN 10 - 6 MON - SAT, 10 - 8 THUR, 11 - 5 SUN.

Factory Shop in a Factory Shopping Village • *Womenswear & Menswear*

Luxury lingerie for men and women which is normally sold through Harvey Nichols, Harrods and Selfridges is available here at reduced prices. For example, a bra which normally retails for £100 would be reduced by 35% - 50%. Sizes range from extra small to extra large and the company specialises in garments for smaller busts, although D-cups are also stocked. Very well known for their mercerised cottons which never fade or shrink.

HARRIETS
11 MARKET PLACE, KNARESBOROUGH, NORTH YORKSHIRE HG5 8AL
☎ (01423) 863375. OPEN 9 - 5 MON, TUE, WED, THUR, 9 - 5.30 FRI, SAT, 1 - 5 SUN.
16 WESTGATE, OTLEY, WEST YORKSHIRE LS29 6HY
☎ (01943) 465258. OPEN 9 - 5 MON - SAT, 10 - 4 SUN.
2 KIRKGATE, THIRSK YO7 1PQ
☎ (01845) 522079. OPEN 9 - 5 MON - THUR, 9 -
☎ (0113) 239 0399. OPEN 9 - 5 MON - SAT, 10 - 4 SUN. 11198.
OPEN 9 - 5.30 MON - SAT, 10 - 4 SUN.
75B NEW ROAD SIDE, HORSFORTH, LEEDS,
WEST YORKSHIRE LS18 4QD
☎ (0113) 239 0399. OPEN 9 - 5 MON - SAT, 10 - 4 SUN.

Permanent Discount Outlet • *Womenswear & Menswear*

Many high street chainstore over-productions at discounted prices. Clothes which are mostly Marks & Spencer seconds and discontinued lines, but also some from Next, Dorothy Perkins and Littlewoods. For example, a Marks & Spencer jacket which would normally cost £85, for sale at £40; skirts less than £20; and coats and jackets to suit everyone from teenagers upwards in sizes 8-20.

HAVENPLAN LTD
THE OLD STATION, STATION ROAD, KILLARMARSH, SHEFFIELD,
SOUTH YORKSHIRE S21 1EN
☎ (0114) 2489972. OPEN 10 - 3 TUE - SAT.
Architectural Salvage • *DIY/Renovation*
Very large stock of architectural antiques, bygones, decorative items ideal for the home and garden, stained glass, doors, lighting, fireplaces, church pews, kitchenalia, stone troughs.

HAWICK CASHMERE COMPANY
20 MONTPELLIER PARADE, HARROGATE, WEST YORKSHIRE HG1 2TG
☎ (01423) 502519. OPEN 9.30 - 5.30 MON - SAT.
Factory Shop • *Womenswear & Menswear*
Hawick offers you the luxury of Scottish knitwear direct from the Scottish borders at prices which are below normal retail prices. You can choose from cashmere, cashmere/silk, merino and lambswool for men and women. Also some trousers, gloves, scarves and handbags.

HIGH SOCIETY
THE MARKET PLACE, EASINGWOLD, YORK,
NORTH YORKSHIRE YO61 3AD
☎ (01347) 822668. WEBSITE: www.highsociety.uk.com
OPEN 10 - 5 MON - SAT.
Dress Agency • *Hire Shop* • *Womenswear Only*
Up to 300 new evening dresses to buy or to hire by After Six, John Charles, Serenade, Simon Ellis, etc. Sale rail with new and ex-hire frocks from £20. Clearance sales take place in January and August to make way for new stock. The dress agency sells secondhand daywear and accessories, from Marks & Spencer to top designers - all in perfect condition, freshly laundered and less than three years old. Stock might include Moschino top £20, Paul Costelloe jacket £45, Valentino jacket £45, K & S shoes £26.

HONEY
HORNSEA FREEPORT, POTTERS WAY, ROLSTON ROAD, HORNSEA,
EAST YORKSHIRE HU18 1UT
☎ (01964) 537394. OPEN 9.30 - 6 MON - SUN.
Factory Shop in a Factory Shopping Village • *Womenswear Only*
Leisure-oriented women's T-shirts, leggings and sweaters at discounts of mostly 30% to 50%.

HOUSE OF FABRICS
HIRST LANE, SALTAIRE, SHIPLEY, WEST YORKSHIRE BD18 4ND
☎ (01274) 595952. OPEN 9 - 5 MON - SAT, 10 - 4 SUN.
Permanent Discount Outlet • *Furniture/Soft Furnishings*
Curtaining and upholstery fabrics from a range which includes plain cotton,

chintz, damasks and heavy upholstery fabric. Prices from £2.99p a metre. The upholstery fabric is sold at greatly reduced prices. There are many brands to choose from, including Rectella, Prestigious and Wilson Wilcox. They can supply all accessories too, such as braid, tiebacks, brassware, corded and uncorded tracks; metal, wood and brass poles; brass tiebacks, holdbacks, embracers, braids, cords and trims, and offer a complete measure, make-up and fitting service, including upholstery.

HOWKEL CARPETS
60 LOWER VIADUCT STREET, HUDDERSFIELD, WEST YORKSHIRE
☎ (01484) 425422. OPEN 9 - 5 MON - FRI, 9 - 4.30 SAT.
Factory Shop • *Furniture/Soft Furnishings*
Warehouse type building on three floors stacked with quality carpets and ends of lines, they specialise in 80% wool twist pile carpets. For example 40 oz wool twist off the roll costs £10 a sq yard. There is a small offshoot shop selling their seconds and offcuts at Blackmoorfoot Road.

JACK & JILL
1 WEST PARK DRIVE, WEST PARK, LEEDS, WEST YORKSHIRE LS16 5AS
☎ (0113) 278 5560.
Hire Shop • *Children*
Part of the Baby Equipment Hirers Association (BEHA), which has more than 100 members countrywide. A range of equipment can be hired from high chairs, cots and travel cots to baby car seats and buggies. Some members also hire out party equipment including child-sized tables and chairs. BEHA run an advice line which will try and answer any queries you have regarding hiring services for children. Phone the Babyline on 0831 310355 for your nearest BEHA shop.

JAEGER FACTORY SHOP
C/O THOMAS BURNLEY, GOMERSAL MILLS, CLECKHEATON,
WEST YORKSHIRE BD19 4LU
☎ (01274) 852292. OPEN 9 - 5 MON - SAT.
MCARTHURGLEN DESIGNER OUTLET VILLAGE, YORK
Factory Shops • *Womenswear & Menswear*
Contemporary classics from Jaeger at excellent prices. Most of the merchandise is previous seasons' stock, but you might also find some special makes. All shops stock tailoring and knitwear for women and men, except for Boundary Mills, which sells womenswear only.

JAGS TRADING
YORKSHIRE
☎ (01274) 425425. WEBSITE: www.jags-online.freeserve.co.uk MAIL ORDER.
Permanent Discount Outlet • *Sportswear & Equipment Womenswear & Menswear*
Designer sportswear at discount prices by mail order. Phone for a brochure.

JAMES BARRY MENSWEAR
THE YORKSHIRE OUTLET, WHITE ROSE WAY, DONCASTER,
SOUTH YORKSHIRE DN4 5JU
☎ (01302) 361127. OPEN 10 - 6 MON - SAT, 11 - 5 SUN.
Factory Shop in a Factory Shopping Village • *Menswear Only*
Range of men's suits, jackets, trousers, socks, belts, briefs and shirts from James Barry, Pierre Cardin, Haggar and Wolsey. Some of the factory shops also stock the Double Two range of brand names. Suits reduced from £175 to £115; casual shirts, £11.95 or two for £20; trousers reduced from £44.95 to £29.95; Pierre Cardin casual and business shirts, knitwear and trouser are available, too.

JANE SHILTON
THE YORKSHIRE OUTLET, WHITE ROSE WAY, DONCASTER,
SOUTH YORKSHIRE DN4 5JH
☎ (01302) 320035. OPEN 10 - 6 MON - SAT, 11 - 5 SUN.
FREEPORT CASTLEFORD DESIGNER OUTLET VILLAGE, CARWOOD ROAD, GLASSHOUGHTON, NR CASTLEFORD,
WEST YORKSHIRE WF10 4BS
☎ (01977) 517710. FAX ☎ (01977) 517762. OPEN 10 - 8 MON - FRI,
10 - 6 SAT, 11 - 5 SUN.
Factory Shop in a Factory Shopping Village • *Womenswear Only*
Merchandise from past seasons' collections or factory seconds at discounts of at least 30% and up to 70% off the original price. There is a wide range of handbags, small leather goods, shoes, luggage umbrellas and travel bags. Example of price reduction: handbags at £24.99 originally £37.

JOHN SMEDLEY LTD
RANDS LANE, ARMTHORPE, DONCASTER, SOUTH YORKSHIRE DN3 3DY
☎ (01302) 832346. OPEN 11 - 3.30 MON - FRI, 10 - 3 SAT.
Factory Shop • *Womenswear & Menswear*
John Smedley knitwear for men and women in wool and cotton, own range wool and cotton underwear, all at greatly reduced prices. There is another, much larger outlet in Matlock, Derbyshire.

JOKIDS LTD
THE YORKSHIRE OUTLET, WHITE ROSE WAY, DONCASTER,
SOUTH YORKSHIRE DN4 5JH
☎ (01302) 760137. OPEN 10 - 6 MON - SAT, 11 - 5 SUN.

Factory Shop in a Factory Shopping Village • *Children*

JoKids is the factory shop trading name for Jeffrey Ohrenstein which sells unusual and attractive clothes for children aged from birth to ten years. This includes pretty party dresses for girls at reductions of up to 40%, all-in-one smocked playsuits, T-shirts, denim shirts, denim dresses, sunhats, shorts, and accessories.

JUMPER

7 KING CHARLES WALK, HEADROW CENTRE, LEEDS,
WEST YORKSHIRE LS1 6JB
☎ (0113) 234 1161. OPEN 9 - 5.30 MON - FRI, 11 - 5 SUN.

Factory Shop • *Womenswear & Menswear*

A wide range of Jumper label sweaters, gloves, scarves, shirts and cardigans for men and women all at discount prices of up to 50% off. Prices start at £2.

KARRIMOR

31 WINDSOR TERRACE, WHITBY, NORTH YORKSHIRE YO21 1ET
☎ (01947) 820945. OPEN 9.3- = 5.30 MON - FRI, 9.30 - 5 SAT, 10 - 4 SUN.

Factory Shop • *Sportswear & Equipment*

Best known for their comprehensive range of rucksacks, Karrimor also make an outstanding range of outdoor equipment for walkers, climbers and campers. The factory shop sells seconds, former display items, samples and clearance stock at discounts of between 15% and 25% and always stocks the current range for the season.

KASTIX MILL SHOP

11 UPPER BRIDGE, WOODHEAD ROAD, HOLMFIRTH, HUDDERSFIELD,
WEST YORKSHIRE
☎ (01484) 681797. OPEN 9 - 5 MON - SAT.

Factory Shop • *Womenswear & Menswear* • *Children*

Kastix manufacture everything on the premises, mostly for the catalogue business, selling an ever-changing mix of shorts, trousers, pedal pushers, jumpers, T-shirts, jackets and fleeces at discounted prices.

LABELS

1 MARKET ROW, BARKERS ARCADE, NORTHALLERTON,
NORTH YORKSHIRE DL7 8LN.
☎ (01609) 779483. OPEN 9.30 - 5 TUE - SAT.

Dress Agency • *Womenswear Only*

Two-storey shop selling designer nearly-new wear from Pangi, Droopy & Browns, Jaeger, Escada and Windsmoor to Cache D'Or at about half the initial shop price. Two-piece suits, wedding outfits, holiday wear, blazers, evening wear cocktail dresses and hats.

LABELS FOR LESS
ALLERTON ROAD, BRADFORD, WEST YORKSHIRE BD15 7AB
☎ (01274) 491311. OPEN 9 - 5.30 MON - SAT.
Permanent Discount Outlet • *Womenswear & Menswear*
Designer shopping outlet within the elegant department store surroundings of the former Hoopers store. Stocks a wide selection of well-known contemporary designer and classic fashion labels for men and women at prices at least 50% below the original selling price. Seen here in the past have been Moschino, Hugo Boss, Christian Lacroix. There is a hair and beauty salon on site and easy parking.

LAURA ASHLEY
HORNSEA FREEPORT SHOPPING VILLAGE, HORNSEA,
WEST YORKSHIRE HU18 1UT
☎ (01964) 536503. OPEN 9.30 - 6 SEVEN DAYS A WEEK.
Factory Shop in a Factory Shopping Village
Furniture/Soft Furnishings
Home furnishings on two floors. Most of the merchandise is made up of perfect carry-overs from the high street shops around the country, though there are also some discontinued lines. Stock reflects the normal high street variety, though at least one season later and with less choice in colours. The shopping village has restaurants, play centres, a vintage car collection, water games, and plenty for the family to do and see.

LE CREUSET
MCARTHURGLEN DESIGNER OUTLET VILLAGE, ST NICHOLAS
AVENUE, NABURN, YORK, YORKSHIRE YO19 4TA
☎ (01904) 630485. OPEN 10 - 6 MON - SAT, 10 - 8 THUR, 11 - 5 SUN.
Factory Shop in a Factory Shopping Village • *Household*
Items from the famous Le Creuset range - casseroles, saucepans, fry pans etc - plus their pottery collection at discounts of at least 30%.

LEE COOPER
FREEPORT OUTLET VILLAGE, CARRWOOD ROAD, GLASSHOUGHTON, CASTLEFORD, OFF JUNCTION 32 OF M52, WEST YORKSHIRE WF10 4SB
☎ (01977) 557011. OPEN 10 - 8 MON - FRI, 10 - 6 SAT, 11 - 5 SUN.
Factory Shop in a Factory Shopping Village
Womenswear & Menswear • *Children*
Denim jeans, jackets and shirts, each ranked by size and gender at discounts of up to 30%. Casual shirts from £9.99, jeans from £14.99, T-shirts and ladieswear. Lee Cooper was founded in 1908 as a workwear manufacturer before becoming a supplier to the armed forces. Most of the stock here is current, discontinued and irregular merchandise, all of which comes straight from Lee Cooper's factories in Europe.

LIGHTWATER VILLAGE AND FACTORY SHOPPING
NORTH STAINLEY, RIPON, WEST YORKSHIRE HG4 3HT
☎ (01765) 635321. OPEN FROM 10 DAILY.
Factory Shop • *Womenswear & Menswear* • *Children* • *Household*
Large complex of retail and factory outlets with a wide range of branded ladies' wear including blouses, skirts, suits, dresses, lingerie, outerwear, shoes and accessories as well as menswear from jeans and outdoor wear (from Tog 24) to formal wear. Shoes, jewellery, home furnishings, crystal and glass, a large range of pottery as well as a seasonal shop, garden products, toys, a bakery, cheese and confectionery. Old Macdonald's farm is open to shoppers all year free of charge. There is a restaurant and coffee shop serving snacks and refreshments, free parking and disabled facilities.

LILLEY & SKINNER
FREEPORT DESIGNER OUTLET VILLAGE, CARRWOOD ROAD, GLASSHOUGHTON, CASTLEFORD, OFF JUNCTION 32 OF M52, WEST YORKSHIRE WF10 4PS
☎ (01977) 510910. OPEN 10 - 8 MON - FRI, 10 - 6 SAT, 11 - 5 SUN.
Factory Shop in a Factory Shopping Village
Womenswear & Menswear • *Children*
Wide range of brand names including Stead & Simpson, Lilley & Skinner, Hobos, Hush Puppies, Lotus, Sterling & Hunt, Richleigh, Scholl, Red Tape, Flexi Country, Padders, Canaletto, Bronx, Frank Wright, Brevitt, Romba Wallace, Rieker, all at discount prices of up to 50%.

LITTLEWOODS CATALOGUE DISCOUNT STORE
602-608 ATTERCLIFFE ROAD, SHEFFIELD, SOUTH YORKSHIRE S9 3QS
☎ (0114) 244 1611. OPEN 9 - 5.30 TUE - SAT.
FREEPORT DESIGNER OUTLET VILLAGE, CARRWOOD ROAD, GLASSHOUGHTON, CASTLEFORD, OFF JUNCTION 32 OF M52 WEST YORKSHIRE WF10 4PS
☎ (01977) 520153 (VILLAGE). OPEN 10 - 8 MON - FRI, 10 - 6 SAT, 11 - 5 SUN. - 8 MON - FRI, 10 - 6 SAT, 11 - 5 SUN.
Permanent Discount Outlet • *Womenswear & Menswear*
Electrical Equipment • *Children*
Littlewoods clearance shops offering up to 50% off the catalogue price for clothing and between 50% and 60% off for electrical goods. Stock changes constantly and varies from day to day but can include well-known brand names such as Berlei and Gossard lingerie, Vivienne Westwood, Pamplemousse leisure wear, Nike and Adidas sports shoes, Workers for Freedom, and Timberland and Caterpillar footwear. Stock depends on the size and location of the shop, so larger shops will get the longer discontinued runs and smaller shops over-runs with only a small amount of colour and size variations left. Littlewoods also run a mobile shop which operates in cities where

they don't have a sale shop. For details of further venues for the sales, which usually take place once a month, contact Melanie Lamb, c/o Crosby DC Kershaw Avenue, Endbutt Lane, Crosby, Merseyside L70 1AH.

LONDON LEATHERS DIRECT
FREEPORT VILLAGE, ROLSTON ROAD, HORNSEA,
EAST YORKSHIRE HU18 1UT
☎ (01964) 535432 . OPEN 9.30 - 6 SEVEN DAYS A WEEK.
CASTLEFORD FREEPORT VILLAGE, CASTLEFORD, WEST YORKSHIRE
☎ (01977) 517550. OPEN 10 - 8 MON - FRI, 10 - 6 SAT, 11 - 5 SUN.
Factory Shop in a Factory Shopping Village • *Womenswear & Menswear*
Very good quality leather and suede jackets, coats and trousers, at discounts of at least 30%, with most at 50% off in this village which features lots of restaurants and fun things for the family to take part in.

LUGGAGE & BAGS
FREEPORT LEISURE VILLAGE, ROLSTON ROAD, HORNSEA,
YORKSHIRE HU18 1UT
☎ (01964) 535651. OPEN 9.30 - 6 SEVEN DAYS A WEEK.
Factory Shop in a Factory Shopping Village • *Food and Leisure*
Luggage and travel-related products and executive cases, handbags, umbrellas from leading brands such as Samsonite, Desley, Head, Taurus and GlobeTrotter. Each product is offered at a substantially reduced price compared to those found on the high street due to being production over-runs, discontinued ranges or colours and last season's products. Discounts range from 30%-75% off high street prices.

MAGNET LTD CLEARANCE CENTRE
ROYDINGS AVENUE, KEIGHLEY, YORKSHIRE BD21 4BY
☎ (01535) 680461. OPEN 8 - 5 MON - FRI, 9 - 1 SAT.
DARLINGTON CLEARANCE CENTRE, ALLINGTON WAY, YARM ROAD INDUSTRIAL ESTATE, DARLINGTON DL1 4XT
☎ (01642) 344564. OPEN 8 - 5 MON - FRI, 9 - 1 SAT.
Factory Shop • *Furniture/Soft Furnishings*
With more than 200 branches countrywide, when Magnet Kitchens discontinue one of their ranges, there are always some shops with spare stock they can no longer sell. This applies to equipment such as ovens, hob, hoods, washing machines, tumble dryers and fridges, too as when manufacturers upgrade their ranges, Magnet customers don't want to buy the old model currently in situ in the showroom. Old stock is sent to three sites in Birmingham, Darlington and the head office factory site in Keighley, West Yorkshire. Prices on average are about 70% less than the high street price. If you are looking for a particular kitchen from the current catalogue, you may need to make three or four trips to buy sufficient quantities. The Darlington outlet has the most stock, followed by Birmingham and then Keighley. Electrical equipment is all

top brands - Neff and Smeg ovens, as well as Magnet's own brand range which is made by Whirlpool. Some is ex-display, some discontinued models, some just overstock which is still boxed. Ovens cost from £120-£400. There are also wood and PVC glazed window frames, conservatory panels (from £25 for panels which normally cost £100), patio doors and French doors.

MANORGROVE
121-123 MAIN STREET, BINGLEY, WEST YORKSHIRE BD16 2ND
☎ (01274) 561933. OPEN 9 - 5.30 MON - SAT.
YOU & YOURS, 105-109 WESTGATE, HECKMONDWIKE WF16 OEW
☎ (01924) 410734. OPEN 9 - 5.30 MON - SAT.
Permanent Discount Outlet • *Womenswear & Menswear* • **Children**
A selection of clearance items from those featured in the Grattan catalogue, which can consist of anything from children's clothes and toys to bedding, electrical equipment and nursery accessories. Each shop sells a slightly different range, so always ring first to check they stock what you want. All items are discounted by up to 50%.

MARY COOPER
GINNEL ANTIQUES CENTRE, OFF PARLIAMENT STREET, HARROGATE, NORTH YORKSHIRE HG1 1DH
☎ (01765) 677483. OPEN 9.30 - 5.30 MON - SAT.
Secondhand and Vintage Clothes • *Womenswear & Menswear*
Mainly sells fans and lace but also stocks vintage clothes up to 1935, with Twenties underwear, beaded dresses, accessories and shawls. Also quilts, samplers, sheets, pillowcases, tablecloths, hats, men's hats, waistcoats and shirts. For men, there are only hats and waistcoats; for children, christening gowns. Beaded dresses, £200-£300. Discounts for cash purchases. Phone before visiting if you have a specific request and Mary will try to get it for you.

MATALAN
THE WHEATLEY CENTRE, WHEATLEY HALL ROAD, DONCASTER, SOUTH YORKSHIRE DN2 4PH
☎ (01302) 760444. OPEN 10 - 8 MON - FRI, 9 - 6 SAT, 11 - 5 SUN.
UNIT 4B, STADIUM WAY RETAIL PARK, PARKGATE, ROTHERHAM S60 1TG
☎ (01709) 780173. OPEN 10 - 8 MON - FRI, 9 - 6 SAT, 11 - 5 SUN.
CLIFTON MOORE CENTRE, YORK YO3 4XZ
☎ (01904) 693080. OPEN 10 - 8 MON - FRI, 9 - 6 SAT, 11 - 5 SUN.
GREENMOUNT RETAIL PARK, PELLON ROAD, HALIFAX HX1 5QN
☎ (01422) 383051. OPEN 10 - 8 MON - FRI, 9 - 6 SAT, 11 - 5 SUN.
KINGSWOOD RETAIL PARK, BUDE ROAD, HULL HU7 4AF
☎ (01482) 832880. OPEN 10 - 8 MON - FRI, 9 - 6 SAT 11 - 5 SUN.
1 WOMBWELL LANE, STAIRFOOT, BARNSLEY S70 3NS
☎ (01226) 733372. OPEN 9.30 - 8 MON - FRI, 9 - 6 SAT, 11 - 5 SUN.

INGS ROAD RETAIL PARK, INGS ROAD, WAKEFIELD WF1 1RF
☎ (01924) 367395. OPEN 10 - 8 MON - FRI, 9 - 6 SAT, 11 - 5 SUN.
FORSTER SQUARE RETAIL PARK, 53 VALLEY ROAD,
BRADFORD BD1 4RN
☎ (01274) 381000. OPEN 10 - 8 MON - FRI, 9 - 6 SAT, 11 - 5 SUN.
LOWER WORTLEY ROAD, OFF LEEDS RING ROAD, LEEDS LS12 4SL
☎ (0113) 290 7400. OPEN 9 - 8 MON - FRI, 9 - 6 SAT, 10 - 4 SUN.
HEELEY INDUSTRIAL PARK, CHESTERFIELD ROAD, SHEFFIELD S8 0RG
☎ (0114) 262 9400. OPEN 10 - 8 MON - FRI, 9 - 6 SAT, 11 - 5 SUN.
RINGWAY INDUSTRIAL ESTATE, HUDDERSFIELD
☎ (01484) 448800. OPEN 9.30 - 8 MON - FRI, 9 - 6 SAT, 11 - 5 SUN.
Permanent Discount Outlet • *Womenswear & Menswear*
Household • *Children*
Matalan is a fashion and homewares value retailer giving customers what they claim to be unbeatable value for money with huge savings on a wide range of products including high quality fashionable clothing for men, women and children at up to 50% off high street prices. Matalan is situated out of town and stores are open seven days a week all year round.

MCARTHURGLEN DESIGNER OUTLET
ST NICHOLAS AVENUE, FULFORD, JUNCTION OF A19 AND A64, YORK,
NORTH YORKSHIRE YO19 4TA
FREEPHONE INFORMATION LINE ☎ 0800 3164532.
☎ (01904) 682700. WEBSITE: www.mcarthurglen.com
OPEN 10 - 6 MON - SAT, 10 - 8 THUR, 11 - 5 SUN.
Factory Shop • *Womenswear & Menswear* • *Household*
Children • *Electrical Equipment* • *Sportswear & Equipment*
Food and Leisure • *Furniture/Soft Furnishings*
This indoor centre three miles outside York has 75 stores offering top brands and designer labels with discounts of between 30% and 50%. Facilities include a food court, an indoor children's play area and free parking. (There is also a free shuttle bus from York station.) Outlets include Adidas, Armani, Ted Baker, Blazer, the Body Shop, Burberry, Calvin Klein Jeans, Cerruti, Chilli Pepper, Cotton Traders, The Designer Room, Daniel Shoes, Descamps, Dolce & Gabbana, Dunhill, Episode, Escada Sport, Flannels, Franchetti Bond, Guess, Hanro, Jaeger/Viyella/Van Heusen, Karrimor, Levi's, Margaret Howell, Hanro, Iceberg, Jackpot, Jacques Vert, Jaeger, Joan & David, Levi, Mulberry, Nine West, Olsen, Oneida, Paul Smith, Pied a Terre, Pilot, Pringle, Proibito, Reebok, Rockport, Sense, Slix, Suits You, Tie Rack, Thomas Pink, Tog 24, Tommy Hilfiger, USC - stocking well-known designer brands - Van Heusen, Vans, Virgin, Viyella, Warners Brothers, Wolford, Woods of Windsor, Ronit Zilkha. Household names include China, China, famous for their twice-yearly china and glass sales in York and now offering a permanent opportunity to buy a huge range of famous-name china and glass at discount prices, Descamps, Le Creuset, Oneida, Prices Candles, Professional

Cookware, Remington, Warner Bros Studio and Whittard Kitchen and Garden. There's also footwear, confectionery, luggage, accessories and gifts.

MEXX INTERNATIONAL
HORNSEA FREEPORT VILLAGE, HORNSEA, YORKSHIRE HU18 1UT
☎ (01964) 537401. OPEN 9 - 6.30 MON - SAT, 11 - 5 SUN.
FREEPORT VILLAGE, GLASSHOUGHTON, CASTLEFORD,
WEST YORKSHIRE WF10 4FB
☎ (01977) 550886. OPEN 10 - 8 MON - FRI, 10 - 6 SAT, 11 - 5 SUN.
Factory Shop in a Factory Shopping Village
Womenswear & Menswear • *Children*

High street fashion at factory outlet prices for men, women, babies and kids, all of which are heavily discounted by more than 30%.

MIDAS CLOTHES
10 LITTLE STONEGATE, YORK, NORTH YORKSHIRE YO1 8AX
☎ (01904) 625870. OPEN 10 - 4 MON - WED, 10 - 5 THUR - SAT.
Dress Agency • *Womenswear Only*

Clothes exchange shop selling designer labels and high street names, shoes, hats, handbags and a small selection of jewellery. The shop is all on one level.

MR BABY
4 ST JOHN'S ROAD, HUDDERSFIELD, WEST YORKSHIRE HD1 5AT
☎ (01484) 515381. OPEN 9 - 5.30 MON - SAT.
Permanent Discount Outlet • *Children*

Sells reconditioned, seconds and former showroom models of the Mamas & Papas range and their nursery equipment, as well as everything for the nursery.

MR VALUE
KILLINGHALL ROAD, BRADFORD, YORKSHIRE BD3 8DN
☎ (01274) 669674. OPEN 9 - 8 MON - FRI, 9 - 5.30 SAT, 10 - 4 SUN.
Permanent Discount Outlet • *Womenswear & Menswear*
Children • *Household* • *Food and Leisure* • *Electrical Equipment*

A discount store offering a wide selection of goods which are catalogue returns, factory rejects, seconds and ends of lines - everything from clothes with the labels cut out to tapes, kettles, TVs, microwaves, irons, toasters, bed-linen, towels, sweets, artificial flowers, batteries, toiletries, crockery, glass, stationery, pots and pans, toys and bins. Kitchen equipment brand names include Russell Hobbs and Morphy Richards. There is now also a department for mobility: wheelchairs, scooters etc.

MULBERRY CLEARANCE SHOP
23 - 25 SWINEGATE, YORK, YORKSHIRE
☎ (01904) 611055. OPEN 10 - 6 MON - SAT.
Permanent Discount Outlet • *Household*
Furniture/Soft Furnishings

Clearance shop for the famous Mulberry brands with some full-price goods also on sale. There's a smaller selection of the goods on sale at the larger Mulberry factory shop in Somerset including leather goods, handbags, filofaxes, wallets, last season's clothes for men and women, cushions, lamps, china, throws, fabric. The shop is all on one level.

MULBERRY HALL
STONEGATE, YORK, NORTH YORKSHIRE YO1 8ZW
☎ (01904) 620736. OPEN 9 - 5.30 MON - SAT.
Designer Sale • *Household*

Mulberry Hall's once a year only, January sale is the greatest sale of top quality china and crystal in the north of England. Held in Mulberry Hall's majestic medieval premises in Stonegate, there are reductions of between 30% and 70% on many thousands of items of tableware including hundreds of dinner and tea services, giftware from leading British manufacturers including Royal Crown Derby, Royal Doulton, Royal Worcester, Spode, Wedgwood, Royal Brierley, Edinburgh Crystal and Stuart Crystal. Phone and put your name on the mailing list.

NIGHTINGALES FACTORY SHOP
13 CHESTERFIELD ROAD, SHEFFIELD, YORKSHIRE S8 ORL
☎ (0114) 255 4623. OPEN 10 - 5 MON - SAT.
Factory Shop • *Womenswear Only*

The mail order company which sells smart but casual clothes for women has a factory shop above their shop in Sheffield. Their catalogue features button-through dresses for about £28.99; mix and match two-pieces, £39.50, cotton camisoles, £17.99; and tucked cotton shirts, £14.99. The factory shop sells a selection of seconds, some returns and ends of lines.

NURSERY NEEDS
43 PIKEPURSE LANE, RICHMOND, YORKSHIRE DL10 4PS
☎ (01748) 824524.
Hire Shop • *Children*

Part of the Baby Equipment Hirers Association (BEHA), which has more than 100 members countrywide. A range of equipment can be hired from high chairs, cots and travel cots to baby car seats and buggies. Some members also hire out party equipment including child-sized tables and chairs. BEHA run an advice line which will try and answer any queries you have regarding hiring services for children. Phone the Babyline on 0831 310355 for your nearest BEHA shop.

ONEIDA
MCARTHURGLEN DESIGNER OUTLET CENTRE, ST NICHOLAS
AVENUE, FULFORD, YORK, YORKSHIRE YO1 4RE
☎ (01904) 610675. OPEN 10 - 6 MON - SAT, 8 ON THUR, 11 - 5 SUN.
Factory Shop in a Factory Shopping Village • *Household*
Oneida is the world's largest cutlery company and originates from the United States of America. In addition to cutlery, it sells silver and silver plate at discounts of between 30% and 50%, plus frames, candlesticks and trays. They now also have their own range of chinaware and glass, also sold here at discounts of 30%-50%.

OPPORTUNITIES
13 PROVIDENCE STREET, WAKEFIELD, WEST YORKSHIRE WF1 3BG
☎ (01924) 290310 OPEN 10 - 5.30 MON - SAT,
EVENINGS BY APPOINTMENT.
Dress Agency • *Womenswear Only* • *Children*
Two floors of nearly-new outfits, from wedding outfits, evening wear and cruise wear to suits and separates for daywear. Larger sizes always in stock. Anything from Louis Feraud and Calvin Klein to Next and Principles. Childrenswear includes Osh Kosh, Oilily, Gap and Mothercare. New and gently-worn jewellery. A large selection of designer shoes, handbags and belts. Free parking. Easy sofas. Coffee and tea.

OSBORNE SILVERSMITHS LTD
WESTWICK WORKS, SOLLY STREET, WEST BAR, SHEFFIELD,
SOUTH YORKSHIRE S1 4BA
☎ (0114) 272 4929. OPEN 9.30 - 4 TUE - THUR, 9.30 - 3 FRI, SAT BY PRIOR ARRANGEMENT; CLOSED END JULY/BEGINNING AUGUST.
Factory Shop • *Household*
For almost 300 years, the Osborne family have been Sheffield craftsmen, and now is one of Britain's leading cutlery manufacturers, supplying many of the top stores in London's West End. The factory shop sells slightly blemished or surplus perfect items of cutlery at special prices direct to the public. Their extensive ranges cover both English and Continental patterns in sterling silver, silver plate and stainless steel. In addition to canteens, place sets or individual pieces, they also manufacture an extensive selection of servicing and accessory items often difficult to find elsewhere.

PACO
FREEPORT CASTLEFORD DESIGNER OUTLET VILLAGE, CARRWOOD ROAD, GLASSHOUGHTON, CASTLEFORD, OFF JUNCTION 32 OF M52, WEST YORKSHIRE WF10 4SB
☎ (01977) 516865. OPEN 10 - 8 MON - FRI, 10 - 6 SAT, 11 - 5 SUN.
Factory Shop in a Factory Shopping Village • *Children Sportswear & Equipment* • *Womenswear & Menswear*

Paco uses bright, distinctive colours and the knack for designing great clothes at affordable prices. For several years, they have also been creating their own brand of sports and leisurewear clothing that shows great verve and energy. This range has a much more everyday living influence. The contrast is a distinct look for the discerning wearer. If you are looking for a great T-shirt or sweatshirt, lightweight jacket or gilet, polar fleece or hooded top, three-quarter length or combat trousers, then you need look no further. Paco now competes with the very best fashion brands in the high street by offering customers high fashion combined with excellent quality, making their clothes real value for money.

PARTRIDGE
FREEPORT VILLAGE YORKSHIRE LTD, CARRWOOD ROAD, GLASSHOUGHTON, CASTLEFORD, WEST YORKSHIRE WF10 4SB
☎ (01977) 555341 . OPEN 10 - 8 MON - FRI, 10 - 6 SAT, 11 - 5 SUN.
Factory Shop in a Factory Shopping Village
Womenswear & Menswear • *Children*

Partridge specialises in fashionable outdoor clothes and accessories. Ranges include waxed jackets, Gore-tex jackets, waterproof jackets, tweeds, quilts, fleece jackets and waistcoats, knitwear, shirts, chinos, cord and moleskin trousers, hats and caps. Discontinued lines are on sale at discounted prices with a minimum of 30% and up to 70% off during promotions.

PEASE & JAY FURNITURE DIRECT
THE FURNITURE FACTORY, LEEDS ROAD, OTLEY, WEST YORKSHIRE LS21 1QX
☎ (01943) 850764. E-MAIL: peaseandjay@bigfoot.com
WEBSITE: wwwpeaseandjay.co.uk
OPEN 9 - 5.30 MON - FRI, 10 - 5 SAT, 11 - 4 SUN. MAIL ORDER.
Permanent Discount Outlet • *Furniture/Soft Furnishings*

High quality traditional English furniture at factory direct prices from this manufacturer with more than 50 years experience in design and production. By cutting out the middleman and selling to customers direct from their factory, they can offer the same high quality products you see in high street shops at significantly lower prices. All their furniture is made in the UK by specialist craftsmen and is available in mahogany or yew. Items on sale include coffee tables, curio cabinets, bow front hall tables, chests of drawers, bedside chests, circular tables, lamp tables, octagonal drum tables, swag and drape chairs, lamp trolleys, desks, bureaux, TV cabinets, hi-fi storage units, sideboards, dining tables, book cases and corner cabinets. Discounted items of furniture are due to Pease & Jay getting better deals on their raw materials and passing the benefits onto customers. They offer a 5-year guarantee and 30-day trial period to deicde whether or not you like the furniture.

PONDEN MILL
COLNE ROAD, STANBURY, NEAR HAWORTH,
WEST YORKSHIRE BD22 OHP
☎ (01535) 643500. OPEN 9.30 - 5.30 MON - SAT, 11 - 5 SUN.
THE YORKSHIRE VILLAGE AT BATLEY, BRADFORD ROAD, BATLEY,
WEST YORKSHIRE WF17 6LZ
☎ (01924) 444948. OPEN 9.30 - 5.30 MON - FRI, 9 - 5.30 SAT, 11 - 5 SUN.
HORNSEA FREEPORT VILLAGE, ROLSTON ROAD, HORNSEA,
EAST YORKSHIRE HU18 1UT
☎ (01964) 537452. OPEN 9.30 - 6 MON - SAT, 11 - 5 SUN.
THE YORKSHIRE OUTLET, WHITE ROSE WAY, DONCASTER,
SOUTH YORKSHIRE DN4 5PH
☎ (01302) 360117. OPEN 10 - 6 MON - SAT, 11 - 5 SUN.
FREEPORT DESIGNER OUTLET, CARWOOD ROAD, GLASSHOUGHTON,
CASTLEFORD, WESTYORKSHIRE WF10 4SB
☎ (01977) 518327. OPEN 10 - 8 MON - FRI, 10 - 6 SAT, 11 - 5 SUN.

Permanent Discount Outlet • *Household* • *Furniture/Soft Furnishings*

A bargain hunter's paradise: piled high with thousands of linen bargains. A massive collection of top brands such as Crown, Coloroll, Broomhill, Jeff Banks Ports-of-Call, to name but a few. They also stock an extensive range of crockery, class, gifts, clothing, books and toys. Licensed restaurant.

POSTOPTICS
ORDER DEPT, FREEPOST, YORK, NORTH YORKSHIRE YO1 8GX
☎ (0800) 038 3333. MAIL ORDER.

Permanent Discount Outlet • *Womenswear Only*

PostOptics is a division of Viewpoint, one of the largest contact lens practices in the UK. Using their massive purchasing power, they are able to offer dramatic savings of up to 33% on contact lens solutions. Their products are supplied by post in three-month packs which are significantly cheaper than the smaller sizes normally found on sale. £2.50 p&p is added to single orders, six month packs are supplied post free.

PREMIER & CAROUSEL
78 STREET LANE, LEEDS, WEST YORKSHIRE LS8 2AL
☎ (0113) 266 6680. OPEN 11 - 5 TUE - FRI, 10 - 5 SAT.

Dress Agency • *Womenswear & Menswear* • *Children*

Premier & Carousel has an extensive range of nearly-new designer and high street fashion for all seasons and occasions at a fraction of the original cost. They stock evening wear, daywear, smart casuals, special occasion outfits, costume jewellery, accessories for men and women.

PRICE'S CANDLES
THE YORKSHIRE OUTLET, WHITE ROSE WAY, DONCASTER,
SOUTH YORKSHIRE DN4 5JH
☎ (01302) 325362. OPEN 10 - 6 MON - SAT, 11 - 5 SUN.
MCARTHURGLEN DESIGNER OUTLET CENTRE, ST NICHOLAS
AVENUE, FULFORD, JUNCTION OF A19 AND A64, YORK YO1 3RE
☎ (01904) 677997. OPEN 10 - 6 MON - SAT, UNTIL 8 ON THUR,
11 - 5 SUN.
Factory Shop in a Factory Shopping Village • *Household*
Everything sold in these shops are seconds, discontinued sizes not available elsewhere, over-runs or candles in old packaging that has now been replaced. There are church candles, lanterns, candles in pots and glass jars, star-shaped candles, floating candles, candlestick holders, serviettes, scented candles and garden torches.

PRIESTLEY'S
1 NORMAN COURT, 11 GRAPE LANE, YORK,
NORTH YORKSHIRE YO1 2HU
☎ (01904) 623114. OPEN 11 - 5 MON - FRI, 9.30 - 5 SAT.
Secondhand and Vintage Clothes • *Womenswear & Menswear*
Period clothing from the 1930s-1970s, pretty and interesting, wearable eveningwear and collectables for men and women. For example, 1950s model dress for £50.

RAINBOW
STATION ROAD, OAKWORTH, KEIGHLEY, WEST YORKSHIRE BD22 ODU
☎ (01535) 644433. OPEN 10 - 5 MON - fri, 10 - 5 SAT.
Hire Shop • *Children*
Retail shop which also hire out baby equipment from wooden cots and car seats to pushchairs, bouncy castles and baby monitors. A wooden cot costs £15 to hire for 1 month, plus a £10 refundable deposit. There is no minimum time limit.

READMANS LTD
ALFRED HOUSE, SPENCE LANE, HOLBECK, LEEDS,
WEST YORKSHIRE LS12 1EF
☎ (0113) 243 6355 CASH AND CARRY. OPEN 9 - 9 MON - FRI, 8.30 - 6 SAT,
10 - 4 SUN.
Permanent Discount Outlet • *Womenswear & Menswear*
Children • *Household*
Mainly women's, men's and children's clothing as well as bedding, textiles, toiletries, footwear, toys, children's books, shoes and towels at prices which are cheaper than the high street. Most of the stock is from Marks & Spencer, but they also sell Calvin Klein, Italian leather shoes, Playtex and Gossard underwear, Dorma bedding. Members of the public can enter with admission card, obtainable on application on a day basis. Cafe on second floor.

REMINGTON
THE YORKSHIRE OUTLET, WHITE ROSE WAY, DONCASTER,
SOUTH YORKSHIRE DN4 5JH
☎ (01302) 366434. OPEN 10 - 6 MON - SAT, 11 - 5 SUN.
MCARTHURGLEN DESIGNER OUTLET CENTRE, YORK.
☎ (01904) 677899. OPEN 10 - 6 MON - SAT, 10 - 8 ON THUR, 11 - 5 SUN.
Factory Shop in a Factory Shopping Village • *Electrical Equipment*
Lots of famous names here from Monogram cutlery to Braun, Philips, Remington, Silencio, Wahl, Krups, Swan and Kenwood small kitchen equipment. There are usually hair, beauty and male grooming accessories as well as kitchen equipment, all at reduced prices. A great place to buy gifts or replenish the kitchen equipment with combi stylers, turbo travel plus hairdryers, air purifiers, liquidisers; food processors; batteries; clocks; and cutlery. Some of the packaging may be damaged but the products are in perfect working order.

RIPON REVIVALS
6 KIRKGATE, RIPON, NORTH YORKSHIRE HG4 1PA
☎ (01765) 604007. OPEN 10 - 5 MON - SAT.
Dress Agency • *Womenswear & Menswear*
Nearly-new clothes for men and women for special occasions: weddings, graduations, evening wear, including Betty Barclay, Betty Jackson, Grace, Olsen, Morgan, Penny Black, Jackpot, Max Mara, Basler, Penny Black, Armani, Escada, Jaeger, Aquascutum. There is a mix of high street and designer wear as well as shoes, bags jewellery, hats and accessories. Sizes 8 - 24.

RL & CM BOND LTD
93 - 99 TOWN STREET, FARSLEY, PUDSEY, NEAR LEEDS,
WEST YORKSHIRE LS28 5HX
☎ (0113) 257 4905. OPEN 9 - 4.30 WED - SAT.
Permanent Discount Outlet • *Furniture/Soft Furnishings*
Two-storey shop selling everything for the needlecraft and cross stitch enthusiast at very competitive prices. There are tapestry kits, silks, zips, threads, buttons, ribbons, cross stitch books galore, as well as a host of items for curtain makers including rufflette tape, braid, trimmings, fringing, bullion fringe, curtain hooks, header tape for Austrian and festoon blinds and tie-backs. All sewing supplies and haberdashery at unbelievable prices.

ROYAL BRIERLEY CRYSTAL
HORNSEA FREEPORT VILLAGE, ROLSTON ROAD, HORNSEA,
EAST YORKSHIRE HU18 1UT
☎ (01964) 532928. OPEN 9.30 - 6 SEVEN DAYS A WEEK.
Factory Shop • *Household*
Sells seconds of Royal Brierley crystal at 30%-50% off retail price, with two special sales. Contact the shop for more information.

SALTS MILL
VICTORIA ROAD, SALTAIRE, SHIPLEY, WEST YORKSHIRE BD18 3LB
☎ (01274) 531163. OPEN 10 - 6 SEVEN DAYS A WEEK.
Factory Shop • *Furniture/Soft Furnishings* • *Household*
Womenswear & Menswear • *Children*

Home to a variety of different businesses including fabrics, kitchen wares, clothes, jewellery and books.

SARROUCHE
28 HARROGATE ROAD, RAWDON, NEAR LEEDS,
WEST YORKSHIRE LS19 6HJ
☎ (0113) 250 9990. OPEN 10 - 5 MON - SAT.
Permanent Discount Outlet • *Womenswear Only*

Full price shop selling Italian and French designers including Gina, Sarrouche, Tricot Lorrain and Ronald Joyce evening wear, also carrying a large selection of sample designerwear at discounted prices. Wedding outfits, shoes and jewellery are also sold.

SCOOPS
41 BARNSLEY ROAD, SOUTH PONTEFRACT, WEST YORKSHIRE WF8 2RN
☎ (01977) 642256. OPEN 9 - 5.30 MON - SAT.
Permanent Discount Outlet • *Womenswear & Menswear*
Electrical • *Household* • *Children*

Grattan catalogue shop. There is a selection of items from those featured in the catalogue, which can consist of anything from children's clothes and toys to bedding, electrical equipment and nursery accessories. Each shop sells a slightly different range, so always ring first to check they stock what you want. All items are discounted by up to 50%.

SCENT TO YOU
THE DESIGNER ROOM, FREEPORT CASTLEFORD DESIGNER OUTLET,
CARRWOOD ROAD, GLASSHOUGHTON, CASTLEFORD, OFF JUNCTION
32 OF M52, WEST YORKSHIRE WF10 4SB
☎ (01977) 519243. OPEN 10 - 8 MON - FRI, 10 - 6 SAT, 11 - 5 SUN.
THE DESIGNER ROOM, FREEPORT HORNSEA OUTLET VILLAGE,
ROLSTON ROAD, HORNSEA, EAST YORKSHIRE HU18 1UT
☎ (01964) 537480. OPEN 9.30 - 6 DAILY.
Factory Shop in a Factory Shopping Village • *Womenswear Only*

Operating within The Designer Room at these outlet villages, Scent to You sells discounted perfume, cosmetics and accessories including body lotions and gels. The company, which has more than thirty branches, buys in bulk and sells more cheaply, relying on a high turnover for profit. Discounts range from 5% to 60%, with greater savings during their twice-yearly sales (phone for details). Most of the leading brand names in perfume are stocked including Christian Lacroix, Armani, Charlie, Givenchy, Anais Anais from Cacherel,

Charlie from Revlon, Coco Chanel, Christian Dior, Elizabeth Taylor, Blue Grass from Elizabeth Arden, Aramis, Lagerfeld. Plus cosmetics from REvlon and Spectacular and skincare from Clarins and Lancome as well as Scent To You's own range of bags, watches, hair brushes and brushkits which is sold under the name S.T.Y. Designs. Stock varies greatly due to the fast turnover and varying supplies so more than one visit may be necessary to obtain the scent of your choice. Or phone first to avoid disappointment.

SCOTTS MILLS FACTORY OUTLET
FACTORY STREET AND TONG STREET, DUDLEY HILL, BRADFORD, WEST YORKSHIRE
☎ (01274) 681238. OPEN 9.30 - 5.30 MON - SAT, 10 - 4 SUN.
Factory Shop • *Furniture/Soft Furnishings Womenswear & Menswear* • *Children*
Factory shop selling a wide range of goods from beds, carpets and pine furniture to clothes for men, women and children. The clothes are divided into those with labels - from names such as Roman, Klass, Just Eleganz and Jamie Oliver - to those without labels from names such as Dorothy Perkins, Next and Principles. There is also an underwear section with lingerie from Camille and a men's department selling Wolsey, Double Two and Fruit of the Loom.

SECOND GLANCE
STABLE COURT, HUDDERSFIELD ROAD, HOLMFIRTH, HUDDERSFIELD, WEST YORKSHIRE
☎ (01484) 684521. OPEN 9 - 5 MON - SAT, 11 - 4 SUN.
Permanent Discount Outlet • *Womenswear & Menswear* • *Children*
Quality chainstore seconds from Marks & Spencer and BhS for men, women and children. The labels are cut out, however.

SHARE YOUR PERKS
☎ (0800) 212577, WEBSITE: www.premierfunds.co.uk
Many companies with stock market valuations offer perks to their shareholders. For example, anyone anyone holding at least 1,000 shares in Barratt homes for 12 months and then buying a Barratt home would save £500 for every £25,000 they spent. Shareholders in Debenhams get 12.5% off goods if they have 2,000 or more shares while Selfridges sends holders of 5000 shares £100 of store vouchers. Airtours shareholders get a 10% discount on holidays and a free bottle of champagne on each flight with Airtours International. Shareholders in Associated British Foods get an £8 sample bags of the company's products when they attend its annual meeting. The perks are not a good reason to buy shares, but be aware that they do exist if you have bought shares. You can find out what your shares might bring you in the way of perks with Premier Asset Management's Perk Guide, cost £2.50, from the above telephone number.

SHEPHERDS FACTORY SHOP
643 CHESTERFIELD ROAD, WOODSEATS, SHEFFIELD,
SOUTH YORKSHIRE S8 0RY
☎ (0114) 255 8418. OPEN 9 - 5 MON - SAT.
Factory Shop • *Womenswear & Menswear* • *Children* • *Household*
Good quality ex-chainstore merchandise from shops such as Marks & Spencer and Next, although all the labels are cut out. Stock includes knitwear, dresses, suits, blouses, skirts, sportswear, nightwear, trousers for women and childrenswear. Also some household goods such as towels. Discounts range up to 50%. There are other branches in Derby, Ilkeston and Lichfield.

SHIRTS TO SUIT
3 MAIN STREET, FULFORD, YORK, NORTH YORKSHIRE YO10 4HJ
☎ (01904) 634508. OPEN 8.30 - 5 MON - THUR, 8.30 - 4.30 FRI, 9.30 - 4 SAT.
Factory Shop • *Womenswear & Menswear*
Makes shirts and blouses for many of the high street department stores, as well as its own range of perfects which it sells in the factory shop at discounts of 30%. Cotton and polycotton blouses cost from £13.95, Viyella ones, £32.95. Also makes extra long sleeved shirts for the taller man from £17.95, sells socks and ties and has a made to measure service.

SMITH'S MILL SHOP
THOMAS STREET, HALIFAX, WEST YORKSHIRE HX1 1QX
☎ (01422) 343432. OPEN 9 - 5 MON - SAT, 10 - 4 SUN.
Permanent Discount Outlet • *Furniture/Soft Furnishings*
Perfect stock and some seconds in a wide range of curtain fabrics at discounts of 50%, as well as tracks, poles and haberdashery. The most expensive fabric in the shop is £9 a square yard, the cheapest £1 and ranges from voiles, chenilles and fur to dress materials. Brands include Prestigious, Ashley Wilde, SMD, Voyage and many more. Full measuring, fitting and sewing service on site.

SOPHIE'S CHOICE
27 NORTH LANE, HEADINGLEY, LEEDS, WEST YORKSHIRE LS6 3HW
☎ (0113) 2743913. OPEN 10 - 5 MON - SAT.
Dress Agency • *Womenswear* • *Children*
Nearly-new ladies and children's clothes which caters for middle to upmarket labels. Also sells shoes, handbags, hats and children's accessories. Navy blue blazers, £35, originally £200; designer shirts, £14.50, usually £80. They specialise in teenage clothing, and have a large range including Morgan, Kookai and Warehouse.

SPENCERS TROUSERS
FRIENDLY WORKS, BURNLEY ROAD, SOWERBY BRIDGE,
WEST YORKSHIRE HX6 2TL
☎ (01422) 833020. WEBSITE: www.spencers-trousers.com
OPEN 9 - 5 MON - SAT.
Factory Shop • *Menswear Only*
Spencers Trousers manufacture better quality trousers in traditional fabrics (cords, moleskin, worsteds) and sell seconds, overstocks, returns and ends of lines at marvellous savings. They occasionally sell plus twos, but phone first to check availablility. The shop is situated on the A646 between Halifax and Hebden Bridgein West Yorkshire and is a traditional factory shop. It also offers a made-to-measure service with next-day delivery on some materials.

SPOILS
UNIT LG9, LG22, PART LG21, PRINCES QUAY, HULL,
EAST YORKSHIRE HU1 2PQ
☎ (01482) 327102. OPEN 9 - 5.30 MON - SAT, 10.30 - 4 SUN.
UNIT 5, ST JOHN'S CENTRE, MERRION STREET, LEEDS LS2 8LQ
☎ (0113) 244 8187. OPEN 9 - 5.30 MON - SAT, 11 - 5 SUN.
UNIT M8U7, WHITE ROSE SHOPPING CENTRE, DEWSBURY ROAD,
LEEDS LS11 8LU
☎ (0113) 271 1433. OPEN 9.30 - 6 MON - FRI, 8 ON WED, 9 - 6 SAT, 11 - 5 SUN.
Permanent Discount Outlet • *Household*
General domestic glassware, non-stick bakeware, non-electrical kitchen gadgets, ceramic oven-to-tableware, textiles, cutting boards, aluminium non-stick cookware, bakeware, plastic kitchenware, plastic storage, woodware, coffee pots/makers, furniture, mirrors and picture frames. Rather than being discounted, all the merchandise is very competitively priced - in fact, the company carry out competitors' checks frequently in order to monitor pricing. With 38 branches, the company is able to buy in bulk and thus negotiate very good prices.

SPORTS SHOES UNLIMITED
YORKSHIRE
☎ (01274) 530530. MAIL ORDER.
Permanent Discount Outlet • *Sportswear & Equipment*
Womenswear & Menswear • *Children*
Sports and training clothes and equipment, many branded names. Newer styles are not discounted but there is usually a range of last season's stock. Phone for a brochure.

SPRINGFIELD CLOTHING
THE MILL SHOP, NORMAN ROAD, DENBY DALE, HUDDERSFIELD,
WEST YORKSHIRE HD8 8TH
☎ (01484 865082). OPEN 9 - 5 MON - SAT, 10 - 5 SUN.
Permanent Discount Outlet • *Womenswear & Menswear*
Children • *Household* • *Furniture/Soft Furnishings*
Located in newly-refurbished premises, Springfield Clothing sells clothes for all the family at up to 50% discount on high street prices such as Marks & Spencer, Principles, Next, Monsoon and Dorothy Perkins. Also stocks men's and women's underwear, a selection of basic bedding, duvets, sheets, pillows, pillow cases as well as tea towels and table cloths and Sheffield cutlery, all at discounted prices.

STAPLES, THE OFFICE SUPERSTORE
UNIT 11B, JUNCTION STREET, CROWN POINT RETAIL PARK, HUNSLET
LANE, LEEDS, WEST YORKSHIRE LS10 1ET
☎ (0113) 2421061. WEBSITE: www.staples.co.uk
OPEN 8 - 8 MON - FRI, 9 - 6 SAT, 11 - 5 SUN. MAIL ORDER ALSO.
Permanent Discount Outlet • *Furniture/Soft Furnishings*
Office equipment and furniture supplier which is aimed at businesses, but is also open to the public. The owner buys in bulk and so is able to sell at very competitive prices a range of goods from paper clips to personal computers. Customers do not have to buy in bulk to make savings. A mail order catalogue is available and delivery is free on purchases over £30 (area permitting). There are more than 70 branches countrywide - for your nearest store, phone Talking Pages on 0800 600 900.

START-RITE
FREEPORT CASTLEFORD DESIGNER OUTLET VILLAGE, CARRWOOD
ROAD, GLASSHOUGHTON, CASTLEFORD, YORKSHIRE WS10 4SB
☎ (01977) 555064. OPEN 10 - 8 MON - FRI, 10 - 6 SAT, 11 - 5 SUN.
Factory Shop • *Children* • *Womenswear & Menswear*
The Children's shoe experts have a large factory shop selling clearance lines at discounts of one third, and rejects at discounts of 50%. They don't stock the full range - it's a matter of choosing from what's available. Rejects are sold at at least half price; end of sales stock with not quite such a high discount. There are also some senior sizes up to 9. Feet are expertly measured by trained staff.

SUMMER GRAND SALE
RIPLEY CASTLE, RIPLEY, NEAR HARROGATE, NORTH YORKSHIRE,
ORGANISER: DAVID HESLAM, PO BOX 4, LECHLADE, GLOS GL7 3YB.
☎ (01367) 860017.
Designer Sale • *Household*
There are now three annual Grand Sales taking place countrywide. The Christmas Grand Sale in London, with over 120 different small companies

selling their merchandise to the public, is the largest. This takes place in mid-November each year. Quality is high and covers everything from dried flowers to bath accessories, Amish quilts to silverware, wooden toys to hand-painted kitchenware, often at discount because they are ends of lines. There is a Spring Grand Sale at Sudeley Castle, Winchcombe, near Cheltenham, Glos every April/May and a Summer Grand Sale at Ripley Castle, near Harrogate, North Yorkshire, in June, both of which feature gardening equipment as well as decorative homes accessories. Phone the above number to put your name on the mailing list; a proportion of the ticket revenue goes to charity.

TAYLOR'S MILL SHOP FACTORY OUTLET
UNIT 19A, NORTONTHORPE MILL, WAKEFIELD ROAD, SCISSETT,
NEAR HUDDERSFIELD, YORKSHIRE HD8 9FB
☎ (01484) 861442. OPEN 10 - 5 MON - SAT, 11 - 5 SUN.
Factory Shop • *Womenswear* • *Children*
Quality chainstore and well-known labels for women and children including Stephen Y, Saloos, Wicked, Frank Saul and Sky. On sale are suits, casualwear, evening wear, raincoats at appropriate times of year, accessories such as handbags, purses and scarves, underwear and hosiery. Also men's sweaters, underwear, pyjamas and socks.

THE BODY SHOP DEPOT
MCARTHURGLEN DESIGNER OUTLET, ST NICHOLAS AVENUE,
FULFORD, YORK, YORKSHIRE YO19 4TA
☎ (01904) 613873. OPEN 10 - 6 MON - SAT, 10 - 8 THUR, 11 - 5 SUN.
Factory Shop in a Factory Shopping Village • *Food and Leisure*
Popular lines from a range of toiletries, The Body Shop Colourings make-up, gifts and accessories, bath, sun and skincare products, all of which are ends of lines sold at 50% less than its high street sites.

THE BOSTON DRESSER
154 HIGH STREET, BOSTON SPA, WETHERBY,
NORTH YORKSHIRE LS23 6BW
☎ (01937) 844944. OPEN 10 - 5 TUE - SAT.
Dress Agency • *Womenswear Only*
New and nearly-new top quality ladieswear in sizes 8 - 24 including names such as Max Mara, Viyella, Yarell, Mondi and Dolce & Gabbana. Hats, belts, handbags and shoes are also available in sizes from 3 to 8.

THE CAPE
CAPE COUNTRY FURNITURE, COMMERCIAL STREET, MORLEY,
WEST YORKSHIRE LS27 8HN
☎ (0113) 253 1024. OPEN 9 - 5 MON - SAT.
Factory Shop • *Household* • *Furniture/Soft Furnishings*
High density pine furniture made in South Africa from trees grown in managed forests, is sold at factory direct prices with home delivery throughout the UK. The range includes beds, wardrobes, blanket boxes, chests of drawers, tallboys, dressing tables, cheval mirrors, headboards, mattresses, a kitchen range, dining room tables, Welsh dressers, hi-fi units, bookcases. Also on sale in this shops is a range of African accessories and artefacts from Zimbabwe encompassing mirrors, prints, serpentine (stone) ornaments, recylced stationery, handmade wirework, candles and other ethnic and traditional gifts. Colour brochure and price list available on 01535 650940.

THE CURTAIN EXCHANGE
162 HIGH STREET, BOSTON SPA, WEST YORKSHIRE LS23 6BW
☎ (01937) 849755. OPEN 10 - 5 MON - SAT.
Secondhand shops • *Furniture/Soft Furnishings*
The Curtain Exchange is a franchised group of shops selling beautiful top quality secondhand curtains, blinds, pelmets, etc at between one-third and one half of the brand new price. Their stock comes from a variety of sources: people who are moving house; people who have curtains made and then feel they are wrong for the room; show houses where the builder wants to recoup some of his outgoings; interior designers' mistakes. Stock changes constantly and ranges from rich brocades, damasks and velvets to chintzes, linens and cottons. Designer names include Colefax & Fowler, Designers Guild, Laura Ashley, Warner, Sanderson, Osborne & Little, Fortuny and Bennison. A team of fitters and alteration experts are available if required. They offer a 24-hour availability. The Curtain Exchange also supply bespoke ranges with samples of curtains hanging. These fabrics are chosen from suppliers all over the world and are an excellent buy. They also offer ready made curtains designed exclusively for them which come in lengths up to 305cm (120"). These are outstanding value, e.g. 80" wide, 120" drop start at £175 including VAT.

THE DARLEY MILL CENTRE
DARLEY, NEAR HARROGATE, NORTH YORKSHIRE HG3 2QQ
☎ (01423) 780857. OPEN 9.30 - 5.30 MON - SAT, 11 - 5 SUN.
Permanent Discount Outlet • *Household*
Furniture/Soft Furnishings • *Food and Leisure*
Womenswear & Menswear
Offers a great day out for the whole family, combining great bargains in clothing, crockery, linens, crafts and exclusive gifts to lots for children to see and do. This 17th century corn mill has one of the largest working water wheels in Yorkshire and there's a licensed restaurant with an outdoor terrace.

THE DAVID MELLOR FACTORY SHOP
THE ROUND BUILDING, HATHERSAGE, SHEFFIELD, YORKSHIRE S32 1BA
☎ (01433) 650220. OPEN 10 - 5 MON - SAT, 11- 5 SUN.
Factory Shop • *Household*
Up to 10% discount on most David Mellor cutlery designs to personal shoppers. The shop, situated in a former industrial workshop at an old gasworks in the Peak District, also sells handthrown pottery with which David Mellor has been involved in design or development at normal prices, as well as kitchen racks, basketware and cutlery boxes. Lots of wooden utensils and good quality kitchenware.

THE FABRIC EMPORIUM
KIDD HOUSE, WHITEHALL ROAD, LEEDS, YORKSHIRE LS12 1AP
☎ (0113) 2458601. OPEN 9.30 - 6 MON - SAT, 10 - 4 SUN.
Permanent Discount Outlet • *Furniture/Soft Furnishings*
Curtain and upholstery own brand fabrics and those from many well-known high street brands such as Laura Ashley, Next and Marks & Spencer. Because they buy job lots from the USA, Europe and the UK, prices range from 99p a metre to £25.99 a metre although the normal recommended retail price of many items ranges from £16 to £30 a metre. Most goods are first quality and the majority of goods are priced in the range of £3.99 to £7.99 a metre. Stock is continually changing and brands include Prestigious, Voyage, Moggashel, Monkwell, and Matthew Stevens. All curtain accessories are available and there is an in-house making up service.

THE FABRIC SHOP
82 MAIN STREET, ADDINGHAM, NEAR ILKLEY,
WEST YORKSHIRE LS29 OPL
☎ (01943) 830982. OPEN 9 - 5 MON - SAT.
Permanent Discount Outlet • *Furniture/Soft Furnishings*
Great fabric bargains in this rabbit warren of interconnecting rooms, stacked high to the ceiling with bolts of perfects and seconds of furnishing fabrics. Brands include Moygashel Monkwell and Designers Guild. Most of the fabric, tapestries and damasks are from Italian and US manufacturers. Prints on the roll cost no more than £8.80 per metre, upholstery fabric costs no more than £15 per metre. Fabrics range from £3-£15 a metre, curtain lining from £2.40 - £3 a metre, tapes from 45p a metre and interlining from £3 a metre. No making up service; telephone orders taken. They also stock seconds of basics such as lining fabrics, muslin and 90" wide sheeting. The staff are very helpful and knowledgeable and there is parking directly outside or in the next side street at the village car park. You can also find the merchandise at York market on a Tuesday and Ripon market on a Thursday.

THE FACTORY SHOP
LAWKHOLME LANE, KEIGHLEY, WEST YORSHIRE BD21 3JQ
☎ (01535) 611703. OPEN 9.30 - 5 MON - SAT, 10.30 - 4.30 SUN.
5 NORTH STREET, RIPON, NORTH YORKSHIRE HG4 1JY
☎ (01765) 601156. OPEN 9 - 5 MON - SAT.
LIGHTWATER VALLEY SHOPPING VILLAGE, NORTH STAINLEY, RIPON, NORTH YORKSHIRE HG4 3HT
☎ (01765) 635438. OPEN 10 - 6 MON - SAT, 11 - 5 SUN.
THE CLOTHES SHOP, PARK ROSE LTD, CARNABY COVERT LANE, CARNABY, BRIDLINGTON, NORTH YORKSHIRE YO15 3QF
☎ (01262) 603518. OPEN 10 - 5 MON - SAT, 10.30 - 4.30 SUN.
WHEATLEY LANE, LEEDS ROAD, ILKLEY, WEST YORKSHIRE LS29 8BS
☎ (01943) 604514. OPEN 9 - 5.30 MON - SAT, 10.30 - 4.30 SUN.
Factory Shop • *Children* • *Womenswear & Menswear* • *Household Furniture/Soft Furnishings* • *Sportswear & Equipment*
Wide range on sale includes men's, ladies and children's clothing and footwear; household textiles; toiletries; hardware; luggage; lighting and bedding, most of which are chainstore and high street brands at discounts of approximately 30%-50%. There are weekly deliveries and brands include many major stars such as Adidas, Nike, Joe Bloggs and Brabantia to name just a few. There are kitchen and furniture displays and a new line in Cape Country furniture on sale. Ranges are continually changing and few factory shops offer such a variety under one roof. Most of the shops have their own car parks or there are nearby car parking facilities. The Lightwater and Bridlington outlets are part of a Shopping and Leisure Park with a host of brand concessions in clothing and homeware plus restaurant. It is free to enter, although the leisure park does make a charge. Car parking is free except in Ripon, where public car parks are pay and display.

THE FACTORY SHOP
NAYLOR JENNINGS, GREEN LANE DYEWORKS, GREEN LANE, YEADON, LEEDS, WEST YORKSHIRE LS19 7XP
☎ (0113) 250 2933. OPEN 9.30 - 4.30 MON - FRI, 10 - 4 SAT, 11 - 4 SUN.
CV CLOTHING, WEST END LANE, ROSSINGTON, DONCASTER, SOUTH YORKSHIRE DN11 OPQ
☎ (01302) 860302. OPEN 10 - 5 MON - SAT, 11 - 4 SUN.
Factory Shop • *Womenswear & Menswear* • *Children* • *Household*
Part of the Coats Viyella group, which makes quality clothing for many of the major high street storres, overstocks and clearance lines are sold through more than 30 of the group's factory shops. Many of you will recognise the garments on sale, despite the lack of well-known labels. Ladieswear includes dresses, blouses, jumpers, cardigans, trousers, nightwear, underwear, lingerie, hosiery, coats and swimwear. Menswear includes trousers, belts, shirts, ties, pullovers, cardigans, T-shirts, underwear, nightwear, hosiery and jackets. Childrenswear includes jackets, trousers, T-shirts, underwear, hosiery, jumpers and babywear.

Although predominantly fashion, there are also curtain linings, cotton chintz and towels on sale. There are regular deliveries to constantly update the range.

THE FAMOUS BRUNSWICK WAREHOUSE
☎ (0191) 217 0084. HEAD OFFICE.
Permanent Discount Outlet • *Womenswear & Menswear*
Children • *Sportswear & Equipment*

Self-service discount store chain with thirty-five branches selling branded sportswear and sports footwear as well as non-branded footwear at discounts of 50%. Also a reasonable selection of clothing and accessories. Phone head office telephone number for your local branch.

THE GREAT CLOTHES FASHION STORE
84 YORK ROAD, LEEDS, WEST YORKSHIRE LS9 9AA
☎ (0113) 2350303. OPEN 9.30 - 9 MON - FRI, 9.30 - 6 SAT, 11 - 5 SUN.
Permanent Discount Outlet • *Hire Shops*
Womenswear & Menswear • *Children*

50,000 square feet of space with clothes for men, women and children from French Connection, Adidas, Berghaus, Pringle, Wolsey, Puma, Nike, Christian Dior to Sonnetti, and including all brands of jeans. There are also accessories such as socks, shoes for adults, hats, scarves and underwear. Formal men's and boyswear includes hire of morning suits and kilts for weddings and a comprehensive 'Big Man's Department' with sizes up to 54" chest. All stock is current season and is discounted by 20%. Free alterations carried out on site and there is a coffee shop and free parking.

THE HARROGATE DRESS AGENCY
3 JOHN STREET, OFF JAMES STREET, HARROGATE,
WEST YORKSHIRE HG1 1JZ
☎ (01423) 521344. OPEN 9.30 - 5 MON - FRI, 10 - 5 SAT.
Dress Agency • *Womenswear & Menswear*

Two-storey shop with men's and women's top quality labels such as Jean Muir, Moschino, Georges Rech, Jaeger, Daks, Boss, Armani as well as some high street names. Also jewellery, shoes, handbags. and any accessory you might need.

THE ILKLEY DRESS AGENCY
THE ALPACA STUDIO, VICTORIAN ARCADE, HAWKSWORTH STREET, ILKLEY, WEST YORKSHIRE
☎ (01943) 600732. OPEN 10 - 4.30 MON - FRI, 10 - 5.30 SAT
Dress Agency • *Womenswear Only*

Ever-changing stock of womenswear by Max Mara, Paul Costelloe, Monsoon, Marks and Spencers etc to sell to you or for you in stylish premises. Luxurious Alpaca knitwear by Spirit of the Andes, costume jewellery, handbags, shoes, hats and accessories for sale.

THE LIGHTING FACTORY SHOP
GELDERD ROAD, LEEDS, WEST YORKSHIRE LS12 6NB
☎ (0113) 276 7491. OPEN 9 - 5 MON - SAT, 10 - 4 SUN.
Factory Shop • *Electrical Equipment*
First quality seconds and end of line lighting for the house and garden at very competitive prices. Large range includes wall lights, spots, fluorescents, table lamps, student and children's lamps, glass shades, party lights, security and garden lighting. Also light bulbs and fluorescent tubes.

THE SHOE FACTORY SHOP
6/7 OSLO ROAD, SUTTON FIELDS, HULL, EAST YORKSHIRE HU7 OYN
☎ (01482) 839292. OPEN 9 - 5 MON - WED, SAT, 9 - 7 THUR, FRI, 10 -4 SUN.
Factory Shop • *Womenswear & Menswear* • *Children*
Men's, women's and children's shoes and accessories which are bought in from other manufacturers including Spanish, Portuguese and Italian companies. All are unbranded. The range covers from mocassins to dressy shoes. Ladies shoes which would cost £35 retail are £29. Children's shoes from size 6 to adult size 5 from £10 upwards. Slippers start at baby size 4 to junior size 2 from £3.50 - £6.50.

THE SHOE SHELTER
UNIT 16A SPRINGFIELD MILLS, DENBY-DALE, HUDDERSFIELD,
WEST YORKSHIRE HD8 9TH
☎ (01484) 866221. OPEN 9.30 - 5 MON - FRI, 9 - 5 SAT,
10 - 5 SUN AND BANK HOLIDAYS.
Permanent Discount Outlet • *Womenswear & Menswear* • *Children*
Wide range of men's, women's and children's shoes with labels such as Ecco, Loake, Gabor, Start-Rite, Elefanten and Lotus, usually sold at up to 50% of normal high street prices.

THE SHUTTLE FABRIC SHOP
BAILDON BRIDGE, OTLEY ROAD, SHIPLEY, YORKSHIRE BD17 7AA
☎ (01274) 587171. OPEN 9 - 5.30 MON - SAT.
Permanent Discount Outlet • *Furniture/Soft Furnishings*
Sells discounted dress fabrics and some furnishing fabrics from well-known designers as well as furnishing sheeting, quilting, curtain lining, plastic fabrics for tablecloths, wadding, patterns and general haberdashery. Many are ends of lines and there are always special offers.

THE SPORTS FACTORY
THE YORKSHIRE OUTLET, WHITE ROSE WAY, DONCASTER,
SOUTH YORKSHIRE DN4 5JH
☎ (01302) 322 663. OPEN 10 - 6 MON - SAT, 11 - 5 SUN.
Factory Shop in a Factory Shopping Village
Sportswear & Equipment • *Womenswear & Menswear* • *Children*
Wide range of sports clothes and accessories, some of which are only stocked in season (for example, cricket bats and tennis rackets in summer only). There

are also tennis rackets, cricket gear, leisure clothing (Kicker, Kangol, Timberland, Mizuno, Champion, and Reggatta). All are discontinued lines and are cheaper than in the high street by between 10% - 40%. and are cheaper than in the high street by between 10%-40%.

THE TEA POTTERY
BUSINESS PARK, HARMBY ROAD, LEYBURN, WENSLEYDALE, NORTH YORKSHIRE DL8 5QA
☎ (01969) 623839. OPEN 9 - 5 SEVEN DAYS A WEEK.
Factory Shop • *Household*
A boon for collectors of novelty teapots, all of which are manufactured on site in up to 57 different designs and in sizes from one cup to five cups. Designs include Welsh dressers, caravans, Agas, cookers, bellboys with luggage, can-can girls, washbasins and a host of others, many of which are collectors' items. Prices range from £9.95 - £45 for perfects, which represents a 10% - 20% savings on retail prices, and up to 50% discounts on seconds. This factory shop has refreshments, a large free car park and access for the disabled, while its sister shop in Keswick is smaller and has no refreshments or disabled facilities.

THE YORKSHIRE MILL VILLAGE
BRADFORD ROAD, BATLEY, WEST YORKSHIRE WF17 5LZ
☎ (01924) 423172. OPEN 9.30 - 5.30 MON - SAT, 11 - 5 SUN.
Factory Shop • *Womenswear & Menswear • Children • Household Furniture/Soft Furnishings • Sportswear & Equipment Food and Leisure • Electrical Equipment*
Launched in September 2000, following a £6 million refurbishment and redevelopment, the Yorkshire Mill Village promises to be the UK's largest and most exciting mill shopping complex. Situated within a fully restored Victorian mill comprising approximately 125,000 square feet of trading space, the complex offers a unique value shopping experience within a stimulating atmospheric and rewarding environment. The extensive retail offer includes branded discounted perfumery, jewellery, accessories, luggage, gifts, menswear, ladieswear, unisex fashions, lingerie, swimwear, shoes, glass and china, cookshop, haberdashery, linens, home accessories, home furnishings, fabrics, lighting, books and CDs. Located at Batley in the heart of West Yorkshire, the complex is easy to access by car, coach and train. Junction 40 of the M1 and junctions 27 and 28 of the M62 are located within 5 and 6 miles of the site respectively. In addition, Batley station is five minutes walk away, providing easy access to Leeds and Manchester from the Trans-Pennine railway. There are over 500 on-site car parking spaces, substantial coach parking and overflow parking in close proximity. On-site, there are children's and male creches, a cybercafe, tourist information centre, cashpoint and disabled access throughout. The site is fully under cover. A contemporary, brasserie-style licensed restaurant offers a wide mixture of European food while the Yorkshire Tea-Room offers cold foods and snacks, self service, in a period setting. The Yorkshire Exhibition celebrates the county of Yorkshire, its

history and people while the Yorkshire Food Emporium, a two-level speciality store, comprises speciality Yorkshire food brands in a Victorian environment. On sale here are Bacchanalia selling glass, china, cutlery and gifts from names such as Dartington, Gleneagles of Edinburgh, Royal Brierley, Johnson Bros, Poole Pottery, TTC, Wedgwood Whitewear seconds and Arthur Price of England; Colway & Sew-On selling industrial and domestic sewing machines, haberdashery and sewing equipment, American patchwork, tapestry, and embroidery; Edinburgh Woollen Mill selling smart and casual fashion, accessories and outerwear together with The Golf Shop offering branded golf wear and equipment at greatly reduced prices; First Choice Decor and Modella Interiors selling wallpaper and co-ordinating furnishing fabrics from major suppliers such as Sandersons, Timney Fowler, Harlequin, Nono, Wilman Interiors, Brian Yates, Villa Nova and Romo as well as offering a full bespoke making up service; Ponden Mill Linens with famous branded bedlinen, duvets, pillows and curtains at direct from the mill prices from names such as Crown, Coloroll, Chortex and Rectella as well as bathroom and kitchen accessories; Skopos Interior Furnishings, one of the world's leading designers and manufacturers of furnishing fabrics who design and manufacture flame-retardant fabrics for leading international hotel groups and interior designers. They now offer end of contract runs, specials and quality seconds direct to the public. Ends of rolls are half price, plus there are 100% cotton furnishing fabrics, sheers, voiles and linings, ex-contract and ex-display curtains, quilted bedspreads, quilted pieces, cushions, haberdashery and remnants. There is also a wide range of gifts, some at normal retail price, some reduced. The furniture showroom also sells ex-display and prototype sofas and armchairs at greatly reduced prices. Bring your measurements for curtains or take advantage of the professional interior design service. There is also a Susan Moore Lighting department selling a superb range of table lamps, lampshades, ceiling fittings and wall lights from most major suppliers including David Hunt and Dar Lighting. Finally, at UBI Ladies Fashions you can find a wide range of stunning outfits and casual separates at a price to suit every pocket. Stephen Y specialises in a co-ordinating range of separates and easy-to-wear informal suits while Ambience, Tagg, Vera Finzzi and Whimsy are just a few of the other brands on offer. Sizes range from 10-26.

THE YORKSHIRE OUTLET
WHITE ROSE WAY, JUNCTION 3 OF M18, DONCASTER LAKESIDE, SOUTH YORKSHIRE DN4 5JH
☎ (01302) 366444. E-MAIL: Outletcentres@mepc.co.uk
WEBSITE: www.theyorkshireoutletcentre.co.uk
OPEN 10 - 6 MON - SAT, 11 - 5 SUN.
Factory Shopping Village • *Womenswear & Menswear* • *Children Household* • *Electrical Equipment* • *Food and Leisure Sportswear & Equipment*
This outlet has 39 shops and four restaurants, children's play areas and wheelchair hire. Built in an E shape without the middle branch, free parking is in

front of the centre. Shops include: Big L, Bookends, Birthdays, Black & Decker, Ciro Citterio, Clarks, Cloverleaf, Cook & Dine, Converse, Discount Clothing Outlet, The Designer Room, Double Two, Event Jewellery, Hardcore jeans, Jane Shilton, JoKids , Linen Cupboard, Outdoor Adventure, Pilot, Sports Factory, Sports Mill, The Suit Company, Tom Sayers, Thorntons, Toyworld, VF, Warners, Windsmoor, XS Sound & Media,

THORNTONS

THE YORKSHIRE OUTLET, DONCASTER, YORKSHIRE DN4 5PH
☎ (01302) 320206. OPEN 10 - 6 MON - SAT, 11 - 5 SUN.
MCARTHURGLEN DESIGNER OUTLET VILLAGE, NABURN RETAIL PARK, FULFORD, YORK YO19 4TA
☎ (01904) 679227. OPEN 10 - 6 MON - SAT, 8 ON THUR, 11 - 5 SUN.
HORNSEA FREEPORT FACTORY OUTLET, ROLSTON ROAD, HORNSEA, EAST YORKSHIRE HU18 1UT
☎ (01964) 536724. OPEN 10 - 6 MON - SAT, 8 ON THUR, 11 - 5 SUN.
CASTLEFORD DESIGNER OUTLET VILLAGE, CARRWOOD ROAD, GLASSHOUGHTON, CASTLEFORD, YORKSHIRE WF10 4SB
☎ (01977) 519746. OPEN 10 - 6 MON - SAT, 8 ON THUR, 11 - 5 SUN.

Factory Shop in a Factory Shopping Village • *Food and Leisure*

The UK's leading specialist confectionery retailer has more than 500 shops and franchises nationwide selling a wide range of boxed and loose, chocolate and sugar confectionery. The factory outlets sell three different categories: misshapes. discounted lines and standard lines. Misshapes are loose chocolates which are the result of new product development, product trials or end of production runs which cannot be packed as Thorntons standard lines. They are packed into assorted bags and offer a saving of 35%-55% over the recommended retail price of standard "loose line" products. Discounted lines are excess to Thorntons' normal retail requirements and can be as a result of excess seasonal or export stock, discontinued lines or packaging changes. These products, when available, are offered at a discount of 25%-50% over the standard retail price. Standard lines from the full Thorntons range are also on sale at normal prices.

TIE RACK

MCARTHURGLEN DESIGNER OUTLET, ST NICHOLAS AVENUE, FULFORD, YORK YORKSHIRE YO19 4TA
☎ (01904) 624431. OPEN 10 - 6 MON, TUE, WED, FRI, SAT, 10 - 8 THUR, 11 - 5 SUN.

Factory Shop in a Factory Shopping Village • *Menswear Only*

Usual range of Tie Rack items including boxer shorts, silk ties, socks, silk scarves and waistcoats, all at up to 50% reductions.
Customer Careline: 0208 230 2333.

TILE CLEARING HOUSE
149-150 CLOUGH ROAD, HULL HU5 1SW
☎ (01482) 470 711. OPEN 8 - 6 MON - FRI, 9 - 6 SAT, 10 - 4 SE,
HIGGINSHAW LANE, ROYTON, OLDHAM OL2 6LH
☎ (0161) 628 9462. OPEN 8 - 6 MON - FRI, 9 - 6 SAT, 10 - 4 SUN.
PEEL RETAIL PARK, CANAL ROAD, BRADFORD,
WEST YORKSHIRE BD1 4RB
☎ (01274) 741 207. OPEN 8 - 6 MON - FRI, 9 - 6 SAT, 10 - 4 SUN.
107 MEADOWHALL ROAD, MEEADOWHALL, SHEFFIELD S9 1HE
☎ (01142) 432 444. OPEN 8 - 6 MON - FRI, 9 - 6 SAT, 10 - 4 SUN.
6 MON - FRI, 9 - 6 SAT, 10 - 4 SUN.
Permanent Discount Outlet • *DIY/Renovation*

Over 500 ranges of top quality ceramic wall and floor tiles permanently in stock, plus a comprehensive range of grouts, adhesives, tools and accessories to complete the job. By buying direct from the manufacturer and passing the savings on to the customer, their prices are very competitive. Moreover, everything you see is in stock, so there's no waiting for orders to be processed. Save up to 75% on manufacturers' recommended selling prices.

TK MAXX
PRINCES QUAY, HULL, EAST YORKSHIRE HU1 2PQ
☎ (01482) 223202. OPEN 9 - 5.30 MON - FRI, 9 - 6 SAT, 10.30 - 4.30 SUN.
THE VICTORIA SHOPPING CENTRE, HARROGATE,
NORTH YORKSHIRE.
☎ (01423) 536636. OPEN 9 - 5.30 MON - SAT, 10.30 - 4.30 SUN.
LEEDS SHOPPING PLAZA, 27 ALBION ARCADE, LEEDS, WEST
YORKSHIRE LS1 5ER
☎ (0113) 246 7990. OPEN 9 - 5.30 MON - WED, 9 - 6 FRI, SAT, 11 - 5 SUN.
ORCHARD SQUARE SHOPPING CENTRE, FARGATE, SHEFFIELD,
SOUTH YORKSHIRE S1 2FB
☎ (0114) 275 1751. OPEN 9 - 6 MON - SAT, UNTIL 7 ON WED, 1 - 5 SUN.
UNIT 2 MONKS CROSS RETAIL PARK, MONKS CROSS DRIVE,
YORK Y032 9GX
☎ (01904) 659996. OPEN 9 - 8 MON, 9 - 6 SAT, 10.30 - 5 SUN.
UNITS 11 & 12, FORSTER SQUARE RETAIL PARER SQUARE RETAIL
PARK, 53 VALLEY ROAD, BRADFORD BD1 4RN
☎ (01274) 738600. OPEN 9.30 - 8 MON - FRI, 9 - 6 SAT, 10.30 - 4.30 SUN.
Permanent Discount Outlet • *Womenswear & Menswear*
Children • *Household* • *Furniture/Soft Furnishings*

Based on an American concept, TK Maxx is situated in easily accessible, often centrally located stores and offers famous label goods with up to 60% savings off recommended retail prices. TK Maxx has fashion for the whole family - women's, men's and childrenswear - accessories, shoes, gifts, kitchenware and home goods. Everything in the store is branded with a choice of well-known high street names to designer labels, and while a small percentage might be clearly marked past season, the great majority of items in store are current season, current stock and still with phenomenal savings. There is a huge choice with 50,000 pieces in store and up to 10,000 new items arriving a week. The stores are simple and unfussy with wide aisles, shopping trolleys and baskets, and a spacious, functional feel to them but there are individual changing rooms, ramps for buggies and wheelchairs and plenty of staff on the shop floor. Every branch accepts all major credit and debit cards and has a liberal refund and return policy.

TOG 24

THE YORKSHIRE OUTLET STORE, WHITE ROSE WAY, DONCASTER LAKESIDE, DONCASTER, YORKSHIRE DN4 5PH
☎ (01302) 364123. OPEN 10 - 6 MON - SAT, 11 - 5 SUN.
HORNSEA FREEPORT SHOPPING VILLAGE, HORNSEA, EAST YORKSHIRE HU18 1UT
☎ (01964) 535308. OPEN 9.30 - 6 SEVEN DAYS A WEEK.
LIGHTWATER VALLEY FACTORY SHOPPING
☎ (01723) 377760. OPEN 9 - 5.30 MON - SAT, 11 - 4 SUN.
93-94 CHURCH STREET, WHITBY, YORKSHIRE YO22 4BH
☎ (01947) 820456. OPEN 10 - 5 EVERY DAY.
MCARTHURGLEN DESIGNER OUTLET VILLAGE, NABURN, YORK YO14 4RE
☎ (01904) 677814. OPEN 10 - 6 MON, TUE, WED, FRI, SAT, 10 - 8 THUR, 11 - 5 SUN.
SPEN VALE MILLS, STATION LANE, HECKMONDWIKE WF16 ONQ
☎ (01924) 409314. OPEN 10 - 5 MON - SAT, 11 WED, FRI, SAT, 10 - 8 THUR, 11 - 5 SUN.
Factory Shop in a Factory Shopping Village
Womenswear & Menswear • Children • Sportswear & Equipment
Tog 24 are the UK's fastest growing brand name in outdoor clothing and leisurewear. They utilise the world's finest performance fabrics including Gore-Tex, Polartec and Burlington MCS, catering for all the family for all seasons, with cosy fleeces and waterproofs for the winter, and trekking ranges, shorts and t-shirts for the summer. With all prices at least 30% below the recommended retail price, you can afford to enter the Tog comfort zone.

TOM SAYERS CLOTHING CO

THE YORKSHIRE OUTLET, WHITE ROSE WAY, DONCASTER, SOUTH YORKSHIRE DN4 5JH
☎ (01302) 364912. OPEN 10 - 6 MON - SAT, 11 - 5 SUN.
Factory Shop in a Factory Shopping Village • *Menswear Only*
Tom Sayers make sweaters for some of the top high street department stores. Unusually for a factory shop, if they don't stock your size, they will try and order it for you from their factory or one of their other factory outlets and send it to you. Most of the stock here is overstock, cancelled orders or last season's and includes jumpers, trousers and shirts at discounts of 30%. The trousers and shirts are bought in to complement the sweaters which they make.

TOMLINSON'S FINE FURNITURE CLUB

TOMLINSON FURNITURE GROUP, MOORSIDE, BETWEEN TOCKWITH
AND COWTHORPE, NEAR YORK, NORTH YORKSHIRE Y26 7QG
☎ (01423) 358777. WEBSITE: www.antique-furniture.co.uk
OPEN 9 - 4.30 SAT AND BANK HOLIDAYS ONLY.

Secondhand shops • *Furniture/Soft Furnishings* • *Household*

One of the North's leading wholesalers and exporters of antique and reproduction furniture and artefacts, with over 5,000 items of antique furniture under one roof. They are open to the public on Saturdays and Bank Holidays only. Membership is £3 to this huge emporium selling everything from antique china services, to original and reproduction nests of tables, rocking horses, dining tables, beds, sideboards and wardrobes. If you see something you like but it needs restoration work, this can be quoted for on site. Bespoke furniture can be made to your requirements.

TOMMY HILFIGER STORE

MCARTHURGLEN DESIGNER OUTLET CENTRE, ST NICHOLAS
AVENUE, FULFORD, JUNCTION OF A19 AND A64, YORK,
NORTH YORKSHIRE YO10 4RE
☎ (01904) 627 247. OPEN 10 - 6 MON - SAT, UNTIL 8 ON THUR,
11 - 5 SUN.

Factory Shop in a Factory Shopping Village • *Womenswear & Menswear*

Sells mainly casual wear and end of season lines, special purchases and cancelled orders at discounts of at least 30%. All stock is perfect.

TOYFACTORY

FREEPORT VILLAGE CASTLEFORD, WEST YORKSHIRE WF10 4SB
☎ (01977) 551900. WEBSITE: www.thetoyfactory.co.uk
OPEN 10 - 8 MON - FRI, 10 - 6 SAT, 11 - 5 SUN.

Factory Shop in a Factory Shopping Village • *Children*

ToyFactory sells a large range of discontinued toys, manufacturers over-runs and excess stock from many famous brand names such as Barbie, Action Man, Lego, Tomy, Fisher-Price and many more at least 30%-60% off high street prices.

TOYWORLD FACTORY OUTLETS LTD

THE YORKSHIRE OUTLET, WHITE ROSE WAY, DONCASTER,
SOUTH YORKSHIRE DN14 5JH
☎ (01302) 365511. WEBSITE: www.toyworldstore.com
OPEN 10 - 6 MON - SAT, 11 - 5 SUN.
MCARTHURGLEN DESIGNER OUTLET VILLAGE, SELBY ROAD,
NABURN, YORK, JUNCTION OF A19 AND A64,
NORTH YORKSHIRE YO19 4TA
☎ (01904) 639 33. OPEN 10 - 6 MON - SAT, 8 ON THUR, 11 - 5 SUN.
UNIT 28, NORTH POINT SHOPPING CENTRE, BRANSHOLME, HULL,
EAST YORKSHIRE HU7 4EE

☎ (01482) 833314. OPEN 9 - 5.30 MON - SAT.
TOYWORLD FACTORY SHOP, BUTTERLEY STREET, LEEDS LS10 1ES
☎ (0113) 234 2221. OPEN 10 - 5 FRI, SAT, 11 - 5 SUN.

Factory Shop in a Factory Shopping Village • *Factory Shop* • *Children*

Toyworld sell a large range of discontinued toys, manufacturers' overruns and excess stock from many famous brand names such as Barbie, Action Man, Lego, Tomy, Fisher-Price and many more at least 30-60% off high street prices. The Leeds outlet also sells a range of TP Activity toys and play frames.

TRADEX

BRADFORD ROAD, PUDSEY, YORKSHIRE LS28 5AS
☎ (0113) 239 3377. OPEN 9.30 - 8.30 MON - FRI, 9 - 5.30 SAT, 10.30 - 4.30 SUN.
CHATSWORTH ROAD, OFF HAREHILLS LANE, HAREHILLS, LEEDS, WEST YORKSHIRE LS8 1QW
☎ (0113) 240 7407. OPEN 9.30 - 8.30 MON - FRI, 9 - 5.30 SAT,
10.30 - 4.30 SUN.

Permanent Discount Outlet • *Household* • *Children*
Womenswear & Menswear

Household goods, clothes for all the family, shoes, foodstuffs, costume jewellery, furniture (at Pudsey only) and alcohol at very competitive prices. You have to be a member - bring two forms of ID including address - you can join instantly for £2. There is a coffee shop on site.

TRAVEL ACCESSORY

MACARTHURGLEN DESIGNER OUTLET CENTRE, ST NICHOLAS AVENUE, FULFORD, YORK, NORTH YORKSHIRE YO19 4TA
☎ (01904) 629978. OPEN 10 - 6 MON - SAT, 8 ON THUR, 11 - 5 SUN.

Factory Shop in a Factory Shopping Village • *Food and Leisure*

Luggage and travel-related products and executive cases, handbags, umbrellas from leading brands such as Samsonite, Desley, Head, Taurus and GlobeTrotter. Each product is offered at a substantially reduced price compared to those found on the high street due to being production over-runs, discontinued ranges or colours and last season's products. Discounts range from 30%-75% off high street prices.

UNITED FOOTWEAR

ROOLEY LANE, DUDLEY ROUNDABOUT, (A6036 RING ROAD),
BRADFORD, WEST YORKSHIRE
☎ (01274) 680322. OPEN 9 - 8 MON - FRI, 9 - 5.30 SAT, 10 - 4 SUN.
178 EASTERLY ROAD, LEEDS, WEST YORKSHIRE
☎ (0113) 249 3244. OPEN 9 - 5.30 MON - SAT, 10 - 4 SUN.

Permanent Discount Outlet • *Womenswear & Menswear* • *Children*

Shoes for all the family as well as clothes, handbags, sports shoes, boots, giftware and household goods, all at discounted prices. Famous brands including Clarks, K Shoes and Elmdale. Part of a national chain.

VF OUTLETS
THE YORKSHIRE OUTLET, WHITE ROSE WAY, DONCASTER,
SOUTH YORKSHIRE DN4 5JH
☎ (01302) 325593. OPEN 10 - 6 MON - SAT, 11 - 5 SUN.
Factory Shop in a Factory Shopping Village
Womenswear & Menswear • *Children*
Men's, women's and children's denim jeans and jackets, cords, T-shirts, shirts, most of which are irregular (ie seconds). T-shirts and shirts are all perfects, as are some jeans. Discounts are about one-third off the normal price. Brand names on sale include Lee, Wrangler and Maverick. Children's range starts at two years. Also sells French underwear by Variance, Jan Sport bags, caps and hats.

VIYELLA
MCARTHURGLEN OUTLET VILLAGE, ST NICHOLAS AVENUE,
FULFORD, YORK, NORTH YORKSHIRE YO19 4TA
☎ (01904) 678680. OPEN 10 - 6 MON - FRI, 8 ON THUR, 9 - 6 SAT, 11 - 5 SUN.
Factory Shop • *Womenswear & Menswear*
Wide range of Viyella clothing at discount prices from 30% on ladies formal wear and casual wear.

W MACHELL & SONS LTD
LOW MILLS, GUISELEY, LEEDS, WEST YORKSHIRE LS20 9LT
☎ (0113) 250 5043. OPEN 8 - 5 MON - FRI, 8 - 12 SAT.
Architectural Salvage • *DIY/Renovation*
One of the country's largest stocks of reclaimed building materials, including recycled oak and pine beams and period reclaimed flooring. Six full-time stone masons handcrafting genuine period stone fireplaces, mullioned window sets, stone doorways, all tailor-made to individual specifications. Period joinery work, including panelling, doors, etc, also undertaken.

WALKLEYS CANALSIDE MILL SHOPPING
BURNLEY ROAD, HEBDEN BRIDGE, YORKSHIRE
☎ (01422) 842061. OPEN 10 - 5 MON - FRI, 10 - 5.30 SAT, SUN.
Permanent Discount Outlet • *Household* • *Womenswear & Menswear*
Three-storey shop selling a wide selection of goods at discount prices: linen, textiles, footwear, clothes, gifts, crafts, china, fine art and collectables. The ground floor houses the clearance stock or merchandise which is bought in bulk and sold at very competitive prices, the first floor clothes for men and women at 30-50% discounts, the third floor houses the china and art shop.

WALTONS MILL SHOP
41 TOWER STREET, HARROGATE, NORTH YORKSHIRE HG1 1HS
☎ (01423) 520980. FAX: (01423) 526855. OPEN 10 - 5 MON - SAT.

THIRTY SIX, PIERCY END, KIRKBYMOORSIDE, YORK,
NORTH YORKSHIRE YO62 6DF
☎ (01751) 433253. OPEN 10 - 5 TUE, WED, FRI, SAT.
Permanent Discount Outlet • *Furniture/Soft Furnishings*
The Harrogate shop is a high street retail outlet which sells international designer fabrics with the emphasis on high class designs with a difference. More unusually, they also stock a vast range of quality trimmings, cords, bullions, tassels, tiebacks, etc. Regular customers really do describe the shop as an Aladdin's Cave, with its tapestries, handmade quilts, Egyptian cotton bedding, throws, cushions and traditional household textiles. Those who have tried the famous Knaresborough linen dishcloth vow never to use anything else again. Most of the stock is overmakes, bankrupt merchandise, bought from the US or imported from all over the world. Tucked away, you have to take the A61 Leeds road into Harrogate, and take the first right hand turn after the Prince of Wales roundabout at the longterm car park sign. The shop is 200 yards up on the left hand side. The Kirkbymoorside shop is small but bursting with incredible soft furnishing bargains, including fabric from as little as £1 a metre and a good selection of trimmings and accessories at budget prices. Making up service available. Kirkbymoorside is a picturesque market town, well served with restaurants and cafes, and perfect for a day out in the North York moors countryside.

WARNERS UK LTD
HORNSEA FREEPORT, ROLSTON ROAD, HORNSEA,
YORKSHIRE HU18 1UT
☎ (01964) 536996. OPEN 9.30 - 6 MON - SUN.
Factory Shop in a Factory Shopping Village • *Womenswear & Menswear*
This shop sells a wide range of women's lingerie from Leisureby, Warners, with bras, slips, thongs, bodies and briefs at discounts from 25% to 70%. Each item is labelled with both the rrp and the discounted prices. For example, bikini brief £6.99 reduced from £17; underwire bra £14.99 reduced from £33; body £24.99 reduced from £65, "Marilyn Monroe" sleepwear £14.99, reduced from £60. Slightly imperfect stock as well as perfect quality, end of season and discontinued merchandise and swimwear are also stocked. Underwear for men, including Calvin Klein briefs for £2.99 is on offer too.

WHITE ROSE CANDLES WORKSHOP
WENSLEY MILL, WENSLEY, LEYBURN, NORTH YORKSHIRE DL8 4HR
☎ (01969) 623544. OPEN 10 - 5 MON, TUE, THUR, FRI, SUN JUNE-NOVEMBER. MAIL ORDER.
Factory Shop • *Household*
Based in an old watermill, this candle workshop has been selling direct to the public for the past 26 years. All types of candles are made in simple shapes from hand-dipped and cast dinner table candles to church candles. Sizes range up to 5 feet high x 3 inches in diameter. There are also aromatherapy candles and a wide range of candle holders.

WINDSMOOR SALE SHOP
THE YORKSHIRE OUTLET, WHITE ROSE WAY, DONCASTER,
SOUTH YORKSHIRE DN4 5JH
☎ (01302) 320531. OPEN 10 - 6 MON - SAT, 11 - 5 SUN.
FREEPORT OUTLET VILLAGE, CARRWOOD ROAD,
GLASSHOUGHTONTON, JUNCTION 32 OF M52 WF10 4SB
OPEN 10 - 8 MON - FRI, 10 - 6 SAT, 11 - 5 SUN.
Factory Shop in a Factory Shopping Village • *Womenswear Only*
Previous season's stock as well as any returned merchandise and overmakes from the Windsmoor, Planet and Precis ranges at discounts averaging about 50% off the original price.

WOLFORD
MCARTHURGLEN DESIGNER OUTLET CENTRE, ST NICHOLAS
AVENUE, FULFORD, YORK, NORTH YORKSHIRE YO19 4TA
☎ (01904) 613877. OPEN 10 - 6 MON - SAT, UNTIL 8 ON THUR,
11 - 5 SUN AND BANK HOLIDAYS. MAIL ORDER ALSO.
Factory Shop in a Factory Shopping Village • *Womenswear Only*
The first factory shop for this Austrian luxury hosiery brand sells discontinued lines and seconds. Previously, these have only been on sale at Wolford's on-site factory shop in Bregenz, Austria, where the brand manufactures and houses its entire range for worldwide distribution and for special purchase sales to retailers twice a year. This factory shop stocks merchandise from Bregenz and not from Wolford's UK shops. There are bodies, swimwear, luxury tights, hold-ups at discounts of up to 60%. You can join the mailing list and order goods by phone with next day delivery.

WRANGLER
HORNSEA FREEPORT SHOPPING VILLAGE, HORNSEA,
EAST YORKSHIRE HU18 1UT
☎ (01964) 532979. OPEN 10 - 5 SEVEN DAYS A WEEK (WINTER),
9.30 - 6 MON - SAT, 11 - 5 SUN (SUMMER).
Factory Shop • *Womenswear & Menswear*
Previous season's stock as well as any seconds and overmakes. Men's and women's jeans from £18, youths from £12. The Shopping Village has plenty to entertain the family with playgrounds, an indoor play centre, restaurants and butterfly world.

WYNSORS WORLD OF SHOES
CLARENCE STREET, YORK, NORTH YORKSHIRE YO3 7EW
☎ (01904) 637611. 9 - 5.30 MON, TUE, WED, SAT, 9 - 8 THUR, FRI, 10 - 4
SUN AND BANK HOLIDAYS.
THORNTON ROAD, BRADFORD, WEST YORKSHIRE
☎ (01274) 495016. 9 - 5.30 MON, TUE, WED, SAT, 9 - 8 THUR, FRI, 10 - 4
SUN AND BANK HOLIDAYS.
THURCROFT, NEAR ROTHERHAM, SOUTH YORKSHIRE
☎ (01709) 540876. 9 - 5.30 MON, TUE, WED, SAT, 9 - 8 THUR, FRI, 10 - 4
SUN AND BANK HOLIDAYS.

MIDDLETON SHOPPING CENTRE, LEEDS, WEST YORKSHIRE
☎ (0113) 2710849. 9 - 5.30 MON, TUE, WED, SAT, 9 - 8 THUR, FRI,
10 - 4 SUN AND BANK HOLIDAYS.
HORNCASTLE STREET, CLECKHEATON, WEST YORKSHIRE
☎ (01274) 851366. 9 - 5.30 MON, TUE, WED, SAT, 9 - 8 THUR, FRI,
10 - 4 SUN AND BANK HOLIDAYS.
INFIRMARY ROAD, SHEFFIELD, SOUTH YORKSHIRE
☎ (0114) 2737903. 9 - 5.30 MON, TUE, WED, SAT, 9 - 8 THUR, FRI,
10 - 4 SUN AND BANK HOLIDAYS.
CLARENCE STREET, YORK, NORTH YORKSHIRE
☎ (01904) 637611. 9 - 5.30 MON, TUE, WED, SAT, 9 - 8 THUR, FRI,
10 - 4 SUN AND BANK HOLIDAYS.
ENTERPRISE WAY, CASTLEFORD, WEST YORKSHIRE
☎ (01977) 514774. 9 - 5.30 MON, TUE, WED, SAT, 9 - 8 THUR, FRI,
10 - 4 SUN AND BANK HOLIDAYS.
HESSEL ROAD, HULL, YORKSHIRE
☎ (01482) 223585. 9 - 5.30 MON, TUE, WED, SAT, 9 - 8 THUR, FRI,
10 - 4 SUN AND BANK HOLIDAYS.

Permanent Discount Outlet • *Womenswear & Menswear* • *Children*

Stocks top brand-name shoes at less than half price. Special monthly offers always available. There are shoes, trainers, slippers, sandals and boots for all the family, with a selection of bags, cleaners and polishes available.

YOU & YOURS

UNIT 9, CROWN POINT RETAIL PARK, HUNSLET ROAD, LEEDS,
WEST YORKSHIRE LS10 1ET
☎ (01132) 341937. OPEN 10 - 6 MON, 10 - 7 TUE - FRI, 9.30 - 6 SAT, 11 - 5 SUN.
INGLEBY ROAD, BRADFORD BD99 2XE, WEST YORKSHIRE.
☎ (01274) 624611. OPEN 10 - 5.30 MON, 10 - 8 TUE - FRI, 9 - 5.30 SAT,
11 - 5 SUN.
98-100 NEW STREET, HUDDERSFIELD HD1 2UD, WEST YORKSHIRE.
☎ (01484) 543301. OPEN 9 - 5.30 MON - SAT.
SCOOPS, SHIRETHORNE CENTRE, 34-43 PROSPECT STREET, HULL HU2 8PX
☎ (01482) 224354. OPEN 9 - 5.30 MON - SAT. SUN.
25 TOWN STREET, ARMLEY, LEEDS, WEST YORKSHIRE LS12 1UX
☎ (0113) 2631825. OPEN 9.30 - 5.30 MON - SAT.
41 BARNSLEY ROAD, SOUTH ELMSALL WF9 2RN
☎ (01977) 642256. OPEN 9 - 5.30 MON - SAT.

Permanent Discount Outlet • *Womenswear & Menswear* • *Children*
Electrical Equipment • *Household* • *Furniture/Soft Furnishings*

Mostly consisting of unsold lines through the Grattan mail order catalogues at the end of the season, but there is also some current season stock. Women's, men's and children's clothing, hardware, plastics and textiles, electrics and some furniture, although the majority is women's fashion, including many famous high street labels. All items in the store retail at a minimum of 30% off the catalogue price, with some items discounted by up to 50%. They also have regular promotional offers.

YORK HANDMADE BRICK CO LTD
FOREST LANE, ALNE, YORK, NORTH YORKSHIRE YO61 1TU
☎ (01347) 838881. E-MAIL: sales@yorkhandmade.co.uk
WEBSITE: www.yorkhandmade.co.uk. OPEN 8.30 - 4.30 MON - FRI, 9 - 12 SAT.
Architectural Salvage • *DIY/Renovation*
One of the few businesses still producing handmade bricks, as well as pavers and terracotta floor tiles. They can provide bricks for archways, slopes, edges, ledges and corners and do all the British Standards specials as well as taking special orders.

YOYO
61 EASTGATE, BEVERLEY, EAST YORKSHIRE HU17 0DR
☎ (01482) 861713. OPEN 10.30 - 3 MON, TUE, 10 - 3 WED - SAT.
Dress Agency • *Children*
YoYo sell good quality, nearly-new childrenswear at prices from one quarter to one third of the original cost. The labels range from marks & Spencer, Debenhams and BhS to Oilily, Patrizia Wigan, Tick Tock, Babi-Mini, Clayeaux and Absorba. Most items are under £10 and generally you can clothe a child for the price of one week's family allowance. Age range from birth to about 10 years. They also sell maternity wear and children's dance wear.

Southern Scotland

ANDREW ELLIOT LTD
DUNSDALE ROAD, FOREST MILL, SELKIRK TD7 5EA
☎ (01750) 20412. OPEN 9 - 5 MON - THUR, 9 - 4 FRI,
SAT MORNS BY ARRANGEMENT.
Factory Shop • *Womenswear & Menswear*
Manufactures short cloth runs for UK clients and here sells tweed fabric by the metre. The factory shop comprises two rooms above the working mill, one set out with lengths of cloth, the other with finished rugs, pashminas and shawls. They also make their own range of rugs, fabric and scarves. This is the place to come if you're handy with a sewing machine as their shooting jacket material and fine lightweight lambswool are excellent quality. Commission weaving undertaken.

ANNE THOMAS NATURAL FIBRE FABRICS
MAINHILL, 43 BRIDGEND, DUNS, BERWICKSHIRE TD11 3ES
☎ (01361) 883030/882633 FAX. OPEN 9 - 5 MON - FRI.
MAIL ORDER ONLY.
Permanent Discount Outlet • *Womenswear Only*
Designer and high quality dress fabrics from well-known British manufacturers, all sold by the metre from £7 per metre. Specialises in natural fibre fab-

rics. No minimum purchase. The Fabric Club allows you to receive six collections of outstanding quality dressmaking fabrics throughout the year for £16, enabling you to purchase top quality fabrics at very low prices. Customers can receive up to 50 samples in each batch. Most of the fabrics are suited to smart daywear, although there are some eveningwear fabrics at Christmas.

ANTHONY HAINES MILL SHOP
UNIT 1, DUNSDALE ROAD, SELKIRK TD7 5EA
☎ (01750) 20046. OPEN 9 - 5.30 MON - FRI.
Factory Shops • *Womenswear & Menswear*
Family-run company specialising in producing quality wool ties from fabric designed and woven in their own mill. Tiny factory shop at the front of the factory selling tartan kilts, skirts, stoles, scarves, rugs, cloth and wool ties.

BALMORAL MILL SHOP
16 CHURCH LANE, GALSTON, AYRSHIRE KA4 8HF
☎ (01563) 820213/821740 FAX. E-MAIL: info@balmoralknitwear.co.uk
WEBSITE: www.balmoralknitwear.co.uk OPEN 9 - 5 MON - SAT, 12 - 5 SUN.
Factory Shops • *Womenswear & Menswear* • *Children*
Sells cashmere and lambswool knitwear, embroidered knitwear, sweatshirts, polo shirts, bowling and golf attire and schoolwear, some of which is brand name and some own label, but all sold at factory direct prices. Ladies, men's, children's and babywear are all stocked. Popular ranges are Alice Collins, Emreco, Lyle and Scott, Farah, Hodgsons and Poppy. Examples of prices include embroidered sweatshirts £14.95, polo shirts £8.95, lambswool jumpers £22.95, Seconds from £1.95. Telephone orders welcome.

D C DAGLEISH LTD
DUNSDALE MILL, SELKIRK TD7 5EB
☎ (01750) 20781. OPEN 9 - 12 AND 1 - 4 MON - FRI.
Factory Shops • *Womenswear & Menswear*
Small shop to the side of the factory which specialises in tartan manufacture. Pure wool headsquares, £3.50; tartan braces; tartan dolls; tartan scarves; Celtic brooches; tartan kilts and waistcoats; knee rugs and woollen rugs.

GRETNA GATEWAY OUTLET VILLAGE
GLASGOW ROAD, GRETNA DG16 6GG
INFORMATION ☎ (01461) 339100. MAIN LINE
☎ (01461) 339028. OPEN 10 - 6 SEVEN DAYS A WEEK.
Factory Shopping Village • *Womenswear & Menswear* • *Children*
Household • *Sportswear & Equipment* • *Food and Leisure*
Twenty-two trading outlets with a planned second phase of 20 shops. Includes Designer Room, DKNY, Edinburgh Woollen Mill, Jane Shilton, Leather Rat (for leather clothing and footwear), LMI baggage, John Partridge, Price's Candles, the largest Polo Ralph Lauren factory shop in Europe (stocking clothes for men,

women and children as well as homewares), Reebok, The Savoy Taylors' Guild, The Golf Company, Tog 24, Tommy Hilfiger, Van Heusen, Whittards, and several more international fashion and sports names due to commit at the time of going to press. There are restaurants, a children's play area and a themed visitor centre.

HAWICK CASHMERE CO LTD
TRINITY MILLS, DUKE STREET, HAWICK TD9 9QA
☎ (01450) 371221. OPEN 9.30 - 5 MON - SAT.
20 BRIDGE STREET, KELSO, SCOTTISH BORDERS TD5 7JD
☎ (01573) 226776. OPEN 9.30 - 5.30 MON - FRI, 9.30 - 5 SAT, 9 - 1 WED.
Factory Shops • *Womenswear & Menswear*
Manufactures high quality ladies and men's knitwear for top department stores and sells ends of lines here at below retail prices. Specialises in such luxury fibres as cashmere, cashmere silk, lambswool and merino in a range which comprises sweaters, capes, cardigans, dresses, skirts, gloves and cushions. Visitor Centre on site.

J & W CARPETS
24 BACK MAIN STREET, AYR KA8 8BZ
☎ (01292) 265539. OPEN 9 - 8 MON - FRI, 9 - 5.30 SAT, 12 - 5 SUN.
UNIT 1, FORGE INDUSTRIAL ESTATE, BONNYTON ROAD, KILMARNOCK
☎ (01563) 535397. OPEN 9 - 8 MON - FRI, 9 - 5.30 SAT, 12 - 5 SUN.
9 PORTLAND ROAD, IRVINE, SCOTLAND KA12 8HY
☎ (01294) 274724. OPEN 9 - 8 MON - FRI, 9 - 5.30 SAT, 12 - 5 SUN.
3 RUTHERGLEN ROAD, RUTHERGLEN G73 1SX
☎ (0141) 647 9442. OPEN 9 - 8 MON - FRI, 9 - 5.30 SAT, 12 - 5 SUN.
WAREHOUSE 1, LOCH STREET, COATBRIDGE ML5 3RT
☎ (01236) 440090. OPEN 9 - 8 MON - FRI, 9 - 5.30 SAT, 12 - 5 SUN.
32 POSSIL ROAD, GLASGOW G4 9SR
☎ (0141) 333 1212. OPEN 9 - 8 MON - FRI, 9 - 5.30 SAT, 12 - 5 SUN
WAREHOUSE 1, CARRON ROAD, FALKIRK FK2 7RR
☎ (01324) 610210. OPEN 9 - 8 MON - FRI, 9 - 5.30 SAT, 12 - 5 SUN
Permanent Discount Outlet • *Furniture/Soft Furnishings*
Sells carpets from polyproplene and wool twists to Axminsters at discounts of up to 50%. They also sell Chinese rugs from £20-£175, representing discounts of 20%-30% on the high street. Carpets range from £1.50 a square yard to £20.

JANE SHILTON
GRETNA GATEWAY OUTLET VILLAGE, GLASGOW ROAD, GRETNA, DUMFRIESSHIRE DG6 5DT
☎ (01461) 339062. FAX (01461) 339061.
OPEN 10 - 6 SEVEN DAYS A WEEK.
Factory Shop in a Factory Shopping Village • *Womenswear Only*
Merchandise from past seasons' collections or factory seconds at discounts of

at least 30% and up to 70% off the original price. There is a wide range of handbags, small leather goods, shoes, luggage umbrellas and travel bags. Example of price reduction: handbags at £24.99 originally £37.

JOHN MOODY,
38 THE SQUARE, KELSO, ROXBURGHSHIRE
☎ (01573) 224400. OPEN 10 - 5 MON - SAT, CLOSED 1.30 - 2 DAILY.
Permanent Discount Outlet • *Womenswear & Menswear*

Cashmere and lambswool sweaters and cardigans for men and women at factory shop prices.

PARTRIDGE
GRETNA GATEWAY OUTLET VILLAGE, ADDRESS AND OPENING HOURS AS BEFORE.
☎ (01461) 338959.
Factory Shop in a Factory Shopping Village
Womenswear & Menswear • *Children*

Partridge specialises in fashionable outdoor clothes and accessories. Ranges include waxed jackets, Gore-tex jackets, waterproof jackets, tweeds, quilts, fleece jackets and waistcoats, knitwear, shirts, chinos, cord and moleskin trousers, hats and caps. Discontinued lines are on sale at discounted prices with a minimum of 30% and up to 70% off during promotions.

PETER SCOTT FACTORY SHOP
11 BUCCLEUCH STREET, HAWICK TD9 OHJ
☎ (01450) 372311. OPEN 10 - 5 MON - FRI, 10 - 4 SAT.
Factory Shops • *Womenswear & Menswear*

Peter Scott is one of the oldest woollen factories in the country. It stocks sweaters for women and men in almost every conceivable material from cotton and merino wool to cashmere and silk. Some of the stock is current season, some discontinued, but there are no seconds. Visit on a weekday and if they haven't got what you want in stock, they can phone up to the factory for it. Opening times are shorter in the winter time so ring first.

PRICE'S CANDLES
GRETNA GATEWAY OUTLET VILLAGE, ADDRESS AND OPENING HOURS AS BEFORE.
☎ (01461) 339050.
Factory Shop in a Factory Shopping Village • *Household*

Everything sold in this shop are seconds, discontinued sizes not available elsewhere, over-runs or candles in old packaging that has now been replaced. There are church candles, lanterns, candles in pots and glass jars, star-shaped candles, floating candles, candlestick holders, serviettes, scented candles and garden torches.

SCENT TO YOU
GRETNA GATEWAY OUTLET VILLAGE, ADDRESS AND OPENING HOURS AS BEFORE.
☎ (01461) 339075.
Factory Shop in a Factory Shopping Village • *Womenswear Only*
Operating within The Designer Room in this outlet village, Scent To You sells discounted perfume, cosmetics and accessories including body lotions and gels. The company, which has more than thirty branches, buys in bulk and sells more cheaply, relying on a high turnover for profit. Discounts range from 5% to 60%, with greater savings during their twice-yearly sales (phone for details). Most of the leading brand names in perfume are stocked including Christian Lacroix, Armani, Charlie, Givenchy, Anais Anais from Cacherel, Charlie from Revlon, Coco Chanel, Christian Dior, Elizabeth Taylor, Blue Grass from Elizabeth Arden, Aramis, Lagerfeld. Plus cosmetics from REvlon and Spectacular and skincare from Clarins and Lancome as well as Scent To You's own range of bags, watches, hair brushes and brushkits which is sold under the name S.T.Y. Designs. Stock varies greatly due to the fast turnover and varying supplies so more than one visit may be necessary to obtain the scent of your choice. Or phone first to avoid disappointment.

SLATERS MENSWEAR
184 HIGH STREET, AYR, AYRSHIRE KA7 1RQ
☎ (01292) 261730. OPEN 8.30 - 5.30 MON - SAT, 7.30 ON THUR.
Permanent Discount Outlets • *Menswear Only*
Full range of men's clothes from underwear and shoes to casualwear, suits and dresswear and including labels such as Odermark, Bulmer, Valentino, Charlie's Co, and Charlton Gray. Men's suits from £79.

THE FACTORY SHOP LTD
DRAKEMYRE, DALRY, AYRSHIRE KA24 5JD
☎ (01294) 832791. OPEN 10 - 5 MON - SAT, 11 - 5 SUN.
54 - 60 HIGH STREET, ANNAN, DUMFRIES DG12 6AJ
☎ (01461) 207687. OPEN 9 - 5 MON - SAT, 10.30 - 4.30 SUN.
STANDALANE STREET, GALSTON, KILMARNOCK KA4 8AY
☎ (01563) 820320. OPEN 10 - 5.30 MON - SAT, 11 - 5 SUN.
Factory Shops • *Children* • *Womenswear & Menswear* • *Household Furniture/Soft Furnishings* • *Sportswear & Equipment*
Wide range on sale includes men's, ladies and children's clothing and footwear; household textiles; toiletries; hardware; luggage; lighting and bedding, most of which are chainstore and high street brands at discounts of approximately 30%-50%. There are weekly deliveries and brands include many major stars such as Adidas, Nike, Joe Bloggs and Brabantia, to name just a few. Lines are continually changing and few factory shops offer such a variety under one roof. The Factory Shop also has kitchen and furniture displays and sells Cape Country Furniture, highest quality pine furniture made exclusively for The

Factory Shop Ltd in the New South Africa. Prices are direct from the factory and there is home delivery service throughout the UK. A colour brochure and price list is available. Tea room with home prepared food and free car park in Dalry, the Galston shop has its own free car park and at Annan there is on road parking and public car parks adjacent.

THORNTONS
GRETNA GREEN GATEWAY OUTLET VILLAGE, GLASGOW ROAD, GRETNA GREEN, AYRSHIRE DG16 5GG
☎ (01461) 339189. OPEN SEVEN DAYS A WEEK.
Factory Shop in a Factory Shopping Village • *Food and Leisure Household*

The UK's leading specialist confectionery retailer has more than 500 shops and franchises nationwide selling a wide range of boxed and loose chocolate and sugar confectionery. The factory outlets sell three different categories: misshapes. discounted lines and standard lines. Misshapes are loose chocolates which are the result of new product development, product trials or end of production runs which cannot be packed as Thorntons standard lines. They are packed into assorted bags and offer a saving of 35%-55% over the recommended retail price of standard "loose line" products. Discounted lines are excess to Thorntons' normal retail requirements and can be as a result of excess seasonal or export stock, discontinued lines or packaging changes. These products, when available, are offered at a discount of 25%-50% over the standard retail price. Standard lines from the full Thorntons range are also on sale at normal prices.

TOG 24
GRETNA GATEWAY OUTLET VILLAGE, ADDRESS AND OPENING HOURS AS BEFORE.
☎ (01461) 339080.

Tog 24 are the UK's fastest growing brand name in outdoor clothing and leisurewear. They utilise the world's finest performance fabrics including Gore-Tex, Polartec and Burlington MCS, catering for all the family for all seasons, with cosy fleeces and waterproofs for the winter, and trekking ranges, shorts and t-shirts for the summer. With all prices at least 30% below the recommended retail price, you can afford to enter the Tog comfort zone.

TOM SCOTT KNITWEAR
DENHOLM, HAWICK TD9 8NJ
☎ (01450) 870531. OPEN 10 - 12 AND 2 - 4.30 MON - FRI, CLOSED JAN.
Factory Shops • *Womenswear & Menswear*

Overmakes, samples and prototypes from this mill shop which operates just a few hundred yards from the factory where the garments are made, about five miles from Hawick. Most of the stock has been made for some of the top designers and couture houses in the world. The shop is crammed with stock so you have to be good at rummaging.

TRAVEL ACCESSORY
GRETNA GATEWAY OUTLET VILLAGE, ADDRESS AND OPENING HOURS AS BEFORE.
☎ (01461) 339019.
Factory Shop in a Factory Shopping Village • *Food and Leisure*
Luggage and travel-related products and executive cases, handbags, umbrellas from leading brands such as Samsonite, Desley, Head, Taurus and GlobeTrotter. Each product is offered at a substantially reduced price compared to those found on the high street due to being production over-runs, discontinued ranges or colours and last season's products. Discounts range from 30%-75% off high street prices.

WHITE OF HAWICK
VICTORIA ROAD, HAWICK TD9 7AH
☎ (01450) 373206. FAX: (01450) 371900. E-MAIL: sales@whiteofhawick.com
WEBSITE: www.whiteofhawick.com
OPEN 9 - 5.15 MON - FRI, 9.30 - 5 SAT. MAIL ORDER ALSO.
Permanent Discount Outlet • *Womenswear & Menswear*
White of Hawick is a privately owned family-run business selling the highest quality cashmere and lambswool at the keenest prices in the UK, including garments manufactured by top names such as Lyle & Scott, Peter Scott, Johnstons and White of Hawick. While their shop is not a discount shop as such, everything there is very competitively priced with many items sold at up to one third of the price of the same merchandise in top London department stores. For example, ladies round-neck, long-sleeved pullover in 100% single cashmere, from £79; ladies high button, long-sleeved cashmere cardigan with contrast trimming, £99; classic long-sleeved turtle neck pullover in 100% single cashmere, from £79; men's long-sleeved, V-neck pullover with saddle shoulders in 100% double cashmere, from £89. Round neck, long-sleeved ladies pullover in 100% shrink resistant single geelong lambswool, £39.95; men's long-sleeved V-neck cardigan with two pockets and saddle shoulders in 100% double lambswool from £39.95. Ladies fringed cape in 100% woven double lambswool, £26.95. The shop also sells cashmere scarves from £15.95 and lambswool scarves from £2, cashmere and lambswool gloves and all-wool rugs. Also available is four-ply chunky cashmere and factory seconds at unbeatable prices. Mail order brochure available.

Central Scotland

A & K CLOTHING LTD
45 ETNA ROAD, FALKIRK, STIRLINGSHIRE FK2 9EG
☎ (01324) 622181. OPEN 10 - 5 MON - SAT, 11 - 5 SUN.
Permanent Discount Outlet • *Womenswear & Menswear* • *Children*
Mostly ladies wear, with some men's and children's clothes which is made up of surplus stock from Marks & Spencer and other high street names such as Principles. There are also vases, teapots, trainers, underwear and shoes and a large stockroom of upholstered furniture.

ANTA SCOTLAND LTD
32 HIGH STREET, THE ROYAL MILE, EDINBURGH
☎ 0131 557 8300. E-MAIL: sales@anta.co.uk WEBSITE: www.anta.co.uk
OPEN 9.30 - 5.30 MON - SAT, 12 - 4 SUN.
Factory Shops • *Furniture/Soft Furnishings*
Anta design everything on site, using tartan check designs in traditional Scottish landscape colours and there are usually seconds and ends of lines available at discounted prices. There are jazzy check woollen rugs, carpets, fabrics, throws, blankets and ceramics (also made on site) on sale at greatly discounted prices. Mail order is not at discount prices.

ANTARTEX VILLAGE VISITOR CENTRE
LOMOND INDUSTRIAL ESTATE, ALEXANDRIA,
DUMBARTONSHIRE G83 OTP
☎ (01389) 752393. OPEN 10 - 6 MON - SUN.
Factory Shop • *Womenswear & Menswear* • *Children*
Large, rambling building, well signposted off the A82, which has a vast retail area and then lots of small workshops where you can watch sheepskin jackets being made, or enjoy whisky tasting. It's difficult to tell how good the prices are as most are not double ticketed to show the original and sale price, but there are bargain sections and lots of baskets of bargains. Edinburgh Woollen Mill has a large area, and other labels on sale include Telemac, Pitlochry, Country Rose and Regatta. As well as clothes for men (new One Valley range of waterproof jackets, Hippo and Progen) and women and children, there are tea towels, toys, books, food, gifts, blankets, mugs, candles, cds and tapes, table mats, sports equipment and countrywear. There is a big golf department selling Wilson, Spalding and Arnold Palmer equipment at discounts of 20%-30% and lots of different workshops. Close to the Loch Lomond Outlet Village.

BABYGRO LTD
GATESIDE INDUSTRIAL ESTATE, OLD PERTH ROAD, COWDENBEATH
☎ (01383) 511105. OPEN 11 - 4.30 MON, 9.30 - 4.30 TUE, WED, THUR,
9.30 - 12.30 FRI, CLOSED 1.30-2.30 DAILY.
Factory Shops • *Children*
Babywear for 0-5 year olds at discounts of up to 50%: all-in-ones, playsuits, shorts, t-shirts, vests, shirts, pyjamas, and rompers at factory shop prices. Pyjamas upwards of £3 - a pair for a 4-year-old cost £6.99 compared with £12.99 for the same make in a high street store. Also does a line of adult leisurewear. Factory sales take place throughout the year and are advertised locally.

BCP AIRPORT PARKING AND TRANSFER SERVICE
GLASGOW
☎ (0870) 0134586. 8AM - 9 PM, 7 DAYS A WEEK.
BCP provides secure, value-for-money car parking at Gatwick, Heathrow, luton, Manchester, Glasgow, Bristol, Birmingham, Cardiff, East Midlands, Southampton, Newcastle, Leeds Bradford, Edinburgh, Prestwick and Belfast, with prices from just £2.50 net per day. For an extra £24.95 (£28.95 at Prestwick and Heathrow), you can save time by being met at the airport terminal on your departure and return as part of BCP's Meet and Greet Parking service. Your car is then taken to the BCP.Co.UK secure car park nearby. Or you can pre-book a chauffeur-driven airport car to and from the airport. This service is ideal if you live within 30 miles of your departure airport - prices start from about £60 return. To book and save at least 15% on the car park gate prices and 10% on lounges and chauffeur-driven cars, phone the BCP reservations line quoting reference 'GDD'. BCP will confirm your booking by post with directions to your car park or details of the pick-up or meeting arrangements as appropriate.

BEE LINE
UNIT 9, LOMOND TRADE CENTRE, LOMOND INDUSTRIAL ESTATE, ALEXANDRIA, DUMBARTONSHIRE G83 OTL
☎ (01389) 756161. OPEN 10 - 5 FRI, SAT, 12 - 5 SUN.
Factory Shops • *Womenswear* • *Children*
Major chainstore overmakes for women and children. Stock depends on the time of year but includes shorts, T-shirts, jogging pants, dresses, skirts and sweaters, smart separates, some underwear, branded sportswear and bags, all sold at 30% less than normal retail prices. Stock is current and last season's.

BELINDA ROBERTSON CASHMERE
22 PALMERSTON PLACE, EDINBURGH EH12 5AL
☎ (0131) 225 1057. OPEN 9 - 5.30 MON - FRI, 10 - 4 SAT,
OR BY APPOINTMENT.

Factory Shops • *Womenswear & Menswear*
Belinda Robertson is an award-winning designer of ladies fashion and classic knitwear in 100% cashmere. The collection is designed and manufactured in Scotland and is sold in boutiques and leading department stores throughout the world. Focusing on the working woman of the Nineties, the designs range from essential pieces to high fashion and can be worn for day and evening. Her showroom in Edinburgh carries ends of ranges, samples and over-runs, all sold at discounted prices, usually between 25%-75% less than retail, and many styles can be ordered on request in a wide range of colours and sizes. There is also a small range of men's classic and handknit sweaters available.

BIRTHDAYS
FREEPORT LEISURE VILLAGE, WEST CALDER, WEST LOTHIAN EH55 8QB
☎ (01501) 762030. OPEN 10 - 6 MON - SAT, 8 ON THUR, 10 - 6 SUN.
Factory Shop in a Factory Shopping Village • *Household*
Cards, notelets, stationery sets, colouring books, soft toys, photo albums, picture frames, gifts, giftwrap, tissue paper, party packs, Christmas crackers, string puppets, fairy lights all at discounts of up to 30%. Some are special purchases, some seconds.

BMJ POWER
280 GREAT WESTERN ROAD, ST GEORGE'S CROSS, GLASGOW G4 9EJ
☎ (0141) 332 8000. OPEN 8.30 - 5 MON - SAT, 9 - 5 WED.
Factory Shops • *DIY/Renovation*
Reconditioned tools and acccessories from the famous Black & Decker range, as well as other power tools from brands such as Matabo, Makito, Flymo and Kress, all with full manufacturer's warranty. This is essentially an after-sales service with a retail outlet. Often, stock consists of goods returned from the shops because of damaged packaging or are part of a line which is being discontinued. Lots of seasonal special offers. There are more than three dozen BMJ service outlets countrywide. Phone 0345 230230 and you can find out where your nearest outlet is.

BUMPSADAISY MATERNITY STYLE
4TH FLOOR, 90 MITCHELL STREET, GLASGOW G1 3NQ
☎ (0141) 221 4808. WEBSITE: www.bumpsadaisy.co.uk
OPEN 9.30 - 5 TUE - SAT.
Hire Shop • *Womenswear Only*
Franchised shops and home-based branches with large range of specialist maternity wear, from wedding outfits to ball gowns, to hire and to buy. Hire costs range from £30 to £100 for special occasion wear. To buy are lots of casual and business wear in sizes 8 - 18. For example, skirts £20-£70; dresses £40-£100. Also four branches run by young mums from their homes, specialising inhiring but also stocking a small retail range (Camberley, Edgbaston, Exeter and Southampton). Phone 0208-789 0329 for details.

BURNTHILL DEMOLITION LTD
FLOORS STREET, JOHNSTONE, RENFREWSHIRE PA5 8QS
☎ (01505) 329644. OPEN 8 - 6 MON - FRI, 8 - 12 SAT.
Architectural Salvage • *DIY/Renovation*
Secondhand timber, roofing tiles, slates, steel and wooden beams and a selection of other reclaimed items.

CAPONES
1- 7 MOLENDINAR STREET, GLASGOW G1 5AT
☎ (0141) 552 4399. OPEN 9 - 5.30 MON - SAT, 10 - 5.30 SUN.
1 - 5, L 710990. OPEN 8 - 8 MON - FRI, 9 - 5 SAT, 10 - 5.30 SUN.
OPEN 8 - 8 MON - FRI, 9 - 5 SAT, 10 - 5.30 SUN.
Permanent Discount Outlet • *DIY/Renovation*
Wallpaper and paint clearance warehouse which also sells paste, borders, tiles, brushes, rollers. Paste free when you buy three rolls of wallpaper. Stocks Crown, Narrar, Berger paints; Crown, Belgravia and wallpaper with thousands of rolls in stock at any one time.

CATALOGUE BARGAIN SHOP
36-38 QUEEN STREET, GLASGOW
OPEN 9 - 5 MON - SAT, 12 - 5 SUN.
THE FORGE SHOPPING CENTRE, PARKHEAD, GLASGOW
☎ (0141) 556 5352. OPEN 9 - 6 MON - SAT, 8 ON THUR, 11 - 5 SUN.
12-16 CADZOW STREET, HAMILTON, LANARKSHIRE ML3 6DG
☎ (01698) 421112. OPEN 9 - 5.30 MON - SAT, 12 - 4 SUN. MON - SAT, 12 - 4 SUN.
Permanent Discount Outlets • *Womenswear & Menswear*
Children • *Household* • *Electrical Equipment*
Catalogue Bargain Shop is a growing national chain of stores which obtains the majority of its goods from mail order giants Great Universal and Kays, and offers a range of clothing for all the family, a wide selection of shoes, bed linen, household goods, electrical equipment and hundreds of other catalogue items at very competitive prices. The merchandise consists of ends of ranges and previous season's stock for which there is no longer storage space when the catalogues change. The Queen Street shop is on the first floor of an office block. The Parkhead branch has a new section selling different types of furniture.

CHARLES CLINKARD
STERLING MILLS DESIGNER OUTLET VILLAGE, DEVONVALE,
TILLICOULTRY, CLACKMANNANSHIRE FK13 6HP
☎ (01259) 753001. OPEN 10 - 6 MON - SAT.
Factory Shop in a Factory Shopping Village • *Children*
Womenswear & Menswear
Footwear for the family at discounts of between 20% and 50%. Labels on sale here include Rockport, Loake, Camel, Bally, Church's, Ecco, Gabor, Rohde,

Van-Dal, Kickers, Clarks, Dr Martens, K Shoes, Lotus and Renata. The telephone number given here is for the centre, not the shop.

CLARKS FACTORY SHOP
UNIT 26, THE FORGE SHOPPING CENTRE, PARKHEAD,
GLASGOW G31 4EB
☎ (0141) 556 5290. OPEN 9.30 - 5.30 MON - SAT,
12 - 4.30 SUN AND BANK HOLIDAYS.
Factory Shops • *Children* • *Womenswear & Menswear*
Clarks International operate a chain of factory shops nationally which specialise in selling discontinued lines and slight sub-standards for children, women and men from Clarks, K Shoes and other famous brands. These shops trade under the name of K Shoes Factory shop or Clarks Factory Shop and while not all are physically attached to a shoe factory, they are treated as factory shops by the company. Customers can expect to find an extensive range of quality shoes, sandals, walking boots, slippers, trainers, handbags, accessories and gifts, while their major outlets also offer luggage, sports clothing, sports equipment and outdoor clothing. Brands stocked include Clarks, K Shoes, Springer, CICA, Hi-Tec, Puma, Mercury, Dr Martens, Nike, LA Gear, Fila, Mizuno, Slazenger, Weider, Antler and Carlton, although not all are sold in every outlet. Discounts are on average 30% off the normal high street price for perfect stock.

CLEARMART
32-33 NEW KIRKGATE, LEITH, EDINBURGH
☎ (0131) 553 3073. OPEN 9.30 - 5 MON - SAT.
Factory Shops • *Womenswear & Menswear*
Damart underwear and merchandise - anything from tights, socks and gloves to dresses, coats, cardigans and jumpers - some of which is current stock sold at full price, some discontinued and ends of lines sold at discount. There several shops selling some discounted stock from the Damart range, known as Damart Extra.

CORSTON SINCLAIR LTD
INDUSTRIAL PROTECTIVE CLOTHING, 36 GLENBURN ROAD,
COLLEGE MILTON NORTH, EAST KILBRIDE G74 5BA
☎ (01355) 222273. OPEN 8.30 - 4.30 MON - THUR, 8.30 - 4 FRI.
Permanent Discount Outlets • *Womenswear & Menswear*
Sportswear & Equipment
Designer trainers from Reebok, Nike, Dunlop and Inter trainers as well as protective clothing (safety helmets, safety footwear, overalls), sports and leisure items: jeans, shorts, sweatshirts, socks and underwear at discounts of between 20% and 30% off normal retail prices.

COSALT INTERNATIONAL LTD
UNIT 7, WEST SHORE TRADING ESTATE, WEST SHORE ROAD,
GRANTON, EDINBURGH EH5 1QF
☎ (0131) 552 0011. OPEN 8 - 5 MON - FRI.
Permanent Discount Outlet • *Womenswear & Menswear*

The company specialises in workwear, safety clothing and marine wear but some of the merchandise is eminently wearable for everyday and is sold at very reasonable prices. They have a wide selection of leisure and outdoor clothes from Doc Martens to padded jackets and denim shirts, dungarees and donkey jackets, safety footwear and hard hats, protective clothing and boiler suits. VAT has to be added to prices. There are catalogues available for you to order from if what you want isn't in stock. They also provide marine safety and liferaft servicing.

DARTINGTON CRYSTAL
STERLING MILL, MOSS ROAD, TILLICOULTRY,
CLACKMANNANSHIRE FK13 6NS
☎ (01259) 755181. OPEN 10 - 6 SEVEN DAYS A WEEK.
Factory Shop in a Factory Shopping Village • *Household*

An extensive range of Dartington Crystal seconds at greatly reduced prices as well as some perfect crystal at full price. Range includes wine suites, sherry glasses, tankards, decanters, rippled glass, fruit and salad bowls.

DENBY FACTORY SHOP
STERLING MILLS DESIGNER OUTLET VILLAGE, MOSS ROAD,
TILLICOULTRY, CLACKMANNANSHIRE FK13 6HN
☎ (01259) 753 939. OPEN 9 - 5.30 MON - SAT (WINTER),
9 - 6 MON - SAT (SUMMER), 11 - 5 SUN.
Factory Shop in a Factory Shopping Village • *Household*

Denby is renowned for its striking colours and glaze effects. The Factory Shops stock first and second quality with seconds discounts starting at 20% off RRP. There are regular "mega bargains" with up to 75% off throughout the year.

DESIGNER SHADES
SCOTTISH DESIGNER OUTLET CENTRE, AVONDALE BOULEVARD,
LIVINGSTON EH54 6QX
☎ (0800) 3164352 CENTRE FREEPHONE INFORMATION LINE.
OPEN 10 -8 MON - FRI, 10 - 7 SAT, 10 - 6 SUN.
Permanent Discount Outlet • *Womenswear & Menswear* • *Children*

Designer Shades offer a wide selection of top-notch sunglasses at more than 30% off typical high street prices. The frames are invitingly displayed on backlit columns - no locked cabinets, messy stickers or hanging labels to contend with. Gucci, Polo Ralph Lauren, Jean Paul Gaultier, Valentino, Police, Christian Dior and Diesel are included in the ever-changing stock of top international brand names. Designer Shades ensure that all their sunglasses have quality lenses which protect against UVA and UVB rays, as well as filtering out damaging reflective blue light. They plan to have 20 shops throughout Europe by the end of 2001. For details of other locations, ring 01423 858007 or email info@designer-shades.net.

EDINBURGH ARCHITECTURAL SALVAGE YARD (E.A.S.Y.)
UNIT 6, COUPER STREET, OFF COBURG STREET, LEITH, EDINBURGH EH6 6HH
☎ (0131) 554 7077. WEBSITE: www.easy-arch-salv.co.uk
OPEN 9 - 5 MON - SAT.
Architectural Salvage • *DIY/Renovation*
Antique fireplaces, fire surrounds, fire inserts, wooden doors, cast iron spiral staircases, original fixtures and fittings, panelled doors, shutters, baths, sinks, radiators, and general architectural salvage.

EDINBURGH CRYSTAL
EASTFIELD, PENICUIK, LOTHIAN EH26 8HB
☎ (01968) 675128. OPEN 9 - 5 MON - SAT, 11 - 5 SUN.
Factory Shops • *Household*
Home to the world's largest collection of Edinburgh crystal, wine glasses, vases and decanters, both perfects and seconds with discounts of up to 75% off normal shop prices. There is a Visitor Centre and tea room on site.

ENCORE
48 WATERSIDE STREET, STRATHAVEN, LANARKSHIRE ML10 6AW
☎ (01357) 529779. OPEN 10 - 5 TUE, THUR, FRI AND SAT.
Dress Agencies • *Womenswear Only*
Encore has a large stock of nearly-new outfits from designers such as Frank Usher, Condici, Basler, Jacques Vert, Escada, Mondi, Tom Bowker, Mansfield and Alexon. Clothes range from daywear and suits to coats and evening wear and there is a large number from which to choose. Good place to find mother of the bride and groom outfits as well as accessories such as hats, bags and shoes.

FREEPORT SCOTLAND OUTLET VILLAGE
FIVE SISTERS, WESTWOOD, WEST CALDER, NEAR JUNCTION 4 OF THE M8, WEST LOTHIAN EH55 8QB
☎ (01501) 763488. OPEN 10 - 6 SEVEN DAYS A WEEK, 8 ON THUR.
Factory Shopping Village • *Womenswear & Menswear* • *Children Household* • *Electrical Equipment* • *Sportswear & Equipment*
Designer Outlet Village with more than 40 outlets offering discounts of 30% and more below high street prices, as well as restaurants, family attractions, free parking and entry. Outlets for women include The Designer Room (selling Donna Karan, Christian Lacroix, Armani and Kenzo), Mexx, Leather

Direct, Versace, Double Two, Christian Lacroix, Camille, Select, Company, Iceberg, Proibito and Honey Fashion offering formal and casual clothes and accessories; Jane Shilton with shoes and handbags and Luggage & Bags with bags, while The Perfume Shop sells top name fragrances. Men's outlets include the Suit Company, Jeanscene, London Leather, Ciro Citerio, Versace, Double Two, Iceberg and Proibito. Sportswear outlets include Russell Athletic and Tog 24 while footwear is covered by the Branded Shoe Warehouse (Ecco, Lotus, Gabor, Loake, Van-Dal and Salamander). Sweet-toothed visitors can savour the chocolates at Thornton's. Shops which stock items for children include Russell Athletic, Tog 24, Card & Gift, Versace, Select Thornton's and the Book Depot, while for teenage girls, there is Shoe Warehouse. There is plenty to keep the children amused with Tropical Rainforest World, Frontierland, Go-Kart track, Monster Trucks, Cheeky Chimp's soft-play jungle and lots of places to eat. Also a good selection of homeware shops offering a wide variety of products including mirrors, picture frames, framed prints, lamps, linens, cushions, rugs, quilts, glass and china gift and tableware as well as soaps, dried flowers, pot pourri etc. These shops include Beautiful Homes, John Jenkins, Ponden Mill and Churchill China. Electrical goods are supplied by Beautiful Homes, which sells an extensive range of household lamps along with other homewares such as mirrors and framed prints. Sports and leisure outlets comprise Russell Athletic with a wide range of sports clothes, shoes and equipment for all the family. Tog 24 has golf, walking and hiking gear for men and women such as waterproofs, day packs and boots as well as fleeces and waterproofs for children. Luggage & Bag stocks a wide selection of luggage and travel accessories.

GLADRAGS

17 HENDERSON ROW, EDINBURGH EH3 5DH

☎ (0131) 557 1916. OPEN 10.30 - 6 TUE - SAT.

Secondhand shops • *Household* • *Womenswear & Menswear*

Gladrags has a unique selection of exquisite vintage clothes, accessories and costume jewellery, lace-edged table and bed linen and paisley shawls. Next door at number 15 is a distinctive specialist shop selling decorative/functional silver, ladies and men's jewellery, porcelain, pottery, glass and metalware.

GLENEAGLES CRYSTAL

9 SIMPSON ROAD, EAST MAIN INDUSTRIAL ESTATE, BROXBURN, LOTHIAN EH52 5NP

☎ (01506) 852566. OPEN 10 - 5 MON - SAT, 11 - 4 SUN.

Factory Shops • *Household*

Hand-cut crystal, wine glasses, tumblers, ornaments, giftware, china and ceramics at discounts of about 15% for seconds. Tableware, dinner sets, complete china range from names such as Villeroy Boch, Wedgwood, Royal Doulton, Royal Worcester, Spode, Denby, Port Merion and Arthur Price cutlery.

HAVEN
473 HILLINGTON ROAD, HILLINGTON INDUSTRIAL ESTATE,
GLASGOW, DUMBARTONSHIRE G52 4QX
☎ (0141) 883 4801. OPEN 8 - 4.20 MON - THUR, 8 - 3 FRI.
Permanent Discount Outlet • *Womenswear & Menswear* • *Children*
A sheltered workshop owned by the Haven Products Trust to whom all the profits go. It sells women's, men's and children's knitwear, many of them high street and brand names at reduced prices.

HAWICK
Renowned for knitwear, Hawick is a cashmere buyer's dream town with four or five shops selling a wide variety of knits at bargain prices. As well as White of Hawick, there's the Cashmere Sweater Store which sells Chas N Whillans, Pringle, Alice Collins leisure wear, Tulchan hand embroidered knitwear, Cross Creek sports hats, rugs and socks. In the high street, there's Peter Scott selling cashmere and lambswool/merini wool for men and women. The Hawick Cashmere Co sells cashmere, lambswool, jackets and cardigans for men and women. Walk around the town and you'll find other knitwear treasures.

HAWICK CASHMERE CO LTD
81, GRASSMARKET, EDINBURGH EH1 2HJ.
☎ (0131) 2258634. OPEN 10 - 5 MON - SAT.
Factory Shops • *Womenswear & Menswear*
Manufactures high quality ladies and men's knitwear for top department stores and sells ends of lines here at below retail prices. Specialises in such luxury fibres as cashmere, cashmere silk, lambswool and merino in a range which comprises sweaters, capes, cardigans, dresses, skirts, gloves and cushions. Visitor Centre on site.

HELCO LTD
53 WILSON PLACE, NERSTON, EAST KILBRIDE, LANARKSHIRE
☎ (01355) 260066. OPEN 8 - 4.20 MON - THUR, 10 - 4 FRI.
Factory Shops • *Womenswear & Menswear*
Helco manufactures fleece jackets and they comprise most of the items on sale here. They also make waxed cotton garments and breathable jackets for Rohan and Barbour, samples and seconds of which are on sale, albeit with the labels cut out. There is another branch in Oldham.

HENDERSON ROOFING SUPPLIES LTD
31 WESTERBURN STREET, CARNTYNE, GLASGOW G32 6AT
☎ (0141)778 3602. OPEN 8 - 4.30 MON - THUR, 8 - 3.30 FRI.
Architectural Salvage • *DIY/Renovation*
Slate merchants and specialists in new and secondhand slates. Free car park.

HERMIONE SPENCER
UNIT 15, LOMOND TRADE CENTRE, ALEXANDRIA,
DUMBARTONSHIRE G83 OTL
☎ (01389) 721542. OPEN 9 - 4 MON - FRI.
Factory Shops • *Womenswear Only*
Knitwear, including cashmere, as well as wool for knitting in this factory which manufactures for all the top designers. Everything on sale here has been made on site, mostly for export to the United States. Phone first to check stock levels.

HONEY
FREEPORT VILLAGE WESTWOOD, WEST CALDER EH55 8PW
☎ (01501) 763222. OPEN 10 - 6 MON - SUN, 10 - 8 THUR.
LOCH LOMOND FACTORY OUTLET, ALEXANDRIA,
DUMBARTONSHIRE G83 ODG
☎ (01389) 607268. OPEN 10 - 6 MON - SUN.
Factory Shop in a Factory Shopping Village • *Womenswear Only*
Leisure-oriented women's T-shirts, leggings and sweaters at discounts of mostly 30% to 50%.

J & W CARPETS
UNIT 1, FORGE INDUSTRIAL ESTATE, BONNYTON ROAD,
KILMARNOCK
☎ (01563) 535397. OPEN 9 - 8 MON - FRI, 9 - 5.30 SAT, 12 - 5 SUN.
9 PORTLAND ROAD, IRVINE, SCOTLAND KA12 8HY
☎ (01294) 274724. OPEN 9 - 8 MON - FRI, 9 - 5.30 SAT, 12 - 5 SUN.
3 RUTHERGLEN ROAD, RUTHERGLEN G73 1SX
☎ (0141) 647 9442. OPEN 9 - 8 MON - FR141) 333 1212.
OPEN 9 - 8 MON - FRI, 9 - 5.30 SAT, 12 - 5 SUN
WAREHOUSE 1, CARRON ROAD, FALKIRK FK2 7RR
☎ (01324) 610210. OPEN 9 - 8 MON - FRI, 9 - 5.30 SAT, 12 - 5 SUN
☎ (0141) 333 1212. OPEN 9 - 8 MON - FRI, 9 - 5.30 SAT, 12 - 5 SUN
WAREHOUSE 1, CARRON ROAD, FALKIRK FK2 7RR
☎ (01324) 610210. OPEN 9 - 8 MON - FRI, 9 - 5.30 SAT, 12 - 5 SUN
Permanent Discount Outlets • *Furniture/Soft Furnishings*
Sells carpets from polyproplene and wool twists to Axminsters at discounts of up to 50%. They also sell Chinese rugs from £20-£175, representing discounts of 20%-30% on the high street. Carpets range from £1.50 a square yard to £20.

JAEGER FACTORY SHOP
TULLIBODY ROAD, LORNSHILL, ALLOA FK10 2EZ
☎ (01259) 218985. OPEN 9 - 5 MON - SAT, 10 - 4 SUN.
15 MUNRO PLACE, BONNYTON INDUSTRIAL ESTATE,
KILMARNOCK KA1 2NP
☎ (01563) 526511. OPEN 9 - 12 AND 2 - 4 MON, THUR, 9 - 4 TUE, WED, FRI, 10 - 4 SAT, SUN.
MCARTHURGLEN OUTLET, LIVINGSTONE, OPENING LATE 2000
Factory Shops • *Womenswear & Menswear*
Contemporary classics from Jaeger at excellent prices. Most of the merchandise is previous seasons' stock, but you might also find some special makes. Both shops stock tailoring and knitwear for women and men. The Alloa shop also sells a wide range of Viyella clothing at discount prices from 30% on ladies formal wear and casual wear, as well as Van Heusen.

JANE SHILTON
FREEPORT VILLAGE, FIVE SISTERS, WESTWOOD, WEST CALDER,
WEST LOTHIAN EH55 8QB
☎ (01501) 762985. OPEN 10 - 6 SEVEN DAYS A WEEK, UNTIL 8 THUR.
Factory Shop • *Womenswear Only*
Merchandise from past seasons' collections or factory seconds at discounts of at least 30% and up to 70% off the original price. There is a wide range of handbags, small leather goods, shoes, luggage umbrellas and travel bags. Example of price reduction: handbags at £24.99 originally £37.

JOHN BAILLIE CARPETS
22 GREENHILL ROAD, PAISLEY PA3 1RN
☎ (0141) 848 5502. OPEN 9 - 8 MON - FRI, 9 - 5.30 SAT, 11 - 5 SUN.
Permanent Discount Outlet • *Furniture/Soft Furnishings*
Sells carpets from polyproplene and wool twists to Axminsters at discounts of up to 50%. Carpets range from £1.50 a square yard to £20. Hardwood flooring also available at discounts of up to 20%. Vinyls start from £4 a square yard, underlay £1.75 to £3.63 per square yard.

JUMPER
FREEPORT SHOPPING AND LEISURE VILLAGE, WESTWOOD,
WEST CALDER, WEST LOTHIAN EH55 8QB
☎ (01501) 763203. OPEN 9.30 - 5.30 MON - SAT, 11 - 5 SUN.
Factory Shop in a Factory Shopping Village • *Womenswear & Menswear*
A wide range of Jumper label sweaters, gloves, scarves, shirts and cardigans for men and women all at discount prices of up to 50% off. Prices start at £2.

LEITH MILLS
70 - 74 BANGOR ROAD, OFF GREAT JUNCTION STREET, LEITH, EDINBURGH EH6 5JU
☎ (0131) 553 5161. OPEN SUMMER: 9 - 5.30 MON - SAT, 10 - 5 SUN, WINTER 10 - 5 MON - SAT, 11 - 5 SUN.
Permanent Discount Outlet • *Womenswear & Menswear*
Leith Mills is one of those places I find hard to place among discounters and factory shops. It's not really a factory shop as the stock is not made on site but bought in from all over Scotland, but it does claim to be very competitively priced. The only time prices may be equal with those in the high street is when the latter is on sale. As I'm not familiar with prices in Edinburgh, I couldn't tell how much of a good deal they were. Leith Mills is a very big outlet with plenty of car parking. It houses the Edinburgh Woollen Mill, James Pringle and the Clan Tartan Centre. The men's department houses Antartex sweaters, Harris Tweed, One Valley, Clan Royal sweaters, Tulchan knitwear, T-shirts and trousers. The women's department has Country Rose knitwear, blouses, shawls, pleated tartan skirts, Arran knits, gloves, scarves, hats, and cashmere. There is a very small children's clothing section and also a department selling tapes, teddies, cushions, books, silver spoons, Edinburgh and Stuart Crystal, Portmeirion china and Caithness giftware but at the normal shop prices. New additions include a shoe department, Ponden Mills and a golf shop. There is a coffee shop on site and a small food gift area.

LILLEY & SKINNER
DESIGNER OUTLET VILLAGE, ALMONDVALE AVENUE, LIVINGSTON, WEST LOTHIAN, JUNCTION 3 OFF THE M8 BETWEEN EDINBURGH AND GLASGOW EH54 6QX
FREEPHONE INFORMATION LINE ☎ 0800 3164352.
WEBSITE: www.mcarthurglen.com
OPEN 10 -8 MON - FRI, 10 - 7 SAT, 10 - 6 SUN.
Factory Shop in a Factory Shopping Village
Womenswear & Menswear • *Children*
Wide range of brand names including Stead & Simpson, Lilley & Skinner, Hobos, Hush Puppies, Lotus, Sterling & Hunt, Richleigh, Scholl, Red Tape, Flexi Country, Padders, Canaletto, Bronx, Frank Wright, Brevitt, Romba Wallace, Rieker, all at discount prices of up to 50%. Opening in late 2000.

LITTLEWOODS CATALOGUE OUTLET STORE
MRCARTHURGLEN OUTLET VILLAGE, DETAILS AS ABOVE.
Factory Shop in a Factory Shopping Village
Womenswear & Menswear • *Children* • *Electrical Equipment*
Ends of line and surplus stock from the Littlewoods catalogue at discounts of 30-50%. Sells clothing, footwear and electricals.

LOCH LOMOND FACTORY OUTLETS
MAIN STREET, ALEXANDRIA, JUNCTION 17 OF M8 THEN A82,
LOCH LOMOND G83 OUG
☎ (01389) 710077. E-MAIL: Outletcentres@mepc.co.uk
WEBSITE: www.lochlomondoutletcentre.co.uk   OPEN 10 - 6 MON - SUN.
**Factory Shopping Village • *Womenswear & Menswear
Children • Household • Sportswear & Equipment***
Just off the A82, the main route between Glasgow and the West Highlands and Islands, and only one mile from Loch Lomond, this factory outlet centre combines history, heritage, adventure and shopping under one roof. Twenty-two Shops include Book Depot, Designer Room (Christian Lacroix, Louis Feraud, Mondi and Maska), Honey, Hornsea Pottery, Jean Scene, Leading Labels, Luggage & Bags (which as well as selling luggage also carries Mulberry bags), Nickleby,s, offering Armani, Valentino, Hugo Boss, DKNY and Dolce & Gabanna; Original Shoe Company; Outdoor Adventure selling Timberland and Rockport brands; Pavers Shoes, Ponden Mill, Room offering homes accessories, ceramics, silverware, glass, rugs, throws, soft furnishings, fabric, lamps and frames; Stuart Crystal; Thorntons; Tog 24, Tom Sayers and XS Music. There is also a Motor Heritage Centre telling the history of the Scottish Motor Car industry.

LONDON LEATHERS DIRECT
FREEPORT VILLAGE, WEST CALDER, WEST LOTHIAN EH55 8QB
☎ (01501) 762405. OPEN 10 - 6 SEVEN DAYS A WEEK.
Factory Shop in a Factory Shopping Village • *Womenswear & Menswear*
Very good quality leather and suede jackets, coats and trousers, at discounts of at least 30%, with most at 50% off in this village which features lots of restaurants and fun things for the family to take part in.

LUGGAGE & BAGS
LOCH LOMOND FACTORY OUTLETS, MAIN STREET, ALEXANDRIA,
JUNCTION 4 OF M8 G83 OUG
☎ (01389) 607 251. OPEN 10 - 6 SEVEN DAYS A WEEK.
FREEPORT VILLAGE. WEST CALDER, WEST LOTHIAN EH55 8QB
☎ (01501) 763 443. OPEN 10 - 6 SEVEN DAYS A WEEK, UNTIL 8 THUR.
SEVEN DAYS A WEEK, UNTIL 8 THUR.
Factory Shop in a Factory Shopping Village • *Food and Leisure*
Luggage and travel-related products and executive cases, handbags, umbrellas from leading brands such as Samsonite, Desley, Head, Taurus and GlobeTrotter. Each product is offered at a substantially reduced price compared to those found on the high street due to being production over-runs, discontinued ranges or colours and last season's products. Discounts range from 30%-75% off high street prices.

MACKINNON MILLS
KIRKSHAW ROAD, COATBRIDGE ML5
☎ (01236) 440702. OPEN 10 - 5.30 MON - FRI, 7 ON THUR,
10 - 6 SAT, SUN.
Factory Shops • *Womenswear & Menswear*
Sportswear & Equipment • *Household*
Working woollen mill that sells seconds and perfect woollens with labels such as Pringle, Lyle & SCott, Antartex and Edinburgh Woollen Mills. They also sell golf equipment, polo shirts, Scottish music tapes, dress jewellery, books, shoes, bags and bedding.

MARSHALLS CHUNKY CHICKEN SHOP
NEWBRIDGE, MIDLOTHIAN EH28 8SW
☎ (0131) 333 3341. OPEN 8.30 - 5 MON - THUR,
8.30 - 4.30 FRI. 8.30 - 12 SAT.
Food and Drink Discounters
Sells whole fresh chickens, minimum four and a half pounds in weight, bags of about two dozen cooked drumsticks; bags of ten cooked thighs and chicken breast fillets. The company supply Marks & Spencer, Tesco and Asda.

MATALAN
SEAFIELD WAY, SEAFIELD ROAD, LEITH, EDINBURGH EH15 1TB
☎ (0131) 657 5045. OPEN 10 - 8 MON - FRI, 9.30 - 5.30 SAT, 10 - 6 SUN.
UNIT 5, CALEDONIAN CENTRE, NEW ASHTREE STREET,
WISHAW ML2 7UR
☎ (01698) 357075. OPEN 10 - 8 MON - FRI, 9.30 - 6.30 SAT, 10 - 6 SUN.
UNIT 7, GLENCAIRN RETAIL PARK, KILMARNOCK KA1 4AY
☎ (01563) 573892. OPEN 10 - 8 MON - FRI, 9.30 - 5.30 SAT, 10 - 6 SUN.
155 SLATEFORD ROAD, EDINBURGH EH14 1NZ
☎ (0131) 455 7224. OPEN 10 - 8 MON - FRI, 9.30 - 5.30 SAT, 10 - 6 SUN.
CARRON ROAD, FALKIRK FK1
☎ (01324) 614130. OPEN 10 - 8 MON - FRI, 10 - 6 SAT, SUN.
CLYDE RETAIL PARK, LIVINGSTONE STREET, CLYDEBANK,
GLASGOW G53 2XA
☎ (0141) 435 7450. OPEN 10 - 8 MON - FRI, 9.30 - 5.30 SAT, 10 - 6 SAT.
NITSHILL ROAD, DARNLEY, GLASGOW G53 7BW
☎ (0141) 880 3900. OPEN 10 - 8 MON - FRI, 9.30 - 5.30 SAT, 10 - 6 SUN.
Permanent Discount Outlets • *Womenswear & Menswear*
Children • *Household*
Matalan is a fashion and homewares value retailer giving customers what they claim to be unbeatable value for money with huge savings on a wide range of products including high quality fashionable clothing for men, women and children at up to 50% off high street prices. Matalan is situated out of town and stores are open seven days a week all year round.

McCALLS OF THE ROYAL MILE
11 THE HIGH STREET, EDINBURGH EH1 1SR
☎ (0131) 557 3979. OPEN 9 - 5.30 MON, WED, FRI, SAT, 9.30 - 5.30 TUE, 9 - 7.30 THUR, 12 - 4 SUN.
Hire Shop • *Menswear Only*
Hire and sell men's formal wear, whether a dinner suit or the full regalia. Kilt, shoes, bow tie, sporran costs £29.50 plus £5 for the shirt, socks £4.95; men's formal dinner suit, £20. Also hires morning suits, jackets, waistcoats, trousers, shirts and cravat or tie, £40; boys outfits, £28.50, but not girls or ladies. However, does sell women's outfits at full retail price.

MCARTHURGLEN DESIGNER OUTLET
ALMONDVALE AVENUE, LIVINGSTON, WEST LOTHIAN, JUNCTION 3 OFF THE M8 BETWEEN EDINBURGH AND GLASGOW EH54 6QX
☎ (0800) 316 4352. WEBSITE: www.mcarthurglen.com
OPEN 10 -8 MON - FRI, 10 - 7 SAT, 10 - 6 SUN.
(BARS AND RESTAURANTS OPEN UNTIL 10).
Factory Shopping Village • *Womenswear & Menswear*
Children • *Household* • *Sportswear & Equipment*
Factory shopping village opening in late 2000, comprising 100 factory shops all selling last season's or excess stock at 30%-50% below usual prices with a food court, cafes and restaurants. There's also an 8-screen licensed cinema, leisure club, a children's play area and parking for 2,500 cars.

FREEPORT VILLAGE
FIVE SISTERS, WESTWOOD, WEST CALDER, NEAR JUNCTION 4 OF THE M8, WEST LOTHIAN EH55 8QB
☎ (01501) 763488. OPEN 10 - 6 SEVEN DAYS A WEEK, UNTIL 8 THUR.
Factory Shop • *Womenswear & Menswear* • *Children*
High street fashion at factory outlet prices for men, women, babies and kids, all of which are heavily discounted by more than 30%. The telephone number given here is for the centre.

NORTH CAPE (SCOTLAND) LTD
ROYAL SCOT LTD, BANDEATH ESTATE, THROSK, NEAR STIRLING FK7 7NP
☎ (01786) 815349. OPEN 1 - 4 MON - FRI.
Factory Shop • *Sportswear & Equipment*
North Cape manufacture a leading range of outdoor clothing, including Rhovyl thermal underwear, silk underwear, Coolmax underwear, Polartec fleece ranges and Cyclone waterproofs as well as making North Cape own-label outdoor wear. The factory shop sells seconds, surplus stock and discontinued lines at discounts of 50% and more.

NORTH FACE OUTLET STORE
53 THE PLAZA, TOWN CENTRE, EAST KILBRIDE G74 1LW
☎ (01355) 238 383. OPEN 9.30 - 5.30 MON - SAT.
Permanent Discount Outlets • *Womenswear & Menswear*
Sportswear & Equipment
Sells first quality discounted North Face clothing and equipment up to 40% off.

PACO
STERLING MILLS, MOSS ROAD, TILLICOULTRY,
CLACKMANNANSHIRE FK13 6HN
☎ (01259) 753933. OPEN 10 - 6 SEVEN DAYS A WEEK.
Factory Shop in a Factory Shopping Village • *Children*
Womenswear Only • *Sportswear & Equipment*
Paco uses bright, distinctive colours and the knack for designing great clothes at affordable prices. For several years, they have also been creating their own brand of sports and leisurewear clothing that shows great verve and energy. This range has a much more everyday living influence. The contrast is a distinct look for the discerning wearer. If you are looking for a great T-shirt or sweatshirt, lightweight jacket or gilet, polar fleece or hooded top, three-quarter length or combat trousers, then you need look no further. Paco now competes with the very best fashion brands in the high street by offering customers high fashion combined with excellent quality, making their clothes real value for money.

PONDEN MILL LINENS
FREEPORT SHOPPING VILLAGE, FIVE SISTERS, WESTWOOD,
WEST CALDER, WEST LOTHIAN EH55 8QB
☎ (01501) 763053. OPEN 10 - 6 SEVEN DAYS A WEEK, UNTIL 8 ON THUR.
LOCH LOMOND FACTORY OUTLET, ARGYLE WORKS, MAIN STREET,
ALEXANDRIA, LOCH LOMOND G83 OUG
☎ (01389) 607200. OPEN 10 - 6 SEVEN DAYS A WEEK.
Factory Shop in a Factory Shopping Village • *Household*
Famous branded products at direct from the mill prices. A fabulous assortment of towels, duvets, pillows, throws, bedspreads, up-to-the-minute coordinated bed linen, from Crown, Coloroll, Jeff Banks Ports-of-Call, to name but a few. Something for every room in the house.

PUTTING ON THE RITZ
THE VICTORIAN VILLAGE, 93 WEST REGENT STREET, GLASGOW G2 2BA
☎ (0141) 332 9808. OPEN 10 - 5 MON - SAT.
Secondhand and Vintage Clothes • *Womenswear & Menswear*
Retro jewellery, marcasite and Fifties silver, nightwear, Paisley shawls, vintage dinner suits and tuxedos, Thirties and Forties sportswear, riding boots, stetsons, 1930s USA football outfits. Jewellery from £5, dinner suits from £15. Unusual gifts, exciting decorative items, interior furnishings, small pieces of furniture, also stocked, as well as Victorian jewellery and original Scottish agate jewellery.

Q MARK WAREHOUSE
CROW ROAD, GLASGOW G11 7DN
☎ (0131) 225 6861. OPEN 10 - 5 MON - SAT, 12 - 5 SUN.
BRAIDHOLM ROAD, GEB
☎ (0141) 633 3636. OPEN 10 - 5 MON - SAT, 12 - 5 SUN.
KERSE ROAD INDUSTRIAL ESTATE, KERSE ROAD, STIRLING
☎ (01786) 474747. OPEN 10 - 5 MON- SAT, 12 - 5 SUN.
Permanent Discount Outlets • *Womenswear & Menswear* • *Children*
Scotland's biggest discount clothing warehouse for women, men and children offers top quality fashions at up to 50% off normal high street prices. Huge selection of homewares also. Regular stock deliveries ensure a constant selection of new styles - often recognised in famous chain stores, but always at ridiculously low prices. Q Mark operate a once-a-year membership fee of £5. All prices are subject to VAT, charged at point of sale.

RE-DRESS
51 EASTWOODMAINS ROAD, GIFFNOCK, GLASGOW G46 6PW
☎ (0141) 638 5090. OPEN 9.30 - 5.30 MON -SAT.
Dress Agencies • *Womenswear Only*
Designer labels on sale here include Escada, Armani, Mondi and Betty Barclay. Day and eveningwear is sold, as well as handbags, shoes, hats, and costume jewellery.

REDRESS
1 PRIESTON ROAD, BRIDGE OF WEIR PA11 3AJ
☎ (01505) 615151. OPEN 9.30 - 5.30 MON - SAT.
Dress Agencies • *Womenswear Only*
Sells both new and nearly-new fashion items at bargain prices. The designers range from high street to top designers, and often feature Parigi, Armani, Versace, Betty Barclay, Puccini, and Jacques Vert. Sells everything from blouses, shirts, suits and dresses to beads, shoes, hats, bags, belts and jewellery. Prices range from £10 upwards and sizes from 8-18.

REDRESS
71 HIGH STREET, NORTH BERWICK, EAST LOTHIAN EH39 4HG
☎ (01620) 895633. OPEN 10 - 4.30 MON - SAT,
CLOSED THUR DURING WINTER.
Dress Agencies • *Womenswear Only*
Established for over six years, this shop has a friendly atmosphere, with clothes arriving daily from all over the country. Names include Escada, Nicole Farhi, Max Mara, Tomasz Starzewski, Moschino, Sisley, Y.S.L., Betty Barclay Jaeger, Geiger, Monsoon, Gucci, Ferragamo and lots more... from casual wear to special occasions, sizes 8-28 when available. They also have a large selection of hats, bags, shoes and jewellery. You can arrange to see their colour and image consultant who will tell you what 'season' you are, and advise you what colours to wear and which to avoid. Also included in the pacage is a makeover and your own personalised pallette to take shopping.

RUMMAGE

5 STEWART STREET, MILNGAVIE G62 6BW
☎ (0141) 956 2333. OPEN 10 - 5 MON - SAT.
Dress Agencies • *Womenswear Only*

New and nearly-new designer clothes from Lagerfeld and Dior to Givenchy as well as items from high street chain stores. There are usually at least 200 special occasion outfits available as well as handbags, shoes and costume jewellery. There's also evening wear, ballgowns, bric a brac, china, ornaments, glassware, hat boxes and hat hire.

SARATOGA TRUNK

THIRD FLOOR, 61 HYDE PARK STREET, GLASGOW G3 8BW
☎ (0141) 221 4433. OPEN 10.30 - 5 MON - FRI, 10.30 - 5 SAT.
Secondhand and Vintage Clothes • *Womenswear Only*

Old-fashioned and antique clothing, Paisley shawls, embroidered shawls, wedding dresses from the Forties and Fifties, and Christening robes. Victorian to 1950s daywear, evening wear and underwear. Accessories including costume jewellery. Patchwork, lace curtains, bedlinen, table covers and collectibles including dolls and teddy bears.

SCENT TO YOU

THE DESIGNER ROOM, STERLING MILLS DESIGNER OUTLET VILLAGE,
TILLICOULTRY, NEAR STIRLING,
MIDWAY BETWEEN M9 AND M90 FK13 6HQ
☎ (01259) 752100. OPEN 10 - 6 SEVEN DAYS A WEEK.
Factory Shop in a Factory Shopping Village • *Womenswear Only*

Operating within The Designer Room at this outlet village, Scent to You sells discounted perfume, cosmetics and accessories including body lotions and gels. The company, which has more than thirty branches, buys in bulk and sells more cheaply, relying on a high turnover for profit. Discounts range from 5% to 60%, with greater savings during their twice-yearly sales (phone for details). Most of the leading brand names in perfume are stocked including Christian Lacroix, Armani, Charlie, Givenchy, Anais Anais from Cacherel, Charlie from Revlon, Coco Chanel, Christian Dior, Elizabeth Taylor, Blue Grass from Elizabeth Arden, Aramis, Lagerfeld. Plus cosmetics from Revlon and Spectacular and skincare from Clarins and Lancome as well as Scent To You's own range of bags, watches, hair brushes and brushkits which is sold under the name S.T.Y. Designs. Stock varies greatly due to the fast turnover and varying supplies so more than one visit may be necessary to obtain the scent of your choice. Or phone first to avoid disappointment.

SCOTTISH FINE SOAPS FACTORY SHOP
UNIT 2, OCHILTERRACE, GROVE INDUSTRIAL ESTATE, CARRON, FALKIRK FK2 8DZ
☎ (01324) 551377. OPEN 1 - 4 MON -THUR, 1 - 3.30 FRI.
Factory Shops • *Household*
Makes soap, pot pourri, bubble bath and a novelty range of soaps in the shape of cats, pigs, elephants and dogs. Prices are half that of the high street for discontinued lines in soaps which are made for many of the major department stores. From 5p to 50p for a bar of soap.

SHELAGH BUCHANAN
65 BATH STREET, GLASGOW G2 2BX
☎ (0141) 331 1862. OPEN 9 - 5 MON - FRI, 9 - 12 SAT.
Dress Agencies • *Womenswear Only*
Situated in the centre of Glasgow, this shop sells anything from shoes to ballgowns, including cocktail dresses, evening wear, suits and outfits, bags and accessories. Designer labels in this outlet can be found on the second floor and include Armani, Versace, Country Casuals, Jaeger, Mondi, Escada, Jean Muir, Jobis and Basler. There is a tailoring alterations service on the premises. Situated near to the bus and train station as well as Buchanan Galleries Shopping Mall.

SLATERS MENSWEAR
165 HOWARD STREET, GLASGOW G1 4HF
☎ (0141) 552 7171. OPEN 8.30 - 5.30 MON - SAT, 7.30 ON THUR.
10 BON ACCORD STREET, ABERDEEN AB11 6EL
☎ (01224) 212334. OPEN 8.30 - 5.30 MON - SAT, 7.30 ON THUR.
Permanent Discount Outlets • *Menswear Only*
Full range of men's clothes from underwear and shoes to casualwear, suits and dresswear and including labels such as Odermark, Bulmer, Valentino, Charlie's Co, and Charlton Gray. Men's suits from £79.

SNOW SENSE
2 HOWE STREET, EDINBURGH EH3 6TD
☎ (0131) 662 4487. OPEN 5.30 - 7.30 TUE AND THUR (MID OCT - END MAR), 10.30 - 5.30 SAT, SUN DURING HIGH SEASON ONLY.
Dress Agencies • *Sportswear & Equipment*
Open only during the ski season, there is everything here that the enthusiastic skier could want from nearly-new salopettes and ski jackets to gloves, goggles and other accessories as well as the hardware: boots, skis and poles. They also stock high quality snowboards and some nearly-new equipment. Now also have a selection of ex-display new clothing from top brand names including Lange, Saloman and Nordica.

SPOILS
UNIT 6/7 RIGHEAD GATE, TOWN CENTRE, EAST KILBRIDE,
GLASGOW G74 1LS
☎ (01355) 579224. OPEN 9 - 5.30 MON - SAT, 12 - 5 SUN.
UNIT MSU2 ST ENOCH CENTRE, GLASGOW G1 4BW
☎ (0141) 221 6044
Permanent Discount Outlets • *Household*

General domestic glassware, non-stick bakeware, kitchen gadgets, ceramic oven-to-tableware, textiles, cutting boards, aluminium non-stick cookware, bakeware, plastic kitchenware, plastic storage, woodware, coffee pots/makers, furniture, mirrors and picture frames. Rather than being discounted, all the merchandise is very competitively priced - in fact, the company carry out competitors' checks frequently in order to monitor pricing. With 38 branches, the company is able to buy in bulk and thus negotiate very good prices.

STARRY STARRY NIGHT
19 - 21 DOWANSIDE LANE, GLASGOW G12 9BZ
☎ (0141) 337 1837. OPEN 10 - 5.30 MON - SAT.
Secondhand and Vintage Clothes • *Womenswear & Menswear*

Retro gear, especially evening gowns, menswear, including morning coats, tails and striped blazers from Victorian through the Twenties and Thirties to Sixties and Seventies gear. Morning suits, £35, dinner suits, £30, leather jackets, £15-£25, evening gowns, £10 upwards, waistcoats, collarless shirts, bow ties and costume jewellery. Also Levi 501s and all types of Levis from £10. Hire service available. They are constantling looking for Seventies stock, in particular Biba, Pucci, Geoff Banks.

STERLING MILLS DESIGNER OUTLET VILLAGE
TILLICOULTRY, NEAR STIRLING,
MIDWAY BETWEEN M9 AND M90 FK13 6HQ
☎ (01259) 752100. WEBSITE: www.sterlingmills.com
OPEN 10 - 6 SEVEN DAYS A WEEK.
Factory Shopping Village • *Womenswear & Menswear* • *Children*
Household • *Food and Leisure* • *Sportswear & Equipment*

This factory shopping centre in Scotland guarantees prices of at least 30% off typical high street prices and sometimes as much as 70%. Outlets so far include Because It's There, clothes for outdoor pursuits; Bed & Bath Works; Book Depot; Claire's Accessories; Cotton Traders; D2, men and women's fashion; Denby Pottery; Designer Room; DKNY; Double Two shirts; Jacadi; Jacques Heim, featuring Whitbread, Jules Verne and men's formal wear; Julian Graves, herbs, spices and nuts; Nike; Nickelbys menswear; Paco for adults and children; Pavers Shoes; Proibito, including Armani and Versace; Roman Originals; Thorntons; Tog 24 outdoor wear; Travel Accessory Outlet; USA Golf Wear House; USC famous casualwear brands; VF Corporation Factory

Store; Winning Line ladieswear and XS Music and more are planned. There's also a restaurant and coffee shop. Across the road is the very large Sterling Furniture Centre.

THE ADDRESS-DESIGNER EXCHANGE
3 ROYAL EXCHANGE COURT, OFF 17 ROYAL EXCHANGE SQUARE, GLASGOW G1 3DB
☎ (0141) 221 6898. OPEN 10 - 5.30 TUE - SAT.

Dress Agencies • *Womenswear Only*

A warm, inviting shop tucked away, yet in the heart of the city centre, which is about to celebrate ten years in business. Sharp-eyed lovers of style travel from afar to this exciting shop which is full of new and nearly-new designer clothes and accessories ranging from Chanel, Armani, Versace and Moschino to high-fashion high street names such as Whistles, Jigsaw, Kookai and Morgan. Stock turns around quickly with new items arriving daily, all of which are personally selected by the owners. Items come from all over the UK, many from well-known celebrities. Customers can browse in a relaxed, fun and low-pressure environment, where an honest opinion is always given. Examples of prices Armani trouser suit £149 from £700, Escada jacket, £99 from £500, Prada bag £120 from £380, Moschino dress £85 from £360, Hermes scarf £45 from £180.

THE COTTON PRINT FACTORY SHOP
58 ADMIRAL STREET, GLASGOW G41 1HU
☎ (0141) 420 1855. OPEN 9 - 5.30 MON - SAT, 10 - 5 SUN.

Factory Shops • *Furniture/Soft Furnishings*

Offers the largest selection of top quality curtain fabric at discount prices in Scotland as well as wallpaper and borders. There are up to 6,000 rolls of curtaining fabric from names such as Ashley Wilde and Leon, heading tapes, tiebacks, curtain pulls, cushion pads, track fabrics. They claim no one in Scotland can beat their prices.

THE MAD HATTER
6 CANNIESBURN TOLL, BEARSDEN, GLASGOW G61 2QU
☎ (0141) 942 1711. OPEN 10 - 5 MON - SAT.
COMMLEYBANK AVENUE, COMMLEYBANK, EDINBURGH
☎ (0131) 315 4111. OPEN 10 - 5 MON - SAT.

Hire Shop • *Womenswear Only*

Hats hired out from a superb selection of 500. Top-name designer hats for Ascot and garden parties. Hire charges from £15 to £75.

THORNTONS
LOCH LOMOND FACTORY OUTLET CENTRE, MAIN STREET, ALEXANDRIA, STRATHCLYDE G83 OUG
☎ (01389) 729994. OPEN 10 - 6 SEVEN DAYS A WEEK.
FREEPORT VILLAGE FIVE SISTERS, WESTWOOD, WEST CALDER, NR LIVINGSTON, WEST LOTHIAN EH55
☎ (01501) 762271. OPEN 10 - 6 SEVEN DAYS A WEEK, 8 ON THUR.
STERLING MILLS FACTORY OUTLET,TILLICOULTRY FK13 6NS
☎ (01259) 753875. OPEN 10 - 6 MON - SAT, 8 ON THUR, 11 - 5 SUN.

Factory Shop in a Factory Shopping Village
Food and Leisure • Household

The UK's leading specialist confectionery retailer has more than 500 shops and franchises nationwide selling a wide range of boxed and loose chocolate and sugar confectionery. The factory outlets sell three different categories: misshapes. discounted lines and standard lines. Misshapes are loose chocolates which are the result of new product development, product trials or end of production runs which cannot be packed as Thorntons standard lines. They are packed into assorted bags and offer a saving of 35%-55% over the recommended retail price of standard "loose line" products. Discounted lines are excess to Thorntons' normal retail requirements and can be as a result of excess seasonal or export stock, discontinued lines or packaging changes. These products, when available, are offered at a discount of 25%-50% over the standard retail price. Standard lines from the full Thorntons range are also on sale at normal prices.

TK MAXX
THE SAUCHIEHALL CENTRE, GLASGOW G2 3ER
☎ (0141) 331 0411. OPEN 9 - 5.30 MON - FRI, 9 - 7 THUR, 9 - 6 SAT, 12 - 5 SUN.
MEADOW BANK RETAIL PARK, EDINBURGH EH17 5TS
☎ (0131) 661 6611. OPEN 9 - 5 MON - FRI, UNTIL 7 ON THUR, 9 - 6 SAT, 12 - 5 SUN.
CALLENDER SQUARE SHOPPING CENTRE, FALKIRK
☎ (01324) 619881. OPEN 9 - 5.30 MON - WED, 9 - 7 THUR, 9 - 6 FRI,
UNIT 42 - 44 MERCAT CENTRE, KIRKCALDY KY1 1N1
☎ (01592) 644488. OPEN 9 - 5 MON - FRI, 9 - 9 THUR, 9 - 6 SAT, 12 - 5 SUN.
UNIT 5 AMONDVALE WEST RETAIL PARK, ALMONDVALE ROAD, LIVINGSTON EH54 6QX
☎ (01506) 462 060. OPEN 10 - 8 MON - FRI, 9 44488. OPEN 9 - 5 MON - FRI, 9 - 9 THUR, 9 - 6 SAT, 12 - 5 SUN.

Permanent Discount Outlets • *Womenswear & Menswear*
Children • Household • Furniture/Soft Furnishings

Based on an American concept, TK Maxx is situated in easily accessible, often centrally located stores and offers famous label goods with up to 60% savings off recommended retail prices. TK Maxx has fashion for the whole family -

women's, men's and childrenswear - accessories, shoes, gifts, kitchenware and home goods. Everything in the store is branded with a choice of well-known high street names to designer labels, and while a small percentage might be clearly marked past season, the great majority of items in store are current season, current stock and still with phenomenal savings. There is a huge choice with 50,000 pieces in store and up to 10,000 new items arriving a week. The stores are simple and unfussy with wide aisles, shopping trolleys and baskets, and a spacious, functional feel to them but there are individual changing rooms, ramps for buggies and wheelchairs and plenty of staff on the shop floor. Every branch accepts all major credit and debit cards and has a liberal refund and return policy.

TOG 24

LOCH LOMOND FACTORY OUTLETS, MAIN STREET, ALEXANDRIA, STRATHCLYDE G83 OUG
☎ (01389) 607175. OPEN 10 - 6 SEVEN DAYS A WEEK.
FREEPORT VILLAGE FIVE SISTERS, WEST CALDER, JUNCTION 4 OF M8, WEST LOTHIAN
☎ (01501) 762823. OPEN 10 - 6 SEVEN DAYS A WEEK, 8 ON THUR.
STERLING MILLS DESIGNER OUTLET VILLAGE, TILLICOULTRY, CLACKMANNANSHIRE
☎ (01259) 753911. OPEN 10 - 6 SEVEN DAYS A WEEK.
LEVEL 3, BUCHANAN GALLERIES SHOPPING CENTRE, 6 SAUCHIEHALL STREET, GLASGOW G2 3GF
☎ (01413) 339377. OPEN 9 - 6 MON - SAT, 8 ON THUR, 11 - 5 SUN.
Factory Shop in a Factory Shopping Village
Womenswear & Menswear • Children • Sportswear & Equipment
Tog 24 are the UK's fastest growing brand name in outdoor clothing and leisurewear. They utilise the world's finest performance fabrics including Gore-Tex, Polartec and Burlington MCS, catering for all the family for all seasons, with cosy fleeces and waterproofs for the winter, and trekking ranges, shorts and t-shirts for the summer. With all prices at least 30% below the recommended retail price, you can afford to enter the Tog comfort zone.

TRAVEL ACCESSORY

STERLING MILLS DESIGNER OUTLET VILLAGE, MOSS ROAD, TILLICOULTRY, CLACKMANNANSHIRE FK13 6HN
☎ (01259) 753884. OPEN 10 - 6 SEVEN DAYS A WEEK.
Factory Shop in a Factory Shopping Village • *Food and Leisure*
Luggage and travel-related products and executive cases, handbags, umbrellas from leading brands such as Samsonite, Desley, Head, Taurus and GlobeTrotter. Each product is offered at a substantially reduced price compared to those found on the high street due to being production over-runs, discontinued ranges or colours and last season's products. Discounts range from 30%-75% off high street prices.

VALLEY TEXTILES
1 CAMPBELL STREET, DARVEL, NEAR KILMARNOCK KA17 OBZ
☎ (01560) 320140. OPEN 8.30 - 5 MON - THUR, 8.30 - 1 FRI.
Factory Shops • *Furniture/Soft Furnishings*
All types of curtaining materials from lace and cotton to voiles, satins and Terylene, as well as a making-up service on site. Fabric costs from £2 - £25 a metre, at least half the normal retail price. They also sell table linens, bedcovers and bed canopies from £25 - £50, as well as swags and tails.

WHAT'S THE LABEL
KINGSGATE RETAIL PARK, GLASGOW ROAD, EAST KILBRIDE, SOUTH LANARK
☎ (01355) 224470. OPEN 9 - 6 MON - WED, SAT, 9 - 8 THUR, FRI, 10.30 - 5.30 SUN.
Permanent Discount Outlets • *Womenswear Only*
Originating from M&S, Dorothy Perkins, Principles, and many more high street stores, the merchandise consists of excess stock. The majority of the shop labels are cut out. There are also branches at Hamilton, Paisley and Rutherglen.

WILD ROSE
15 HENDERSON ROW, EDINBURGH EH3 5DH
☎ (0131) 557 1916. OPEN 10.30 - 6 TUE - SAT.
Secondhand shops • *Household*
A distinctive specialist shop selling decorative/functional silver, ladies and men's jewellery, porcelain, pottery, glass and metalware. Next door at number 17 is Gladrags which has a unique selection of exquisite vintage clothes, accessories and costume jewellery, lace-edged table and bed linen, paisley shawls.

Scottish Highlands & Islands

ANTA SCOTLAND LTD
FEARN, TAIN, ROSS-SHIRE IV20 1XW
☎ (0186) 283 2477. FAX 0186 283 266. E-MAIL: sales@anta.co.uk
WEBSITE: www.anta.co.uk
OPEN 9.30 - 5.30 MON - SAT, 12 - 4 SUN. ALSO MAIL ORDER.
Factory Shops • *Furniture/Soft Furnishings*
Anta design everything on site, using tartan check designs in traditional Scottish landscape colours and there are usually seconds and ends of lines available at discounted prices. There are jazzy check woollen rugs, carpets, fabrics, throws, blankets and ceramics (also made on site) on sale at greatly discounted prices. Mail order is not at discount prices.

BABYGRO LTD
HAYFIELD INDUSTRIAL ESTATE, KIRKCALDY, FIFE KY2 5DN
☎ (01592) 647800. OPEN 10.30 - 1.30 AND 2 - 4.30 MON,
9.30 - 1.30 AND 2 - 4.30 TUE - SAT, 12.30 - 4.30 SUN.
Factory Shops • *Children*
Babywear for 0-5 year olds at discounts of up to 50%: all-in-ones, playsuits, shorts, t-shirts, vests, shirts, pyjamas, and rompers at factory shop prices. Pyjamas upwards of £3 - a pair for a 4-year-old cost £6.99 compared with £12.99 for the same make in a high street store. Also does a line of adult leisurewear. Factory sales take place throughout the year and are advertised locally.

BLUE MOON AT BELMONT STUDIOS
FIRST FLOOR, 11 BELMONT STREET, ABERDEEN AB10 1JR
☎ (01224) 641741. OPEN 9.30 - 5 TUE - SAT, 9.30 - 7 THUR.
Dress Agencies • *Womenswear Only*
Designer bridal wear sold at discounted prices. Some new dresses, some once-worn, but all in immaculate condition. New samples and ex-display dresses also sold as well as accessories such as bridesmaids dresses, veils, shoes. Up to 200 dresses in stock at any one time from labels such as Tray Connop, Alan Hannah, Richards Designs, Pretty Maid and many more. It's advisable to book an appointment.

CAITHNESS GLASS VISITOR CENTRE
INVERALMOND INUSTRIAL ESTATE, PERTH PH1 3TZ
☎ (01738) 637373. OPEN 9 - 5 MON - SAT, 10 - 5 SUN IN SUMMER,
12 - 5 WINTER.
VISITORS CENTRE, AIRPORT INDUSTRIAL ESTATE, WICK,
CAITHNESS KW1 5BP
☎ (01955) 602286. OPEN 9 - 5 MON - SAT, 11 - 5 SUN EASTER-DECEMBER.
FACTORY SHOP, THE WATERFRONT CENTRE, RAILWAY PIER, OBAN,
ARGYLL PA34 4LW
☎ (01631) 563386. OPEN 9 - 5 MON - SAT IN MARCH - OCTOBER,
9 - 7.30 IN MAY - OCTOBER, 11 - 5 SUN IN APRIL - OCTOBER
Factory Shops • *Household*
Well stocked factory shop with many bargains all year round in glass and crystal, giftware and tableware. Also selection of Royal Doulton products and other great gift ideas to choose from. Special offers throughout the year.

CASHMERE AT LOCHLEVEN
LOCHLEVEN MILLS, KINROSS KY13 8DH
☎ (01577) 863521. OPEN 9 - 5.30 MON - SAT.
Factory Shops • *Womenswear & Menswear* • *Sportswear & Equipment*
For over 100 years Todd & Duncan have been spinning finest cashmere yarn by the side of picturesque Loch Leven in Kinross. Their adjacent factory shop acts as an ideal focal point for those eager to purchase sophisticated cashmere

lines at affordable prices. Visitors will be captivated by The Cashmere Story, a visually stimulating pictorial history of the journey taken by cashmere from the barren plains of Mongolia, through the traditional Scottish yarn spinning processes, and on to its final destination - the catwalks of the world's leading fashion designers. The shop provides a terrific selection of clothing of perfect quality, with no damaged goods or seconds. Labels stocked include their own popular Kinross Cashmere label, as well as complementary classics from famed collections such as Daks, Henri White, Barrie etc. and the full Pringle range of both men and women's fashion sportswear. The shop and visitors' centre is located about half an hour's drive from Edinburgh and just five minutes from the M90 motorway.

CATALOGUE BARGAIN SHOP
315-317 HIGH STREET, COWDENBEATH, FIFE KY4 9QJ
☎ (01383) 611054. OPEN 9 - 5.30 MON - SAT, 11 - 4 SUN.
Permanent Discount Outlets • *Womenswear & Menswear Children* • *Household* • *Electrical Equipment*
Catalogue Bargain Shop is a growing national chain of stores which obtains the majority of its goods from mail order giants Great Universal and Kays, and offers a range of clothing for all the family, a wide selection of shoes, bed linen, household goods, electrical equipment and hundreds of other catalogue items at very competitive prices. The merchandise consists of ends of ranges and previous season's stock for which there is no longer storage space when the catalogues change. The Queen Street shop is on the first floor of an office block. The Parkhead branch has a new section selling different types of furniture.

DAMART
36-40 MARKET STREET, ABERDEEN, SCOTLAND
☎ (01124) 571146. OPEN 9.30 - 5 MON - SAT.
Factory Shops • *Womenswear & Menswear*
Damart underwear and merchandise - anything from tights, socks and gloves to dresses, coats, cardigans and jumpers - some of which is current stock sold at full price, some discontinued and ends of lines sold at discount. There several shops selling some discounted stock from the Damart range, known as Damart Extra.

DARTINGTON CRYSTAL
STUART CRYSTAL, MUTHILL ROAD, CRIEFF, PERTHSHIRE PH7 4HQ
☎ (01764) 655632. OPEN 10 - 6 SEVEN DAYS A WEEK JUNE - SEPT, 10 - 5 REST.
Factory Shop in a Factory Shopping Village • *Household*
An extensive range of Dartington Crystal seconds at greatly reduced prices as well as some perfect crystal at full price. Range includes wine suites, sherry glasses, tankards, decanters, rippled glass, fruit and salad bowls.

ELYSEES DRESS AGENCY
129 HORLBURN STREET, ABERDEEN
☎ (01224) 582257. OPEN 10.30 - 4.30 MON - WED, FRI,
10.30 - 6.30 THUR, 10.30 - 5 SAT.
Dress Agencies • *Womenswear Only*
Now moved to much larger premises with more stock available. New and nearly-new clothes including ends of ranges and designer samples as well as a few high street names. Daywear, evening wear and accessories and very extensive 'Mother of the Bride' and hat selection.

FOOTWEAR DISCOUNT CENTRE
JOHN STREET, OBAN PA34 5NI
☎ (01631) 563633. OPEN 9 - 5.30 MON - SAT, 11 - 4 SUN.
Permanent Discount Outlets • *Womenswear & Menswear* • *Children*
Two floors of more than 10,000 pairs of quality branded footwear such as Lotus, Nil Simile and Equity, which are seconds, discontinued lines, factory directs and Italian imports. Ladies shoes, fashion courts to leather walking shoes, from size 2 to 9. Men's leather shoes in sizes 5-13, including walking boots, trainers, work boots and safety boots. Children's shoes and Wellingtons.

GLENEAGLES KNITWEAR COMPANY
ABBEY ROAD, AUCHTERARDER, TAYSIDE PH3 1DP
☎ (01764) 662112. OPEN 9 - 5 MON - SAT.
Factory Shops • *Womenswear & Menswear*
Perfect knitwear for women and men including cardigans, jumpers, socks. Also stocks coats and jackets by Burberry and Daks; sweaters by Jaeger and cashmere made to order.

INNOVATIONS
5 ABBOT STREET, PERTH PH2 OEB
☎ (01738) 638568. OPEN 10 - 4 MON - SAT.
Dress Agencies • *Womenswear Only*
Small, friendly shop where customers speak to each other over countless cups of coffee sipped by ladies who come from afar to snap up some of the wonderful clothes which come and go on a daily basis. Prices are kept low to maintain a high turnover. Stocks ballgowns, wedding outfits, business suits and casual/holiday wear, all at less than one third of the original price. Examples of prices include Weill suit for £120, originally £425, Cerruti suit £130, originally £700, Wolford body £18, originally £79. There are usually hundreds of different outfits in stock in sizes 8-24, plus lots of costume jewellery, scarves, handbags, and some shoes. Half-price sales take place in January and July.

JOHNSTONS OF ELGIN
CASHMERE VISITORS CENTRE, NEW MILL, ELGIN 1V30 4AF
☎ (01343) 554099. OPEN 9 - 5.30 MON - SAT, 11 - 5 SUN JUNE - OCTOBER.
Factory Shops • *Womenswear & Menswear*

A factory shop with an on-site visitors mill, where you can watch raw wool being made into luxurious cashmere from the dyeing and blending through to the spinning, winding and weaving. Cashmere sweaters sold from £75 - £250, plus regular bargain baskets.

LABELS
36 BROOMHILL ROAD, ABERDEEN AB1 6HT
☎ (01224) 213345. OPEN 10 - 5 WED - SAT.
Dress Agencies • *Womenswear Only*

Small but interesting shop which stocks both high street and designer names including Versace, Moschino, Jasper Conran, Country Casuals, Principles, Wallis, Next and Jaeger. Stock is constantly changing and there is always something different to see on each visit. There are also shoes, handbags, hats and jewellery. Clothes range from daywear and holiday wear to ballgowns, evening wear and business outfits. Coffee always available!

LABELS FOR LESS
78 HIGH STREET, AUCHTERARDER, PERTHSHIRE PH3 18J
☎ (01764) 664482. OPEN 10 - 5 MON - SAT, WED 10 - 4.30, CLOSED 1 - 3.
Dress Agencies • *Womenswear Only*

The agency with a touch of class and top quality designers in abundance. Attention to layout and display is second to none and prices for gently worn garments very competitive. Lynne Francis, the owner accepts new garments in pristine condition daily. Well worth a visit.

MACGILLIVRAY & CO
BALIVANICH, BENBECULA, WESTERN ISLES HS7 5LA
☎ (01870) 602525. OPEN 9.30 - 5 MON - FRI, CLOSED 1 - 2, 9.30 - 4 SAT. MAIL ORDER.
Factory Shops • *Womenswear & Menswear*

The MacGillivray Company has been selling handwoven Harris tweed and hand-knitted sweaters all over the world since 1941. Usually hand-knitted sweaters in pure new wool cost from £60 and 72cm (28") wide Harris tweed costs £11.55 a metre (£10.50 a yard). They sometimes hold a stock of special offer fabrics, which they obtain from various mills throughout Britain. Because these are surplus stock, cancelled export orders or out of season fabrics, they can be sold at less than half the original selling price. These can range from Scottish tweeds, Shetlands, Donegals, dress and fancy fabrics, suitings and coatings. Send for a brochure.

MATALAN
CONSTITUTION STREET, ABERDEEN AB24 5ET
☎ (01224) 650690. OPEN 10 - 6 MON - FRI, 9.30 - 5900.
OPEN 10 - 8 MON - FRI, 9.30 - 5.30 SAT, 10 - 6 SUN.
INSHES RETAIL PARK, INVERNESS IV2 3T OPEN 10 - 8 MON - FRI,
9.30 - 5.30 SAT, 10 - 6 SUN.
Permanent Discount Outlets • *Womenswear & Menswear*
Children • *Household*
Matalan is a fashion and homewares value retailer giving customers what they claim to be unbeatable value for money with huge savings on a wide range of products including high quality fashionable clothing for men, women and children at up to 50% off high street prices. Matalan is situated out of town and stores are open seven days a week all year round.

ORCHID
110 ST CLAIR'S STREET, KIRKCALDY, FIFE KY1 2BZ
☎ (01592) 655364. OPEN 10 - 5 TUE - SAT.
Permanent Discount Outlets • *Womenswear Only*
Samples and cancelled orders of a wide range of German, Italian, French, Irish and British designers at reduced prices. Names cannot be mentioned here as confidentiality is demanded by the suppliers to this shop. Day and evening wear is stocked in sizes 10-22.

OUT LINES
TRINITY GASK, AUCHTERARDER, PERTHSHIRE PH3 1LG
☎ (01764) 683733. FAX (01764) 683462. OPEN 9.30 - 5 MON - FRI, 9 - 1 SAT.
E-mail northwood@mcmail.com
Permanent Discount Outlets • *Furniture/Soft Furnishings*
Two businesses, one selling current ranges of furnishing fabrics and wallpapers to order, while the one next door stocks discontinued fabrics and wallpapers from £1.99 a metre or £5 a roll. Fabric names include Designers Guild, Osborne & Little, Baker's, Zoffany, Marvic, Titley & Marr, Warner's, etc. There are also linings, cushions, heading tapes, remnants and accessories. Prices are about one half to one third of the normal price. Many of the fabrics are flameproofed and are suitable for hotels as well as for private houses. The shop will deliver in the UK by carrier and can arrange for making up. There is a vast amount of stock in the shop, which is well worth a visit. Telephone for directions. Parking facilities are available.

RE-DRESS
43 NEW ROW, OFF GLASGOW ROAD, PERTH PH1 5QA
☎ (01738) 444447. OPEN 10 - 4.30 MON - SAT.
Dress Agencies • *Womenswear Only*

Situated in a discreet area in the town of Perth, Re-dress stocks a range of middle to top name nearly-new designer labels and some new clothes. There are wedding outfits and matching accessories at about one third of the original price, as well as evening wear, and a large selection of daywear, shoes and hats. You can choose from labels such as Laurel, Mondi, Louis Feraud, Escada, MaxMara, Paul Costelloe, Caroline Charles, Basler, Geiger, Oui Set, Betty Barclay and Austin Reed. Clearance sales are usually held twice a year. Stock changes constantly.

REJECTS
123 ST CLAIR STREET, KIRKCALDY, FIFE KY1 2BS
☎ (01592) 655955. OPEN 9 - 5.30 MON - SAT, 12.30 - 4.30 SUN.
Permanent Discount Outlets • *Furniture/Soft Furnishings*

Rejects Department Store sells curtain and dress fabric, china, pottery, carpets, silk flower, glassware, home decoration equipment and materials, lighting, basketware, carpet and flooring and has a cookshop. The shop is 100,000 sq feet and claims to be the best value department store in the UK, although it isn't a discount store as such. For example, in the curtain shop, which is larger than Harrods curtain department with thousands of rolls of material, fabric costs from £10.99 to £29.95 a metre. There is a particularly large selection of pottery and china seconds, bedding, cushions, pictures, mirrors, wallpaper, paint, hardware and garden tools. The shop also has a self-service cafe.

ROYAL LOCHNAGAR DISTILLERY
CRATHIE, BALLATER, ABERDEENSHIRE AB35 5TB
☎ (013397) 42273. OPEN 10 - 5 MON - SAT, 12 - 4 SUN IN SUMMER, NOVEMBER - EASTER 10 - 5 MON - FRI. MAIL ORDER.

Spend £4 on a distillery tour and you get a £3 voucher to spend against any 70cl bottle of malt whisky at the shop attached to the distillery. While prices for these classic malts - sixty of Scotland's finest - aren't rock bottom, they are likely to be cheaper than you'll find elsewhere.

SCENT TO YOU
UNIT 12A, BON ACCORD CENTRE, GEORGE STREET,
ABERDEEN AB15 1HZ
☎ (01224) 625340. OPEN 9 - 5.30 MON - SAT, 8 ON THUR, 12 - 4 SUN.
Permanent Discount Outlets • *Womenswear Only*

Discounted perfume, cosmetics and accessories including body lotions and gels. The company, which has more than thirty branches, buys in bulk and sells more cheaply, relying on a high turnover for profit. Discounts range from 5% to 60%, with greater savings during their twice-yearly sales (phone for details). Most of the leading brand names in perfume are stocked including Christian Lacroix, Armani, Charlie, Givenchy, Anais Anais from Cacherel, Charlie from Revlon, Coco Chanel, Christian Dior, Elizabeth Taylor, Blue Grass from Elizabeth Arden, Aramis, Lagerfeld. Plus cosmetics from REvlon and Spectacular and skincare from Clarins and Lancome as well as Scent To You's own range of bags, watches, hair brushes and brushkits which is sold under the name S.T.Y. Designs. Stock varies greatly due to the fast turnover and varying supplies so more than one visit may be necessary to obtain the scent of your choice. Or phone first to avoid disappointment.

SELLERS
2 CROWN LANE, OFF CROWN TERRACE, ABERDEEN AB1 2HF
☎ (01224) 582528. OPEN 10.30 - 5 TUE - SAT, UNTIL 7 ON THUR.
Dress Agencies • *Womenswear Only*
This long established dress agency is now under new ownership. It sells a wide selection of day and evening wear from Louis Feraud and Paul Costelloe to Mondi and Jaeger at between one third and one half of the original price as well as hats, jewellery, accessories and some shoes. Wide selection of special occasion wear. Stock is a mixture of new and nearly-new as some designer merchandise is bought in from boutiques' ends of ranges. Aromatherapy by Ann Lowd is available.

SHAW'S DUNDEE SWEET FACTORY
THE KEILLERS BUILDING, 34 MAINS LOAN, DUNDEE DD4 7BT
☎ (01382) 461435. CLOSED JAN - FEB. OPEN 10.30 - 4 WED IN MAR - MAY,
11 - 4 MON - FRI IN JUN - AUG, CLOSED LAST WEEK JULY,
FIRST AUGUST. OPEN 1.30 - 4 WED IN SEPT - DEC.
Food and Drink Discounters • *Food and Leisure*
Large self-service shop with a wall of 100 jars of sweets to pick and mix from. Specialises in fudge, toffees and boiled sweets, and Scottish Tablet. You can taste the sweets while they are still hot and freshly made. Special offers always available. Free car and coach park, disabled facilities.

SLATERS MENSWEAR
10 BON ACCORD STREET, ABERDEEN AB11 6EL
☎ (01224) 212334. OPEN 8.30 - 5.30 MON - SAT, 7.30 ON THUR.
Permanent Discount Outlets • *Menswear Only*
Full range of men's clothes from underwear and shoes to casualwear, suits and dresswear and including labels such as Odermark, Bulmer, Valentino, Charlie's Co, and Charlton Gray. Men's suits from £79.

STUART CRYSTAL
MUTHILL ROAD, CRIEFF, PERTHSHIRE PH7 4HQ
☎ (01764) 654004. OPEN 10 - 6 SEVEN DAYS A WEEK JUNE-SEPT,
10 - 5 OTHERWISE.
Factory Shops • *Household*

Seconds of Stuart Crystal sold at about 25% discount. The selection includes wine glasses, flower holders, perfume holders, everyday tableware, salt and pepper sets, ice buckets, wine coolers, cutlery and candle lamps. Also seasonal special offers. First quality is also for sale at the appropriate price.

THE MILL TRAIL, CLACKMANNANSHIRE
ARGYLL, THE ISLES, LOCH LOMOND, STIRLING AND TROSSACHS
TOURIST BOARD, OLD TOWN JAIL, ST JOHN STREET,
STIRLING FK8 1EA
☎ (01786) 445222. E-MAIL: info@scottish.heartlands.org
WEBSITE: www.scottish.heartlands.org
PHONE FOR INFORMATION BOOKLET.

Follow the mill trail and you're guaranteed a great shopping experience. You can pick up comprehensive Mill Trail booklets at tourist information centres in Clackmannanshire and the different shops are also signposted. The booklet gives details of where to stay, where to eat, plus lots of shops - some factory shops, some not - where you can buy anything from cashmere to chocolate, art to jewellery.

TK MAXX
WELLGATE SHOPPING CENTRE, DUNDEE DD1 2DF
☎ (01382)322288. OPEN 9 - 5.30 MON - WED, FRI, SAT, 9 - 8 THUR,
12 - 5 SUN.
Permanent Discount Outlets • *Womenswear & Menswear*
Children • *Household* • *Furniture/Soft Furnishings*

Based on an American concept, TK Maxx is situated in easily accessible, often centrally located stores and offers famous label goods with up to 60% savings off recommended retail prices. TK Maxx has fashion for the whole family - women's, men's and childrenswear - accessories, shoes, gifts, kitchenware and home goods. Everything in the store is branded with a choice of well-known high street names to designer labels, and while a small percentage might be clearly marked past season, the great majority of items in store are current season, current stock and still with phenomenal savings. There is a huge choice with 50,000 pieces in store and up to 10,000 new items arriving a week. The stores are simple and unfussy with wide aisles, shopping trolleys and baskets, and a spacious, functional feel to them but there are individual changing rooms, ramps for buggies and wheelchairs and plenty of staff on the shop floor. Every branch accepts all major credit and debit cards and has a liberal refund and return policy.

WALKER'S SHORTBREAD FACTORY SHOP
ABERLOUR-ON-SPEY, OFF A95, MORAY AB38 9PD
☎ (01340) 871555. E-MAIL: enquiries@walkers-shortbread.co.uk
WEBSITE: www.walkersshortbread.com
OPEN 8.30 - 5 MON - THUR, 8.30 - 4.30 FRI, 9 - 2 SAT.
Factory Shops • *Food and Leisure*

Misshapes and ends of lines of these famous shortbread biscuits and Scotch oatcakes, plus a wide variety of other tasty cakes and biscuits. Many of the products are in presentation boxes and packs and make excellent gifts. The factory shop is on the banks of the River Spey and on the well publicised Malt Whisky trail. Joseph Walker's original bakery shop is further along the high street in Aberlour and this, along with other bakery shops in Elgin and Grantown on Spey also carry a reduced range of factory shop products.

South Wales

ALEXON SALE SHOP
CARDIFF ROAD, HAWTHORN, PONTYPRIDD, MID GLAMORGAN
☎ (01443) 480673. OPEN 10 - 5 MON - SAT.
Permanent Discount Outlet • *Womenswear Only*

Alexon, Eastex, Ann Harvey and Calico from last season at 40% less than the original price; during sale time in January and June, the reductions are as much as 70%. Stock includes separates, skirts, jackets, blouses; there is no underwear or night clothes. The Pontypridd branch is situated at the back of the factory itself.

BEULAH DRESS AGENCY
3B BEULAH ROAD, RHIWBINA, CARDIFF CF14 6LT
☎ (02920) 691039. OPEN 10 - 5 MON - SAT.
Secondhand and Vintage Clothes • *Womenswear Only*

Top quality, nearly new ladies clothing - high street labels and some designer wear. Also stocks accessories, shoes, hats and jewellery.

BIG L FACTORY OUTLET
MCARTHURGLEN DESIGNER OUTLET VILLAGE, THE DERWEN,
BRIDGEND, JUNCTION 35 OF M4 CF32 9FU
☎ (01656) 767335. OPEN 10 - 8 MON - THUR, 10 - 6 SAT, 11 - 5 SUN.
Factory Shop in a Factory Shopping Village • *Womenswear & Menswear*

Men's and women's Levi jeans, jackets, cord and Sherpa fleece jackets, T-shirts and shirts but no children's, all at discount prices.

BIRTHDAYS
UNIT 24, FESTIVAL PARK, VICTORIA, EBBW VALE, GWENT NP23 5EX
☎ (01495) 306434. OPEN 9.30 - 5.30 MON - SAT, 11 - 5 SUN.
Factory Shop in a Factory Shopping Village • *Household*
Cards, notelets, stationery sets, colouring books, soft toys, photo albums, picture frames, gifts, giftwrap, tissue paper, party packs, Christmas crackers, string puppets, fairy lights all at discounts of up to 30%. Some are special purchases, some seconds.

BOOKENDS
DOCK STREET, NEWPORT, MONMOUTHSHIRE NP9 1FU
☎ (01633) 222086. OPEN 9 - 5.30 MON - SAT.
Secondhand shops • *Food and Leisure*
Secondhand and damaged books and publishers' returns, as well as new and review copies, including recently published books, usually half price and below.

BROADSPEED ENGINEERING AND CAR PRICES
☎ (01206) 263 377. ☎ 020-8387 9121 24-HOUR INFORMATION LINE.
☎ 0906 960 8888 PERSONAL ADVICE LINE, WEBSITE: www.car-prices.com
Broadspeed offer a range of options enabling you to import a car from abroad, usually Holland or Ireland: car cruises which take you to a dealer and allow you to drive back; self-import (fly out, ferry home and register the car yourself) or deliver to your door up to a distance of 100 miles from Colchester. The charge is betwen £750-£1,000 incl VAT.

BURBERRY
YNYSWEN ROAD, TREOCHY, RHONDDA, MID GLAMORGAN
☎ (01443) 772020. OPEN 9 - 4 TUES - THUR, 9 - 2 FRI, 9 - 1.30 SAT.
Factory Shop • *Womenswear & Menswear* • *Children*
This Burberry factory shop is quite difficult to find as it is some way up the Rhondda Valley. However, GDD readers have written to tell me it is definitely worth the trip - although rather olde world, it has some good merchandise at extremely good prices. It sells seconds and overmakes of the famous name raincoats and duffle coats as well as accessories such as the distinctive umbrellas, scarves and handbags. All carry the Burberry label and discounts are about one third off the normal retail price. Childrenswear tends to be thin on the ground, but there are usually plenty of gift items such as Burberry brand name teas, coffees and marmalade. The shop is midway between Treochy and Treherbert - phone for directions.

CARDIFF RECLAMATION
SITE 7, TREMORFA INDUSTRIAL ESTATE, CARDIFF CF2 2SD
☎ 029 20 458995. OPEN 9 - 5 MON - FRI, 9 - 1 SAT, 10 - 1SUN.
Architectural Salvage • *DIY/Renovation*
Flagstones, Victorian fireplaces, pine doors, church pews, handrails, chimney pots, quarry tiles, oak beams and lots more.

CATALOGUE BARGAIN SHOP
BRYN FERTH ROAD, RHY-Y-BLEW, EBBW VALE, GWENT NP3 5YD
☎ (01495) 309297. OPEN 9 - 8 MON - THUR, SAT, 9 - 9 FRI, 10 - 4 SUN.
61 HIGH STREET, MERTHYR TYDFIL, MID GLAMORGAN CF47 8DE
☎ (01685) 385653. OPEN 9 - 5.30 MON - SAT, 10.30 - 4.30 SUN.
31 STATION ROAD, PORT TALBOT, WEST GLAMORGAN SA13 1NN
☎ (01639) 899419. OPEN 9 - 5.30 MON - SAT, 10 - 4 SUN.
FFALDS ROAD SHOPPING CENTRE, PYLE CROSS, PYLE,
BRIDGEND CF33 6BH
☎ (01656) 746426. OPEN 9 - 8 MON - SAT, 10.30 - 4.30 SUN.
229-230 HIGH STREET, SWANSEA, WEST GLAMORGAN SA1 ANY
☎ (01792) 456748. OPEN 9 - 5.30 MON - SAT, 10.30 - 4.30 SUN.
Permanent Discount Outlet • *Womenswear & Menswear*
Children • *Household* • *Electrical Equipment*

Catalogue Bargain Shop is a growing national chain of stores which obtains the majority of its goods from mail order giants Great Universal and Kays, and offers a range of clothing for all the family, a wide selection of shoes, bed linen, household goods, electrical equipment and hundreds of other catalogue items at very competitive prices. For example, a three-piece leather suite, £899, reduced from £1,600. The merchandise consists of ends of ranges and previous season's stock for which there is no longer storage space when the catalogues change.

CHANGES DRESS AGENCY
27A HIGH STREET, COWBRIDGE, VALE OF GLAMORGAN CF71 7AG
☎ (01446) 772184. OPEN 10 - 5 TUE - SAT, CLOSED MON.
Dress Agency • *Womenswear Only*

Designer and high quality labels such as MaxMara, Cerruti, Mani, Jaeger, Frank Usher, Nicole Farhi, Karen Millen, Jobis and Basler. All the outfits are bought and sold on a commission basis at a fraction of the original price.

CLASSIC CHOICE FURNISHINGS LIMITED
BRYNMENYN INDUSTRIAL ESTATE, BRYNMENYN, BRIDGEND,
GLAMORGAN CF32 9TD
☎ (01656) 725111. SHOWROOM: OPEN 10 - 4 SEVEN DAYS A WEEK.
MAIL ORDER.
Permanent Discount Outlet • *Furniture/Soft Furnishings*

Save money on high quality furniture by purchasing direct. Choose from modern and traditional designs in suites or separates - all fully guaranteed for quality and supplied with a twenty-one day, full refund, no-quibble guarantee. There is an excellent choice of fabric and leather furniture in a wide choice of covers. Phone or write for free catalogue. Once a month, a selection of furniture is set out in hotels countrywide for customers to try out.

COSALT INTERNATIONAL LTD
THE DOCKS, MILFORD HAVEN, PEMBROKESHIRE SA73 3AF
☎ (01646) 692032. OPEN 8 - 5 MON - FRI, 9 - 12 SAT.
Permanent Discount Outlet • *Womenswear & Menswear*
The company specialises in workwear, safety clothing and marine wear but some of the merchandise is eminently wearable for everyday and is sold at very reasonable prices. This particular outlet specialises in guy cotton French wet weather clothing, fishermen's gear (bib and brace trousers and smocks), personal protective equipment and safety footwear, although there is a limited amount of donket jackets and dungarees. VAT has to be added to prices. There are catalogues available for you to order from if what you want isn't in stock. They also provide marine safety and life-raft servicing.

CRAZY MAC'S
PONTARDULAIS ROAD, FFOREST FACH, SWANSEA SA5 4BA
☎ (01792) 585828 OPEN 9 - 5.30 MON - SAT, 10 - 4 SUN.
Permanent Discount Outlet • *Womenswear & Menswear* • *Household Children* • *Electrical Equipment* • *DIY/Renovation* • *Food and Leisure Furniture/Soft Furnishings* • *Sportswear & Equipment*
An Aladdin's cave of "salvaged" stock for the avid bargain hunter, most of which has been the subject of bankruptcy, insurance claims, fire or flood. Regular visitors have found anything from half-price Kenwood Chefs, typewriters and telephones to furniture, kitchen items and designer clothes. Yves St Laurent, Ungaro, MaxMara, Chloe, Agnes B and Mondi are just some the labels (though they are often cut out) to appear. Discounts range from 50%-75%. Phone first to check stock.

DEWHIRST IMPRESSIONS
UNIT 22, THE KINGSWAY, FFORESTFACH INDUSTRIAL ESTATE, FFORESTFACH, SWANSEA SA5 4HY
☎ (01792) 584621. OPEN 9 - 5.30 MON - SAT, 11 - 5 SUN.
Factory Shop • *Children* • *Womenswear & Menswearear*
Sells garments from the manufacturing side of the business direct to the public as part of the Dewhirst Group plc which manufactures ladies, men's and childrenswear for a leading high street retailer. You can choose from a huge selection of surplus production and slight seconds at bargain prices, making savings of more than 50% of the normal retail cost. For men there is a wide range of suits, formal shirts and casual wear. For example, suits from £60, formal and casual shirts from £7. For ladies there's a selection of blouses, smart tailoring and casual wear that includes a denim range. You can find ladies jackets from £50, skirts, trousers and blouses from £8. Children's clothes start at £3. High street quality and style at wholesale prices.

DIVANI
MAERDY INDUSTRIAL ESTATE, RYHMNEY NP22 5YD
☎ (01685) 844444. FAX (01685) 844911. MAIL ORDER ONLY.
Factory Shop • *Furniture/Soft Furnishings*
Divani manufacture and supply direct from their factory in South Wales with no retail overheads of margins to cover. Thus you pay factory prices direct from the manufacturer. Owned and managed by the same family for the past 18 years, they offer products made with hardwood frames which have all passed the relevant BS Standards and come with a two-year guarantee. There are six styles in a variety of fabrics and colours, including three-seaters, two-seaters, sofabeds, chairs, footstool as well as extra scatter cushions and arm caps. Prices for the chairs range from £200-£225; for two-seaters from £299-£349 and for the three-seaters from £349-£399. Orders take four weeks to manufacture and deliver and you have 21 days following delivery to return the product if you change your mind. Phone for a brochure and fabric swatches.

DYFED ANTIQUES & ARCHITECTURAL SALVAGE
WESLEYAN CHAPEL, PERROTS ROAD, HAVERFORDWEST, PEMBROKESHIRE
☎ (01437) 760496. OPEN 10 - 5 MON - SAT.
Architectural Salvage • *DIY/Renovation*
Slate slabs, quarry tiles, oak beams and flooring, doors, Victorian fireplaces, tiled insets, surrounds in wood, marble and cast iron, antique furniture, many huge dressers and curios, gardenware including urns. Furniture and fire surrounds made to measure in new or old wood.

ECCO
MACARTHURGLEN DESIGNER OUTLET, THE DERWEN, BRIDGEND CF32 3SU
☎ (01656) 767202. OPEN 10 - 8 MON - THUR, 10 - 6 FRI AND SAT, 11 - 5 SUN.
Factory Shop in a Factory Shopping Village
Womenswear & Menswear • *Children*
Ladies', men's and children's shoes, all discounted by at least 25%. Phone 0800 387368 for a catalogue. Other outlets in Wiltshire, Somerset and Cheshire.

ELLE
41A HIGH STREET, COWBRIDGE, VALE OF GLAMORGAN CF7 7AE
☎ (01446) 775687. OPEN 10.30 - 5 TUE - SAT.
Dress Agency • *Womenswear Only*
Nearly-new Jasper Conran, Escada, Laurel, Mondi, Christian Dior and occasionally Louis Feraud, Jean Paul Gaultier and Armani are on sale at this centrally located shop. Prices tend to be below £100. There are a lot of separates and good office wear and half-price sales in January and July. Also mother of the bride outfits and hats to buy or hire and they have recently opened a Bridal Room.

FAMOUS FOOTWEAR
DESIGNER OUTLET VILLAGE, BRIDGEND, JUNCTION 35 OF M4
☎ (01656) 657779. OPEN 10 - 8 MON, THUR, 10 - 6 FRI, SAT, 11 - 5 SUN.
Factory Shop in a Factory Shopping Village • *Womenswear & Menswear*
Wide range of brand names including Stead & Simpson, Lilley & Skinner, Hobos, Hush Puppies, Lotus, Sterling & Hunt, Richleigh, Scholl, Red Tape, Flexi Country, Padders, Canaletto, Bronx, Frank Wright, Brevitt, Romba Wallace, Rieker, all at discount prices of up to 50%.

FESTIVAL PARK FACTORY OUTLET SHOPPING VILLAGE
FESTIVAL PARK, VICTORIA, EBBW VALE, GWENT NP23 8FP
☎ (01495) 350010. FAX ☎ (01495) 307363. OPEN 9.30 - 5.30 MON - SAT, TILL 7 THUR, 11 - 5 SUN.
Factory Shopping Village • *Womenswear & Menswear*
Children • *Household* • *Sportswear & Equipment*
Factory shopping village with 36 shops offering a wide range of top brand goods and designer labels, many at half the recommended retail price. Factory shops include: fashion and golf equipment from Edinburgh Woollen Mill, accessories from Claire's and Jane Shilton; luggage from Antler; fashion from Windsmoor, Designer Room and Roman Originals; shoes from Paver, Start - Rite and Jane Shilton; china and crystal from Royal Worcester, Wedgwood and Edinburgh Crystal; chocolates and dried fruit from Thorntons and Julian Graves and much more. Built on the former site of the National Garden Festival of there are over 70 acres of woodland and parkland to explore either on foot or on the land train which runs throughout the summer. Within the park you can visit the tropical plant house, forge, woodland craft centre and owl sanctuary. There is a new 200 seat restaurant with panoramic views over the valley serving both snacks and cooked meals. The car park is free with disabled spaces, free wheelchair hire and baby changing facilities.

GAINSBOROUGH
12 SWANSEA ROAD, LLANGYFELACH, SWANSEA SA5 7JD
☎ (01792) 790922. OPEN 10 - 5 MON - SAT.
Dress Agency • *Womenswear Only*
This shop stocks currently fashionable flawless outfits from top labels such as Frank Usher, Jacques Vert, Kasper, Betty Barclay, Condici, Tom Bowker, Mani and Louis Feraud, all at savings of between 55% and 80% off the original price. There is plenty of day and evening wear and special occasion wear, including ballgowns and hats and more than 300 wedding outfits. Stock changes constantly. There is also an alteration service.

GLAMOURLINE BLINDS
UNIT 2, CAMBRIAN PARK, CLYDACH VALE, TONYPANDY CF40 2XX
☎ (01443) 433232. OPEN 9 - 5 MON - THUR, 9 - 2 FRI,
CLOSED 1 - 1.30 DAILY, 9 - 12 SAT.
Factory Shop • *Household*
Specialise in blinds of all types - Venetian, roller, vertical, Austrian and conservatory - as well as awnings which are sold by mail order and to high street department stores, as well as some curtains. Made to measure vertical blinds are available at up to 50% less than normal retail prices. Catalogue returns are also sometimes available. Operates a home visit and fitting service.

GLYN WEBB
PONTARDULAIS ROAD, CADLE, SWANSEA SA5 4BA
☎ (01792) 579955 . OPEN 9 - 8 MON - SAT, 11 - 5 SUN AND BANK HOLS.
Permanent Discount Outlet • *DIY/Renovation*
Stockists of all your home improvement needs from wallpaper to paint, furniture to flooring, tiles to textiles, housewares to lighting - in fact, almost everything for your home, with 25 branches in the North-West, Midlands and Yorkshire. Specialists in discontinued mail order, slightly imperfect branded stocks as well as perfect quality superior products. They carry top brands such as Dulux, Crown Paints and Vymura and Coloroll wall coverings, Rectella and Norwood textiles and much more in store. To find your nearest branch, phone Head Office on 0161 621 4500.

GOSSARD FACTORY SHOP
PENMAEN ROAD, PONTLLANFRAITH, BLACKWOOD, GWENT NP2 2DL
☎ (01495) 221103. OPEN 9.30 - 5.30 MON - SAT.
Factory Shop • *Womenswear Only*
Factory shop sells seconds and discontinued ranges of Gossard and Berlei underwear including bras, briefs, suspender belts and bodies at discounted prices (no nightwear or long-line slips). Most of the stock is last year's trade catalogue styles at discounts of between 25%-75%. Free parking; ramp for wheelchairs.

HYPER VALUE HOLDINGS LTD
BROWN LENNOX RETAIL PARK, YUYSANGHARAD ROAD,
PONTYPRIDD CF37 4DA
☎ (01443) 480115. OPEN 9 - 6 MON - WED, SAT, 9 - 8 THUR, FRI, 11 - 5 SUN.
Permanent Discount Outlet • *Household*

Housed in old supermarket premises, this Aladdin's cave holds a huge array of just about everything, some of which is tat, some great value finds. Dig around among the frames, mirror, socks, tights, toiletries, tools, carpets, stationery, shirts, ornaments, paint, wallpaper borders and garden furniture and you may find the odd gem such as the natural canvas parasol, Habitat-style, £20, or Christian Dior tights, 40p. There are 22 branches in South Wales, 24 in total, some in retail parks, others in stand-alone shops. Phone 01446 721200 for details of your nearest outlet.

JAEGER FACTORY SHOP
MCARTHURGLEN DESIGNER OUTLET VILLAGE, THE DERWEN,
BRIDGEND, JUNCTION 35 OF M4 CF32 95U
☎ (01656) 665700. OPEN 10 - 8 MON - THUR, 11 - 5 SUN.
Factory Shop in a Factory Shopping Village • *Womenswear & Menswear*

Contemporary classics from Jaeger at excellent prices. Most of the merchandise is previous seasons' stock, but you might also find some special makes. The telephone number given here is for the centre, not the shop.

JANE SHILTON
FESTIVAL PARK SHOPPING CENTRE, VICTORIA ROAD, EBBW VALE,
MID-GLAMORGAN NP3 6OH
☎ (01495) 302216. OPEN 10 - 6 MON - SAT, 11 - 5 SUN.
Factory Shop in a Factory Shopping Village • *Womenswear Only*

Merchandise from past seasons' collections or factory seconds at discounts of at least 30% and up to 70% off the original price. There is a wide range of handbags, small leather goods, shoes, luggage umbrellas and travel bags. Example of price reduction: handbags at £24.99 originally £37.

JOJO MAMAN BEBE
UNIT 9, LLANTARNAM INDUSTRIAL PARK, CWMBRAN,
GWENT NP44 3AX
☎ (01633) 484343. OPEN 10 - 3.30 WED ONLY.
Factory Shop • *Womenswear Only* • *Children*

Maternity wear and children's and baby clothes as well as some gifts, toys and nursery equipment. These are end of ranges, seconds and samples from the company's catalogue. The type and amount of stock varies from week to week so if there's something in particular that you're looking for, phone first.

JOKIDS
MCARTHURGLEN DESIGNER VILLAGE, THE DERWEN,
BRIDGEND CF32 9SU
☎ (0800) 316 4352. OPEN 10 - 8 MON - THUR, 10 - 6 FRI, SAT, 11 - 5 SUN.
Factory Shop in a Factory Shopping Village • *Children*
This shop sells childrenswear for 0-10-year-olds including everdaywear like t-shirts, jogwear, various denim styles and accessories. For special occasions there are pretty hand-smocked party dresses and rompers. Reductions are up to 40%. The telephone number given here is for the centre, not the shop.

KIDS PLAY FACTORY
MCARTHURGLEN DESIGNER OUTLET VILLAGE, BRIDGEND,
JUNCTION 35 OF M4, MID-GLAMORGAN
☎ (01656) 652265. OPEN 10 - 8 MON - THUR, 10 - 6 FRI, SAT, 11 - 5 SUN.
Factory Shop in a Factory Shopping Village • *Children*
This shop sells a wide range of well-known children's brand names: Little Tikes, Corgi, Crayola, Tomy, Lego, Hasbro, Playskool, Mattel and Fisher-Price at discounts of up to 50%. They also stock a wide range of soft toys including TY Beanie Babies.

KIRKDALE DIRECT FURNITURE
VIADUCT WORKS, CRUMLIN ROAD, CRUMLIN, GWENT MP11 3PL
☎ (01495) 243999. MAIL ORDER.
Permanent Discount Outlet • *Furniture/Soft Furnishings*
Sells a range of luxury upholstery at prices below those you would expect to pay in the shops. By choosing not to supply retailers and sell direct to the customer, they can offer more value for money. Offer 21-day trial period. On sale are sofas, incliners, high back chairs, armchairs, storage stools, footstools and sofa beds. Phone for mail order brochure.

LEE COOPER
MCARTHURGLEN DESIGNER OUTLET CENTRE, THE DERWEN,
BRIDGEND, JUNCTION 36 OFF THE M4 CF32 9SU
☎ (01656) 645992. OPEN 10 - 8 MON - THUR, 10 - 6 FRI, SAT, 11 - 5 SUN.
Factory Shop in a Factory Shopping Village
Womenswear & Menswear • *Children*
Denim jeans, jackets and shirts, each ranked by size and gender at discounts of up to 30%. Casual shirts from £9.99, jeans from £14.99, T-shirts and ladieswear. Lee Cooper was founded in 1908 as a workwear manufacturer before becoming a supplier to the armed forces. Most of the stock here is current, discontinued and irregular merchandise, all of which comes straight from Lee Cooper's factories in Europe.

LEGS CLOTHING CO
UNIT 1, THE BARN CENTRE, ALEXANDRA ROAD,
ABERYSTWYTH SY23 1LF
☎ (01970) 611897. OPEN 9 - 5 MON - FRI, 9 - 4 SAT, 11 - 5 BANK HOLS.
Factory Shop • *Children*

Exclusive outlet for Europe's largest trouser manufacturer sells ends of lines, cancelled orders and samples of jeans, trousers and shorts for all the family at factory direct prices. Also available are ancillary lines of casual wear at bargain prices.

LITTLEWOODS CATALOGUE DISCOUNT STORE
MCARTHURGLEN DESIGNER OUTLET THE DERWEN,
BRIDGEND CF32 9SU
☎ (01656) 665700. OPEN 10 - 8 MON - THUR, 10 - 6 FRI, SAT, 11 - 5 SUN.
Factory Shop • *Womenswear & Menswear* • *Children*
Electrical Equipment

Littlewoods clearance shops offering up to 50% off the catalogue price for clothing and between 50% and 60% off for electrical goods. Stock changes constantly and varies from day to day but can include well-known brand names such as Berlei and Gossard lingerie, Vivienne Westwood, Pamplemousse leisure wear, Nike and Adidas sports shoes, Workers for Freedom, and Timberland and Caterpillar footwear. Stock depends on the size and location of the shop, so larger shops will get the longer discontinued runs and smaller shops over-runs with only a small amount of colour and size variations left. Littlewoods also run a mobile shop which operates in cities where they don't have a sale shop. For details of further venues for the sales, which usually take place once a month, contact Melanie Lamb, c/o Crosby DC Kershaw Avenue, Endbutt Lane, Crosby, Merseyside L70 1AH.

MATALAN
UNIT 8, GLAMORGAN VALE RETAIL PARK, LLANTRISANT,
MID-GLAMORGAN CF7 8RP
☎ (01443) 224854. OPEN 10 - 8 MON - FRI, 9 - 6 SAT, 11 - 5 SUN.
FOUNDRY ROAD, MORRISTON, SWANSEA SA6 8DU
☎ (01792) 792229. OPEN 10 - 8 MON - FRI, 9 - 6 SAT, 11 - 5 SUN.
UNIT 4B, CWMBRAN RETAIL PARK, CWMBRAN DRIVE, CWMBRAN,
GWENT NP44 3JQ
☎ (01633) 866944. OPEN 9.30 - 8 MON - FRI, 9 - 6 SAT, 11 - 5 SUN.
UNIT 2, 383-384 NEWPORT ROAD, CARDIFF CF3 7AE
☎ (029) 20 491781. OPEN 10 - 8 MON - FRI, 9 - 6 SAT, 11 - 5 SUN.
Permanent Discount Outlet • *Children*
Womenswear & Menswear • *Household*

Matalan is a fashion and homewares value retailer giving customers what they claim to be unbeatable value for money with huge savings on a wide range of products including high quality fashionable clothing for men, women and children at up to 50% off high street prices. Matalan is situated out of town and stores are open seven days a week all year round.

MCARTHURGLEN DESIGNER OUTLET

THE DERWEN, BRIDGEND, JUNCTION 36 OFF THE M4 CF32 9SU
☎ (0800) 316 4352. WEBSITE: www.mcarthurglen.com
OPEN 10 - 8 MON - THUR, 10 - 6 FRI, SAT, 11 - 5 SUN.

Factory Shopping Village • *Womenswear & Menswear* • *Children*
Household • *Electrical Equipment* • *Food and Leisure*
Sportswear & Equipment • *Furniture/Soft Furnishings*

Ninety stores offering discounts of 30%-50% with an Odeon multi-screen cinema and food court as part of the centre. Shops for women include BhS for Less, Big L (Levi,s), Bookends, Calvin Klein, Chilli Pepper/Watsons, Claire,s Accessories; Clarks shoes; Ciro pearls; Cotton Traders leisurewear, Donnay, Ecco, Elle, Etam, Famous Footwear, Helly Hansan, Jacques Vert, Jaeger, John Partridge countrywear, Karrimor, Knickerbox, Lee Cooper, Littlewoods, Mexx, Monet jewellery, Next, Nickelbys, Nike, Paco, Pepe Jeans, Pilot, Reebok, Roman Originals, Soled Out, The Designer Room (top designer labels), The Watch Store, Tog 24 outdoor and walking wear, U Wear/I Wear underwear; Vans footwear, Viyella, Warners, Winning Line, Woodies offering top designer ladies and menswear and footwear. For men, Ben Sherman, BhS for Less, Big L, Calvin Klein, Ciro Citterio suits, Clarks shoes, Cotton Traders, Ecco, Famous Footwear, Helly Hansen, HKA Casualwear, Lee Cooper jeans, Jaeger, John Partridge countrywear, Mexx, Nickelbys, Nike, Overland casualwear, Pepe Jeans, Petroleum, Red/Green everyday sailing wear, Reebok, Soled Out, Suits You, Ted Baker, The Suit Company, Tie Rack, Timberland, Tog 24 outdoorwear, Van Heusen, Vans footwear, Woodies. Shops for children include Big L (Levi,s), Ecco, JoKids, Kids Play Factory, Mexx, Next to Nothing, Pepe Jeans, Nike, Reebok, Tammy Girl, Sidoli,s confectionery, Soled Out footwear, Thorntons, Tog 24 outdoor and walking wear. Shops for the home include Bed & Bath Works towels and bedlinen; Carphone Warehouse; Clover House tablemats and kitchenware; Edinburgh Crystla; Dixons; Mondian glass; Price,s Candles; Royal Doulton; Royal Worcester; Spiegelau glass, The Craft Outlet; The Garden Outlet; Wedgwood china; Whittard of Chelsea,s wide range of colourful kitchenware and china. Electrical shops include Remington selling everything from knives and saucepans to hairdryers and shavers and Dixons. Leisure shops include Antler luggage; Bookends; Carphone Warehouse; Dixons; Julian Graves; Remington; Thorntons; Travel Accessories and XS Music and Video selling CDs and tapes. Sports shops and footwear include Clarks, Donnay, Ecco, Elle, Famous Footwear, Nike, Red/Green everyday sailing wear, Reebok, Soled Out and Tog 24 outdoor and walking wear. There are two cafes and seven different places to eat in the foodcourt.

MEXX INTERNATIONAL
MCARTHURGLEN DESIGNER OUTLET, THE DERWEN,
BRIDGEND CF32 9SU
☎ (01656) 766870. OPEN 10 - 8 MON - THUR, 10 - 6 FRI, SAT, 11 - 5 SUN.
Factory Shop in a Factory Shopping Village
Womenswear & Menswear • Children

High street fashion at factory outlet prices for men, women, babies, and kids, all of which are heavily discounted by more than 30%.

NEXT TO NOTHING
MCARTHURGLEN DESIGNER OUTLET VILLAGE, BRIDGEND CF32 9SU
☎ (01656) 641950. OPEN 10 - 8 MON - THUR, 10 - 6 FRI, SAT, 11 - 5 SUN.
Factory Shop in a Factory Shopping Village
Womenswear & Menswear • Children

Sells perfect surplus stock from Next stores and the Next Directory catalogue - from belts, jewellery and underwear to day and evening wear - at discounts of 50% or more. The ranges are usually last season's and overruns. Stock consists of women's, men's and children's clothing, with some homeware and shoes. Stock is replenished three times a week and there is plenty of it.

ODEON FURNITURE COMPANY
GWALIA WORKS, FACTORY ROAD, BRYNMAWR, GWENT NP23 4DP
☎ (01495) 717170. OPEN 10 - 4 MON - FRI BY APPOINTMENT ONLY.
Factory Shop • *Furniture/Soft Furnishings*

A manufacturer which also offers a mail order and a showroom service. They offer four, three and two-seaters, sofabeds, recliners, high back and club chairs and footstools. Four-seaters cost £499, three seaters, £399 and two seaters £349 from any one of the six models. Phone for a brochure or visit them at the factory showroom.

OAKRIDGE DIRECT
MAERDY INDUSTRIAL ESTATE, RHYMNEY NP22 5YP
☎ (01685) 844944. MAIL ORDER. OPEN 9 - 4.30 MON - FRI.
Permanent Discount Outlet • *Furniture/Soft Furnishings*

Suites delivered direct at comfortable prices. Showroom shared with Divani sofas.

PACO
MCARTHURGLEN DESIGNER OUTLET THE DERWEN, BRIDGEND,
JUNCTION 36 OFF THE M4 CF32 9SU
☎ (01656) 651372. OPEN 10 - 8 MON - THUR, 10 - 6 FRI, SAT, 11 - 5 SUN.
Factory Shop in a Factory Shopping Village
Womenswear & Menswear • Children • Sportswear & Equipment

Paco uses bright, distinctive colours and the knack for designing great clothes at affordable prices. For several years, they have also been creating their own brand of sports and leisurewear clothing that shows great verve and energy. This range has a much more everyday living influence. The contrast is a distinct look for the discerning wearer. If you are looking for a great T-shirt or sweatshirt, lightweight jacket or gilet, polar fleece or hooded top, three-quarter length or combat trousers, then you need look no further. Paco now competes with the very best fashion brands in the high street by offering customers high fashion combined with excellent quality, making their clothes real value for money.

PARTRIDGE
DESIGNER OUTLET CENTRE, DERWEN, BRIDGEND CF32 9ST
☎ (01656) 667461. OPEN 10 - 8 MON - THUR, 10 - 6 FRI, SAT, 11 - 5 SUN.
Factory Shop in a Factory Shopping Village
Womenswear & Menswear • *Children*
Partridge specialises in fashionable outdoor clothes and accessories. Ranges include waxed jackets, Gore-tex jackets, waterproof jackets, tweeds, quilts, fleece jackets and waistcoats, knitwear, shirts, chinos, cord and moleskin trousers, hats and caps. Discontinued lines are on sale at discounted prices with a minimum of 30% and up to 70% off during promotions.

PEGGY SUE DRESS AGENCY
28 BRIDGE STREET, USK, GWENT NP15 1BG
☎ (01291) 673309. OPEN 10 - 5 MON - SAT, CLOSED 1 WED.
Dress Agency • *Womenswear Only*
Popular labels here include Escada, Jacques Vert and Windsmoor, although they also stock Marks & Spencer. As well as ballgowns, jewellery and hats, there is new bridal wear.

PERIOD TIMBER FLOORING
MONMOUTHSHIRE, WALES
☎ (01291) 690709. RING FOR APPOINTMENT.
Architectural Salvage • *DIY/Renovation*
Original Victorian pitch pine and pine floorboards, panelling, doors and beams. Ancient oak timbers and floorboards and other original re-claimed flooring. There isn't really a showroom and the barns are hard to find so it's best to ring up first to get directions and make sure someone will be there. The outlet is near Monmouth.

PONDEN MILL LINENS
FESTIVAL PARK SHOPPING VILLAGE, VICTORIA, EBBW VALE NP3 6FP
☎ (01495) 302 765. OPEN 9.30 - 5.30 MON - S AT, TILL 7 ON THUR, 11 - 5 SUN.
Factory Shop in a Factory Shopping Village • *Household*
Famous branded products at direct from the mill prices. A fabulous assortment of towels, duvets, pillows, throws, bedspreads, up-to-the-minute coordinated bed linen, from Crown, Coloroll, Jeff Banks Ports-of-Call, to name but a few. Something for every room in the house.

PRICE'S CANDLES
MCARTHURGLEN DESIGNER OUTLET THE DERWEN, BRIDGEND,
JUNCTION 35 OF M4 CF31 1PF
☎ (01656) 767001. OPEN 10 - 8 MON - THUR, 10 - 6 FRI, SAT, 11 - 5 SUN.
Factory Shop in a Factory Shopping Village • *Household*
Everything sold in this shop are seconds, discontinued sizes not available elsewhere, over-runs or candles in old packaging that has now been replaced. There are church candles, lanterns, candles in pots and glass jars, star-shaped candles, floating candles, candlestick holders, serviettes, scented candles and garden torches.

REDGREEN
MCARTHURGLEN OUTLET VILLAGE, THE DERWEN,
BRIDGEND CF32 9ST
☎ (01656) 645464. OPEN 10 - 8 MON - THUR, 10 - 6 FRI, SAT, 11 - 5 SUN.
Factory Shop in a Factory Shopping Village
Womenswear & Menswear • *Sportswear & Equipment*
RedGreen is Scandinavian leisure wear for men and women. The high quality and classic design has a nautical heritage but a stylish look. The collection includes outerwear, sweaters, shirts, trousers, skirts, dresses, sweatshirts, T-shirts, tailored jackets, footwear and accessories. In addition to the main collection, you will also find a broad RedGreen golf collection for men and women and also the younger and more casual First Gear Collection. Discounts offered are between 25% and 70%.

REMINGTON
MCARTHURGLEN OUTLET VILLAGE, BRIDGEND CF32 9SU
☎ (01656) 766722. OPEN 10 - 8 MON - THUR, 10 - 6 FRI, SAT, 11 - 5 SUN.
Factory Shop in a Factory Shopping Village • *Electrical Equipment*
Specialise in haircare, personal hygiene and small kitchen items at 30% off high street prices. Lots of famous names here from Monogram cutlery to Braun, Philips, Remington, Clairol, Wahl, Krups and Kenwood small kitchen equipment. It's a great place to buy gifts or replenish the kitchen equipment with combi stylers, turbo travel plus hairdryers, air purifiers, liquidisers; food processors; batteries; clocks; and cutlery. Some of the packaging may be damaged but the products are in perfect working order.

ROYAL WORCESTER & SPODE FACTORY SHOP
FESTIVAL PARK FACTORY OUTLET CENTRE, VICTORIA,
EBBW VALE, GWENT NP3 6FP
☎ (01495) 308155. OPEN 9.30 - 5.30 MON - SAT, 11 - 5 SUN.
Factory Shop in a Factory Shopping Village • *Household*
Infinitesimally flawed porcelain and china seconds at 25% less than "perfect" prices. The Festival Park outlet stocks Mayflower, Langham Glass, Clover Leaf and Pimpernel table mats, Lakeland Plaques, Paw Prints, Fo-Frame,

Collectible World, Country Artists and Six Trees. There is a vast range with special offers throughout the year on anything from crystal decanters and bowls to figurines, cookware and dinner sets. Shipping arrangements worldwide can be organised.

ROYAL WORCESTER & SPODE FACTORY SHOP
MCARTHURGLEN DESIGNER OUTLET, THE DERWEN,
BRIDGEND CF32 9SU
☎ (01656) 651444. OPEN 10 - 8 MON - THUR, 10 - 6 FRI, SAT, 11 - 5 SUN.
Factory Shop in a Factory Shopping Village • *Household*
Infinitesimally flawed porcelain and china seconds at 25% less than "perfect" prices. This outlet stocks Langham Glass, Country Artists, Paw Prints, Bowbrook, Ornamental Studio, Collectible World, Fo-Frame, Six Trees and Pimpernel table mats. There is a vast range with special offers throughout the year on anything from crystal decanters and bowls to figurines, cookware and dinner sets. Shipping arrangements worldwide can be organised.

SCENT TO YOU
THE DESIGNER ROOM, MERMAID QUAYS, CARDIFF CF10 5BZ
☎ (0292) 0485626.
Factory Shop • *Womenswear Only*
Operating within The Designer Room, Scent to You sells discounted perfume, cosmetics and accessories including body lotions and gels. The company, which has more than thirty branches, buys in bulk and sells more cheaply, relying on a high turnover for profit. Discounts range from 5% to 60%, with greater savings during their twice-yearly sales (phone for details). Most of the leading brand names in perfume are stocked including Christian Lacroix, Armani, Charlie, Givenchy, Anais Anais from Cacherel, Charlie from Revlon, Coco Chanel, Christian Dior, Elizabeth Taylor, Blue Grass from Elizabeth Arden, Aramis, Lagerfeld. Plus cosmetics from Revlon and Spectacular and skincare from Clarins and Lancome as well as Scent To You's own range of bags, watches, hair brushes and brushkits which is sold under the name S.T.Y. Designs. Stock varies greatly due to the fast turnover and varying supplies so more than one visit may be necessary to obtain the scent of your choice. Or phone first to avoid disappointment.

SECOND TO NONE
17 HIGH STREET, CHEPSTOW, MONMOUTHSHIRE NP6 5LG
☎ (01291) 622424. OPEN 9 - 5 MON - SAT, SOME BANK HOLS.
Permanent Discount Outlet • *Children* • *Womenswear & Menswear*
In the South West for twenty-seven years, this company has built a reputation for giving excellent customer service and for selling goods which are of a quality and value second to none! This famous chainstore and branded clearing lines include surplus stocks of branded goods such as Fabrizio, Zorbit, Naturana and many more. They stock a large range of ladies and children's and baby wear (including baby bedding and accessories), leisurewear, sports

clothes and some menswear, and an extensive range of underwear and nightwear for all the family. You can save up to 75% off recommended retail prices and they offer a seven-day money back guarantee.

SECONDS AHEAD
CNWCAU, CILGERRAN, CARDIGAN, PEMBROKESHIRE SA43 2SN
☎ (01239) 612721. OPEN 9.30 - 5.30 MON - FRI, 9 - 5.30 SAT.
Permanent Discount Outlet • *Womenswear & Menswear* • *Children*
A family owned store selling clothing from chainstore seconds in ladies, men's and childrenswear at discounted prices at over 20 shops throughout England and Wales. If you phone (01239) 621867, they will give you the address of your nearest branch. There are branches at Cardigan, Haverfordwest, Milford Haven, Pembroke, Fishguard, Barry, Bridgend, Maesteg, Newtown, Newcastle Emlyn, Abergavenny, Welsh Pool, Leominster, Aberdere, Newport, Neath, Llandovery; also at Shrewsbury, Gloucester, Street, Wellington, Market Drayton, Ammanford and Ludlow.

SLATERS MENSWEAR
116 ST MARY'S STREET, CARDIFF CF1 1DY
☎ (029) 20 384186. OPEN 8.30 - 5.30 MON - SAT, 7.30 ON THUR.
Permanent Discount Outlet • *Menswear Only*
Full range of men's clothes from underwear and shoes to casualwear, suits and dresswear and including labels such as Odermark, Bulmer, Valentino, Charlie's Co, and Charlton Gray. Men's suits from £79.

SOFA WORKSHOP DIRECT
COED CAE LANE, PONTYCLUN CF72 9DX
☎ (01443) 238699. WEBSITE: www.sofaworkshopdirect.co.uk MAIL ORDER.
Factory Shop • *Furniture/Soft Furnishings*
Based in Wales, Sofa Workshop Direct have been making furniture for 14 years and supplying direct to the customer at factory prices. There are nine ranges from which to choose in a variety of fabrics, both loose cover and fixed, with a choice of large or small sofa, sofabed, chair or footstool. Fabric options range from brushed cotton twill and soft chenille to a striking patterned chenille to a chunky plain cotton with a textured floral pattern. Chairs cost from £229 - £299 and large sofas (up to 220cms long) from £379-£499. Phone for a brochure or visit the website.

START-RITE
FESTIVAL SHOPPING VILLAGE, VICTORIA ROAD, EBBW VALE, GWENT NP23 6UF
☎ (01495) 305700. OPEN 9.30 - 5.30 MON - FRI, SAT, 7 ON THUR, 11 - 5 SUN.
Factory Shop • *Children* • *Womenswear & Menswear*
The children's shoe experts have a large factory shop selling clearance lines at discounts of one third, and rejects at discounts of 50%. They don't stock the full range - it's a matter of choosing from what's available. Rejects are sold at at least half price; end of sales stock with not quite such a high discount. There are also some senior sizes up to 9. Feet are expertly measured by trained staff.

STEWART'S
12 PIER STREET, ABERSTWYTH, CEREDIGION SY23 2LJ
☎ (01970) 611437. OPEN 9 - 5.30 MON - SAT, 10.30 - 4.30 SUN IN SUMMER.
RIVERSIDE, CARDIGAN, CEREDIGION SA43 3AD
☎ (01239) 621880. FAX 01239 621919. OPEN 9 - 5.30 MON - SAT.
14 NOTTS SQUARE, CARMARTHEN SA31 3PQ
☎ (01267) 222294. OPEN 9 - 5.30 MON - SAT.
21-22 GREYFRIARS, CARMARTHEN SA31 3NB.
☎ (01267) 232208. OPEN 9 - 5.30 MON, SAT.
GLAMORE TERRACE, NEW QUAY, CEREDIGION SA45 9PL
☎ (01545) 560740. OPEN 9.30- 5.30 MON - SAT, 10 - 5.30 SUN.
HARFORD SQUARE, LAMPETER, CEREDIGION SA48 7HD
☎ (01570) 422205. OPEN 9.30 - 5.30 MON - SAT.
52 STEPNEY STREET, LLANELLI, CARMARTHENSHIRE SA15 3TR
☎ (01554) 776957. OPEN 9 - 5 MON - SAT.
UNIT 4, BETHEL SQUARE SHOPPING CENTRE, BRECON, POWYS LD3 7HU
☎ (01874) 610260. OPEN 9 - 6 5.30 SUN.
79A TAFF STREET, PONTYPRIDD, MID GLAMORGAN CF37 4SU
☎ (01443) 402225. OPEN 9.30 - 5.30 MON - SAT.
2-4 CARDIFF ROAD, Y TWYN, CAERPHILLY, MID GLAMORGAN CF8 1JN
☎ (02920) 888054. OPEN 9.30 - 5.30 MON - SAT.
MARLAS ROAD, PYLE CROSS, NR BRIDGENYFED SA69 9HG.
☎ (01834) 813169. OPEN 9.30 - 5.30 SEVEN DAYS A WEEK.
228-230 OXFORD STREET, SWANSEA
☎ (01792) 410906. OPEN 9.30 - 5.30 MON - SAT.
7-11 MONNOW STREET, MONMOUTH, MONMOUTHSIRE
☎ (01600) 716926. OPEN 9.30 - 5.30 MON - SAT.
THE STRAND, SAUNDERSFOOT, PEMBROKESHIRE SA69 9GE.
☎ (01834) 812579. 9 - 5.30 MON - SAT, 10 - 5.30 SUN.
Factory Shop • *Household* • *Womenswear & Menswear*
Children • *Sportswear & Equipment*
Branded merchandise from most of the major UK chain stores, all well-known high street department store names, offered at a discount of 40%-70% off normal high street prices. The garments are selected with great care by experienced buyers direct from factories worldwide to bring customers top quality merchandise at highly competitive prices.

STUART CRYSTAL
BRIDGE STREET, CHEPSTOW, MONMOUTHSHIRE NP16 5EZ
☎ (01291) 620135. OPEN 9 - 5 MON - SAT APRIL - SEPTEMBER,
10 - 5 OCTOBER - MARCH, 11 - 5 SUN.
Factory Shop • *Household*

Opposite the castle with its handy car park, this large factory shop also has a coffee shop on site. It sells Waterford crystal and Arthur Price cutlery and giftware. There is a crystal gift engraving service and chip repair service, display of old china and picnic area. Seconds of Stuart Crystal sold at about 25% discount. The selection includes wine glasses, flower holders, perfume holders, everyday tableware, salt and pepper sets, ice buckets, wine coolers, cutlery and candle lamps. Also seasonal special offers. First quality is also for sale at the appropriate price.

THE ABBEY WOOLLEN MILLS
MUSEUM SQUARE, MARITIME QUARTER, SWANSEA SA1 1SN
☎ (01792) 650351. OPEN 10 - 5 TUE - SUN,
CLOSED MON EXCEPT FOR BANK HOLIDAYS.
Permanent Discount Outlet • *Household*

Housed in the Swansea Maritime and Industrial Museum because its products are woven on the restored nineteenth century looms housed there, Abbey Woollen Mills makes blankets woven from the raw fleece of the Welsh Radno breed of sheep. The Mills dye, lubricate, card and spin the fleece into yarn which is woven using traditional colours and patterns. Unlike blankets which are acrylic or wool blends and can therefore use a cheap fleece, these products are hard-wearing, long-lasting and wash well. Only available through the on-site shop, you can save at least 50% on shop prices of the same quality blankets. The mills specialise in pure wool shawls, rugs and blankets, which are sold at discounts of one third off the normal retail price, with occasional seconds selling at half price. Scarves start at £4.99, picnic rugs from £13-£20, large throw 100"x 70", £40 in various colours and patterns. Savings can be as much as 50% off retail price. There is a small tea room open from easter to the end of September.

THE FACTORY SHOP LTD
FESTIVAL PARK FACTORY OUTLET SHOPPING CENTRE, VICTORIA,
EBBW VALE, GWENT NP3 6FP
☎ (01495) 352533. OPEN 9.30 - 5.30 MON - SAT, 9.30 - 7 THUR, 11 - 5 SUN.
SNOWDROP LANE, HAVERFORDWEST, PEMBROKESHIRE SA61 1ET
☎ (01437) 766000. OPEN 9 - 5.30 MON - SAT, 10.30 - 4.30 SUN.
Factory Shop in a Factory Shopping Village • *Furniture/Soft Furnishings*
Children • *Womenswear & Menswear* • *Household*
Sportswear & Equipment

Wide range on sale includes men's, ladies and children's clothing and footwear; household textiles; electricals; toiletries; hardware; luggage; lighting, Cape

Country Furniture and bedding, most of which are chainstore and high street brands at discounts of approximately 30%-50%. There are weekly deliveries and brands include many major stars such as Adidas, Nike, Joe Bloggs and Brabantia, to name just a few. There are kitchen and furniture displays and a new line in Cape Country furniture on sale. Ranges are continually changing and few factory shops offer such a variety under one roof. There is a free car park. This shop is part of Wales first factory outlet centre with a host of brand concessions in clothing and homeware plus restaurants. The telephone number given here is for the centre.

THE SOFA SERVICE
UNIT H2, GELLIHIRION INDUSTRIAL ESTATE, PONTYPRIDD,
MID-GLAMORGAN CF37 55X
☎ (01443) 841144. OPEN 9 - 5 MON - FRI, 10 - 4 SAT, SUN.
Factory Shop • *Furniture/Soft Furnishings*
The Sofa Service claims to beat prices on the high street by manufacturing at their own factory, cutting out the middleman, and passing the benefits onto the customer. A three year guarantee comes with all their products and all their fabrics are tested to BS 2543. The sofas are handcrafted in frames manufactured from wood sourced from managed forests. Steel serpentine springs are used in the seats and fixed backs. Fabric swatches are available and extra material can be bought to make matching curtains; covers can be loose or fixed. Delivery is within 28 days and they will unpack the sofa in the room in which it will be placed. There is a 21-day change-your-mind option, too. There are small and large sofas, sofabeds, chairs in six different styles, each with a variety of fabric choices. Prices range from £199-£269 for a chair to £299-£399 for a large sofa. Phone for a brochure.

THORNTONS
MCARTHURGLEN OUTLET CENTRE, BRIDGEND,
GLAMORGAN CF32 9SU
☎ (01656) 657104. OPEN 10 - 6 MON - SAT, 8 ON THUR, 11 - 5 SUN.
FESTIVAL PARK FACTORY SHOPPING CENTRE, VICTORIA, EBBW VALE,
GWENT NP3 6FP
☎ (01495) 305099. OPEN 10 - 6 MON - SAT, 11 - 5 SUN.
Factory Shop in a Factory Shopping Village • *Food and Leisure Household*
The UK's leading specialist confectionery retailer has more than 500 shops and franchises nationwide selling a wide range of boxed and loose, chocolate and sugar confectionery. The factory outlets sell three different categories: misshapes. discounted lines and standard lines. Misshapes are loose chocolates which are the result of new product development, product trials or end of production runs which cannot be packed as Thorntons standard lines. They are packed into assorted bags and offer a saving of 35%-55% over the recommended retail price of standard "loose line" products. Discounted lines are

excess to Thorntons' normal retail requirements and can be as a result of excess seasonal or export stock, discontinued lines or packaging changes. These products, when available, are offered at a discount of 25%-50% over the standard retail price. Standard lines from the full Thorntons range are also on sale at normal prices.

TIMBERLAND

MCARTHURGLEN OUTLET VILLAGE, DERWEN, BRIDGEND CF32 9SU
☎ (01656) 663545. OPEN 10 - 8 MON - THUR, 10 - 6 FRI, 9 - 6 SAT, 11 - 5 SUN AND BANK HOLS.

Factory Shop in a Factory Shopping Village • *Womenswear & Menswear*

Footwear, clothing and outdoor gear from the well-known Timberland range at discounts of 30% or more. Most of the stock is last season's or discontinued lines, but not seconds. All stock is last season's excess stock in limited ranges and sizes. As most of Timberland's stock is from a core range which rarely changes, there are few discontinued lines.

TK MAXX

UNIT 25, GREYFRIARS SHOPPING CENTRE, BLUE STREET, CARMARTHEN
☎ (01267) 220934. OPEN 9 - 6 MON, TUE, 9 - 6 WED, FRI, SAT, 9 - 8 THUR, 10 - 4 SUN.
QUEENS WEST SHOPPING CENTRE, CARDIFF
☎ (029) 20 341290. OPEN 9 - 5.30 MON, TUE, 9 - 6 WED, FRI, SAT, 9 - 8 THUR, 11 - 5 SUN.

Permanent Discount Outlet • *Womenswear & Menswear*
Children • *Household* • *Furniture/Soft Furnishings*

Based on an American concept, TK Maxx is situated in easily accessible, often centrally located stores and offers famous label goods with up to 60% savings off recommended retail prices. TK Maxx has fashion for the whole family - women's, men's and childrenswear - accessories, shoes, gifts, kitchenware and home goods. Everything in the store is branded with a choice of well-known high street names to designer labels, and while a small percentage might be clearly marked past season, the great majority of items in store are current season, current stock and still with phenomenal savings. There is a huge choice with 50,000 pieces in store and up to 10,000 new items arriving a week. The stores are simple and unfussy with wide aisles, shopping trolleys and baskets, and a spacious, functional feel to them but there are individual changing rooms, ramps for buggies and wheelchairs and plenty of staff on the shop floor. Every branch accepts all major credit and debit cards and has a liberal refund and return policy.

TOG 24

MCARTHURGLEN DESIGNER OUTLET VILLAGE, BRIDGEND,
JUNCTION 35 OF M4, MID GLAMORGAN CF32 9SU
☎ (01656) 767033. OPEN 10 - 8 MON - THUR, 10 - 6 FRI, SAT, 11 - 5 SUN.
FESTIVAL PARK OUTLET CENTRE, VICTORIA, EBBW VALE,
GWENT NP23 8FP
☎ (01495) 301902. OPEN 9.30 - 5.30 MON - SAT, 7 ON THUR, 11 - 5 SUN.
Factory Shop in a Factory Shopping Village
Womenswear & Menswear • Children • Sportswear & Equipment
Tog 24 are the UK's fastest growing brand name in outdoor clothing and leisurewear. They utilise the world's finest performance fabrics including Gore-Tex, Polartec and Burlington MCS, catering for all the family for all seasons, with cosy fleeces and waterproofs for the winter, and trekking ranges, shorts and t-shirts for the summer. With all prices at least 30% below the recommended retail price, you can afford to enter the Tog comfort zone.

TOGS

6 MONNOW STREET, MONMOUTH NP25 3EE
☎ (01600) 772629. OPEN 9.30 - 5 MON - SAT.
Permanent Discount Outlet • *Womenswear Only*
Togs has been established in Thame High Street for more than 15 years and now has three outlets. Here, you will find quality, value-for-money ladies separates, most of which are priced beween £10 and £15. Catering for all ages, they introduce new lines frequently. Regulars drop in often to see what's new or just for a chat. Staff are friendly and helpful and will always advise honestly on what suits each customer. Each of the three shops is situated in a building full of character with dark green paintwork and a distinctive oval signboard. Wide range of casual wear for women at competitive prices, including labels such as Viz-A-Viz, Adini and Poppy. Sizes range from 10 - 18 for women. All items are perfects and current fashion.

TOM SAYERS CLOTHING CO

FESTIVAL SHOPPING CENTRE, VICTORIA ROAD, EBBW VALE NP3 6AU
☎ (01495) 301414. OPEN 9.30 - 5.30 MON - SAT, 11 - 5 SUN.
Factory Shop in a Factory Shopping Village • *Menswear Only*
Tom Sayers make sweaters for some of the top high street department stores. Unusually for a factory shop, if they don't stock your size, they will try and order it for you from their factory or one of their other factory outlets and send it to you. Most of the stock here is overstock, cancelled orders or last season's and includes jumpers, trousers and shirts at discounts of 30%. The trousers and shirts are bought in to complement the sweaters which they make.

TRAVEL ACCESSORY
MACARTHURGLEN DESIGNER OUTLET VILLAGE, PEN-Y-CAE,
JUNCTION 35 OF M4, BRIDGEND CF32 9ST
☎ (01656) 767770. OPEN 10 - 8 MON - THUR, 10 - 6 FRI, SAT, 11 - 5 SUN.
Factory Shop in a Factory Shopping Village • *Food and Leisure*
Luggage and travel-related products and executive cases, handbags, umbrellas from leading brands such as Samsonite, Desley, Head, Taurus and GlobeTrotter. Each product is offered at a substantially reduced price compared to those found on the high street due to being production over-runs, discontinued ranges or colours and last season's products. Discounts range from 30%-75% off high street prices.

VIYELLA
MCARTHURGLEN WELSH DESIGNER OUTLET VILLAGE, PEN-Y-CAR LANE, BRIDGEND, JUNCTION 35 OF M4 CF32 9ST
☎ (01656) 648660. OPEN 10 - 6 MON - FRI, 8 ON THUR, 9 - 6 SAT, 11 - 5 SUN.
Factory Shop in a Factory Shopping Village • *Womenswear & Menswear*
Wide range of Viyella clothing at discount prices from 30% on ladies formal wear and casual wear.

WHITTARD
MCARTHURGLEN DESIGNER OUTLET, THE DERWEN, BRIDGEND, MID GLAMORGAN CF32 9SU
☎ (01656) 658434. OPEN 10 - 8 MON - THUR, 10 - 6 FRI - SAT, 11 - 5 SUN.
Factory Shop in a Factory Shopping Village • *Household*
Sells tea, coffee, coffee-making equipment (cafetieres and stove-top espressos), wide range of china, colourful tableware, corkscrews, trays, bins, kitchen containers at discount prices.

North Wales

ABAKHAN FABRICS
LLANERCH-Y-MOR, COAST ROAD, MOSTYN, FLINTSHIRE CH8 9DX
☎ (01745) 562100. OPEN 9 - 5.15 MON - SAT, 8 ON THUR, 10.30 - 4.30 SUN.
Factory Shop • *Furniture/Soft Furnishings* • *Food and Leisure*
DIY/Renovation
With five outlets in the North West, Abakhan Fabrics are as well known for the emphasis they put on value for money as they are for the huge variety of fabrics, needlecrafts, haberdashery, gifts and knitting yarns, soft furnishings, all gathered from around the world. The large mill shop complex in Clwyd has a new Home and Garden Department, baskets of remnant fabrics, wools, yarns and unrivalled selections of fabrics sold by the metre from evening wear, bridal wear and crepe de Chine to curtaining, nets and velvets. Here in this historic

building, there are more than ten tonnes of remnant fabrics and 10,000 rolls, all at mill shop prices. Abakhan is able to offer such bargains through bulk buying, or selling clearance lines, job lots and seconds. There is a coffee shop and free parking at the Flintshire outlet and coach parties are welcome provided they pre-book. Free information pack available: ring 01745 562100.

ANGLESEY NURSERY HIRE
10 GORWEL DEG, RHOSTREHWFA, LLANGEFNI, ANGLESEY LL77 7JR
☎ (01248) 723181.
Hire Shop • *Children*
Part of the Baby Equipment Hirers Association (BEHA), which has more than 100 members countrywide. A range of equipment can be hired from high chairs, cots and travel cots to baby car seats and buggies. Some members also hire out party equipment including child-sized tables and chairs. BEHA run an advice line which will try and answer any queries you have regarding hiring services for children. Phone the Babyline on 0831 310355.

CATALOGUE BARGAIN SHOP
6-8 MADOC STREET, LLANDUDNO, GWYNEDD LL30 2TP
☎ (01492) 877561. OPEN 9 - 5 MON - SAT, 10.30 - 4.30 SUN.
OLD KERRY ROAD, NEWTOWN, POWYS SY16 1BJ
☎ (01686) 628283. OPEN 9 - 5 MON - SAT, 10 - 4 SUN.
Permanent Discount Outlet • *Womenswear & Menswear* • *Children* *Household* • *Electrical Equipment*
Catalogue Bargain Shop is a growing national chain of stores which obtains the majority of its goods from mail order giants Great Universal and Kays, and offers a range of clothing for all the family, a wide selection of shoes, bed linen, household goods, electrical equipment and hundreds of other catalogue items at very competitive prices. For example, a three-piece leather suite, £899, reduced from £1,600. The merchandise consists of ends of ranges and previous season's stock for which there is no longer storage space when the catalogues change.

CHINA CHASE
LONG BYRE, BORRAS HEAD, WREXHAM, NORTH WALES LL13 9TL
☎ (01978) 856400. CALL OR SEND LETTER AND SAE FOR DETAILS.
Rather like a marriage agency, China Chase matches up those who've lost or broken an item of china with those who've got one to sell. They can help if you need to replace a piece or pieces of tableware, wish to increase your service even though it is no longer available from the manufacturer, want to increase the number of place settings, or would like to build up stock against future breakages. As well as holding large stocks of obsolete patterns, they constantly buy at auction and from clients disposing of unwanted family China and have A database of over 1,500 clients wishing to buy or sell. There is a one-off registration fee of £6 where you are put in touch with a match and do the deal yourself with no extra commission to pay.

DARTINGTON CRYSTAL
C/O JAMES PRINGLE WEAVERS, HOLYHEAD ROAD,
LLANFAIRPWLLGWYNGYLL, ANGLESEY LL61 5UJ
☎ (01248) 715255. OPEN 9 - 5.30 MON - SAT, 11 - 5 SUN.
TWEEDMILL, LLANERCH PARK, ST ASAPH LL17 OUY
☎ (01745) 730072. OPEN 9.30 - 6 MON - SAT, 11 - 5 SUN.
Factory Shop • *Household*

An extensive range of Dartington Crystal seconds at greatly reduced prices as well as some perfect crystal at full price. Range includes wine suites, sherry glasses, tankards, decanters, rippled glass, fruit and salad bowls.

DEESIDE FURNITURE LTD
UNIT 47 GREENFIELD BUSINESS PARK, BAGILLT ROAD,
HOLYWELL, FLINTSHIRE CH8 7FF
☎ (01352) 711196. OPEN 7.30 - 4.30 TUE - THUR, 7.30 - 12.30 FRI,
9 - 2 SAT, 10 - 2 SUN.
Permanent Discount Outlet • *Furniture/Soft Furnishings*

Large furniture warehouse selling sofas, curtains and soft furnishings at factory direct prices. Many of the sofas are made for top high street stores.

HARRY TUFFINS SUPERMARKET AND PETROL STATION
NIGHTON SHELL GARAGE, POWYS
☎ (01547) 528645. OPEN 8 - 6 MON - WED, SAT, 8 - 8 THUR, FRI, 10 - 4 SUN.
Permanent Discount Outlet • *Food and Leisure*

Supermarket selling foodstuffs, garden furniture, household goods at incredibly competitive prices. Newly refurbished with the looks and service of a Sainsbury's and the prices are better. There's a vast range of tinned food, pickles, sauces, dried foods, soups, cereals, wine, household cleaning products, kitchen equipment, stationery and diy. The fruit and veg sections outside the main shop are not run by Tuffins and are not always a bargain.

KIDS STOCK AND EXCHANGE
UNIT 2, WELLINGTON ROAD, RHYL, CLWYD LL18 1BD
☎ (01745) 330115. OPEN 10 - 5 MON - SAT.
Secondhand shops • *Hire Shop* • *Children*

Sells nearly-new baby equipment and also hires out. There are buggies, stair gates, parasols, raincovers, cots, prams, Moses baskets - and everything parents of young children could want, including items with famous brand names such as Cosatto. Old prams are exchanged for nearly-new or new. Hire charges start at £1.50 per day for a baby walker, £2.50 for a pushchair. No children's clothes are stocked.

LEGS CLOTHING CO
39 HIGH STREET, BUILTH WELLS, POWYS LD2 3AB
☎ (01982) 551043. OPEN 9 - 5 MON - FRI, 9 - 4 SAT, 11 - 5 BANK HOLS.
21 BROAD STREET, NEWTOWN, POWYS SY16 2NE
☎ (01686) 624388. OPEN 9 - 5 MON - FRI, 9 - 4 SAT.
BROAD STREET, KNIGHTON, POWYS LD7 1BL
☎ (01547) 520649. OPEN 9 - 5 MON - FRI, 9 - 4 SAT.
25 HIGH STREET, BRECON, POWYS LD3 7LA
☎ (01874) 611432. OPEN 9 - 5 MON - FRI, 9 - 4 SAT, 11 - 5 SUN, EASTER TO CHRISTMAS, BANK HOLS.
Factory Shop • *Children*
Exclusive outlet for Europe's largest trouser manufacturer sells ends of lines, cancelled orders and samples of jeans, trousers and shorts for all the family at factory direct prices. Also available are ancillary lines of casual wear at bargain prices.

MATALAN
UNIT 1A & 1B, CAEMARFON ROAD, BANGOR LL57 4SU.
☎ (01248) 362778. OPEN 9.30 - 8 MON - FRI, 9 - 6 SAT, 11 - 5 SUN.
UNIT E, WREXHAM RETAIL PARK, PLAS COCH ROAD, WREXHAM LL1 2UD
☎ (01978) 340900. OPEN 10 - 8 MON - FRI, 9 - 6 SAT, 11 - 5 SUN.
Permanent Discount Outlet • *Children* • *Womenswear & Menswear Household*
Matalan is a fashion and homewares value retailer giving customers what they claim to be unbeatable value for money with huge savings on a wide range of products including high quality fashionable clothing for men, women and children at up to 50% off high street prices. Matalan is situated out of town and stores are open seven days a week all year round.

PHOEBE'S DRESS AGENCY
45 HIGH STREET, MENAI BRIDGE
☎ (01248) 717454. OPEN 10 - 5.30 TUE, WED, FRI, 10 - 3 SAT.
Dress Agency • *Womenswear Only*
New and nearly-new shop selling high quality designer labels such as Basler, Armani, Alexon, Louis Feraud, Jaeger, Jobis and Dolce & Gabbana and many more. Car park at rear of shop.

PYJAMA TOPS
HIGH STREET, BALA, LL23 7AD
☎ (01678) 520348. OPEN 10.30 - 4.30 MON - SAT, EASTER TO OCTOBER.
Permanent Discount Outlet • *Children*
Excellent selection of children's pyjamas, most of which are ends of lines from shops such as BhS, Mothercare, Tesco, Woolworth's and Littlewoods, at savings of about 50%. Sizes range from six months to 13 years. Many of the pyjamas are character PJs with, for example, Postman Pat and Toy Story and Barbie designs.

SIMON BOYD
ISLAND GREEN SHOPPING CENTRE, WREXHAM, CLWYD LL13 7NW
☎ (01978) 313628. OPEN 9.30 - 5.30 MON - SAT, 10 - 4 SUN.
Permanent Discount Outlet • *Furniture/Soft Furnishings*

Stocks thousands of rolls of curtain fabric including chenilles, tapestries, cotton satin and chintzes from brands such as Monkwell, Sanderson and Crowson. For example a chenille costing £25 a yard costs £15.99 here. Also tie-backs, cushions, throws, ready-made curtains. Free measuring, plus making-up service available.

STEWART'S
Y MAES, PWLLHELI, GWYNEDD LL53 5HG
☎ (01758) 701130. OPEN 9 - 5.30 MON - SAT.
BREWERY TERRACE, SAUNDERSFOOT, DYFED SA69 9HG.
☎ (01834) 813169. OPEN 9.30 - 5.30 SEVEN DAYS A WEEK.
144 HIGH STREET, PORTHMADOG, GWYNEDD LL49 9NU
☎ (01766) 514166. OPEN 9 - 5.30 MON - SAT.
23 MOSTYN STREET, LLANDUDNO, GWYNEDD LL30 2NL
☎ (01492) 870733. OPEN 9.30 - 5.30 MON - SAT.
Factory Shop • *Household* • *Womenswear & Menswear*
Children • *Sportswear & Equipment*

Branded merchandise from most of the major UK chain stores, all well-known high street department store names, offered at a discount of 40%-70% off normal high street prices. The garments are selected with great care by experienced buyers direct from factories worldwide to bring customers top quality merchandise at highly competitive prices.

THE TWEEDMILL FACTORY OUTLETS
LLANNERCH PARK, ST ASAPH, DENBIGHSHIRE, (OFF A55) LL17 OUY
☎ (01745) 730072. E-MAIL: enquiries@tweedmill.co.uk
OPEN 9.30 - 6 MON - SAT, 11 - 5 SUN.
Factory Shop • *Womenswear & Menswear* • *Household*

Has a wide range of clothes for both men and women, luggage, giftware, handbags and home accessories with savings of up to 50% off normal high street prices. Selling directly to the public from the manufacturers, there are always at least 50,000 garments in stock and 5,000 pairs of shoes as well as 100,000 homeware items, all of which are perfects. Labels on sale include Regatta, Klass, Roman, Wolsey, French Connection, Easy Jeans, Glenmuir, Levi's, James Barry, Double Two, Timberland, Lotus, Salisbury's and Farah for clothes and shoes; Coloroll, Staffordshire Tableware, Price's Candles, Clover Leaf and Dartington Crystal for homewares. Everything has the original retail price on it so you can see the discounts of up to 50%.

TK MAXX
UNIT 12, ISLAND GREEN, WREXHAM, CLWYD LL13 7LW
☎ (01978) 261133 . OPEN 9 - 5.30 MON - FRI, 9 - 6 SAT, 11 - 5 SUN.
Permanent Discount Outlet • *Womenswear & Menswear* • *Children Household* • *Furniture/Soft Furnishings*

Based on an American concept, TK Maxx is situated in easily accessible, often centrally located stores and offers famous label goods with up to 60% savings off recommended retail prices. TK Maxx has fashion for the whole family - women's, men's and childrenswear - accessories, shoes, gifts, kitchenware and home goods. Everything in the store is branded with a choice of well-known high street names to designer labels, and while a small percentage might be clearly marked past season, the great majority of items in store are current season, current stock and still with phenomenal savings. There is a huge choice with 50,000 pieces in store and up to 10,000 new items arriving a week. The stores are simple and unfussy with wide aisles, shopping trolleys and baskets, and a spacious, functional feel to them but there are individual changing rooms, ramps for buggies and wheelchairs and plenty of staff on the shop floor. Every branch accepts all major credit and debit cards and has a liberal refund and return policy.

TREFRIW WOOLLEN MILLS LTD
TREFRIW, CONWAY LL27 ONQ
☎ (01492) 640462. OPEN 9.30 - 5 MON - FRI, 10 - 5 SAT.
Factory Shop • *Furniture/Soft Furnishings*

Sells products manufactured on the premises: traditional Welsh "tapestry" bedspreads from £80, travel rugs from £25, wool, tweed fabrics from £14.90 a metre, tapestries, mohair coats; tweed sports jackets, ruanas and knitting wool at £2.95 per 100g.

VELMORE LTD
1-2 JAEGER HOUSE, 141 HOLT ROAD, WREXHAM, CLWYD LL13 9DY
☎ (01978) 363456. OPEN 10.30 - 3 MON, WED, FRI.
Factory Shop • *Womenswear Only*

Seconds of skirts, dresses, suits, jackets and trousers originally made for the most famous high street name at very cheap prices.

Northern Ireland

ADRIA LTD
BEECHMOUNT AVENUE, MELMONT ROAD, STRABANE, COUNTY TYRONE, NORTHERN IRELAND BT82 9BG
☎ (028) 7138 2568. OPEN 9 - 5 MON - FRI, 9 - 2 SAT.
CARNBANE INDUSTRIAL ESTATE, NEWRY, CO DOWN
☎ (028) 3025 4448
Factory Shop • *Womenswear & Menswear* • *Children*
Manufacturer of tights and socks for Marks & Spencer, this shop sells hosiery which consists of Marks & Spencer seconds, Charnos lingerie, seconds in menswear, children's and women's clothes. Seconds in tights cost 45p.

ALEXANDER THE GRATE
126-128 DONEGAL PASS, BELFAST, NORTHERN IRELAND BT7 1BZ
☎ (028 90) 232041. OPEN 10 - 5 MON - SAT.
Architectural Salvage • *DIY/Renovation*
A specialist in antique fireplaces, as well as leaded windows, doors and general architectural salvage. There is also garden furniture in the spring and summer. The owner also runs an antiques market on the first floor of the same premises every Saturday from 9.30 - 5 with 4 different stallholders.

ANNE STOREY OUTLET SHOP
THE LINEN GREEN, 17 WEAVING SHEDS, MAIN ROAD, MOYGASHEL, DUNGANNON, NORTHERN IRELAND BT71 7HB
☎ (028) 8772 9770. OPEN 9.30 - 5.30 MON -SAT.
Factory Shop • *Womenswear Only*
Modern designer collection of easy clothes for women of today. Currently no other outlet store in Northern ireland or the UK for Anne Storey. Reductions from 30%.

CANCER RESEARCH CAMPAIGN
50 HIGH STREET, NEWTOWNARDS, COUNTY DOWN, NORTHERN IRELAND BT23 3HZ
☎ (028) 9182 0268. OPEN 9 - 5 MON - SAT.
Dress Agency • *Womenswear* • *Children*
Charity shop with a difference. Ground floor sells everything that you would expect to find in such a shop. The first floor caters specifically for the bridal market and sells wedding dresses, bridesmaids dresses and pageboy outfits, with accessories. All of the stock is donated by the public or the manufacturers.

CV HOME FURNISHINGS
MAYDOWN INDUSTRIAL ESTATE, CARROWKEEL DRIVE, MAYDOWN,
LONDONDERRY BT47 6UQ
☎ (028) 7185 2108. OPEN 9 - 4.30 MON - SAT, 1 - 5.30 SUN.

Factory Shop • *Womenswear & Menswear* • *Children* • *Household*

Part of the Coats Viyella group, which makes quality clothing for many of the major high street storres, overstocks and clearance lines are sold through more than 30 of the group's factory shops. Many of you will recognise the garments on sale, despite the lack of well-known labels. Ladieswear includes dresses, blouses, jumpers, cardigans, trousers, nightwear, underwear, lingerie, hosiery, coats and swimwear. Menswear includes trousers, belts, shirts, ties, pullovers, cardigans, T-shirts, underwear, nightwear, hosiery and jackets. Childrenswear includes jackets, trousers, T-shirts, underwear, hosiery, jumpers and babywear. There is also a range of quality towels. There are regular deliveries to constantly update the range.

DESMOND & SONS LTD
THE MAIN STREET, CLAUDY, LONDONDERRY,
NORTHERN IRELAND BT47 3SD
☎ (028) 7133 8441. OPEN 10 - 5 MON - SAT.
KEVLIN ROAD, OMAGH
☎ (028) 8224 1560. OPEN 10 - 5 MON - SAT.
MILL STREET, ENNISKILLEN
☎ (028) 6632 5467. OPEN 10 - 5 MON - SAT.
BALLYQUINN ROAD, DUNGIVEN
☎ (028) 7174 2068. OPEN 10 - 5 MON - SAT.
31 GARVAGH ROAD, SWATRAGH
☎ (028) 7940 1639. OPEN 10 - 5 MON - SAT.

Factory Shop • *Womenswear & Menswear* • *Children* • *Household*

Large range of men's, women's and childrenswear including trousers, jeans, plain and round-neck lambswool and cotton sweaters, nightwear and knitwear. Most of the stock is seconds and is sold at discounts of one third. They also buy in some imperfects of household items such as handtowels and bath towels which are sold at competitive prices.

DISCOUNT DRESSING
70 BLOOMFIELD AVENUE, BELFAST, NORTHERN IRELAND BT5 5AE
☎ (028) 9073 8853. OPEN 9.30 - 5.30 MON - SAT.

Permanent Discount Outlet • *Womenswear Only*

A veritable Aladdin's Cave of designer bargains, Discount Dressing sells mostly German, Italian and French designer labels at prices at least 50% and up to 90% below those in normal retail outlets. All items are brand new and perfect. A team of buyers all over Europe purchase stock directly from the manufacturer for this growing chain of discount shops. This enables Discount Dressing to by-pass the importers and wholesalers and, of course, their mark-up. They also buy bankrupt stock in this country. Their agreement with their suppliers means that they are not able to advertise brand names for obvious reasons, but they are all well-known for their top quality and style. So confident is Discount Dressing that you will be unable to find the same item cheaper elsewhere, that they guarantee to give the outfit to you free of charge should you perform this miracle. Merchandise includes raincoats, dresses, suits, trousers, blouses, evening wear, special occasion outfits and jackets, in sizes 6-24 and in some cases larger. GDD readers can obtain a further 10% discount if they visit the shop taking a copy of this book with them. There are other branches in Lincolnshire, London and Hertfordshire.

HAWKES BAY APPAREL
16 COMBER ROAD, NEWTOWNARDS, COUNTY DOWN BT23 4HY
☎ (028) 9180 0200. OPEN 9.30 - 5.30 MON - WED, 9.30 - 8.30 THUR, FRI, 9.30 - 5.30 SAT, 1 - 6 SUN.
Factory Shop • *Womenswear & Menswear* • *Children*
Men's, women's and children's own-brand jeans, jackets, T-shirts, hats and sweatshirts at 30% - 50% savings. Also childrenswear, casual men's and ladieswear at competitive prices from designers such as Calvin Klein, Versace and Armani.

JEREMIAH AMBLER (ULSTER) LTD
BARN MILLS, TAYLOR AVENUE, CARRICKFERGUS,
COUNTY ANTRIM BT38 7HQ
☎ (028) 9336 1011. OPEN 11 - 1 AND 2 - 4 MON - FRI.
ALSO MAIL ORDER.
Factory Shop • *Womenswear Only*
Hand-knitting wools, especially mohair at 30%- 50% less than retail. Also wool fabric and accessories including rugs, and travel rugs.

LINIAN KNITWEAR
SPAMOUNT MILLS, CASTLEDERG, CO TYRONE BT81 7NB
☎ (028) 8167 1181. OPEN 10 - 5 MON - SAT.
Factory Shop • *Womenswear & Menswear* • *Children*
Irish woollens, knitted on the premises, seconds of which are sold in the factory shop. Ends of lines and last season's garments are sold at up to 50% discounts against normal prices.

LOTUS LTD
34 BRIDGE STREET, BANBRIDGE, COUNTY DOWN BT32 3JL
☎ (028) 4062 2480. OPEN 9 - 5.30 MON - SAT.
Factory Shop • *Womenswear & Menswear*
This manufacturer for well-known chainstores sells all sizes and styles of Lotus shoes - from smart fashion shoes to walking shoes - at discounted prices for discontinued lines and rejects. Prices from £20 - £50 for men's shoes and from £12 - £35 for women's shoes. They also have a bridal shoe department with prices from £25 and a range of matching handbags.

OCTOPUS SPORTSWEAR MFG LTD
UNIT 1, DUBLIN ROAD INDUSTRIAL ESTATE, STRABANE,
COUNTY TYRONE BT82 9EA
☎ (028) 7188 2320. OPEN 9 - 5.30 MON - THUR, 10 - 4 FRI - SAT.
Factory Shop • *Sportswear & Equipment* • *Children*
Manufactures own-brand sportswear: shorts, jerseys, socks, pants, hooded tops, sweatshirts and sell seconds and clearance lines at discounts of up 50%-75%.

ONEIDA
BALLOO SOUTH INDUSTRIAL ESTATE, ENTERPRISE ROAD, BANGOR,
COUNTY DOWN BT19 7TA
☎ (028) 9147 4747. OPEN 10 - 5 MON - FRI.
Factory Shop • *Household*
Oneida is the world's largest cutlery company and originates from the United States of America. This shop is attached to the warehouse and sells ends of ranges and discontinued lines as well as cancelled orders of cutlery, silver and silver plate at discounts of between 30% and 75%.

PAUL COSTELLOE FACTORY STORE
THE WORKSHOP, 9 LINEN GREEN, MAIN ROAD, MOYGASHEL,
DUNGANNON, COUNTY TYRONE BT71 7HB
☎ (028) 8775 3867. OPEN 9.30 - 5.30 MON - SAT.
Factory Shop • *Womenswear & Menswear*
A wide range of 1,500 garments, consisting of special purchases, seconds, samples and past season stocks at substantial savings on original prices. The comprehensive selection encompasses business and special occasion designs and menswear as well as a more casual range for relaxed weekend wear. Now the sole stockist of Paul Costelloe womens' footwear in Ireland.

SPOILS
UNITS 55, 56, 57, CASTLE COURT SHOPPING CENTRE, BELFAST BT1 1DD
☎ (028) 9032 8512. OPEN 9.30 - 6 MON - SAT, 9 ON THUR, 1 - 6 SUN.
Permanent Discount Outlet • *Household*
General domestic glassware, non-stick bakeware, kitchen gadgets, ceramic oven-to-tableware, textiles, cutting boards, aluminium non-stick cookware, bakeware, plastic kitchenware, plastic storage, woodware, coffee pots/makers, furniture, mirrors and picture frames. Rather than being discounted, all the merchandise is very competitively priced - in fact, the company carry out competitors' checks frequently in order to monitor pricing. With 38 branches, the company is able to buy in bulk and thus negotiate very good prices.

THE COURTAULDS FACTORY SHOP
PORTADOWN ROAD, LURGAN, COUNTY ARMAGH BT66 8RB
☎ (028) 3831 6747. OPEN 9.30 - 6 MON - FRI, UNTIL 8 ON THUR,
9 - 6 SAT, 1 - 6 SUN.
Factory Shop • *Womenswear & Menswear* • *Children* • *Household*
Sells a wide range of ladies, men's and childrens high street fashions at between 30% and 50% below high street prices. Also stocks a wide range of household textiles and accessories.

THE ELLIOTT DESIGNER SALE STORE
10 MAIN STREET, HILLSBOROUGH, COUNTY DOWN BT26 6AE
☎ (028) 9268 9992. OPEN 10 - 5 MON - SAT.
Permanent Discount Outlet • *Womenswear Only*
Sells brand new designer clothes from some of the best known names at very competitive prices. Labels include Ramsay of Dublin, Gerard Darel, Philippe Adec, Caractere, as well as other designers from time to time. There are skirts, blouses, dresses, sweaters, waistcoats, coats and jackets, and traditional knitwear, including Arran and some jewellery. Recently extended to include separates from the Continent also with accessories and shoes. Sizes range from 8-18.

THE FACTORY SHOP OUTLET
CV HOME FURNISHINGS, 36 MAGHERALANE ROAD, RANDALSTOWN,
COUNTY ANTRIM BT41 2NT
☎ (028) 3844 4102. OPEN 9 - 4.30 MON - SAT.
53 MAIN STREET, DONAGHCLONEY, CRAIGAVON,
CO ARMAGH BT66 7LX
☎ (028) 3888 2923. OPEN 10 - 4.30 MON - SAT, 1 - 5 SUN, BANK HOLS.
CV HOME FURNISHINGS, MAYDOWN INDUSTRIAL ESTATE,
CARROWKEEL DRIVE, MAYDOWN BT47 6UQ
☎ (028) 7185 2108. OPEN 9 - 4.30 MON - SAT, 1 - 5.30 SUN.
Part of the Coats Viyella group, which makes quality clothing for many of the major high street storres, overstocks and clearance lines are sold through more than 30 of the group,s factory shops. Many of you will recognise the garments on sale, despite the lack of well-known labels. Ladieswear includes dresses, blouses, jumpers, cardigans, trousers, nightwear, underwear, lingerie, hosiery, coats and swimwear. Menswear includes trousers, belts, shirts, ties, pullovers, cardigans, T-shirts, underwear, nightwear, hosiery and jackets. Childrenswear includes jackets, trousers, T-shirts, underwear, hosiery, jumpers and babywear. There is also a range of quality towels. There are regular deliveries to constantly update the range.

THE LIGHTHOUSE COLLECTION
THE MEWS, 12 MAIN STREET, HILLSBOROUGH,
COUNTY DOWN BT26 6AE
☎ (02892) 688188. WEBSITE: www.lighthousecollection.com
OPEN 10 - 5 MON - FRI.
Permanent Discount Outlet • *Household*
The Lighthouse Collection of teak furniture is made from teak exclusively grown on the plantations of East Java and not in the tropical forest. These plantations are under the control of the Indonesian Government and are strictly managed by the Forest Commission. The Lighthouse Collection currently manufactures teak garden furniture. They encourage price comparisons with other suppliers of teak furniture as they claim to be by far the best value for money. They also sell a large selection of quality American cotton bath towels and various bathroom accessories. Prices range from £5 for a hand towel to £23 for a large bath sheet, a third off normal retail prices. The garden furniture is available by mail order - phone for a catalogue and price list.

TK MAXX
FIRST FLOOR, CASTLECOURT SHOPPING CENTRE, BELFAST BT1 1DD
☎ (028) 9033 1151. OPEN 9 - 6 MON - SAT, 9 - 9 THUR, 1 - 6 SUN.
UNIT 31, RUSHMERE SHOPPING CENTRE, CRAIGAVON BT64 1AA
☎ (028) 3834 4544.
Permanent Discount Outlet • *Children* • *Womenswear & Menswear* • *Household* • *Furniture/Soft Furnishings*
Based on an American concept, TK Maxx is situated in easily accessible, often centrally located stores and offers famous label goods with up to 60% savings off recommended retail prices. TK Maxx has fashion for the whole family - women's, men's and childrenswear - accessories, shoes, gifts, kitchenware and home goods. Everything in the store is branded with a choice of well-known high street names to designer labels, and while a small percentage might be clearly marked past season, the great majority of items in store are current season, current stock and still with phenomenal savings. There is a huge choice with 50,000 pieces in store and up to 10,000 new items arriving a week. The stores are simple and unfussy with wide aisles, shopping trolleys and baskets, and a spacious, functional feel to them but there are individual changing rooms, ramps for buggies and wheelchairs and plenty of staff on the shop floor. Every branch accepts all major credit and debit cards and has a liberal refund and return policy.

TYRONE CRYSTAL LTD
KILLYBRACKEY, DUNGANNON, COUNTY TYRONE BT71 6TT
☎ (028) 8772 5335. OPEN 9 - 5 MON - SAT. MAIL ORDER.
Factory Shop • *Household*
Factory shop selling the full range of Tyrone crystal including non-current range items discounted by up to thirty percent off normal retail prices and slight imperfects discounted by up to forty percent.

ULSTER WEAVERS
44 MONTGOMERY ROAD, CASTLEREAGH, BELFAST BT6 9QZ
☎ (028) 9079 5569. OPEN 9.30 - 5 MON - SAT.
Factory Shop • *Household*
Ulster Weaver products at discounts of 20% as well as quality giftware from all corners of Ireland.

Channel Islands

CAMELEON
65 NEW ST, ST HELIER, JERSEY JE2 3RA
☎ (01534) 722438. OPEN 10 - 4 TUE - FRI, 10 - 5 SAT.
Dress Agency • *Womenswear & Menswear* • *Furniture/Soft Furnishings*
An interesting fashion agency for men and women covering high street and designer labels, including accessories. A blend of old and new, Cameleon also stocks vintage clothing and collectables. Madhatters new hats are available in stock and to order.

CINDERELLA'S WARDROBE
10 CONWAY ST, ST HELIER, JERSEY JE2 3NT
☎ (01534) 618545. OPEN 10 - 5.30 MON - SAT.
Dress Agency • *Womenswear Only*
Sells nearly-new and new designer outfits, shoes, hats and accessories. Labels are top quality: Maxmara, Ralph Lauren, Louis Feraud, Escada, Chanel, Byblos and Krizia.

STONELAKE LTD
5 SMITH STREET, ST PETER PORT, GUERNSEY,
CHANNEL ISLANDS GY1 2JN
☎ (01481) 720053. FAX 0148 713808. OPEN 9 - 5.15 MON - SAT.
MAIL ORDER AVAILABLE.
Permanent Discount Outlet • *Womenswear Only* • *Household*
Family-run business which has operated in Guernsey for more than 80 years serving both locals and tourists alike. In recent years, they have added a mail order service. They have two shops - one a pharmacy and perfumery, the other selling perfumery and cosmetics - and specialise in fragrance bargains from UK and French companies, in aftershaves, cosmetics, perfumes, toilet waters, soaps, and talcs. Being duty-free, and with no VAT, they have competitive prices on standard ranges and by buying excess stocks and ends of lines, they have a large list of extra special offers including ranges no longer sold in the UK. Brand names stocked include YSL, Elizabeth Taylor, Paloma Picasso, Cacharel, Boss, Georgio, Paco Rabanne, Gucci, Safari, Elizabeth Arden, Givenchy, Oscar de la Renta, Nina Ricci, and Roc cosmetics. Free postage and packaging on mail orders over £40.

SUMMERLAND FACTORY SHOP
GOREY WOOLLEN MILL, GOREY, JERSEY
☎ (01534) 858024. OPEN 9 - 5 MON - FRI, 9.30 - 4 SAT,
10 - 4 SUN IN SUMMER.
ST AUBINS WOOLLEN MILL, JERSEY
☎ (01534) 445043. OPEN 9 - 5.30 MON - FRI, 9 - 4.30 SAT, 10 - 5 SUN.
INTERNATIONAL HOUSE, THE PARADE, ST HELIER, JERSEY
☎ (01534) 625698. OPEN 9 - 5.30 MON - SAT, IN SUMMER WEEKDAY
EVENINGS 7.30 - 9.30.
NORTH ESPLANADE, GUERNSEY
☎ (01481) 701336. OPEN 9 - 5.30 MON - SAT.
Permanent Discount Outlet • *Womenswear & Menswear*
Sells a large range of men's and ladies wear at factory direct prices. The ladies range includes underwear, skirts, blouses, classic and fashon knitwear and footwear. The men's range includes underwear, shirts, silk ties, trousers, knitwear, casual shirts and footwear. Labels sold include Wolsey, Jockey, Baumler, Peter England, Pierre Balmain and Pierre Cardin at discounts of up to 50%.

THE FABRIC FACTORY
35 HILGROVE STREET, ST HELIER, JERSEY JE2 4SL
☎ (01534) 739551. OPEN 9 - 5.30 MON - SAT.
Permanent Discount Outlet • *Furniture/Soft Furnishings*
The Fabric Factory sells dress and furnishing fabrics at discounted prices. Stock is regular and clearance, and they also sell tracks, poles, and offer a made-to-measure service.

THE FROCK EXCHANGE
CHEAPSIDE, ST HELIER, JE2 3PG
☎ (01534) 768324. OPEN 10 - 4 MON, TUE, THUR, SAT, 11 - 5 WED, FRI.
Dress Agency • *Womenswear Only*
Sells everything from blouses and skirts to ballgowns (at Christmas) and bikinis. Labels range from high street to good quality middle market names such as Jaeger and Jacques Vert. When we visited, we saw a Jacques Vert blouse and skirt, £24, and blouses from £6-£18. Jewellery, handbags, hats are also on sale with new and secondhand shoes from £8 upwards. Please phone before making a special journey during holiday periods.

EUROPE
Eire

PATAGONIA INTERNATIONAL INC
24-26 EXCHEQUER STREET, DUBLIN 2, EIRE
☎ (00 353 1) 6705748. OPEN 10 - 6 MON - FRI, 8 ON THUR, 9.30 - 6 SAT.
Factory Shop • *Sportswear & Equipment* • *Womenswear & Menswear*
'Green' outlet shop selling outdoor clothing, fleeces, ski wear and casual wear which is made up mainly of discontinued stock, surplus merchandise and occasional seconds. All cotton is organically grown and 1% of sales is donated to the preservation and restoration of the natural environment.

PONDEN MILL LINENS
KILLARNEY OUTLET CENTRE, KILLARNEY, COUNTY KERRY, EIRE
☎ (00 353) 6430091. OPEN 10 - 6 MON - SAT, 12 - 6 SUN.
Factory Shopping Village • *Household* • *Furniture/Soft Furnishings*
Famous branded products at direct from the mill prices. A fabulous assortment of towels, duvets, pillows, throws, bedspreads, up-to-the-minute coordinated bed linen, from Crown, Coloroll, Jeff Banks Ports-of-Call, to name but a few. Something for every room in the house.

SPOILS
UNITS 7 & 8, THE JERVIS CENTRE, DUBLIN
☎ (00 353 1) 878 0717 . OPEN 9 - 5.30 MON - SAT, 10.30 - 4 SUN.
Permanent Discount Outlet • *Household*
General domestic glassware, non-stick bakeware, non-electrical kitchen gadgets, ceramic oven-to-tableware, textiles, cutting boards, aluminium non-stick cookware, bakeware, plastic kitchenware, plastic storage, woodware, coffee pots/makers, furniture, mirrors and picture frames. Rather than being discounted, all the merchandise is very competitively priced - in fact, the company carry out competitors' checks frequently in order to monitor pricing. With 38 branches, the company is able to buy in bulk and thus negotiate very good prices.

TK MAXX
BLANDCHARDSTOWN RETAIL PARK, DUBLIN, EIRE 15
☎ (00 353 1) 8219410. OPEN 9 - 6 MON - WED, FRI, SAT, 9 - 8 THUR, 12 - 6 SUN.
Permanent Discount Outlet • *Womenswear & Menswear* • *Children*
Household • *Furniture/Soft Furnishings*
Based on an American concept, TK Maxx is situated in easily accessible, often centrally located stores and offers famous label goods with up to 60% savings

off recommended retail prices. TK Maxx has fashion for the whole family - women's, men's and childrenswear - accessories, shoes, gifts, kitchenware and home goods. Everything in the store is branded with a choice of well-known high street names to designer labels, and while a small percentage might be clearly marked past season, the great majority of items in store are current season, current stock and still with phenomenal savings. There is a huge choice with 50,000 pieces in store and up to 10,000 new items arriving a week. The stores are simple and unfussy with wide aisles, shopping trolleys and baskets, and a spacious, functional feel to them but there are individual changing rooms, ramps for buggies and wheelchairs and plenty of staff on the shop floor. Every branch accepts all major credit and debit cards and has a liberal refund and return policy.

Austria

MCARTHURGLEN DESIGNER OUTLET PARNDORF GmbH

INDUSTRIE UND GEWERBEZENTRUM,
PARNDORF, A-7111, AUSTRIA
☎ 00 43 2166 3614. WEBSITE: www.mcarthurglen.com
OPEN 9.30 - 7 MON - FRI, 9 - 5 SAT.

Factory Shopping Village • *Womenswear & Menswear* • *Children Household* • *Sportswear & Equipment*

This is Austria's first designer outlet with a foodcourt, restaurants, cafe, children's play area and free parking. More than 50 shops here sell top international brands and designer labels at discounts of between 30% and 50% off retail prices. Situated near the tourist resort of Neusiedler See, east of Vienna. Stores include Aigner, Cerruti, Chevignon, Designer Room, Designer Shades selling top of the range designer sunglasses, cases and chains; DKNY, In Wear, Jaques Helm, Karrimor, Lee Cooper, Mexx, Nike, Reebok, Red/Green, Timberland, Tool Man, Travel Accessory Outlet, Villeroy & Boch and many more.

TRAVEL ACCESSORY

PARNDORF GmbH, INDUSTRIE UND GEWERBEGEBIET,
7111 PARNDORF, AUSTRIA.
☎ 00432 1662634.

Factory Shop in a Factory Shopping Village • *Food and Leisure*

Luggage and travel-related products and executive cases, handbags, umbrellas from leading brands such as Samsonite, Desley, Head, Taurus and GlobeTrotter. Each product is offered at a substantially reduced price compared to those found on the high street due to being production over-runs, discontinued ranges or colours and last season's products. Discounts range from 30%-75% off high street prices.

France

MCARTHURGLEN DESIGNER OUTLET VILLAGE: BOUTIQUE DE FABRICANTS

44 MAIL DE LANNOY, 59100 ROUBAIX, NEAR LILLE,
A1 MOTORWAY FROM PARIS TO LILLE, FRANCE
☎ 0033 3 28 33 36 00. WEBSITE: www.mcarthurglen.com
OPEN 10 - 7 MON - FRI, 9.30 - 7 SAT.

Factory Shopping Village • *Womenswear & Menswear*
Children • *Household*

Located in the heart of the town of Roubaix on the outskirts of Lille, near the German border, this outlet is linked by both tram and metro. There are 45 stores selling top brands and designer labels at between 30% and 50% off normal retail prices. Fashion shops include Adidas, Blanc Blue, Brenda & Moore, Bruce Field, Cacharel, Carbone, Complices, Courreges, Dome, Donaldson, Eminence, Fila and Gallus shoes, Gossard, Jacqueline Riu, Jacques helm, Jean Dresses, Lafuma sportswear, Laura Scott, Old River, Olympia, Petit Boy, Reebok, River Woods. You can buy luggage at Samsonite and there are stores selling childrenswear, gifts, lingerie and bed linen; there's even a hairdresser. The Metro station is just in front of the Designer Village and there are 1,500 parking spaces.

MCARTHURGLEN DESIGNER OUTLET VILLAGE: BOUTIQUES DE FABRICANTS

ZONE DES MAGASINS D'USINE NORD, 10150 PONT SAINTE MARIE,
TROYES, JUNCTION 20 OF A5, EXIT PONT-STE-MARIE.
FROM CALAIS JUNCTION 31 OF THE A26, FRANCE
☎ 0033 3 25 70 47 10. WEBSITE: www.mcarthurglen.com
OPEN 2 - 7 MON, 10 - 7 TUE - FRI, 9.30 - 7 SAT.

Factory Shopping Village • *Womenswear & Menswear* • *Children*
Household • *Sportswear & Equipment*

Fifteen minutes from the medieval town of Troyes, this area is well known for its factory shops. As you'd expect from a French site, most of the big bargains in this 80-shop village are fashion companies - Aigle, Armani, Bally, Blanc Bleu, Cacharel, CK Jeans, Damart, Diesel, Fedora, Francoise Saget, Guess, Jacques Helm, Jean Bourget, Kookai, Lacoste, Lee Cooper, Lulu Castagnette, Marlborough Classics, Mephisto, Mexx, Morgan, Naf Naf, Nike, Petit Bateau, Polo Ralph Lauren, Quiksilver, Rech, Reebok, Sinequanone, Status, Timberland, Versace, Villeroy & Boch, Warners, Well, to name just a few of the newer boutiques. There are restaurants, a children's play area, free parking and expected savings of up to 50% on accessories, clothes, luggage and linen.

Germany

B5 DESIGNER OUTLET CENTRE
BERLIN, GERMANY DUE TO OPEN IN 2000.
Shops here include Designer Shades offering top of the range designer sunglasses, cases and chains.

VILLINGEN OUTLET CENTRE
THE BLACK FOREST, GERMANY DUE TO OPEN IN 2001.

ZWEIBRUCKEN DESIGNER OUTLET CENTER
GERMANY
Mixture of factory shops, cafes, bars and restaurants. Due to open spring 2001.

Holland

TK MAXX
SHOPPING CENTRE GOOISE BRINK, UNIT 31 & 32,
KERK STRAAT 63, HILVERSUM, NETHERLANDS 1211CL
☎ (0031) 356233 455. OPEN 1- 6 MON , 9.30 - 6 TUE, WED, FRI,
9.30 - 9 THUR, 9 - 5 SAT.
Permanent Discount Outlet • *Womenswear & Menswear* • *Children Household* • *Furniture/Soft Furnishings*
Based on an American concept, TK Maxx is situated in easily accessible, often centrally located stores and offers famous label goods with up to 60% savings off recommended retail prices. TK Maxx has fashion for the whole family - women's, men's and childrenswear - accessories, shoes, gifts, kitchenware and home goods. Everything in the store is branded with a choice of well-known high street names to designer labels, and while a small percentage might be clearly marked past season, the great majority of items in store are current season, current stock and still with phenomenal savings. There is a huge choice with 50,000 pieces in store and up to 10,000 new items arriving a week. The stores are simple and unfussy with wide aisles, shopping trolleys and baskets, and a spacious, functional feel to them but there are individual changing rooms, ramps for buggies and wheelchairs and plenty of staff on the shop floor. Every branch accepts all major credit and debit cards and has a liberal refund and return policy.

Italy

MCARTHURGLEN DESIGNER OUTLET VILLAGE
SERRAVALLE SCRIVIA, ALESSANDRIA, ON THE A7 MOTORWAY
BETWEEN GENOA AND MILAN, NORTHERN ITALY 15069
WEBSITE: www.mcarthurglen.com
OPEN 10 - 9 JUNE TO SEPTEMBER, 10 -7 OCTOBER - MAY,
SEVEN DAYS A WEEK.
Factory Shopping Village • *Womenswear & Menswear* • *Children*
The first designer outlet village in Italy, this is an easy drive from Genoa, Milan and Turin and located in the wine region of Gavi and Berlucchi above Portofino and Rapallo. The 60 factory shops sell top brands and designer labels at discounts of between 30% and 50% off normal retail prices. Stores include mens', women's and childrenswear from Italian and international designers and home-grown Designer Shades, offering top of the range designer sunglasses, cases and chains. There's a spectacular circular food court with bars and restaurants, coach parking and over 3,000 car parking spaces.

Spain

LA ROCA
30KM FROM BARCELONA, OFF EXIT 12 OF THE A7, SPAIN
☎ 34 93 842 39 39. OPEN 11 - 8.30 MON - FRI, 10 - 9 SAT.
Factory Shopping Village • *Womenswear & Menswear* • *Children*
Household • *Sportswear & Equipment*
Over 35 shops selling a wide range of local and global brands at discount prices. For the home, Cotton Corner offers Catalan quality towels and sheets in vivid colours while established names such as Descamps and Price's Candles provide familiar products in an unfamiliar setting. Other shops here include Cacharel French clothing for men and women; Catimini quality French chiildrenswear; Champion, the US sportswear comany; Dockers; Eleonora Silvestri's quality leather goods, knitwear and accessories; Espacio de Creadores offering a selection of top Spanish designer labels; Farrutx's Spanish designer shoes for women; Gianfranco Ferre; Globe which offers contemporary Spanish fashion for women; IKKS Compagnie for quality children's sportswear; John Partridge's traditional British country clothing for men, women and children; K&E Factory Store with classic Spanish designer clothes for men and women; Levi's; Old Ridel fashion for men and women; Nike; Pepe Jeans; Petit Bateau French childrenswear; Ray Ban sunglasses; Red/Green nautical-style casualwear; Sergio Tacchini sportswear; The Designer Room; Timberland; Travel Accessory Outlet; Vans famous American skate, surf and snowboard gear; Versace; Warner's lingerie and Yanko handmade shoes.

TRAVEL ACCESSORY
LA ROCA COMPANY STORES, SANTA AGNES DE MALANYANES 08430, LA ROCA, DEL VALLES, BARCELONA, SPAIN
☎ 00349 38 45 60 61.
Factory Shop in a Factory Shopping Village • *Food and Leisure*
Luggage and travel-related products and executive cases, handbags, umbrellas from leading brands such as Samsonite, Desley, Head, Taurus and GlobeTrotter. Each product is offered at a substantially reduced price compared to those found on the high street due to being production over-runs, discontinued ranges or colours and last season's products. Discounts range from 30%-75% off high street prices.

Sweden

ARLANDASTAD OUTLET VILLAGE
NEAR SIGTUNA, ON ROAD BETWEEN STOCKHOLM CITY CENTRE AND THE AIRPORT, SWEDEN
Among the companies here at Sweden's first factory outlet centre are Nike, Diesel, Diesel Footwear, Fjall Raven and Vanity Fair, manufacturer of Wrangler, Lee and JanSport.

TRAVEL ACCESSORY
BARKERBY OUTLET VILLAGE, MAJORSVAGEN 2-4, S- 17738, JARFALLA, STOCKHOLM, SWEDEN
☎ 0046 870 842 6875.
Factory Shop in a Factory Shopping Village • *Food and Leisure*
Luggage and travel-related products and executive cases, handbags, umbrellas from leading brands such as Samsonite, Desley, Head, Taurus and GlobeTrotter. Each product is offered at a substantially reduced price compared to those found on the high street due to being production over-runs, discontinued ranges or colours and last season's products. Discounts range from 30%-75% off high street prices.

Index of
Mail Order Discounters

A C Computer Warehouse	21
Anne Thomas Natural Fibre Fabrics	564
Anta Scotland Ltd	510, 571, 594
Aynsley China	394
Baby Barn	500
Bibliophile Books	243
Bridgewater	395
Cannock Gates Factory Shop	396
Cannock Gates Ltd	396
Cd & Book & Video Selections	101
Charles Tyrwhitt Shirts	250
China Matching Replacements	431
Chinamatch	502
Chinasearch	459
Classic Choice Furnishings Ltd	605
Classical Passions	369
Croft Mill	192
Dakota Marketing	352
Dartington Crystal	62, 67, 76, 93, 101, 140, 151, 193, 376, 398, 483, 502, 518, 576, 596, 626
Denner Cashmere	254
Designer Fine Fragrances	193
Direct Cosmetics Ltd	224
Divani	607
Edgcumbe Tea and Coffee	449
Elite Lighting	172
English Country Pottery	126
Essential Items	343
Gerards Frozen Food Centre	196
Hartleys Mail Order Ltd	198
Hollin Hall Craft & Sewing Centre	199
Hybury China	378
Jags Trading	528
Jeremiah Ambler (Ulster) Ltd	632
Just Fabrics	112, 356
Just Fabrics at Inscape	62
Keystones	404
Kid's Stuff Mail Order Ltd	129
Kirkdale Direct Direct Furniture	611
LBS Horticulture	202
Leigh Lighting Company	113
Linton Tweeds Ltd	69
M & M Sports	152
Macgillivray & Co	598
Mrs Pickering's Dolls Clothes	316
Northampton Footwear Distributors Ltd	323
Oakridge Direct	614
Odeon Furniture Company	614
Optilabs	438
Pease & Jay Furniture Direct	538
Postoptics	539
Postscript	280
Power Plus Direct	57
Renahall Ltd	452
Royal Lochnagar Distillery	600
Royal Worcester Porcelain	506
Screenface	287
Screwfix Direct	387
Shipton & Heneage	289
Siesta Cork Tiles	440
Silver Editions	10
Sofa Workshop Direct	618
Sports Shoes Unlimited	545
Springvale Leather Furniture	211
Staples the Office Superstore	546
Stonelake Ltd	636
Sundaes Sandals	236
Swimgear	292
T G Green Pottery Factory Outlet	86
Tablewhere?	292
The Craft Company	465
The East Lancashire Towel Company	214
The Garden Factory	414
The Lighthouse Collection	635
The Red House	362
The Tool Shop	426
Tracks and Trimmings	183
Tyrone Crystal Ltd	635
Universal Direct	47
V & F Parker Ltd	480
White of Hawick	570
White Rose Candles Workshop	561
Wilkinsons Home and Garden Stores	419

Index of
Brand Names

Well-known brand names and some factory shops and permanent discount shops which are known by well-known brand names, such as Timberland, Levi's and Paul Costelloe, are listed below with the pages on which they appear. Brand names with two words to their name such as Paul Costelloe are listed under P for Paul and not C for Costelloe; those with the word The in front of them are listed under their second word. Bear in mind that if these names appear in dress agencies, the shop may not carry them all year round as it depends on whether clients bring in these particular brands. The same is true of secondhand curtain shops.

Adidas	21, 34, 35, 55, 59, 65, 70, 72, 82, 88, 109, 119, 135, 138, 142, 152, 161, 181, 203, 207, 209, 213, 228, 229, 234, 237, 292, 320, 346, 348, 355, 389, 414, 426, 442, 453, 455, 456, 462, 472, 495, 507, 508, 531, 534, 550, 551, 568, 612, 621, 640
AEG	145, 189, 340, 439, 452
AGA	92, 154
Alexon	9, 42, 126, 138, 143, 151, 169, 170, 185, 230, 313, 324, 330, 376, 393, 421, 429, 445, 466, 481, 489, 499, 509, 523, 577, 603, 627
Amanda Wakeley	6, 9, 39, 126, 244, 296, 508
Anna French	77, 165, 306, 432
Antler	36, 68, 84, 92, 177, 186, 189, 201, 341, 352, 375, 483, 489, 490, 513, 515, 575, 608, 613
Arthur Price of England	21, 53, 172, 186, 385, 394, 419, 462, 554, 578, 620
Aquascutum	69, 107, 153, 155, 239, 321, 349, 350, 376, 481, 489, 541
Armani	5, 10, 11, 27, 28, 29, 35, 42, 49, 55, 63, 97, 107, 110, 113, 116, 123, 126, 136, 137, 138, 144, 164, 173, 182, 187, 193, 209, 214, 239, 243, 247, 248, 250, 255, 256, 258, 266, 267, 268, 273, 276, 279, 281, 287, 288, 289, 294, 297, 298, 301, 307, 335, 341, 345, 346, 354, 361, 362, 386, 398, 410, 427, 433, 434, 438, 440, 445, 448, 453, 463, 469, 470, 478, 484, 490, 495, 504, 516, 519, 521, 534, 541, 542, 551, 568, 577, 583, 587, 588, 589, 590, 591, 601, 608, 617, 627, 632, 640
Aynsley China	394
Axminster	200, 330, 501, 507
Bally	108, 314, 514, 574, 640
Barbour	163. 331, 376, 579
Bebe Confort	10, 115, 162, 178, 383, 438, 464, 505
Berghaus	152, 161, 317, 551
Berlei	3, 34, 55, 68, 82, 161, 203, 234, 243, 339, 462, 472, 531, 609, 612
Black & Decker	51, 99, 334, 374, 376, 467, 511, 555, 573
Blazer	2, 35, 167, 351, 371, 374, 534
Braun	40, 86, 334, 385, 494, 541, 616
Bridgewater Pottery	92, 395, 424,
Britax	10, 115, 162, 178, 383, 438, 464, 500, 505
Burberry	10, 23, 25, 107, 110, 229, 246, 258, 328, 350, 351, 398, 482, 512, 513, 534, 597, 604
Byblos	33, 484, 636
Caithness Crystal	314, 582, 595
Calvin Klein	6, 7, 12, 25, 61, 107, 110, 112, 122, 132, 137, 166, 187, 193, 220, 244, 301, 335, 346, 348, 362, 365, 376, 398, 438, 444, 453, 464, 470, 489, 499, 519, 534, 537, 540, 561, 613, 632,
Carmen	206, 476
Caroline Charles	10, 49, 136, 138, 170, 247, 297, 421, 425, 435, 521, 600
Cerruti	4, 10, 28, 55, 166, 250, 265, 305, 346, 350, 351, 448, 484, 490, 494, 534, 597, 605, 639
Charnos	76, 630

THE GOOD DEAL DIRECTORY

Christian Dior	63, 96, 97, 109, 116, 124, 138, 140, 144, 164, 209, 287, 386, 410, 478, 518, 543, 551, 568, 576, 588, 601, 608, 610, 617
Christian Lacroix	63, 96, 109, 110, 116, 144, 164, 209, 258, 281, 287, 350, 386, 410, 530, 542, 568, 577, 578, 583, 588, 599, 616
Clairol	40, 86, 385, 616
Colefax & Fowler	19, 44, 64, 118, 140, 165, 224, 253, 295, 337, 362, 367, 388, 425, 433, 437, 454, 491, 495, 548
Dannimac	61, 108, 223, 307, 339, 509
Dartington Crystal	62, 67, 68, 76, 83, 93, 101, 140, 151, 188, 193, 195, 376, 388, 398, 419, 483, 502, 518, 523, 576, 596, 626, 628
Dash	169, 509, 521
David Charles	253
David Fielden	432
Delsey	68, 92, 107, 165, 201, 335, 483
Descamps	351, 351, 534, 642
Designers guild	19, 44, 58, 64, 118, 140, 165, 224, 295, 362, 367, 388, 425, 433, 456, 491, 495, 548, 549, 599
Dolce & Gabbana	255, 269, 484
Doc Martens	163, 341, 352, 375, 397, 514, 515, 575
Donna Karan	35, 49, 256, 259, 268, 279, 289, 296, 297, 330, 350, 434, 577
Dorma	58, 192, 205, 335, 540
DKNY	7, 27, 35, 54, 122, 137, 214, 248, 250, 267, 298, 301, 365, 440, 444, 498, 565, 583, 590, 639
Eastex	8, 124, 138, 143, 151, 169, 185, 230, 235, 313, 376, 393, 481, 509, 523, 603
Ecco	28, 35, 83, 90, 107, 142, 156, 158, 166, 167, 177, 377, 397, 484, 489, 490, 515, 552, 574, 576, 607, 613
Elefanten	107, 156, 552
Escada	10, 11, 48, 52, 53, 69, 122, 126, 128, 136, 138, 143, 155, 171, 178, 182, 214, 215, 236, 239, 255, 267, 268, 279, 288, 341, 350, 361, 366, 379, 420, 421, 427, 433, 434, 439, 440, 445, 449, 452, 466, 467, 494, 521, 529, 534, 541, 577, 587, 589, 591, 600, 608, 615, 636
Fendi	35, 276, 289
French Connection	5, 54, 77, 169, 172, 240, 241, 247, 267, 275, 350, 358, 429, 459, 489, 509, 521, 551, 628
Gap	30, 35, 36, 122, 139, 142, 155, 173, 177, 212, 243, 267, 282, 294, 312, 324, 345, 355, 385, 429, 448, 450, 474, 485, 489, 537
Georgina von Etzdorf	296, 485
Gianfranco Ferre	187, 265, 271, 281, 288, 350, 642
Givenchy	63, 96, 116, 136, 144, 164, 209, 224, 287, 297, 324, 386, 410, 542, 568, 588, 586, 601, 617, 636
Gossard	2, 34, 55, 70, 82, 161, 189, 203, 234, 243, 335, 376, 462, 472, 495, 512, 523, 531, 540, 540, 609, 612, 640
Gucci	5, 107, 109, 140, 167, 168, 187, 243, 248, 255, 256, 257, 260, 261, 266, 269, 279, 287, 289, 290, 297, 298, 307, 361, 425, 439, 484, 490, 518, 576, 587, 636
Hobbs	35, 126, 247, 312, 350, 354
Hom	351, 364, 376, 391, 498
Hush Puppies	29, 114, 176, 179, 522, 531, 582, 608
Ideal Standard	313
In Wear	169, 240, 265, 355, 429, 639
Isis Ceramics	355, 450
Jaeger	3, 5 10, 11, 17, 31, 35, 41, 42, 49, 67, 69, 77, 80, 84, 100, 103, 106, 122, 123, 126, 132, 133, 138, 144, 151, 155, 170, 171, 172, 200, 226, 239, 258, 259, 276, 278, 315, 324, 350, 354, 355, 360, 361, 366, 374, 376, 378, 423, 425, 427, 430, 435, 440, 442, 445, 447, 450, 453, 466, 478, 485, 486, 489, 496, 504, 527, 529, 534, 541, 551, 581, 587, 589, 597, 598, 601, 610, 613, 627, 629, 637
Jane Churchill	79, 128, 170, 224, 253, 379

BRAND NAME INDEX   647

Jeff Banks	*15, 39, 57, 71, 85, 104, 118, 143, 152, 159, 163, 179, 181, 207, 334, 389, 408, 493, 506, 539, 586, 615, 638*
Joan & David	*350, 356, 534*
Jockey	*45, 54, 216, 255, 637*
Joe Bloggs	*32, 35, 39, 58, 65, 72, 98, 109, 111, 119, 135, 154, 181, 215, 228, 237, 320, 334, 346, 389, 414, 426, 442, 456, 456, 459, 507, 550, 568, 621*
John Smedley	*81, 296, 528*
Kangol	*35, 69, 335, 390, 553*
Karen Millen	*126, 182, 244, 261, 307, 350, 360, 440, 605*
Karrimor	*35, 36, 82, 163, 201, 230, 490, 529, 534, 613, 639*
Kasper	*260, 609*
Kenwood	*86, 142, 215, 313, 385, 494, 541, 606, 616*
Kenzo	*112, 294, 307, 486, 576*
Krups	*86, 478, 494, 541, 616*
LA Gear	*341, 352, 375, 515, 575*
Le Creuset	*113, 175, 177, 488, 489, 490, 530, 534*
Lego	*46, 60, 88, 94, 109, 112, 149, 160, 167, 175, 183, 219, 282, 335, 339, 391, 417, 487, 508, 558, 559, 611*
Levis	*429, 590*
Liberty	*41, 69, 76, 77, 79, 95, 117, 165, 172, 231, 278, 280*
Lowe Alpine	*162*
Lyle & Scott	*88, 229, 348, 376, 570, 584*
Louis Feraud	*41, 46, 49, 53, 70, 97, 109, 123, 124, 138, 258, 260, 276, 305, 361, 366, 401, 420, 425, 442, 445, 478, 484, 490, 499, 521, 536, 583, 600, 601, 608, 609, 627, 636*
Maclaren	*10, 36, 115, 162, 178, 383, 438, 464, 474, 500, 505*
Magnet	*473, 532, 533*
Mamas & Papas	*10, 36, 106, 115, 162, 178, 382, 438, 464, 500, 505, 535*
Marks & Spencer	*4, 11, 14, 26, 31, 56, 80, 88, 102, 124, 129, 132, 134, 137, 151, 170, 172, 173, 192, 194, 221, 225, 226, 228, 243, 267, 282, 307, 309, 324, 332, 335, 342, 348, 354, 364, 374, 420, 442, 455, 456, 459, 465, 469, 470, 472, 478, 491, 504, 522, 525, 526, 540, 542, 544, 546, 549, 564, 571, 584, 615, 630*
Max Factor	*166, 224, 257*
MaxMara	*146, 294, 361, 470, 541, 547, 551, 587*
Miele	*145, 452*
Minton	*292, 398, 406, 410, 459, 476*
Mondi	*3, 10,11, 28, 42, 70, 100, 124, 134, 155, 170, 171, 182, 216, 236, 239, 260, 276, 313, 324, 332, 374, 423, 425, 429, 433, 434, 437, 439, 440, 442, 449, 469, 470, 478, 485, 547, 577, 583, 587, 589, 600, 601, 606, 608*
Monkwell	*41, 43, 79, 99, 150, 170, 231, 306, 352, 371, 389, 432, 456, 516, 549, 628*
Monsoon	*15, 124, 226, 261, 294, 314, 350, 358, 360, 375, 381, 421, 429, 448, 453, 474, 546, 551, 587*
Morlands	*382*
Moschino	*5, 25, 27, 29, 35, 55, 105, 110, 113, 122, 146, 187, 214, 215, 235, 255, 258, 259, 263, 273, 276, 281, 294, 297, 341, 345, 362, 434, 440, 466, 469, 470, 478, 484, 489, 490, 516, 526, 530, 551, 587, 591, 598*
Moss Bros	*45, 54, 150, 216, 252, 274, 335, 363, 432*
Mothercare	*35, 36, 88, 212, 243, 324, 521, 537, 627*
Moulinex	*478*
Mulberry	*5, 6, 10, 124, 137, 296, 382, 534, 536, 583*
Neff	*3, 145, 188, 189, 313, 439, 452, 473, 533*
Next	*4, 14, 17, 29, 35, 36, 51, 52, 53, 56, 67, 70, 108, 122, 124, 127, 134, 139, 146, 155, 157, 166, 170, 195, 205, 212, 228, 235, 250, 251, 261, 275, 312, 314, 329, 332, 335, 342, 344, 348, 360, 361, 374, 376, 382, 385, 401, 410, 424, 425, 429, 432, 442, 448, 450, 470, 474, 475, 489, 490, 491, 522, 523, 525, 537, 543, 544, 546, 548, 598, 613, 614*

Nicole Farhi	9, 11, 20, 52, 55, 132, 136, 137, 147, 151, 166, 169, 240, 244, 247, 248, 250, 259, 266, 275, 296, 345, 350, 358, 360, 362, 398, 424, 429, 432, 434, 445, 453, 504, 508, 518, 587, 605
Nike	34,35,36, 37, 39, 55, 59, 65, 70, 72, 82, 88, 109, 110, 119, 135, 142, 152, 154, 161, 177, 181, 189, 203, 207, 215, 228, 229, 234, 236, 320, 341, 346, 348, 352, 355, 375, 389, 414, 426, 442, 452, 454, 456, 462, 472, 489, 490, 491, 495, 507, 512, 515, 523, 531, 550, 551, 568, 575, 590, 612, 621, 639, 640, 642, 643
Nintendo	461
Nobel	92, 386
Osborne & Little	19, 44, 64, 118, 278, 295, 352, 362, 367, 388, 425, 433, 436, 456, 491, 495, 548, 599
Osh Kosh b' Gosh	155, 282, 284, 324, 398, 428, 448, 450, 452, 474, 537
Paddy Campbell	6, 9, 267
Paloma Picasso	636
Panasonic	31, 145, 198, 264, 418
Paul Costelloe	5, 9, 11, 20, 46, 55, 123, 128, 132, 140, 172, 228, 258, 276, 297, 398, 423, 427, 598, 518, 526, 551, 600, 601, 633
Paul Smith	137, 187, 214, 250, 276, 279, 296, 297, 298, 345, 349, 534
Petit Bateau	294, 351, 385, 640, 642
Philips	31, 40, 86, 123, 141, 198, 313, 334, 385, 398, 418, 494, 541, 616
Pied a Terre	35, 534
Pierre Cardin	32, 42, 45, 75, 76, 99, 172, 216, 297, 327, 335, 432, 528, 637
Pifco	206, 476
Planet	3, 49, 53, 61, 77, 100, 123, 126, 155, 172, 183, 221, 239, 307, 330, 354, 376, 392, 401, 425, 442, 445, 494, 500, 509, 562
Polo Ralph Lauren	25, 109, 140, 188, 350, 359, 489, 518, 565, 576, 640
Portmeirion	93, 125, 281, 408, 459, 582
Precis	49, 61, 77, 100, 172, 183, 221, 239, 307, 376, 392, 499, 500, 509, 562
Pringle	333, 339, 534, 551, 579, 582, 584, 596, 626
Puma	68, 90, 92, 201, 229, 335, 341, 352, 375, 483, 515, 551, 575
Rayburn	92, 386
Reebok	35, 36, 39, 88, 109, 110, 152, 177, 189, 350, 375, 455, 512, 534, 566, 575, 613, 639, 640
Rigby & Peller	324
Royal Brierley	54, 56, 376, 410, 475, 476, 523, 536, 541, 554
Royal Crown Derby	86, 406, 410, 476, 536,
Royal Grafton	404,
Royal Worcester	21, 36, 41, 83, 139, 180, 186, 209, 283, 292, 376, 385, 410, 431, 459, 475, 476, 494, 502, 504, 506, 536, 578, 608, 613, 616, 617
Russell Hobbs	206, 476, 535
Samsonite	47, 51, 69, 82, 88, 92, 106, 109, 122, 141, 165, 166, 177, 201, 203, 332, 335, 350, 483, 505, 532, 58, 570, 583, 593, 624, 639, 640, 643
Sanderson	19, 41, 44, 58, 64, 79, 94, 103, 112, 118, 140, 170, 209, 231, 234, 256, 261, 280, 295, 308, 352, 362, 367, 371, 388, 425, 435, 456, 495, 516, 548, 554, 628
Siemens	3, 145, 452
Slazenger	68, 92, 201, 335, 341, 352, 375, 483, 515, 575
Spode	41, 180, 209, 282, 292, 385, 388, 410, 412, 424, 431, 459, 476, 494, 504, 536, 578, 616, 617
Start-Rite	156, 258, 319, 546, 552, 618
Stuart Crystal	104, 172, 376, 419, 478, 490, 536, 582, 583, 596, 601, 620
Swan	40, 478, 494, 541
Telemac	100, 153, 571
Timberland	34, 35, 36, 39, 46, 55, 70, 75, 82, 109, 113, 161, 166, 179, 203, 217, 234, 355, 390, 462, 472, 490, 497, 531, 553, 583, 612, 613, 622, 628, 639, 640, 642
Tomasz Starzewski	244, 288, 587
Ton Sur Ton	84, 113

Tower	206, 476
Triumph	90, 243, 351, 364, 376, 391, 490, 498
Ungaro	28, 69, 215, 276, 297, 313, 606
Valentino	27, 28, 100, 109, 122, 126, 140, 166, 173, 182, 210, 243, 258, 267, 268, 273, 276, 278, 279, 281, 287, 294, 297, 305, 336, 350, 361, 362, 374, 433, 449, 464, 469, 477, 478, 495, 518, 526, 568, 576, 583, 588, 601, 618
Versace	5, 27, 28, 34, 107, 110, 112, 138, 166, 187, 193, 215, 235, 255, 265, 266, 273, 276, 281, 298, 300, 307, 346, 350, 378, 433, 466, 470, 478, 489, 519, 578, 587, 589, 590, 591, 598, 632, 640, 642
Villeroy & Boch	21, 36, 48, 142, 149, 186, 251, 306, 351, 364, 459, 490, 498, 578, 639, 640
Viyella	5, 35, 48, 79, 80, 84, 100, 106, 138, 178, 220, 236, 343, 374, 376, 378, 392, 421, 450, 452, 464, 490, 499, 534, 544, 547, 550, 560, 581, 613, 624, 631, 634
Vymura	26, 30, 80, 110, 185, 197, 226, 233, 253, 256, 307, 370, 402, 524, 609
Wallis	11, 35, 49, 51, 52, 53, 124, 134, 226, 228, 235, 236, 239, 314, 335, 348, 360, 398, 401, 409, 428, 453, 466, 499, 598
Warners	36, 61, 90, 128, 138, 220, 335, 348, 351, 365, 379, 435, 491, 534, 555, 560, 561, 612, 640
Wedgwood	21, 93, 97, 110, 139, 142, 166, 172, 177, 186, 281, 283, 292, 351, 376, 398, 419, 431, 459, 490, 504, 523, 536, 554, 578, 608, 613
Whirlpool	256, 313, 473, 533
Whistles	244, 248, 250, 263, 294, 312, 350, 360, 591
White of Hawick	570, 579
Wilton	200, 262, 286, 330, 418, 487, 499
Windsmoor	3, 49, 53, 54, 61, 69, 77, 90, 100, 103, 109, 122, 123, 124, 155, 172, 173, 183, 221, 226, 235, 238, 259, 307, 339, 354, 376, 392, 401, 421, 423, 425, 445, 466, 469, 470, 485, 490, 496, 499, 500, 509, 523, 529, 555, 562, 608, 615
Wolsey	32, 45, 54, 75, 77, 88, 153, 157, 172, 216, 223, 229, 335, 348, 528, 543, 551, 628, 636
Wrangler	12, 66, 88, 163, 220, 229, 308, 376, 523, 560, 562, 643
Yarell	146, 236, 276, 305, 429, 447, 478, 547
Yves St Laurent	6, 12, 215, 228, 243, 258, 288, 313, 420, 439, 449, 465, 484, 490, 606
Zanussi	145, 313, 340, 411, 439, 452, 467

THE GOOD DEAL DIRECTORY

THANKS
TO GOOD DEAL DIRECTORY
READERS

My grateful thanks to the following readers who all contributed information about discount shops they have visited which has helped to make this edition of this book the definitive guide to bargain shopping.

Andrea Barham, *Essex*

E. D. Boys-Stones, *South London*

H. M. Bridges, *Suffolk*

S Cammush, *Warwickshire*

Trevor Copestake, *Staffordshire*

Mrs B Cunningham, *West Midlands*

Mrs J Demmen, *Swindon*

Gillian Dicken, *Cardiff*

Mrs Marie Gray, *Powys*

A. E. Gregory, *West Midlands*

Mrs D. L. Healey, *West Yorkshire*

Patricia L. Jones, *Hampshire*

Patricia Longdon, *Surrey*

Mrs M. McLeod, *Lanarkshire*

Rita Moudarri, *Surrey*

Mrs Sonya Nesbitt, *Wiltshire*

Janette Rickman, *Cambridgeshire*

Mrs J. Rowe, *Essex*

Audrey Simpson, *Brighton*

Miss Josephine Smith, *Glasgow*

Jayne Stewart, *South London*

Denise Strang, *Glasgow*

Mrs S Thomas, *Gloucestershire*

Mrs P.A. Thompson, *South London*

Mrs S. Townley, *Northamptonshire*

Ann Ward, *Lincoln*

Mrs Jean Ward, *Birmingham*

Sheila Whiteman, *Shropshire*

Shirley Wood, *Northumberland*

THE GOOD DEAL DIRECTORY

REPORT FORM
EARN £10

Write and tell us about a Good Deal shop you have visited and, if we publish details based on your information, we'll send you a cheque for £10.

TO: **The Good Deal Directory
PO Box 4, Lechlade, Glos GL7 3YB**

Name of Outlet ....

....

Address ....

....

....

Telephone number ....

Type of Merchandise ....

....

....

Comments
(please write as much as possible, explaining in detail the type of goods sold, quality, any brand names, whether labels are cut out, discounts, car parking facilities etc)

THE GOOD DEAL DIRECTORY

Signed ....

Name (capitals please) ....

Address ....

....

....

Tel No. ....

e-mail ....

Date ....

THE GOOD DEAL DIRECTORY

REPORT FORM
EARN £10

Write and tell us about a Good Deal shop you have visited and, if we publish details based on your information, we'll send you a cheque for £10.

TO: **The Good Deal Directory
PO Box 4, Lechlade, Glos GL7 3YB**

Name of Outlet ....

....

Address ....

....

....

Telephone number ....

Type of Merchandise ....

....

....

Comments
(please write as much as possible, explaining in detail the type of goods sold, quality, any brand names, whether labels are cut out, discounts, car parking facilities etc)

THE GOOD DEAL DIRECTORY

Signed ....

Name (capitals please) ....

Address ....

....

....

Tel No. ....

e-mail ....

Date ....

THE GOOD DEAL DIRECTORY

REPORT FORM
EARN £10

Write and tell us about a Good Deal shop you have visited and, if we publish details based on your information, we'll send you a cheque for £10.

TO: **The Good Deal Directory**
PO Box 4, Lechlade, Glos GL7 3YB

Name of Outlet ....

....

Address ....

....

....

Telephone number ....

Type of Merchandise ....

....

....

Comments
(please write as much as possible, explaining in detail the type of goods sold, quality, any brand names, whether labels are cut out, discounts, car parking facilities etc)

THE GOOD DEAL DIRECTORY

REPORT FORM
EARN £10

Write and tell us about a Good Deal shop you have visited and, if we publish details based on your information, we'll send you a cheque for £10.

TO: **The Good Deal Directory**
PO Box 4, Lechlade, Glos GL7 3YB

Name of Outlet

Address

Signed

Name (capitals please)

Telephone number

Address

Type of Merchandise

Comments
(please write as much as possible, explaining in detail the type of discounts, car parking facilities etc)

Tel No.

e-mail

Date

THE GOOD DEAL DIRECTORY

REPORT FORM
EARN £10

Write and tell us about a Good Deal shop you have visited and, if we publish details based on your information, we'll send you a cheque for £10.

TO: **The Good Deal Directory
PO Box 4, Lechlade, Glos GL7 3YB**

Name of Outlet ....

....

Address ....

....

....

Telephone number ....

Type of Merchandise ....

....

....

Comments
(please write as much as possible, explaining in detail the type of goods sold, quality, any brand names, whether labels are cut out, discounts, car parking facilities etc)

THE GOOD DEAL DIRECTORY

Signed ....

Name (capitals please) ....

Address ....

....

....

Tel No. ....

e-mail ....

Date ....